STATUTORY INSTRUMENTS 1968

PART I

(in two Sections)

SECTION 2

Published by Authority

LONDON

HER MAJESTY'S STATIONERY OFFICE

1968

NOL

NOL:

© *Crown copyright* 1968

PRINTED AND PUBLISHED BY HER MAJESTY'S STATIONERY OFFICE

To be purchased from

49 High Holborn, LONDON, W.C.1 423 Oxford Street, LONDON, W.1
13a Castle Street, EDINBURGH, 2 109 St. Mary Street, CARDIFF CF1 1JW
Brazennose Street, MANCHESTER, 2 50 Fairfax Street, BRISTOL, BS1 3DE
258/9 Broad Street, BIRMINGHAM, 1 7 – 11 Linenhall Street, BELFAST BT2 8AY

or through any Bookseller

1968

Price: £7 7s. 0d. the two Sections: the Volume, complete, £22 1s. 0d.

PRINTED IN ENGLAND

SBN 11 840005 3

Contents of the Volume

PART I, Section 1

PART I, Section 2

PART II

PART III

STATUTORY INSTRUMENTS

1968 No. 333

EXCHANGE CONTROL

The Exchange Control (Scheduled Territories) (Amendment) Order 1968

Made - - -	*6th March* 1968
Laid before Parliament	*11th March* 1968
Coming into Operation	*12th March* 1968

The Treasury, in exercise of the powers conferred upon them by sections 1(3)(*b*) and 36(5) of the Exchange Control Act 1947(**a**), hereby make the following Order :—

1. Schedule 1 to the Exchange Control Act 1947, as amended by the Exchange Control (Scheduled Territories) Order 1967(**b**), shall be further amended by inserting after paragraph 21 the following paragraph :—

"21A. Mauritius."

2. This Order shall extend to the Channel Islands, and any reference in this Order to the Exchange Control Act 1947 includes a reference to that Act as extended by the Exchange Control (Channel Islands) Order 1947(**c**).

3. The Interpretation Act 1889(**d**) shall apply for the interpretation of this Order as it applies for the interpretation of an Act of Parliament.

4. This Order may be cited as the Exchange Control (Scheduled Territories) (Amendment) Order 1968, and shall come into operation on 12th March 1968.

E. *Alan Fitch,*
B. K. *O'Malley,*
Two of the Lords Commissioners
of Her Majesty's Treasury.

6th March 1968.

EXPLANATORY NOTE

(This Note is not part of the Order.)

This Order amends the list of Scheduled Territories contained in the First Schedule to the Exchange Control Act 1947 by the inclusion by name of Mauritius, previously included by definition.

(**a**) 1947 c. 14.   (**b**) S.I. 1967/1767 (1967 III, p. 4736).
(**c**) S.R. & O. 1947/2034 (Rev. VI, p. 1001: 1947 I, p. 660).
(**d**) 1889 c. 63.

STATUTORY INSTRUMENTS

1968 No. 338

WEIGHTS AND MEASURES

ADMINISTRATION

The Weights and Measures (Amendment) Regulations 1968

Made - - - -	*7th March* 1968
Laid before Parliament	*14th March* 1968
Coming into Operation	*15th March* 1968

The Board of Trade, in pursuance of the powers conferred upon them by sections 11(3), 14(1) and 58 of the Weights and Measures Act 1963(a) and all other powers enabling them in that behalf, hereby make the following Regulations:—

1. The Weights and Measures Regulations 1963(b), as amended (c), shall have effect as if for paragraph 3(a) of Part III of Schedule 1 to those Regulations there were substituted the following paragraph:—

" 3. *Metric system*

　(a) Metric weights, other than carat (metric) weights:—

Purported value	Error in excess only (or, in relation to the obliteration of stamps, error in excess or deficiency)	
	Weights made of iron	Weights not made of iron
1 milligramme	—	0.1 milligramme
2 milligrammes	—	0.2 milligramme
5 milligrammes	—	0.2 milligramme
10 milligrammes	—	0.5 milligramme
20 milligrammes	—	1 milligramme
50 milligrammes	—	2 milligrammes
100 milligrammes	—	2 milligrammes
200 milligrammes	—	2 milligrammes
300 milligrammes	—	2 milligrammes
400 milligrammes	—	2 milligrammes
500 milligrammes	—	2 milligrammes
1 gramme	—	2 milligrammes
2 grammes	—	5 milligrammes
3 grammes	—	5 milligrammes
4 grammes	—	5 milligrammes
5 grammes	—	5 milligrammes
10 grammes	—	5 milligrammes
20 grammes	—	10 milligrammes
50 grammes	—	15 milligrammes

(a) 1963 c. 31.　　　　(b) S.I. 1963/1710 (1963 III, p. 3286).
(c) The amendments have no relevance to the present Regulations.

Purported value	Error in excess only (or, in relation to the obliteration of stamps, error in excess or deficiency)	
	Weights made of iron	Weights not made of iron
100 grammes	40 milligrammes	20 milligrammes
200 grammes	100 milligrammes	50 milligrammes
500 grammes	200 milligrammes	100 milligrammes
1 kilogramme	400 milligrammes	200 milligrammes
2 kilogrammes	600 milligrammes	300 milligrammes
5 kilogrammes	1 gramme	500 milligrammes
10 kilogrammes	2 grammes	1 gramme
20 kilogrammes	3 grammes	1.5 grammes ".

2. These Regulations may be cited as the Weights and Measures (Amendment) Regulations 1968 and shall come into operation on 15th March 1968.

Gwyneth Dunwoody,
Parliamentary Secretary to
the Board of Trade.

7th March 1968.

EXPLANATORY NOTE

(This Note is not part of the Regulations.)

The Weights and Measures (Additional Metric Weights) Order 1968 (S.I. 1968/320) which came into operation on 12th March 1968, adds weights of 4 grammes, 3 grammes, 400 milligrammes and 300 milligrammes to the list of metric weights which may lawfully be used for trade purposes. These Regulations amend the Weights and Measures Regulations 1963 by prescribing limits of error for weights of those denominations.

STATUTORY INSTRUMENTS

1968 No. 339

WEIGHTS AND MEASURES

ADMINISTRATION

The Weights and Measures (Local Standards: Limits of Error) (Amendment) Regulations 1968

Made - - - -	*7th March* 1968
Laid before Parliament	*14th March* 1968
Coming into Operation	*15th March* 1968

The Board of Trade, in pursuance of the powers conferred upon them by sections 4(4) and 58 of the Weights and Measures Act 1963(a) and all other powers enabling them in that behalf, hereby make the following Regulations:—

1. The Weights and Measures (Local Standards: Limits of Error) Regulations 1963(b) shall have effect as if for paragraph 2(*a*) of Part III of the Schedule to those Regulations, there were substituted the following paragraph:—

" 2. *Metric system*

(*a*) *Metric weights other than carat (metric) weights*

	Error in excess or in deficiency
20 kilogrammes	150 milligrammes
10 kilogrammes	100 milligrammes
5 kilogrammes	50 milligrammes
2 kilogrammes	30 milligrammes
1 kilogramme	20 milligrammes
500 grammes, 200 grammes	10 milligrammes
100 grammes	4 milligrammes
50 grammes	3 milligrammes
20 grammes	2 milligrammes
10 grammes, 5 grammes, 4 grammes, 3 grammes, 2 grammes	1 milligramme
1 gramme, 500 milligrammes, 400 milligrammes, 300 milligrammes, 200 milligrammes, 100 milligrammes, 50 milligrammes	0.4 milligramme
20 milligrammes	0.2 milligramme
10 milligrammes	0.1 milligramme
5 milligrammes, 2 milligrammes, 1 milligramme	0.04 milligramme ".

(a) 1963 c. 31.   (b) S.I. 1963/1711 (1963 III, p. 3329).

2. These Regulations may be cited as the Weights and Measures (Local Standards: Limits of Error) (Amendment) Regulations 1968 and shall come into operation on 15th March 1968.

Gyneth Dunwoody,
Parliamentary Secretary to
7th March 1968.   the Board of Trade.

EXPLANATORY NOTE

(This Note is not part of these Regulations.)

The Weights and Measures (Additional Metric Weights) Order 1968 (S.I. 1968/320), which came into operation on 12th March 1968, adds weights of 4 grammes, 3 grammes, 400 milligrammes and 300 milligrammes to the list of metric weights which may lawfully be used for trade purposes. These Regulations amend the Weights and Measures (Local Standards: Limits of Error) Regulations 1963 by prescribing limits of error for local standards of weights of those denominations.

STATUTORY INSTRUMENTS

1968 No. 342

INDUSTRIAL TRAINING

The Industrial Training Levy (Ceramics, Glass and Mineral Products) Order 1968

Made - - - -	*7th March* 1968
Laid before Parliament	*18th March* 1968
Coming into Operation	*1st April* 1968

The Minister of Labour after approving proposals submitted by the Ceramics, Glass and Mineral Products Industry Training Board for the imposition of a further levy on employers in the ceramics, glass and mineral products industry and by virtue of the powers conferred on him by section 4 of the Industrial Training Act 1964(a) and of all other powers enabling him in that behalf hereby makes the following Order:—

Title and commencement

1. This Order may be cited as the Industrial Training Levy (Ceramics, Glass and Mineral Products) Order 1968 and shall come into operation on 1st April 1968.

Interpretation

2.—(1) In this Order unless the context otherwise requires:—

(a) " an appeal tribunal " means an industrial tribunal established under section 12 of the Industrial Training Act 1964;

(b) " assessment " means an assessment of an employer to the levy;

(c) " the Board " means the Ceramics, Glass and Mineral Products Industry Training Board;

(d) " business " means any activities of industry or commerce;

(e) " ceramics, glass and mineral products establishment " means an establishment in Great Britain engaged in the second base period wholly or mainly in the ceramics, glass and mineral products industry for a total of twenty-seven or more weeks or, being an establishment that commenced to carry on business in the second base period, for a total number of weeks exceeding one-half of the number of weeks in the part of the said period commencing with the day on which business was commenced and ending on the last day thereof;

(f) " the ceramics, glass and mineral products industry " means any one or more of the activities which, subject to the provisions of paragraph 2 of Schedule I to the industrial training order, are specified in paragraph 1 of that Schedule as the activities of the ceramics, glass and mineral products industry;

(g) " dock work " and " registered dock worker " have the same meanings as in the Scheme contained in the Second Schedule to the Dock Workers (Regulation of Employment) (Amendment) Order 1967(b);

(a) 1964 c. 16.   (b) S.I.1967/1252 (1967 II, p. 3623).

(h) " emoluments " means all emoluments assessable to income tax under Schedule E (other than pensions), being emoluments from which tax under that Schedule is deductible, whether or not tax in fact falls to be deducted from any particular payment thereof;

(i) " employer " means a person who is an employer in the ceramics, glass and mineral products industry at any time in the second levy period, but does not include a person in whose case the sum of the emoluments paid or payable to all persons in, or deemed under the provisions of this Article to have been in, his employment in the second base period is less than £5,000;

(j) " the industrial training order " means the Industrial Training (Ceramics, Glass and Mineral Products Board) Order 1965(a);

(k) " the levy " means the levy imposed by the Board in respect of the second levy period;

(l) " local authority " means—

(i) in relation to England and Wales, a local authority within the meaning of the Local Government Act 1933(b) or the Common Council of the City of London, and includes a joint board or joint committee of such authorities;

(ii) in relation to Scotland, a county council, town council or district council, and includes any joint board or joint committee of such authorities appointed under any enactment, order or scheme;

(m) " notice " means notice in writing;

(n) " the second base period " means the period of twelve months that commenced on 6th April, 1966;

(o) " the second levy period " means the period of twelve months commencing on 1st April 1968 and ending on 31st March 1969.

(2) In the case where a ceramics, glass and mineral products establishment is taken over (whether directly or indirectly) by an employer in succession to, or jointly with, another person, a person employed at any time in the second base period at or from the establishment shall be deemed, for the purposes of this Order, to have been so employed by the employer carrying on the said establishment on 1st April 1968.

(3) Any reference in this Order to an establishment that commences to carry on business or that ceases to carry on business shall not be taken to apply where the location of the establishment is changed but its business is continued wholly or mainly at or from the new location, or where the suspension of activities is of a temporary or seasonal nature.

(4) The Interpretation Act 1889(c) shall apply to the interpretation of this Order as it applies to the interpretation of an Act of Parliament.

Imposition of the Levy

3.—(1) The levy to be imposed by the Board on employers in respect of the second levy period shall be assessed in accordance with the provisions of this Article.

(2) The levy shall be assessed by the Board separately in respect of each ceramics, glass and mineral products establishment of an employer, but in agreement with the employer one assessment may be made in respect of any number of such establishments, in which case those establishments shall be deemed for the purposes of that assessment to constitute one establishment.

(3) Subject to the provisions of this Article, the levy assessed in respect of a ceramics, glass and mineral products establishment of an employer shall be an amount equal to 0·75 per cent. of the sum of the emoluments of all the persons following, that is to say—

(a) S.I. 1965/1391 (1965 II, p. 4062).   (b). 1933 c. 51.   (c) 1889 c. 63.

(a) any persons employed by the employer at or from that establishment in the second base period;

(b) any persons deemed to have been so employed under the provisions of Article 2(2) of this Order.

(4) In respect of any ceramics, glass and mineral products establishment described in the Schedule to this Order the amount of the levy shall be twice the amount determined in accordance with the foregoing paragraph.

(5) The amount of the levy imposed in respect of a ceramics, glass and mineral products establishment that ceases to carry on business in the second levy period shall be in the same proportion to the amount that would otherwise be due under paragraph (3) or (4) of this Article as the number of days between the commencement of the said levy period and the date of cessation of business (both dates inclusive) bears to the number of days in the said levy period.

(6) For the purposes of this Article no regard shall be had to the emoluments of any person employed as follows:—

(a) by a local authority in any activities specified in paragraph 1(m) of Schedule 1 to the industrial training order;

(b) by a harbour authority within the meaning of the Harbours Act 1964(a) when acting in that capacity;

(c) wholly as a registered dock worker in dock work;

(d) wholly in the supply of food or drink for immediate consumption.

Assessment Notices

4.—(1) The Board shall serve an assessment notice on every employer assessed to the levy, but one notice may comprise two or more assessments.

(2) An assessment notice shall state the amount of the levy payable by the person assessed to the levy, and that amount shall be equal to the total amount (rounded down where necessary to the nearest £1) of the levy assessed by the Board under Article 3 of this Order in respect of each establishment included in the notice.

(3) An assessment notice shall state the Board's address for the service of a notice of appeal or of an application for an extension of time for appealing.

(4) An assessment notice may be served on the person assessed to the levy either by delivering it to him personally or by leaving it, or sending it to him by post, at his last known address or place of business in the United Kingdom or, if that person is a corporation, by leaving it, or sending it by post to the corporation, at such address or place of business or at its registered or principal office.

Payment of the Levy

5.—(1) Subject to the provisions of this Article and of Articles 6 and 7, the amount of the levy payable under an assessment notice served by the Board shall be payable to the Board in two instalments, equal to one-third and two-thirds of the said amount respectively, and the said instalments shall be due respectively one month and five months after the date of the notice.

(2) The amount of an instalment mentioned in the foregoing paragraph may be rounded up or down by the Board to a convenient figure, but so that the aggregate amount of both instalments shall be equal to the amount of the levy stated in the assessment notice in accordance with Article 4(2) of this Order.

(3) An instalment of an assessment shall not be recoverable by the Board until there has expired the time allowed for appealing against the assessment by Article 7(1) of this Order and any further period or periods of time that the Board or an appeal tribunal may have allowed for appealing under paragraph (2) or

---

(3) of that Article, or, where an appeal is brought, until the appeal is decided or withdrawn.

Withdrawal of Assessment

6.—(1) The Board may, by a notice served on the person assessed to the levy in the same manner as an assessment notice, withdraw an assessment if that person has appealed against that assessment under the provisions of Article 7 of this Order and the appeal has not been entered in the Register of Appeals kept under the appropriate Regulations specified in paragraph (5) of that Article.

(2) The withdrawal of an assessment shall be without prejudice—

    (a) to the power of the Board to serve a further assessment notice in respect of any establishment to which that assessment related and, where the withdrawal is made by reason of the fact that an establishment has ceased to carry on business in the second levy period, the said notice may provide that the whole amount payable thereunder in respect of the establishment shall be due one month after the date of the notice; or

    (b) to any other assessment included in the original assessment notice, and such notice shall thereupon have effect as if any assessment withdrawn by the Board had not been included therein.

Appeals

7.—(1) A person assessed to the levy may appeal to an appeal tribunal against the assessment within one month from the date of the service of the assessment notice or within any further period or periods of time that may be allowed by the Board or an appeal tribunal under the following provisions of this Article.

(2) The Board by notice may for good cause allow a person assessed to the levy to appeal to an appeal tribunal against the assessment at any time within the period of four months from the date of the service of the assessment notice or within such further period or periods as the Board may allow before such time as may then be limited for appealing has expired.

(3) If the Board shall not allow an application for extension of time for appealing, an appeal tribunal shall upon application made to the tribunal by the person assessed to the levy have the like powers as the Board under the foregoing paragraph.

(4) In the case of an establishment that ceases to carry on business in the second levy period on any day after the date of the service of the relevant assessment notice, the foregoing provisions of this Article shall have effect as if for the period of four months from the date of the service of the assessment notice mentioned in paragraph (2) of this Article there were substituted the period of six months from the date of the cessation of business.

(5) An appeal or an application to an appeal tribunal under this Article shall be made in accordance with the Industrial Tribunals (England and Wales) Regulations 1965(**a**) as amended by the Industrial Tribunals (England and Wales) (Amendment) Regulations 1967(**b**) except where the establishment to which the relevant assessment relates is wholly in Scotland in which case the appeal or application shall be made in accordance with the Industrial Tribunals (Scotland) Regulations 1965(**c**) as amended by the Industrial Tribunals (Scotland) (Amendment) Regulations 1967(**d**).

(6) The powers of an appeal tribunal under paragraph (3) of this Article may be exercised by the President of the Industrial Tribunals (England and Wales) or by the President of the Industrial Tribunals (Scotland) as the case may be.

(a) S.I. 1965/1101 (1965 II, p. 2805).   (b) S.I. 1967/301 (1967 I, p. 1040).
(c) S. I. 1965/1157 (1965 II, p. 3266).   (d) S. I. 1967/302 (1967 I, p. 1050).

Evidence

8.—(1) Upon the discharge by a person assessed to the levy of his liability under an assessment the Board shall if so requested issue to him a certificate to that effect.

(2) The production in any proceedings of a document purporting to be certified by the Secretary of the Board to be a true copy of an assessment or other notice issued by the Board or purporting to be a certificate such as is mentioned in the foregoing paragraph of this Article shall, unless the contrary is proved, be sufficient evidence of the document and of the facts stated therein.

7th March 1968.

R. J. Gunter,
Minister of Labour.

SCHEDULE

Establishments to which Article 3(4) *of this Order applies*

1. Any ceramics, glass and mineral products establishment that was engaged wholly or mainly in the activities specified in paragraph 2 of this Schedule.

2. The said activities are the activities following or any of them, that is to say—

    (*a*) the manufacture of glass;

    (*b*) the manufacture of articles or other products wholly or mainly from glass;

    (*c*) the calibrating, graduating or toughening of glass or glass articles;

    (*d*) the milling, grinding or mixing of any material for the purpose of the manufacture of pottery;

    (*e*) the manufacture of pottery;

    (*f*) when carried out in conjunction with any of the foregoing activities, any of the following activities, being incidental or ancillary thereto, that is to say—

        (i) research, development, design or drawing;

        (ii) operations in connection with sale, packing, warehousing, distribution or transport;

        (iii) work done at any office or laboratory, at any store, warehouse or similar place or at a garage.

3. In this Schedule—

    (*a*) " pottery " includes vitreous china, porcelain, earthenware, wall tiles, sanitary fire clay ware, sanitary earthenware and similar wares;

    (*b*) other expressions have the same meaning as in Schedule 1 to the industrial training order or in Article 2 of this Order.

EXPLANATORY NOTE

(This Note is not part of the Order.)

This Order gives effect to proposals submitted to the Minister of Labour by the Ceramics, Glass and Mineral Products Industry Training Board for the imposition of a further levy upon employers in the ceramics, glass and mineral products industry for the purpose of raising money towards the expenses of the Board.

The levy is to be imposed in respect of the second levy period commencing on 1st April 1968 and ending on 31st March 1969. The levy will be assessed by the Board and there will be a right of appeal against an assessment to an industrial tribunal.

STATUTORY INSTRUMENTS

1968 No. 343

INDUSTRIAL TRAINING

The Industrial Training Levy (Agricultural, Horticultural and Forestry) Order 1967 (Amendment) Order 1968

Made - - -	*7th March* 1968
Laid before Parliament	*18th March* 1968
Coming into Operation	*1st April* 1968

The Minister of Labour after approving proposals submitted by the Agricultural, Horticultural and Forestry Industry Training Board for the amendment of the Industrial Training Levy (Agricultural, Horticultural and Forestry) Order 1967(**a**) (which Order, hereinafter referred to as the "principal Order", makes provision in respect of the first levy period commencing on 13th December 1967 and ending on 31st August 1968 as to the levy to be imposed by the Board on employers in the agricultural, horticultural and forestry industry) and by virtue of the powers conferred on him by section 4 of the Industrial Training Act 1964(**b**) and of all other powers enabling him in that behalf hereby makes the following Order:—

Title and Commencement

1.—(1) This Order may be cited as the Industrial Training Levy (Agricultural, Horticultural and Forestry) Order 1967 (Amendment) Order 1968 and shall come into operation on 1st April 1968.

(2) The Interpretation Act 1889(**c**) shall apply to the interpretation of this Order as it applies to the interpretation of an Act of Parliament and as if this Order and the principal Order were Acts of Parliament.

Amendment of principal Order

2. In paragraph (3) of Article 3 of the principal Order (which paragraph provides that the levy to be assessed in respect of an establishment shall be an amount equal to that obtained by multiplying the sum of £6 by the number of certain regular whole-time employees) for the reference to £6 there shall be substituted a reference to £3.

7th March 1968.

R. J. Gunter,
Minister of Labour.

(**a**) 1967/1747 (1967 III, p. 4660).   (**b**) 1964 c. 16.
(**c**) 1889 c. 63.

EXPLANATORY NOTE

(This Note is not part of the Order.)

This Order gives effect to proposals submitted by the Agricultural, Horticultural and Forestry Industry Training Board to the Minister of Labour for the amendment of the Industrial Training Levy (Agricultural, Horticultural and Forestry) Order 1967 which makes provision for the imposition of a levy on employers in the agricultural, horticultural and forestry industry in respect of the first levy period commencing on 13th December 1967 and ending on 31st August 1968. The amount of the levy to be imposed in respect of that period is halved.

STATUTORY INSTRUMENTS

1968 No. 344

LAND REGISTRATION

The Land Registration (District Registries) Order 1968

Made - - -	*5th March* 1968
Coming into Operation	*1st April* 1968

I, Gerald, Baron Gardiner, Lord High Chancellor of Great Britain, in exercise of the powers conferred on me by sections 132 and 133 of the Land Registration Act 1925(**a**), and with the concurrence of the Treasury, hereby make the following Order :—

Title, commencement, revocation and interpretation

1.—(1) This Order may be cited as the Land Registration (District Registries) Order 1968 and shall come into operation on 1st April 1968.

(2) The Interpretation Act 1889(**b**) shall apply to the interpretation of this Order as it applies to the interpretation of an Act of Parliament.

(3) The Land Registration (District Registries) (No. 2) Order 1967(**c**) and the Land Registration (District Registries) (No. 3) Order 1967(**d**) are hereby revoked.

(4) In this Order, unless the context otherwise requires :—

"the Act" means the Land Registration Act 1925 ;

"application" means an application made or delivered under the Land Registration Rules 1925(**e**) and the Land Registration Rules 1930(**f**), as amended(**g**), and includes a notice or other instrument so made or delivered ;

"district registry" means a district registry of the Land Registry within the meaning of section 132 of the Act.

District Registries

2.—(1) There shall continue to be district registries bearing the names and at the places specified in column 1 of the Schedule to this Order.

(2) Each district registry shall be the proper office for the registration of titles to land and for the delivery of any application relating to land in its district, which shall comprise the administrative areas specified opposite its name in columns 2 and 3 of the said Schedule.

(3) The district registrar appointed for each district shall have the powers and indemnity conferred by section 133 of the Act :

Provided that :—

   (*a*) nothing in this paragraph shall be construed as giving a district registrar any powers or duties which are exercisable only by the Chief Land Registrar ; and

   (*b*) all powers and duties of the district registrar shall be exercised under the general direction and authority of the Chief Land Registrar.

(**a**) 1925 c. 21.   (**b**) 1889 c. 63.   (**c**) S.I. 1967/1385 (1967 III, p. 4043).
(**d**) S.I. 1967/1929 (1967 III, p. 5370).
(**e**) S.R. & O. 1925/1093 (Rev. XII, p. 81: 1925, p. 717).
(**f**) S.R. & O. 1930/211 (Rev. XII, p. 167: 1930, p. 798).
(**g**) The relevant amending instrument is S.R. & O. 1936/1302 (Rev. XII, p. 167: 1936 I, p. 1537).

Delivery of instruments and applications at the proper office

3. No application shall be duly delivered until it is delivered at the proper office, namely :—

    (*a*) where an application relates to land wholly within a district, the district registry for that district ;

    (*b*) where an application relates to land in two or more districts, any one of the district registries for those districts.

Dated 1st March 1968.

                                    Gardiner, C.

We concur.

                                  Joseph Harper,

                                  J. McCann,

                Two of the Lords Commissioners of
                        Her Majesty's Treasury.

Dated 5th March 1968.

SCHEDULE

DISTRICT REGISTRIES

1 District Registry	2 Administrative Counties	3 County Boroughs, London Boroughs, etc.
The Croydon District Land Registry at Croydon		Bexley Bromley Croydon Greenwich Kingston upon Thames Lambeth Lewisham Merton Richmond upon Thames Southwark Sutton Wandsworth
The Durham District Land Registry at Durham	Durham Northumberland Yorkshire, East Riding Yorkshire, North Riding Yorkshire, West Riding	Barnsley Bradford Darlington Dewsbury Doncaster Gateshead Halifax Hartlepool Huddersfield Kingston upon Hull Leeds Newcastle upon Tyne Rotherham Sheffield South Shields Sunderland Teesside Tynemouth Wakefield York
The Gloucester District Land Registry at Gloucester	Gloucestershire Hampshire Isle of Wight Oxford	Bournemouth Bristol Gloucester Oxford Portsmouth Southampton

1 District Registry	2 Administrative Counties	3 County Boroughs, London Boroughs, etc.
The Harrow District Land Registry at Harrow-on-the-Hill		The City of London The Inner Temple and the Middle Temple Barking Barnet Brent Camden City of Westminster Ealing Enfield Hackney Hammersmith Haringey Harrow Havering Hillingdon Hounslow Islington Kensington and Chelsea Newham Redbridge Tower Hamlets Waltham Forest
The Lytham District Land Registry at Lytham St. Annes	Chester Cumberland Herefordshire Lancaster Monmouthshire Salop Westmorland All the counties in Wales	Barrow-in-Furness Birkenhead Blackburn Blackpool Bolton Bootle Burnley Bury Carlisle Chester Liverpool Manchester Newport Oldham Preston Rochdale St. Helens Salford Southport Stockport Wallasey Warrington Wigan All the county boroughs in Wales

1 District Registry	2 Administrative Counties	3 County Boroughs, London Boroughs, etc.
The Nottingham District Land Registry at Nottingham	Derbyshire Leicester Nottinghamshire Staffordshire Warwickshire Worcestershire	Birmingham Burton upon Trent Coventry Derby Dudley Leicester Nottingham Solihull Stoke-on-Trent Walsall Warley West Bromwich Wolverhampton Worcester
The Plymouth District Land Registry at Plymouth	Cornwall Devon Dorset Somerset Wiltshire	Bath Exeter Plymouth Torbay

The Stevenage District Land Registry at Stevenage	Bedfordshire
	Buckingham
	Cambridgshire and
	    Isle of Ely
	Essex
	Hertfordshire
	Huntingdon and
	    Peterborough
	Lincoln, parts of Holland
	Lincoln, parts of Kesteven
	Lincoln, parts of Lindsey
	Norfolk
	Northamptonshire
	Rutland
	Suffolk, East
	Suffolk, West
		Great Yarmouth
		Grimsby
		Ipswich
		Lincoln
		Luton
		Northampton
		Norwich
		Southend-on-Sea

The Tunbridge Wells District Land Registry at Tunbridge Wells	Berkshire Kent Surrey Sussex, East Sussex, West	Brighton Canterbury Eastbourne Hastings Reading

EXPLANATORY NOTE
(This Note is not part of the Order.)

This Order, which replaces the Land Registration (District Registries) (No. 2) Order 1967 and revokes that Order and the Land Registration (District Registries) (No. 3) Order 1967, transfers responsibility for the registration of titles in Wiltshire from the Gloucester to the Plymouth District Land Registry. The areas of the remaining district registries at Croydon, Durham, Harrow, Lytham St. Annes, Nottingham, Stevenage and Tunbridge Wells are unchanged : the Order does not reproduce the provisions of the Land Registration (District Registries) (No. 3) Order 1967 transferring responsibility for the registration of titles in Staffordshire and certain county boroughs from the Nottingham to the Gloucester District Land Registry.

The Order continues the requirement that applications for the registration of titles shall be delivered at the appropriate district registry as defined in the Order.

STATUTORY INSTRUMENTS

1968 No. 345

EDUCATION, ENGLAND AND WALES

The Remuneration of Teachers (Farm Institutes) Order 1968

Made - - -	*8th March* 1968
Coming into Operation	*8th March* 1968

Whereas—

(1) in pursuance of section 2(2) of the Remuneration of Teachers Act 1965(a) (hereinafter referred to as "the Act") the Committee constituted under section 1 of the Act for the purpose of considering the remuneration of teachers in farm institutes and teachers of agricultural subjects on the staff of local education authorities (hereinafter referred to as "the Committee") have transmitted to the Secretary of State for Education and Science (hereinafter referred to as "the Secretary of State") recommendations agreed on by them with respect to the remuneration of such teachers ;

(2) in pursuance of section 2(3) of the Act, the Secretary of State has prepared a draft document setting out the scales and other provisions required for determining the remuneration of teachers of the description aforesaid in the form in which, in his opinion, those scales and provisions should be so as to give effect to those recommendations ;

(3) the Secretary of State, as required by section 2(4) of the Act, has consulted the Committee with respect to the draft document and the Committee has made no representations with respect thereto ; and

(4) the Secretary of State has arranged for a document setting out the requisite scales and other provisions in the form of the draft to be published by Her Majesty's Stationery Office under the title "SCALES OF SALARIES FOR THE TEACHING STAFF OF FARM INSTITUTES AND FOR TEACHERS OF AGRICULTURAL (INCLUDING HORTICULTURAL) SUBJECTS, ENGLAND AND WALES, 1967".

Now therefore the Secretary of State, in pursuance of section 2(4) of the Act, hereby orders as follows :—

Citation

1. This Order may be cited as the Remuneration of Teachers (Farm Institutes) Order 1968.

Interpretation

2. The Interpretation Act 1889(b) shall apply for the interpretation of this Order as it applies for the interpretation of an Act of Parliament.

(a) 1965 c. 3.   (b) 1889 c. 63.

Remuneration of Teachers

3. The remuneration payable from 1st July 1967 to full-time teachers employed as members of the teaching staff of farm institutes maintained by local education authorities or as teachers of agricultural subjects (including horticultural and related subjects) on the staff of local education authorities shall be determined in accordance with the scales and other provisions set out in the document published by Her Majesty's Stationery Office as aforesaid.

Revocation

4. The Remuneration of Teachers (Farm Institutes) Order 1965(a) is hereby revoked and section 38(2) of the Interpretation Act 1889 (which relates to the effect of repeals) shall have effect in relation to that Order as if it were an enactment repealed by an Act.

Given under the Official Seal of the Secretary of State for Education and Science on 8th March 1968.

(L.S.)

Patrick Gordon Walker,
Secretary of State for Education
and Science.

EXPLANATORY NOTE
(This Note is not part of the Order.)

This Order brings into operation the scales and other provisions relating to the remuneration of full-time teachers in farm institutes and teachers of agricultural subjects on the staff of local education authorities contained in a document published by Her Majesty's Stationery Office. This document gives effect to the recommendations agreed on by the Committee for the consideration of the remuneration of such teachers.

Clause 3 provides that the Order shall have effect as from 1st July 1967 ; this provision is made in exercise of the power conferred by section 7(3) of the Act.

(a) S.I. 1965/2029 (1965 III, p. 6005).

STATUTORY INSTRUMENTS

1968 No. 348

LOCAL GOVERNMENT, ENGLAND AND WALES
The Inner London (Needs Element) Regulations 1968

Made - - -		*8th March* 1968
Laid before Parliament		*21st March* 1968
Coming into Operation		*1st April* 1968

The Minister of Housing and Local Government, after consultation with the association which appeared to him to be representative of the councils of the inner London boroughs and with the Common Council of the City of London and the Greater London Council, in exercise of his powers under paragraph 11 of Part I of Schedule 1 to the Local Government Act 1966(a) and of all other powers enabling him in that behalf, hereby makes the following regulations:—

1.—(1) These regulations may be cited as the Inner London (Needs Element) Regulations 1968 and shall come into operation on 1st April 1968.

(2) The Interpretation Act 1889(b) applies to the interpretation of these regulations as it applies to the interpretation of an Act of Parliament.

2. Forty per cent. of the amount of the needs element of the rate support grants for the year 1968-69 and subsequent years payable to the council of each inner London borough or to the Common Council of the City of London shall be payable to the Greater London Council instead of to the council aforesaid.

3. The Inner London (Needs Element) Regulations 1967(c) are hereby revoked except in so far as they apply to amounts of the needs element for the year 1967-68.

Given under the official seal of the Minister of Housing and Local Government on 8th March 1968.

(L.S.)

Anthony Greenwood,
Minister of Housing
and Local Government.

(a) 1966 c. 42.   (b) 1889 c. 63.   (c) S.I. 1967/446 (1967 I, p. 1378).

EXPLANATORY NOTE
(This Note is not part of the Regulations.)

The needs element of the rate support grants is not payable to the Greater London Council unless the Minister of Housing and Local Government determines by regulations under paragraph 11(1) of Part I of Schedule 1 to the Local Government Act 1966 that any proportion of the amount of that element for any year which apart from that paragraph would be payable to the council of an inner London borough or the Common Council of the City of London shall be payable instead to the Greater London Council.

These regulations increase from one-ninth to forty per cent. the amount of the needs element for any year which the Greater London Council is to receive and which would otherwise be payable to the councils of the inner London boroughs or to the Common Council of the City of London.

The inner London boroughs are—
Camden, Greenwich, Hackney, Hammersmith, Islington, Kensington and Chelsea, Lambeth, Lewisham, Southwark, Tower Hamlets, Wandsworth and Westminster.

STATUTORY INSTRUMENTS

1968 No. 354

FACTORIES

The Abstract of Factories Act (Docks, etc.) Order 1968

Made - - -	*11th March* 1968	
Coming into Operation	*25th March* 1968	

The Minister of Labour by virtue of the powers conferred on him by sections 138(1) and 180(3) of the Factories Act 1961(a) and of all other powers enabling him in that behalf, hereby makes the following Order :—

1.—(1) This Order may be cited as the Abstract of Factories Act (Docks, etc.) Order 1968 and shall come into operation on 25th March 1968.

(2) The Abstract of Factories Act (Docks, etc.) Order 1963(b) is hereby revoked.

2. The Interpretation Act 1889(c) shall apply to the interpretation of this Order as it applies to the interpretation of an Act of Parliament, and as if this Order and the Order hereby revoked were Acts of Parliament.

3. The abstract of the Factories Act 1961 required by section 138(1) of that Act to be kept posted at the principal entrances of a factory at which employed persons enter shall, in the case of premises to which provisions of that Act apply by virtue of section 125 thereof (docks, etc.), be in the form set out in the Schedule to this Order.

Signed by order of the Minister of Labour.

11th March 1968.

P. H. St. J. Wilson,
Deputy Secretary,
Ministry of Labour.

Article 3
F 2

SCHEDULE

Abstract of the Factories Act 1961 prescribed by the Minister of Labour by virtue of section 138(1) of that Act for Docks, Wharves, Quays and certain Warehouses.
Certain provisions of the Factories Act 1961 including those mentioned below, apply by virtue of section 125 of that Act (A) to every dock, wharf or quay (including any warehouse belonging to the owners, trustees or conservators of the dock, wharf or quay and any line or siding used in connection with and for the purposes of the dock, wharf or quay and not forming part of a railway or tramway*) ; (B) to every other warehouse (not forming part of a factory) in or for the purposes of which mechanical power is used ; (C) to the processes of loading, unloading or coaling of any ship in any dock, harbour or canal and to all machinery or plant (including gangways or ladders) used in those processes. Certain additional (General Safety) provisions apply to every warehouse by virtue of section 125 sub-section (6) as if it were a factory. The provisions of Part II of the Act with respect to steam boilers apply except as regards liability (see para. 31 below).

(a) 1961 c. 34.   (b) 1963/525 (1963 I, p. 586).   (c) 1889 c. 63.

SAFETY

Docks, Wharves, Quays, Warehouses; Loading, Unloading and Coaling of Ships

1. STEAM BOILERS.—Every part of every steam boiler must be of good construction, sound material, adequate strength and free from patent defect. Detailed requirements are laid down as to the valves and other fittings.

Steam boilers and their fittings must be properly maintained and (unless the Minister provides otherwise in an exemption order) must be thoroughly examined by a competent person at least once in every 14 months and after extensive repairs†. A report of each examination must be attached to the General Register. New boilers must be certified and all boilers must be examined before being taken into use. (Sections 32 to 35, 37 and 38 and Sixth Schedule, para. (3).)

2. NOTIFICATION OF ACCIDENTS AND DANGEROUS OCCURRENCES.—Accidents causing loss of life or disabling a worker for more than three days from earning full wages at the work at which he was employed must be reported on form F43 forthwith to the District Inspector and entered in the General Register. Certain dangerous occurrences must also be reported whether disablement is caused or not, e.g. the bursting of a revolving vessel, wheel or grindstone moved by mechanical power, the collapse or failure of a crane, hoist or other lifting appliance, or any part thereof (except the breaking of chain or rope slings), or the overturning of a crane; and explosions or fires in certain circumstances. (Sections 80, 81 and 140, and regulations.)

3. DANGEROUS CONDITIONS AND PRACTICES.—A magistrate's court or sheriff may by order prohibit work or require remedial action to be taken if satisfied that dangerous conditions or practices exist. (Sections 54 and 55.)

Warehouses—(Additional Provisions)

4. FENCING.—Every part of the transmission machinery and every dangerous part of other machinery, and all parts of electric generators, motors, rotary converters, and flywheels directly connected to them, must be securely fenced unless in such a position or of such construction as to be as safe to every person employed or working on the premises as if securely fenced. A male person over 18 may, however, approach unfenced machinery in motion in certain strictly limited contingencies and subject to conditions specified in regulations. (Sections 12 to 15.)

5. Moving parts of other prime movers, and flywheels directly connected to them must be securely fenced irrespective of their position. (Section 12.)

6. All fencing must be of substantial construction and maintained in an efficient state. (Section 16.)

7. FURTHER REQUIREMENTS IN CONNECTION WITH TRANSMISSION MACHINERY.—Devices or appliances for promptly cutting off the power from the transmission machinery must be provided in every room or place where work is carried on. Efficient mechanical appliances must be provided to move driving belts to and from fast and loose pulleys. Driving belts must not rest or ride on revolving shafts when the belt is not in use. (Section 13.)

8. NEW MACHINES.—New power-driven machines must not be sold, let on hire, or used unless certain parts are effectively guarded. (Section 17.)

9. **CLEANING MACHINERY.**—A woman or young person must not clean (a) a prime mover or transmission machinery while it is in motion or (b) any part of any machine if there is risk of injury from any moving part of that machine or of any adjacent machinery. (Section 20.)

10. **TRAINING OF YOUNG PERSONS.**—A young person must not work at any machine specified by the Minister to be dangerous unless (i) he has been fully instructed as to the dangers and precautions and (ii) he has received sufficient training in the work or is under adequate supervision by an experienced person. (Section 21.)

11. **HOISTS AND LIFTS.**—Every hoist or lift must be of good mechanical construction, sound material and adequate strength and must be properly maintained. It must be thoroughly examined every six months by a competent person whose report must be entered in or attached to the General Register.

Every hoistway must be efficiently protected by a substantial enclosure and landing gates, with efficient interlocking or other devices. The safe working load must be marked conspicuously on each hoist. Additional safeguards (e.g. devices to prevent overrunning) must be provided on hoists used for carrying persons, whether with goods or otherwise. The requirements are somewhat less stringent in the case of hoists constructed before the 30th July 1937, hoists not connected with mechanical power, and continuous hoists. (Sections 22, 23 and 25.)

12. **CHAINS, ROPES AND LIFTING TACKLE.**—No chain, rope or lifting tackle used for raising or lowering persons or goods may be used unless it is of good construction, sound material and adequate strength and free from patent defect. Tables of safe working loads must be posted in the stores and elsewhere, but need not cover any lifting tackle the safe working load of which is marked on the tackle itself. No tackle shall be used for any load exceeding its stated safe working load. Chains, ropes and lifting tackle in use must be thoroughly examined by a competent person every six months, and must not (excepting fibre ropes and fibre rope slings) be taken into use for the first time in the warehouse unless they have been tested and certified.

Periodic annealing is required except in the case of ropes and rope slings and other tackle exempted by HM Chief Inspector.

A register of all chains, etc. and also the certificates of tests, must be kept. (Section 26.)

13. **CRANES, ETC.**—All parts and working gear (including anchoring appliances) of cranes and other lifting machines must be of good construction, sound material, adequate strength and free from patent defect and must be properly maintained. A thorough examination of all such parts and gear by a competent person must be made every 14 months. A lifting machine must not be taken into use for the first time unless it has been tested and certified. A register of examinations and tests must be kept. The safe working load or loads must be shown on every lifting machine; in the case of cranes with a derricking jib an automatic indicator or a table of safe working loads must be attached to the crane. No lifting machine shall be loaded above its stated safe working load.

Rails and tracks of travelling cranes and transporters must be of proper size and construction. If any person is working near the wheel-track of an overhead travelling crane steps must be taken to ensure that the crane does not approach within 20 feet.

Effective measures should also be taken to give warning of the approach of such a crane to anyone working above floor level and liable to be struck by it or by its load. (Section 27.)

14. CONSTRUCTION OF FLOORS, ETC..—Floors, steps, stairs, passages and gangways, must be soundly constructed, properly maintained and so far as is reasonably practicable, kept free from obstruction and any substance likely to cause persons to slip. Handrails must be provided for stairs. All ladders must be soundly constructed and properly maintained. Openings in floors should, wherever practicable, be securely fenced. (Section 28.)

HEALTH

15. LEAD PROCESSES.—A woman or young person must not be employed in certain lead processes or in cleaning workrooms where any of the processes are carried on. (Section 74.)

Where women or young persons are employed in any other process which involves the use of a lead compound producing dust or fume, or if they are liable to be splashed with any lead compound, (a) the dust or fume produced must be drawn away by an efficient exhaust draught; (b) they must undergo medical examination as prescribed and may be suspended from further employment in lead processes; (c) no food, drink, or tobacco may be brought into the workroom; (d) protective clothing must be provided by the occupier and worn; (e) suitable cloakroom, mess-room and washing accommodation must be provided as prescribed; and (f) all tools and apparatus must be kept clean. (Section 75.)

16. NOTIFICATION OF INDUSTRIAL POISONING OR DISEASE.— Cases of poisoning by beryllium, cadmium, lead, phosphorus, arsenic, mercury, carbon bisulphide, manganese, or aniline; chronic poisoning by benzene; compressed air illness; anthrax; toxic jaundice due to tetrachloroethane or nitro- or amido-derivatives of benzene or other poisonous substance; toxic anaemia; epitheliomatous ulceration, and chrome ulceration, must be reported on form F41 to the District Inspector and to the Appointed Factory Doctor and entered in the General Register. (Sections 82 and 140 and regulations.)

EMPLOYMENT OF YOUNG PERSONS

Hours and Holidays (Section 116)

17. The provisions set out in paragraphs 18-27 apply to young persons employed—

(1) in collecting, carrying or delivering goods, carrying messages or running errands, in connection with any business carried on at a dock, wharf or quay or any warehouse (except a warehouse which forms part of a factory or to which the Shops Act 1950, applies), if employed by a person having the use or occupation of the dock, wharf, quay or warehouse or of premises within it or forming part of it;

(2) in or in connection with any process (except certain specified processes‡ in a ship in harbour or wet dock) carried on at any dock, wharf, quay or warehouse, and by a person having such use or occupation;

(3) in or in connection with the processes of loading, unloading or coaling of any ship in any dock, harbour or canal.

18. WEEKLY HOURS.—The total hours worked by such a young person in any week (exclusive of intervals for meals and rest) must not exceed 48 (apart from overtime—see below). The total weekly hours worked by a young person under 16 must not exceed 44.

19. INTERVALS FOR MEALS AND REST.—The young person must not be employed for more than 5 hours without an interval of at least half-an-hour. Where the hours of employment include the hours from 11.30 a.m. to 2.30 p.m. an interval of not less than 45 minutes must be allowed between these hours.

20. PROHIBITION OF NIGHT EMPLOYMENT.—An interval of at least 11 consecutive hours, including 10 p.m. to 6 a.m., must be allowed between midday on one day and midday on the next day.

21. SHORT DAY.—On at least one weekday in each week, to be notified in the prescribed form and manner (F15) the young person must not be employed after 1 p.m.

22. SUNDAY EMPLOYMENT is prohibited (subject to a special exception where both employer and the employee observe the Jewish sabbath).

23. OVERTIME (work in excess of 48 hours in a week) may be worked by young persons **aged 16 or over** on occasions of seasonal or other special pressure or in cases of emergency. The overtime worked by any young person must not exceed **6 hours** in any week, or **50 hours** in any calendar year ; and when the employer has employed overtime any young persons to whom these provisions apply in **12 weeks** (whether consecutive or not) in any calendar year, neither he nor any person succeeding to his business may employ any such young persons (whether the same young persons or not) overtime during the remainder of that year.

24. HOLIDAYS.—Young persons must be allowed as holidays in each year (1) in **England and Wales,** Christmas Day, Good Friday and every bank holiday unless the occupier not less than three weeks before any one of those days gives notice substituting another weekday ; (2) in **Scotland,** six weekdays specified in a notice given not less than three weeks before the holiday (in Burghs two of these days, not less than three months apart, are to be fixed by the Town Council). At least half of the holidays must be allowed between 15th March and 1st October.

25. OTHER EMPLOYMENT UNDER THE SAME EMPLOYER.—In reckoning the above hours of employment, and also for the purpose of allowing the intervals, any other employment of the young person by the same employer must be taken into account.

26. RECORDS.—The employer must keep in the prescribed form and manner a record (F38) of the prescribed particulars as to each young person including particulars of the hours worked and the intervals allowed for meals and rest.

27. ALTERNATIVE HOURS.—The employer may on giving notice in form F16 to the District Inspector, adopt, instead of the above provisions, the provisions of the Act regulating the hours of employment of young persons in ordinary factories.

28. Where application is made to the Minister he may, if he is satisfied that it is desirable to do so in the public interest to maintain or increase the efficiency of industry or transport, and after undertaking the consultations provided for exempt the employment of young persons aged 16 and over from any of the provisions summarised in paragraphs 17-27 above. (Section 117.)

Certificate of Fitness

29. No young person under 18 years of age may remain in any of the following employments after a period of 14 days unless he had been medically examined by the Appointed Factory Doctor and given a certificate of fitness for it :
(1) employment in harbour or wet dock in constructing, reconstructing, repairing, refitting, painting, finishing or breaking-up a ship ; scaling,

scurfing or cleaning boilers (including combustion chambers and smoke boxes) in a ship; cleaning, in a ship, bilges or oil-fuel tanks or any tank last used for oil of any description carried as cargo;

(2) employment in or in connection with the processes of loading, unloading or coaling any ship in any dock, harbour or canal.

For the purpose of reckoning the period of 14 days, a young person shall be treated as remaining in the same employment if he continues to be employed by the same employer in employment within the same group, either (1) or (2) above. The certificate must be renewed every 12 months or earlier if the doctor so directs and details of the certificate entered in the General Register. (Sections 125 and 126 and Order.)

MISCELLANEOUS

30. GENERAL REGISTER.—The person having the actual use or occupation of the premises must keep a General Register in the prescribed form (F35). (Section 140.)

31. LIABILITY.—Any person having the actual use of a dock, wharf or quay, or of any warehouse having mechanical power, is regarded for the purposes of the Act as the occupier of a factory and responsible for any contravention of the provisions of the Act relating to docks, wharves, quays and warehouses, except in respect of steam boilers when the owner of the steam boiler is responsible. (Section 125.)

32. EXCEPTIONS.—The safety provisions of Part II of the Act do not apply to any steam boiler which is on board a ship and is the property of the ship owner.

The power of a magistrate's court or sheriff to make orders as to dangerous conditions and practices do not apply in respect of any plant or machinery which is on board a ship and is the property of the ship owner.

The provisions of Part VI of the Act, relating to the medical examination of young persons and the provisions of Part XI of the Act with regard to appointed factory doctors, do not apply to a member of the crew of a ship. (Section 125.)

33. SPECIAL REGULATIONS AND WELFARE REGULATIONS made for particular industries, processes, plant, etc. must be observed, and printed copies of prescribed abstracts of all such regulations which apply must be kept posted on the premises. (Section 139.)

34. PROHIBITION OF DEDUCTIONS FROM WAGES.—The occupier must not make a deduction from wages in respect of anything he has to do or provide in pursuance of the Act, or permit any person in his employment to receive payment from other employees for such services. (Section 136.)

35. DUTIES OF PERSONS EMPLOYED.—A person employed must not wilfully interfere with or misuse any means, appliance, convenience or other thing provided in pursuance of the Act for securing health, safety or welfare and he must use any means or appliance for securing health or safety provided for his use under the Act. He must not wilfully and without reasonable cause do anything likely to endanger himself or others. (Section 143.)

36. INSPECTION.—HM Inspectors have power to inspect every part of the premises by day or by night. They may require the production of registers, certificates and other papers. They may examine any person found on the premises, either alone or in the presence of any other person as they think fit,

and may require him to sign a declaration of the truth of the matters about which he is examined. They may also exercise such other powers as may be necessary for carrying the Act into effect. Every person obstructing an Inspector is liable to a penalty. (Sections 146 and 147.)

---

* "Railway" means any railway used for the purposes of public traffic whether passenger, goods, or other traffic and includes any works of the railway companies connected with the railway. "Tramway" means a tramway authorised by or under any Act of Parliament and used for the purpose of public traffic.

† When section 33 (2) and (3) is brought into operation, the present requirements regarding examinations will be superseded by regulations.

‡ The excepted processes (hours of employment which are governed by different provisions under section 126 of the 1961 Act) are constructing, reconstructing, repairing, refitting, painting, finishing or breaking up a ship; scaling, scurfing or cleaning boilers (including combustion chambers and smoke boxes) in a ship; cleaning, in a ship, bilges or oil-fuel tanks or any tank last used for oil of any description carried as cargo.

EXPLANATORY NOTE
(*This Note is not part of the Order.*)

This Order prescribes the abstract of the Factories Act 1961, required by section 138(1) of that Act to be kept posted at the principal entrances of a factory at which employed persons enter, for use in the case of any dock, wharf, quay, warehouse, line or siding to which section 125 of that Act applies.

The abstract prescribed by this Order is in substitution for that prescribed by the Abstract of Factories Act (Docks, etc.) Order 1963 which is revoked.

STATUTORY INSTRUMENTS

1968 No. 355

ROAD TRAFFIC

The Road Vehicles (Index Marks) (Amendment)

Regulations 1968

Made - - -	*7th March* 1968	
Laid before Parliament	*19th March* 1968	
Coming into Operation	*1st April* 1968	

The Minister of Transport, in exercise of the powers conferred upon her by section 16 of the Vehicles (Excise) Act 1962(a) and of all other powers her enabling in that behalf, hereby makes the following Regulations :—

1. These Regulations shall come into operation on the 1st April 1968, and may be cited as the Road Vehicles (Index Marks) (Amendment) Regulations 1968.

2. The Road Vehicles (Index Marks) Regulations 1964(b), as amended (c), shall have effect as though in Schedule 2 thereto :—

(*a*) there were substituted for the word "Berks" in the first column the word "Berkshire" ;

(*b*) there were inserted after the reference to the Council of the County Borough of Swansea a reference to the Council of the County Borough of Teesside ;

(*c*) there were specified in relation to the Council of the County Borough of Teesside the index marks specified in relation to the Council of the County Borough of Middlesbrough ;

(*d*) the reference to the Council of the County Borough of Middlesbrough and all the index marks specified in relation thereto were deleted ;

(*e*) there were inserted after the reference to the Council of the County Borough of Teesside a reference to the Council of the County Borough of Torbay ;

(*f*) there were specified in relation to the Council of the County Borough of Torbay the following index marks (each such mark being preceded for the purposes of the said Schedule by a symbol as shown below) :—

"†AXF, †BXF, †CXF, †DXF, †EXF, †FXF, †GXF, †HXF, †JXF, †KXF, †LXF, †MXF, †NXF, †OXF, †PXF, †RXF, †SXF, †TXF, †UXF, †VXF, †WXF, †XXF & †YXF".

(**a**) 10 & 11 Eliz. 2. c. 13.   (**b**) S.I. 1964/404 (1964 I, p. 635).
(**c**) S.I. 1965/237, 1966/250, 1967/315 (1965 I, p. 593; 1966 I, p. 574; 1967 I, p. 1091).

Given under the Official Seal of the Minister of Transport the 7th March 1968.

(L.S.)   *Barbara Castle,*
                                                                   Minister of Transport.

<hr>

EXPLANATORY NOTE

(This Note is not part of the Regulations.)

These Regulations further amend the Road Vehicles (Index Marks) Regulations 1964, which allocated to certain Councils index marks to be assigned to vehicles upon their registration under the Vehicles (Excise) Act 1962. The principal changes are: —

  (a) to allot to the Council of the new County Borough of Teesside the index marks of the dissolved County Borough Council of Middlesbrough ; and

  (b) to allot to the Council of the new County Borough of Torbay specified index marks.

STATUTORY INSTRUMENTS

1968 No. 357

DENTISTS

The Ancillary Dental Workers Regulations 1968

Laid before Parliament in draft

Made - - - - 8*th March* 1968

Coming into Operation 1st September 1969

ARRANGEMENT OF REGULATIONS

The General Dental Council in exercise of the powers conferred upon them by section forty-one of the Dentists Act, 1957(a), and of all other powers enabling them in that behalf hereby make the following regulations:

PART I

CITATION, COMMENCEMENT AND INTERPRETATION

1.—(1) These regulations may be cited as the Ancillary Dental Workers Regulations 1968, and shall come into force on the 1st day of September 1969.

(2) The Interpretation Act, 1889(b), shall apply to the interpretation of these regulations as it applies to the interpretation of an Act of Parliament.

(3) In these regulations, unless the context otherwise requires:

" the Act " means the Dentists Act, 1957 ;

" the Committee " means the Ancillary Dental Workers Committee set up by the Council in accordance with the provisions of section forty-five of the Act ;

" the Council " means the General Dental Council.

(4) The Ancillary Dental Workers Regulations 1957(c), and the Dental Auxiliaries Regulations 1961(d), are hereby revoked.

(a) 5 & 6 Eliz. 2. c. 28.
(c) S.I. 1957/1423 (1957 I, p. 639).
(b) 52 & 53 Vict. c. 63.
(d) S.I. 1961/1365 (1961 II, p. 2578).

PART II

THE ROLLS AND ENROLMENT

2. The Registrar shall keep a separate roll for each class of ancillary dental workers established by the Council in accordance with sub-section (1) of section forty-one of the Act, and shall enter in such roll, in respect of every person entitled to have his name entered therein, the name, the address, the date on which the entry is made and particulars of the certificate by virtue of which the entry is made.

3.—(1) A person shall be entitled to have his name entered in the roll for a class of ancillary dental workers if he has paid the appropriate fee prescribed in regulation 6 of these regulations and has shown to the satisfaction of the Registrar that he is of good character, that he holds a certificate conferring a right to the inclusion of his name in that roll as defined in regulation 7 of these regulations and that he has complied with any other requirements specified in these or any other regulations made by the Council relating to that class.

(2) Where the Council are satisfied that a person who holds a certificate other than the certificate described in paragraph (3) of regulation 7 of these regulations has taken such courses of study and passed such examinations as furnish sufficient guarantee of that person's possessing the requisite knowledge and skill to practise dentistry to the extent permitted by the regulations for a class of ancillary dental workers, the Council may direct that he shall be entitled to have his name entered in the roll for that class as if his certificate were a certificate granted in accordance with regulation 7 of these regulations.

4.—(1) Except where a name has been erased in accordance with the provisions of these regulations the Registrar shall retain in the appropriate roll of ancillary dental workers the name of any enrolled person in respect of whom he has received before the thirty-first day of March in every year a signed application for retention of the name until the thirty-first day of March in the next following year, accompanied by the appropriate fee.

(2) Not later than the fourteenth day of March in every year, the Registrar shall send to every person whose name is entered in a roll of ancillary dental workers a form of application for retention of a name in that roll, together with a notice of the fee payable and a warning that non-payment entails erasure, but failure to receive a form or notice shall not of itself constitute a ground for retention or restoration of a name.

(3) Where the Registrar on the thirty-first day of March in any year shall not have received from any person whose name is entered in a roll of ancillary dental workers a fee for the retention of that person's name in that roll for the ensuing year, the Registrar shall erase that name from the roll.

(4) The provisions of the foregoing paragraph shall not apply, except by leave of the chairman of the Committee, to any person who is the subject of a submission by the Registrar to the chairman of the Committee in accordance with the provisions of paragraph (1) of regulation 9 of these regulations.

5. The Registrar may restore to a roll of ancillary dental workers a name erased from that roll other than a name erased in accordance with the provisions of Part IV of these regulations upon receipt of an application in the form provided by the Council for the purpose, accompanied by (*a*) the fee for restoration, (*b*) the fee for retention in the roll and (*c*) where the name of the applicant has not been entered in the roll in any of the five years immediately preceding the date of the application, a certificate of identity and good character signed by a Justice of the Peace, or a minister of religion, or a registered medical practitioner or a registered dentist.

Fees Payable for Enrolments, etc.

6. The following are the fees prescribed by the Council under sub-section (7) of section forty-one of the Act:

	£	s.	d.
For first enrolment of a name	2	0	0
For the retention of a name under regulation 4 of these regulations	1	0	0
For restoration of a name under regulation 5 of these regulations	1	0	0

Part III

Training and Examinations

7.—(1) Subject to the provisions of these regulations, the Council may approve courses of instruction held by any of the dental authorities or by such other bodies as the Council may think fit for the purpose of training persons to become members of a class of ancillary dental workers established by regulations made by the Council, and the arrangements for such training:

Provided that the Council shall not approve arrangements under this paragraph unless they are satisfied that the arrangements do not materially impair the facilities for the training of dental students.

(2) The Council may approve examinations held by any of the dental authorities or by such other bodies as the Council may think fit for the purpose of testing the fitness of persons to become members of a class of ancillary dental workers as aforesaid, and the arrangements for such examinations.

(3) Subject to the provisions of the next following paragraph, a certificate granted by a dental authority or other body providing approved examinations for a particular class of ancillary dental workers, which purports to attest the fitness of the person to whom it is granted to practise dentistry to the extent permitted by the regulations for that class, shall be a certificate conferring the right to the inclusion of the name of the person to whom it is granted in the appropriate roll of the class of ancillary dental workers specified in the certificate.

(4) Where in accordance with the provisions of this regulation the Council have approved arrangements made by a dental authority or other body and it subsequently appears to the Council that the arrangements are materially impairing the facilities for the training of dental students or that courses of instruction or examinations held under the arrangements are defective, the Council may withdraw their approval from the arrangements or from the courses of instruction or from the examinations (as the case may be) and a certificate granted by the dental authority or other body concerned after the date on which approval was withdrawn shall not be a certificate for the purposes of the last foregoing paragraph.

8.—(1) The Council shall from time to time appoint a visitor or visitors to visit places where instruction is given and to visit examinations held in accordance with the provisions of the last foregoing regulation.

(2) A visitor appointed under this regulation shall, in relation to each of the places which he visits, report to the Council (a) on the sufficiency of the instruction given ; (b) on the examinations held ; (c) whether the arrangements materially impair the facilities for the training of dental students ; and (d) on any other matters which may be specified by the Council either generally or in any particular case ; but no visitor shall interfere with the giving of any instruction or with any examinations.

(3) A visitor under this regulation shall be entitled to be paid fees and expenses as if he were a visitor appointed in accordance with the provisions of section nine of the Act.

(4) The report of a visitor or visitors appointed under paragraph (1) of this regulation shall be considered by the Council before any decision is taken to withdraw the Council's approval under paragraph (4) of regulation 7 of these regulations.

PART IV

DISCIPLINARY ERASURE OF A NAME FROM A ROLL

9.—(1) Where it is brought to the notice of the Council that an enrolled ancillary dental worker (in this part of these regulations referred to as " the respondent ") either before or after his name has been entered in a roll (a) has been convicted of an offence which if committed in England would be triable on indictment or (b) is alleged to have been guilty of any misconduct, the Registrar, after making such further inquiries as he considers necessary, shall submit the matter to the chairman of the Committee, who shall, if after consultation with the President of the General Dental Council he thinks fit, bring it before the Committee.

Provided that the chairman may after consultation with the President decline to proceed with the matter unless the evidence in support of the charge (except in the case of a conviction) is supported by statutory declaration.

(2) Where the chairman decides to bring a case before the Committee, the Registrar shall invite the respondent to furnish any written statement or explanation which he may desire to offer.

(3) Where a case has been brought before the Committee by the chairman the Committee shall, having regard to any declarations or statements or explanations received with reference thereto, decide whether or not the matter should proceed to a hearing.

(4) The Committee may at any time take the advice of a solicitor appointed by the Council and may instruct him to obtain proofs of evidence in support of the allegations against the respondent.

10. If the Committee decide that the matter should proceed to a hearing, the solicitor shall send to the respondent a " notice of inquiry " specifying the matter alleged against the respondent in the form of a charge or charges and stating the day, time and place appointed for the hearing, together with a copy of these regulations, in a registered letter or in a letter sent by the recorded delivery service addressed to the respondent at the address entered against his name in the roll or at his last known address.

11.—(1) At any hearing held in accordance with these regulations, the respondent shall be entitled to be represented by a friend or by counsel or a solicitor.

(2) If the respondent does not attend, either personally or by representative, the Committee may proceed to hear and determine the case in his absence, so long as they are satisfied that all practicable steps have been taken to bring the notice of inquiry to the attention of the respondent and that (whether he is shown to have received it or not) the substance of the matters alleged therein and the likelihood of an inquiry resulting therefrom have been made known to him.

12. At the hearing of the case, the solicitor or other person appointed by the Committee for the purpose shall first state to the Committee the facts of the case and the charge alleged against the respondent, and shall then adduce evidence in support of the charge, and the respondent or his representative shall be entitled to cross-examine any witness appearing against him on matters relevant to the charge.

13. When the statement of the charge and the evidence in support thereof are concluded, the respondent, or his representative, shall be invited by the chairman to address the Committee and to adduce evidence in answer to the charge, and the solicitor or other person appointed by the Committee for the purpose shall be entitled to cross-examine any witness tendered in answer to the charge.

14. If the Committee find the charges against the respondent proved either in whole or in part, the chairman—

(*a*) may invite the solicitor or other person appointed by the Committee for the purpose to address the Committee and to adduce evidence as to the character and previous history of the respondent, and

(*b*) shall then invite the respondent to address the Committee by way of mitigation and to adduce evidence as aforesaid.

15.—(1) Upon the conclusion of the case the Committee shall, after consideration of the relevant evidence, pronounce their decision either forthwith or at a later date in writing or at a subsequent meeting.

(2) If the Committee determine not to postpone their decision they shall decide whether the Registrar shall be directed to erase the name of the respondent from any roll in which it is entered.

(3) If the Committee postpone their decision to a later date they may invite the respondent to furnish the Registrar shortly before that date with the names and addresses of persons to whom reference may be made confidentially as to his character and conduct and any information received from any such person in consequence of such reference may be considered by the Committee.

(4) As soon as the Committee pronounce their decision, the Registrar shall communicate that decision to the respondent by registered letter or by a letter sent by the recorded delivery service.

16. The Committee may, if they think fit, appoint a barrister, advocate or solicitor to advise them on questions of law arising in any proceedings under this Part of these regulations.

17. Where in the exercise of their powers under sub-paragraph (8) of paragraph 14 of Part II of the First Schedule to the Act the Committee have appointed a sub-committee to deal with disciplinary questions connected with members of a class of ancillary dental workers, the provisions of this Part and of the next following Part of these regulations shall apply as if references to the Committee were references to the sub-committee so appointed.

PART V
RESTORATION AFTER DISCIPLINARY ERASURE

18.—(1) Where the name of an enrolled ancillary dental worker has been removed from a roll under Part IV of these regulations any application for its restoration to the roll shall be made in writing addressed to the Registrar and signed by the applicant, stating the gounds on which the application is made.

(2) The application shall contain the names and addresses of two or more persons, of whom two shall be Justices of the Peace, or ministers of religion, or registered medical practitioners, or registered dentists, or ancillary dental workers whose names have been enrolled for five years or more, or other persons of standing, able and willing to identify the applicant and give evidence as to his character and the nature of his employment both before and since the date of the removal of his name. The Registrar may invite any of the persons aforesaid to furnish information, to be received in confidence, as to the character and conduct of the applicant both before and since the date of the removal of his name.

(3) The Registrar shall thereafter refer the application to the chairman of the Committee, who may require the applicant to support by a statutory declaration any statement made in his application or any further statement which he may think necessary. Subject to the next following paragraph he shall then refer the application to the Committee and shall advise the applicant of his right to attend in person at a meeting of the Committee (the date of which will be notified to him) at which the application will be considered.

(4) The chairman shall not refer to the Committee and the Committee shall not consider any application made within five months from the date of erasure or from the date of any previous application.

19. If, upon consideration of the application and of the evidence furnished in support of it, the Committee are satisfied that the name of the applicant should be restored to the roll, they may direct the Registrar accordingly, and, upon payment where applicable of the fee prescribed in regulation 6 of these regulations for retention of a name in a roll, his name shall be restored to the roll. When considering the application the Committee may take into account any information received under paragraph (2) of the foregoing regulation.

20. The provisions of regulation 16 of these regulations shall apply also to proceedings under this Part of these regulations.

PART VI
DENTAL HYGIENISTS

21. There shall continue to be a class of ancillary dental workers who shall be called dental hygienists. The roll for this class kept by the Registrar in accordance with the provisions of regulation 2 of these regulations shall be called the roll of dental hygienists.

22. In accordance with the provisions of sub-section (4) of section forty one of the Act, a person enrolled in the roll of dental hygienists (hereafter called a dental hygienist) shall be authorised to use the title " dental hygienist ".

23.—(1) Subject to the provisions of this regulation, a dental hygienist shall be permitted to carry out dental work (amounting to the practice of dentistry) of the following kinds:

(*a*) cleaning and polishing teeth ;

(*b*) scaling teeth (that is to say, the removal of tartar, deposits, accretions and stains from those parts of the teeth which are exposed or which are directly beneath the free margins of the gums, including the application of medicaments appropriate thereto) ;

(*c*) the application to the teeth of solutions of sodium or stannous fluoride or such other similar prophylactic solutions as the Council may from time to time determine ;

(*d*) giving advice within the meaning of subsection (1) of section thirty-three of the Act on matters relating to oral hygiene ;

but shall not be permitted to carry out dental work amounting to the practice of dentistry of any other kind.

(2) A dental hygienist shall not be permitted to carry out such dental work authorised as aforesaid except under the direction of a registered dentist and after the registered dentist has examined the patient and has indicated to the dental hygienist the course of treatment to be provided for the patient.

(3) Except in the course of providing national or local authority health services, a dental hygienist shall carry out such dental work authorised as aforesaid only under the direct personal supervision of a registered dentist who is on the premises at which the hygienist is carrying out such work at the time at which it is being carried out.

24. Courses of instruction for the dental hygienist class shall not be approved by the Council for the purposes of paragraph (1) of regulation 7 of these regulations unless such courses extend over a period of at least nine months.

25. The possessor of the Minister of Health's Certificate of Proficiency in Oral Hygiene shall be entitled to have his name entered in the roll of dental hygienists as if that certificate were a certificate granted in accordance with regulation 7 of these regulations.

PART VII

DENTAL AUXILIARIES

26. There shall be established a class of ancillary dental workers who shall be called dental auxiliaries. The roll for this class kept by the Registrar in accordance with the provisions of regulation 2 of these regulations shall be called the roll of dental auxiliaries.

27. In accordance with the provisions of sub-section (4) of section forty-one of the Act, a person enrolled in the roll of dental auxiliaries (hereafter called a dental auxiliary) shall be authorised to use the title " dental auxiliary ".

28.—(1) Subject to the provisions of this regulation, a dental auxiliary shall be permitted to carry out dental work (amounting to the practice of dentistry) of the following kinds:

(a) extracting deciduous teeth under local infiltration anaesthesia ;

(b) undertaking simple dental fillings ;

(c) cleaning and polishing teeth ;

(d) scaling teeth (that is to say, the removal of tartar, deposits, accretions and stains from those parts of the surfaces of the teeth which are exposed or which are directly beneath the free margins of the gums, including the application of medicaments appropriate thereto) ;

(e) the application to the teeth of solutions of sodium or stannous fluoride or such other similar prophylactic solutions as the Council may from time to time determine ;

(f) giving advice within the meaning of sub-section (1) of section thirty-three of the Act, such as may be necessary to the proper performance of the dental work referred to in this regulation, and on matters relating to oral hygiene ;

but shall not be permitted to carry out dental work amounting to the practice of dentistry of any other kind.

(2) A dental auxiliary shall not be permitted to carry out such dental work authorised as aforesaid except (a) in the course of providing national or local authority health services (b) under the direction of a registered dentist and (c) after the registered dentist has examined the patient and has indicated in writing to the dental auxiliary the specific treatment to be provided for the patient by the said auxiliary.

29. Courses of instruction for the dental auxiliary class shall not be approved by the Council for the purposes of paragraph (1) of regulation 7 of these regulations unless such courses extend over a period of at least two academic years.

30. The possessor of the Council's Certificate of Proficiency as a Dental Auxiliary shall be entitled to have his name entered in the roll of dental auxiliaries as if that certificate were a certificate granted in accordance with regulation 7 of these regulations.

The Common Seal of the General Dental
Council was hereto affixed in the presence
of : —

ROBERT BRADLAW, *President,*

DAVID HINDLEY-SMITH, *Registrar,*

this 8th day of March, 1968.

EXPLANATORY NOTE

(This Note is not part of the Regulations.)

These regulations contain in Parts II to V general provisions governing the enrolment of classes of ancillary dental workers, including provisions as to the training and examinations leading to enrolment and the machinery for removing a name from the roll and for restoring it.

Parts VI and VII provide for the establishment of specific classes of ancillary dental workers to be known as "dental hygienists" and "dental auxiliaries" and regulations 23 and 28 specify the kinds of dental work dental hygienists and dental auxiliaries may undertake and the conditions under which they may undertake such work.

The regulations were approved in draft:—

(*a*) by the Privy Council on the 12th day of January, 1968.

(*b*) by a resolution of the House of Lords on the 27th day of February, 1968.

(*c*) by a resolution of the House of Commons on the 15th day of February, 1968.

STATUTORY INSTRUMENTS

1968 No. 361 (C.6)

ADMINISTRATION OF ESTATES

The Finance Act 1967 (Section 10) Appointed Day Order 1968

Made - - - *12th March* 1968

The Lord Chancellor and the Secretary of State for Scotland, in exercise of the powers conferred on them by section 10 of the Finance Act 1967(a), hereby make the following order :—

1. The day appointed for the purposes of section 10 of the Finance Act 1967 shall be 1st April 1968.

2. This order may be cited as the Finance Act 1967 (Section 10) Appointed Day Order 1968.

Dated 8th March 1968.

Gardiner, C.

Dated 12th March 1968.

William Ross.

EXPLANATORY NOTE

(*This Note is not part of the Order.*)

This order appoints 1st April 1968 as the day from which the enactments specified in Part V of Schedule 16 to the Finance Act 1967 are to cease to have effect ; these enactments confer on the Commissioners of Customs and Excise functions in respect of grants of representation in the case of small estates.

(a) 1967 c. 54.

STATUTORY INSTRUMENTS

1968 No. 362

ROAD TRAFFIC

The Motor Vehicles (Construction and Use) (Amendment) Regulations 1968

Made - - - -	*11th March* 1968
Laid before Parliament	*25th March* 1968
Coming into Operation	*1st July* 1968

The Minister of Transport, in exercise of her powers under section 64(1) of the Road Traffic Act 1960(a) as amended by section 51 of, and Schedule 4 to, the Road Traffic Act 1962(b) and of all other powers her enabling in that behalf, and after consultation with representative organisations in accordance with the provisions of section 260(2) of the said Act of 1960, hereby makes the following Regulations:—

1.—(1) These Regulations shall come into operation on 1st July 1968, and may be cited as the Motor Vehicles (Construction and Use) (Amendment) Regulations 1968.

(2) The Interpretation Act 1889(c) shall apply for the interpretation of these Regulations as it applies for the interpretation of an Act of Parliament.

(3) In these Regulations the expression "the Principal Regulations" means the Motor Vehicles (Construction and Use) Regulations 1966(d), as amended(e).

2. The Principal Regulations shall be varied by inserting in Regulation 3(1) next after the definition of the expression "dual-purpose vehicle", the two following definitions:—

" "engineering plant" has the same meaning as in Part III of the Motor Vehicles (Authorisation of Special Types) General Order 1966(f);

"exhaust brake" means a device with which a vehicle is fitted as a means of using cylinder pressure or exhaust back pressure so as to provide for the vehicle a retarding force greater than would ordinarily result for a vehicle not so fitted;."

3. The Principal Regulations shall be varied by inserting next after Regulation 21 the following Regulation:—

(a) 8 & 9 Eliz. 2. c. 16.
(c) 52 & 53 Vict. c. 63.
(e) There is no relevant amending instrument.

(b) 10 & 11 Eliz. 2. c. 59.
(d) S.I. 1966/1288 (1966 III. p. 3493).
(f) S.I. 1966/1289 (1966 III. p. 3579).

"Noise

21A.—(1) Except as provided in the next following paragraph of this Regulation, every motor vehicle registered after 1st April 1970 shall be so constructed that, at a time when the noise emitted by it is measured under the specified conditions by an apparatus of the kind prescribed by paragraph (3) of this Regulation, the sound level (A weighting) in decibels indicated by that apparatus in relation to the said noise so measured does not exceed the sound level which appears in Column 2 of Schedule 9 as the maximum sound level (A weighting) in decibels permitted for the relevant class or description of vehicle shown against that sound level in Column 1 of that Schedule.

(2) This Regulation shall not apply—

(*a*) to a motor vehicle proceeding to a place where, by previous arrangement—

(i) noise emitted by it is about to be measured for the purpose of ascertaining whether or not that vehicle complies with this Regulation, or

(ii) the vehicle is about to be mechanically adjusted, modified or equipped for the purpose of securing that it so complies, or

(*b*) to a motor vehicle returning from such a place immediately after the noise has been so measured, or the vehicle has been so adjusted, modified or equipped, or

(*c*) to a road roller.

(3) The apparatus prescribed for the purposes of paragraph (1) of this Regulation shall be a noise meter—

(*a*) which, at the time when it is used for those purposes, is in good working order and complies with the requirements laid down by the British Standards Institution for vehicle noise meters in Part I of the British Standard Specification for Sound Level Meters published on 7th September 1962 under the number B.S. 3539: 1962, and

(*b*) of which the overall performance and calibration have been checked as provided by clause 7 of that British Standard in a test of the meter conducted not more than 12 months before the date of the measurement made in accordance with the said paragraph (1), and

(*c*) in respect of which a certificate recording the date on which the calibration has been so checked has been issued by the National Phsyical Laboratory, the British Standards Institution or the Minister.

(4) In this Regulation, "the specified conditions" means the method of measuring the noise emitted by motor vehicles (excluding signalling devices) which is described by the British Standard Method for the Measurement of Noise Emitted by Motor Vehicles published on 24th June 1966 under the number B.S. 3425: 1966.

(5) The definition of sound level (A weighting) in decibels contained in clause 2 of the British Standard numbered B.S. 3539: 1962 shall apply for the purposes of this Regulation and Schedule 9."

4. The Principal Regulations shall have effect as though from Regulation 86 (which relates to excessive noise) there were omitted the words "either directly or indirectly as a result of" (which occur in the second and third lines of the Regulation) and the two sub-paragraphs (*a*) and (*b*) which immediately follow those words.

5. The Principal Regulations shall be varied by inserting next after Regulation 87 the following Regulation:—

"Limitation of noise by measurement

87A.—(1) Except as provided in paragraph (4) of this Regulation, this Regulation applies to any vehicle which is a motor vehicle registered on or after 1st January 1931 or which is a trailer.

(2) Subject to the following provisions of this Regulation, no person shall use or cause or permit to be used on a road any vehicle to which this Regulation applies if—

(*a*) at a time when the noise emitted by that vehicle is measured under the conditions set out in Schedule 10 by an apparatus of the kind prescribed by paragraph (5) of this Regulation, there is indicated by that apparatus in relation to the said noise so measured a sound level (A weighting) in decibels which exceeds the maximum sound level permitted in relation to that vehicle by the next following paragraph, and

(*b*) the sound level of such noise as is described in paragraph 4 of Schedule 10 when measured in accordance with the provisions of that paragraph is found to be at least 10 decibels (A weighting) below the sound level indicated as hereinbefore provided by the said apparatus in relation to the noise emitted by the vehicle.

(3) The maximum permitted sound level for the purposes of the last preceding paragraph shall be—

(*a*) if the vehicle to which this Regulation applies is a motor vehicle registered before 1st November 1970, the sound level (A weighting) in decibels which appears in Column 3 of Schedule 9 as the maximum sound level permitted for the relevant class or description of vehicle shown against that sound level in Column 1 of that Schedule, and

(*b*) if the vehicle to which this Regulation applies is a motor vehicle registered on or after 1st November 1970, the sound level (A weighting) in decibels which appears in Column 4 of Schedule 9 as the maximum sound level permitted for the relevant class or description of vehicle shown against that sound level in Column 1 of that Schedule.

(4) This Regulation shall not apply—

(*a*) to a motor vehicle proceeding to a place where, by previous arrangement—

(i) noise emitted by it is about to be measured for the purpose of ascertaining whether or not that vehicle complies with Regulation 21A, or

(ii) the vehicle is about to be mechanically adjusted, modified or equipped for the purpose of securing that it so complies, or (*b*) to a motor vehicle returning from such a place immediately after the noise has been so measured, or the vehicle has been so adjusted, modified or equipped, or

(*c*) to a vehicle at a time when it is stationary otherwise than through enforced stoppage owing to the necessities of traffic and at the same time Regulation 88, by virtue of the proviso thereto, does not apply in relation to that vehicle, or

(*d*) to a motor vehicle registered before the date mentioned in paragraph (3)(*a*) of this Regulation at a time when an exhaust brake with which that vehicle is fitted is in operation, or

(*e*) to a road roller.

(5) The apparatus prescribed for the purposes of paragraph (2) of this Regulation shall be a noise meter of the same kind as that prescribed for the purposes of paragraph (1) of Regulation 21A and paragraph (3) of that Regulation shall have effect in relation to this Regulation as if any references therein to paragraph (1) of Regulation 21A were references to paragraph (2) of this Regulation.

(6) It shall be a good defence to proceedings taken in respect of the use of a vehicle which does not comply with this Regulation to prove the matters which would, by virtue of either proviso (i) or proviso (ii) to Regulation 86, constitute a good defence to proceedings taken in respect of the use of a motor vehicle which does not comply with that Regulation.

(7) The definition of sound level (A weighting) in decibels specified in Regulation 21A (5) shall apply for the purposes of this Regulation and Schedules 9 and 10.

(8) In this Regulation and Schedule 10, any reference to noise emitted by a vehicle shall be construed as including a reference to noise howsoever arising which is attributable to any load, burden or goods carried on or by the vehicle or to anything (other than an audible warning instrument fitted in accordance with Regulation 20(1) or an instrument or apparatus fitted in accordance with Regulation 20(5)) fitted to it, or attributable to the manner in which the vehicle is loaded or fitted.

(9) Where any motor vehicle to which this Regulation applies is drawing a trailer, this Regulation and Schedules 9 and 10 shall have effect in relation to that motor vehicle as if any reference to it were a reference both to the motor vehicle and to the trailer drawn thereby."

6. The Principal Regulations shall be varied by adding after Schedule 8 the following Schedules:—

SCHEDULE 9

Maximum Sound Levels (A weighting) in Decibels (dBA)

Column 1	Column 2	Column 3	Column 4
Class or description of vehicle	Regulation 21A Maximum (dBA)	Regulation 87A(3)(*a*) Maximum (dBA)	Regulation 87A(3)(*b*) Maximum (dBA)
1. Motor cycle of which the cylinder capacity of the engine does not exceed 50 cubic centimetres	77	80	80
2. Motor cycle of which the said cylinder capacity exceeds 125 cubic centimetres	86	90	89
3. Any other motor cycle	82	90	85
4. Goods vehicle to which Regulation 28 applies and which is equipped with a plate complying with the requirements of paragraph (2) of that Regulation and showing particulars of a maximum gross weight of more than 3½ tons	89	92	92
5. Goods vehicle registered before 1st January 1968 which complies with the requirements of Regulation 70(3)(*c*) and is equipped with such a plate as aforesaid notwithstanding that Regulation 28 does not apply to that vehicle by reason only that it was so registered	89	92	92
6. Motor tractor	89	92	92
7. Locomotive	89	92	92
8. Land tractor	89	92	92
9. Works truck	89	92	92
10. Engineering plant	89	92	92

Column 1	Column 2	Column 3	Column 4
Class or description of vehicle	Regulation 21A Maximum (dBA)	Regulation 87A(3)(a) Maximum (dBA)	Regulation 87A(3)(b) Maximum (dBA)
11. Passenger vehicle constructed for the carriage of more than 12 passengers exclusive of the driver	89	92	92
12. Any other passenger vehicle	84	87	87
13. Motor car within the meaning of section 253(2)(b) of the 1960 Act not being a goods vehicle of either of the kinds described in paragraphs 4 and 5 of this Column	85	88	88
14. Any other vehicle not elsewhere classified or described in this column	85	92	88

SCHEDULE 10

Conditions mentioned in Regulation 87A(2)

1. At the time when the noise emitted by the vehicle is measured, the microphone of the apparatus shall be so placed that the top of the microphone is set at a height of not less than 3 feet 9 inches and not more than 4 feet 1 inch above a point at ground level which is not less than 17 feet away from the nearest part of the carriageway on which the vehicle is being used.

2.—(1) For the purposes of this paragraph, the area in the vicinity of the microphone shall be treated as comprising areas the situation and extent of which shall be determined by reference to a line joining a point at ground level above which the microphone is placed to the said nearest part of the carriageway and in accordance with the diagram at the end of this Schedule including the directions contained therein; and the said areas shown marked I, II, III or IV on the said diagram are hereafter in this Schedule respectively referred to as the areas so marked.

(2) At the time when the noise is measured there shall not be:—

    (*a*) in the area marked I, any physical object higher than 2 feet above ground level;

    (*b*) in the area marked II, any physical object higher than 3 feet above ground level; and

    (*c*) in the areas marked III or IV, any physical object higher than 5 feet above ground level:

Provided that the requirements at (*c*) above shall not apply in relation to the following objects or to any of them, that is to say:—

    (i) to plants, shrubs, trees or any other kind of vegetation, or

    (ii) to any physical object, of which a continuous surface less than 1 foot wide over all its height would be visible in daylight, to a person looking at it from the point above which the microphone is placed and whose eye level is at the height of the microphone.

(3) For the purpose of sub-paragraph (2) of this paragraph, neither the vehicle nor any part thereof, nor any person nor thing in or on the vehicle, nor the apparatus nor any part thereof, nor any persons being less than 3 in number attending the apparatus, shall be taken into account.

3. At the time when the noise emitted by the vehicle is measured, the vehicle shall be wholly or partly on a part of the road which falls within the area marked IV on the said diagram.

4. As soon as the vehicle has left the area marked IV on the said diagram the apparatus shall be used to measure the sound level (A weighting) in decibels of such noise as is then capable of affecting the sound level indications of the apparatus, such measurement being carried out in the manner in which the measurement of the sound emitted by the vehicle was carried out and under the conditions applicable under the foregoing provisions of this Schedule, excluding paragraphs 2(2)(*c*) and 3.

DIAGRAM

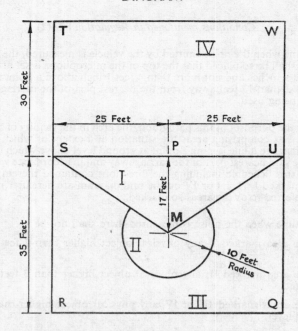

DIAGRAM DIRECTIONS (*including Key and Dimensions*)

M = a point at ground level above which the microphone is placed.

P = the nearest part of the carriageway to the microphone.

The area marked I consists of the triangle MSU.

The area marked II consists of so much of the circle of radius 10 feet with centre at M as does not enclose any part of the area marked I.

The area marked III consists of so much of the rectangle RSUQ as does not enclose any parts of the areas marked I or II.

The area marked IV consists of the rectangle STWU.

DIMENSIONS

The distance MP is not less than 17 feet.

The lengths of SR, and UQ are each 35 feet.

The lengths of TW, SU, and RQ are each 50 feet.

The lengths of SP, and PU are each 25 feet.

The lengths of TS, and WU are each 30 feet.

Given under the official Seal of the Minister of Transport the 11th March 1968.

(L.S.)

Barbara Castle,
Minister of Transport.

EXPLANATORY NOTE

(This Note is not part of the Regulations.)

These Regulations further amend the Motor Vehicles (Construction and Use) Regulations 1966 by—

(i) requiring that every motor vehicle registered after 1st April 1970 shall be so constructed that when the noise emitted by it is measured under specified conditions by an apparatus of a prescribed kind the sound level indicated by the apparatus in relation to that noise does not exceed the maximum sound level (A weighting) in decibels which appears in Schedule 9 for the class or description of motor vehicle to which it belongs—(Regulation 21A(1));

(ii) providing for Regulation 21A not to apply to vehicles undertaking journeys for certain purposes and to road rollers—(Regulation 21A(2));

(iii) prescribing as the kind of apparatus mentioned in (i) above a noise meter, its specification, performance and calibration—(Regulation 21A(3));

(iv) defining the specified conditions referred to in paragraph (i) above as the method of measuring the noise emitted by motor vehicles described by British Standard B.S. 3425:1966 and prescribing the definition of "sound level (A weighting) in decibels" to apply for the purposes of this Regulation and of Schedule 9 (Regulation 21A(4) and (5));

(v) omitting from Regulation 86 certain provisions with regard to potential causes of excessive noise;

(vi) requiring that there shall not be used or permitted to be used on a road a motor vehicle registered after 1930 or trailer if—

(a) when the noise emitted by it is measured under the conditions set out in Schedule 10 by an apparatus of a prescribed kind there is indicated by the apparatus in relation to that noise a sound level which exceeds, in the case of a motor vehicle registered before 1st November 1970 the maximum sound level prescribed in column 3 of Schedule 9 and in the case of a motor vehicle registered after 31st October 1970 the level prescribed in column 4 of Schedule 9, and

(b) the sound level of such noise as is described in paragraph 4 of Schedule 10 and measured in accordance with that paragraph is found to be at least 10 decibels (A weighting) below the sound level indicated by the apparatus in relation to the noise emitted by the vehicle—(Regulation 87A(2) and (3));

(vii) providing for Regulation 87A not to apply to vehicles undertaking journeys for certain purposes, to road rollers and to certain vehicles while stationary or while using an exhaust brake—(Regulation 87A(4));

(viii) prescribing as the kind of apparatus mentioned in (vi) above a noise meter as provided by Regulation 21A(3) see paragraph (iii) above—(Regulation 87A(5));

(ix) providing certain defences in the event of proceedings, making provision for a definition of the expression "sound level (A weighting) in decibels" for the purposes of Regulation 87A and Schedules 9 and 10, and for the way in which references in Regulation 87A and Schedule 10 to the expression "noise emitted by a vehicle" are to be construed—(Regulation 87A(6),(7) and (8));

(x) providing for the case where a motor vehicle is drawing a trailer that Regulation 87A and Schedules 9 and 10 are to have effect in relation to the motor vehicle as if references to it were references both to that vehicle and to the trailer drawn by it—(Regulation 87A(9));

(xi) setting out the maximum sound levels permitted for each listed class or description of vehicle—(Schedule 9); and lastly

(xii) providing the conditions under which noise is measured for the purposes of Regulation 87A(2) (Schedule 10).

STATUTORY INSTRUMENTS

1968 No. 366

HOUSING, ENGLAND AND WALES

The Assistance for House Purchase and Improvement (Qualifying Lenders) Order 1968

Made - - - -	12*th March* 1968
Coming into Operation	20*th March* 1968

The Minister of Housing and Local Government, in exercise of his powers under sections 27 and 32(2) of the Housing Subsidies Act 1967(a), and after consultation with the Chief Registrar of Friendly Societies as required by section 27(2) of the said Act, hereby orders as follows:

1. This order may be cited as the Assistance for House Purchase and Improvement (Qualifying Lenders) Order 1968 and shall come into operation on 20th March 1968.

2. The Interpretation Act 1889(b) shall apply for the interpretation of this order as it applies for the interpretation of an Act of Parliament.

3. The Elsecar, Hoyland and Wentworth Benefit Building Society shall be a qualifying lender for the purposes of all the provisions of Part II of the Housing Subsidies Act 1967.

Given under the official seal of the Minister of Housing and Local Government on 12th March 1968.

(L.S.)

J. E. Beddoe,
Under Secretary,
Ministry of Housing and Local Government.

(a) 1967 c. 29.   (b) 1889 c. 63.

EXPLANATORY NOTE
(This Note is not part of the Order.)

By this order, the Minister of Housing and Local Government, after appropriate consultation, prescribes a further body as a qualifying lender for the purpose of operating the Option Mortgage Scheme. This body is additional to the bodies already jointly prescribed by previous orders made by the Minister, the Secretary of State for Scotland and the Secretary of State for Wales, all local authorities with powers to lend for house purchase and improvement, all building societies designated under section 1 of the House Purchase and Housing Act 1959 (c. 33) (i.e. those with "trustee" status), all development corporations, the Commission for the New Towns and the three Ministers themselves, all these being already designated as qualifying lenders by section 27(1) of the Housing Subsidies Act 1967 itself.

STATUTORY INSTRUMENTS

1968 No. 370

CUSTOMS AND EXCISE

The Export of Goods (Control) (Amendment No. 2) Order 1968

Made - - -	13*th March* 1968
Coming into Operation	27*th March* 1968

The Board of Trade, in exercise of the powers conferred upon them by section 1 of the Import, Export and Customs Powers (Defence) Act 1939(a), hereby order as follows :—

1. The Export of Goods (Control) Order 1967(b), as amended (c), shall have effect as if Part I of Schedule 1 thereto were amended as provided in the Schedule hereto.

2. The Interpretation Act 1889(d) shall apply to the interpretation of this Order as it applies to the interpretation of an Act of Parliament.

3. This Order may be cited as the Export of Goods (Control) (Amendment No. 2) Order 1968 and shall come into operation on 27th March 1968.

R. L. Davies,
An Assistant Secretary
of the Board of Trade.

13th March 1968.

SCHEDULE

Amendments to Part 1 of Schedule 1

1. In Group 6 :—
   delete the entry relating to pipe and tubing (metal) and substitute :—
   "Pipe and tubing, the following :—
       (1) Pipe and tubing made of polytetrafluoroethylene or polychlorotrifluoroethylene whether or not reinforced with another material.

(a) 1939 c. 69.   **(b)** S.I. 1967/675 (1967 I, p. 2080).
(c) S.I. 1968/132 (1968 I, p. 353).   **(d)** 1889 c. 63.

(2) Pipe and tubing made of any material lined with or covered with polytetrafluoroethylene or polychlorotrifluoroethylene."

2. In Group 7:—
delete the entries relating to fork and other lift trucks and to mechanically propelled road vehicles or chassis, and substitute:—

"Automotive road vehicles, tractors, fork and other lift trucks possessing or built to military specifications differing materially from normal commercial specifications".

EXPLANATORY NOTE

(This Note is not part of the Order.)

This Order further amends the Export of Goods (Control) Order 1967 (hereinafter referred to as "the principal Order"). The changes are as follows:—

(1) Export control is removed (except for exports to Southern Rhodesia) from civilian type multi-axle-drive vehicles and tractors.

(2) The description of metal pipe and tubing referred to in Schedule 1, Group 6 to the principal Order has been amended.

STATUTORY INSTRUMENTS

1968 No. 373 (S. 34)

POLICE

The Police (Common Police Services) (Scotland) Order 1968

Made - - - -	11*th March* 1968
Laid before Parliament	21*st March* 1968
Coming into Operation	22*nd March* 1968

In exercise of the powers conferred on me by section 36(5) of the Police (Scotland) Act 1967(a), and of all other powers enabling me in that behalf, and after consultation with the associations appearing to me representative of police authorities, I hereby order as follows:—

1. This order may be cited as the Police (Common Police Services) (Scotland) Order 1968 and shall come into operation on 22nd March 1968.

2. The Police (Common Police Services) (Scotland) Order 1964(b) is hereby revoked.

3. Section 36(4) of the Police (Scotland) Act 1967 (which provides for the recovery by the Secretary of State from police authorities and joint police committees of one-half of the expenses incurred by the Secretary of State in establishing and maintaining any central training institution) shall apply to the expenses incurred by me for the purposes of police forces generally, on or in connection with—

(a) the Police (Scotland) Examinations Board.

(b) police representative and negotiating machinery.

(c) the Scottish Criminal Record Office.

(d) attendance at meetings of the International Criminal Police Organisation.

(e) attendance of officers at the Police College for England and Wales.

(f) the National Forensic Science Laboratory for Scotland.

(g) the Standard Entrance Examination for entry to police forces in Scotland.

William Ross,
One of Her Majesty's
Principal Secretaries of State.

St. Andrew's House,
Edinburgh, 1.
11th March 1968.

(a) 1967 c. 77.   (b) S.I. 1964/2030 (1964 III, p. 5104).

EXPLANATORY NOTE
(*This Note is not part of the Order.*)

This Order revokes and re-enacts with additions the Police (Common Police Services) (Scotland) Order 1964. The two new services are the National Forensic Science Laboratory for Scotland and the Standard Entrance Examination for all entrants to Scottish police forces.

STATUTORY INSTRUMENTS

1968 No. 375

EDUCATION, ENGLAND AND WALES

The Remuneration of Teachers (Primary and Secondary Schools) Amending Order 1968

Made - - - -	*13th March* 1968
Coming into Operation	*14th March* 1968

Whereas—

(1) in pursuance of section 2(2) of the Remuneration of Teachers Act 1965(a) (hereinafter referred to as "the Act") the Committee constituted under section 1 of the Act for the purpose of considering the remuneration payable to teachers in primary and secondary schools maintained by local education authorities (hereinafter referred to as "the Committee") have transmitted to the Secretary of State for Education and Science (hereinafter referred to as "the Secretary of State") certain recommendations agreed on by them with respect to the remuneration of such teachers;

(2) there is in force an order made under section 2(4) of the Act with respect to the remuneration of such teachers, namely, the Remuneration of Teachers (Primary and Secondary Schools) Order 1967(b);

(3) it appears to the Secretary of State that effect can more conveniently be given to the recommendations of the Committee by amending the scales and other provisions set out in the document referred to in the said Order, namely, the document published by Her Majesty's Stationery Office under the title "SCALES OF SALARIES FOR TEACHERS IN PRIMARY AND SECONDARY SCHOOLS, ENGLAND AND WALES, 1967";

(4) in pursuance of section 2(5) of the Act the Secretary of State has prepared a draft Order setting out the amendments of the scales and other provisions contained in the said document which, in his opinion, are requisite for giving effect to the recommendations of the Committee; and

(5) the Secretary of State, as required by section 2(6) of the Act, has consulted the Committee with respect to the draft order and the Committee have made no representations with respect thereto.

Now therefore the Secretary of State, in pursuance of section 2(6) of the Act, hereby orders as follows—

Citation and Commencement

1. This Order may be cited as the Remuneration of Teachers (Primary and Secondary Schools) Amending Order 1968 and shall come into operation on 14th March 1968.

(a) 1965 c. 3.   (b) S.I. 1967/1305 (1967 III, p. 3916).

Interpretation

2. The Interpretation Act 1889(a) shall apply for the interpretation of this Order as it applies for the interpretation of an Act of Parliament.

Amendment of Document

3. The scales and other provisions set out in the document published by Her Majesty's Stationery Office as aforesaid are hereby amended—

> (a) with effect from 1st July 1967, in the manner specified in Schedule 1 to this Order; and

> (b) with effect from 1st April 1968, in the manner specified in Schedule 2 to this Order.

SCHEDULE 1

AMENDMENTS EFFECTIVE FROM 1ST JULY 1967

1. In Section N of the document (which relates to allowances for heads of departments) the following paragraph shall be substituted for paragraph 3:—

"3. In Special Schools in which there is a substantial number of senior pupils the Local Education Authority may establish posts of Head of Department of such number as the Authority deems appropriate. Posts so established shall be Grade A except that an Authority may, in its discretion, establish posts Grade B in schools in Group 6(S) or above."

2. In Part A of Appendix IV of the document (which specifies the qualifications entitling a qualified assistant teacher to receive an addition to the appropriate salary scale)—

> (a) the following qualification shall be added to paragraph 2(c):—

"Leicester Diploma in the Teaching of Science"; and

> (b) the following course shall be substituted for that specified in paragraph 3(a)(i):—

"(i) A course of initial training in teaching as defined by Regulation 6 of the Training of Teachers Regulations 1967 (or the corresponding provisions of the appropriate regulations in force from time to time) of at least one year's full-time duration, or the equivalent part-time."

3. In Appendix V of the document (which specifies the qualifications entitling a qualified assistant teacher to be placed in Group II or Group III)—

> (a) the following qualifications shall be substituted for those specified in paragraph VIII(13) and paragraph VIII(41) respectively of Part B:—

"(13) Professional Associateship of the Royal Institution of Chartered Surveyors (formerly Professional Associate of the Surveyors Institution) by examination provided that:

> (i) the course for Associate Membership was entered upon on or after 1st October 1966, and the Associate Member satisfied the General Educational Requirements for enrolment to Student Membership introduced by the Institution with effect from that date, or

> (ii) where the course was entered upon before 1st October 1966, the Associate Member has had four years' professional experience after passing the examination (see paragraph 5 of Part A of this Appendix)."; and

"(41) (a) The Extra Master's Certificate of Competency of the Board of Trade (or Ministry of Transport) by examination passed after 1st March 1931.

(b) The Extra First Class Engineer's Certificate of Competency of the Board of Trade (or Ministry of Transport).";

(a) 1889 c. 63.

(*b*) the following qualification shall be added to paragraph VIII of Part B:—

"(43) Associate Membership of the Institute of Quantity Surveyors by examination, provided that the course for Associate Membership was entered upon on or after 1st October 1966, and the Associate Member satisfied the General Education Requirements for enrolment to Student Membership introduced by the Institute with effect from that date."

(*c*) the following degrees shall be added to Part D:—

"Leeds

Degree
Bachelor of Education (B.Ed.)

Higher degree
Master of Philosophy (M.Phil.)

Newcastle upon Tyne

Higher degree
Master of Fine Art (M.A.)":— and

(*d*) the higher degree of Bachelor of Education (Ed. B.) of the University of Glasgow shown in Part D shall be such a degree conferred under the Ordinances of the University relating thereto prior to that of 1966.

4. In Appendix VII of the document (which relates to unit totals and review averages)—

(*a*) the following paragraph shall be substituted for paragraph 3 of Part A:—

"3. In the case of Special Schools (including Hospital Schools), a procedure similar to that described in paragraph 1 above shall be followed. The further classification of the enrolled pupils shall be on the basis of the specific handicap of the individual pupil and not according to the age of the pupil. Where a pupil has multiple handicaps, the handicap from which he/she is suffering which attracts the highest unit value shall count for this purpose.

For the purposes of this document the unit total (S) for 1967 and subsequent years shall be calculated as follows:

	For each pupil count
Delicate or Educationally sub-normal children	4 units
Blind, Partially sighted, Epileptic or Physically Handicapped children	5 units
Deaf, Partially hearing, Maladjusted or children suffering from Speech Defect	6 units

The unit total (S) for 1965 and 1966 shall be calculated in accordance with the provisions of paragraph 3 of Part A of Appendix VII to the Primary and Secondary Salaries Document 1965.";

(*b*) the following paragraph shall be substituted for paragraph 1 of Part B:—

"1. Subject to the conditions of paragraph 2 immediately following, the Head Teacher Scale and the Deputy Head Teacher Allowance shall be determined as follows:

(*a*) for the period from 1st July 1967 to 31st March 1970 on the review average for 1967 in the case of schools other than Special Schools and on the review average for 1967 or the unit total for 1967, whichever is the greater, in the case of Special Schools;

(*b*) for the three years beginning 1st April 1970 on the review average for 1970;

(*c*) for every three years thereafter beginning 1st April the procedure in (b) above shall apply with appropriate adjustment of dates."; and
2c

(c) the following paragraph shall be substituted for paragraph 1 of Part C:—

"1. Subject to the Conditions of paragraph 2 immediately following, the "score" for graded posts for a school or department shall be calculated as follows:

(a) for the period from 1st July 1967 to 31st March 1970 on the review average for 1967 in the case of schools other than Special Schools and on the unit total for 1967 in the case of Special Schools;

(b) for the three years beginning 1st April 1970 on the review average for 1970;

(c) for every three years thereafter beginning 1st April the procedure in (b) above shall apply with appropriate adjustment of dates."

SCHEDULE 2

AMENDMENT EFFECTIVE FROM 1ST APRIL 1968

The following Section shall be inserted in the document after the existing Section S:—

"SECTION SS

ADDITIONAL PAYMENTS FOR TEACHERS IN SCHOOLS OF EXCEPTIONAL DIFFICULTY

1. The following additional payments shall be made to teachers employed in a school of exceptional difficulty—

(a) to a qualified teacher: £75 per annum; and

(b) to any other teacher: £60 per annum.

2.—(1) For the purposes of this Section a school of exceptional difficulty shall be a school which, having regard to one or more of the criteria mentioned in sub-paragraph (2) below, is recognised by the Secretary of State as such a school on the recommendation of the Local Education Authority.

(2) For the purposes of sub-paragraph (1) above the criteria shall be:—

(a) the social and economic status of the parents of children at the school;

(b) the absence of amenities in the homes of children attending the school;

(c) the proportion of children in the school receiving free meals or belonging to families in receipt of supplementary benefits under the Ministry of Social Security Act 1966; and

(d) the proportion of children in the school with serious linguistic difficulties.

(3) A school of exceptional difficulty shall—

(a) be recognised as such a school from 1st April 1968 or from such later date as may be specified by the Secretary of State in giving notice of his recognition to the Local Education Authority; and

(b) cease to be recognised as such a school on its reorganisation or on 31st March 1970, whichever shall be the earlier.

3. The provisions of Section Q of this document shall not apply in relation to an additional payment under this Section."

Given under the Official Seal of the Secretary of State for Education and Science
on 13th March 1968.

(L.S.)   *Patrick Gordon Walker,*
                                 Secretary of State for Education and Science.

EXPLANATORY NOTE

(This Note is not part of the Order)

This Order amends the scales and other provisions relating to the remuneration of teachers in primary and secondary schools maintained by local education authorities in accordance with recommendations agreed on by the Committee for the consideration of the remuneration of such teachers.

The amendments set out in Schedule 1 have retrospective effect by virtue of section 7(3) of the Remuneration of Teachers Act 1965.

STATUTORY INSTRUMENTS

1968 No. 378

LANDLORD AND TENANT

The Agriculture (Calculation of Value for Compensation) Amendment Regulations 1968

Made - - -		13*th March* 1968
Laid before Parliament		21*st March* 1968
Coming into Operation		25*th March* 1968

The Minister of Agriculture, Fisheries and Food, in exercise of the powers conferred on him by section 51 of the Agricultural Holdings Act 1948(a), and of all other powers enabling him in that behalf, with the advice of the Committee appointed under the provisions of section 79 of the Act, hereby makes the following regulations:—

1. These regulations may be cited as the Agriculture (Calculation of Value for Compensation) Amendment Regulations 1968, and shall come into operation on 25th March 1968.

2.—(1) In these regulations
" the Act " means the Agricultural Holdings Act 1948;
" the principal regulations " means the Agriculture (Calculation of Value for Compensation) Regulations 1959(b).

(2) The Interpretation Act 1889(c) shall apply to the interpretation of these regulations as it applies to the interpretation of an Act of Parliament.

3. These regulations shall apply in relation to the calculation of the value of improvements in any case where the tenancy of the tenant claiming compensation for such improvements by virtue of the provisions of the Act terminates on or after the day on which these regulations come into operation.

4. Subject to the provisions of Regulation 3 above Part 1 of the schedule to the principal regulations shall have effect as if for Tables 1, 2, 3 and 4 there were substituted Tables 1, 2, 3, and 4 in the schedule to these regulations.

In witness whereof the Official Seal of the Minister of Agriculture, Fisheries and Food is hereunto affixed on 13th March 1968.

(L.S.)   *Frederick Peart*,
                                        Minister of Agriculture, Fisheries and Food.

(a) 11 & 12 Geo. 6 c. 63. For change of title of the Minister see S.I. 1955/554 (1955 I, p. 1200).
(b) S.I. 1959/496 (1959 I, p. 1528).   (c) 52 & 53 Vict. c. 63.

SCHEDULE

TABLE 1

Unit Values of 1 per cent. of a ton of Manure

	After one crop has been taken from the land	After two crops have been taken from the land	After three crops have been taken from the land	After four crops have been taken from the land
	s. d.	s. d.	s. d.	s. d.
Nitrogen:				
(a) Inorganic N	NIL	NIL	NIL	NIL
Phosphoric acid:				
(b) P_2O_5 soluble in water or in citric acid	10 0	5 0	2 6	NIL
(c) P_2O_5 insoluble in water or of unspecified solubility	5 0	2 6	1 3	NIL
Potash:				
(d) Total K_2O	4 0	2 0	NIL	NIL

Notes:

  (i) The unit values in this Table are inclusive of the cost of delivery and spreading.

  (ii) Unit values per ton are to be calculated to the nearest shilling.

TABLE 2

Unit Values of 1 per cent. of a ton of Basic Slag

	After one crop has been taken from the land	After two crops have been taken from the land	After three crops have been taken from the land	After four crops have been taken from the land
	s. d.	s. d.	s. d.	s. d.
Phosphoric acid:				
(a) P_2O_5 soluble in citric acid	10 0	5 0	2 6	NIL
(b) P_2O_5 insoluble in citric acid	5 0	2 6	1 3	NIL

Notes:

  (i) The unit values in this Table are inclusive of the cost of delivery and spreading.

  (ii) Unit values per ton are to be calculated to the nearest shilling.

TABLE 3

Unit Values of 1 per cent of a ton of Manure

	After one crop has been taken from the land	After two crops have been taken from the land	After three crops have been taken from the land	After four crops have been taken from the land
	s. d.	s. d.	s. d.	s. d.
Nitrogen:				
(a) N in dried blood ...	NIL	NIL	NIL	NIL
(b) Organic N other than dried blood	7 6	3 9	NIL	NIL
Phosphoric acid:				
(c) Total P_2O_5 in bone products	7 6	3 9	1 10½	NIL
(d) Total P_2O_5 in other materials	5 0	2 6	1 3	NIL

Notes:

(i) The unit values in this Table are inclusive of the cost of delivery and spreading.

(ii) Unit values per ton are to be calculated to the nearest shilling.

TABLE 4

	Value per ton of feedingstuff consumed	
	Before one crop has been taken from the land	After one crop has been taken from the land
	£ s. d.	£ s. d.
1. Decorticated cotton cake ...	3 0 0	1 10 0
2. Undecorticated cotton cake (Egyptian)	1 18 0	19 0
3. Undecorticated cotton cake (Bombay)	1 18 0	19 0
4. Linseed cake	2 1 0	1 0 6
5. Linseed	1 12 0	16 0
6. Soya bean cake...	2 8 0	1 4 0
7. Palmnut cake	1 1 0	10 6
8. Coconut cake	1 14 0	17 0
9. Earthnut cake	2 13 0	1 6 6
10. Rape cake	2 5 0	1 2 6
11. Meat meal	3 15 0	1 17 6
12. Fish meal	5 4 0	2 12 0
13. Beans	1 11 0	15 6
14. Peas	1 6 0	13 0
15. Wheat	16 0	8 0
16. Barley	15 0	7 6
17. Oats	15 0	7 6
18. Maize	13 0	6 6
19. Rice meal	14 0	7 0
20. Locust beans	14 0	7 0
21. Malt	16 0	8 0
22. Malt culms	2 0 0	1 0 0
23. Bran and other offals of wheat	2 3 0	1 1 6
24. Brewers' grains (dried) ...	1 6 0	13 0
25. Brewers' grains (wet) ...	7 0	3 6
26. Clover hay	1 1 0	10 6
27. Meadow hay	17 0	8 6
28. Dried grass and meal	1 5 0	12 6
29. Mangolds	3 0	1 6
30. Swedes	3 0	1 6
31. Turnips	3 0	1 6
32. Sugar-beet pulp (dry)	9 0	4 6
33. Sugar-beet pulp (wet) ...	2 0	1 0
34. Potatoes	6 0	3 0
35. Straw, pea straw and pods ...	16 0	8 0
36. Compound cakes and meal for each 1 per cent. of albuminoid (proteins)	1 6	9
Thus 18 per cent. albuminoids	1 7 0	13 6
24 per cent. albuminoids	1 16 0	18 0
30 per cent. albuminoids	2 5 0	1 2 6

Note: In the case of straw mechanical value has been taken into account.

EXPLANATORY NOTE

(This Note is not part of the Regulations.)

These Regulations, which amend the Agriculture (Calculation of Value for Compensation) Regulations 1959 (S.I. 1959/496), are made by the Minister of Agriculture, Fisheries and Food under section 51 of the Agricultural Holdings Act 1948 on the advice of the Committee on Agricultural Valuation appointed under section 79 of the Act.

New tables of unit values for manure and feedingstuffs are substituted for those in the Regulations now amended. The new tables are to take effect in relation to claims for compensation for the value of improvements arising under the provisions of the Act in the case of tenancies which terminate on or after 25th March 1968.

1968 No. 379

OPTICIANS

The General Optical Council (Registration and Enrolment Rules) (Amendment) Order of Council 1968

Made - - - - 15*th March* 1968

At the Council Chamber, Whitehall, the 15th day of March 1968

By the Lords of Her Majesty's Most Honourable Privy Council

Whereas in pursuance of section 7 of the Opticians Act 1958(**a**), the General Optical Council have made rules entitled "The Registration and Enrolment (Amendment) Rules 1968 ":

And whereas by subsection (5) of the said section such rules shall not come into force until approved by Order of the Privy Council:

Now, therefore, Their Lordships, having taken the said rules into consideration, are hereby pleased to approve the same as set out in the Schedule to this Order.

This Order may be cited as the General Optical Council (Registration and Enrolment Rules) (Amendment) Order of Council 1968.

W. G. Agnew.

SCHEDULE

The Registration and Enrolment (Amendment) Rules 1968

The General Optical Council, in exercise of their powers under section 7 of the Opticians Act 1958, hereby make the following rules:—

1. These rules may be cited as the Registration and Enrolment (Amendment) Rules 1968.

2. Rule 22 of the Registration and Enrolment Rules 1959, scheduled to the General Optical Council (Registration and Enrolment Rules) Order of Council 1959(**b**), as amended by the rules scheduled to the General Optical Council (Registration and Enrolment Rules) (Amendment) Order of Council 1963(**c**), and the General Optical Council (Registration and Enrolment Rules) (Amendment) Order of Council 1965(**d**), is hereby revoked and replaced by the following Rule:—

" 22. The registration fee shall cover the inclusion in the register of particulars inserted under paragraphs (*a*), (*b*), (*d*) and (*e*) of Rule 4 of these rules, but shall be increased by £1 for each address entered under paragraph (*c*) of that Rule."

(**a**) 1958 c. 32.
(**c**) S.I. 1963/1222 (1963 II, p. 2033).
(**b**) S.I. 1959/1432 (1959 II, p. 1984).
(**d**) S.I. 1965/259 (1965 I, p. 648).

3. These rules shall come into operation on the 1st day of April 1968.

Sealed on the 31st day of January 1968.

Attested by:

L.S.

G. R. ROUGIER, *Member of Council.*

RONALD RUSSELL, *Member of Council.*

A. T. GERARD, *Registrar.*

EXPLANATORY NOTE

(This Note is not part of the Order.)

The rules approved by this Order abolish from 1st April 1968 the fees payable for inserting, at the request of a registered optician, in the appropriate opticians register additional qualifications accepted for this purpose by the General Optical Council.

1968 No. 384

CUSTOMS AND EXCISE

The Anti-Dumping Duty Order 1968

Made - - - - - 14th *March* 1968
Laid before the House of Commons 18th *March* 1968
Coming into Operation - - 19th *March* 1968

Whereas it appears to the Board of Trade—

(1) that goods of the descriptions specified in the Schedule hereto have been imported into the United Kingdom in circumstances in which, under the provisions of the Customs Duties (Dumping and Subsidies) Act 1957(a), they are to be regarded as having been dumped; and

(2) that, having regard to all the circumstances, it would be in the national interest to impose a duty of customs to meet the dumping of such goods:

Now, therefore, the Board of Trade in pursuance of the powers conferred upon them by sections 1, 2 and 3 of the Customs Duties (Dumping and Subsidies) Act 1957 hereby make the following Order:—

1. There shall be charged on the import into the United Kingdom of any goods of a description specified in the first column in the Schedule hereto a duty of customs at the relevant rate specified in the second column.

2. Section 3 of the Customs Duties (Dumping and Subsidies) Act 1957 (which provides for giving relief from any duty imposed under that Act) shall apply in relation to the duty imposed by this Order.

3. This Order may be cited as the Anti-Dumping Duty Order 1968 and shall come into operation on 19th March 1968.

Gwyneth Dunwoody,
Parliamentary Secretary to
the Board of Trade.

14th March 1968.

(a) 1957 c. 18.

SCHEDULE

Description of Goods	Rate of Duty
Copolymers of methylsiloxane blocks with oxyalkylenes in which the oxyalkylene portion consists of oxyethylene and oxy-1,2-propylene units in molar proportions between 70:30 and 30:70, originating in the United States of America and being a product of the Union Carbide Corporation or of the Dow Corning Corporation.	5s. 9d. per lb.

EXPLANATORY NOTE

(This Note is not part of the Order.)

This Order imposes an anti-dumping duty of 5s. 9d. per lb. on copolymers, of descriptions specified in the Schedule to the Order (which include some silicone polyether copolymer surfactants), originating in the U.S.A. and being a product of the Union Carbide Corporation or of the Dow Corning Corporation.

STATUTORY INSTRUMENTS

1968 No. 386

PROBATION AND AFTER-CARE
The Probation (Conditions of Service) (Amendment) Rules 1968

Made - - - -	*14th March* 1968
Coming into Operation	*1st April* 1968

In pursuance of the powers conferred on me by Schedule 5 to the Criminal Justice Act 1948(a), I hereby make the following Rules:—

1. For Schedule 1 to the Probation (Conditions of Service) Rules 1965(b), as substituted by Rule 2(1) of the Probation (Conditions of Service) (Amendment) Rules 1967(c), there shall be substituted the following Schedule:—

"SCHEDULE 1   Rule 2

TABLE

SCALE OF ANNUAL SALARY FOR SENIOR PROBATION OFFICERS

Column 1 Length of Service	Column 2 Rate of Annual Salary
	£
Up to 1 year's service	1,715
Over 1 and up to 2 years' service ...	1,770
Over 2 and up to 3 years' service ...	1,830
Over 3 and up to 4 years' service ...	1,890
Over 4 years' service	1,950"

2. For Schedule 1 to the said Rules of 1965 as substituted by Rule 1 of these Rules, there shall be substituted on and after 1st April 1969 the following Schedule:—

(a) 1948 c. 58.   (b) S.I. 1965/722 (1965 I, p. 2230).
(c) S.I. 1967/869 (1967 II, p. 2606).

Rule 2

"SCHEDULE 1

TABLE

SCALE OF ANNUAL SALARY FOR SENIOR PROBATION OFFICERS

Column 1 Length of Service	Column 2 Rate of Annual Salary
	£
Up to 1 year's service	1,770
Over 1 and up to 2 years' service ...	1,830
Over 2 and up to 3 years' service ...	1,890
Over 3 and up to 4 years' service ...	1,950
Over 4 years' service	2,015"

3. For Schedule 2 to the said Rules of 1965 as substituted by Rule 2 of the Probation (Conditions of Service) Rules 1966(a), there shall be substituted the following Schedule:—

Rule 3(1)

"SCHEDULE 2

TABLE

SCALE OF ANNUAL SALARY FOR PROBATION OFFICERS

Column 1 Length of Service	Column 2 Rate of Annual Salary
	£
Up to 1 year's service	870
Over 1 and up to 2 years' service ...	925
Over 2 and up to 3 years' service ...	975
Over 3 and up to 4 years' service ...	1,030
Over 4 and up to 5 years' service ...	1,080
Over 5 and up to 6 years' service ...	1,135
Over 6 and up to 7 years' service ...	1,190
Over 7 and up to 8 years' service ...	1,245
Over 8 and up to 9 years' service ...	1,305
Over 9 and up to 10 years' service ...	1,360
Over 10 and up to 11 years' service ...	1,420
Over 11 and up to 12 years' service ...	1,480
Over 12 and up to 13 years' service ...	1,540
Over 13 years' service	1,600"

(a) S.I. 1966/273 (1966 I, p. 734).

4. These Rules may be cited as the Probation (Conditions of Service) (Amendment) Rules 1968 and shall come into operation on 1st April 1968.

James Callaghan,
One of Her Majesty's Principal
Secretaries of State.

Home Office,
Whitehall.
14th March 1968.

EXPLANATORY NOTE
(This Note is not part of the Rules.)

The Rules amend the Probation (Conditions of Service) Rules 1965 by introducing higher scales of annual salary, in the case of senior probation officers on 1st April 1968 and 1st April 1969, and in the case of probation officers on 1st April 1968.

STATUTORY INSTRUMENTS

1968 No. 388 (L. 7)
SUPREME COURT OF JUDICATURE, ENGLAND
MATRIMONIAL CAUSES
COUNTY COURTS
The Matrimonial Causes Fees Order 1968

Made - - - - 14*th March* 1968
Coming into Operation 11*th April* 1968

The Lord Chancellor and the Treasury, in exercise of the powers conferred on them by section 8 of the Matrimonial Causes Act 1967(a) and sections 2 and 3 of the Public Offices Fees Act 1879(b), hereby make and concur in the following Order:—

1. This Order may be cited as the Matrimonial Causes Fees Order 1968 and shall come into operation on 11th April 1968.

2.—(1) In this Order—

(*a*) expressions used in the Matrimonial Causes Rules 1968(c) have the same meaning as in those rules;

(*b*) a rule referred to by number means the rule so numbered in the Matrimonial Causes Rules 1968 and a form referred to by number means the form so numbered in Appendix II to those rules;

(*c*) "the County Court Fees Order" means the County Court Fees Order 1959(d), as amended(e), and a fee referred to by a number prefixed by the letters "C.C." means the fee so numbered in the Schedule to that Order;

(*d*) "the Supreme Court Fees Order" means the Supreme Court Fees Order 1961(f), as amended(g), and a fee referred to by number prefixed by the letters "S.C." means the fee so numbered in the First Schedule to that Order.

(2) The Interpretation Act 1889(h) shall apply for the interpretation of this Order as it applies for the interpretation of an Act of Parliament.

3. The fees specified in Schedule 1 to this Order shall be taken in all matrimonial proceedings, whether in the High Court or a divorce county court.

4. In addition to the fees specified in Schedule 1, the fees specified in the first column of Schedule 2 to this Order (being fees prescribed by the County Court Fees Order and the Supreme Court Fees Order) shall be taken in the matrimonial proceedings specified opposite thereto in the second column, subject to the directions contained in the notes to that Schedule.

5. Any fee prescribed by this Order shall be taken—

(*a*) in the divorce registry, by judicature fee stamps impressed on the appropriate document;

(*b*) in a divorce county court or district registry, in cash.

(**a**) 1967 c. 56.   (**b**) 1879 c. 58.
(**c**) S.I. 1968/219.   (**d**) S.I. 1959/1262 (1959 I, p. 803).
(**e**) S.I. 1961/355, 1961/1894, 1963/897, 1965/395, 1966/243 (1961 I, p. 565; III, p. 3554; 1963 II, p. 1508; 1965 I, p. 1099; 1966 I, p. 496).
(**f**) S.I. 1961/2307 (1961 III, p. 4055).   (**g**) There are no relevant amendments.
(**h**) 1889 c. 63.

6. If any question arises with regard to the amount or payment of any fee prescribed by this Order, the registrar may report the matter to the Lord Chancellor and obtain his directions thereon.

7. Where it appears to the Lord Chancellor that the payment of any fee prescribed by this Order would, owing to the exceptional circumstances of the particular case, involve undue hardship, the Lord Chancellor may reduce or remit the fee in that case.

8. The Supreme Court Fees Order shall have effect subject to the amendments set out in Schedule 3 to this Order, but those amendments shall not affect any fee due or payable before the commencement of this Order.

9. Where a cause begun by petition has not been set down for trial before the commencement of this Order, a fee of £5 shall be payable on a request for directions for trial or, if the registrar's certificate has been granted under the rules relating to matrimonial proceedings hitherto in force, on receipt of a demand by the registrar for payment of such fee.

Dated 14th March 1968.

Gardiner, C.

E. Alan Fitch,   } Lords Commissioners
B. K. O'Malley, } of Her Majesty's
                  } Treasury.

SCHEDULE 1
Fees to be Taken in all Matrimonial Proceedings

Fee	Amount
1. On filing an originating application or on sealing an originating summons	£2
2. On presenting a petition except in a case to which rule 12(3) applies	£10
3. On filing a notice in Form 8 or 9 except where the terms of any agreement as to the order which the court is to be asked to make are set out in the notice	£2
4. On making a search in the index of decrees absolute kept under rule 66(2)	2s. 6d.
5. On a request for a photographic or office copy of a decree or of a certificate that a decree has been made absolute	5s. 0d.
6. On a certificate under the hand of a judge or registrar	5s. 0d.
7. On the issue of a notice under rule 55	£2

SCHEDULE 2

Fees to be Taken in Specified Matrimonial Proceedings

Fee	Proceedings in which fee to be taken
C.C. Fees Nos. 4*, 20, 35, 37, 39 to 44, 46, 49, 54, 66†, 67, 70 and 71	Proceedings in a divorce county court
C.C. Fees Nos. 62 and 69	Proceedings in a divorce county court other than the divorce registry
C.C. Fees Nos. 50, 51 and 53	All proceedings, whether in the High Court or a divorce county court
S.C. Fees Nos. 9(b), 15, 23, 62, 63, 69†, 70†, 72, 73, 81, 82 and 95	Proceedings in the Supreme Court
S.C. Fees Nos. 74 to 77	Proceedings in the divorce registry, whether pending in the High Court or treated as pending in a divorce county court, and proceedings in a district registry

Notes

* This fee is payable only in respect of a document requiring personal service.
† This fee does not apply to a copy in respect of which Fee No. 5 in Schedule 1 above is payable.

SCHEDULE 3

Amendments of Supreme Court Fees Order 1961

1. S.C. Fees Nos. 20, 49 to 53, 65(b) and 71 shall be revoked.

2. In S.C. Fee No. 5 the words "Fee No. 49 or" shall be omitted.

3. In S.C. Fee No. 6 the words "or a notice under Rule 36(1) of the Matrimonial Causes Rules, 1957" shall be omitted.

4. In S.C. Fee No. 7 the words "(other than a petition on which Fee No. 49 has been paid or is payable)" shall be omitted.

5. In S.C. Fee No. 19(a) the words "(including a notice under Rule 36(1) of the Matrimonial Causes Rules, 1957)" shall be omitted.

6. In the proviso to S.C. Fee No. 64 the word "or" at the end of paragraph (b) shall be deleted and paragraphs (c), (d) and (e) shall be omitted.

7. In S.C. Fee No. 69 the words "(other than a copy on which Fee No. 71 is payable)" shall be omitted.

EXPLANATORY NOTE
(*This Note is not part of the Order.*)

This Order prescribes the fees to be taken in matrimonial proceedings in the High Court and divorce county courts. A fee of £2 is to be charged on issuing an originating application or originating summons and a fee of £10 on presenting a petition. In most cases no further fee will be payable except on an application for ancillary relief (for which a fee of £2 is prescribed by Schedule 1) or on the taxation of costs or the enforcement of any order (for which the ordinary county court and Supreme Court fees will be payable by virtue of Schedule 2).

STATUTORY INSTRUMENTS

1968 No. 389

FOOD AND DRUGS

The Welfare Foods Order 1968

Made - - - -	15th *March* 1968
Laid before Parliament	25th *March* 1968
Coming into Operation	31st *March* 1968

The Minister of Health and the Secretary of State, acting jointly in exercise of the powers conferred on them by sections 4 and 7 of the Emergency Laws (Re-enactments and Repeals) Act 1964(a) and of all other powers enabling them in that behalf, hereby order as follows:—

PART I

PRELIMINARY

Title, commencement and extent

1.—(1) This order may be cited as the Welfare Foods Order 1968 and shall come into operation on 31st March 1968.

(2) This order shall not extend to Northern Ireland.

Interpretation

2.—(1) In this order, unless the context otherwise requires—

"beneficiary" means any of the following persons in Great Britain, namely, a young child, a handicapped child, an expectant mother or a nursing mother;

"dried milk" means National Dried Milk;

"enactment" includes any instrument made under an Act;

"handicapped child" in England and Wales means a child (other than a young child) who—

    (*a*) is less than 16 years of age and is not in paid employment,

    (*b*) is declared by the local education authority to be unable by reason of disability of mind or body to become a registered pupil of a school (other than a special school within the meaning of the Education Act 1944(b)),

    (*c*) is not a registered pupil of such a special school, and

    (*d*) is not in attendance at a full-time training centre;

and in Scotland means a child (other than a young child) who—

    (i) is less than 16 years of age and is not in paid employment, and

    (ii) is declared by the education authority to be unable by reason of disability of mind or body to become a pupil of a school (including a special school) within the meaning of the Education (Scotland) Act 1962(c);

"large family" means a family in which the number of beneficiaries entitled to welfare milk exceeds two;

(a) 1964 c. 60.   (b) 1944 c. 31.
(c) 1962 c. 47.

"milk" means liquid cows' milk, but does not include separated milk, skimmed milk, condensed milk or evaporated milk;

"Milk Order" means the order for the time being in force under section 6 of the Emergency Laws (Re-enactments and Repeals) Act 1964 (which provides for controlling maximum prices of milk);

"the Minister" means in relation to England and Wales the Minister of Health and in relation to Scotland the Secretary of State;

"nursing mother" means a woman who has given birth to a child within the preceding 30 weeks and is herself suckling the child;

"registered day nursery" means a day nursery which is for the time being registered by the Minister for the purposes of this order;

"standard price", in relation to milk, means the lowest of the maximum prices per pint specified in the Milk Order;

"supplier" means a person who supplies milk under this order;

"token" means a token for welfare milk, free welfare milk or any other welfare food issued by the Minister under article 8;

"vitamin tablets" means vitamin A and D tablets;

"week" means a week ending at midnight between Saturday and Sunday;

"welfare food" means milk, dried milk, concentrated orange juice, cod liver oil or vitamin tablets;

"welfare milk", in relation to a beneficiary, means the milk or dried milk which he is entitled to obtain under Part II of this order;

"welfare price", in relation to milk, means a price of 6d. per pint, increased, where the supplier would be entitled under the Milk Order to charge the beneficiary for the milk supplied a price which exceeds the standard price, by the amount of the difference between these prices;

"young child" in England and Wales means a child aged not more than 5 years and 1 month, and in Scotland means a child aged not more than 5 years, so however that a child who does not attain the age of 5 years on a fixed date for commencing school attendance shall for the purpose of such attendance be deemed to attain that age on the fixed date next following the fifth anniversary of his birth.

(2) Where any provision in this order (other than a provision in article 19 or 20) requires or enables anything to be done by or in respect of a beneficiary, and that beneficiary is a young child or a handicapped child, the provision shall, unless the context otherwise requires, be deemed to refer to one of his parents or his guardian or the person having custody of him.

(3) Any reference in this order to a numbered article or schedule shall, unless the reference is to an article of or a schedule to a specified enactment, be construed as a reference to the article or schedule bearing that number in this order.

(4) In this order, unless the context otherwise requires, any reference to any enactment shall be construed as a reference to that enactment as amended by or under any subsequent enactment.

PART II

ENTITLEMENT TO WELFARE FOODS

Meaning of a family in special circumstances

3.—(1) For the purposes of this order, a beneficiary shall be deemed to belong to a family in special circumstances in respect of any period during which his requirements exceed his resources when calculated or estimated by the Minister according to the provisions of paragraphs 3 and 7 to 29 of schedule 2 to the Ministry of Social Security Act 1966(a), subject to the following modifications—

    (a) in sub-paragraph (a) of paragraph 23 (which relates to the calculation of weekly earnings) for the expression "20s." there shall be substituted the expression "40s."; and

    (b) his requirements shall be deemed to include also—
        (i) such amounts in respect of hire purchase transactions and mortgage repayments as the Minister may allow; and
        (ii) the cost of welfare foods; and
        (iii) any further amounts which the Minister may in special circumstances allow.

(2) Where by virtue of the said paragraph 3 the resources of the beneficiary would be aggregated with those of some other person, the requirements and resources of that other person when calculated as aforesaid shall be deemed to be the requirements and resources of the beneficiary.

Entitlement to welfare milk

4.—(1) Subject to the provisions of this article, welfare milk shall be available, on application, to all beneficiaries at a rate for each beneficiary of 7 pints per week of liquid milk or one 20 oz. pack per week of dried milk, in the case of a beneficiary described in paragraph (2) of this article free of charge, and in any other case at a charge—

    (a) for liquid milk, as provided in article 10, and

    (b) for dried milk, of 2s. 4d. per 20 oz. pack:

Provided that where a nursing mother applies for welfare milk in respect of a young child whom she is suckling, she shall not be entitled under this paragraph to welfare milk in respect both of herself and the child; but nothing in article 20 shall prohibit her from consuming any welfare milk obtained for the child.

(2) The beneficiaries who are entitled to welfare milk free of charge under paragraph (1) of this article are—

    (a) all but two of the beneficiaries in a large family, and

    (b) all the beneficiaries in a family in special circumstances.

(3) Dried milk, additional to that to which he is entitled under paragraph (1) of this article, and on the same conditions as to payment, shall be available, on application, for a young child under one year of age who is being fed mainly on dried milk, in the quantities specified in column (2) of schedule 1 in relation to his age at the time of application as specified in column (1).

Entitlement to welfare foods other than liquid milk

5. A beneficiary described in column (1) of schedule 2 may buy the welfare foods specified in respect of him in column (2) at the price so specified in column (3), and where the beneficiary belongs to a family in special circumstances he shall be entitled to receive free of charge the quantity of those welfare foods so specified in column (4).

Milk for children attending registered day nurseries

6. The Minister may make arrangements for each young child attending a registered day nursery to receive (without prejudice to his entitlement under article 4) one third of a pint of milk, or dried milk made up to provide one third of a pint, in respect of each day of attendance, at a reduced price or free of charge.

(a) 1966 c. 20.

Part III

Supply of Welfare Foods

Application forms

7. Application for welfare foods shall be made by a beneficiary on a form supplied for the purpose by the Minister.

Issue of Tokens

8. The Minister shall issue tokens to enable beneficiaries to obtain welfare milk under article 4 and welfare foods free of charge under article 5.

Use of Tokens

9.—(1) To obtain the welfare foods to which he is entitled under this order, a beneficiary shall use the relevant tokens in the manner described in this article.

(2) A token for welfare milk may be used—

(a) to obtain 7 pints of milk during the week ending on the date specified on the token or during any of the four succeeding weeks, or

(b) to obtain a 20 oz. pack of dried milk during the period beginning one month before and ending one month after the date so specified;

and a token shall not be used in any other manner.

(3) A token for additional supplies of dried milk may be used to obtain a 20 oz. pack of dried milk when a token for welfare milk is used to obtain dried milk.

(4) A token for free welfare milk shall be used together with, and in the same manner as, a token for welfare milk, but where a date is specified on a token for free welfare milk it may be used only with a token for welfare milk bearing the same date.

(5) A token for free additional supplies of dried milk may be used only with a token for additional supplies of dried milk.

(6) Tokens for concentrated orange juice, cod liver oil and vitamin tablets may be used by a beneficiary in a family in special circumstances to obtain free of charge the quantities of those welfare foods specified in respect of him in column (4) of schedule 2.

Part IV

Distribution of Milk

Suppliers of and charges for milk

10.—(1) Where any supplier has accepted from any beneficiary a token for welfare milk he shall (unless he has returned it to the beneficiary before it became valid) supply 7 pints of milk to the beneficiary against that token, during the period of validity of the token; and he may charge the beneficiary the welfare price for milk so supplied.

(2) Where any supplier has accepted from any beneficiary, together with a token for welfare milk, a token for free welfare milk, he shall (unless he has returned both tokens to the beneficiary before they became valid) supply 7 pints of milk to the beneficiary against the said tokens during the period of validity of the token for welfare milk; and—

(a) in any case where he would not be entitled under the Milk Order to charge for the milk supplied a price exceeding the standard price, he shall make no charge; and (*b*) in any other case, he may charge the beneficiary for milk so supplied at a rate not exceeding the difference between the standard price and the price which he would be entitled to charge under the Milk Order.

(3) A supplier may accept tokens from a beneficiary before they have become valid; but he shall on demand return to the beneficiary all tokens in respect of which no milk has been supplied.

(4) If a supplier is prevented by circumstances beyond his control from supplying milk under this article, he shall be deemed not to have contravened this article.

Absence for less than a week

11. Where any beneficiary is absent from his usual place of residence for more than one day but less than 7 days during the period of validity of any token for welfare milk which a supplier has accepted from him, and the supplier has supplied against that token some, but not all, of the requisite 7 pints, the supplier shall, if the beneficiary so requests within the said period of validity, forthwith pay or allow the beneficiary, in respect of each pint not supplied, a sum equal to the standard price reduced by 6d. or, if the token was accepted together with a token for free welfare milk, not so reduced.

Absence for a week

12. Where a young child or handicapped child is absent from his usual place of residence for any period of 7 consecutive days during which the person for the time being in charge of that child has provided him with 7 pints of milk, that person shall, notwithstanding anything to the contrary in this order, be entitled to retain a token for welfare milk issued in respect of the child and to use it free from all restrictions as to the use of the milk so obtained.

Submission of tokens by suppliers

13. A supplier shall, in such manner as the Minister may from time to time direct, submit to the Minister all tokens against which the supplier has supplied 7 pints of milk.

PART V
TOKENS

Property in tokens

14. Every token is and shall remain the property of the Minister.

Replacement of tokens

15.—(1) The Minister may replace tokens which have been lost.

(2) Where a supplier or a beneficiary to or in respect of whom replacement tokens have been issued subsequently finds the tokens supposed to have been lost, he shall deliver the latter forthwith to any office of the Ministry of Social Security.

Validity and cancellation of tokens

16.—(1) Tokens shall be valid only if used by or on behalf of a beneficiary, and within the periods and in the manner specified in this order.

(2) The Minister may cancel any token which cannot be validly used under this order.

Return of tokens

17.—(1) Any beneficiary or supplier holding tokens shall, when requested by the Minister, produce or deliver all tokens in his possession within such time and to such place as the Minister may direct.

(2) Where any beneficiary holding tokens ceases to be entitled thereto under this order, he shall forthwith deliver them to any office of the Ministry of Social Security.

(3) When a beneficiary dies, any person who has, or comes into, possession of any token issued in respect of that beneficiary shall deliver it forthwith to any office of the Ministry of Social Security or, where death resulted from an infectious or contagious disease, in accordance with the instructions of the Medical Officer of Health.

Supplier losing possession of tokens

18.—(1) Where a supplier accepts any token for welfare milk or free welfare milk from a beneficiary but, before supplying milk against it or returning it to the beneficiary as provided for in article 10, loses possession of it (whether through accidental loss, theft or otherwise), he shall notify the Minister forthwith.

(2) Where—

> (*a*) a supplier loses possession, as described in the last preceding paragraph, of a token and
>
> (*b*) the Minister replaces that token pursuant to article 15(1),

the Minister may (unless satisfied that it has not been and can not be used by any person other than the beneficiary) require the supplier to pay to him—

> (i) in respect of each such token which is a token for welfare milk, a sum equal to 7 times the difference between the standard price and 6d., and
>
> (ii) in respect of each such token which is a token for free welfare milk, a sum of 3s. 6d.

(3) Any sum required to be paid under this article may be recovered as a civil debt.

(4) Where the Minister receives payment of a sum under this article but subsequently becomes satisfied that any tokens in respect of which payment was made were not misused, he shall make a refund to the supplier accordingly.

PART VI

MISCELLANEOUS

Restrictions on supply of welfare foods

19.—(1) No person shall obtain any welfare food unless he is a beneficiary or is obtaining that food on behalf of a beneficiary.

(2) A beneficiary or a person acting on behalf of a beneficiary shall not obtain welfare milk pursuant to article 4 or welfare foods free of charge pursuant to article 5 in quantities exceeding those to which the beneficiary is entitled thereunder, or otherwise than in exchange for tokens pursuant to article 9.

(3) A beneficiary or a person acting on behalf of a beneficiary shall not obtain free welfare milk pursuant to article 4 otherwise than in exchange for tokens pursuant to article 9.

Use of welfare foods

20. Where any welfare food is obtained by or on behalf of a beneficiary, it shall not be consumed otherwise than by that beneficiary unless—

> (*a*) if the food is liquid milk or dried milk, the beneficiary has consumed a

quantity of milk approximately equal to the quantity of welfare milk obtained in respect of him; or

(b) any such consumption is reasonably necessary to avoid waste or is trifling in amount; or

(c) the food is welfare milk referred to in the proviso to article 4(1).

Northern Ireland tokens to be valid in Great Britain

21. Any token issued by a department of the Government of Northern Ireland under the provisions of the Welfare Foods (Northern Ireland) Order 1968 (a) shall be valid in Great Britain as if it had been issued by the Minister under this order.

Revocations

22. The orders specified in schedule 3 are hereby revoked:
Provided that—

(a) such revocation shall not affect any right or liability acquired or incurred, or anything duly done or suffered, under those orders;

(b) such revocation shall not affect any legal proceedings in respect of any contravention of those orders, but any such proceedings may be continued or commenced as if this order had not been made;

(c) such revocation shall not affect any declaration, registration or authorisation made or granted under those orders, and every such declaration, registration or authorisation shall, so far as it could have been made or granted under this order, have effect as if it had been so made or granted.

Article 4(3)   **SCHEDULE 1**

Additional supplies of dried milk for a young child under one year of age who is being fed mainly on dried milk.

Age of child at time of application (1)	Amount (2)
Not exceeding 3 months	31 20 oz. packs
3 months but not exceeding 4 months	28 ,, ,, ,,
4 ,, ,, ,, ,, 5 ,, ...	24 ,, ,, ,,
5 ,, ,, ,, ,, 6 ,, ...	20 ,, ,, ,,
6 ,, ,, ,, ,, 7 ,, ...	16 ,, ,, ,,
7 ,, ,, ,, ,, 8 ,, ...	12 ,, ,, ,,
8 ,, ,, ,, ,, 9 ,, ...	8 ,, ,, ,,
9 ,, ,, ,, ,, 10 ,, ...	8 ,, ,, ,,
10 ,, ,, ,, ,, 11 ,, ...	4 ,, ,, ,,
11 ,, ,, ,, ,, 12 ,, ...	2 ,, ,, ,,

Article 5

SCHEDULE 2

Entitlement to welfare foods other than liquid milk.

(1) Class of beneficiary	(2) Welfare food	(3) Price	(4) Quantity of welfare food supplied free of charge to beneficiaries in a family in special circumstances
All beneficiaries	Dried milk	4s. 0d. per 20 oz. pack	As specified in article 4(1)
Young child	Concentrated orange juice	1s. 6d. per bottle	From birth to 6 months of age at the rate of 3 bottles every 13 weeks. From 6 months to 2 years of age at the rate of 7 bottles every 13 weeks
	Cod liver oil	1s. 0d. per bottle	At the rate of 2 bottles every 13 weeks
Expectant mother	Concentrated orange juice	1s. 6d. per bottle	At the rate of 10 bottles every 13 weeks
	Vitamin tablets	6d. per packet of 45 tablets	At the rate of 2 packets of 45 tablets every 13 weeks
Nursing mother	Concentrated orange juice	1s. 6d. per bottle	At the rate of 10 bottles every 13 weeks
	Vitamin tablets	6d. per packet of 45 tablets	5 packets of 45 tablets

In this schedule "bottle" means a bottle containing not less than 6 oz.

Article 22 SCHEDULE 3

Orders revoked (1)	References (2)
The Welfare Foods (Great Britain) Order 1954 ...	S.I. 1954/1401 (1954 II, p. 2119).
The Welfare Foods (Great Britain) (Amendment) Order 1955	S.I. 1955/1369 (1955 II, p. 2511).
The Welfare Foods (Great Britain) Amendment (No. 2) Order 1955	S.I. 1955/1796 (1955 II, p. 2512).
The Welfare Foods (Great Britain) Amendment Order 1956	S.I. 1956/1130 (1956 II, p. 2266).
The Welfare Foods (Great Britain) Amendment Order 1957	S.I. 1957/411 (1957 II, p. 2343).
The Welfare Foods (Great Britain) Amendment (No. 2) Order 1957	S.I. 1957/1759 (1957 II, p. 2344).
The Welfare Foods (Great Britain) Amendment Order 1961	S.I. 1961/352 (1961 I, p. 561).

Given under the official seal of the Minister of Health on 15th March 1968.

(L.S.)

Kenneth Robinson,
Minister of Health.

Given under the seal of the Secretary of State for Scotland on 14th March 1968.

(L.S.)

William Ross,
Secretary of State for Scotland.

EXPLANATORY NOTE
(This Note is not part of the Order.)

This Order re-enacts with amendments the Orders relevant to the administration of the welfare foods scheme operated in Great Britain by the Minister of Health and the Secretary of State.

The principal matters dealt with in the Order include:—

(1) a description of the beneficiaries (expectant and nursing mothers, children under 5 and handicapped children) and a list of the foods to which each is entitled;

(2) the method of using, and the period of validity of, the tokens by which welfare foods are obtainable;

(3) restrictions on the use of welfare foods by non-beneficiaries;

(4) the prices to be charged for welfare foods.

The price of milk supplied under the scheme to beneficiaries is 6d. per pint of milk normally sold at the lowest of the maximum controlled prices for milk (which, currently, is 10d. per pint). If the beneficiary takes milk which would normally be sold at a price higher than that price, he pays the balance also.

The principal changes from the revoked Orders are that—

(a) a definition is provided of beneficiaries who are to receive free welfare foods—namely, beneficiaries in families in special circumstances, defined by reference to criteria employed by the Ministry of Social Security in the payment of benefit;

(b) the provision for welfare milk to be supplied free is extended to all but two of the beneficiaries in large families (those containing three or more beneficiaries);

(c) provision is made for the obligations of the supplier in respect of lost tokens;

(d) some drafting changes are necessary because the Order is not made under the same enabling powers as the revoked Orders. Certain of the penal provisions hitherto applicable (mainly with respect to misuse of tokens) are now contained in the enabling Act—namely the Emergency Laws (Re-enactments and Repeals) Act 1964.

STATUTORY INSTRUMENTS

1968 No. 390

MEDICAL PROFESSION

The Abortion Regulations 1968

Made - - -	*15th March* 1968
Laid before Parliament	*1st April* 1968
Coming into Operation	*27th April* 1968

The Minister of Health, in exercise of the powers conferred on him by section 2 of the Abortion Act 1967(**a**) and of all other powers enabling him in that behalf, hereby makes the following regulations :—

Citation and commencement

1. These regulations may be cited as the Abortion Regulations 1968, and shall come into operation on 27th April 1968.

Interpretation

2.—(1) In these regulations "the Act" means the Abortion Act 1967 and "practitioner" means a registered medical practitioner.

(2) The Interpretation Act 1889(**b**) shall apply to the interpretation of these regulations as it applies to the interpretation of an Act of Parliament.

Certificate of opinion

3.—(1) Any opinion to which section 1 of the Act refers shall be certified in the appropriate form set out in Schedule 1 to these regulations.

(2) Any certificate of an opinion referred to in section 1(1) of the Act shall be given before the commencement of the treatment for the termination of the pregnancy to which it relates.

(3) Any certificate of an opinion referred to in section 1(4) of the Act shall be given before the commencement of the treatment for the termination of the pregnancy to which it relates or, if that is not reasonably practicable, not later than 24 hours after such termination.

(4) Any such certificate as is referred to in paragraphs (2) and (3) of this regulation shall be preserved by the practitioner who terminated the pregnancy to which it relates for a period of three years beginning with the date of such termination and may then be destroyed.

Notice of termination of pregnancy and information relating thereto

4.—(1) Any practitioner who terminates a pregnancy shall within 7 days of the termination give to the Chief Medical Officer of the Ministry of Health notice thereof and the other information relating to the termination in the form set out in Schedule 2 to these regulations.

(**a**) 1967 c. 87.   (**b**) 1889 c. 63.

(2) Any such notice and information shall be sent in a sealed envelope to the Chief Medical Officer, Ministry of Health, Alexander Fleming House, Elephant and Castle, London, S.E.1.

Restriction on disclosure of information

5. A notice given or any information furnished to the Chief Medical Officer in pursuance of these regulations shall not be disclosed except that disclosure may be made—

(*a*) for the purposes of carrying out their duties,

   (i) to an officer of the Ministry of Health authorised by the Chief Medical Officer of that Ministry, or

   (ii) to the Registrar General or a member of his staff authorised by him ; or

(*b*) for the purposes of carrying out his duties in relation to offences against the Act or the law relating to abortion, to the Director of Public Prosecutions or a member of his staff authorised by him ; or

(*c*) for the purposes of investigating whether an offence has been committed against the Act or the law relating to abortion, to a police officer not below the rank of superintendent or a person authorised by him ; or

(*d*) for the purposes of criminal proceedings which have begun ; or

(*e*) for the purposes of bona fide scientific research ; or

(*f*) to the practitioner who terminated the pregnancy ; or

(*g*) to a practitioner, with the consent in writing of the woman whose pregnancy was terminated.

SCHEDULE 1

IN CONFIDENCE   **Certificate A**

Not to be destroyed within three years of the date of operation

ABORTION ACT 1967

CERTIFICATE TO BE COMPLETED BEFORE AN ABORTION IS
PERFORMED UNDER SECTION 1(1) OF THE ACT

I,..
(Name and qualifications of practitioner in block capitals)

of ....

....
(Full address of practitioner)

and I,..
(Name and qualifications of practitioner in block capitals)

of ....

....
(Full address of practitioner)

hereby certify that we are of the opinion, formed in good faith, that in the

case of..
(Full name of pregnant woman in block capitals)

of ....

....
(Usual place of residence of pregnant woman in block capitals)

1. the continuance of the pregnancy would involve risk to the life of the pregnant woman greater than if the pregnancy were terminated;

2. the continuance of the pregnancy would involve risk of injury to the physical or mental health of the pregnant woman greater than if the pregnancy were terminated;

3. the continuance of the pregnancy would involve risk of injury to the physical or mental health of the existing child(ren) of the family of the pregnant woman greater than if the pregnancy were terminated;

4. there is a substantial risk that if the child were born it would suffer from such physical or mental abnormalities as to be seriously handicapped.

(Ring appropriate number(s))

This certificate of opinion is given before the commencement of the treatment for the termination of pregnancy to which it refers.

Signed ....

Date...

Signed ....

Date...

SCHEDULE 1

IN CONFIDENCE   **Certificate B**

Not to be destroyed within three years of the date of operation

ABORTION ACT 1967

CERTIFICATE TO BE COMPLETED IN RELATION TO ABORTION PERFORMED
IN EMERGENCY UNDER SECTION 1(4) OF THE ACT

I,...
(Name and qualifications of practitioner in block capitals)

of ....,

....
(Full address of practitioner)

hereby certify that I *am/was of the opinion formed in good faith that it *is/was
necessary immediately to terminate the pregnancy of

....
(Full name of pregnant woman in block capitals)

of ....

....
(Usual place of residence of pregnant woman in block capitals)

in order 1.   to save the life of the pregnant woman; or

         2.   to prevent grave permanent injury to the physical or mental health
of the pregnant woman.

This certificate of opinion is given—

A. before the commencement of the treatment for the termination of the
pregnancy to which it relates; or,

if that is not reasonably practicable, then

B. not later than 24 hours after such termination.

Signed ....

Date...

*Delete as appropriate

2d

IN CONFIDENCE

SCHEDULE 2

ABORTION ACT 1967

NOTIFICATION TO THE CHIEF MEDICAL OFFICER OF AN ABORTION
PERFORMED UNDER SECTION 1 OF THE ACT

I,...

(Name and qualifications of practitioner in block capitals)

of ....

....

(Full address of practitioner)

hereby give notice that I terminated the pregnancy of

....

(Full name of pregnant woman in block capitals)

of ....

....

(Usual place of residence of pregnant woman in block capitals)

The grounds for terminating the pregnancy were certified as:—

1. the continuance of the pregnancy would have involved risk to the life of the pregnant woman greater than if the pregnancy were terminated;

2. the continuance of the pregnancy would have involved risk of injury to the physical or mental health of the pregnant woman greater than if the pregnancy were terminated;

(Ring appropriate number)

3. the continuance of the pregnancy would have involved risk of injury to the physical or mental health of the existing child(ren) of the family of the pregnant woman greater than if the pregnancy were terminated;

4. there was a substantial risk that if the child had been born it would have suffered from such physical or mental abnormalities as to be seriously handicapped;

In case of emergency

The grounds for terminating the pregnancy were:—

5. it was necessary to save the life of the pregnant woman; *or*

6. it was necessary to prevent grave permanent injury to the physical or mental health of the pregnant woman.

Place of termination

The pregnancy was terminated at: 1.   N.H.S. hospital

                                        2.   Approved place

                                        3.   Other place.

(Ring appropriate number)

(address) ....

....

on (date) ....

Signature of practitioner who terminated pregnancy

In all non-emergency cases, particulars of the practioner(s) who joined in giving the certificate required for the purposes of section 1 should be shown below in the appropriate space(s):—

If the operating practitioner joined in giving certificate, insert at A. particulars of the other certifying practitioner.

     A. Name ....

           Address..

           ....

           Qualifications ....

If the operating practioner did not join in giving certificate, insert at A. & B. particulars of the two certifying practitioners.

     B. Name ....

           Address..

           ....

           Qualifications ....

	For official use only

Other information relating to the termination
(Items 1 to 8 to be completed to the best of the knowledge and belief of the operating practitioner):

1. N.H.S. Number of woman...

2. Maiden name of woman...

3. Date of birth of woman..

4. Marital status of woman:
       1. Single   2. Married   3. Widowed
       4. Divorced or separated   5. Not known
         (Ring appropriate number)

5. Occupation ....
   NOTE: (a) If woman is married, specify husband's occupation
        (b) If woman is unmarried, specify her own occupation

6. Date of woman's last menstrual period...............................

7. Previous pregnancies of woman:
       Number of live-births...
               stillbirths...
               abortions ....
       If applicable, date of last termination of pregnancy under the above-mentioned Act

8. Number of woman's existing children* ....

9. Date of admission to place of termination of pregnancy ....

10. Date of discharge from place of termination of pregnancy ....

11. Grounds for termination of pregnancy ....
   (a) Medical condition of woman:
       Obstetric disease (specify) ....
       Non-obstetric disease (specify) ....
   (b) Suspected medical condition of foetus (specify) ....
   (c) Non-medical grounds for termination of pregnancy (specify) ....

*children mean a woman's natural children and any adopted, foster or step-children, up to the age of 16 years living with her.

	For official use only

12. Type of termination of pregnancy:

    1.   Dilation and evacuation

    2.   Hysterotomy—abdominal

    3.   Hysterotomy—vaginal

    4.   Hysterectomy

    5.   Vacuum aspiration

    6.   Other (specify)...

         (Ring appropriate number)

13. Was sterilization performed?...

14. Complications or death prior to notification:

    1.   None

    2.   Sepsis

    3.   Haemorrhage

    4.   Death

    5.   Other (specify)...

         (Ring appropriate number)

15. In the case of death, specify cause...

....

....

NOTE: This form is to be completed by the operating practitioner and sent in a sealed envelope within seven days of the termination of the pregnancy to the Chief Medical Officer, Ministry of Health, Alexander Fleming House, Elephant and Castle, London, S.E.1.

Given under the official seal of the Minister of Health on 15th March 1968.

(L.S.)   *Kenneth Robinson,*

Minister of Health.

EXPLANATORY NOTE

(This Note is not part of the Regulations.)

These Regulations, made under the Abortion Act 1967,

(a) prescribe forms for the purpose of certifying opinions under section 1 of the Act and the time for such certification (regulation 3(1), (2) and (3) and Schedule 1);

(b) provide for the preservation and disposal of such certificates (regulation 3(4));

(c) require the notification of the abortion and prescribe the information relevant thereto to be given to the Chief Medical Officer (regulation 4 and Schedule 2); and

(d) restrict the disclosure of such notices and information (regulation 5).

STATUTORY INSTRUMENTS

1968 No. 391 (S.37)

AGRICULTURE

AGRICULTURAL MARKETING

The Scottish Milk Marketing Scheme (Amendment) Approval Order 1968

Made - - -	*14th March* 1968
Coming into Operation	*1st April* 1968

Whereas the Scottish Milk Marketing Board (hereinafter referred to as "the Board") submitted to the Secretary of State in accordance with the provisions of section 2 of and Schedule 1 to the Agricultural Marketing Act 1958(a), an amendment to the Scottish Milk Marketing Scheme 1933, as amended, approved by the Scottish Milk Marketing Scheme (Approval) Order 1933(b), as amended (c) :

And Whereas no objections were made to the amendment so submitted :

And Whereas the amendment so submitted is set out in the Schedule to this Order :

Now therefore, in exercise of the powers conferred on him by the said section 2 and Schedule 1, the Secretary of State hereby orders as follows :—

1.—(1) This Order may be cited as the Scottish Milk Marketing Scheme (Amendment) Approval Order 1968 and shall come into operation on 1st April 1968.

(2) The Interpretation Act 1889(d) shall apply for the interpretation of this Order as it applies for the interpretation of an Act of Parliament.

2. The amendment to the Scottish Milk Marketing Scheme 1933, as amended, set out in the Schedule to this Order is hereby approved.

William Ross,
One of Her Majesty's Principal
Secretaries of State.

St. Andrew's House,
Edinburgh, 1.

14th March 1968.

(a) 1958 c. 47.

(b) S.R. & O. 1933/479 (Rev. I, p. 263: 1933, p. 51).

(c) The relevant amending orders are S.I. 1956/650, 1965/2193 (1956 I, p. 103; 1965 III, p. 6413).

(d) 1889 c. 63.

SCHEDULE

AMENDMENT TO THE SCOTTISH MILK MARKETING SCHEME 1933

Section 16 (*Prohibition of Sale except to or through the Board and the Board's Obligation to accept Milk*)

In subsection (2) delete the proviso and substitute therefor: —

(c) in any case where the milk tendered by a registered producer during any period of sixty-four consecutive days has failed on seven occasions during that period to satisfy such tests relating to hygienic quality as may have been determined by the Board, within the twenty-one days immediately following the expiry of said period, give written notice to the producer that his milk will not be accepted by the Board (i) for a period of three days reckoned from twenty-four hours after the date of posting the said notice and (ii) for any immediately succeeding period during which his milk does not satisfy the said tests, and may refuse to accept his milk accordingly:

Provided, however, that, before exercising the power of refusal in subsection (2)(b) hereof, the Board shall notify the registered producer in writing of the action they propose to take thereunder, and if so requested by the registered producer within seven days of the service of such notification shall give him an opportunity of showing cause why such action should not be taken.

EXPLANATORY NOTE

(This Note is not part of the Order.)

This Order approves an amendment to the Scottish Milk Marketing Scheme. The amendment empowers the Board to refuse milk tendered by a registered producer whose milk has failed on seven occasions during a period of sixty-four consecutive days to comply with hygienic standards.

STATUTORY INSTRUMENTS

1968 No. 392 (S.38)

TOWN AND COUNTRY PLANNING, SCOTLAND

The Town and Country Planning (Grants) (Scotland) Regulations 1968

Made - - -	13*th March* 1968
Laid before Parliament	26*th March* 1968
Coming into Operation	27*th March* 1968

In exercise of the powers conferred on me by section 8 of the Local Government (Scotland) Act 1966**(a)** as read with section 89(4) to (6) and section 91 of the Town and Country Planning (Scotland) Act 1947**(b)**, and of all other powers enabling me in that behalf, I hereby, with the consent of the Treasury and after consultation with such associations of local authorities as appear to me to be concerned, make the following regulations:—

Citation and commencement

1. These regulations may be cited as the Town and Country Planning (Grants) (Scotland) Regulations 1968 and shall come into operation on 27th March 1968.

Interpretation

2.—(1) In these regulations, except where the context otherwise requires:—
"the Act of 1945" means the Town and Country Planning (Scotland) Act 1945**(c)**;

"the Act of 1947" means the Town and Country Planning (Scotland) Act 1947;

"the Act of 1959" means the Town and Country Planning (Scotland) Act 1959**(d)**;

"the Act of 1966" means the Local Government (Scotland) Act 1966;

"approved expenditure" means expenditure eligible for grant under regulation 5 of these regulations and includes any expenditure, not being expenditure on the acquisition of land for major redevelopment or land situated within an area to which a Town Development Scheme as defined in Part II of the Housing and Town Development (Scotland) Act 1957**(e)** relates, deemed to be approved expenditure by virtue of regulation 7;

"approved land" means land approved by the Secretary of State for the purposes of these regulations and includes any land deemed to be so approved by virtue of regulation 7;

"clearing" in relation to any approved land, means the removal of buildings or materials from the land, and the levelling of the surface of the land and includes the following operations—

(*a*) the disconnection and filling-in or removal of sewers, mains, pipes, cables or other apparatus in, on, over or under the land;

(a) 1966 c. 51.   (b) 1947 c. 53.   (c) 1945 c. 33.   (d) 1959 c. 70.   (e) 1957 c. 38.

(b) the carrying out of the prescribed requirements with respect to the removal and reinterment of any human remains and the disposal of monuments, tombstones and other memorials, and of fixtures and furnishings under section 27 of the Act of 1945;

"notional loan charges" means, in relation to any expenditure, the amount of the annual payment that would be required to repay that expenditure if it had been borrowed from the Public Works Loan Commissioners on the relevant date in relation to the defrayal of the expenditure and were repayable, together with interest at the rate appropriate to such a borrowing (being the appropriate rate fixed by the Treasury for loans from the Local Loans Fund, or, where there are 2 rates so fixed, the higher of those rates), by equal annual instalments of principal and interest combined over a period of 60 years;

"relevant date" in relation to an act or event means the 16th November occurring in the same financial year as that in which the act or event occurred;

"preliminary development" in relation to any approved land means the carrying out of any work determined by the Secretary of State, either generally or in relation to particular land, to be—

(a) work preparatory to the development or redevelopment of the land for the purposes for which it was acquired or appropriated, or

(b) work comprised in the initial stages of such development.

(2) The Interpretation Act 1889(a) shall apply for the interpretation of these regulations as it applies for the interpretation of an Act of Parliament.

(3) References in these regulations to any enactment are references to that enactment as amended by any subsequent enactment.

General conditions

3. The payment of grant under these regulations, including grant in respect of expenditure incurred in terms of regulation 7 (2) and (3) thereof, shall be dependent upon the fulfilment of the following conditions—

(a) the approval of the Secretary of State shall have been obtained for the land to be the subject of grant and for the use to which it is to be put;

(b) the local planning authority shall have kept such records and furnished such information and returns as may be required by the Secretary of State in connection with his functions under these regulations;

(c) the local planning authority shall have produced to the auditor of their accounts, and when called upon to do so to an authorised officer of the Secretary of State, the said records and copies of the said information and returns, together with any references, plans or other relative documents, certificates and vouchers which the said auditor or authorised officer may require;

(d) the local planning authority shall, where the carrying out of any works by them is necessary to achieve the purpose for which the land was acquired, carry out the works in a reasonably expeditious manner and shall, in a case where disposal of the land is necessary to achieve the said purpose, effect its disposal in a manner approved by the Secretary of State.

General provisions as to payment of grant

4.—(1) Claims in respect of any grant payable under these regulations shall be submitted at such times and in such form as the Secretary of State may

(a) 1889 c. 63.

determine and an advance or advances of such proportion as the Secretary of
State may determine of the estimated amount of the grant payable in accordance
with these regulations may be paid on account. The balance of the grant payable
shall be paid and any excess of advances over grant payable shall be recoverable
after—

(a) the accounts of the expenditure in respect of which the claim was made
have been audited and certified, and

(b) the grant payable has been ascertained.

(2) Where in any year there is, on applying the provisions of sub-paragraphs
(a), (b) and (c) of regulation 6(1) of these regulations to such approved land as
the Secretary of State may determine, an excess of the amount arrived at under
the said sub-paragraph (c) over the total of the amounts arrived at under the
said sub-paragraphs (a) and (b), the Secretary of State may for the purpose of
calculating grant under these regulations in respect of any other approved land
of the local authority apply the excess in reduction of any amount in respect of
which grant would, but for the reduction, be payable for that year.

(3) Where the development or redevelopment of any approved land has been
completed and the Secretary of State is satisfied that it is expedient that the
amount of grant remaining payable towards the approved expenditure in respect
of that land should be paid as a single capital sum and not as 2 or more periodical
grants, the Secretary of State may, after consultation with the local planning
authority concerned, determine that the said amount shall be so paid; and in
determining the amount to be paid in such a case the Secretary of State shall
have regard to the amounts which, but for this paragraph, would have been
payable under the provisions of regulation 6 of these regulations.

(4) Any grant payable under these regulations shall be calculated to the
nearest pound, a fraction of a pound in the final result being ignored or reckoned
as a pound according as it is or is not less than 10s.

Expenditure eligible for grant

5.—(1) For the year 1967/68 and subsequent years, grant shall be payable
by the Secretary of State to local planning authorities in respect of expenditure
incurred by them, whether before or after 16th May 1967, in connection with—

(a) the acquisition of approved land under any such enactment as is mentioned
in paragraph (4) of this regulation, being land concerning which the
Secretary of State is satisfied that it is required for or in connection with—

(i) the development or redevelopment as a whole of any area (whether
or not defined in a Development Plan as an area of comprehensive
development); or

(ii) the relocation of population or industry, or the replacement of open
space, in the course of or in consequence of such development or
redevelopment, and

(b) the clearing and preliminary development of any land falling within the
last foregoing sub-paragraph.

(2) For the purposes of these regulations land appropriated by a local planning
authority for a purpose, being a purpose in respect of which grant would be
payable thereunder in connection with the acquisition of the land had it been
acquired for that purpose, shall be treated as if it had been acquired for that purpose, and at a cost of such amount as shall be determined by the Secretary of State.

(3) The expenditure which may be reckoned as expenditure incurred in connection with the acquisition, clearing and preliminary development of approved land, shall for the purpose of these regulations be such as may be determined by the Secretary of State, with the consent of the Treasury, after deduction of such contributions, receipts, credits or other items received by or due to the local planning authority in respect of the land concerned as the Secretary of State with such consent may determine, and such expenditure may include any sums or any parts of sums paid by local planning authorities in connection with any restriction imposed on the development or use of the land by or under any enactment (whether by way of compensation or by way of contribution towards damage or expense incurred in consequence of the restriction), provided that grant has not been paid or become payable in respect thereof under these regulations or any regulations made under section 89 of the Act of 1947.

(4) The enactments referred to in paragraph (1) (*a*) of this regulation are any of the following enactments, that is to say—

(*a*) Part I of the Act of 1945 or section 35 or section 37 of the Act of 1947, including land acquired by virtue of section 17 of the Act of 1947;

(*b*) section 38 of the Act of 1959;

(*c*) (i) sections 156 and 157 of the Local Government (Scotland) Act 1947(**a**) in any case where land is acquired for the purpose of sections 1 and 2 of the Local Government (Development and Finance) (Scotland) Act 1964(**b**);

(ii) any corresponding provision of any Local Act.

Calculation and amount of grant

6.—(1) Subject to the provisions of paragraphs (2) and (3) of regulation 4 of these regulations grant in respect of approved land shall be payable annually for such a period in relation to any approved expenditure as the Secretary of State may from time to time determine (but not exceeding 60 years), and shall in respect of each year be 50 per cent of the amount arrived at by—

(*a*) taking in respect of approved expenditure defrayed out of money borrowed by the local planning authority the amount of the notional loan charges calculated by reference to the expenditure so defrayed up to the end of the year for which the grant is being calculated;

(*b*) taking in respect of approved expenditure defrayed otherwise than out of money borrowed by the local planning authority the amount of the notional loan charges calculated by reference to so much as the Secretary of State may consider appropriate of such expenditure so defrayed up to the end of the year for which the grant is being calculated and adding to that amount the balance of any approved expenditure defrayed in that year otherwise than out of money so borrowed;

(*c*) taking the amount of the annual equivalent of the capital value of so much of the approved land as the Secretary of State shall at the end of each year determine, plus the amount of any income received during that year in respect of the balance of the approved land; and

(*d*) subtracting from the total of the amounts arrived at under sub-paragraphs (*a*) and (*b*) of this paragraph the total amount arrived at under sub-paragraph (*c*) thereof.

(**a**) 1947 c. 43.   (**b**) 1964 c. 67.

(2) In this regulation "the annual equivalent of the capital value" means the amount of the annual payment that would be required to repay the amount represented by the capital value, if that last mentioned amount had been borrowed from the Public Works Loan Commissioners on the relevant date in relation to the appropriation, sale or disposal, and were repayable, together with interest at the rate appropriate to such a borrowing (being the appropriate rate fixed by the Treasury for loans from the Local Loans Fund, or, where there are 2 rates so fixed, the higher of those rates), by equal annual instalments of principal and interest combined over a period of 60 years.

Revocation and Saving

7.—(1) The Town and Country Planning (Grants) (Scotland) Regulations 1960(a) and the General Grant (Relevant Expenditure) (Scotland) Regulations 1963(b) are hereby revoked.

(2) Any expenditure approved by the Secretary of State under the said regulations of 1960 or under any regulations revoked by the said regulations, being expenditure in respect of which grant is payable under these regulations, shall be deemed to be approved expenditure for the purpose of these regulations.

(3) Where land had been acquired before 16th May 1967, under any enactment referred to in paragraph 5(1)(a) of Part I of Schedule 1 to the Local Government and Miscellaneous Financial Provisions (Scotland) Act 1958(c) for the purposes of the development or redevelopment of any area as a whole and the acquisition, clearing and preliminary development of that land had not been completed before that date, any expenditure incurred before that date on the acquisition, clearing and preliminary development of that land, not being expenditure on the acquisition of land for major redevelopment or land situated within an area to which a Town Development Scheme as defined in Part II of the Housing and Town Development (Scotland) Act 1957, relates, being expenditure by reference to which relevant expenditure was ascertained for the purposes of the said Act of 1958, shall be deemed to be approved expenditure, and the land shall be deemed to be approved land, for the purposes of these regulations.

William Ross,
One of Her Majesty's Principal
Secretaries of State.

St. Andrew's House,
Edinburgh, 1.
11th March 1968.

We consent.

B. K. O'Malley,
E. Alan Fitch,
Two of the Lords Commissioners
of Her Majesty's Treasury.

13th March 1968.

(a) S.I. 1960/2433 (1960 III, p. 3300).   (b) S.I. 1963/1165 (1963 II, p. 1995).
(c) 1958 c. 64.

EXPLANATORY NOTE
(This Note is not a part of the Regulations.)

These regulations replace the Town and Country Planning (Grants) (Scotland) Regulations 1960, in consequence of the revocation and replacement of section 89(1) of the Town and Country Planning (Scotland) Act 1947 (which provided for the payment of Exchequer grants to local authorities in connection with major redevelopment and restrictions imposed by or under planning legislation), by section 8 of the Local Government (Scotland) Act 1966.

These regulations

(i) provide for the payment of Exchequer grants to local authorities in respect of expenditure incurred in connection with the acquisition, clearing and preliminary development of land acquired for the development or redevelopment of areas as a whole and any consequential relocation of population or industry or replacement of open space;

(ii) determine the basis and method of calculation of such grants and lay down the terms and conditions of payment; and

(iii) make consequential savings in consequence of the revocation of the General Grant (Relevant Expenditure) (Scotland) Regulations 1963.

STATUTORY INSTRUMENTS

1968 No. 397

FIRE SERVICES

The Firemen's Pension Scheme (Amendment) (No. 2) Order 1968

Made - - - -	*15th March* 1968
Laid before Parliament	*22nd March* 1968
Coming into Operation	*1st April* 1968

In exercise of the powers conferred upon me by section 26 of the Fire Services Act 1947(a), as amended and extended by sections 1 and 2(1) of the Fire Services Act 1951(b), section 42 of the Reserve and Auxiliary Forces (Protection of Civil Interests) Act 1951(c), section 8 of the Fire Services Act 1959(d) and section 12 of the Superannuation (Miscellaneous Provisions) Act 1967(e), with the approval of the Treasury and after consultation with the Central Fire Brigades Advisory Council and the Scottish Central Fire Brigades Advisory Council, and solely in connection with a transfer of functions in accordance with the said section 12, I hereby make the following Order:—

1.—(1) For paragraph (1)(*d*) of Article 66 of the Firemen's Pension Scheme 1966 set out in the Appendix to the Firemen's Pension Scheme Order 1966(f), as amended(g), (which relates to temporary employment in connection with the provision of fire services) there shall be substituted the following provision:—

"(*d*) employment entered upon in pursuance of arrangements made by the Secretary of State or the Minister of Overseas Development in connection with the training and organisation of fire fighting forces in such an overseas territory as is mentioned in paragraph (3).".

(2) For paragraph (2) of the said Article 66 there shall be substituted the following provisions:—

"(2) In the case of such a person as is mentioned in paragraph (1), the employment therein mentioned (hereafter in this paragraph referred to as 'the relevant employment') shall be treated for the purposes of this Scheme as employment as a member of a brigade and this Scheme shall apply in relation to that employment as if—

(*a*) he were a regular fireman and his duties were his duties as such;

(*b*) his pay and rank were the same as they would have been had he not ceased to perform duties as such a fireman or, where section 10 of the Fire Services Act 1959 applies in his case, the same as his pay and rank as a member of a fire brigade;

(*c*) any reference to a brigade were a reference to the relevant employment;

(a) 1947 c. 41.   (b) 1951 c. 27.   (c) 1951 c. 65.
(d) 1959 c. 44.   (e) 1967 c. 28.
(f) S.I. 1966/1045 (1966 II, p. 2504).
(g) The amending Orders are not relevant to the subject matter of this Order.

(*d*) the reference to a court of quarter sessions in Article 47(1) were a reference to the court of quarter sessions for any county or borough which constitutes or is wholly or partly included in the area of the fire authority by whom he was employed immediately before entering the relevant employment;

(*e*) the reference to the sheriff in Article 47(5) were a reference to the sheriff having jurisdiction in the place where he served as a fireman immediately before entering the relevant employment; and

(*f*) Articles 51, 73 and 74 were omitted;

and, except where the relevant employment is such as is mentioned in paragraph 1(*d*)—

(*g*) any reference to a fire authority were a reference to the Secretary of State.

(2A) Without prejudice to paragraph (2), in the case of such a person as is mentioned in paragraph (1) whose relevant employment is such as is mentioned in paragraph 1(*d*), this Scheme shall apply in relation to that employment as if—

(*a*) any reference to a fire authority were a reference to the Secretary of State or the Minister of Overseas Development; and

(*b*) any reference in Article 46 or Schedule 8 to the Secretary of State were a reference to the Secretary of State or the Minister of Overseas Development.".

2. This Order may be cited as the Firemen's Pension Scheme (Amendment) (No. 2) Order 1968 and shall come into operation on 1st April 1968.

James Callaghan,
One of Her Majesty's Principal
Secretaries of State.

14th March 1968.

We approve,

Joseph Harper,
B. K. O'Malley,
Two of the Lords Commissioners
of Her Majesty's Treasury.

15th March 1968.

EXPLANATORY NOTE
(*This Note is not part of the Order.*)

This Order contains amendments to the Firemen's Pension Scheme 1966 in connection with the transfer, in accordance with section 12 of the Superannuation (Miscellaneous Provisions) Act 1967, of certain functions relating to firemen with overseas service from the Secretary of State to the Minister of Overseas Development.

STATUTORY INSTRUMENTS

1968 No. 398

AGRICULTURE

GUARANTEED PRICES AND ASSURED MARKETS

The Fatstock (Guarantee Payments) (Amendment) Order 1968

Made - - -		*13th March* 1968
Laid before Parliament		*26th March* 1968
Coming into Operation		*1st April* 1968

The Minister of Agriculture, Fisheries and Food and the Secretaries of State respectively concerned with agriculture in Scotland and Northern Ireland, acting jointly, in exercise of the powers conferred upon them by sections 1, 9(4) and 35(3) of the Agriculture Act 1957(a) and of all other powers enabling them in that behalf, with the consent of the Treasury and after consultation with such bodies of persons as appear to the said Ministers to represent the interests of producers of fatstock, hereby make the following order:—

1.—(1) This order may be cited as the Fatstock (Guarantee Payments) (Amendment) Order 1968; and shall come into operation on 1st April 1968.

(2) The Interpretation Act 1889(b) shall apply to the interpretation of this order as it applies to the interpretation of an Act of Parliament.

2. The Fatstock (Guarantee Payments) Order 1964(c) shall be amended as follows:—

    (*a*) by deleting article 14 thereof (which empowers the Minister to provide a separate guaranteed price for pigs of a quality premium grade);

    (*b*) by substituting for sub-paragraph (*b*) of article 15(3) thereof the following sub-paragraph:—

        " (*b*) the producer has made a declaration that it has been sold by private treaty; or ";

    (*c*) by substituting for paragraph (4) of article 15 thereof the following paragraph:—

        " (4) No carcase shall be certified unless the producer has made a declaration that—

            (*a*) it has been sold; or

            (*b*) it will be sold by or on behalf of the producer in a butchery business and is not intended for consumption in the producer's household; or

            (*c*) it has been or will be transferred by the producer from the carcase owner's agricultural undertaking to another undertaking (not being an agricultural undertaking) in the same ownership for consumption therein.

    In any case where a declaration has been made pursuant to sub-paragraph (*c*) above the carcase shall not be certified unless the Minister is satisfied that the carcase owner's agricultural undertaking is managed as a separate concern.";

(**a**) 1957 c. 57.   (**b**) 1889 c. 63.
(**c**) S.I. 1964/463 (1964 I, p. 746).

(*d*) by inserting immediately after article 16 thereof the following article:—

"16A. The Minister may, to such extent and in such manner as he may from time to time direct, delegate to the Meat and Livestock Commission (established under section 1 of the Agriculture Act 1967(**a**)) any of the functions in relation to Great Britain (other than the function of determining guaranteed prices or factors relevant to the operation of such prices) conferred or imposed on him by this order.";

(*e*) by substituting in Part IV of the Schedule thereto for the words " articles 12 and 14 " the words " article 12 " and in sub-paragraph (*b*) of that Part for the words " articles 13(1) and 14 " the words " article 13(1) " and by deleting in that sub-paragraph the words " as the case may be".

In Witness whereof the Official Seal of the Minister of Agriculture, Fisheries and Food is hereunto affixed on 8th March 1968.

(L.S.)

Frederick Peart,
Minister of Agriculture, Fisheries and Food.

Given under the Seal of the Secretary of State for Scotland on 12th March 1968.

(L.S.)

William Ross,
Secretary of State for Scotland.

Given under the hand of the Secretary of State for the Home Department on 12th March 1968.

James Callaghan,
Secretary of State for the Home Department.

We consent　　　　　　　　　　　　　*B. K. O'Malley,*
13th March 1968.　　　　　　　　　　*E. Alan Fitch,*
　　　　　　　　　　　　Two of the Lords Commissioners of
　　　　　　　　　　　　　　　　Her Majesty's Treasury.

EXPLANATORY NOTE

(This Note is not part of the Order.)

This order amends the Fatstock (Guarantee Payments) Order 1964 to enable the Minister of Agriculture, Fisheries and Food and the Secretary of State for Scotland to delegate to the Meat and Livestock Commission in Great Britain certain of the functions conferred or imposed on them by that order.

It deletes article 14 of that order, which empowered the provision of a separate guaranteed price for pigs of a quality premium grade.

It also makes minor amendments to certification procedures.

(**a**) 1967 c. 22.

STATUTORY INSTRUMENTS

1968 No. 399

AGRICULTURE

GUARANTEED PRICES AND ASSURED MARKETS

The Fatstock (Protection of Guarantees) (Amendment) Order 1968

Made - - -	*12th March* 1968
Laid before Parliament	*26th March* 1968
Coming into Operation	*1st April* 1968

The Minister of Agriculture, Fisheries and Food and the Secretaries of State respectively concerned with agriculture in Scotland and Northern Ireland, acting jointly, in exercise of the powers conferred upon them by sections 5 (as amended by sections 3(2) and 70(1) of the Agriculture Act 1967(a)), 9(4) and 35(3) of the Agriculture Act 1957(b), and of all other powers enabling them in that behalf, hereby make the following order:—

1.—(1) This order may be cited as the Fatstock (Protection of Guarantees) (Amendment) Order 1968; and shall come into operation on 1st April 1968.

(2) The Interpretation Act 1889(c) shall apply to the interpretation of this order as it applies to the interpretation of an Act of Parliament.

2. The Fatstock (Protection of Guarantees) Order 1958(d), as amended(e), shall be further amended as follows:—

(*a*) by adding at the end of article 3 thereof the words " and in addition, if the appropriate Minister so requires, the ear or ears of any approved carcase shall be removed or mutilated.";

(*b*) by substituting for sub-paragraphs (*a*) and (*b*) of article 6(1) thereof the following sub-paragraphs:—
  " (*a*) by virtue of the Movement of Animals (Records) Order 1960(f), as amended(g), or the Transit of Animals (Amendment) (Northern Ireland) Order 1941(h) or the Movements of Animals (Records) Order (Northern Ireland) 1962(i), as amended(j), to keep or retain a record of the movement of animals, or
  (*b*) by virtue of the Swine Fever Order 1963(k) or the Swine Fever Order (No. 2) (Northern Ireland) 1959(l), to keep a register or record of his transactions in pigs,";

(**a**) 1967 c. 22.
(**c**) 1889 c. 63.
(**e**) S.I. 1960/293 (1960 I, p. 103).
(**g**) S.I. 1961/1493 (1961 II, p. 3016).
(**i**) S.R. & O. (N.I.) 1962/100.
(**k**) S.I. 1963/286 (1963 I, p. 239).

(**b**) 1957 c. 57.
(**d**) S.I. 1958/958 (1958 I, p. 84).
(**f**) S.I. 1960/105 (1960 I, p. 302).
(**h**) S.R. & O. (N.I.) 1941/145.
(**j**) S.R. & O. (N.I.) 1966/199.
(**l**) S.R. & O. (N.I.) 1959/71.

(*c*) by inserting immediately after article 10 thereof the following article:—

" 10A. The appropriate Minister may, to such extent and in such manner as he may from time to time direct, delegate to the Meat and Livestock Commission (established under section 1 of the Agriculture Act 1967(**a**)) any of the functions in relation to Great Britain conferred or imposed on him by this order.";

(*d*) by deleting from paragraph 4(*b*) of the Schedule thereto the words " and in addition the ear or ears of the carcase to be removed or mutilated ".

In Witness whereof the Official Seal of the Minister of Agriculture, Fisheries and Food is hereunto affixed on 8th March 1968.

(L.S.)

Frederick Peart,
Minister of Agriculture, Fisheries and Food.

Given under the Seal of the Secretary of State for Scotland on 12th March 1968.

(L.S.)

William Ross,
Secretary of State for Scotland.

Given under the hand of the Secretary of State for the Home Department on 12th March 1968.

James Callaghan,
Secretary of State for the Home Department.

EXPLANATORY NOTE

(This Note is not part of the Order.)

This order amends the Fatstock (Protection of Guarantees) Order 1958, as amended, to enable the Minister of Agriculture, Fisheries and Food and the Secretary of State for Scotland to delegate to the Meat and Livestock Commission in Great Britain functions conferred or imposed on them by that order.

It provides for the marking of any approved carcase by the removal or mutilation of an ear or ears if the appropriate Minister so requires.

It also extends the provision for access to records kept under other orders, by the addition of two Northern Ireland Orders to those already specified.

(**a**) 1967 c. 22.

STATUTORY INSTRUMENTS

1968 No. 400

SUGAR

The Sugar Beet (Research and Education) Order 1968

Made - - -	*14th March* 1968
Laid before Parliament	*25th March* 1968
Coming into Operation	*1st April* 1968

The Minister of Agriculture, Fisheries and Food and the Secretary of State in exercise of the powers conferred upon them by section 18(1) and (2) of the Sugar Act 1956(a), and of all other powers them enabling in that behalf, after consultation with the British Sugar Corporation Limited and with such bodies as in their opinion are substantially representative of growers of home-grown beet and having prepared a programme for carrying out research and education in matters affecting the growing of home-grown beet, hereby jointly make the following order:—

1.—(1) This order may be cited as the Sugar Beet (Research and Education) Order 1968; and shall come into operation on 1st April 1968.

(2) The Interpretation Act 1889(b), shall apply to the interpretation of this order as it applies to the interpretation of an Act of Parliament.

2. The programme of research and education set out in the Schedule to this order together with the expenditure estimated to be incurred in carrying it out shall be the programme for the year beginning on 1st April 1968.

3. The contributions from the British Sugar Corporation Ltd. (hereinafter referred to as " the Corporation ") and every grower of home-grown beet who delivers beet to the Corporation during the year beginning on 1st April 1968, towards defraying the expenditure to be incurred in carrying out the aforesaid programme shall be assessed as follows:—

(a) in the case of any grower of home-grown beet, the contribution shall be at the rate of threepence halfpenny for every ton of home-grown beet sold by him for delivery to the Corporation in that year;

(b) in the case of the Corporation the contribution shall be at the rate of threepence halfpenny for every ton of home-grown beet purchased by them for delivery in that year.

4.—(1) All contracts made between the Corporation and any grower for the sale of home-grown beet for delivery to the Corporation during the year beginning on 1st April 1968 shall provide that the total amount of the grower's contribution assessed in accordance with the foregoing provisions of this order shall be payable by the grower to the Corporation out of any sums standing to the credit of that grower in account with the Corporation and be deducted by the Corporation from the amount payable to the grower.

(a) 1956 c. 48. (b) 1889 c. 63.

(2) The Corporation shall pay the proceeds, together with the amount of the contribution from the Corporation assessed in accordance with sub-paragraph (*b*) of Article 3 of this order, to the Minister of Agriculture, Fisheries and Food within that year.

5. The amount of any contribution which has not been paid to the Minister of Agriculture, Fisheries and Food during the year within which it is due shall become a debt due to that Minister.

In witness whereof the Official Seal of the Minister of Agriculture, Fisheries and Food is hereunto affixed on 13th March 1968.

(L.S.)   *Frederick Peart,*
                             Minister of Agriculture, Fisheries and Food.

Given under the Seal of the Secretary of State for Scotland on 14th March 1968.

(L.S.)   *William Ross,*
                             Secretary of State for Scotland.

SCHEDULE

Projects of research and education in matters affecting the growing of home-grown beet to be carried out by the persons or bodies described in relation thereto and estimates of expenditure to be incurred in carrying them out.

	£	£
A. RESEARCH		
1. Plant Breeding: Plant Breeding Institute, Cambridge		45,720
2. Variety Trials: National Institute of Agricultural Botany		15,750
3. Diseases Investigations, Fertilizer and Seed Production Experiments: Broom's Barn Experimental Station		64,306
4. Crop Husbandry: Norfolk Agricultural Station ...		12,010
5. Machinery and Cultivation Experiments: National Institute of Agricultural Engineering		9,660
6. Scottish Trials and Experiments		3,310
7. Agronomic Experiments: School of Agriculture, University of Nottingham...		2,139
8. Physiology:—		
(*a*) Imperial College of Science and Technology, London ...	4,674	
(*b*) Rothamsted Experimental Station	3,520	
(*c*) School of Agricultural Sciences, University of Leeds	551	
		8,745

	£	£

B. EDUCATION

9. Publicity, British Sugar Corporation Ltd.:—

    (a) British Sugar Beet Review 3,550

    (b) Films 1,050

    (c) Virus Yellows 2,375

                             6,975

10. Demonstrations:—

    (a) Cultivation 14,450

    (b) Harvest Machinery 1,500

    (c) Scottish 850

    (d) Spring Mechanisation 3,000

                             19,800

C. GENERAL

11. Travelling and Subsistence Expenses of Members and Officers of the Sugar Beet Research and Education Committee and its sub-committees ... 300

12. Administrative Charges:—

    (a) Ministry of Agriculture, Fisheries and Food ... 1,355

    (b) Department of Agriculture and Fisheries for Scotland 100

    (c) Exchequer and Audit Department 75

                             1,530

13. Institut International de Recherches Betteravières:—

    (a) Subscriptions 1,100

    (b) Expenses and Visits 1,100

                             2,200

14. Other Items:—

    (a) Docking Disorder, Aerial Photographic Survey 850

    (b) Visits Abroad 350

    (c) Contingencies 1,355

                             2,555

               Total 195,000

EXPLANATORY NOTE

(This Note is not part of the Order.)

This order provides for the assessment and collection of contributions in 1968 from the British Sugar Corporation Ltd., and growers of home-grown beet towards the programme of research and education set out in the Schedule to the Order. The contributions in 1968 remain at 3½d. per ton.

1968 No. 404 (L. 8)

COUNTY COURTS

The County Court Districts (Aldershot and Farnham) Order 1968

Made - - - -	18*th March* 1968
Coming into Operation	1*st April* 1968

I, Gerald, Baron Gardiner, Lord High Chancellor of Great Britain, in exercise of the powers conferred on me by section 2 of the County Courts Act 1959(a), do hereby order as follows:—

1.—(1) The districts of the Aldershot and Farnham County Courts shall be consolidated and a court shall be held for the consolidated district at Aldershot by the name of the Aldershot and Farnham County Court:

Provided that no process shall be invalid if the court is described therein as the Aldershot County Court or the Farnham County Court.

(2) The Aldershot and Farnham County Court shall have jurisdiction in proceedings commenced in the Aldershot County Court or the Farnham County Court before this Order comes into operation.

2.—(1) The County Court Districts Order 1949(b), as amended (c), shall have effect as further amended by this Order.

(2) This Order may be cited as the County Court Districts (Aldershot and Farnham) Order 1968, and shall come into operation on 1st April 1968.

Dated 18th March 1968.

Gardiner, C.

EXPLANATORY NOTE

(This Note is not part of the Order.)

This Order consolidates the districts of the Aldershot and Farnham County Courts, and provides for the court for the consolidated district to be held at Aldershot, by the name of the Aldershot and Farnham County Court.

(a) 1959 c. 22.   (b) S.I. 1949/2058 (1949 I, p. 955).
(c) The relevant amending instrument is S.I. 1952/1380 (1952 I, p. 633).

STATUTORY INSTRUMENTS

1968 No. 405

CUSTOMS AND EXCISE

The Composite Goods (Amendment) Order 1968

Made - - - -	*19th March 1968*
Laid before the House of Commons	*19th March 1968*
Coming into Operation	*20th March 1968*

Whereas on 19th March 1968 a resolution was passed by the House of Commons increasing the duty of customs on hydrocarbon oils, which resolution has statutory effect under the Provisional Collection of Taxes Act 1968(**a**):

Now, therefore, the Lords Commissioners of Her Majesty's Treasury, by virtue of the powers conferred on them by Schedule 2 to the Finance Act 1957(**b**) and in view of the said resolution, hereby make the following Order: —

1. As from the date of the coming into operation of this Order, the Composite Goods Order 1964(**c**) shall have effect with the substitution in Article 2 thereof and in the Schedule thereto of 8 per cent for 5½ per cent.

2. The Composite Goods (Amendment) Order 1967(**d**) is hereby revoked.

3.—(1) This Order may be cited as the Composite Goods (Amendment) Order 1968.

(2) This Order shall come into operation on the 20th March 1968.

B. K. O'Malley,

Joseph Harper,

Two of the Lords Commissioners
of Her Majesty's Treasury.

19th March 1968.

EXPLANATORY NOTE

(This note is not part of the Order.)

This Order increases the rate of hydrocarbon oil duty, chargeable on imported goods of the categories specified in the Schedule to the Composite Goods Order 1964, as amended by the Composite Goods (Amendment) Order 1967, from 7 per cent to 8 per cent ad valorem. This increase reflects the change in the rate of customs duty on hydrocarbon oils made by resolution of the House of Commons on 19th March 1968.

(**a**) 1968 c. 2.   (**b**) 1957 c. 49.
(**c**) S.I. 1964/1341 (1964 II, p. 3056).   (**d**) S.I. 1967/574 (1967 I, p. 1781).

STATUTORY INSTRUMENTS

1968 No. 407

CHILDREN AND YOUNG PERSONS

The Approved Schools (Contributions by Local Authorities) Regulations 1968

Made - - -	*15th March* 1968
Coming into Operation	*1st April* 1968

In pursuance of the power conferred upon me by section 90(1) of the Children and Young Persons Act 1933(**a**), I, the Right Honourable James Callaghan, one of Her Majesty's Principal Secretaries of State, hereby make the following Regulations :—

1. In Regulation 1 of the Approved Schools (Contributions by Local Authorities) Regulations 1962(**b**), as amended (**c**) (which provides that the contributions to be made by the local authority named in an approved school order to the expenses of the managers of an approved school throughout the time, except in certain specified circumstances, during which the person to whom the order relates is under the care of the said managers, shall be at the rate of eleven pounds five shillings and ninepence a week) for the words "eleven pounds five shillings and ninepence" there shall be substituted the words "twelve pounds fifteen shillings and sixpence".

2. The Approved Schools (Contributions by Local Authorities) Regulations 1967(**c**) are hereby revoked.

3. The Interpretation Act 1889(**d**) shall apply to the interpretation of these Regulations as it applies to the interpretation of an Act of Parliament.

4. These Regulations may be cited as the Approved Schools (Contributions by Local Authorities) Regulations 1968 and shall come into operation on 1st April 1968.

James Callaghan,
One of Her Majesty's Principal
Secretaries of State.

Home Office,
   Whitehall.
15th March 1968.

(**a**) 1933 c. 12.	(**b**) S.I. 1962/623 (1962 I, p. 612).
(**c**) S.I. 1967/334 (1967 I, p. 1157).	(**d**) 1889 c. 63.

EXPLANATORY NOTE

(This Note is not part of the Regulations.)

These Regulations raise from £11 5s. 9d. a week to £12 15s. 6d. a week the contributions to be made by the local authority named in an approved school order towards the expenses of the managers of the school in respect of the person to whom the order relates during the time when that person is under the care of those managers.

STATUTORY INSTRUMENTS

1968 No. 414

EXCHEQUER

The Treasury Bills Regulations 1968

Made - - - -	*18th March* 1968
Laid before Parliament	*21st March* 1968
Coming into Operation	*1st April* 1968

The Treasury, in exercise of the powers conferred upon them by section 9 of the Treasury Bills Act 1877(a) and section 5 of the National Debt Act 1889(b), and of all other powers enabling them in that behalf, hereby make the following Regulations:—

Mode of Issue of Treasury bills

1. Treasury bills may be issued in the following ways :—

(a) by inviting tenders and issuing Treasury bills to persons whose tenders are accepted ; or

(b) by issue at a fixed rate of discount, determined by the Treasury, to the National Debt Commissioners or to such other persons as may be willing to buy them.

Invitations to tender and tenders

2.—(1) An invitation to tender for Treasury bills shall be given by notice in the London Gazette not less than two clear days before the date on which tenders are to be delivered, and such notice shall specify—

(a) the date on which, and the place at which, tenders are to be delivered, and

(b) the period for which, and the terms and conditions subject to which, the bills are to be issued.

(2) Tenders for Treasury bills shall be in a form approved by the Treasury and shall be opened at the Bank of England in the presence of such person or persons as may from time to time be appointed by the Treasury.

(3) The Treasury may refuse any tender if they think fit.

Form of bills

3.—(1) Treasury bills—

(a) shall be in the form set out in Schedule 1 to these Regulations, and

(b) shall have printed on them a facsimile of the signature of one of the Secretaries to the Treasury for the time being.

(2) Treasury bills issued in any financial year shall be numbered consecutively in accordance with their order of issue in that financial year.

(a) 1877 c. 2. (b) 1889 c. 6.

Preparation and delivery of bills

4.—(1) When any tenders for Treasury bills have been accepted by the Treasury, or when the National Debt Commissioners or any other persons have signified their willingness to buy Treasury bills at a fixed rate of discount, the Treasury shall issue a warrant authorising the Bank of England to prepare bills, in denominations of £5,000 or multiples thereof as may be necessary, for such total amount as is specified in the warrant, and the warrant shall be transmitted to the Comptroller and Auditor General for his counter-signature.

(2) The Treasury bills, when ready for issue, shall upon receipt of the sums payable in respect of them, be delivered by the Bank of England, under the authority of the Treasury warrant, to the order of the persons entitled to them.

Issue of amount of discount out of the National Loans Fund

5. In respect of any Treasury bills issued, the Treasury shall from time to time issue to the Bank of England out of the National Loans Fund a sum equal to the amount of discount on the bills, and such sum shall be paid by the Bank of England into the National Loans Fund, together with the sums actually received in respect of the bills.

Mode of payment and discharge

6.—(1) The principal sum payable in respect of a Treasury bill shall be paid at the head office of the Bank of England.

(2) Where the Bank of England require a discharge to be given upon the payment of a Treasury bill, it shall be given by means of an acknowledge-ment of receipt given on the back of the bill or on a schedule showing the number and amount of the bill.

Cancellation of bills

7.—(1) Where a Treasury bill has been paid off by the Bank of England, it shall be cancelled by perforation of the signature on the bill.

(2) Cancelled Treasury bills shall from time to time be destroyed by the Bank of England, and the Chief Cashier of the Bank of England shall give particulars to the Treasury of the total nominal value of the Treasury bills so destroyed and of the dates between which they were paid off and cancelled.

Defaced, lost and destroyed bills

8. Where a Treasury bill has been defaced, lost or destroyed, the Bank of England may issue a duplicate bill on such terms as to evidence and indemnity as the Bank of England may require.

Interpretation

9. The Interpretation Act 1889(**a**) shall apply for the interpretation of these Regulations as it applies for the interpretation of an Act of Parliament, and as if these Regulations and the instruments hereby revoked were Acts of Parliament.

(**a**) 1889 c. 63.

Revocations

10. The instruments specified in Schedule 2 to these Regulations are hereby revoked.

Citation and commencement

11. These Regulations may be cited as the Treasury Bills Regulations 1968, and shall come into operation on 1st April 1968.

B. K. O'Malley,
E. Alan Fitch,
Two of the Lords Commissioners
of Her Majesty's Treasury.

18th March 1968.

SCHEDULE 1

Regulation 3

FORM OF TREASURY BILL

TREASURY BILL

Due ....

Issued under the Treasury Bills Act 1877 and the National Loans Act 1968.
£ ....   [000000]

London, ... 19......

This Treasury Bill entitles* ....
....
or Order to Payment of .... Pounds at the Bank of England
out of the National Loans Fund on the .... 19......

.... £...............

Secretary to the Treasury.

[000000]

* If this blank is not filled in, the Bill will be paid to bearer.

SCHEDULE 2

Regulation 10

Instruments revoked	References
Treasury Minute dated 31st May 1889 prescribing regulations as to the preparation, issue and cancellation of Treasury bills.	S.R. & O. Rev. XXIII, p. 289.
Treasury Minute dated 24th January 1904 amending the regulations laid down in the Treasury Minute of 31st May 1889.	H. of C. Paper 1 (2nd February 1904).
Treasury Minute dated 13th April 1915 prescribing further regulations.	H. of C. Paper 199 (15th April 1915).

EXPLANATORY NOTE

(This Note is not part of the Regulations.)

These Regulations, which consolidate with amendments the instruments specified in Schedule 2, provide for the mode of issue of Treasury bills, their form, the mode of their payment, their cancellation, and the replacement of lost bills.

The principal changes are :—

(*a*) the minimum period between invitation to tender and date of tender is reduced from three to two clear days ; and

(*b*) the form of Treasury bills is altered to facilitate their handling.

STATUTORY INSTRUMENTS

1968 No. 416

DANGEROUS DRUGS

The Dangerous Drugs (Supply to Addicts) Regulations 1968

Made - - -	18*th March* 1968
Laid before Parliament	25*th March* 1968
Coming into Operation	16*th April* 1968

In exercise of the powers conferred on me by section 11 of the Dangerous Drugs Act 1965(**a**) as extended by section 1(1) of the Dangerous Drugs Act 1967(**b**) and sections 5 and 8(3) of the said Act of 1967, I hereby make the following Regulations :—

1.—(1) Subject to paragraph (3) of this Regulation, a medical practitioner shall not administer, supply or authorise the administration or supply to persons addicted to any drug, or prescribe for such persons, any substance to which this Regulation applies except—

(*a*) for the purpose of relieving pain due to organic disease or injury ; or

(*b*) under the authority and in accordance with the conditions of a licence issued to him by the Secretary of State in pursuance of these Regulations.

(2) For the purposes of the preceding paragraph, a person shall be regarded as addicted to a drug only if, as a result of repeated administration, he has become so dependent upon the drug that he has an overpowering desire for the administration of it to be continued.

(3) Paragraph (1) of this Regulation shall not apply to the administration or supply by a medical practitioner of a substance to which this Regulation applies if the administration or supply is authorised by another medical practitioner under the authority and in accordance with the conditions of a licence issued to him in pursuance of these Regulations.

(4) This Regulation applies to—

(*a*) cocaine, its salts and any preparation, admixture, extract or other substance containing any proportion of cocaine or its salts other than a preparation for the time being falling within paragraph 10 of the Schedule to the Dangerous Drugs Act 1965 ;

(*b*) diamorphine, its salts and any preparation, admixture, extract or other substance containing any proportion of diamorphine or its salts.

2. A licence issued for the purposes of Regulation 1 of these Regulations shall be valid for such period and subject to such conditions as may be specified in the licence and may be revoked by the Secretary of State at any time.

(**a**) 1965 c. 15.   (**b**) 1967 c. 82.

3. These Regulations and, in relation only to the requirements of these Regulations, sections 1, 2 and 3 of the Dangerous Drugs Act 1967 and sections 16 and 20 of the Dangerous Drugs Act 1965 shall apply to servants and agents of the Crown.

4.—(1) In these Regulations the expression "drug" means any substance for the time being specified in Part I of the Schedule to the Dangerous Drugs Act 1965.

(2) The Interpretation Act 1889(**a**) shall apply to the interpretation of these Regulations as it applies to the interpretation of an Act of Parliament.

5. These Regulations shall not extend to Northern Ireland.

6. These Regulations may be cited as the Dangerous Drugs (Supply to Addicts) Regulations 1968 and shall come into operation on 16th April 1968.

James Callaghan,
One of Her Majesty's Principal
Secretaries of State.

Home Office,
Whitehall.

18th March 1968.

EXPLANATORY NOTE
(This Note is not part of the Regulations.)

These Regulations prohibit a medical practitioner from administering, supplying or authorising the administration or supply to drug addicts, or prescribing for drug addicts, cocaine or diamorphine (commonly known as heroin) except for the purpose of relieving pain due to organic disease or injury, or under and in accordance with a licence issued by the Secretary of State in pursuance of the Regulations. Their provisions, and such of the provisions of the Dangerous Drugs Acts of 1965 and 1967 as are necessary to implement them, are applied to servants and agents of the Crown.

(**a**) 1889 c. 63.

STATUTORY INSTRUMENTS

1968 No. 418 (S. 39)

PROBATION OF OFFENDERS

The Probation (Scotland) Amendment Rules 1968

Made - - -		18*th March* 1968
Coming into Operation—		
Rules 1, 2 *and* 3 -		1*st April* 1968
Rule 4 - - -		1*st April* 1969

In exercise of the powers conferred on me by paragraph 7 of Schedule 3 to the Criminal Justice (Scotland) Act 1949(a), and by section 1 of the Police, Fire and Probation Officers Remuneration Act 1956(b), and of all other powers enabling me in that behalf, I hereby make the following Rules:—

Citation, commencement and interpretation

1.—(1) These Rules may be cited as the Probation (Scotland) Amendment Rules 1968.

(2) This Rule and Rules 2 and 3 of these Rules shall come into operation on 1st April 1968 and Rule 4 of these Rules shall come into operation on 1st April 1969.

(3) In these Rules the expression " the principal Rules " means the Probation (Scotland) Rules 1967(c) as amended by the Probation (Scotland) Amendment Rules 1967(d).

(4) The Interpretation Act 1889(e) applies for the interpretation of these Rules as it applies for the interpretation of an Act of Parliament.

Salary of probation officers

2. For Schedule 2 to the principal Rules there shall be substituted the following Schedule.

(a) 1949 c. 94.   (b) 1956 c. 1.   (c) S.I. 1967/65 (1967 I, p. 129).
(d) S.I. 1967/908 (1967 II, p. 2727).   (e) 1889 c. 63.

Rule 44(1)   " SCHEDULE 2

SCALE OF ANNUAL SALARY FOR WHOLE-TIME PROBATION OFFICERS

TABLE

		£
Up to 1 year's service	.. ..	870
Over 1 and up to 2 years' service	.. ..	925
„ 2 „ „ „ 3 „ „	.. ..	975
„ 3 „ „ „ 4 „ „	.. ..	1,030
„ 4 „ „ „ 5 „ „	.. ..	1,080
„ 5 „ „ „ 6 „ „	.. ..	1,135
„ 6 „ „ „ 7 „ „	.. ..	1,190
„ 7 „ „ „ 8 „ „	.. ..	1,245
„ 8 „ „ „ 9 „ „	.. ..	1,305
„ 9 „ „ „ 10 „ „	.. ..	1,360
„ 10 „ „ „ 11 „ „	.. ..	1,420
„ 11 „ „ „ 12 „ „	.. ..	1,480
„ 12 „ „ „ 13 „ „	.. ..	1,540
Over 13 years' service	.. ..	1,600 "

Salary of senior probation officers

3. For Schedule 3 to the principal Rules as amended by the Probation (Scotland) Amendment Rules 1967 there shall be substituted the following Schedule:—

Rule 46(1)   " SCHEDULE 3

SCALE OF ANNUAL SALARY FOR SENIOR PROBATION OFFICERS

TABLE

		£
Up to 1 year's service	.. ..	1,715
Over 1 and up to 2 years' service	.. ..	1,770
„ 2 „ „ „ 3 „ „ ..	.. ..	1,830
„ 3 „ „ „ 4 „ „ ..	.. ..	1,890
„ 4 years' service	.. ..	1,950 "

4. For the said Schedule 3, as amended by Rule 3 of these Rules, there shall be substituted the following Schedule:—

" SCHEDULE 3   Rule 46(1)

SCALE OF ANNUAL SALARY FOR SENIOR PROBATION OFFICERS

TABLE

	£
Up to 1 year's service	1,770
Over 1 and up to 2 years' service..	1,830
„ 2 „ „ „ 3 „ „	1,890
„ 3 „ „ „ 4 „ „	1,950
„ 4 years' service	2,015 "

William Ross,

One of Her Majesty's Principal
Secretaries of State.

St. Andrew's House,
Edinburgh 1.
18th March 1968.

EXPLANATORY NOTE

(This Note is not part of the Rules.)

The Rules amend the Probation (Scotland) Rules 1967 by introducing higher scales of annual salary, in the case of senior probation officers on 1st April 1968 and 1st April 1969, and in the case of probation officers on 1st April 1968.

STATUTORY INSTRUMENTS

1968 No. 420 (S.41)

EDUCATION, SCOTLAND

The Remuneration of Teachers (Scotland) Order 1968

Made - - -	14*th March* 1968
Coming into Operation	1*st April* 1968

Whereas—

(1) under section 1 of the Remuneration of Teachers (Scotland) Act 1967(a) (hereinafter referred to as "the Act") the Scottish Teachers Salaries Committee (hereinafter referred to as "the Committee") have been constituted for the purpose of considering the remuneration of teachers and the Secretary of State has directed them to consider the remuneration of the following descriptions of teachers—(*a*) teachers employed whole-time by education authorities in the provision of primary and secondary education under the Education (Scotland) Acts 1939 to 1967 and duly qualified for appointment other than a temporary appointment in terms of regulations for the time being in force under the said Acts ; and (*b*) teachers employed whole-time by education authorities in the provision of further education under the said Acts ;

(2) under section 2(2) of the Act the Committee have transmitted to the Secretary of State recommendations agreed on by them with respect to the remuneration of teachers of the said descriptions;

(3) under section 2(3) of the Act the Secretary of State has prepared a draft memorandum setting out the scales and other provisions required for determining the remuneration of teachers of the said descriptions in the form in which, in his opinion, those scales and provisions should be so as to give effect to the recommendations of the Committee;

(4) the Secretary of State, as required by section 2(4) of the Act, has consulted the Committee with respect to the draft memorandum and has made such modifications thereof as were requisite for giving effect to representations made by the Committee; and

(5) the Secretary of State has arranged for a memorandum setting out the requisite scales and other provisions in the form of the draft as modified as aforesaid to be published by Her Majesty's Stationery Office under the title "SCOTTISH TEACHERS' SALARIES MEMORANDUM 1968";

Now, Therefore, in exercise of the powers conferred on me by section 2(4) of the Act, and of all other powers enabling me in that behalf, I hereby order as follows:—

Citation and Commencement

1. This order may be cited as the Remuneration of Teachers (Scotland) Order 1968 and shall come into operation on 1st April 1968.

(a) 1967 c. 36.

Interpretation

2.—(1) In this order—

"education authority" has the meaning assigned to it by the Education (Scotland) Act 1962(**a**);

"registered" has the meaning assigned to it by the Teaching Council (Scotland) Act 1965(**b**); and

"regulations of 1966" means the Teachers' Salaries (Scotland) Regulations 1966(**c**)

(2) The Interpretation Act 1889(**d**) shall apply for the interpretation of this order as it applies for the interpretation of an Act of Parliament.

(3) Section 38 of the Interpretation Act 1889 shall apply as if this order were an Act of Parliament and as if the regulations revoked by this order were an Act of Parliament repealed by an Act of Parliament.

Remuneration of Teachers

3. The remuneration payable to teachers employed whole-time by education authorities solely or mainly in or in connection with (*a*) primary and secondary education under the Education (Scotland) Acts 1939 to 1967 and who are registered teachers, or (*b*) further education under the said Acts shall be determined in accordance with the scales and other provisions set out in the memorandum published by Her Majesty's Stationery Office as aforesaid.

Revocation

4.—(1) The regulations of 1966 are hereby revoked: provided that such revocation shall not prevent the Secretary of State or the education authority from exercising any of their functions under the said regulations in respect of employment of any teachers to which the said regulations apply in the period during which the said regulations were in operation.

(2) Notwithstanding the provisions of the last foregoing paragraph any power, whether under the regulations of 1966 or under regulations made before the regulations of 1966, to reassess the length of service of a teacher for the purpose of the calculation of his salary in respect of employment in the period during which the regulations of 1966, or the regulations made before the regulations of 1966, were in operation shall not be exercised save in exceptional circumstances.

St. Andrews' House,
Edinburgh, 1.
14th March 1968.

William Ross,
One of Her Majesty's
Principal Secretaries of State.

(**a**) 1962 c. 47.   (**b**) 1965 c. 19.
(**c**) S.I. 1966/831 (1966 II, p. 1919).   (**d**) 1889 c. 63.

EXPLANATORY NOTE

(This Note is not part of the Order.)

This order brings into operation from 1st April 1968 the scales and other provisions contained in a memorandum published by Her Majesty's Stationery Office relating to the remuneration of registered teachers employed whole-time by education authorities in primary and secondary schools and of teachers employed whole-time by education authorities in further education centres. The memorandum gives effect to agreed recommendations made to the Secretary of State by the Scottish Teachers Salaries Committee.

Article 4 of the order revokes the Teachers' Salaries (Scotland) Regulations 1966 but provides for the continued exercise by the Secretary of State and education authorities of functions under the 1966 Regulations in relation to employment during the currency of those regulations.

1968 No. 422

WAGES COUNCILS

The Wages Regulation (Aerated Waters) (England and Wales) Order 1968

Made - - -	18*th March* 1968
Coming into Operation	15*th April* 1968

Whereas the Minister of Labour (hereafter in this Order referred to as "the Minister") has received from the Aerated Waters Wages Council (England and Wales) the wages regulation proposals set out in Schedules 1 and 2 hereof ;

Now, therefore, the Minister by virtue of the powers conferred on him by section 11 of the Wages Councils Act 1959(a), and of all other powers enabling him in that behalf, hereby makes the following Order :—

1. This Order may be cited as the Wages Regulation (Aerated Waters) (England and Wales) Order 1968.

2.—(1) In this Order the expression "the specified date" means the 15th April 1968, provided that where, as respects any worker who is paid wages at intervals not exceeding seven days, that date does not correspond with the beginning of the period for which the wages are paid, the expression "the specified date" means, as respects that worker, the beginning of the next such period following that date.

(2) The Interpretation Act 1889(b) shall apply to the interpretation of this Order as it applies to the interpretation of an Act of Parliament and as if this Order and the Orders hereby revoked were Acts of Parliament.

3. The wages regulation proposals set out in Schedules 1 and 2 hereof shall have effect as from the specified date and as from that date the Wages Regulation (Aerated Waters) (England and Wales) Order 1966(c) and the Wages Regulation (Aerated Waters) (England and Wales) (Amendment) Order 1966(d) shall cease to have effect.

Signed by order of the Minister of Labour.
18th March 1968.

A. S. Marre,
Deputy Secretary,
Ministry of Labour.

(a) 1959 c. 69.   (b) 1889 c. 63.
(c) S.I. 1966/551 (1966 II, p. 1134).   (d) S.I. 1966/1491 (1966 III, p. 4098).

SCHEDULE 1

The following minimum remuneration shall be substituted for the statutory minimum remuneration fixed by the Wages Regulation (Aerated Waters) (England and Wales) Order 1966(a) (Order A. (71)) as amended by the Wages Regulation (Aerated Waters) (England and Wales) (Amendment) Order 1966(b) (Order A. (73)).

STATUTORY MINIMUM REMUNERATION

PART I

GENERAL

1.—(1) The minimum remuneration payable to a worker, other than a driver-salesman or delivery worker, to whom this Schedule applies for all work, except work to which a minimum overtime rate applies under Part V, is—

(a) in the case of a worker employed as a time worker, the hourly general minimum time rate applicable to the worker under the provisions of Part II or IV of this Schedule;

(b) in the case of a worker employed on piece work, piece rates each of which would yield, in the circumstances of the case, to an ordinary worker at least the same amount of money as the hourly general minimum time rate which would be payable to the worker under Part II of this Schedule if he were a time worker.

(2) The minimum remuneration payable to a driver-salesman or delivery worker is the remuneration payable to the worker under the provisions of Part III of this Schedule.

(3) For the purposes of this Schedule the expression "hourly general minimum time rate" means the general minimum time rate applicable to the worker under Part II or IV of this Schedule divided by 42½.

PART II

WORKERS OTHER THAN DRIVER-SALESMEN, DELIVERY WORKERS AND MATES

MALE WORKERS—GENERAL MINIMUM TIME RATES

2. The general minimum time rates applicable to all male workers (other than driver-salesmen, delivery workers and mates) are as follows:—

	Per week of 42½ hours
	s. d.
Aged 21 years or over	210 0
„ 20 and under 21 years	171 6
„ 19 „ „ 20 „	155 0
„ 18 „ „ 19 „	136 0
„ 17 „ „ 18 „	115 6
„ 16 „ „ 17 „	96 6
„ under 16 years	80 6

(a) S.I. 1966/551 (1966 II, p. 1134).   (b) S.I. 1966/1491 (1966 III, p. 4098).

FEMALE WORKERS

GENERAL MINIMUM TIME RATES

3. The general minimum time rates applicable to all female workers (other than driver-salesmen, delivery workers and mates) are as follows:—

	Per week of 42½ hours	
	s.	d.
Aged 19 years or over	155	0
„ 18 and under 19 years	130	0
„ 17 „ „ 18 „	115	6
„ 16 „ „ 17 „	96	6
„ under 16 years	80	6

PART III

DRIVER-SALESMEN AND DELIVERY WORKERS
MALE OR FEMALE WORKERS

A—FULL TIME WORKERS

4.—(1) Subject to the provisions of this paragraph, the minimum remuneration payable to a full time driver-salesman or a full time delivery worker for any week in which he is employed, whether he performs any work for his employer in the week or not, is the remuneration specified in the table set out in paragraph 5 applicable to the worker in that week and in addition the amount (if any) payable to the worker in respect of overtime worked in the week under the provisions of paragraph 8:

Provided that no remuneration shall be payable to the worker for any week throughout which he is not capable of, or not available for, work.

(2) The minimum remuneration payable in respect of any week under the foregoing provisions of this paragraph shall be reduced in respect of any day in the week—

(a) allowed to the worker as a day of annual holiday under the provisions of a wages regulation order, by the amount of holiday remuneration paid in respect of the day;

(b) throughout which the worker is absent from work by reason of illness or accident or without the consent of his employer—

(i) where the worker normally works for the employer on six days a week and the day of absence is not the worker's weekly short day, by two-elevenths or,

(ii) where the worker normally works for the employer on six days a week and the day of absence is the worker's weekly short day, by one-eleventh or,

(iii) where the worker normally works for the employer on five days a week only, by one-fifth

of the remuneration specified in the table set out in paragraph 5 applicable to the worker;

(c) on which the worker performs some work but is absent from work without the consent of his employer for some part of the day, being a part of the day during which the worker is required by or under his contract of employment to work for his employer, by an amount equal to the remuneration which would be payable to the worker if he were paid in respect of the time during which he was so absent from work at the hourly rate of two eighty-fifths of the remuneration specified in the table set out in paragraph 5 applicable to the worker.

(3) Where under the provisions of this paragraph a worker is entitled to remuneration in any week in which he does no work for his employer, the remuneration specified in the table set out in paragraph 5 normally applicable to the worker shall for the purposes of this paragraph be deemed to be the remuneration so specified applicable to the worker in that week.

(4) Where in any week a worker to whom this paragraph applies is in charge of more than one of the types of vehicles specified in the table set out in paragraph 5, the remuneration applicable to him for the purposes of this paragraph in that week shall be the highest set out in the table applicable to him during the week.

5. The table of remuneration referred to in paragraph 4 is as follows:—

Class of worker	Mechanically propelled vehicle with carrying capacity of	Horse-drawn vehicle	Remuneration
			s. d.
DRIVER-SALESMEN of any age ..	Any weight	One or two horse	220 0
DELIVERY WORKERS—			
aged 21 years or over ..	1 ton or less		220 0
„ 20 & under 21 years			185 6
„ 19 „ „ 20 „			164 0
„ 18 „ „ 19 „			146 6
„ under 18 years ..			128 6
of any age ..	Over 1 ton and up to 2 tons	One horse ..	220 0
	Over 2 tons and up to 5 tons	Two horse ..	226 0
	Over 5 tons and up to 8 tons		232 0
	Over 8 tons and up to 12 tons		236 0
	Over 12 tons		240 0

B—OTHER THAN FULL TIME WORKERS

6. The minimum remuneration payable to a driver-salesman or a delivery worker, other than a full time worker, is the hourly rate increased by 4d. per hour. For the purposes of this paragraph the hourly rate is the amount obtained by dividing by 42½ the remuneration specified in the table in paragraph 5 which would be applicable to the worker if he were a full time worker.

PART IV

MATES

MALE OR FEMALE WORKERS

GENERAL MINIMUM TIME RATES

7. The general minimum time rates applicable to male or female workers employed as mates are as follows:—

	Per week of 42½ hours	
	s.	d.
Aged 21 years or over	210	0
„ 20 and under 21 years	171	6
„ 19 „ „ 20 „	155	0
„ 18 „ „ 19 „	136	0
„ 17 „ „ 18 „	115	6
„ 16 „ „ 17 „	96	6
„ under 16 years	80	6

PART V

OVERTIME AND WAITING TIME

ALL WORKERS

MINIMUM OVERTIME RATES

8. Subject to the provisions of paragraph 4 and of this paragraph, overtime is payable at the following minimum rates:—

(1) To any worker other than a driver-salesman or delivery worker—

(a) on a Sunday or customary holiday, for all time worked .. .. **double time**

(b) on the weekly short day, for all time worked in excess of 4 hours .. .. **time-and-a-half**

(c) in any week, exclusive of any time in respect of which a minimum overtime rate is payable under the foregoing provisions of this sub-paragraph—

(i) for the first 2 hours worked in excess of 42½ hours .. .. **time-and-a-quarter**

(ii) thereafter .. .. **time-and-a-half**

(2) To a driver-salesman or delivery worker—

(a) on a Sunday or customary holiday, for all time worked .. .. **double time**

(b) on a Saturday, for all time worked in excess of 4 hours .. .. **time-and-a-half**

(c) in any week, exclusive of any time in respect of which a minimum overtime rate is payable under (a) or (b) of this sub-paragraph—

(i) for the first 8 hours worked in excess of 42½ hours .. .. **time-and-a-quarter**

(ii) thereafter .. .. **time-and-a-half**

WAITING TIME

9.—(1) A worker is entitled to payment of the minimum remuneration specified in this Schedule for all time during which he is present on the premises of his employer unless he is present thereon in any of the following circumstances:—

(a) without the employer's consent, express or implied ;

(b) for some purpose unconnected with his work and other than that of waiting for work to be given to him to perform ;

(c) by reason only of the fact that he is resident thereon ;

(d) during normal meal times in a room or place in which no work is being done, and he is not waiting for work to be given to him to perform.

(2) The minimum remuneration payable under sub-paragraph (1) of this paragraph to a piece worker when not engaged on piece work is that which would be applicable if he were a time worker.

PART VI

DEFINITIONS

10. For the purposes of this Schedule—

"CARRYING CAPACITY" means the weight of the maximum load normally carried by a mechanically propelled vehicle, and such carrying capacity when so established shall not be affected either by variations in the weight of the load resulting from collections or deliveries or emptying of containers during the course of the journey, or by the fact that on any particular journey a load greater or less than the established carrying capacity is carried.

Where a trailer is attached to the vehicle the load shall be the loads of the vehicle and the trailer combined.

"CUSTOMARY HOLIDAY" means—

(1) Christmas Day (or, if Christmas Day falls on a Sunday, such weekday as may be appointed by national proclamation, or, if none is so appointed, the next following Tuesday), Boxing Day, Good Friday, Easter Monday, Whit Monday (or where another day is substituted therefor by national proclamation, that day), August Bank Holiday and any day proclaimed as an additional Bank Holiday or as a public holiday throughout England and Wales, or

(2) in the case of each of the said days such weekday as may be substituted therefor, being either a day recognised by local custom as a day of holiday in substitution for the said day or a day agreed between the employer and the worker or his representative.

"DELIVERY WORKER" means a worker who normally is in charge of and wholly or mainly engaged in driving a mechanically propelled or horse-drawn vehicle and in work in connection with the vehicle and its load (if any) while on the road and, if so required by the employer, in washing the vehicle when not on the road : provided that where a worker who is not normally employed as a delivery worker is in any week called upon to perform the work of a delivery worker the worker shall for that week be regarded as a delivery worker.

"DRIVER-SALESMAN" means a worker who normally is wholly or mainly engaged in the duties of a delivery worker as defined above and in the sale of goods to and the collection of monies from customers : provided that where a worker who is not normally employed as a driver-salesman is in any week called upon to perform the work of a driver-salesman the worker shall for that week be regarded as a driver-salesman.

"FULL TIME WORKER" means a driver-salesman or a delivery worker who normally works for the employer for at least 30 hours per week and performs some work to which statutory minimum remuneration applies.

"MATE" means a worker, other than a driver-salesman or delivery worker, who is required to travel on or to accompany a mechanically propelled or horse-drawn vehicle for the purpose of assisting the driver-salesman or delivery worker in charge of the vehicle.

"TIME-AND-A-QUARTER", "TIME-AND-A-HALF" and "DOUBLE TIME" mean respectively : —

(a) in the case of workers other than delivery workers and driver-salesmen —one and a quarter times, one and a half times and twice the minimum remuneration payable to the worker for work to which a minimum overtime rate does not apply,

(b) in the case of full time delivery workers and full time driver-salesmen —one and a quarter times, one and a half times and twice the rate obtained by dividing the remuneration specified in the table in paragraph 5 by 42½,

(c) in the case of delivery workers and driver-salesmen other than full time workers—one and a quarter times, one and a half times and twice the rate calculated in accordance with paragraph 6.

"WAGES REGULATION ORDER" means an order made by the Minister to give effect to wages regulation proposals submitted to him by the Aerated Waters Wages Council (England and Wales).

"WEEK" means pay week.

"WEEKLY SHORT DAY" means Saturday or (except where in the case of a woman or young person such substitution is unlawful) any day, other than Sunday, which may be substituted therefor by agreement in writing between the employer and the worker.

PART VII

APPLICABILITY OF STATUTORY MINIMUM REMUNERATION

11. This Schedule applies to workers in relation to whom the Aerated Waters Wages Council (England and Wales) operates, that is to say, workers employed in England and Wales in the trade specified in the Schedule to the Aerated Waters Wages Council (England and Wales) (Variation) Order 1948(a), that is to say : —

(1) The manufacture, wherever carried on, of mineral or aerated waters, non-alcoholic cordials, flavoured syrups, unfermented sweet drinks, and other similar beverages, and the manufacture in unlicensed premises of brewed liquors,

Including—

(a) the operations of bottle washing, bottling and filling, and all other operations preparatory to the sale of any of the aforesaid beverages or liquors in bottles, jars, syphons, casks, or other similar receptacles ; and

(b) the transport and delivery of any of the aforesaid beverages or liquors (and operations incidental thereto including the collection of empty bottles or containers) when carried on as an activity of the undertaking engaged in the manufacture thereof, by persons in the employment of that undertaking, and operations involved in the sale by retail of any of such beverages or liquors when sold in the course of a delivery round by a driver-salesman or delivery salesman employed in the undertaking which manufactures the said beverages or liquors.

(a) S.I. 1948/705 (Rev. XXIII, p. 451: 1948 I, p. 4395).

(2) The following operations when carried on in association or in conjunction with any of the operations specified in (a) of sub-paragraph (1) of this paragraph so as to form a common or interchangeable form of employment for workers and whether carried on simultaneously with those operations or not, that is to say all subsidiary operations preparatory to the sale in bottles, jars or other similar receptacles of cider, ale, stout, porter or other alcoholic beers, including the operations of bottle washing, bottling and filling.

SCHEDULE 2

HOLIDAYS AND HOLIDAY REMUNERATION

The Aerated Waters Wages Council (England and Wales) Wages Regulation (Holidays) Order 1954(a) (Order A. 51)) shall have effect as if in the Schedule thereto for sub-paragraph (2) of paragraph 2 (which relates to customary holidays) there were substituted the following: —

"(2) The said customary holidays are: —

(a) Christmas Day (or, if Christmas Day falls on a Sunday, such weekday as may be appointed by national proclamation, or, if none is so appointed, the next following Tuesday), Boxing Day, Good Friday, Easter Monday, Whit Monday (*or where another day is substituted therefor by national proclamation, that day*), August Bank Holiday and any day proclaimed as an additional Bank Holiday or as a public holiday throughout England and Wales, or

(b) in the case of each of the said days such weekday as may be substituted therefor, being either a day recognised by local custom as a day of holiday in substitution for the said day or a day agreed between the employer and the worker or his representative."

EXPLANATORY NOTE

(This Note is not part of the Order.)

This Order has effect from 15th April 1968. Schedule 1 sets out the statutory minimum remuneration payable in substitution for that fixed by the Wages Regulation (Aerated Waters) (England and Wales) Order 1966 (Order A. (71)) as amended by the Wages Regulation (Aerated Waters) (England and Wales) (Amendment) Order 1966 (Order A. (73)), which Orders are revoked. Schedule 2 amends the Aerated Waters Wages Council (England and Wales) Wages Regulation (Holidays) Order 1954 (Order A. (51)) by providing that a nationally proclaimed holiday may be substituted for Whit Monday.

New provisions are printed in Italics.

(a) S.I. 1954/609 (1954 II, p. 2491).

STATUTORY INSTRUMENTS

1968 No. 423

CIVIL AVIATION

The Civil Aviation (Navigation Services Charges) (Second Amendment) Regulations 1968

Made - - - -	*19th March* 1968
Laid before Parliament	*25th March* 1968
Coming into Operation	*1st April* 1968

The Board of Trade in exercise of their powers under section 4 of the Civil Aviation (Eurocontrol) Act 1962(a) as having effect by virtue of the Transfer of Functions (Civil Aviation) Order 1966(b) and of all other powers enabling them in that behalf, and with the consent of the Treasury, hereby make the following Regulations:—

1. These Regulations may be cited as the Civil Aviation (Navigation Services Charges) (Second Amendment) Regulations 1968, and shall come into operation on 1st April 1968.

2. The Interpretation Act 1889(c) applies for the purpose of the interpretation of these Regulations as it applies for the purpose of the interpretation of an Act of Parliament.

3. The Civil Aviation (Navigation Services Charges) Regulations 1964(d), as amended (e), shall be further amended as follows:

In Regulation 4—

   (*a*) in paragraph (2) for the words "subparagraph (1) of this paragraph" there shall be substituted the words "paragraph (1) of this Regulation";

   (*b*) the following paragraph shall be added after paragraph (2)—

   "(3) Where the flight of an aircraft taking off or landing, as the case may be, is a flight to or from a place outside the United Kingdom, Channel Islands and the Isle of Man, or a flight which is part of a through journey of the aircraft to or from a place outside those countries, for the references to "the standard charge" in paragraphs (1) and (2) of this Regulation there shall be substituted references to "112½% of the standard charge." "

	J. P. W. Mallalieu,
19th March 1968.	Minister of State
	Board of Trade.

(a) 1962 c. 8.
(c) 1889 c. 63.
(e) S.I. 1966/465 (1966 I, p. 982).

(b) S.I. 1966/741 (1966 II p. 1732).
(d) S.I. 1964/1071 (1964 II, p. 2367).

We consent to the making of these Regulations.

                                                    B. K. O'Malley,
                                                    E. Alan Fitch,
19th March 1968.   Lords Commissioners
                                                    of Her Majesty's Treasury.

EXPLANATORY NOTE

(*This Note is not part of the Regulations.*)

These Regulations amend the Civil Aviation (Navigation Services Charges) Regulations 1964 as amended. In addition to making a minor drafting amendment the Regulations increase by 12½% the standard charge payable by operators of aircraft taking off or landing in the course of international journeys.

STATUTORY INSTRUMENTS

1968 No. 424

CIVIL AVIATION

The Air Navigation (Fees) (Third Amendment) Regulations 1968

Made - - - -	*19th March* 1968
Coming into Operation	*1st April* 1968

The Board of Trade with the consent of the Treasury and in exercise of their powers under Article 77 of the Air Navigation Order 1966(a), as amended (b), and of all other powers enabling them in that behalf, hereby make the following Regulations.

1. These Regulations shall come into operation on 1st April 1968 and may be cited as the Air Navigation (Fees) (Third Amendment) Regulations 1968.

2. The Interpretation Act 1889(c), shall apply for the purpose of the interpretation of these Regulations as it applies for the purpose of the interpretation of an Act of Parliament.

3. The Schedule to the Air Navigation (Fees) Regulations 1966(d), as amended(b), shall be further amended as follows:

(1) In paragraph 2 for "10s. 0d." there shall be substituted "£1";

(2) In paragraph 3—

    (*a*) for "10s. 0d." there shall be substituted "£1";

    (*b*) for items (i), (ii), (iii) and (iv) in sub-paragraph (1)(*c*) of the proviso there shall be substituted:

"(i) when the maximum total weight does not exceed 2,000 lb., in respect of each 1,000 lb. or part thereof 5 0 0

(ii) when the maximum total weight exceeds 2,000 lb., in respect of each 1,000 lb. or part thereof ... ... 7 0 0"

    (*c*) In paragraph 5 for sub-paragraphs (*a*) and (*b*) and the proviso there shall be substituted:

	£	s.	d.
" (*a*) When the maximum total weight authorised for the aircraft does not exceed 2,000 lb., in respect of each 1,000 lb. or part thereof	5	0	0
(*b*) When the maximum total weight authorised for the aircraft exceeds 2,000 lb. but does not exceed 5,000 lb., in respect of each 1,000 lb. or part thereof	7	0	0
(*c*) When the maximum total weight authorised for the aircraft exceeds 5,000 lb., in respect of each 1,000 lb. or part thereof ...	9	0	0"

(a) S.I. 1966/1184 (1966 III, p.3073).
(b) There is no amendment expressly relating to the subject matter of these Regulations.
(c) 1889 c. 63.   (d) S.I. 1966/1255 (1966 III, p. 3404).

19th March 1968.

J. H. Riddoch,
An Under-Secretary of
the Board of Trade.

We consent to the making of these Regulations.

B. K. O'Malley,
E. Alan Fitch,
Lords Commissioners of
Her Majesty's Treasury.

19th March 1968.

EXPLANATORY NOTE

(This Note is not part of the Regulations.)

These Regulations amend the Air Navigation (Fees) Regulations 1966, as amended, by increasing the fees payable in connection with permits to fly and certificates of airworthiness.

1968 No. 425

BORROWING AND SECURITIES

The Savings Certificates (Amendment) Regulations 1968

Made - - - -	*19th March* 1968
Laid before Parliament	*20th March* 1968
Coming into Operation	*22nd March* 1968

The Treasury, in exercise of the powers conferred upon them by section 12 of the National Debt Act 1958(a) and of all other powers enabling them in that behalf, hereby make the following Regulations :—

1. Regulation 4 of the Savings Certificates Regulations 1933(b), as substituted by Regulation 1 of the Savings Certificates (Amendment) Regulations 1966(c) and amended by the Savings Certificates (Amendment) Regulations 1967(d), shall be further amended by substituting for the figures " 750 " in paragraph (1) (g) of the said Regulation the figures " 1,000 ".

2. The Interpretation Act 1889(e) shall apply for the interpretation of these Regulations as it applies for the interpretation of an Act of Parliament.

3. The Savings Certificates (Amendment) Regulations 1967 are hereby revoked.

4. These Regulations may be cited as the Savings Certificates (Amendment) Regulations 1968, and shall come into operation on 22nd March 1968.

B. K. O'Malley,
Joseph Harper,

Two of the Lords Commissioners
of Her Majesty's Treasury.

19th March 1968.

EXPLANATORY NOTE

(This Note is not part of the Regulations.)

These Regulations further amend Regulation 4 of the Savings Certificates Regulations 1933, as substituted by Regulation 1 of the Savings Certificates (Amendment) Regulations 1967. They increase the maximum permitted holding of National Savings Certificates of the Twelfth Issue from 750 unit certificates (purchase price £750) to 1,000 unit certificates (purchase price £1,000) as from 22nd March 1968.

(a) 7 & 8 Eliz. 2. c. 6.
(b) S.R. & O. 1933/1149 (Rev. XV, p. 309 : 1933, p. 1406).
(c) S.I. 1966/216 (1966 I, p. 419).   (d) S.I. 1967/578 (1967 I, p. 1786).   (e) 1889 c. 63.

STATUTORY INSTRUMENTS

1968 No. 426

ROAD TRAFFIC

The Motor Vehicles (Construction and Use) (Amendment) (No. 2) Regulations 1968

Made - - -		*14th March* 1968
Laid before Parliament		*27th March* 1968
Coming into Operation		*8th April* 1968

The Minister of Transport, in exercise of her powers under section 64(1) of the Road Traffic Act 1960(a), as amended by section 51 of and Schedule 4 to the Road Traffic Act 1962(b), and of all other enabling powers, and after consultation with representative organisations in accordance with the provisions of section 260(2) of the said Act of 1960, hereby makes the following Regulations:—

1.—(1) These Regulations shall come into operation on 8th April 1968 and may be cited as the Motor Vehicles (Construction and Use) (Amendment) (No. 2) Regulations 1968.

(2) The Interpretation Act 1889(c) shall apply for the interpretation of these Regulations as it applies for the interpretation of an Act of Parliament.

2. The Motor Vehicles (Construction and Use) Regulations 1966(d), as amended (e), shall have effect as though—

(1) in Regulation 7(1), for the figures and word "13 metres", there were substituted the figures and word "15 metres";

(2) for Regulation 19 there were substituted the following Regulations:—

"Windscreen wipers

19.—(1) The windscreen of every motor vehicle, which is so constructed that the driver cannot obtain an adequate view to the front of the vehicle without looking through the windscreen by opening the windscreen or otherwise, shall be fitted with one or more efficient automatic windscreen wipers.

(2) Subject to the next following paragraph the windscreen wipers required by the last preceding paragraph shall be capable of clearing the windscreen so that the driver has an adequate view of the road in front of the near and off sides of the vehicle in addition to an adequate view to the front of the vehicle.

(3) The last preceding paragraph shall apply in the case of vehicles registered on or after the 1st October 1969 on and after that date, and, in the case of vehicles registered before that date, on and after 1st October

---

(a) 8 & 9 Eliz. 2.c.16.   (b) 10 & 11 Eliz.2.c.59.
(c) 52 & 53 Vict. c.63.
(e) There is no relevant amending instrument. (d) S.I. 1966/1288 (1966 III, p.3493).

1972, being in either case vehicles such as are described in paragraph (1) of this Regulation.

Windscreen Washers

19A.—(1) Subject to the following paragraph every motor vehicle, the windscreen of which is required to be fitted with one or more efficient automatic windscreen wipers by virtue of Regulation 19 of these Regulations or Regulation 46 of the Public Service Vehicles (Conditions of Fitness) Regulations 1958(a), as amended (b), shall be fitted with a windscreen washer capable of clearing, in conjunction with those windscreen wipers, the area of the windscreen swept by those windscreen wipers of mud or other similar deposit.

(2) This Regulation shall not apply to land tractors, vehicles which are incapable by reason of their construction of exceeding 20 miles per hour on the level under their own power or vehicles being used for the time being as stage carriages or on any journey incidental to such use and shall apply in respect of the vehicles specified in paragraph (3) of the last preceding regulation as from the dates specified therein in relation to those vehicles." ;

(3) For Regulation 58 (Overall length of Trailers) there were substituted the following Regulation:—

"Overall length

58.—(1) Save as provided in paragraph (2) of this Regulation, the overall length of a trailer shall not exceed 7 metres :
Provided that the said maximum length may be 12 metres in the case of a trailer which—
  (a) has not less than 4 wheels and where the distance between the centres of the respective areas of contact with the road of the foremost and the rearmost wheels on the same side of the trailer is not less than three-fifths of its overall length ; and
  (b) is drawn by a motor vehicle having an unladen weight of 2 tons or more.

(2) This Regulation shall not apply—
  (a) to a trailer constructed and normally used for the conveyance of indivisible loads of exceptional length :
  (b) to a land implement ;
  (c) to a trailer forming part of an articulated vehicle ;
  (d) to any broken down vehicle which is being drawn by a motor vehicle in consequence of the breakdown ;
  (e) to a trailer which is a trolley vehicle in course of construction or delivery ; or
  (f) to any trailer which is drying or mixing plant designed for the production of asphalt or of bituminous or tar macadam and used mainly for the construction, repair or maintenance of roads or which is a road planing machine used as aforesaid if, in any such case, the overall length of the trailer together with that of the motor vehicle by which it is drawn does not exceed 60 feet.

(3) For the purposes of this Regulation, the overall length of a trailer shall be treated as excluding any part of the trailer designed primarily for use as a means of attaching it to another vehicle and any fitting designed for use in connection with any such part." ;

(a) S.I. 1958/473 (1958 II, p.2014).   (b) There is no relevant amending instrument.

(4) in Regulation 106, after paragraph (2), there were inserted the following paragraph:—

"(2A) Where a motor vehicle is drawing two trailers only one such trailer may exceed 7 metres in overall length, and, where a motor vehicle is drawing three trailers, no trailer in the combination of vehicles shall exceed 7 metres in overall length.";

(5) in Regulation 109—

(*a*) in sub-paragraph (5)(*b*), after the word "road", there were inserted the words and figures "before 1st October 1968";

(*b*) after sub-paragraph (5)(*b*), there were inserted the following sub-paragraphs:—

"(*bb*) has a rearward projection exceeding 3 feet 6 inches in length but not exceeding 6 feet in length, shall be used on a road on or after 1st October 1968 unless the condition specified in paragraph 4 of the said Schedule has been complied with ;
(*bbb*) has a rearward projection exceeding 6 feet in length but not exceeding 10 feet in length, shall be used on a road on or after 1st October 1968 unless the condition specified in paragraph 3 of the said Schedule has been complied with; or";

(*c*) in sub-paragraph (6)(*b*), after the figures and words "10 feet in length,", there were inserted the words and figures "before 1st October 1968,";

(*d*) after sub-paragraph (6)(*b*), there were inserted the following sub-paragraphs:—

"(*bb*) where the load has a rearward projection exceeding 3 feet 6 inches in length but not exceeding 6 feet in length, on or after 1st October 1968, unless the condition specified in paragraph 4 of the said Schedule has been complied with;
(*bbb*) where the load has a rearward projection exceeding 6 feet in length but not exceeding 10 feet in length, on or after 1st October 1968, unless the condition specified in paragraph 3 of the said Schedule has been complied with; and"; and

(*e*) after sub-paragraph 6(*c*), there were inserted the following sub-paragraph:—

"(*d*) on and after 1st July 1968 where the load is carried on an articulated vehicle not exceeding 15 metres in overall length and which is not constructed and normally used for the conveyance of indivisible loads of exceptional length where the overall length of the articulated vehicle together with any forward or rearward projections of the load exceeds 55 feet, unless the condition specified in paragraph 1 of the said Schedule has been complied with;"; and

(6) in Schedule 8, in Part I—

(*a*) in paragraph 3, after sub-paragraph (*g*), there were inserted the following proviso:—
"Provided that the conditions in sub-paragraph (*b*) so far as it relates to side projection surfaces in sub-paragraph (*d*) shall not apply by reason only that a vehicle has a special appliance or apparatus, or is carrying a load, which has a rearward projection exceeding 6 feet in length but not exceeding 10 feet in length." ; and

(*b*) in paragraph 4, in the definition of "relevant projection", after the words "in sub-paragraph (*b*), there were inserted "or (*bb*)".

Given under the Official Seal of the Minister of Transport the 14th March 1968.

(L.S.)

Barbara Castle,
Minister of Transport.

EXPLANATORY NOTE
(This Note is not part of the Regulations.)

These Regulations further amend the Motor Vehicles (Construction and Use) Regulations 1966 by—

1. increasing the maximum permitted overall length of articulated vehicles from 13 metres to 15 metres (Regulation 2(1)) ;

2. varying the existing provision as to windscreen wipers so as to require the windscreens of all motor vehicles, with some exceptions, to be fitted with one or more efficient automatic windscreen wipers capable of clearing the windscreen so that the driver has an adequate view of the road to the front and in front of the near and off sides of the vehicle; and requiring all motor vehicles which are required to be fitted with automatic windscreen wipers, other than land tractors, certain slow moving vehicles and stage carriages, to be fitted with a windscreen washer capable of clearing, in conjuction with the windscreen wipers, the area of the windscreen swept by the windscreen wipers, of mud or other similar deposit; these requirements apply to vehicles registered on or after 1st October 1969 on and after that date and to those registered before that date on and after 1st October 1972 (Regulation 2(2));

3. increasing, subject to specified conditions, the maximum permitted overall length of draw-bar trailers from 7 metres to 12 metres (Regulation 2(3)) ;

4. restricting the overall length of trailers when two or more are being drawn by a motor vehicle (Regulation 2(4));

5. requiring vehicles having projections to the rear or carrying loads which project to the rear of a vehicle which are more than 6 feet in length instead of 10 feet to indicate the projection by means of the marker board prescribed in paragraph 3 of Part I to Schedule 8, on and after 1st October 1968 (Regulation 2(5)(a) to (d) and 2(6)) ; and

6. requiring the police to be given advance notification of the movement of certain articulated vehicles not exceeding 15 metres in length where the overall length of the articulated vehicle and its load exceeds 55 feet, on and after 1st July 1968 (Regulation 2(5)(e)).

STATUTORY INSTRUMENTS

1968 No. 427

FOOD AND DRUGS

The Welfare Foods (Northern Ireland) Order 1968

Made - - -	19*th March* 1968
Laid before Parliament	26*th March* 1968
Coming into Operation	31*st March* 1968

The Secretary of State in exercise of the powers conferred on him by sections 4 and 7 of the Emergency Laws (Re-enactments and Repeals) Act 1964(a) hereby orders as follows:—

PART I

PRELIMINARY

Title, commencement and extent

1.—(1) This Order may be cited as the Welfare Foods (Northern Ireland) Order 1968 and shall come into operation on 31st March 1968.

(2) This Order shall extend only to Northern Ireland.

Interpretation

2.—(1) In this Order, unless the context otherwise requires—

" appropriate local education authority " means the local education authority constituted under section 2 of the Education Act (Northern Ireland) 1947(b);

" beneficiary " means any of the following persons in Northern Ireland, namely, a young child, a handicapped child, an expectant mother or a nursing mother;

" dried milk " means National Dried Milk;

" enactment " includes any instrument made under an Act;

" handicapped child " means a child (other than a young child) who—

(*a*) is less than 16 years of age and is not in paid employment,

(*b*) is declared by the appropriate local education authority to be unable by reason of disability of mind or body to become a registered pupil of a school, and

(*c*) is not in attendance at a full-time training centre;

" large family " means a family in which the number of beneficiaries entitled to welfare milk exceeds two;

" milk " means liquid cows' milk, but does not include separated milk, skimmed milk, condensed milk or evaporated milk;

" Milk Order " means the Milk (Northern Ireland) Order 1965(c) or any order amending or revoking and replacing that Order;

(a) 1964 c. 60.   (b) 1947 c. 3 (N.I.).
(c) S.I. 1965/1412 (1965 II, p. 4176).

" the Ministry " means the Ministry of Health and Social Services for Northern Ireland;

" nursing mother " means a woman who has given birth to a child within the preceding 30 weeks and is herself suckling the child;

" standard price ", in relation to milk, means the lower of the maximum prices per pint set out in the Schedule to the Milk Order;

" supplier " means a person who supplies milk under this Order;

" token " means a token for welfare milk, free welfare milk or any other welfare food issued by the Ministry under Article 8, and includes a book of tokens or any part of such a book;

" vitamin tablets " means vitamin A and D tablets;

" week " means a week ending at midnight between Saturday and Sunday;

" welfare food " means milk, dried milk, concentrated orange juice, cod liver oil or vitamin tablets;

" welfare milk ", in relation to a beneficiary, means the milk or dried milk which he is entitled to obtain under Part II of this Order;

" welfare price ", in relation to milk, means a price of 6d. per pint, increased, where the supplier would be entitled under the Milk Order to charge the beneficiary for the milk supplied a price which exceeds the standard price, by the amount of the difference between these prices;

" young child " means a child aged not more than 5 years and 1 month.

(2) Where any provision in this Order (other than a provision in Article 18 or 19) requires or enables anything to be done by or in respect of a beneficiary, and that beneficiary is a young child or a handicapped child, the provision shall, unless the context otherwise requires, be deemed to refer to one of his parents or his guardian or the person having custody of him.

(3) Any reference in this Order to a numbered Article or Schedule shall, unless the reference is to an Article of or a Schedule to a specified enactment, be construed as a reference to the Article or Schedule bearing that number in this Order.

(4) In this Order, unless the context otherwise requires, any reference to any enactment shall be construed as a reference to that enactment as amended by or under any subsequent enactment.

PART II

ENTITLEMENT TO WELFARE FOODS

Meaning of a family in special circumstances

3.—(1) For the purposes of this Order, a beneficiary shall be deemed to belong to a family in special circumstances in respect of any period during which his requirements exceed his resources when calculated or estimated by the Ministry under the Supplementary Benefits etc. Act (Northern Ireland) 1966(a) subject to the following modifications—

    (*a*) the first 40s. 0d. of any weekly earnings shall be disregarded; and

    (*b*) his requirements shall be deemed to include also—

        (i) such amounts in respect of hire purchase transactions and mortgage repayments as the Ministry may allow;

        (ii) the cost of welfare foods; and

(a) 1966 c. 28 (N.I.).

(iii) any further amounts which the Ministry may in special circumstances allow.

(2) Where under the said Act the resources of the beneficiary would be aggregated with those of some other person, the requirements and resources of that other person when calculated as aforesaid shall be deemed to be the requirements and resources of the beneficiary.

Entitlement to welfare milk

4.—(1) Subject to the provisions of this Article, welfare milk shall be available, on application, to all beneficiaries at a rate for each beneficiary of 7 pints per week of liquid milk or one 20 oz. pack per week of dried milk, in the case of a beneficiary described in paragraph (2) of this Article free of charge, and in any other case at a charge—

(a) for liquid milk, as provided in Article 9, and

(b) for dried milk, of 2s. 4d. per 20 oz. pack:

Provided that where a nursing mother applies for welfare milk in respect of a young child whom she is suckling, she shall not be entitled under this paragraph to welfare milk in respect both of herself and the child; but nothing in Article 19 shall prohibit her from consuming any welfare milk obtained for the child.

(2) The beneficiaries who are entitled to welfare milk free of charge under paragraph (1) of this Article are—

(a) all but two of the beneficiaries in a large family, and

(b) all the beneficiaries in a family in special circumstances.

(3) Dried milk, additional to that to which he is entitled under paragraph (1) of this Article, and on the same conditions as to payment, shall be available, on application, for a young child under one year of age who is being fed mainly on dried milk, in the quantities specified in column (2) of Schedule 1 in relation to his age at the time of application as specified in column (1).

Entitlement to welfare foods other than liquid milk

5. A beneficiary described in column (1) of Schedule 2 may buy the welfare foods specified in respect of him in column (2) at the price so specified in column (3), and where the beneficiary belongs to a family in special circumstances he shall be entitled to receive free of charge the quantity of those welfare foods so specified in column (4).

PART III

SUPPLY OF WELFARE FOODS

Application forms

6. Application for welfare foods shall be made by a beneficiary on a form supplied for the purpose by the Ministry.

Issue of tokens

7. The Ministry shall issue tokens to enable beneficiaries to obtain welfare milk under Article 4 and welfare foods free of charge under Article 5.

Use of tokens

8.—(1) To obtain the welfare foods to which he is entitled under this Order, a beneficiary shall use the relevant tokens in the manner described in this Article.

(2) A token for welfare milk may be used—

(*a*) to obtain 7 pints of milk during the week ending on the date specified on the token or during any of the four succeeding weeks, or

(*b*) to obtain a 20 oz. pack of dried milk during the period beginning one month before and ending one month after the date so specified;

and a token shall not be used in any other manner.

(3) A token for additional supplies of dried milk may be used to obtain a 20 oz. pack of dried milk when a token for welfare milk is used to obtain dried milk.

(4) A token for free welfare milk shall be used together with, and in the same manner as, a token for welfare milk, but where a date is specified on a token for free welfare milk it may be used only with a token for welfare milk bearing the same date.

(5) A token for free additional supplies of dried milk may be used only with a token for additional supplies of dried milk.

(6) Tokens for concentrated orange juice, cod liver oil and vitamin tablets may be used by a beneficiary in a family in special circumstances to obtain free of charge the quantities of those welfare foods specified in respect of him in column (4) of Schedule 2.

PART IV

DISTRIBUTION OF MILK

Suppliers of and charges for milk

9.—(1) Where any supplier of milk has accepted from any beneficiary a token for welfare milk he shall (unless he has returned it to the beneficiary before it became valid) supply 7 pints of milk to the beneficiary against that token, during the period of validity of the token; and he may charge the beneficiary the welfare price for milk so supplied.

(2) Where any supplier of milk has accepted from any beneficiary, together with a token for welfare milk, a token for free welfare milk, he shall (unless he has returned both tokens to the beneficiary before they became valid) supply 7 pints of milk to the beneficiary against the said tokens during the period of validity of the token for welfare milk; and—

(*a*) in any case where he would not be entitled under the Milk Order to charge for the milk supplied a price exceeding the standard price, he shall make no charge; and

(*b*) in any other case, he may charge the beneficiary for milk so supplied at a rate not exceeding the difference between the standard price and the price which he would be entitled to charge under the Milk Order.

(3) A supplier may accept tokens from a beneficiary before they have become valid; but he shall on demand return to the beneficiary all tokens in respect of which no milk has been supplied.

(4) If a supplier is prevented by circumstances beyond his control from supplying milk under this Article, he shall be deemed not to have contravened this Article.

Absence for less than a week

10. Where any beneficiary is absent from his usual place of residence for more than one day but less than 7 days during the period of validity of any token for welfare milk which a supplier has accepted from him, and the supplier has supplied against that token some, but not all, of the requisite 7 pints, the supplier shall, if the beneficiary so requests within the said period of validity, forthwith pay or allow the beneficiary, in respect of each pint not supplied, a sum equal to the standard price reduced by 6d. or, if the token was accepted together with a token for free welfare milk, not so reduced.

Absence for a week

11. Where a handicapped child or young child is absent from his usual place of residence for any period of 7 consecutive days during which the person for the time being in charge of that child has provided him with 7 pints of milk, that person shall, notwithstanding anything to the contrary in this Order, be entitled to retain a token for welfare milk issued in respect of the child and to use it free from all restriction as to the use of the milk so obtained.

Submission of tokens by suppliers

12. A supplier shall, in such manner as the Ministry may from time to time direct, submit to the Milk Marketing Board for Northern Ireland all tokens against which the supplier has supplied 7 pints of milk.

Part V

Tokens

Property in tokens

13. Every token is and shall remain the property of the Ministry.

Replacement of tokens

14.—(1) The Ministry may replace tokens which have been lost.

(2) Where a supplier or a beneficiary to or in respect of whom replacement tokens have been issued subsequently finds the tokens supposed to have been lost, he shall deliver the latter forthwith to any local office of the Ministry.

Validity and cancellation of tokens

15.—(1) Tokens shall be valid only if used by or on behalf of a beneficiary, and within the periods and in the manner specified in this Order.

(2) The Ministry may cancel any token which cannot be validly used under this Order.

Return of tokens

16.—(1) Any beneficiary or supplier holding tokens shall, when requested by the Ministry, produce or deliver all tokens in his possession within such time and to such place as the Ministry may direct.

(2) Where any beneficiary holding tokens ceases to be entitled thereto under this Order, he shall forthwith deliver them to any office of the Ministry.

(3) When a beneficiary dies, any person who has, or comes into, possession of any token issued in respect of that beneficiary shall deliver it forthwith to any office of the Ministry or, where death resulted from an infectious or contagious disease, in accordance with the instructions of the Medical Officer of Health.

Supplier losing possession of tokens

17.—(1) Where a supplier accepts any token for welfare milk or free welfare milk from a beneficiary but, before supplying milk against it or returning it to the beneficiary as provided for in Article 9, loses possession of it (whether through accidental loss, theft or otherwise), he shall notify the Ministry forthwith.

(2) Where—

(a) a supplier loses possession, as described in the last preceding paragraph, of a token, and

(b) the Ministry replaces that token pursuant to Article 14(1),

the Ministry may (unless satisfied that it has not been and can not be used by any person other than the beneficiary) require the supplier to pay to him—

(i) in respect of each such token which is a token for welfare milk, a sum equal to 7 times the difference between the standard price and 6d., and

(ii) in respect of each such token which is a token for free welfare milk, a sum of 3s. 6d.

(3) Any sum required to be paid under this Article may be recovered as a civil debt.

(4) Where the Ministry receives a sum under this Article but subsequently becomes satisfied that any tokens in respect of which payment was made were not misused, he shall make a refund to the supplier accordingly.

PART VI

MISCELLANEOUS

Restrictions on supply of welfare foods

18.—(1) No person shall obtain any welfare food unless he is a beneficiary or is obtaining that food on behalf of a beneficiary.

(2) A beneficiary or a person acting on behalf of a beneficiary shall not obtain welfare milk pursuant to Article 4 or welfare foods free of charge pursuant to Article 5 in quantities exceeding those to which the beneficiary is entitled thereunder, or otherwise than in exchange for tokens pursuant to Article 8.

(3) A beneficiary or a person acting on behalf of a beneficiary shall not obtain free welfare milk pursuant to Article 4 otherwise than in exchange for tokens pursuant to Article 8.

Use of welfare foods

19. Where any welfare food is obtained by or on behalf of a beneficiary, it shall not be consumed otherwise than by that beneficiary unless—

(a) if the food is liquid milk or dried milk, the beneficiary has consumed a quantity of milk approximately equal to the quantity of welfare milk obtained in respect of him; or

(b) any such consumption is reasonably necessary to avoid waste or is trifling in amount; or

(c) the food is welfare milk referred to in the proviso to Article 4(1).

Tokens issued in Great Britain to be valid in Northern Ireland

20. Any token issued in Great Britain by the Minister of Health under the provisions of the Welfare Foods Order 1968(a) shall be valid in Northern Ireland as if it had been issued by the Ministry under this Order.

Revocations

21. The Orders specified in Schedule 3 are hereby revoked:
Provided that—

(a) such revocation shall not affect any right or liability acquired or incurred, or anything duly done or suffered, under those Orders;

(b) such revocation shall not affect any legal proceedings in respect of any contravention of those Orders, but any such proceedings may be continued or commenced as if this Order had not been made;

(c) such revocation shall not affect any declaration, registration or authorisation made or granted under those Orders, and every such declaration, registration or authorisation shall, so far as it could have been made or granted under this Order, have effect as if it had been so made or granted.

James Callaghan,
One of Her Majesty's Principal
Secretaries of State.

Home Office,
Whitehall.

19th March 1968.

(a) S.I. 1968/389 (1968 I, p.1050).

SCHEDULE 1

Article 4(3)

Additional supplies of dried milk for a young child under one year of age who is being fed mainly on dried milk

Age of child at time of application (1)	Amount (2)
Not exceeding 3 months	31 20 oz. packs.
3 months but not exceeding 4 months ..	28 ,, ,, ,,
4 ,, ,, ,, ,, 5 ,, ..	24 ,, ,, ,,
5 ,, ,, ,, ,, 6 ,, ..	20 ,, ,, ,,
6 ,, ,, ,, ,, 7 ,, ..	16 ,, ,, ,,
7 ,, ,, ,, ,, 8 ,, ..	12 ,, ,, ,,
8 ,, ,, ,, ,, 9 ,, ..	8 ,, ,, ,,
9 ,, ,, ,, ,, 10 ,, ..	8 ,, ,, ,,
10 ,, ,, ,, ,, 11 ,, . ..	4 ,, ,, ,,
11 ,, ,, ,, ,, 12 ,, ..	2 ,, ,, ,,

SCHEDULE 2

Entitlement to welfare foods other than liquid milk

Class of beneficiary (1)	Welfare food (2)	Price (3)	Quantity of welfare food supplied free of charge to beneficiaries in a family in special circumstances (4)
All beneficiaries	Dried milk	4s. 0d. per 20 oz. pack	As specified in Article 4(1).
Young child	Concentrated orange juice	1s. 6d. per bottle	From birth to 6 months of age at the rate of 3 bottles every 13 weeks. From 6 months to 2 years of age at the rate of 7 bottles every 13 weeks.
Expectant mother	Cod liver oil	1s. 0d. per bottle	At the rate of 2 bottles every 13 weeks.
	Concentrated orange juice	1s. 6d. per bottle	At the rate of 10 bottles every 13 weeks.
	Vitamin tablets	6d. per packet of 45 tablets	At the rate of 2 packets of 45 tablets every 13 weeks.
Nursing mother	Concentrated orange juice	1s. 6d. per bottle	At the rate of 10 bottles every 13 weeks.
	Vitamin tablets	6d. per packet of 45 tablets	5 packets of 45 tablets.

In this Schedule "bottle" means a bottle containing not less than 6 oz.

SCHEDULE 3 Article 21

Orders revoked (1)	References (2)
The Welfare Foods (Northern Ireland) Order 1954.	S.I. 1954/1402 (1954 II, p. 2131).
The Welfare Foods (Northern Ireland) (Amendment) Order 1955.	S.I. 1955/1370 (1955 II, p. 2514).
The Welfare Foods (Northern Ireland) (Amendment) Order 1957.	S.I. 1957/415 (1957 II, p. 2346).
The Welfare Foods (Northern Ireland) (Amendment No. 2) Order 1957.	S.I. 1957/1760 (1957 II, p. 2348).
The Welfare Foods (Northern Ireland) (Amendment) Order 1961.	S.I. 1961/367 (1961 I, p. 567).
The Welfare Foods (Northern Ireland) (Amendment No. 2) Order 1961.	S.I. 1961/2074 (1961 III, p. 3788).

EXPLANATORY NOTE

(This Note is not part of the Order.)

This Order re-enacts with amendments the orders relevant to the administration of the welfare foods scheme operated in Northern Ireland by the Ministry of Health and Social Services.

The principal matters dealt with in the Order include—

(1) a description of the beneficiaries (expectant and nursing mothers, children under 5 and handicapped children) and a list of the foods to which each is entitled;

(2) the method of using, and the period of validity of, the tokens by which welfare foods are obtainable;

(3) restrictions on the use of welfare foods by non-beneficiaries;

(4) the price to be charged for welfare foods.

The price of milk supplied under the scheme to beneficiaries is 6d. per pint of milk normally sold at the lower of the maximum controlled prices for milk (which currently is 10d. per pint). If the beneficiary takes milk which would normally be sold at a price higher than that price, he pays the balance also.

The principal changes from the revoked Orders are that—

(a) a definition is provided of beneficiaries who are to receive free welfare foods—namely, beneficiaries in families in special circumstances, defined by reference to criteria employed by the Ministry of Health and Social Services in the payment of benefit;

(b) the provision for welfare milk to be supplied free is extended to all but two of the beneficiaries in large families (those containing three or more beneficiaries);

(c) provision is made with respect to the obligations of the supplier in respect of lost tokens;

(*d*) some drafting changes are necessary because the Order is not made under the same enabling powers as the revoked Orders. Certain of the penal provisions hitherto applicable (mainly with respect to misuse of tokens) are now contained in the enabling Act—namely, the Emergency Laws (Re-enactments and Repeals) Act 1964.

STATUTORY INSTRUMENTS

1968 No. 428

INCOME TAX

The Ulster and Colonial Savings Certificates (Income Tax Exemption) (Amendment) Regulations 1968

Made - - - -	19*th March* 1968
Coming into Operation	22*nd March* 1968

The Treasury, in exercise of the powers conferred upon them by section 193 of the Income Tax Act 1952(a) and of all other powers enabling them in that behalf, hereby make the following Regulations :—

1. Regulation 3 of the Ulster and Colonial Savings Certificates (Income Tax Exemption) Regulations 1956(b), as substituted by the Ulster and Colonial Savings Certificates (Income Tax Exemption) (Amendment) Regulations 1967(c), shall be amended by substituting for the figures " 750 " in paragraph (g) of the said Regulation the figures " 1,000 ".

2. The Interpretation Act 1889(d) shall apply for the interpretation of these Regulations as it applies for the interpretation of an Act of Parliament.

3. These Regulations may be cited as the Ulster and Colonial Savings Certificates (Income Tax Exemption) (Amendment) Regulations 1968, and shall come into operation on 22nd March 1968.

B. K. O'Malley,
Joseph Harper,
Two of the Lords Commissioners
of Her Majesty's Treasury.

9th March 1968.

EXPLANATORY NOTE

(This Note is not part of the Regulations.)

These Regulations amend Regulation 3 of the Ulster and Colonial Savings Certificates (Income Tax Exemption) Regulations 1956, as substituted by Regulation 1 of the Ulster and Colonial Savings Certificates (Income Tax Exemption) (Amendment) Regulations 1967. They increase, by the addition of 250 unit certificates issued on or after 28th March 1966, the maximum holding of Ulster, Colonial and certain other Savings Certificates, the interest on which is in certain circumstances exempt from income tax under section 193 of the Income Tax Act 1952.

(a) 1952 c. 10.	(b) S.I. 1956/715 (1956 I, p. 1086).
(c) S.I. 1967/579 (1967 I, p. 1787).	(d) 1889 c. 63.

STATUTORY INSTRUMENTS

1968 No. 430

FOOD AND DRUGS

COMPOSITION AND LABELLING

The Fish and Meat Spreadable Products Regulations 1968

Made - - -	*15th March* 1968
Laid before Parliament	*27th March* 1968
Coming into Operation	*15th March* 1971

The Minister of Agriculture, Fisheries and Food and the Minister of Health, acting jointly, in exercise of the powers conferred on them by sections 4, 7, 123 and 136(2) of, and paragraph 2(2) of Schedule 12 to, the Food and Drugs Act 1955(a) and of all other powers enabling them in that behalf, hereby make the following regulations after consultation with such organisations as appear to them to be representative of interests substantially affected by the regulations and reference to the Food Hygiene Advisory Council under section 82 of the said Act (insofar as the regulations are made in exercise of the powers conferred by the said section 7) :—

PART I

PRELIMINARY

Citation and commencement

1. These regulations may be cited as the Fish and Meat Spreadable Products Regulations 1968 ; and shall come into operation on 15th March 1971.

Interpretation

2.—(1) In these regulations, unless the context otherwise requires—

"the Act" means the Food and Drugs Act 1955 ;

"binder" means flour, or starch derived therefrom, of any non-leguminous starchy grain, non-leguminous root or non-leguminous tuber or of any physical modification of any such grain, root or tuber, and includes any soya flour, soya starch, groundnut flour or groundnut lipoprotein ;

"butter-fat content" means the total weight of butter-fat contained in a paste expressed as a percentage of the total weight of the paste, and "content of butter-fat" shall be construed accordingly ;

"container" includes any form of packaging of food for sale as a single item, whether by way of wholly or partly enclosing the food or by way of attaching the food to some other article, and in particular includes a wrapper or confining band ;

"fish" means the edible portion of any fish including edible molluscs and crustacea ;

(a) 4 & 5 Eliz. 2. c. 16.

"fish content" means the total weight of fish when raw contained in any fish paste expressed as a percentage of the total weight of that fish paste, and "content of fish" shall be construed accordingly ;

"fish paste" means any readily spreadable product intended for sale for human consumption of which fish is a major ingredient and includes potted fish, chopped fish, minced fish, flaked fish and pâté intended, in each case, for a use similar to any normal use of fish paste ;

"food" means food intended for sale for human consumption and includes drink, chewing gum and other products of a like nature and use, and articles and substances used as ingredients in the preparation of food or drink or of such products, but does not include—

(a) water, live animals or birds,

(b) fodder or feeding stuffs for animals, birds or fish, or

(c) articles or substances used only as drugs ;

"food and drugs authority" has the meaning assigned to it by section 83 of the Act ;

"human consumption" includes use in the preparation of food for human consumption ;

"lean meat content" means the total weight of lean meat, free of visible fat, when raw, contained in meat paste expressed as a percentage of the total weight of that meat paste ;

"meat" means the flesh, including fat, and the skin, rind, gristle and sinew in amounts naturally associated with the flesh used, of any animal or bird which is normally used for human consumption and includes cured meat and permitted offal, but does not include fish ;

"meat content" means the total weight of meat when raw contained in any meat paste expressed as a percentage of the total weight of that meat paste, and "content of meat" shall be construed accordingly ;

"meat paste" means any readily spreadable product intended for sale for human consumption of which meat is a major ingredient and includes potted meat, chopped meat, minced meat, flaked meat and pâté intended, in each case, for a use similar to any normal use of meat paste ;

"paste" means fish paste or meat paste ;

"permitted offal" means any offal other than offal prohibited to be used in any uncooked open meat product by the Offals in Meat Products Order 1953(a) ;

"sell" includes offer or expose for sale or have in possession for sale, and "sale" and "sold" shall be construed accordingly ;

"sell by retail" means sell to a person buying otherwise than for the purpose of re-sale, and "sold by retail" shall be construed accordingly ;

AND other expressions have the same meaning as in the Act.

(2) The Interpretation Act 1889(b) shall apply to the interpretation of these regulations as it applies to the interpretation of an Act of Parliament and as if these regulations and the orders hereby revoked were Acts of Parliament.

(3) All percentages mentioned in these regulations are percentages calculated by weight.

(a) S.I. 1953/246 (1953 I, p. 686).   (b) 1889 c. 63.

(4) Any reference in these regulations to a label borne on a container shall be construed as including a reference to any legible marking on the container however effected.

(5) For the purposes of these regulations, the supply of food, otherwise than by sale, at, in or from any place where food is supplied in the course of a business shall be deemed to be a sale of that food, and references to purchasing and purchaser shall be construed accordingly.

(6) Any reference in these regulations to any order or other regulations shall be construed as a reference to such order or regulations as amended by any subsequent order or regulations.

Exemptions

3. The following provisions of these regulations shall not apply to any paste—

(*a*) sold, consigned or delivered for exportation to any place outside the United Kingdom ; or

(*b*) supplied under Government contracts for consumption by Her Majesty's forces or supplied for consumption by a visiting force within the meaning of any of the provisions of Part I of the Visiting Forces Act 1952(**a**) ; or

(*c*) sold, consigned or delivered to a manufacturer for the purposes of his manufacturing business or to a caterer for the purposes of his catering business.

PART II

DESCRIPTION AND COMPOSITION OF MEAT PASTE AND FISH PASTE

Description and composition of meat paste

4.—(1) Subject to the provisions of regulation 6 hereof, any meat paste sold, consigned or delivered shall bear one of the following descriptions and comply with the compositional requirements specified in relation to that description, save that the appropriate description need be borne by any meat paste sold, consigned or delivered otherwise than in a container only when such meat paste is sold by retail :—

(*a*) "meat paste" if the meat paste has a meat content of not less than 70 per cent. :

Provided that in place of the word "meat" there may be substituted the name of any meat characterising the meat paste, and in place of the word "paste" the word "pâté" in the case of a meat paste which has the characteristics of a pâté ;

(*b*) "X spread", the description being completed by inserting at "X" the name of any meat, if the meat paste has a meat content of such meat of not less than 70 per cent. :

Provided that in the place of the word "spread" there may be substituted the word "pâté" in the case of a meat paste which has the characteristics of a pâté ;

(*c*) "potted meat", "chopped meat", "minced meat" or "flaked meat" if the meat paste has a meat content of not less than 95 per cent. and does not contain any added binder ;

(**a**) 1952 c. 67.

(*d*) "potted X", "chopped X", "minced X" or "flaked X", the description being completed by inserting at "X" the name of any meat, if the meat paste has a meat content of such meat of not less than 95 per cent. and does not contain any added binder ;

(*e*) "potted meat and Y", "chopped meat and Y", "minced meat and Y" or "flaked meat and Y", the description being completed by inserting at "Y" the name of another main ingredient, if the meat paste has a meat content of not less than 80 per cent. and a content of meat and that other main ingredient, taken together, of not less than 95 per cent. and does not contain any added binder;

(*f*) "potted X and Y", "chopped X and Y", "minced X and Y" or "flaked X and Y", the description being completed by inserting at "X" the name of any meat and at "Y" the name of another main ingredient, if the meat paste has a meat content of such meat of not less than 80 per cent. and a content of such meat and that other main ingredient, taken together, of not less than 95 per cent. and does not contain any added binder :

Provided that in any description mentioned in this or the last preceding sub-paragraph there may be substituted for the word "and" the word "in" or "with" ;

(*g*) "chopped meat in jelly", "minced meat in jelly" or "flaked meat in jelly" if the meat paste contains added jelly but no added binder and has a meat content of not less than 70 per cent.;

(*h*) "chopped X in jelly", "minced X in jelly" or "flaked X in jelly", the description being completed by inserting at "X" the name of any meat, if the meat paste contains added jelly but no added binder and has a meat content of such meat of not less than 70 per cent.;

(*j*) "brawn" without any word or words stating or implying that the meat paste with jelly has a meat content of not less than 70 per cent., if the meat paste contains added jelly but no added binder and has a meat content of not less than 60 per cent.;

(*k*) any description mentioned in sub-paragraph (*a*) or (*b*) hereof followed by the words "and butter" or "with butter" if the meat paste has a butter-fat content of not less than 6 per cent. and complies with the requirements specified in the said sub-paragraph (*a*) or (*b*), as the case may be, in relation to that description ;

(*l*) any description mentioned in sub-paragraph (*c*) or (*d*) hereof followed by the words "and butter" or "with butter" if the meat paste does not contain any added binder and has a butter-fat content of not less than 6 per cent. and either a meat content and butter-fat content, taken together, of not less than 96 per cent. or, in a case where the description includes the name of any meat, a meat content of the meat so named and a butter-fat content, taken together, of not less than 96 per cent.;

(*m*) any description mentioned in sub-paragraph (*e*) or (*f*) hereof followed by the words "and butter" or "with butter" if the meat paste does not contain any added binder and has a butter-fat content of not less than 6 per cent. and either a meat content of not less than 80 per cent. or, in a case where the description includes the name of any meat, a meat content of the meat so named of not less than 80 per cent. and, in any case, a content of meat, butter-fat and the other main ingredient, taken together of not less than 96 per cent. .

(2) Where any meat paste is sold, consigned or delivered in a container under any description mentioned in sub-paragraph (g) or (h) of the last preceding paragraph and has a net weight of more than 3 ounces, the words "for spreading" shall appear clearly and legibly on a label on the container in immediate proximity to, and as prominently as, the description.

(3) The lean meat content of any meat paste shall be not less than 60 per cent. of the minimum meat content specified in relation to that meat paste in this regulation:

Provided that this paragraph shall not apply to any meat paste bearing a description which includes the word "pâté" in accordance with paragraph (1) (a) or (b) of this regulation.

(4) No person shall sell, consign or deliver any meat paste in contravention of this regulation.

Description and composition of fish paste

5.—(1) Subject to the provisions of regulation 6 hereof, any fish paste sold, consigned or delivered shall bear one of the following descriptions and comply with the compositional requirements specified in relation to that description, save that the appropriate description need be borne by any fish paste sold, consigned or delivered otherwise than in a container only when such fish paste is sold by retail:—

(a) "fish paste" if the fish paste has a fish content of not less than 70 per cent.:

Provided that in place of the word "fish" there may be substituted the name of any fish characterising the fish paste, and in place of the word "paste" the word "pâté" in the case of a fish paste which has the characteristics of a pâté;

(b) "X spread", the description being completed by inserting at "X" the name of any fish, if the fish paste has a fish content of such fish of not less than 70 per cent.:

Provided that in place of the word "spread" there may be substituted the word "pâté" in the case of a fish paste which has the characteristics of a pâté;

(c) "potted fish", "chopped fish", "minced fish" or "flaked fish" if the fish paste has a fish content of not less than 95 per cent. and does not contain any added binder;

(d) "potted X", "chopped X", "minced X" or "flaked X", the description being completed by inserting at "X" the name of any fish, if the fish paste has a fish content of such fish of not less than 95 per cent. and does not contain any added binder;

(e) "potted fish and Y", "chopped fish and Y", "minced fish and Y" or "flaked fish and Y", the description being completed by inserting at "Y" the name of another main ingredient, if the fish paste has a fish content of not less than 80 per cent. and a content of fish and that other main ingredient, taken together, of not less than 95 per cent. and does not contain any added binder;

(f) "potted X and Y", "chopped X and Y", "minced X and Y" or "flaked X and Y", the description being completed by inserting at "X" the name of any fish and at "Y" the name of another main ingredient, if the fish paste has a fish content of such fish of not less than 80 per cent. and a content of such fish and that other main ingredient, taken together, of not less than 95 per cent. and does not contain any added binder:

Provided that in any description mentioned in this or the last preceding sub-paragraph there may be substituted for the word "and" the word "in" or "with";

(g) "dressed crab" if the fish paste has a fish content, consisting wholly of crab meat, of not less than 93 per cent. ;

(h) any description mentioned in sub-paragraph (a) or (b) hereof followed by the words "and butter" or "with butter" if the fish paste has a butter-fat content of not less than 6 per cent. and complies with the requirements specified in the said sub-paragraph (a) or (b), as the case may be, in relation to that description ;

(j) any description mentioned in sub-paragraph (c) or (d) hereof followed by the words "and butter" or "with butter" if the fish paste does not contain any added binder and has a butter-fat content of not less than 6 per cent. and either a fish content and butter-fat content, taken together, of not less than 96 per cent. or, in a case where the description includes the name of any fish, a fish content of the fish so named and a butter-fat content, taken together, of not less than 96 per cent.;

(k) any description mentioned in sub-paragraph (e) or (f) hereof followed by the words "and butter" or "with butter" if the fish paste does not contain any added binder and has a butter-fat content of not less than 6 per cent. and either a fish content of not less than 80 per cent., or, in a case where the description includes the name of any fish, a fish content of the fish so named of not less than 80 per cent. and, in any case, a content of fish, butter-fat and the other main ingredient, taken together, of not less than 96 per cent. .

(2) No person shall sell, consign or deliver any fish paste in contravention of this regulation.

Pastes which require grilling

6. Regulations 4 and 5 of these regulations shall not apply to any paste if such paste, when sold, consigned or delivered, bears the words "requires grilling".

Sales by description

7.—(1) No person shall sell any food under such a description as to lead an intending purchaser to believe that he is purchasing any kind of paste for which compositional requirements are specified in these regulations unless the food complies with the appropriate compositional requirements specified in these regulations in relation to that kind of paste.

(2) Where a person sells any food to a purchaser in response to a request for any kind of paste for which compositional requirements are specified in these regulations, he shall be deemed to sell paste of that kind and under such a description as is specified in these regulations in relation to that kind of paste unless he clearly notifies the purchaser at the time of sale that the food is not that kind of paste.

Requirements as to presentation of descriptions

8. Any description, name or word required or permitted by virtue of regulation 4, 5 or 6 of these regulations to be borne on any paste shall appear, when the said paste is—

(*a*) sold, consigned or delivered in a container, on a label borne on the container of the said paste ;

(*b*) sold by retail otherwise than in a container, on a ticket placed on or in immediate proximity to the said paste so as to be clearly visible to an intending purchaser ;

and such description, name or word shall appear as or as part of, or in close proximity to, the name of the paste, and the provisions of paragraphs 1 and 2 of Schedule 4 to the Labelling of Food Regulations 1967(**a**) shall apply in relation to any description, name or word required by virtue of this regulation to appear on a label borne on the container as they apply in relation to an appropriate designation or common or usual name for the purposes of those regulations and the provisions of paragraph 6 of the said Schedule 4 shall apply in relation to any description, name or word required by virtue of this regulation to appear on a ticket as they apply in relation to a statement required by regulation 9 (1) or (2) of those regulations.

Labelling and advertisement of paste

9. No person shall—

(*a*) give with any paste sold by him any label, whether attached to or borne on the container or not, or display with any paste offered or exposed by him for sale any ticket, or

(*b*) publish, or be a party to the publication of, any advertisement for paste,

being a label, ticket or advertisement, as the case may be, which bears or includes any description required or permitted to be used by virtue of regulation 4 or 5 of these regulations, or any description substantially similar to such description, unless such paste conforms to the compositional requirements specified in regulation 4 or 5 of these regulations in relation to that description.

PART III

ADMINISTRATION AND GENERAL

Penalties and enforcement

10.—(1) If any person contravenes or fails to comply with any of the foregoing provisions of these regulations he shall be guilty of an offence and shall be liable to a fine not exceeding one hundred pounds or to imprisonment for a term not exceeding three months, or to both, and, in the case of a continuing offence, to a further fine not exceeding five pounds for each day during which the offence continues after conviction.

(2) Each food and drugs authority shall enforce and execute such provisions in their area.

(3) The requirement of section 109(3) of the Act (which requires notice to be given to the Minister of Agriculture, Fisheries and Food of intention to institute proceedings for an offence against any provisions of these regulations made under section 7 of the Act) shall not apply as respects any proceedings instituted by a council for an offence against any such provisions of these regulations.

(**a**) S.I. 1967/1864 (1967 III, p. 5013).

Defences

11.—(1) In any proceedings for an offence against these regulations in relation to the publication of an advertisement, it shall be a defence for the defendant to prove that, being a person whose business it is to publish, or arrange for the publication of, advertisements, he received the advertisement for publication in the ordinary course of business.

(2) In any proceedings against the manufacturer or importer of any paste for an offence against these regulations in relation to the publication of an advertisement, it shall rest on the defendant to prove that he did not publish, and was not a party to the publication of, the advertisement.

Application of various sections of the Act

12.—(1) Sections 108 (3) and (4) (which relate to prosecutions), 110 (1), (2) and (3) (which relate to evidence of analysis), 112 (which relates to the power of a court to require analysis by the Government Chemist), 113 (which relates to a contravention due to some person other than the person charged), 115 (2) (which relates to the conditions under which a warranty may be pleaded as a defence) and 116 (which relates to offences in relation to warranties and certificates of analysis) of the Act shall apply for the purposes of these regulations as if references therein to proceedings, or a prosecution, under or taken or brought under the Act included references to proceedings, or a prosecution as the case may be, taken or brought for an offence under these regulations and as if the reference in the said section 112 to subsection (4) of section 108 included a reference to that subsection as applied by these regulations.

(2) Paragraph (*b*) of the proviso to section 108 (1) of the Act shall apply for the purposes of these regulations as if the reference therein to section 116 of the Act included a reference to that section as applied by these regulations.

Revocation

13. The orders specified in the Schedule to these regulations are hereby revoked.

In Witness whereof the Official Seal of the Minister of Agriculture, Fisheries and Food is hereunto affixed on 13th March 1968.

    (L.S.)   *Frederick Peart.*
                            Minister of Agriculture, Fisheries and Food.

Given under the official seal of the Minister of Health on 15th March 1968.

    (L.S.)   *Kenneth Robinson,*
                            Minister of Health.

SCHEDULE

Regulation 13

Orders revoked	References
The Food Standards (Fish Paste) Order 1951.	S.I. 1951/1456 (1951 III, p. 16).
The Food Standards (Meat Paste) Order 1951.	S.I. 1951/1457 (1951 III, p. 20).
The Food Standards (Fish Paste) (Amendment) Order 1951.	S.I. 1951/2241 (1951 III, p. 18).
The Food Standards (Meat Paste) (Amendment) Order 1951.	S.I. 1951/2242 (1951 III, p. 22).

EXPLANATORY NOTE

(This Note is not part of the Regulations.)

These regulations, which apply to England and Wales only, supersede the Food Standards (Fish Paste) Order 1951, as amended, and the Food Standards (Meat Paste) Order 1951, as amended. They specify requirements for the description, composition, labelling and advertisement of meat paste and fish paste. They come into operation on 15th March 1971.

The regulations do not apply to any meat paste or fish paste sold for export, supplied for consumption by Her Majesty's forces or a visiting force or for use for manufacturing or catering purposes.

STATUTORY INSTRUMENTS

1968 No. 431

CLEAN AIR

The Clean Air (Measurement of Grit and Dust) Regulations 1968

Made - - -	*20th March* 1968
Laid before Parliament	*3rd April* 1968
Coming into Operation	*1st May* 1968

The Minister of Housing and Local Government, in exercise of his powers under section 7(2) of the Clean Air Act 1956(**a**) and of all other powers enabling him in that behalf, hereby makes the following regulations :—

1. These regulations may be cited as the Clean Air (Measurement of Grit and Dust) Regulations 1968 and shall come into operation on 1st May 1968.

2. The Interpretation Act 1889(**b**) applies for the interpretation of these regulations as it applies for the interpretation of an Act of Parliament.

3. Where, by virtue of a direction served by the local authority under section 7(1) of the Clean Air Act 1956, the provisions of subsection (2) of that section apply to a furnace, the occupier of the building in which the furnace is situated shall comply with the requirements set out in the schedule hereto.

SCHEDULE

ADAPTATIONS TO CHIMNEYS AND PROVISION AND
MAINTENANCE OF APPARATUS

1.—(1) Where the occupier receives not less than 6 weeks notice in writing from the local authority requiring adaptations to the chimney serving a furnace and the provision of apparatus for the purpose of making and recording the measurements of grit and dust emitted from the furnace, he shall, within the period specified in the notice, make such adaptations to the chimney as are necessary for the making and recording of such measurements by one of the methods described in British Standard 3405, 1961, published by the British Standards Institution, and provide the apparatus therein mentioned.

(2) All apparatus provided for the purpose of this paragraph shall be maintained in good working order.

(**a**) 1956 c. 52.   (**b**) 1889 c. 63.

MAKING AND RECORDING MEASUREMENTS

2.—(1) When the requirements of paragraph 1 of this Schedule have been complied with the occupier, on receiving not less than 28 days notice in writing from the local authority requiring him to make and record measurements of grit and dust emitted from a furnace, shall within the period specified in the notice, make and record such measurements in accordance with the method detailed in pages 13 to 26 of the publication "Measurement of Solids in Flue Gases" by P. G. W. Hawksley, S. Badzioch and J. H. Blackett, published in 1961 by the British Coal Utilization Research Association.

(2) Before making any measurements the occupier shall give to the local authority not less than 48 hours notice in writing of the date on which and the time at which he proposes to commence to do so.

(3) The occupier shall, in relation to each chimney to which these regulations apply, keep a written record containing the following particulars—

    (a) the date on which any measurements were made ;

    (b) the number of furnaces discharging into the chimney on that date ;

    (c) the measurements in terms of pounds per hour of grit and dust emitted, and in the case of solid fuel fired boilers the percentage of grit contained in the solids emitted ;

and shall transmit a copy of such particulars to the local authority within 7 days from the making of the measurements in respect of which the particulars are recorded.

(4) A notice served for the purpose of this paragraph may require the making of measurements from time to time or at stated intervals:

Provided that an occupier shall not be required to make measurements in respect of any one chimney more than once in any period of 3 months unless in the opinion of the local authority the true level of emission of grit and dust cannot be determined without the making of further measurements.

3. Anything required to be done by an occupier under the provisions of this schedule may be done on his behalf by any other person.

Given under the official seal of the Minister of Housing and Local Government on 20th March 1968.

(L.S.)   *Anthony Greenwood,*

Minister of Housing and Local Government.

EXPLANATORY NOTE

(This Note is not part of the Regulations.)

Under section 7 of the Clean Air Act 1956 occupiers of buildings in which certain furnaces are situated may be directed by the local authority to make and record measurements of the grit and dust emitted from the furnace in accordance with requirements prescribed by the Minister of Housing and Local Government. These regulations prescribe the requirements to be observed.

British Standard 3405, 1961 may be obtained from British Standards Institution, British Standards House, 2 Park Street, London, W.1, and "Measurements of Solids in Flue Gases" may be obtained from the British Coal Utilisation Research Association, Randalls Road, Leatherhead, Surrey.

STATUTORY INSTRUMENTS

1968 No. 434 (S.42)

TOWN AND COUNTRY PLANNING, SCOTLAND

The Town and Country Planning (Building Preservation Order) (Scotland) Amendment Regulations 1968

Made - - - - *19th March* 1968

Laid before Parliament *27th March* 1968

Coming into Operation *1st April* 1968

In exercise of the powers conferred on me by sections 27 and 107 of the Town and Country Planning (Scotland) Act 1947(a), and section 10 of the Civic Amenities Act 1967(b), and of all other powers enabling me in their behalf, I hereby make the following regulations:—

1.—(1) These regulations may be cited as the Town and Country Planning (Building Preservation Order) (Scotland) Amendment Regulations 1968, and these regulations and the Town and Country Planning (Building Preservation Order) (Scotland) Regulations 1948(c) may be cited together as the Town and Country Planning (Building Preservation Order) (Scotland) Regulations 1948 and 1968.

(2) These regulations shall come into operation on 1st April 1968.

(3) The Interpretation Act 1889(d) shall apply for the interpretation of these regulations as it applies for the interpretation of an Act of Parliament.

2. The Town and Country Planning (Building Preservation Order) (Scotland) Regulations 1948 are hereby amended as follows:—

(a) In regulation 2(1), after the definition of "the Act" there shall be added the following definition—

"'the Act of 1967' means the Civic Amenities Act 1967;";

(b) In regulation 5, for the words "A notice given or served under paragraph (c) or (d) of the last preceding regulation shall state" there shall be substituted—

"A notice given or served under paragraph (c) or (d) of the last preceding regulation shall, in any case where the order contains a direction under section 10 (procedure for making building preservation orders) of the Act of 1967, state the effect of the direction, and shall in all cases also state";

(c) In paragraph (c) of regulation 8, the words "(except where the order is confirmed provisionally under the proviso to sub-section (4) of section 27 of the Act)" shall be deleted, and at the end there shall be added the following words—

"and (d) in any case where the order contains a direction under section 10 of the Act of 1967 and the Secretary of State, within the period of six

(a) 1947 c. 53.
(c) S.I. 1948/2096 (Rev. XXII, p.897: 1948 I, p. 4241).
(b) 1967 c. 69.
(d) 1889 c. 63.

months beginning with the date on which the order was made, notifies the local planning authority that he does not propose to confirm it, serve copies of that notice on the presons on whom notices have been served under paragraph (*d*) of regulation 4 hereof.".

William Ross.
One of Her Majesty's Principal
Secretaries of State.

St. Andrew's House,
    Edinburgh, 1.
19th March 1968.

EXPLANATORY NOTE

(This Note is not part of the Regulations.)

These regulations amend the 1948 regulations governing the form, and procedure for the submission and confirmation, of building preservation orders made under section 27 of the Town and Country Planning (Scotland) Act 1947. They provide that where, by direction of a local planning authority, an order is to take immediate effect provisionally under section 10 of the Civic Amenities Act 1967, proper notice is given of the effect of the direction and (where appropriate) of any decision of the Secretary of State that the order should not be confirmed.

STATUTORY INSTRUMENTS

1968 No. 435 (S. 43)

TOWN AND COUNTRY PLANNING, SCOTLAND

The Town and Country Planning (Tree Preservation Order) (Scotland) Amendment Regulations 1968

Made - - - -	*19th March* 1968
Laid before Parliament	*27th March* 1968
Coming into Operation	*1st April* 1968

In exercise of the powers conferred on me by sections 26 and 107 of the Town and Country Planning (Scotland) Act 1947(**a**), and section 16 of the Civic Amenities Act 1967(**b**), and of all other powers enabling me in that behalf, I hereby make the following regulations:—

1.—(1) These regulations may be cited as the Town and Country Planning (Tree Preservation Order) (Scotland) Amendment Regulations 1968, and these regulations and the Town and Country Planning (Tree Preservation Order) (Scotland) Regulations 1948(**c**) may be cited together as the Town and Country Planning (Tree Preservation Order) (Scotland) Regulations 1948 and 1968.

(2) These regulations shall come into operation on 1st April 1968.

(3) The Interpretation Act 1889(**d**) shall apply for the interpretation of these regulations as it applies for the interpretation of an Act of Parliament.

2. The Town and Country Planning (Tree Preservation Order) (Scotland) Regulations 1948 are hereby amended as follows:—

(*a*) In regulation 2(1), after the definition of "the Act" there shall be added the following definition—

" 'the Act of 1967' means the Civic Amenities Act 1967;";

(*b*) In regulation 5, for the words "A notice given or served under sub-paragraphs (*b*) or (*c*) of the last preceding regulation shall state" there shall be substituted—

"A notice given or served under sub-paragraph (*b*) or (*c*) of the last preceding regulation shall, in any case where the order contains a direction under section 16 (procedure for making tree preservation orders) of the Act of 1967, state the effect of the direction, and shall in all cases also state";

(*c*) In sub-paragraph (*b*) of regulation 8, the words "(except where the order is confirmed provisionally under the proviso to sub-section (5) of section 26 of the Act)" shall be deleted and at the end there shall be added the following words—

"and (*c*) in any case where the order contains a direction under section 16 of the Act of 1967 and the Secretary of State, within the period of six

---

(**a**) 1947 c. 53.
(**c**) S.I. 1948/1781 (Rev. XXII, p.895: 1948 I, p. 4346).

(**b**) 1967 c. 69.
(**d**) 1889 c. 63.

months beginning with the date on which the order was made, notifies the local planning authority that he does not propose to confirm it, serve copies of that notice on the persons on whom notices have been served under sub-paragraph (c) of regulation 4 hereof.".

William Ross,
One of Her Majesty's Principal
Secretaries of State.

St. Andrew's House,
   Edinburgh, 1.
19th March 1968.

EXPLANATORY NOTE

(This Note is not part of the Regulations.)

These regulations amend the 1948 regulations governing the form, and procedure for the submission and confirmation, of tree preservation orders made under section 26 of the Town and Country Planning (Scotland) Act 1947. They provide that where, by direction of a local planning authority, an order is to take immediate effect provisionally under section 16 of the Civic Amenities Act 1967, proper notice is given of the effect of the direction and (where appropriate) of any decision of the Secretary of State that the order should not be confirmed.

1968 No. 436 (C.7)

HARBOURS, DOCKS, PIERS AND FERRIES

The Docks and Harbours Act 1966 (Commencement No. 9) Order 1968

Made - - - *19th March* 1968

The Minister of Labour in exercise of the powers conferred on him by section 60 of the Docks and Harbours Act 1966(a) and of all other powers enabling him in that behalf, hereby makes the following Order:—

1. Part II (which relates to welfare amenities for ports) of the Docks and Harbours Act 1966 shall come into operation on 1st April 1968.

2. This Order may be cited as the Docks and Harbours Act 1966 (Commencement No. 9) Order 1968.

Signed by order of the Minister of Labour.
19th March 1968.

P. H. St. J. Wilson,
Deputy Secretary,
Ministry of Labour.

EXPLANATORY NOTE

(This Note is not part of the Order.)

This Order brings into operation Part II of the Docks and Harbours Act 1966 which deals with the provision of welfare amenities for the ports specified in Schedule 1 to that Act in accordance with welfare amenity schemes prepared under the said Part II.

(a) 1966 c. 28.

STATUTORY INSTRUMENTS

1968 No. 438

ROAD TRAFFIC

The Motor Vehicles (Authorisation of Special Types) (Amendment) Order 1968

Made - - -		*15th March* 1968
Coming into Operation		*8th April* 1968

The Minister of Transport, in exercise of her powers under section 64(4) of the Road Traffic Act 1960(a) as amended by section 51 of and Schedule 4 to the Road Traffic Act 1962(b) and under subsections (5) and (6) of the said section 64 and of all other powers her enabling in that behalf, hereby makes the following Order :—

1.—(1) This Order shall come into operation on 8th April 1968 and may be cited as the Motor Vehicles (Authorisation of Special Types) (Amendment) Order 1968.

(2) The Interpretation Act 1889(c) shall apply for the interpretation of this Order as it applies for the interpretation of an Act of Parliament.

2. The Motor Vehicles (Authorisation of Special Types) General Order 1966(d) shall have effect as though—

(1) Article 11 (Showmen's trailers) were deleted ; and

(2) in Article 20 (Interpretation), for the definition of "abnormal indivisible load", there were substituted the following definition—
" "abnormal indivisible load" means a load—
    (a) which cannot without undue expense or risk of damage be divided into two or more loads for the purpose of carriage on roads, and
    (b) which—
        (i) owing to its dimensions, cannot be carried by a heavy motor car or trailer or a combination of a heavy motor car and trailer complying in all respects with the requirements of the Construction and Use Regulations, or
        (ii) owing to its weight cannot be carried by a heavy motor car or trailer or a combination of a heavy motor car and trailer having a total laden weight of less than 24 tons and complying in all respects with the requirements of the Construction and Use Regulations ;".

Given under the Official Seal of the Minister of Transport the 15th March 1968.

(L.S.)

J. R. Madge,
An Under Secretary of the
Ministry of Transport.

(a) 8 & 9 Eliz. 2. c. 16.   (b) 10 & 11 Eliz. 2. c. 59.
(c) 52 & 53 Vict. c. 63.   (d) S.I. 1966/1289 (1966 III, p. 3579).

EXPLANATORY NOTE

(This Note is not part of the Order.)

This Order amends the Motor Vehicle (Authorisation of Special Types) General Order 1966 by—

1. deleting Article 11 relating to the use of showmen's trailers as these provisions are now included in Regulation 58 of the Motor Vehicles (Construction and Use) Regulations 1966 (S.I. 1966/1288), as amended by the Motor Vehicles (Construction and Use) (Amendment) (No. 2) Regulations 1968 (S.I. 1968/426) (Article 2(1)); and

2. redefining the meaning of "abnormal indivisible load" in Article 20 to authorise the use of special vehicles manufactured on or after 1st December 1966 to carry such loads with a gross weight of between 24 and 32 tons (Article 2(2)).

STATUTORY INSTRUMENTS

1968 No. 439

ROAD TRAFFIC

The Road Vehicles (Duration of Licences) Order 1968

Made -	-	-	-	*19th March* 1968
Coming into Operation				*20th March* 1968

The Minister of Transport, in exercise of her powers under section 3 of the Vehicles (Excise) Act 1962(a) and of all other powers her enabling in that behalf, hereby makes the following Order :—

1.—(1) This Order shall come into operation on the 20th March 1968, and may be cited as the Road Vehicles (Duration of Licences) Order 1968.

(2) The Interpretation Act 1889(b) shall apply for the interpretation of this Order as it applies for the interpretation of an Act of Parliament, and as if for the purposes of section 38 of that Act this Order were an Act of Parliament.

2. Section 2(1) of the Vehicles (Excise) Act 1962 shall have effect as though the words " eight pounds " were substituted for the words " four pounds " in paragraph (c) thereof.

Given under the Official Seal of the Minister of Transport the 19th March 1968.

(L.S.)

J. R. Madge,
An Under Secretary of
the Ministry of Transport.

EXPLANATORY NOTE

(This Note is not part of the Order.)

Section 2(1)(c) of the Vehicles (Excise) Act 1962 provides that a four monthly excise licence may be taken out for a vehicle the annual rate of duty for which exceeds four pounds. This order amends section 2(1)(c) and provides that four monthly excise licences may be taken out only where the annual rate of duty exceeds eight pounds.

(a) 10 & 11 Eliz. 2. c. 13.   (b) 52 & 53 Vict. c. 63.

STATUTORY INSTRUMENTS

1968 No. 440

PRISONS

ENGLAND AND WALES

The Prison (Amendment) Rules 1968

Made - - -	*19th March* 1968
Laid before Parliament	*27th March* 1968
Coming into Operation	*1st April* 1968

In pursuance of section 47 of the Prison Act 1952(**a**), as amended by sections 23 and 41 of, and Schedule 4 to, the Criminal Justice Act 1961(**b**) and sections 66 and 103 of, and Schedule 7 to, the Criminal Justice Act 1967(**c**), I hereby make the following Rules:—

1. For Rule 5 of the Prison Rules 1964(**d**) (hereafter in these Rules referred to as " the principal Rules ") there shall be substituted the Rule set out in the Schedule to these Rules.

2. Rules 50 and 51 of the principal Rules shall be amended by omitting, in paragraph (*g*) of each of those Rules, the words—

" or, in the case of a prisoner serving a sentence of corrective training or preventive detention and not having been recalled after release on licence, postponement of his eligibility for release on licence for ".

3. Rule 52 of the principal Rules shall be amended by omitting in paragraph (3) the words " subject to paragraph (4) of this Rule " and " or postponement ", and by omitting paragraphs (4), (5) and (6).

4. Rule 53 of the principal Rules (which relates to corporal punishment) shall be omitted.

5. In Rule 54 of the principal Rules, for the words " restricted diet or corporal punishment " there shall be substituted the words " or restricted diet ".

6. Rules 65 to 71 of the principal Rules (which relate to corrective training and preventive detention) shall be omitted.

7. These Rules may be cited as the Prison (Amendment) Rules 1968 and shall come into operation on 1st April 1968.

James Callaghan,

One of Her Majesty's Principal
Secretaries of State.

Home Office,
  Whitehall.
19th March 1968.

(a) 1952 c. 52.	(b) 1961 c. 39.
(c) 1967 c. 80.	(d) S.I. 1964/388 (1964 I, p. 591).

SCHEDULE

RULE TO BE SUBSTITUTED FOR RULE 5 OF THE PRINCIPAL RULES

Remission of sentence

5.—(1) A prisoner serving a sentence of imprisonment for an actual term of more than one month may, on the ground of his industry and good conduct, be granted remission in accordance with the provisions of this Rule:

Provided that this Rule shall not permit the reduction of the actual term to less than thirty-one days, or in the case of a prisoner (other than a prisoner within paragraph (2)(*b*) of this Rule) who has been released on licence and recalled to prison, permit his release before the thirtieth day following his return to prison on recall.

(2) The remission granted under this Rule shall not exceed—

  (*a*) one-third of the total of the actual term and any period spent in custody by the prisoner after his conviction awaiting sentence which is taken into account under section 67 of the Criminal Justice Act 1967 (which relates to the computation of a sentence of imprisonment); or

  (*b*) in the case of a prisoner in respect of whom an extended sentence certificate was issued when sentence was passed on him or who was under the age of twenty-one when sentence was passed on him and who has been released on licence and recalled to prison, one-third of that part of his sentence unexpired at the time of his recall.

(3) For the purposes of this Rule—

  (*a*) a person committed to prison in default of payment of a sum adjudged to be paid by a conviction shall be treated as serving a sentence of imprisonment; and

  (*b*) consecutive terms of imprisonment shall be treated as one term.

(4) This Rule shall have effect subject to any disciplinary award of forfeiture of remission, and shall not apply to a prisoner serving a sentence of imprisonment for life.

(5) In this Rule—

  (*a*) " actual term " means the term of a sentence of imprisonment as reduced by section 67 of the Criminal Justice Act 1967;

  (*b*) " forfeiture of remission " includes, in the case of a disciplinary award made before 1st April 1968, postponement of eligibility for release on licence;

  (*c*) a reference to a person being recalled to prison shall include a reference to the revocation of a licence by a court;

  (*d*) a reference to the said section 67 shall, in the case of a sentence passed before 1st October 1967, include a reference to section 17(2) of the Criminal Justice Administration Act 1962(**a**).

(**a**) 1962 c. 15.

EXPLANATORY NOTE

(This Note is not part of the Rules.)

These Rules amend the Prison Rules 1964 to take account of the abolition by the Criminal Justice Act 1967 of corrective training, preventive detention and corporal punishment in prisons.

The Rule relating to remission, set out in the Schedule, has been amended to make special provision for the case of prisoners released on licence and recalled to prison.

STATUTORY   INSTRUMENTS

1968 No. 443

NATIONAL HEALTH SERVICE, ENGLAND AND WALES

The National Health Service (General Dental Services) Amendment Regulations 1968

Made - - -	*20th March* 1968
Laid before Parliament	*27th March* 1968
Coming into Operation	*1st April* 1968

The Minister of Health, in exercise of the powers conferred on him by section 40 of the National Health Service Act 1946(a), as amended by the National Health Service (Amendment) Act 1949(b), and of all other powers enabling him in that behalf, hereby makes the following regulations :—

1.—(1) These regulations may be cited as the National Health Service (General Dental Services) Amendment Regulations 1968 and shall come into operation on 1st April 1968.

(2) The Interpretation Act 1889(c) applies to the interpretation of these regulations as it applies to an Act of Parliament.

2. For paragraphs 1 and 3 of schedule 6 to the National Health Service (General Dental Services) Regulations 1967(d) (Remuneration of Salaried Practitioners) there shall be respectively substituted the following paragraphs :—

"1.   Rates applicable to whole-time employment at a health centre :—

Grade	Scale of Remuneration
I	Commencing at £2,390 per annum and rising to £3,020 per annum by annual increments as follows : —

£
2,390
2,480
2,570
2,660
2,750
2,840
2,930
3,020

(a) 1946 c. 81.
(c) 1889 c. 63.
(b) 1949 c. 93.
(d) S.I. 1967/937 (1967 II, p. 2816).

II   Commencing at £1,725 per annum and rising to £2,535 per
     annum by annual increments as follows:—

£

1,725
1,795
1,865
1,945
2,025
2,105
2,185
2,265
2,355
2,445
2,535"

"3. Rates of sessional remuneration:—

Grade	Fees per session of 3 hours
I	£6 6s. 0d.
II	£5 0s. 0d.".

Given under the official seal of the Minister of Health on 20th March 1968.

(L.S.)   *Kenneth Robinson,*
                                         Minister of Health.

EXPLANATORY NOTE

(This Note is not part of the Regulations.)

These Regulations amend the National Health Service (General Dental
Services) Regulations 1967 by providing for increased rates of remuneration
for salaried dental practitioners practising at a health centre.

STATUTORY INSTRUMENTS

1968 No. 444

LOCAL GOVERNMENT, ENGLAND AND WALES

The Rate Support Grants (Health Authorities) (Pooling Arrangements) Regulations 1968

Made - - -	*20th March* 1968
Laid before Parliament	*26th March* 1968
Coming into Operation	*29th March* 1968

The Minister of Health, in exercise of the powers conferred upon him by paragraph 13 of Part I of Schedule 1 to the Local Government Act 1966(**a**), and of all other powers enabling him in that behalf, hereby makes the following regulations :—

Title and commencement

1. These regulations may be cited as the Rate Support Grants (Health Authorities) (Pooling Arrangements) Regulations 1968, and shall come into operation on 29th March 1968.

Interpretation

2.—(1) In these regulations—

"authority" means local health authority ; and

"the Minister" means the Minister of Health.

(2) In these regulations, any reference to a numbered regulation is to the regulation bearing that number in these regulations.

(3) The Interpretation Act 1889(**b**) shall apply for the interpretation of these regulations as it applies for the interpretation of an Act of Parliament.

Notification of expenditure

3.—(1) Every authority shall in each year, in relation to expenditure incurred by the authority to which these regulations apply, make to the Minister in such form as he may direct—

(*a*) not later than 21st October, an estimate of—

    (i) the expenditure incurred for the previous financial year ; and

    (ii) the expenditure likely to be incurred for the ensuing financial year ; and

(*b*) as soon as practicable after the authority's accounts have been audited, an account of the expenditure incurred for the year to which the audit relates ;

and every such estimate or account shall be certified by the chief financial officer of the authority.

(**a**) 1966 c. 42.   (**b**) 1889 c. 63.

(2) These regulations apply to expenditure incurred—

(a) in the training of persons to become health visitors or in respect of persons who are being so trained ; and

(b) in the training of persons to become midwives or in respect of persons who are being so trained.

Apportionment of expenditure

4.—(1) The aggregate of the expenditure incurred in relation to the matters referred to in regulation 3(2)(a) shall be so apportioned among authorities that each authority's share of the aggregate of that expenditure shall be in the ratio which in the relevant financial year the population of the area of the authority bears to the aggregate of the population of the areas of all authorities.

(2) The aggregate of the expenditure incurred in relation to the matters referred to in regulation 3(2)(b) shall be so apportioned among authorities that each authority's share of the aggregate of that expenditure shall be in the ratio which in the relevant financial year the number of domiciliary births in the area of the authority bears to the aggregate of the number of domiciliary births in the areas of all authorities.

(3) For the purposes of this regulation—

(a) "the population" means the population as at 30th June in the relevant financial year, as estimated by the Registrar-General for England and Wales ; and

(b) "the number of domiciliary births" means the number of births (including still-births) occurring elsewhere than in hospitals or maternity homes, as estimated by the Minister for the purposes of this regulation upon the best information available and notified by him to the authority.

Adjustment of needs element

5. The Minister shall ascertain the amount by which the needs element payable to each authority ought to be increased or decreased by comparing the expenditure of each authority in relation to the matters referred to in regulation 3 with its apportioned share in relation to those matters ; and he shall notify each authority accordingly.

Certificates of adjustments to the needs element

6.—(1) The Minister shall in each year certify to the Minister of Housing and Local Government—

(a) not later than 31st December, the estimated amount of the increases and decreases of the needs element which ought to be made for—
(i) the preceding financial year and
(ii) the ensuing financial year ; and

(b) as soon as practicable after he has received the audited accounts of each authority, the actual amount of those increases and decreases.

(2) In making any estimate for the purposes of sub-paragraph (a) above the Minister may modify any estimate submitted by an authority under regulation 3 if, after consulting the authority, he is satisfied that in respect of any class of expenditure the expenditure likely to be incurred by the authority is substantially more or less than the amount shown in the estimate.

Given under the official seal of the Minister of Health on 20th March 1968.

(L.S.)

Kenneth Robinson,
Minister of Health.

EXPLANATORY NOTE

(This Note is not part of the Regulations.)

These Regulations provide for the pooling, for the purposes of rate support grants paid under the Local Government Act 1966, of expenditure incurred by local health authorities in the training of health visitors and midwives, and for apportioning the total between authorities on the basis of, respectively, population and the number of domiciliary births.

STATUTORY INSTRUMENTS

1968 No. 448

BRITISH NATIONALITY

The British Nationality (Amendment) Regulations 1968

Made - - - - 20*th March* 1968

Coming into Operation 1*st April* 1968

In exercise of the powers conferred on me by section 29(1) of the British Nationality Act 1948(**a**), as amended and extended by section 1 of the South Africa Act 1962(**b**) and Schedule 1 thereto, section 6(2) of the British Nationality (No. 2) Act 1964(**c**), section 5(2) of the British Nationality Act 1965(**d**), and section 12 of the West Indies Act 1967(**e**) and Schedule 3 thereto, I hereby make with the consent, so far as Regulation 5 is concerned, of the Treasury the following Regulations:—

1. Regulation 5 of the principal Regulations (which relates to the form of a notice under the South Africa Act 1962 given before the end of the year 1965) is hereby revoked.

2. In Regulation 9(2) of the principal Regulations (which relates to the authorities to whom applications and notices are to be made or given) the reference to Regulation 5 thereof shall be omitted.

3. After Regulation 26 of the principal Regulations there shall be inserted the following Regulation:—

"*Application in relation to associated states*

26A.—(1) Any reference in these Regulations to a colony shall be construed as including a reference to an associated state but in relation to such a state any reference to the Governor shall be construed as a reference to the Secretary of State or, where he has issued a relevant direction under paragraph 4 of Schedule 3 to the West Indies Act 1967, to the person, or the person for the time being holding the office, specified in the direction.

(2) In accordance with paragraph (1), by reason of the issue of such directions as aforesaid, any reference in these Regulations to the Governor shall be construed—

    (*a*) in relation to the associated state of Antigua, of Dominica, of Saint Christopher, Nevis and Anguilla or of Saint Lucia, as a reference to the person holding the office of Secretary to the Cabinet;

(**a**) 1948 c. 56.   (**b**) 1962 c. 23.   (**c**) 1964 c. 54.
(**d**) 1965 c. 34.   (**e**) 1967 c. 4.

(*b*) in relation to the associated state of Grenada, as a reference to the person holding the office of Permanent Secretary to the Premier.

(3) Regulation 12(3) shall have effect as if the reference therein to section 10(2) of the Act of 1948 included a reference to paragraph 5 of Schedule 3 to the West Indies Act 1967.".

4. Schedule 7 to the principal Regulations (which relates to the form of a notice under the South Africa Act 1962 given before the end of the year 1965) is hereby revoked.

5. For Schedule 14 to the principal Regulations (which relates to the fees which may be taken) there shall be substituted the Schedule set out in the Appendix to these Regulations.

6. In these Regulations any reference to the principal Regulations is a reference to the British Nationality Regulations 1965(a).

7. These Regulations may be cited as the British Nationality (Amendment) Regulations 1968 and shall come into operation on 1st April 1968.

James Callaghan,
One of Her Majesty's Principal
Secretaries of State.

15th March 1968.

We consent to Regulation 5 of these Regulations.

Joseph Harper,
E. Alan Fitch,
Two of the Lords Commissioners
of Her Majesty's Treasury.

20th March 1968.

APPENDIX

"Regulation 25(1)

SCHEDULE 14
TABLE OF FEES

Matter in which fee may be taken	Amount of fee	To whom fee is to be paid
	£ s. d.	
Registration of a woman who is a British protected person or an alien as a citizen under s.6(2) of the British Nationality Act 1948.	2 0 0	Into the Exchequer in accordance with Treasury directions.
Registration of a woman as a British subject under s.1 of the British Nationality Act 1965.	2 0 0	The same.
Registration of a minor who is a British protected person or an alien as a citizen under s.7 of the British Nationality Act 1948—		
Subject as hereinafter provided, where the minor is a British protected person;	7 10 0	The same.
Subject as hereinafter provided, where the minor is an alien;	15 0 0	

(a) S.I. 1965/1753 (1965 III, p. 4956).

Matter in which fee may be taken	Amount of fee	To whom fee is to be paid
	£ s. d.	
If the application for the minor's registration was made at the same time as an application by one of his parents for a certificate of naturalisation;	2 0 0	
If the application for the minor's registration was made at the same time as an application for the registration of another minor child of the same parent, except in the case of the first child registered in pursuance of those applications.	2 0 0	The same.
Registration of a stateless person as a citizen under s.1 of the British Nationality (No. 2) Act 1964.	2 0 0	The same.
Grant of a certificate of naturalisation- To a British protected person; To an alien.	15 0 0 30 0 0	The same.
Grant of a certificate of citizenship in case of doubt.	15 0 0	The same.
Witnessing the signing of an application or declaration mentioned in Regulation 23 of these Regulations.	5 0	In England or Northern Ireland, if the application or declaration is witnessed, or the oath administered, by a commissioner or notary public to the commissioner or notary public.
Administering the oath of allegiance	5 0	In Scotland, if the application or declaration is witnessed, or the oath administered, by a sheriff or sheriff-substitute, to the sheriff clerk or to any of his deputes, and if by a notary public, to the notary public.
Registration of a declaration of intention to resume British nationality.	2 0 0	Into the Exchequer in accordance with Treasury directions.
Registration of a declaration of renunciation of citizenship other than a declaration made in the circumstances mentioned in s.1(1)(a) of the British Nationality Act 1964.	2 0 0	The same.
Supplying a certified true copy of any notice, certificate, order, declaration or entry given, granted or made by or under the British Nationality Act 1948.	10 0	The same.

For the purposes of this Schedule—

(a) any reference to a child and his parent includes a reference to a step-child and his step-parent, to an illegitimate child and his mother and to an adopted child and his adoptive parent, and

(b) where two or more children of the same parent are registered on the same occasion, the eldest of those children shall be treated as the first child registered on that occasion."

2g

EXPLANATORY NOTE
(This Note is not part of the Regulations.)

These Regulations amend the British Nationality Regulations 1965.

Regulations 1, 2 and 4 revoke certain provisions of the Regulations of 1965 which are now spent.

Regulation 3 makes provision for the application of the Regulations of 1965 in relation to an associated state. In relation to such a state the British Nationality Acts 1948 to 1965 have effect subject to the provisions of Schedule 3 to the West Indies Act 1967 and account is taken of directions issued under paragraph 4 of that Schedule for the performance by specified office holders of functions under the enactments mentioned in sub-paragraph (3) thereof.

Regulation 5 provides for increases in certain fees.

STATUTORY INSTRUMENTS

1968 No. 449 (S.44)

EDUCATION, SCOTLAND

The Grant-Aided Secondary Schools (Scotland) Grant (Amendment) Regulations 1968

Made - - - -	*20th March* 1968
Laid before Parliament	*28th March* 1968
Coming into Operation	*1st April* 1968

In exercise of the powers conferred upon me by sections 75(3) and (4)(e) and 76(1) of the Education (Scotland) Act 1962(a), and of all other powers enabling me in that behalf, I hereby make the following regulations, a draft of which has been published and a copy of such draft sent to every education authority in accordance with the provisions of section 144(2) of the said Act:—

Citation, commencement and interpretation

1.—(1) These regulations may be cited as the Grant-Aided Secondary Schools (Scotland) Grant (Amendment) Regulations 1968 and shall come into operation on 1st April 1968.

(2) These regulations shall be construed as one with the Grant-Aided Secondary Schools (Scotland) Grant Regulations 1959(b) (in these regulations referred to as " the principal regulations ").

Amendment of the principal regulations

2.—(1) Subject to the provisions of paragraph (2) of this regulation, the principal regulations shall be amended as follows:—

(i) in regulation 3(5) thereof there shall be added at the end of the definition of " secondary school " the words " and includes a group of such schools under the same management." ;

(ii) in regulation 4 thereof there shall be substituted for paragraph (1) the following paragraph:—

" (1) Subject to the conditions prescribed in these regulations the Secretary of State may pay to the Managers of a recognised secondary school in aid of their approved expenditure on the maintenance of the school in respect of each financial year of the school beginning after 1st April 1968 a grant of the amount specified in column (2) of the Schedule to these regulations opposite the name of the school in column (1) of that Schedule:

Provided that if the Secretary of State considers that the circumstances of any particular case justify him in so doing he may in lieu of the amount specified in column (2) of the said Schedule pay

---

(a) 1962 c. 47. (b) S.I. 1959/833 (1959 I, p. 1104).

such sum as he may determine being a sum not exceeding the sum whereby the said approved expenditure exceeds the income of the Managers from sources other than grants after deduction from the said income of any sums approved as being required for purposes other than the maintenance of the school." ;

(iii) the Schedule to these regulations shall be the Schedule to the principal regulations.

(2) Nothing in this regulation shall affect the payment of grant in respect of any financial year of a recognised secondary school beginning before 2nd April 1968.

3. For the purposes of the principal regulations in relation to any financial year of a recognised secondary school beginning before 2nd April 1968, approved expenditure shall not include any increase in teachers' salaries payable in respect of any period after 31st March 1968.

Revocation of regulation 6 of the principal regulations

4. Regulation 6 of the principal regulations is hereby revoked.

William Ross,

One of Her Majesty's Principal
Secretaries of State.

St. Andrew's House,
  Edinburgh, 1.
20th March 1968.

Regulation 2

SCHEDULE

Column (1) Name of School	Column (2) Grant (£)
Albyn School for Girls	44,675
Convent of the Sacred Heart	23,215
Robert Gordon's College	101,115
St. Margaret's School	28,430
High School of Dundee	95,670
Merchant Company Schools:	
Daniel Stewart's College	
Mary Erskine School for Girls	363,510
George Watson's College	
George Watson's Ladies' College	
George Heriot's School	101,010
John Watson's School	29,635
Melville College	37,770
St. Mary's Cathedral Choir School	4,685
Craigholme School	45,605
Hutchesons' Grammar School	145,950
Kelvinside Academy	42,425
Laurel Bank School	54,640
St. Aloysius' College	63,860
Westbourne School	43,695
Troon, Marr College	80,805
Dollar Academy	83,480
Benedictine Convent School	15,405
St. Joseph's College	29,775
Morrison's Academy, Crieff	83,240
Morrison's Academy for Girls	
Girls' School Company Limited:	
The Park School, Glasgow	
St. Bride's School, Helensburgh	126,435
St. Columba's School, Kilmacolm	

EXPLANATORY NOTE

(This Note is not part of the Regulations.)

These regulations amend the provisions of the Grant-Aided Secondary Schools (Scotland) Grant Regulations 1959, empowering the Secretary of State to pay to the Managers of secondary schools not managed by education authorities grants in aid of their expenditure on the maintenance of the schools. They provide that the amount of grant which may be paid to the Managers of each school, or group of schools, in respect of the financial year of that school, or group of schools, beginning after 1st April 1968 and subsequent years, shall, save in particular circumstances, be the amount set out in the Schedule. They also provide that any increase in teachers' salaries after 31st March 1968 will not attract grant under the 1959 Regulations.

These regulations also revoke Regulation 6 of the 1959 Regulations which dealt with the payment of transitional grant.

STATUTORY INSTRUMENTS

1968 No. 454

INCOME TAX

DOUBLE TAXATION RELIEF

The Non-Residents' Transitional Relief from Income Tax on Dividends (Extension of Period) Order 1968

Laid before the House of Commons in draft

Made - - -	*21st March* 1968
Coming into Operation	*6th April* 1968

Whereas a draft of this Order was laid before the Commons House of Parliament and approved by resolution:

Now, therefore, the Lords Commissioners of Her Majesty's Treasury, in exercise of the power conferred on them by section 31(1) of the Finance Act 1966(a) hereby make the following Order :—

1. This Order may be cited as the Non-Residents' Transitional Relief from Income Tax on Dividends (Extension of Period) Order 1968.

2. The period referred to in section 31(1) of the Finance Act 1966 shall be extended to comprise the year 1968/69 in relation to dividends paid to residents in all the overseas territories with the Governments of which the Double Taxation Agreements mentioned in Schedule 9 to the said Act are made.

E. Alan Fitch,
Harry Gourlay,

Two of the Lords Commissioners of
Her Majesty's Treasury.

21st March 1968.

(a) 1966 c. 18.

EXPLANATORY NOTE

(This Note is not part of the Order.)

This Order extends by one year the period during which relief is available under section 31, Finance Act 1966. This section gives relief from United Kingdom income tax on dividends paid by United Kingdom companies to residents of the overseas territories with which the United Kingdom has the Double Taxation Agreements listed in Schedule 9 to the same Act. The relief was originally given for the years 1966/67 and 1967/68, but provision was made in subsection 1 of the section for the extension of this period.

STATUTORY INSTRUMENTS

1968 No. 455

INCOME TAX

DOUBLE TAXATION RELIEF

The Transitional Relief for Interest and Royalties paid to Non-Residents (Extension of Period) Order 1968

Laid before the House of Commons in draft

Made - - - *21st March* 1968

Coming into Operation *1st April* 1968

Whereas a draft of this Order was laid before the Commons House of Parliament and approved by resolution:

Now, therefore, the Lords Commissioners of Her Majesty's Treasury, in exercise of the power conferred on them by section 32(1) of the Finance Act 1966(a) hereby make the following Order:—

1. This Order may be cited as the Transitional Relief for Interest and Royalties paid to Non-Residents (Extension of Period) Order 1968.

2. The period referred to in section 32(1) of the Finance Act 1966 shall be extended to comprise the financial year 1968 in relation to residents in all overseas territories.

E. Alan Fitch,
Harry Gourlay,

Two of the Lords Commissioners of
Her Majesty's Treasury.

21st March 1968.

(a) 1966 c. 18.

EXPLANATORY NOTE
(This Note is not part of the Order.)

This Order extends by one year the period during which relief is available under section 32, Finance Act 1966. This section ensures that certain payments to non-residents which are relieved from United Kingdom income tax under a Double Taxation Agreement are not treated as distributions for corporation tax purposes in the hands of the United Kingdom company making them. The relief was originally given for the financial years 1966 and 1967, but provision was made in subsection 1 of the section for the extension of this period.

STATUTORY INSTRUMENTS

1968 No. 456
DIPLOMATIC SERVICE
Consular Fees (No. 2) Regulations 1968

Made - - -		21*st March* 1968
Coming into Operation		22*nd March* 1968

Her Majesty's Principal Secretary of State for Foreign Affairs, in the exercise of the powers conferred upon him by Section 2(2) of the Consular Salaries and Fees Act 1891(a) and Section 8(2) of the Fees (Increase) Act 1923(b), and of all other powers enabling him in that behalf, hereby makes, with the approval of the Treasury, the following Regulations :

Commencement and citation

1. These Regulations shall come into operation on 22nd March 1968 and may be cited as the Consular Fees (No. 2) Regulations 1968.

Interpretation and revocation

2.—(1) The Interpretation Act 1889(c) shall apply for the interpretation of these Regulations as it applies for the interpretation of an Act of Parliament and as if these Regulations and the Regulations hereby revoked were Acts of Parliament.

(2) In these Regulations—

(*a*) "consular officer" has the same meaning as in Section 3 of the Consular Salaries and Fees Act 1891. It also includes where the context so requires public officers, any person authorized to act as a marriage officer under the Foreign Marriage Act 1892(d), and any person authorized under Section 6 of the Commissioners for Oaths Act 1889(e), as amended by Section 2 of the Commissioners for Oaths Act 1891(f), to perform the acts set out in that section ;

(*b*) "public officer" means a public officer in Great Britain acting under the authority of the Secretary of State ;

(*c*) "fee" means any fee fixed by the Consular Fees Order 1968(g) including any Order amending the said Order (hereinafter referred to as "the Order") ;

(*d*) "applicant" means any person making application to a consular officer for any matter or thing to be done by him in the execution of his office.

(3) The Consular Fees Regulations 1968(h) are hereby revoked.

Payment in local currency

3. Fees shall be paid in currency circulating at the place of payment, except that a consular officer shall have discretion to accept, in lieu of such currency, a cheque, money order, or other means of effecting payment in terms of that currency. The equivalents of fees in terms of a foreign currency shall be calculated at a rate of exchange sufficient to cover the cost of remittance to London.

(a) 1891 c. 36.
(b) 1923 c. 4.
(c) 1889 c. 63.
(d) 1892 c. 23.
(e) 1889 c. 10.
(f) 1891 c. 50.
(g) S.I. 1968/114 (1968 I, p. 328).
(h) S.I. 1968/137 (1968 I, p. 377).

Levy of fees in advance

4. Fees shall be levied in advance, except where—

   (*a*) a master of a British ship does not have sufficient funds ;

   (*b*) the applicant, in the case of fee 83, does not have sufficient funds ;

   (*c*) a fee cannot be calculated in advance ;

   (*d*) in the opinion of the consular officer, it is impracticable to levy a fee in advance.

In such cases, before any matter or thing is done in respect of which a fee is to be levied, the applicant shall be required to signify his agreement to pay that fee, which shall be claimed subsequently in accordance with instructions issued from time to time by the Secretary of State.

Travelling and other expenses

5. Before travelling or other expenses are incurred in the performance of any matter or thing for which a fee is to be levied, the applicant shall be required to signify his agreement to pay such expenses which shall be recovered by the consular officer when the fee is taken. Travelling expenses shall not be charged by the consular officer for attendance at the consular office or residence.

Use of fee stamps

6.—(1) On receipt of any fee, fee stamps to the amount of the fee shall be affixed—

   (*a*) by a consular officer, either in accordance with any instruction contained in the Schedule to these Regulations or to the appropriate document, or, if there is no such instruction or document, to a receipt, issued to the person paying the fee ;

   (*b*) by a public officer, except in respect of fees 36, 49, 50, 51, 52, 53, 54, 55, 56, 58 and 60, to the appropriate document, or, if there is no such document, to a receipt.

(2) Fee stamps shall not be affixed to any consular register or retained in any consular archives in respect of any fee paid.

Cancellation of fee stamps

7. Fee stamps, on being affixed in accordance with Regulation 6, shall be cancelled by the consular officer with the date stamp supplied for the purpose, in such manner that as much as possible of the date and name of the post or date and wording on the date stamp will appear on each stamp cancelled.

Authority to waive fees

8. The consular officer is authorized to waive fees as follows :—

   (*a*) where the consular officer so decides on the ground of proved destitution ;

   (*b*) where the consular officer so decides as a matter of international courtesy ;

   (*c*) in respect of any matter or thing done in connexion with the official duty of any official of Her Majesty's Government in the United Kingdom ;

   (*d*) where the fee would be borne by any Government within the Commonwealth ;

(*e*) in respect of any matter or thing done in connexion with British yachts owned by British clubs mentioned in the Navy List whose owners are in possession of warrants to fly a special ensign issued by the Secretary of State for Defence, provided that it is ascertained from the Master or otherwise that

(i) the warrant is carried on board and

(ii) the owner holding the warrant is on board or in effective control of the yacht when she is in harbour or at anchor near the shore,

for which, but for this Article, fees numbers 1 to 16, 21, 22, 24, 25, 28 and any fee for the certification of a foreign bill of health would be taken ;

(*f*) for any matter or thing done for candidates or for a holder of a British Council scholarship in connexion with such scholarship ;

(*g*) where the Secretary of State with the consent of the Treasury so directs.

Procedure when fee is waived

9. Where, but for Regulation 8, a consular officer would have levied a fee and would have affixed a fee stamp to a document or receipt in accordance with Regulation 6 of these Regulations, he shall add "Gratis" near his signature on the document or receipt.

Recording of fees

10. A consular officer shall record each fee on receipt, and each occasion on which a fee is waived by reason of Regulation 8, in a Fee Cash Book.

Accounts

11.—(1) All fees shall be accounted for to the Secretary of State.

(2) A consular officer shall include with each account separate statements showing the total value of fees levied and of fees waived by reason of Regulation 8.

21st March 1968.

Approved.

Michael Stewart,
Her Majesty's Principal Secretary
of State for Foreign Affairs.

We approve these Regulations.

21st March 1968.

B. K. O'Malley,
Harry Gourlay,
Two of the Lords Commissioners
of Her Majesty's Treasury.

SCHEDULE

Fee stamps shall be affixed in respect of—

Fee	
2	to the agreement with the crew and not to the certificate of registry, a note being made on the agreement of the matter or thing in respect of which the fee is paid ;
7	to the certificate of sale and not the bill of sale or certificate of registry ;
8 to 12	beside the endorsement on the agreement with the crew ;
14	beside the entry of the result of the examination in the official log-book ;
16	beside the signature of the consular officer on the agreement with the European seamen where there are separate agreements with the European seamen and with the non-European seamen and the endorsement is made on both agreements, a note to this effect being made on the other agreement ;
18	to the first copy, if any, required by the person asking for the extension and paying the fee, and on this copy the consular officer shall write the words "First copy gratis" beside his attesting signature ;
19	to the order of survey ;
20	to the first copy, if any, required by the person asking for the survey and paying for the survey and fee, and on this copy the consular officer shall write the words "First copy gratis" beside his attesting signature ;
21	to the top left-hand corner of the front page of the copy of the agreement which is signed by the crew and delivered to the master.

EXPLANATORY NOTE

(This Note is not part of the Regulations.)

Section 2(2) of the Consular Salaries and Fees Act 1891 provides that all fees to be taken by a consular officer shall be levied, accounted for, and applied, and may be remitted, in accordance with regulations issued by the Secretary of State with the approval of the Treasury.

These Regulations prescribe the manner in which a consular officer should carry out these duties. They replace the Consular Fees Regulations 1968 and make minor amendments, in particular to Regulations 1, 6, 7, 9, and 10 thereof.

The Fees referred to in the Regulations are those which form the Schedule to the Consular Fees Order 1968.

STATUTORY INSTRUMENTS

1968 No. 457

FOOD AND DRUGS

MILK AND DAIRIES

The Milk (Great Britain) (Amendment) Order 1968

Made - - - -	21st *March* 1968
Laid before Parliament	29th *March* 1968
Coming into Operation	31st *March* 1968

The Minister of Agriculture, Fisheries and Food and the Secretary of State, acting jointly in exercise of the powers conferred on them by sections 6 and 7 of the Emergency Laws (Re-enactments and Repeals) Act 1964(a) and of all other powers enabling them in that behalf, hereby make the following order:—

Citation and commencement

1. This order may be cited as the Milk (Great Britain) (Amendment) Order 1968; and shall come into operation on 31st March 1968.

Amendment of the principal order

2. The Milk (Great Britain) Order 1967(b) shall be amended by substituting for Schedules 1 and 2 thereto respectively Schedules 1 and 2 to this order.

In Witness whereof the Official Seal of the Minister of Agriculture, Fisheries and Food is hereunto affixed on 20th March 1968.

(L.S.)   *Frederick Peart,*
Minister of Agriculture, Fisheries and Food.

Given under the Seal of the Secretary of State for Scotland on 21st March 1968.

(L.S.)   *William Ross,*
Secretary of State for Scotland.

(a) 1964 c. 60.   (b) S.I. 1967/455 (1967 I, p. 1398).

SCHEDULE 1

MAXIMUM PRICES OF MILK IN ENGLAND AND WALES

1. Subject to the provisions of this Schedule, the maximum price of milk on a sale in England and Wales shall be a price in accordance with whichever of the following tables is appropriate:—

TABLE A

Milk other than Channel Islands Milk or South Devon Milk	Maximum Price (Rate per Pint)	
	From 31st March 1968 to 29th June 1968 inclusive	On and after 30th June 1968
	d.	s. d.
Untreated Milk Farm Bottled	11½	1 0
Ultra Heat Treated milk	10½	11
Sterilised milk	10½	11
Homogenised milk	10½	11
Untreated milk	10	10½
Pasteurised milk	10	10½
Ordinary milk (that is to say, milk in respect of which a maximum price is not for the time being otherwise applicable in accordance with this Schedule) ...	10	10½

TABLE B

Channel Islands Milk and South Devon Milk	Maximum Price (Rate per Pint)		
	From 31st March 1968 to 28th December 1968 inclusive	From 29th December 1968 to 29th March 1969 inclusive	From 30th March 1969 to 27th September 1969 inclusive
	s. d.	s. d.	s. d.
Channel Islands Untreated Milk Farm Bottled	1 0½	1 1	1 0½
Other Channel Islands milk ...	1 0	1 0½	1 0
South Devon Untreated Milk Farm Bottled	1 0½	1 1	1 0½
Other South Devon milk	1 0	1 0½	1 0

2. A reasonable charge may be made by the seller in addition to the appropriate maximum price specified in either of the above tables for milk sold by him as Kosher milk or Kedassia milk if—

(a) such milk is sold in a container distinctly labelled "Kosher" or "Kedassia", as the case may be; and

(b) such milk has been prepared for consumption in accordance with the appropriate Jewish practice relating thereto.

SCHEDULE 2

MAXIMUM PRICES OF MILK IN SCOTLAND

1. Subject to the provisions of this Schedule, the maximum price of milk on a sale in Scotland, excluding the islands other than the islands of Islay, Coll and Gigha in the County of Argyll and those in the Counties of Bute and Orkney, shall be a price in accordance with whichever of the following tables is appropriate:—

TABLE A

Milk other than Channel Islands Milk or South Devon Milk	Maximum Price (Rate per Pint)	
	From 31st March 1968 to 29th June 1968 inclusive	On and after 30th June 1968
	d.	s. d.
Premium milk	11½	1 0
Ultra Heat Treated milk	10½	11
Sterilised milk	10½	11
Homogenised milk	10½	11
Standard milk	10	10½
Pasteurised milk	10	10½
Ordinary milk (that is to say, milk in respect of which a maximum price is not for the time being otherwise applicable in accordance with this Schedule) ...	10	10½

TABLE B

Channel Islands Milk and South Devon Milk	Maximum Price (Rate per Pint)		
	From 31st March 1968 to 28th December 1968 inclusive	From 29th December 1968 to 29th March 1969 inclusive	From 30th March 1969 to 27th September 1969 inclusive
	s. d.	s. d.	s. d.
Channel Islands Premium milk ...	1 0½	1 1	1 0½
Other Channel Islands milk ...	1 0	1 0½	1 0
South Devon Premium milk ...	1 0½	1 1	1 0½
Other South Devon milk	1 0	1 0½	1 0

2. A reasonable charge may be made by the seller in addition to the appropriate maximum price specified in either of the above tables for milk sold by him as Kosher milk or Kedassia milk if—

(a) such milk is sold in a container distinctly labelled "Kosher" or "Kedassia", as the case may be; and

(b) such milk has been prepared for consumption in accordance with the appropriate Jewish practice relating thereto.

EXPLANATORY NOTE

(This Note is not part of the order.)

This amending order, which comes into operation on 31st March 1968, amends the Milk (Great Britain) Order 1967—

(a) by increasing by ½d. per pint from 30th June 1968 the maximum prices of milk on sales in Great Britain other than sales of Channel Islands milk and South Devon milk, and

(b) by prescribing a new scale of maximum prices for Channel Islands milk and South Devon milk for the period from 31st March 1968 to 27th September 1969 which incorporates the increase of ½d. per pint.

STATUTORY INSTRUMENTS

1968 No. 458

BORROWING AND SECURITIES

The Local Loans (Procedure) Regulations 1968

Made - - -	*22nd March* 1968
Laid before Parliament	*29th March* 1968
Coming into Operation	*1st April* 1968

The Public Works Loan Commissioners, in exercise of the powers conferred upon them by section 41 of the Public Works Loans Act 1875(a) and of all other powers enabling them in that behalf, with the approval of the Treasury, hereby make the following Regulations :—

Meetings of the Commissioners

1.—(1) Meetings of the Public Works Loan Commissioners (hereinafter referred to as "the Commissioners") shall be convened by the Secretary to the Commissioners from time to time, as the business to be transacted may require.

(2) If at any meeting the chairman is not present, the deputy chairman shall be the chairman of the meeting ; if neither the chairman nor the deputy chairman is present, the Commissioners present shall choose one of their number to be the chairman of the meeting.

(3) Three Commissioners shall form a quorum.

(4) All questions arising at any meeting shall be decided by a majority of votes, and in the event of an equality of votes the chairman of the meeting shall have a second or casting vote.

(5) A minute book shall be kept, in which applications for loans and minutes of the proceedings of the Commissioners shall be recorded.

Applications for loans

2. Applications for loans shall be in the form required by the Commissioners, and the Commissioners may require applicants to provide such information as they think necessary for their consideration of the applications.

Payment of loans

3.—(1) The Secretary to the Commissioners shall from time to time certify to the Treasury the amount required for the purpose of local loans to be made by the Commissioners and the date on which such loans are to be made.

(a) 1875 c. 89.

(2) There shall be established a Public Works Loans (Advances) Account at the Bank of England under the control of the Commissioners, and, on receipt of a certificate given under paragraph (1) of this Regulation, the Treasury shall, on or before the day on which the loans are due to be made, issue from the National Loans Fund to the Public Works Loans (Advances) Account the sum specified in that certificate.

(3) The Secretary to the Commissioners shall sign orders to the Cashiers of the Bank of England for payment out of the Public Works Loans (Advances) Account to the agents specified therein of the amount of the loans which the agents are authorised to receive. No order shall be delivered by the Secretary to the agent named therein unless that agent has paid the amount of the fees and disbursements payable in respect of the loan or loans to which the order relates.

Repayment of loans

4. All sums payable or applicable in or towards the discharge of the principal or interest of any loan made by the Commissioners shall be paid by the borrower or his agent into the Bank of England to the credit of the Public Works Loans Account, being an account kept by direction of the Treasury under section 43 of the Public Works Loans Act 1875, and such payments are to be made under an authority to be obtained at the office of the Commissioners empowering the Bank of England to receive the sum therein mentioned.

Receipts and discharges

5. Any receipt required to be given by or on behalf of the Commissioners, and any receipt or further discharge to be given when all money due in respect of a loan has been fully paid, shall be given by the Secretary to the Commissioners.

Powers of Secretary

6. All documents of the Commissioners shall, if purporting to be signed by their Secretary, be deemed, until the contrary is proved, to be made or issued by the Commissioners ; and all directions given or acts done by the Secretary shall be deemed, until the contrary is proved, to be given or done by the Commissioners ; and all documents may be proved by the production of a copy or extract purporting to be certified by the Secretary to be true. For the purpose of this Regulation no proof shall be required of the handwriting or official position of the person purporting to be the Secretary.

Powers of other officers

7. The Assistant Secretary to the Commissioners, and not more than two other officers authorised by the Commissioners for the purpose, shall be competent to perform any act authorised by these Regulations to be performed by their Secretary.

Interpretation

8. The Interpretation Act 1889(a) shall apply for the interpretation of these Regulations as it applies for the interpretation of an Act of Parliament.

Revocation

9. The Regulations specified in the Schedule to these Regulations are hereby revoked.

(a) 1889 c. 63.

Citation and Commencement

10. These Regulations may be cited as the Local Loans (Procedure) Regulations 1968, and shall come into operation on 1st April 1968.

A. H. M. Hillis,
Secretary.

Public Works Loan Board.

22nd March 1968.

Approved.

B. K. O'Malley,
Harry Gourlay,
Two of the Lords Commissioners
of Her Majesty's Treasury.

22nd March 1968.

Regulation 9

SCHEDULE

Regulations revoked	References
The following Regulations made by the Public Works Loan Commissioners and approved by the Treasury under section 41 of the Public Works Loans Act 1875:—	
1. Regulations dated 1st April 1876.	Rev. XVIII, p.899.
2. Regulations dated 18th December 1879.	Rev. XVIII, p.901.
3. Regulations dated 12th June 1945.	S.R. & O. 1945/722 (Rev. XVIII, p.903).
4. The Public Works Loan Commissioners (Officers' Powers) Regulations 1959.	S.I. 1959/1253 (1959 I, p.306).

EXPLANATORY NOTE

(This Note is not part of the Regulations.)

These Regulations consolidate with amendments the earlier Regulations made by the Public Works Loan Commissioners for carrying into effect the Public Works Loans Act 1875. Apart from the omission of various provisions which have become unnecessary with the passage of time, the main amendment is the revision of the procedure for the financing of loans by the Commissioners, to take account of the establishment of the National Loans Fund under the National Loans Act 1968.

STATUTORY INSTRUMENTS

1968 No. 463

CARIBBEAN AND NORTH ATLANTIC TERRITORIES

The Bermuda Constitution (Amendment) Order 1968

Made - - - -	*22nd March* 1968
Laid before Parliament	*28th March* 1968
Coming into Operation	*29th March* 1968

At the Court at Buckingham Palace, the 22nd day of March 1968

Present,

The Queen's Most Excellent Majesty in Council

Her Majesty, by virtue and in exercise of the powers vested in Her in that behalf by section 1 of the Bermuda Constitution Act 1967(a), is pleased, by and with the advice of Her Privy Council, to order, and it is hereby ordered, as follows:—

1.—(1) This Order may be cited as the Bermuda Constitution (Amendment) Order 1968, and the Bermuda Constitution Order 1968(b) and this Order may be cited together as the Bermuda Constitution Orders 1968. *(Citation and commencement.)*

(2) This Order shall come into force on 29th March 1968.

2. Paragraph (*a*) of section 43(2) of the Constitution set out in Schedule 2 to the Bermuda Constitution Order 1968 is amended by the substitution of the word " four " for the word " fourteen ". *(Amendment of section 43 of the Constitution of Bermuda.)*

W. G. Agnew.

EXPLANATORY NOTE

(*This Note is not part of the Order.*)

This Order corrects a typographical error in the Bermuda Constitution Order 1968 relating to the quorum of the Legislative Council for Bermuda.

(a) 1967 c. 63.   (b) S.I. 1968/182 (1968 I, p. 436).

STATUTORY INSTRUMENTS

1968 No. 464

DIPLOMATIC AND INTERNATIONAL IMMUNITIES AND PRIVILEGES

The Commonwealth Countries and Republic of Ireland (Immunities) (Amendment) Order 1968

Made - - - -	*22nd March* 1968
Laid before Parliament	*28th March* 1968
Coming into Operation	*29th March* 1968

At the Court at Buckingham Palace, the 22nd day of March 1968

Present,

The Queen's Most Excellent Majesty in Council

Her Majesty, in exercise of the powers conferred on Her by section 1(2) of the Diplomatic Immunities (Commonwealth Countries and Republic of Ireland) Act 1952(a) and of all other powers enabling Her in that behalf, is pleased, by and with the advice of Her Privy Council, to order, and it is hereby ordered, as follows: —

1.—(1) This Order may be cited as the Commonwealth Countries and Republic of Ireland (Immunities) (Amendment) Order 1968.

(2) This Order shall come into operation on 29th March 1968.

(3) The Interpretation Act 1889(b) shall apply, with the necessary adaptations, for the interpretation of this Order as it applies for the interpretation of an Act of Parliament.

2. In Part I of Schedule 1 to the Commonwealth Countries and Republic of Ireland (Immunities) (No. 2) Order 1967(c) after the entry " The Regional Welfare Officer, Manchester " shall be inserted the sub-heading " Malawi " followed by the entry: —

" The Chief Buying and Trade Agent,".

W. G. Agnew.

EXPLANATORY NOTE

(This Note is not part of the Order.)

This Order adds an additional office to Part I of Schedule 1 to the Commonwealth Countries and Republic of Ireland (Immunities) (No. 2) Order 1967, namely the office of the Chief Buying and Trade Agent for Malawi. It confers on the person holding this office the like immunity from suit and legal process and the like inviolability of official archives as are accorded to consular officers of a foreign sovereign Power, and restricts powers of entry into the official premises of such a person.

(a) 1952 c. 18.   (b) 1889 c. 63.   (c) S.I. 1967/815 (1967 II, p. 2431).

STATUTORY INSTRUMENTS

1968 No. 465

ARABIA

The Aden, Perim and Kuria Muria Islands Act 1967 (Modification of Enactments) Order 1968

Made - - - -	*22nd March* 1968
Laid before Parliament	*28th March* 1968
Coming into Operation	*29th March* 1968

At the Court at Buckingham Palace, the 22nd day of March 1968

Present,

The Queen's Most Excellent Majesty in Council

Her Majesty, by virtue and in exercise of the powers in that behalf by section 3 of the Aden, Perim and Kuria Muria Islands Act 1967(a) in Her Majesty vested, and being satisfied that it is necessary or expedient so to order in consequence of Aden and Perim having ceased to form part of Her Majesty's dominions, is pleased, by and with the advice of Her Privy Council, to order, and it is hereby ordered, as follows:

1.—(1) This Order may be cited as the Aden, Perim and Kuria Muria Islands Act 1967 (Modification of Enactments) Order 1968.

(2) This Order shall come into operation on 29th March 1968.

(3) In this Order " appointed day " means 30th November 1967.

(4) The Interpretation Act 1889(b) shall apply, with the necessary adaptations, for the purpose of interpreting this Order and otherwise in relation thereto as it applies for the purpose of interpreting and in relation to Acts of the Parliament of the United Kingdom.

2. The Schedule to this Order shall have effect as from the appointed day in relation to the enactments mentioned in that Schedule.

W. G. Agnew.

SCHEDULE

Conveyancing (Scotland) Act 1874

1. Section 51 of the Conveyancing (Scotland) Act 1874(c) shall apply in relation to any probate of the will or other testamentary settlement of a person deceased, issued before the appointed day by the Supreme Court of Aden, as if that section had not ceased to apply to Aden.

Colonial Prisoners Removal Act 1884

2. Any person who, before the appointed day, was removed from Aden under the Colonial Prisoners Removal Act 1884(d) may be detained under that Act after that day, and the provisions of that Act shall have effect in relation to any such person as if it had not ceased to apply to Aden.

(a) 1967 c. 71.   (b) 1889 c. 63.   (c) 1874 c. 94.   (d) 1884 c. 31.

Provided that so much of subsection (1) of section 8 as relates to the questioning of the conviction, judgment and sentence of a prisoner removed under that Act, and to the remission of his sentence and the ordering of his discharge, shall not apply in relation to any such person.

Colonial Probates Act 1892

3. Any probate or letters of administration granted in respect of the estate of a deceased person granted before the appointed day by a court in Aden having jurisdiction in matters of probate may be sealed in the United Kingdom under section 2 of the Colonial Probates Act 1892(a), and the provisions of the Act shall have effect in relation to such grants as if it had not ceased to apply to Aden.

Copyright Acts 1911 and 1956

4. If the Copyright Act 1911(b), so far as in force in the laws of Aden and Perim immediately before the appointed day, is repealed or amended by either of these laws at any time when sub-paragraph (2) of paragraph 39 of Schedule 7 to the Copyright Act 1956(c) (which applies certain provisions of that Act in relation to countries to which the said Act of 1911 extended) is in force in relation to Aden and Perim, the said sub-paragraph (2) shall thereupon cease to have effect in relation thereto.

EXPLANATORY NOTE

(This Note is not part of the Order.)

This Order modifies certain Acts of Parliament in consequence of Aden and Perim having ceased to form part of Her Majesty's dominions. In accordance with section 3(2) of the Aden, Perim and Kuria Muria Islands Act 1967 these modifications are to take effect as from 30th November 1967, the day appointed by Order in Council (S.I. 1967/1761) in relation to Aden and Perim for the purposes of section 1 of that Act.

(a) 1892 c. 6.   (b) 1911 c. 46.   (c) 1956 c. 74.

STATUTORY INSTRUMENTS

1968 No. 467

MERCHANT SHIPPING

The Merchant Shipping (Safety Convention Countries) (Various) Order 1968

Made - - -	*22nd March* 1968
Laid before Parliament	*28th March* 1968
Coming into Operation	*4th April* 1968

At the Court at Buckingham Palace, the 22nd day of March 1968

Present,

The Queen's Most Excellent Majesty in Council

Whereas by section 31 of the Merchant Shipping (Safety Convention) Act 1949(a) as amended by section 1 of the Merchant Shipping Act 1964(b) it is enacted that Her Majesty, if satisfied that the government of any country has accepted the International Convention for the Safety of Life at Sea 1960 (hereinafter referred to as "the 1960 Convention"), may by Order in Council make a declaration to that effect :

And whereas Her Majesty is satisfied that the governments of the countries specified in the Schedule to this Order have accepted the 1960 Convention :

Now, therefore, Her Majesty, in pursuance of the powers conferred upon Her by the aforesaid sections and of all other powers enabling Her in that behalf, by and with the advice of Her Privy Council, is pleased to order, and it is hereby ordered, as follows :—

1. It is hereby declared that the governments of the countries specified in the Schedule to this Order have accepted the 1960 Convention.

2. This Order may be cited as the Merchant Shipping (Safety Convention Countries) (Various) Order 1968, and shall come into operation on 4th April 1968.

W. G. Agnew.

SCHEDULE

Commonwealth of Australia
People's Republic of Bulgaria
Czechoslovak Socialist Republic
Islamic Republic of Mauritania
Republic of Nicaragua
Republic of South Africa

(a) 1949 c. 43.   (b) 1964 c. 47.

STATUTORY INSTRUMENTS

1968 No. 468

MERCHANT SHIPPING

The Oil in Navigable Waters (Convention Countries) (Nigeria) Order 1968

Made - - -	*22nd March* 1968
Laid before Parliament	*28th March* 1968
Coming into Operation	*22nd April* 1968

At the Court at Buckingham Palace, the 22nd day of March 1968

Present,

The Queen's Most Excellent Majesty in Council

Whereas by section 18(3) of the Oil in Navigable Waters Act 1955(a) it is enacted that for the purposes of that section Her Majesty may, if satisfied that the government of any country has accepted the International Convention for the Prevention of Pollution of the Sea by Oil 1954, by Order in Council make a declaration to that effect :

And whereas Her Majesty is satisfied that the Government of the Federal Republic of Nigeria has accepted the said Convention :

Now, therefore, Her Majesty, in pursuance of the powers conferred upon Her by the said section 18(3) and of all other powers enabling Her in that behalf, is pleased, by and with the advice of Her Privy Council, to order, and it is hereby ordered, as follows :—

1. For the purposes of section 18 of the Oil in Navigable Waters Act 1955 it is hereby declared that the Government of the Federal Republic of Nigeria has accepted the International Convention for the Prevention of Pollution of the Sea by Oil 1954.

2. This Order may be cited as the Oil in Navigable Waters (Convention Countries) (Nigeria) Order 1968 and shall come into operation on 22nd April 1968.

W. G. Agnew.

(a) 1955 c. 25.

1968 No. 469 (C.8)

CIVIL AVIATION

The Tokyo Convention Act 1967 (Commencement) Order 1968

Made - - - *22nd March* 1968

At the Court at Buckingham Palace, the 22nd day of March 1968

Present,

The Queen's Most Excellent Majesty in Council

Her Majesty, in exercise of the powers conferred upon Her by section 9(3) of the Tokyo Convention Act 1967(a) and of all other powers enabling Her in that behalf, is pleased, by and with the advice of Her Privy Council, to order, and it is hereby ordered, as follows:

1. The Tokyo Convention Act 1967, with the exception of section 2, shall come into force on 1st April 1968.

2. This Order may be cited as the Tokyo Convention Act 1967 (Commencement) Order 1968.

W. G. Agnew.

(a) 1967 c. 52.

STATUTORY INSTRUMENTS

1968 No. 470

TRUSTEES

The Trustee Investments (Additional Powers) Order 1968

Made - - - -	*22nd March* 1968
Laid before Parliament	*28th March* 1968
Coming into Operation	*1st April* 1968

At the Court at Buckingham Palace, the 22nd day of March 1968

Present,

The Queen's Most Excellent Majesty in Council

Her Majesty, in exercise of the powers conferred upon Her by section 12 of the Trustee Investments Act 1961(**a**) and of all other powers enabling Her in that behalf, is pleased, by and with the advice of Her Privy Council, to order, and it is hereby ordered, as follows :—

1. The powers of investment conferred by section 1 of the Trustee Investments Act 1961 shall be extended by adding British Savings Bonds to paragraph 1 of Part I of the First Schedule thereto.

2. The Interpretation Act 1889(**b**) shall apply for the interpretation of this Order as it applies for the interpretation of an Act of Parliament.

3. This Order may be cited as the Trustee Investments (Additional Powers) Order 1968, and shall come into operation on 1st April 1968.

W. G. Agnew

EXPLANATORY NOTE

(This Note is not part of the Order.)

This Order adds British Savings Bonds to the list of " Narrower-Range Investments not Requiring Advice " set out in Part I of Schedule 1 to the Trustee Investments Act 1961.

(**a**) 1961 c. 62. (**b**) 1889 c. 63.

1968 No. 471

PENSIONS

The Superannuation (Transfers between the Civil Service and Public Boards) (Amendment) Rules 1968

Made - - -	*22nd March* 1968	
Laid before Parliament	*28th March* 1968	
Coming into Operation	*29th March* 1968	

The Treasury, in exercise of the powers conferred on them by sections 2 and 15 of the Superannuation (Miscellaneous Provisions) Act 1948(**a**), and of all other powers enabling them in that behalf, hereby make the following Rules:—

1.—(1) The Superannuation (Transfers between the Civil Service and Public Boards) Rules 1950(**b**) (hereafter in these Rules referred to as "the principal Rules"), as amended(**c**), shall be further amended as follows:—

    (*a*) by substituting for sub-paragraph (*d*) of paragraph (1) of Rule 7 thereof the following sub-paragraph:—

        "(*d*) has not become eligible for a pension under the Superannuation Act 1965(**d**), or, if he has become so eligible, has not been granted a pension under that Act; and";

    (*b*) by inserting after Rule 8 thereof the following Rule:—

        "8A. Where the officer on ceasing to be employed as a civil servant is eligible for a pension under the Superannuation Act 1965, he shall, upon the Treasury's paying a transfer value in respect of him under Rule 8 of these Rules, cease to be so eligible."

(2) Rule 5 of the Superannuation (Transfers between the Civil Service and Public Boards) (Amendment) Rules 1955(**e**) (which provides for the application of Part III of the principal Rules to a person entering the National Industrial Fuel Efficiency Service after ceasing to be employed as a civil servant where he has become eligible for, but has not been awarded, a pension under the Superannuation Act 1965) shall cease to have effect.

(**a**) 1948 c. 33.   (**b**) S.I. 1950/1539 (1950 II, p. 291).

(**c**) The relevant amending instruments are S.I. 1955/127, 1966/454 (1955 II, p. 1822; 1966 I, p. 974).

(**d**) 1965 c. 74.   (**e**) S.I. 1955/127 (1955 II, p. 1822).

2.—(1) The principal Rules shall have effect as if the following body were added to the Schedule thereto, that is to say:—

The British Airports Authority

(2) In their application to any person who becomes employed as a civil servant after ceasing to be in the pensionable employment of the British Airports Authority the principal Rules shall have effect as if—

(a) the references to the date of the making of the principal Rules in Rule 3(1)(d) and (e) thereof were references to the date of the making of these Rules; and

(b) the references to the coming into operation of the principal Rules in Rule 3(2) thereof were references to the coming into operation of these Rules.

(3) In their application to any person who enters the pensionable employment of the British Airports Authority after ceasing to be employed as a civil servant the principal Rules shall have effect as if—

(a) the reference to the date of the making of the principal Rules in Rule 7(1)(e) thereof were a reference to the date of the making of these Rules; and

(b) the references to the coming into operation of the principal Rules in Rule 7(2) thereof were references to the coming into operation of these Rules.

3. The Interpretation Act 1889(a) shall apply for the interpretation of these Rules as it applies for the interpretation of an Act of Parliament.

4. These Rules may be cited as the Superannuation (Transfers between the Civil Service and Public Boards) (Amendment) Rules 1968, and shall come into operation on 29th March 1968.

B. K. O'Malley,
Harry Gourlay,
Two of the Lords Commissioners
of Her Majesty's Treasury.

22nd March 1968.

(a) 1889 c. 63.

EXPLANATORY NOTE
(This Note is not part of the Rules.)

These Rules amend the Superannuation (Transfers between the Civil Service and Public Boards) Rules 1950. The principal Rules provide for the aggregation of service and for a single superannuation award in cases where a person transfers from an established post in the Civil Service to pensionable service with one of the bodies specified in the Schedule to those Rules or vice versa, and these Rules extend the Treasury's power to pay transfer values so as to allow for their payment where a former civil servant enters the employment of one of these bodies after reaching the age at which he is eligible for a pension under the Superannuation Act 1965, provided that he has not been granted a pension under that Act.

These Rules also add the British Airports Authority to the list of bodies in the Schedule to the principal Rules, and under the powers of section 2(5) of the Superannuation (Miscellaneous Provisions) Act 1948 the principal rules are applied, subject to certain conditions, to persons who have transferred between the Civil Service and the British Airports Authority before the coming into operation of these rules.

STATUTORY INSTRUMENTS

1968 No. 480

BUILDING SOCIETIES

The Building Societies (Designation for Trustee Investment) (Amendment) Regulations 1968

Made - - - -	*25th March* 1968
Laid before Parliament	*28th March* 1968
Coming into Operation	*1st April* 1968

The Treasury, in exercise of the powers conferred upon them by section 1(1) of the House Purchase and Housing Act 1959(**a**), and of all other powers enabling them in that behalf, hereby make the following regulations :—

1. The Schedule to the Building Societies (Designation for Trustee Investment) Regulations 1964(**b**) shall, subject to regulation 2 hereof, be amended as follows—

(*a*) in paragraph 1, for the words " five hundred thousand " substitute the words " one million " ;

(*b*) for paragraph 4, substitute the following paragraph—

" 4.—(1) The reserves of the society are not less than the proportion of the assets of the society hereinafter stated, that is to say—

$2\frac{1}{2}$ per cent. of its assets not exceeding £100 million ;

2 per cent. of its assets exceeding £100 million but not exceeding £500 million ;

$1\frac{1}{2}$ per cent. of its assets exceeding £500 million but not exceeding £1,000 million ;

$1\frac{1}{4}$ per cent. of its assets exceeding £1,000 million.

(2) In the preceding sub-paragraph the following expressions have the meanings hereby respectively assigned to them—

" reserves " means the amount of the reserves (other than reserves which have been set aside for a particular purpose) together with the amount of any provision against depreciation of or losses on investments, less the aggregate of—

(*a*) any amount by which the total book value of the society's investments exceeds their total market value, and

(*b*) any amount recommended by the society's directors for distribution as interest, dividend or bonus, and not provided for in the annual return ;

(**a**) 1959 c. 33   (**b**) S.I. 1964/1354 (1964 II, p. 3075).

" assets " means the total amount of the assets less the aggregate of—

    (i) the total amount owing by the society in respect of any loans made to it under the House Purchase and Housing Act 1959,

    (ii) any amount by which the total book value of the society's investments exceeds their total market value, and

    (iii) the total amount of any reserves set aside for a particular purpose, other than any reserve against depreciation of or losses on investments."

2. The amendment effected by paragraph (*a*) of regulation 1 hereof shall not operate so as to affect the requirements to be fulfilled by a building society for the purpose of designation under section 1 of the House Purchase and Housing Act 1959 if the society has applied in writing to the Chief Registrar for such designation before the date of the laying of these regulations before Parliament and is designated by him before the 1st January 1969.

3. Regulation 1 of the Building Societies (Designation for Trustee Investment) Regulations 1964, in its application to a building society as defined in section 1(4) of the Building Societies Act (Northern Ireland) 1967(**a**), shall be construed as if for references to sections 22(2)(*b*), 23 and 88 of the Building Societies Act 1962(**b**) there were substituted references to sections 22(2)(*b*), 23 and 88 of the said Act of 1967.

4. The Interpretation Act 1889(**c**) shall apply for the interpretation of these regulations as it applies for the interpretation of an Act of Parliament.

5. These regulations may be cited as the Building Societies (Designation for Trustee Investment) (Amendment) Regulations 1968, and shall come into operation on 1st April 1968.

25th March 1968.

> *J. McCann,*
> *Joseph Harper,*
> Two of the Lords Commissioners
> of Her Majesty's Treasury.

EXPLANATORY NOTE

(This Note is not part of the Regulations.)

These Regulations alter the requirements laid down in the Building Societies (Designation for Trustee Investment) Regulations 1964, which have to be fulfilled by building societies, including building societies registered in Northern Ireland, in order to qualify them for designation under Section 1 of the House Purchase and Housing Act 1959.

They raise to £1 million the minimum assets to be held and lay down a sliding scale of reserves. They also make certain transitional provisions.

(**a**) 1967 c. 31 (N.I.).   (**b**) 1962 c. 37.   (**c**) 1889 c. 63.

STATUTORY   INSTRUMENTS

1968 No. 481

CUSTOMS AND EXCISE

The Import Duty Drawbacks (No. 3) Order 1968

Made - - - -	*25th March* 1968
Laid before the House of Commons - -	*29th March* 1968
Coming into Operation -	*4th April* 1968

The Lords Commissioners of Her Majesty's Treasury, by virtue of the powers conferred on them by sections 9 and 13 of, and Schedule 5 to, the Import Duties Act 1958(a) and section 2(5) of the Finance Act 1965(b), and of all other powers enabling them in that behalf, on the recommendation of the Board of Trade hereby make the following Order:—

1.—(1) Schedule 2 to the Import Duty Drawbacks (No. 6) Order 1966(c) (which relates to the drawbacks to be allowed on the exportation of goods produced or manufactured from imported articles) shall be amended in accordance with the following provisions of this Article.

(2) In the entry relating to foodstuffs, canned or bottled, the rate of drawback specified in column 3 (being a rate inserted by paragraph 3 of the Schedule to the Import Duty Drawbacks (No. 4) Order 1967(d)) shall be omitted.

(3) The entry relating to printed drip mats shall be omitted.

(4) In the entry relating to quebracho extract and blends thereof (being an entry inserted by paragraph 7 of the Schedule to the said Order of 1967), the following shall be inserted in column 1, at the end of paragraph 3—

" (G) sulphite cellulose, in which the content by weight of insoluble quebracho extract is 50 per cent."

2. In consequence of the amendments made by paragraphs (2) and (3) of Article 1 above—

(*a*) paragraph 2 of Schedule 3 to the said Order of 1966 shall be amended by omitting the words " Foodstuffs " and " Printed drip mats ", and

(*b*) paragraph 3 of the Schedule to the said Order of 1967 is hereby revoked.

3.—(1) This Order may be cited as the Import Duty Drawbacks (No. 3) Order 1968.

(2) The Interpretation Act 1889(e) shall apply for the interpretation of this Order as it applies for the interpretation of an Act of Parliament.

(3) This Order shall come into operation on 4th April 1968.

E. Alan Fitch,

Harry Gourlay,

Two of the Lords Commissioners of Her Majesty's Treasury.

25th March 1968.

(a) 1958 c. 6.
(b) 1965 c. 25.
(c) S.I. 1966/921 (1966 II, p. 2207).
(d) S.I. 1967/651 (1967 I, p. 2045).
(e) 1889 c. 63.

EXPLANATORY NOTE

(This Note is not part of the Order)

This Order—

(i) revokes the existing fixed rate of drawback of import duty for canned or bottled foodstuffs and provides for drawback to be related to the duty paid on the imported tomato purée actually used in the manufacture of the exported goods;

(ii) revokes the provision for the allowance of drawback of import duty on printed drip mats manufactured from imported wood pulp board; and

(iii) extends the scope of the existing provisions for the drawback of import duty in respect of blends of quebracho extract manufactured from imported quebracho extract.

STATUTORY INSTRUMENTS

1968 No. 488

LONDON GOVERNMENT

The London Authorities (Staff) Order 1968

Made - - -	26*th March* 1968
Laid before Parliament	2*nd April* 1968
Coming into Operation	8*th April* 1968

The Minister of Housing and Local Government, in exercise of his powers under sections 84 and 90 of the London Government Act 1963(**a**) and of all other powers enabling him in that behalf, hereby makes the following order :—

1. This order may be cited as the London Authorities (Staff) Order 1968, and shall come into operation on 8th April 1968.

2.—(1) The Interpretation Act 1889(**b**) applies to the interpretation of this order as it applies to the interpretation of an Act of Parliament.

(2) In this order—

"the Council" means the Greater London Council ;

"officer" includes the holder of any place, situation or employment.

3. Article 4 shall apply where—

(*a*) any person employed at a sewage disposal works ;

(*b*) any person employed wholly or substantially so in connection with any such works or any public sewer,

being a sewage disposal works or a public sewer, as the case may be, in relation to which the Council make a declaration under section 35(5) or (6) of the London Government Act 1963, immediately after leaving such employment enters the employment of the Council ; and in that article "relevant date" means the date specified in the declaration as the date of vesting of the works.

4. Every officer entering the employment of the Council as specified in article 3 shall, so long as he continues in that employment by virtue of the contract under which he enters therein, enjoy terms and conditions of employment not less favourable than those he enjoyed immediately before the relevant date :

Provided that this paragraph shall apply to the scale of the salary or remuneration of the officer only so long as he is engaged in duties reasonably comparable to those in which he was engaged immediately before the relevant date.

Any question whether duties are reasonably comparable as aforesaid shall be determined by a tribunal established under section 12 of the Industrial Training Act 1964(**c**).

(**a**) 1963 c. 33.   (**b**) 1889 c. 63.   (**c**) 1964 c. 16.

5. In the London Authorities (Superannuation) Order 1965(**a**), in article 3 (Definition of transferred employee) the following item shall be added—

"(*ccc*) any officer entering the employment of the Greater London Council as specified in article 3 of the London Authorities (Staff) Order 1968,".

Given under the official seal of the Minister of Housing and Local Government on 26th March 1968.

(L.S.)

Anthony Greenwood,
Minister of Housing and Local Government.

EXPLANATORY NOTE
(*This Note is not part of the Order.*)

This Order makes provision for the protection of interests of certain persons employed at sewage disposal works or in connection with such works or a public sewer as to which the Greater London Council, under the London Government Act 1963, make a declaration vesting the works or sewer in the Council.

(**a**) S.I. 1965/621 (1965 I, p. 1970).

STATUTORY INSTRUMENTS

1968 No. 490

NATIONAL HEALTH SERVICE, ENGLAND AND WALES

HOSPITAL AND SPECIALIST SERVICES

The National Health Service (Designation of London Teaching Hospitals, etc.) Order 1968

Made - - -	*26th March* 1968
Coming into Operation	*1st April* 1968

The Minister of Health, in exercise of the powers conferred on him by sections 11 and 75 of the National Health Service Act 1946(a) and of all other powers enabling him in that behalf, and after consultation with the University of London, hereby orders as follows:—

1. This order may be cited as the National Health Service (Designation of London Teaching Hospitals, etc.) Order 1968 and shall come into operation on 1st April 1968.

2.—(1) In this order—

" the Act " means the National Health Service Act 1946;

" the appointed day " means 1st April 1968;

" Board of Governors " means a Board of Governors specified in column (4) of the schedule;

" Hospital Board " means a Regional Hospital Board specified in column (2) of the schedule;

" Management Committee " means a Hospital Management Committee specified in column (3) of the schedule and, for the purposes of article 12 of this order, includes the old Committee;

" the Minister " means the Minister of Health;

" the new Committee " means the St. Charles's Group Hospital Management Committee;

" the new scheme " means the new scheme providing for the termination of the functions of the old Committee and the appointment of the new Committee to exercise those functions submitted to the Minister by the North-West Metropolitan Regional Hospital Board under section 11(5) of the Act and approved by the Minister with effect from the appointed day;

" the old Committee " means the Paddington Group Hospital Management Committee;

(a) 1946 c. 81.

" the principal order " means the National Health Service (Designation of London Teaching Hospitals) Order 1957(a) as amended(b);

" the schedule " means the schedule to this order;

" the transferred hospitals " means the hospitals whose names are added to column (2) of schedule 1 to the principal order by article 7 of this order and whose names appear in column (1) of the schedule.

(2) The Interpretation Act 1889(c) shall apply to the interpretation of this order as it applies to the interpretation of an Act of Parliament.

3. As from the appointed day, the old Committee shall be dissolved.

4. The sum of £16,203, being the apportioned share in the net capital sum of the Hospital Endowments Fund calculated with reference to values on 5th July 1948 and allotted to the old Committee, shall on the appointed day be re-allotted to the new Committee.

5. On the appointed day there shall be transferred to and vest without further conveyance in the new Committee—

(a) any property held immediately before the appointed day by the old Committee—

    (i) under section 59 of the Act for the purposes of any hospital or hospitals (other than the Paddington General Hospital and the National Temperance Hospital) managed by it, and

    (ii) under section 60 of the Act so far as practicable for the purposes of any such hospital or hospitals (other than those excluded in sub-paragraph (a)(i) of this article);

(b) any other property held by the old Committee and any rights and liabilities (other than property, rights and liabilities in respect of the hospitals excluded in sub-paragraph (a)(i) of this article) to which it was entitled or subject immediately before the appointed day;

(c) any such property as is mentioned in paragraphs (a) and (b) of this article held by the Central Middlesex Group Hospital Management Committee for the purposes of the Marlborough Day Hospital, 38, Marlborough Place, London, N.W.8.

6. The new Committee shall be responsible for closing the accounts of the old Committee and with respect to these accounts references in regulation 19 of the National Health Service (Hospital Accounts and Financial Provisions) Regulations 1948(d) to " the Chief financial officer ", " the Secretary " and " the Committee " shall be deemed to be references to the chief financial officer and the secretary of the new Committee and to the new Committee respectively.

7. Column 2 of schedule 1 to the principal order (which column prescribes hospitals or groups of hospitals designated as teaching hospitals) shall be further amended as follows:—

(1) Opposite the name " The Hospital for Sick Children " in column (1) there shall be added the words " Queen Elizabeth Hospital for Children, Hackney Road, E.2. (including the Little Folks Home, Bexhill and the Queen Elizabeth Hospital for Children, Banstead Branch) ";

(a) S.I. 1957/488 (1957 I, p. 1452).   (b) S.I. 1964/453 (1964 I, p. 723).
(c) 1889 c. 63.   (d) S.I. 1948/1414 (Rev. XV. p. 734: 1948 I, p. 2083).

(2) Opposite the name " The London Hospital " in column (1) there shall be added the words " Mile End Hospital, E.1." and the words " St. Clement's Hospital, Bow ";

(3) Opposite the name " The Royal Free Hospital " in column (1) there shall be added the words " New End Hospital, N.W.3." and the words " Coppetts Wood Hospital, N.10 ";

(4) Opposite the name " St. Mary's Hospital " in column (1) there shall be added the words " Paddington General Hospital, W.9.";

(5) Opposite the name " University College Hospital " in column (1) there shall be added the words " National Temperance Hospital, N.W.1.";

(6) Opposite the name " St. Thomas' Hospital " in column (1) there shall be added the words " South-Western Hospital, S.W.9." and the words " 'Holmhurst', 46, Half Moon Lane, Herne Hill, S.E.24.".

8.—(1) All officers employed immediately before the appointed day solely at or for the purposes of a transferred hospital being officers of a Hospital Board specified against the name of that hospital in the schedule shall on that day be transferred to and become officers of the Board of Governors similarly specified.

(2) The provisions of paragraph (1) of this article shall apply in like manner to all medical and dental officers employed immediately before the appointed day partly at or for the purposes of such transferred hospital and partly at or for the purposes of any other hospital who shall on the appointed day become officers of such Board of Governors in relation to their work at such transferred hospital and all rights and liabilities under their contract in relation thereto with such Hospital Board shall be transferred to such Board of Governors.

(3) Any other officer of such Hospital Board who is employed immediately before the appointed day partly at or for the purposes of such transferred hospital and who receives before that day notice in writing from that Hospital Board that he is to be transferred to such Board of Governors shall on that day be transferred to and become an officer of that Board of Governors.

(4) Any officer who is transferred to a Board of Governors under this article and whose employment was whole-time shall continue to be subject to the remuneration and other conditions of service applicable to a whole-time officer so long as his employment for both such Hospital Board and such Board of Governors amounts in the aggregate to whole-time employment.

9. On the appointed day there shall be transferred to and vest without further conveyance in a Board of Governors—

    (a) any property held immediately before the appointed day by the Hospital Board or the Management Committee specified against the name of that Board of Governors in the Schedule—

        (i) under Section 59 of the Act for the purposes of the transferred hospital specified against the name of such Board of Governors, and

        (ii) under Section 60 of the Act so far as practicable for the purposes of such transferred hospital; and

    (b) any other property held by such Hospital Board or such Management Committee and any rights and liabilities by which either of them were entitled or subject immediately before the appointed day so far as these relate solely to such transferred hospital.

10. On the appointed day capital assets equivalent to assets of the Hospital Endowments Fund with a market value on 5th July 1948 of the amount specified in column (5) of the schedule against the name of the transferred hospital specified in column (1) thereof shall be transferred from the said Fund to the Board of Governors specified against the name of such transferred hospital in column (4) thereof and the respective shares of the Hospital Board and of the Management Committee specified against the name of such transferred hospital in columns (2) and (3) thereof in the net capital sum referred to in the National Health Service (Apportionment of Hospital Endowment Fund) Regulations 1949(a) shall be reduced by the amount specified against the name of such transferred hospital in column (6) thereof.

11. Any action or proceeding or any cause of action or proceeding, pending or existing at the appointed day, by, or against, a Hospital Board or a Management Committee solely in respect of any property, right or liability in connection with a transferred hospital shall not be prejudicially affected by reason of this order, and may be continued, prosecuted and enforced by, or against, the Board of Governors specified against the name of such Hospital Board or such Management Committee in the schedule.

12. Any officer employed immediately before the appointed day at or for the purposes of any hospital managed by a Management Committee who suffers loss of employment or loss or diminution of emoluments which is attributable to the making of the new scheme or of this order shall be entitled to have his case considered for the payment of compensation at the like rate and in the like manner and subject to the like conditions as if he had been entitled to claim compensation under the Local Government (Executive Councils) (Compensation) Regulations 1964(b) as amended(c); and those regulations (except regulations 3, 4 and 5 thereof) shall apply for this purpose as if they had been set out in this order with the modifications that—

(a) references to the " material date " shall be construed as references to the appointed day, and

(b) references to " any such provision as is mentioned in Regulation 4 of these regulations " shall be construed as references to the new scheme 'or to this order.

Given under the official seal of the Minister of Health on 26th March 1968.

(L.S.)

J. Hauff,
Under Secretary,
Ministry of Health.

(a) S.I. 1949/482 (1949 I, p. 2595).   (b) S.I. 1964/1177 (1964 II, p. 2696).
(c) S.I. 1966/254 (1966 I, p. 653).

SCHEDULE

Hospital (1)	Regional Hospital Board (2)	Hospital Management Committee (3)	Board of Governors (4)	Funds transferred to Board of Governors (5)	Funds transferred from (6) R.H.B.	Funds transferred from (6) H.M.C.
Queen Elizabeth Hospital for Children, Hackney Road, E.2. (including the Little Folks Home, Bexhill and the Queen Elizabeth Hospital for Children, Banstead Branch) ...	North-East Metropolitan	Hackney and Queen Elizabeth Group	The Hospital for Sick Children	£11,642	£5,821	£5,821
Mile End Hospital, E.1. ...	North-East Metropolitan	East London Group	The London Hospital	£23,872	£11,936	£11,936
St. Clement's Hospital, Bow.	North-East Metropolitan	Thames Group	The London Hospital	£2,144	£1,072	£1,072
New End Hospital, N.W.3. ...	North-West Metroppitan	North London Group	The Royal Free Hospital	£10,928	£5,464	£5,464
Coppetts Wood Hospital, N.10.	North-West Metropolitan	North London Group	The Royal Free Hospital	£6,052	£3,026	£3,026
Paddington General Hospital, W.9.	North-West Metropolitan	Paddington Group	St. Mary's Hospital	£28,116	£14,058	£14,058
National Temperance Hospital, N.W.1	North-West Metropolitan	Paddington Group	University College Hospital	£6,640	£3,320	£3,320
South-Western Hospital, S.W.9.	South-West Metropolitan	South-West London Group	St. Thomas' Hospital	£12,566	£6,283	£6,283

EXPLANATORY NOTE

(This Note is not part of the Order.)

This Order amends the National Health Service (Designation of London Teaching Hospitals) Order 1957 by allocating eight additional hospitals between six of the groups of London Teaching Hospitals.

The Order dissolves the Paddington Group Hospital Management Committee, which is replaced by the St. Charles's Group Hospital Management Committee to whom the management of the Marlborough Day Hospital is transferred from the Central Middlesex Hospital Management Committee.

It also provides for consequential matters relating to officers and property connected with the transferred hospitals.

STATUTORY INSTRUMENTS

1968 No. 491

RATING AND VALUATION

The Rate Product Rules 1968

Made - - -	*27th March* 1968
Laid before Parliament	*29th March* 1968
Coming into Operation	*1st April* 1968

The Minister of Housing and Local Government, after consultation with the local authorities and the associations of local authorities with whom consultation appeared to him to be desirable, in exercise of his powers under section 113 of the General Rate Act 1967(a) and of all other powers enabling him in that behalf, hereby makes the following rules:—

Citation, commencement and interpretation

1.—(1) These rules may be cited as the Rate Product Rules 1968 and shall come into operation on 1st April 1968.

(2) The Interpretation Act 1889(b) applies to the interpretation of these rules as it applies to the interpretation of an Act of Parliament.

Precepts

2. The schedule to these rules shall apply in relation to precepts under sections 12 and 13 of the General Rate Act 1967 (provisions as to precepts by county councils, the Greater London Council, the Receiver of the Metropolitan Police District and other authorities).

Resources element of rate support grants

3.—(1) Subject to the following paragraphs of this rule, the product of a rate of one penny in the pound for any area for the purposes of Part II of Schedule 1 to the Local Government Act 1966(c) (which relates to the resources element of the rate support grants) shall be ascertained in accordance with the provisions of the schedule to these rules.

(2) In determining the product of a rate of one penny in the pound for any area for the said purposes there shall be disregarded—

(a) any relief afforded under section 2 and any grant paid under section 5 of the Rating (Interim Relief) Act 1964(d); and

(b) any rebate under section 49 of the General Rate Act 1967 and any grant under section 9 of the Rating Act 1966(e).

(3) The product of a rate of one penny in the pound for the area of a county council or the Greater London Council shall be determined by aggregating the product of a rate of one penny in the pound for all the rating areas within the area.

(a) 1967 c. 9.	(b) 1889 c. 63.	(c) 1966 c. 42.
(d) 1964 c. 18.	(e) 1966 c. 9.	

Expenditure not specifically authorised

4.—(1) Subject to the following paragraph of this rule, the product of a rate of one penny in the pound for any area for the purposes of section 6 of the Local Government (Financial Provisions) Act 1963(**a**) (which relates to the power of a local authority to incur expenditure in the interests of their area or its inhabitants but not otherwise authorised) shall be ascertained in accordance with the provisions of the schedule to these rules.

(2) In ascertaining the product of a rate of one penny in the pound for any area for the said purposes there shall be disregarded any rebate under section 49 of the General Rate Act 1967 and any grant under section 9 of the Rating Act 1966.

Amendment of enactments

5.—(1) In section 6(6) of the Local Government (Financial Provisions) Act 1963—

   (*a*) for the words from "in the case of an area" to "Local Government Act 1958" there shall be substituted the words "in accordance with rules made under section 113 of the General Rate Act 1967";

   (*b*) for the words "for the purposes of the said section 9(2)" there shall be substituted the words "under the said section 113".

(2) In section 10(1) of the Rating Act 1966, the words from "or section 6" to the end of the subsection shall be omitted.

Repeals and revocations

6.—(1) Subject as hereinafter provided—

   (*a*) the following provisions are hereby repealed—
      (i) section 10(2) (*b*) of the Rating Act 1966; and
      (ii) section 49(10) of the General Rate Act 1967;

   (*b*) the following instruments are hereby revoked—

      (i) the Rate-product Rules 1959(**b**);

      (ii) the Rate-product Rules 1960(**c**); and

      (iii) the Rate-product (Amendment) Rules 1966(**d**).

(2) The repeals and revocations contained in the preceding paragraph of this rule shall not affect any determination of the product of a rate of one penny in the pound to be made at any time after the coming into operation of these rules in respect of the year ending on 31st March 1967 or any previous year.

SCHEDULE

PRECEPTS AND DETERMINATION OF THE PRODUCT OF A RATE OF ONE PENNY IN THE POUND

Determination of product of a penny rate

1. Each rating authority shall as soon as may be after the close of any year determine the product of a rate of one penny in the pound for that year for the rating area, and where a precept is issuable in respect of a part only of the rating area the product of a rate of one penny in the pound for that year for such part.

(a) 1963 c. 46.   (b) S.I. 1959/258 (1959 II, p.2288).   (c) S.I. 1960/1530 (1960 III, p. 2831).
(d) S.I. 1966/1132 (1966 III, p. 2733).

Manner of determination

2. The product of a rate of one penny in the pound for any area for any year shall be determined by deducting from the gross rate income the cost of collection and the loss on collection and dividing the remainder (hereinafter called "the total rate product") by the total of the pence in the pound of the rate or rates made in respect of the year (disregarding any reductions in poundage made in pursuance of section 48 of the principal Act):

Provided that if the total of the pence in the pound of the rates is not the same throughout the area the rating authority shall so calculate the product of a rate of one penny in the pound separately for each part of the area in which a different total has been levied, and the product of a rate of one penny in the pound for the area shall be taken to be the sum of the products of rates of one penny in the pound for the several parts as so calculated and in the case of a rating area as a whole of a rate of one penny in the pound on any gas and electricity hereditaments.

Gross rate income

3.—(1) The gross rate income for any area for any year shall be ascertained by adding together the following amounts—

(a) the total of the amounts produced by calculating, from the rateable value of each hereditament in the area shown in the rates record, the gross liability of the hereditament to rates for the year (having regard to reductions in poundage made in pursuance of section 48 of the principal Act) less the total amount of any reliefs granted in respect of such hereditaments under section 40 or 47 of the principal Act;

(b) the total of the amounts by way of contributions in aid of rates which, under sections 37 and 38 of the principal Act fall to be taken into account in respect of hereditaments, or former hereditaments, in the area for the purpose of ascertaining the proceeds of any rate for the year;

(c) the total of the amounts of any payments receivable in respect of the year, or any portion thereof, under section 133 of the Lands Clauses Act 1845(a) or section 27 of the Compulsory Purchase Act 1965(b), in respect of hereditaments, or former hereditaments, in the area;

(d) the total of amounts by way of rates for an earlier year found during the year to be recoverable in respect of hereditaments or former hereditaments, in the area under section 79 of the principal Act or in respect of adjustments of domestic relief under section 48 or rebates under section 49 of that Act or in respect of rates written off as irrecoverable;

(e) where the area for which the gross rate income is being ascertained is the whole of a rating area, the amounts receivable for the year under section 32(5) of the principal Act, together with any such amounts in respect of a previous year which may have been notified to the rating authority by the Minister at the time of ascertainment; and where the said area is part of a rating area, the sum which has to such amounts the same proportion as the aggregate rateable value of all the hereditaments in that part, as shown in the Valuation List at the beginning of the year, has to the aggregate rateable value of all the hereditaments (other than gas and electricity hereditaments) in the rating area, as so shown;

(f) the amount of any grant under section 5 of the Rating (Interim Relief) Act 1964, paid in the year as if received under section 32(5) of the principal Act;

(g) where the area for which the gross rate income is being ascertained is the whole of a rating area, the amount of any grant payable to the rating authority in respect of the year under section 9 of the Rating Act 1966; and where the said area is part of a rating area, the sum which has to such amount the same proportion as the aggregate amount of any rebates under section 49 of the principal Act afforded during the year in respect of hereditaments in the part has to the aggregate amount of such rebates so afforded in respect of hereditaments in the whole of the rating area;

(a) 1845 c. 18.   (b) 1965 c. 56.

(*h*)   where the area for which the gross rate income is being ascertained is the whole of a rating area, the amount receivable by the rating authority for the year in respect of the domestic element of the rate support grants as last notified to the authority by the Minister at the time of ascertainment subject to any adjustment of the domestic element for any previous year notified by him since the ascertainment of the gross rate income for the preceding year; and where the said area is part of a rating area, the proportion of the said amounts which the domestic rateable value for the year of that part of the rating area has to the domestic rateable value of the whole of the area.

(2) For the purposes of head (*h*) of the foregoing sub-paragraph, the domestic rateable value for any year of any area shall be the sum of—

(*a*)   the amount, divided by two, of the aggregate of the rateable values as at 1st April and 31st March in the year of dwellinghouses in the area as ascertained by the rating authority from the rates record; and

(*b*)   a proportion of the amount, divided by two, of the aggregate rateable values as at 1st April and 31st March in the year of mixed hereditaments in the area; the proportion being that which the amount in the pound of the reduction in rates for the year made by the rating authority under section 48 (1) (*b*) has to that made under section 48(1) (*a*) of the principal Act.

(3) In the application of sub-paragraph (1) of this paragraph to the City of London—

(*a*)   in head (*a*), the reference to reductions of rates made in pursuance of section 48 of the principal Act shall be read as a reference to reductions of the poor rate made in pursuance of regulations for the time being in force under section 48(4) of the principal Act;

(*b*)   in head (*e*), the reference to the amounts receivable for the year under section 32(5) of the principal Act shall be read as a reference to the proportion of those amounts which is, under any order for the time being in force under paragraph 4(4) of Part II of Schedule 5 to the principal Act, to be taken into account in computing a poor rate of one penny in the pound;

(*c*)   in head (*h*), the reference to the amount receivable by the rating authority for the year in respect of the domestic element of the rate support grants shall be read as a reference to the proportion of that amount which is, in pursuance of the said regulations, to be treated as the proceeds of the poor rate.

Cost of collection

4.—(1) The cost of collection for any area for any year shall be determined—

(*a*)   in the case of a rating area as a whole, by ascertaining the net cost of making, collecting and recovering rates during the year, including a proper proportion of such expenses as are attributable in part to the matters aforesaid and in part to other matters, but not including any proportion of any allowances made to owners or occupiers;

(*b*)   in the case of part of a rating area, by calculating the sum which bears to the cost of the collection in the rating area as a whole the same proportion as the aggregate rateable value of all the hereditaments in such part, as shown in the Valuation List at the beginning of the year, has to the aggregate rateable value of all the hereditaments (other than gas and electricity hereditaments) in the rating area, as so shown.

(2) For the purposes of this paragraph, the net cost of making, collecting and recovering rates during the year includes any sums properly paid by the rating authority during the year as compensation for the loss of employment or diminution of emoluments of any person whose remuneration is, or would, had he continued to be employed by the rating authority, have been, chargeable as part of such net cost, or properly borne by the general rate fund, or in the case of the City of London out of the poor rate, in respect of any injury allowance or gratuity payable to or in respect of any such person under statutory provision or in respect of any increase of any annual pension or superannuation allowance, retirement grant, widow's pension or death grant payable to or in respect of any such person arising from statutory provision for such increase or from the treatment, under such provision, of non-contrbuting service as contributing service.

Loss on collection

5.—(1) The loss on collection for any area for any year shall be ascertained by adding together the following amounts—

   (a) the total in the rates record for the year of rates written off in respect of hereditaments, or former hereditaments, in the area other than allowances made by way of discount under section 51 or 54 of the principal Act;

   (b) the amount of relief afforded in the year under section 2 of the Rating (Interim Relief) Act 1964 in relation to hereditaments, or former hereditaments, in the area;

   (c) the amount of any rebates granted in respect of the year under section 49 of the principal Act in relation to hereditaments, or former hereditaments, in the area.

(2) Where the provisions of Schedule 1 to the principal Act apply in their area, the rating authority in calculating the total referred to in head (a) of the preceding sub-paragraph shall have regard to payments received in respect of the rating of unoccupied property.

Ascertainment of amount due under precept

6.   The amount due under a precept shall be taken to be the product of a rate of one penny in the pound for the rating area or for the part thereof in respect of which the precept has been issued, as the case may be, multiplied by the number of pence specified in the precept.

Excess of amount due over payments required

7.   Where the amount due under a precept exceeds the aggregate amount of the payments required by the precept, the rating authority, subject to their obligation under paragraph (a) of section 12(7) of the principal Act, may defer payment of any sum not exceeding that which has to the amount due under the precept the same proportion as the amount of arrears carried forward at the close of the year and for the time being still outstanding has to the total rate-product.

Estimates

8.—(1) Any estimate of the product of a rate of one penny in the pound in the next ensuing year which a rating authority are required to transmit to a precepting authority before 1st February in each year shall be calculated in accordance with the preceding provisions of this schedule.

(2) In calculating such estimate the rating authority shall take the latest ascertained figures available for the area to which the estimate relates and shall modify those figures to such extent as appears to them to be necessary having regard to any alteration in total rateable value which may reasonably be anticipated and to any other material circumstances.

Audit

9.   The calculations required by this schedule for any year shall be included in the accounts submitted by a rating authority to the district auditor, and the auditor's certificate allowing the accounts shall be construed as a certificate that, subject to any amendments made by him, such calculations have been properly and correctly made, and any necessary consequential adjustments shall be made in the accounts between the rating authority and the precepting authority.

Definitions

10.   In this schedule—

   "gas and electricity hereditaments" means hereditaments which a Gas Board is, under section 33(3) or by virtue of a direction made by the Minister under section 33(5), or an Electricity Board is, under section 34(3), of the principal Act, to be treated as occupying in the rating area;

"the Minister" means the Minister of Housing and Local Government;
"mixed hereditament" has the meaning assigned to it by section 48(5) of the principal
    Act;
"the principal Act" means the General Rate Act 1967;
"year" means a period of twelve months beginning with 1st April.

Given under the official seal of the Minister of Housing and Local Government on
27th March 1968.

(L.S.)   *Anthony Greenwood,*
                                        Minister of Housing and Local Government.

EXPLANATORY NOTE
(This Note is not part of the Rules.)

These rules, which apply to England and Wales, deal primarily with precepting
by county councils and the Greater London Council on rating authorities. They
provide for the way in which the amount due under the precept is to be calculated, namely by ascertaining the product of a rate of one penny in the pound in
the relevant area and multiplying that amount by the number of pence in the
pound specified in the precept. The rules also provide for the way in which the
product of a rate of one penny in the pound for any area is to be determined for
the purpose of (i) deciding entitlement to, and the amount to be paid in respect
of, the resources element of the rate support grants; and (ii) ascertaining the
amount a local authority may spend annually in the interests of their area or its
inhabitants under section 6 of the Local Government (Financial Provisions) Act
1963.

The schedule to the rules re-enacts existing rules with drafting amendments and
amendments necessary to take account of the introduction by the Local Government Act 1966 of the domestic element of the rate support grants. A further
change is that the schedule does not include a provision, contained in the existing
rules, precluding a rating authority, in ascertaining the product of a rate of one
penny in the pound for precepting and other purposes, from deducting from the
gross rate income, as part of the cost of collection of the rate, expenses incurred
in making or objecting to proposals for the alteration of the current valuation
list.

Certain statutory provisions which become unnecessary in consequence of the
rules are repealed and amendments which are appropriate in consequence of the
rules are made in certain other statutory provisions. The rules re-enacted in the
schedule to these rules are revoked.

STATUTORY INSTRUMENTS

1968 No. 497

LONDON GOVERNMENT

The London Borough Council Elections Rules 1968

Made - - - -	*25th March* 1968
Laid before Parliament	*3rd April* 1968
Coming into Operation	*9th May* 1968

In pursuance of the powers conferred upon me by paragraph 13 of Schedule 3 to the London Government Act 1963(a), I hereby make the following Rules:—

1. In the application of the local elections rules contained in Schedule 2 to the Representation of the People Act 1949(b) to an election of London borough councillors, adaptations, alterations and exceptions shall be made therein so that the said local elections rules shall read as set out in the Schedule hereto.

2. Rule 1 of and Schedule 1 to the London Borough Council and Greater London Council Elections Rules 1963(c) and Rule 1 of the London Borough Council and Greater London Council Elections Rules 1964(d) are hereby revoked.

3.—(1) These Rules may be cited as the London Borough Council Elections Rules 1968 and shall come into operation on 9th May 1968:

Provided that for the purpose of all proceedings preliminary or relating to an election to be held on or after that day these Rules shall come into operation forthwith.

(2) The Interpretation Act 1889(e) shall apply to the interpretation of these Rules as it applies to the interpretation of an Act of Parliament.

James Callaghan,
One of Her Majesty's Principal
Secretaries of State.

Home Office,
 Whitehall.
25th March 1968.

(a) 1963 c. 33.
(c) S.I. 1963/1864 (1963 III, p. 3455).
(e) 1889 c. 63.

(b) 1949 c. 68.
(d) S.I. 1964/454 (1964 I, p. 725).

SCHEDULE

LOCAL ELECTIONS RULES

Arrangement of rules

PART I

PROVISIONS AS TO TIME

Rule
1. Timetable
2. Computation of time.
3. Hours of poll.

PART II

STAGES COMMON TO CONTESTED AND UNCONTESTED ELECTIONS

4. Notice of election.
5. Nomination of candidates.
6. Subscription of nomination paper.
7. Consent to nomination.
8. Place for delivery of nomination papers.
9. Decisions as to validity of nomination papers.
10. Publication of nominations.
11. Withdrawal of candidates.
12. Nomination in more than one ward.
13. Method of election.

PART III

CONTESTED ELECTIONS

General provisions

14. Poll to be taken by ballot.
15. The ballot papers.
16. The official mark.
17. Prohibition of disclosure of vote.
18. Use of schools and public rooms.

Action to be taken before the poll

19. Notice of poll.
20. Death of candidate.
21. Postal ballot papers.
22. Provision of polling stations.
23. Appointment of presiding officers and clerks.
24. Special lists.
25. Equipment of polling stations.
26. Appointment of polling and counting agents.
27. Declaration of secrecy.

The poll

PART I

PROVISIONS AS TO TIME

Timetable

1. The proceedings at the election shall be conducted in accordance with the following Table.

TIMETABLE

Proceeding	Time
Publication of notice of election ...	Not later than the twentieth day before the day of election.
Delivery of nomination papers ...	Not later than noon on the fourteenth day before the day of election.
Despatch of notice of decisions on nominations and publication of statement as to persons nominated	Not later than noon on the thirteenth day before the day of election.
Delivery of notices of withdrawals of candidature	Not later than noon on the twelfth day before the day of election.
Notice of poll	Not later than the fifth day before the day of election.
Notice of appointment of polling or counting agents	Not later than the third day before the day of election.
Polling	On the day of election.

Computation of time

2. In computing any period of time for the purposes of the Timetable, a Sunday, Christmas Day, Good Friday, bank holiday or day appointed for public thanksgiving or mourning and the Saturday before and the Tuesday after Easter Day or Whit Sunday shall be disregarded and any such day shall not be treated as a day for the purpose of any proceedings up to the completion of the poll nor shall the returning officer be obliged to proceed with the counting of the votes thereon:

Provided that where under Part III of these rules a person ought to proceed with the preparation of special lists or the issue of postal ballot papers on the said Saturday before or Tuesday after Easter Day or Whit Sunday, nothing in this rule shall absolve him from that duty.

Hours of poll

3. The poll shall commence at eight o'clock in the morning and be kept open till nine o'clock in the evening of the same day and no longer.

PART II

STAGES COMMON TO CONTESTED AND UNCONTESTED ELECTIONS

Notice of election

4.—(1) Notice of the election in the prescribed form shall be prepared, signed and published by the returning officer.

(2) The notice shall be published by causing it to be affixed to the town hall and to be exhibited at such places in the ward as the returning officer may determine.

Nomination of candidates

5.—(1) Each candidate shall be nominated by a separate nomination paper in the prescribed form, delivered at the place fixed for the purpose.

(2) The nomination paper shall state the full names, place of residence and description of the candidate and the surname shall be placed first in the list of his names.

(3) The description shall not refer to the candidate's political activities, and need not refer to his rank, profession or calling so long as, with the other particulars of the candidate, it is sufficient to identify him.

(4) If the description is unduly long, the returning officer after consultation (if possible) with the candidate or his election agent, proposer or seconder, may shorten it or substitute another.

Subscription of nomination paper

6.—(1) The nomination paper shall be subscribed by two electors for the ward as proposer and seconder, and by eight other electors for the ward as assenting to the nomination.

(2) Where a nomination paper bears the signatures of more than the required number of persons as proposing, seconding or assenting to the nomination of a candidate, the signature or signatures (up to the required number) appearing first on the paper in each category shall be taken into account to the exclusion of any others in that category.

(3) The returning officer shall provide nomination papers and shall supply any elector for the ward with as many nomination papers as may be required and shall, at the request of any such elector, prepare for signature a nomination paper.

(4) No person shall—

(a) subscribe more nomination papers than there are vacancies to be filled in the ward; or

(b) subscribe a nomination paper for more than one ward; or

(c) subscribe more than one nomination paper in respect of the same candidate:

Provided that a person shall not be prevented from subscribing a nomination paper by reason only of his having subscribed that of a candidate who has died or withdrawn before delivery of the first-mentioned paper.

(5) If any person subscribes nomination papers in contravention of the last foregoing paragraph, his signature shall be inoperative in all but those papers (up to the permitted number) which are first delivered.

(6) In this rule, the expression "elector for the ward" means a person who is registered as a local government elector for the ward in the register to be used at the election or who, pending the publication of that register, appears from the electors lists therefor as corrected by the registration officer to be entitled to be so registered:

Provided that, in relation to an election at which the date fixed for the poll falls within the period beginning with 16th February in any year and ending with 1st October in that year, the said expression shall not include a person who, by virtue of section 2(1) of the Electoral Registers Act 1949(a) as amended by section 1(2) of the Electoral Registers Act 1953(b) (which relates to persons coming of age during the currency of the register), is registered as a local government elector for the ward in the register to be used at that election or who, by virtue of that subsection, appears from the electors lists for that register to be entitled to be so registered.

Consent to nomination

7.—(1) A person shall not be validly nominated unless his consent to nomination, given in writing on or within one month before the day fixed as the last day for the delivery of nomination papers and attested by one witness, is delivered at the place and within the time appointed for the delivery of nomination papers:

(a) 1949 c. 86.   (b) 2 & 3 Eliz. 2. c. 8.

Provided that in the case of an election to fill a casual vacancy, if the returning officer is satisfied that owing to the absence of a person from the United Kingdom it has not been reasonably practicable for his consent in writing to be given as aforesaid, a telegram consenting to his nomination and purporting to have been sent by him shall be deemed, for the purpose of this rule, to be consent in writing given by him on the day on which it purports to have been sent, and attestation of his consent shall not be required.

(2) A candidate's consent given under this rule shall contain a statement that he is qualified as required by law to be elected to and hold the office in question, and the statement shall give particulars of his qualification.

Place for delivery of nomination papers

8. Every nomination paper shall be delivered at the place fixed by the returning officer.

Decisions as to validity of nomination papers

9.—(1) Where a nomination paper and the candidate's consent thereto are delivered in accordance with these rules, the candidate shall be deemed to stand nominated unless and until the returning officer decides that the nomination paper is invalid, or proof is given to the satisfaction of the returning officer of the candidate's death, or the candidate withdraws.

(2) The returning officer shall be entitled to hold a nomination paper invalid only on one of the following grounds, that is to say,—

(a) that the particulars of the candidate or the persons subscribing the paper are not as required by law; and

(b) that the paper is not subscribed as so required.

(3) As soon as practicable after the latest time for the delivery of nomination papers, the returning officer shall examine the nomination papers, and decide whether the candidates have been validly nominated in accordance with these rules.

(4) Where he decides that a nomination paper is invalid, he shall endorse and sign on the paper the fact and the reasons for his decision.

(5) The decision of the returning officer that a nomination paper is valid shall be final and shall not be questioned in any proceeding whatsoever.

(6) Subject to the last foregoing paragraph, nothing in this rule shall prevent the validity of a nomination being questioned on an election petition.

(7) The returning officer shall send notice of his decision to each candidate at his place of residence as stated on his nomination paper.

Publication of nominations

10.—(1) The returning officer shall prepare and publish a statement in the prescribed form showing the persons who have been and stand nominated and any other persons who have been nominated, with the reason why they no longer stand nominated.

(2) The statement shall show the names, addresses and descriptions of the persons nominated as given in their nomination papers.

(3) The statement shall show the persons standing nominated arranged alphabetically in the order of their surnames, and, if there are two or more of them with the same surnames, of their other names.

(4) In the case of a person nominated by more than one nomination paper, the returning officer shall take the particulars required by the foregoing provisions of this rule from such one of the papers as the candidate or the returning officer in default of the candidate may select.

(5) The statement as to persons nominated shall be published by causing it to be affixed to the place appointed for the delivery of nomination papers.

Withdrawal of candidates

11.—(1) A candidate may withdraw his candidature by notice of withdrawal signed by him and attested by one witness and delivered at the place appointed for the delivery of nomination papers.

(2) In the case of a candidate who is outside the United Kingdom, a notice of withdrawal signed by his proposer and accompanied by a written declaration also so signed of the candidate's absence from the United Kingdom shall be of the same effect as a notice of withdrawal signed by the candidate:

Provided that where the candidate stands nominated by more than one nomination paper a notice of withdrawal under this paragraph shall be effective if, but only if,—

(a) it and the accompanying declaration are signed by all the proposers except any who is, and is stated in the said declaration to be, outside the United Kingdom; or

(b) it is accompanied, in addition to the said declaration, by a written statement signed by the candidate that the proposer giving the notice is authorised to do so on the candidate's behalf during his absence from the United Kingdom.

Nomination in more than one ward

12. A candidate who is validly nominated for more than one ward must duly withdraw from his candidature in all those wards except one, and if he does not so withdraw he shall be deemed to have withdrawn from his candidature in all those wards.

Method of election

13.—(1) If the number of persons remaining validly nominated for the ward after any withdrawals under these rules exceeds the number of vacancies, the councillors shall be elected from among them at a poll under Part III of these rules.

(2) If the said number does not exceed the number of vacancies, the person or persons (if any) deemed to be elected under the following provisions of this rule shall be declared elected in accordance with Part IV of these rules.

(3) The person or persons (if any) remaining validly nominated for the ward after any withdrawals under these rules shall be deemed to be elected.

(4) If, at an ordinary election of councillors, no person remains validly nominated as aforesaid, or the number of persons so remaining validly nominated is less than the number of vacancies, such of the retiring councillors for the ward as were highest on the poll at the last ordinary election, or as filled the places of councillors who were highest on the poll at that election, or if the poll was equal or there was no poll, as may be determined by the drawing of lots conducted under the direction of the returning officer, shall be deemed to be elected to fill up the vacancies not filled under paragraph (3) of this rule.

PART III

CONTESTED ELECTIONS

GENERAL PROVISIONS

Poll to be taken by ballot

14. The votes at the poll shall be given by ballot, the result shall be ascertained by counting the votes given to each candidate, and the candidate or candidates to whom the majority of votes have been given shall be declared to have been elected.

The ballot papers

15.—(1) The ballot of every voter shall consist of a ballot paper, and the persons remaining validly nominated for the ward after any withdrawals under these rules, and no others, shall be entitled to have their names inserted in the ballot paper.

(2) Every ballot paper shall be in the form in the Appendix and shall be printed in accordance with the directions therein, and—

(a) shall contain the names and other particulars of the candidates as shown in the statement of persons nominated;

(b) shall be capable of being folded up;

(c) shall have a number printed on the back;

(d) shall have attached a counterfoil with the same number printed on the face.

(3) The order of the names in the ballot paper shall be the same as in the statement of persons nominated.

The official mark

16.—(1) Every ballot paper shall be marked with an official mark, which shall be either embossed or perforated.

(2) The official mark shall be kept secret, and an interval of not less than seven years shall intervene between the use of the same official mark at elections for the same London borough.

Prohibition of disclosure of vote

17. No person who has voted at the election shall, in any legal proceeding to question the election, be required to state for whom he voted.

Use of schools and public rooms

18.—(1) The returning officer may use, free of charge, for the purpose of taking the poll or counting the votes—

(a) a room in a school maintained or assisted by a local education authority or a school in respect of which grants are made out of moneys provided by Parliament to the person or body of persons responsible for the management of the school;

(b) a room the expense of maintaining which is payable out of any rate.

(2) The returning officer shall make good any damage done to, and defray any expense incurred by the persons having control over, any such room as aforesaid by reason of its being used for the purpose of taking the poll or of counting the votes.

(3) The use of a room in an unoccupied house for the purpose of taking the poll or of counting the votes shall not render that person liable to be rated or to pay any rate for that house.

(4) The election shall not be held in a church, chapel or other place of public worship.

ACTION TO BE TAKEN BEFORE THE POLL

Notice of poll

19.—(1) Notice of the poll shall be published by the returning officer at the places at which the notice of election is required to be published under rule 4 of these rules.

(2) Notice of the poll shall specify—

(a) the day and hours fixed for the poll;

(b) the number of councillors to be elected;

(c) the particulars of each candidate remaining validly nominated (the names and other particulars of the candidates, and the order of the names of the candidates, being the same as in the statement of persons nominated);

(d) the names of the proposer and seconder signing a candidate's nomination paper;

(e) a description of the polling districts (if any); and

(f) the situation of each polling station and the description of the persons entitled to vote thereat.

(3) In the case of a candidate nominated by more than one nomination paper, the nomination paper mentioned in sub-paragraph (d) of paragraph (2) of this rule shall be that from which the names and other particulars of the candidate shown in the statement of persons nominated are taken, but the candidate may require the returning officer to include in the notice the names of the proposer and seconder signing a second and third nomination paper.

Death of candidate

20. If before the poll is commenced proof is given to the satisfaction of the returning officer—

(a) that a person remaining validly nominated has died after the latest time for delivery of nomination papers, or

(b) that a person shown in the statement of persons nominated as standing nominated had in fact died before the latest time for delivery of nomination papers,

the returning officer shall countermand the poll and the provisions of section 36(2) of the Representation of the People Act 1949 shall apply to any further election ordered under the Local Government Act 1933(a).

Postal ballot papers

21. The returning officer shall as soon as practicable send to those entitled to vote by post, at the addresses furnished by them for the purpose, a ballot paper and a declaration of identity in the prescribed form, together with an envelope for their return.

Provision of polling stations

22.—(1) The returning officer shall provide a sufficient number of polling stations and, subject to the following provisions of this rule, shall allot the electors to the polling stations in such manner as he thinks most convenient.

(2) One or more polling stations may be provided in the same room.

(3) The polling station allotted to electors from any parliamentary polling district wholly or partly within the ward shall, in the absence of special circumstances, be in the parliamentary polling place for that district, unless the polling place is outside the ward.

(4) The returning officer shall provide each polling station with such number of compartments as may be necessary in which the voters can mark their votes screened from observation.

Appointment of presiding officers and clerks

23.—(1) The returning officer shall appoint and pay a presiding officer to attend at each polling station and such clerks as may be necessary for the purposes of the election, but he shall not appoint any person who has been employed by or on behalf of a candidate in or about the election.

(a) 1933 c. 51.

(2) The returning officer may, if he thinks fit, preside at a polling station and the provisions of these rules relating to a presiding officer shall apply to a returning officer so presiding with the necessary modifications as to things to be done by the returning officer to the presiding officer or by the presiding officer to the returning officer.

(3) A presiding officer may do, by the clerks appointed to assist him, any act (including the asking of questions) which he is required or authorised by these rules to do at a polling station except order the arrest, exclusion or removal of any person from the polling station.

Special lists

24. The registration officer shall as soon as practicable prepare the following special lists, namely—

    (a) a list (in these rules referred to as "the absent voters list") giving the name and number on the register of every person entitled to vote at the election as an absent voter;

    (b) a list (in these rules referred to as "the list of proxies") giving—

        (i) the names and numbers on the register of the electors for whom proxies have been appointed; and

        (ii) the names and addresses of the persons appointed;

    (c) a list of any persons entitled to vote by post as proxy at the election.

Equipment of polling stations

25.—(1) The returning officer shall provide each presiding officer with such number of ballot boxes and ballot papers as in the opinion of the returning officer may be necessary.

(2) Every ballot box shall be so constructed that the ballot papers can be put therein, but cannot be withdrawn therefrom, without the box being unlocked.

(3) The returning officer shall provide each polling station with—

    (a) materials to enable voters to mark the ballot papers;

    (b) instruments for stamping thereon the official mark;

    (c) copies of the register of electors for the ward or such part thereon as contains the names of the electors allotted to the station;

    (d) the parts of any special lists prepared for the election corresponding to the register of electors for the ward or part thereof provided under the last foregoing sub-paragraph.

(4) A notice in the form in the Appendix, giving directions for the guidance of the voters in voting, shall be printed in conspicuous characters and exhibited outside every polling station and in every compartment of every polling station.

Appointment of polling and counting agents

26.—(1) Each candidate may, before the commencement of the poll, appoint polling agents to attend at polling stations for the purpose of detecting personation and counting agents to attend at the counting of the votes:

Provided that—

    (a) the returning officer may limit the number of counting agents, so however that the number shall be the same in the case of each candidate and the number allowed to a candidate shall not (except in special circumstances) be less than the number obtained by dividing the number of clerks employed on the counting by the number of candidates;

    (b) the appointment of a polling agent may be on behalf of more than one candidate;

(c) not more than one polling agent shall be appointed to attend on behalf of the same candidate at a polling station;

(d) not more than three or, if the number of candidates exceeds twenty, four polling agents shall be appointed to attend at any polling station.

(2) If the number of polling agents appointed to attend at a polling station exceeds the permitted number, only those polling agents, up to the permitted number, whose appointments are signed by or on behalf of the greater number of candidates, or, in the event of an equality in the number of signatures, only such of those polling agents as may be determined by the returning officer, shall be deemed to have been duly appointed.

(3) Notice in writing of the appointment, stating the names and addresses of the persons appointed, shall be given by the candidate to the returning officer and shall be so given not later than the time appointed for that purpose in the Timetable.

(4) If an agent dies, or becomes incapable of acting, the candidate may appoint another agent in his place, and shall forthwith give to the returning officer notice in writing of the name and address of the agent appointed.

(5) The foregoing provisions of this rule shall be without prejudice to the requirements of section 60(1) of the Representation of the People Act 1949 as to the appointment of paid polling agents, and counting agents may be appointed and the notice of appointment given to the returning officer by the candidate's election agent, instead of by the candidate.

(6) In the following provisions of these rules references to polling and counting agents shall be taken as references to agents whose appointments have been duly made and notified and, where the number of agents is restricted, who are within the permitted number.

(7) Any notice required to be given to a counting agent by the returning officer may be delivered at or sent by post to the address stated in the notice of appointment.

(8) A candidate may himself do any act or thing which any polling or counting agent of his, if appointed, would have been authorised to do, or may assist his agent in doing any such act or thing.

(9) Where by these rules any act or thing is required or authorised to be done in the presence of the polling or counting agents, the non-attendance of any agents or agent at the time and place appointed for the purpose, shall not, if the act or thing is otherwise duly done, invalidate the act or thing done.

Declaration of secrecy

27.—(1) Before the opening of the poll a declaration of secrecy in the form in paragraph (4) of this rule, or in a form as near thereto as circumstances admit, shall be made by—

(a) the returning officer;

(b) every officer or clerk authorised to attend at a polling station or the counting of the votes;

(c) every candidate attending at a polling station or at the counting of the votes and every election agent so attending;

(d) every candidate's wife or husband attending at the counting of the votes;

(e) every polling agent and counting agent;

(f) every person permitted by the returning officer to attend at the counting of the votes, though not entitled to do so.

(2) Notwithstanding anything in the foregoing paragraph, the following persons attending at the counting of the votes, that is to say:—

(a) any candidate;

(b) any election agent, or any candidate's wife or husband attending by virtue of the rule authorising election agents and candidates' wives or husbands to attend as such;

(c) any person permitted by the returning officer to attend, though not entitled to do so;

need not make the declaration before the opening of the poll but shall make it before he or she is permitted to attend the counting, and a polling or counting agent appointed after the opening of the poll shall make the declaration before acting as such agent.

(3) The returning officer shall make the declaration in the presence of a Justice of the Peace, and any other person shall make the declaration in the presence either of a Justice of the Peace or of the returning officer, and subsections (1), (2), (3) and (6) of section 53 of the Representation of the People Act 1949 shall be read to the declarant by the person taking the declaration.

(4) The declaration shall be as follows—

"I solemnly promise and declare that I will not do anything forbidden by subsections (1), (2), (3) and (6) of section 53 of the Representation of the People Act 1949, which have been read to me.".

The Poll

Admission to polling station

28.—(1) The presiding officer shall regulate the number of voters to be admitted to the polling station at the same time, and shall exclude all other persons except—

(a) the candidates and their election agents;

(b) the polling agents appointed to attend at the polling station;

(c) the clerks appointed to attend at the polling station;

(d) the constables on duty; and

(e) the companions of blind voters.

(2) A constable or person employed by a returning officer shall not be admitted to vote in person elsewhere than at his own polling station under the provisions of the Representation of the People Act 1949 in that behalf, except on production and surrender of a certificate as to his employment, which shall be in the prescribed form and signed by the prescribed officer of police or by the returning officer, as the case may be.

(3) Any certificate surrendered under this rule shall forthwith be cancelled.

Keeping of order in station

29.—(1) It shall be the duty of the presiding officer to keep order at his polling station.

(2) If a person misconducts himself in a polling station, or fails to obey the lawful orders of the presiding officer, he may immediately, by order of the presiding officer, be removed from the polling station by a constable in or near that station or by any other person authorised in writing by the returning officer to remove him, and the person so removed shall not, without the permission of the presiding officer, again enter the polling station during the day.

(3) Any person so removed may, if charged with the commission in the polling station of an offence, be dealt with as a person taken into custody by a constable for an offence without a warrant.

(4) The powers conferred by this rule shall not be exercised so as to prevent a voter who is otherwise entitled to vote at a polling station from having an opportunity of voting at that station.

Sealing of ballot boxes

30. Immediately before the commencement of the poll, the presiding officer shall show the ballot box empty to such persons, if any, as are present in the polling station, so that they may see that it is empty, and shall then lock it up and place his seal on it in such manner as to prevent its being opened without breaking the seal, and shall place it in his view for the receipt of ballot papers, and keep it so locked and sealed.

Questions to be put to voters

31.—(1) The presiding officer may, and if required by a candidate or his election or polling agent shall, put to any person applying for a ballot paper at the time of his application, but not afterwards, the following questions, or either of them, that is to say—

(*a*) in the case of a person applying as an elector—

(i) Are you the person registered in the register of local government electors now in force for this ward as follows [*read the whole entry from the register*]?

(ii) Have you already voted at the present election [*adding in the case of an election for several wards* in this or any other ward] otherwise than as proxy for some other person?

(*b*) in the case of a person applying as proxy—

(i) Are you the person whose name appears as A.B. in the list of proxies for this election as entitled to vote as proxy on behalf of C.D.?

(ii) Have you already voted here or elsewhere at the present election as proxy on behalf of C.D.?

(2) A ballot paper shall not be delivered to any person required to answer the above questions or any of them unless he has answered the questions or question satisfactorily.

(3) Save as by this rule authorised, no inquiry shall be permitted as to the right of any person to vote.

Challenge of voter

32.—(1) If at the time a person applies for a ballot paper for the purpose of voting in person, or after he has applied for a ballot paper for that purpose and before he has left the polling station, a candidate or his election or polling agent declares to the presiding officer that he has reasonable cause to believe that the applicant has committed an offence of personation and undertakes to substantiate the charge in a court of law, the presiding officer may order a constable to arrest the applicant, and the order of the presiding officer shall be sufficient authority for the constable so to do.

(2) A person against whom a declaration is made under this rule shall not by reason thereof be prevented from voting.

(3) A person arrested under the provisions of this rule shall be dealt with as a person taken into custody by a constable for an offence without a warrant.

Voting procedure

33.—(1) A ballot paper shall be delivered to a voter who applies therefor, and immediately before delivery—

(*a*) the ballot paper shall be stamped with the official mark, either embossed or perforated;

(*b*) the number, name and description of the elector as stated in the copy of the register of electors shall be called out;

(*c*) the number of the elector shall be marked on the counterfoil;

(*d*) a mark shall be placed in the register of electors against the number of the elector to denote that a ballot paper has been received but without showing the particular ballot paper which has been received; and

(*e*) in the case of a person applying for a ballot paper as proxy, a mark shall also be placed against his name in the list of proxies.

(2) The voter, on receiving the ballot paper, shall forthwith proceed into one of the compartments in the polling station and there secretly mark his paper and fold it up so as to conceal his vote, and shall then show to the presiding officer the back of the paper so as to disclose the official mark, and put the ballot paper so folded up into the ballot box in the presence of the presiding officer.

(3) The voter shall vote without undue delay, and shall leave the polling station as soon as he has put his ballot paper into the ballot box.

(4) Notwithstanding anything in the foregoing provisions of this rule in the case of an election at which the date fixed for the poll falls within the period beginning with 16th February in any year and ending with 1st October in that year, no ballot paper shall be delivered to a person who, by virtue of section 2(1) of the Electoral Registers Act 1949 as amended by section 1(2) of the Electoral Registers Act 1953 (which relates to persons coming of age during the currency of the register), is registered in the register to be used at the election or to his proxy, except where the part of the register in which his name appears is being used at the election by virtue of section 1(6) of the said Act (which relates to registers not published by the required time):

Provided that this paragraph shall not apply to a person applying for a ballot paper as proxy of a person entitled, apart from section 2 of the said Act as so amended, to vote.

Votes marked by presiding officer

34.—(1) The presiding officer, on the application of—

   (a) a voter who is incapacitated by blindness or other physical cause from voting in manner directed by these rules; or

   (b) if the poll is taken on a Saturday, a voter who declares that he is a Jew, and objects on religious grounds to vote in manner directed by these rules; or

   (c) a voter who declares orally that he is unable to read;

shall, in the presence of the polling agents, cause the vote of the voter to be marked on a ballot paper in manner directed by the voter, and the ballot paper to be placed in the ballot box.

(2) The name and number on the register of electors of every voter whose vote is marked in pursuance of this rule, and the reason why it is so marked, shall be entered on a list (in these rules called "the list of votes marked by the presiding officer").

In the case of a person voting as proxy for an elector, the number to be entered together with the name of the voter shall be the number of the elector.

Voting by blind persons

35.—(1) If a voter makes an application to the presiding officer to be allowed on the ground of blindness to vote with the assistance of another person by whom he is accompanied (in these rules referred to as "the companion"), the presiding officer shall require the voter to declare orally whether he is so incapacitated by his blindness as to be unable to vote without assistance.

(2) If the presiding officer is satisfied that the voter is so incapacitated and is also satisfied by a written declaration made by the companion (in these rules referred to as "the declaration made by the companion of a blind voter") that the companion is a qualified person within the meaning of this rule and has not previously assisted more than one blind person to vote at the election, the presiding officer shall grant the application, and thereupon anything which is by these rules required to be done to or by the said voter in connection with the giving of his vote may be done to, or with the assistance of, the companion.

(3) For the purposes of this rule, a person shall be qualified to assist a blind voter to vote, if that person is either—

   (a) a person who is entitled to vote as an elector at the election; or

   (b) the father, mother, brother, sister, husband, wife, son or daughter of the blind voter and has attained the age of twenty-one years.

(4) The name and number in the register of electors of every voter whose vote is given in accordance with this rule and the name and address of the companion shall be entered on a list (in these rules referred to as "the list of blind voters assisted by companions").

In the case of a person voting as proxy for an elector, the number to be entered together with the name of the voter shall be the number of the elector.

(5) The declaration made by the companion—

(a) shall be in the form in the Appendix;

(b) shall be made before the presiding officer at the time when the voter applies to vote with the assistance of a companion and shall forthwith be given to the presiding officer who shall attest and retain it.

(6) No fee or other payment shall be charged in respect of the declaration.

Tendered ballot papers

36.—(1) If a person, representing himself to be—

(a) a particular elector named on the register and not named in the absent voters list; or

(b) a particular person named in the list of proxies as proxy for an elector and not named in the list of persons entitled to vote by post as proxy,

applies for a ballot paper after another person has voted in person either as the elector or his proxy, the applicant shall, on satisfactorily answering the questions permitted by law to be asked at the poll, be entitled, subject to the following provisions of this rule, to mark a ballot paper (in these rules referred to as "a tendered ballot paper") in the same manner as any other voter.

(2) A tendered ballot paper shall—

(a) be of a colour differing from the other ballot papers;

(b) instead of being put into the ballot box, be given to the presiding officer and endorsed by him with the name of the voter and his number in the register of electors, and set aside in a separate packet.

(3) The name of the voter and his number on the register of electors shall be entered on a list (in these rules referred to as the "tendered votes list").

(4) In the case of a person voting as proxy for an elector, the number to be endorsed or entered together with the name of the voter shall be the number of that elector.

Spoilt ballot papers

37. A voter who has inadvertently dealt with his ballot paper in such manner that it cannot be conveniently used as a ballot paper may, on delivering it to the presiding officer and proving to his satisfaction the fact of the inadvertence, obtain another ballot paper in the place of the ballot paper so delivered (in these rules referred to as "a spoilt ballot paper"), and the spoilt ballot paper shall be immediately cancelled.

Adjournment of poll in case of riot

38. For the purpose of the adjournment of the poll in the event of riot or open violence, a presiding officer shall have the power by law belonging to a presiding officer at a parliamentary election.

Procedure on close of poll

39.—(1) As soon as practicable after the close of the poll, the presiding officer shall, in the presence of the polling agents, make up into separate packets, sealed with his own seal and the seals of such polling agents as desire to affix their seals—

(a) each ballot box in use at the station, sealed so as to prevent the introduction of additional ballot papers and unopened, but with the key attached;

(b) the unused and spoilt ballot papers placed together;

(c) the tendered ballot papers;

(d) the marked copies of the register of electors and of the list of proxies;

(e) the counterfoils of the used ballot papers and the certificates as to employment on duty on the day of the poll;

(f) the tendered votes list, the list of blind voters assisted by companions, the list of votes marked by the presiding officer, a statement of the number of voters whose votes are so marked by the presiding officer under the heads "physical incapacity", "Jews", and "unable to read", and the declarations made by the companions of blind voters;

and shall deliver the packets to the returning officer to be taken charge of by him.

(2) The marked copies of the register of electors and of the list of proxies shall be in one packet but shall not be in the same packet as the counterfoils of the used ballot papers and the certificates as to employment on duty on the day of the poll.

(3) The packets shall be accompanied by a statement (in these rules referred to as "the ballot paper account") made by the presiding officer showing the number of ballot papers entrusted to him, and accounting for them under the heads of ballot papers in the ballot box, unused, spoilt and tendered ballot papers.

COUNTING OF VOTES

Attendance at counting of votes

40.—(1) The returning officer shall make arrangements for counting the votes in the presence of the counting agents as soon as practicable after the close of the poll, and shall give to the counting agents notice in writing of the time and place at which he will begin to count the votes.

(2) No person other than—

(a) the returning officer and his clerks;

(b) the candidates and their wives or husbands;

(c) the election agents;

(d) the counting agents;

may be present at the counting of the votes, unless permitted by the returning officer to attend.

(3) The returning officer shall give the counting agents all such reasonable facilities for overseeing the proceedings, and all such information with respect thereto, as he can give them consistently with the orderly conduct of the proceedings and the discharge of his duties in connection therewith.

(4) In particular, where the votes are counted by sorting the ballot papers according to the candidate for whom the vote is given and then counting the number of ballot papers for each candidate, the counting agents shall be entitled to satisfy themselves that the ballot papers are correctly sorted.

The count

41.—(1) Before the returning officer proceeds to count the votes, he shall—

(a) in the presence of the counting agents open each ballot box and, taking out the ballot papers therein, count and record the number thereof;

(b) count such of the postal ballot papers as have been duly returned and record the number counted; and

(c) then mix together the whole of the ballot papers mentioned in the foregoing sub-paragraphs.

(2) A postal ballot paper shall not be deemed to be duly returned, unless it is returned in the proper envelope so as to reach the returning officer before the close of the poll and is accompanied by the declaration of identity duly signed and authenticated.

(3) The returning officer shall not count any tendered ballot paper.

(4) The returning officer, while counting and recording the number of ballot papers and counting the votes, shall keep the ballot papers with their faces upwards and take all proper precautions for preventing any person from seeing the numbers printed on the back of the papers.

(5) The returning officer shall, so far as practicable, proceed continuously with counting the votes, allowing only time for refreshment:

Provided that he may, in so far as he and the agents agree, exclude the hours between nine o'clock in the evening and nine o'clock on the following morning.

For the purposes of this proviso the agreement of a candidate or his election agent shall be as effective as the agreement of his counting agents.

(6) During the excluded time the returning officer shall place the ballot papers and other documents relating to the election under his own seal and the seals of such of the counting agents as desire to affix their seals and shall otherwise take proper precautions for the security of the papers and documents.

Re-count

42.—(1) A candidate or his election agent may, if present when the counting or any re-count of the votes is completed, require the returning officer to have the votes re-counted or again re-counted but the returning officer may refuse to do so if in his opinion the request is unreasonable.

(2) No step shall be taken on the completion of the counting or any re-count of votes until the candidates and election agents present at the completion thereof have been given a reasonable opportunity to exercise the right conferred by this rule.

Rejected ballot papers

43.—(1) Any ballot paper—

(a) which does not bear the official mark; or

(b) on which votes are given for more candidates than the voter is entitled to vote for; or

(c) on which anything is written or marked by which the voter can be identified except the printed number on the back; or

(d) which is unmarked or void for uncertainty;

shall, subject to the provisions of this rule, be void and not counted.

(2) Where the voter is entitled to vote for more than one candidate, a ballot paper shall not be deemed to be void for uncertainty as respects any vote as to which no uncertainty arises and that vote shall be counted.

(3) A ballot paper on which a vote is marked—

(a) elsewhere than in the proper place; or

(b) otherwise than by means of a cross; or

(c) by more than one mark;

shall not by reason thereof be deemed to be void (either wholly or as respects that vote), if an intention that the vote shall be for one or other of the candidates clearly appears and the way the paper is marked does not of itself identify the voter and it is not shown that he can be identified thereby.

(4) The returning officer shall endorse—

(a) the word "rejected" on any ballot paper which under this rule is not to be counted; and

(b) in the case of a ballot paper on which any vote is counted under paragraph (2) of this rule, the words "rejected in part" and a memorandum specifying the votes counted;

and shall add to the endorsement the words "rejection objected to" if an objection is made by a counting agent to his decision.

(5) The returning officer shall draw up a statement showing the number of ballot papers rejected, including those rejected in part, under the several heads of—

(a) want of official mark;

(b) voting for more candidates than voter is entitled to;

(c) writing or mark by which voter could be identified;

(d) unmarked or wholly void for uncertainty;

(e) rejected in part;

and any counting agent may copy the statement.

Decisions on ballot papers

44. The decision of the returning officer on any question arising in respect of a ballot paper shall be final, but shall be subject to review on an election petition.

Equality of votes

45. Where, after the counting of the votes (including any re-count) is completed, an equality of votes is found to exist between any candidates and the addition of a vote would entitle any of those candidates to be declared elected, the returning officer shall forthwith decide between those candidates by lot, and proceed as if the candidate on whom the lot falls had received an additional vote.

PART IV

FINAL PROCEEDINGS IN CONTESTED AND UNCONTESTED ELECTIONS

Declaration of result

46.—(1) In a contested election, when the result of the poll has been ascertained the returning officer shall forthwith declare to be elected the candidate or candidates for whom the majority of votes have been given, and shall as soon as possible publish the name or names of the candidate or candidates elected and the total number of votes given for each candidate, whether elected or not.

(2) In an uncontested election, the returning officer shall, not later than eleven o'clock in the morning on the day of election, publish the name or names of the person or persons elected.

PART V

DISPOSAL OF DOCUMENTS

Verification of ballot paper account

47.—(1) On the completion of the counting at a contested election the returning officer shall seal up in separate packets the counted and rejected ballot papers, including ballot papers rejected in part.

(2) The returning officer shall then in the presence of the counting agents verify each ballot paper account by comparing it with the number of ballot papers recorded by him, and the unused and spoilt ballot papers in his possession and the tendered votes list (opening and resealing the packets containing the unused and spoilt ballot papers and the tendered votes list) and shall draw up a statement as to the result of the verification, which any counting agent may copy.

(3) The returning officer shall not open the sealed packets of tendered ballot papers or of counterfoils and certificates as to employment on duty on the day of the poll, or of marked copies of the register of electors and lists of proxies.

Marking of packets

48. The returning officer shall endorse on each of the following packets, that is to say—

(a) the packets of ballot papers in his possession;

(b) the ballot paper accounts and the statements of rejected ballot papers and of the result of the verification of the ballot paper accounts;

(c) the tendered votes lists, the lists of blind voters assisted by companions, the lists of votes marked by the presiding officer and the statements relating thereto, and the declarations made by the companions of blind voters;

(d) the packets of counterfoils and certificates as to employment on duty on the day of the poll;

(e) the packets containing marked copies of registers and of lists of proxies,

a description of its contents, the date of the election to which they relate and the name of the ward for which the election was held.

Orders for production of documents

49.—(1) An order—

(a) for the inspection or production of any rejected ballot papers, including ballot papers rejected in part; or

(b) for the opening of a sealed packet of counterfoils and certificates as to employment on duty on the day of the poll or for the inspection of counted ballot papers,

may be made by either a county court having jurisdiction in the London Borough or any part thereof or an election court, if the court is satisfied by evidence on oath that the order is required for the purpose of instituting or maintaining a prosecution for an offence in relation to ballot papers, or for the purpose of an election petition.

(2) The order may be made subject to such conditions as to persons, time, place and mode of inspection, production or opening as the court making the order may think expedient and may direct the town clerk having custody of the ballot papers and the sealed packets of counterfoils and certificates to retain them intact for such period as may be specified in the order:

Provided that in making and carrying into effect the order, care shall be taken that the way in which the vote of any particular elector has been given shall not be disclosed until it has been proved that his vote was given and the vote has been declared by a competent court to be invalid.

(3) An appeal shall lie to the High Court from any order of a county court made under this rule.

(4) Any power given under this rule to a county court may be exercised by any judge of the court otherwise than in open court.

(5) Where an order is made for the production by the town clerk of any document in his possession relating to any specified election, the production by him or his agent of the document ordered, in such manner as may be directed by that order shall be conclusive evidence that the document relates to the specified election; and any endorsement on any packet of ballot papers so produced shall be prima facie evidence that the ballot papers are what they are stated to be by the endorsement.

(6) The production from proper custody of a ballot paper purporting to have been used at any election, and of a counterfoil marked with the same printed number and having a number marked thereon in writing, shall be prima facie evidence that the elector whose vote was given by that ballot paper was the person who at the time of the election has affixed to his name in the register of electors the same number as the number written on the counterfoil.

(7) Save as by this rule provided, no person shall be allowed to inspect any rejected or counted ballot papers in the possession of the town clerk or to open any sealed packets of counterfoils and certificates.

Retention and public inspection of documents

50.—(1) The town clerk shall retain for six months among the records of the London borough all documents relating to an election which were held by him as returning officer and then, unless otherwise directed by an order under the last foregoing rule, shall cause them to be destroyed.

(2) The said documents, except ballot papers, counterfoils and certificates as to employment on duty on the day of the poll, shall during a period of six months from the day of election be open to public inspection at such time and in such manner as may be determined by the council of the London borough with the consent of the Secretary of State.

(3) The town clerk shall, on request, supply copies of or extracts from the documents open to public inspection on payment of such fees, and subject to such conditions, as may be determined by the council of the London borough with the consent of the Secretary of State.

Supplemental provisions as to documents

51. Subject to the provisions of these rules, the town clerk shall, in respect of the custody and destruction of ballot papers and other documents coming into his possession in pursuance of these rules, be subject to the directions of the council of the London borough.

PART VI

SUPPLEMENTAL

General duty of returning officer

52. It shall be the general duty of the returning officer to do any act or thing that may be necessary for effectually conducting the election under these rules.

APPENDIX

Note.—The forms contained in this Appendix may be adapted so far as circumstances require.

Rule 15

BALLOT PAPER

Form of Front of Ballot Paper

Counterfoil
No.

The counterfoil is to have a number to correspond with that on the back of the Ballot Paper.

1 | **BROWN**
(JOHN EDWARD Brown, of 52 George Street, Bristol, merchant.)

2 | **BROWN**
(THOMAS WILLIAM Brown, of 136 London Road, Swindon, salesman.)

3 | **JONES**
(William David Jones, of High Elms, Wilts., gentleman.)

4 | **MERTON**
(Hon. George Travis, commonly called Viscount Merton of Swanworth, Berks.)

5 | **SMITH**
(Mary Smith, of 72 High Street, Bath, married woman.)

Form of Back of Ballot Paper

No.

Election for the   ward of the London borough of
              day of   , 19 .

Note.—The number on the ballot paper is to correspond with that on the counterfoil.

Directions as to printing the ballot paper

1. Nothing is to be printed on the ballot paper except in accordance with these directions.

2. So far as practicable, the following arrangements shall be observed in the printing of the ballot paper:—

(*a*) no word shall be printed on the face except the particulars of the candidates;

(b) no rule shall be printed on the face except the horizontal rules separating the particulars of the candidates from one another and the vertical rules separating those particulars from the numbers on the left-hand side and the spaces on the right where the vote is to be marked;

(c) the whole space between the top and bottom of the paper shall be equally divided between the candidates by the rules separating their particulars.

3. The surname of each candidate shall in all cases be printed by itself in large capitals, and his full particulars shall be set out below it and shall be printed in ordinary type except that small capitals shall be used—

(a) if his surname is the same as another candidate's, for his other names; and

(b) if his other names are also the same as the other candidate's, either for his residence or for his description unless each of them is the same as that of another candidate with the same surname and other names.

4. The number on the back of the ballot paper shall be printed in small characters.

Rule 25   DIRECTIONS FOR THE GUIDANCE OF THE VOTERS IN VOTING

1. The voter may vote for not more than   candidate(s).

2. The voter should see that the ballot paper, before it is handed to him, is stamped with the official mark.

3. The voter will go into one of the compartments and, with the pencil provided in the compartment, place a cross on the right-hand side of the ballot paper, opposite the name of each candidate for whom he votes, thus X.

4. The voter will then fold up the ballot paper so as to show the official mark on the back, and leaving the compartment will, without showing the front of the paper to any person, show the official mark on the back to the presiding officer, and then, in the presence of the presiding officer, put the paper into the ballot box, and forthwith leave the polling station.

5. If the voter inadvertently spoils a ballot paper he can return it to the officer, who will, if satisfied of such inadvertence, give him another paper.

6. If the voter votes for more than   candidate(s) or places any mark on the paper by which he may afterwards be identified, his ballot paper will be void, and will not be counted.

7. If the voter fraudulently takes a ballot paper out of a polling station or fraudulently puts into the ballot box any paper other than the one given to him by the officer, he will be liable on conviction to imprisonment for a term not exceeding six months, or to a fine not exceeding twenty pounds or to both such imprisonment and such fine.

Rule 35   DECLARATION TO BE MADE BY THE COMPANION OF A
                            BLIND VOTER

I, A.B., of   , having been requested to assist C.D. [in the case of a blind person voting as proxy add voting as proxy for G.H.], who is numbered on the register of local government electors for the ward of the London borough of   , to record his vote at the election now being held for the said ward, do hereby declare that [I am entitled to vote as an elector at the said election] [I am the*   of the said voter and have attained the age of twenty-one years] and that I have not previously assisted any blind person [except E.F., of   ] to vote at the said election.

(Signed) A. B.

day of   , 19 .

*State the relationship of the companion to the voter.

I, the undersigned, being the presiding officer for the polling station for the
ward of the London Borough of   do hereby
certify that the above declaration, having been first read to the above-named declarant
was signed by the declarant in my presence.

(Signed) X. Y.

          day of   , 19 , at   minutes past   o'clock
[a.m.] [p.m.]

Note.—*If the person making the above declaration knowingly and wilfully makes
therein a statement false in a material particular, he will be guilty of an offence.*

EXPLANATORY NOTE

(This Note is not part of the Rules.)

These Rules provide for the application of the local elections rules contained
in Schedule 2 to the Representation of the People Act 1949 to an election of
London borough councillors, subject to the necessary adaptations, alterations
and exceptions.

STATUTORY INSTRUMENTS

1968 No. 505 (S. 49)

MEDICAL PROFESSION

The Abortion (Scotland) Regulations 1968

Made - - -	*27th March* 1968
Laid before Parliament	*3rd April* 1968
Coming into Operation	*27th April* 1968

In exercise of the powers conferred on me by section 2 of the Abortion Act 1967(a), and of all other powers enabling me in that behalf, I hereby make the following regulations:—

Citation and commencement

1. These regulations may be cited as the Abortion (Scotland) Regulations 1968, and shall come into operation on 27th April 1968.

Interpretation

2.—(1) In these regulations "the Act" means the Abortion Act 1967 and "practitioner" means a registered medical practitioner.

(2) The Interpretation Act 1889(b) shall apply for the interpretation of these regulations as it applies for the interpretation of an Act of Parliament.

Certificate of opinion

3.—(1) Any opinion to which section 1 of the Act refers shall be certified in the appropriate form set out in Schedule 1 to these regulations.

(2) Any certificate of an opinion referred to in section 1(1) of the Act shall be given before the commencement of the treatment for the termination of the pregnancy to which it relates.

(3) Any certificate of an opinion referred to in section 1(4) of the Act shall be given before the commencement of the treatment for the termination of the pregnancy to which it relates or, if that is not reasonably practicable, not later than 24 hours after such termination.

(4) Any such certificate as is referred to in paragraphs (2) and (3) of this regulation shall be preserved by the practitioner who terminated the pregnancy to which it relates for a period of three years beginning with the date of such termination and may then be destroyed.

Notice of termination of pregnancy and information relating thereto

4.—(1) Any practitioner who terminates a pregnancy shall within seven days of the termination give to the Chief Medical Officer of the Scottish Home and Health Department notice thereof and the other information relating to the termination in the form set out in Schedule 2 to these regulations.

(a) 1967 c. 87.   (b) 1889 c. 63.

(2) Any such notice and information shall be sent in a sealed envelope to the Chief Medical Officer, Scottish Home and Health Department, St. Andrew's House, Edinburgh, 1.

Restriction on disclosure of information

5. A notice given or any information furnished to the Chief Medical Officer in pursuance of these regulations shall not be disclosed except that disclosure may be made:—

(a) for the purposes of carrying out his duties to an officer of the Scottish Home and Health Department authorised by the Chief Medical Officer of that Department; or

(b) for the purposes of carrying out his duties in relation to offences against the Act or the law relating to abortion, to the Lord Advocate or Procurator Fiscal or a member of the staff of either of them authorised by them; or

(c) for the purposes of investigating whether an offence has been committed against the Act or the law relating to abortion, to a police officer not below the rank of superintendent or a person authorised by him; or

(d) for the purposes of criminal proceedings which have begun; or

(e) for the purposes of bona fide scientific research; or

(f) to the practitioner who terminated the pregnancy; or

(g) to a practitioner, with the consent in writing of the woman whose pregnancy was terminated.

William Ross,
One of Her Majesty's
Principal Secretaries of State.

St. Andrew's House,
Edinburgh.
27th March 1968.

SCHEDULE 1

IN CONFIDENCE   **Certificate A**

*Not to be destroyed within three years of
the date of the operation*

ABORTION ACT 1967

CERTIFICATE TO BE COMPLETED IN RELATION TO ABORTION
UNDER SECTION 1(1) OF THE ACT

I, ...

(Name and qualifications of practitioner in block capitals)

of ....

....

(Full address of practitioner)

and I, ...

(Name and qualifications of practitioner in block capitals)

of ....

....

(Full address of practitioner)

hereby certify that we are of the opinion, formed in good faith, that in the

case of ....

(Full name of pregnant woman in block capitals)

of ....

....

(Usual place of residence of pregnant woman in block capitals)

(1)   the continuance of the pregnancy would involve risk to the life of the   (Ring
pregnant woman greater than if the pregnancy were terminated;   appropriate number(s))

(2)   the continuance of the pregnancy would involve risk of injury to the
physical or mental health of the pregnant woman greater than if
the pregnancy were terminated;

(3)   the continuance of the pregnancy would involve risk of injury to the
physical or mental health of the existing child(ren) of the family of
the pregnant woman greater than if the pregnancy were terminated;

(4)   there is a substantial risk that if the child were born it would suffer
from such physical or mental abnormalities as to be seriously
handicapped.

This certificate of opinion is given before the commencement of the treatment
for the termination of pregnancy to which it refers.

Signed ....

         Date ....

Signed ....

         Date ....

IN CONFIDENCE   **Certificate B**

*Not to be destroyed within three years of
the date of the operation*

ABORTION ACT 1967

CERTIFICATE TO BE COMPLETED IN RELATION TO ABORTION PERFORMED
IN EMERGENCY UNDER SECTION 1(4) OF THE ACT

I, ...

(Name and qualifications of practitioner in block capitals)

of ....

....

(Full address of practitioner)

hereby certify that I *am/was of the opinion formed in good faith that it *is/was
necessary immediately to terminate the pregnancy of

....

(Full name of pregnant woman in block capitals)

of ....

....

(Usual place of residence of pregnant woman in block capitals)

(Ring
appropriate
number)

in order (1) to save the life of the pregnant woman; or

(2) to prevent grave permanent injury to the physical or mental health
of the pregnant woman.

This certificate of opinion is given—

A. before the commencement of the treatment for the termination of the
pregnancy to which it relates; or, if that is not reasonably practicable,
then

B. not later than 24 hours after such termination.

Signed ....

Date...

*Delete as appropriate.

SCHEDULE 2

IN CONFIDENCE

ABORTION ACT 1967: ABORTION (SCOTLAND) REGULATIONS 1968

NOTIFICATION OF AN ABORTION PERFORMED
UNDER SECTION 1 OF THE ACT

I, ...
(Name and qualifications of practitioner)

of ....

BLOCK CAPITALS

....
(Full address of practitioner)

hereby give notice that I terminated the pregnancy of

....
(Full name of pregnant woman)

of ....

....
(Usual place of residence of pregnant woman)

The statutory grounds certified for terminating the pregnancy were:—

OTHERWISE THAN IN EMERGENCY

(1) the continuance of the pregnancy would have involved risk to the life of the pregnant woman greater than if the pregnancy were terminated; **(Ring appropriate number(s))**

(2) the continuance of the pregnancy would have involved risk of injury to the physical or mental health of the pregnant woman greater than if the pregnancy were terminated;

(3) the continuance of the pregnancy would have involved risk of injury to the physical or mental health of the existing child(ren) of the family of the pregnant woman greater than if the pregnancy were terminated;

(4) there was a substantial risk that if the child had been born it would have suffered from such physical or mental abnormalities as to be seriously handicapped;

IN CASE OF EMERGENCY

(5) it was necessary to save the life of the pregnant woman; *or*

(6) it was necessary to prevent grave permanent injury to the physical or mental health of the pregnant woman.

THE PREGNANCY WAS TERMINATED AT (to be completed for all terminations)

Name of hospital/approved place/other place ....
   (address) ....
   ....
   on (date) ....
Signature of practitioner who terminated pregnancy
....

   In all non-emergency cases, particulars of the practitioner(s) who joined in
giving the certificate required for the purposes of section 1 should be shown
below in the appropriate space(s):—

If the operating practitioner ⎫   A.   Name ....
joined in giving certificate   ⎪   Address ....
insert at A. particulars of   ⎬   ....
the other certifying   ⎪
practitioner.   ⎭

If the operating practitioner ⎫   B.   Name ....
did not join in giving   ⎪   Address ....
certificate insert at A. & B. ⎬   ....
particulars of the two   ⎪
certifying practitioners.   ⎭

   NOTE: This form is to be completed by the operating practitioner and sent
            within seven days of the termination of the pregnancy in a sealed
            envelope marked 'In confidence' to the Chief Medical Officer,
            Scottish Home and Health Department, St. Andrew's House,
            Edinburgh, 1.

Part II (ALL QUESTIONS TO BE ANSWERED
            to the best of the notifying practitioner's knowledge and belief)

ADDITIONAL PARTICULARS OF PATIENT

1.   Maiden surname ....
2.   Date of birth ....
3.   Hospital case reference number ....
4.   Marital status of woman:

       1. Single   2. Married   3. Widowed
            4. Divorced/separated   5. Not known
                    (Ring appropriate number)

5.   Husband's occupation ....
6.   Patient's occupation (if any) ....

PREVIOUS OBSTETRIC HISTORY   CURRENT PREGNANCY

7.   Total no. of pregnancies ....   13.   Estimated duration of gestation
8.   No. of live births.................................   ....
9.   No. of still births ....   14.   Date of admission for termin-
10. No. of abortions ....   ation ....
11. No. of surviving children ....   15.   Date of discharge (if known) ....
12. Date of last termination under Act (where applicable)...............................

SPECIFIC INDICATIONS FOR TERMINATION OF PREGNANCY
(Enter reasons in appropriate section(s) below)

16.   Obstetric and/or gynaecological conditions in mother...

17.   Other organic and/or psychiatric conditions in mother ....

18.   Risk of abnormality of foetus ....

19.   Medico-social reasons ....

20.   TYPE OF TERMINATION (ring appropriate number)
        1. Dilation and evacuation   2. Abdominal hysterotomy
        3. Vaginal hysterotomy   4. Vacuum aspiration
        5. Other (specify) ....

21. Was HYSTERECTOMY or OTHER STERILISATION carried out
(specify) ....

22. COMPLICATIONS PRIOR TO NOTIFICATION (ring appropriate
number(s))
    1. None   2. Sepsis   3. Haemorrhage
    4. Other (specify) ....

23.   In Case of DEATH specify cause ....

EXPLANATORY NOTE

(*This Note is not part of the regulations.*)

These regulations, made under the Abortion Act 1967,

    (*a*) prescribe forms for the purpose of certifying opinions under section 1 of the Act and the time for such certification (regulation 3(1), (2) and (3) and Schedule 1);

    (*b*) provide for the preservation and disposal of such certificates (regulation 3(4));

    (*c*) require the notification of the abortion and prescribe the information relevant thereto to be given to the Chief Medical Officer (regulation 4 and Schedule 2); and

    (*d*) restrict the disclosure of such notices and information (regulation 5).

STATUTORY INSTRUMENTS

1968 No. 514

AGRICULTURE

AGRICULTURAL AND HORTICULTURAL MARKETING

The Market Development Scheme (Extension of Period) Order 1968

Made	- - -	20th February 1968
Laid before Parliament		28th February 1968
Coming into Operation		27th March 1968

The Minister of Agriculture, Fisheries and Food and the Secretary of State, acting jointly in exercise of the powers conferred upon them by section 9(6) of the Agriculture (Miscellaneous Provisions) Act 1963(a), hereby make the following order:—

1. This order may be cited as the Market Development Scheme (Extension of Period) Order 1968; and shall come into operation on the day after it has been approved by resolution of each House of Parliament.

2. The period during which approvals may be given under section 9 of the Agriculture (Miscellaneous Provisions) Act 1963 (which relates to schemes for the payment of grants for the promotion of efficient marketing of agricultural and horticultural produce) was extended until the end of March 1968 by the Market Development Scheme (Extension of Period) Order 1965(b) and that period as so extended is hereby further extended until the end of March 1971.

In Witness whereof the Official Seal of the Minister of Agriculture, Fisheries and Food is hereunto affixed on 19th February 1968.

(L.S.)

Frederick Peart,
Minister of Agriculture, Fisheries and Food.

Given under the Seal of the Secretary of State for Scotland on 20th February 1968.

(L.S.)

William Ross,
Secretary of State for Scotland.

(a) 1963 c. 11.   (b) S.I.1965/638 (1965 I, p.2020).

EXPLANATORY NOTE

(This Note is not part of the order.)

The Market Development Scheme (Extension of Period) Order 1965 extended by three years, ending on 31st March 1968 the period during which approvals may be given by the appropriate Minister under section 9 of the Agriculture (Miscellaneous Provisions) Act 1963. This order further extends such period by three years, ending on 31st March 1971. These approvals relate to proposals under the Market Development Scheme 1964 (S.I. 1964/456) and any other such scheme under that section for grant-aiding the promotion of efficient marketing of agricultural and horticultural produce.

In accordance with section 9(10) of the Act, this order was approved by a resolution of the House of Commons on 26th March 1968 and a resolution of the House of Lords on 26th March 1968.

STATUTORY INSTRUMENTS

1968 No. 516 (S.50)

LOCAL GOVERNMENT, SCOTLAND
The Rate Support Grant (Increase) (Scotland) Order 1968

Made - - -		*4th March* 1968
Laid before the Commons		
House of Parliament		*7th March* 1968
Coming into Operation		*27th March* 1968

The Secretary of State, with the consent of the Treasury and after consultation with such associations of local authorities as appear to him to be concerned, in exercise of his powers under section 4 of the Local Government (Scotland) Act 1966(**a**) and of all other powers enabling him in that behalf, hereby makes the following order :—

1. This order may be cited as the Rate Support Grant (Increase) (Scotland) Order 1968 and shall come into operation on the day following the day on which it is approved by a resolution of the Commons House of Parliament.

2. The Interpretation Act 1889(**b**) shall apply for the interpretation of this order as it applies for the interpretation of an Act of Parliament.

3. For the amounts prescribed by the Rate Support Grant (Scotland) Order 1967(**c**) for the purposes of rate support grants for the years 1967-68 and 1968-69 in respect of the matters indicated in column (1) of the following table, being the amounts set out in column (2) thereof, there shall be substituted the amounts specified in column (3) thereof—

TABLE

column (1)	column (2) £	column (3) £
As the aggregate amount of rate support grants—		
For the year 1967-68	149,790,000	155,440,000
For the year 1968-69	159,210,000	167,740,000
As the amount of the needs element—		
For the year 1967-68	110,200,000	114,410,000
For the year 1968-69	115,060,000	121,380,000
As the amount of the resources element—		
For the year 1967-68	36,740,000	38,140,000
For the year 1968-69	38,350,000	40,460,000

(**a**) 1966 c. 51.   (**b**) 1889 c. 63.
(**c**) S.I. 1967/270 (1967 I, p. 981).

	column (1)	column (2) £	column (3) £
As the amount of the domestic element—			
For the year 1967-68		2,850,000	2,890,000
For the year 1968-69		5,800,000	5,900,000

WILLIAM ROSS,
One of Her Majesty's Principal
Secretaries of State.

St. Andrew's House,
Edinburgh, 1.
4th March 1968.

We consent.

B. K. O'MALLEY,
J. McCANN,
Two of the Lords Commissioners
4th March 1968.   of Her Majesty's Treasury.

EXPLANATORY NOTE

(This Note is not part of the Order.)

This order increases the aggregate amounts of the rate support grants and the amounts of the needs, resources and domestic elements payable for the years 1967-68 and 1968-69 under Part I of the Local Government (Scotland) Act 1966 to county and town councils in Scotland and replaces the order laid before the House of Commons on 21st December 1967.

STATUTORY INSTRUMENTS

1968 No. 523

ROAD TRAFFIC

The Motor Vehicles (Construction and Use) (Amendment) (No.3) Regulations 1968

Made - - -	*27th March* 1968
Laid before Parliament	*9th April* 1968
Coming into Operation	*30th April* 1968

The Minister of Transport, in exercise of her powers under section 64(1) of the Road Traffic Act 1960(a) as amended by section 51 of and Schedule 4 to the Road Traffic Act 1962(b), and of all other powers her enabling in that behalf, and after consultation with representative organisations in accordance with the provisions of section 260(2) of the said Act of 1960, hereby makes the following Regulations:—

1.—(1) These Regulations shall come into operation on the 30th April 1968 and may be cited as the Motor Vehicles (Construction and Use) (Amendment) (No. 3) Regulations 1968.

(2) The Interpretation Act 1889(c) shall apply for the interpretation of these Regulations as it applies for the interpretation of an Act of Parliament.

2. The Motor Vehicles (Construction and Use) Regulations 1966(d) as amended(e) shall have effect as though

(1) for Regulation 51 there were substituted the following Regulation:—

" *Seat belts and anchorage points.*

51.—(1) Except as provided by paragraph (2) of this Regulation, this Regulation applies:—

(a) to every motor car registered on or after 1st April 1967;

(b) on and after 30th June 1968 to every motor car registered on or after 1st January 1966; and

(c) on and after 31st December 1968 to every motor car registered on or after 1st January 1965.

(2) This Regulation does not apply:—

(a) to a goods vehicle unless it was constructed on or after 1st September 1966, is registered on or after 1st April 1967, and has an unladen weight not exceeding 30 hundredweight;

(b) to a passenger vehicle or a dual-purpose vehicle being in either case a vehicle adapted to carry more than twelve passengers exclusive of the driver;

(c) to a land tractor or a motor tractor;

(a) 8 & 9 Eliz. 2. c. 16.   (b) 10 & 11 Eliz. 2. c. 59.
(c) 52 & 53 Vict. c. 63.   (d) S.I. 1966/1288 (1966 III, p. 3493).
(e) The only relevant amending Instrument is S.I. 1967/1665 (1967 III, p. 4563).

(d) to a works truck;

(e) to an electrically propelled goods vehicle;

(f) to a pedestrian controlled vehicle;

(g) until 30th June 1968 to a vehicle constructed before 1st September 1966;

(h) to a vehicle in respect of which, under section 23 of the Purchase Tax Act 1963(a), any tax has been remitted and has not subsequently become payable;

(i) to a vehicle constructed before 30th June 1964; or

(j) to a vehicle which has been used on roads outside Great Britain and has been imported into Great Britain, whilst it is being driven after its importation into Great Britain on the journey from the place where it has arrived in Great Britain to a place of residence of the owner or driver of the vehicle, and on the journey from any such place to a place where, by previous arrangement, the vehicle will be provided with such anchorage points and seat belts as will comply with the requirements of this Regulation.

(3) Every motor car to which this Regulation applies shall be provided with anchorage points designed to hold body-restraining seat belts securely in position on the vehicle for—

(a) the driver's seat; and

(b) the specified passenger's seat:

Provided that this paragraph shall not apply so as to require anchorage points to be provided for any seat which is a seat with integral seat belt anchorages.

(4) Every motor car to which this Regulation applies shall be provided with—

(a) a body-restraining seat belt designed for use by an adult for the driver's seat; and

(b) a body-restraining seat belt for the specified passenger's seat:

Provided that this paragraph shall not apply to a vehicle—

(a) while it is being used under a trade licence within the meaning of the Vehicles (Excise) Act 1962(b); or

(b) while it is being driven from premises of the manufacturer by whom it was made, or of a distributor of vehicles or dealer in vehicles—

(i) to premises of a distributor of vehicles, dealer in vehicles or purchaser thereof, or

(ii) to premises of a person obtaining possession thereof under a hiring agreement or hire-purchase agreement.

(5) Every seat belt provided in pursuance of this Regulation shall, if the seat for which it is provided is a seat with integral seat belt anchorages, be properly secured to the integral seat belt anchorage points forming part thereof, or, if the seat for which it is provided is not such a seat, be properly secured to the structure of the vehicle by the anchorage points provided for it under paragraph (3) of this Regulation.

(6) (a) Every vehicle constructed on or after 1st September 1966 and

_____

(a) 1963 c. 9.   (b) 10 & 11 Eliz. 2. c. 13.

registered on or after 1st April 1967 which is provided with seat belt anchorage points in pursuance of paragraph (3) of this Regulation shall be legibly and permanently marked with the specification number of the British Standard for seat belt anchorage points, namely B.S. AU48: 1965;

(b) where in the case of any motor car to which this Regulation applies and which was registered on or after 1st April 1967 the driver's seat or the specified passenger's seat is a seat with integral seat belt anchorages, such seat shall be legibly and permanently marked with the specification number of the British Standard for Seats with Integral Seat Belt Anchorages followed by the suffix " 1 ", namely B.S. AU140/1: 1967;

(c) if any seat with integral seat belt anchorages is provided on or after 1st January 1969 for a motor car to which this Regulation applies and which was constructed on or after 1st September 1966 and registered on or after 1st April 1967 the vehicle for which it is so provided shall be legibly and permanently marked with the said specification number, namely B.S. AU140: 1967; and

(d) each seat belt provided for any person in any motor car to which this Regulation applies shall be legibly and permanently marked with the specification number of the British Standard for Seat Belt Assemblies for Motor Vehicles namely B.S 3254: 1960, and the registered certification trade mark of the British Standards Institution.

(7) Nothing in this Regulation shall be taken to authorise any person to apply a specification number or registered certification trade mark to a vehicle, seat or seat belt in contravention of the Merchandise Marks Act 1887 to 1953(a).

(8) In this Regulation—
" body-restraining seat belt " means a seat belt designed to provide restraint for both the upper and lower parts of the trunk of the wearer in the event of an accident to the vehicle;
" seat belt " means a belt intended to be worn by a person in a vehicle and designed to prevent or lessen injury to its wearer in the event of an accident to the vehicle and includes, in the case of a restraining device for a young person, any special chair to which the belt is attached; and
" specified passenger's seat " means—

(a) in the case of a vehicle which has one forward-facing front seat alongside the driver's seat, such seat, and in the case of a vehicle which has more than one such seat, the one furthest from the driver's seat; or

(b) if the vehicle has no seat which is the specified passenger's seat under the last preceding sub-paragraph, the forward-facing front seat for a passenger which is foremost in the vehicle and furthest from the driver's seat, unless there is a fixed partition separating such seat from the space in front of it alongside the driver's seat."; and

(2) in Regulation 95, in the proviso, after paragraph (b), there were added the following paragraph:—

(a) 50 & 51 Vict. c. 28; 54 & 55 Vict. c. 15; 57 & 58 Vict. c. 19; 1 & 2 Geo. 5. c. 31; 16 & 17 Geo. 5. c. 53; 1 & 2 Eliz. 2. c. 48.

" or (c) a vehicle when it is being used for police or ambulance purposes.".

Given under the Official Seal of the Minister of Transport the 27th March 1968.

(L.S.)

Barbara Castle,
Minister of Transport,

EXPLANATORY NOTE

(This Note is not part of the Regulations.)

These Regulations further amend the Motor Vehicles (Construction and Use) Regulations 1966, as amended, by:—

(1) (a) extending (except in the case of light vans) the existing requirement that most motor cars first registered on or after 1st April 1967 shall be provided with anchorage points and seat belts for the driver and front seat passenger, (i) on and after 30th June 1968, to vehicles first registered on or after 1st January 1966, and (ii) on and after 31st December 1968, to vehicles first registered on or after 1st January 1965; and

(b) exempting used imported vehicles from the requirement to have anchorage points and seat belts while they are being driven from the place of their arrival in Great Britain to a residence of the owner or driver of the vehicle and from there to a place where, by previous arrangement, anchorage points and seat belts are to be provided (Regulation 2(1)); and

(2) exempting vehicles being used for police or ambulance purposes from the prohibition in Regulation 95 against an unattended vehicle having its engine running (Regulation 2(2)).

STATUTORY INSTRUMENTS

1968 No. 524

SOCIAL SECURITY

The Family Allowances, National Insurance and Industrial Injuries (Consequential) Regulations 1968

Made - - - -	*29th March* 1968
Laid before Parliament	*4th April* 1968
Coming into Operation	*8th April* 1968

The Minister of Social Security, acting in conjunction with the Treasury, in exercise of the powers conferred by the provisions set out in column 1 of the Schedule to these regulations, and the National Insurance Joint Authority and the Industrial Injuries Joint Authority in exercise of the powers respectively conferred by the provisions set out in columns 2 and 3 of that Schedule, in each case in consequence of the Family Allowances and National Insurance Act 1967(a) and of all other powers enabling them in that behalf, hereby make the following regulations:—

PART I

GENERAL

Citation, commencement and interpretation

1.—(1) These regulations may be cited as the Family Allowances, National Insurance and Industrial Injuries (Consequential) Regulations 1968, and shall come into operation on 8th April 1968.

(2) In these regulations, unless the context otherwise requires—

" the Insurance Act " means the National Insurance Act 1965(b);

" the Industrial Injuries Act " means the National Insurance (Industrial Injuries) Act 1965(c);

" the 1967 Act " means the Family Allowances and National Insurance Act 1967;

"family allowance" means an allowance payable under the Family Allowances Act 1965(d);

and other expressions have the same meaning as in the Insurance Act, the Industrial Injuries Act or the Family Allowances Act 1965, as the case may require.

(3) References in these regulations to any enactment or regulation shall, except in so far as the context otherwise requires, be construed as references to that enactment or regulation as amended or extended by or under any other enactment, order or regulation.

(4) The rules for the construction of Acts of Parliament contained in the Interpretation Act 1889(e) shall apply for the purpose of the interpretation of these regulations as they apply for the purpose of the interpretation of an Act of Parliament.

(a) 1967 c. 90.   (b) 1965 c. 51.   (c) 1965 c. 52.   (d) 1965 c. 53.
(e) 1889 c. 63.

PART II

NATIONAL INSURANCE

Amendments of the National Insurance (General Benefit) Regulations

2.—(1) The National Insurance (General Benefit) Regulations 1948(a), as amended(b), (hereinafter in this regulation called " the General Benefit Regulations "), shall be further amended in accordance with the following provisions of this regulation.

(2) After regulation 5A of the General Benefit Regulations, there shall be inserted the following regulation: —

" Children treated as included in a family for increase of certain benefits

5B. For the purposes of section 41(3) of the National Insurance Act 1965 (treating certain children as included in a man's family for the purpose of an increase of unemployment benefit, sickness benefit or a retirement pension) the prescribed rate shall be a rate equal to the amount for the time being specified in column 5 of Schedule 3 to the said Act in relation to the benefit in question, being the amount of the increase for a third or additional qualifying child."

(3) For paragraph (2) of regulation 5C of the General Benefit Regulations, there shall be substituted the following paragraph: —

" (2) Where, for the purposes of section 40 of the National Insurance Act 1965, a person has a family which includes children, one or more of whom is, or are, treated as included in his family only by virtue of the provisions of section 41(3) of that Act (which child or children are hereafter in this paragraph referred to as a " treated child " or " treated children "), and there is, or are, also another child or other children living with that person who is, or are, included or treated as included in his family otherwise than by virtue of the said section 41(3) (which child or children are hereafter in this paragraph referred to as the " said other child or children "), that person shall in relation to an increase of sickness benefit, unemployment benefit or retirement pension in respect of a treated child be deemed to be contributing to the cost of providing for that child for the purposes of section 42(1)(b) of that Act at a weekly rate not less than that required in the case of that child by that section if he contributes to the cost of providing for that child at a rate not less than the rate which would be appropriate in the circumstances of the case if the said other child or children were older than the treated child or (if there is more than one treated child) any of the treated children."

(4) Regulation 5B of the General Benefit Regulations shall apply in relation to an increase of retirement pension with effect from 8th April 1968 and in relation to an increase of unemployment benefit or sickness benefit with effect from 10th April 1968.

Amendment of the National Insurance (Widows Benefit and Retirement Pensions) Regulations

3. For paragraph (1) of regulation 6 of the National Insurance (Widows Benefit and Retirement Pensions) Regulations 1948(c), as amended(d), there shall be substituted the following paragraph: —

(a) S.I. 1948/1278 (Rev. XVI, p. 179: 1948 I, p. 2626).   (b) The relevant amending instruments are S.I. 1966/388, 1967/1228 (1966 I, p. 875; 1967 II, p. 3579).
(c) S.I. 1948/1261 (Rev. XVI, p. 207: 1948 I, p. 2704).   (d) The relevant amending instruments are S.I. 1963/394, 1965/40, 1967/1228 (1963 I, p. 424; 1965 I, p. 47; 1967 II, p. 3579).

" Priority between a man and his wife to increase of retirement pension for a child

6.—(1) Where but for Section 41(4)(*b*) of the National Insurance Act 1965 a man and his wife would, for the same period, both be entitled to an increase under Section 40(1) of that Act in respect of the same child or, in respect of different children, to such an increase at the rate applicable to an only, elder or eldest child, or to such an increase at the rate applicable to a second child, the following provisions shall apply : —

(*a*) if and so long as the man and his wife are living together, the man shall, and his wife shall not, be entitled to the increase, or, as the case may be, to the increase at the rate applicable to an only, elder or eldest child or the increase at the rate applicable to a second child ;

(*b*) if and so long as they are not living together such one of them shall, and such other of them shall not, be entitled to the increase or, as the case may be, to the increase at the rate applicable to an only, elder or eldest child or the increase at the rate applicable to a second child, as the Minister may in his discretion from time to time determine."

PART III

INDUSTRIAL INJURIES

Amendments of the National Insurance (Industrial Injuries) (Benefit) Regulations

4.—(1) The National Insurance (Industrial Injuries) (Benefit) Regulations 1964(**a**), as amended(**b**), (hereinafter in this regulation called " the Benefit Regulations ") shall be further amended in accordance with the following provisions of this regulation : —

(2) In regulation 4(2)(*b*) of the Benefit Regulations (injury benefit rates for children of school age), for the figure £1 5s. 0d. there shall be substituted the figure £1 8s. 0d.

(3) After regulation 12 of the Benefit Regulations there shall be inserted the following regulation : —

" Children treated as included in family for increase of certain benefits

13. For the purposes of section 17(3) of the National Insurance (Industrial Injuries) Act 1965 (treating certain children as included in a man's family for the purpose of an increase of injury benefit or disablement pension) the prescribed rate shall be a rate equal to the amount for the time being specified in Schedule 3, paragraph 7, sub-paragraph (*c*) to the said Act, being the amount of the increase for an additional child of the beneficiary's family after the second."

(4) For paragraph (2) of regulation 14 of the Benefit Regulations (contribution towards cost of providing for child) there shall be substituted the following paragraph : —

" (2) Where for the purposes of section 17(1) of the National Insurance (Industrial Injuries) Act 1965, a person has a family which includes children, one or more of whom is, or are, treated as included in his family only by virtue of the provisions of section 17(3) of that Act (which child or children are hereafter in this paragraph referred to as a " treated child " or " treated children "), and there is, or are, also another child

(**a**) S.I. 1964/504 (1964 I, p. 833).   (**b**) The relevant amending instruments are S.I. 1966/389, 1967/1223, 1228 (1966 I, p. 876; 1967 II, pp. 3565, 3579).

or other children living with that person who is, or are, included or treated as included in his family otherwise than by virtue of the said section 17(3) (which child or children are hereafter in this paragraph referred to as the " said other child or children "), that person shall in relation to an increase of injury benefit or disablement pension in respect of a treated child be deemed to be contributing to the cost of providing for that child for the purposes of section 17(4)(*b*) of that Act at a weekly rate not less than that required in the case of that child by that section if he contributes to the cost of providing for that child at a rate not less than the rate which would be appropriate in the circumstances of the case if the said other child or children were older than the treated child or (if there is more than one treated child) any of the treated children."

(5) For regulation 25 of the Benefit Regulations there shall be substituted the following regulation: —

" *Priority of title to allowance or allowances under section* 21

25. Where in respect of the same death each of two or more persons satisfies the conditions of section 21 of the Act for the receipt of—

(*a*) an allowance in respect of the same child ; or

(*b*) an allowance at the rate applicable to an only, elder or eldest child in respect of different children ; or

(*c*) an allowance at the rate applicable to a second child in respect of different children ;

the person entitled to the allowance, or, as the case may be, the allowance at the rate applicable to an only, elder or eldest child or the allowance at the rate applicable to a second child, shall as between such persons be determined, subject to the provisions of Schedule 5, paragraph 1(*c*), of the Act (priority of title to such an allowance of a person who is entitled to death benefit as the widow or widower of the deceased), in accordance with the order of priority specified in Schedule 8 to these regulations ".

PART IV

MISCELLANEOUS AND TRANSITIONAL PROVISIONS

Persons not ordinarily resident in Great Britain

5.—(1) Notwithstanding the provisions of these or any other regulations, but subject to the provisions of this regulation, a person who is not ordinarily resident in Great Britain immediately before 9th April 1968 (in this regulation referred to as " the said date ") shall, unless and until that person becomes ordinarily resident in Great Britain, be disqualified for receiving in respect of any child: —

(*a*) in the case of a woman who immediately before the said date is a married woman and had not retired from regular employment, any additional retirement pension by virtue of her husband's insurance, if the husband before the said date had retired from regular employment and was not ordinarily resident in Great Britain ;

(*b*) in the case of a woman who immediately before the said date is a widow, any additional retirement pension by virtue of her husband's insurance, if her husband had died before the said date ;

(c) in any other case, any additional retirement pension (not. being additional retirement pension to which either of the two foregoing subparagraphs apply) if that person had retired from regular employment before the said date:

Provided that the disqualification for the receipt of additional retirement pension contained in this sub-paragraph shall not apply to a woman in relation to a retirement pension by virtue of her husband's insurance, if that husband had not retired from regular employment before the said date and either—

(i) he was her husband immediately before that date, or

(ii) she married him on or after that date ;

(d) any additional widow's benefit, if her husband had died or retired before the said date ;

(e) any additional child's special allowance, if her former husband had died before the said date.

(2) Notwithstanding as aforesaid, if immediately before the said date a person is not ordinarily resident in Great Britain but that person has, or would, but for the absence of any child from Great Britain, have in his family immediately before the said date a child in relation to whom the conditions for guardian's allowance specified in section 29 of the Insurance Act are satisfied, that person and any other person who would otherwise be entitled to any additional guardian's allowance in respect of that child shall be disqualified for receiving any additional guardian's allowance in respect of that child unless and until the child becomes (or is) included in the family of a person who is ordinarily resident in Great Britain.

(3) A widow who—

(a) is not ordinarily resident in Great Britain immediately before the said date, and was entitled to widow's benefit immediately before attaining pensionable age, or who would, but for any provision of the Insurance Act disqualifying her for the receipt of such benefit have been so entitled ; and

(b) is or becomes entitled to a retirement pension by virtue of her own insurance the right to which is calculated by taking into account under section 33 of the Insurance Act, her husband's contributions ;

shall be disqualified for receiving any additional retirement pension in respect of any child the right to which is so calculated unless and until she becomes ordinarily resident in Great Britain—

(i) if her husband died before the said date ; or

(ii) if before the said date he had retired from regular employment and was not ordinarily resident in Great Britain.

(4) The disqualification for the receipt of additional benefit contained in this regulation shall not apply to a person for any period during which he is in Great Britain.

(5) For the purposes of this regulation references to additional benefit of any description in respect of any child are to be construed as referring to additional benefit of that description in respect of that child under the Insurance Act by virtue (either directly or indirectly) of section 1(2) (modified rates of benefit) of the 1967 Act.

(6) In regulation 5 of the National Insurance (Increase of Benefit and Miscellaneous Provisions) Regulations 1967(a) (which contains provisions corresponding to the foregoing provisions of this regulation) there shall, as from the said date, be inserted, at the end of paragraph (1)(c), the following : —

(a) S.I. 1967/1265 (1967 II, p. 3673).

" Provided that the disqualification for the receipt of additional retirement pension contained in this sub-paragraph shall not apply to a woman in relation to a retirement pension by virtue of her husband's insurance, if that husband had not retired from regular employment before the said date and either—

(i) he was her husband immediately before that date, or

(ii) she married him on or after that date."

Continuation of previous rates of benefit

6.—(1) In this regulation—

" benefit " means a retirement pension, widow's allowance, widowed mother's allowance or child's special allowance under the Insurance Act or an allowance under section 21 of the Industrial Injuries Act (death benefit in respect of children) ;

" continuing beneficiary " means a person who, being entitled to receive any benefit in respect of any child or children immediately before the qualifying date, continues without a break to be entitled to receive benefit in respect of that child or both or all those children (as the case may be) and does not become so entitled in respect of any other child or children ;

" eldest child " means a child in respect of whom a continuing beneficiary is entitled to benefit at a rate applicable to an only, elder or eldest child ;

" old rate " means a rate of benefit or of family allowance in force at the passing of the 1967 Act ;

" payable " means payable to the continuing beneficiary or to any other person and, in relation to a family allowance, includes an allowance which would be, or would have been, so payable if duly claimed ;

" period " means a continuous period commencing with the qualifying date ; and

" qualifying date ", in relation to a continuing beneficiary, means the earliest day on which any weekly rate of benefit to which he is then entitled is, or but for the provisions of this regulation would be, reduced by the operation of section 1 of the 1967 Act.

(2) For any period during which the aggregate weekly rate of—

(*a*) the benefit in respect of children to which a continuing beneficiary would but for the provisions of this regulation be entitled, and

(*b*) the family allowances payable in respect of the same children,

is less than it would have been if the old rates had continued in force, the reductions in benefit rates under section 1 of the 1967 Act shall be excluded in his case to the extent necessary to enable effect to be given to the following paragraph :

Provided that this paragraph shall not, save in such cases as the Minister in his discretion may permit, have effect in relation to a person who does not before 9th October 1968 give to the Minister notice in writing that he is or claims to be a person entitled to the continuation of an old rate of benefit.

(3) During any period during which the foregoing paragraph has effect in relation to a continuing beneficiary, the weekly rate of benefit to which he is entitled in respect of each child (other than an eldest child) successively according to age shall be such sum as—

(*a*) does not exceed that which would have been applicable —

(i) if the old rates had continued in force, and

(ii) if he had not become entitled in respect of that child (where he has so become) to any benefit of which immediately before the qualifying date the rate was higher than that of the benefit to which he was then entitled, but had instead continued to be entitled to the benefit to which he was then entitled ; and

(b) suffices, so far as possible, to secure that the aggregate weekly rate of—

(i) the benefit to which he is entitled in respect of that child and any older children, and

(ii) the benefit to which he would be entitled in respect of any children younger than that child if this regulation did not affect the rate thereof, and

(iii) the family allowances payable in respect of all the children in respect of whom he is entitled to benefit,

is not less than the aggregate weekly rate of the benefit to which he would be entitled in respect of all those children and of the family allowances which would be payable in respect of them if the old rates had continued in force.

Effect of existing awards of family allowances

7. Where a family allowance previously awarded has not terminated by 9th April 1968, and the award does not provide for it to be paid as from that date at the rate provided for by the 1967 Act, it shall not become payable at that rate for any period before—

(a) the expiry of any book of allowance orders for the payment of sums on account of that allowance which is current at that date ; or

(b) 8th April 1969 if there is no such book ;

save in so far as sums on account thereof are made receivable before 9th October 1969.

Condition relating to payment of additional benefit under awards made before changes in rates take effect

8.—(1) Where an award of any benefit under the Insurance Act or the Industrial Injuries Act, the weekly rate of which is affected by the 1967 Act, has been made before the date when the change in the weekly rate takes effect and the award does not provide in accordance with sub-paragraph (2) of paragraph 3 of Schedule 3 to the 1967 Act for the benefit to be paid as from the date when the change in the weekly rate takes effect at the rate appropriate under or by virtue of that Act, paragraph 3 of Schedule 3 to the 1967 Act shall, if the period to which the award relates has not ended before the said date, have effect subject to the condition set out in the following paragraph.

(2) Notwithstanding the provisions of regulation 12 of the National Insurance (Claims and Payments) Regulations 1948(a), as amended(b), or regulation 20 of the National Insurance (Industrial Injuries) (Claims and Payments) Regulations 1964(c), as amended(d) (extinguishment of the right to sums payable by way of benefit), the right to any sum which, by virtue of the said paragraph 3 of Schedule 3, becomes payable under the award by way of additional benefit shall, as respects the period beginning with the said date and ending—

(a) S.I. 1948/1041 (Rev. XVI, p. 313: 1948 I, p. 2709). (b) The relevant amending instruments are S.I. 1952/1207, 1957/578, 1961/557 (1952 II, p. 2122; 1957 I, p. 1516; 1961 I, p. 1228). (c) S.I. 1964/73 (1964 I. p. 115).
(d) There is no amendment which relates expressly to the subject matter of these regulations.

(*a*) in a case where a book of serial orders (as defined in regulation 1(2) of the said Regulations) for the payment of benefit to which the award relates has been issued to the beneficiary and is current on the said date, with the date of the expiration of that book ; or

(*b*) in any other case with the expiration of 12 months from the said date ;

be extinguished if payment thereof is not obtained within the period of 18 months (or such longer period as the Minister may determine in the circumstances of any particular case) from the said date.

Given under the official seal of the National Insurance Joint Authority.

(L.S.)

D. J. Carter,
Secretary,
National Insurance Joint Authority.

27th March 1968.

Given under the official seal of the Industrial Injuries Joint Authority.

(L.S.)

D. J. Carter,
Secretary,
Industrial Injuries Joint Authority.

27th March 1968.

Judith Hart,
Minister of Social Security.

27th March 1968.

E. Alan Fitch,
B. K. O'Malley,
Two of the Lords Commissioners
of Her Majesty's Treasury.

29th March 1968.

SCHEDULE
POWERS EXERCISED IN MAKING THESE REGULATIONS

Minister of Social Security (1)	National Insurance Joint Authority (2)	Industrial Injuries Joint Authority (3)
The National Insurance Act 1965, sections 41(3) and 49(1); the National Insurance (Industrial Injuries) Act 1965, section 17(3); the Family Allowances and National Insurance Act 1967, Schedule 3, paragraphs 2(1), 3(1) and 6.	The National Insurance Act 1965, sections 41(4) and 55(1).	The National Insurance (Industrial Injuries) Act 1965, sections 34(1), 78(2) and Schedule 5, paragraph 1(d).

EXPLANATORY NOTE

(This Note is not part of the Regulations.)

These Regulations are made in consequence of the Family Allowances and National Insurance Act 1967 and in accordance with Schedule 3 paragraph 7 of that Act have not been referred to the National Insurance Advisory Committee or the Industrial Injuries Advisory Council.

Part I of the Regulations contains provisions relating to their interpretation ; Part II makes consequential amendments to provisions of the National Insurance (General Benefit) Regulations and the National Insurance (Widows Benefit and Retirement Pensions) Regulations relating to increases of certain benefits payable in respect of children ; Part III increases the rate of injury benefit payable to children of school age and makes amendments to the National Insurance (Industrial Injuries) (Benefit) Regulations corresponding with those made in Part II ; and Part IV contains miscellaneous and transitional provisions, in particular provisions relating to persons not ordinarily resident in Great Britain and to continuation of previous rates of benefit in special cases.

STATUTORY INSTRUMENTS

1968 No. 525

WAGES COUNCILS

The Wages Regulation (Milk Distributive) (England and Wales) Order 1968

Made - - - -	*28th March* 1968
Coming into Operation	*28th April* 1968

Whereas the Minister of Labour (hereafter in this Order referred to as "the Minister") has received from the Milk Distributive Wages Council (England and Wales) the wages regulation proposals set out in the Schedule hereto;

Now, therefore, the Minister by virtue of the powers conferred on him by section 11 of the Wages Councils Act 1959(a), and of all other powers enabling him in that behalf, hereby makes the following Order:—

1. This Order may be cited as the Wages Regulation (Milk Distributive) (England and Wales) Order 1968.

2.—(1) In this Order the expression "the specified date" means the 28th April 1968, provided that where, as respects any worker who is paid wages at intervals not exceeding seven days, that date does not correspond with the beginning of the period for which the wages are paid, the expression "the specified date" means, as respects that worker, the beginning of the next such period following that date.

(2) The Interpretation Act 1889(b) shall apply to the interpretation of this Order as it applies to the interpretation of an Act of Parliament and as if this Order and the Order hereby revoked were Acts of Parliament.

3. The wages regulation proposals set out in the Schedule hereto shall have effect as from the specified date and as from that date the Wages Regulation (Milk Distributive) (England and Wales) Order 1966(c) shall cease to have effect.

Signed by order of the Minister of Labour.

28th March 1968.

> *D. C. Barnes,*
> Secretary,
> Ministry of Labour.

ARRANGEMENT OF SCHEDULE

PART I

STATUTORY MINIMUM REMUNERATION

	Paragraphs
General	1
General minimum time rates	2–3
Workers on two or more areas	4
Overtime	5
Work on a customary holiday	6–7
Waiting time	8
Overtime being night work	9
Night work	10

(a) 1959 c. 69.　　　　　(b) 1889 c. 63.
(c) S.I. 1966/1516 (1966 III, p. 4203).

PART II

HOLIDAYS AND HOLIDAY REMUNERATION

PART III

GENERAL

SCHEDULE

The following minimum remuneration and provisions as to holidays and holiday remuneration shall be substituted for the statutory minimum remuneration and the provisions as to holidays and holiday remuneration fixed by the Wages Regulation (Milk Distributive) (England and Wales) Order 1966(a) (Order M.D. (107)).

PART I

STATUTORY MINIMUM REMUNERATION

GENERAL

1.—(1) The minimum remuneration payable to a worker to whom this Schedule applies is the sum of the amounts calculated in accordance with the provisions of (a)(i) or (a)(ii) and (b) and (c) below:—

(a) For all work except overtime,

(i) in the case of a time worker, the amount yielded by the hourly general minimum time rate applicable to the worker under the provisions of this Schedule; or,

(ii) in the case of a worker employed on piece work, the amount yielded by piece rates, each of which would yield, in the circumstances of the case, to an ordinary worker at least the same amount of money as the hourly general minimum time rate which would be applicable if the worker were a time worker;

(b) For all overtime including work on a customary holiday and any waiting time, the amount payable under paragraphs 5, 6, 7, 8 and 9; and

(c) Any further amount payable under paragraph 10.

(2) In this Schedule the expression "hourly general minimum time rate" means the general minimum time rate applicable to the worker under the provisions of the paragraphs 2, 3 and 4 divided by 42.

(a) S.I. 1966/1516 (1966 III, p. 4203).

GENERAL MINIMUM TIME RATES

MALE WORKERS

2. The general minimum time rates applicable to male workers employed in Area A, Area B or Area C are respectively as follows:—

	Area A	Area B	Area C
	Per week	Per week	Per week
	s. d.	s. d.	s. d.
(1) Foreman	246 6	252 0	258 6
(2) Sterilizers (other than assistant sterilizers), being workers aged 21 years or over	232 6	235 6	239 6
(3) Clerks, being workers aged:—			
21 years or over	232 6	235 6	239 6
20 and under 21 years	203 6	206 0	209 6
19 ,, ,, 20 ,, ...	186 6	188 6	191 6
18 ,, ,, 19 ,, ...	168 6	170 6	173 6
17 ,, ,, 18 ,, ...	139 6	141 6	143 6
16 ,, ,, 17 ,, ...	122 0	123 6	125 6
Under 16 years	110 6	112 0	114 0
(4) Rounds Salesmen, being workers aged:—			
21 year or over	237 6	240 0	244 0
20 and under 21 years	214 0	216 0	219 6
19 ,, ,, 20 ,, ...	196 0	198 0	201 6
18 ,, ,, 19 ,, ...	178 0	180 0	183 0
Under 18 years	154 6	156 0	158 6
(5) Shop Assistants, Assistant Rounds Salesmen, Pasteurizers, Assistant Sterilizers, and **Any Other Workers** not specified in the foregoing provisions of this Table, being workers aged:—			
21 year or over	228 0	230 6	234 6
20 and under 21 years	199 6	201 6	205 0
19 ,, ,, 20 ,, ...	182 6	184 6	187 6
18 ,, ,, 19 ,, ...	165 6	167 0	170 0
17 ,, ,, 18 ,, ...	137 0	138 6	140 6
16 ,, ,, 17 ,, ...	119 6	121 0	123 0
Under 16 years	108 6	109 6	111 6

FEMALE WORKERS

3. The general minimum time rates applicable to female workers employed in Area A, Area B or Area C are respectively as follows:—

	Area A	Area B	Area C
	Per week	Per week	Per week
	s. d.	s. d.	s. d.
(1) Rounds Saleswomen, being workers aged:—			
21 years or over	224 0	226 0	231 6
20 and under 21 years	201 6	203 6	208 6
19 ,, ,, 20 ,,	185 0	186 6	191 0
18 ,, ,, 19 ,,	168 0	169 6	173 6
Under 18 years	145 6	147 0	150 6
(2) Clerks, being workers aged:—			
21 years or over	180 0	180 6	187 0
20 and under 21 years	166 6	167 0	173 0
19 ,, ,, 20 ,,	153 0	153 6	159 0
18 ,, ,, 19 ,,	139 6	140 0	145 0
17 ,, ,, 18 ,,	121 6	122 0	126 0
16 ,, ,, 17 ,,	108 0	108 6	112 0
Under 16 years	94 6	95 0	98 0
(3) All Other Workers, being workers aged:—			
21 years or over	180 6	182 0	186 0
20 and under 21 years	167 0	168 6	172 0
19 ,, ,, 20 ,,	153 6	154 6	158 0
18 ,, ,, 19 ,,	140 0	141 0	144 0
17 ,, ,, 18 ,,	122 0	123 0	125 6
16 ,, ,, 17 ,,	108 6	109 0	111 6
Under 16 years	95 0	95 6	97 6

MALE OR FEMALE WORKERS IN TWO OR MORE AREAS

4. The general minimum time rate applicable to any worker in any week in which he works in Area A, Area B and Area C or in any two of those areas is:—

(1) in the case of a rounds salesman or rounds saleswomen, the rate which would be applicable if he worked solely in that Area in which is served the majority of the customers on his round;

(2) in the case of any other worker, the rate which would be applicable if he worked solely at his depot.

OVERTIME, WORK ON A CUSTOMARY HOLIDAY AND WAITING TIME

OVERTIME

5. Subject to the provisions of paragraph 9, the following minimum remuneration is payable to any worker for overtime:—

(1) On any week day, not being a rest day or a customary holiday, for all time worked in excess of 8½ hours ... ... time-and-a-half

(2) On a Sunday, not being a rest day or a customary holiday—

(*a*) for any time worked not exceeding 5 hours   ...   time-and-a-half for 5 hours

(*b*) for all time worked in excess of 5 hours   ...   time-and-a-half

(3) On a Sunday, being also a rest day but not being a customary holiday—

(*a*) for any time worked not exceeding 6 hours   ...   double time for 6 hours

(*b*) for all time worked in excess of 6 hours   ...   double time

(4) On a rest day, not being a Sunday or a customary holiday, for all time worked   ...   .   time-and-a-half

WORK ON A CUSTOMARY HOLIDAY

6. Subject to the provisions of paragraphs 7 and 9, the following minimum remuneration is payable for work on a customary holiday:—

(1) To any worker who normally works for an employer for not less than 21 hours per week—

(*a*) On a customary holiday not being the worker's rest day—

(i) for any time worked not exceeding 6 hours   double time for 6 hours

(ii) for all time worked in excess of 6 hours   double time

(*b*) On a customary holiday being also the worker's rest day—

(i) for any time worked not exceeding 6 hours   treble time for 6 hours

(ii) for all time worked in excess of 6 hours   treble time

(2) To all other workers—
for all time worked   ...   .   double time

7. Where a worker to whom the provisions of paragraph 11 apply is required to work on a customary holiday, and it is mutually agreed between the employer and the worker (in accordance with the provisions of sub-paragraph (4) of paragraph 11) that a holiday in lieu of the customary holiday shall not be allowed to the worker, the minimum remuneration payable to the worker in respect of work on that day shall be:—

(1) the amount to which the worker is entitled in accordance with the provisions of paragraph 6 for working on a customary holiday,

and in addition,

(2) an amount equal to the holiday remuneration to which the worker would have been entitled under the provisions of paragraph 15 had he been allowed a holiday on that day.

WAITING TIME

8.—(1) A worker is entitled to payment of the minimum remuneration specified in this Schedule for all time during which he is present on the premises of his employer, unless he is present thereon in any of the following circumstances—

(a) without the employer's consent, express or implied;

(b) for some purpose unconnected with his work and other than that of waiting for work to be given to him to perform;

(c) by reason only of the fact that he is resident thereon;

(d) during normal meal times in a room or place in which no work is being done, and he is not waiting for work to be given to him to perform.

(2) The minimum remuneration payable under sub-paragraph (1) of this paragraph to a piece worker when not engaged on piece work is that which would be applicable if he were a time worker.

OVERTIME BEING NIGHT WORK

9.—(1) In the application of the provisions of paragraphs 5, 6 and 7 to a worker to whom an additional minimum time rate is payable for night work under the provisions of paragraph 10—

(a) the minimum remuneration for overtime shall be payable only in respect of hours of overtime within the same turn of duty and

(b) a day shall be deemed to be any period of 24 hours commencing at noon.

(2) Where a worker is ordinarily employed on a spell of duty which starts before and ends after midnight the provisions of paragraphs 6 and 7 shall be applicable to time worked during the period of 24 hours commencing at noon on the day prior to the customary holiday.

ADDITIONAL MINIMUM REMUNERATION

NIGHT WORK

10. In addition to the minimum remuneration payable to a worker under paragraphs 5, 6, 7, 8 and 9, minimum remuneration at the rate of 11d. per hour is payable to a worker for any time worked between the hours of 9 p.m. and 5 a.m.:

Provided that where a worker commences a spell of work between the hours of 9 p.m. and 5.am. and works for less than 4 hours between those hours he shall be paid as remuneration under this paragraph the sum of 3s. 8d. instead of at the rate of 11d. per hour.

PART II

HOLIDAYS AND HOLIDAY REMUNERATION

CUSTOMARY HOLIDAYS

11.—(1) Subject to the provisions of this paragraph, and, except in the circumstances provided for in sub-paragraph (3) of this paragraph, the employer shall in each year on the days specified in the next following sub-paragraph or in sub-paragraph (5) of this paragraph as the case may be allow a holiday (hereinafter referred to as a "customary holiday") to any worker in his employment who—

(a) normally works for the employer for not less than 21 hours a week, and

(b) unless excused by the employer or absent by reason of proved illness or injury of the worker, worked for the employer throughout the last working day on which work was available to him immediately prior to the customary holiday.

(2) The said customary holidays are Christmas Day, Boxing Day, Good Friday, Easter Monday, Whit Monday (*or where another day is substituted therefor by national proclamation, that day*), August Bank Holiday and any day proclaimed as an additional Bank Holiday or as a public holiday, or where it is the custom in any locality instead of any of the said days to observe some other day as a holiday each such other day shall, for the purposes of this Schedule be treated in that locality as a customary holiday instead of the day for which it is substituted.

(3) Notwithstanding the preceding provisions of this paragraph, an employer may (except where in the case of a women or young person such a requirement would be unlawful) require a worker who is otherwise entitled to any customary holiday under the preceding provisions of this paragraph to work thereon and, in lieu of any customary holiday on which he so works, the employer shall (except in the case provided for in sub-paragraph (4) of this paragraph) allow to the worker a day's holiday (hereinafter referred to as "a holiday in lieu of a customary holiday") on a week day being:—

(a) a day mutually agreed between the employer and the worker, and

(b) a day on which the worker would normally work and

(c) a day before the commencement of the next holiday season or before the commencement of the holiday season in the next succeeding year:

Provided that in the absence of agreement between the employer and the worker a holiday in lieu of a customary holiday shall be allowed on the last day on which the worker would normally work prior to the commencement of the next holiday season or as the case may require the holiday season in the next succeeding year.

(4) Where a worker otherwise entitled to be allowed a customary holiday or holiday in lieu thereof under the foregoing provisions of this paragraph, is required to work on a customary holiday and it is mutually agreed between the employer and the worker before the customary holiday on which the worker works (for which he is to receive not less than the remuneration calculated in accordance with paragraph 7) that a holiday in lieu thereof shall not be allowed, the employer shall not be required to allow the worker a holiday in lieu of the customary holiday.

(5) Where a worker is ordinarily employed on a spell of duty which starts before and ends after midnight, he shall be allowed—

(a) as a customary holiday in his case the period of 24 hours commencing at noon on the day prior to the customary holiday;

(b) as a holiday in lieu of a customary holiday a period of 24 hours commencing at noon.

ANNUAL HOLIDAY

12.—(1) Subject to the provisions of this paragraph, an employer shall, between the date on which the provisions of this Schedule become effective and 31st October 1968, and in each succeeding year between 1st April and 31st October allow a holiday (hereinafter referred to as an "annual holiday") to every worker in his employment to whom this Schedule applies who was employed by him during the 12 months immediately preceding the commencement of the holiday season for any one of the periods of employment set out in the Table below and the duration of the annual holiday shall in the case of each such worker be related to that period as follows:—

Period of employment	Duration of annual holiday where the worker's normal working week is:—		
	5 days	4 days	3 days
At least 5 weeks but less than 6	1 day	—	—
„ „ 6 „ „ „ „ 7	1 „	1 day	—
„ „ 7 „ „ „ „ 8	1 „	1 „	—
„ „ 8 „ „ „ „ 10	1 „	1 „	1 day
„ „ 10 „ „ „ „ 11	2 days	1 „	1 „
„ „ 11 „ „ „ „ 12	2 „	1 „	1 „
„ „ 12 „ „ „ „ 14	2 „	2 days	1 „
„ „ 14 „ „ „ „ 15	2 „	2 „	1 „
„ „ 15 „ „ „ „ 16	3 „	2 „	1 „
„ „ 16 „ „ „ „ 18	3 „	2 „	2 days
„ „ 18 „ „ „ „ 20	3 „	3 „	2 „
„ „ 20 „ „ „ „ 21	4 „	3 „	2 „
„ „ 21 „ „ „ „ 24	4 „	3 „	2 „
„ „ 24 „ „ „ „ 25	4 „	4 „	3 „
„ „ 25 „ „ „ „ 28	1 normal working week	4 „	3 „
„ „ 28 „ „ „ „ 30	1 „ „ „	4 „	3 „
„ „ 30 „ „ „ „ 32	1 „ „ „ and 1 day	5 „	3 „
„ „ 32 „ „ „ „ 35	1 „ „ „ „ 1 „	5 „	4 „
„ „ 35 „ „ „ „ 36	1 „ „ „ „ 2 days	5 „	4 „
„ „ 36 „ „ „ „ 39	1 „ „ „ „ 2 „	6 „	4 „
„ „ 39 „ „ „ „ 40	1 „ „ „ „ 2 „	6 „	4 „
„ „ 40 „ „ „ „ 42	1 „ „ „ „ 3 „	6 „	5 „
„ „ 42 „ „ „ „ 44	1 „ „ „ „ 3 „	7 „	5 „
„ „ 44 „ „ „ „ 45	1 „ „ „ „ 3 „	7 „	5 „
„ „ 45 „ „ „ „ 46	1 „ „ „ „ 4 „	7 „	5 „
„ „ 46 „ „ „ „ 48	1 „ „ „ „ 4 „	7 „	5 „
„ „ 48 „ „ „ „ 49	1 „ „ „ „ 4 „	8 „	6 „
„ „ 49 „ „ „ „ 50	1 „ „ „ „ 4 „	8 „	6 „
„ „ 50	2 normal working weeks	8 „	6 „

(2) In this Schedule the expression "holiday season" means in relation to an annual holiday during the year 1968, the period commencing on 1st April 1968, and ending on 31st October 1968, and in relation to each subsequent year, the period commencing on 1st April and ending on 31st October in that year.

(3) Notwithstanding the provisions of sub-paragraph (1) of this paragraph:—

(a) the number of days of annual holiday which an employer is required to allow to a worker in any holiday season shall not exceed in the aggregate twice the number of days constituting the worker's normal working week;

(b) where before the expiration of any holiday season a worker enters into an agreement in writing with his employer that the annual holiday or part thereof shall be allowed on a specified date or dates after the expiration of the holiday season but before the commencement of the next following holiday season, then any day or days of annual holiday so allowed shall for the purposes of this Schedule be treated as having been allowed during the holiday season;

(c) the duration of the worker's annual holiday during the holiday season ending on 31st October 1968, shall be reduced by any days of annual holiday duly allowed to him by the employer under the provisions of Order M.D. (107) between 1st April 1968 and the date on which the provisions of this Schedule become effective.

(4) A night worker shall be allowed as a day of annual holiday in his case, a period of 24 hours commencing at noon.

13.—(1) An annual holiday shall be allowed on consecutive working days, being days on which the worker is normally called upon to work for the employer, and days of annual holiday shall be treated as consecutive notwithstanding the intervention of a customary holiday on which the worker is not required to work or of some other holiday:

Provided that where the number of days of annual holiday for which a worker has qualified exceeds the number of days constituting his normal working week, the holiday may at the written request of the worker and with the agreement of the employer be allowed in two periods of consecutive working days; so however that when a holiday is so allowed, one of the periods shall consist of a number of such days not less than the number of days constituting the worker's normal working week.

(2) A day of annual holiday under this Schedule may be allowed on a day on which the worker is entitled to a day of holiday or to a half-holiday under any enactment other than the Wages Councils Act 1959.

14. An employer shall give to a worker reasonable notice of the commencing date or dates and of the duration of his annual holiday. Such notice may be given individually to the worker or by the posting of a notice in the place where the worker is employed.

HOLIDAY REMUNERATION

15.—(1) (a) Subject to the provisions of this paragraph, for each customary holiday or day in lieu of a customary holiday, which a worker is entitled to be allowed under this Schedule, he shall be paid by the employer one day's holiday pay as defined in paragraph 20:

Provided, however, that payment of the above-mentioned remuneration is subject to the condition that the worker presents himself for employment at the usual starting hour on the first working day following the holiday or day in lieu, or, if he fails to do so, failure is by reason of the proved illness or injury of the worker or with the consent of the employer, and

Provided also that when two customary holidays on both of which the worker is not required to work occur on successive days or so that no working day intervenes, the above proviso shall apply only to the second customary holiday.

(b) Subject to the provisions of this paragraph, holiday remuneration in respect of any customary holiday or day in lieu of a customary holiday shall be paid by the employer to the worker on the pay day on which the wages for the first working day following the holiday or day in lieu are paid:

Provided that if a worker ceases to be employed before being allowed a holiday in lieu of a customary holiday to which he is entitled the said payment shall be made immediately upon the termination of his employment.

(2) Subject to the provisions of paragraph 16, a worker qualified to be allowed an annual holiday under this Schedule shall be paid by his employer, on the last pay day preceding such annual holiday, one day's holiday pay as defined in paragraph 20 in respect of each day thereof.

(3) Where under the provisions of paragraph 13 an annual holiday is allowed in more than one period the holiday remuneration shall be apportioned accordingly.

16. Where any accrued holiday remuneration has been paid by the employer to the worker in accordance with paragraph 17 of this Schedule or with Order M.D. (107) in respect of employment during any of the periods referred to in that paragraph or that Order respectively, the amount of holiday remuneration payable by the employer in respect of any annual holiday for which the worker has qualified by reason of employment during the said period shall be reduced by the amount of the said accrued holiday remuneration unless that remuneration has been deducted from a previous payment of holiday remuneration made under the provisions of this Schedule or of Order M.D. (107).

ACCRUED HOLIDAY REMUNERATION PAYABLE ON TERMINATION OF EMPLOYMENT

17. Where a worker ceases to be employed by an employer after the provisions of this Schedule become effective the employer shall, immediately on the termination of the employment (hereinafter referred to as "the termination date"), pay to the worker as accrued holiday remuneration:—

(1) in respect of employment in the 12 months up to the end of the preceding March, a sum equal to the holiday remuneration for any days of annual holiday for which he has qualified, except days of annual holiday which he has been allowed or has become entitled to be allowed before leaving the employment; and

(2) in respect of any employment since the end of the preceding March, a sum equal to the holiday remuneration which would have been payable to him if he could have been allowed an annual holiday in respect of that employment at the time of leaving it:

Provided that—

(a) no worker shall be entitled to the payment by his employer of accrued holiday remuneration if he is dismissed on the grounds of misconduct and is so informed by the employer at the time of dismissal;

(b) where a worker is employed under a contract of service under which he is required to give not less than one week's notice before terminating his employment and the worker without the consent of his employer terminates his employment:—

(i) without having given not less than one week's notice, or

(ii) before one week has expired from the beginning of such notice,

the amount of accrued holiday remuneration payable to the worker shall be the amount payable under the foregoing provisions of this paragraph, less an amount equal to one day's holiday pay multiplied, in the case of (i), by the number of days constituting the worker's normal working week or, in the case of (ii), by the number of days which at the termination date would complete a normal working week commencing at the beginning of the notice.

CALCULATION OF EMPLOYMENT

18. For the purposes of calculating any period of employment qualifying a worker for an annual holiday or for any accrued holiday remuneration under this Schedule, the worker shall be treated—

(1) as if he were employed for a week in respect of any week in which—

(a) he has worked for the employer for not less than 21 hours and has performed some work for which statutory minimum remuneration is payable; or

(b) he has worked for the employer for less than 21 hours, or has performed no work, solely by reason of the proved illness of or accident to the worker (provided that the number of weeks which may be treated as weeks of employment for such reason shall not exceed eight in any such period as aforesaid); and

(2) as if he were employed on any day of annual holiday allowed under the provisions of this Schedule and for the purpose of the provisions of sub-paragraph (1) of this paragraph, a worker who is absent on such a holiday shall be treated as having worked thereon for the employer for the number of hours ordinarily worked by him on that day of the week on work for which statutory minimum remuneration is payable.

OTHER HOLIDAY AGREEMENTS

19. The provisions of this Schedule are without prejudice to any agreement for the allowance of any further holidays with pay or for the payment of additional holiday remuneration.

PART III
GENERAL
DEFINITIONS

20. In this Schedule, the following expressions have the meanings hereby assigned to them respectively, that is to say—

(1) "AREA A" comprises—

(a) each area in England and Wales which is administered by a Rural District Council; and

(b) each area in England and Wales which at the date of the 1961 census was administered by a Municipal Borough Council or an Urban District Council and which, according to the census had a population not exceeding 10,000,

but does not include any area within the Metropolitan Police District.

(2) "AREA B" comprises the whole of England and Wales other than Area A and Area C.

(3) "AREA C" comprises the Metropolitan Police District as defined in the London Government Act 1963(a), the City of London, the Inner Temple and the Middle Temple.

(4) "CLERK" means a person employed, wholly or mainly, on clerical work.

(5) "CUSTOMARY HOLIDAY" has the meaning assigned to it in sub-paragraph (2) of paragraph 11.

(6) "FOREMAN" means a person to whom is deputed the duty of exercising supervisory authority over workers exceeding 5 in number (exclusive of the foreman).

(7) "HOURLY GENERAL MINIMUM TIME RATE" has the meaning assigned to it in sub-paragraph (2) of paragraph 1.

(8) "NIGHT WORKER" means a worker who is ordinarily employed on a spell of duty which starts before and ends after midnight.

(9) "NORMAL WORKING WEEK" means:—

(a) in the case of a rota worker the total number of days (excluding rest days) on which the worker has ordinarily worked for the employer during the periods of rota during the 12 months immediately preceding the commencement of the holiday season, or where under paragraph 17 accrued holiday remuneration is payable, during the 12 months immediately preceding the termination date, divided by the total number of weeks in the said periods of rota;

(a) 1963 c. 33.

(b) in the case of any other worker the number of days (excluding rest days) on which it has been usual for the worker to work for the employer in a week during the 12 months immediately preceding the commencement of the holiday season, or where under paragraph 17 accrued holiday remuneration is payable, during the 12 months immediately preceding the termination date: provided that in either case—

    (i) for the purpose of calculating the normal working week part of a day shall count as a day;

    (ii) except in the case of a rota worker's rest days, no account shall be taken of any week in which the worker did not perform any work for which statutory minimum remuneration has been fixed;

    (iii) in the case of a night worker a day is a period of 24 hours commencing at noon.

(10) "ONE DAY'S HOLIDAY PAY" means, where the worker's normal working week is:—

5 days—one-fifth of
4 days—one-quarter of
3 days—one-third of

the remuneration which the worker would be entitled to receive from his employer at the date of the annual holiday or at the termination date, as the case may be, for work for which statutory minimum remuneration is payable, either:—

    (a) for the number of hours normally worked by him for the employer in his normal working week, or

    (b) for 42 hours,

whichever number of hours is the less, if paid at the appropriate hourly general minimum time rate for that number of hours' work.

(11) "OVERTIME" means work for which minimum remuneration is payable under paragraphs 5, 6, 7 and 8.

(12) "REST DAYS" means two days in each week which have been notified to the worker by the employer before the commencement of the week as rest days, or, failing such notification, the last two days in the week; and "REST DAY" means one of these days:

Provided that in the case of a rota worker "REST DAYS" means any such days calculated at the rate of two days for each week in the period of rota.

(13) "ROTA WORKER" means a worker employed under an agreement which provides that his rest days should be taken according to a rota over a period not exceeding 12 weeks.

(14) "ROUNDS SALESMAN" or "ROUNDS SALESWOMAN" means a person who is employed, wholly or mainly, as a salesman on a defined or established route, and is responsible for keeping account of his retail sales to customers and of any cash or tokens received in payment and is not accompanied, save in exceptional circumstances, by any other person who exercises control or supervision.

(15) "SHOP ASSISTANT" means a person employed, wholly or mainly, in a shop in serving customers or in checking in and out or in both such operations.

(16) "SPELL OF DUTY" means a period of work broken only by intervals for meals.

(17) "STATUTORY MINIMUM REMUNERATION" means minimum remuneration (other than holiday remuneration) fixed by a wages regulation

order made by the Minister to give effect to proposals submitted to him by the Milk Distributive Wages Council (England and Wales).

(18) "TIME-AND-A-HALF", "DOUBLE TIME" and "TREBLE TIME" mean respectively one and a half times, twice and three times the hourly general minimum time rate (exclusive of any amount payable under paragraph 10 in respect of time worked between 9 p.m. and 5 a.m.) which would be payable to the worker for work other than overtime.

(19) "WEEK" means pay week.

WORKERS TO WHOM THE SCHEDULE APPLIES

21. This Schedule applies to workers in relation to whom the Milk Distributive Wages Council (England and Wales) operates, that is to say, workers employed in England and Wales in the trade specified in the Schedule to the Trade Boards (Milk Distributive Trade, England and Wales) (Constitution and Proceedings) Regulations 1928(a), which reads as follows:—

"1. Subject as hereinafter provided the Milk Distributive Trade shall consist of the following operations:—

    (i) the wholesale and retail sale of milk;

    (ii) the sale of other goods by workers mainly employed in the sale specified in paragraph 1(i) hereof;

    (iii) all work incidental to the sale specified in paragraph 1(i) hereof.

2. Work incidental to the sale specified in paragraph 1(i) hereof shall include, *inter alia*:—

    (*a*) collecting, delivering, despatching;

    (*b*) pasteuring, sterilising, homogenising, humanising, cooling, separating and all work performed in connection with any other processes in the preparation of milk;

    (*c*) blending, testing and sampling of milk;

    (*d*) cleaning of utensils, receptacles, vehicles, premises, plant, machinery;

    (*e*) stoking, attending to boiler, plant or machinery, fire lighting, portering of coal or other fuel;

    (*f*) horse keeping and harness cleaning;

    (*g*) portering, lift or hoist-operating, time-keeping, storing, stock-keeping, warehousing;

    (*h*) boxing, parcelling, labelling, weighing, measuring, checking, bottling, packing and unpacking;

    (*i*) clerical work or canvassing carried on in conjunction with the work specified in paragraph 1 hereof.

3. Notwithstanding any of the foregoing provisions, the Milk Distributive Trade shall not include any of the following operations:—

    (*a*) the wholesale sale of milk (and operations incidental thereto) from an establishment at which milk products are manufactured and from which unseparated milk is not ordinarily sold as such;

    (*b*) the wholesale sale of milk direct from the farm where the milk was produced and all operations incidental thereto;

    (*c*) the sale of milk in restaurants, shops or similar premises by waiters or shop assistants who are not mainly engaged upon such sale;

    (*d*) the transport of goods by common carriers;

(a) S.R. & O. 1928/480 (1928, p. 1281).

(e) carting and operations incidental thereto where the business carried on consists exclusively of such operations;

(f) work done by or on behalf of the Post Office.

4. For the purpose of this Schedule the expression 'milk' means milk other than dried or condensed milk."

EXPLANATORY NOTE

(This Note is not part of the Order.)

This Order, which has effect from 28th April 1968, sets out the statutory minimum remuneration payable and the holidays to be allowed to workers in substitution for the statutory minimum remuneration and holidays provided for by the Wages Regulation (Milk Distributive) (England and Wales) Order 1966 (Order M.D. (107)), which is revoked.

New provisions are printed in italics.

1968 No. 530

POLICE

The Police Pensions (Amendment) Regulations 1968

Laid before Parliament in draft

Made - - -	*29th March* 1968

Coming into Operation—

for the purposes of Part III	*9th April* 1968
for all other purposes	*1st April* 1968

In exercise of the powers conferred on me by sections 1, 3 and 5(4) of the Police Pensions Act 1948(**a**), as extended and amended by section 43 of the Reserve and Auxiliary Forces (Protection of Civil Interests) Act 1951(**b**), section 5(3) of the Overseas Service Act 1958(**c**) and Schedule 2 thereto, section 1(1) of the Police Pensions Act 1961(**d**), sections 40, 43(4), 45(4) and 63 of the Police Act 1964(**e**) and Schedules 6 and 9 thereto, section 12(4) of the Superannuation (Miscellaneous Provisions) Act 1967(**f**), and sections 35 and 38(4) of the Police (Scotland) Act 1967(**g**), and after consultation with the Police Council for Great Britain, I hereby, with the consent of the Treasury and, so far as Part I is concerned, solely in connection with a transfer of functions in accordance with section 12 of the Superannuation (Miscellaneous Provisions) Act 1967, make the following Regulations, a draft of which has been laid before Parliament and has been approved by resolution of each House of Parliament :—

PART I

PROVISIONS RELATING TO THE TRANSFER OF FUNCTIONS TO THE MINISTER OF OVERSEAS DEVELOPMENT AND COMING INTO OPERATION ON 1ST APRIL 1968

1. In Regulations 3(1)(*c*), 57, 59(3), 63(3) and (4), 86 and 100(1) of the principal Regulations (which relate to persons who are not members of home police forces) for the words "the Secretary of State", wherever they occur, there shall be substituted the words "the appropriate Minister".

2. For Regulation 100(5) of the principal Regulations (which assigns meanings to certain expressions in relation to persons who are not members of home police forces) there shall be substituted the following provisions :—

"(5) Any reference in Regulation 54(2) and paragraphs 2 and 7 of Schedule 6 to the Secretary of State shall be construed, in relation to an overseas policeman, as a reference to the Secretary of State or the Minister of Overseas Development.

(a) 1948 c. 24.   (b) 1951 c. 65.   (c) 1958 c. 14.
(d) 1961 c. 35.   (e) 1964 c. 48.   (f) 1967 c. 28.
(g) 1967 c. 77.

(6) Any reference in these Regulations to the police authority or to the appropriate Minister shall be construed—

(*a*) in relation to an overseas policeman, as a reference to the Secretary of State or the Minister of Overseas Development, or

(*b*) in relation to an inspector or assistant inspector of constabulary or to a central police officer, as a reference to the Secretary of State.".

PART II

OTHER PROVISIONS COMING INTO OPERATION
ON 1ST APRIL 1968

3. For Regulation 14(4) of the principal Regulations (which relates to a widow's augmented award where the husband's death results from an attack or injury received in effecting an arrest) there shall be substituted the following provision :—

"(4) The gratuity under paragraph (3) shall be of an amount equal to twice the annual pensionable pay, at the date of the death of the person in respect of whom the gratuity is payable, of a man—

(*a*) holding the rank of constable in the metropolitan police force or, where the death occurred before 1st April 1968, in the police force of which that person was a member, and

(*b*) entitled to reckon 30 years' service for the purposes of pay.".

4. After Regulation 96 of the principal Regulations (which, as set out in the Police Pensions (Amendment) Regulations 1967(a), relates to Lincolnshire) there shall be inserted the following Regulation :—

"River Tyne police force

96A.—(1) This Regulation shall have effect in the event of the dissolution of the River Tyne police force and the transfer of the members thereof to the police force for the police area comprising the county borough of South Shields by a harbour reorganisation scheme confirmed by the Minister of Transport under section 18 of the Harbours Act 1964(b).

(2) In relation to a person who has served as a member of the River Tyne police force, whether he ceased so to serve before the dissolution of that force or is transferred as aforesaid, the police force, police authority and police fund for the police area comprising the county borough of South Shields shall, for the purposes of these Regulations, be deemed to be the same force, authority and fund as the force, authority and fund for the River Tyne police area.

(3) If the chief constable of the River Tyne police force is transferred as aforesaid and suffers reduction in rank attributable to the provisions of the Scheme by which he is transferred, Regulation 66 shall apply as though he had not suffered such reduction in rank, unless he elects otherwise by notice in writing to the police authority.".

(a) S.I. 1967/453 (1967 I, p. 1395).   (b) 1964 c. 40.

5. At the end of Regulation 97(3) of the principal Regulations (which relates to alterations in police areas) there shall be added the following provision :—

"(c) a reference to the combination of a police area with another police area includes a reference to the inclusion of a police area in a county or county borough police area, on or after 1st April 1968, on a date on which an order affecting the area, made under Part II of the Local Government Act 1958(a), comes into force and, in such case, a reference to the combined police area shall be construed as a reference to the county or, as the case may be, the county borough police area.".

PART III

PROVISIONS COMING INTO OPERATION ON 9TH APRIL 1968

6. Regulation 27 of the principal Regulations (which relates to the child of a member of a police force who died before 5th July 1948) is hereby revoked.

7.—(1) For paragraph 1(4) of Part III of Schedule 3 to the principal Regulations (which, as set out in Regulation 5 of the Police Pensions (Amendment) (No. 2) Regulations 1967(b), provides, in certain cases, for the increase of a child's allowance up to 42s. 6d. a week) there shall be substituted the following provision :—

"(4) Where both parents of the child are dead and the parent in respect of whose death an ordinary or special allowance is payable was the child's father and he had attained the age of 65 years on 5th July 1948, then in respect of any week during which—

(a) no person is receiving a guardian's allowance under the National Insurance Act 1965(c) in respect of the child ;

(b) the child is included in a family within the meaning of the Family Allowances Act 1965(d) or of the Family Allowances Act 1945(e), either as originally enacted or as amended by any subsequent enactment ;

(c) where the allowance is a special allowance, no allowance is payable under section 21 of the National Insurance (Industrial Injuries) Act 1965(f) in respect of the child ;

(d) no armed forces pension or award is payable to or for the child in pursuance of any Royal Warrant or other instrument ; and

(e) no grant is payable to or in respect of the child under any scheme made under the Personal Injuries (Emergency Provisions) Act 1939(g),

the amount of the allowance may, without prejudice to the provisions of the preceding sub-paragraphs but subject to Part IV of this Schedule, be increased under sub-paragraph (1) to an amount not exceeding 45s. 6d.".

(a) 1958 c. 55.   (b) S.I. 1967/1500 (1967 III, p. 4204).
(c) 1965 c. 51.   (d) 1965 c. 53.   (e) 1945 c. 41.
(f) 1965 c. 52.   (g) 1939 c. 82.

(2) For paragraph 2(2) of the said Part III (which, as set out as aforesaid, provides that the appropriate weekly amount up to which a child's allowance may, in certain cases, be increased shall be 42s. 6d. for the first child, 39s. 6d. for the second child, 37s. 6d. for the third child, and 35s. 0d. for each subsequent child, included in a family) there shall be substituted the following provision :—

"(2) The appropriate amount referred to in the preceding sub-paragraph shall be—

(a) irrespective of the date of the father's death, 45s. 6d. in the case of the only or eldest child included in a family within the meaning of the Family Allowances Act 1965 or of the Family Allowances Act 1945, either as originally enacted or as amended by any subsequent enactment ;

(b) where the father dies on or after 9th April 1968—

(i) 35s. 6d., in the case of the second child so included, and

(ii) 33s. 6d., in the case of each subsequent child so included ;

(c) where the father died before 9th April 1968—

(i) 39s. 6d., in the case of the second child so included,

(ii) 37s. 6d., in the case of the third child so included, and

(iii) 35s. 0d., in the case of each subsequent child so included.".

8. Parts V and VI of Schedule 3 to the principal Regulations (which, as amended by Regulation 6 of the Police Pensions (Amendment) (No. 2) Regulations 1967, relate to the child of a member of a police force who died before 5th July 1948) are hereby revoked.

PART IV
GENERAL

9. In these Regulations a reference to the principal Regulations is a reference to the Police Pensions Regulations 1966(**a**), as amended (**b**).

10. These Regulations shall come into operation—

(a) except for the purposes of Part III thereof, on 1st April 1968 ;

(b) for the purposes of Part III thereof, on 9th April 1968.

11. These Regulations may be cited as the Police Pensions (Amendment) Regulations 1968.

James Callaghan,
One of Her Majesty's Principal
Secretaries of State.

27th March 1968.

We consent,

B. K. O'Malley,

E. Alan Fitch,

Two of the Lords Commissioners of
Her Majesty's Treasury.

29th March 1968.

(a) S.I. 1966/1582 (1966 III, p. 4894).
(b) The relevant amending Regulations are S.I. 1967/1500 (1967 III, p. 4204).

EXPLANATORY NOTE

(This Note is not part of the Regulations.)

These Regulations amend the Police Pensions Regulations 1966.

Part I contains amendments in connection with the transfer, in accordance with section 12 of the Superannuation (Miscellaneous Provisions) Act 1967, of certain functions relating to policemen with overseas service from the Secretary of State to the Minister of Overseas Development. The operative date for Part I is 1st April 1968 (Regulation 10).

Part II, which comes into operation on the same date, contains amendments relating to other matters. Regulation 3 provides that where a policeman dies on or after that date in circumstances which entitle his widow to a gratuity in addition to a special pension, the gratuity shall be calculated by reference to the rate of pay of a constable in the metropolitan police force, whether or not the policeman was a member of that force. Regulations 4 and 5 make provision as respects the application of the 1966 Regulations in the event of the dissolution of the River Tyne police force by a scheme under the Harbours Act 1964 or of the inclusion of a police area in a county or county borough police area in consequence of an order under the Local Government Act 1958.

Part III, which comes into operation on 9th April 1968, contains amendments relating to children's allowances. Regulations 6 and 8 revoke certain spent provisions. Regulation 7 varies the amounts up to which children's allowances may be increased in those cases where discretionary increases are permitted. In the case of the only or eldest child in a family where only the father is dead, or in the case of any child in a family where both parents are dead, the child's allowance may be increased to 45s. 6d. instead of 42s. 6d. In the case of second and subsequent children in a family where only the father is dead, no change is made in the permitted increase except where he dies on or after 9th April 1968, in which case the permitted increases are reduced.

STATUTORY INSTRUMENTS

1968 No. 531

AGRICULTURE

LIVESTOCK INDUSTRIES

The Calf Subsidies (United Kingdom) Scheme 1968

Laid before Parliament in draft

Made - - - - 28th March 1968

Coming into Operation 1st April 1968

The Minister of Agriculture, Fisheries and Food and the Secretary of State, acting jointly, being the appropriate Minister in relation to a joint scheme for the whole of the United Kingdom, in exercise of the power conferred on them by sections 1 and 4 of the Agriculture (Calf Subsidies) Act 1952(a) as amended by section 10 of the Agriculture Act 1967(b), by the said section 10 and of all other powers enabling them in that behalf, with the approval of the Treasury, hereby make the following scheme: —

Citation, extent and commencement

1. This scheme, which may be cited as the Calf Subsidies (United Kingdom) Scheme 1968, shall apply to the United Kingdom and shall come into operation on 1st April 1968.

Interpretation

2.—(1) In this scheme the following expressions have the meanings hereby respectively assigned to them: —

" the Act " means the Agriculture (Calf Subsidies) Act 1952 ;

" carcases " means carcases of cattle ;

" the Fatstock (Guarantee Payments) Order " means the Fatstock (Guarantee Payments) Order 1964(c), including any order amending or replacing it ;

" the Minister " means the Minister of Agriculture, Fisheries and Food ;

" proper officer " means for any of the purposes of this scheme the person for the time being authorised to act for that purpose, in England and Wales by the Minister, in Scotland by the Secretary of State and in Northern Ireland by the Ministry of Agriculture for Northern Ireland.

(2) For the purposes of Part I of this scheme the limit of age at which an animal ceases to be a calf shall (subject to paragraph 6(2) below) be the age when it cuts its first permanent incisor tooth.

(3) The Interpretation Act 1889(d) applies to the interpretation of this scheme as it applies to the interpretation of an Act of Parliament.

(a) 1952 c. 62. For change of title of the Minister, see S.I. 1955/554 (1955 I, p. 1200).
(b) 1967 c. 22.   (c) S.I. 1964/463 (1964 I, p. 746).   (d) 1889 c. 63.

Applications for subsidy

3. It shall be a condition of the payment of a subsidy under this scheme that any person who desires to be paid in accordance with the provisions of this scheme shall apply in writing in such form applicable to Part I or Part II thereof and at such time as in relation to England and Wales the Minister, to Scotland the Secretary of State and to Northern Ireland the Ministry of Agriculture for Northern Ireland may from time to time respectively require.

PART I

Stage A—Calves

Rates of subsidy

4. Subject to the provisions of this scheme, the Minister or the Secretary of State may pay to the person who is the owner of a calf to which this part of this scheme applies at the time when the calf is certified to be a calf of the description specified in this part of this scheme—

(a) in the case of a heifer calf, a subsidy of £9 0s. 0d., or

(b) in the case of a steer calf, a subsidy of £11 5s. 0d.

Eligible calves

5. The description of calf specified in this part of this scheme is any steer or heifer calf, except a heifer calf of the Guernsey, Jersey, Friesian or Ayrshire breeds, which has been reasonably well reared and is, or will after further rearing be, suitable for beef production or, if a heifer calf, for use for breeding for beef production, being in any case an animal which, if slaughtered either immediately or after a period of further rearing and fattening, would be likely to yield a carcase of reasonably good quality beef.

Conditions of subsidy

6.—(1) A calf to which this part of this scheme applies is a calf which—

(a) was born in the United Kingdom within the period beginning with 30th October 1967 and ending with 29th October 1970,

(b) has been certified by a proper officer to be of the description specified in paragraph 5 above,

(c) had not been previously so certified under either this scheme or a corresponding provision of any earlier scheme made under the Act, and

(d) had not at the time of certification attained the age at which it ceases to be a calf for the purposes of this part of this scheme.

(2) Sub-paragraph (1)(d) above shall not apply in the case of an animal as respects which the Minister or the Secretary of State is satisfied that the animal in question would have been certified under this part of this scheme before it attained the age referred to in that sub-paragraph had certification not been delayed in order to avoid the risk of the introduction or spreading of animal disease.

(3) It shall be a condition of the payment of a subsidy under this part of this scheme that any person who desires to be paid in accordance with the provisions thereof in respect of any calves shall collect and properly secure them at a convenient place for the purposes of examination and marking in accordance with any order made under section 11 of the Agriculture Act 1967, and shall assist the person appointed for those purposes.

PART II

Stage B—Carcases

Subsidies in respect of carcases

7.—(1) Subject to the provisions of this part of this scheme the Minister or the Secretary of State may pay to the person who is the producer of a carcase to which this part of this scheme applies a subsidy at the rate determined in accordance with paragraph 10 below.

(2) This part of this scheme applies to any carcase which—

(a) is of fat cattle of a guarantee class in respect of which guarantee payments may be made under the Fatstock (Guarantee Payments) Order, and

(b) is not the carcase of an animal in respect of which a subsidy has been paid under Part I of this scheme (or any earlier scheme made under the Act) or which has been imported into the United Kingdom.

(3) In this paragraph " producer " means the person in whose name the carcase is presented for certification under this part of this scheme.

Conditions of subsidy

8. It shall be a condition of the payment of subsidy under this part of this scheme that—

(a) the carcase is presented for certification at the same time and place as it is presented for certification under such arrangements as are in force for payments to be made in respect of fat cattle under the Fatstock (Guarantee Payments) Order ;

(b) the carcase is certified by a proper officer to be a carcase of the description specified in paragraph 7(2)(a) above ; and

(c) such proper officer is satisfied that subsidy under any scheme made under the Act, whether as originally enacted or as amended by sections 10 and 11 of the Agriculture Act 1967, has not previously been paid in respect of the animal in question, either as a calf or a carcase.

Period for presentation

9. Subsidy shall not be payable under this part of this scheme unless the carcase is certified in accordance with paragraph 8(b) above within the period beginning with 1st April 1968 and ending with 31st March 1971.

Amount of subsidy

10. The rates of subsidy in respect of carcases of animals eligible for subsidy under this part of this scheme shall be such amounts as the Minister and the Secretary of State, with the approval of the Treasury, determine as being approximately equivalent on the average to the rates of subsidy which would have been payable under Part I of this scheme (or any earlier scheme made under the Act) if the animals in question had been certified for subsidy under the said Part I (or any such earlier scheme).

For the purposes of this paragraph the fact that heifer calves of certain breeds are excepted under paragraph 5 of this scheme (or a corresponding provision of any such earlier scheme) shall be disregarded.

Delegation to Meat and Livestock Commission

11. The Minister and the Secretary of State may, to such extent and in such manner as they may from time to time direct, delegate to the Meat and Livestock Commission established under section 1 of the Agriculture Act 1967 any of their functions in relation to Great Britain conferred on them by this part of this scheme.

In Witness whereof the Official Seal of the Minister of Agriculture, Fisheries and Food is hereunto affixed on 26th March 1968.

(L.S.)

Frederick Peart,
Minister of Agriculture,
Fisheries and Food.

Given under the Seal of the Secretary of State for Scotland on 27th March 1968.

(L.S.)

William Ross,
Secretary of State
for Scotland.

We approve,

B. K. O'Malley,
E. Alan Fitch,
Two of the Lords Commissioners
of Her Majesty's Treasury.

28th March 1968.

EXPLANATORY NOTE
(This Note is not part of the scheme.)

Part I of this scheme (Stage A), which applies to calves born in the United Kingdom between 30th October 1967 and 29th October 1970, continues provision for the payment of calf subsidies under the Agriculture (Calf Subsidies) Act 1952. The amounts payable per head are £9 for heifers and £11 5s. for steers. Apart from a provision enabling calves to be certified for the subsidy later than would otherwise be permissible, where the reason for late certification was in order to avoid the risk of animal disease, Part I of the scheme is substantially similar to earlier schemes.

Part II of the scheme (Stage B), made under the extended powers conferred by section 10 of the Agriculture Act 1967, provides for the payment of subsidy to producers of certain carcases. Such carcases must be of a class in respect of which guarantee payments may be made under the fatstock guarantee scheme but must not be of animals in respect of which subsidy has been paid at Stage A, or which have been imported into the United Kingdom. Carcases must be presented for certification at the same time as they are presented under the fatstock guarantee scheme, and they must be certified between 1st April 1968 and 31st March 1971.

The rates of subsidy at Stage B are such amounts as are determined to be approximately equivalent on the average to the rates which would have been payable at Stage A if the animals in question had been certified (while calves) at Stage A.

The scheme, which applies to the whole of the United Kingdom, contains provision enabling the Stage B functions in Great Britain to be delegated to the Meat and Livestock Commission.

STATUTORY INSTRUMENTS

1968 No. 533

POST OFFICE

The Inland Post Amendment (No. 1) Regulations 1968

Made - - -	29*th March* 1968
Laid before Parliament	8*th April* 1968
Coming into Operation	1*st May* 1968

I, The Right Honourable Edward Watson Short, M.P., Her Majesty's Post-master General, by virtue of the powers conferred upon me by sections 5, 8, 15 and 81 of the Post Office Act 1953(a) (as amended or substituted by section 28 of and the Schedule to the Post Office Act 1961(b)), and all other powers enabling me in this behalf, do hereby make the following regulations :

Interpretation

1.—(1) These regulations shall be read as one with the Inland Post Regulations 1967(c) (hereinafter called "the principal regulations").

(2) The Interpretation Act 1889(d) applies for the interpretation of these regulations as it applies for the interpretation of an Act of Parliament.

Transmission of parcels in bulk

2.—(1) In Part V of the principal regulations there shall be inserted immediately after regulation 32 the following regulation :

"32A—(1) The Postmaster General may make arrangements with any senders of parcels for the acceptance and transmission of unregistered parcels (other than cash on delivery packets) as bulk postings under this regulation and such arrangements shall operate and continue in force at such times and during such periods as the Postmaster General may from time to time consider expedient.

(2) The senders of parcels under this regulation shall comply with such conditions as the Postmaster General may consider appropriate either generally or in the particular case and regulation 20(1) shall not apply to such parcels.

(3) There shall be charged and paid on parcels accepted for transmission under this regulation such rates of postage as the Postmaster General may fix ; and different rates may be fixed for different circumstances.

(4) Postage on parcels accepted for transmission under this regulation shall be paid and denoted in such manner and at such time as the Postmaster General may require or permit and regulation 10(3) shall not apply to such parcels."

(a)	1953 c. 36.	(b)	1961 c. 15.
(c)	S.I. 1967/1416 (1967 III, p. 4077).	(d)	1889 c. 63.

(2) For regulation 3 of the principal regulations there shall be substituted the following regulation :

"3. There shall be charged and paid upon the postal packets specified in the first column of Schedule 1 (other than parcels accepted for transmission under regulation 32A) the rates of postage respectively specified in the second column thereof, upon unaddressed packets the rates of postage fixed under regulation 25, and upon parcels accepted for transmission under regulation 32A the rates of postage fixed under that regulation."

(3) In regulation 21(2) of the principal regulations, as substituted by regulation 56(2) of the principal regulations, (which provides for the delivery of parcels free of customs duty and other charges in the Republic of Ireland) there shall be inserted after the word "Ireland" the words "(other than a parcel accepted for transmission under the provisions of regulation 32A)".

Citation and commencement

3. These regulations may be cited as the Inland Post Amendment (No. 1) Regulations 1968, and shall come into operation on 1st May 1968.

Dated 29th March 1968.

Edward Short,
Her Majesty's Postmaster General.

EXPLANATORY NOTE
(This Note is not part of the Regulations.)

These regulations provide for the acceptance and transmission of parcels in bulk.

STATUTORY INSTRUMENTS

1968 No. 534

EDUCATION, ENGLAND AND WALES

The Provision of Milk and Meals Amending Regulations 1968

Made - - - -	1st April 1968
Laid before Parliament	9th April 1968
Coming into Operation	10th April 1968

The Secretary of State for Education and Science, in exercise of the powers conferred upon him by section 49 of the Education Act 1944(a) as amended by the Secretary of State for Education and Science Order 1964(b) and section 3 of the Public Expenditure and Receipts Act 1968(c), hereby makes the following regulations :—

Citation, commencement and interpretation

1.—(1) These regulations may be cited as the Provision of Milk and Meals Amending Regulations 1968 and shall come into operation on 10th April 1968.

(2) The Interpretation Act 1889(d) shall apply for the interpretation of these regulations as it applies for the interpretation of an Act of Parliament.

Amendment of regulations

2.—(1) The Provision of Milk and Meals Regulations 1945(e) as amended(f) shall have effect subject to the substitution for the proviso to regulation 8 (remission of charge for school dinner) of the following proviso :

" Provided that the parent shall be entitled to remission of the charge in accordance with approved arrangements—

    (*a*) if he is unable to pay it without financial hardship ; and

    (*b*) in respect of any child of a family which includes three other dependent children under 19 in respect of whom the charge is not remitted under this subparagraph."

(2) As respects any school paragraph (1) shall not take effect until the beginning of the summer term 1968.

    Given under the Official Seal of the Secretary of State for Education and Science on 1st April 1968.

    (L.S.)   *Patrick Gordon Walker*,
                                     Secretary of State for Education and Science.

(a) 1944 c. 31.   (b) S.I. 1964/490 (1964 I, p. 800).   (c) 1968 c. 14.
(d) 1889 c. 63.   (e) S.R. & O. 1945/698 (Rev. VI, p. 380: 1945 I, p. 366).
   (f) The relevant amending instrument is S.I. 1959/409 (1959 I, p. 1029).

EXPLANATORY NOTE

(This Note is not part of the Regulations.)

These regulations provide for the remission of the charge for school dinners payable in respect of children belonging to large families.

STATUTORY INSTRUMENTS

1968 No. 541

CIVIL DEFENCE

The Civil Defence Corps (Revocation) Regulations 1968

Laid before Parliament in draft

Made - - - - *29th March* 1968
Coming into Operation *1st April* 1968

In exercise of the powers conferred on me by section 2 of the Civil Defence Act 1948(a), I hereby make the following Regulations, a draft of which has been laid before Parliament and approved by resolution of each House of Parliament: —

1. The following Regulations are hereby revoked, namely,

The Civil Defence Corps Regulations 1949(b),

The Civil Defence Corps (Scunthorpe) Regulations 1951(c).

2.—(1) Section 38 of the Interpretation Act 1889(d) shall apply as if these Regulations were an Act of Parliament and as if the Regulations revoked by these Regulations were Acts of Parliament repealed by an Act of Parliament.

(2) These Regulations may be cited as the Civil Defence Corps (Revocation) Regulations 1968 and shall come into operation on 1st April 1968.

James Callaghan,
One of Her Majesty's Principal
Secretaries of State.

Home Office,
Whitehall.
29th March 1968.

EXPLANATORY NOTE

(This Note is not part of the Regulations.)

These Regulations revoke the Civil Defence Corps Regulations 1949, as amended which provide for the organisation by local authorities of divisions of the Civil Defence Corps.

(a) 12, 13 & 14 Geo. 6. c. 5.   (b) S.I. 1949/1433 (1949 I, p. 639).
(c) S.I. 1951/1259 (1951 I, p. 256).   (d) 1889 c. 63.

STATUTORY INSTRUMENTS

1968 No. 542

CIVIL DEFENCE

The Civil Defence (Fire Services) Regulations 1968

Laid before Parliament in draft

Made - - - - *29th March* 1968
Coming into Operation *1st April* 1968

In exercise of the powers conferred on me by section 2 of the Civil Defence Act 1948(**a**), I hereby make the following Regulations, a draft of which has been laid before Parliament and approved by resolution of each House of Parliament: —

1. For paragraph (*a*) of Regulation 2 of the Civil Defence (Fire Services) Regulations 1949(**b**) there shall be substituted the following paragraph—

" (*a*) to employ such additional persons, if any, as members of the fire brigade for the purposes of civil defence as may be authorised from time to time by the Secretary of State ; ".

2.—(1) These Regulations may be cited as the Civil Defence (Fire Services) Regulations 1968 and shall come into operation on 1st April 1968.

(2) These Regulations shall not apply to Scotland.

James Callaghan,
One of Her Majesty's Principal
Secretaries of State.

Home Office,
Whitehall.
29th March 1968.

EXPLANATORY NOTE

(This Note is not part of the Regulations.)

These Regulations amend the Civil Defence (Fire Services) Regulations 1949 by providing that it shall be the function of a fire authority to employ only such additional persons as members of the fire brigade for the purposes of civil defence as may be authorised by the Secretary of State. This replaces the existing unrestricted power of a fire authority to employ additional persons and in particular auxiliary firemen.

(**a**) 12, 13 & 14 Geo. 6. c. 5.　　　　　(**b**) S.I. 1949/2120 (1949 I, p. 658).

STATUTORY INSTRUMENTS

1968 No. 544

NATIONAL HEALTH SERVICE,

ENGLAND AND WALES

The National Health Service (Charges for Dental Treatment) Regulations 1968

Made - - -		*29th March* 1968
Laid before Parliament		*10th April* 1968
Coming into Operation		*1st May* 1968

The Minister of Health, in exercise of his powers under section 2 of the National Health Service Act 1952(**a**) and section 2 of the National Health Service Act 1961(**b**), and of all other powers enabling him in that behalf, hereby makes the following regulations :—

1.—(1) These regulations may be cited as the National Health Service (Charges for Dental Treatment) Regulations 1968 and shall come into operation on 1st May 1968.

(2) The Interpretation Act 1889(**c**) applies to the interpretation of these regulations as it applies to the interpretation of an Act of Parliament.

2. The amount of one pound authorised by section 2(2) of the National Health Service Act 1952 (which provides for a maximum charge of one pound for certain general dental services other than those for which a charge is payable under the National Health Service Act 1951(**d**)) as a charge for dental treatment is hereby increased to thirty shillings.

3. These regulations apply in respect of any services provided in pursuance of a contract or arrangement under which the first examination took place after the coming into operation of these regulations.

4. Any reference in the National Health Service (General Dental Services) Regulations 1967(**e**) to a charge authorised by section 2 of the National Health Service Act 1952 shall include a reference to such charge as varied by these regulations.

Given under the official seal of the Minister of Health on 29th March 1968.

(L.S.)
Kenneth Robinson,
Minister of Health.

(**a**) 1952 c. 25.   (**b**) 1961 c. 19.   (**c**) 1889 c. 63.
(**d**) 1951 c. 31.   (**e**) S.I. 1967/937 (1967 II, p. 2816).

EXPLANATORY NOTE

(This Note is not part of the Regulations.)

These Regulations increase from one pound to thirty shillings the maximum amount payable by patients in respect of treatment, other than the supply of dentures, provided under general dental services.

STATUTORY INSTRUMENTS

1968 No. 545

NATIONAL HEALTH SERVICE, ENGLAND AND WALES

HOSPITAL AND SPECIALIST SERVICES

The National Health Service (Hydestile Hospital) Order 1968

Made - - -	*29th March* 1968
Coming into Operation	*1st April* 1968

The Minister of Health, in exercise of the powers conferred on him by sections 11 and 75 of the National Health Service Act 1946(a) and of all other powers enabling him in that behalf, and after consultation with the University of London, hereby orders as follows:—

1. This order may be cited as the National Health Service (Hydestile Hospital) Order 1968 and shall come into operation on 1st April 1968.

2.—(1) In this order—

" the Act " means the National Health Service Act 1946;

" the appointed day " means 1st April 1968;

" the Board of Governors " means the Board of Governors of St. Thomas' Hospital;

" the Hospital Board " means the South-West Metropolitan Regional Hospital Board;

" the Management Committee " means the Guildford and Godalming Group Hospital Management Committee;

" the transferred hospital " means the hospital named in article 3 hereof.

(2) The Interpretation Act 1889(b) shall apply to the interpretation of this order as it applies to the interpretation of an Act of Parliament.

3. Column 2 of schedule 1 to the National Health Service (Designation of London Teaching Hospitals) Order 1957(c) as amended(d) (which column prescribes hospitals or groups of hospitals designated as teaching hospitals), shall be further amended by deleting from the names of hospitals listed against the name of St. Thomas' Hospital in column 1 the words " (including St. Thomas' Hospital, Hydestile, Godalming, Surrey)."

4.—(1) All officers of the Board of Governors employed immediately before the appointed day solely at or for the purposes of the transferred hospital shall on that day be transferred to and become officers of the Hospital Board.

(2) All medical and dental officers of the Board of Governors employed immediately before the appointed day partly at and for the purposes of the

---

(a) 1946 c. 81.
(b) 1889 c. 63.
(c) S.I. 1957/488 (1957 I, p. 1452).
(d) S.I. 1964/453 (1964 I, p. 723).

transferred hospital and partly at and for the purposes of any other hospital shall on that day become officers of the Hospital Board in relation to their work at the transferred hospital and all rights and liabilities under their contract in relation thereto with the Board of Governors shall be transferred to the Hospital Board.

(3) Any other officer of the Board of Governors who is employed immediately before the appointed day partly at or for the purposes of the transferred hospital and who receives before that day notice in writing from the Board of Governors that he is to be transferred to the Hospital Board shall on that day be transferred to and become an officer of the Hospital Board.

(4) Any officer who is transferred to the Hospital Board under this article and whose employment was whole-time shall continue to be subject to the remuneration and other conditions of service applicable to a whole-time officer so long as his employment for both the Board of Governors and the Hospital Board amounts in the aggregate to whole-time employment.

5. On the appointed day there shall be transferred to and vest without further conveyance in the Hospital Board or the Management Committee—

    (*a*) any property held immediately before the appointed day by the Board of Governors—

        (i) under section 59 of the Act for the purposes of the transferred hospital, and

        (ii) under section 60 of the Act so far as practicable for the purposes of the transferred hospital; and

    (*b*) any other property held by the Board of Governors and any rights and liabilities to which the Board was entitled or subject immediately before the appointed day so far as these relate to the transferred hospital.

6. On the appointed day capital assets equivalent to assets of the Hospital Endowments Fund with a market value on 5th July 1948 of such sum as may be determined by agreement between the Board of Governors and the Hospital Board (or in default of agreement such sum, if any, as may be decided by the Minister) shall be transferred from the Board of Governors to the Fund, and the respective shares of the Hospital Board and the Management Committee in the net capital sum referred to in the National Health Service (Apportionment of Hospital Endowment Fund) Regulations 1949(**a**) shall each be increased by one half of the assets so transferred.

7. Any officer employed immediately before the appointed day at or for the purposes of the transferred hospital who suffers loss of employment or loss or diminution of emoluments which is attributable to this order shall be entitled to have his case considered for the payment of compensation at the like rate and in the like manner and subject to the like conditions as if he had been entitled to claim compensation under the Local Government (Executive Councils) (Compensation) Regulations 1964(**b**) as amended(**c**); and those regulations (except regulations 3, 4 and 5 thereof) shall apply for this purpose as if they had been set out in this order with the modifications that—

    (*a*) references to the " material date " shall be construed as references to the appointed day, and

    (*b*) references to " any such provision as is mentioned in regulation 4 of these regulations " shall be construed as references to this order.

(a) S.I. 1949/482 (1949 I, p. 2595).   (b) S.I. 1964/1177 (1964 II, p. 2696).
(c) S.I. 1966/254 (1966 I, p. 653).

2k

8. Any action or proceeding or any cause of action or proceeding, pending or existing at the appointed day, by, or against, the Board of Governors solely in respect of any property, right or liability transferred by this order shall not be prejudicially affected by reason of this order, and may be continued, prosecuted and enforced by, or against, the Hospital Board or the Management Committee.

Given under the official seal of the Minister of Health on 29th March 1968.

(L.S.)

J. P. Dodds,
Under Secretary,
Ministry of Health.

EXPLANATORY NOTE

(*This Note is not part of the Order.*)

This Order amends the National Health Service (Designation of London Teaching Hospitals) Order 1957 by excluding St. Thomas' Hospital, Hydestile, Godalming, Surrey, from the group of hospitals designated as St. Thomas' Hospital and provides for consequential matters relating to officers and property connected with that hospital.

STATUTORY INSTRUMENTS

1968 No. 547 (S. 51)

CIVIL DEFENCE

The Civil Defence Corps (Scotland) (Revocation) Regulations 1968

Laid before Parliament in draft

Made - - -		*29th March* 1968
Coming into Operation		*1st April* 1968

In exercise of the powers conferred on me by section 2 as read with the proviso to subsection (2) of section 9 of the Civil Defence Act 1948(a) and of all other powers enabling me in that behalf, I hereby make the following regulations, a draft of which has been laid before Parliament and approved by resolution of each House of Parliament:—

1. These regulations may be cited as the Civil Defence Corps (Scotland) (Revocation) Regulations 1968 and shall come into operation on 1st April 1968.

2. The Interpretation Act 1889(b) shall apply for the interpretation of these regulations as it applies for the interpretation of an Act of Parliament.

3. The Civil Defence Corps (Scotland) Regulations 1949(c) are hereby revoked.

William Ross,

One of Her Majesty's Principal
Secretaries of State.

St. Andrew's House,
   Edinburgh, 1.
29th March 1968.

EXPLANATORY NOTE

(This Note is not part of the regulations.)

These regulations revoke the Civil Defence Corps (Scotland) Regulations 1949 which made it the function of certain local authorities to organise divisions of the Civil Defence Corps.

(a) 12, 13 & 14 Geo. 6, c. 5.   (b) 1889 c. 63.   (c) S.I. 1949/1417 (1949 I, p. 645).

STATUTORY INSTRUMENTS

1968 No. 548 (S. 52)

CIVIL DEFENCE

The Civil Defence (Fire Services) (Scotland) Amendment Regulations 1968

Laid before Parliament in draft

Made - - -	*29th March* 1968
Coming into Operation	*1st April* 1968

In exercise of the powers conferred on me by section 2 as read with the proviso to subsection (2) of section 9 of the Civil Defence Act 1948(a) and of all other powers enabling me in that behalf, I hereby make the following regulations, a draft of which has been laid before Parliament and approved by resolution of each House of Parliament:—

1. These regulations may be cited as the Civil Defence (Fire Services) (Scotland) Amendment Regulations 1968 and shall come into operation on 1st April 1968.

2. The Interpretation Act 1889(b) shall apply for the interpretation of these regulations as it applies for the interpretation of an Act of Parliament.

3. The Civil Defence (Fire Services) (Scotland) Regulations 1949(c) (hereinafter referred to as the principal regulations) shall be amended as follows:—

For paragraph (i) of regulation 4 of the principal regulations (which relates to the employment of additional and auxiliary members of fire brigades) there shall be substituted the following:—

" (i) to employ such additional persons if any as members of the fire brigade for the purposes of civil defence as may be authorised from time to time by the Secretary of State."

William Ross,

One of Her Majesty's Principal Secretaries of State.

St. Andrew's House,
  Edinburgh, 1.
29th March 1968.

(a) 12, 13 & 14 Geo. 6, c. 5.   (b) 1889 c. 63.   (c) S.I. 1949/2167 (1949 I, p. 659).

EXPLANATORY NOTE
(This Note is not part of the regualtions.)

These regulations amend the Civil Defence (Fire Services) (Scotland) Regulations 1949 by providing that, with effect from 1st April 1968, only such additional persons as may be authorised by the Secretary of State may be employed by a fire authority for the purposes of civil defence. The function of a fire authority to enrol auxiliary firemen for such purposes is removed.

STATUTORY INSTRUMENTS

1968 No. 549

LAND COMMISSION

The Betterment Levy (Rate of Interest) Order 1968

Made - - -	*2nd April* 1968
Laid before the House of Commons	*10th April* 1968
Coming into Operation	*11th April* 1968

The Treasury, in exercise of the powers conferred upon them by section 51(2) of the Land Commission Act 1967(a) and of all other powers enabling them in that behalf, hereby make the following Order :—

1. The rate of interest for the purposes of section 51 of the Land Commission Act 1967 shall be 7½ per cent. per annum.

2. The Betterment Levy (Rate of Interest) (No. 5) Order 1967(b) is hereby revoked.

3. The Interpretation Act 1889(c) shall apply for the interpretation of this Order as it applies for the interpretation of an Act of Parliament.

4. This Order may be cited as the Betterment Levy (Rate of Interest) Order 1968, and shall come into operation on 11th April 1968.

B. K. O'Malley,
E. Alan Fitch,
Two of the Lords Commissioners
of Her Majesty's Treasury.

2nd April 1968.

EXPLANATORY NOTE

(This Note is not part of the Order.)

Section 51 of the Land Commission Act 1967 provides that interest shall be paid on unpaid or overpaid betterment levy. This Order decreases the rate of interest from 8 per cent. to 7½ per cent. per annum and revokes the Betterment Levy (Rate of Interest) (No. 5) Order 1967.

(a) 1967 c. 1.   (b) S.I. 1967/1765 (1967 III, p. 4734).   (c) 1889 c. 63.

STATUTORY INSTRUMENTS

1968 No. 551

AGRICULTURE

The Price Stability of Imported Products (Levy Revocation) Order 1968

Made - - - -	*2nd April* 1968
Coming into Operation	*5th April* 1968

The Minister of Agriculture, Fisheries and Food, in exercise of the powers conferred upon him by section 1(2), (4), (5), (6) and (7) of the Agriculture and Horticulture Act 1964(a) and of all other powers enabling him in that behalf, hereby makes the following order :—

1.—(1) This order may be cited as the Price Stability of Imported Products (Levy Revocation) Order 1968 ; and shall come into operation on 5th April 1968.

(2) The Interpretation Act 1889(b) shall apply to the interpretation of this order as it applies to the interpretation of an Act of Parliament and as if this order and the order hereby revoked were Acts of Parliament.

2. The Price Stability of Imported Products (Rates of Levy) Order 1966(c) is hereby revoked.

In Witness whereof the Official Seal of the Minister of Agriculture, Fisheries and Food is hereunto affixed on 2nd April 1968.

(L.S.)

A. C. Sparks,
Authorised by the Minister.

EXPLANATORY NOTE

(This Note is not part of the order.)

This order, which comes into operation on 5th April 1968, by revoking the Price Stability of Imported Products (Rates of Levy) Order 1966 (S.I. 1966/518) removes the general levy of 15s. per ton on imports of maize meal.

(a) 1964 c. 28.　　　(b) 1889 c. 63.　　　(c) S.I. 1966/518 (1966 II, p. 1103).

STATUTORY INSTRUMENTS

1968 No. 552

POLICE

ENGLAND AND WALES

The Police (Amendment) Regulations 1968

Made - - -		*2nd April* 1968
Laid before Parliament		*9th April* 1968
Coming into Operation		*11th April* 1968

In exercise of the powers conferred on me by section 33 of the Police Act 1964(a), and after consulting the Police Council for Great Britain in accordance with section 45(4) of that Act, I hereby make the following Regulations :—

1. For paragraph 3(3) of Part I of Schedule 3 to the Police Regulations 1968(b) (which contains scales of pay for men) there shall be substituted the following provision :—

"(3) Where the pay of a man falls to be determined in accordance with this sub-paragraph, his annual pay shall be determined in accordance with the scale set out in the column of the Table in sub-paragraph (4) appropriate to his police force by reference to his relevant service for the purposes of this sub-paragraph, that is to say, by reference to his service after the commencement of the last anniversary of the day of his birth falling on or before 1st March 1967:

Provided that—

(a) in the case of a man who, on or before 1st March 1967, had not completed 2 years' service reckonable for the purposes of his scale of pay, until he has completed 2 years of such service his annual pay, determined as aforesaid, shall be reduced by £35 ;

(b) in the case of a man who, on or before 1st March 1967, had completed 2 years' but not 3 years' service so reckonable and had not attained the age of 24 years, until he has completed a year's relevant service his annual pay, determined as aforesaid, shall be reduced by £35.".

2. For paragraph 3(3) of Part II of Schedule 3 to the Police Regulations 1968 (which contains scales of pay for women) there shall be substituted the following provision :—

"(3) Where the pay of a woman falls to be determined in accordance with this sub-paragraph, her annual pay shall be determined in accordance with the scale set out in the column of the Table in sub-paragraph (4) appropriate to

---

(a) 1964 c. 48.   (b) S.I. 1968/26 (1968 I, p. 38).

her police force by reference to her relevant service for the purposes of this sub-paragraph, that is to say, by reference to her service after the commencement of the last anniversary of the day of her birth falling on or before 1st March 1967:

Provided that—

    (a) in the case of a woman who, on or before 1st March 1967, had not completed 2 years' service reckonable for the purposes of her scale of pay, until she has completed 2 years of such service her annual pay, determined as aforesaid, shall be reduced by £30;

    (b) in the case of a woman who, on or before 1st March 1967, had completed 2 years' but not 3 years' service so reckonable and had not attained the age of 24 years, until she has completed a year's relevant service her annual pay, determined as aforesaid, shall be reduced by £30.".

3. These Regulations may be cited as the Police (Amendment) Regulations 1968 and shall come into operation on 11th April 1968.

James Callaghan,
One of Her Majesty's Principal
Secretaries of State.

Home Office,
    Whitehall.
    2nd April 1968.

EXPLANATORY NOTE

(This Note is not part of the Regulations.)

These Regulations substitute for paragraph 3(3) of Part I and paragraph 3(3) of Part II of Schedule 3 to the Police Regulations 1968 (which contain scales of pay) provisions which reproduce the corresponding provisions of the Regulations revoked by those Regulations (set out in Appendix 1 to the Police (Amendment) (No. 3) Regulations 1967—S.I. 1967/923).

STATUTORY INSTRUMENTS

1968 No. 557 (S.53)

NATIONAL HEALTH SERVICE, SCOTLAND

The National Health Service (Charges for Dental Treatment) (Scotland) Regulations 1968

Made - - -	*2nd April* 1968
Laid before Parliament	*10th April* 1968
Coming into Operation	*1st May* 1968

In exercise of the powers conferred on me by section 2 of the National Health Service Act 1952(a) and section 2 of the National Health Service Act 1961(b), and of all other powers enabling me in that behalf, I hereby make the following regulations :—

1. These regulations may be cited as the National Health Service (Charges for Dental Treatment) (Scotland) Regulations 1968 and shall come into operation on 1st May 1968.

2. The Interpretation Act 1889(c) applies for the interpretation of these regulations as it applies for the interpretation of an Act of Parliament.

3. The amount of one pound authorised by section 2(2) of the National Health Service Act 1952 (which provides for a maximum charge of one pound for certain general dental services other than those for which a charge is payable under the National Health Service Act 1951(d)) as a charge for dental treatment is hereby increased to thirty shillings.

4. These regulations apply in respect of any services provided in pursuance of a contract or arrangement under which the first examination took place after the coming into operation of these regulations.

5. Any reference in the National Health Service (General Dental Services) (Scotland) Regulations 1966(e) to a charge authorised by section 2 of the National Health Service Act 1952 shall include a reference to such charge as varied by these regulations.

William Ross,
One of Her Majesty's Principal
Secretaries of State.

St. Andrew's House,
Edinburgh, 1.
2nd April 1968.

(a) 1952 c. 25.   (b) 1961 c. 19.   (c) 1889 c. 63.
(d) 1951 c. 31.   (e) S.I. 1966/1449 (1966 III, p. 3802).

EXPLANATORY NOTE

(This Note is not part of the regulations.)

These regulations increase from one pound to thirty shillings the maximum amount payable by patients in respect of treatment, other than the supply of dentures, provided under general dental services.

STATUTORY INSTRUMENTS

1968 No. 565

TRANSPORT

The London Transport Board (Borrowing Powers) Order 1968

Laid before the House of Commons in draft

Made - - -	*4th April* 1968
Coming into Operation	18th *April* 1968

The Minister of Transport, in exercise of her powers under section 19(3) of the Transport Act 1962(**a**) and of all other enabling powers, hereby makes the following Order, a draft of which has been approved by a resolution of the Commons House of Parliament :—

1.—(1) This Order shall come into operation on the 18th April 1968 and may be cited as the London Transport Board (Borrowing Powers) Order 1968.

(2) The Interpretation Act 1889(**b**) shall apply for the interpretation of this Order as it applies for the interpretation of an Act of Parliament.

2. The aggregate amount outstanding in respect of—

(*a*) the principal of any money borrowed by the London Transport Board under section 19 of the Transport Act 1962, and

(*b*) the commencing capital debt, as defined in section 39 of that Act, of that Board,

taken together shall not exceed the sum of two hundred and seventy million pounds.

Sealed with the Official Seal of the Minister of Transport the 4th April 1968.

(L.S.)

Barbara Castle,
Minister of Transport.

(**a**) 10 & 11 Eliz. 2. c. 46.   (**b**) 52 & 53 Vict. c. 63.

EXPLANATORY NOTE

(This Note is not part of the Order.)

This Order under section 19(3) of the Transport Act 1962 increases the
borrowing powers of the London Transport Board. The Act prescribes a limit
of £200m. for the outstanding total of the principal of any money borrowed by
the Board and the Board's commencing capital debt to the Minister (prescribed
by S.I. 1964/448). The Minister is empowered by section 19(3) to increase
this limit from time to time up to a maximum of £270m. The London Transport Board (Borrowing Powers) Order 1965 (S.I. 1965/1979) increased the
limit to £250m. and this Order increases it further to £270m.

STATUTORY INSTRUMENTS

1968 No. 570

PETROLEUM

The Petroleum (Inflammable Liquids) Order 1968

Made - - - *8th* April 1968

Coming into Operation *1st August* 1968

At the Court at Windsor Castle, the 8th day of April 1968

Present,

The Queen's Most Excellent Majesty in Council

Her Majesty, in exercise of the powers conferred on Her by section 19 of the Petroleum (Consolidation) Act 1928(a), is pleased, by and with the advice of Her Privy Council, to order, and it is hereby ordered, as follows :—

1. Sections 6, 13(2) and (3), 14, 15, 16 and 18 of the Petroleum (Consolidation) Act 1928 shall apply to—

(a) the substances specified in the first column of the Table in Part I of the Schedule to this Order, being substances which are known also by the name or names (if any) mentioned in the second column of the said Table ;

(b) any solution or mixture (not being a mixture of petroleum as defined in the Schedule to the Petroleum (Mixtures) Order 1929(b)) which contains any of the said substances and which gives off an inflammable vapour at a temperature below seventy-three degrees Fahrenheit ; and

(c) any substance specified in Part II of the Schedule to this Order which gives off an inflammable vapour at a temperature below seventy-three degrees Fahrenheit.

2. In the Petroleum (Inflammable Liquids and Other Dangerous Substances) Order 1947(c)—

(a) in Article 1, the words "Parts I and II of" and the words from "and to any mixture" to the end shall be omitted ; and

(b) in the Schedule, Part I shall be omitted.

3.—(1) Nothing in this Order shall render invalid any order, notice, direction or warrant made, given or issued, or other thing done, under any provision of the Petroleum (Consolidation) Act 1928 as applied by the Petroleum (Inflammable Liquids and Other Dangerous Substances) Order 1947, and any such order, notice, direction, warrant or thing which could have been made, given, issued or done under any such provision as applied by this Order and in force or having effect at the date when this Order comes into operation shall be deemed to have been made, given, issued or done under that provision as applied by this Order.

(2) The Interpretation Act 1889(d) shall apply to the interpretation of this Order as it applies to the interpretation of an Act of Parliament.

4. This Order may be cited as the Petroleum (Inflammable Liquids) Order 1968 and shall come into operation on 1st August 1968, except that for the purpose of making any regulations under section 6 of the Petroleum (Consolidation) Act 1928 as applied by this Order to come into operation on or after the said date this Order shall come into operation forthwith.

W. G. Agnew.

(a) 1928 c. 32.   (b) S.R. & O. 1929/993 (Rev. XVIII, p. 7: 1929, p. 1143).
(c) S.R. & O. 1947/1443 (Rev. XVIII, p. 5: 1947 I, p. 1677).   (d) 1889 c. 63.

SCHEDULE

PART I

Name of substance	Alternative name or names
Acetaldehyde	Ethanal
Acetaldehyde oxime	Acetaldoxime
Acetone	Dimethyl ketone Propanone
Acrylaldehyde	Acraldehyde Acrolein Allyl aldehyde Propenal
Acrylonitrile	Propenenitrile Vinyl cyanide
Allyl acetate	
Allyl alcohol	Prop-2-en-l-ol 2-Propen-l-ol
Allylamine	2-Propenylamine
Allyl bromide	3-Bromoproprene
Allyl chloride	3-Chloropropene
Allyl ethyl ether	3-Ethoxypropene
Allyl formate	2-Propenyl methanoate
Benzenethiol	Thiophenol
Benzotrifluoride	Trifluoromethylbenzene
Bicycloheptadiene	
Boron trifluoride diethyl etherate	
2-Bromobutane	*sec*Butyl bromide
1-Bromo-2, 3-epoxypropane	Epibromohydrin
2-Bromoethyl ethyl ether	
1-Bromo-3-methylbutane	*iso*Amyl bromide
1-Bromo-2-methylpropane	*iso*Butyl bromide
2-Bromo-2-methylpropane	*tert*Butyl bromide
2-Bromopentane	*sec*Amyl bromide
1-Bromopropane	Propyl bromide
2-Bromopropane	*iso*Propyl bromide
3-Bromopropyne	Propargyl bromide
Butanedione	Diacetyl
Butane-1-thiol	n-Butane thiol Butyl mercaptan
Butan-2-ol	*sec*Butanol *sec*Butyl alcohol
Butanone	Ethyl methyl ketone
But-3-en-2-one	3-Butene-2-one Methyl vinyl ketone
Butyl acetate	2-Butanol acetate
*iso*Butyl acetate	
*sec*Butyl acetate	
Butylamine	1-Aminobutane
*iso*Butylamine	1-Amino-2-methylpropane
*sec*Butylamine	2-Aminobutane

SCHEDULE—*continued*

PART I—*continued*

Name of substance	*Alternative name or names*
*tert*Butylamine	{ 2-Amino-2-methylpropane 2-Amino *iso*butane
Butyl ethyl ether	1-Ethoxybutane
Butyl formate	Butyl methanoate
*iso*Butyl formate	
Butyl methyl ether	1-Methoxybutane
Butyl nitrite	
*iso*Butyl propionate	
Butyl vinyl ether	
*iso*Butyl vinyl ether	
But-2-yne	{ 2-Butine Crotonylene Dimethyl acetylene
Butyraldehyde	Butanal
*iso*Butyraldehyde	2-Methyl propanal
Butyronitrile	Propyl cyanide
Butyryl chloride	Butanoyl chloride
*iso*Butyryl chloride	*iso*Butanoyl chloride
1-Chlorobutane	Butyl chloride
2-Chlorobutane	*sec*Butyl chloride
1-Chloro-3-methylbutane	*iso*Amyl chloride
2-Chloro-2-methylbutane	*tert*Amyl chloride
Chloromethyl ethyl ether	
Chloromethyl methyl ether	{ Chlorodimethyl ether Chloromethoxy methane
1-Chloro-2-methylpropane	*iso*Butyl chloride
2-Chloro-2-methylpropane	*tert*Butyl chloride
3-Chloro-2-methylprop-1-ene	
1-Chloropentane	Amyl chloride
1-Chloropropane	Propyl chloride
2-Chloropropane	*iso*Propyl chloride
Crotonaldehyde	{ 2-Butenal β-Methyl acrolein Propyl aldehyde Propylene aldehyde
Cycloheptatriene	
Cyclohexene	Tetrahydrobenzene
Cyclohexylamine	Aminocyclohexane
Cyclo-octatetraene	
Diacetone alcohol	{ Diacetone, technical 4-Hydroxy-2-keto-4-methylpentane 4-Hydroxy-4-methylpentan-2-one
Diallylamine	Di-2-propenylamine
Diallyl ether	

SCHEDULE—*continued*

PART I—*continued*

Name of substance	Alternative name or names
Di*iso*butene	Di*iso*butylene
Di*iso*butylamine	
1,1-Dichloroethane	Ethylidene chloride
1,2-Dichloroethane	Ethylene dichloride
1,1-Dichloroethylene	Vinylidene chloride
1,2-Dichloroethylene	Acetylene dichloride
1,2-Dichloropropane	{ Propylene chloride { Propylene dichloride
Di (dimethylamino) ethane	Tetramethyl ethylene diamine
1,1-Diethoxyethane	{ Acetal { Diethyl acetal { Ethylidene diethyl ether
Diethoxymethane	{ Diethyl formal { Ethylal methylene diethyl ether { Formaldehyde diethyl acetal
3,3-Diethoxypropene	Acrolein acetal
Diethylamine	
Diethyl ether	{ Diethyl oxide { Ethoxyethane { Ethyl ether
Diethyl sulphide	
2,3-Dihydropyran	
1,1-Dimethoxyethane	{ Dimethyl acetal { Ethylidene dimethyl ether
Dimethoxymethane	{ Methylal { Methylene dimethyl ether
2-Dimethylaminoacetonitrile	2-Dimethylaminoethyl cyanide
1,3-Dimethylbutylamine	2-Amino-4-methylpentane
Dimethyl carbonate	Methyl carbonate
Dimethyldichlorosilane	
Dimethyldiethoxysilane	
Dimethyl disulphide	
NN'-Dimethylhydrazine	1,1-Dimethylhydrazine
Dimethyl sulphide	{ Methanthiomethane { Methyl sulphide
1,4-Dioxan	{ 1,4-Diethylene dioxide { Dioxan { Dioxyethylene ether
Dioxolane	
Dipropylamine	
Di*iso*propylamine	
Dipropyl ether	
Di*iso*propyl ether	{ 2-*iso*Propoxypropane { *iso*Propyl ether
Divinyl ether	Vinyl ether

Name of substance	Alternative name or names
Ethane thiol	Ethyl mercaptan
Ethanol	Ethyl alcohol
Ethyl acetate	
Ethyl acrylate	Ethyl propenoate
2-Ethylbutyraldehyde	Diethyl acetaldehyde
Ethyl *iso*butyrate	{ *iso*Butyric ether Ethyl 2-methylpropanoate
Ethyl chloroformate	Ethyl chlorocarbonate
Ethyl crotonate	
Ethyldichlorosilane	
Ethyleneimine	{ Aziridene Dimethyleneimine
Ethyl formate	Ethyl methanoate
Ethyl nitrite	
1-Ethylpiperidine	N-Ethyl piperidine
Ethyl propronate	
Ethyltrichlorosilane	
Ethyl vinyl ether	
Fluorobenzene	
2-Fluorotoluene	o-Fluorotoluene
3-Fluorotoluene	m-Fluorotoluene
Furan	
Fusel oil	
2-Iodobutane	*sec*Butyl iodide
1-Iodo-2-methylpropane	*iso*Butyl iodide
2-Iodo-2-methylpropane	*tert*Butyl iodide
1-Iodopropane	Propyl iodide
2-Iodopropane	*iso*Propyl iodide
Iron carbonyl	Iron pentacarbonyl
Isoprene monomer	2-Methyl-1,3-butadiene
Methacraldehyde	{ α-Methacrolein 2-Methylpropenal
Methanol	Methyl alcohol
Methyl acetate	
Methyl acetone	
Methyl acrylate	
3-Methylbutane-1-thiol	{ Amyl mercaptan Pentanethiol
2-Methylbutan-2- ol	{ *tert*Amyl alcohol Ethyl dimethyl carbinol 2-Methyl-2-butanol

SCHEDULE—*continued*

PART I—*continued*

Name of substance	Alternative name or names
3-Methylbutan-1- ol	*iso*Amyl alcohol
3-Methylbutan-2-one	{ 3-Methyl-2-butanone Methyl *iso*propyl ketone
Methyl butyrate	
Methyl chloroformate	Methyl chlorocarbonate
Methyldichlorosilane	
N-Methylformamide	Form-methylamide
Methyl formate	
Methyl hydrazine	
Methylhydrogendichlorosilane	
Methyl methacrylate, monomer	
2-Methylpentan-2-ol	
4-Methylpentan-2-one	{ *iso*Butyl methyl ketone Hexone 4-Methyl-2-pentanone
1-Methylpiperidine	N-Methylpiperidine
2-Methylpropan-2-ol	{ *tert*Butanol *tert*Butyl alcohol 2-Methyl-2-propanol Trimethyl carbinol
Methyl propionate	
Methyltrichlorosilane	
2-Methylvaleraldehyde	α-Methylvaleraldehyde
Methyl *iso*valerate	
Nickel carbonyl	Nickel tetracarbonyl
Paraldehyde	
Pentan-1-ol	{ n-Amyl alcohol Butyl carbinol 1-Pentanol
Pentan-2-ol	{ *sec*Amyl alcohol Methyl propyl carbinol 2-Pentanol
Pentan-2-one	{ Ethyl acetone Methyl propyl ketone 2-Pentanone
Pentan-3-one	{ Diethyl ketone Ethyl propionyl Metacetone Propione
*iso*Pentyl acetate	*iso*Amyl acetate

SCHEDULE—*continued*

PART I—*continued*

Name of substance	*Alternative name or names*
Pentylamine	{ 1-Aminopentane { n-Amylamine
*iso*Pentylamine	*iso*Amylamine
Pentyl nitrite	n-Amyl nitrite
*iso*Pentyl nitrite	*iso*Amyl nitrite
1-Phenylpropane-1,2-Dione	
Piperidine	
Propane-1-thiol	Propyl mercaptan
Propane-2-thiol	*iso*Propyl mercaptan
Propan-1-ol	{ 1-Propanol { Propyl alcohol
Propan-2-ol	{ Dimethyl carbinol { 2-Propanol { *iso*Propyl alcohol { *sec*Propyl alcohol
*iso*Propenyl acetate	
Propionaldehyde	
Propionitrile	Ethyl cyanide
Propyl acetate	
*iso*Propyl acetate	
Propylamine	
*iso*Propylamine	
*iso*Propyl butyrate	
*iso*Propyl *iso*Butyrate	
*iso*Propyl chloroformate	
Propyleneimine	
Propylene oxide	{ 1,2-Epoxy propane { Methyloxiran { Propene oxide
Propyl formate	
*iso*Propyl formate	
Propyl nitrate	
*iso*Propyl nitrate	
*iso*Propyl propionate	
Pyridine	
Pyrrolidine	
Tetrahydrofuran	
1,2,3,6-Tetrahydropyridine	
Tetrahydrothiophen	Tetramethylene sulphide
Tetrapropyl orthotitanate	
Thioacetic acid	
Thiophen	
Triethylamine	
Triethyl borate	{ Ethylborate { Triethoxyboron

SCHEDULE—*continued*

PART I—*continued*

Name of substance	*Alternative name or names*
Trimethoxyborine	Trimethoxyboroxine
Trimethyl borate	
Trimethylchlorosilane	
*iso*Valeraldehyde	{ *iso*Amyl aldehyde { 3-Methyl butanal { β-Methyl valeraldehyde
Vinyl acetate	
Vinyltrichlorosilane	

PART II

Dimethylamine solution in alcohol or water.
Ethylamine solution in alcohol or water.
Glyceryl trinitrate (otherwise known as nitroglycerine) solution in alcohol, not exceeding 5 per cent. of glyceryl trinitrate.
Methylamine solution in alcohol or water.
Trimethylamine solution in alcohol or water.

EXPLANATORY NOTE

(This Note is not part of the Order.)

This Order applies certain provisions of the Petroleum (Consolidation) Act 1928 to the inflammable substances specified in Part I of the Schedule ; and also to a solution or mixture containing any of those substances or a substance specified in Part II of the Schedule, if it gives off an inflammable vapour at a temperature below 73°F. Under the provisions as applied the Secretary of State is empowered to make regulations as to the conveyance of the inflammable liquids by road and for protecting persons and property from danger in connection with such conveyance. In addition, the provisions as applied require notice of certain accidents in connection with the inflammable liquids to be given to the Secretary of State, empower him to direct an inquiry to be made in regard thereto, make provision in regard to inquests and confer certain powers on magistrates' courts and on government inspectors in relation to the inflammable liquids.

The same provisions of the Act of 1928 already apply to certain of the inflammable liquids specified in the Schedule to this Order, as well as to certain other dangerous substances, by virtue of the Petroleum (Inflammable Liquids and Other Dangerous Substances) Order 1947 which is therefore amended by this Order so as to exclude references to those inflammable liquids.

1968 No. 571

PETROLEUM

The Petroleum (Carbon Disulphide) Order 1968

Made - - -	*8th April* 1968
Coming into Operation	*1st August* 1968

At the Court at Windsor Castle, the 8th day of April 1968

Present,

The Queen's Most Excellent Majesty in Council

Her Majesty, in exercise of the powers conferred on Her by section 19 of the Petroleum (Consolidation) Act 1928(a), is pleased, by and with the advice of Her Privy Council, to order, and it is hereby ordered, as follows:—

1. For paragraph (2) of Article 1 of the Petroleum (Carbon Disulphide) Order 1958(b) (which specifies the modifications to be made in section 5 of the Petroleum (Consolidation) Act 1928 in the application of that section to carbon disulphide) there shall be substituted the following paragraph:—

'(2) The said section 5 shall have effect as if—

(*a*) in subsection (1)—

(i) the words "(*b*) is sent or conveyed between any two places in Great Britain; or", the words "(ii) in the case of petroleum-spirit sent or conveyed, the name and address of the sender;" and, in the proviso, paragraph (*b*) were omitted;

(ii) in the words required by the subsection to be shown on the label referred to therein, the words "Carbon Disulphide" were substituted for the words "Petroleum-Spirit";

(*b*) in subsection (2) the words "sends, conveys," were omitted.'.

2. This Order may be cited as the Petroleum (Carbon Disulphide) Order 1968 and shall come into operation on 1st August 1968, except that for the purpose of making any regulations under section 6 of the Petroleum (Consolidation) Act 1928 as applied by the Petroleum (Carbon Disulphide) Order 1958 as amended by this Order to come into operation on or after the said date this Order shall come into operation forthwith.

W. G. Agnew.

(a) 1928 c. 32.   (b) S.I. 1958/257 (1958 II, p. 1888).

EXPLANATORY NOTE

(This Note is not part of the Order.)

The provisions of section 5 of the Petroleum (Consolidation) Act 1928 relating to the labelling of vessels containing petroleum-spirit are, by the Petroleum (Carbon Disulphide) Order 1958, applied to carbon disulphide, subject to certain modifications. This Order provides for a further modification of section 5, the effect of which is that the labelling requirements of section 5 will no longer apply to carbon disulphide being sent or conveyed between any two places in Great Britain.

STATUTORY INSTRUMENTS

1968 No. 572

INCOME TAX

The Double Taxation Relief (Shipping and Air Transport Profits) (Brazil) Order 1968

Laid before the House of Commons in draft
Made -   -   -   -   8th April 1968

At the Court at Windsor Castle, the 8th day of April 1968

Present,

The Queen's Most Excellent Majesty in Council

Whereas a draft of this Order was laid before the Commons House of Parliament in accordance with the provisions of section 347(6) of the Income Tax Act 1952(a), and an Address has been presented to Her Majesty by that House praying that an Order may be made in the terms of this Order :

Now, therefore, Her Majesty, in exercise of the powers conferred upon Her by section 347(1) of the said Income Tax Act 1952, as amended by section 64 of the Finance Act 1965(b), and of all other powers enabling Her in that behalf, is pleased, by and with the advice of Her Privy Council, to order, and it is hereby ordered, as follows :—

1. This Order may be cited as the Double Taxation Relief (Shipping and Air Transport Profits) (Brazil) Order 1968.

2. It is hereby declared—

(a) that the arrangements specified in the Schedule to this Order have been made with the Government of Brazil with a view to affording relief from double taxation in relation to income tax or corporation tax and taxes of a similar character imposed by the laws of Brazil ; and

(b) that it is expedient that those arrangements should have effect.

W. G. Agnew.

SCHEDULE

(1) The Government of Brazil shall in accordance with Article 22 of the Income Tax Regulations (Decree 58.400 of 10th May, 1965) exempt all income derived from the business of shipping and air transport in international traffic by United Kingdom undertakings engaged in such business from all taxes which are covered by the Federal income tax law and all similar Federal taxes on income or profits which are, or may become, chargeable in Brazil.

(2) The Government of the United Kingdom shall exempt all income derived from the business of shipping and air transport in international traffic by Brazilian undertakings engaged in such business from income tax and corporation tax and all other taxes on income or profits which are, or may become, chargeable in the United Kingdom.

(a) 15 & 16 Geo. 6 & 1 Eliz. 2. c. 10.   (b) 1965 c. 25.

(3) (*a*) The expression " United Kingdom undertakings " means the Government of the United Kingdom and companies managed and controlled in the United Kingdom, provided that they have their Head Offices in the United Kingdom.

(*b*) The expression " Brazilian undertakings " means the Government of Brazil and companies managed and controlled in Brazil, provided that they are established in accordance with Brazilian law and have their Head Offices in Brazil.

(4) The exemptions provided for in paragraphs (1) and (2) above shall apply to all income earned from 1st January 1967.

(5) The exemptions from tax provided for in paragraphs (1) and (2) above shall continue until either

(*a*) Brazilian law ceases to provide for the exemption from tax referred to in paragraph (1) above, or

(*b*) the Government of the United Kingdom terminates the exemption from tax referred to in paragraph (2) above by giving six months' notice in writing to the Government of Brazil.

(6) This Agreement between the two Governments may be extended by a further Exchange of Notes to any territory for the international relations of which the Government of the United Kingdom are responsible.

EXPLANATORY NOTE
(*This Note is not part of the Order.*)

Under the arrangements with Brazil scheduled to this Order shipping and air transport profits derived from one country by an undertaking of the other country are (subject to certain conditions) to be exempt from tax in the former country.

The arrangements apply to income earned from 1st January 1967.

STATUTORY INSTRUMENTS

1968 No. 573

INCOME TAX

The Double Taxation Relief (Taxes on Income) (British Honduras) Order 1968

Laid before the House of Commons in draft

Made - - - *8th April* 1968

At the Court at Windsor Castle, the 8th day of April 1968

Present,

The Queen's Most Excellent Majesty in Council

Whereas a draft of this Order was laid before the Commons House of Parliament in accordance with the provisions of section 347 (6) of the Income Tax Act 1952(**a**), and an Address has been presented to Her Majesty by that House praying that an Order may be made in the terms of this Order :

Now, therefore, Her Majesty, in exercise of the powers conferred upon Her by section 347 (1) of the said Income Tax Act 1952, as amended by section 64 of the Finance Act 1965(**b**), and of all other powers enabling Her in that behalf, is pleased, by and with the advice of Her Privy Council, to order, and it is hereby ordered, as follows :—

1. This Order may be cited as the Double Taxation Relief (Taxes on Income) (British Honduras) Order 1968.

2. It is hereby declared—

(*a*) that the arrangements specified in the Arrangement set out in the Schedule to this Order have been made with the Government of British Honduras with a view to affording relief from double taxation in relation to income tax or corporation tax and taxes of a similar character imposed by the laws of British Honduras varying the arrangements set out in the Schedule to the Double Taxation Relief (Taxes on Income) (British Honduras) Order 1947(**c**) ; and

(*b*) that it is expedient that those arrangements should have effect.

W. G. Agnew.

(**a**) 15 & 16 Geo. 6 & 1 Eliz. 2. c. 10.   (**b**) 1965 c. 25.
(**c**) S.R. & O. 1947/2866 (Rev. X, p. 363: 1947 1, p. 1084).

SCHEDULE

ARRANGEMENT BETWEEN HER MAJESTY'S GOVERNMENT AND THE GOVERNMENT
OF BRITISH HONDURAS TO AMEND THE EXISTING ARRANGEMENT FOR THE
AVOIDANCE OF DOUBLE TAXATION AND THE PREVENTION OF FISCAL
EVASION WITH RESPECT TO TAXES ON INCOME

1. The Arrangement made in 1947 between His Majesty's Government and
the Government of British Honduras for the avoidance of double taxation and
the prevention of fiscal evasion with respect to taxes on income (hereinafter
referred to as "the existing Arrangement") shall be amended—

(*a*) by the addition at the end of paragraph 6 of the following new sub-
paragraph—

"(3) If the recipient of a dividend is a company which owns 10 per
cent. or more of the class of shares in respect of which the dividend
is paid then sub-paragraph (1) shall not apply to the dividend to the
extent that it can have been paid only out of profits which the company
paying the dividend earned or other income which it received in a
period ending twelve months or more before the relevant date. For
the purposes of this sub-paragraph the term "relevant date" means the
date on which the beneficial owner of the dividend became the owner
of 10 per cent. or more of the class of shares in question.

Provided that this sub-paragraph shall not apply if the beneficial
owner of the dividend shows that the shares were acquired for *bona
fide* commercial reasons and not primarily for the purpose of securing
the benefit of this paragraph." ; and

(*b*) by the substitution for sub-paragraphs (1) and (2) of paragraph 13 of
the following two new sub-paragraphs—

"(1) Subject to the provisions of the law of the United Kingdom
regarding the allowance as a credit against United Kingdom tax of tax
payable in a territory outside the United Kingdom (which shall not
affect the general principle hereof)—

(*a*) Colonial tax payable under the laws of the Colony and in accordance with this Arrangement, whether directly or by deduction, on
profits or income from sources within the Colony shall be allowed
as a credit against any United Kingdom tax computed by reference
to the same profits or income by reference to which the Colonial
tax is computed.

Provided that in the case of a dividend the credit shall only take
into account such tax in respect thereof as is additional to any
tax payable by the company on the profits out of which the
dividend is paid and is ultimately borne by the recipient without
reference to any tax so payable.

(*b*) Where a company which is a resident of the Colony pays a
dividend to a company resident in the United Kingdom which
controls directly or indirectly at least 10 per cent. of the voting
power in the first-mentioned company, the credit shall take into
account (in addition to any Colonial tax for which credit may be
allowed under (*a*) of this sub-paragraph) the Colonial tax payable
by that first-mentioned company in respect of the profits out of
which such dividend is paid.

(2) Subject to the provisions of the law of the Colony regarding the allowance as a credit against Colonial tax of tax payable in a territory outside the Colony (which shall not affect the general principle hereof)—

(*a*) United Kingdom tax payable under the laws of the United Kingdom and in accordance with this Arrangement, whether directly or by deduction, on profits or income from sources within the United Kingdom shall be allowed as a credit against any Colonial tax computed by reference to the same profits or income by reference to which the United Kingdom tax is computed.

Provided that in the case of a dividend the credit shall only take into account such tax in respect thereof as is additional to any tax payable by the company on the profits out of which the dividend is paid and is ultimately borne by the recipient without reference to any tax so payable.

(*b*) Where a company which is a resident of the United Kingdom pays a dividend to a company resident in the Colony which controls directly or indirectly at least 10 per cent. of the voting power in the first-mentioned company, the credit shall take into account (in addition to any United Kingdom tax for which credit may be allowed under (*a*) of this sub-paragraph) the United Kingdom tax payable by that first-mentioned company in respect of the profits out of which such dividend is paid."

2. This Arrangement shall enter into force when the last of all such things shall have been done in the United Kingdom and the Colony as are necessary to give the Arrangement the force of law in the United Kingdom and the Colony respectively, and the new sub-paragraph (3) of paragraph 6 of the existing Arrangement shall have effect immediately, and the new sub-paragraphs (1) and (2) of paragraph 13 thereof shall have effect—

(*a*) in the United Kingdom:

(i) as respects income tax (including surtax), for any year of assessment beginning on or after 6 April, 1968 ; and

(ii) as respects corporation tax, for any financial year beginning on or after 1 April, 1968 ;

(*b*) in the Colony:
as respects Colonial tax, for any year of assessment beginning on or after 1 January, 1968.

EXPLANATORY NOTE

(This Note is not part of the Order.)

This Arrangement makes two amendments to the Arrangement between the United Kingdom and British Honduras which is scheduled to the Double Taxation Relief (Taxes on Income) (British Honduras) Order 1947.

First it provides that the exemption of dividends from any tax chargeable in addition to the tax on the paying company's profits is not to be allowed in certain cases where the shareholder is a company having a substantial holding in the paying company. The restriction does not apply to dividends on shares acquired for *bona fide* commercial reasons.

Secondly, it amends paragraph 13 of the 1947 Arrangement in its application to dividends by providing that credit for tax on the profits out of which dividends are paid, whether that tax is deducted from the dividends or not, is to be given only where the recipient is a company which holds not less than 10 per cent of the voting power in the paying company. So far as United Kingdom income tax is concerned this provision takes effect from the year of assessment 1968/69.

STATUTORY INSTRUMENTS

1968 No. 574

INCOME TAX

The Double Taxation Relief (Taxes on Income) (British Solomon Islands Protectorate) Order 1968

Laid before the House of Commons in draft

Made - - - - *8th April* 1968

At the Court at Windsor Castle, the 8th day of April 1968

Present,

The Queen's Most Excellent Majesty in Council

Whereas a draft of this Order was laid before the Commons House of Parliament in accordance with the provisions of section 347(6) of the Income Tax Act 1952(a), and an Address has been presented to Her Majesty by that House praying that an Order may be made in the terms of this Order:

Now, therefore, Her Majesty, in exercise of the powers conferred upon Her by section 347(1) of the said Income Tax Act 1952, as amended by section 64 of the Finance Act 1965(b) and of all other powers enabling Her in that behalf, is pleased, by and with the advice of Her Privy Council, to order, and it is hereby ordered, as follows:—

1. This Order may be cited as the Double Taxation Relief (Taxes on Income) (British Solomon Islands Protectorate) Order 1968.

2. It is hereby declared—

   (*a*) that the arrangements specified in the Arrangement set out in the Schedule to this Order have been made with the Government of the British Solomon Islands Protectorate with a view to affording relief from double taxation in relation to income tax or corporation tax and taxes of a similar character imposed by the laws of the British Solomon Islands Protectorate varying the arrangements set out in the Schedule to the Double Taxation Relief (Taxes on Income) (British Solomon Islands Protectorate) Order 1950(c); and

   (*b*) that it is expedient that those arrangements should have effect.

W. G. Agnew.

(a) 15 & 16 Geo. 6 & 1 Eliz. 2. c. 10.   (b) 1965 c. 25.
(c) S.I. 1950/748 (1950 I, p. 997).

SCHEDULE

ARRANGEMENT BETWEEN HER MAJESTY'S GOVERNMENT AND THE GOVERNMENT OF THE BRITISH SOLOMON ISLANDS PROTECTORATE TO AMEND THE EXISTING ARRANGEMENT FOR THE AVOIDANCE OF DOUBLE TAXATION AND THE PREVENTION OF FISCAL EVASION WITH RESPECT TO TAXES ON INCOME

1. The Arrangement made in 1950 between His Majesty's Government and the Government of the British Solomon Islands Protectorate for the avoidance of double taxation and the prevention of fiscal evasion with respect to taxes on income (hereinafter referred to as "the existing Arrangement") shall be amended—

(a) by the addition at the end of paragraph 6 of the following new sub-paragraph—

"(3) If the recipient of a dividend is a company which owns 10 per cent. or more of the class of shares in respect of which the dividend is paid then sub-paragraph (1) shall not apply to the dividend to the extent that it can have been paid only out of profits which the company paying the dividend earned or other income which it received in a period ending twelve months or more before the relevant date. For the purposes of this sub-paragraph the term "relevant date" means the date on which the beneficial owner of the dividend became the owner of 10 per cent. or more of the class of shares in question.

Provided that this sub-paragraph shall not apply if the beneficial owner of the dividend shows that the shares were acquired for *bona fide* commercial reasons and not primarily for the purpose of securing the benefit of this paragraph."; and

(b) by the substitution for sub-paragraphs (1) and (2) of paragraph 13 of the following two new sub-paragraphs—

"(1) Subject to the provisions of the law of the United Kingdom regarding the allowance as a credit against United Kingdom tax of tax payable in a territory outside the United Kingdom (which shall not affect the general principle hereof)—

(a) Protectorate tax payable under the laws of the Protectorate and in accordance with this Arrangement, whether directly or by deduction, on profits or income from sources within the Protectorate shall be allowed as a credit against any United Kingdom tax computed by reference to the same profits or income by reference to which the Protectorate tax is computed.

Provided that in the case of a dividend the credit shall only take into account such tax in respect thereof as is additional to any tax payable by the company on the profits out of which the dividend is paid and is ultimately borne by the recipient without reference to any tax so payable.

(b) Where a company which is a resident of the Protectorate pays a dividend to a company resident in the United Kingdom which controls directly or indirectly at least 10 per cent. of the voting power in the first-mentioned company, the credit shall take into account (in addition to any Protectorate tax for which credit may be allowed under (a) of this sub-paragraph) the Protectorate tax payable by that first-mentioned company in respect of the profits out of which such dividend is paid.

(2) Subject to the provisions of the law of the Protectorate regarding the allowance as a credit against Protectorate tax of tax payable in a territory outside the Protectorate (which shall not affect the general principle hereof)—

(a) United Kingdom tax payable under the laws of the United Kingdom and in accordance with this Arrangement, whether directly or by deduction, on profits or income from sources within the United Kingdom shall be allowed as a credit against any Protectorate tax computed by reference to the same profits or income by reference to which the United Kingdom tax is computed.

Provided that in the case of a dividend the credit shall only take into account such tax in respect thereof as is additional to any tax payable by the company on the profits out of which the dividend is paid and is ultimately borne by the recipient without reference to any tax so payable.

(b) Where a company which is a resident of the United Kingdom pays a dividend to a company resident in the Protectorate which controls directly or indirectly at least 10 per cent. of the voting power in the first-mentioned company, the credit shall take into account (in addition to any United Kingdom tax for which credit may be allowed under (a) of this sub-paragraph) the United Kingdom tax payable by that first-mentioned company in respect of the profits out of which such dividend is paid."

2. This Arrangement shall enter into force when the last of all such things shall have been done in the United Kingdom and the Protectorate as are necessary to give the Arrangement the force of law in the United Kingdom and the Protectorate respectively, and the new sub-paragraph (3) of paragraph 6 of the existing Arrangement shall have effect immediately and the new sub-paragraphs (1) and (2) of paragraph 13 thereof shall have effect—

(a) in the United Kingdom:

    (i) as respects income tax (including surtax), for any year of assessment beginning on or after 6 April, 1968; and

    (ii) as respects corporation tax, for any financial year beginning on or after 1 April, 1968;

(b) in the Protectorate:

as respects income tax, for any year of assessment beginning on or after 1 January, 1968.

EXPLANATORY NOTE

(This Note is not part of the Order.)

This Arrangement makes two amendments to the Arrangement between the United Kingdom and the British Solomon Islands which is scheduled to the Double Taxation Relief (Taxes on Income) (British Solomon Islands Protectorate) Order 1950.

First it provides that the exemption of dividends from any tax chargeable in addition to the tax on the paying company's profits is not to be allowed in certain cases where the shareholder is a company having a substantial holding in the paying company. The restriction does not apply to dividends on shares acquired for *bona fide* commercial reasons.

Secondly, it amends paragraph 13 of the 1950 Arrangement in its application to dividends by providing that credit for tax on the profits out of which dividends are paid, whether that tax is deducted from the dividends or not, is to be given only where the recipient is a company which holds not less than 10 per cent of the voting power in the paying company. So far as United Kingdom income tax is concerned this provision takes effect from the year of assessment 1968/69.

1968 No. 575

INCOME TAX

The Double Taxation Relief (Taxes on Income) (Falkland Islands) Order 1968

Laid before the House of Commons in draft

Made - - - *8th April* 1968

At the Court at Windsor Castle, the 8th day of April 1968

Present,

The Queen's Most Excellent Majesty in Council

Whereas a draft of this Order was laid before the Commons House of Parliament in accordance with the provisions of section 347(6) of the Income Tax Act 1952(a), and an Address has been presented to Her Majesty by that House praying that an Order may be made in the terms of this Order :

Now, therefore, Her Majesty, in exercise of the powers conferred upon Her by section 347(1) of the said Income Tax Act 1952, as amended by section 64 of the Finance Act 1965(b), and of all other powers enabling Her in that behalf, is pleased, by and with the advice of Her Privy Council, to order, and it is hereby ordered, as follows :—

1. This Order may be cited as the Double Taxation Relief (Taxes on Income) (Falkland Islands) Order 1968.

2. It is hereby declared—

(*a*) that the arrangements specified in the Arrangement set out in the Schedule to this Order have been made with the Government of the Falkland Islands with a view to affording relief from double taxation in relation to income tax or corporation tax and taxes of a similar character imposed by the laws of the Falkland Islands varying the arrangements set out in the Schedule to the Double Taxation Relief (Taxes on Income) (Falkland Islands) Order 1949(c) ; and

(*b*) that it is expedient that those arrangements should have effect.

W. G. Agnew.

(a) 15 & 16 Geo. 6 & 1 Eliz. 2. c. 10.   (b) 1965 c. 25.
(c) S.I. 1949/360 (1949 I, p. 2262).

SCHEDULE

ARRANGEMENT BETWEEN HER MAJESTY'S GOVERNMENT AND THE GOVERNMENT OF THE FALKLAND ISLANDS TO AMEND THE EXISTING ARRANGEMENT FOR THE AVOIDANCE OF DOUBLE TAXATION AND THE PREVENTION OF FISCAL EVASION WITH RESPECT TO TAXES ON INCOME

1. The Arrangement made in 1949 between His Majesty's Government and the Government of the Falkland Islands for the avoidance of double taxation and the prevention of fiscal evasion with respect to taxes on income (hereinafter referred to as "the existing Arrangement") shall be amended—

(*a*) by the addition at the end of paragraph 6 of the following new sub-paragraph—

"(3) If the recipient of a dividend is a company which owns 10 per cent. or more of the class of shares in respect of which the dividend is paid then sub-paragraph (1) shall not apply to the dividend to the extent that it can have been paid only out of profits which the company paying the dividend earned or other income which it received in a period ending twelve months or more before the relevant date. For the purposes of this sub-paragraph the term "relevant date" means the date on which the beneficial owner of the dividend became the owner of 10 per cent. or more of the class of shares in question.

Provided that this sub-paragraph shall not apply if the beneficial owner of the dividend shows that the shares were acquired for *bona fide* commercial reasons and not primarily for the purpose of securing the benefit of this paragraph." ; and

(*b*) by the substitution for sub-paragraphs (1) and (2) of paragraph 13 of the following two new sub-paragraphs—

"(1) Subject to the provisions of the law of the United Kingdom regarding the allowance as a credit against United Kingdom tax of tax payable in a territory outside the United Kingdom (which shall not affect the general principle hereof)—

(*a*) Colonial tax payable under the laws of the Colony and in accordance with this Arrangement, whether directly or by deduction, on profits or income from sources within the Colony shall be allowed as a credit against any United Kingdom tax computed by reference to the same profits or income by reference to which the Colonial tax is computed.

Provided that in the case of a dividend the credit shall only take into account such tax in respect thereof as is additional to any tax payable by the company on the profits out of which the dividend is paid and is ultimately borne by the recipient without reference to any tax so payable.

(*b*) Where a company which is a resident of the Colony pays a dividend to a company resident in the United Kingdom which controls directly or indirectly at least 10 per cent. of the voting power in the first-mentioned company, the credit shall take into account (in addition to any Colonial tax for which credit may be allowed under (*a*) of this sub-paragraph) the Colonial tax payable by that first-mentioned company in respect of the profits out of which such dividend is paid.

(2) Subject to the provisions of the law of the Colony regarding the allowance as a credit against Colonial tax of tax payable in a territory outside the Colony (which shall not affect the general principle hereof)—

(a) United Kingdom tax payable under the laws of the United Kingdom and in accordance with this Arrangement, whether directly or by deduction, on profits or income from sources within the United Kingdom shall be allowed as a credit against any Colonial tax computed by reference to the same profits or income by reference to which the United Kingdom tax is computed.

Provided that in the case of a dividend the credit shall only take into account such tax in respect thereof as is additional to any tax payable by the company on the profits out of which the dividend is paid and is ultimately borne by the recipient without reference to any tax so payable.

(b) Where a company which is a resident of the United Kingdom pays a dividend to a company resident in the Colony which controls directly or indirectly at least 10 per cent. of the voting power in the first-mentioned company, the credit shall take into account (in addition to any United Kingdom tax for which credit may be allowed under (a) of this sub-paragraph) the United Kingdom tax payable by that first-mentioned company in respect of the profits out of which such dividend is paid."

2. This Arrangement shall enter into force when the last of all such things shall have been done in the United Kingdom and the Colony as are necessary to give the Arrangement the force of law in the United Kingdom and the Colony respectively, and the new sub-paragraph (3) of paragraph 6 of the existing Arrangement shall have effect immediately and the new sub-paragraphs (1) and (2) of paragraph 13 thereof shall have effect—

(a) in the United Kingdom:

    (i) as respects income tax (including surtax), for any year of assessment beginning on or after 6 April, 1968 ; and

    (ii) as respects corporation tax, for any financial year beginning on or after 1 April, 1968 ;

(b) in the Colony:

as respects Colonial tax, for any year of assessment beginning on or after 1 January, 1968.

EXPLANATORY NOTE
(This Note is not part of the Order.)

This Arrangement makes two amendments to the Arrangement between the United Kingdom and the Falkland Islands which is scheduled to the Double Taxation Relief (Taxes on Income) (Falkland Islands) Order 1949.

First it provides that the exemption of dividends from any tax chargeable in addition to the tax on the paying company's profits is not to be allowed in certain cases where the shareholder is a company having a substantial holding in the paying company. The restriction does not apply to dividends on shares acquiring for *bona fide* commercial reasons.

Secondly, it amends paragraph 13 of the 1949 Arrangement in its application to dividends by providing that credit for tax on the profits out of which dividends are paid, whether the tax is deducted from the dividends or not, is to be given only where the recipient is a company which holds not less than 10 per cent. of the voting power in the paying company. So far as United Kingdom income tax is concerned this provision takes effect from the year of assessment 1968/69.

STATUTORY INSTRUMENTS

1968 No. 576

INCOME TAX

The Double Taxation Relief (Taxes on Income) (Montserrat) Order 1968

Laid before the House of Commons in draft

Made - - - - *8th April* 1968

At the Court at Windsor Castle, the 8th day of April 1968

Present,

The Queen's Most Excellent Majesty in Council

Whereas a draft of this Order was laid before the Commons House of Parliament in accordance with the provisions of section 347(6) of the Income Tax Act 1952(a), and an Address has been presented to Her Majesty by that House praying that an Order may be made in the terms of this Order:

Now, therefore, Her Majesty, in exercise of the powers conferred upon Her by section 347(1) of the said Income Tax Act 1952, as amended by section 64 of the Finance Act 1965(b), and of all other powers enabling Her in that behalf, is pleased, by and with the advice of Her Privy Council, to order, and it is hereby ordered, as follows:—

1. This Order may be cited as the Double Taxation Relief (Taxes on Income) (Montserrat) Order 1968.

2. It is hereby declared—

  (*a*) that the arrangements specified in the Arrangement set out in the Schedule to this Order have been made with the Government of Montserrat with a view to affording relief from double taxation in relation to income tax or corporation tax and taxes of a similar character imposed by the laws of Montserrat varying the arrangements set out in the Schedule to the Double Taxation Relief (Taxes on Income) (Montserrat) Order 1947(c); and

  (*b*) that it is expedient that those arrangements should have effect.

W. G. Agnew.

(a) 15 & 16 Geo. 6 & 1 Eliz. 2. c. 10.　　　　(b) 1965 c. 25.
(c) S.R. & O. 1947/2869 (Rev. X, p. 433: 1947 I, p. 1119).

SCHEDULE

ARRANGEMENT BETWEEN HER MAJESTY'S GOVERNMENT AND THE GOVERNMENT OF MONTSERRAT TO AMEND THE EXISTING ARRANGEMENT FOR THE AVOIDANCE OF DOUBLE TAXATION AND THE PREVENTION OF FISCAL EVASION WITH RESPECT TO TAXES ON INCOME

1. The Arrangement made in 1947 between His Majesty's Government and the Government of the Presidency of Montserrat for the avoidance of double taxation and the prevention of fiscal evasion with respect to taxes on income (hereinafter referred to as "the existing Arrangement") shall be amended—

(*a*) by the deletion from the title and paragraph 1(1)(*b*) of the words "the Presidency of";

(*b*) by the deletion of paragraph 2(1)(*b*);

(*c*) by the substitution for the references therein to "the Presidency", "Presidential enterprise" and "Presidential tax" of references to "Montserrat", "Montserrat enterprise" and "Montserrat tax" respectively;

(*d*) by the addition at the end of paragraph 6 of the following new sub-paragraph—

"(3) If the recipient of a dividend is a company which owns 10 per cent. or more of the class of shares in respect of which the dividend is paid then sub-paragraph (1) shall not apply to the dividend to the extent that it can have been paid only out of profits which the company paying the dividend earned or other income which it received in a period ending twelve months or more before the relevant date. For the purposes of this sub-paragraph the term "relevant date" means the date on which the beneficial owner of the dividend became the owner of 10 per cent. or more of the class of shares in question.

Provided that this sub-paragraph shall not apply if the beneficial owner of the dividend shows that the shares were acquired for *bona fide* commercial reasons and not primarily for the purpose of securing the benefit of this paragraph."; and

(*e*) by the substitution for sub-paragraphs (1) and (2) of paragraph 13 of the following two new sub-paragraphs—

"(1) Subject to the provisions of the law of the United Kingdom regarding the allowance as a credit against United Kingdom tax of tax payable in a territory outside the United Kingdom (which shall not affect the general principle hereof)—

(*a*) Montserrat tax payable under the laws of Montserrat and in accordance with this Arrangement, whether directly or by deduction, on profits or income from sources within Montserrat shall be allowed as a credit against any United Kingdom tax computed by reference to the same profits or income by reference to which Montserrat tax is computed.

Provided that in the case of a dividend the credit shall only take into account such tax in respect thereof as is additional to any tax payable by the company on the profits out of which the dividend is paid and is ultimately borne by the recipient without reference to any tax so payable.

(*b*) Where a company which is a resident of Montserrat pays a dividend to a company resident in the United Kingdom which controls directly or indirectly at least 10 per cent. of the voting power in the first-mentioned company, the credit shall take into account (in addition to any Montserrat tax for which credit may be allowed under (*a*) of this sub-paragraph) the Montserrat tax payable by that first-mentioned company in respect of the profits out of which such dividend is paid.

(2) Subject to the provisions of the law of Montserrat regarding the allowance as a credit against Montserrat tax of tax payable in a territory outside Montserrat (which shall not affect the general principle hereof)—

(*a*) United Kingdom tax payable under the laws of the United Kingdom and in accordance with this Arrangement, whether directly or by deduction, on profits or income from sources within the United Kingdom shall be allowed as a credit against any Montserrat tax computed by reference to the same profits or income by reference to which the United Kingdom tax is computed.

Provided that in the case of a dividend the credit shall only take into account such tax in respect thereof as is additional to any tax payable by the company on the profits out of which the dividend is paid and is ultimately borne by the recipient without reference to any tax so payable.

(*b*) Where a company which is a resident of the United Kingdom pays a dividend to a company resident in Montserrat which controls directly or indirectly at least 10 per cent. of the voting power in the first-mentioned company, the credit shall take into account (in addition to any United Kingdom tax for which credit may be allowed under (*a*) of this sub-paragraph) the United Kingdom tax payable by that first-mentioned company in respect of the profits out of which such dividend is paid."

2. This Arrangement shall enter into force when the last of all such things shall have been done in the United Kingdom and Montserrat as are necessary to give the amendments the force of law in the United Kingdom and Montserrat respectively, and the new sub-paragraph (3) of paragraph 6 of the existing Arrangement shall have effect immediately and the new sub-paragraphs (1) and (2) of paragraph 13 thereof shall have effect—

(*a*) in the United Kingdom:

(i) as respects income tax (including surtax), for any year of assessment beginning on or after 6 April, 1968; and

(ii) as respects corporation tax, for any financial year beginning on or after 1 April, 1968;

(*b*) in Montserrat:

as respects Montserrat tax, for any year of assessment beginning on or after 1 January, 1968.

EXPLANATORY NOTE

(This Note is not part of the Order.)

This Arrangement makes two amendments to the Arrangement between the United Kingdom and Montserrat which is scheduled to the Double Taxation Relief (Taxes on Income) (Montserrat) Order 1947.

First it provides that the exemption of dividends from any tax chargeable in addition to the tax on the paying company's profits is not to be allowed in certain cases where the shareholder is a company having a substantial holding in the paying company. The restriction does not apply to dividends on shares acquired for *bona fide* commercial reasons.

Secondly, it amends paragraph 13 of the 1947 Arrangement in its application to dividends by providing that credit for tax on the profits out of which dividends are paid, whether that tax is deducted from the dividends or not, is to be given only where the recipient is a company which holds not less than 10 per cent of the voting power in the paying company. So far as United Kingdom income tax is concerned this provision takes effect from the year of assessment 1968/69.

STATUTORY INSTRUMENTS

1968 No. 577

INCOME TAX

The Double Taxation Relief (Taxes on Income) (Netherlands) Order 1968

Laid before the House of Commons in draft

Made - - - *8th April* 1968

At the Court at Windsor Castle, the 8th day of April 1968

Present,

The Queen's Most Excellent Majesty in Council

Whereas a draft of this Order was laid before the Commons House of Parliament in accordance with the provisions of section 347(6) of the Income Tax Act 1952(a), and an Address has been presented to Her Majesty by that House praying that an Order may be made in the terms of this Order:

Now, therefore, Her Majesty, in exercise of the powers conferred upon Her by section 347(1) of the said Income Tax Act 1952, as amended by section 39 and section 64 of the Finance Act 1965(b), and of all other powers enabling Her in that behalf, is pleased, by and with the advice of Her Privy Council, to order, and it is hereby ordered, as follows:—

1. This Order may be cited as the Double Taxation Relief (Taxes on Income) (Netherlands) Order 1968.

2. It is hereby declared—

(*a*) that the arrangements specified in the Convention set out in the Schedule to this Order have been made with the Government of the Kingdom of the Netherlands with a view to affording relief from double taxation in relation to income tax, corporation tax, or capital gains tax and taxes of a similar character imposed by the laws of the Netherlands; and

(*b*) that it is expedient that those arrangements should have effect.

W. G. Agnew.

(a) 15 & 16 Geo. 6 & 1 Eliz. 2. c. 10.   (b) 1965 c. 25.

SCHEDULE

CONVENTION BETWEEN THE GOVERNMENT OF THE UNITED KINGDOM OF GREAT BRITAIN
AND NORTHERN IRELAND AND THE GOVERNMENT OF THE KINGDOM OF THE
NETHERLANDS FOR THE AVOIDANCE OF DOUBLE TAXATION AND THE PREVENTION
OF FISCAL EVASION WITH RESPECT TO TAXES ON INCOME AND CAPITAL

The Government of the United Kingdom of Great Britain and Northern Ireland
and the Government of the Kingdom of the Netherlands;

Desiring to conclude a new Convention for the avoidance of double taxation and
the prevention of fiscal evasion with respect to taxes on income and capital;

Have agreed as follows:—

ARTICLE 1

Persons Covered

This Convention shall apply to persons who are residents of one or both of the
States.

ARTICLE 2

Taxes Covered

(1) The taxes which are the subject of this Convention are:

(a) In the United Kingdom of Great Britain and Northern Ireland:
the income tax including surtax, the corporation tax and the capital gains
tax
(hereinafter referred to as "United Kingdom tax").

(b) In the Netherlands:
the income tax (*inkomstenbelasting*), the wages tax (*loonbelasting*), the
company tax (*vennootschapsbelasting*), the dividend tax (*dividendbelasting*),
the tax on fees of directors of companies (*commissarissenbelasting*) and
the capital tax (*vermogensbelasting*)
(hereinafter referred to as "Netherlands tax").

(2) This Convention shall also apply to any identical or substantially similar future
taxes which are imposed in addition to, or in place of, the existing taxes by either State.
The taxation authorities of the States shall notify to each other any substantial changes
which have been made in their respective taxation laws.

ARTICLE 3

General Definitions

(1) In this Convention, unless the context otherwise requires—

(a) the term "United Kingdom" means Great Britain and Northern Ireland,
including any area outside the territorial sea of the United Kingdom which
in accordance with international law has been or may hereafter be designated,
under the laws of the United Kingdom concerning the Continental Shelf,
as an area within which the rights of the United Kingdom with respect to the
sea bed and sub-soil and their natural resources may be exercised;

(b) the term "Netherlands" comprises the part of the Kingdom of the Netherlands
that is situated in Europe and the part of the sea bed and its sub-soil under the
North Sea over which the Kingdom of the Netherlands has sovereign rights
in accordance with international law;

(c) the term "State" means the United Kingdom or the Netherlands, as the
context requires; the term "States" means the United Kingdom and the
Netherlands;

(d) the term "person" comprises an individual, a company and any other body
of persons;

(e) the term "company" means any body corporate or any entity which is treated as a body corporate for tax purposes;

(f) the terms "enterprise of one of the States" and "enterprise of the other State" mean respectively an enterprise carried on by a resident of one of the States and an enterprise carried on by a resident of the other State;

(g) the term "taxation authorities" means, in the case of the United Kingdom, the Commissioners of Inland Revenue or their authorised representative; in the case of the Netherlands, the Minister of Finance or his authorised representative;

(h) the term "tax" means United Kingdom tax or Netherlands tax as the context requires;

(i) the term "international traffic" includes any voyage of a ship or aircraft other than a voyage solely between places in the State which is not the State of which the person deriving the profits from the operation of the ship or aircraft is a resident.

(2) As regards the application of the Convention by one of the States any term not otherwise defined shall, unless the context otherwise requires, have the meaning which it has under the laws of that State relating to the taxes which are the subject of the Convention.

ARTICLE 4

Residence

(1) For the purposes of this Convention, the term "resident of one of the States" means any person who, under the law of that State, is liable to taxation therein by reason of his domicile, residence, place of management or any other criterion of a similar nature but the term does not include any person who is liable to tax in that State only if he derives income from sources therein. The terms "resident of the United Kingdom" and "resident of the Netherlands" shall be construed accordingly.

(2) Where by reason of the provisions of paragraph (1) an individual is a resident of both States, then his status shall be determined in accordance with the following rules:

(a) he shall be deemed to be a resident of the State in which he has a permanent home available to him. If he has a permanent home available to him in both States, he shall be deemed to be a resident of the State with which his personal and economic relations are closest (centre of vital interests);

(b) if the State in which he has his centre of vital interests cannot be determined, or if he has not a permanent home available to him in either State, he shall be deemed to be a resident of the State in which he has an habitual abode;

(c) if he has an habitual abode in both States or in neither of them, he shall be deemed to be a resident of the State of which he is a national;

(d) if he is a national of both States or of neither of them, the taxation authorities of the States shall settle the question by mutual agreement.

(3) Where by reason of the provisions of paragraph (1) a person other than an individual is a resident of both States, then it shall be deemed to be a resident of the State in which its place of effective management is situated.

ARTICLE 5

Permanent Establishment

(1) For the purposes of this Convention, the term "permanent establishment" means a fixed place of business in which the business of the enterprise is wholly or partly carried on.

(2) The term "permanent establishment" shall include especially:

(a) a place of management;

(b) a branch;

(c) an office;

(d) a factory;

(e) a workshop;

(f) a mine, quarry or other place of extraction of natural resources;

(g) a building site or construction or assembly project which exists for more than twelve months.

(3) The term "permanent establishment" shall not be deemed to include:

(a) the use of facilities solely for the purpose of storage, display or delivery of goods or merchandise belonging to the enterprise;

(b) the maintenance of a stock of goods or merchandise belonging to the enterprise solely for the purpose of storage, display or delivery;

(c) the maintenance of a stock of goods or merchandise belonging to the enterprise solely for the purpose of processing by another enterprise;

(d) the maintenance of a fixed place of business solely for the purpose of purchasing goods or merchandise, or for collecting information, for the enterprise;

(e) the maintenance of a fixed place of business solely for the purpose of advertising, for the supply of information, for scientific research or for similar activities which have a preparatory or auxiliary character, for the enterprise.

(4) A person acting in one of the States on behalf of an enterprise of the other State—other than an agent of an independent status to whom paragraph (5) applies—shall be deemed to be a permanent establishment in the first-mentioned State if he has, and habitually exercises in that State, an authority to conclude contracts in the name of the enterprise, unless his activities are limited to the purchase of goods or merchandise for the enterprise.

(5) An enterprise of one of the States shall not be deemed to have a permanent establishment in the other State merely because it carries on business in that other State through a broker, general commission agent or any other agent of an independent status, where such persons are acting in the ordinary course of their business.

(6) The fact that a company which is a resident of one of the States controls or is controlled by a company which is a resident of the other State, or which carries on business in that other State (whether through a permanent establishment or otherwise), shall not of itself constitute either company a permanent establishment of the other.

ARTICLE 6
Limitation of Relief

Where under any provision of this Convention income is relieved from Netherlands tax and, under the law in force in the United Kingdom, an individual, in respect of the said income, is subject to tax by reference to the amount thereof which is remitted to or received in the United Kingdom and not by reference to the full amount thereof, then the relief to be allowed under the Convention in the Netherlands shall apply only to so much of the income as is remitted to or received in the United Kingdom.

ARTICLE 7
Immovable Property

(1) Income from immovable property may be taxed in the State in which such property is situated.

(2) (a) The term "immovable property" shall, subject to sub-paragraph (b) below, be defined in accordance with the law of the State in which the property in question is situated.

(*b*) The term "immovable property" shall in any case include property accessory to immovable property, livestock and equipment used in agriculture and forestry, rights to which the provisions of general law respecting landed property apply, usufruct of immovable property and rights to variable or fixed payments as consideration for the working of, or the right to work, mineral deposits, sources and other natural resources; ships, boats and aircraft shall not be regarded as immovable property.

(3) The provisions of paragraph (1) shall apply to income derived from the direct use, letting, or use in any other form of immovable property.

(4) The provisions of paragraphs (1) to (3) shall also apply to the income from immovable property of an enterprise and to income from immovable property used for the performance of professional services.

ARTICLE 8

Business Profits

(1) The profits of an enterprise of one of the States shall be taxable only in that State unless the enterprise carries on business in the other State through a permanent establishment situated therein. If the enterprise carries on business as aforesaid, the profits of the enterprise may be taxed in the other State but only so much of them as is attributable to that permanent establishment.

(2) Where an enterprise of one of the States carries on business in the other State through a permanent establishment situated therein, there shall in each State be attributed to that permanent establishment the profits which it might be expected to make if it were a distinct and separate enterprise engaged in the same or similar activities under the same or similar conditions and dealing at arm's length with the enterprise of which it is a permanent establishment.

(3) In the determination of the profits of a permanent establishment, there shall be allowed as deductions expenses of the enterprise (other than expenses which would not be deductible if the permanent establishment were a separate enterprise) which are incurred for the purposes of the permanent establishment including executive and general administrative expenses so incurred, whether in the State in which the permanent establishment is situated or elsewhere.

(4) In so far as it has been customary under the law of one of the States which is in force at the date of signature of this Convention to determine the profits to be attributed to a permanent establishment of a life assurance company on the basis of an apportionment of the total income and expenses of the enterprise nothing in paragraph (2) shall preclude that State from determining the profits to be taxed by such an apportionment. The method of apportionment adopted shall, however, be such that the result shall be in accordance with the principles of this Article.

(5) No profits shall be attributed to a permanent establishment by reason of the mere purchase by that permanent establishment of goods or merchandise for the enterprise.

(6) For the purposes of the preceding paragraphs, the profits to be attributed to the permanent establishment shall be determined by the same method year by year unless there is good and sufficient reason to the contrary.

(7) Where profits include items which are dealt with separately in other Articles of this Convention, then the provisions of those Articles shall not be affected by the provisions of this Article.

ARTICLE 9

Shipping and Air Transport

Profits which a resident of one of the States derives from the operation of ships or aircraft in international traffic shall be taxable only in that State.

ARTICLE 10

Associated Enterprises

Where

(a) an enterprise of one of the States participates directly or indirectly in the management, control or capital of an enterprise of the other State, or

(b) the same persons participate directly or indirectly in the management, control or capital of an enterprise of one of the States and an enterprise of the other State,

and in either case conditions are made or imposed between the two enterprises in their commercial or financial relations which differ from those which would be made between independent enterprises, then any profits which would, but for those conditions, have accrued to one of the enterprises, but, by reason of those conditions, have not so accrued, may be included in the profits of that enterprise and taxed accordingly.

ARTICLE 11

Dividends

(1) Dividends derived from a company which is a resident of one of the States by a resident of the other State may be taxed in that other State.

(2) However, such dividends may be taxed in the State of which the company paying the dividends is a resident, and according to the law of that State, but where such dividends are beneficially owned by a resident of the other State the tax charged shall not exceed:

(a) 5 per cent of the gross amount of the dividends if the beneficial owner is a company the capital of which is wholly or partly divided into shares and it controls directly or indirectly at least 25 per cent of the voting power in the company paying the dividends;

(b) in all other cases 15 per cent of the gross amount of the dividends.

This paragraph shall not affect the taxation of the company in respect of the profits out of which the dividends are paid.

(3) The term "dividends" as used in this Article means income from shares, *jouissance* shares or *jouissance* rights, mining shares, founders' shares or other rights, not being debt-claims, participating in profits, as well as income from other corporate rights treated in the same manner as income from shares by the taxation law of the State of which the company making the distribution is a resident (other than interest or royalties taxable only in one of the States according to Article 12 or Article 13) and also the excess part of any payment of interest or royalties mentioned in paragraph (5) of Article 12 or paragraph (5) of Article 13 to the extent that it is treated as a distribution under the taxation law of the State of which the company making the payment is a resident.

(4) If the beneficial owner of dividends being a resident of one of the States owns 10 per cent or more of the class of shares in respect of which the dividends are paid and does not suffer tax thereon in that State then paragraph (2) of this Article shall not apply to the dividends to the extent that they can have been paid only out of profits which the company paying the dividends earned or other income which it received in a period ending twelve months or more before the relevant date. For the purposes of this paragraph the term "relevant date" means the date on which the beneficial owner of the dividends became the owner of 10 per cent or more of the class of shares in question.

Provided that this paragraph shall apply only if the shares were acquired primarily for the purpose of securing the benefit of this Article and not for bona fide commercial reasons.

(5) The provisions of paragraphs (1) and (2) shall not apply if the recipient of the dividends, being a resident of one of the States, has in the other State, of which the company paying the dividends is a resident, a permanent establishment and the

holding by virtue of which the dividends are paid is effectively connected with the business carried on through such permanent establishment. In such a case the provisions of Article 8 shall apply.

(6) Where a company which is a resident of one of the States derives profits or income from the other State, that other State may not impose any tax on the dividends paid by the company to persons who are not residents of that other State, or subject the company's undistributed profits to a tax on undistributed profits, even if the dividends paid or the undistributed profits consist wholly or partly of profits or income arising in such other State.

(7) Not later than five years after the date of the entry into force of this Convention the taxation authorities shall consult together to study the possibility of an amendment of this Convention which would reduce the rate mentioned in paragraph (2)(a) of this Article.

ARTICLE 12

Interest

(1) Interest derived and beneficially owned by a resident of one of the States shall be taxable only in that State.

(2) The term "interest" as used in this Article means income from Government securities, bonds or debentures, whether or not secured by mortgage and whether or not carrying a right to participate in profits, and other debt-claims of every kind as well as all other income assimilated to income from money lent by the taxation law of the State in which the income arises.

(3) The provisions of paragraph (1) of this Article shall not apply if the recipient of the interest, being a resident of one of the States, has in the other State a permanent establishment and the debt-claim giving rise to the interest is effectively connected with the business carried on through such permanent establishment. In such a case the provisions of Article 8 shall apply.

(4) Any provision in the law of one of the States which relates only to interest paid to a non-resident company with or without any further requirement, or which relates only to interest payments between interconnected companies, with or without any further requirement, shall not operate so as to require such interest paid to a company which is a resident of the other State to be left out of account as a deduction in computing the taxable profits of the company paying the interest as being a distribution.

(5) Where, owing to a special relationship between the payer and the recipient or between both of them and some other person, the amount of the interest paid, having regard to the debt-claim for which it is paid, exceeds the amount which would have been agreed upon by the payer and the recipient in the absence of such relationship, the provisions of this Article shall apply only to the last-mentioned amount. In that case, the excess part of the payment shall remain taxable according to the law of each State, due regard being had to the other provisions of this Convention.

(6) The provisions of this Article shall not apply if the debt-claim in respect of which the interest is paid was created or assigned mainly for the purpose of taking advantage of this Article and not for bona fide commercial reasons.

ARTICLE 13

Royalties

(1) Royalties derived and beneficially owned by a resident of one of the States shall be taxable only in that State.

(2) The term "royalties" as used in this Article means payments of any kind received as a consideration for the use of, or the right to use, any copyright of literary, artistic or scientific work (including cinematograph films and films or tapes for radio or television broadcasting), any patent, trade mark, design or model, plan, secret formula

or process, or for the use of, or the right to use, industrial, commercial, or scientific equipment, or for information concerning industrial, commercial or scientific experience and shall include gains derived from the sale or exchange of any right or property giving rise to such royalties.

(3) The provisions of paragraph (1) of this Article shall not apply if the recipient of the royalties, being a resident of one of the States has in the other State a permanent establishment and the right or property giving rise to the royalties is effectively connected with the business carried on through such permanent establishment. In such a case the provisions of Article 8 shall apply.

(4) Any provision in the law of one of the States which requires royalties paid by a company to be left out of account as a deduction in computing the company's taxable profits as being a distribution shall not operate in relation to royalties paid to a resident of the other State.

(5) Where, owing to a special relationship between the payer and the recipient or between both of them and some other person, the amount of the royalties paid, having regard to the use, right or information for which they are paid, exceeds the amount which would have been agreed upon by the payer and the recipient in the absence of such relationship, the provisions of this Article shall apply only to the last-mentioned amount. In that case, the excess part of the payments shall remain taxable according to the law of each State, due regard being had to the other provisions of this Convention.

(6) The provisions of this Article shall not apply if the right or property giving rise to the royalties was created or assigned mainly for the purpose of taking advantage of this Article and not for bona fide commercial reasons.

ARTICLE 14

Application of Articles 11, 12 and 13

(1) The reductions and exemptions from tax in the State of source given by Articles 11, 12 and 13 shall be carried out in accordance with the mode of application determined (having due regard to the taxation laws of that State) by the taxation authorities of the States.

(2) Where tax has been deducted at the source in excess of the amount of tax chargeable under the provisions of Articles 11, 12 or 13 the excess amount of tax shall be refunded upon application to the taxation authorities concerned, provided that the application is made within a period of six years after the end of the calendar year in which the tax was deducted.

(3) The provisions of paragraph (2) of Article 11, paragraph (1) of Article 12 and paragraph (1) of Article 13 shall not apply if:

(a) the holding, security or asset giving rise to the income in question was obtained in virtue of any contract, option or any arrangement under which the beneficial owner agreed, or might be obliged, to sell again or to transfer again the holding, security or asset or to sell or transfer a similar holding, security or asset, or

(b) the beneficial owner of the holding, security or asset giving rise to the income in question sells the holding, security or asset within three months from the date on which he acquired it.

ARTICLE 15

Capital Gains

(1) Gains from the alienation of any property forming part of the business property of a permanent establishment which an enterprise of one of the States has in the other State or of any property pertaining to a fixed base available to a resident of one of the States in the other State for the purpose of performing professional services, including such gains from the alienation of such a permanent establishment (alone or together with the whole enterprise) or of such a fixed base, may be taxed in the other State.

(2) Notwithstanding paragraph (1) of this Article, gains derived by a resident of one of the States from the alienation of ships and aircraft operated in international traffic and movable property pertaining to the operation of such ships and aircraft shall be taxable only in that State.

(3) Gains from the alienation of any property other than those mentioned in paragraph (1) shall be taxable only in the State of which the alienator is a resident.

(4) The provisions of paragraph (3) shall not affect the right of either of the States to levy according to its own law a tax on gains from the alienation of any property derived by an individual who is a resident of the other State and has been a resident of the first-mentioned State at any time during the five years immediately preceding the alienation of the property.

ARTICLE 16

Independent Personal Services

(1) Income derived by a resident of one of the States in respect of professional services or other independent activities of a similar character shall be taxable only in that State unless he has a fixed base regularly available to him in the other State for the purpose of performing his activities. If he has such a fixed base, the income may be taxed in the other State but only so much of it as is attributable to that fixed base.

(2) The term "professional services" includes independent scientific, literary, artistic, educational or teaching activities as well as the independent activities of physicians, lawyers, engineers, architects, dentists and accountants.

ARTICLE 17

Employments

(1) Subject to the provisions of Articles 18, 20 and 21, salaries, wages and other similar remuneration derived by a resident of one of the States in respect of an employment shall be taxable only in that State unless the employment is exercised in the other State. If the employment is so exercised, such remuneration as is derived therefrom may be taxed in that other State.

(2) Notwithstanding the provisions of paragraph (1), remuneration derived by a resident of one of the States in respect of an employment exercised in the other State shall be taxable only in the first-mentioned State if:

   (a) the recipient is present in the other State for a period or periods not exceeding in the aggregate 183 days in the fiscal year concerned, and

   (b) the remuneration is paid by, or on behalf of, an employer who is not a resident of the other State, and

   (c) the remuneration is not borne by a permanent establishment or a fixed base which the employer has in the other State.

(3) Notwithstanding the preceding provisions of this Article, remuneration in respect of an employment exercised aboard a ship or aircraft shall be taxable only in the State of which the employee is a resident, provided that such remuneration may be taxed in the State of which the person deriving the profits from the operation of the ship or aircraft is a resident if that remuneration is paid in respect of a voyage solely between places in that State, or in respect of regular voyages between a port in that State and an overseas port involving an absence from that State of less than forty-eight hours.

ARTICLE 18

Directors' Fees

(1) Directors' fees and similar payments derived by a resident of the Netherlands in his capacity as a member of the board of directors of a company which is a resident of the United Kingdom may be taxed in the United Kingdom.

(2) Remuneration derived by a resident of the United Kingdom in his capacity as a *commissaris* of a company which is a resident of the Netherlands and remuneration

other than a fixed salary derived by a resident of the United Kingdom in his capacity as a *bestuurder* of a company which is a resident of the Netherlands may be taxed in the Netherlands.

ARTICLE 19
Artistes and Athletes

Notwithstanding the provisions of Articles 16 and 17, income derived by public entertainers, such as theatre, motion picture, radio or television artistes, and musicians, and by athletes, from their personal activities as such may be taxed in the State in which these activities are exercised.

ARTICLE 20
Pensions

(1) Subject to the provisions of Article 21, pensions and other similar remuneration paid in consideration of past employment to a resident of one of the States and any annuity paid to such a resident, shall be taxable only in that State.

(2) The term "annuity" means a stated sum payable periodically at stated times during life or during a specified or ascertainable period of time under an obligation to make the payments in return for adequate and full consideration in money or money's worth.

ARTICLE 21
Governmental Functions

(1) Remuneration, including pensions, paid by, or out of funds created by, the Netherlands or a political sub-division or a local authority thereof to any individual in respect of services rendered to the Government of the Netherlands, or a political sub-division, or a local authority thereof, in the discharge of functions of a governmental nature, may be taxed in the Netherlands.

(2) Remuneration, including pensions, paid by, or out of funds created by, the United Kingdom or Northern Ireland or any local authority in the United Kingdom to any individual in respect of services rendered to the Government of the United Kingdom or Northern Ireland, or a local authority in the United Kingdom, in the discharge of functions of a governmental nature, may be taxed in the United Kingdom.

(3) The provisions of Articles 17, 18 and 20 shall apply to remuneration or pensions in respect of services rendered in connection with any trade or business carried on by the Netherlands or a political sub-division, or a local authority thereof, or by the United Kingdom or Northern Ireland or any local authority in the United Kingdom.

ARTICLE 22
Students

A student or business apprentice who is or was immediately before visiting one of the States a resident of the other State and is present in the first-mentioned State solely for the purpose of his education or training shall not be taxed in that first-mentioned State on payments which he receives for the purpose of his maintenance, education or training provided that such payments are made to him from sources outside that first-mentioned State.

ARTICLE 23
Income not Expressly Mentioned

Items of income of a resident of one of the States being income of a class or from sources not expressly mentioned in the foregoing Articles of this Convention shall be taxable only in that State.

ARTICLE 24

Capital

(1) Capital represented by immovable property, as defined in paragraph (2) of Article 7, may be taxed in the State in which such property is situated.

(2) Capital represented by movable property forming part of the business property of a permanent establishment of an enterprise, or by movable property pertaining to a fixed base used for the performance of professional services, may be taxed in the State in which the permanent establishment or fixed base is situated.

(3) Notwithstanding paragraph (2) of this Article, ships and aircraft operated in international traffic and movable property pertaining to the operation of such ships and aircraft shall be taxable only in the State of which the operator is a resident.

(4) All other elements of capital of a resident of one of the States shall be taxable only in that State.

ARTICLE 25

Personal Allowances

(1) Individuals who are residents of the Netherlands shall be entitled to the same personal allowances, reliefs and reductions for the purposes of United Kingdom tax as British subjects not resident in the United Kingdom.

(2) Individuals who are residents of the United Kingdom shall be entitled to the same personal allowances, reliefs and reductions for the purposes of Netherlands tax as Netherlands nationals resident in the United Kingdom.

ARTICLE 26

Elimination of Double Taxation

(1) Subject to the provisions of the law of the United Kingdom regarding the allowance as a credit against United Kingdom tax of tax payable in a territory outside the United Kingdom (which shall not affect the general principle hereof)

(a) Netherlands tax payable under the laws of the Netherlands and in accordance with this Convention, whether directly or by deduction, on profits, income or chargeable gains from sources within the Netherlands (excluding in the case of a dividend, tax payable in respect of the profits out of which the dividend is paid) shall be allowed as a credit against any United Kingdom tax computed by reference to the same profits, income or chargeable gains by reference to which the Netherlands tax is computed;

(b) In the case of a dividend paid by a company which is a resident of the Netherlands to a company which is a resident of the United Kingdom and which controls directly or indirectly at least 10 per cent of the voting power in the Netherlands company, the credit shall take into account (in addition to any Netherlands tax creditable under sub-paragraph (a)) the Netherlands tax payable by the company in respect of the profits out of which such dividend is paid if, at the time when the dividend is paid, a company which is a resident of the Netherlands the capital of which is wholly or partly divided into shares is exempt from Netherlands tax in respect of dividends received from a company which is a resident of the United Kingdom in which its holding of shares is related to its normal business.

(2) (a) The Netherlands, when imposing tax on its residents, may include in the basis upon which such taxes are imposed (i.e. the *onzuivere inkomen* in the case of Netherlands income tax or the *winst* in the case of Netherlands company tax) the items of income or capital, which according to the provisions of this Convention may be taxed in the United Kingdom.

(b) Without prejudice to the application of the provisions concerning the compensation of losses in the unilateral regulations for the avoidance of double taxation the Netherlands shall allow a deduction from the amount of tax computed in conformity with paragraph (2)(a) of this Article equal to such part of that tax which bears the same proportion to the aforesaid tax, as the part of the income or capital which is included in the basis mentioned in paragraph (2)(*a*) of this Article and may be taxed in the United Kingdom according to Articles 7, 8, 11 (paragraph (5)), 12 (paragraph (3)), 13 (paragraph (3)), 15 (paragraph (1)), 16, 17 (paragraphs (1) and (3)), 18 (paragraph (1)), 19, 21 (paragraphs (2) and (3)), and 24 (paragraphs (1) and (3)) of this Convention bears to the total income or capital which forms the basis mentioned in paragraph (2)(*a*) of this Article.

Further, the Netherlands shall allow a deduction from the Netherlands tax so computed for such items of income, as may be taxed in the United Kingdom according to Articles 11 (paragraph (2)) and 15 (paragraph (4)) and are included in the basis mentioned in paragraph (2)(*a*) of this Article.   The amount of this deduction shall be the lesser of the following amounts:

> (i) the amount equal to the United Kingdom tax;
> (ii) the amount of the Netherlands tax which bears the same proportion to the amount of tax computed in conformity with paragraph (2)(*a*) of this Article, as the amount of the said items of income bears to the amount of income which forms the basis mentioned in paragraph (2)(*a*) of this Article.

(3) For the purposes of paragraph (1) of this Article, income and chargeable gains owned by a resident of the United Kingdom which may be taxed in the Netherlands in accordance with this Convention shall be deemed to arise from sources in the Netherlands.

ARTICLE 27

Non-discrimination

(1) The nationals of one of the States shall not be subjected in the other State to any taxation or any requirement connected therewith which is other or more burdensome than the taxation and connected requirements to which nationals of that other State in the same circumstances are or may be subjected.

(2) The term "national" means:

(*a*) in relation to the United Kingdom:

> (i) all British subjects deriving their status as such from connection with the United Kingdom and all British subjects and British protected persons residing in the United Kingdom;
> (ii) all legal persons, partnerships, associations and other entities deriving their status as such from the law of the United Kingdom;

(*b*) in relation to the Netherlands:

> (i) all individuals possessing the Netherlands nationality;
> (ii) all legal persons, partnerships, associations and other entities deriving their status as such from the law in force in the Netherlands.

(3) The taxation on a permanent establishment which an enterprise of one of the States has in the other State shall not be less favourably levied in that other State than the taxation levied on enterprises of that other State carrying on the same activities.

Nothing contained in this paragraph shall be construed as obliging either State to grant to individuals not resident in that State any of the personal allowances and reliefs for tax purposes which are granted to individuals so resident, nor as conferring any exemption from tax in a State in respect of dividends paid to a company which is a resident of the other State.

(4) Enterprises of one of the States, the capital of which is wholly or partly owned or controlled, directly or indirectly, by one or more residents of the other State, shall not be subjected in the first-mentioned State to any taxation or any requirement connected therewith which is other or more burdensome than the taxation and connected requirements to which other similar enterprises of that first-mentioned State are or may be subjected.

(5) In determining for the purpose of United Kingdom tax whether a company is a close company, the term "recognized stock exchange" shall include any stock exchange in the Netherlands which is a stock exchange within the meaning of the Netherlands law relating to stock exchanges.

(6) In this Article the term "taxation" means taxes of every kind and description.

ARTICLE 28

Mutual Agreement

(1) Where a resident of one of the States considers that the actions of one or both of the States result or will result for him in taxation not in accordance with this Convention, he may, notwithstanding the remedies provided by the national laws of those States, present his case to the taxation authority of the State of which he is a resident or a national.

(2) The taxation authority shall endeavour, if the objection appears to it to be justified and if it is not itself able to arrive at an appropriate solution, to resolve the case by mutual agreement with the taxation authority of the other State, with a view to the avoidance of taxation not in accordance with the Convention.

(3) The taxation authorities of the States shall endeavour to resolve by mutual agreement any difficulties or doubts arising as to the interpretation or application of the Convention. In particular the taxation authorities may consult together to endeavour to resolve disputes arising out of the application of paragraph (2) of Article 8 or Article 10.

ARTICLE 29

Exchange of Information

(1) The taxation authorities of the States shall exchange such information (being information which such authorities have at their disposal) as is necessary for carrying out the provisions of this Convention or for the prevention of fraud or for the administration of statutory provisions against legal avoidance in relation to the taxes which are the subject of the Convention. Any information so exchanged shall be treated as secret and shall not be disclosed to any persons other than persons (including a Court or administrative body) concerned with the assessment or collection of, or prosecution in respect of, or the determination of appeals in relation to, the taxes which are the subject of the Convention.

(2) In no case shall the provisions of paragraph (1) be construed so as to impose on the taxation authority of either State the obligation:

(a) to carry out administrative measures at variance with the laws or administrative practice prevailing in that or the other State ;

(b) to supply particulars which are not obtainable under the laws or in the normal course of the administration in that or the other State ; or

(c) to supply information which would disclose any trade, business, industrial, commercial or professional secret or trade process, or information the disclosure of which would be contrary to public policy in that or the other State.

ARTICLE 30

Territorial Extension

(1) This Convention may be extended, either in its entirety or with any necessary modifications, to any territory for whose international relations the United Kingdom of Great Britain and Northern Ireland is responsible as well as to either or both of the countries of Surinam or the Netherlands Antilles, if the territory or country concerned imposes taxes substantially similar in character to those to which this Convention applies. Any such extension shall take effect from such date and

subject to such modifications and conditions, including conditions as to termination, as may be specified and agreed in notes to be exchanged through diplomatic channels.

(2) Unless otherwise agreed the termination of this Convention shall not also terminate the application of this Convention to any territory or country to which it has been extended under this Article.

ARTICLE 31

Entry into Force

(1) This Convention shall be ratified and the instruments of ratification shall be exchanged at The Hague as soon as possible.

(2) This Convention shall enter into force after the expiration of a period of thirty days following the date on which the instruments of ratification are exchanged(a) and shall, subject to paragraph (5) of this Article, thereupon have effect—

(a) In the United Kingdom—

(i) in respect of income tax (including surtax) and capital gains tax for any year of assessment beginning on or after 6th April, 1968 ;

(ii) in respect of corporation tax for any financial year beginning on or after 1st April, 1964.

(b) In the Netherlands—

in respect of any taxes for taxable years and periods beginning on or after 1st January, 1968.

(3) Subject to paragraph (4) of this Article the Convention for the Avoidance of Double Taxation and the Prevention of Fiscal Evasion with respect to Taxes on Income between the United Kingdom of Great Britain and Northern Ireland and the Kingdom of the Netherlands signed at London on 15th October, 1948 shall terminate and cease to be effective as respects taxes to which this Convention in accordance with paragraph (2) above applies.

(4) Subject to paragraph (5) of this Article where any provision of the Convention signed at London on 15th October, 1948 would have afforded any greater relief from tax any such provision as aforesaid shall continue to have effect for any year of assessment or financial year or taxable year or period beginning before the entry into force of this Convention.

(5) The provisions of sub-paragraphs (a) and (b) of paragraph (2), of paragraph (3) and of paragraph (4) shall not apply in relation to dividends but the provisions of this Convention shall have effect, and the provisions of the Convention signed at London on 15th October, 1948 shall cease to be effective, in relation to dividends paid on or after the date of entry into force of this Convention.

(6) The following agreements between the United Kingdom and the Kingdom of the Netherlands shall not have effect for any year or period for which this Convention has effect, that is to say,

(a) the Agreement dated 20th May, 1926, for the reciprocal exemption from income tax in certain cases of profits accruing from the business of shipping ;

(b) the Convention dated 6th June, 1935, for reciprocal exemption from taxes in certain cases ; and

(c) the Agreement constituted by the Exchange of Notes dated 27th August, 1936, for reciprocal exemptions from certain taxation in respect of the business of air transport.

(7) This Convention shall not affect any agreement in force extending the Convention signed at London on 15th October, 1948 in accordance with Article XIX thereof.

(a) Instruments of ratification were exchanged on 14th March 1968.

ARTICLE 32

Termination

This Convention shall continue in effect indefinitely but either State may, on or before the thirtieth day of June in any calendar year after the year 1971 give, through diplomatic channels, notice of termination to the other State and, in such event, this Convention shall cease to be effective—

(a) In the United Kingdom:

    (i) as respects income tax (including surtax) and capital gains tax for any year of assessment beginning on or after 6th April in the calendar year next following that in which the notice is given ;

    (ii) as respects corporation tax, for any financial year beginning on or after 1st April in the calendar year next following that in which the notice is given ;

(b) In the Netherlands:

    for any taxable year or period beginning after the end of the calendar year in which the notice is given.

In witness whereof the undersigned, duly authorised thereto, have signed this Convention.

Done in duplicate at London this thirty-first day of October, 1967 in the English and Netherlands languages, both texts being equally authoritative.

For the Government of the United Kingdom of Great Britain and Northern Ireland:

                    CHALFONT

For the Government of the Kingdom of the Netherlands:

                    J. H. VAN ROIJEN

STATUTORY INSTRUMENTS

1968 No. 577

INCOME TAX

The Double Taxation Relief (Taxes on Income) (Netherlands) Order 1968

CORRECTION

On page 16*, in the Explanatory Note, in the first paragraph, *delete* the sentence beginning "Government salaries".

*p. 1341 in the 1968 volume of Statutory Instruments.

August 1972

LONDON: HER MAJESTY'S STATIONERY OFFICE

EXPLANATORY NOTE

(This Note is not part of the Order.)

Under the Convention with the Netherlands scheduled to this Order (which is to replace the Convention signed in London on 15th October, 1948(a)) shipping and air transport profits, certain trading profits not arising through a permanent establishment, interest, royalties, pensions (other than Government pensions) and the earnings of temporary business visitors are (subject to certain conditions) to be taxed only in the country of the taxpayer's residence. ~~Government salaries and pensions are normally to be taxed by the paying Government only.~~ Payments made for the maintenance of visiting students are (subject to certain conditions) to be exempt in the country visited.

The rate of tax in the source country on dividends paid to residents of the other country is, in general, not to exceed 5 per cent if the recipient is a company which controls at least 25 per cent of the voting power in the paying company or 15 per cent in other cases. Where income continues to be taxable in both countries, relief from double taxation is to be given by the country of the taxpayer's residence. In the case of a dividend paid by a Netherlands company, credit for the tax on the profits out of which the dividend is paid is, while certain provisions of the Netherlands law are in force, to be given for United Kingdom tax purposes where the recipient of the dividend is a United Kingdom company which controls not less than 10 per cent of the voting power of the paying company. Capital gains are normally to be taxed only in the country of the taxpayer's residence unless they arise from the disposal of the assets of a permanent establishment which the taxpayer has in the other country. There are provisions safeguarding nationals and enterprises of one country against discriminatory taxation in the other country, and for the exchange of information and consultation between the taxation authorities of the two countries.

The Convention is in general to take effect in the United Kingdom for all years for corporation tax, and for 1968–69 and subsequent years for income tax, surtax and capital gains tax.

(a) S.I. 1950/1196 (1950 I, p. 1044).

STATUTORY INSTRUMENTS

1968 No. 578

INCOME TAX

The Double Taxation Relief (Taxes on Income) (Virgin Islands) Order 1968

Laid before the House of Commons in draft
Made - - - - 8th April 1968

At the Court at Windsor Castle, the 8th day of April 1968

Present,

The Queen's Most Excellent Majesty in Council

Whereas a draft of this Order was laid before the Commons House of Parliament in accordance with the provisions of section 347(6) of the Income Tax Act 1952(a), and an Address has been presented to Her Majesty by that House praying that an Order may be made in the terms of this Order:

Now, therefore, Her Majesty, in exercise of the powers conferred upon Her by section 347(1) of the said Income Tax Act 1952, as amended by section 64 of the Finance Act 1965(b), and of all other powers enabling Her in that behalf, is pleased, by and with the advice of Her Privy Council, to order, and it is hereby ordered, as follows: —

1. This Order may be cited as the Double Taxation Relief (Taxes on Income) (Virgin Islands) Order 1968.

2. It is hereby declared—

(a) that the arrangements specified in the Arrangement set out in the Schedule to this Order have been made with the Government of the Virgin Islands with a view to affording relief from double taxation in relation to income tax or corporation tax and taxes of a similar character imposed by the laws of the Virgin Islands varying the arrangements set out in the Schedule to the Double Taxation Relief (Taxes on Income) (Virgin Islands) Order 1947(c); and

(b) that it is expedient that those arrangements should have effect.

W. G. Agnew.

(a) 15 & 16 Geo. 6 & 1 Eliz. 2. c. 10.   (b) 1965 c. 25.
(c) S.R. & O. 1947/2874 (Rev. X, p. 537: 1947 I, p. 1191).

SCHEDULE

ARRANGEMENT BETWEEN HER MAJESTY'S GOVERNMENT AND THE GOVERNMENT OF THE VIRGIN ISLANDS TO AMEND THE EXISTING ARRANGEMENT FOR THE AVOIDANCE OF DOUBLE TAXATION AND THE PREVENTION OF FISCAL EVASION WITH RESPECT TO TAXES ON INCOME

1. The Arrangement made in 1947 between His Majesty's Government and the Government of the Presidency of the Virgin Islands for the avoidance of double taxation and the prevention of fiscal evasion with respect to taxes on income (hereinafter referred to as " the 1947 Arrangement ") shall be amended—

(a) by the deletion from the title and paragraph 1(1)(b) of the words " the Presidency of " ;

(b) by the deletion of paragraph 2(1)(b) ;

(c) subject to sub-paragraph (a) above by the substitution for the references therein to " Presidency " and " Presidential " of references to " Virgin Islands " ;

(d) by the addition at the end of paragraph 6 of the following new sub-paragraph—

   " (3) If the recipient of a dividend is a company which owns 10 per cent. or more of the class of shares in respect of which the dividend is paid then sub-paragraph (1) shall not apply to the dividend to the extent that it can have been paid only out of profits which the company paying the dividend earned or other income which it received in a period ending twelve months or more before the relevant date. For the purposes of this sub-paragraph the term " relevant date " means the date on which the beneficial owner of the dividend became the owner of 10 per cent. or more of the class of shares in question.

   Provided that this sub-paragraph shall not apply if the beneficial owner of the dividend shows that the shares were acquired for *bona fide* commercial reasons and not primarily for the purpose of securing the benefit of this paragraph." ; and

(e) by the substitution for sub-paragraphs (1) and (2) of paragraph 13 of the following two new sub-paragraphs—

   " (1) Subject to the provisions of the law of the United Kingdom regarding the allowance as a credit against United Kingdom tax of tax payable in a territory outside the United Kingdom (which shall not affect the general principle hereof)—

   (a) Virgin Islands tax payable under the laws of the Virgin Islands and in accordance with this Arrangement, whether directly or by deduction, on profits or income from sources within the Virgin Islands shall be allowed as a credit against any United Kingdom tax computed by reference to the same profits or income by reference to which the Virgin Islands tax is computed.

   Provided that in the case of a dividend the credit shall only take into account such tax in respect thereof as is additional to any tax payable by the company on the profits out of which the dividend is paid and is ultimately borne by the recipient without reference to any tax so payable.

   (b) Where a company which is a resident of the Virgin Islands pays a dividend to a company resident in the United Kingdom which controls directly or indirectly at least 10 per cent. of the voting power in the first-mentioned company, the credit shall take into account (in addition to any Virgin Islands tax for which credit may be allowed under (a) of this sub-paragraph) the Virgin Islands tax payable by that first-mentioned company in respect of the profits out of which such dividend is paid.

(2) Subject to the provisions of the law of the Virgin Islands regarding the allowance as a credit against Virgin Islands tax of tax payable in a territory outside the Virgin Islands (which shall not affect the general principle hereof)—

(a) United Kingdom tax payable under the laws of the United Kingdom and in accordance with this Arrangement, whether directly or by deduction, on profits or income from sources within the United Kingdom shall be allowed as a credit against any Virgin Islands tax computed by reference to the same profits or income by reference to which the United Kingdom tax is computed.

Provided that in the case of a dividend the credit shall only take into account such tax in respect thereof as is additional to any tax payable by the company on the profits out of which the dividend is paid and is ultimately borne by the recipient without reference to any tax so payable.

(b) Where a company which is a resident of the United Kingdom pays a dividend to a company resident in the Virgin Islands which controls directly or indirectly at least 10 per cent. of the voting power in the first-mentioned company, the credit shall take into account (in addition to any United Kingdom tax for which credit may be allowed under (a) of this sub-paragraph) the United Kingdom tax payable by that first-mentioned company in respect of the profits out of which such dividend is paid."

2. This Arrangement shall enter into force when the last of all such things shall have been done in the United Kingdom and the Virgin Islands as are necessary to give the Arrangement the force of law in the United Kingdom and the Virgin Islands respectively, and the new sub-paragraph (3) of paragraph 6 of the 1947 Arrangement shall have effect immediately and the new sub-paragraphs (1) and (2) of paragraph 13 thereof shall have effect—

(a) in the United Kingdom:
   (i) as respects income tax (including surtax), for any year of assessment beginning on or after 6 April, 1968 ; and
   (ii) as respects corporation tax, for any financial year beginning on or after 1 April, 1968 ;

(b) in the Virgin Islands:
   as respects income tax, for any year of assessment beginning on or after 1 January, 1969.

EXPLANATORY NOTE
(This Note is not part of the Order.)

This Arrangement makes two amendments to the Arrangement between the United Kingdom and the Virgin Islands which is scheduled to the Double Taxation Relief (Taxes on Income) (Virgin Islands) Order 1947.

First it provides that the exemption of dividends from any tax chargeable in addition to the tax on the paying company's profits is not to be allowed in certain cases where the shareholder is a company having a substantial holding in the paying company. The restriction does not apply to dividends on shares acquired for *bona fide* commercial reasons.

Secondly, it amends paragraph 13 of the 1947 Arrangement in its application to dividends by providing that credit for tax on the profits out of which dividends are paid, whether that tax is deducted from the dividends or not, is to be given only where the recipient is a company which holds not less than 10 per cent of the voting power in the paying company. So far as United Kingdom income tax is concerned this provision takes effect from the year of assessment 1968/69.

STATUTORY INSTRUMENTS

1968 No. 579 (L.9)

SUPREME COURT OF JUDICATURE, ENGLAND

OFFICERS AND OFFICES

The District Registries Order in Council 1968

Made	-	-	-	*8th April* 1968
Coming into Operation				*23rd April* 1968

At the Court at Windsor Castle, the 8th day of April 1968

Present,

The Queen's Most Excellent Majesty in Council

Her Majesty, in exercise of the powers conferred on Her by section 84 of the Supreme Court of Judicature (Consolidation) Act 1925(a) and of all other powers enabling Her in that behalf, is pleased, by and with the advice of Her Privy Council, to order, and it is hereby ordered, as follows :—

1. The District Registries Order in Council 1966(b) (which provides that there shall be district registries of the High Court at the places and for the districts specified in the Schedule thereto) shall have effect subject to the amendments set out in the Schedule to this Order.

2.—(1) This Order may be cited as the District Registries Order in Council 1968 and shall come into operation on 23rd April 1968.

(2) The Interpretation Act 1889(c) shall apply for the interpretation of this Order as it applies for the interpretation of an Act of Parliament.

W. G. Agnew.

SCHEDULE

1. In this Schedule any reference to an entry relating to a district registry is a reference to that entry in the Schedule to the District Registries Order in Council 1966 and any reference to the first or second column is a reference to that column in that Schedule.

2. In the entry relating to the Derby District Registry, the word "Ashbourne" in the second column shall be deleted.

3. In the entry relating to the Guildford District Registry, for the words "Aldershot" and "Farnham" in the second column, there shall be substituted the words "Aldershot and Farnham".

(a) 1925 c. 49.   (b) S.I. 1966/1189 (1966 III, p. 3188).   (c) 1889 c. 63.

4. The entry relating to the Hanley District Registry shall be deleted.

5. After the entry relating to the Stockton-on-Tees District Registry, there shall be inserted the following new entry:—

First Column	*Second Column*
"Stoke on Trent	Congleton
	Leek
	Newcastle-under-Lyme
	Stoke on Trent
	Uttoxeter".

6. In the entry relating to the Northampton District Registry, the words "Bletchley and Buckingham" and "Leighton Buzzard" in the second column shall be deleted, and the words "Bletchley and Leighton Buzzard" shall be inserted therein above the word "Kettering".

7. In the entry relating to the Scunthorpe District Registry, the words "Barton-on-Humber" in the second column shall be deleted.

8. In the entry relating to the Torquay District Registry, the word "Totnes" in the second column shall be deleted.

9. The entry relating to the West Hartlepool District Registry shall be deleted.

10. After the entry relating to the Harrogate District Registry, there shall be inserted the following new entry:—

First Column	*Second Column*
"Hartlepool	Hartlepool".

11. In the entry relating to the Worcester District Registry, the word "Bromyard" in the second column shall be deleted.

12. In the entry relating to the Yeovil District Registry, the words "Axminster" and "Chard" in the second column shall be deleted, and the words "Axminster and Chard" shall be inserted above the word "Bridport".

EXPLANATORY NOTE

(This Note is not part of the Order.)

This Order amends the District Registries Order in Council 1966 by altering the names of the Hanley District Registry and the West Hartlepool District Registry, which will in future be known as the Stoke on Trent District Registry and the Hartlepool District Registry respectively. It also takes account of certain changes which have been made in the names and districts of county courts.

STATUTORY INSTRUMENTS

1968 No. 580

MERCHANT SHIPPING

The Merchant Shipping (Light Dues) Order 1968

Laid before Parliament in draft

Made - - -		*8th April* 1968
Laid before Parliament		*17th April* 1968
Coming into Operation		*22nd April* 1968

At the Court at Windsor Castle, the 8th day of April 1968

Present,

The Queen's Most Excellent Majesty in Council

Her Majesty in exercise of the powers conferred upon Her by section 5 of the Merchant Shipping (Mercantile Marine Fund) Act 1898(a), and of all other powers enabling Her in that behalf, is pleased, by and with the advice of Her Privy Council, to order, and it is hereby ordered, as follows:—

1. The scale of payments and rules relating to the levying of light dues contained in Schedule 2 to the Merchant Shipping (Mercantile Marine Fund) Act 1898, as altered **(b)**, shall be further altered as follows:—

(a) for the scale of payments set out therein there shall be substituted the scale set out in the Schedule to this Order;

(b) in the proviso to Rule 1 for "one shilling and fourpence half-penny" and "one shilling and a penny half-penny" there shall be substituted respectively "7s. 2.625d." and "5s. 10.875d."; and

(c) in the proviso to Rule 7 for "one penny" there shall be substituted "5.25d.".

2. The Merchant Shipping (Light Dues) Order 1965(c) and Article 2 of the Merchant Shipping (Light Dues) Order 1953(d) are hereby revoked.

3.—(1) The Interpretation Act 1889(e) shall apply to the interpretation of this Order as it applies to the interpretation of an Act of Parliament and as if this Order and the Order and the part of an Order hereby revoked were Acts of Parliament.

(2) This Order shall come into operation at the expiration of 14 days from the date hereof and may be cited as the Merchant Shipping (Light Dues) Order 1968.

W. G. Agnew.

(a) 1898 c. 44. (b) S.I. 1953/392; 1965/318 (1953 I, p. 1065; 1965 I, p. 783).
(c) S.I. 1965/318 (1965 I, p. 783). (d) S.I. 1953/392 (1953 I, p. 1065). (e) 1889 c. 63.

SCHEDULE
SCALE OF PAYMENTS

(Substituted for the scale set out in Schedule 2 to the Merchant Shipping (Mercantile Marine Fund) Act 1898)

1. Home-trade sailing ships: 5.25d. per ton per voyage.
2. Foreign-going sailing ships: 11.8125d. per ton per voyage.
3. Home-trade steamers: 7.875d. per ton per voyage.
4. Foreign-going steamers:

    Full rate: 1s. 2.4375d. per ton per voyage.

    Reduced rate (visiting cruise ships): 8d. per ton per voyage.

A ship shall be treated as a visiting cruise ship if and only if it makes a call at one or more ports in the United Kingdom, Isle of Man or Republic of Ireland for the purpose of disembarking passengers for a visit ashore and for subsequent re-embarkation (whether or not at the same port) and at no time during that cruise does the ship—

(a) embark or disembark any other passengers; or

(b) load or discharge any cargo or mails—
at any such port.

5. In the place of payments per voyage, the following payments:—

(a) for pleasure yachts which the general lighthouse authority is satisfied are ordinarily kept or used outside any of the following countries and territories (including the territorial waters adjacent thereto), namely the United Kingdom, Isle of Man, Republic of Ireland, a payment in respect of any visit of 5.25d. per ton for every period of 30 days or less comprised in such visit;

(b) for tugs and pleasure yachts not included in sub-paragraph (a) of this paragraph an annual payment of 5s. 3d. per ton.

EXPLANATORY NOTE
(This Note is not part of the Order.)

This Order consolidates the scale of light dues at present in force under section 5 of the Merchant Shipping (Mercantile Marine Fund) Act 1898. It reduces from 1s. 2.4375d. to 8d. per ton per voyage the dues payable by a foreign-going steamer calling at one or more ports in the United Kingdom and other specified territories for the sole purpose of disembarking passengers for visits ashore and for subsequent re-embarkation.

STATUTORY INSTRUMENTS

1968 No. 585

ANIMALS

DISEASES OF ANIMALS

The Foot-and-Mouth Disease (Imported Meat) (No. 2) Order 1968

Made - - - -	*9th April* 1968
Coming into Operation	*15th April* 1968

The Minister of Agriculture, Fisheries and Food and the Secretary of State, acting jointly, in exercise of the power vested in them under sections 1, 20 and 85 of the Diseases of Animals Act 1950(a), as read with the Transfer of Functions (Animal Health) Order 1955(b), and all their other enabling powers hereby order as follows:—

Citation, extent and commencement

1. This order, which may be cited as the Foot-and-Mouth Disease (Imported Meat) (No. 2) Order 1968, shall apply to Great Britain and shall come into operation on 15th April 1968.

Interpretation

2.—(1) In this order—

" carcases " in relation to a single carcase, includes part of a carcase;

" the Minister " means in the application of this order to England and Wales, the Minister of Agriculture, Fisheries and Food, and, in its application to Scotland, the Secretary of State.

(2) The Interpretation Act 1889(c) applies to the interpretation of this order as it applies to the interpretation of an Act of Parliament, and as if this order and the order hereby revoked were Acts of Parliament.

Prohibition of movement of imported meat and offal

3.—(1) No person shall in connection with any trade or business which is carried on remove from the place of storage or other place where it is for the time being stored or situated any fresh or refrigerated meat or offal to which this article applies except in accordance with a licence issued by the Minister.

(2) This article applies to mutton, lamb and ovine offal landed in or obtained from carcases which have been landed in Great Britain from Argentina, Brazil, Chile or Uruguay.

Licences

4.—(1) The Minister may attach to any licence issued under this order any conditions he may think fit for the purpose of preventing the introduction or spread of disease.

(a) 1950 c. 36.   For change of title of the Minister see S.I. 1955/554 (1955 I, p. 1200).
(b) S.I. 1955/958 (1955 I, p. 1184).
(c) 1889 c. 63.

(2) If any person contravenes or fails to comply with any condition subject to which any licence is issued under this order he shall be guilty of an offence against the Diseases of Animals Act 1950.

Local Authority to enforce order

5. This order, except where the Minister otherwise directs, shall be executed and enforced by the local authority.

Revocation

6. The Foot-and-Mouth Disease (Imported Meat) Order 1968(a) is hereby revoked.

In Witness whereof the Official Seal of the Minister of Agriculture, Fisheries and Food is hereunto affixed on 9th April 1968.

(L.S.)

Cledwyn Hughes,
Minister of Agriculture, Fisheries and Food.

Given under the Seal of the Secretary of State for Scotland on 9th April 1968.

(L.S.)

William Ross,
Secretary of State for Scotland.

EXPLANATORY NOTE

(This Note is not part of the Order.)

This order prohibits the removal from store of all fresh or refrigerated mutton, lamb or ovine offal landed in or obtained from carcases landed in Great Britain from Argentina, Brazil, Chile or Uruguay, except in accordance with a licence issued by the Minister of Agriculture, Fisheries and Food or the Secretary of State for Scotland.

(a) S.I. 1968/94 (1968 I, p. 270).

STATUTORY INSTRUMENTS

1968 No. 586

SUGAR

The Sugar (Rates of Surcharge and Surcharge Repayments) (No. 2) Order 1968

Made - - - -,	*9th April* 1968
Laid before Parliament	*16th April* 1968
Coming into Operation	*17th April* 1968

The Minister of Agriculture, Fisheries and Food, in exercise of the powers conferred on him by sections 7(4), 8(6) and 33(4) of the Sugar Act 1956(a) having effect subject to the provisions of section 3 of, and Part II of Schedule 5 to, the Finance Act 1962(b), and of all other powers enabling him in that behalf, with the concurrence of the Treasury, on the advice of the Sugar Board, hereby makes the following order:—

1.—(1) This order may be cited as the Sugar (Rates of Surcharge and Surcharge Repayments) (No. 2) Order 1968; and shall come into operation on 17th April 1968.

(2) The Interpretation Act 1889(c) shall apply for the interpretation of this order as it applies for the interpretation of an Act of Parliament.

2. Notwithstanding the provisions of Article 2 of the Sugar (Rates of Surcharge and Surcharge Repayments) Order 1968(d), the rates of surcharge payable under and in accordance with the provisions of section 7 of the Sugar Act 1956, having effect as aforesaid, in respect of sugar and invert sugar imported or home produced or used in the manufacture of imported composite sugar products shall on and after 17th April 1968 be those rates specified in Schedule 1 to this order.

3. For the purpose of section 8(3)(b) of the Sugar Act 1956, having effect as aforesaid, the rates of surcharge repayments in respect of invert sugar produced in the United Kingdom from materials on which on or after 17th April 1968 sugar duty has been paid or, by virtue of paragraph 1 of Part II of Schedule 5 to the Finance Act 1962, is treated as having been paid shall, notwithstanding the provisions of Article 3 of the Sugar (Rates of Surcharge and Surcharge Repayments) Order 1968 be those specified in Schedule 2 to this order.

(a) 1956 c. 48. (b) 1962 c. 44.
(c) 1889 c. 63. (d) S.I. 1968/285 (1968 I, p. 876).

In Witness whereof the Official Seal of the Minister of Agriculture Fisheries and Food is hereunto affixed on 9th April 1968.

(L.S.)   *R. P. Fraser,*

Authorised by the Minister.

We concur.

9th April 1968.

B. K. O'Malley,
Joseph Harper,

Two of the Lords Commissioners of
Her Majesty's Treasury.

SCHEDULE 1

PART I

SURCHARGE RATES FOR SUGAR

Polarisation	Rate of Surcharge per cwt.	
	s.	d.
Exceeding—		
99°	35	0
98° but not exceeding 99°	33	0
97° ,, ,, ,, 98°	32	2·4
96° ,, ,, ,, 97°	31	4·3
95° ,, ,, ,, 96°	30	6·2
94° ,, ,, ,, 95°	29	8·1
93° ,, ,, ,, 94°	28	10
92° ,, ,, ,, 93°	28	0
91° ,, ,, ,, 92°	27	1·9
90° ,, ,, ,, 91°	26	3·8
89° ,, ,, ,, 90°	25	5·7
88° ,, ,, ,, 89°	24	7·6
87° ,, ,, ,, 88°	23	11·2
86° ,, ,, ,, 87°	23	2·8
85° ,, ,, ,, 86°	22	7·3
84° ,, ,, ,, 85°	21	11·7
83° ,, ,, ,, 84°	21	4·2
82° ,, ,, ,, 83°	20	8·6
81° ,, ,, ,, 82°	20	1·9
80° ,, ,, ,, 81°	19	7·2
79° ,, ,, ,, 80°	19	0·4
78° ,, ,, ,, 79°	18	5·7
77° ,, ,, ,, 78°	17	11
76° ,, ,, ,, 77°	17	4·3
Not exceeding 76°	16	9·6

PART II
SURCHARGE RATES FOR INVERT SUGAR

Sweetening matter content by weight	Rate of Surcharge per cwt.
	s. d.
70 per cent. or more	22 2
Less than 70 per cent. and more than 50 per cent.	15 11
Not more than 50 per cent.	7 10

SCHEDULE 2
SURCHARGE REPAYMENT RATES FOR INVERT SUGAR

Sweetening matter content by weight	Rate of Surcharge Repayment per cwt.
	s. d.
More than 80 per cent.	26 3
More than 70 per cent. but not more than 80 per cent.	22 2
More than 60 per cent. but not more than 70 per cent.	15 11
More than 50 per cent. but not more than 60 per cent.	12 8
Not more than 50 per cent. and the invert sugar not being less in weight than 14 lb. per gallon	7 10

EXPLANATORY NOTE

(This Note is not part of the Order.)

This order prescribes—

(a) increases equivalent to 2s. 4d. per cwt. of refined sugar in the rates of surcharge payable on sugar and invert sugar which become chargeable with surcharge on or after 17th April 1968;

(b) correspondingly increased rates of surcharge repayment in respect of invert sugar produced in the United Kingdom from materials on which surcharge has been paid.

STATUTORY   INSTRUMENTS

1968 No. 587

SUGAR

The Composite Sugar Products (Surcharge and Surcharge Repayments—Average Rates) (No. 2) Order 1968

Made - - - -		*9th April* 1968
Laid before Parliament		*16th April* 1968
Coming into Operation		*17th April* 1968

Whereas the Minister of Agriculture, Fisheries and Food (hereinafter called " the Minister ") has on the recommendation of the Commissioners of Customs and Excise (hereinafter called " the Commissioners ") made an order(a) pursuant to the powers conferred upon him by sections 9(1) and 9(4) of the Sugar Act 1956(b), having effect subject to the provisions of section 3 of, and Part II of Schedule 5 to, the Finance Act 1962(c) and to the provisions of section 52(2) of the Finance Act 1966(d), providing that in the case of certain descriptions of composite sugar products surcharge shall be calculated on the basis of an average quantity of sugar or invert sugar taken to have been used in the manufacture of the products, and that certain other descriptions of composite sugar products shall be treated as not containing any sugar or invert sugar, and that in the case of certain descriptions of goods in the manufacture of which sugar or invert sugar is used, surcharge repayments shall be calculated on the basis of an average quantity of sugar or invert sugar taken to have been so used:

Now, therefore, the Minister, on the recommendation of the Commissioners and in exercise of the powers conferred upon him by sections 9(1), 9(4) and 33(4) of the Sugar Act 1956, having effect as aforesaid, and of all other powers enabling him in that behalf, hereby makes the following order:—

1.—(1) This order may be cited as the Composite Sugar Products (Surcharge and Surcharge Repayments—Average Rates) (No. 2) Order 1968; and shall come into operation on 17th April 1968.

(2) The Interpretation Act 1889(e) shall apply for the interpretation of this order as it applies for the interpretation of an Act of Parliament.

2. Surcharge payable on or after 17th April 1968 under and in accordance with the Sugar Act 1956, having effect as aforesaid, in respect of sugar and invert sugar used in the manufacture of the descriptions of imported composite sugar products specified in column 2 of Schedule 1 to this order shall, notwithstanding the provisions of the Sugar (Rates of Surcharge and Surcharge Repayments) (No. 2) Order 1968(f) and the Composite Sugar Products (Surcharge and Surcharge Repayments—Average Rates) Order 1968(a), be calculated by reference to the weight or value, as the case may be, of the products at the rates specified in relation thereto in column 3 of the said Schedule.

(a) S.I. 1968/286 (1968 I, p. 879).   (b) 1956 c. 48.   (c) 1962 c. 44.
(d) 1966 c. 18.   (e) 1889 c. 63.   (f) S.I. 1968/586
(1968 I, p. 1351).

3. Imported composite sugar products other than those of a description specified in Schedules 1 and 2 to this order shall be treated as not containing any sugar or invert sugar for the purposes of surcharge payable on or after 17th April 1968.

4. Surcharge repayments payable on and after 17th April 1968 under and in accordance with the provisions of section 8 of the Sugar Act 1956, having effect as aforesaid, in respect of sugar and invert sugar used in the manufacture of the descriptions of goods specified in column 1 of Schedule 3 to this order shall, notwithstanding the provisions of the Sugar (Rates of Surcharge and Surcharge Repayments) (No. 2) Order 1968(a) and the Composite Sugar Products (Surcharge and Surcharge Repayments—Average Rates) Order 1968(b), be calculated by reference to the quantity of the goods at the rates specified in relation thereto in column 2 of the said Schedule.

In Witness whereof the Official Seal of the Minister of Agriculture, Fisheries and Food is hereunto affixed on 9th April 1968.

(L.S.)

R. P. Fraser,
Authorised by the Minister.

SCHEDULE 1

In this Schedule:—

" Tariff heading " means a heading or, where the context so requires, a subheading of the Customs Tariff 1959 (see paragraph (1) of Article 1 of the Import Duties (General) (No. 11) Order 1966(c)).

" Per cent." means, where it occurs in relation to any rate of surcharge, per cent. of the value for customs duty purposes of the product to which it relates.

Tariff heading	Description of Imported Composite Sugar Products	Rate of Surcharge
		per cwt. s. d.
04.02	Milk and cream, preserved, concentrated or sweetened containing more than 10 per cent. by weight of added sweetening matter	15 6
17.02 (B) (2) and 17.05 (B)	Syrups containing sucrose sugar, whether or not flavoured or coloured, but not including fruit juices containing added sugar in any proportion:—	
	containing 70 per cent. or more by weight of sweetening matter	22 3
	containing less than 70 per cent., and more than 50 per cent., by weight of sweetening matter...	16 0
	containing not more than 50 per cent. by weight of sweetening matter	7 9

(a) S.I. 1968/586 (1968 I, p. 1351). (b) S.I. 1968/286 (1968 I, p. 879).
(c) S.I. 1966/1555 (1966 III, p. 4405).

Tariff heading	Description of Imported Composite Sugar Products	Rate of Surcharge
		per cwt. s. d.
17.02 (F) ...	Caramel:—	
	Solid	35 0
	Liquid	24 6
17.04	Sugar confectionery, not containing cocoa	28 6
18.06	Chocolate and other food preparations containing cocoa:—	
	Chocolate couverture not prepared for retail sale; chocolate milk crumb, liquid	15 6
	Chocolate milk crumb, solid	19 2
	Other	20 3
		per cent.
19.08	Pastry, biscuits, cakes and other fine bakers' wares containing added sweetening matter:—	
	Biscuits	7½
	Other	4½
20.01	Vegetables and fruit, prepared or preserved by vinegar or acetic acid, containing added sweetening matter	10½
20.03	Fruit preserved by freezing, containing added sugar	3¾
		per cwt. s. d.
20.04	Fruit, fruit-peel and parts of plants, preserved by sugar (drained, glacé or crystallised)	23 0
20.05	Jams, fruit jellies, marmalades, fruit purée and fruit pastes, being cooked preparations, containing added sweetening matter	22 0
		per cent.
20.06 (A) and (B)	Fruit otherwise prepared or preserved, containing added sweetening matter:—	
	Ginger	15
	Other	3¾

SCHEDULE 2

Tariff heading	Description of Imported Composite Sugar Products
17.05 (A) and (B)	Sugar and invert sugar, flavoured or coloured.

SCHEDULE 3

Description of goods	Rate of surcharge repayment per bulk barrel of 36 gallons
Lager	1s. 5·5d.
All beer other than lager	1s. 3·6d.

EXPLANATORY NOTE

(*This Note is not part of the Order.*)

This order provides for increases on and after 17th April 1968 in the average rates of surcharge payable on imported composite sugar products of the descriptions specified in Schedule 1 and in the average rates of surcharge repayment in respect of exported goods of the descriptions specified in Schedule 3. These correspond to the increases in surcharge rates effected by the Sugar (Rates of Surcharge and Surcharge Repayments) (No. 2) Order 1968 (S.I. 1968/586). Provision is also made for certain imported composite sugar products to be treated as not containing any sugar or invert sugar.

STATUTORY INSTRUMENTS

1968 No. 588

EDUCATION, ENGLAND AND WALES

The Independent Schools Tribunal (Amendment) Rules 1968

Made - - -	*9th April* 1968
Coming into Operation	*25th April* 1968

I, Gerald, Baron Gardiner, Lord High Chancellor of Great Britain, in exercise of the powers conferred on me by section 75(1) of the Education Act 1944(a), after consultation with the Council on Tribunals in accordance with section 8 of the Tribunals and Inquiries Act 1958(b) and with the approval of the Treasury, do hereby make the following Rules with the concurrence of the Lord President of the Council:—

1.—(1) These Rules may be cited as the Independent Schools Tribunal (Amendment) Rules 1968, and shall come into operation on 25th April 1968.

(2) The Interpretation Act 1889(c), shall apply to the interpretation of these Rules as it applies to the interpretation of an Act of Parliament.

2. Paragraph (2) of the Second Schedule to the Independent Schools Tribunal Rules 1958(d) shall be amended as follows:—

(*a*) in sub-paragraph (*a*) for the figures "5s. 6d." and "12s." there shall be substituted the figures "6s. 6d." and "14s." respectively;

(*b*) in sub-paragraph (*b*) for the words "48s. 6d. for each night" there shall be substituted the following words:—

"(i) for each night spent within 4 miles of Charing Cross, £4 8s.;

(ii) for each night spent elsewhere, £4."

Dated 9th April 1968.   *Gardiner, C.*

I concur,

R. H. S. Crossman,
Lord President of the Council.

We approve the allowances prescribed by these Rules.

Joseph Harper, } Lords Commissioners of
J. McCann,   } Her Majesty's Treasury.

(a) 1944 c. 31.   (b) 1958 c. 66.   (c) 1889 c. 63.   (d) S.I. 1958/519 (1958 I, p. 1006).

EXPLANATORY NOTE

(This Note is not part of the Rules.)

These Rules increase the subsistence allowances payable to the chairmen and members of Independent Schools Tribunals, set up under section 72 of the Education Act 1944.

STATUTORY INSTRUMENTS

1968 No. 590 (S. 55)

POLICE

The Police Federation (Scotland) Amendment Regulations 1968

Made - - - -   *5th April* 1968
Laid before Parliament   *19th April* 1968
Coming into Operation   *30th April* 1968

In exercise of the powers conferred on me by section 44 of the Police Act 1964(a), and of all other powers enabling me in that behalf, and after consultation with the three Central Committees of the Police Federation for Scotland sitting together as a Joint Committee, I hereby make the following regulations:—

1. These regulations may be cited as the Police Federation (Scotland) Amendment Regulations 1968 and shall come into operation on 30th April 1968.

2. The Police Federation (Scotland) Regulations 1966(b) (hereinafter referred to as "the principal regulations"), shall have effect subject to the amendments specified in regulation 3 of these regulations.

3. In regulation 11 of the principal regulations (which relates to central committees)—

(*a*) there shall be substituted in sub-paragraph (*a*) of paragraph (2) the figure "3" for the figure "2"; and

(*b*) in sub-paragraph (*c*) of paragraph (2) there shall be substituted the figure "1" for the figure "2".

William Ross,
One of Her Majesty's Principal
Secretaries of State.

St. Andrew's House,
Edinburgh, 1.
5th April 1968.

EXPLANATORY NOTE

(*This Note is not part of the Regulations.*)

These regulations amend the Police Federation (Scotland) Regulations 1966.

Regulation 3 amends the number of male members of each central committee to be elected by delegates to the three central conferences from the various groups of police forces in Scotland so that 3 members shall be from county police forces, 2 from Glasgow, and 1 from the police forces of burghs other than Glasgow.

(a) 1964 c. 48.   (b) S.I. 1966/132 (1966 I, p. 241).

STATUTORY INSTRUMENTS

1968 No. 592

JUVENILE COURTS AND OFFENDERS
The Juvenile Courts (London) Order 1968

Made	- - -	*9th April* 1968
Coming into Operation		*1st May* 1968

In pursuance of the powers conferred on me by paragraphs 14 and 20 of Schedule 2 to the Children and Young Persons Act 1933(**a**), as amended by section 17(1) of the Children and Young Persons Act 1963(**b**) and section 12(1) of the Administration of Justice Act 1964(**c**), I hereby make the following Order :—

1. In the Schedule to the Juvenile Courts (London) Order 1965(**d**), as amended(**e**), for the entry in column 2 relating to the place of sitting of the juvenile court for the South Western London division there shall be substituted the following entry :—

<blockquote>
"Anchor Mission,
273, Garratt Lane,
Wandsworth, S.W.18.

The Town Hall,
Municipal Buildings,
Wandsworth, S.W.18.".
</blockquote>

2. This Order may be cited as the Juvenile Courts (London) Order 1968 and shall come into operation on 1st May 1968.

James Callaghan,
One of Her Majesty's Principal
Secretaries of State.

Home Office,
Whitehall.
9th April 1968.

EXPLANATORY NOTE
(This Note is not part of the Order.)

This Order amends the Juvenile Courts (London) Order 1965 (which assigned divisions and places of sitting to the juvenile courts for the inner London area and the City of London) by adding the Town Hall, Wandsworth in addition to the Anchor Mission, Wandsworth as a place of sitting for the juvenile court for the South Western division.

(**a**) 1933 c. 12.   (**b**) 1963 c. 37.
(**c**) 1964 c. 42.   (**d**) S.I. 1965/584 (1965 I, p. 1833).
(**e**) The amending Order is not relevant to the subject matter of this Order.

STATUTORY INSTRUMENTS

1968 No. 593

TELEGRAPHS

The Telephone Amendment (No. 4) Regulations 1968

Made - - - -	10*th April* 1968
Laid before Parliament	11*th April* 1968
Coming into Operation	16*th April* 1968

I, The Right Honourable Roy Mason, M.P., Her Majesty's Postmaster General, by virtue of the power vested in me by section 1 of the Telephone Act 1951(a), as amended by sections 16 and 28 of the Post Office Act 1961(b), and of every other power enabling me in this behalf, do hereby make the following regulations:—

Interpretation

1.—(1) These regulations shall be read as one with the Telephone Regulations 1965(c) as amended(d).

(2) The Interpretation Act 1889(e) applies for the interpretation of these regulations as it applies for the interpretation of an Act of Parliament.

Connection charge

2. In Schedule 5 of the Telephone Regulations 1965 (which specifies maximum connection charges), for item 1 there shall be substituted:—

		£	s.	d.
" 1. Exchange line of which the chargeable length does not exceed 3 miles		20	–	– "

Citation and commencement

3. These regulations may be cited as " The Telephone Amendment (No. 4) Regulations 1968 " and shall come into operation on the 16th April 1968.

Dated 10th April 1968.

Roy Mason,
Her Majesty's Postmaster General.

(a) 1951 c. 52.   (b) 1961 c. 15.   (c) S.I. 1965/225 (1965 I, p. 518).
(d) The relevant amending instruments are S.I. 1965/1191, 1966/857, 1967/433 (1965 II, p. 3388; 1966 II, p. 2042; 1967 I, p. 1369).   (e) 1889 c. 63.

EXPLANATORY NOTE

(This Note is not part of the Regulations.)

These regulations increase the maximum connection charges for exchange lines.

STATUTORY INSTRUMENTS

1968 No. 594

ROAD TRAFFIC

The Road Vehicles (Registration and Licensing) (Amendment) Regulations 1968

Made - - -	*8th April* 1968
Laid before Parliament	*22nd April* 1968
Coming into Operation	*24th April* 1968

The Minister of Transport in exercise of his powers under paragraph 6 of Schedule 4 to the Vehicles (Excise) Act 1962(a), and of all other enabling powers, hereby makes the following Regulations:—

1.—(1) These Regulations shall come into operation on the 24th April 1968 and may be cited as the Road Vehicles (Registration and Licensing) (Amendment) Regulations 1968.

(2) The Interpretation Act 1889(b) shall apply for the interpretation of these Regulations as it applies for the interpretation of an Act of Parliament.

2. The Road Vehicles (Registration and Licensing) Regulations 1964(c), as amended(d), shall have effect as though after Regulation 47 there were inserted the following Regulation:—

"Exemption of agricultural machines from duty as goods vehicles in certain cases—

47A (1) This Regulation applies to vehicles which are agricultural machines (as defined in Part I of Schedule 3 to the Act) which do not draw trailers and which are constructed or adapted for use and used for the conveyance in removable appliances fitted to the vehicle of goods or burden the haulage of which is permissible under paragraphs (*a*) to (*e*) of paragraph 2(1) of that Part of that Schedule.

(2) An appliance, not being a tined appliance, which has an external width not exceeding 8 feet 2 inches, an external length not exceeding 5 feet 2 inches and an external height not exceeding 2 feet 2 inches and which does not satisfy condition (*b*) in paragraph 5(2) of Part I of Schedule 4 to the Act, is hereby prescribed for the purposes of sub-paragraphs (2), (3) and (4) of paragraph 6 of that Part of that Schedule.

(3) Paragraph 5(2) of Part I of Schedule 4 to the Act shall not apply to a vehicle to which this Regulation applies which is fitted with an appliance of the description prescribed by paragraph (2) of this Regulation unless the appliance is used in the following circumstances, namely:—

(*a*) another appliance with the same dimensions shall be fitted at the opposite end of the vehicle;

(a) 10 & 11 Eliz. 2. c. 13.   (b) 52 & 53 Vict. c. 63.
(c) S.I. 1964/1178 (1964 II, p. 2722).   (d) There is no relevant amending instrument.

(b) each such appliance shall be so fitted to the vehicle that its longitudinal axis lies in the same vertical plane as the longitudinal axis of the vehicle;

(c) the weight of any goods or burden carried in each such appliance shall not exceed 6½ cwt.;

(d) the weight of any goods or burden carried in the two appliances shall be distributed equally between them;

(e) the goods or burden carried in each appliance shall not be above the highest point of that appliance; and

(f) the vehicle shall not proceed on a public road at a speed exceeding 10 miles per hour.

(4) Paragraph 5(2)(b) of Part I of Schedule 4 to the Act shall not have effect in relation to appliances of the description prescribed by paragraph (2) of this Regulation, but in relation thereto paragraph 5(4) of that Part of that Schedule shall have effect with the substitution of the distance of three miles for the distance of fifteen miles specified therein."

Given under the Official Seal of the Minister of Transport the 8th April 1968.

(L.S.)

Richard Marsh,
Minister of Transport.

EXPLANATORY NOTE
(This Note is not part of the Regulations.)

Schedule 4 to the Vehicles (Excise) Act 1962, contains provision that agricultural machines when used for the conveyance of goods or burden in removable appliances which are constructed and used in accordance with conditions laid down in the Schedule, or which may be prescribed in Regulations, shall be chargeable with the lower rate of duty as agricultural machines under Schedule 3 instead of the higher rate as goods vehicles under Schedule 4.

These Regulations, which further amend the Road Vehicles (Registration and Licensing) Regulations 1964, prescribe such an appliance and the conditions under which it may be used.

STATUTORY INSTRUMENTS

1968 No. 597 (C. 9)

METROPOLITAN AND CITY POLICE DISTRICTS

The London Cab Act 1968 (Commencement) Order 1968

Made - - - - *9th April* 1968

In exercise of the powers conferred on me by section 4(6) of the London Cab Act 1968(a), I hereby make the following Order :—

1. The provisions of section 4, other than subsection (6), of the London Cab Act 1968 shall come into operation on 15th July 1968.

2. This Order may be cited as the London Cab Act 1968 (Commencement) Order 1968.

James Callaghan,
One of Her Majesty's Principal
Secretaries of State.

Home Office,
Whitehall.
9th April 1968.

EXPLANATORY NOTE

(*This Note is not part of the Order.*)

This Order brings into operation on 15th July 1968 those provisions of the London Cab Act 1968 which have not already been brought into force by the Act itself, namely, section 4(1) to (5) (which relate to the prohibition of the display of certain signs or notices on, and the issue of certain advertisements in connection with, private hire-cars).

(a) 1968 c. 7.

STATUTORY INSTRUMENTS

1968 No. 598 (C.10)

SOCIAL SECURITY

NATIONAL INSURANCE

The Public Expenditure and Receipts Act 1968 (Commencement) Order 1968

Made - - - -	10*th April* 1968
Laid before Parliament	16*th April* 1968
Coming into Operation	17*th April* 1968

The Minister of Social Security, in exercise of powers conferred by section 1(4) of the Public Expenditure and Receipts Act 1968(a) and of all other powers enabling her in that behalf, hereby makes the following Order :—

Citation and commencement

1. This Order may be cited as the Public Expenditure and Receipts Act 1968 (Commencement) Order 1968 and shall come into operation on the 17th April 1968.

Appointed date

2. The date appointed for the coming into force of section 1(1) of the Public Expenditure and Receipts Act 1968 shall be the 6th May 1968.

Judith Hart,
Minister of Social Security.

10th April 1968.

EXPLANATORY NOTE

(This Note is not part of the Order.)

This Order appoints the 6th May 1968 for the coming into force of section 1(1) of the Public Expenditure and Receipts Act 1968, which increases the contributions payable under the National Insurance Act 1965.

By section 2 of the Public Expenditure and Receipts Act 1968 increased contributions under the National Health Service Contributions Act 1965 will become payable as from the same day.

(a) 1968 c. 14.

1968 No. 599

TERMS AND CONDITIONS OF EMPLOYMENT

The Redundancy Fund (Advances out of the National Loans Fund) Order 1968

Laid before Parliament in draft

Made - - - -	*9th April* 1968
Coming into Operation	*25th April* 1968

The Minister of Labour with the consent of the Treasury in exercise of the powers conferred upon her by section 35(2) of the Redundancy Payments Act 1965(a) and of all other powers enabling her in that behalf hereby makes the following Order, a draft of which has been laid before Parliament and approved by a resolution of each House of Parliament.

1.—(1) This Order may be cited as the Redundancy Fund (Advances out of the National Loans Fund) Order 1968 and shall come into operation on 25th April 1968.

(2) The Redundancy Fund (Advances out of the Consolidated Fund) Order 1967(b) is hereby revoked.

2. The Interpretation Act 1889(c) shall apply to the interpretation of this Order as it applies to the interpretation of an Act of Parliament, and as if this Order and the Order hereby revoked were Acts of Parliament.

3. The aggregate amount outstanding at any time during the period of one year beginning on 25th April 1968 by way of principal in respect of sums advanced under the said section 35 out of the National Loans Fund for the purposes of the Redundancy Fund shall not exceed £15 million.

8th April 1968.

Barbara Castle,
Minister of Labour.

We consent.

B. K. O'Malley,
Joseph Harper,

9th April 1968.

Two of the Lords Commissioners of Her Majesty's Treasury.

(a) 1965 c. 62.
(c) 1889 c. 63.

(b) S.I. 1967/1165 (1967 II, p. 3409).

EXPLANATORY NOTE

(This Note is not part of the Order.)

This Order increases to £15 million the aggregate amount that may be outstanding at any time during the period of one year beginning on 25th April 1968 by way of principal in respect of sums advanced out of the National Loans Fund for the purposes of the Redundancy Fund, and revokes the Redundancy Fund (Advances out of the Consolidated Fund) Order 1967 which increased the said aggregate amount from £8 million to £12 million for a period of one year beginning on 15th August 1967.

1968 No. 600 (S.56)

SEA FISHERIES

The Sea Fisheries (Scotland) Byelaw (No. 80) 1968

Made - - - -	*22nd February* 1968
Coming into Operation	*9th April* 1968

The Secretary of State in exercise of the powers conferred upon him by section 6 of the Herring Fishery (Scotland) Act 1889(a), and of all other powers enabling him in that behalf, hereby makes the following Byelaw:—

Citation, commencement and interpretation

1.—(1) This Byelaw may be cited as the Sea Fisheries (Scotland) Byelaw (No. 80) 1968.

(2) This Byelaw shall come into operation on the date of its confirmation by the Secretary of State.

(3) The Interpretation Act 1889(b) shall apply for the interpretation of this Byelaw as it applies for the interpretation of an Act of Parliament.

Revocation of Byelaw (No. 72) 1965

2. The Sea Fisheries (Scotland) Byelaw (No. 72) 1965(c) is hereby revoked.

Method of fishing permitted in a defined area in the Firth of Clyde

3. It shall be lawful to use the method of fishing known as otter trawling in that area of the Firth of Clyde lying inside a line drawn from Corsewall Point in the County of Wigtown to the Mull of Kintyre in the County of Argyll, except within three miles of low water mark of any part of the coast, which area is hereinafter referred to as "the defined area", subject to the following conditions:—

(*a*) such method of fishing shall be so lawful during the period from the date of coming into operation of this Byelaw until 5th July 1968 and for the purpose of capturing nephrops norvegicus;

(*b*) any boat from which such method of fishing is used within the defined area shall not exceed 70 feet in length overall;

(*c*) the number of otter boards used on any occasion in such method of fishing shall not exceed two;

(*d*) any otter board so used shall not exceed one inch in thickness and shall be of such other dimensions that if placed on a level surface with the towing bracket upwards the product of the maximum length and the maximum breadth of the surface so covered shall not exceed 16 square feet;

(*e*) the surface area of the cross-section of any metal keel or shoe forming part of any otter board so used shall not exceed three square inches;

(**a**) 1889 c. 23.   (**b**) 1889 c. 63.   (**c**) S.I. 1965/1417 (1965 II, p. 4193).

(f) it shall not be lawful for any boat carrying any otter board which does not comply with the provisions of the foregoing conditions (d) and (e) to be engaged in using such method of fishing within the defined area;

(g) no landing at the termination of a voyage by a boat which has been engaged in such method of fishing within the defined area at any time during such voyage shall contain more than 25 per centum by weight of fish other than nephrops norvegicus.

Made by the Secretary of State 22nd February 1968.

A. J. Aglen,
Fisheries Secretary.

Confirmed by the Secretary of State 9th April 1968.

A. J. Aglen,
Fisheries Secretary.

St. Andrew's House,
Edinburgh, 1.

EXPLANATORY NOTE

(This Note is not part of the Byelaw.)

This Byelaw replaces Byelaw (No. 72) 1965. It permits, on certain conditions, the use of a trawl net for the capture of Norway Lobsters in certain specified waters in the Firth of Clyde from the date of coming into operation of this Byelaw to 5th July 1968. It provides a method of measuring otter boards of irregular shape and removes a previous restriction which required that such boards should be made of wood.

STATUTORY INSTRUMENTS

1968 No. 601

ROAD TRAFFIC

The Goods Vehicles (Plating and Testing) Regulations 1968

Made - - - -	10*th April* 1968
Laid before Parliament	25*th April* 1968
Coming into Operation	1*st August* 1968

ARRANGEMENT OF REGULATIONS

PART I—GENERAL

PART II—REGULATIONS GOVERNING FIRST EXAMINATIONS

PART III—REGULATIONS GOVERNING GOODS VEHICLE TESTS REQUIRED TO BE CARRIED OUT AT INTERVALS

PART IV—REGULATIONS GOVERNING NOTIFIABLE ALTERATIONS, AMENDMENTS OF PLATING CERTIFICATES AND RE-EXAMINATIONS IN CONNECTION THEREWITH

PART V—MISCELLANEOUS MATTERS

PART VI—REGULATION RELATING TO CROWN VEHICLES

PART VII—EXEMPTIONS

SCHEDULES

The Minister of Transport (hereinafter referred to as "the Minister") in exercise of his powers under sections 9 and 14(8) of the Road Safety Act 1967(a) and of all other powers him enabling in that behalf, and after consultation with representative organisations in accordance with the provisions of section 260(2) of the Road Traffic Act 1960(b), as applied by section 29(6) of the said Act of 1967, hereby makes the following Regulations:—

PART I—GENERAL

Commencement and citation

1. These Regulations shall come into operation on the 1st August 1968, and may be cited as the Goods Vehicles (Plating and Testing) Regulations 1968.

Interpretation

2.—(1) In these Regulations, except where the context otherwise requires, the following expressions have the meanings hereby respectively assigned to them:—

"the 1960 Act" means the Road Traffic Act 1960;

"the 1967 Act" means the Road Safety Act 1967;

"the Construction and Use Regulations" means the Motor Vehicles (Construction and Use) Regulations 1966(c), as amended(d);

"articulated vehicle" and "registered" have the same meanings respectively as in the Construction and Use Regulations;

"examination appointment card" means a notice mentioned in Regulation 13, 19(3), 25(4), 26(4), 30, 32(3), 40 or 41;

"first examination", in relation to a vehicle, means an examination being both an examination for plating and a first goods vehicle test;

"Ministry plate" means a plate issued by the Minister for a goods vehicle following the issue or amendment of a plating certificate under these Regulations and in the form in, and containing the particulars required by, Schedule 11 to the Construction and Use Regulations;

"Part II re-test", in relation to a vehicle, means an examination, being both an examination for plating and a goods vehicle test, carried out on a vehicle under Part II of these Regulations subsequent to a first examination of that vehicle;

"Part III re-test", in relation to a vehicle, means a goods vehicle test carried out on a vehicle under Part III of these Regulations subsequent to a periodical test of that vehicle;

"Part IV test", in relation to a vehicle, means a re-examination carried out on a vehicle under Part IV of these Regulations;

"periodical test", in relation to a vehicle, means a goods vehicle test carried out by virtue of Part III of these Regulations on a vehicle in respect of which a goods vehicle test certificate has been issued for that vehicle on a first examination thereof or as a result of a Part II re-test following that examination or as a result of an appeal under Regulation 25, 26 or 52 following that examination or re-test;

"re-test", in relation to a vehicle, means either a Part II re-test or a Part III re-test;

"plated particulars" means those particulars which are required to be shown in a Ministry plate by Schedule 11 to the Construction and Use

(a) 1967 c. 30. (b) 8 & 9 Eliz. 2. c. 16. (c) S.I. 1966/1288 (1966 III, p. 3493).
(d) The relevant amending instruments are S.I. 1967/1270, 1665, 1666, 1753, 1968/426, 602 (1967 II, p. 3698; III, p. 4563; 4567; 4667; 1968 I, p. 1114, 1415).

Regulations and "plated weights" means such of the plated particulars relating to gross weight, axle weight for each axle and train weight required to be shown in column (2) of the said plate ;

"Scottish based vehicle" means a motor vehicle having a base or centre in Scotland from which the use of the vehicle on a journey is normally commenced ;

"semi-trailer" means a trailer which is constructed or adapted to form part of an articulated vehicle ;

"tester" means a person appointed by the Minister to carry out or assist in the carrying out of examinations for plating or of goods vehicle tests under the directions of a goods vehicle examiner ;

"the standard lists" means lists—

(a) prepared by the Minister after consultation with representative organisations of the motor manufacturing and road transport industries and other connected organisations ;

(b) published by Her Majesty's Stationery Office on the 21st February 1968, and on the 12th and 29th March 1968 ; and

(c) showing as respects goods vehicles of a make, model and type specified in the lists and complying in the case of motor vehicles with certain particulars relating to the engine, transmission, brakes and dimensions so specified and in the case of trailers with certain particulars relating to type of coupling, dimensions, brakes and tyres so specified (the said particulars being hereinafter referred to in these Regulations as the "constructional particulars") the gross weight for, and the axle weight for each axle of, vehicles of that make, model and type and, in the case of motor vehicles constructed or adapted to form part of an articulated vehicle, the train weight for vehicles of that make, model and type, the said weights being weights at or below which the Minister considers vehicles of that make, model and type could safely be driven on roads having regard to—

(i) the weights at which vehicles of that make, model and type were originally designed to operate ; and

(ii) in the case of motor vehicles the requirements as to brakes of Regulations 11, 43 and 48 of the Construction and Use Regulations prior to their amendment by the Motor Vehicles (Construction and Use) (Amendment) (No. 4) Regulations 1968 (which requirements relate to vehicles for which plating certificates have not been issued) ;

(iii) in the case of trailers the requirements of Regulation 60 of the Construction and Use Regulations ; and

(iv) in the case of trailers the provisions of Schedule 1 as respects braking force for trailers ;

"vehicle testing station" means a station provided by the Minister under section 24 of the 1967 Act.

(2) In these Regulations, any reference to a vehicle of a make, model and type shall, in relation to a trailer, include a reference to a vehicle of a make and bearing a serial number.

(3) For the purpose of these Regulations, in counting the number of axles of a vehicle, where the centres of the areas of contact between all the wheels and the road surface can be included between any two vertical planes at right angles to the longitudinal axis of the vehicle less than 3 feet 4 inches apart, those wheels shall be treated as constituting one axle.

(4) Any reference in these Regulations to a numbered Regulation or Schedule is a reference to the Regulation or Schedule bearing that number in these Regulations except where otherwise expressly provided.

(5) The Interpretation Act 1889(a) shall apply for the interpretation of these Regulations as it applies for the interpretation of an Act of Parliament.

Application of Regulations

3.—(1) Subject to paragraph (2) of this Regulation, these Regulations apply to goods vehicles of any of the following classes, that is to say—

(*a*) heavy motor cars and motor cars registered before the 1st January 1968 or, if not so registered, manufactured before that date and not registered before the 1st January 1969, and constructed or adapted for the purpose of forming part of an articulated vehicle ;

(*b*) other heavy motor cars registered before the 1st January 1968 ;

(*c*) other motor cars registered before the 1st January 1968, the weight of which unladen exceeds 30 hundredweight ;

(*d*) other heavy motor cars manufactured before the 1st January 1968 and not registered before the 1st January 1969 ;

(*e*) other motor cars manufactured before the 1st January 1968 and not registered before the 1st January 1969, the weight of which unladen exceeds 30 hundredweight ;

(*f*) semi-trailers manufactured before the 1st January 1968 ;

(*g*) other trailers manufactured before the 1st January 1968 and the weight of which unladen exceeds 1 ton.

(2) Nothing in these Regulations shall apply to a goods vehicle of any of the classes of vehicle specified in Schedule 2.

Prescribed statutory requirements for goods vehicle tests

4.—(1) Subject to the provisions of these Regulations, every goods vehicle to which these Regulations apply submitted for a goods vehicle test in accordance with the provisions of these Regulations shall be examined for the purpose of ascertaining whether, where that vehicle is a motor vehicle, the construction and use requirements specified in Part I of Schedule 3 (except any such requirement as, by virtue of any provision in the regulation containing that requirement, does not apply to that vehicle) are complied with in the case of that vehicle and, where that vehicle is a trailer, the construction and use requirements specified in Part II of the said Schedule (except as aforesaid) are complied with in the case of that trailer.

(2) The statutory requirements specified in Schedule 3 are in these Regulations referred to as " the prescribed construction and use requirements " and for the purposes of these Regulations the applicability of any such statutory requirement to a vehicle at the date of its goods vehicle test shall not be affected by Regulation 4(8A) of the Construction and Use Regulations.

Supervision of tests

5. Subject to the provisions of these Regulations, every examination for plating and every goods vehicle test shall be carried out by or under the direction of a goods vehicle examiner.

Authority to drive

6. A vehicle examiner or a tester by whom is carried out a first examination of a vehicle, a re-test of a vehicle, a periodical test of a vehicle

---

or a Part IV test of a vehicle, an area mechanical engineer by whom is carried out a re-examination of a vehicle on an appeal under section 9(3) of the 1967 Act and an officer appointed by the Minister to carry out a re-examination of a vehicle under section 9(4) of the 1967 Act are authorised to drive the vehicle, whether on a road or elsewhere.

Duties of driver of goods vehicle

7. The driver of a goods vehicle submitted for a first examination of the vehicle, a re-test of the vehicle, a periodical test of the vehicle, a Part IV test of the vehicle, or a re-examination of the vehicle on an appeal under section 9(3) or (4) of the 1967 Act shall, except so far as permitted to be absent by the person carrying out any such examination, be present throughout the whole of the said first examination, re-test, periodical test, Part IV test or re-examination, as the case may be, and shall drive the vehicle when directed to do so, and shall operate the controls in accordance with any directions given to him, by that person, and a contravention of a requirement of this Regulation is hereby declared to be an offence.

Conditions subject to which vehicles accepted for examinations

8.—(1) In this Regulation and the next succeeding Regulation, except where the context otherwise requires—

" examination " means either a first examination of a vehicle, a re-test of a vehicle, a periodical test of a vehicle, a Part IV test of a vehicle or a re-examination of a vehicle under section 9(3) or (4) of the 1967 Act ;

" examiner " means, in relation to an examination being either a first examination of a vehicle, a re-test of a vehicle, a periodical test of a vehicle or a Part IV test of a vehicle, a goods vehicle examiner, and, in relation to a re-examination under section 9(3) of the 1967 Act, an area mechanical engineer, and in relation to a re-examination under section 9(4) of the 1967 Act the officer appointed by the Minister to carry out that re-examination.

(2) The conditions, subject to which goods vehicles, being motor vehicles, will be accepted for an examination are the following conditions set out in this Regulation.

(3) An examiner shall not be under an obligation to proceed with the carrying out of an examination of a goods vehicle, being a motor vehicle, in any of the following cases, that is to say—

(*a*) if a vehicle is not submitted for the examination within thirty minutes after the time fixed under these Regulations for the examination ;

(*b*) where on the submission of a vehicle for the examination the applicant for the examination does not, after being requested to do so, produce the examination appointment card (if any) relating to the examination, and either the registration book relating to the vehicle or other evidence as to the date of its first registration or, in the case of a vehicle not registered before the 1st January 1969, evidence as to its date of manufacture ;

(*c*) where on the submission of a vehicle for an examination the particulars relating to the vehicle and shown in any application form relevant to that examination are found to be substantially incorrect ;

(*d*) where the vehicle is one as respects which it has been stated in the said application form it is to be used on roads to draw a trailer and in the last examination appointment card preceding the examination it was requested that the vehicle be accompanied by a trailer which is to be drawn by the vehicle, and the vehicle is not accompanied by such a trailer ;

(e) where the vehicle is not marked with the chassis or serial number shown in the registration book relating to that vehicle, or where if no such number is so shown or exists, the vehicle is not marked with an identification mark which shall have been allotted to the vehicle by the Minister in the examination appointment card relating to the first examination of the vehicle, or where that number or mark is not permanently affixed to the chassis or the main structure of the vehicle in a conspicuous and easily accessible position so as to be readily legible ;

(f) where the vehicle or any part thereof or any of its equipment or any trailer by which it is accompanied or any part of the trailer or any of its equipment is in such a dirty or dangerous condition as to make it unreasonable for the examination to be carried out in accordance with the provisions of these Regulations or of any directions given under section 9(7) of the 1967 Act, or where the applicant for the examination does not produce any certificate, required by the last examination appointment card preceding the examination, that a vehicle used for carrying toxic, corrosive or inflammable loads has been properly cleaned or otherwise rendered safe ;

(g) where an examiner is not able with the facilities and apparatus available to that examiner at the vehicle testing station or other place at which the examination would otherwise be carried out to complete the examination without the vehicle being driven and the vehicle is not when submitted for examination provided with fuel and oil to enable it to be driven to such extent as may be necessary for the purposes of the carrying out of the examination ;

(h) where on the submission of a vehicle for the examination that vehicle or any trailer which accompanies it is not in such a condition as respects the presence thereon or the absence thereon of a load as may have been specified for the purposes of that examination in the last examination appointment card preceding that examination.

9.—(1) The conditions, subject to which goods vehicles, being trailers, will be accepted for an examination are the following conditions set out in this Regulation.

(2) An examiner shall not be under an obligation to proceed with the carrying out of an examination of a goods vehicle, being a trailer, in any of the following cases, that is to say—

(a) if a trailer is not submitted for the examination within thirty minutes after the time fixed under these Regulations for the examination ;

(b) where on the submission of a trailer for the examination, the applicant for the examination does not, after being requested to do so, produce the examination appointment card (if any) relating to the examination and evidence as to the date of manufacture of the trailer ;

(c) where on the submission of a trailer for an examination the particulars relating to the trailer and shown in any application form relevant to that examination are found to be substantially incorrect ;

(d) where the trailer is not accompanied by a motor vehicle suitable as to its construction and equipment for drawing that trailer ;

(e) where the trailer is not marked with an identification mark which shall have been allotted to the trailer by the Minister in the examination appointment card (if any) relating to the first examination of the trailer or shall have otherwise been allotted to the trailer by the Minister under these Regulations prior to that first examination, or where that mark is not permanently affixed to the chassis or the main structure of the trailer in a conspicuous and easily accessible position so as to be readily legible ;

(f) where the trailer or any part thereof or any of its equipment or any motor vehicle which accompanies it or any part of that vehicle or any of its equipment is in such a dirty or dangerous condition as to make it unreasonable for the examination to be carried out in accordance with the provisions of these Regulations or of any directions given under section 9(7) of the 1967 Act, or where the applicant for the examination does not produce any certificate, required by the last examination appointment card preceding the examination, that a vehicle used for carrying toxic, corrosive or inflammable loads has been properly cleaned or otherwise rendered safe ;

(g) where an examiner is not able with the facilities and apparatus available to that examiner at the vehicle testing station or other place at which the examination would otherwise be carried out to complete the examination without the motor vehicle which accompanies the trailer being driven and that motor vehicle is not provided with fuel and oil to enable it to be driven to such extent as may be necessary for the purposes of the carrying out of the examination ;

(h) where an examiner is not able with the facilities and apparatus available to that examiner at the vehicle testing station or other place at which the examination would otherwise be carried out to complete the examination without the motor vehicle which accompanies the trailer being driven on a public road and that motor vehicle cannot be so used without contravention of section 7 of the Vehicles (Excise) Act 1962(a), because no licence under that Act is in force for the vehicle ;

(i) where on the submission of a trailer for the examination that trailer is not in such a condition as respects the presence thereon or the absence thereon of a load as may have been specified for the purposes of that examination in the last examination appointment card (if any) preceding that examination or shall have otherwise been requested by the Minister under these Regulations.

PART II—REGULATIONS GOVERNING FIRST EXAMINATIONS

Dates by which vehicles to be submitted for first examinations

10.—(1) Every goods vehicle to which these Regulations apply, being a motor vehicle of a class specified in column 1 of Part I of Schedule 4 but not being a Scottish based vehicle, shall be submitted for a first examination by the date specified in relation to that class in column 3 of the said Part.

(2) Every goods vehicle to which these Regulations apply, being a motor vehicle of a class specified in column 1 of Part II of Schedule 4 and being a Scottish based vehicle, shall be submitted for a first examination by the date specified in relation to that class in column 3 of the said Part.

(3) Every goods vehicle to which these Regulations apply, being a trailer of a class specified in column 1 of Part III of Schedule 4, shall be submitted for a first examination by the date specified in relation to that class in column 3 of the said Part.

(a) 10 & 11 Eliz. 2. c. 13.

(4) Nothing in the foregoing provisions of this Regulation shall be taken to prevent the Minister authorising a goods vehicle of a class specified in Schedule 4 being submitted for a first examination on or after the date by which a goods vehicle of that class is required by those provisions to be submitted for such an examination.

Manner of making applications for first examinations and fees therefor

11.—(1) Subject to the provisions of these Regulations, any person wishing to have a first examination carried out on a goods vehicle to which these Regulations apply shall make an application for that purpose in accordance with the following provisions of this Regulation to the Minister at the Goods Vehicle Centre, Swansea :

Provided that such an application may be made in the case of a trailer direct to a vehicle testing station, if the written consent of the Minister (which consent may provide for the marking of, and load to be carried by, a trailer on its examination) to the application being so made has first been obtained from that Centre, and upon the receipt of the application the person in charge of the station shall arrange a date and time for the first examination to be carried out.

(2) Every such application shall be made on a form approved by the Minister, shall contain the particulars required by that form and shall be accompanied by a fee of the amount shown in column 2 of Part I of Schedule 5 in relation to the class of vehicle specified in column 1 in that Part.

Time within which applications to be made

12. Every application for a first examination of a goods vehicle to which these Regulations apply and of a class specified in Schedule 4 shall be made at least one month before the date the applicant desires to submit the vehicle for a first examination and on or after the date specified in relation to that class in column 2 of Schedule 4 :

Provided that such an application may be accepted and dealt with, notwithstanding it was not made in accordance with the foregoing provisions of this Regulation, if the Minister is satisfied there were reasonable grounds for the application not having been so made.

Notice of place and time for first examinations

13.—(1) As soon as reasonably practicable after the date of the receipt of an application for a first examination for a vehicle to which these Regulations apply, the Minister shall send to the applicant for that examination a notice stating the address of the vehicle testing station at which the examination is to take place and the date and time reserved by the Minister for that examination :

Provided that the Minister shall not be required to send to the applicant such a notice in a case where the application is made direct to a vehicle testing station by virtue of Regulation 11.

(2) In stating any address, date or time under the provisions of the last paragraph the Minister shall so far as is reasonably practicable have regard to any preference as to that address, date or time expressed by the applicant in the application made by him for the first examination of the vehicle.

Examination for plating

14. For the purpose of determining the plated weights for a goods vehicle submitted for an examination for plating, a goods vehicle examiner shall first cause the vehicle to be examined in order to determine whether it is a vehicle of a make, model and type to which the standard lists apply, whether the constructional particulars relating to that make, model and type are substantially complied with by the vehicle and whether the weights shown in the lists are applicable to the vehicle, and for this purpose the examiner shall have regard to—

(a) the particulars as respects the vehicle shown in the application mentioned in Regulation 11 relating to the vehicle ; and

(b) any information which may have been supplied by the Minister subsequent to the publication of the standard lists as to the applicability of any of the weights shown in those lists.

15. In the event of it being determined by the goods vehicle examiner that the goods vehicle submitted for an examination for plating is one of a make, model and type and otherwise one to which the weights shown in the standard lists are applicable there shall be determined in respect of the vehicle—

(a) as its plated weights relating to gross weight and axle weight for each axle the equivalent weights shown as design weights in the standard lists for vehicles of that make, model and type :

Provided that if the use on roads of the vehicle at any such equivalent weight as is mentioned in this paragraph would render—

(i) a motor vehicle, when not drawing a trailer, liable to be used in contravention of Regulation 70 of the Construction and Use Regulations ;

(ii) a trailer, to which Regulation 71(3) of the said Regulations does not apply, liable to be used in contravention of Regulation 71(1) and (2) ;

(iii) a trailer, to which the said Regulation 71(3) does apply, when drawn by a prior 1968 vehicle as defined in Regulation 71(4) of the said Regulations, liable to be used in contravention of the said Regulation 71(3) ; or

(iv) a motor vehicle or trailer liable to be used in contravention of Regulation 74 or 123 of the said Regulations,

then such equivalent weight shall for the purpose of the determination of a plated weight under this Regulation be reduced to such extent as is necessary to ensure compliance with any such Regulation ;

(b) if the vehicle is a motor vehicle constructed or adapted to form part of an articulated vehicle, as its plated weight relating to train weight, the equivalent weight shown as a design weight in the standard lists for vehicles of that make, model and type :

Provided that, if any such equivalent weight is in excess of 32 tons in the case of a motor vehicle, being a prior 1968 vehicle as defined in Regulation 73(3) of the Construction and Use Regulations or in the case of any other motor vehicle in excess of 24 tons, then such equivalent weight shall for the purpose of the determination of a plated weight relating to train weight under this Regulation be reduced in the first mentioned case to 32 tons and in the second mentioned case to 24 tons.

16.—(1) In the event of it being determined by the goods vehicle examiner that the goods vehicle submitted for an examination for plating is not one of a make, model and type or otherwise one to which the weights shown in the standard lists are applicable, he shall determine the plated weights.

(2) In reaching the determination under the last paragraph as respects a goods vehicle, the goods vehicle examiner shall have regard—

(a) to any information which may have been supplied by the Minister as to the plated weights which have been determined for similar vehicles under these Regulations as a result of an examination thereof for plating ;

(b) to its design, construction and equipment and the stresses to which it is likely to be subject when in use on roads ;

(c) to any information which may be available about the weights at which the vehicle was originally designed to be driven on roads ;

(d) in a case where the vehicle or its equipment has, or appears to have been, altered since the date of its manufacture, to the likely effect of any such alteration in making the vehicle fit to be driven safely on roads at weights different from those at which it appears to the examiner the vehicle was originally designed to be so driven ;

(e) in the case of the vehicle being a motor vehicle, to the requirements as to brakes specified in the definition of " standard lists " in Regulation 2(1) ;

(f) in the case of the vehicle being a trailer, to the requirements of Regulation 60 of the Construction and Use Regulations ;

(g) in the case of the vehicle being a trailer, to the provisions of Schedule 1 as respects braking force for trailers ; and

(h) to the need for the vehicle to comply with the requirements of Regulations 70, 71, 74 and 123 of the Construction and Use Regulations and with the requirement that no plated weight relating to train weight for a motor vehicle constructed or adapted to form part of an articulated vehicle shall exceed, in the case of a motor vehicle, being a prior 1968 vehicle as defined in Regulation 73(3) of the Construction and Use Regulations, 32 tons or, in any other case 24 tons.

17. After the determination of the plated weights for a goods vehicle submitted for an examination for plating, there shall be issued for that vehicle a plating certificate, unless there is a refusal for the vehicle of a goods vehicle test certificate.

Provision for goods vehicle test

18.—(1) After an examination for plating in respect of a goods vehicle has been carried out, a goods vehicle examiner shall arrange for the vehicle to undergo a goods vehicle test.

(2) After a goods vehicle test has been completed as respects a vehicle there shall be issued—

(a) where the vehicle is found to comply with the prescribed construction and use requirements, a goods vehicle test certificate and also a plating certificate for that vehicle, and

(b) where the vehicle is found not to comply with the prescribed construction and use requirements, a notification of the refusal of a goods vehicle test certificate and in that event no plating certificate shall be issued for the vehicle.

Application for Part II re-tests

19.—(1) Where under Regulation 18(2)(b) a notification of the refusal of a goods vehicle test certificate is issued for a vehicle and accordingly no plating certificate is issued for the vehicle, it may be submitted and, if need be, from time to time be submitted at a vehicle testing station for a Part II re-test in accordance with the following provisions of this Regulation.

(2) Where it is desired to submit a vehicle for a Part II re-test at the same vehicle testing station as that at which it was submitted for its first examination within a period of fourteen days after the date it was submitted for that examination, the applicant for the re-test shall first make arrangements in writing or otherwise with the person in charge of the station for a date and time at which the vehicle is to be submitted for the re-test.

(3) Where it is desired to submit a vehicle for a Part II re-test (not being a re-test falling within the next paragraph) at the vehicle testing station mentioned in the last preceding paragraph but otherwise than within the period therein mentioned or at a vehicle testing station different from that at which it was submitted for its first examination, the applicant for the re-test shall first make a written application to the Goods Vehicle Centre, Swansea, for a time at which the vehicle may be submitted for the re-test and every such application shall be made on a form approved by the Minister and shall contain the particulars required by that form, and upon receipt of the application the Minister shall send to the applicant a notice stating where and when the re-test is to take place and in this connection shall have regard so far as is reasonably practicable to any preference expressed by the applicant as to when and where the re-test should take place.

(4) Where it is desired to submit a vehicle for a further Part II re-test at the same vehicle testing station as that at which it was submitted for a re-test under the last preceding paragraph within a period of 14 days after the date it was submitted for the last mentioned re-test, the applicant for the further Part II re-test shall first make arrangements in writing or otherwise with the person in charge of the station for a date and time at which the vehicle is to be submitted for that re-test.

Fees for Part II re-tests

20.—(1) The fee payable for a Part II re-test of a vehicle carried out in accordance with arrangements made under Regulation 19(2) or (4) shall be of the amount specified in paragraph 1 of Part II of Schedule 5:

Provided that no fee shall be payable for such a re-test of a vehicle submitted within the relevant time, if it is the first re-test of the vehicle carried out following the first examination of the vehicle or following an earlier Part II re-test of the vehicle in respect of which a fee has been paid under this Regulation.

In this paragraph " relevant time " means the same day as that on which the said first examination or the said Part II re-test was completed or the next following day on which the vehicle testing station is open.

(2) The fee payable under the last preceding paragraph shall be paid to the Minister on the submission of the vehicle for the Part II re-test to be carried out in accordance with the arrangements made under Regulation 19(2) or (4), and may be paid in cash.

(3) The fee payable for a Part II re-test of a vehicle carried out by virtue of Regulation 19(3) shall be of the amount specified in paragraph 2 of Part II of Schedule 5.

(4) The said fee shall be paid to the Minister at the same time as the written application mentioned in Regulation 19(3) is made.

Part II re-tests

21.—(1) Where a vehicle is submitted for a Part II re-test at a vehicle testing station in accordance with the arrangements mentioned in Regulation 19(2) or (4) a goods vehicle examiner shall—

(*a*) in a case where after examination of the vehicle he is satisfied that no alteration has been made to the vehicle or its equipment which would render the plated weights, where determined under Regulation 15, for the vehicle on its first examination inapplicable, determine for the vehicle as its plated weights the weights so determined ;

(*b*) in a case where he is not so satisfied, determine the plated weights for the vehicle having regard to the matters specified in Regulation 16(2) ;

(*c*) in a case where at the first examination of the vehicle or at its last Part II re-test the plated weights were determined under Regulation 16, determine the plated weights for the vehicle having regard to the matters specified in Regulation 16(2) ; and

(*d*) in carrying out a goods vehicle test be under an obligation only to examine the vehicle for the purpose of ascertaining whether it complies with such of the particular items of the prescribed construction and use requirements as respects which it was shown in the last notification of a refusal of a test certificate not to comply.

(2) Where a goods vehicle examiner finds that the vehicle complies with such of the particular items of the prescribed construction and use requirements mentioned in sub-paragraph (*d*) of the last preceding paragraph and has no reason to believe that the prescribed construction and use requirements as respects other items are not complied with in relation to the vehicle, there shall be issued a goods vehicle test certificate and also a plating certificate for the vehicle.

(3) Where a goods vehicle examiner does not find that the vehicle complies with the particular items of the prescribed construction and use requirements mentioned in sub-paragraph (*d*) of paragraph (1) of this Regulation or finds that the prescribed construction and use requirements as respects other items are not complied with in relation to the vehicle, there shall be issued a notification of the refusal of a test certificate and in that event no plating certificate shall be issued for the vehicle.

(4) Where a vehicle is submitted for a re-test at a vehicle testing station as a result of the application mentioned in Regulation 19(3) a goods vehicle examiner shall—

(*a*) in a case where after examination of the vehicle he is satisfied that no alteration has been made to the vehicle or its equipment which would render the plated weights, where determined under Regulation 15, for the vehicle on its first examination inapplicable, determine for the vehicle as its plated weights the weights so determined ;

(*b*) in a case where he is not so satisfied, determine the plated weights for the vehicle having regard to the matters specified in Regulation 16(2) ;

(*c*) in a case where at the first examination of the vehicle or at its last re-test, the plated weights were determined under Regulation 16, determine the plated weights for the vehicle having regard to the matters specified in Regulation 16(2) ; and

(*d*) arrange for the vehicle to undergo a goods vehicle test.

(5) Where the goods vehicle test mentioned in the last preceding paragraph has been completed as respects the vehicle there shall be issued—

(*a*) where the vehicle is found to comply with the prescribed construction and use requirements, a goods vehicle test certificate and also a plating certificate for that vehicle ; and

(b) where the vehicle is found not to comply with the prescribed construction and use requirements, a notification of the refusal of a goods vehicle test certificate and in that event no plating certificate shall be issued for the vehicle.

Particulars to be contained in plating certificates

22. Every plating certificate issued for a vehicle under the foregoing provisions of these Regulations shall contain—

    (a) particulars of the plated weights determined for that vehicle under Regulation 15, 16 or 21 ;

    (b) where any such plated weight determined under Regulation 15 is less than the equivalent weight shown as a design weight in the standard lists, particulars of that equivalent weight ;

    (c) where any such plated weight determined under Regulation 16 or having regard to the matters specified in Regulation 16(2) is less than the weight that would have been otherwise determined but for sub-paragraph (h) of paragraph (2) of Regulation 16, particulars of the last mentioned weight which shall be shown as a design weight ;

    (d) particulars of the other plated particulars ascertained from the application mentioned in Regulation 11 and an inspection of the vehicle ;

    (e) particulars of any alteration in the vehicle or its equipment which is required by these Regulations to be notified to the Minister ;

    (f) particulars of the sizes of the tyres fitted to the wheels of the vehicle at the time of the issue of the certificate, and of the particular conditions, if any, in which a vehicle when used on roads at or below its plated weights and fitted with those tyres properly maintained should as respects such tyres so maintained be driven ;

    (g) the date on which it is issued and the number allotted by the Minister to the vehicle testing station at which it is issued ;

and shall be signed by the goods vehicle examiner who carried out, or under whose direction was carried out, the examination for plating or shall be signed on behalf of that examiner by a person authorised in that behalf by the examiner.

Particulars to be contained in test certificates and notifications of refusal thereof

23.—(1) Every goods vehicle test certificate issued for a vehicle under the foregoing provisions of these Regulations shall contain—

    (a) a statement that the vehicle was found to comply with the prescribed construction and use requirements ; and

    (b) the period of validity of the certificate.

(2) Every notification of the refusal of a goods vehicle test certificate issued for a vehicle under the foregoing provisions of these Regulations shall contain a written notification of the refusal of a goods vehicle test certificate and of the grounds of such refusal.

(3) In addition to the particulars required by paragraph (1) or (2) of this Regulation, every such goods vehicle test certificate and every such notification of the refusal of a goods vehicle test certificate shall contain the following particulars—

    (a) in the case of a certificate or notification issued for a motor vehicle, the registration mark (if any) exhibited on the vehicle or, if no such mark is so exhibited, the chassis or serial number marked on the vehicle or, if no such number is so marked, the identification mark which shall have been allotted to the vehicle by the Minister in the examination appointment card relating to the first examination of the vehicle ;

(*b*) in the case of a certificate or notification issued for a trailer, the identification mark which shall have been allotted to the trailer by the Minister in the examination appointment card (if any) relating to the first examination of the trailer or shall have otherwise been allotted to the trailer by the Minister under these Regulations ;

(*c*) the name and address of the applicant for the goods vehicle test to which the certificate or notification relates ;

(*d*) the date on which the certificate or the notification is issued and the number allotted by the Minister to the vehicle testing station at which it is issued ;

and shall be signed by the goods vehicle examiner who carried out, or under whose direction was carried out, the goods vehicle test or shall be signed on behalf of that examiner by a person authorised in that behalf by the examiner.

Period of validity of first goods vehicle test certificate

24. Where a goods vehicle test certificate is issued for a goods vehicle, as a result of a first examination or a Part II re-test of that vehicle or an appeal under Regulation 25 or 26, the certificate shall be valid from the date of its issue until the last day (inclusive of that day) by which that vehicle is required by virtue of Part III of these Regulations to be submitted for a periodical test.

Appeals to area mechanical engineer

25.—(1) Any person aggrieved by a determination made on a first examination of a vehicle or a Part II re-test of a vehicle by the person in charge of the examination may appeal to an area mechanical engineer appointed by the Minister to act for the traffic area in which that examination was made.

(2) Any such appeal shall be lodged at the office of the traffic area not later than 10 days from the date of the determination.

(3) Every appeal shall be made on a form approved by the Minister and shall contain the particulars required by that form and shall be accompanied by a fee of fifteen pounds.

(4) As soon as reasonably practicable after the date of the receipt of the appeal, the area mechanical engineer shall send a notice stating where and when a re-examination for the purposes of determining the issues raised on the appeal is to take place addressed to the appellant at the address of the appellant stated in the form of appeal.

(5) The place to be selected by the area mechanical engineer for the re-examination for the purposes of the appeal may be either a vehicle testing station or such other place as he may consider convenient for the purpose of carrying out that re-examination.

(6) The vehicle shall be submitted for the re-examination at the place and time specified in the notice sent to the appellant under paragraph (4) of this Regulation, unless arrangements are made with the agreement of the area mechanical engineer for the carrying out of the examination at some other place and time.

(7) On the submission of a goods vehicle for a re-examination for the purposes of an appeal the person submitting the vehicle for the re-examination

shall, if requested to do so by the area mechanical engineer, produce to that officer—

(a) if the appeal relates to a determination made on an examination for plating, as a result of which a plating certificate was issued, that certificate ;

(b) if the appeal relates to a determination made on a goods vehicle test, the notification of the refusal of a goods vehicle test certificate issued as a result of that test.

(8) On the submission of a goods vehicle for a re-examination for the purposes of an appeal, the person submitting the vehicle for the re-examination shall, if requested to do so by the area mechanical engineer, give that officer such information as he may reasonably require relating to any alteration made or repairs carried out, or any accident or other event occurring, since the date of the determination appealed against, which may have affected the vehicle or its equipment.

(9) The said area mechanical engineer shall not be required to proceed with the carrying out of the re-examination unless the person submitting the vehicle for the re-examination complies with the provisions of paragraphs (7) and (8) of this Regulation and nothing in this paragraph shall be taken to be in derogation of the provisions of Regulation 8 or 9.

(10) Upon completion of the said re-examination the area mechanical engineer shall make such determination in the matter as he thinks fit, and may—

(a) where the appeal relates to a determination made on an examination for plating as respects which a plating certificate was issued, either determine that such certificate was properly issued or issue a different plating certificate upon the surrender of the first mentioned certificate ;

(b) if the appeal relates to a determination made on a goods vehicle test, issue either a goods vehicle test certificate and a plating certificate for the vehicle or a notification of the refusal of a goods vehicle test certificate stating the grounds thereof and in that event no plating certificate shall be issued for the vehicle.

(11) Plating certificates, goods vehicle test certificates and notifications of the refusal of a goods vehicle test certificate issued under the foregoing provisions of this Regulation shall contain—

(a) the same particulars as are appropriate in the case of plating certificates, goods vehicle test certificates and notifications of the refusal of a goods vehicle test certificate mentioned in Regulation 22 or 23, subject nevertheless to such modifications as may be appropriate and subject in the case of a plating certificate to that certificate showing particulars of the plated weights determined for that vehicle by the area mechanical engineer carrying out the examination for the purpose of the appeal ;

(b) in the case of a plating certificate—

(i) where the vehicle is of a make, model and type and otherwise one to which the standard lists apply and any plated weight so determined by the area mechanical engineer is less than the equivalent weight shown as a design weight in such lists, particulars of that equivalent weight ; and

(ii) where any plated weight so determined is less than the weight that would have been otherwise determined under Regulation 16(2) but for sub-paragraph (h) of paragraph (2) of Regulation 16, particulars of the last mentioned weight which shall be shown as a design weight ; and

shall be signed by that area mechanical engineer.

Appeals to Minister

26.—(1) Any person aggrieved by the determination of an area mechanical engineer under the last foregoing Regulation may appeal to the Minister.

(2) Any such appeal shall be lodged at the Goods Vehicle Centre, Swansea, not later than 14 days from the date of the determination and shall be accompanied by a fee of twenty-five pounds.

(3) Every appeal shall be made on a form approved by the Minister and shall contain the particulars required by that form.

(4) As soon as reasonably practicable after the date of the receipt of the appeal, the Minister shall send a notice stating where and when a re-examination for the purposes of determining the issues raised on appeal is to take place addressed to the appellant at the address of the appellant stated in the form of appeal.

(5) The place to be selected by the Minister for the re-examination for the purposes of the appeal may be either a vehicle testing station or such other place as he may consider convenient for the purpose of carrying out that re-examination.

(6) The vehicle shall be submitted for re-examination at the place and time specified in the notice sent to the appellant under paragraph (4) of this Regulation, unless arrangements are made with the agreement of the Minister for the carrying out of the re-examination at some other place and time.

(7) On the submission of a goods vehicle for a re-examination for the purposes of an appeal the person submitting the vehicle for the re-examination shall, if requested to do so by the officer appointed by the Minister to re-examine the vehicle, produce to that officer—

(a) if the appeal relates to a determination made by an area mechanical engineer in connection with any such plating certificate as is mentioned in Regulation 25(10), that certificate ;

(b) if the appeal relates to a determination made by an area mechanical engineer in connection with a notification of the refusal of a goods vehicle test certificate issued under Regulation 25(10)(b), that notification.

(8) On the submission of a goods vehicle for a re-examination for the purposes of an appeal, the person submitting the vehicle for the re-examination shall, if requested to do so by the officer appointed by the Minister to re-examine the vehicle, give that officer such information as he may reasonably require relating to any alteration made or repairs carried out, or any accident or other event occurring, since the date of the determination appealed against, which may have affected the vehicle or its equipment.

(9) The said officer shall not be required to proceed with the carrying out of the re-examination unless the person submitting the vehicle for the re-examination complies with the provisions of paragraphs (7) and (8) of this Regulation and nothing in this paragraph shall be taken to be in derogation of the provisions of Regulation 8 or 9.

(10) Upon completion of the said re-examination the Minister shall make such determination on the basis of the re-examination as he thinks fit, and may—

(a) where the appeal relates to a determination made in connection with an examination for plating as respects which a plating certificate was issued, either determine that such certificate was properly issued or issue a different plating certificate upon surrender of the first mentioned certificate ; and

(b) where the appeal relates to a determination made by an area mechanical engineer in connection with a notification of the refusal of a goods vehicle test certificate, issue either a goods vehicle test certificate and a plating certificate for the vehicle or a notification of the refusal of a goods vehicle test certificate stating the grounds thereof and in that event no plating certificate shall be issued for the vehicle.

(11) Plating certificates, goods vehicle test certificates and notifications of the refusal of a goods vehicle test certificate issued under the foregoing provisions of this Regulation shall contain—

(a) the same particulars as are appropriate in the case of plating certificates, goods vehicle test certificates and notifications of the refusal of a goods vehicle test certificate mentioned in Regulation 22 or 23, subject nevertheless to such modifications as may be appropriate and subject in the case of a plating certificate to that certificate showing particulars of the plated weights determined for that vehicle by the Minister ;

(b) in the case of a plating certificate—

(i) where the vehicle is of a make, model and type and otherwise one to which the standard lists apply and any plated weight so determined by the Minister is less than the equivalent weight shown as a design weight in such lists, particulars of that equivalent weight ; and

(ii) where any plated weight so determined is less than the weight that would have been otherwise determined under Regulation 16(2) but for sub-paragraph (h) of paragraph (2) of Regulation 16, particulars of the last mentioned weight which shall be shown as a design weight ; and

shall be signed on behalf of the Minister by an officer appointed by him for the purpose.

PART III—REGULATIONS GOVERNING GOODS VEHICLE TESTS REQUIRED TO BE CARRIED OUT AT INTERVALS

Dates by which goods vehicles to be submitted for periodical tests

27.—(1) A goods vehicle to which these Regulations apply and registered before the 1st January 1968, being a motor vehicle in respect of which a goods vehicle test certificate has been issued prior to the 1st April 1970—

(a) shall be submitted for a periodical test, subject to the provisions of sub-paragraphs (b) and (c) of this paragraph, not later than the end of the month in the first renewal period in which month falls the anniversary of the date on which it was registered and not later than the end of the month in each succeeding renewal period in which month falls the said anniversary ;

(b) where a vehicle is submitted for a first periodical test before the 1st April 1970 earlier than two months before the last date in the first renewal period by which it is required by sub-paragraph (*a*) of this Regulation to be submitted for that test, then it shall be submitted for a periodical test in the first renewal period not later than the end of the month, and in each succeeding renewal period not later than the end of the month in each such period, which corresponds with the same month in which it was submitted for the first periodical test ;

(*c*) where a vehicle is submitted for a first periodical test on or after the 1st April 1970 earlier than two months before the last date in the first renewal period by which it is required by sub-paragraph (*a*) of this Regulation to be submitted for that test, then it shall be submitted for a periodical test in each succeeding renewal period not later than the end of the month in that period corresponding with the same month in the first renewal period in which it was submitted for the first periodical test.

For the purposes of this paragraph and paragraph (4) of this Regulation, " the first renewal period " means the period of twelve months beginning on the 1st April 1970 and " succeeding renewal period " means a period of twelve months beginning on the 1st April in 1971 or on the 1st April in each calendar year thereafter.

(2) A goods vehicle to which these Regulations apply and registered before the 1st January 1968, being a motor vehicle in respect of which its first goods vehicle test certificate has been issued during a month after the 31st March 1970, shall be submitted for a periodical test not later than the end of the next month in a calendar year in which month falls the anniversary of the date on which it was registered and in each following calendar year not later than the end of the month in which falls the said anniversary.

(3) A goods vehicle to which these Regulations apply and to which paragraph 4 of Part I of Schedule 4 or paragraph 3 of Part II of that Schedule applies, being a motor vehicle in respect of which its first goods vehicle test certificate has been issued in any calendar year shall be submitted for a periodical test in each following calendar year not later than the end of the month in which falls the anniversary of the date of issue of that first goods vehicle test certificate.

(4) A goods vehicle to which these Regulations apply, being a trailer in respect of which its first goods vehicle test certificate has been issued prior to the 1st April 1970, shall be submitted for a periodical test not later than the end of the relevant month in the first renewal period, and in each succeeding renewal period not later than the end of the relevant month in that period.

(5) A goods vehicle to which these Regulations apply, being a trailer in respect of which its first goods vehicle test certificate has been issued during a month after the 31st March 1970, shall be submitted for a periodical test not later than the end of the next relevant month in a calendar year, and in each following calendar year not later than the end of the relevant month.

For the purposes of paragraphs (4) and (5), " relevant month " means the month indicated by the last figure or the two last figures where they are 10, 11 or 12 included in the Ministry of Transport identification mark which was allotted to the trailer by the Minister in the examination appointment card (if any) relating to the first examination of the trailer or shall have otherwise been allotted to the trailer by the Minister under these Regulations prior to that first examination.

(6) Nothing in the foregoing provisions of this Regulation shall be taken to prevent the Minister authorising a goods vehicle to which these Regula-

tions apply being submitted for a periodical test on or after the date by which that goods vehicle is required by those provisions to be submitted for such a test.

Manner of making applications for periodical tests and fees therefor

28.—(1) Subject to the provisions of these Regulations, any person wishing to have a periodical test carried out on a goods vehicle to which these Regulations apply shall make an application for the purpose in accordance with the following provisions of this Regulation to the Minister at the Goods Vehicle Centre, Swansea:

Provided that such an application may be made in the case of a trailer direct to a vehicle testing station, if the written consent of the Minister (which consent may provide for the load to be carried by a trailer on the examination) to the application being so made has first been obtained from that Centre and upon receipt of the application the person in charge of the station shall arrange a date and time for the periodical test to be carried out.

(2) Every such application shall be on a form approved by the Minister and shall be accompanied by a fee of the amount shown in column 2 in Part III of Schedule 5 in relation to the class of vehicle specified in column 1 in that Part.

Time within which applications to be made

29. Every application for a periodical test of a goods vehicle to which these Regulations apply shall be made not earlier than 3 months nor later than two weeks before the last day by which the periodical test for that vehicle is by Regulation 27 required to be carried out:

Provided that such an application may be accepted and dealt with, notwithstanding it was not made in accordance with the foregoing provisions of this Regulation, if the Minister is satisfied that there were reasonable grounds for the application not having been so made.

Notice of place and time for periodical test

30.—(1) As soon as reasonably practicable after the date of the receipt of an application for a periodical test for a vehicle to which these Regulations apply, the Minister shall send to the applicant for that test a notice stating the address of the vehicle testing station at which the test is to take place and the date and time reserved by the Minister for that test:

Provided that the Minister shall not be required to send to the applicant such a notice in a case where the application is made direct to a vehicle testing station by virtue of Regulation 28.

(2) In stating any address, date or time under the provisions of the last paragraph the Minister shall so far as is reasonably practicable have regard to any preference as to that address, date or time expressed by the applicant in the application made by him for the periodical test of the vehicle.

Provision for periodical test

31.—(1) On the submission of a goods vehicle to which these Regulations apply for a periodical test, a goods vehicle examiner shall arrange for the vehicle to undergo the test.

(2) After a periodical test has been carried out on a vehicle, a goods vehicle examiner shall—

(a) where it is found to comply with the prescribed construction and use requirements, issue a goods vehicle test certificate, and

(b) where it is found not to comply with the prescribed construction and use requirements, issue a notification of the refusal of a goods vehicle test certificate.

Application for Part III re-tests

32.—(1) Where under Regulation 31(2)(*b*) a notification of the refusal of a goods vehicle test certificate is issued for a vehicle, it may be submitted and, if need be, from time to time be submitted at a vehicle testing station for a Part III re-test in accordance with the following provisions of this Regulation.

(2) Where it is desired to submit a vehicle for a Part III re-test at the same vehicle testing station as that at which it was submitted for the last periodical test within a period of fourteen days after the date it was submitted for that periodical test, the applicant for the Part III re-test shall first make arrangements in writing or otherwise with the person in charge of the station for a date and time at which the vehicle is to be submitted for the re-test.

(3) Where it is desired to submit a vehicle for a Part III re-test (not being a re-test falling within the next paragraph) at the vehicle testing station mentioned in the last preceding paragraph but otherwise than within the period therein mentioned or at a vehicle testing station different from that at which it was submitted for the last periodical test, the applicant for the Part III re-test shall first make a written application to the Goods Vehicle Centre, Swansea, for a date and time at which the vehicle may be submitted for the re-test and every such application shall be made on a form approved by the Minister, and upon receipt of the application the Minister shall send to the applicant a notice stating where and when the re-test is to take place and in this connection shall have regard so far as is reasonably practicable to any preference expressed by the applicant as to when and where the re-test should take place.

(4) Where it is desired to submit a vehicle for a further Part III re-test at the same vehicle testing station as that at which it was submitted for a Part III re-test under the last preceding paragraph within a period of 14 days after the date it was submitted for the last mentioned re-test, the applicant for the further Part III re-test shall first make arrangements in writing or otherwise with the person in charge of the station for a date and time at which the vehicle is to be submitted for the further re-test.

Fees for Part III re-tests

33.—(1) The fee payable for a Part III re-test of a vehicle carried out in accordance with arrangements made under Regulation 32(2) or (4) shall be of the amount specified in paragraph 1 of Part IV of Schedule 5:

Provided that no fee shall be payable for such a re-test of a vehicle submitted within the relevant time, if it is the first re-test of the vehicle carried out following the last periodical test of the vehicle or following an earlier Part III re-test of the vehicle in respect of which a fee has been paid under this Regulation.

In this paragraph "relevant time" means the same day as that on which the said periodical test or the said Part III re-test was completed or the next following day on which the vehicle testing station is open.

(2) The fee payable under the last preceding paragraph shall be paid to the Minister on the submission of the vehicle for the Part III re-test to be carried out in accordance with the arrangements made under Regulation 32(2) or (4) and may be paid in cash.

(3) The fee payable for a Part III re-test of a vehicle carried out by virtue of Regulation 32(3) shall be of the amount specified in paragraph 2 of Part IV of Schedule 5.

(4) The said fee shall be paid to the Minister at the same time as the written application mentioned in Regulation 32(3) is made.

Part III re-tests

34.—(1) Where a vehicle is submitted for a Part III re-test at a vehicle testing station in accordance with the arrangements mentioned in Regulation 32(2) or (4), a goods vehicle examiner shall in carrying out a goods vehicle test be under an obligation only to examine the vehicle for the purpose of ascertaining whether it complies with such of the particular items of the prescribed construction and use requirements as respects which it was shown in the last notification of a refusal of a test certificate not to comply.

(2) Where a goods vehicle examiner finds that the vehicle complies with such of the particular items of the prescribed construction and use requirements mentioned in the preceding paragraph and has no reason to believe that the prescribed construction and use requirements as respects other items are not complied with in relation to the vehicle, there shall be issued a goods vehicle test certificate.

(3) Where a goods vehicle examiner does not find that the vehicle complies with the particular items of the prescribed construction and use requirements mentioned in paragraph (1) of this Regulation or finds that the prescribed construction and use requirements as respects other items are not complied with in relation to the vehicle, there shall be issued a notification of the refusal of a test certificate.

(4) Where a vehicle is submitted for a re-test at a vehicle testing station as a result of the application mentioned in Regulation 32(3) a goods vehicle examiner shall arrange for the vehicle to undergo a goods vehicle test.

(5) Where the goods vehicle test mentioned in the last preceding paragraph has been completed as respects a vehicle there shall be issued—

(a) where the vehicle is found to comply with the prescribed construction and use requirements, a goods vehicle test certificate ; and

(b) where the vehicle is found not to comply with the prescribed construction and use requirements, a notification of the refusal of a goods vehicle test certificate.

Form of certificates etc.

35. Goods vehicle test certificates and notifications of the refusal of a goods vehicle test certificate issued under Regulation 31 or 34 shall contain the same particulars as are appropriate in the case of goods vehicle test certificates and notifications of the refusal of a goods vehicle test certificate mentioned in Regulation 23 and shall be signed in the same manner as is provided in Regulation 23.

Period of validity of goods vehicle test certificate issued on periodical tests

36. Where a goods vehicle test certificate is issued for a goods vehicle, as a result of a periodical test of a vehicle, a Part III re-test of that vehicle or an appeal under Regulation 37, the certificate shall be valid from the date of its issue until the last day (inclusive of that day) by which that vehicle is required by virtue of Regulation 27 to be submitted again for a periodical test.

Appeals following periodical tests

37.—(1) Any person aggrieved by a determination made on a periodical test of a vehicle or a Part III re-test of a vehicle by the person in charge of that periodical test or that Part III re-test may appeal to an area mechanical engineer appointed by the Minister to act for the traffic area in which that periodical test or, as the case may be, that Part III re-test was made.

(2) The provisions of Regulation 25(2) to (11) shall apply in relation to any appeal under the last paragraph as they apply in relation to an appeal under that Regulation relating to a determination made on a goods vehicle test, and for the purposes of such application of the said provisions each reference in Regulation 25(10)(b) to a plating certificate shall be treated as being omitted.

(3) Any person aggrieved by the determination of an area mechanical engineer under the preceding paragraphs of this Regulation may appeal to the Minister.

(4) The provisions of Regulation 26(2) to (11) shall apply in relation to any appeal under the last preceding paragraph as they apply in relation to an appeal under that Regulation relating to a determination made by an area mechanical engineer in connection with a notification of the refusal of a goods vehicle test certificate issued under Regulation 25(10)(b), and for the purposes of such application of the said provisions the reference in Regulation 26(7)(b) to Regulation 25(10)(b) shall be treated as a reference to Regulation 25(10)(b) as applied by paragraph (2) of this Regulation and each reference in Regulation 26(10)(b) to a plating certificate shall be treated as being omitted.

PART IV—REGULATIONS GOVERNING NOTIFIABLE ALTERATIONS, AMENDMENTS OF PLATING CERTIFICATES AND RE-EXAMINATIONS IN CONNECTION THEREWITH

Interpretation

38. In this Part of the Regulations "notifiable alteration", in relation to a goods vehicle to which these Regulations apply, means—

(a) an alteration made in the structure or fixed equipment of the vehicle which varies the carrying capacity of the vehicle ;

(b) an alteration, otherwise than by way of replacement of a part, adversely affecting any part of a braking system with which the vehicle is equipped or of the means of operation of that system ; or

(c) any other alteration made in the structure or fixed equipment of the vehicle which materially renders the vehicle unsafe to travel on roads at any weight equal to any plated weight shown in the plating certificate for that vehicle.

Minister to be informed of notifiable alterations

39. On a notifiable alteration being made to a goods vehicle to which these Regulations apply and in respect of which a plating certificate has been issued under these Regulations, particulars of that alteration shall be sent on a form approved by the Minister to the Minister at the Goods Vehicle Centre, Swansea, before the vehicle to which the alteration has been made is used on roads, and any such form may also contain a request by the sender thereof (hereinafter referred to as "the sender") for an amendment to be made as respects a plated weight shown on the plating certificate for the said vehicle.

Provision as to re-examination

40.—(1) Where particulars of a notifiable alteration made to a goods vehicle are sent to the Minister in the form mentioned in the last preceding Regulation and such a request as is therein mentioned is made in the form, the Minister shall require the vehicle to be submitted for a re-examination at a place, date and time specified in a notice sent by him to the sender and in this connection shall have regard so far as is reasonably practicable to any preference expressed by the sender as to when and where the re-examination should take place.

(2) Where particulars of a notifiable alteration made to a goods vehicle are sent to the Minister in the said form and no such request is made therein, the Minister shall determine whether the vehicle shall be required to be re-examined.

(3) In the event of the Minister determining under the last preceding paragraph—

(a) that no re-examination of the vehicle is required, he shall notify in writing the sender accordingly ; or

(b) that a re-examination of the vehicle is required, he shall by notice inform the sender accordingly and in such notice specify the place, date and time at which the vehicle is to be submitted for the re-examination and in this connection shall have regard so far as is reasonably practicable to any preference expressed by the sender as to when and where the re-examination should take place.

41.—(1) Where otherwise than by reason of a notifiable alteration, any particular (with reference to a plated weight or any other matter) contained in a plating certificate for a goods vehicle to which these Regulations apply may have become no longer applicable to that vehicle, an application on a form approved by the Minister may be made to him at the Goods Vehicle Centre, Swansea, for the purpose of having the vehicle re-examined with a view to having that particular amended.

(2) On receipt of the said form, the Minister shall require the vehicle to be submitted for a re-examination at a place, date and time specified in a notice sent by him to the person forwarding the said form (which person is also hereinafter referred to as " the sender ") and in this connection shall have regard so far as is reasonably practicable to any preference expressed by the sender as to when and where the re-examination should take place.

Fee for re-examination

42. Where such a request as is mentioned in Regulation 39 is contained in the form mentioned in that Regulation or where an application mentioned in Regulation 41 is made, a fee of five pounds shall be sent to the Minister with that form or, as the case may be, with that application.

Conditions subject to which vehicles accepted for re-examination

43. A goods vehicle examiner shall not be under an obligation to proceed with the carrying out of a re-examination of a vehicle under this Part of the Regulations where on the submission of a vehicle for the re-examination the sender does not, after being required to do so, produce to the examiner the plating certificate relating to the vehicle, and nothing in this paragraph shall be taken to be in derogation of Regulation 8 or 9.

Re-examination

44.—(1) On the submission of a vehicle for a re-examination under this Part of the Regulations, a goods vehicle examiner shall in a case where the re-examination is carried out by reason of a notifiable alteration examine the vehicle for the purpose of determining to what extent that notifiable alteration has rendered the plated weights shown in the plating certificate relating to that vehicle no longer appropriate and in any other case examine the vehicle for the purpose of determining to what extent any particular contained in the said plating certificate is no longer applicable.

(2) On the completion of the re-examination, the goods vehicle examiner shall either—

(a) notify in writing the sender that—

(i) the said notifiable alteration has not rendered the plated weights shown in the said plating certificate no longer appropriate, or

(ii) the said particular is still applicable ;

(b) amend the plating certificate to show any new plated weights or any new particular which the examiner has determined for the vehicle ; or

(c) if he thinks fit issue a new plating certificate in the place of the plating certificate produced under Regulation 43 which shall be marked as cancelled by the vehicle examiner.

(3) Any goods vehicle examiner amending or cancelling a plating certificate shall authenticate the amendment or cancellation by showing on the certificate his name, the address of the place at which the certificate was amended or cancelled and the date of such amendment or cancellation.

(4) Where a new plating certificate is issued for a vehicle it shall contain—

(a) particulars of any plated weights determined for the vehicle under this Regulation ;

(b) where the vehicle is of a make, model and type and otherwise one to which the standard lists apply and any such plated weight so determined is less than the equivalent weight shown as a design weight in such lists, particulars of that equivalent weight ;

(c) where any such plated weight so determined is less than the weight that would have been otherwise determined under Regulation 16(2) but for sub-paragraph (h) of paragraph (2) of Regulation 16, particulars of the last mentioned weight which shall be shown as a design weight ;

(d) any other new particular determined for the vehicle under this Regulation ;

(e) subject as aforesaid, the same particulars as are appropriate in the case of the plating certificate mentioned in Regulation 22, but with such modifications as may be appropriate.

(5) A new plating certificate shall be signed by the goods vehicle examiner who carried out or under whose direction the re-examination was carried out or shall be signed on behalf of that examiner by a person authorised in that behalf by that examiner.

Appeals following re-examinations

45.—(1) Any person aggrieved by a determination made on a re-examination of a vehicle under this Part of the Regulations by the person in charge of that re-examination may appeal to an area mechanical engineer appointed by the Minister to act for the traffic area in which that re-examination took place.

(2) The provisions of Regulation 25(2) to (9) shall apply in relation to an appeal under the last paragraph as they apply to an appeal under that Regulation, but for the purposes of such application of the said provisions paragraph (7) of Regulation 25 shall have effect as though sub-paragraphs (a) and (b) were omitted and for those paragraphs there were substituted a reference to any plating certificate relevant to the appeal.

(3) Upon completion of the re-examination of the vehicle for the purposes of the appeal, the area mechanical engineer shall make such determination in the matter as he thinks fit and may issue a different plating certificate upon the surrender of any plating certificate previously issued for the vehicle.

(4) Any different plating certificate issued under the last preceding paragraph shall contain—

(a) the same particulars as are appropriate in the case of the plating certificate mentioned in Regulation 22, subject nevertheless to such modifications as may be appropriate and subject to the certificate showing particulars of the plated weights determined for that vehicle by the area mechanical engineer carrying out the re-examination for the purposes of the appeal in a case where any such plated weight is so determined ;

(b) where the vehicle is of a make, model and type and otherwise one to which the standard lists apply and any such plated weight so determined is less than the equivalent weight shown as a design weight in such lists, particulars of that equivalent weight ;

(c) where any such plated weight so determined is less than the weight that would have been otherwise determined under Regulation 16(2) but for sub-paragraph (h) of paragraph (2) of Regulation 16, particulars of the last mentioned weight which shall be shown as a design weight ;

and shall be signed by that area mechanical engineer.

(5) Any person aggrieved by the determination of an area mechanical engineer under paragraph (3) of this Regulation may appeal to the Minister.

(6) The provisions of Regulation 26(2) to (9) shall apply in relation to an appeal under the last preceding paragraph as they apply in relation to an appeal under that Regulation, but for the purposes of such application of the said provisions paragraph (7) of Regulation 26 shall have effect as though sub-paragraphs (a) and (b) were omitted and for those paragraphs there were substituted a reference to any plating certificate relevant to the appeal.

(7) Upon completion of the re-examination for the purposes of the appeal, the Minister shall make such determination on the basis of the re-examination as he thinks fit and may issue a different plating certificate upon the surrender of any plating certificate previously issued for the vehicle.

(8) Any different plating certificate issued under the last preceding paragraph shall contain—

(a) the same particulars as are appropriate in the case of the plating certificate mentioned in Regulation 22, subject nevertheless to such modifications as may be appropriate and subject to the certificate showing particulars of the plated weights determined for that vehicle by the Minister in a case where any such plated weight is so determined ;

(b) where the vehicle is of a make, model and type and otherwise one to which the standard lists apply and any such plated weight so determined is less than the equivalent weight shown as a design weight in such lists, particulars of that equivalent weight ;

(c) where any such plated weight so determined is less than the weight that would have been otherwise determined under Regulation 16(2) but for sub-paragraph (h) of paragraph (2) of Regulation 16, particulars of the last mentioned weight which shall be shown as a design weight ;

and shall be signed on behalf of the Minister by an officer appointed by him for the purpose.

Part V—Miscellaneous Matters

Method of payment of fees

46. Except where by these Regulations provision is made for fees to be payable to the Minister in cash, all fees payable to the Minister under these Regulations shall be paid by cheque, money order or postal order.

General provision as to fees

47.—(1) Where any fee payable in accordance with the foregoing provisions of these Regulations on an application for a first examination of a vehicle, a re-test of a vehicle to be carried out by virtue of Regulation 19(3) or Regulation 32(3), a periodical test of a vehicle or a Part IV test of a vehicle has been paid to the Minister at the Goods Vehicle Centre, Swansea, or at a vehicle testing station, the said fee shall be payable notwithstanding the vehicle is not submitted for any such examination (hereinafter referred to as " the original examination ") on the day and within thirty minutes after the time fixed under these Regulations for that examination.

(2) Where at the time of the notice hereinafter mentioned a request is made for another examination of the same kind as the original examination to be carried out at another time, the said fee may be treated as payable in respect of that other examination:—

(*a*) if the applicant for the original examination has not less than 14 days (or not less than 3 days in the case of a Part IV test) before the day fixed under these Regulations for the carrying out of the original examination given the Minister notice (whether in writing or otherwise) at the said Goods Vehicle Centre that the applicant does not propose to submit the vehicle for examination on the said day ; or

(*b*) if the said applicant satisfies the Minister that the vehicle could not be submitted for the original examination on the day and within 30 minutes of the time fixed for the carrying out of the original examination owing to an accident involving the vehicle arising not more than 14 days (or not more than 3 days in the case of a Part IV test) before the said time and of which notice is given to the Minister whether in writing or otherwise within 3 days of the happening thereof.

48. Where any fee payable in accordance with the foregoing provisions of these Regulations for a first examination of a vehicle, a re-test of a vehicle, a periodical test of a vehicle or a Part IV test of a vehicle or a re-examination of the vehicle under section 9(3) or (4) of the 1967 Act has been paid to the Minister, the said fee shall be payable notwithstanding any such examination is not carried out by reason of any of the provisions contained in Regulation 8 or 9 so, however, that nothing in this Regulation shall be taken as affecting the provisions of Regulation 47(2).

Particular provision as to fees on appeal

49.—(1) After the completion of a re-examination for the purposes of an appeal under section 9(3) or (4) of the 1967 Act the Minister may repay to the appellant, as he thinks fit, either the whole or part of the fee paid on the appeal, where it appears to him there were substantial grounds for contesting the whole or part of the determination appealed from.

(2) A fee payable on an appeal in accordance with the foregoing provisions of these Regulations shall be payable notwithstanding that the vehicle is not submitted for re-examination in accordance with Regulation 25(6) or 26(6) or in accordance with either such Regulation as applied by any other Regulation contained in these Regulations:

Provided that, if the appellant has before the time fixed under the said Regulation 25 or 26 or under either such Regulation as so applied for the carrying out of the re-examination given the Minister not less than two clear days' notice (whether in writing or otherwise) at the office at which his appeal was lodged that the appellant does not propose to submit the vehicle for re-examination at that time, the appeal shall be treated for the purposes of this Regulation as one in respect of which no fee is payable and any amount previously paid in respect of such a fee shall be repaid by the Minister to the appellant unless another time is arranged for the carrying out of the re-examination.

Applications for replacements for plates, plating certificates and test certificates

50.—(1) If a Ministry plate, plating certificate or a goods vehicle test certificate has been lost or defaced, an application for the issue of a replacement for the plate or certificate lost or defaced may be made in writing to the Goods Vehicle Centre, Swansea.

(2) On the receipt of such an application and being paid a fee of one pound, where the application relates to a Ministry plate or a plating certificate, or ten shillings, where the application relates to a goods vehicle test certificate, the Minister shall issue to the applicant a replacement for the plate or certificate to which the application relates and any such replacement shall have the same effect as the plate or certificate which it replaces.

Provision as to notices under Regulations

51.—(1) Except as otherwise provided in these Regulations, every notice under these Regulations shall be in writing and may be given by post.

(2) For the purposes of calculating the period of any notice which may be given under these Regulations Saturdays, Sundays and public holidays shall be excluded from that period.

PART VI—REGULATION RELATING TO CROWN VEHICLES

Provision as to Crown Vehicles

52.—(1) In relation to goods vehicles in the public service of the Crown which are registered or are liable to be registered under the Vehicles (Excise) Act 1962, being goods vehicles to which these Regulations apply, and to trailers in the public service of the Crown while drawn by goods vehicles (whether or not in the public service of the Crown) which are required to be so registered, being trailers to which these Regulations apply, these Regulations shall apply subject to the modifications hereinafter contained in this Regulation.

(2) A first examination of a vehicle, a periodical test of a vehicle or a Part IV test of a vehicle may be made by or under the direction of an examiner (hereinafter referred to as an "authorised examiner") authorised for the purpose by the Minister instead of by or under the direction of a goods vehicle examiner, and in relation to any such examination made by an authorised examiner these Regulations shall apply as if—

(a) Regulations 5, 8, 9, 11, 12, 13, 19, 25, 28, 29, 30, 32, 37 and 45 were omitted ;

(b) subject to the preceding sub-paragraph, any reference in the Regulations to a goods vehicle examiner were a reference to an authorised examiner and any reference in the Regulations to a vehicle testing station were a reference to premises approved by the Minister as suitable for the carrying out of examinations under these Regulations by authorised examiners ;

(c) in Regulation 14(a) and Regulation 22(d) the reference to the application therein mentioned were a reference to a form approved by the Minister for the purpose of an application for an examination under these Regulations by an authorised examiner ; and

(d) in Regulation 23(3)(a) and (b) and in Regulation 27(5) the reference to the identification mark were a reference to an identification mark allotted by the Minister for the purpose of an examination under these Regulations by an authorised examiner.

(3) Any person aggrieved by a determination of an authorised examiner on a first examination of a vehicle, a periodical test of a vehicle or a Part IV test of a vehicle may appeal to the Minister and on the appeal the Minister shall cause the vehicle to be re-examined by an officer appointed by him for the purpose and may make such determination on the basis of the re-examination as he thinks fit and, where appropriate, may issue a plating certificate, a goods vehicle test certificate or a notification of the refusal of a goods vehicle test certificate.

PART VII—EXEMPTIONS

Exemption from s. 14(1) of the 1967 Act of the use of vehicles for certain purposes

53.—(1) The use of a goods vehicle to which these Regulations apply for any of the purposes specified in the following provisions of this Regulation is exempted from section 14(1) of the 1967 Act.

(2) The use of a vehicle—

(a) for the purpose of submitting it by previous arrangement for, or bringing it away from, an examination under Part II of these Regulations or under section 9(3) or (4) of the 1967 Act ; or

(b) in the course of any such examination for the purpose of taking it to, or bringing it away from, any place where a part of the examination is to be or, as the case may be, has been carried out, or of carrying out any part of the examination, the person so using it being a goods vehicle examiner or a person carrying out the examination under his direction or a person driving the vehicle in pursuance of a requirement to do so under these Regulations ; or

(c) where a goods vehicle test certificate is refused on such an examination—

(i) for the purpose of delivering it by previous arrangement at, or bringing it away from, a place where work is to be or has been done on it to remedy the defects on the grounds of which the certificate was refused ; or

(ii) for the purpose of delivering it, by towing it, to a place where the vehicle is to be broken up.

(3) The use of a vehicle unladen when driven, or drawn by a vehicle driven, under a trade licence issued under section 12 of the Vehicles (Excise) Act 1962, for the purpose of delivering it at, or bringing it away from, a place where work of repair or inspection is to be or has been done on it for the purposes of enabling the prescribed construction and use requirements to be complied with, or to be ascertained as complied with, in the case of the vehicle.

(4) The use of a vehicle for or in connection with any purpose for which it is authorised to be used on roads by an order under section 64(4) of the 1960 Act, being an order authorising that vehicle or any class or description of vehicles comprising that vehicle to be so used notwithstanding that it

does not comply with the prescribed construction and use requirements or with such of the said requirements as are specified in the said order.

(5) The use of a vehicle for the purpose of removing it in pursuance of section 20 of the Civic Amenities Act 1967(a), of moving or removing it in pursuance of regulations under section 20 of the Road Traffic Regulation Act 1967(b) as altered by the Removal and Disposal of Vehicles (Alteration of Enactments) Order 1967(c), or of removing it from a parking place in pursuance of an order under section 31(1) of the Road Traffic Regulation Act 1967, an order relating to a parking place designated under section 35 thereof, or a provision of a designation order having effect by virtue of section 39(2) thereof.

(6) The use of a vehicle, which has been detained or seized by a police constable, for police purposes connected with such detention or seizure.

(7) The use by an Officer of Customs and Excise, or by any other person authorised generally or specially in that behalf in writing by the Commissioners of Customs and Excise, of any vehicle removed, detained, seized or condemned as forfeited under any provision of the Customs and Excise Act 1952(d).

Exemption from s. 14(2) of the 1967 Act of the use of vehicles for certain purposes

54.—(1) The use of a goods vehicle to which these Regulations apply for any of the purposes specified in the following provisions of this Regulation is exempted from section 14(2) of the 1967 Act.

(2) The use of a vehicle—

(*a*) for the purpose of submitting it by previous arrangement for, or bringing it away from, an examination under Part II, III or IV of these Regulations or under section 9(3) or (4) of the 1967 Act ; or

(*b*) in the course of any such examination for the purpose of taking it to, or bringing it away from, any place where a part of the examination is to be or, as the case may be, has been carried out, or of carrying out any part of the examination, the person so using it being a goods vehicle examiner or a person carrying out the examination under his direction or a person driving the vehicle in pursuance of a requirement to do so under these Regulations ; or

(*c*) where a goods vehicle test certificate is refused on such an examination—

(i) for the purpose of delivering it by previous arrangement at, or bringing it away from, a place where work is to be or has been done on it to remedy the defects on the grounds of which the certificate was refused ; or

(ii) for the purpose of delivering it, by towing it, to a place where the vehicle is to be broken up.

(3) The use of a vehicle for any of the purposes specified in paragraphs (3) to (7) of the last preceding Regulation.

Exemption from s. 14(1) and (2) of the 1967 Act of the use of vehicles in certain areas

55.—(1) The use of a goods vehicle to which these Regulations apply in any area to which this Regulation applies is exempted from section 14(1) and (2) of the 1967 Act.

(a) 1967 c. 69.   (b) 1967 c. 76.   (c) S.I. 1967/1900 (1967 III, p. 5191).
(d) 15 & 16 Geo. 6. & 1 Eliz. 2. c. 44.

(2) This Regulation applies to any island and to any area mainly surrounded by water, being an island or area from which motor vehicles not constructed for special purposes can at no time be conveniently driven to a road in any other part of Great Britain by reason of the absence of any bridge, tunnel, ford or other way suitable for the passage of such motor vehicles:

Provided that this Regulation does not apply to any of the following islands, namely, the Isle of Wight, the islands of Lewis, Mainland (Orkney), Mainland (Shetland) and Skye or to any other island or area from which motor vehicles not constructed for special purposes can either at all times or at some times be conveniently driven to a road in any of the aforesaid islands by reason of the existence of a bridge, tunnel, ford or other way suitable for the passage of such motor vehicles.

Exemption from s. 14(5) of the 1967 Act

56. The following class of goods vehicles, namely, motor vehicles not constructed or adapted to form part of an articulated vehicle, is exempted from section 14(5) of the 1967 Act.

Given under the Official Seal of the Minister of Transport the 10th April 1968.

(L.S.)

Richard Marsh,
Minister of Transport.

SCHEDULE 1 (see Regulations 2(1) and 16(2))

PROVISIONS AS TO BRAKING FORCE FOR TRAILERS

1. In this Schedule—

the letter " W " represents—

(a) in the case of a trailer so designed that part of the weight of the trailer is imposed on the drawing vehicle, the axle weight, or, as the case may be, the sum of the axle weights which is or are to be determined for the trailer on an examination for plating;

(b) in any other case the gross weight of the trailer which is to be so determined.

2. The minimum braking force capable of being developed by the brakes of a trailer manufactured before 1st January 1968 should in the case of—

(a) a trailer, not being a semi-trailer, be .4W;

(b) a semi-trailer for which a gross weight of 6 tons or more is to be determined for the vehicle on an examination for plating, be .35W;

(c) a semi-trailer for which a gross weight of less than 6 tons is to be so determined, be .32W.

SCHEDULE 2 (see Regulation 3)

CLASSES OF VEHICLE TO WHICH REGULATIONS DO NOT APPLY

1. Dual-purpose vehicles not constructed or adapted to form part of an articulated vehicle.

2. Mobile cranes as defined in Schedule 3 to the 1962 Act.

3. Break-down vehicles.

4. Engineering plant.

5. Trailers being drying or mixing plant designed for the production of asphalt or of bituminous or tar macadam.

6. Tower wagons as defined in Schedule 4 to the 1962 Act.

7. Road construction vehicles as defined in section 6(8) of the 1962 Act and road rollers.

8. Vehicles designed for fire fighting or fire salvage purposes.

9. Works trucks, straddle carriers used solely as works trucks, and works trailers.

10. Electrically-propelled motor vehicles.

11. Motor vehicles used solely for clearing frost, ice or snow from roads by means of a snow plough or similar contrivance, whether forming part of the vehicle or not.

12. Vehicles constructed or adapted for, and used solely for spreading material on roads to deal with frost, ice or snow.

13. Motor vehicles used for no other purpose that the haulage of lifeboats and the conveyance of the necessary gear of the lifeboats which are being hauled.

14. Living vans.

15. Vehicles constructed or adapted for, and used primarily for the purpose of, carrying equipment permanently fixed to the vehicle which equipment is used for medical, dental, veterinary, health, educational, display or clerical purposes, such use not directly involving the sale, hire or loan of goods from the vehicle.

16. Trailers which have no other brakes than a parking brake and brakes which automatically come into operation on the over-run of the trailer.

17. Vehicles exempted from duty under the 1962 Act by virtue of section 6(6) of that Act and any trailer drawn by such a vehicle.

18. Land implements, land locomotives and land tractors.

19. Agricultural trailers drawn on roads only by a land tractor.

20. Vehicles to which paragraph 5 or paragraph 6 of Schedule 13 to the 1960 Act applies.

21. Vehicles used solely for the purposes of funerals.

22. Goods vehicles to which any of the prescribed construction and use requirements do not apply by virtue of either of the following provisions of the Construction and Use Regulations namely—
    (*a*) Regulation 4(3) (which relates to vehicles proceeding to a port for export) ;
    (*b*) Regulation 4(7) (which relates to vehicles in the service of a visiting force or of a headquarters).

23. Vehicles equipped with new or improved equipment or types of equipment and used, solely by a manufacturer of vehicles or their equipment or by an importer of vehicles, for or in connection with the test or trial of any such equipment.

24. Motor vehicles temporarily in Great Britain to which a registration mark is assigned under paragraph (1) of Regulation 2 of the Motor Vehicles (International Circulation) Regulations 1965(a), or under provisions applying in Northern Ireland and corresponding to the provisions of that paragraph or under Regulation 4(2) of the said Regulations, a period of twelve months not having elapsed since the mark was so assigned.

25. Motor vehicles for the time being licensed under the Vehicles (Excise) Act (Northern Ireland) 1954(b).

26. Vehicles having a base or centre in any of the following islands, namely, Arran, Bute, Great Cumbrae, Islay, Mull or North Uist from which the use of the vehicle on a journey is normally commenced.

27. Trailers temporarily in Great Britain a period of twelve months not having elapsed since the vehicle in question was last brought into Great Britain.

(a) S.I. 1965/329 (1965 I, p. 1067).   (b) 1954 c. 17 (N.I.).

28. Track laying vehicles.

29. Steam propelled vehicles.

30. Motor vehicles registered before 1st January 1940 used unladen and not drawing a laden trailer, and trailers manufactured before 1st January 1940 and used unladen.

31. Vehicles designed for use, and used solely by a local authority or highway authority or a person acting in pursuance of a contract with such an authority, for the purpose of street cleansing, the collection or disposal of refuse, the collection or disposal of the contents of gullies or cesspools or the testing of weighbridges.

32. Vehicles designed and used for the purpose of servicing or controlling aircraft, while so used on an aerodrome within the meaning of the Airports Authority Act 1965(a) or on roads to such extent as is essential for the purpose of proceeding directly from one part of such an aerodrome to another part thereof or, subject as aforesaid, outside such an aerodrome unladen and not drawing a laden trailer.

33. Vehicles provided for police purposes and maintained in workshops approved by the Minister as suitable for such maintenance, being vehicles provided in England and Wales by a police authority or the Receiver for the metropolitan police district, or, in Scotland, by a police authority or a joint police committee.

Interpretation

In this Schedule the following expressions have the meanings hereby respectively assigned to them : —

" the 1962 Act " means the Vehicles (Excise) Act 1962 ;

" agricultural trailer ", " dual-purpose vehicle ", " land implement ", " land locomotive ", " land tractor ", " straddle carrier ", " track laying " and " works trailer " have the same meanings respectively as in Regulation 3(1) of the Construction and Use Regulations ;

" break-down vehicle " means a motor vehicle on which is mounted apparatus designed to lift a disabled vehicle ;

" engineering plant " means movable plant or equipment being a motor vehicle or trailer (not constructed primarily to carry a load) especially designed and constructed for the special purposes of engineering operations ;

" works truck " means a motor vehicle designed for use in private premises and used on a road only in delivering goods from or to such premises to or from a vehicle on a road in the immediate neighbourhood, or in passing from one part of any such premises to another or to other private premises in the immediate neighbourhood or in connection with road works while at or in the immediate neighbourhood of the site of such works.

SCHEDULE 3 (see Regulation 4)

The Prescribed Construction and Use Requirements

Part I

The construction and use requirements which are prescribed for the purposes of a goods vehicle test in the case of a motor vehicle are the requirements specified in each of the following sections : —

Section 1

The requirements contained in the following provisions of the Construction and Use Regulations : —

1. Regulation 81 (relating to maintenance of silencer).

2. Regulation 83 (relating to the use of vehicles so as not to emit smoke).

(a) 1965 c. 16.

3. Regulation 118 (relating to Ministry plate).

4. Regulation 75(1) in so far as that Regulation provides that a motor vehicle and all parts and accessories of such vehicle shall at all times be in such condition that no danger is caused or is likely to be caused to any person in or on the vehicle or on a road and in so far as that provision relates to the following parts and accessories of a motor vehicle provided thereon, namely: —

    (a) spare wheel carrier

    (b) means of attaching trailer

    (c) the chassis

    (d) the wiring of the electrical system

    (e) engine mounting

    (f) fuel tank and fuel pipes

    (g) the propeller shaft and its associated couplings and bearings

    (h) exhaust system

    (i) battery.

Section II

The requirements contained in the following provisions of the Construction and Use Regulations: —

5. Regulation 79(1) (relating to steering gear).

6. Regulation 82 (relating to maintenance of tyres).

7. Regulation 123 (relating to strength of tyres).

8. Regulation 75(1) in so far as that Regulation provides that a motor vehicle and all parts and accessories of such vehicle shall at all times be in such condition that no danger is caused or is likely to be caused to any person in or on the vehicle or on a road and in so far as that provision relates to the following parts and accessories of a motor vehicle provided thereon, namely: —

    (a) wheels

    (b) the suspension system

    (c) axles

    (d) shock absorbers.

Section III

The requirements contained in the following provisions of the Construction and Use Regulations: —

9. Regulation 13 (speedometer).

10. Regulation 16 (relating to view to the front).

11. Regulation 17 (relating to mirrors).

12. Regulation 19 (relating to windscreen wiper).

13. Regulation 20(1) and 20(3) (relating to audible warning instrument).

14. Regulation 77 (relating to maintenance of glass).

15. Regulation 79(2) (relating to maintenance of windscreen wiper).

16. Regulation 75(1) in so far as that Regulation provides that a motor vehicle and all parts and accessories of such vehicle shall at all times be in such condition that no danger is caused or is likely to be caused to any person in or on the vehicle or on a road and in so far as that provision relates to the following parts and accessories of a motor vehicle provided thereon, namely: —

    (a) bumpers

    (b) wings

    (c) the cab

(*d*) the driving seat

(*e*) the body

(*f*) driving controls other than those of brakes and steering

(*g*) cab steps or step rings

(*h*) glass or other transparent material.

Section IV

The requirements contained in the following provisions of the Construction and Use Regulations:—

17. Regulation 11 (relating to parking brakes).
18. Regulation 12 (relating to vacuum or pressure braking systems).
19. Regulation 43(6) and (7) (relating to brakes).
20. Regulation 48(6) and (7) (relating to brakes).
21. Regulation 78(1) (relating to maintenance of brakes).

Section V

The requirement contained in the following provision of the Construction and Use Regulations:—

22. Regulation 75(1) in so far as that Regulation provides that a motor vehicle and all parts and accessories of such vehicle shall at all times be in such condition that no danger is caused or is likely to be caused to any person in or on the vehicle or on a road and in so far as that provision relates to direction indicators provided on the vehicle.

The requirements contained in the following provisions of the Road Transport Lighting Act 1957(**a**) and the Road Vehicles Lighting Regulations 1964(**b**), as amended(**c**):—

23. Section 1(1) and (2) of the said Act (relating to lights and reflectors).
24. Regulations 4, 5, 8, 9, 13 and 20 of the said Regulations.
25. The requirements contained in the Road Vehicles (Headlamps) Regulations 1967(**d**).

PART II

The construction and use requirements which are prescribed for the purposes of a goods vehicle test in the case of a trailer are the requirements specified in each of the following sections:—

Section I

The requirements contained in the following provisions of the Construction and Use Regulations:—

1. Regulation 118 (relating to Ministry plate).
2. Regulation 75(1) in so far as that Regulation provides that a trailer and all parts and accessories of such trailer shall at all times be in such condition that no danger is caused or is likely to be caused to any person in or on the trailer or on a road and in so far as that provision relates to the following parts and accessories of a trailer provided thereon, namely:—

     (*a*) spare wheel carrier

     (*b*) means of attachment to another vehicle

     (*c*) the chassis

     (*d*) the wiring of the electrical system.

(a) 5 & 6 Eliz. 2. c. 51.   (b) S.I. 1964/205 (1964 I, p. 345).
(c) The relevant amending instruments are S.I. 1965/870, 1966/30, 1967/1934
                    (1965 I, p. 2367; 1966 I, p. 45; 1967 III, p. 5387).
(d) S.I. 1967/1933 (1967 III, p. 5382).

Section II

The requirements contained in the following provisions of the Construction and Use Regulations:—

3. Regulation 82 (relating to maintenance of tyres).

4. Regulation 123 (relating to strength of tyres).

5. Regulation 75(1) in so far as that Regulation provides that a trailer and all parts and accessories of such trailer shall at all times be in such condition that no danger is caused or is likely to be caused to any person in or on the trailer or on a road and in so far as that provision relates to the following parts and accessories of a trailer provided thereon, namely:—

    (a) wheels

    (b) the suspension system

    (c) axles and steering gear

    (d) shock absorbers.

Section III

The requirement contained in the following provision of the Construction and Use Regulations:—

6. Regulation 75(1) in so far as that Regulation provides that a trailer and all parts and accessories of such trailer shall at all times be in such condition that no danger is caused or is likely to be caused to any person in or on the trailer or on a road and in so far as that provision relates to the following parts and accessories of a trailer provided thereon, namely:—

    (a) bumpers

    (b) wings

    (c) the body

    (d) glass or other transparent material.

Section IV

The requirements contained in the following provisions of the Construction and Use Regulations:—

7. Regulation 60(1) (relating to brakes).

8. Regulation 78(1)(a) (relating to maintenance of brakes).

Section V

The requirement contained in the following provision of the Construction and Use Regulations:—

9. Regulation 75(1) in so far as that Regulation provides that a trailer and all parts and accessories of such trailer shall at all times be in such condition that no danger is caused or is likely to be caused to any person in or on the trailer or on a road and in so far as that provision relates to direction indicators provided on the trailer.

The requirements contained in the following provisions of the Road Transport Lighting Act 1957 and the Road Vehicles Lighting Regulations 1964, as amended:—

10. Section 1(1)(b) and (2) of the said Act (relating to lights and reflectors).

11. Regulations 13 and 20 of the said Regulations.

SCHEDULE 4 (see Regulation 10)

DATES BY WHICH GOODS VEHICLES TO WHICH THESE REGULATIONS APPLY ARE
REQUIRED TO BE SUBMITTED FOR FIRST EXAMINATION

PART I

Dates relating to motor vehicles other than Scottish based vehicles

1. Class of vehicle	2. Date on or after which application may be made for first examination	3. Date by which to be submitted for first examination
1. Vehicles registered before 1st January 1958, the weight of which unladen exceeds 3 tons	1st August 1968...	1st December 1968
2. Vehicles registered before 1st January 1958, the weight of which unladen exceeds 30 cwt. but does not exceed 3 tons	1st October 1968	1st February 1969
3. Vehicles registered on or after 1st January 1958 and before 1st January 1961	1st December 1968	1st April 1969
4. Vehicles manufactured before 1st January 1968 and not registered before 1st January 1969	1st January 1969	1st April 1969
5. Vehicles registered in the month of April in any of the calendar years 1961 to 1967 inclusive	1st February 1969	1st May 1969
6. Vehicles registered in the month of May in any of the calendar years 1961 to 1967 inclusive	1st March 1969 ...	1st June 1969
7. Vehicles registered in the month of June in any of the calendar years 1961 to 1967 inclusive	1st April 1969 ...	1st July 1969
8. Vehicles registered in the month of July in any of the calendar years 1961 to 1967 inclusive	1st May 1969 ...	1st August 1969
9. Vehicles registered in the month of August in any of the calendar years 1961 to 1967 inclusive	1st June 1969 ...	1st September 1969
10. Vehicles registered in the month of September in any of the calendar years 1961 to 1967 inclusive	1st July 1969 ...	1st October 1969
11. Vehicles registered in the month of October in any of the calendar years 1961 to 1967 inclusive	1st August 1969...	1st November 1969

SCHEDULE 4—*continued*
PART I—*continued*

1. Class of vehicle	2. Date on or after which application may be made for first examination	3. Date by which to be submitted for first examination
12. Vehicles registered in the month of November in any of the calendar years 1961 to 1967 inclusive	1st September 1969	1st December 1969
13. Vehicles registered in the month of December in any of the calendar years 1961 to 1967 inclusive	1st October 1969	1st January 1970
14. Vehicles registered in the month of January in any of the calendar years 1961 to 1967 inclusive	1st November 1969	1st February 1970
15. Vehicles registered in the month of February in any of the calendar years 1961 to 1967 inclusive	1st December 1969	1st March 1970
16. Vehicles registered in the month of March in any of the calendar years 1961 to 1967 inclusive	1st January 1970	1st April 1970

PART II
Dates relating to motor vehicles being Scottish based vehicles

1. Class of vehicle	2. Date on or after which application may be made for first examination	3. Date by which to be submitted for first examination
1. Vehicles registered before 1st January 1958, the weight of which unladen exceeds 3 tons	1st November 1968	1st February 1969
2. Vehicles registered before 1st January 1958, the weight of which unladen exceeds 30 cwt. but does not exceed 3 tons	1st January 1969	1st April 1969
3. Vehicles manufactured before 1st January 1968 and not registered before 1st January 1969	1st January 1969	1st April 1969
4. Vehicles registered in the month of April in any of the calendar years 1958 to 1967 inclusive	1st February 1969	1st May 1969

SCHEDULE 4—*continued*
PART II—*continued*

1. Class of vehicle	2. Date on or after which application may be made for first examination	3. Date by which to be submitted for first examination
5. Vehicles registered in the month of May in any of the calendar years 1958 to 1967 inclusive	1st March 1969 ...	1st June 1969
6. Vehicles registered in the month of June in any of the calendar years 1958 to 1967 inclusive	1st April 1969 ...	1st July 1969
7. Vehicles registered in the month of July in any of the calendar years 1958 to 1967 inclusive	1st May 1969 ...	1st August 1969
8. Vehicles registered in the month of August in any of the calendar years 1958 to 1967 inclusive	1st June 1969 ...	1st September 1969
9. Vehicles registered in the month of September in any of the calendar years 1958 to 1967 inclusive	1st July 1969 ...	1st October 1969
10. Vehicles registered in the month of October in any of the calendar years 1958 to 1967 inclusive	1st August 1969...	1st November 1969
11. Vehicles registered in the month of November in any of the calendar years 1958 to 1967 inclusive	1st September 1969	1st December 1969
12. Vehicles registered in the month of December in any of the calendar years 1958 to 1967 inclusive	1st October 1969	1st January 1970
13. Vehicles registered in the month of January in any of the calendar years 1958 to 1967 inclusive	1st November 1969	1st February 1970
14. Vehicles registered in the month of February in any of the calendar years 1958 to 1967 inclusive	1st December 1969	1st March 1970
15. Vehicles registered in the month of March in any of the calendar years 1958 to 1967 inclusive	1st January 1970	1st April 1970

SCHEDULE 4—*continued*

PART III

Dates relating to trailers

1. Class of trailer	2. Date on or after which application may be made for first examination	3. Date by which to be submitted for first examination
1. Trailers manufactured before 1st January 1959	1st November 1968	1st February 1969
2. Trailers manufactured on or after 1st January 1959 and before 1st January 1960	1st December 1968	1st March 1969
3. Trailers manufactured on or after 1st January 1960 and before 1st January 1961	1st January 1969	1st April 1969
4. Trailers manufactured on or after 1st January 1961 and before 1st January 1962	1st February 1969	1st May 1969
5. Trailers manufactured on or after 1st January 1962 and before 1st January 1963	1st March 1969 ...	1st June 1969
6. Trailers manufactured on or after 1st January 1963 and before 1st January 1964	1st April 1969 ...	1st July 1969
7. Trailers manufactured on or after 1st January 1964 and before 1st January 1965	1st May 1969 ...	1st August 1969
8. Trailers manufactured on or after 1st January 1965 and before 1st January 1966	1st June 1969 ...	1st September 1969
9. Trailers manufactured on or after 1st January 1966 and before 1st January 1967	1st July 1969 ...	1st November 1969
10. Trailers manufactured on or after 1st January 1967 and before 1st January 1968	1st September 1969	1st January 1970

SCHEDULE 5 (see Regulations 11, 20, 28 and 33)
FEES PAYABLE ON EXAMINATIONS

PART I
Fees payable on first examinations

1. Class of vehicle	2. Amount of fee
1. Motor vehicle with 2 axles	£5
2. Motor vehicle with 3 axles	£6
3. Motor vehicle with 4 or more axles	£7
4. Trailer with 1 axle	£3
5. Trailer with 2 or more axles	£4

PART II
Fees payable on Part II re-tests

1. Subject to Regulation 20(1), the fee for a Part II re-test of a vehicle carried out under Regulation 19(2) or (4) shall be £2, together with an additional amount of £1 for each section (in excess of one) in which falls a prescribed construction and use requirement with which the vehicle was found not to comply when last undergoing either a first examination or a Part II re-test, so, however, that no such fee shall exceed the fee which would be payable for that vehicle were that vehicle submitted for a Part II re-test to be carried out under Regulation 19(3).

2. The fee for a Part II re-test of a vehicle carried out under Regulation 19(3) shall be of the same amount as was payable in respect of a first examination of that vehicle.

PART III
Fees payable on periodical tests

1. Class of vehicle	2. Amount of fee
1. Motor vehicle with 2 axles	£5
2. Motor vehicle with 3 axles	£6
3. Motor vehicle with 4 or more axles	£7
4. Trailer with 1 axle	£3
5. Trailer with 2 or more axles	£4

PART IV
Fees payable on Part III re-tests

1. Subject to Regulation 33(1), the fee for a Part III re-test of a vehicle carried out under Regulation 32(2) or (4) shall be £2, together with an additional amount of £1 for each section (in excess of one) in which falls a prescribed construction and use requirement with which the vehicle was found not to comply when last undergoing either a periodical test or a Part III re-test, so, however, that no such fee shall exceed the fee which would be payable for that vehicle were that vehicle submitted for a Part III re-test to be carried out under Regulation 32(3).

2. The fee for a Part III re-test of a vehicle carried out under Regulation 32(3) shall be of the same amount as was payable in respect of a periodical test of that vehicle.

EXPLANATORY NOTE

(This Note is not part of the Regulations.)

These Regulations make provision for the examination at vehicle testing stations provided by the Minister of Transport of goods vehicles of prescribed classes for the purpose of determining particulars (including particulars as to maximum weights) applicable to those vehicles and for the purpose of ascertaining whether the vehicles comply with prescribed construction and use requirements. By the Motor Vehicles (Construction and Use) (Amendment) (No. 4) Regulations 1968 (S.I. 1968/602) provision is made for the particulars (hereafter referred to as " the plated particulars ") determined for a vehicle on such an examination to be marked on it by means of a plate and for weights so determined not to be exceeded.

Regulation 3 specifies the classes of goods vehicles, being motor vehicles or trailers, to which the Regulations apply and provides that vehicles of the classes set out in Schedule 2 will not be liable to examination.

Regulation 4 and Schedule 3 prescribe the construction and use requirements in relation to which a vehicle is to be examined.

Part II of the Regulations governs " first examinations " of a vehicle. These are examinations for determining the plated particulars for a vehicle and comprise a goods vehicle test, which is an examination for the purpose of ascertaining whether it complies with the prescribed construction and use requirements. Where a vehicle is found to comply with these requirements, Regulations 18 and 21 provide for the issue of a goods vehicle test certificate, and a plating certificate which by virtue of Regulation 22 is to contain the plated particulars determined for that vehicle. Regulation 10 and Schedule 4 specify the dates by which goods vehicles to which these Regulations apply are to be submitted for first examinations. These dates are relevant in relation to subsections (1) and (2) of section 14 of the Road Safety Act 1967 which respectively make it an offence for goods vehicles to which these Regulations apply to be used on roads on or after those dates without a plating certificate and a goods vehicle test certificate being in force.

Part III of the Regulations contains provision for vehicles for which a first goods vehicle test certificate has been issued to be submitted for subsequent goods vehicle tests at intervals. In particular, Regulation 27 fixes the dates by which vehicles are to be submitted for these tests.

Part IV of the Regulations requires certain alterations to a vehicle or its fixed equipment to be notified to the Minister. Under section 14(6) of the Road Safety Act 1967 it is an offence to use on a road a goods vehicle when such an alteration has been made to it and not been notified to the Minister. Part IV also provides in certain cases for re-examinations of vehicles to be carried out and for new plating certificates to be issued, when a notifiable alteration has been made to the vehicle or any particulars contained in its plating certificate may have become no longer applicable to the vehicle.

Part V of the Regulations deals with various matters and, in particular, matters concerning the fees which are payable in respect of examinations and the amounts of which are, in general, specified in Schedule 5. The amount of fees payable for appeals against determinations on examinations are set out in Regulations 25(3) and 26(2).

Part VI of the Regulations contains modifications of the Regulations for the purpose of their application to examinations of Crown vehicles.

Part VII contains exemptions from section 14(1) and (2) of the Road Safety Act 1967 of vehicles used for certain purposes or in certain areas and also exempts a class of motor vehicles from section 14(5) of the 1967 Act (which provides that a goods vehicle for which a plating certificate has been issued must not draw a trailer unless a maximum laden weight for that vehicle and trailer is shown in that certificate).

STATUTORY INSTRUMENTS

1968 No. 602

ROAD TRAFFIC

The Motor Vehicles (Construction and Use) (Amendment) (No. 4) Regulations 1968

Made	- - -	*10th April* 1968
Laid before Parliament		*25th April* 1968
Coming into Operation		*1st August* 1968

The Minister of Transport, in exercise of his powers under section 64(1) of the Road Traffic Act 1960(**a**), as amended by section 51 of and Schedule 4 to the Road Traffic Act 1962(**b**) and as extended by section 8 of the Road Safety Act 1967(**c**), and of all other powers him enabling in that behalf, and after consultation with representative organisations in accordance with the provisions of section 260(2) of the said Act of 1960, hereby makes the following Regulations:—

1.—(1) These Regulations shall come into operation on the 1st August 1968, and may be cited as the Motor Vehicles (Construction and Use) (Amendment) (No. 4) Regulations 1968.

(2) The Interpretation Act 1889(**d**) shall apply for the interpretation of these Regulations as it applies for the interpretation of an Act of Parliament.

2. The Motor Vehicles (Construction and Use) Regulations 1966(**e**), as amended(**f**), shall be further amended in accordance with the following provisions of these Regulations.

3. Regulation 3 of the said Regulations shall have effect as though—

(*a*) in paragraph (1), after the definition of " pedestrian controlled vehicle " there were inserted the following definition:—

" ' plating certificate ', in relation to a vehicle, means a plating certificate issued for that vehicle under the Goods Vehicles (Plating and Testing) Regulations 1968(**g**) and which shows therein the following particulars, namely, the gross weight for the vehicle, the axle weight for each axle of the vehicle and in the case of a motor vehicle constructed or adapted to form part of an articulated vehicle, the train weight for that motor vehicle;";

(*b*) in paragraph (5) after the words " axles of " there were inserted the words " and in determining the sum of the weights transmitted to the road surface by any one axle of "

4. Regulation 4 of the said Regulations shall have effect as though—

(*u*) in paragraph (5) after the words " any Regulation hereof " there were

---

(a) 8 & 9 Eliz. 2. c. 16.   (b) 10 & 11 Eliz. 2. c. 59.   (c) 1967 c. 30.
(d) 52 & 53 Vict. c. 63.   (e) S.I. 1966/1288 (1966 III, p. 3493).
(f) The relevant amending instruments are S.I. 1967/1270, 1665, 1666 (1967 II, p. 3698; III, 4563, 4567).
(g) S.I. 1968/601 (1968 I, p. 1372).

inserted the words " (other than a regulation contained in Part V of these Regulations)";

(b) after paragraph 8 there were inserted the following paragraph:—

" (8A) Part II of these Regulations and Regulations 64 to 86 inclusive and Regulation 110 shall not apply to a motor vehicle or trailer which has been submitted for an examination either under regulations under section 9 of the Road Safety Act 1967 or under section 9(3) or (4) of that Act while it is being used on a road in connection with the carrying out of that examination and is being so used by a person who is empowered under the said regulations to carry out that examination, or by a person acting under the direction of a person so empowered.".

5. After Part IV of the said Regulations, there shall be added Part V set out in Schedule 1 to these Regulations.

6. After Schedule 10 to the said Regulations, there shall be added Schedule 11 set out in Schedule 2 to these Regulations.

Given under the Official Seal of the Minister of Transport the 10th April 1968.

(L.S.)

Richard Marsh,
Minister of Transport.

SCHEDULE 1

PART V

PARTICULAR REGULATIONS RELATING TO VEHICLES FOR WHICH PLATING CERTIFICATES HAVE BEEN ISSUED

Interpretation

116. In this Part of these Regulations, unless the context otherwise requires, the following expressions have the meanings hereby assigned to them respectively, that is to say—

" axle weight ", in relation to each axle of a motor vehicle or trailer, means the sum of the weights transmitted to the road surface by all the wheels of that axle;

" design gross weight ", in relation to a vehicle, means the gross weight of the vehicle at or below which in the opinion of the Minister or of a person authorised in that behalf by the Minister the vehicle could safely be driven on roads;

" design ", in relation to the gross weight, each axle weight or the train weight of a motor vehicle or trailer, means any such weight is one at or below which in the opinion of the Minister or of a person authorised in that behalf by the Minister the vehicle could safely be driven on roads;

" gross weight ", in relation to a motor vehicle, means the sum of the weights transmitted to the road surface by all the wheels of the vehicle;

" gross weight ", in relation to a trailer, means the sum of the weights transmitted to the road surface by all the wheels of the trailer and includes any weight of the trailer imposed on the drawing vehicle;

" Ministry plate " means a plate issued by the Minister for a goods vehicle following the issue or amendment of a plating certificate under the plating and testing regulations and in the form in, and containing the particulars required by, Schedule 11, the said particulars being those shown in the plating certificate for the vehicle;

" the plating and testing regulations " means the Goods Vehicles (Plating and Testing) Regulations 1968;

" the 1967 Act " means the Road Safety Act 1967;

" train weight ", in relation to a motor vehicle which may draw a trailer, means the maximum laden weight for the motor vehicle together with any trailer which may be drawn by it.

Application of Part V

117. This Part of these Regulations applies to goods vehicles, being goods vehicles of a class to which the plating and testing regulations apply, for which a plating certificate has been issued.

Ministry plates for goods vehicles

118. Every goods vehicle to which this Part of the Regulations applies shall as from the relevant date as defined in section 14(1) of the 1967 Act be equipped with a Ministry plate securely affixed to the vehicle in the cab thereof in a conspicuous and readily accessible position or, if the vehicle is constructed without a cab, in a conspicuous and readily accessible position elsewhere on the vehicle, and the said plate shall at all times be readily legible.

Weight restrictions

119.—(1) As respects a goods vehicle to which this Part of the Regulations applies, whether laden or unladen and whether drawing or being drawn by another vehicle, the following provisions of this paragraph shall apply as from the said relevant date, namely,—

(*a*) the gross weight shown in column (2) of the plating certificate for that vehicle shall not be exceeded;

(*b*) the axle weight for each axle shown in column (2) of the plating certificate for that vehicle shall not be exceeded:

Provided that this sub-paragraph shall not apply in the case of any axle being one of two or more axles to which the following sub-paragraph applies;

(c) where any two or more axles are fitted with a compensating arrangement in accordance with Regulation 9, the sum of the axle weights for all the axles so fitted shall not exceed the sum of such weights for those axles as are shown in column (2) of the said plating certificate.

(2) As respects a goods vehicle to which this Part of these Regulations applies, being a motor vehicle, the train weight (if any) shown in column (2) of the plating certificate for that vehicle shall not be exceeded.

(3) Nothing in any plate mentioned in Regulation 28 with which a goods vehicle to which this Part of the Regulations applies is equipped or in Regulation 70, 71, 72, 73 or 74 shall be taken to permit any such weight as is mentioned in the preceding provisions of this Regulation to be exceeded.

Additional markings

120.—(1) Without prejudice to the provisions of Regulation 118, any weight which by virtue of Regulation 119 may not be exceeded in the case of a goods vehicle to which this Part of the Regulations applies may be marked on the near side of the vehicle, the off side of the vehicle or on both sides thereof.

(2) Where at any time by virtue of any provision contained in Regulation 70 or 71 a goods vehicle to which this Part of these Regulations applies may not be used in excess of a weight, being a weight equal to the sum of the weights transmitted to the road surface by all the wheels of the vehicle and less than the gross weight which may not be exceeded by that vehicle by virtue of Regulation 119, the first mentioned weight may be marked on the near side of the vehicle, the off side of the vehicle or on both sides thereof.

(3) Where at any time by virtue of any provision contained in Regulation 72 or 73 a goods vehicle to which this Part of these Regulations applies is drawing, or being drawn by, another vehicle and those vehicles may not be used together in excess of a laden weight applicable to those vehicles by virtue of any such provision, that weight may be marked on the near side of that goods vehicle, the off side of that vehicle or on both sides thereof.

Alteration of braking requirements

121. In relation to a goods vehicle, being a motor vehicle to which this Part of these Regulations applies and to which paragraph (6) or (7) of either Regulation 43 or Regulation 48 applies, each such paragraph shall as from the date a plating certificate is issued for the vehicle have effect as though there were added at the end of that paragraph the following provision:—

" In the application of this paragraph to a motor vehicle, being a vehicle for which a plating certificate has been issued, the aforesaid requirements as to total braking efficiencies shall not be treated as being complied with unless such efficiencies are capable of being produced when the sum of the weights transmitted to the road surface by all the wheels of the vehicle is either equal to the design gross weight shown in that plating certificate or, if no such weight is so shown, equal to the gross weight shown in column (2) of that certificate."

Additional provisions as to braking requirements

122.—(1) In this Regulation " original braking requirements " means the requirements of Regulations 43(6), 43(7), 48(6) and (7), as read prior to their amendment by Regulation 121 and with Regulation 78(1)(d).

(2) Notwithstanding the said amendment, no person shall use or cause or permit to be used on a road a goods vehicle, being a motor vehicle to which this Part of these Regulations applies, as from the date a plating certificate is issued for the vehicle, if it does not also comply with the original braking requirements.

Tyres

123. Each axle of every goods vehicle to which this Part of these Regulations applies shall as from the date a plating certificate is issued for the vehicle be equipped with tyres which, as respects strength, are designed and maintained adequately to support the axle weight shown in column (2) of that certificate for that axle.

MINISTRY PLATE

MINISTRY OF TRANSPORT

Road Safety Act 1967, Sections 8 and 9
Examination of Goods Vehicles

PLATE	REGISTRATION/IDENTIFICATION MARK (where applicable)	CHASSIS/SERIAL NO. (where marked on vehicle)	YEAR OF ORIGINAL REGISTRATION (where applicable)	YEAR OF MANUFACTURE	MAKE	MODEL (where applicable)	Serial No.

(1) DESCRIPTION OF WEIGHTS APPLICABLE TO VEHICLE	(2) WEIGHTS NOT TO BE EXCEEDED IN GREAT BRITAIN		(3) DESIGN WEIGHTS (if higher than shown in col. (2))		Space for Authenticating Stamp
	TONS	KILOGRAM EQUIVALENT	TONS	KILOGRAM EQUIVALENT	
AXLE WEIGHT (Axles numbered from front to rear) — AXLE 1					
AXLE 2					
AXLE 3					
AXLE 4					
GROSS WEIGHT (see warning opposite)					
TRAIN* WEIGHT (see warning opposite)					DATE OF ISSUE OF PLATING CERTIFICATE

WARNING

1. A reduced gross weight may apply in certain cases to a vehicle towing or being towed by another.
2. A reduced train weight may apply depending on the type of trailer drawn.
3. All weights shown are subject to fitting of correct tyres.

* *Note:* Entries in respect of train weight are required in the case of only motor vehicles constructed or adapted to form part of an articulated vehicle.

EXPLANATORY NOTE

(This Note is not part of the Regulations.)

These Regulations further amend the Motor Vehicles (Construction and Use) Regulations 1966. The principal change is to add a new Part to those Regulations, being Part V (containing Regulations 116 to 123) which is set out in Schedule 1 to these Regulations and relates to goods vehicles for which a plating certificate has been issued under the Goods Vehicles (Plating and Testing) Regulations 1968 (S.I. 1968/601).

Regulation 118 provides that goods vehicles for which a plating certificate has been issued (hereafter referred to as " plated vehicles ") must from the date they are required to be submitted for examination for plating by the above mentioned regulations of 1968 be equipped with a Ministry plate in the form set out in Schedule 2 to these Regulations.

Regulation 119 provides that as from the above date plated vehicles must not be used in excess of weights specified in their plating certificate, and Regulation 120 authorises the marking of vehicles with various weights.

Regulation 121 introduces more stringent braking requirements for plated vehicles (being motor vehicles), but Regulation 122 provides that those plated vehicles must also not be used unless their brakes can produce the braking efficiencies which are required of those brakes when the vehicle is in any condition of load.

Regulation 123 requires plated vehicles to be equipped with tyres adequate in strength to support the axle weights specified in their plating certificates.

STATUTORY INSTRUMENTS

1968 No. 614

FIRE SERVICES

The Fire Services (Appointments and Promotion) (Amendment) Regulations 1968

Made - - -	11*th April* 1968
Laid before Parliament	23*rd April* 1968
Coming into Operation	1*st May* 1968

In exercise of the powers conferred on me by section 18(1) of the Fire Services Act 1947(**a**), as amended by the Fire Services Act 1959(**b**), I hereby, after consultation with the Central Fire Brigades Advisory Council, make the following Regulations :—

1. In Regulation 4(1) of the principal Regulations (which relates to qualifications for promotion to a rank higher than that of fireman) for the words "is neither an auxiliary fireman nor" there shall be substituted the words "is not".

2. In Regulation 7(2) of the principal Regulations (which authorises the Fire Services Central Examinations Board to delegate certain functions to the Local Government Examinations Board) for the words "the Local Government Examinations Board" there shall be substituted the words "the Local Government Training Board".

3. Regulation 8(1)(*a*) of the principal Regulations (which defines the expression "auxiliary fireman") is hereby revoked.

4. In these Regulations any reference to the principal Regulations is a reference to the Fire Services (Appointments and Promotion) Regulations 1965(**c**), as amended(**d**).

5. These Regulations may be cited as the Fire Services (Appointments and Promotion) (Amendment) Regulations 1968 and shall come into operation on 1st May 1968.

James Callaghan,
One of Her Majesty's Principal
Secretaries of State.

Home Office,
  Whitehall.
11th April 1968.

(**a**) 1947 c. 41.
(**c**) S.I. 1965/577 (1965 I, p. 1817).

(**b**) 1959 c. 44.
(**d**) The amending Regulations are not relevant to the subject matter of these Regulations.

EXPLANATORY NOTE

(This Note is not part of the Regulations.)

These Regulations amend the Fire Services (Appointments and Promotion) Regulations 1965.

By reason of the Civil Defence (Fire Services) Regulations 1968 (S.I. 1968/542) it is no longer the function of fire authorities to enrol auxiliary firemen. Regulations 1 and 3 remove references to such firemen from the Regulations of 1965.

The Regulations of 1965 provide that the Fire Services Central Examinations Board may delegate certain functions thereunder to the Local Government Examinations Board. The last mentioned Board has been replaced by the Local Government Training Board and Regulation 2 makes a consequential amendment.

STATUTORY INSTRUMENTS

1968 No. 615

EDUCATION, ENGLAND AND WALES

The County and Voluntary Schools (Notices) Regulations 1968

Made - - -	10*th April* 1968
Laid before Parliament	23*rd April* 1968
Coming into Operation	24*th April* 1968

The Secretary of State for Education and Science, in exercise of the powers conferred upon him by section 13(3) of the Education Act 1944(a) hereby makes the following regulations :—

Citation, commencement and interpretation

1.—(1) These regulations may be cited as the County and Voluntary Schools (Notices) Regulations 1968 and shall come into operation on 24th April 1968.

(2) The Interpretation Act 1889(b) shall apply for the interpretation of these regulations as it applies for the interpretation of an Act of Parliament.

Public notices

2. Public notice shall be given in the following manner of any proposals to which section 13(3) of the Education Act 1944 (public notice of proposals relating to schools) applies :—

(*a*) by publishing the notice in at least one newspaper circulating in the area served or, as the case may be, to be served by the school ;

(*b*) by posting the notice in some conspicuous place or places within that area ;

(*c*) in the case of an existing school, by posting the notice at or near any main entrance to the school ; and

(*d*) in such other manner, if any, as appears to the authority or persons by whom the proposals were submitted to be desirable for giving publicity to the notice.

Revocation

3. The County and Voluntary Schools (Notices) Regulations 1945(c) and the County and Voluntary Schools (Notices) Amending Regulations 1953(d) are hereby revoked.

(a) 1944 c. 31.   (b) 1889 c. 63.
(c) S. R. & O. 1945/248 (Rev. VI, p. 375: 1945 I, p. 291).   (d) S.I. 1953/1230 (1953 I, p. 604).

Given under the Official Seal of the Secretary of State for Education and Science on 10th April 1968.

(L.S.)   *Edward Short,*
                                    Secretary of State for Education and Science.

EXPLANATORY NOTE

(This Note is not part of the Regulations.)

These regulations prescribe the manner in which public notice must be given of proposals for the establishment, discontinuance or alteration of county and voluntary schools.

STATUTORY INSTRUMENTS

1968 No. 616

PRICES AND INCOMES

The Prices and Incomes (General Considerations) Order 1968

Made - - - -	*16th April* 1968
Laid before Parliament	*22nd April* 1968
Coming into Operation	*23rd April* 1968

The Secretary of State, in exercise of the powers conferred on her by section 4 of the Prices and Incomes Act 1966(a) and after consultation, in accordance with subsection (3) of that section, with organisations appearing to her to represent to a substantial extent the interests of those particularly concerned, hereby makes the following Order :—

1.—(1) This Order, which may be cited as the Prices and Incomes (General Considerations) Order 1968, shall come into operation on 23rd April 1968.

(2) The Interpretation Act 1889(b) shall apply for the interpretation of this Order as it applies for the interpretation of an Act of Parliament, and as if for the purposes of section 38 of that Act this Order were an Act of Parliament and the Order revoked by Article 3 of this Order were an Act of Parliament thereby repealed.

2. The considerations set out in the Schedule to this Order (which reproduces a memorandum entitled " Productivity, Prices and Incomes Policy in 1968 and 1969 "(c) which was presented to Parliament by the Secretary of State by Command of Her Majesty in April 1968) shall be substituted for the considerations set out in Schedule 2 to the said Act of 1966 (as substituted by the Schedule to the Prices and Incomes (General Considerations) Order 1967(d)) as the considerations to which the National Board for Prices and Incomes are to have regard in accordance with section 4 of that Act.

3. The Prices and Incomes (General Considerations) Order 1967 is hereby revoked.

Given under the Hand of the First Secretary of State and Secretary of State for Employment and Productivity on 16th April 1968.

Barbara Castle,
First Secretary of State and Secretary of
State for Employment and Productivity.

(a) 1966 c. 33.   (b) 1889 c. 63.   (c) Cmnd. 3590.   (d) S.I. 1967/642 (1967 I, p. 1975).

SCHEDULE

PRODUCTIVITY, PRICES AND INCOMES POLICY IN 1968 AND 1969

I. INTRODUCTION—THE POLICY AND STATUTORY POWERS

1. We now have a real basis for putting our balance of payments into substantial surplus and paying off our debts abroad, and an opportunity for the economy to sustain a faster rate of growth and a higher level of employment than was possible before devaluation.

2. But paying our way abroad means consuming less of what we produce ourselves. We shall be able to take these opportunities only if there is a big transfer of resources from home consumption to producing goods for export and import saving, and if the competitive advantage gained by devaluation is not eroded by an inflation of costs. The action taken in the Budget is intended to achieve the first of these tasks and this will mean a temporary fall in personal consumption. The prices and incomes policy is vitally important in maintaining the competitive edge of devaluation.

3. Over the next two years it is of paramount importance for the national economic strategy after devaluation to raise productivity and efficiency and to obtain substantial restraint from all sections of the community in order to keep incomes more in line with the expected growth of national output and prevent them rising with the cost of living.

4. The Government's firm intention is to continue the development of the policy for productivity, prices and incomes to the fullest extent practicable on a voluntary basis, in consultation with the Confederation of British Industry and the Trades Union Congress.

5. The economy cannot yet afford any automatic increase in personal incomes, and all increases or other significant improvements must continue to be justified against the criteria and considerations which are set out below.

6. The new feature of the policy will be a ceiling of 3½ per cent on wage, salary and dividend increases. But the Government wish to encourage agreements which genuinely raise productivity and efficiency, thereby helping to stabilise or reduce prices, and the policy provides for an exception to the ceiling for such agreements.

7. There will be unavoidable increases in prices because of devaluation and the Budget, but it is essential that there should be continuing efforts to contain cost increases by improvements in efficiency and greater productivity, to prevent unjustifiable price increases and to reduce prices where practicable.

8. There must be protection for the poorest section of the community and there must be restraint, not only on employment incomes, but also on incomes from property.

9. The Government believe that it is necessary in the circumstances now facing the country, and in the light of experience since 1966, to have available

statutory powers. The powers at present available to the Government derive from Part II of the Prices and Incomes Act 1966, as extended by the Prices and Incomes Act 1967, and are exercisable in the context of references to the National Board for Prices and Incomes. These powers enable the Government to require statutory notification of proposed increases in prices and pay, and to defer increases for a maximum of seven months.

10. The relevant sections of the 1967 Act will expire on 11th August 1968, and Part II of the 1966 Act will lapse at the same time unless renewed by Order in Council. The Government have decided to introduce legislation to replace the powers under the expiring sections of the 1967 Act so as to:—

(i) lengthen the maximum delaying power on price and pay increases to 12 months in the context of reference to the N.B.P.I.;

(ii) require reductions in existing prices where this is recommended by the N.B.P.I.;

(iii) moderate and phase housing rent increases;

(iv) require notification of dividend increases, and prevent excessive distributions.

The powers will be sought for eighteen months, with provision for renewal should this prove necessary.

11. All these powers will be held in reserve, and will be used only to the extent necessary where the voluntary arrangements are not being properly observed. The notification arrangements for price, pay and dividend increases will be on a voluntary basis provided that they operate satisfactorily.

12. Full support of this policy for productivity, prices and incomes will enable us to seize the opportunities in the new situation after devaluation and so ensure the basis for a lasting improvement in living standards for the whole community.

II. PRICES AND CHARGES

13. The continuing objectives of the policy for domestic prices are to encourage industry and commerce to contain cost increases by improvements in efficiency and greater productivity, to prevent unjustifiable price increases and to stabilise or reduce prices where practicable. Greater price competitiveness will enhance the advantage for home-produced over imported goods. Increased costs will need to be avoided if the opportunities for development of our export trade which devaluation has provided are to be fully exploited.

Price Increases

14. It is inescapable after devaluation that price increases will occur where costs of manufacturing and distribution have been unavoidably increased as the result of higher costs of imported foodstuffs, materials and components. Similarly there will be some increases in prices as a result of direct action by the Government, such as increased taxation. There may also be unavoidable increases in prices as a result of the factors set out

in paragraph 16. But it is essential that increases in manufacturers' and distributors' prices due to any of these causes should do no more than cover the overall increases in costs that have been sustained.

15. Increased prices, particularly of foodstuffs, due to changes in supply for seasonal or other reasons are unavoidable, but where prices rise for these reasons they should fall again when supplies are plentiful.

Criteria for Price Increases

16. Every effort should be made to absorb increases in costs by means of increased efficiency, and price increases should take place only where strictly justified by one or more of the following criteria: —

(i) if output per employee cannot be increased sufficiently to allow wages and salaries to increase at a rate consistent with the criteria for incomes* without some increase in prices, and no offsetting reductions can be made in non-labour costs per unit of output or in the return sought on investment;

(ii) if there are unavoidable increases in non-labour costs such as materials, fuel, services or marketing costs per unit of output which cannot be offset by reductions in labour or capital costs per unit of output or in the return sought on investment;

(iii) if there are unavoidable increases in capital costs per unit of output which cannot be offset by reductions in non-capital costs per unit of output or in the return sought on investment;

(iv) if, after every effort has been made to reduce costs, the enterprise is unable to secure the capital required to meet home and overseas demand.

Price Reductions

17. The need in the present economic circumstances to increase price competitiveness makes even more necessary efforts by all concerned in determining prices to reduce prices wherever possible. During the next two years increased productivity and efficiency should make some price reductions possible and should help to keep other prices stable.

Criteria for Price Reductions

18. The criteria for price reductions specified in the White Paper on Prices and Incomes Policy after 30th June 1967 (Cmnd. 3235) will continue to apply. These require price reductions: —

(i) if output per employee is increasing faster than the rate of increase in wages and salaries which is consistent with the criteria for incomes*, and there are no offsetting and unavoidable increases in non-labour costs per unit of output;

(ii) if the costs of materials, fuel or services per unit of output are falling and there are no offsetting and unavoidable increases in labour or capital costs per unit of output;

* The reference to the criteria for incomes in paragraphs 16(i) and 18(i) must now be taken to include the application of the ceiling and the incomes policy considerations set out in the incomes section (Part III).

(iii) if capital costs per unit of output are falling and there are no offsetting and unavoidable increases in non-capital costs per unit of output ;

(iv) if profits are based on excessive market power.

Prices Supervision

19. The Government intend that the early warning arrangements for notification of proposed increases in prices should continue, and, where necessary, be extended in co-operation with industry and commerce. These arrangements enable the Government to maintain a watch on the trend of prices over a wide range of goods of economic significance, including those of importance in the cost of living.

20. The voluntary early warning system is described in the White Paper on Prices and Incomes Policy: An " Early Warning " System (Cmnd. 2808). The goods and services to which these arrangements currently apply are listed in Part A of Appendix I, and, as announced in Parliament recently, the Government are in consultation with industry on the addition of further items to this list.

21. Proposals for increases notified under these arrangements will be scrutinised to ensure that they are consistent with the policy set out in this White Paper, and appropriate cases will be referred to the N.B.P.I. for examination.

22. There are also arrangements to keep watch over the trend of manufacturers' prices of certain goods where advance notice of individual price increases is not practicable, e.g. because of fluctuations in raw material prices (Part B of Appendix I). Where possible these will be extended. The arrangements for keeping a constant watch on the prices of a number of basic foodstuffs will continue (Part C of Appendix I).

23. These arrangements for the supervision of prices are primarily concerned with the prices of manufacturing industry. The Government also intend to keep generally under review the trend of retail prices because of their direct importance to the consumer, and of the need to ensure at the retail stage, as well as at other stages, that unjustifiable increases in prices are avoided. The number of individual prices in the economy makes detailed supervision of all prices impracticable. Where appropriate, Government Departments will follow up with those concerned the movement of prices of particular products.

24. The N.B.P.I. has concluded in a recent report* on prices recommended by manufacturers for the resale of their goods that in general in such circumstances a reduction in distributors' percentage margins should be made where the manufacturer's price has to be increased because of devaluation. The Government consider that in principle there should be no automatic maintenance of distributors' percentage margins when their prices are increased to take account of higher costs.

---

* Report No. 55 on Distributors' Margins in Relation to Manufacturers' Recommended Prices (Cmnd. 3546).

Application of Prices Policy

25. The criteria and considerations set out above are intended to be applied by all concerned, including wholesalers and retailers, in the determination of prices for the sale of goods, and charges for the performance of services, on the home market in both the private and public sectors. This includes all concerned in the negotiation of prices under individual contract.

26. The Government will continue to refer to the N.B.P.I. any question relating to prices where independent examination is desirable, and will not hesitate to use their strengthened delaying powers to prevent unjustifiable increases in prices.

III. INCOMES

Employment Incomes

27. For the reasons set out in Part I above substantial restraint is required over the next two years, and the Government propose to take power to delay increases in pay for up to 12 months in the context of reference to the N.B.P.I. All increases in pay, or other significant improvements, will need to be justified against the criteria and considerations of the policy. In addition the Government have decided that for all wage and salary settlements reached on or after 20th March, 1968, which satisfy these criteria and considerations there will be a ceiling of $3\frac{1}{2}$ per cent.

The Ceiling

28. The ceiling will be applied as an annual rate ; thus if in a particular case the criteria permit an increase, and more than a year has elapsed since the pay of the particular group was last adjusted, the ceiling on any such increase will be correspondingly higher than $3\frac{1}{2}$ per cent, though large increases will still need to be staged.

29. Wages and salary earnings are largely determined by reference to rates or scales of pay which may apply to the time worked, or to units of work or output, or to a combination of both. The $3\frac{1}{2}$ per cent ceiling is intended to be applied to increases in these rates or scales and other elements referred to in paragraph 30, having regard to the effect on earnings. But it is not intended to be applied to increases in earnings which are due to necessary increases in hours worked or in the amount of work done.

30. This means that the ceiling should cover increases in basic pay rates and allowances (including basic pay scales or ranges), rates for overtime, night or shift working, etc. Improvements in fringe benefits, normal or standard hours or holiday entitlement must also be taken into account for the purpose of applying the ceiling.

31. There will be increases in earnings under payment by results systems resulting directly from increased output. Changes in payment by results systems, and changes within such systems, including changes in piecework rates, bonus rates or standard times, should not, however, result in higher earnings unless they can be justified on grounds of increased effort or other direct contribution towards increasing productivity from the employees

concerned. It is expected that the forthcoming report of the N.B.P.I. on payment by results will offer guidance on the application of incomes policy to these systems of payment.

32. Changes in rates or scales may be settled at national, local, firm or plant level, but where groups benefit from increases or improvements settled at more than one level, the application of the ceiling requires that the overall increase should not exceed the $3\frac{1}{2}$ per cent ceiling. In considering increases settled at national level account must be taken of probable increases at local, company and plant level ; conversely, increases in rates setted at the plant level should take account of relevant increases settled at other levels.

33. Where a settlement covers the pay of one or more groups of workers, or a wage or salary structure is considered as a whole, the ceiling should be applied to the settlement as a whole, thus permitting flexibility of adjustment of rates within the group or structure.

Criteria for Incomes Policy

34. Over the next two years the criteria contained in Cmnd. 3235 will continue to apply. These provide for increases in the following circumstances : —

    (i) where the employees concerned, for example by accepting more exacting work or a major change in working practices, make a direct contribution towards increasing productivity in the particular firm or industry. Even in such cases some of the benefit should accrue to the community as a whole in the form of lower prices ;

    (ii) where it is essential in the national interest to secure a change in the distribution of manpower (or to prevent a change which would otherwise take place) and a pay increase would be both necessary and effective for this purpose ;

    (iii) where there is general recognition that existing wage and salary levels are too low to maintain a reasonable standard of living ;

    (iv) where there is widespread recognition that the pay of a certain group of workers has fallen seriously out of line with the level of remuneration for similar work and needs in the national interest to be improved.

35. These criteria will need to be applied firmly and should be read in conjunction with the considerations which are set out below, and where appropriate with the reports of the N.B.P.I.

36. It is of continuing importance to encourage increased productivity and efficiency, and so help stabilise or reduce prices, and priority will continue to be given to increases which are justified under the productivity criterion. Reorganisations of wage and salary structures which can be justified on grounds of economic efficiency and increased productivity may be justified under this criterion. There may also be productivity agreements or major reorganisations of wage and salary structures which, as exceptions, justify above-ceiling increases (see paragraph 43).

37. It will be necessary to ensure that increases under the low pay criterion are confined to low paid workers. Low paid workers will be able

to benefit up to the ceiling if their claims satisfy this criterion. Moreover there can be above-ceiling increases for low paid workers under a settlement which, though covering a wider group of workers, is within the ceiling. In addition the purpose of the new arrangements for family allowances is to ensure that help is given specifically to low paid workers with two or more children.

38. The criterion justifying increases on grounds of comparability needs to be applied selectively, and must not be used to spread pay increases into areas of employment where the original justification does not apply.

39. The criterion justifying pay increases on manpower grounds is retained, but there is a growing acceptance on both sides of industry that the most effective way of remedying a labour shortage is to use existing manpower more efficiently.

40. The ceiling and the criteria described above do not apply to existing arrangements for increasing pay with age, as with apprentices or juveniles, or by means of regular increments within a fixed range or scale, or progressions based on added experience, increased responsibility or special effort, or to increases resulting from promotion to work at a higher level, whether with the same or a different employer. It would be contrary to the policy for posts to be regraded without proper justification as a means of raising pay.

Cost of Living

41. Pay increases based on a rise in the cost of living are not justified under the criteria, and should not be conceded. Not only would this be self-defeating since it would result in further increases in costs and prices, but it could set off a wage–price spiral that would damage our competitive position. Cost of living sliding scales are of diminishing importance in industry, and pay increases resulting from such existing arrangements should be taken fully into account in applying the ceiling to the pay of the group covered.

Interval between Settlements

42. The period which should elapse between the operative dates of successive settlements should be at least twelve months.

Exception to the Ceiling

43. There will be an exception to the ceiling for agreements which genuinely raise productivity and increase efficiency sufficiently to justify a pay increase above $3\frac{1}{2}$ per cent. The guidelines (reproduced in Appendix II) laid down by the N.B.P.I. in their Report No. 36 on " Productivity Agreements " provide the basis for determining the justification for such increases. Major reorganisations of wage and salary structures which can be justified on productivity and efficiency grounds may also qualify for this exceptional treatment.

Staging

44. It was stated in paragraph 24 of Cmnd. 3235 that in some cases it is appropriate for substantial improvements in pay or conditions to be achieved by stages, even though justified under the criteria. The application of the ceiling should considerably reduce the number of cases where large increases are justified, but they may still occur where a much longer interval than twelve months has elapsed since the previous increase or improvement. The

need to consider staging in such cases will be particularly important now that the majority of workers will be able to receive only limited increases.

Application of The Policy

45. The ceiling and criteria for incomes policy and the considerations set out above are intended to be applied by all concerned with the determination of employment incomes in the private and public sectors, whether at national, local, company or plant level and including arbitrators, independent review bodies and statutory wage fixing bodies.

46. It will continue to be the aim of the Government in consultation with the C.B.I. and the T.U.C., and with the assistance of the parties, and of the N.B.P.I. in appropriate cases, to secure the effective and consistent application of the policy both in the private and public sectors.

Notification of Claims and Proposed Settlements

47. Under the existing early warning arrangements described in Cmnd. 2808 the Government receive information on a voluntary basis about claims and proposals to increase pay from the C.B.I. and the T.U.C., from organisations which are not members of either of these bodies, and directly from firms and employers' organisations in the case of local and company negotiations. There are similar arrangements for the public sector.

48. It is intended that these arrangements will continue, and consequently information about claims and proposed settlements, whether at national, local, company or plant level, will continue to be required. While all settlements are subject to the requirements of the policy, the information to be submitted under the early warning arrangements relates to claims and proposed settlements which might be significant (e.g. because of the nature of the claim, or the possible repercussions on the pay of other groups) and, in any case, to all those involving more than 100 workers.

49. The information about claims should specify the nature and terms of the claim, the proposed date of implementation, the number and category or workers covered, and the date and terms of the previous settlement covering this group of workers. The notification should also include an assessment of the justification for the proposed improvement against the criteria and considerations set out in paragraphs 34–44. The information about proposed settlements should give details of the way in which the ceiling has been calculated and applied.

Other Forms of Employment Income

50. Many individual salaries and other forms of remuneration, including that of company directors and executives, are fixed outside the usual process of collective bargaining. The principles of incomes policy should however be applied equally to them as to other forms of income. The Companies Act of 1967 has provisions concerning the disclosure of the remuneration of directors and executives.

51. The incomes and scales of charges and fees of self-employed persons, including all forms of professional fees, are expected to conform with the policy. The Government have referred to the N.B.P.I. the remuneration of solicitors, and architects' costs and fees. The Board's report on solicitors' remuneration was published in February, and its recommendations are being considered by the Government.

Non-Employment Incomes

52. The Government are committed to use their fiscal powers or other appropriate means to correct any excessive growth in aggregate profits, whether distributed or not, as compared with the growth of total wages and salaries, after allowing for short-term fluctuations. The Budget provides for the rate of Corporation Tax to be increased by $2\frac{1}{2}$ per cent to $42\frac{1}{2}$ per cent, and for a special charge, which is expected to yield a revenue of £100 million, to be made on the investment income of an individual for 1967–68 where this exceeds £3,000.

53. The Government will also refer for examination prices cases where the growth of profits or dividends is based on excessive market power.

54. As already announced in the Chancellor of the Exchequer's Budget Statement the Government propose to take statutory powers relating to notification of dividend increases and prevention of excessive distributions. All companies are asked not to increase dividends without good reason, and to limit any essential increase. In any case total ordinary dividends in respect of a company account year should be limited to:—

  (i) not more than $3\frac{1}{2}$ per cent above the amount of ordinary dividends declared in respect of the preceding account year ; or

 (ii) not more than the amount in respect of the account year before that ; or

(iii) where dividends in each of the last two account years were abnormally low, and subject to examination and approval by the Treasury, not more than the amount in respect of an earlier account year.

55. This requirement affects all companies incorporated in the United Kingdom with the exception of unit trusts, investment trusts, those close companies which increase distributions to meet the requirements of the Finance Act 1965, and companies wholly owned by other companies where ordinary dividend payments are exclusively inter-company transactions. It affects all distributions in respect of paid-up ordinary share capital which are recommended after 19th March 1968.

56. The call for dividend restraint is addressed to all other companies, and in order to achieve its objectives the Government will institute early warning arrangements in the main company sector comparable to the arrangements made in the field of prices and pay. All quoted companies are therefore asked to notify the Treasury whenever an intended distribution would involve any increase at all above total declarations in respect of the preceding company accounts year, and such companies should not take irrevocable action upon such intentions without the Treasury's consent.

IV. RENTS AND RATES

Rents of Houses

57. House rents are a large item in the family budgets of workers, and sharp changes in rent levels are, therefore, of significance for incomes policy.

58. Many private rents are still rigidly controlled under the Rent Act 1957. For those subject to rent regulation under the Rent Act 1965, fair rents are determined by Rent Officers or Rent Assessment Committees. In certain cases these can give rise to sharp increases, and it is therefore proposed that in the present situation the Housing Ministers should be empowered to make Regulations for phasing increases above a stipulated minimum amount over a period not exceeding three years.

59. Most local authorities have followed Government advice and kept increases in the rents of their houses to no more than has been needed to meet increases in costs. Many have adopted or improved rent rebate schemes. Some, however, have raised rents more sharply, for example on a scale designed to secure sufficient revenue now to cover cost increases over several years ahead. In present circumstances this is not compatible with prices and incomes policy.

60. The Government have decided therefore to take powers to require early warning of rent increases, and to enable them to direct local authorities to moderate or phase rent increases which they regard as too high in present circumstances.

61. The need for moderation in rent increases applies also to housing owned by new towns and the Scottish Special Housing Association. The responsible Ministers are able under existing arrangements to ensure that any necessary increases are moderated or phased.

Rates

62. Rates as a form of taxation are outside the scope of prices and incomes policy: they are necessary to help pay for the range of services provided by local authorities. Better services are bound to cost more money, but the Government have taken steps to reduce the impact of rates on householders by providing special grants which have reduced the amount in the £ they have to pay, by 5d. in the £ last year and 10d. in the £ this year. As a result of this, and of the savings made by local authorities, most householders during 1967–68 paid little, if any, more in rates than they did in the previous year. There is every reason to believe that this will also be the case in 1968–69, though larger increases may be unavoidable in some areas. In addition the income limits for rate rebates are being raised from next October and this will help many householders with small incomes, particularly those with large families.

63. In Scotland rates are fixed much later in the year and it is not yet possible to say what their level will be in 1968–69. However, special grants will reduce the amount householders have to pay by 1s. 8d. in the £ compared with 10d. in 1967–68, and the higher income limits for rate rebates will also apply from next October.

V. NATIONAL BOARD FOR PRICES AND INCOMES

64. The work of the National Board for Prices and Incomes and its role as an independent statutory body in furthering the objectives of the productivity, prices and incomes policy will be of increasing importance.

65. The Government will continue to exercise the statutory powers in relation to prices and pay through the process of reference to the N.B.P.I. The Board has been strengthened to enable it to deal with an increased volume of work covering the expected increase in post-devaluation prices and incomes references, and it will be further strengthened if this should prove necessary.

66. In consultation with the C.B.I., the T.U.C. and other interested bodies, the Government will continue to refer to the Board appropriate cases relating to the application of the productivity, prices and incomes policy and matters of longer term importance to the policy.

APPENDIX I

PART A

Goods and Services Subject to Early Warning Arrangements

Ministry of Agriculture, Fisheries and Food

Bread
Flour
Biscuits
Cakes
Breakfast cereals
Sausages
Meat pies
Canned fruit
Canned vegetables
Jams and marmalade
Margarines and cooking fats
Milk products (including condensed milk)
Pickles and sauces
Processed vegetables
Quick-frozen foods
Ice-cream
Soft drinks
Chocolate and sugar confectionery
Soups
Table jellies
Tea
Processed coffee
Manufactured pet foods
Animal feeding stuffs
Beer
Cider and perry
Wines and spirits

Ministry of Technology

Domestic refrigerators (electric)
Gas cookers
Electric cookers
Washing machines
Vacuum cleaners
Gas fires
Electric storage heaters
Domestic boilers

Domestic water-heaters
Electric lamps—coil and fluorescent
Household electrical wiring components
Cash registers
Office photocopying machines
Typewriters
Domestic sewing machines
Industrial sewing machines
Chain link fencing
Domestic electric power tools and their attachments
Electric motors
Primary cells and primary batteries
Secondary batteries
Contractors' plant
Agricultural machinery
Tractors
Commercial vehicles
Motor cars
Bicycles and motorcycles
Radio and television electronic components (including valves and cathode ray tubes)
Copper cylinders and boilers
Galvanised steel cisterns and tanks
Plastic cold water tanks

Board of Trade

Fertilisers
Glass jars and bottles
Insurance premiums
Man-made staple fibre and filament yarn
Sewing thread
Building and decorative paints
Paper and board
Wallpaper
National daily and Sunday newspapers
Polyethylene
Polyvinyl chloride
Rubber footwear
Tyres
Household soaps and detergents
Acetylene and oxygen
Coastal shipping rates (freight and passenger)

Ministry of Public Building and Works

Asbestos cement
Cement
Bricks
Glass
Glazed floor tiles
Ceramic sanitaryware
Plaster and plaster board
Pitch fibre pipes
Roofing felt
Clay pipes

Ministry of Power

Petrol
Derv
Fuel oils

Bottled gas
Coal
Coke
Manufactured fuel
Iron and steel products
Gas
Electricity (England and Wales)

Scottish Development Department

Electricity (Scotland)

Ministry of Transport

Rail fares (country-wide charges outside London Passenger Transport Area)
Rail freight charges (published scales for parcels and sundries; and other
country-wide charges)
B.R.S. Parcels Ltd. (published scale of country-wide charges for parcels)

PART B

Goods of which the Trend of Manufacturers' Prices is kept under review

Board of Trade

Carpets, mats and matting
Cotton and man-made fibre spun yarns
Footwear (other than rubber)
Electric power cables
Wool yarns for weaving and hosiery
Knitting wool
Clothing
General chemicals
Hosiery and knitwear
Leather

Ministry of Public Building and Works

Building blocks
Sand and gravel
Ready mixed concrete

PART C

Foodstuffs subject to Constant Watch

Ministry of Agriculture, Fisheries and Food

Carcase meat and offal
Bacon and ham
Poultry (including broilers)
Eggs
Fresh fruit
Fresh vegetables (including potatoes)
Lard, cooking and edible oils
Fish
Sugar
Cheese
Butter
Cream

APPENDIX II
NATIONAL BOARD FOR PRICES AND INCOMES GUIDELINES FOR PRODUCTIVITY AGREEMENTS

The guidelines for productivity agreements in the N.B.P.I. report No. 36 (Cmnd. 3311) are as follows:—

(i) It should be shown that the workers are making a direct contribution towards increasing productivity by accepting more exacting work or a major change in working practices.

(ii) Forecasts of increased productivity should be derived by the application of proper work-standards.

(iii) An accurate calculation of the gains and the costs should normally show that the total cost per unit of output, taking into account the effect on capital, will be reduced.

(iv) The scheme should contain effective controls to ensure that the projected increase in productivity is achieved, and that payment is made only as productivity increases or as changes in working practice take place.

(v) The undertaking should be ready to show clear benefits to the consumer through a contribution to stable prices.

(vi) An agreement covering part of an undertaking should bear the cost of consequential increases elsewhere in the same undertaking, if any have to be granted.

(vii) In all cases negotiators should beware of setting extravagant levels of pay which would provoke resentment outside.

EXPLANATORY NOTE
(*This Note is not part of the Order.*)

This Order sets out the considerations to which the National Board for Prices and Incomes are required to have regard in examining questions relating to prices, incomes and other matters referred to them under section 2 of the Prices and Incomes Act 1966 and in complying with instructions to keep such questions under continuous review under section 3.

The Order provides that, from the date of its coming into operation, the said considerations shall be those set out in the Schedule to this Order (which reproduces the White Paper " Productivity, Prices and Incomes Policy in 1968 and 1969 "—Cmnd. 3590) in substitution for those set out in the Schedule to the Prices and Incomes (General Considerations) Order 1967 (S.I. 1967/642).

1968 No. 617

PLANT BREEDERS' RIGHTS

The Plant Breeders' Rights (Perennial Chrysanthemums) Scheme 1968

Made - - -	*9th April* 1968
Laid before Parliament	*25th April* 1968
Coming into Operation	*26th April* 1968

The Minister of Agriculture, Fisheries and Food, the Secretary of State for Scotland and the Secretary of State for the Home Department (being the Secretary of State concerned with agriculture in Northern Ireland), acting jointly, in exercise of the powers conferred on them by sections 1 and 3 of, and paragraph 1 of Schedule 3 to, the Plant Varieties and Seeds Act 1964(a), as extended to Northern Ireland by the Plant Varieties and Seeds (Northern Ireland) Order 1964(b), and of all other powers enabling them in that behalf, after consultation with the Controller of Plant Variety Rights and with representatives of such interests as appear to them to be concerned, hereby make the following Scheme :—

Citation and Commencement

1. This Scheme may be cited as the Plant Breeders' Rights (Perennial Chrysanthemums) Scheme 1968 and shall come into operation on 26th April 1968.

Interpretation

2.—(1) In this Scheme, unless the context otherwise requires—
"the Act" means the Plant Varieties and Seeds Act 1964 as extended to Northern Ireland ;

"plant breeders' rights" means rights which may be granted in accordance with Part I of the Act ;

"plant variety" means any clone, line, hybrid or genetic variant.

(2) The Interpretation Act 1889(c) shall apply to the interpretation of this Scheme as it applies to the interpretation of an Act of Parliament.

Plant Varieties for which Plant Breeders' Rights may be granted

3. There are prescribed for the purposes of the grant of plant breeders' rights all plant varieties of perennial chrysanthemums which conform with the characteristics of cultivated plant varieties of the genus *Chrysanthemum* of the following species or groups :—

Chrysanthemum morifolium Ramatuelle ; *C. indicum* Auct. non L.;

C. sinense Sabine ; *C. chinense* Hort.; *C. hortorum* W. Miller ;

C. japonense (Makino) Nakai ; *C. vestitum* (Hemsley) Stapf ;

C. makinoi Matsumura and Nakai ; *C. sibiricum* (DC.) Fischer ex Turcz.;

(a) 1964 c. 14.   (b) S.I. 1964/1574 (1964 III, p. 3543).   (c) 1889 c. 63.

C. zawadskii Herbich and varieties ; *C. rubellum* Sealy (*C. erubescens* Hort. non Stapf) ; *C. cuneifolium* Kitamura ; *C. okiense* Kitamura ;

C. boreale (Makino) Makino ; *C. aphrodite* Kitamura ; *C. articum* Auct. non L.; *C. ornatum* Hemsley ; *C. koreanum* (coreanum) Hort.;

C. yezoense Maekawa ; Korean chrysanthemums ; Konji chrysanthemums and Cascade chrysanthemums.

Period for which Rights are Exercisable

4. The period for which plant breeders' rights shall be exercisable in respect of the plant varieties referred to in the last preceding paragraph shall be 15 years.

Additional Rights

5. Plant breeders' rights exercisable in respect of the plant varieties referred to in paragraph 3 of this Scheme shall include the exclusive right to produce or propagate and to authorise others to produce or propagate any such plant variety for the purpose of selling cut blooms of that plant variety.

In Witness whereof the official seal of the Minister of Agriculture, Fisheries and Food is hereunto affixed on 4th April 1968.

(L.S.)   *Frederick Peart,*
                            Minister of Agriculture, Fisheries and Food.

Given under the seal of the Secretary of State for Scotland on 8th April 1968.

(L.S.)   *William Ross,*
                                    Secretary of State for Scotland.

Given under the hand of the Secretary of State for the Home Department on 9th April 1968.

                                            James Callaghan,
                            Secretary of State for the Home Department.

EXPLANATORY NOTE
(*This Note is not part of the Scheme.*)

This Scheme, made under the Plant Varieties and Seeds Act 1964, prescribes the varieties of perennial chrysanthemums in respect of which grants of plant breeders' rights may be made and also prescribes the period of 15 years as that during which the rights may be exercised.

Plant breeders' rights in respect of any variety of perennial chrysanthemums to which the Scheme applies are extended to the production or propagation of the variety for the purpose of selling cut blooms.

STATUTORY INSTRUMENTS

1968 No. 618

PLANT BREEDERS' RIGHTS

The Plant Breeders' Rights (Raspberries) Scheme 1968

Made - - -		*9th April* 1968
Laid before Parliament		*25th April* 1968
Coming into Operation		*26th April* 1968

The Minister of Agriculture, Fisheries and Food, the Secretary of State for Scotland and the Secretary of State for the Home Department (being the Secretary of State concerned with agriculture in Northern Ireland), acting jointly, in exercise of the powers conferred on them by sections 1, 3 and 7 of, and paragraph 1 of Schedule 3 to, the Plant Varieties and Seeds Act 1964(a), as extended to Northern Ireland by the Plant Varieties and Seeds (Northern Ireland) Order 1964(b), and of all other powers enabling them in that behalf, after consultation with the Controller of Plant Variety Rights and with representatives of such interests as appear to them to be concerned, hereby make the following Scheme :—

Citation and Commencement

1. This Scheme may be cited as the Plant Breeders' Rights (Raspberries) Scheme 1968 and shall come into operation on 26th April 1968.

Interpretation

2.—(1) In this Scheme, unless the context otherwise requires—

"the Act" means the Plant Varieties and Seeds Act 1964 as extended to Northern Ireland ;

"the Controller" means the Controller of Plant Variety Rights ;

"plant breeders' rights" means rights which may be granted in accordance with Part I of the Act ;

"plant variety" means any clone, line, hybrid or genetic variant.

(2) The Interpretation Act 1889(c) shall apply to the interpretation of this Scheme as it applies to the interpretation of an Act of Parliament.

Plant Varieties for which Plant Breeders' Rights may be granted

3. There are prescribed for the purposes of the grant of plant breeders' rights all plant varieties of raspberries which conform with the characteristics of cultivated plant varieties of the species *Rubus idaeus, Rubus strigosus* and *Rubus occidentalis.*

Period for which Rights are Exercisable

4. The period for which plant breeders' rights shall be exercisable in respect of the plant varieties referred to in the last preceding paragraph shall be 20 years.

(a) 1964 c. 14.   (b) S.I. 1964/1574 (1964 III, p. 3543).   (c) 1889 c. 63.

Period Prescribed for the Purposes of Section 7(2) of the Act

5. In relation to the plant varieties referred to in paragraph 3 of this Scheme, the period prescribed for the purposes of section 7(2) of the Act (which enables a provision to be made whereby a compulsory licence granted by the Controller as respects a plant variety of a species or group specified in a scheme shall not have effect for a prescribed period after the grant of rights in that plant variety) shall be 2 years.

Additional Rights

6. Plant breeders' rights exercisable in respect of the plant varieties referred to in paragraph 3 of this Scheme shall include the exclusive right to produce or propagate and to authorise others to produce or propagate any such plant variety for the purpose of selling fruit of that plant variety.

In Witness whereof the official seal of the Minister of Agriculture, Fisheries and Food is hereunto affixed on 4th April 1968.

(L.S.)   *Frederick Peart,*
Minister of Agriculture, Fisheries and Food.

Given under the seal of the Secretary of State for Scotland on 8th April 1968.

(L.S.)   *William Ross,*
Secretary of State for Scotland.

Given under the hand of the Secretary of State for the Home Department on 9th April 1968.

James Callaghan,
Secretary of State for the Home Department.

EXPLANATORY NOTE

(This Note is not part of the Scheme.)

This Scheme, made under the Plant Varieties and Seeds Act 1964, prescribes the varieties of raspberries in respect of which grants of plant breeders' rights may be made and also prescribes the period of 20 years as that during which the rights may be exercised.

This Scheme also provides that a compulsory licence granted by the Controller of Plant Variety Rights in respect of a variety of raspberry shall not have effect during a period of 2 years from the date of the grant of rights in that variety.

Plant breeders' rights in respect of any variety of raspberry to which the Scheme applies are extended to the production or propagation of the variety for the purpose of selling fruit.

STATUTORY INSTRUMENTS

1968 No. 619

PLANT BREEDERS' RIGHTS

The Plant Breeders' Rights (Fees) Regulations 1968

Made - - - -	10*th April* 1968
Laid before Parliament	25*th April* 1968
Coming into Operation	26*th April* 1968

The Minister of Agriculture, Fisheries and Food, the Secretary of State for Scotland and the Secretary of State for the Home Department (being the Secretary of State concerned with agriculture in Northern Ireland), acting jointly, in exercise of the powers vested in them by sections 9 and 36 of the Plant Varieties and Seeds Act 1964(a), as extended to Northern Ireland by the Plant Varieties and Seeds (Northern Ireland) Order 1964(b) and of all other powers enabling them in that behalf, with the approval of the Treasury, hereby make the following Regulations:—

Citation and Commencement

1. These Regulations may be cited as the Plant Breeders' Rights (Fees) Regulations 1968 and shall come into operation on 26th April 1968.

Revocation of Previous Regulations

2. The Regulations specified in Schedule 1 to these Regulations are hereby revoked.

Interpretation

3.—(1) In these Regulations, unless the context otherwise requires,—

"the Act" means the Plant Varieties and Seeds Act 1964 as extended to Northern Ireland, except Parts II and III thereof;

"the Controller" means the Controller of Plant Variety Rights;

"plant breeders' rights" means rights which may be granted in accordance with Part I of the Act;

"the principal Regulations" means the Plant Breeders' Rights Regulations 1965(c) as amended (d);

and other expressions have the same meaning as they have in the Act.

(2) The Interpretation Act 1889(e) shall apply to the interpretation of these Regulations as it applies to the interpretation of an Act of Parliament and as if these Regulations and the Regulations hereby revoked were Acts of Parliament.

(a) 1964 c. 14.   (b) S.I. 1964/1574 (1964 III, p. 3543).
(c) S.I. 1965/65 (1965 I, p. 96).
(d) S.I. 1967/1530, 1968/255, 622 (1967 III, p. 4295; 1968 I, p. 769, 1456).
(e) 1889 c. 63.

Payment of Fees

4. There shall be paid to the Controller in respect of the matters relating to plant breeders' rights arising under the Act or the principal Regulations the fees of the amounts set out in the fourth column of Schedule 2 to these Regulations opposite the respective references to those matters set out in the second column of the said Schedule, which fees shall be paid at the time or times specified in respect of each such matter as set out in the third column of the said Schedule.

Renewal Fees

5.—(1) The fee payable in respect of the continued exercise of plant breeders' rights in a plant variety (hereinafter referred to as the "renewal fee") shall be paid only by the holder of those rights or by a person acting on his behalf, being either an agent duly authorised in accordance with Regulation 15 of the principal Regulations or a person who shall deliver to the Controller with the fee an authority in writing to pay the same, signed by the holder of the rights.

(2) If any such fee is tendered or paid otherwise than in accordance with the last preceding paragraph, the liability to pay the same shall not be regarded as having been thereby discharged.

(3) In a case where the period for which any plant breeders' rights are exercisable has been terminated in accordance with the principal Regulations on the ground that a renewal fee has not been paid there shall only be recoverable by the Controller such a proportion of the said fee as the period during which the said rights have continued to be enjoyed since the date when the said fee became payable bears to the period of 12 months.

(4) Notwithstanding Regulation 4 of these Regulations and the last preceding paragraph of this Regulation, in a case where the period for which any plant breeders' rights are exercisable has been terminated in accordance with the principal Regulations on the ground that a renewal fee has not been paid and

(*a*) the person entitled to exercise those rights shall, not later than 14 days before the date when the said fee became payable, have informed the Controller that he did not propose to exercise any of such rights at any time after such date, and

(*b*) such person shall not have exercised any of the said rights during the period beginning with the date when the said fee became payable and ending with the date when the said period was terminated,

the Controller shall not be entitled to recover from such person, by any legal proceedings or otherwise, the said fee or any part thereof.

In Witness whereof the official seal of the Minister of Agriculture, Fisheries and Food is hereunto affixed on 4th April 1968.

(L.S.)   *Frederick Peart,*
                              Minister of Agriculture, Fisheries and Food.

Given under the seal of the Secretary of State for Scotland on 8th April 1968.

(L.S.)

William Ross,
Secretary of State for Scotland.

Given under the hand of the Secretary of State for the Home Department on 9th April 1968.

James Callaghan,
Secretary of State for the Home Department.

Approved on 10th April 1968.

B. K. O'Malley,
E. Alan Fitch,
Two of the Lords Commissioners of
Her Majesty's Treasury.

SCHEDULE 1

Regulations revoked	References
The Plant Breeders' Rights (Fees) Regulations 1965	S.I. 1965/66 (1965 I, p. 112).
The Plant Breeders' Rights (Fees) (Amendment) Regulations 1966	S.I. 1966/641 (1966 II, p. 1443).
The Plant Breeders' Rights (Fees) (Amendment No. 2) Regulations 1966	S.I. 1966/1224 (1966 III, p. 3284).
The Plant Breeders' Rights (Fees) (Amendment) Regulations 1967	S.I. 1967/1455 (1967 III, p. 4139).
The Plant Breeders' Rights (Fees) (Amendment) Regulations 1968	S.I. 1968/256 (1968 I, p. 772).

SCHEDULE 2   Regulation 4

FEES

No.	Matter	When Payable	Amount
			£ s. d.
1	Application for a grant of plant breeders' rights.	On making the application.	10 0 0
2	Application for an extension of the period for which plant breeders' rights are exercisable.	On making the application.	10 0 0
3	Application for a compulsory licence.	On making the application.	5 0 0
4	Application to extend, limit, vary or revoke a compulsory licence.	On making the application.	5 0 0
5	Application to amend a document in any application or proceeding.	On making the application.	1 0 0
6	Application to rectify an error or omission in the register of plant varieties.	On making the application.	1 0 0
7	Application for extension of time for the service or delivery of a document or thing or for the doing of an act.	On making the application.	1 0 0
8	Making representations in writing to the Controller, by any person other than the applicant, in connection with any application.	On delivering the representations.	10 0
9	Making representations in writing to the Controller, by any person other than the holder of plant breeders' rights in connection with a proposal to terminate those rights or to revoke or terminate any extension of such rights.	On delivering the representations.	10 0
10	On attending to be heard by the Controller or by a person appointed by him for the purpose.	Before the hearing.	5 0 0
11	The grant of plant breeders' rights	Before the issue of the document constituting evidence of the grant.	20 0 0
12	The grant of an extension of the period for which plant breeders' rights are exercisable.	Before the issue of the document constituting evidence of the extension.	10 0 0

SCHEDULE 2—Continued

No.	Matter	When Payable	Amount
			£ s. d.
13	The giving of a protective direction.	Before the issue of the document constituting evidence of the giving of the protective direction.	3 0 0
14	Continuance of the exercise of plant breeders' rights.	Annually on, but not more than three months before, the anniversary of the grant of plant breeders' rights or within such later period as may have been allowed.	25 0 0
15	Application for an extension of the period for payment of a renewal fee.	On making the application.	5 0 0
16	Payment of a renewal fee after the expiration of 7 days from the date when it fell due, except in a case where an application has been made for the period for payment to be extended.	On payment of the renewal fee.	2 10 0
17	Application for the approval of a substituted name for a plant variety.	On making the application.	5 0 0
18	Application for the amendment of the register of plant varieties, except in a case where the plant breeders' rights are transferred to another person.	On making the application.	1 0 0
19	Registration of title and amendment of the register of plant varieties on a transfer of plant breeders' rights or a share in such rights.	On making the application for registration.	5 0 0
20	Trials of a plant variety which is the subject of an application for a grant of plant breeders' rights, being	Within 14 days of demand made by the Controller, but on not more than one occasion in any year.	
	(a) a cereal variety		30 0 0
	(b) a potato variety		20 0 0
	(c) a rose variety		15 0 0
	(d) a dahlia variety		15 0 0
	(e) a perennial delphinium variety		15 0 0
	(f) a rhubarb variety		15 0 0
	(g) a strawberry variety		15 0 0

SCHEDULE 2—Continued

No.	Matter	When Payable	Amount
			£ s. d.
	(h) (i) an apple variety other than a variety of a rootstock of *Malus* spp.:—		
	(a) for each year before that in which one or more of the trees undergoing trials first comes into fruit		5 0 0
	(b) for each succeeding year		15 0 0
	(ii) an apple variety being a variety of a rootstock of *Malus* spp.		15 0 0
	(i) (i) a pear variety other than a variety of a rootstock of *Pyrus* spp.:—		
	(a) for each year before that in which one or more of the trees undergoing trials first comes into fruit		5 0 0
	(b) for each succeeding year		15 0 0
	(ii) a pear variety being a variety of a rootstock of *Pyrus* spp.		15 0 0
	(j) a pea variety		30 0 0
	(k) a French bean variety		30 0 0
	(l) a ryegrass variety		35 0 0
	(m) a lucerne variety		35 0 0
	(n) a rhododendron variety		15 0 0
	(o) a carnation variety		15 0 0
	(p) a perennial chrysanthemum variety		15 0 0
	(q) a black currant variety		15 0 0
	(r) a raspberry variety		15 0 0
	(s) a plum or damson variety other than a variety of a rootstock of the species *Prunus domestica*, *Prunus cerasifera* or *Prunus insititia* or of a hybrid derived from two or all of those species—		
	(a) for each year before that in which one or more of the trees undergoing trials first comes into fruit		5 0 0
	(b) for each succeeding year		15 0 0

SCHEDULE 2—Continued

No.	Matter	When Payable	Amount
			£ s. d.
	(*t*) a plum or damson variety, being a variety of a rootstock of the species *Prunus domestica, Prunus cerasifera* or *Prunus insititia* or of a hybrid derived from two or all of those species		15 0 0
21	Inspection of the register of plant varieties or of a document in the possession of the Controller.	Before the inspection.	5 0
22	Supplying copies of documents, (*a*) foolscap or smaller, per page (*b*) larger than foolscap, per page.	Before the delivery of the copies	1 0 1 6
23	Supplying a duplicate of a document constituting evidence of a grant of plant breeders' rights or protective direction or of an extension of the period for which plant breeders' rights are exercisable.	On ordering the duplicate.	2 0 0

EXPLANATORY NOTE

(This Note is not part of the Regulations.)

These Regulations, made under the Plant Varieties and Seeds Act 1964, prescribe the fees payable to the Controller of Plant Variety Rights in regard to matters arising out of the application for and granting of plant breeders' rights.

These Regulations consolidate, with amendments, the Plant Breeders' Rights (Fees) Regulations 1965, as already amended. The new amendments prescribe the fees payable for the trials of further plant varieties for which plant breeders' rights may be granted.

1968 No. 620

PLANT BREEDERS' RIGHTS

The Plant Breeders' Rights (Plums and Damsons) Scheme 1968

Made - - - -	*9th April* 1968
Laid before Parliament	*25th April* 1968
Coming into Operation	*26th April* 1968

The Minister of Agriculture, Fisheries and Food, the Secretary of State for Scotland and the Secretary of State for the Home Department (being the Secretary of State concerned with agriculture in Northern Ireland), acting jointly, in exercise of the powers conferred on them by sections 1, 3, 5 and 7 of, and paragraph 1 of Schedule 3 to, the Plant Varieties and Seeds Act 1964(a), as extended to Northern Ireland by the Plant Varieties and Seeds (Northern Ireland) Order 1964(b), and of all other powers enabling them in that behalf, after consultation with the Controller of Plant Variety Rights and with representatives of such interests as appear to them to be concerned, hereby make the following Scheme:—

Citation and Commencement

1. This Scheme may be cited as the Plant Breeders' Rights (Plums and Damsons) Scheme 1968 and shall come into operation on 26th April 1968.

Interpretation

2.—(1) In this Scheme, unless the context otherwise requires—
"the Act" means the Plant Varieties and Seeds Act 1964 as extended to Northern Ireland;
"the Controller" means the Controller of Plant Variety Rights;
"plant breeders' rights" means rights which may be granted in accordance with Part I of the Act;
"plant variety" means any clone, line, hybrid or genetic variant.

(2) The Interpretation Act 1889(c) shall apply to the interpretation of this Scheme as it applies to the interpretation of an Act of Parliament.

Plant Varieties for which Plant Breeders' Rights may be Granted

3. There are prescribed for the purposes of the grant of plant breeders' rights all plant varieties of plums which conform with the characteristics of cultivated plant varieties of the species *Prunus domestica* or *Prunus cerasifera*, all plant varieties of damsons, bullaces and mirabelles which conform with the characteristics of cultivated plant varieties of the species *Prunus insititia* and all plant varieties of plum and damson rootstocks of the species *Prunus domestica*, *Prunus cerasifera* or *Prunus insititia* including hybrids derived from any two or all of those species.

(a) 1964 c. 14.   (b) S.I. 1964/1574 (1964 III, p. 3543).   (c) 1889 c. 63.

Period for which Rights are Exercisable

4. The period for which plant breeders' rights shall be exercisable in respect of the plant varieties referred to in the last preceding paragraph shall be 25 years.

Class of Plant Varieties for the Purposes of Section 5(7) of the Act

5. In relation to the plant varieties referred to in paragraph 3 of this Scheme, the class of plant varieties prescribed for the purposes of section 5(7) of the Act (which enables classes of plant varieties to be prescribed in connection with the use of names likely to deceive or cause confusion) consists of all plant varieties of plums, damsons, bullaces and mirabelles and of plum and damson rootstocks.

Period Prescribed for the Purposes of Section 7(2) of the Act

6. In relation to the plant varieties referred to in paragraph 3 of this Scheme, the period prescribed for the purposes of section 7(2) of the Act (which enables a provision to be made whereby a compulsory licence granted by the Controller as respects a plant variety of a species or group specified in a scheme shall not have effect for a prescribed period after the grant of rights in that plant variety) shall be 3 years.

Additional Rights

7. Plant breeders' rights exercisable in respect of the plant varieties, other than plum and damson rootstocks, referred to in paragraph 3 of this Scheme shall include the exclusive right to produce or propagate and to authorise others to produce or propagate any such plant variety for the purpose of selling fruit of that plant variety.

In Witness whereof the official seal of the Minister of Agriculture, Fisheries and Food is hereunto affixed on 4th April 1968.

(L.S.)   *Frederick Peart,*
                               Minister of Agriculture, Fisheries and Food.

Given under the seal of the Secretary of State for Scotland on 8th April 1968.

(L.S.)   *William Ross,*
                               Secretary of State for Scotland.

Given under the hand of the Secretary of State for the Home Department on 9th April 1968.

                               James Callaghan,
                          Secretary of State for the Home Department.

EXPLANATORY NOTE

(This Note is not part of the Scheme.)

This Scheme, made under the Plant Varieties and Seeds Act 1964, prescribes the varieties of plums, damsons, bullaces and mirabelles and of plum and damson rootstocks in respect of which grants of plant breeders' rights may be made and also prescribes the period of 25 years as that during which the rights may be exercised.

The aforesaid Act, as read with this Scheme, provides that infringements of the rights in the registered name of a variety of plum, damson, bullace or mirabelle or plum and damson rootstock may be the subject of legal proceedings when committed in connection with any other variety of plum, damson, bullace or mirabelle or plum and damson rootstock.

This Scheme also provides that a compulsory licence granted by the Controller of Plant Variety Rights in respect of a variety of plum, damson, bullace or mirabelle or plum and damson rootstock shall not have effect during a period of 3 years from the date of the grant of rights in that variety.

Plant breeders' rights in respect of any variety of plum, damson, bullace or mirabelle to which the Scheme applies are extended to the production or propagation of the variety for the purpose of selling fruit.

STATUTORY INSTRUMENTS

1968 No. 621

PLANT BREEDERS' RIGHTS
The Plant Breeders' Rights (Black Currants) Scheme 1968

Made - - -	*9th April* 1968
Laid before Parliament	*25th April* 1968
Coming into Operation	*26th April* 1968

The Minister of Agriculture, Fisheries and Food, the Secretary of State for Scotland and the Secretary of State for the Home Department (being the Secretary of State concerned with agriculture in Northern Ireland), acting jointly, in exercise of the powers conferred on them by sections 1, 3 and 7 of, and paragraph 1 of Schedule 3 to, the Plant Varieties and Seeds Act 1964(a), as extended to Northern Ireland by the Plant Varieties and Seeds (Northern Ireland) Order 1964(b), and of all other powers enabling them in that behalf, after consultation with the Controller of Plant Variety Rights and with representatives of such interests as appear to them to be concerned, hereby make the following Scheme:—

Citation and Commencement

1. This Scheme may be cited as the Plant Breeders' Rights (Black Currants) Scheme 1968 and shall come into operation on 26th April 1968.

Interpretation

2.—(1) In this Scheme, unless the context otherwise requires—

"the Act" means the Plant Varieties and Seeds Act 1964 as extended to Northern Ireland;

"the Controller" means the Controller of Plant Variety Rights;

"plant breeders' rights" means rights which may be granted in accordance with Part I of the Act;

"plant variety" means any clone, line, hybrid or genetic variant.

(2) The Interpretation Act 1889(c) shall apply to the interpretation of this Scheme as it applies to the interpretation of an Act of Parliament.

Plant Varieties for which Plant Breeders' Rights may be Granted

3. There are prescribed for the purposes of the grant of plant breeders' rights all plant varieties of black currants which conform with the characteristics of cultivated plant varieties of the species *Ribes nigrum, Ribes ussuriense* and *Ribes dikuscha*.

Period for which Rights are Exercisable

4. The period for which plant breeders' rights shall be exercisable in respect of the plant varieties referred to in the last preceding paragraph shall be 20 years.

(a) 1964 c. 14. (b) S.I. 1964/1574 (1964 III, p. 3543). (c) 1889 c. 63.

Period Prescribed for the Purposes of Section 7(2) of the Act

5. In relation to the plant varieties referred to in paragraph 3 of this Scheme, the period prescribed for the purposes of section 7(2) of the Act (which enables a provision to be made whereby a compulsory licence granted by the Controller as respects a plant variety of a species or group specified in a scheme shall not have effect for a prescribed period after the grant of rights in that plant variety) shall be 2 years.

Additional Rights

6. Plant breeders' rights exercisable in respect of the plant varieties referred to in paragraph 3 of this Scheme shall include the exclusive right to produce or propagate and to authorise others to produce or propagate any such plant variety for the purpose of selling fruit of that plant variety.

In Witness whereof the Official Seal of the Minister of Agriculture, Fisheries and Food is hereunto affixed on 4th April 1968.

(L.S.)   *Frederick Peart,*
                    Minister of Agriculture, Fisheries and Food.

Given under the Seal of the Secretary of State for Scotland on 8th April 1968.
(L.S.)   *William Ross,*
                                  Secretary of State for Scotland.

Given under the hand of the Secretary of State for the Home Department on 9th April 1968.

James Callaghan,
                    Secretary of State for the Home Department.

EXPLANATORY NOTE
(*This Note is not part of the Scheme.*)

This Scheme, made under the Plant Varieties and Seeds Act 1964, prescribes the varieties of black currants in respect of which grants of plant breeders' rights may be made and also prescribes the period of 20 years as that during which the rights may be exercised.

This Scheme also provides that a compulsory licence granted by the Controller of Plant Variety Rights in respect of a variety of black currant shall not have effect during a period of 2 years from the date of the grant of rights in that variety.

Plant breeders' rights in respect of any variety of black currant to which the Scheme applies are extended to the production or propagation of the variety for the purpose of selling fruit.

STATUTORY INSTRUMENTS

1968 No. 622

PLANT BREEDERS' RIGHTS

The Plant Breeders' Rights (Amendment No. 2) Regulations 1968

Made - - -	*9th April* 1968
Laid before Parliament	*25th April* 1968
Coming into Operation	*26th April* 1968

The Minister of Agriculture, Fisheries and Food, the Secretary of State for Scotland and the Secretary of State for the Home Department (being the Secretary of State concerned with agriculture in Northern Ireland, acting jointly, in exercise of the powers vested in them by sections 9 and 36 of the Plant Varieties and Seeds Act 1964(a), as extended to Northern Ireland by the Plant Varieties and Seeds (Northern Ireland) Order 1964(b) and of all other powers enabling them in that behalf, hereby make the following Regulations:

Citation and Commencement

1.—(1) These Regulations may be cited as the Plant Breeders' Rights (Amendment No. 2) Regulations 1968 and shall come into operation on 26th April 1968.

(2) These Regulations shall be read as one with the Plant Breeders' Rights Regulations 1965(c), as amended(d) (hereinafter referred to as "the principal Regulations").

Amendment of Principal Regulations

2. The principal Regulations are hereby further amended as follows:

    (*a*) For paragraph (17) of Regulation 12 there shall be substituted the following paragraph:—

        "(17) The Controller shall publish in the gazette notice of his decision in respect of an application, from the decision upon which an appeal lies to the Tribunal, and of a proposal to terminate the period for which plant breeders' rights are exercisable or to revoke or, if it has begun, terminate any extension of such period."

    (*b*) At the end of Schedule 2 to those Regulations there shall be added 8 further Parts as follows:

"PART XV
RHODODENDRONS

Quantity

(1) *All varieties except varieties of azaleas to be flowered under glass*

Two visually healthy shrubs, typical of the variety, each at least 5 but not more than 7 years old, shall be delivered.

(2) *Varieties of azaleas to be flowered under glass*

Two visually healthy shrubs, typical of the variety, each at least 3 but not

---

(a) 1964 c. 14.   (b) S.I. 1964/1574 (1964 III, p. 3543).
(c) S.I. 1965/65 (1965 I, p. 96).   (d) S.I. 1967/1530, 1968/255 (1967 III, p. 4295; 1968 I, p.769).

more than 5 years old and each furnished with flower buds and all natural lateral growth, shall be delivered.

PART XVI
CARNATIONS

Quantity

(1) *Border carnations and pinks*

Nine visually healthy young plants, typical of the variety, shall be delivered.

(2) *Perpetual flowering carnations*

Seventy-five unrooted, visually healthy cuttings, each furnished with at least 4 but not more than 5 clearly visible internodes, shall be delivered.

PART XVII
PERENNIAL CHRYSANTHEMUMS

Quantity

(1) *Varieties to be flowered in the open*

Fourteen visually healthy rooted cuttings, typical of the variety, shall be delivered.

(2) *Varieties to be flowered under glass*

Twenty-five visually healthy rooted cuttings, typical of the variety, shall be delivered.

PART XVIII
BLACKCURRANTS

Quantity

Twelve visually healthy 2-year old bushes shall be delivered.

PART XIX
RASPBERRIES

Quantity

Twenty-five visually healthy canes shall be delivered.

PART XX
PLUMS AND DAMSONS

1. *Quantity*

Three trees on Myrobalan B or St. Julian A rootstocks shall be delivered. The trees shall not be less than 2 and not more than 3 years old. Alternatively, if the Controller shall so allow, scion or bud wood sufficient to produce 4 trees may be delivered instead of the 3 trees as mentioned above.

2. *Health*

    (1) *Complete trees*

        (*a*) The trees shall not show symptoms of any virus disease.

        (*b*) The trees shall be healthy. They shall not be lacking in vigour or affected by any pest or disease.

    (2) *Scion or bud wood*

    Scion or bud wood shall be the produce of a healthy tree of the variety which satisfies the requirements set out in paragraph 2(1)(*a*) and (*b*) above.

PART XXI
PLUM AND DAMSON ROOTSTOCKS

1. *Quantity*

Twenty-five well-rooted rootstocks of not less than 7 mm. in diameter selected from the stool or layer bed shall be delivered.

2. *Health*

    (*a*) The rootstocks shall not show symptoms of any virus disease.

    (*b*) The rootstocks shall be healthy. They shall not be lacking in vigour or affected by any pests or diseases.

PART XXII
PEAR ROOTSTOCKS

1. *Quantity*

Twenty-five well-rooted rootstocks of not less than 7 mm. in diameter selected from the stool or layer bed shall be delivered.

2. *Health*

    (*a*) The rootstocks shall not show symptoms of any virus disease.

    (*b*) The rootstocks shall be healthy. They shall not be lacking in vigour or affected by any pests or diseases."

In Witness whereof the official seal of the Minister of Agriculture, Fisheries and Food is hereunto affixed on 4th April 1968.

(L.S.)   *Frederick Peart,*

Minister of Agriculture, Fisheries and Food.

Given under the seal of the Secretary of State for Scotland on 8th April 1968.

(L.S.)   *William Ross,*

Secretary of State for Scotland.

Given under the hand of the Secretary of State for the Home Department on 9th April 1968.

James Callaghan,

Secretary of State for the Home Department.

EXPLANATORY NOTE

(This Note is not part of the Regulations.)

Schemes having been made to enable plant breeders' rights to be granted in respect of rhododendrons, carnations, chrysanthemums, black currants, raspberries, plums and damsons (with their rootstocks) and pear rootstocks, these Regulations amend the Plant Breeders' Rights Regulations 1965 to 1968 by specifying the reproductive and other plant material to be delivered accordingly to the Controller of Plant Variety Rights when an application is made for a grant of plant breeders' rights.

A minor amendment is also made in connection with the advertisement of certain decisions and proposals of the Controller of Plant Variety Rights.

STATUTORY INSTRUMENTS

1968 No. 623

PLANT BREEDERS' RIGHTS

The Plant Breeders' Rights (Rhododendrons) Scheme 1968

Made - - -	*9th April* 1968
Laid before Parliament	*25th April* 1968
Coming into Operation	*26th April* 1968

The Minister of Agriculture, Fisheries and Food, the Secretary of State for Scotland and the Secretary of State for the Home Department (being the Secretary of State concerned with agriculture in Northern Ireland), acting jointly, in exercise of the powers conferred on them by sections 1, 3 and 7 of the Plant Varieties and Seeds Act 1964(a), as extended to Northern Ireland by the Plant Varieties and Seeds (Northern Ireland) Order 1964(b) and of all other powers enabling them in that behalf, after consultation with the Controller of Plant Variety Rights and with representatives of such interests as appear to them to be concerned, hereby make the following Scheme :—

Citation and Commencement

1. This Scheme may be cited as the Plant Breeders' Rights (Rhododendrons) Scheme 1968 and shall come into operation on 26th April 1968.

Interpretation

2.—(1) In this Scheme, unless the context otherwise requires—

"the Act" means the Plant Varieties and Seeds Act 1964 as extended to Northern Ireland ;

"the Controller" means the Controller of Plant Variety Rights ;

"plant breeders' rights" means rights which may be granted in accordance with Part I of the Act ;

"plant variety" means any clone, line, hybrid or genetic variant.

(2) The Interpretation Act 1889(c) shall apply to the interpretation of this Scheme as it applies to the interpretation of an Act of Parliament.

Plant Varieties for which Plant Breeders' Rights may be granted

3. There are prescribed for the purposes of the grant of plant breeders' rights all plant varieties of rhododendrons, azaleas and azaleodendrons which conform with the characteristics of cultivated plant varieties of the genus *Rhododendron*.

Period for which Rights are Exercisable

4. The period for which plant breeders' rights shall be exercisable in respect of the plant varieties referred to in the last preceding paragraph shall be 20 years.

(a) 1964 c. 14.
(c) 1889 c. 63.

(b) S.I. 1964/1574 (1964 III, p. 3543).

Period Prescribed for the Purposes of Section 7(2) of the Act

5. In relation to the plant varieties referred to in paragraph 3 of this Scheme, the period prescribed for the purposes of section 7(2) of the Act (which enables a provision to be made whereby a compulsory licence granted by the Controller as respects a plant variety of a species or group specified in a scheme shall not have effect for a prescribed period after the grant of rights in that plant variety) shall be 3 years.

In Witness whereof the official seal of the Minister of Agriculture, Fisheries and Food is hereunto affixed on 4th April 1968.

(L.S.)   *Frederick Peart,*
Minister of Agriculture, Fisheries and Food.

Given under the seal of the Secretary of State for Scotland on 8th April 1968.

(L.S.)   *William Ross,*
Secretary of State for Scotland.

Given under the hand of the Secretary of State for the Home Department on 9th April 1968.

James Callaghan,
Secretary of State for the Home Department.

EXPLANATORY NOTE

(This Note is not part of the Scheme.)

This Scheme, made under the Plant Varieties and Seeds Act 1964, prescribes the varieties of rhododendrons, azaleas and azaleodendrons in respect of which grants of plant breeders' rights may be made and also prescribes the period of 20 years as that during which the rights may be exercised.

This Scheme also provides that a compulsory licence granted by the Controller of Plant Variety Rights in respect of a variety of rhododendron, azalea or azaleodendron shall not have effect during a period of 3 years from the date of the grant of rights in that variety.

STATUTORY INSTRUMENTS

1968 No. 624

PLANT BREEDERS' RIGHTS

The Plant Breeders' Rights (Carnations) Scheme 1968

Made - - -	*9th April* 1968
Laid before Parliament	*25th April* 1968
Coming into Operation	*26th April* 1968

The Minister of Agriculture, Fisheries and Food, the Secretary of State for Scotland and the Secretary of State for the Home Department (being the Secretary of State concerned with agriculture in Northern Ireland), acting jointly, in exercise of the powers conferred on them by sections 1 and 3 of, and paragraph 1 of Schedule 3 to, the Plant Varieties and Seeds Act 1964(a), as extended to Northern Ireland by the Plant Varieties and Seeds (Northern Ireland) Order 1964(b), and of all other powers enabling them in that behalf, after consultation with the Controller of Plant Variety Rights and with representatives of such interests as appear to them to be concerned, hereby make the following Scheme :—

Citation and Commencement

1. This Scheme may be cited as the Plant Breeders' Rights (Carnations) Scheme 1968 and shall come into operation on 26th April 1968.

Interpretation

2.—(1) In this Scheme, unless the context otherwise requires—

"the Act" means the Plant Varieties and Seeds Act 1964 as extended to Northern Ireland ;

"plant breeders' rights" means rights which may be granted in accordance with Part I of the Act ;

"plant variety" means any clone, line, hybrid or genetic variant.

(2) The Interpretation Act 1889(c) shall apply to the interpretation of this Scheme as it applies to the interpretation of an Act of Parliament.

Plant Varieties for which Plant Breeders' Rights may be granted

3. There are prescribed for the purposes of the grant of plant breeders' rights all plant varieties of carnations and pinks which conform with the characteristics of cultivated plant varieties of the genus *Dianthus* excluding the species *Dianthus barbatus*.

Period for which Rights are Exercisable

4. The period for which plant breeders' rights shall be exercisable in respect of the plant varieties referred to in the last preceding paragraph shall be 15 years.

(a) 1964 c. 14.　　　　　　(b) S.I. 1964/1574 (1964 III, p. 3543).
(c) 1889 c. 63.

Additional Rights

5. Plant breeders' rights exercisable in respect of the plant varieties referred to in paragraph 3 of this Scheme shall include the exclusive right to produce or propagate and to authorise others to produce or propagate any such plant variety for the purpose of selling cut blooms of that plant variety.

In Witness whereof the official seal of the Minister of Agriculture, Fisheries and Food is hereunto affixed on 4th April 1968.

(L.S.)   *Frederick Peart,*
                         Minister of Agriculture, Fisheries and Food.

Given under the seal of the Secretary of State for Scotland on 8th April 1968.

(L.S.)   *William Ross,*
                         Secretary of State for Scotland.

Given under the hand of the Secretary of State for the Home Department on 9th April 1968.

                           James Callaghan,
                         Secretary of State for the Home Department.

EXPLANATORY NOTE

(This Note is not part of the Scheme.)

This Scheme, made under the Plant Varieties and Seeds Act 1964, prescribes the varieties of carnations and pinks in respect of which grants of plant breeders' rights may be made and also prescribes the period of 15 years as that during which the rights may be exercised.

Plant breeders' rights in respect of any variety of carnation or pink to which the Scheme applies are extended to the production or propagation of the variety for the purpose of selling cut blooms.

STATUTORY INSTRUMENTS

1968 No. 626

WAGES COUNCILS

The Wages Regulation (Hollow-ware) Order 1968

Made - - -	16*th April* 1968
Coming into Operation	6*th May* 1968

Whereas the Minister of Labour (hereafter in this Order referred to as "the Minister") has received from the Hollow-ware Wages Council (Great Britain) the wages regulation proposals set out in Schedules 1 and 2 hereof ;

Now, therefore, the Minister by virtue of the powers conferred on her by section 11 of the Wages Councils Act 1959(a), and of all other powers enabling her in that behalf, hereby makes the following Order : —

1. This Order may be cited as the Wages Regulation (Hollow-ware) Order 1968.

2.—(1) In this Order the expression "the specified date" means the 6th May 1968, provided that where, as respects any worker who is paid wages at intervals not exceeding seven days, that date does not correspond with the beginning of the period for which the wages are paid, the expression "the specified date" means, as respects that worker, the beginning of the next such period following that date.

(2) The Interpretation Act 1889(b) shall apply to the interpretation of this Order as it applies to the interpretation of an Act of Parliament and as if this Order and the Order hereby revoked were Acts of Parliament.

3. The wages regulation proposals set out in Schedules 1 and 2 hereof shall have effect as from the specified date and as from that date the Wages Regulation (Hollow-ware) Order 1967(c) shall cease to have effect.

Signed by order of the Minister of Labour.

D. C. Barnes,
Secretary,
Ministry of Labour.

16th April 1968.

(a) 1959 c. 69.   (b) 1889 c. 63.
(c) S.I. 1967/1198 (1967 II, p. 3506).

SCHEDULE 1

The following minimum remuneration shall be substituted for the statutory minimum remuneration fixed by the Wages Regulation (Hollow-ware) Order 1967(a) (Order H.(94)).

STATUTORY MINIMUM REMUNERATION
PART I
GENERAL

1. The minimum remuneration payable to a worker to whom this Schedule applies for all work except work to which a minimum overtime rate applies under Part IV is:—

(1) in the case of a time worker, the general minimum time rate payable to the worker under Part II or Part III of this Schedule ;

(2) in the case of a worker employed on piece work, piece rates each of which would yield, in the circumstances of the case, to an ordinary worker at least the same amount of money as the piece work basis time rate applicable to the worker under Part II or Part III of this Schedule.

PART II
MALE WORKERS
TIME WORKERS

2. The general minimum time rates payable to male time workers are as follows:—

	General minimum time rates per hour
	s. d.
(1) Workers aged 21 years or over and employed in the enamel ware section of the trade as—	
(a) Fusers' helpers who work in association with fusers	
(b) Annealers, or	5 7¼
(c) Scalers	
(2) All other workers except learners	5 5¼
(3) Learners, being aged—	
20 and under 21 years	4 6⅛
19 ,, ,, 20 ,,	3 8⅞
18 ,, ,, 19 ,,	3 3⅝
17 ,, ,, 18 ,,	2 9¼
16 ,, ,, 17 ,,	2 3¼
under 16 years	1 11⅛

Provided that the general minimum time rate otherwise payable to a learner who enters, or has entered, the trade for the first time when aged not less than 17 but less than 21 years shall, during his first 12 months' employment in the trade or until he attains the age of 21 years, whichever period is the lesser, be reduced as follows:—

(a) during the first six months of such employment or until he attains the age of 21 years, whichever period is the lesser, by 1d. per hour ;

(b) during the second six months of such employment or until he attains the age of 21 years, whichever period is the lesser, by ½d. per hour.

(a) S.I. 1967/1198 (1967 II, p. 3506).

PIECE WORKERS

3. The piece work basis time rates applicable to male piece workers are as follows:—

	Piece work basis time rates per hour
	s. d.
(1) Workers (other than learners) employed—	
(a) as fusers' helpers or dippers in the enamel ware section of the trade .. .. }	5 7¾
(b) otherwise than as such fusers' helpers or dippers .. }	
(2) Learners employed—	
(a) as fusers' helpers or dippers in the enamel ware section of the trade, being aged—	
20 and under 21 years	4 8¼
19 " " 20 "	3 10¾
18 " " 19 "	3 5¼
17 " " 18 "	2 10½
16 " " 17 "	2 5
under 16 years	1 11⅞
(b) otherwise than as such fusers' helpers or dippers, being aged—	
20 and under 21 years	4 8
19 " " 20 "	3 10¾
18 " " 19 "	3 4⅝
17 " " 18 "	2 10⅜
16 " " 17 "	2 5
under 16 years	1 10⅝

Part III

FEMALE WORKERS

TIME WORKERS

4. The general minimum time rates payable to female time workers are as follows:—

	General minimum time rates per hour	
	s.	d.
(1) Workers other than learners	4	6¼
(2) Learners, being aged—		
17 and under 18 years	3	9⅛
16 „ „ 17 „	2	8⅝
under 16 years	2	3½
Provided that the general minimum time rates payable during her first 12 months' employment in the trade to a learner who enters, or has entered, the trade for the first time at or over the age of 16 years shall be—		
during the first six months of such employment	2	2¾
during the second six months of such employment	2	3½

PIECE WORKERS

5. The piece work basis time rates applicable to female piece workers are as follows:—

	Piece work basis time rates per hour	
	s.	d.
(1) Workers other than learners	4	7½
(2) Learners, being aged—		
17 and under 18 years	3	10⅜
16 „ „ 17 „	2	11⅜
under 16 years	2	4⅛
Provided that the piece work basis time rates applicable during her first 12 months' employment in the trade to a learner who enters, or has entered, the trade for the first time at or over the age of 16 years shall be—		
during the first six months of such employment	2	3⅜
during the second six months of such employment	2	4¼

PART IV

OVERTIME AND WAITING TIME

MINIMUM OVERTIME RATES

6.—(1) The following minimum overtime rates are payable to all workers other than male workers employed as fusers' helpers, dippers, annealers or scalers in the enamel ware section of the trade:—

(a) on a Sunday or a customary holiday—
for all time worked .. .. double time

(b) on a Saturday, not being a customary holiday—
for all time worked in excess of 4 hours .. time-and-a-half

(c) in any week exclusive of any time in respect of which a minimum overtime rate is payable under the foregoing provisions of this sub-paragraph—
for all time worked in excess of 40 hours .. time-and-a-quarter

(2) The following minimum overtime rates are payable to male workers employed as fusers' helpers, dippers, annealers or scalers in the enamel ware section of the trade:—

(a) on a Sunday or a customary holiday—
for all time worked in excess of 2 hours .. double time

(b) in any week exclusive of any time in respect of which double time is payable under (a) of this sub-paragraph—
for all time worked in excess of 40 hours .. time-and-a-quarter

7. In this Part of this Schedule,

(1) the expression "customary holiday" means:—

(a) (i) in England and Wales—

Christmas Day (or, if Christmas Day falls on a Sunday, such week-day as may be appointed by national proclamation, or, if none is so appointed, the next following Tuesday), Boxing Day, Good Friday, Easter Monday, Whit Monday (or where another day is substituted therefor by national proclamation, that day), August Bank Holiday and two other days (being days on which the worker normally works) in the course of a calendar year, to be fixed by the employer and notified to the worker not less than three weeks before the holiday ;

(ii) in Scotland—

New Year's Day (or, if New Year's Day falls on a Sunday, the following Monday); the local Spring holiday, the local Autumn holiday ; and five other days (being days on which the worker normally works) in the course of a calendar year, to be fixed by the employer and notified to the worker not less than three weeks before the holiday ;

or (b) in the case of each of the said days (other than a day fixed by the employer and notified to the worker as aforesaid), a day substituted therefor, being either a day recognised by local custom as a day of holiday in substitution for the said day, or a day fixed by agreement between the employer and the worker or his agent.

(2) the expressions "time-and-a-quarter", "time-and-a-half" and "double time" mean respectively—

(a) in the case of a time worker, one and a quarter times, one and a half times and twice the general minimum time rate otherwise payable to the worker ;

(b) in the case of a piece worker, such piece rates as would each yield respectively, in the circumstances of the case, to an ordinary worker at least the same amount of money as one and a quarter times, one and a half times and twice the piece work basis time rate otherwise applicable to the worker.

WAITING TIME

8.—(1) A worker is entitled to payment of the minimum remuneration specified in this Schedule for all time during which he is present on the premises of his employer, unless he is present thereon in any of the following circumstances : —

(a) without the employer's consent, express or implied ;

(b) for some purpose unconnected with his work and other than that of waiting for work to be given to him to perform ;

(c) by reason only of the fact that he is resident thereon ;

(d) during normal meal times in a room or place in which no work is being done and he is not waiting for work to be given to him to perform.

(2) The minimum remuneration payable under sub-paragraph (1) of this paragraph to a piece worker when not engaged in piece work, is that which would be payable if the worker were a time worker.

PART V

INTERPRETATION

9. In this Schedule the expression "learner" means : —

(1) in the case of a male worker, a worker aged under 21 years and employed under conditions which, in the circumstances of the case, afford a reasonable prospect of advancement to the position of a worker other than a learner ;

(2) in the case of a female worker, a worker aged under 18 years, or a worker aged 18 years or over having less than 12 months' experience in the trade, the worker being employed in either case under conditions which, in the circumstances of the case, afford a reasonable prospect of advancement to the position of a worker other than a learner.

APPLICABILITY OF STATUTORY MINIMUM REMUNERATION

10.—(1) This Schedule does not apply to workers employed as watchmen, but save as aforesaid applies to workers in relation to whom the Hollow-ware Wages Council (Great Britain) operates, that is to say, workers employed in Great Britain in the operations in the Hollow-ware Branch of the Hollow-ware Making trade specified in the Schedule to the Trade Boards (Hollow-ware Trade, Great Britain) (Constitution and Proceedings) Regulations 1937(a), namely : —

(a) all work in connection with—

(i) the manufacture from sheet iron or sheet steel (hereinafter called black plate) of articles of hollow-ware or parts thereof ;

(ii) the manufacture of baths and dustbins from black plate or from black plate coated with any metal, of an average thickness not exceeding .0392 of an inch (20 Birmingham Gauge);

(iii) the manufacture from any iron or steel of forged, stamped or pressed mountings or fittings or parts thereof, for articles specified in (a) (i) and (ii) of this sub-paragraph when done by workers wholly or mainly so engaged, or in association or conjunction with the manufacture specified in (a) (i) and (ii) of this sub-paragraph ;

(a) S.R. & O. 1937/325 (1937, p. 2335).

(b) all work in connection with—

    (i) the manufacture of kegs, drums, tapers, taper-necked cans and painters' pots, or parts thereof;

        from black plate of an average thickness less than .125 of an inch (10 Birmingham Gauge), or

        from black plate coated with any metal and of an average thickness exceeding .01745 of an inch (27 Birmingham Gauge) but less than .125 of an inch (10 Birmingham Gauge),

        and the repair thereof;

        when done in a department mainly engaged on work specified in (a) of this sub-paragraph;

    (ii) the manufacture from any iron or steel of forged, stamped or pressed mountings or fittings, or parts thereof, for the articles to the manufacture or repair of which (b) (i) of this sub-paragraph applies.

(2) Work in connection with the manufacture specified in sub-paragraph (1) of this paragraph includes—

    (a) finishing;

    (b) the work of persons employed in the factory or workshop in counting or weighing materials handed to workers and articles or parts thereof received from workers;

    (c) packing, warehousing, despatching, the work of inside messengers, yard-workers and stokers and work of a similar nature.

(3) Notwithstanding anything in this paragraph the following operations are not operations in the Hollow-ware branch of the Hollow-ware making trade:—

    (a) work specified in sub-paragraph (1) of this paragraph when performed in an establishment, branch or department mainly engaged on other work and in which the jointing and finishing of the articles or parts of articles specified in sub-paragraph (1) of this paragraph are done by workers mainly employed in jointing and finishing other articles;

    (b) finishing (other than enamelling) when performed in a department mainly engaged in the finishing of articles other than articles specified in sub-paragraph (1) of this paragraph and in which no manufacture specified in sub-paragraph (1) of this paragraph is carried on;

    (c) packing, warehousing, despatching, the work of inside messengers, yard-workers and stokers, and work of a similar nature when performed in an establishment not otherwise engaged in operations in the hollow-ware branch of the hollow-ware making trade;

    (d) the manufacture of baths or dustbins from black plate or from black plate coated with any metal, of an average thickness exceeding .0392 of an inch (20 Birmingham Gauge);

    (e) the manufacture referred to in (a) (ii) of sub-paragraph (1) of this paragraph in an establishment, branch or department mainly engaged in the operations specified in (d) of this sub-paragraph or in operations other than those specified in sub-paragraph (1) of this paragraph or both in such operations and such manufacture;

    (f) the manufacture of component parts of motor vehicles, motor plants, aircraft, cycles or motor cycles;

    (g) the manufacture of any article or part of any article when made in an establishment mainly engaged in the manufacture of motor vehicles, motor plants, aircraft, cycles or motor cycles or of component parts thereof;

    (h) all clerical work other than work specified in (b) of sub-paragraph (2) of this paragraph;

(*i*) the manufacture of tin rollers, tin roller drums, card cases, coiler cans and other articles for use with textile or other machinery ;

(*j*) all work in connection with the maintenance or upkeep of premises, machinery or plant ;

(*k*) all work included under the Trade Boards (Keg and Drum Trade, Great Britain) (Constitution and Proceedings) Regulations 1928(**a**) ;

(*l*) all work included under the Trade Boards (Tin Box Trade, Great Britain) (Constitution and Proceedings) Regulations 1928(**b**).

(4) The expression "finishing" includes operations of coating (including the processes of galvanising, tinning, enamelling, painting, japanning, lacquering and varnishing), polishing and cleaning articles.

SCHEDULE 2

HOLIDAYS AND HOLIDAY REMUNERATION

The Wages Regulation (Hollow-ware) (Holidays) Order 1966(**c**) (Order H. (92)) shall have effect as if in the Schedule thereto for sub-paragraph (2) (*a*) (i) of paragraph 2 (which relates to customary holidays) there were substituted the following :—

"(2) The said customary holidays are : —

(*a*) (i) in England and Wales—

Christmas Day (or, if Christmas Day falls on a Sunday, such week-day as may be appointed by national proclamation, or, if none is so appointed, the next following Tuesday), Boxing Day, Good Friday, Easter Monday, Whit Monday (or where another day is substituted therefor by national proclamation, that day), August Bank Holiday and two other days (being days on which the worker normally works) in the course of a calendar year, to be fixed by the employer and notified to the worker not less than three weeks before the holiday ;"

EXPLANATORY NOTE

(*This Note is not part of the Order.*)

This Order has effect from 6th May 1968. Schedule 1 sets out the statutory minimum remuneration payable in substitution for that fixed by the Wages Regulation (Hollow-ware) Order 1967 (Order H.(94)), which Order is revoked. Schedule 2 repeats without alteration the amendment to the Wages Regulation (Hollow-ware) (Holidays) Order 1966 (Order H.(92)), contained in (H.(94)).

New provisions are printed in italics.

(**a**) S.R. & O. 1928/844 (1928, p. 1276).   (**b**) S.R. & O. 1928/847 (1928, p. 1289).
(**c**) S.I. 1966/669 (1966 II, p. 1506).

STATUTORY INSTRUMENTS

1968 No. 639 (S.60)

SHERIFF COURT, SCOTLAND

SITTINGS AND DISTRIBUTION OF BUSINESS

The Sheriff Courts (Peterhead) Order 1968

Made - - -	*19th April* 1968
Coming into Operation	*3rd May* 1968

In exercise of the powers conferred on him by sections 18 and 19 of the Sheriff Courts (Scotland) Act 1907(a), as read with the Secretaries of State Act 1926(b), the Secretary of State hereby orders as follows:—

1. This order may be cited as the Sheriff Courts (Peterhead) Order 1968 and shall come into operation on 3rd May 1968.

2. Without prejudice to anything duly done under the order by The Right Honourable Sir William Vernon Harcourt, one of Her Majesty's Principal Secretaries of State dated 10th June 1885 so much of that order as directs that Courts shall be held at Peterhead and Fraserburgh on stated days is hereby revoked and shall cease to have effect as from the date of the coming into operation of this order.

3. Ordinary Courts and Small Debt Courts shall be held at Peterhead on Friday of each week.

4. This order shall be recorded in the Sheriff Court Books at Peterhead and shall be intimated on the walls of the Sheriff Court House there.

Given under the seal of the Secretary of State for Scotland.

(L.S.)

H. H. A. Whitworth,
Under Secretary.

Scottish Home and Health Department,
St. Andrew's House,
Edinburgh, 1.
19th April 1968.

(a) 1907 c. 51.　　　　　　　　　　　　　　(b) 1926 c. 18.

STATUTORY   INSTRUMENTS

1968 No. 641

CUSTOMS AND EXCISE

The Import Duties (Temporary Exemptions) (No. 2) Order 1968

Made - - - -	*22nd April* 1968
Laid before the House of Commons	*26th April* 1968
Coming into Operation	*2nd May* 1968

The Lords Commissioners of Her Majesty's Treasury, by virtue of the powers conferred on them by sections 3(6) and 13 of the Import Duties Act 1958(a), and of all other powers enabling them in that behalf, on the recommendation of the Board of Trade hereby make the following Order:—

1.—(1) Until the beginning of 1st January 1969 or, in the case of goods in relation to which an earlier day is specified in Schedule 1 to this Order, until the beginning of that day, any import duty which is for the time being chargeable on goods of a heading of the Customs Tariff 1959 specified in that Schedule shall not be chargeable in respect of goods of any description there specified in relation to that heading.

(2) The period for which the goods of the headings of the Customs Tariff 1959 and descriptions specified in Schedule 2 to this Order are exempt from import duty shall be extended until the beginning of 1st January 1969, or in the case of goods in relation to which an earlier day is specified in that Schedule, until the beginning of that day.

(3) Any entry in column 2 in Schedule 1 or 2 to this Order is to be taken to comprise all goods which would be classified under an entry in the same terms constituting a subheading (other than the final subheading) in the relevant heading in the Customs Tariff 1959.

(4) For the purposes of classification under the Customs Tariff 1959, in so far as that depends on the rate of duty, any goods to which paragraph (1) or (2) above applies shall be treated as chargeable with the same duty as if this Order had not been made.

2.—(1) This Order may be cited as the Import Duties (Temporary Exemptions) (No. 2) Order 1968.

(2) The Interpretation Act 1889(b) shall apply for the interpretation of this Order as it applies for the interpretation of an Act of Parliament.

(3) This Order shall come into operation on 2nd May 1968.

Joseph Harper,
J. McCann,
Two of the Lords Commissioners
of Her Majesty's Treasury.

22nd April 1968.

(a) 1958 c. 6.   (b) 1889 c. 63.

SCHEDULE 1

Goods Temporarily Exempt from Import Duty

Tariff Heading	Description
28.38	Thallous sulphate
28.47	Sodium tungstate containing not more than 0·0003 per cent. by weight of arsenic compounds calculated as As and not more than 0·005 per cent. by weight of molybdenum compounds calculated as Mo
29.01	Nonane
29.02	Benzotrifluoride
29.03	Sodium 2-bromoethanesulphonate
29.08	2-[2,2-Di-(2-hydroxyethoxymethyl)butoxy]ethanol
29.13	$3H,3H$-Hexafluoroacetylacetone
29.14	3-(2-Chloroethoxy)-9α-fluoro-11β,21-dihydroxy-20-oxo-16α,17α-*iso*propylidenedioxypregna-3,5-diene-6-carbaldehyde 21-acetate (until 5th September 1968)
	Vinyl chloroacetate
29.22	1,6-Diaminotrimethylhexane, mixed 2,2,4- and 2,4,4- isomers
29.25	N-(3-Chloro-*p*-tolyl)-2-methylvaleramide
29.27	Cyanoacetamide
	Methacrylonitrile
29.29	Benzylideneaminoguanidinium tartrate
29.31	Di-(4-chlorophenyl) sulphone
29.35	Acetoguanamine
	Clorazepic acid, dipotassium salt
	Methyl 7-diethylamino-4-hydroxy-6-propylquinoline-3-carboxylate
29.36	5-Chloroaniline-2,4-disulphonamide
29.43	Fructose tetranicotinate, mixed isomers
70.18	Optical glass in the form of sheets, slabs or moulded lens blanks, having, with reference to the D line of sodium, a refractive index (n_D) not less than 1·5625 and not greater than 1·5650 and a dispersive power (v_D) not less than 60·0 and not greater than 61·5
83.13	Tinplate caps for sealing jars, of an internal diameter on the rim of not less than 1·580 inches and not more than 1·610 inches and a maximum depth of not less than 0·415 inch and not more than 0·425 inch stamped from tinplate of nominal thickness of 0·0066 inch, with an internal curl, a vinyl coating applied to the internal surface and a plasticised lining compound deposited on the internal side wall and top sealing panel to form a sealing gasket
90·01	Lenses, prisms, mirrors and other optical elements, not optically worked, of thallium bromide-iodide

SCHEDULE 2

Tariff Heading	*Description*
27.07	Naphthalene (until 4th July 1968)
28.18	Barium oxide (until 4th July 1968)
28.39	Nickel nitrate (until 7th November 1968)
29.01	Biphenyl (until 4th July 1968) Naphthalene (until 4th July 1968)
29.04	Tridecyl alcohol, mixed isomers (until 4th July 1968)
29.13	Indanetrione hydrate (until 4th July 1968)

29.14	Chloroacetyl chloride
	Palmitoyl chloride containing
	   (*a*) not more than 100 parts per million by weight of phosphorus compounds calculated as P,
	   (*b*) not more than 100 parts per million by weight of sulphur compounds calculated as S, and
	   (*c*) not more than 10 parts per million by weight of heavy metals calculated as Pb (until 4th July 1968)

29.15	Dimethyl adipate (until 4th July 1968) Phthalic anhydride (until 4th July 1968)
29.16	Ethyl sodioacetoacetate (until 7th November 1968)
29.22	*N*-2-Amino-3,5-dibromobenzyl-*N*-cyclohexylmethylammonium chloride
29.25	α-Chloro-*N*-*iso*propylacetanilide (until 4th July 1968) 3,4,4′-Trichloro-*NN*′-diphenylurea (until 4th July 1968)
76.16	Aluminium can ends, having a diameter of not less than 2·9 inches nor more than 3 inches, and incorporating a riveted tab for opening along scored lines (until 4th July 1968)

EXPLANATORY NOTE

(*This Note is not part of the Order.*)

This Order provides that the goods listed in Schedule 1 shall be temporarily exempt from import duty, and those listed in Schedule 2 shall continue to be exempt from import duty, both until 1st January 1969, except for items for which an earlier day is specified.

STATUTORY INSTRUMENTS

1968 No. 642

CUSTOMS AND EXCISE

The Import Duties (General) (No. 2) Order 1968

Made - - - -	*22nd April* 1968
Laid before the	
House of Commons	*26th April* 1968
Coming into Operation	*2nd May* 1968

The Lords Commissioners of Her Majesty's Treasury, by virtue of the powers conferred on them by sections 1, 2 and 13 of the Import Duties Act 1958(a), and of all other powers enabling them in that behalf, on the recommendation of the Board of Trade hereby make the following Order:—

1. Schedule 1 to the Import Duties (General) (No. 11) Order 1966(b) (which Schedule by reference to the Customs Tariff 1959 sets out the import duties chargeable under the Import Duties Act 1958) shall be amended in accordance with the Schedule to this Order.

2.—(1) This Order may be cited as the Import Duties (General) (No. 2) Order 1968.

(2) The Interpretation Act 1889(c) shall apply for the interpretation of this Order as it applies for the interpretation of an Act of Parliament.

(3) This Order shall come into operation on 2nd May 1968.

B. K. O'Malley,

J. McCann,

Two of the Lords Commissioners
of Her Majesty's Treasury,

22nd April 1968.

(a) 1958 c. 6.   (b) S.I. 1966/1555 (1956 III, p. 4405).   (c) 1889 c. 63.

SCHEDULE

AMENDMENTS OF IMPORT DUTIES (GENERAL) (No. 11) ORDER 1966

1. In heading 12.07, in subheading (A), the following shall be inserted in the appropriate alphabetical positions:—

Agrimony herb
Aletris root
Angelica root
Balmony herb and leaves
Bayberry bark
Belladonna herb and leaves
Beth root
Black cohosh root
Black haw bark
Blue cohosh root
Blood root
Boneset herb
Calamus rhizome
Comfrey leaves and roots
Cubeb berries

Drosera
Echinacea root
Elder leaves and flowers
Euonymus bark
Fringe tree bark
Galanga root
Henbane (Hyoscyamus niger)
Lavender flowers
Lime tree flowers
Marshmallow leaves and roots
Nux vomica seeds
Pleurisy root
Prickly ash bark and berries
Quince seeds
Rhus aromaticus bark

2. In heading 13.02, in subheading (B), there shall be inserted in the appropriate alphabetical position the words " gum euphorbium ".

EXPLANATORY NOTE

(This Note is not part of the Order.)

This Order removes the import duty on certain plants and parts of plants primarily used in the production of medicinal preparations, and on gum euphorbium.

STATUTORY INSTRUMENTS

1968 No. 643

CUSTOMS AND EXCISE

The Import Duties (General) (No. 3) Order 1968

Made - - - -	*22nd April* 1968
Laid before the	
House of Commons -	*26th April* 1968
Coming into Operation -	*2nd May* 1968

The Lords Commissioners of Her Majesty's Treasury by virtue of the powers conferred on them by sections 1, 2 and 13 of the Import Duties Act 1958(a), and of all other powers enabling them in that behalf, on the recommendation of the Board of Trade hereby make the following Order:—

1. Schedule 1 to the Import Duties (General) (No. 11) Order 1966(b) (which Schedule by reference to the Customs Tariff 1959 sets out the import duties chargeable under the Import Duties Act 1958) shall be amended as follows—

(*a*) in subheading (B)(3) of heading 37.07 (film of a width of 16 millimetres, with double perforation but without sound track of any description), after " 16 millimetres " there shall be inserted " bearing not more than one frame across the width ";

(*b*) in the Notes to Chapter 27, for special note (*b*), there shall be inserted the following—

" (*b*) ' light oils ' has the meaning given by section 195(1) of the Customs and Excise Act 1952 as for the time being in force."

2.—(1) This Order may be cited as the Import Duties (General) (No. 3) Order 1968.

(2) The Interpretation Act 1889(c) shall apply for the interpretation of this Order as it applies for the interpretation of an Act of Parliament.

(3) This Order shall come into operation on 2nd May 1968.

B. K. O'Malley,
J. McCann,
Two of the Lords Commissioners
of Her Majesty's Treasury.

22nd April 1968.

(a) 1958 c. 6.   (b) S.I. 1966/1555 (1966 III, p. 4405).   (c) 1889 c. 63.

EXPLANATORY NOTE

(This Note is not part of the Order.)

This Order re-imposes an import duty of 1d. per linear foot (full rate), 2/9ths. of 1d. per linear foot (Commonwealth Preference Area rate) and NIL (E.F.T.A. and Irish Republic rates) on cinematograph film of a width of 16 millimetres bearing two positive prints, each of 8 millimetres, across the width.

It also redefines the term " light oils " to bring the definition for import duty purposes into line with that already applied to revenue duties by an amendment made in the Finance Act 1967 (Section 1(5) and Schedule 5).

STATUTORY INSTRUMENTS

1968 No. 644

CUSTOMS AND EXCISE

The Import Duty Drawbacks (No. 4) Order 1968

Made - - - -	*22nd April* 1968
Laid before the House of Commons	*26th April* 1968
Coming into Operation	*2nd May* 1968

The Lords Commissioners of Her Majesty's Treasury, by virtue of the powers conferred on them by sections 9 and 13 of, and Schedule 5 to, the Import Duties Act 1958(a), and section 2(5) of the Finance Act 1965(b), and of all other powers enabling them in that behalf, on the recommendation of the Board of Trade hereby make the following Order:—

1.—(1) Schedule 2 to the Import Duty Drawbacks (No. 6) Order 1966(c) (which relates to the drawbacks to be allowed on the exportation of goods produced or manufactured from imported articles) shall be amended as follows—

(a) in the entry relating to fruit cakes and other goods made with dried fruit, the rates of drawback specified in column 3 shall be omitted;

(b) in the entry beginning " Linseed oil ", the rate of drawback specified in column 3 against paragraph 2 (being a rate inserted by paragraph 2(1)(b) of the Schedule to the Import Duty Drawbacks (No. 2) Order 1968(d)) shall be omitted;

(c) in the entry relating to sugar refined in the United Kingdom, there shall be added after paragraph (b) in column (1) (with no rate of drawback specified against it in column 3)—

" (c) in the form of fine white powder, not flavoured, containing not less than 8 per cent. and not more than 10 per cent. invert sugar ".

(2) In consequence of the amendment made by paragraph (1)(b) above, paragraph 2 of Schedule 3 to the said Order of 1966 shall be amended by substituting for the words " Linseed oil (paragraphs 2 to 12 only) " the words " Linseed oil (paragraphs 3 to 12 only) ", and paragraph 2(1)(b) of the Schedule to the said Order of 1968 is hereby revoked.

(a) 1958 c. 6.
(c) S.I. 1966/921 (1966 II, p. 2207).

(b) 1965 c. 25.
(d) S.I. 1968/251 (1968 I, p. 763).

2.—(1) This Order may be cited as the Import Duty Drawbacks (No. 4) Order 1968.

(2) The Interpretation Act 1889(a) shall apply for the interpretation of this Order as it applies for the interpretation of an Act of Parliament.

(3) This Order shall come into operation on 2nd May 1968.

B. K. O'Malley,

J. McCann,

Two of the Lords Commissioners
of Her Majesty's Treasury.

22nd April 1968.

EXPLANATORY NOTE

(This Note is not part of the Order)

This Order—

(i) revokes the existing fixed rate of drawback of import duty for the following exported goods manufactured from the imported materials shown and provides for the drawback to be related to the duty paid on the quantity of imported materials actually used in their manufacture—

Exported goods	*Imported materials*
Fruit cakes, fruit puddings, biscuits and sweetmeat confectionery	Raisins, sultanas, currants and other dried grapes, and dried figs
Mincemeat, pickles, sauces and chutneys	Raisins, sultanas, currants and other dried grapes
Fig jam	Dried figs
Linseed oil, refined or heat treated or both; certain mixtures; adducts of linseed oil; and putty	Linseed oil

(ii) provides for the allowance of drawback of import duty on the exportation of a form of powdered sugar manufactured from imported sugar.

(a) 1889 c. 63.

STATUTORY INSTRUMENTS

1968 No. 645

ANIMALS

PREVENTION OF CRUELTY

The Spring Traps Approval (Amendment) Order 1968

Made - - -	10th *April* 1968
Coming into Operation	1st *May* 1968

The Minister of Agriculture, Fisheries and Food, in exercise of the powers vested in him by section 8 of the Pests Act 1954(a) and of all other powers enabling him in that behalf, hereby makes the following Order :—

Citation, Commencement and Interpretation

1.—(1) This Order may be cited as the Spring Traps Approval (Amendment) Order 1968 and shall come into operation on 1st May 1968.

(2) The Interpretation Act 1889(b) shall apply to the interpretation of this Order as it applies to the interpretation of an Act of Parliament.

Amendment of Principal Order

2. The Spring Traps Approval Order 1957(c), as amended by the Spring Traps Approval (Amendment) Order 1966(d), is hereby further amended by adding at the end of the first column of the Schedule thereto (in which are set out the types and makes of trap approved for the purposes of section 8 of the Pests Act 1954) the following description—

"Lloyd Trap, manufactured under the authority of the National Research Development Corporation, and specified in Patent Specification No. 987113"

and by adding at the end of the second column of the said Schedule (in which are set out the conditions as to the animals for which or the circumstances in which approved traps may be used), opposite the aforesaid description, the following conditions—

"The trap shall be used only

(*a*) for the purpose of killing or taking grey squirrels and stoats, weasels, rats, mice or other small ground vermin, and set in natural tunnels or in artificial tunnels constructed for the purpose, or

(*b*) for the purpose of killing or taking rats or mice and set in the open on their runs".

In Witness whereof the official seal of the Minister of Agriculture, Fisheries and Food is hereunto affixed on 10th April 1968.

(L.S.)

Cledwyn Hughes,
Minister of Agriculture, Fisheries and Food.

(a) 1954 c. 68.　　　　　　　　　　　　(b) 1889 c. 63.
(c) S.I. 1957/2216 (1957 I, p. 146).　　　(d) S.I. 1966/849 (1966 II, p. 1988).

EXPLANATORY NOTE

(This Note is not part of the Order.)

By virtue of section 8 of the Pests Act 1954 it is an offence to use for the killing or taking of animals a spring trap other than one approved by the Minister of Agriculture, Fisheries and Food. This Order adds the Lloyd Trap to those already approved by the Minister in the Spring Traps Approval Order 1957 and in the Spring Traps Approval (Amendment) Order 1966 and specifies the animals for which and the circumstances in which it may be used.

STATUTORY INSTRUMENTS

1968 No. 652 (S.61)

WATER SUPPLY, SCOTLAND
The Water Byelaws (Extension of Operation) Order 1968

Made - - -		18*th April* 1968
Coming into Operation		18*th April* 1968

The Secretary of State in exercise of his powers under section 62(4) of the Water (Scotland) Act 1946(a), and of all other powers enabling him in that behalf, hereby orders as follows:—

1. This order may be cited as the Water Byelaws (Extension of Operation) Order 1968.

2. Any byelaws made under section 61 of the Water (Scotland) Act 1946 (which confers power to make byelaws for preventing pollution of water), being byelaws which would, but for this order, cease to have effect before 31st December 1968 as a consequence of section 62(4) of the said Act, shall remain in force until that day.

Given under the seal of the Secretary of State for Scotland.

(L.S.)

R. A. Dingwall-Smith,

Under-Secretary.

Scottish Development Department,
  St. Andrew's House,
    Edinburgh, 1.
18th April 1968.

(a) 1946 c. 42.

STATUTORY INSTRUMENTS

1968 No. 653

CUSTOMS AND EXCISE

The European Free Trade Association (Origin of Goods) (Amendment) Regulations 1968

Made - - - -	*24th April* 1968
Laid before the House of Commons	*30th April* 1968
Coming into Operation	*1st May* 1968

The Board of Trade, in pursuance of the powers conferred upon them by section 1(1) of the European Free Trade Association Act 1960(**a**), hereby make the following Regulations: —

1. The European Free Trade Association (Origin of Goods) Regulations 1964(**b**), as amended(**c**), shall have effect as if in Schedule 1, after the entry in relation to tariff heading 29.35, there were inserted the following: —

" 1	2
Tariff heading & description	*Qualifying process*
29.35 Furfuryl alcohol	Manufacture from furfuraldehyde."

2. The Interpretation Act 1889(**d**) shall apply to the interpretation of these Regulations as it applies to the interpretation of an Act of Parliament.

3. These Regulations may be cited as the European Free Trade Association (Origin of Goods) (Amendment) Regulations 1968 and shall come into operation on 1st May 1968.

Gwyneth Dunwoody,
Parliamentary Secretary to
the Board of Trade.

24th April 1968.

EXPLANATORY NOTE

(*This Note is not part of the Regulations.*)

These Regulations further amend the European Free Trade Association (Origin of Goods) Regulations 1964. They provide that furfuryl alcohol may be eligible for E.F.T.A. tariff treatment if it has undergone in the E.F.T.A. area the process of manufacture from furfuraldehyde.

(a) 1960 c. 19.   (b) S.I. 1964/1966 (1964 III, p. 4296).
(c) There is no amendment which relates expressly to the subject matter of these Regulations.
(d) 1889 c. 63.

STATUTORY INSTRUMENTS

1968 No. 656

TRIBUNALS AND INQUIRIES

The Fees for Inquiries (Variation) Order 1968

Made - - -		*23rd April* 1968
Laid before Parliament		*29th April* 1968
Coming into Operation		*1st May* 1968

The Treasury, in exercise of the powers conferred on them by section 5 of, and paragraph 6 of Schedule 3 to, the Public Expenditure and Receipts Act 1968(a), and of all other powers enabling them in that behalf, hereby make the following Order :—

1. The enactments specified in column 1 of the Schedule to this Order (which specify the maximum amount of payments in respect of the services of officers of government departments engaged in certain inquiries) shall be amended by substituting for the sums specified in column 2 of that Schedule the sums specified in column 3 thereof.

2. The Interpretation Act 1889(b) shall apply for the interpretation of this Order as it applies for the interpretation of an Act of Parliament.

3. This Order may be cited as the Fees for Inquiries (Variation) Order 1968, and shall come into operation on 1st May 1968.

J. Harper,
H. Gourlay,
Two of the Lords Commissioners
of Her Majesty's Treasury.

23rd April 1968.

(a) 1968 c. 14.   (b) 1889 c. 63.

SCHEDULE

Enactments Amended

1 Enactments specifying maximum payments	2 Old maximum payment per day	3 New maximum payment per day
The Fees (Increase) Act 1923 (c.4) section 9.	£5 5 0	£30
The Local Government Act 1933 (c.51) section 290(4).	£5 5 0	£30
The Road and Rail Traffic Act 1933 (c.53) section 47(2).	£5 5 0	£30
The Local Government (Scotland) Act 1947 (c.43) section 355(8).	£5 5 0	£30
The Road Traffic Act 1960 (c.16) section 249(1)(d).	£5 5 0	£30
The Transport Act 1962 (c.46) section 90(2).	£5 5 0	£30

EXPLANATORY NOTE

(*This Note is not part of the Order.*)

The enactments set out in the Schedule to this Order specify the maximum amount of fees payable per day for the services of officers of government departments engaged in certain inquiries. With a view to securing from the fees a net return corresponding more nearly with the costs incurred, the Order amends the enactments by increasing the maximum amount of the fees.

STATUTORY INSTRUMENTS

1968 No. 657

BUILDING SOCIETIES

The Building Societies (Authorised Investments) (Amendment) Order 1968

Made - - - - -	*24th April* 1968
Laid before Parliament	*2nd May* 1968
Coming into Operation	*6th May* 1968

The Chief Registrar of Friendly Societies, with the consent of the Treasury, in exercise of the powers conferred upon him by section 58 of the Building Societies Act 1962(a) and of all other powers enabling him in that behalf, hereby makes the following Order:—

1.—(1) This Order may be cited as the Building Societies (Authorised Investments) (Amendment) Order 1968, and shall come into operation on 6th May 1968.

(2) The Interpretation Act 1889(b) shall apply to the interpretation of this Order as it applies to the interpretation of an Act of Parliament.

2. The Building Societies (Authorised Investments) Order 1962(c), as amended (d) (which prescribes the manner in which a building society may invest funds which are not immediately required for its purposes) shall be amended by:—

(a) in paragraph (1) of article 2, for the words "the following article" the substitution of the words "articles 3 and 3A of this Order"

(b) after article 3, the insertion of the following article:—

"3A.—(1) Funds kept in cash or on current account with or on temporary loan to a bank (being a bank authorised under section 59 of the Building Societies Act 1962 to hold funds of building societies) shall, for the purposes of determining whether an investment in a manner specified in Part II or Part III of the Schedule to this Order may be made, be deemed to be investments of a kind specified in Part I of the said Schedule.

(2) The expression "temporary loan" in the preceding sub-paragraph means a loan which is repayable—

(a) in not more than six months after the date on which the investment referred to in the preceding sub-paragraph is to be made, or

(b) by notice to the bank requiring it to repay the loan, such notice being a notice which will expire in not more than six months from the giving thereof and which may be given at any time after the said date."

(a) 1962 c. 37.   (b) 1889 c. 63.   (c) S.I. 1962/2044 (1962 III, p. 2461).
(d) The amending instruments are S.I. 1964/671 (1964 II, p. 1268) and S.I. 1966/1338 (1966 III, p. 3667).

(c) in paragraph 1 of the Schedule, after the words "Ulster Development Bonds" the insertion of the words "British Savings Bonds"

(d) at the end of sub-paragraph (g) of paragraph 2 of the Schedule, the addition of the words "or securities issued in the United Kingdom by the Inter-American Development Bank"

(e) in the definition of "local authority" in paragraph 10 of the Schedule, for the word "metropolitan" the substitution of the word "London" and after the words "a parish" the insertion of the words "the Greater London Council"

(f) in the definition of "marketable fixed-interest securities" in paragraph 10 of the Schedule, after the words "Belfast Stock Exchange" the insertion of the words "or bonds issued by a local authority in whole or in part to a bank, discount house, issuing house, or broker in the City of London".

Dated 24th April 1968.

S. D. Musson,
Chief Registrar of Friendly Societies.

We consent to this Order.
Dated 24th April 1968.

Joseph Harper,
Harry Gourlay,
Two of the Lords Commissioners of
Her Majesty's Treasury.

EXPLANATORY NOTE

(This Note is not part of the Order.)

This Order amends the Building Societies (Authorised Investments) Order 1962 by adding to the classes of securities in which building societies may invest. The additions include British Savings Bonds and local authority bonds which have been issued in whole or in part to discount houses and others. It also allows building societies to take into account cash and short term deposits when determining whether they may make medium and long term investments under the Order of 1962.

STATUTORY INSTRUMENTS

1968 No. 658

COMMON

The Commons Registration (General) (Amendment) Regulations 1968

Made - - - -	*24th April* 1968
Laid before Parliament	*2nd May* 1968
Coming into Operation	*9th May* 1968

The Minister of Housing and Local Government and the Secretary of State, in exercise of their respective powers under sections 3 and 19 of the Commons Registration Act 1965(a), as read with the Ministry of Land and Natural Resources (Dissolution) Order 1967(b) and of all other powers enabling them in that behalf, hereby make the following Regulations:—

1. These Regulations may be cited as the Commons Registration (General) (Amendment) Regulations 1968 and shall come into operation on 9th May, 1968.

2.—(1) In these Regulations—

(a) " the principal regulations " means the Commons Registration (General) Regulations 1966(c);

(b) a regulation or form referred to by number in the Schedule to these Regulations is the regulation or form so numbered in the principal regulations.

(2) The Interpretation Act 1889(d) shall apply for the interpretation of these Regulations as it applies for the interpretation of an Act of Parliament.

3. The principal regulations shall be amended in the manner specified in the Schedule to these Regulations.

4.—(1) Nothing in these Regulations shall affect the validity of any application for the registration of land as common land or as a town or village green, or of any application for the registration of a right of common over or of a claim to the ownership of such land, and nothing herein shall affect the validity of any other application which is made before 1st July 1968.

(2) In this regulation " application " includes a statutory declaration in support of an application.

SCHEDULE

1. The following shall be substituted for regulation 7:—

" *Applications in special cases*

7.—(1) Where a right of common is attached to any land, and is comprised in a tenancy of the land, an application for the registration of that right may be made by the landlord, the tenant, or both of them jointly.

(2) Where a right of common belongs to an ecclesiastical benefice of the Church of England which is vacant an application for the registration of that right may be made by the Church Commissioners.

(a) 1965 c. 64.   (b) S.I. 1967/156 (1967 I, p. 258).
(c) S.I. 1966/1471 (1966 III, p. 3978).   (d) 1889 c. 63.

(3) Where any land registered under the Act belongs to an ecclesiastical benefice of the Church of England which is vacant an application for the registration of a claim to the ownership of that land may be made by the Church Commissioners.

(4) The foregoing provisions of this regulation do not affect the right of any person entitled, apart from those provisions, to make any application under the Act.".

2. In regulation 8—

(a) in paragraph 1(b) after the words " signed by " there shall be inserted the words " or on behalf of ";

(b) in paragraph (1)(c) for the words " every person who has signed the application " there shall be substituted the words " every applicant ";

(c) after paragraph (2) insert the following paragraph:—

" (3) An application for the registration of a right of common, or of a claim to the ownership of any land, made by a person who is not the owner of the right or, as the case may be, of the land, shall, unless that person is entitled by virtue of any provision of regulation 7 above to make the application, be supported by such further evidence (if any) of his right to make it as, after considering the application and the declaration in support, the registration authority may reasonably require.".

3. In regulation 27—

(a) the following shall be substituted for paragraph (2):—

" (2) An application under this regulation may be made by the person who, at the date of the application, would have been entitled (whether or not by virtue of any provision of these Regulations) to apply under section 4 of the Act for the registration of a claim to the ownership of the land if at that date such an application could have been made.";

(b) in paragraph 3(b) after the words " signed by " there shall be inserted the words " or on behalf of ".

4. In regulation 29—

(a) the following shall be substituted for paragraph (2):—

" (2) (a) An application under this regulation may be made by any person having an interest under the apportionment, variation, extinguishment, release or transfer.

(b) For the purposes of this regulation the following are included in the expression " person having an interest ", but without prejudice to the generality of that expression:—

(i) in the case of an apportionment, variation or transfer, any person who, at the date of the application under this regulation, would have been entitled (whether or not by virtue of any provision of these Regulations) to apply under section 4 of the Act for the registration of the right as apportioned, varied or transferred, if at that date such an application could have been made;

(ii) in the case of an extinguishment or release, any person who, at the date of the application under this regulation, would have been entitled (whether or not by virtue of any provision of these Regulations) to apply under the said section 4 for the registration of a claim to the ownership of any part of the land over which the

---

right extinguished or released was formerly exercisable, if at that date such an application could have been made.";

(b) in paragraph 3(b) after the words " signed by " there shall be inserted the words " or on behalf of ".

5. After regulation 31 insert:—

"Applications signed by agents

31A. Any application signed by an agent on behalf of an individual applicant shall be supported by such evidence (if any) of the agent's authority as, after considering the application, the registration authority may reasonably require.".

6. In Form 7—

(a) the following shall be substituted for the marginal note [3] at the end of the application:—

" [3] *If the applicant is a body corporate or unincorporate the application must be signed by the secretary or some other duly authorised officer.*";

(b) in paragraph 1 of the Statutory Declaration in Support, after " 1.", there shall be inserted the reference " [2] ", and, in the same paragraph, " made " shall be substituted for " signed ";

(c) at the end of paragraph 3 of that Declaration, there shall be inserted the reference " [3A] ", and against paragraph 3 there shall be added the following marginal note:—

" [3A] *The words " unless it is a town or village green as defined in the Commons Registration Act* 1965 " *may be added here if the applicant can only declare to a belief that the land is one or the other. This will avoid inconsistency if the applicant intends to apply to have the land registered also as a town or village green.*".

7. In Form 8—

(a) the following shall be substituted for the marginal note [3] at the end of the application:—

" [3] *If the applicant is a body corporate or unincorporate the application must be signed by the secretary or some other duly authorised officer.*";

(b) in paragraph 1 of the Statutory Declaration in Support, after " 1.", there shall be inserted the reference " [2] ", and, in the same paragraph, " made " shall be substituted for " signed ";

(c) at the end of paragraph 3 of that Declaration, there shall be inserted the reference " [3A] ", and against paragraph 3 there shall be added the following marginal note:—

" [3A] *The words " unless it is common land as defined in the Commons Registration Act* 1965 " *may be added here if the applicant can only declare to a belief that the land is one or the other. This will avoid inconsistency if the applicant intends to apply to have the land registered also as common land.*".

8. In Form 9—

(a) the following shall be substituted for the marginal note [3] at the end of the application:—

" [3] *If the applicant is a body corporate or charity trustees the application must be signed by the secretary or some other duly authorised officer.*";

(b) in paragraph 1 of the Statutory Declaration in Support, after " 1.", there shall be inserted the reference " ² ", and, in the same paragraph " made " shall be substituted for " signed ";

(c) the following shall be substituted for paragraph 2 of that Declaration and for the marginal note ³ thereto:—

> ³ *Insert capacity in which acting and adapt as necessary.*   " 2. ²I am³   to the applicant(s) and am authorised [by the applicant(s)] [in manner stated in the application] to make the foregoing application on [his] [their] behalf.";

(d) in the first paragraph of Note 2, for the words " (a) by the owner of the right;" there shall be substituted the words " (a) by the owner of the right or in certain cases (see below) by someone on his behalf or in his stead;";

(e) the following shall be substituted for the last paragraph of Note 2:—

> " In certain cases a person may be entitled to apply on behalf of the owner of the right or in his stead. Examples are (a) a receiver appointed under section 105 of the Mental Health Act 1959(a); (b) charity trustees where the right of common is vested in the Official Custodian for Charities; (c) trustees for the purposes of the Settled Land Act 1925(b) authorised by order under section 24 of that Act. In such cases mention should so far as possible be made in part 3 of (a) the Act of Parliament, statutory instrument, order of court or other authority under which the applicant claims to be entitled to apply; (b) the capacity in which he applies; and (c) the name and address of the person on whose behalf or in whose stead the application is made, and whether that person is owner, landlord or tenant. The registration authority has power to call for such further evidence of the right of the applicant to make the application as it may reasonably require.
>
> Where charity trustees apply (whether the right is vested in themselves or in the Official Custodian) the fact should be stated, and the name of the charity given, in part 3."

9. In Form 10—

(a) the following shall be substituted for the marginal note ² at the end of the application:—

> " ² *If the applicant is a body corporate or charity trustees the application must be signed by the secretary or some other duly authorised officer.*";

(b) in paragraph 1 of the Statutory Declaration in Support, after " 1.", there shall be inserted the reference " ² ", and, in the same paragraph " made " shall be substituted for " signed ";

(c) the following shall be substituted for paragraph 2 of that Declaration and for the marginal note ³ thereto:—

> ³ *Insert capacity in which acting and adapt as necessary.*   " 2. ²I am³   to the applicant(s) and am authorised [by the applicant(s)] [in manner stated in the application] to make the foregoing application on [his] [their] behalf.";

(d) in paragraph 3 of that Declaration, after the word " entitled " there shall be inserted the words:—

> " [, in the capacity or respective capacities stated in the application,] ";

(a) 1959 c. 72.   (b) 1925 c. 18.

(e) the following shall be substituted for Note 1 :—

" 1. **Who may apply for registration.**

An application for the registration of a claim to the ownership of any land registered under the Act may be made by the owner of the land or, where the land belongs to an ecclesiastical benefice of the Church of England which is vacant, by the Church Commissioners.

In certain cases a person may be entitled to apply on behalf of the owner of the land or in his stead. Examples are (a) a receiver appointed under section 105 of the Mental Health Act 1959; (b) charity trustees where the land is vested in the Official Custodian for Charities; (c) trustees for the purposes of the Settled Land Act 1925 authorised by order under section 24 of that Act. In such cases mention should so far as possible be made in part 1 of (a) the Act of Parliament, statutory instrument, order of court or other authority under which the applicant claims to be entitled to apply; (b) the capacity in which he applies; and (c) the name and address of the person (i.e. the owner of the land) on whose behalf or in whose stead the application is made. The registration authority has power to call for such further evidence of the right of the applicant to make the application as it may reasonably require.

The ownership of any land, for the purposes of the Act, means the ownership of the legal estate in fee simple in that land. It follows that applications made by, on behalf of or instead of persons not having the legal estate in fee simple cannot be entertained. Thus, for example, an application by or on behalf of a lessee, mortgagee, or person having only an equitable interest in the land must be rejected. Anyone who is not sure whether he is entitled to apply should obtain legal advice.

Where the Church Commissioners apply with respect to land belonging to a vacant benefice, the fact should be stated, and the name of the benefice given, in part 1.

In all cases where charity trustees apply (not only where the land is vested in the Official Custodian) the fact should be stated, and the name of the charity given, in part 1.".

10. In Form 16—

(a) the following shall be substituted for the last sentence of the marginal note to part 1 of the application:—

" *Application may only be made by the person entitled to the relevant right or interest, unless the right or interest belongs to a vacant Church of England benefice, when application may be made by the Church Commissioners. In that case the fact should be stated here and the name of the benefice given. Where charity trustees apply the fact should be stated here and the name of the charity given.)* ";

(b) the following shall be substituted for the marginal note [3] opposite the signature space:—

"[3] *If the applicant is a body corporate or charity trustees the application must be signed by the secretary or some other duly authorised officer.*".

11. In Form 17—

(a) the following shall be substituted for the footnote [2] at the end of the application:—

" [2] *If the applicant is a body corporate or charity trustees the application must be signed by the secretary or some other duly authorised officer.*";

(*b*) in paragraph 1 of the Statutory Declaration in Support, after " 1.", there shall be inserted the reference " ² ", and, in the same paragraph, " made " shall be substituted for " signed ";

(*c*) the following shall be substituted for paragraph 3 of that Declaration:—

" 3. (I) (We) have read the Notes on the back of the application form and believe—

(a) that (I) (we) (the applicant(s)) (am) (are) (is) the owner of the legal estate in fee simple in the land described in the application, and

(a) that the owner(s) of the legal estate in fee simple in the land described in the application (is) (are) the person(s) therein named as such, and that under or by virtue of the matters therein stated (I) (we) (am) (are) entitled, in the capacity or respective capacities therein mentioned, to make this application, and

* Delete all but one of these alternatives.

(a) that the land described in the application belongs to the benefice therein mentioned, that the said benefice is vacant, and

(*b*) that the said land ceased to be (common land) (a town or village green) on the date and in the manner therein stated.";

(*d*) the following shall be substituted for Note 1:—

" 1. **Who may apply for the removal of land from a register.**

An application for the removal of land from a register maintained under the Act may be made by the owner of the land or, where the land belongs to an ecclesiastical benefice of the Church of England which is vacant, by the Church Commissioners.

In certain cases a person may be entitled to apply on behalf of the owner of the land or in his stead. Examples are (*a*) a receiver appointed under section 105 of the Mental Health Act 1959; (*b*) charity trustees where the land is vested in the Official Custodian for Charities; (*c*) trustees for the purposes of the Settled Land Act 1925 authorised by order under section 24 of that Act. In such cases mention should so far as possible be made in part 1 of (*a*) the Act of Parliament, statutory instrument, order of court or other authority under which the applicant claims to be entitled to apply; (*b*) the capacity in which he applies; and (*c*) the name and address of the person (i.e. the owner of the land) on whose behalf or in whose stead the application is made. The registration authority has power to call for such further evidence of the right of the applicant to make the application as it may reasonably require.

The ownership of any land, for the purposes of the Act, means the ownership of the legal estate in fee simple in that land. It follows that applications made by, on behalf or instead of persons not having the legal estate in fee simple cannot be entertained. Thus, for example, an application by or on behalf of a lessee, mortgagee, or person having only an equitable interest in the land must be rejected. Anyone who is not sure whether he is entitled to apply should obtain legal advice.

Where the Church Commissioners apply with respect to land belonging to a vacant benefice, the fact should be stated, and the name of the benefice given, in part 1.

In all cases where charity trustees apply (not only where the land is vested in the Official Custodian) the fact should be stated, and the name of the charity given, in part 1.".

12. In Form 19—

(a) the following shall be substituted for the footnote [2] at the end of the application:—

" [2] *If the applicant is a body corporate or charity trustees the application must be signed by the secretary or some other duly authorised officer.*";

(b) in paragraph 1 of the Statutory Declaration in Support, after " 1.", there shall be inserted the reference " [2] ", and, in the same paragraph " made " shall be substituted for " signed ";

(c) the following shall be substituted for paragraph 3 of that Declaration:—

" 3. (I) (We) have read the Notes on the back of the application form and believe—

Delete all but one of these alternatives.

*that (I) (we) (the applicant(s)) (am) (are) (is) entitled to the interest mentioned in the application, and

*that the person(s) entitled to the interest mentioned in the application (is) (are) the person(s) therein stated to be so entitled, that, under or by virtue of the matters referred to therein (I) (we) (am) (are) authorised, in the capacity or respective capacities therein mentioned, to make this application, and

*that the land described in the application belongs to the benefice therein mentioned, that the said benefice is vacant, and

that, by reason of the facts therein stated, the register to which the application relates ought to be amended accordingly.";

(d) the following shall be substituted for Note 2:—

" 2. **Who may apply.**

An application may be made by any person having an interest under the apportionment, variation, extinguishment, release or transfer. " Having an interest " means having gained a benefit or advantage by the transaction. Thus, for example, in the case of an apportionment, each of the persons entitled to any part of the apportioned right would be entitled to apply. In the case of an extinguishment or release, the applicant would generally be the soil owner. In the case of a variation, any person benefited by the variation, and in the case of a transfer, the transferee, would be entitled to apply. Where the relevant interest belongs to an ecclesiastical benefice of the Church of England which is vacant, the Church Commissioners may make the application and, where they do so, the fact should be stated, and the name of the benefice given, in part 1.

There are certain other cases where a person may be entitled to apply on behalf of the owner of the relevant interest or in his stead. Examples are (a) a receiver appointed under section 105 of the Mental Health Act 1959; (b) charity trustees where the relevant interest is vested in the Official Custodian for Charities; (c) trustees for the purposes of the Settled Land Act 1925 authorised by order under section 24 of that Act. In such cases mention should so far as possible be made, either in part 1 or in part 6 as may be most convenient, of (*a*) the Act of Parliament, statutory instrument, order of court or other authority under which the applicant claims to be entitled to apply; (*b*) the capacity in which he applies; and (*c*) the name and address of the person on whose behalf or in whose stead the application is made, that is to say the person having the necessary interest as explained in the preceding paragraph. The registration authority has power to call for such further evidence of the right of the applicant to make the application as it may reasonably require.

In all cases where charity trustees apply (not only where the right is vested in the Official Custodian) the fact should be stated, and the name of the charity given, in part 1 or 6 as convenient.".

(*e*) the following shall be substituted for the heading to Note 6:—
" 6. **Objections and amendment applications contrasted** ".

Given under the official seal of the Minister of Housing and Local Government on 23rd April, 1968.

(L.S.)   *Anthony Greenwood*,
                                Minister of Housing and Local Government.

                                                George Thomas,
                        Qne of Her Majesty's Principal Secretaries of State.
                                                        Welsh Office.
24th April 1968.

EXPLANATORY NOTE

(This Note is not part of the Regulations.)

These Regulations amend the Commons Registration (General) Regulations 1966 (1) by providing for applications to be made in appropriate cases by persons other than the owner of the relevant right or interest, and for the forms to be signed if necessary by an agent, and (2) by facilitating applications by the same person for the provisional registration of land both as common land and as a town or village green in a case where that person can only declare to a belief that the land is one or the other. The Regulations make revisions to the forms prescribed for these purposes, but the forms as originally prescribed may be used where suitable—

(*a*) in the case of applications for the registration of land as common land or as a town or village green, of rights of common over or claims to the ownership of such land, until 2nd January 1970 (the last date specified under the Commons Registration (Time Limits) Order 1966 (S.I. 1966/1470 (1966 III, p. 3976)) for making such applications), and

(*b*) in the case of applications for a note to be made in a register, for the amendment of a register in relation to a right of common, and for the removal of land from a register, until 30th June 1968, after which date the revised forms must be used.

STATUTORY INSTRUMENTS

1968 No. 659

PUBLIC OFFICE

The Companies Registration Office (Business Names) (Fees) Order 1968

Made - - - -		*24th April* 1968
Coming into Operation		*1st May* 1968

The Treasury, in exercise of the powers conferred on them by sections 2 and 3 of the Public Offices Fees Act 1879(a) and of all other powers enabling them in that behalf, hereby make the following Order:—

1.—(1) Subject to the provisions of the next following paragraph, the fees payable to the Registrar of Companies under the Registration of Business Names Act 1916(b) shall be collected in money.

(2) During the period of six months beginning with the coming into operation of this Order, such of the fees referred to in the last preceding paragraph as are either—

(*a*) specified in paragraph (*a*), (*b*), (*c*) or (*f*) of Rule 9 of the Business Names Rules 1949(c) and payable to the Registrar of Companies in England, or

(*b*) payable to the Registrar of Companies in Scotland,

shall be collected either in money or by means of postage stamps.

2. The Interpretation Act 1889(d) shall apply for the interpretation of this Order as it applies for the interpretation of an Act of Parliament.

3. Article 3 of the Companies Registration Office (Fees) (No. 2) Order 1963(e) is hereby revoked.

4. This Order may be cited as the Companies Registration Office (Business Names) (Fees) Order 1968, and shall come into operation on 1st May 1968.

Joseph Harper,
Harry Gourlay,
Two of the Lords Commissioners
of Her Majesty's Treasury.

24th April 1968.

(**a**) 1879 c. 58. (**b**) 1916 c. 58.
(**c**) S.I. 1949/2441 (1949 I, p. 531). (**d**) 1889 c. 63.
(**e**) S.I. 1963/596 (1963 I, p. 680).

EXPLANATORY NOTE
(This Note is not part of the Order.)

This Order, which replaces article 3 of the Companies Registration Office (Fees) (No. 2) Order 1963, provides for all fees payable to the Registrars of Companies in England and Scotland under the Registration of Business Names Act 1916 to be collected in money. Hitherto, some of these fees have been collected in postage stamps, and the Order provides that during an initial period of six months such fees shall be collected either in money or in postage stamps.

STATUTORY INSTRUMENTS

1968 No. 660

WAGES COUNCILS

The Wages Regulation (Ready-made and Wholesale Bespoke Tailoring) Order 1968

Made - - - -	24*th April* 1968
Coming into Operation	17*th May* 1968

Whereas the Minister of Labour (hereafter in this Order referred to as "the Minister") has received from the Ready-made and Wholesale Bespoke Tailoring Wages Council (Great Britain) the wages regulation proposals set out in Schedules 1 and 2 hereof;

Now, therefore, the Minister by virtue of the powers conferred on her by section 11 of the Wages Councils Act 1959(a), and of all other powers enabling her in that behalf, hereby makes the following Order:—

1. This Order may be cited as the Wages Regulation (Ready-made and Wholesale Bespoke Tailoring) Order 1968.

2.—(1) In this Order the expression "the specified date" means the 17th May 1968, provided that where, as respects any worker who is paid wages at intervals not exceeding seven days, that date does not correspond with the beginning of the period for which the wages are paid, the expression "the specified date" means, as respects that worker, the beginning of the next such period following that date.

(2) The Interpretation Act 1889(b) shall apply to the interpretation of this Order as it applies to the interpretation of an Act of Parliament and as if this Order and the Order hereby revoked were Acts of Parliament.

3. The wages regulation proposals set out in Schedules 1 and 2 hereof shall have effect as from the specified date and as from that date the Wages Regulation (Ready-made and Wholesale Bespoke Tailoring) Order 1966(c) shall cease to have effect.

Signed by order of the Minister of Labour.

24th April 1968.

D. C. Barnes,
Secretary,
Ministry of Labour.

SCHEDULE 1

The following minimum remuneration shall be substituted for the statutory minimum remuneration fixed by the Wages Regulation (Ready-made and Wholesale Bespoke Tailoring) Order 1966 (Order R.M. (81)).

(a) 1959 c. 69.   (b) 1889 c. 63.   (c) S.I. 1966/779 (1966 II, p. 1789).

STATUTORY MINIMUM REMUNERATION

PART I

GENERAL

1. The minimum remuneration payable to a worker to whom this Schedule applies for all work except work to which a minimum overtime rate applies under Part IV of this Schedule is:—

    (1) in the case of a time worker, the general minimum time rate payable to the worker under Part II or Part III of this Schedule;

    (2) in the case of a worker employed on piece work, piece rates each of which would yield, in the circumstances of the case, to an ordinary worker (that is to say, a worker of ordinary skill and experience in the class of work in question) at least the same amount of money as the piece work basis time rate applicable to the worker under Part II or Part III of this Schedule.

PART II

MALE WORKERS

GENERAL MINIMUM TIME RATES AND PIECE WORK BASIS TIME RATES

2.—(1) Subject to the provisions of this Schedule, the general minimum time rates payable to male workers with the qualification specified in Column 2 of the next following Table when employed on time work and the piece work basis time rates applicable to such workers when employed on piece work are those set out in Columns 3 and 4 respectively of the said Table:—

Column 1	Column 2	Column 3	Column 4
		General Minimum Time Rates	Piece Work Basis Time Rates
Class of Worker	Qualifying Period of Employment or Age of Worker	Per hour s. d.	Per hour s. d.
(a) MEASURE CUTTER, that is to say, a person employed in any process of measure cutting who is capable of taking a complete set of measures and of cutting all garments for a male person from patterns, and with sufficient technical knowledge to draft men's trousers and alter the balance and distribution of widths, lengths, etc., for any garment for a male person:	Not less than three years' employment after the age of 18 years as a measure cutter ...	5 9¼	6 1¼
Provided that where the worker is employed in the London District and is not wholly or mainly engaged in the making of heavy cotton clothing the said rates shall be	... ...	5 11½	6 3¼

Column 1	Column 2	Column 3	Column 4
Class of Worker	Qualifying Period of Employment or Age of Worker	General Minimum Time Rates	Piece Work Basis Time Rates
		Per hour s. d.	Per hour s. d.
(*b*) CUTTER or TRIMMER, that is to say, a person substantially employed in one or more of the following processes:— (i) marking-in or marking-up cloth or linings or other materials; (ii) laying-up, hooking-up or folding cloth or linings or other materials; (iii) cutting cloth or linings or other materials or cutting out patterns of any description to be used afterwards for the cutting out of garments; and (iv) dividing (that is to say, the process ordinarily carried on by cutters or their assistants of dividing, parting or separating the parts of garments after being cut and of assembling them into suitable bundles for making up), other than a measure cutter to whom the minimum rates specified in (*a*) of this Table apply or a knife cutter or knifeman:	Not less than three years' employment after the age of 18 years as a cutter of any of the classes specified in Column 1 or as a knifeman	5 7½	5 11¼
Provided that where the worker is employed in the London District and is not wholly or mainly engaged in the making of heavy cotton clothing the said rates shall be	... ...	5 9¼	6 1¼
(*c*) KNIFE CUTTER or KNIFEMAN, that is to say, a person wholly or mainly employed on band, electric or hand-knife processes:	Not less than three years' employment after the age of 18 years as a cutter of any of the classes specified in Column 1 or as a knifeman	5 7½	5 11¼
Provided that where the worker is employed in the London District and is not wholly or mainly engaged in the making of heavy cotton clothing the said rates shall be	... ...	5 9¼	6 1¼
(*d*) FITTER-UP, that is to say, a person employed in fitting-up (which is a process between that of cutting and that of sewing, baisting or machining, and which consists of preparing or fitting accurately the various parts of the garments before being baisted, sewn or machined, such work of preparing or fitting being always done by shears or knives or other cutting appliances—sewing, baisting or machining forming no part or	Not less than three years' employment after the age of 18 years as a fitter-up or tailor ...	5 7½	5 11¼

Column 1	Column 2	Column 3	Column 4
		General Minimum Time Rates	Piece Work Basis Time Rates
Class of Worker	Qualifying Period of Employment or Age of Worker	Per hour s. d.	Per hour s. d.
(e) TAILOR, that is to say, a person employed in sewing by hand in a process of:— (i) making a garment or portion of a garment, or (ii) altering, repairing, renovating or re-making a garment or portion of a garment, when such processes are carried out in a factory.	Not less than three years' employment after the age of 18 years as a tailor	5 7¼	5 11¼
(f) PRESSER, that is to say, a person employed in pressing-off by hand or by machine.	Not less than three years' employment after the age of 18 years in the processes of pressing-off or under-pressing	5 7¼	5 11¼
(g) MACHINIST, that is to say, a person employed in machining other than as a plain machinist and capable of machining any one garment or portion of a garment.	Not less than three years' employment after the age of 18 years as a machinist	5 7¼	5 11¼
(h) PASSER, that is to say, a person employed in examining garments, either in the course of being made up or upon completion.	Not less than three years' employment after the age of 18 years as a passer or tailor... ...	5 7¼	5 11¼
(i) UNDER-PRESSER, that is to say, a person employed in pressing processes other than pressing-off.	Not less than three years' employment after the age of 18 years as an under-presser or presser...	5 4	5 8
(j) PLAIN MACHINIST, that is to say, a person employed in the process of making up plain sleeves, facings, linings, inside pockets, quilting or padding.	Not less than three years' employment after the age of 18 years as a plain machinist or machinist	5 4	5 8
(k) WAREHOUSEMAN, that is to say, a person employed, wholly or mainly, upon one or more of the following operations:—assembling, keeping, storing and distributing stock, and cutting off lengths of cloth, linings or other materials, except where such operations are mainly connected with the sale of finished garments.	Not less than three years' employment as a warehouseman after the age of 18 years. ...	5 5½	5 9¼

Column 1	Column 2	Column 3	Column 4
Class of Worker	Qualifying Period of Employment or Age of Worker	General Minimum Time Rates	Piece Work Basis Time Rates
		Per hour s. d.	Per hour s. d.
(*l*) PACKER, that is to say, a person employed, wholly or mainly, in packing goods and materials.	Not less than three years' employment as a packer after the age of 18 years	5 4½	5 8½
(*m*) PORTER, that is to say, a person employed, wholly or mainly, upon one or more of the operations of unpacking, moving, loading, or unloading goods or materials.	21 years of age or over	5 2½	5 6¼
(*n*) LEARNERS (as defined in paragraph 9)	Aged 21 years or over	5 1½	5 6¼
	„ 20 and under 21 years	4 7¼	
	„ 19 „ „ 20 „	4 2¼	
	„ 18 „ „ 19 „	3 9½	
	„ 17 „ „ 18 „	3 5¼	
	„ 16 „ „ 17 „	2 11¾	
	„ under 16 years	2 6¼	
Provided that the general minimum time rate payable during his first year's employment to a learner who enters, or has entered, the trade for the first time at or over the age of 19 years shall be	(i) Aged under 21 years	3 11	
	(ii) „ 21 years or over	4 3¼	

(2) For the purposes of this paragraph:—

(*a*) "The London District" means the Metropolitan Police District as defined in the London Government Act 1963(a), the City of London, the Inner Temple and the Middle Temple.

(*b*) "Heavy cotton clothing" means articles of clothing for male persons made, wholly or mainly, of cords, moles or other fustians, jeans, drills or other similar cotton material, but excluding gabardine raincoats.

(a) 1963 c. 33.

Part III

FEMALE WORKERS

GENERAL MINIMUM TIME RATES

3. Subject to the provisions of this Schedule, the general minimum time rates payable to female time workers are as follows:—

	Per hour	
	s.	d.

(1) CONVEYOR BELT MACHINISTS (that is to say, female workers employed in machining any work conveyed directly to or from them on a mechanical conveyor belt) not being learners to whom (3) of this paragraph applies **4   1**

(2) FEMALE CUTTERS, TRIMMERS or FITTERS-UP (as defined in paragraph 9) being workers aged—

	s.	d.
Under 19 years	3	11½
19 and under 20 years	4	0
20 years or over	4	0½

Provided that where the worker is employed as a cutter, trimmer or fitter-up for the first time at or over the age of 19 years the general minimum time rate payable during the first two months of such employment shall be 1d. per hour less than the general minimum time rate otherwise payable.

(3) LEARNERS (as defined in paragraph 9) during the following periods of employment in the trade:—

	s.	d.
First six months	2	3¼
Second six months	2	6¼
Second year	3	0
Third year	3	5

Provided that a worker who enters, or has entered, the trade for the first time at or over the age of 18 years shall be treated for the purposes of this paragraph as though she had, at the date of her entry, completed one year of employment as a learner.

(4) ALL OTHER WORKERS **3   11½**

PIECE WORK BASIS TIME RATES

4. The piece work basis time rates applicable to female workers employed on piece work are as follows:—

	Per hour	
	s.	d.

(1) FEMALE CUTTERS, TRIMMERS or FITTERS-UP (as defined in paragraph 9) being workers aged—

	s.	d.
Under 19 years	4	3
19 and under 20 years	4	3½
20 years or over	4	4

(2) ALL OTHER WORKERS irrespective of age (including home-workers) **4   3**

Part IV

OVERTIME AND WAITING TIME

NORMAL NUMBER OF HOURS

5. Subject to the provisions of this Part of this Schedule, the minimum overtime rates set out in paragraph 6 are payable to a worker in respect of any time worked—

(1) in excess of the hours following, that is to say,

(a) in any week ... ... **40 hours**

(b) on any day other than a Saturday, Sunday or customary
    holiday—

        where the normal working hours exceed 8½ ...   ...   9 hours
        or
        where the normal working hours are more than 8 but
            not more than 8½   ...   .   8½ hours
        or
        where the normal working hours are not more than 8   8 hours

  (2) On a Saturday, Sunday or customary holiday.

MINIMUM OVERTIME RATES

6.—(1) Minimum overtime rates are payable to any worker as follows:—

    (a) on any day other than a Sunday or customary holiday—

        (i) for the first 2 hours of overtime worked   ...   time-and-a-quarter
        (ii) for the next 2 hours   ...   .   time-and-a-half
        (iii) thereafter ...   .   double time

    (b) on a Sunday or customary holiday—
        for all time worked   ...   .   double time

Provided that where it is the practice in a Jewish undertaking for the employer
to require attendance on Sunday instead of Saturday the provisions of this
paragraph shall apply as if in such provisions the word "Saturday" were substituted for "Sunday", except where such substitution is unlawful.

    (c) in any week, exclusive of any time in respect of which any minimum
        overtime rate is payable under the foregoing provisions of this sub-
        paragraph—
        for all time worked in excess of 40 hours ...   ...   time-and-a-quarter

  (2) The minimum overtime rates set out in sub-paragraph (1)(a) or (b) of this
paragraph are payable in any week whether or not the minimum overtime rate
set out in sub-paragraph (1)(c) is also payable.

7. In this Part of this Schedule—

  (1) the expression "customary holiday" means—

    (a) (i) in England and Wales—

        Christmas Day (or, if Christmas Day falls on a Sunday, such weekday as
        may be appointed by national proclamation, or, if none is so appointed,
        the next following Tuesday), Boxing Day, Good Friday, Easter Monday,
        Whit Monday (*or where another day is substituted therefor by national
        proclamation, that day*), August Bank Holiday and one other day (being a
        day of the week on which the worker normally works for the employer)
        in the course of a calendar year, to be fixed by the employer and notified
        to the worker not less than three weeks before the holiday;

        (ii) in Scotland—

        New Year's Day (or, if New Year's Day falls on a Sunday, the following
        Monday);
        the local Spring holiday;
        the local Autumn holiday; and
        four other days (being days of the week on which the worker normally
        works for the employer) in the course of a calendar year, to be fixed by the
        employer and notified to the worker not less than three weeks before the
        holiday;

    or, (b) in the case of each of the said days a day substituted by the employer
        therefor, being a day recognised by local custom as a day of holiday in
        substitution for the said day.

(2) the expressions "time-and-a-quarter", "time-and-a-half" and "double time" mean respectively—

(*a*) in the case of a time worker, one and a quarter times, one and a half times and twice the general minimum time rate otherwise payable to the worker;

(*b*) in the case of a male worker aged 21 years or over who is employed on piece work or of a female worker (not being a learner) who is employed on piece work,

   (i) a time rate equal respectively to one quarter, one half and the whole of the piece work basis time rate applicable to the worker and, in addition thereto,

   (ii) the piece rates otherwise payable to the worker under paragraph 1(2);

(*c*) in the case of a male worker aged less than 21 years who is employed on piece work or of a female learner who is employed on piece work,

   (i) a time rate equal respectively to one quarter, one half and the whole of the general minimum time rate which would be payable if the worker were a time worker and a minimum overtime rate did not apply and, in addition thereto,

   (ii) the piece rates otherwise payable to the worker under paragraph 1(2).

WAITING TIME

8.—(1) A worker is entitled to payment of the minimum remuneration specified in this Schedule for all time during which he is present on the premises of his employer unless he is present thereon in any of the following circumstances:—

(*a*) without the employer's consent, express or implied;

(*b*) for some purpose unconnected with his work and other than that of waiting for work to be given to him to perform;

(*c*) by reason only of the fact that he is resident thereon;

(*d*) during normal meal times in a room or place in which no work is being done and he is not waiting for work to be given to him to perform.

(2) The minimum remuneration payable under sub-paragraph (1) of this paragraph to a piece worker when not engaged on piece work is that which would be payable if he were a time worker.

PART V

INTERPRETATION

9. In this Schedule—

(1) A FEMALE CUTTER, TRIMMER or FITTER-UP is a worker substantially occupied in one or more of the following processes:—

(*a*) marking-in or marking-up cloth, or linings or other materials;

(*b*) laying-up, hooking-up or folding cloth or linings or other materials;

(*c*) cutting cloth or linings or other materials;

(*d*) trimming (that is to say, the process as ordinarily carried on of cutting and assembling together the linings and fittings of garments);

(*e*) dividing (that is to say, the process as ordinarily carried on by cutters or their assistants, of dividing, parting or separating the parts of garments after being cut, and of assembling them into suitable bundles for making-up); and (*f*) fitting-up (which is a process between that of cutting and that of-sewing, baisting or machining, and which consists of preparing and fitting accurately the various parts of the garment before being baisted, sewn or machined, such work of preparing and fitting being always done by shears or knives or other cutting appliances—sewing, baisting or machining forming no part or process of fitting-up).

(2) A LEARNER is a worker who:—

(*a*) is employed during the whole or a substantial part of his time in learning any branch or process of the trade by an employer who provides him with reasonable facilities for such learning; and

(*b*) does not work in a room used for dwelling purposes, except where he is in the employment of his parent or guardian.

(3) "THE TRADE" means the trade of ready-made and wholesale bespoke tailoring as specified in paragraph 11.

RECKONING OF EMPLOYMENT

10. For the purpose of determining whether a worker has completed any period of employment specified in paragraph 2 or paragraph 3, there shall be taken into account—

(1) any such employment as a worker in relation to whom there operated one or more of the following Wages Councils (or of the Trade Boards which respectively preceded them), that is to say, the Ready-made and Wholesale Bespoke Tailoring Wages Council (Great Britain), the Retail Bespoke Tailoring Wages Councils for England and Wales and for Scotland and the Wholesale Mantle and Costume Wages Council (Great Britain) and

(2) in the case of a male worker employed as a cutter of any description or as a knifeman any such employment in the rubberised waterproof trade.

APPLICABILITY OF STATUTORY MINIMUM REMUNERATION

11. Subject to the provisions of paragraph 12, this Schedule applies to workers in relation to whom the Ready-made and Wholesale Bespoke Tailoring Wages Council (Great Britain) operates, that is to say, workers employed in Great Britain in those branches of work in the tailoring trade which are specified in the Trade Boards (Ready-made and Wholesale Bespoke Tailoring Trade, Great Britain) (Constitution and Proceedings) Regulations 1929(a), namely:—

"Men's and boys' ready-made and wholesale bespoke tailoring; and all men's and boys' retail bespoke tailoring carried on in a factory where garments are made up for three or more retail establishments; and any other branch of men's and boys' tailoring which is not included within the scope of the Regulations, dated 6th August, 1924, with respect to the Constitution and Proceedings of the Trade Boards in England and Wales and Scotland(b) respectively for Retail Bespoke Tailoring;

INCLUDING:—

(1) (*a*) The altering, repairing, renovating, or re-making of men's or boys' tailored garments, except where included within the scope of the above-mentioned Regulations with respect to Retail Bespoke Tailoring;

(*b*) The cleaning of such garments where carried out in association with or in conjunction with the altering, repairing, renovating or re-making of the garments;

(a) S.R. & O. 1929/765 (1929, p. 1371).
(b) S.R. & O. 1924/835, 836 (1924, pp. 1769, 1772).

(2) The lining with fur of the above-mentioned garments where carried out in association with or in conjunction with the making of such garments;

(3) All processes of embroidery or decorative needlework where carried out in association with or in conjunction with the above-mentioned branches of tailoring;

(4) All warehousing, packing, and other operations incidental to or appertaining to any of the branches of tailoring in question;

BUT EXCLUDING:—

(1) The making of head-gear;

(2) The making of rubberised or oilskin garments;

(3) The making of boys' ready-made washing suits or sailor suits where carried out in association with or in conjunction with the making of garments to be worn by women or girls or by children without distinction of sex."

TRAINING UNDER THE GOVERNMENT VOCATIONAL TRAINING SCHEME

12. Notwithstanding anything hereinbefore contained, this Schedule shall not apply to—

(1) male stock cutters and fitters-up,

(2) male pressers,

(3) male or female tailors and shapers, hand sewers or finishers,

(4) male or female machinists

during any period in respect of which they are in receipt of allowances as provided under the Government Vocational Training Scheme for resettlement training if they are trainees who have been placed by the Ministry of Labour with the employer for a period of approved training and if the requirements of the said Scheme are duly complied with.

SCHEDULE 2

HOLIDAYS AND HOLIDAY REMUNERATION

The Wages Regulation (Ready-made and Wholesale Bespoke Tailoring) (Holidays) Order 1966(a) (Order R.M. (82)) shall have effect as if in the Schedule thereto for sub-paragraph (2)(a)(i) of paragraph 2 (which relates to customary holidays) there were substituted the following:—

"(2) The said customary holidays are:—

(a) (i) In England and Wales—

Christmas Day (or, if Christmas Day falls on a Sunday, such weekday as may be appointed by national proclamation, or, if none is so appointed, the next following Tuesday), Boxing Day, Good Friday, Easter Monday, Whit Monday (or where another day is substituted therefor by national proclamation, that day), August Bank Holiday, and one other day (being a day of the week on which the worker normally works for the employer) in the course of a calendar year, to be fixed by the employer and notified to the worker not less than three weeks before the holiday;"

(a) S.I. 1966/1493 (1966 III, p. 4112).

EXPLANATORY NOTE

(This Note is not part of the Order.)

This Order has effect from 17th May 1968. Schedule 1 sets out the statutory minimum remuneration payable in substitution for that fixed by the Wages Regulation (Ready-made and Wholesale Bespoke Tailoring) Order 1966 (Order R.M. (81)) which is revoked. Schedule 2 amends the Wages Regulation (Ready-made and Wholesale Bespoke Tailoring) (Holidays) Order 1966 (Order R.M. (82)), by providing that a nationally proclaimed holiday may be substituted for Whit Monday.

New provisions are printed in italics.

STATUTORY INSTRUMENTS

1968 No. 668

EXCHANGE CONTROL

The Exchange Control (Authorised Dealers and Depositaries) (Amendment) (No. 2) Order 1968

Made - - -	*25th April* 1968
Coming into Operation	*30th April* 1968

The Treasury, in exercise of the powers conferred upon them by sections 36(5) and 42(1) of the Exchange Control Act 1947(**a**), hereby make the following Order :—

1. Schedule 2 to the Exchange Control (Authorised Dealers and Depositaries) Order 1967(**b**), as amended (**c**), shall be further amended as follows :—

(*a*) by substituting the words "American Express International Banking Corporation." for the words "American Express Company Inc." ;

(*b*) by substituting the words "National Provincial & Rothschild (International) Ltd." for the words "National Provincial & Rothschild (London) Ltd." ;

(*c*) by inserting the words "Western American Bank (Europe) Ltd." after the words "Warburg & Co., Ltd., S.G.".

2. This Order shall extend to the Channel Islands, and any reference in this Order to the Exchange Control Act 1947 includes a reference to that Act as extended by the Exchange Control (Channel Islands) Order 1947(**d**).

3. The Interpretation Act 1889(**e**) shall apply for the interpretation of this Order as it applies for the interpretation of an Act of Parliament.

4. This Order may be cited as the Exchange Control (Authorised Dealers and Depositaries) (Amendment) (No. 2) Order 1968, and shall come into operation on 30th April 1968.

25th April 1968.

J. McCann,

E. Alan Fitch,

Two of the Lords Commissioners
of Her Majesty's Treasury.

(**a**) 1947 c. 14.　　　　　　　　　　(**b**) S.I. 1967/1583 (1967 III, p. 4391).
(**c**) S.I. 1967/1946, 1968/159 (1967 III, p. 5397; 1968 I, p. 391).
(**d**) S.R. & O. 1947/2034 (Rev. VI, p. 1001: 1947 I, p. 660).
(**e**) 1889 c. 63.

EXPLANATORY NOTE

(This Note is not part of the Order.)

This Order amends the list of persons authorised by the Treasury under the Exchange Control Act 1947 to act as dealers in gold and foreign currencies and as depositaries for the purpose of the deposit of securities.

STATUTORY INSTRUMENTS

1968 No. 676 (S.64)

ANIMALS

PREVENTION OF CRUELTY

The Spring Traps Approval (Scotland) Amendment Order 1968

Made - - -	29*th April* 1968
Coming into Operation	1*st May* 1968

In exercise of the powers conferred upon me by section 50(3) and 85(3) of the Agriculture (Scotland) Act 1948(a) as amended by section 10 of the Pests Act 1954(b), and of all other powers enabling me in that behalf, I hereby make the following order:—

Citation, commencement and interpretation

1.—(1) This order may be cited as the Spring Traps Approval (Scotland) Amendment Order 1968 and shall come into operation on 1st May 1968.

(2) The Interpretation Act 1889(c) shall apply for the interpretation of this order as it applies for the interpretation of an Act of Parliament.

Amendment of order

2. The Schedule to the Spring Traps Approval (Scotland) Order 1958(d) as amended by the Spring Traps Approval (Scotland) Amendment Order 1966(e) (which sets out the types and makes of traps approved for the purposes of section 50 of the Agriculture (Scotland) Act 1948 as amended by section 10 of the Pests Act 1954 and the conditions as to the animals for which and the circumstances in which traps so approved may be used) shall be further amended by making the following addition thereto:—

"*Type and Make of Trap*

Lloyd Trap, manufactured under the authority of the National Research Development Corporation and specified in Patent Specification No. 987113.

Conditions

The trap shall be used only—

(*a*) for the purpose of killing or taking grey squirrels or stoats, weasels, or other small ground vermin, and for that purpose shall be set only in tunnels whether natural or constructed for the purpose,

or

(*b*) for the purpose of killing or taking rats or mice and for that purpose shall be set only in the

(a) 1948 c. 45.
(c) 1889 c. 63.
(b) 1954 c. 68.
(d) S.I. 1958/1780 (1958 I, p. 160).
(e) S.I. 1966/844 (1966 II, p. 1983).

open on their runs or in-tunnels whether natural or constructed for the purpose."

William Ross,

One of Her Majesty's Principal Secretaries of State.

St. Andrew's House,
Edinburgh, 1.
    29th April 1968.

EXPLANATORY NOTE

(This Note is not part of the order.)

It is an offence under section 50 of the Agriculture (Scotland) Act 1948 as amended by section 10 of the Pests Act 1954, to use for the purpose of killing or taking animals any spring trap other than one of a type and kind approved by the Secretary of State. By the Spring Traps Approval (Scotland) Order 1958 as amended by the Spring Traps Approval (Scotland) Amendment Order 1966, the Secretary of State specified certain traps as approved and the conditions under which such traps might be lawfully used. This Amendment Order has the effect of adding the Lloyd Trap to those already specified.

STATUTORY INSTRUMENTS

1968 No. 677

LAND CHARGES
The Land Charges Fees Order 1968

Made - - - -	*26th April* 1968
Coming into Operation	*1st June* 1968

The Lord Chancellor and the Treasury, in exercise of the powers conferred on them by section 19 of the Land Charges Act 1925(a) and sections 2 and 3 of the Public Offices Fees Act 1879(b), hereby make and concur in the following instrument:—

1.—(1) This instrument may be cited as the Land Charges Fees Order 1968 and shall come into operation on 1st June 1968.

(2) The Interpretation Act 1889(c) shall apply to this instrument as it applies to the interpretation of an Act of Parliament.

(3) In this instrument, unless the context otherwise requires—
"the Act" means the Land Charges Act 1925;
"fee" means a fee specified in the Schedule;
"the Schedule" means the Schedule to this instrument.

2. The fees specified in the Schedule shall be payable under the Act.

3. Except as provided in the next following paragraph, every fee shall be prepaid in cash or by means of Land Registry adhesive stamps.

4. Every fee payable in respect of registration in a local deeds registry under section 10(6) of the Act (as amended by section 7 of the Law of Property (Amendment) Act 1926(d)) shall be prepaid in cash or by cheque or postal or money order, made payable to the registrar of that registry.

5. The fees numbered 12 and 13 in the Schedule shall not apply to any local deeds registry.

6. Where the amount payable in respect of a fee is not immediately ascertainable, such deposit shall be made as the Registrar shall direct.

7. The Land Charges Fees Order 1927(e) is hereby revoked.

Dated 26th April 1968.

Gardiner, C.

E. Alan Fitch,	Lords Commissioners of
J. McCann,	Her Majesty's Treasury.

(a) 1925 c. 22.　　　　　　　　　　(b) 1879 c. 58.
(c) 1889 c. 63.　　　　　　　　　　(d) 1926 c. 11.
(e) S.R. & O. 1927/1185 (Rev. XI p. 814; 1927, p. 651).

SCHEDULE

Fee	Amount
	s. *d.*
1. Registration or renewal of registration ... ... per name	2　6
2. Entry of priority notice ... ... per name	2　6
3. Entry of satisfaction, cesser, discharge, vacation or cancellation of a registration ... ... per name	2　6
4. Certificate of satisfaction, cesser or discharge ... per name	2　6
5. Modification or rectification of an entry ... ... per name	2　6
6. Personal search in the alphabetical index ... ... per name	2　6
7. Personal search in any register ... ... per name	2　6
8. Official search in the alphabetical index (including issue of certificate) ... ... per name	2　6
9. Official search in any register (including issue of certificate) ... ... per name	2　6
10. Office copy of an entry in any register (not including a copy or extract of any plan or document filed in the Registry)	2　6
11. Office copy of any plan or document filed in the Registry:—such further fee, according to the time and labour employed, as the Registrar shall direct, with a minimum fee of	2　6
12. Expediting an official search (additional fee per application) ...	2　6
13. Telegraphing or telephoning the result of an official search:— such fee (additional to the fee of 2*s*. 6*d*. per name searched) as the Registrar considers reasonable having regard to the cost of the telegram or telephone call, with a minimum of:—	
in the case of a telegram	7　6
in the case of a telephone call	5　0

EXPLANATORY NOTE
(This Note is not part of the Order.)

This instrument, which supersedes the Land Charges Fees Order 1927, amends the fees payable in connection with the registration and disclosure of land charges. A standard fee of 2*s*. 6*d*. is prescribed for all items except the minimum fees for telegraphing and telephoning the result of an official search, which are fixed at 7*s*. 6*d*. and 5*s*. 0*d*. respectively.

1968 No. 678

AGRICULTURE

The Agricultural Credits Fees Order 1968

Made - - - *26th April* 1968

Coming into Operation *1st June* 1968

The Lord Chancellor and the Treasury, in exercise of the powers conferred on them by section 9 of the Agricultural Credits Act 1928(**a**), and sections 2 and 3 of the Public Offices Fees Act 1879(**b**), hereby make and approve the following instrument :—

1.—(1) This instrument may be cited as the Agricultural Credits Fees Order 1968 and shall come into operation on 1st June 1968.

(2) The Interpretation Act 1889(**c**) shall apply to this instrument as it applies to the interpretation of an Act of Parliament.

(3) In this instrument, unless the context otherwise requires—

"the Act" means the Agricultural Credits Act 1928 ;

"fee" means a fee specified in the Schedule ;

"the Schedule" means the Schedule to this instrument.

2. The fees specified in the Schedule shall be payable under the Act.

3. Every fee shall be prepaid in cash or by means of Land Registry adhesive stamps.

4. Where the amount payable in respect of a fee is not immediately ascertainable, such deposit shall be made as the Registrar shall direct.

5. The Agricultural Credits Fees Order 1928(**d**) is hereby revoked.

Dated 26th April 1968.

Gardiner, C.

E. Alan Fitch, } Lords Commissioners of
J. McCann, } Her Majesty's Treasury.

(**a**) 1928 c. 43.　　　(**b**) 1879 c. 58.　　　(**c**) 1889 c. 63.
(**d**) S.R. & O. 1928/668 (Rev. I. p. 94; 1928, p. 3).

SCHEDULE

Fee		Amount
		s. d.
1. Entry in, cancellation or rectification of the register	per name	2 6
2. Certificate of cancellation of a registration ..	per name	2 6
3. Personal search in the register or of a memorandum filed thereunder (except where the inspection is made by or on behalf of a bank)	per name	2 6
4. Official search of the register (including issue of certificate)	per name	2 6
5. Certified copy of any memorandum filed under section 9(3) of the Act	per name	2 6
6. Expediting an official search (additional fee per application)		2 6
7. Telegraphing or telephoning the result of an official search:— such fee (additional to the fee of 2s. 6d. per name searched) as the Registrar considers reasonable having regard to the cost of the telegram or telephone call, with a minimum of:—		
in the case of a telegram		7 6
in the case of a telephone call		5 0

EXPLANATORY NOTE

(*This Note is not part of the Order.*)

This instrument, which supersedes the Agricultural Credits Fees Order 1928, amends the fees payable in connection with the registration and disclosure of agricultural charges under the Agricultural Credits Act 1928. A standard fee of 2s. 6d. is prescribed for all items except the minimum fees for telegraphing and telephoning the result of an official search, which are fixed at 7s. 6d. and 5s. 0d. respectively.

STATUTORY INSTRUMENTS

1968 No. 679

CUSTOMS AND EXCISE

The Import Duties (General) (No. 4) Order 1968

Made - - - -	30th April 1968
Laid before the House of Commons	14th May 1968
Coming into Operation	1st July 1968

The Lords Commissioners of Her Majesty's Treasury, by virtue of the powers conferred on them by sections 1, 2 and 13 of the Import Duties Act 1958(a), and of all other powers enabling them in that behalf, on the recommendation of the Board of Trade hereby make the following Order:—

1.—(1) The form of customs tariff set out in column 1 of Schedule 1 to this Order (being the form prescribed by the Import Duties (General) (No. 11) Order 1966(b) as amended by subsequent Orders under the Import Duties Act 1958(c), and with other amendments required to give effect to the Geneva agreements, or consisting of the omission of unnecessary subheadings or other minor modifications) may continue to be referred to as the Customs Tariff 1959 and to be used in classifying goods for customs purposes in cases where some other method is not required under any enactment.

In this paragraph " the Geneva agreements " means the agreements dated 30th June 1967(d) entered into at Geneva between Her Majesty's Government in the United Kingdom and the Governments of certain other countries and amending the General Agreement on Tariffs and Trade concluded in Geneva in 1947(e).

(2) The form so set out shall be interpreted and applied in accordance with the interpretative rules preceding it in the said Schedule 1, but the Index of General Definitions etc. appended to those rules shall not be taken as part of that form or affect its interpretation.

(3) Where goods are to be classified in accordance with that form and the classification depends on the rate of duty, then, unless the contrary intention appears, account shall be taken of all customs duties for the time being chargeable, other than duty under the Customs Duties (Dumping and Subsidies) Act 1957(f), and the classification shall be made by a comparison of the amounts chargeable on goods not qualifying for any preferential rate of duty.

2.—(1) Where in any heading or subheading of Schedule 1 to this Order a rate of duty is shown in column 2, then, on the importation into the United Kingdom of goods classified in that heading or subheading, there shall, subject to the following provisions of this Article, be charged an import duty at the rate so shown:

Provided that—

(a) no import duty shall be charged in the case of goods of the Republic of Ireland consigned to the United Kingdom from that country;

(b) in the case of goods qualifying for Commonwealth preference (not being goods falling within paragraph (a) above), no import duty shall be charged

---

(a) 1958 c. 6.   (b) S.I. 1966/1555 (1966 III, p. 4405).
(c) See the Orders revoked by Art. 3(3) of this Order.   (d) Cmnd. 3347.
(e) Cmd. 7258.   (f) 1957 c. 18.

unless a rate is shown in column 3 prefixed by the letter " C " and, if a rate is so shown, import duty shall be charged at that rate;

(c) in the case of goods of Convention area origin within the meaning of the European Free Trade Association Act 1960(a), but subject to section 2 of that Act, no import duty shall be charged unless a rate is shown in the said column 3 prefixed by the letter " E " and, if a rate is so shown, import duty shall be charged at that rate; and

(d) where a heading or subheading limits a rate of duty to a specified period, or shows different rates for different periods, the duty shall be charged accordingly.

(2) Goods falling within both paragraph (b) and paragraph (c) of the proviso to paragraph (1) above shall, if less import duty would be chargeable if they were treated as falling solely within one of those paragraphs than if they were treated as falling solely within the other, be treated for the purposes of this Order as excluded from that other paragraph.

(3) Where—

(a) any import duty is by this Order expressed to be chargeable on goods of any description, and

(b) any goods of that description are chargeable with a revenue duty (not being a duty in addition to which the import duty is expressed to be chargeable) but those goods are not exempt from import duties,

then import duty shall be charged on those goods at a rate less by the amount of any such revenue duty chargeable on them than the rate at which the import duty is expressed to be chargeable or, if that amount is equal to or greater than the duty at the last-mentioned rate, shall not be charged on those goods.

(4) Any reference in Schedule 1 to this Order to a percentage, in relation to a rate of duty, is a reference to a percentage of the value of the goods; and the expression " full rate ", where used in column 3 of that Schedule in relation to goods of any description, means the rate shown for goods of that description in column 2.

(5) In this Article, and in Schedule 1 to this Order, " revenue duty " means a duty of customs chargeable under any enactment other than the Import Duties Act 1958(b) and the Customs Duties (Dumping and Subsidies) Act 1957(c).

3.—(1) This Order may be cited as the Import Duties (General) (No. 4) Order 1968.

(2) The Interpretation Act 1889(d) shall apply for the interpretation of this Order as it applies for the interpretation of an Act of Parliament.

(3) The Import Duties (General) Orders specified in Schedule 2 to this Order are hereby revoked.

(4) Nothing in this Order shall be construed as affecting the operation of any instrument made under the Import Duties Act 1958 and not revoked by the foregoing paragraph, or as affecting any relief to which any person is or may become entitled under any provisions of that Act.

(5) This Order shall come into operation on 1st July 1968.

B. K. O'Malley,
Harry Gourlay,
Two of the Lords Commissioners
of Her Majesty's Treasury.

30th April 1968.

(a) 1960 c. 19.   (b) 1958 c. 6.   (c) 1957 c. 18.   (d) 1889 c. 63.

SCHEDULE 1

FORM OF CUSTOMS TARIFF, AND RATES OF IMPORT DUTY

[For list of section and chapter titles, see end of Schedule.]

INTERPRETATIVE RULES

1. The titles of Sections, Chapters and sub-Chapters are provided for ease of reference only; for legal purposes, classification (as between headings) shall be determined according to the terms of the headings and any relative Section or Chapter notes and, provided such headings or notes do not otherwise require, according to Rules 2 to 5 below.

2. Any reference in a heading to a material or substance shall be taken to include a reference to mixtures or combinations of that material or substance with other materials or substances. Any reference to goods of a given material or substance shall be taken to include a reference to goods consisting wholly or partly of such material or substance. The classification of goods consisting of more than one material or substance shall be according to the principles of Rule 3.

3. When for any reason, goods are, *prima facie*, classifiable under two or more headings, classification shall be effected as follows:

(a) The heading which provides the most specific description shall be preferred to headings providing a more general description (subheadings being disregarded).

(b) Mixtures and composite goods which consist of different materials or are made up of different components and which cannot be classified by reference to (a) shall be classified as if they consisted of the material or component which gives the goods their essential character, in so far as this criterion is applicable.

(c) When goods cannot be classified by reference to (a) or (b), they shall be classified under the heading which involves the highest rate of duty.

4. Where in a note to a Section or Chapter it is provided that certain goods are not covered by that Section or Chapter, a reference being made parenthetically to another Section or Chapter or to a particular heading, the note shall, except in so far as the context requires otherwise, be taken to refer to all the goods falling within that other Section or Chapter or heading notwithstanding that only certain of those goods are referred to by description in the note.

5. Goods not falling within any heading of the Schedule shall be classified under the heading appropriate to the goods to which they are most akin.

6. Except as provided in a note to a Section or Chapter expressed to be a special note applying to subheadings only, the classification of goods within a heading is to be determined by applying as between subheadings the like Rules as are to be applied between headings, and, except in so far as the contrary intention appears, terms used in a subheading are to be interpreted in the same way as in the heading.

Index of General Definitions etc.

Phrase or matter	Defined or explained in
1. Alloys (how classified in Sections XIV and XV)	Chapter 71, Note 5 / Section XV, Note 3
2. Artificial fur	Chapter 43, Note 5
3. Base metal	Section XV, Notes 4, and 7
4. Composition leather	Chapter 41, Note 2
5. Embroidery	Chapter 58, Note 5
6. Fine animal hair	Note to Chapter 53
7. Furskins	Chapter 43, Note 1
8. Glass	Chapter 70, Note 3
9. Horsehair	Chapter 5, Note 4
10. Hydrocarbon oils	Chapter 27, Special Note
11. Ivory	Chapter 5, Note 3
12. Light oils	Chapter 27, Special Note
13. Made up (used of textiles in Section XI)	Section XI, Note 6
14. Man-made fibres	Chapter 51, Note 1
15. Mixed textiles (how classified in Chapters 50 to 57)	Section XI, Note 2
16. Parts of general use (of base metal)	Section XV, Note 2
17. Pearls	Chapter 71, Note 4
18. Precious metal	Chapter 71, Notes 4, and 7
19. Put up for retail sale (used of yarn in Chapters 50, 51 and 53 to 56)	Section XI, Note 4
20. Rubber	Chapter 40, Notes 1 and
21. Sweetening matter	Chapter 4, Special Note / Special Note to Section IV
22. Twine, cordage, ropes and cables (in Section XI)	Section XI, Note 3
23. Waste and scrap (used of base metal in Section XV)	Section XV, Note 6

SECTION I

LIVE ANIMALS; ANIMAL PRODUCTS

Chapter 1

Live Animals

Notes

1. This Chapter does not cover fish, crustaceans, molluscs or microbial cultures.

2. Any reference in this Chapter to a particular genus or species, except where the context otherwise requires, includes a reference to the young of that genus or species.

Tariff Heading	Full	Commonwealth (C) E.F.T.A. (E)	
1.01 Live horses, asses, mules and hinnies ...	—	—	
1.02 Live animals of the bovine species ...	—	—	
1.03 Live swine	—	—	
1.04 Live sheep and goats	—	—	
1.05 Live poultry, that is to say, fowls, ducks, geese, turkeys and guinea fowls	10%	C E	— 10%
1.06 Other live animals: (A) Quadrupeds	—	—	
(B) Bees	—	—	
(C) Other	10%	C E	— 10%

Rate of Import Duty (if any) spans Full and Commonwealth/E.F.T.A columns.

Chapter 2
Meat and Edible Meat Offals

Note

This Chapter does not cover:

(a) Products of the kinds described in headings Nos. 02.01, 02.02, 02.03, 02.04 and 02.06 unfit or unsuitable for human consumption;

(b) Guts, bladders or stomachs of animals (heading No. 05.04) and animal blood of heading No. 05.15; or

(c) Animal fat, other than products of heading No. 02.05 (Chapter 15).

Tariff Heading	Rate of Import Duty (if any)		
	Full	Commonwealth (C) E.F.T.A. (E)	
02.01 Meat and edible offals of the animals falling within heading No. 01.01, 01.02, 01.03 or 01.04, fresh, chilled or frozen:			
(A) Meat:			
(1) Beef and veal:			
(a) Boned or boneless	20%	C	—
		E	20%
(b) Other:			
(i) Chilled	¼d. per lb.	C	—
		E	¼d. per lb.
(ii) Fresh or frozen	⅜d. per lb.	C	—
		E	⅜d. per lb.
(2) Mutton and lamb	—		—
(3) Horsemeat	8%	C	—
		E	8%
(4) Other	10%	C	—
		E	10%
(B) Edible offals:			
(1) Beef and veal:			
(a) Sweetbreads and tongues ...	—		—
(b) Other	16%	C	—
		E	16%
(2) Other	—		—
02.02 Dead poultry (that is to say, fowls, ducks, geese, turkeys and guinea fowls) and edible offals thereof (except liver), fresh, chilled or frozen:			
(A) Dead poultry:			
(1) Guinea fowl	10%	C	—
		E	10%
(2) Other	3d. per lb.	C	—
		E	3d. per lb.
(B) Edible poultry offals	10%	C	—
		E	10%
02.03 Poultry liver, fresh, chilled, frozen, salted or in brine	10%	C	—
		E	10%
02.04 Other meat and edible meat offals, fresh, chilled or frozen:			
(A) Rabbit, fresh	5%	C	—
		E	5%
(B) Edible meat offals	—		—
(C) Whale meat	10%		—
(D) Other	10%	C	—
		E	10%

Tariff Heading	Rate of Import Duty (*if any*)	
	Full	*Commonwealth (C) E.F.T.A. (E)*
2.05 Unrendered pig fat free of lean meat and unrendered poultry fat, fresh, chilled, frozen, salted, in brine, dried or smoked	10%	C — E 10%
2.06 Meat and edible meat offals (except poultry liver), salted, in brine, dried or smoked: (A) Meat: (1) Beef and veal: (a) Boned or boneless	20%	C — E 20%
(b) Other	⅔d. per lb.	C — E ⅔d. per lb.
(2) Mutton and lamb	—	—
(3) Hams, whole: (a) In airtight containers	10%	C — E 10%
(b) Other	—	—
(4) Other: (a) Pork (including ham and bacon), not canned or bottled	10%	—
(b) Horsemeat	8%	C — E 8%
(c) Other	10%	C — E 10%
(B) Edible offals: (1) Beef and veal: (a) Sweetbreads and tongues ...	—	—
(b) Other	20%	C — E 20%
(2) Other	—	—

Chapter 3

Fish, Crustaceans and Molluscs

Note

This Chapter does not cover:

(a) Marine mammals (heading No. 01.06) or meat thereof (heading No. 02.04 or 02.0€

(b) Fish (including livers and roes thereof), crustaceans and molluscs, dead, unfit unsuitable for human consumption either by reason of their species or their conditic (Chapter 5); or

(c) Caviar or caviar substitutes (heading No. 16.04).

Tariff Heading	Rate of Import Duty (if any)		
	Full	Commonwealth (C E.F.T.A. (E	
03.01 Fish, fresh (live or dead), chilled or frozen:			
(A) Salmon, chilled or frozen	—	—	
(B) Fish roes	5%	C	
		E	5%
(C) Other:			
(1) Fillets, chilled or frozen; portions, weighing not less than 1 ounce each, prepared by cutting blocks of fillets, chilled or frozen	10%	—	
(2) Other	10%	C	
		E	10%
03.02 Fish, salted, in brine, dried or smoked:			
(A) Wet salted split fish	—	—	
(B) Fish roes	5%	C	
		E	5%
(C) Other	10%	C	
		E	10%
03.03 Crustaceans and molluscs, whether in shell or not, fresh (live or dead), chilled, frozen, salted, in brine or dried; crustaceans, in shell, simply boiled in water:			
(A) Clams, cockles, crabs, crawfish, crayfish, lobsters, mussels, Norway lobsters (Dublin Bay prawns), scallops (including queen scallops), shrimps, whelks, winkles:			
(1) Frozen or dried	10%	C	
		E	10%
(2) Other	30%	C	
		E	30%
(B) Oysters:			
(1) In shell:			
(a) Of the kind *Ostrea virginica* from 1st June to last day of February	15%	C	
		E	15%
(b) Other kinds ... from 1st June to last day of February	30%	C	
		E	30%
(2) Not in shell	30%	C	
		E	30%

Tariff Heading	Rate of Import Duty (*if any*)		
	Full	Commonwealth (C) E.F.T.A. (E)	
03.03 Crustaceans and molluscs, etc.—*contd.*			
(C) Prawns:			
(1) Peeled prawns, chilled or frozen...	10%		
(2) Other	10%	C E	— 10%
(D) Other	10%	C E	— 10%

Chapter 4

Dairy Produce; Birds' Eggs; Natural Honey

Notes

1. The expression " milk " means whole milk (full cream) or skimmed milk (separated) buttermilk, whey, and kephir, yoghourt and similar fermented milk.

2. Milk and cream put up in hermetically sealed cans are regarded as preserved within the meaning of heading No. 04.02. However, milk and cream are not regarded as so preserved merely by reason of being pasteurised, sterilised or peptonised, if they are not put up in hermetically sealed cans.

Special note applying to subheadings only

The expression " sweetening matter " includes only glucose, sucrose and invert sugar For the purposes of this Chapter the weight of sweetening matter contained in any good shall be determined as follows: in so far as the sweetening matter is sucrose the weight shall be taken to be the actual weight of the sucrose or, if the sucrose is of a polarisation not exceeding 98°, 95 per cent. of the actual weight of the sucrose; in so far as it is liquid glucose the weight shall be taken to be 48 per cent. of the actual weight of the glucose and in so far as it is solid glucose or invert sugar the weight shall be taken to be 75 per cent. of the actual weight of the glucose or sugar.

Tariff Heading	Rate of Import Duty (*if any*)		
	Full	*Commonwealth (C)* *E.F.T.A.* (E)	
04.01 Milk and cream, fresh, not concentrated or sweetened	10%	C E	— 10%
04.02 Milk and cream, preserved, concentrated or sweetened:			
(A) Milk (other than buttermilk, whey, and kephir, yoghourt and similar fermented milk):			
(1) Evaporated or condensed:			
(*a*) Whole:			
(i) Not containing added sweetening matter	6s. per cwt.	C E	— 6s. per cwt.
(ii) Other	7s. 7d. per cwt.	C E	— 7s. 7d. per cwt.
(*b*) Skimmed	10%	C E	— 10%
(2) Dried milk, block milk and other...	6s. per cwt.	C E	— 6s. per cwt.
(B) Other:			
(1) Canned cream	10%		—
(2) Other	10%	C E	— 10%
04.03 Butter	—		—
04.04 Cheese and curd:			
(A) Cheese:			
(1) Blue veined	10%		—
(2) Other	15%	C E	— 15%
(B) Curd	10%	C E	— 10%

| | Rate of Import Duty (*if any*) | |
Tariff Heading	Full	Commonwealth (C) E.F.T.A. (E)
4.05 Birds' eggs and egg yolks, fresh, dried or otherwise preserved, sweetened or not:		
(A) Eggs in shell:		
(1) Not exceeding 14 lb. in weight per 120 ...	1s. per 120	C — E 1s. per 120
(2) Over 14 lb. but not exceeding 17 lb. in weight per 120	1s. 6d. per 120	C — E 1s. 6d. per 120
(3) Over 17 lb. in weight per 120 ...	1s. 9d. per 120	C — E 1s. 9d. per 120
(B) Eggs not in shell and egg yolks ...	10%	C — E 10%
4.06 Natural honey	5s. per cwt.	C — E 5s. per cwt.

Chapter 5

Products of Animal Origin, not elsewhere specified or included

Notes

1. This Chapter does not cover:

(a) Edible products (other than guts, bladders and stomachs of animals, whole and piec
thereof, and animal blood, liquid or dried);

(b) Hides or skins (including furskins) other than goods falling within heading N
05.05, 05.06 or 05.07 (Chapter 41 or 43);

(c) Animal textile materials, other than horsehair and horsehair waste (Section XI);

(d) Prepared knots or tufts for broom or brush making (heading No. 96.03).

2. For the purposes of heading No. 05.01, the sorting of hair by length (provided the ro
ends and tip ends respectively are not arranged together) shall be deemed not to constitu
working.

3. Throughout this Schedule elephant, mammoth, mastodon, walrus, narwhal and wi
boar tusks, rhinoceros horns and the teeth of all animals are regarded as ivory.

4. Throughout this Schedule, references to " horsehair " are to be taken to include n
only references to the hair of the manes and tails of equine animals but also such hair
bovine animals.

Tariff Heading	Rate of Import Duty (if any)		
	Full	Commonwealth (C E.F.T.A. (E	
05.01 Human hair, unworked, whether or not washed or scoured; waste of human hair	—	—	
05.02 Pigs', hogs' and boars' bristles or hair; badger hair and other brush making hair; waste of such bristles and hair:			
(A) Raw, whether or not cleaned or washed	—	—	
(B) Bristles in bundles or bunches, consisting exclusively of bristles laid parallel	—	—	
(C) Other	9%	—	
05.03 Horsehair and horsehair waste, whether or not put up in a layer or between two layers of other material:			
(A) Raw, whether or not cleaned or washed	—	—	
(B) Other	9%	—	
05.04 Guts, bladders and stomachs of animals (other than fish), whole and pieces thereof:			
(A) Sausage casings:			
(1) Hog...	—	—	
(2) Other	10%	C E	— 10%
(B) Other:			
(1) Of bovine animals:			
(a) Edible	16%	—	
(b) Other	10%	C E	— 10%
(2) Other:			
(a) Of sheep and pigs			
(b) Other	6%	C E	— 6%

Tariff Heading	Rate of Import Duty (*if any*)	
	Full	Commonwealth (C) E.F.T.A. (E)
.05 Fish waste:		
(A) Herring offals	—	—
(B) Other	8%	—
.06 Sinews and tendons; parings and similar waste, of raw hides or skins	—	—
.07 Skins and other parts of birds, with their feathers or down, feathers and parts of feathers (whether or not with trimmed edges) and down, not further worked than cleaned, disinfected or treated for preservation; powder and waste of feathers or parts of feathers:		
(A) Skins and pieces thereof, with their down	—	—
(B) Feathers in bales, sacks or similar packages, without internal containers; down:		
(1) Cleaned to the standard prescribed in paragraph 8 of Part 12 of British Standard 1425 : 1960	8%	—
(2) Other	—	—
(C) Barbs, quills and scapes	8%	—
(D) Other	16%	—
.08 Bones and horn-cores, unworked, defatted, simply prepared (but not cut to shape), treated with acid or degelatinised; powder and waste of these products:		
(A) Ossein	—	—
(B) Other	8%	—
.09 Horns, antlers, hooves, nails, claws and beaks of animals, unworked or simply prepared but not cut to shape, and waste and powder of these products; whalebone and the like, unworked or simply prepared but not cut to shape, and hair and waste of these products	8%	—
.10 Ivory, unworked or simply prepared but not cut to shape; powder and waste of ivory	—	—
.11 Tortoise-shell (shells and scales), unworked or simply prepared but not cut to shape; claws and waste of tortoise-shell	8%	—

Tariff Heading	Rate of Import Duty (if any)	
	Full	Commonwealth (C) E.F.T.A. (E)
05.12 Coral and similar substances, unworked or simply prepared but not otherwise worked; shells, unworked or simply prepared but not cut to shape; powder and waste of shells:		
(A) Mother of pearl, trochus and other hard shells (including fresh water shells) which possess the characteristic nacre of pearl shell	—	—
(B) Other	6%	—
05.13 Natural sponges	4½%	—
05.14 Ambergris, castoreum, civet and musk; cantharides; bile, whether or not dried; animal products, fresh, chilled or frozen, or otherwise provisionally preserved, of a kind used in the preparation of pharmaceutical products:		
(A) Pancreas glands	—	—
(B) Other	10%	—
05.15 Animal products not elsewhere specified or included; dead animals of Chapter 1 or Chapter 3, unfit for human consumption:		
(A) Cochineal	—	—
(B) Salted fish roes	10%	—
(C) Blood powder and blood plasma ...	10%	—
(D) Other	10%	C —
		E 10%

SECTION II

VEGETABLE PRODUCTS

Chapter 6

Live Trees and Other Plants; Bulbs, Roots and the Like; Cut Flowers and Ornamental Foliage

Notes

1. This Chapter covers only live trees and goods (including seedling vegetables) of a kind commonly supplied by nursery gardeners or florists for planting or for ornamental use; nevertheless it does not include potatoes, onions, shallots or garlic (Chapter 7).

2. Any reference in heading No. 06.03 or 06.04 to goods of any kind shall be construed as including a reference to bouquets, floral baskets, wreaths and similar articles made wholly or partly of goods of that kind, account not being taken of accessories of other materials.

3. In this Chapter, " gross " means inclusive of the weight of any earth or other growing medium in which the goods are imported.

Tariff Heading	Rate of Import Duty (*if any*)		
	Full	*Commonwealth* (*C*) *E.F.T.A.* (*E*)	
06.01 Bulbs, tubers, tuberous roots, corms, crowns and rhizomes, dormant, in growth or in flower:			
(A) Dry:			
(1) Lily of the valley crowns and roots	10%	C E	— 10%
(2) Bulbs, corms, rhizomes and tubers:			
(*a*) Begonia and gloxinia	8%	C E	— 8%
(*b*) Other	10%	C E	— 10%
(3) Other, including dahlia and other tuberous roots	1s. 3d. per lb.	C E	— 1s. 3d. per lb.
(B) Other:			

(1) Ixia ...   .
      Narcissus (polyanthus types) ...
      Roman hyacinth ...   .
      Snowdrop ...   .
      Star of Bethlehem   ...   ...
	4½d. per lb. (gross)	C
		E
			—
			4½d. per lb. (gross)

(2) Ranunculus	7d. per lb. (gross)	C E	— 7d. per lb. (gross)
(3) Hyacinth (other than roman hyacinth), iris, narcissus (other than polyanthus types but including daffodil), tulip			
from 1st December to last day of February	2s. 10d. per lb. (gross)	C E	— 2s. 10d. per lb. (gross)
from 1st March to 30th April ...	2s. 3d. per lb. (gross)	C E	— 2s. 3d. per lb. (gross)
from 1st May to 30th November	1s. 8d. per lb. (gross)	C E	— 1s. 8d. per lb. (gross)

Tariff Heading	Rate of Import Duty (if any)	
	Full	Commonwealth (C) E.F.T.A. (E)
06.01 Bulbs, tubers, tuberous roots, etc.—contd. (B) Other:—contd. (4) Freesia		
from 1st September to 30th April	25%	C — E 25%
from 1st May to 31st August ...	10%	C — E 10%
(5) Other	1s. 8d. per lb. (gross)	C — E 1s. 8d. per lb. (gross)
06.02 Other live plants, including trees, shrubs, bushes and roots; buds, eyes and stems for grafting and budding; cuttings and slips; mushroom spawn:		
(A) Buds, eyes and stems for grafting and budding; cuttings and slips; mushroom spawn	10%	C — E 10%

(B) Rose stocks and rose trees, shrubs, bushes and plants:
(1) Rose stocks neither budded nor grafted, the following:
    Rosa canina rooted single stems, not less than 4 feet in length
    Rosa canina seedlings
    Rosa laxa seedlings
    Rosa rugosa rooted single stems, not less than 4 feet in length
	8%	C —
		E 8%

(2) Other: (a) Standard trees, including half standards, quarter standards and weeping standards	£12 per 100	C — E £12 per 100
(b) Other	£3 per 100	C — E £3 per 100
(C) Fruit stocks and fruit trees, shrubs, bushes and plants	£2 5s. per cwt. (gross)	C — E £2 5s. per cwt (gross)
(D) Azalea indica: (1) Not in flower	—	—
(2) In flower	1s. 8d. per lb. (gross)	C — E 1s. 8d. per lb. (gross)
(E) Broussonetia papyrifera (paper mulberry) and grafts on Broussonetia papyrifera stock; sweet bays	10%	C — E 10%
(F) Other: (1) Not in flower: (a) Trees, shrubs and bushes ...	£2 5s. per cwt. (gross)	C — E £2 5s. per cwt (gross)
(b) Other	1s. 3d. per lb. (gross)	C — E 1s. 3d. per lb. (gross)

Tariff Heading	Rate of Import Duty (*if any*)	
	Full	Commonwealth (*C*) E.F.T.A. (*E*)

.02 Other live plants, etc.—*contd.*
  (F) Other:—*contd.*
    (2) In flower:
      (*a*) Gypsophila ... ...
         Heather... ... ...
         Marguerite ... ...
         Marigold ... ...
         Stock ... ...
	4¼d. per lb.
	(gross)
		C —
		E 4½d. per lb.
		     (gross)

(*b*) Other	1s. 8d. per lb. (gross)	C — E 1s. 8d. per lb. (gross)
.03 Cut flowers and flower buds of a kind suitable for bouquets or for ornamental purposes, fresh, dried, dyed, bleached, im- pregnated or otherwise prepared: (A) Mimosa	2d. per lb.	C — E 2d. per lb.

(B) Gypsophila ... ...
      Heather ... ...
      Ixia ... ...
      Marguerite ... ...
      Marigold ... .:.
      Roman hyacinth ... ...
      Snowdrop ... ...
      Star of Bethlehem ...
      Stock ... ...
	4¼d. per lb.	C —
		E 4¼d. per lb.

(C) Lilac	5¼d. per lb.	C — E 5¼d. per lb.

(D) Narcissus (polyanthus types)... ...
      Peony ... ...
      Ranunculus ... ...
	7d. per lb.	C —
		E 7d. per lb.

(E) Hyacinth (other than roman hyacinth), iris, narcissus (other than polyanthus types, but including daffodil), tulip *from* 1*st December to last day of February*	2s. 10d. per lb.	C — E 2s. 10d. per lb.
from 1*st March to* 30*th April*	2s. 3d. per lb.	C — E 2s. 3d. per lb.
from 1*st May to* 30*th November* ...	1s. 8d. per lb.	C — E 1s. 8d. per lb.

(F) Freesia
    from 1*st September to* 30*th April*
      (*a*) Of a value exceeding 18s. per lb.
	7s. per lb.	C —
		E 7s. per lb.

(*b*) Other	25%	C — E 25%
from 1*st May to* 31*st August*	2s. 6d. per lb.	C — E 2s. 6d. per lb.

(G) Anemone ... ...
      Carnation ... ...
      Rose ... ...
	2s. 6d. per lb.	C —
		E 2s. 6d. per lb.

(H) Other	2s. per lb.	C — E 2s. per lb.

Tariff Heading	Rate of Import Duty (if any)	
	Full	Commonwealth (C E.F.T.A. (E

06.04 **Foliage, branches and other parts (other than flowers or buds) of trees, shrubs, bushes and other plants, and mosses, lichens and grasses, being goods of a kind suitable for bouquets or ornamental purposes, fresh, dried, dyed, bleached, impregnated or otherwise prepared:**
(A) Foliage:
  (1) Cycas ... ...
      Magnolia ... ...
      Holly ... ...
      Mistletoe ... ...
      Golden palm ... ...
	10%	C —
		E 10%

(2) Asparagus	1s. 8d. per lb.	C — E 1s. 8d. per lb.
(3) Other	4½d. per lb.	C — E 4½d. per lb.
(B) Branches (other than foliage) and other parts	10%	C — E 10%
(C) Mosses and lichens	4½d. per lb.	C — E 4½d. per lb.

(D) Grasses:
  (1) Agrostis ... ...
      Erianthus ... ...
      Eulalia ... ...
      Pampas ... ...
      Stipa ... ...
      Tropini (lagurus) ... ...
	10%	C —
		E 10%

(2) Other	4½d. per lb.	C — E 4½d. per lb.

Chapter 7

Edible Vegetables and Certain Roots and Tubers

te

In heading No. 07.01, the word " vegetables " is to be taken to include edible mushrooms, ffles, rhubarb, olives, capers, tomatoes, potatoes, salad beetroot, cucumbers, gherkins, rrows, pumpkins, aubergines, *Capsicum grossum* (sweet capsicum), fennel, parsley, rvil, tarragon, cress, sweet marjoram, horse-radish and garlic.   In headings Nos. 07.02, 03 and 07.04, the word " vegetables " is to be taken to apply to all products which in ir fresh state are classified in heading No. 07.01.   Dried leguminous vegetables, shelled, wever, are to be classified in heading No. 07.05, ground *Capsicum grossum* (sweet capsi- m) in heading No. 09.04, flours of the dried leguminous vegetables of heading No. 07.05 heading No. 11.03, and flour, meal and flakes of potato in heading No. 11.05.

Tariff Heading	Rate of Import Duty (if any)	
	Full	Commonwealth (C) E.F.T.A. (E)
01 Vegetables, fresh or chilled:		
(A) Asparagus		
from 16th April to 30th June ...	£2 16s. per cwt.	C — E £2 16s. per cwt.
from 1st July to 15th April ...	10%	C — E 10%
(B) Broccoli and cauliflowers		
from 1st March to 30th June ...	8s. per cwt.	C — E 8s. per cwt.
from 1st July to last day of February	6s. per cwt.	C — E 6s. per cwt.
(C) Carrots		
from 1st April to 30th April ...	10%	C — E 10%
from 1st May to 30th June ...	£1 per cwt.	C — E £1 per cwt.
from 1st July to 31st October ...	10%	C — E 10%
from 1st November to 31st March	8%	C — E 8%
(D) Cucumbers (other than gherkins)		
from 1st March to 30th September	£1 per cwt.	C — E £1 per cwt.
from 1st October to last day of February	10%	C — E 10%
(E) Green peas, unshelled		
from 1st June to 31st July ...	18s. 8d. per cwt.	C — E 18s. 8d. per cwt.
from 1st August to 31st May ...	10%	C — E 10%
(F) Lettuce and endive		
from 1st March to 30th April ...	£1 10s. per cwt.	C — E £1 10s. per cwt.
from 1st May to 31st May ...	£1 per cwt.	C — E £1 per cwt.

Tariff Heading	Rate of Import Duty (if any)	
	Full	Commonwealth (C) E.F.T.A. (E)
07.01 Vegetables, fresh or chilled—*contd.*		
(F) Lettuce and endive: *contd.*		
from 1st June to 31st October ...	16s. per cwt.	C — E 16s. per cwt.
from 1st November to last day of February	10s. per cwt.	C — E 10s. per cwt.
(G) Chicory (salad)		
from 1st November to 31st March	8s. per cwt.	C — E 8s. per cwt.
from 1st April to 31st October ...	10%	C — E 10%
(H) Mushrooms		
from 1st October to 30th April...	20%	C — E 20%
from 1st May to 30th September	10%	C — E 10%
(IJ) Potatoes		
from 16th May to 30th June:		
(a) New Potatoes	9s. 4d. per cwt.	C — E 9s. 4d. per cwt.
(b) Other	1s. per cwt.	C — E 1s. per cwt.
from 1st July to 31st August ...	2s. per cwt.	C — E 2s. per cwt.
from 1st September to 15th May	1s. per cwt.	C — E 1s. per cwt.
(K) Tomatoes		
from 1st May to 15th May:		
(a) Of a value exceeding £7 per cwt.	£1 17s. 4d. per cwt.	C — E £1 17s. 4d. per cwt.
(b) Other	10%	C — E 10%
from 16th May to 31st May:		
(a) Of a value exceeding £5 12s. per cwt.	£2 16s. per cwt.	C — E £2 16s. per cwt.
(b) Other	10%	C — E 10%
from 1st June to 15th June ...	£2 16s. per cwt.	C — E £2 16s. per cwt.
from 16th June to 31st July ...	£2 6s. 8d. per cwt.	C — E £2 6s. 8d. per cwt.
from 1st August to 31st August	£1 17s. 4d. per cwt.	C — E £1 17s. 4d. per cwt.
from 1st September to 31st October	18s. 8d. per cwt.	C — E 18s. 8d. per cwt.
from 1st November to 15th November	10%	C — E 10%
from 16th November to 31st March	9%	C — E 9%

Tariff Heading	Rate of Import Duty (if any)	
	Full	**Commonwealth (C) E.F.T.A. (E)**
.01 Vegetables, fresh or chilled—*contd.*		
(K) Tomatoes: *contd.*		
from 1st April to 30th April ...	10%	C —
		E 10%
(L) Dry-bulb onions and shallots		
from 1st February to 30th June...	8%	C —
		E 8%
from 1st July to 31st July ...	10%	C —
		E 10%
from 1st August to 30th November	4s. 8d. per cwt.	C —
		E 4s. 8d. per cwt.
from 1st December to 31st January	10%	C —
		E 10%
(M) Horse-radish ... ...·	4%	C —
		E 4%
(N) Herbs	4½d. per lb.	C —
		E 4½d. per lb.
(O) Garlic	10%	C —
(P) Celery	8%	C —
		E 8%
(Q) Other	10%	C —
		E 10%
.02 Vegetables (whether or not cooked), preserved by freezing	10%	C —
		E 10%
.03 Vegetables provisionally preserved in brine, in sulphur water or in other preservative solutions, but not specially prepared for immediate consumption:		
(A) Cauliflowers in brine, not being in airtight containers	6s. per cwt. of the vegetable content	C —
		E 6s. per cwt. of the vegetable content
(B) Other	10%	C —
		E 10%
.04 Dried vegetables, whole, cut, sliced, broken or in powder, but not further prepared:		
(A) Horse-radish	4%	C —
		E 4%
(B) Herbs, not in powder	4½d. per lb.	C —
		E 4½d. per lb.
(C) Garlic, tomatoes and leeks:		
(1) Garlic or leeks in airtight containers	13%	—
(2) Other	10%	—
(D) Other:		
(1) Vegetables (other than asparagus) in airtight containers	15%	C —
		E 15%
(2) Other	10%	C —
		E 10%

Tariff Heading	Rate of Import Duty (if any)	
	Full	Commonwealth (C E.F.T.A. (E
07.05 Dried leguminous vegetables, shelled, whether or not skinned or split: (A) Peas: (1) Split peas	15%	C — E 15%
(2) Whole peas (other than peas of the varieties commonly known as maple peas, dun peas and yellow or white peas)	7s. 6d. per cwt. or 10%, whichever is the greater	C — E 7s. 6d. per cv or 10%, whic ever is t greater
(3) Other	10%	C — E 10%
(B) Beans, dried, white (including haricot) other than butter	6%	C — E 6%
(C) Other	8%	C — E 8%
07.06 Manioc, arrowroot, salep, Jerusalem artichokes, sweet potatoes and other similar roots and tubers with high starch or inulin content, fresh or dried, whole or sliced; sago pith: (A) Manioc	—	—
(B) Other	8%	C — E 8%

Chapter 8

Edible Fruit and Nuts; Peel of Melons or Citrus Fruit

Notes

1. This Chapter does not cover inedible nuts or fruits.
2. The word " fresh " is to be taken to extend to goods which have been chilled.

Tariff Heading	Rate of Import Duty (*if any*)	
	Full	*Commonwealth (C)* *E.F.T.A.* (*E*)
.01 Dates, bananas, coconuts, Brazil nuts, cashew nuts, pineapples, avocados, mangoes, guavas and mangosteens, fresh or dried, shelled or not:		
(A) Brazil nuts and coconuts, shelled or not, whole	—	—
(B) Bananas, fresh	7s. 6d. per cwt.	C — E 7s. 6d. per cwt.
(C) Pineapples, dried	5%	C — E 5%
(D) Dates:		
(1) Unstoned:		
(*a*) Of a value of less than £1 5s. per cwt.	—	—
(*b*) Other	6%	C — E 6%
(2) Stoned	—	—
(E) Mangoes, guavas, mangosteens, avocados	8%	C — E 8%
(F) Other	10%	C — E 10%
.02 Citrus fruit, fresh or dried:		
(A) Fresh:		
(1) Grapefruit	5s. per cwt.	C — E 5s. per cwt.
(2) Oranges, clementines, mandarins and tangerines		
from 1st *April to* 30th *November*	3s. 6d. per cwt.	C — E 3s. 6d. per cwt.
from 1st *December to* 31st *March*	8%	C — E 8%
(3) Other	8%	C — E 8%
(B) Dried	13%	C — E 13%
.03 Figs, fresh or dried:		
(A) Fresh	4s. 9½d. per cwt.	—
(B) Dried	6s. per cwt.	C — E 6s. per cwt.
.04 Grapes, fresh or dried:		
(A) Currants	2s. per cwt.	C — E 2s. per cwt.
(B) Raisins, sultanas and other dried grapes	6s. 8d. per cwt.	C — E 6s. 8d. per cwt.

Tariff Heading	Rate of Import Duty (if any)	
	Full	Commonwealth (C) E.F.T.A. (E)
08.04 Grapes, fresh or dried—*contd.* (C) Other: (1) Hothouse		
from 1st February to 30th June...	14s. per cwt.	C — / E 14s. per cwt.
from 1st July to 31st January ...	20%	C — / E 20%
(2) Other *from 1st February to 30th June...*	14s. per cwt.	C — / E 14s. per cwt.
from 1st July to 31st August ...	10%	C — / E 10%
from 1st September to 31st January	8%	C — / E 8%
08.05 Nuts other than those falling within heading No. 08.01, fresh or dried, shelled or not: (A) Hazel nuts, not in shell; almonds, not in shell; pecans	—	—
(B) Almonds, in shell, and chestnuts ...	10%	—
(C) Other	10%	C — / E 10%
08.06 Apples, pears and quinces, fresh: (A) Apples *from 16th April to 15th August*	4s. 6d. per cwt.	C — / E 4s. 6d. per cwt
(B) Pears *from 1st February to 31st July...*	4s. 6d. per cwt.	C — / E 4s. 6d. per cwt
from 1st August to 31st January	3s. per cwt.	C — / E 3s. per cwt.
(C) Quinces	10%	C — / E 10%
08.07 Stone fruit, fresh: (A) Cherries *from 1st June to 15th August ...*	£1 17s. 4d. per cwt.	C — / E £1 17s. 4d. pe cwt
from 16th August to 31st May...	10%	C — / E 10%
(B) Peaches and nectarines: (1) Hothouse *from 1st April to 30th November*	10%	C — / E 10%
from 1st December to 31st March	14s. per cwt.	C — / E 14s. per cwt.
(2) Other *from 1st April to 30th November*	8%	C — / E 8%
from 1st December to 31st March	14s. per cwt.	C — / E 14s. per cwt.

Tariff Heading	Rate of Import Duty (if any)	
	Full	Commonwealth (C) E.F.T.A. (E)
.07 Stone fruit, fresh—contd.		
(C) Plums (including bullace, damsons, greengages and mirabelles)		
from 1st April to 15th June ...	8%	C — E 8%
from 16th June to 31st October...	16s. 9d. per cwt.	C — E 16s. 9d. per cwt.
from 1st November to 30th November	8%	C — E 8%
from 1st December to 31st March	9s. 4d. per cwt.	C — E 9s. 4d. per cwt.
(D) Other	10%	C — E 10%
.08 Berries, fresh:		
(A) Bilberries	—	—
(B) Currants		
from 16th June to 31st August ...	£1 17s. 4d. per cwt.	C — E £1 17s. 4d. per cwt.
from 1st September to 15th June	10%	C — E 10%
(C) Gooseberries		
from 1st May to 31st July ...	18s. 8d. per cwt.	C — E 18s. 8d. per cwt.
from 1st August to 30th April ...	8%	C — E 8%
(D) Strawberries		
from 1st June to 9th June ...	£1 17s. 4d. per cwt.	C — E £1 17s. 4d. per cwt.
from 10th June to 31st July ...	£2 16s. per cwt.	C — E £2 16s. per cwt.
from 1st August to 31st May ...	10%	C — E 10%
(E) Raspberries and loganberries		
from 1st July to 31st August ...	10%	C — E 10%
from 1st September to 30th June	8%	C — E 8%
(F) Other	8%	C — E 8%
.09 Other fruit, fresh:		
(A) Melons	8%	—
(B) Other	8%	C — E 8%

Tariff Heading	Rate of Import Duty (if any)	
	Full	Commonwealth (C E.F.T.A. (E
08.10 Fruit (whether or not cooked), preserved by freezing, not containing added sugar:		
(A) Apples:		
(1) Pulp...	3s. 6d. per cwt. or 15%, whichever is the less	C — E 3s. 6d. per cw or 15%, whic ever is the le
(2) Other	3s. 6d. per cwt. or 25%, whichever is the less	C — E 3s. 6d. per cw or 25%, whic ever is the le
(B) Bilberries; grapefruit; orange, clementine, mandarin or tangerine pulp not containing the peel	—	
(C) Strawberries	15s. per cwt.	C — E 15s. per cwt.
(D) Other	15%	C — E 15%
08.11 Fruit provisionally preserved (for example, by sulphur dioxide gas, in brine, in sulphur water or in other preservative solutions), but unsuitable in that state for immediate consumption:		
(A) Apples:		
(1) Pulp...	3s. 6d. per cwt. or 15%, whichever is the less	C — E 3s. 6d. per cw or 15%, whic ever is the le
(2) Other	3s. 6d. per cwt. or 25%, whichever is the less	C — E 3s. 6d. per cw or 25%, whic ever is the le
(B) Bilberries and nuts	10%	C — E 10%
(C) Cherries	—	—
(D) Citrus fruits:		
(1) Grapefruit; orange, clementine, mandarin or tangerine pulp not containing the peel	—	—
(2) Other fruits:		
(a) In brine...	—	—
(b) Otherwise preserved ...	12½%	C — E 12½%
(E) Strawberries	15s. per cwt.	C — E 15s. per cwt.
(F) Other	15%	C — E 15%
08.12 Fruit, dried, other than that falling within heading No. 08.01, 08.02, 08.03, 08.04 or 08.05:		
(A) Apples, pears, peaches, nectarines, prunes and bilberries	—	—

Tariff Heading	Rate of Import Duty (if any)		
	Full	Commonwealth (C) E.F.T.A. (E)	
8.12 Fruit, dried, etc.—contd.			
(B) Apricots:			
(1) Pulp...	13%	C E	— 13%
(2) Other	8s. per cwt.	C E	— 8s. per cwt.
(C) Other	13%	C E	— 13%
8.13 Peel of melons and citrus fruit, fresh, frozen, dried, or provisionally preserved in brine, in sulphur water or in other preservative solutions	—		—

Chapter 9

Coffee, Tea, Maté and Spices

Notes

1. Mixtures of the products of headings Nos. 09.04 to 09.10 are to be classified as follow:

(a) Mixtures of two or more of the products falling within the same heading are to b classified in that heading;

(b) Mixtures of two or more of the products falling within different headings are to b classified under heading No. 09.10.

The addition of other substances to the mixtures referred to in paragraph (a) or (b) abov shall not affect their classification provided that the essential character of the mixtu remains unchanged. Otherwise the mixtures are not classified in the present Chapte those constituting mixed condiments or mixed seasonings are classified in heading N 21.04.

2. This Chapter does not cover:

(a) Capsicum grossum (sweet capsicum), unground (Chapter 7); or

(b) Pepper of the variety Cubeba officinalis Miquel or Piper cubeba (heading No. 12.07).

Tariff Heading	Rate of Import Duty (if any)	
	Full	Commonwealth (C E.F.T.A. (E
09.01 Coffee, whether or not roasted or freed of caffeine; coffee husks and skins; coffee substitutes containing coffee in any proportion:		
(A) Coffee, unmixed:		
(1) Roasted or ground	10s. per cwt.	C 7s. 5d. per cw E 10s. per cwt.
(2) Other	7s. 5d. per cwt.	C — E 7s. 5d. per cw
(B) Coffee husks and skins	8%	C — E 8%
(C) Coffee and chicory, roasted and ground, mixed but without other ingredients	£1 2s. 3d. per cwt.	C £1 per cwt. E £1 2s. 3d. per cw
(D) Other	10%	C — E 10%
09.02 Tea	—	—
09.03 Maté	—	—
09.04 Pepper of the genus Piper; pimento of the genus Capsicum or the genus Pimenta:		
(A) Peppercorns, the fruit of Piper nigrum, unground	2s. 8d. per cwt.	C — E 2s. 8d. per cwt
(B) Other	10%	C — E 10%
09.05 Vanilla	10%	C — E 10%
09.06 Cinnamon and cinnamon-tree flowers ...	8%	C — E 8%
09.07 Cloves (whole fruit, cloves and stems) ...	10%	C — E 10%

Tariff Heading	Rate of Import Duty (if any)	
	Full	Commonwealth (C) E.F.T.A. (E)
.08 Nutmeg, mace and cardamoms	10%	C — E 10%
.09 Seeds of anise, badian, fennel, coriander, cumin, caraway and juniper: (A) Caraway seeds ... ... (B) Other	— 6%	— — C — E 6%
.10 Thyme, saffron and bay leaves; other spices: (A) Saffron (*Crocus sativus*) stigmas and styles, dried but not chopped, ground, manufactured or prepared (B) Thyme and bay leaves, not ground ... (C) Other	— 4½d. per lb. 10%	— C — E 4½d. per lb. C — E 10%

Chapter 10

Cereals

NOTE

Headings in this Chapter, except heading No. 10.06, are to be taken not to apply to grains which have been ground to remove the husk or pericarp or otherwise worked. Heading No. 10.06 is to be taken to apply to unworked rice and also rice, husked, glazed, polished or broken, but not otherwise worked.

Tariff Heading	Rate of Import Duty (*if any*)	
	Full	*Commonwealth (C)* *E.F.T.A.* (E)
10.01 Wheat and meslin (mixed wheat and rye):		
(A) Wheat	—	—
(B) Meslin	10%	C — E 10%
10.02 Rye	10%	C — E 10%
10.03 Barley	10%	C — E 10%
10.04 Oats	3s. per cwt.	C — E 3s. per cwt.
10.05 Maize:		
(A) Flat white	10%	C — E 10%
(B) Sweet corn on the cob	8%	C — E 8%
(C) Other	—	—
10.06 Rice:		
(A) Whole, further processed after husking	4s. 9d. per cwt.	C — E 4s. 9d. per cwt
(B) Other	—	—
10.07 Buckwheat, millet, canary seed and grain sorghum; other cereals	10%	C — E 10%

Chapter 11

Products of the Milling Industry; Malt and Starches; Gluten; Inulin

NOTE

This Chapter does not cover:

(*a*) Roasted malt put up as coffee substitutes (heading No. 09.01 or 21.01);

(*b*) Flours modified (for example, by heat-treatment) for infants' food or for dietetic purposes (heading No. 19.02). Flours which have been heat-treated merely to improve their baking qualities are, however, to be classified in the present Chapter;

(*c*) Corn flakes and other products falling within heading No. 19.05;

(*d*) Pharmaceutical products (Chapter 30); or

(*e*) Starches having the character of perfumery, cosmetics or toilet preparations falling within heading No. 33.06.

Tariff Heading	Rate of Import Duty (*if any*)	
	Full	*Commonwealth* (C) *E.F.T.A.* (E)
11.01 Cereal flours:		
(A) Oat flour	5s. per cwt.	C — E 5s. per cwt.
(B) Other	10%	C — E 10%
11.02 Cereal groats and cereal meal; other worked cereal grains (for example, rolled, flaked, polished, pearled or kibbled, but not further prepared), except husked, glazed, polished or broken rice; germ of cereals, whole, rolled, flaked or ground:		
(A) Oat groats; oatmeal; oats, ground, rolled or flaked	5s. per cwt.	C — E 5s. per cwt.
(B) Pearled barley (including blocked, pot and pearl barley); flaked barley	20%	C — E 20%
(C) Other	10%	C — E 10%
11.03 Flours of the leguminous vegetables falling within heading No. 07.05	10%	C — E 10%
11.04 Flours of the fruits falling within any heading in Chapter 8	10%	C — E 10%
11.05 Flour, meal and flakes of potato	10%	C — E 10%
11.06 Flour and meal of sago and of manioc, arrowroot, salep and other roots and tubers falling within heading No. 07.06:		
(A) Of manioc ... ... (B) Of sago	— 3%	— C — E 3%
(C) Other	10%	C — E 10%
11.07 Malt, roasted or not	10%	—

Tariff Heading	Rate of Import Duty (if any)		
	Full	Commonwealth (•) E.F.T.A. (.)	
11.08 Starches; inulin:			
(A) Rice, millet and buckwheat starches...	7s. 6d. per cwt.	C	—
		E	7s. 6d. per c
(B) Maize and milo starches	7½%	C	—
		E	7½%
(C) Sago starch	5%	C	—
		E	5%
(D) Manioc starch	—		—
(E) Potato starch (farina)	—		—
(F) Other	10%	C	—
		E	10%
11.09 Gluten and gluten flour, roasted or not ...	10%	C	—
		E	10%

Chapter 12

Oil Seeds and Oleaginous Fruit; Miscellaneous Grains, Seeds and Fruit;
Industrial and Medical Plants; Straw and Fodder

NOTES

1. Heading No. 12.01 is to be taken to apply, *inter alia*, to ground-nuts, soya beans, mustard seeds, oil poppy seeds, poppy seeds and copra. It is to be taken not to apply to coconuts (heading No. 08.01) or olives (Chapter 7 or Chapter 20).

2. (i) Subject to paragraph (ii) below, heading No. 12.03 is to be taken to apply, *inter alia*, to beet seed, grass and other herbage seeds, seeds of ornamental flowers, vegetable seeds, seeds of forest trees, seeds of fruit trees, seeds of vetches and of lupines.

(ii) Heading No. 12.03 is to be taken not to apply to goods falling within heading No. 07.05 (dried leguminous vegetables), within any heading in Chapter 9 (which relates, *inter alia*, to spices), within any heading in Chapter 10 (which relates to cereals), within heading No. 12.01 or within heading No. 12.07.

3. Heading No. 12.07 is to be taken to apply, *inter alia*, to the following plants or parts thereof: basil, borage, hyssop, all species of mint, rosemary, rue, sage and wormwood.

Heading No. 12.07 is, however, to be taken not to apply to:

(a) Oil seeds and oleaginous fruit (heading No. 12.01);
(b) Medicaments falling within Chapter 30;
(c) Perfumery or toilet preparations falling within Chapter 33; or
(d) Disinfectants, insecticides, fungicides, weed-killers or similar products falling within heading No. 38.11.

Tariff Heading	Rate of Import Duty (if any)	
	Full	Commonwealth (C) E.F.T.A. (E)
12.01 Oil seeds and oleaginous fruit, whole or broken:		
(A) Cotton seed; rape seed; tung nuts...	—	—
(B) Soya beans		
(C) Sesamum seed...	5%	C — E 5%
(D) Castor seed	7½%	C — E 7½%
(E) Mustard seed	10%	—
(F) Other	10%	C — E 10%
12.02 Flours or meals of oil seeds or oleaginous fruit, non-defatted (excluding mustard flour)	10%	C — E 10%
12.03 Seeds, fruit and spores, of a kind used for sowing:		
(A) Seeds of coniferous species	8%	—
(B) Other	10%	C — E 10%
12.04 Sugar beet, whole or sliced, fresh, dried or powdered; sugar cane	10%	C — E 10%
12.05 Chicory roots, fresh or dried, whole or cut, unroasted	19s. per cwt.	C 16s. 9½d. per cwt. E 19s. per cwt.

Tariff Heading	Rate of Import Duty (if any)	
	Full	Commonwealth (C E.F.T.A. (E
12.06 Hop cones and lupulin:		
(A) Hops	£4 per cwt.	C £2 13s. 4d. p cwt. E £4 per cwt.
(B) Lupulin	10%	C — E 10%
12.07 Plants and parts (including seeds and fruit) of trees, bushes, shrubs or other plants, being goods of a kind used primarily in perfumery, in pharmacy, or for insecticidal, fungicidal or similar purposes, fresh or dried, whole, cut, crushed, ground or powdered:		
(A) The following in a dried state, not ground or powdered:	—	—
Aconite root		
Agrimony herb		
Aletris root		
Angelica root		
Arnica flowers		
Balmony herb and leaves		
Bayberry bark		
Bearberry (Uva ursi) leaves		
Belladonna root, herb and leaves		
Beth root		
Black cohosh root		
Black haw bark		
Blood root		
Blue cohosh root		
Boldo leaves		
Boneset herb		
Burdock root		
Calamus rhizome		
Calumba root		
Cascara sagrada bark		
Cassia pods		
Cocillana bark		
Colchicum corms and seeds		
Colocynth pulp		
Comfrey leaves and roots		
Condurango bark		
Cubeb berries		
Damiana leaves		
Dandelion root		
Datura metel leaves, tops and seeds		
Deer tongue leaves		
Digitalis leaves and seeds		
Drosera		
Echinacea root		
Elder leaves and flowers		
Ephedra stems and branches		
Ergot of rye		
Euonymus bark		
Frangula bark		

Tariff Heading	Rate of Import Duty (*if any*)	
	Full	Commonwealth (C) E.F.T.A. (E)

.07 Plant and parts, etc.—*contd.*

(A) The following in a dried state, not ground or powdered:—*contd.*

  Fringe tree bark
  Galanga root
  Gelsem root
  Gentian root
  Grindelia leaves and flowers
  Henbane (*Hyoscyamus muticus*)
  Henbane (*Hyoscyamus niger*)
  Horehound
  Hydrastis rhizomes
  Ipomoea (Orizaba jalap) root
  Jaborandi leaves
  Jalap root
  Kava kava rhizomes
  Krameria root
  Lavender flowers
  Leptandra root
  Lime tree flowers
  Liquorice root
  Lobelia
  Male fern (*Dryopteris filix-mas*) rhizomes
  Marshmallow leaves and roots
  Nux vomica seeds
  Orris root
  Passion flower
  Pichi tops
  Pleurisy root
  Podophyllum and Indian podophyllum rhizomes
  Prickly ash bark and berries
  Quince seeds
  Rauwolfia vomitoria root and root bark
  Rhubarb (*Rheum palmatum*) rhizomes
  Rhubarb (*Rheum rhaponticum*) rhizomes
  Rhus aromaticus bark
  Sabadilla seeds
  Sarsaparilla root
  Sassafras bark
  Saw palmetto berries
  Scammony root
  Scullcap
  Senna leaves and pods
  Serpentaria root
  Slippery elm bark
  Squills
  Stillingia root
  Stone root

Tariff Heading	Rate of Import Duty (if any)	
	Full	Commonwealth (C E.F.T.A. (E

12.07 Plant and parts, etc.—contd.

(A) The following in a dried state, not ground or powdered:—contd.

Stramonium leaves

Tonquin beans (or Cumaru seeds)

Valerian root

White pine bark

Wild cherry bark

Witch hazel (*Hamamelis*) bark and leaves

Yerba Santa leaves

(B) Araroba, crude; chamomile flowers, dried; cinchona bark; coca leaves; cubé (*Lonchocarpus nicou*) bark and root; ipecacuanha root; pyrethrum flowers — —

(C) Basil, borage, mint (excluding dried peppermint and penny royal), rosemary and sage:

	Full	C/E
(1) Not ground or powdered... ...	4½d. per lb.	C — E 4½d. per lb.
(2) Ground or powdered	10%	C — E 10%
(D) Other	10%	—

12.08 Locust beans, fresh or dried, whether or not kibbled or ground, but not further prepared; fruit kernels and other vegetable products of a kind used primarily for human food, not falling within any other heading:

	Full	C/E
(A) Locust bean kernels, whole	—	—
(B) Other	10%	C — E 10%

12.09 Cereal straw and husks, unprepared, or chopped but not otherwise prepared — —

12.10 Mangolds, swedes, fodder roots; hay, lucerne, clover, sainfoin, forage kale, lupines, vetches and similar forage products:

	Full	C/E
(A) Hay	—	—
(B) Other	10%	C — E 10%

Chapter 13

Raw Vegetable Materials of a Kind Suitable for Use in Dyeing or in Tanning;
Lacs; Gums, Resins and Other Vegetable Saps and Extracts

ᴺOTE

Heading No. 13.03 is to be taken to apply, *inter alia*, to liquorice extract and extract of
ᴘrethrum, extract of hops, extract of aloes and opium. The heading is to be taken not
apply to:

(*a*) Liquorice extract containing more than ten per cent. by weight of sugar or when
put up as confectionery (heading No. 17.04);

(*b*) Malt extract (heading No. 19.01);

(*c*) Extracts of coffee, tea or maté (heading No. 21.02);

(*d*) Alcoholic saps and extracts constituting beverages, and compound alcoholic preparations (known as " concentrated extracts ") for the manufacture of beverages (Chapter
22);

(*e*) Camphor (heading No. 29.13) or glycyrrhizin (heading No. 29.41);

(*f*) Medicaments falling within heading No. 30.03;

(*g*) Tanning or dyeing extracts (heading No. 32.01 or 32.04);

(*h*) Essential oils and resinoids (heading No. 33.01) or aqueous distillates and aqueous
solutions of essential oils (heading No. 33.05); or

(*ij*) Rubber, balata, gutta-percha or similar natural gums (heading No. 40.01).

Tariff Heading	Rate of Import Duty (if any)	
	Full	Commonwealth (C) E.F.T.A. (E)
.01 Raw vegetable materials of a kind used primarily in dyeing or in tanning:		
(A) Persian berries; gall nuts; sumach leaves; myrobalans	—	—
(B) Henna leaves, dried, not chopped or ground	—	—
(C) Tara (*Caesalpinia spinosa*) pods and powder	—	—
(D) Other	8%	—
.02 Shellac, seed lac, stick lac and other lacs; natural gums, resins, gum-resins and balsams:		
(A) Shellac, seed lac, stick lac and other lacs; solid natural resins (other than gum resins and damar); balsam of Copaiba, balsam of Peru and balsam of Tolu; storax, crude	—	—
(B) Gum arabic; gum ammoniacum; gum asafetida; gum euphorbium; gum galbanum; gum myrrh; gum oliba-num; gum opoponax; gum tragacanth	—	—
(C) Other	8%	—

Tariff Heading	Rate of Import Duty (if any)	
	Full	Commonwealth (C) E.F.T.A. (E
13.03 Vegetable saps and extracts; pectic substances, pectinates and pectates; agar-agar and other mucilages and thickeners, derived from vegetable products:		
(A) Aloes; cassia pulp; liquorice extract	—	—
(B) Hop extracts	£4	C £2 13s. 4d. E —
	for every cwt. of hops which, in the opinion of the Commissioners of Customs and Excise, has been used in the manufacture of the extract.	
(C) Agar-agar	8%	—
(D) Other	10%	—

Chapter 14

*Vegetable Plaiting and Carving Materials; Vegetable Products not
elsewhere specified or included*

Notes

1. This Chapter does not cover vegetable materials or fibres of vegetable materials of a kind used primarily in the manufacture of textiles, however prepared, or other vegetable materials which have undergone treatment so as to render them suitable only for use in the manufacture of textiles (Section XI).

2. Heading No. 14.01 is to be taken to apply, *inter alia*, to split osier, reeds, bamboos and the like, to rattan cores and to drawn or split rattans. The heading is to be taken not to apply to chipwood (heading No. 44.09).

3. Heading No. 14.02 is to be taken not to apply to wood wool (heading No. 44.12).

4. Heading No. 14.03 is to be taken not to apply to prepared knots or tufts for broom or brush making (heading No. 96.03).

Tariff Heading	Rate of Import Duty (*if any*)	
	Full	Commonwealth (C) E.F.T.A. (E)
14.01 Vegetable materials of a kind used primarily for plaiting (for example, cereal straw, cleaned, bleached or dyed, osier, reeds, rushes, rattans, bamboos, raffia and lime bark):		
(A) Raffia	—	—
(B) Common reeds (*Phragmites communis*)	—	—
(C) Rattan cane	7½%	—
(D) Other	10%	—
14.02 Vegetable materials, whether or not put up in a layer or between two layers of other material, of a kind used primarily as stuffing or as padding (for example, kapok, vegetable hair and eel-grass):		
(A) Eel-grass	—	—
(B) Vegetable hair, being fibres of the dwarf palm *Chamaerops humilis*	5%	—
(C) Kapok (being the seed hairs of the *Eriodendron anfractuosum* or *Bombax pentandrum*) and milkweed (*Asclepias syriaca* and *Asclepias incarnata*)	6½%	—
(D) Other	8%	—
14.03 Vegetable materials of a kind used primarily in brushes or in brooms (for example, sorgho, piassava, couch-grass and istle), whether or not in bundles or hanks:		
(A) Vegetable fibres of the following varieties, not further dressed after scutching or decorticating: Bahia piassava (*Attalea funifera*) Para piassava (*Leopoldinia piassaba*) Gumati or Gomuti fibre (*Arenga saccharifera*) Madagascar fibre (*Dictyosperma fibrosum*)	—	—

Tariff Heading	Rate of Import Duty (if any)	
	Full	Commonwealth (C) E.F.T.A. (E)
14.03 Vegetable materials etc.—*contd.*		
(B) Mexican fibre or istle (*Agave leche-guilla* or *Agave funkiana*) scutched, decorticated, sorted to approximate length, or put up into tails with the butt end cut and the flag end untrimmed or roughly tip-trimmed, but not further prepared or dressed	—	—
(C) Broomcorn and broomcorn tops (*Sorghum vulgare*)	—	—
(D) Other	8%	—
14.04 Hard seeds, pips, hulls and nuts, of a kind used for carving (for example, corozo and dom)	8%	—
14.05 Vegetable products not elsewhere specified or included:		
(A) Esparto, albardin grass and diss or vine-tie grass (*Ampelodesma tenax*)	—	—
(B) Seaweed, raw, unground, dried or bleached, but not further prepared or treated	—	—
(C) Quillaia bark, in a dried state, not ground or powdered	—	—
(D) Other	8%	—

SECTION III

ANIMAL AND VEGETABLE FATS AND OILS AND THEIR CLEAVAGE PRODUCTS; PREPARED EDIBLE FATS; ANIMAL AND VEGETABLE WAXES

Chapter 15

Animal and Vegetable Fats and Oils and their Cleavage Products; Prepared Edible Fats; Animal and Vegetable Waxes

Notes

1. This Chapter does not cover:

(a) Unrendered pig fat or unrendered poultry fat (heading No. 02.05);

(b) Cocoa butter (heading No. 18.04);

(c) Greaves (heading No. 23.01); oil-cake, residual olive pulp or similar residues from the extraction of vegetable oils (heading No. 23.04);

(d) Fatty acids in an isolated state, prepared waxes, medicaments, paints, varnishes, soap, perfumery, cosmetics or toilet preparations, sulphonated oils or other goods falling within any heading in Section VI; or

(e) Factice derived from oils (heading No. 40.02).

2. Soapstocks, oil foots and dregs, stearin, wool grease and glycerol residues are to be taken to fall in heading No. 15.17.

Tariff Heading	Rate of Import Duty (if any)	
	Full	Commonwealth (C) E.F.T.A. (E)
15.01 Lard and other rendered pig fat; rendered poultry fat:		
(A) Lard	—	—
(B) Other	10%	C — E 10%
15.02 Unrendered fats of bovine cattle, sheep or goats; tallow (including "*premier jus*") produced from those fats	10%	C — E 10%
15.03 Lard stearin, oleostearin and tallow stearin; lard oil, oleo-oil and tallow oil, not emulsified or mixed or prepared in any way	10%	C — E 10%
15.04 Fats and oils, of fish and marine mammals, whether or not refined:		
(A) Whale oil (not including sperm oil) ...	—	—
(B) Cod liver oil:		
(1) Imported in casks, drums or other receptacles capable of holding at least 20 gallons and without internal containers	1s. per gallon	—
(2) Other	1s. 4d. per gallon	—
(C) Herring oil	8%	—
(D) Other	10%	—
15.05 Wool grease and fatty substances derived therefrom (including lanolin)	8%	—

Tariff Heading	Rate of Import Duty (if any)		
	Full	Commonwealth (C) E.F.T.A. (E)	

15.06 Other animal oils and fats (including neat's-foot oil and fats from bones or waste):
(A) Bone oil; neat's-foot oil	10%		
(B) Other	10%	C E	— 10%

15.07 Fixed vegetable oils, fluid or solid, crude, refined or purified:
(A) Oiticica oil, raw; stillingia oil (tallow-seed oil), raw; tung oil (china wood oil), raw	—		—
(B) Castor oil	12½%	C E	— 12½%
(C) Coconut oil; ground-nut oil; linseed oil; rape oil; sesamum oil; soya bean oil; sunflower seed oil; safflower seed oil	15%	C E	— 15%
(D) Olive oil extracted by means of solvents	10%		
(E) Other	10%	C E	— 10%

15.08 Animal and vegetable oils, boiled, oxidised, dehydrated, sulphurised, blown or polymerised by heat in vacuum or in inert gas, or otherwise modified:
(A) Whale oil (not including sperm oil) ...	—		—
(B) Castor oil	12½%		—
(C) Coconut oil; ground-nut oil; linseed oil; rape oil; sesamum oil; soya bean oil; sunflower seed oil; safflower seed oil	15%		—
(D) Other	10%		

15.09 Degras ...   .

	8%		—

15.10 Fatty acids; acid oils from refining; fatty alcohols:
(A) Normal aliphatic alcohols containing eight or more carbon atoms in the molecule and having an iodine value not greater than 10	20%		—
(B) Other ... ... · ...	10%		

15.11 Glycerol and glycerol lyes ...   .

	8%		—

15.12 Animal or vegetable oils and fats, wholly or partly hydrogenated, or solidified or hardened by any other process, whether or not refined, but not further prepared:
(A) Whale oil (not including sperm oil) ...	—		—
(B) Coconut oil; ground-nut oil; linseed oil; rape oil; sesamum oil; soya bean oil; sunflower seed oil; safflower seed oil	15%	C E	— 15%

Tariff Heading	Rate of Import Duty (if any)	
	Full	Commonwealth (C) E.F.T.A. (E)
15.12 Animal or vegetable oils and fats, etc.— *contd.* (C) Other: (1) Fats and oils wholly obtained from fish or marine mammals	10%	—
(2) Other	10%	C — E 10%
15.13 Margarine, imitation lard and other prepared edible fats	10%	C — E 10%
15.14 Spermaceti, crude, pressed or refined, whether or not coloured	8%	—
15.15 Beeswax and other insect waxes, whether or not coloured	8%	—
15.16 Vegetable waxes, whether or not coloured: (A) Carnauba wax; candelilla wax; ouricury wax	—	—
(B) Other	6½%	—
15.17 Residues resulting from the treatment of fatty substances or animal or vegetable waxes	6½%	—

SECTION IV

PREPARED FOODSTUFFS; BEVERAGES, SPIRITS AND VINEGAR; TOBACCO

Special note applying to subheadings only

The expression " sweetening matter " includes only glucose, sucrose and invert sugar. For the purposes of this Section the weight of sweetening matter contained in any goods shall be determined as follows: in so far as the sweetening matter is sucrose the weight shall be taken to be the actual weight of the sucrose or, if the sucrose is of a polarisation not exceeding 98°, 95 per cent. of the actual weight of the sucrose; in so far as it is liquid glucose the weight shall be taken to be 48 per cent. of the actual weight of the glucose; and in so far as it is solid glucose or invert sugar the weight shall be taken to be 75 per cent. of the actual weight of the glucose or sugar.

Chapter 16

Preparations of Meat, of Fish, of Crustaceans or Molluscs

Note

This Chapter does not cover meat, fish, crustaceans or molluscs falling within any heading in Chapter 2 or 3.

Tariff Heading	Rate of Import Duty (*if any*)		
	Full	*Commonwealth (C)* *E.F.T.A.*	*(E)*
16.01 Sausages and the like, of meat, meat offal or animal blood	18%	C E	— 18%
16.02 Other prepared or preserved meat or meat offal: (A) Pastes; poultry liver:			
(1) Pastes wholly of pork (including ham and bacon) apart from any curing or seasoning ingredients, in airtight containers	5%	C E	— 5%
(2) Pastes of meat offal, not canned...	18%		
(3) Other	18%	C E	— 18%
(B) Other: (1) In airtight containers:			
(*a*) Pigs' tongues	—		
(*b*) Ground or chopped pork (including ham and bacon):			
(i) Wholly of pork (including ham and bacon) apart from any curing or seasoning incredients	5%		
(ii) With beef or veal... ...	11%	C E	— 11%
(iii) Other:			
(I) Wholly of pork (including ham and bacon) and farinaceous fillers apart from any curing or seasoning ingredients	10%		—
(II) Other...	10%	C E	— 10%

Tariff Heading	Rate of Import Duty (*if any*)	
	Full	*Commonwealth* (C) *E.F.T.A.* (E)
6.02 Other prepared or preserved meat or meat offal:—*contd.*		
(B) Other:—*contd.*		
(1) In airtight containers:—*contd.*		
(c) Beef and veal (including edible offals, but excluding tongues and jellied veal)	18%	C — E 18%
(d) Poultry (not including guinea fowl)	3d. per lb.	C — E 3d. per lb.
(e) Other	10%	C — E 10%
(2) Not in airtight containers:		
(a) Hams, whole	—	—
(b) Other	15%	C — E 15%
6.03 Meat extracts and meat juices:		
(A) Wholly or in part derived from beef or veal	16%	C — E 16%
(B) Whale meat extract	10%	— -
(C) Other	10%	C — E 10%
6.04 Prepared or preserved fish, including caviar and caviar substitutes:		
(A) Caviar and caviar substitutes ...	30%	—
(B) Other roes	5%	—
(C) Salmon, canned	4%	—
(D) Tuna, canned	8%	—
(E) Other	10%	—
6.05 Crustaceans and molluscs, prepared or preserved:		
(A) Oysters	15%	—
(B) Clams, cockles, crabs, crawfish, crayfish, lobsters, mussels, Norway lobsters (Dublin Bay prawns), scallops (including queen scallops), shrimps, whelks and winkles:		
(1) Shrimps, canned	7½%	—
(2) Other:		
(a) Frozen, or preserved in vinegar or airtight containers	10%	—
(b) Other	30%	—
(C) Prawns, canned	7½%	—
(D) Other	10%	—

Chapter 17

Sugars and Sugar Confectionery

Notes

1. This Chapter does not cover:

(a) Sugar confectionery containing cocoa (heading No. 18.06);

(b) Chemically pure sugars other than sucrose, glucose and lactose (heading No. 29.43); or

(c) Pharmaceutical products (Chapter 30).

2. Chemically pure sucrose, whatever its origin, is to be classified in heading No. 17.01.

Tariff Heading	Rate of Import Duty (*if any*)	
	Full	Commonwealth (C) E.F.T.A. (E)
17.01 Beet sugar and cane sugar, solid:		
(A) Sugar of which the polarisation has at any time been reduced either as a result of the sugar having been treated (whether by the addition of invert sugar or otherwise) or as the result of the development of invert sugar or other substance in the sugar	6s. 10·8d. per cwt.	C 1s. 0·8d. per cwt. E 6s. 10·8d. per cwt.
(B) Other :		
Of a polarisation:		
Exceeding—		
99°	6s. 10·8d. per cwt.	C 1s. 0·8d. per cwt. E 6s. 10·8d. per cwt.
98° but not exceeding 99° ...	6s. 10·8d. per cwt.	
97° but not exceeding 98° ...	3s. 11·3d. per cwt.	
96° but not exceeding 97° ...	3s. 10·0d. per cwt.	
95° but not exceeding 96° ...	3s. 8·8d. per cwt.	
94° but not exceeding 95° ...	3s. 7·6d. per cwt.	
93° but not exceeding 94° ...	3s. 6·3d. per cwt.	
92° but not exceeding 93° ...	3s. 5·1d. per cwt.	
91° but not exceeding 92° ...	3s. 3·9d. per cwt.	
90° but not exceeding 91° ...	3s. 2·6d. per cwt.	
89° but not exceeding 90° ...	3s. 1·4d. per cwt.	
88° but not exceeding 89° ...	3s. 0·2d. per cwt.	
87° but not exceeding 88° ...	2s. 11·1d. per cwt.	C — E As full rate
86° but not exceeding 87° ...	2s. 10·1d. per cwt.	
85° but not exceeding 86° ...	2s. 9·2d. per cwt.	
84° but not exceeding 85° ...	2s. 8·3d. per cwt.	
83° but not exceeding 84° ...	2s. 7·3d. per cwt.	
82° but not exceeding 83° ...	2s. 6·4d. per cwt.	
81° but not exceeding 82° ...	2s. 5·6d. per cwt.	
80° but not exceeding 81° ...	2s. 4·8d. per cwt.	
79° but not exceeding 80° ...	2s. 4·0d. per cwt.	
78° but not exceeding 79° ...	2s. 3·1d. per cwt.	
77° but not exceeding 78° ...	2s. 2·3d. per cwt.	
76° but not exceeding 77° ...	2s. 1·5d. per cwt.	
Not exceeding 76°	2s. 0$\frac{3}{4}$d. per cwt.	

Tariff Heading	Rate of Import Duty (if any)	
	Full	Commonwealth (C) E.F.T.A. (E)
17.02 Other sugars; sugar syrups; artificial honey (whether or not mixed with natural honey); caramel:		
(A) Sucrose sugar, solid, which can be completely tested by the polariscope:		
(1) Sugar of which the polarisation has at any time been reduced either as a result of the sugar having been treated (whether by the addition of invert sugar or otherwise) or as the result of the development of invert sugar or other substance in the sugar	6s. 10·8d. per cwt.	C 1s. 0·8d. per cwt. E 6s. 10·8d. per cwt.
(2) Other:		
Of a polarisation:		
Exceeding—		
99°	6s. 10·8d. per cwt.	C 1s. 0·8d. per cwt E 6s. 10·8d. per cwt.
98° but not exceeding 99°...	6s. 10·8d. per cwt.	
97° but not exceeding 98°...	3s. 11·3d. per cwt.	
96° but not exceeding 97°...	3s. 10·0d. per cwt.	
95° but not exceeding 96°...	3s. 8·8d. per cwt.	
94° but not exceeding 95°...	3s. 7·6d. per cwt.	
93° but not exceeding 94°...	3s. 6·3d. per cwt.	
92° but not exceeding 93°...	3s. 5·1d. per cwt.	
91° but not exceeding 92°...	3s. 3·9d. per cwt.	
90° but not exceeding 91°...	3s. 2·6d. per cwt.	
89° but not exceeding 90°...	3s. 1·4d. per cwt.	
88° but not exceeding 89°...	3s. 0·2d. per cwt.	
87° but not exceeding 88°...	2s. 11·1d. per cwt.	C — E As full rate
86° but not exceeding 87°...	2s. 10·1d. per cwt.	
85° but not exceeding 86°...	2s. 9·2d. per cwt.	
84° but not exceeding 85°...	2s. 8·3d. per cwt.	
83° but not exceeding 84°...	2s. 7·3d. per cwt.	
82° but not exceeding 83°...	2s. 6·4d. per cwt.	
81° but not exceeding 82°...	2s. 5·6d. per cwt.	
80° but not exceeding 81°...	2s. 4·8d. per cwt.	
79° but not exceeding 80°...	2s. 4·0d. per cwt.	
78° but not exceeding 79°...	2s. 3·1d. per cwt.	
77° but not exceeding 78°...	2s. 2·3d. per cwt.	
76° but not exceeding 77°...	2s. 1·5d. per cwt.	
Not exceeding 76°	2s. 0⅔d. per cwt.	
(B) Invert sugar; syrups containing sucrose:		
(1) Concentrated cane juice, partly inverted, of the kind known as high test, invert or fancy molasses	—	—
(2) Other:		
(a) Containing 70 per cent. or more by weight of sweetening matter	3s. 8½d. per cwt.	C — E 3s. 8½d. per cwt.

Tariff Heading	Rate of Import Duty (if any)	
	Full	Commonwealth (C E.F.T.A. (E
17.02 Other sugars; sugar syrups, etc.—*contd.*		
(B) Invert sugar; syrups containing sucrose:—*contd.*		
(2) Other:—*contd.*		
(b) Containing less than 70 per cent. and more than 50 per cent. by weight of sweetening matter	2s. 8d. per cwt.	C — E 2s. 8d. per cw
(c) Containing not more than 50 per cent. by weight of sweetening matter	1s. 3½d. per cwt.	C — E 1s. 3½d. per cv
(C) Other sucrose and extracts from sucrose, other than dextrose, which cannot be completely tested by the polariscope	—	—
(D) Glucose:		
(1) Solid	3s. 8½d. per cwt.	C — E 3s. 8½d. per cv
(2) Liquid	2s. 8d. per cwt.	C — E 2s. 8d. per cv
(E) Artificial honey (whether or not mixed with natural honey)	5s. per cwt.	C — E 5s. per cwt.
(F) Caramel:		
(1) Solid	5s. 10d. per cwt.	C — E 5s. 10d. per cw
(2) Liquid	4s. 1d. per cwt.	C — E 4s. 1d. per cv
(G) Other:		
(1) Lactose	3d. per lb.	C — E 3d. per lb.
(2) Other	10%	C — E 10%
17.03 olasses, whether or not decolourised ...	—	—
17.04 Sugar confectionery, not containing cocoa:		
(A) Fondants, pastes, creams and similar intermediate products, in bulk, containing 80 per cent. or more by weight of added sweetening matter:		
(1) Not flavoured or coloured ...	4s. 9d. per cwt.	C — E 4s. 9d. per cv
(2) Other	4s. 9d. per cwt. plus 10%, in addition to any revenue duty	C — E 4s. 9d. per c plus 10%, in addition to a revenue duty
(B) Other	4s. 9d. per cwt. plus 10%, in addition to any revenue duty	—

Tariff Heading	Rate of Import Duty (if any)	
	Full	Commonwealth (C) E.F.T.A. (E)
17.05 Flavoured or coloured sugars, syrups and molasses, but not including fruit juices containing added sugar in any proportion: (A) Sucrose sugar, solid, which can be completely tested by the polariscope: (1) Sugar of which the polarisation has at any time been reduced either as a result of the sugar having been treated (whether by the addition of invert sugar or otherwise) or as the result of the development of invert sugar or other substance in the sugar	6s. 10·8d. per cwt.	C 1s. 0·8d. per cwt. E 6s. 10·8d. per cwt.
(2) Other: Of a polarisation: Exceeding— 99°	6s. 10·8d. per cwt.	C 1s. 0·8d. per cwt. E 6s. 10·8d. per cwt.
98° but not exceeding 99°...	6s. 10·8d. per cwt.	
97° but not exceeding 98°...	3s. 11·3d. per cwt.	
96° but not exceeding 97°...	3s. 10·0d. per cwt.	
95° but not exceeding 96°...	3s. 8·8d. per cwt.	
94° but not exceeding 95°...	3s. 7·6d. per cwt.	
93° but not exceeding 94°...	3s. 6·3d. per cwt.	
92° but not exceeding 93°...	3s. 5·1d. per cwt.	
91° but not exceeding 92°...	3s. 3·9d. per cwt.	
90° but not exceeding 91°...	3s. 2·6d. per cwt.	
89° but not exceeding 90°...	3s. 1·4d. per cwt.	
88° but not exceeding 89°...	3s. 0·2d. per cwt.	
87° but not exceeding 88°...	2s. 11·1d. per cwt.	C — F As full rate
86° but not exceeding 87°...	2s. 10·1d. per cwt.	
85° but not exceeding 86°...	2s. 9·2d. per cwt.	
84° but not exceeding 85°...	2s. 8·3d. per cwt.	
83° but not exceeding 84°...	2s. 7·3d. per cwt.	
82° but not exceeding 83°...	2s. 6·4d. per cwt.	
81° but not exceeding 82°...	2s. 5·6d. per cwt.	
80° but not exceeding 81°...	2s. 4·8d. per cwt.	
79° but not exceeding 80°...	2s. 4·0d. per cwt.	
78° but not exceeding 79°...	2s. 3·1d. per cwt.	
77° but not exceeding 78°...	2s. 2·3d. per cwt.	
76° but not exceeding 77°...	2s. 1·5d. per cwt.	
Not exceeding 76°	2s. 0¾d. per cwt.	
(B) Invert sugar; syrups containing sucrose: (1) Containing 70 per cent. or more by weight of sweetening matter	3s. 8½d. per cwt.	C — E 3s. 8½d. per cwt.
(2) Containing less than 70 per cent. and more than 50 per cent. by weight of sweetening matter	2s. 8d. per cwt.	C — E 2s. 8d. per cwt.
(3) Containing not more than 50 per cent. by weight of sweetening matter	1s. 3½d. per cwt.	C — E 1s. 3½d. per cwt.

Tariff Heading	Rate of Import Duty (if any)	
	Full	Commonwealth (C) E.F.T.A. (E)
17.05 Flavoured or coloured sugars, syrups and molasses, etc.—contd.		
(C) Molasses; other sucrose and extracts from sucrose, other than dextrose, which cannot be completely tested by the polariscope	—	—
(D) Glucose:		
(1) Solid	3s. 8½d. per cwt.	C — E 3s. 8½d. per cwt.
(2) Liquid	2s. 8d. per cwt.	C — E 2s. 8d. per cwt.
(E) Other:		
(1) Lactose	3d. per lb.	C — E 3d. per lb.
(2) Other	10%	C — E 10%

Chapter 18

Cocoa and Cocoa Preparations

Notes

1. This Chapter does not cover goods described in heading No. 19.02, 19.08, 22.02, 22.09 30.03.

2. Heading No. 18.06 includes sugar confectionery containing cocoa and, subject to Note 1 of this Chapter, other food preparations containing cocoa.

Tariff Heading	Rate of Import Duty (*if any*)	
	Full	*Commonwealth* (C) *E.F.T.A.* (E)
.01 Cocoa beans, whole or broken, raw or roasted:		
(A) Raw	1s. 4½d. per cwt.	C —
		E 1s. 4½d. per cwt.
(B) Roasted	1s. 9½d. per cwt.	C —
		E 1s. 9½d. per cwt.
.02 Cocoa shells, husks, skins and waste	—	—
.03 Cocoa paste (in bulk or in block), whether or not defatted	1s. 9½d. per cwt.	—
.04 Cocoa butter (fat or oil)	1s. 4½d. per cwt.	—
.05 Cocoa powder, unsweetened	1s. 9½d. per cwt.	—
.06 Chocolate and other food preparations containing cocoa:		
(A) Chocolate milk crumb	6s. per cwt.	—
(B) Cocoa powder with added sweetening matter	5s. per cwt.	—
(C) Other:		
(1) Consisting wholly of cocoa and one or more of the following: added sweetening matter, milk, coffee, chicory, saccharin, salt, vanilla, vanillin and lecithin	4s. per cwt.	—
(2) Other	4s. per cwt. plus 10%, in addition to any revenue duty	—

Chapter 19

Preparations of Cereals, Flour or Starch; Pastrycooks' Products

Notes

1. This Chapter does not cover:

(a) Preparations of flour, starch or malt extract, of a kind used as infant food or for dietetic or culinary purposes, containing 50 per cent. or more by weight of cocoa (heading No. 18.06);

(b) Biscuits or other articles made from flour or from starch, specially prepared for use as animal feeding stuffs (heading No. 23.07); or

(c) Pharmaceutical products (Chapter 30).

2. In this Chapter the expression " flour " includes the flour of fruits or of vegetables, and products of such flour are to be classified with similar products of cereal flour.

Tariff Heading	Rate of Import Duty (*if any*)	
	Full	Commonwealth (C) E.F.T.A. (E)
19.01 Malt extract	10%	—
19.02 Preparations of flour, starch or malt extract, of a kind used as infant food or for dietetic or culinary purposes, containing less than 50 per cent. by weight of cocoa	10%	—
19.03 Macaroni, spaghetti and similar products...	10%	C — E 10%
19.04 Tapioca and sago; tapioca and sago substitutes obtained from potato or other starches:		
(A) Tapioca; sago	3%	C — E 3%
(B) Other	6%	C — E 6%
19.05 Prepared foods obtained by the swelling or roasting of cereals or cereal products (puffed rice, corn flakes and similar products)	10%	—
19.06 Communion wafers, empty cachets of a kind suitable for pharmaceutical use, sealing wafers, rice paper and similar products	10%	—
19.07 Bread, ships' biscuits and other ordinary bakers' wares, not containing sugar, honey, eggs, fats, cheese or fruit:		
(A) Ships' biscuits, crumbs and rusks ...	10%	—
(B) Other	10%	C — E 10%
19.08 Pastry, biscuits, cakes and other fine bakers' wares, whether or not containing cocoa in any proportion:		
(A) Biscuits, wafers, rusks, cakes without covering or filling, and pastry of the kind known as Danish pastry	10%	—
(B) Other	10%	C — E 10%

Chapter 20

Preparations of Vegetables, Fruit or Other Parts of Plants

Notes

1. This Chapter does not cover:

(a) Vegetables or fruit falling within any heading in Chapter 7 or 8; or

(b) Fruit jellies, fruit pastes or the like in the form of sugar confectionery (heading No. 17.04) or chocolate confectionery (heading No. 18.06).

2. For the purposes of headings Nos. 20.01 and 20.02, the word " vegetables " is to be taken to apply, and apply only, to products which, when in their fresh state, are classified in heading No. 07.01.

3. Edible plants, parts of plants and roots of plants conserved in syrup (for example, ginger and angelica) are to be classified with the preserved fruit falling under heading No. 20.06; roasted ground-nuts are also to be classified in heading No. 20.06.

4. Tomato juice the dry weight content of which is 7 per cent. or more is to be classified under heading No. 20.02.

Tariff Heading	Rate of Import Duty (if any)		
	Full	Commonwealth (C) E.F.T.A. (E)	
20.01 Vegetables and fruit, prepared or preserved by vinegar or acetic acid, with or without sugar, whether or not containing salt, spices or mustard	10%	C E	— 10%
20.02 Vegetables prepared or preserved otherwise than by vinegar or acetic acid:			
(A) Olives:			
(1) Olives in brine imported in a container when the gross weight (including the weight of the container) does not exceed 1 cwt.	12%	—	
(2) Other	9%	—	
(B) Tomato juice	8%	C E	— 8%
(C) Other:			
(1) In airtight containers:			
(a) Asparagus; beans (not being beans in pods); peas	10%	C E	— 10%
(b) Tomatoes:			
(i) Pulp or paste, wholly of tomato and water apart from salt or any other preserving, seasoning or flavouring ingredients, the dry weight of the tomato in any container being not less than 25 per cent. of the weight of its entire contents	8%	—	
(ii) Other	8%	C E	— 8%
(c) Potato crisps	15%	C	—
(d) Other	15%	E	15%
(2) Not in airtight containers:			
(a) Potato crisps	10%	—	
(b) Other	10%	C E	— 10%

Tariff Heading	Rate of Import Duty (*if any*)	
	Full	*Commonwealth (C)* *E.F.T.A.* (E)
20.03 Fruit preserved by freezing, containing added sugar: (A) Strawberries in containers, the contents of each weighing not less than 12 lb.	16s. per cwt.	C — E 16s. per cwt.
(B) Other	15%	C — E 15%
20.04 Fruit, fruit-peel and parts of plants, preserved by sugar (drained, glacé or crystallised): (A) Apricots; figs; plums (including bullace, damsons, greengages and mirabelles, but not prunes)	9s. 6d. per cwt.	C — E 9s. 6d. per cwt
(B) Cherries; fruit peels	21%	C — E 21%
(C) Other	10%	C — E 10%
20.05 Jams, fruit jellies, marmalades, fruit purée and fruit pastes, being cooked preparations, whether or not containing added sugar	10%	C — E 10%
20.06 Fruit otherwise prepared or preserved, whether or not containing added sugar or spirit: (A) Apples: (1) Containing added sweetening matter	2s. 9d. per cwt.	C — E 2s. 9d. per cwt
(2) Other	3s. 6d. per cwt. or 25%, whichever is the less	C — E 3s. 6d. per cw or 25%, which ever is the les
(B) Apricots: (1) Containing added sweetening matter	12%	C — E 12%
(2) Other: (a) Canned ... ... (b) Not canned	— 9%	C — E 9%
(C) Cherries: (1) Containing added sweetening matter: (a) Not stoned: ... ... (i) In a solution of sulphur dioxide	10%	C — E 10%
(ii) Other	15%	C — E 15%

Tariff Heading	Rate of Import Duty (*if any*)	
	Full	Commonwealth (C) E.F.T.A. (E)
0.06 Fruit otherwise prepared, etc.—contd.		
(C) Cherries—contd.		
(b) Stoned	10%	C — E 10%
(2) Other:		
(a) Canned	—	—
(b) Not canned	15%	C — E 15%
(D) Ginger:		
(1) Containing added sweetening matter	10%	C — E 10%
(2) Other	13%	C — E 13%
(E) Grapefruit	—	—
(F) Loganberries:		
(1) Containing added sweetening matter	4s. 9d. per cwt.	C — E 4s. 9d. per cwt.
(2) Other	15%	C — E 15%
(G) Nuts	12%	—
(H) Oranges, clementines, mandarins and tangerines:		
(1) Pulp not containing the peel ...	—	—
(2) Other	12%	C — E 12%
(IJ) Peaches:		
(1) Containing added sweetening matter	9½%	C — E 9½%
(2) Other:		
(a) Canned...	—	—
(b) Not canned	9%	C — E 9%
(K) Pears:		
(1) Containing added sweetening matter	12%	C — E 12%
(2) Other	15%	C — E 15%
(L) Pineapples	5s. 6d. per cwt.	C — E 5s. 6d. per cwt.
(M) Strawberries:		
(1) Containing added sweetening matter	15%	C — E 15%
(2) Other	15s. per cwt.	C — E 15s. per cwt.
(N) Mixtures of fruit (including fruit pulp) which contain not less than four separate descriptions of fruit (no one of which exceeds 60 per cent. by weight of the fruit in the mixture) and not less than 25 pieces of fruit per four ounce portion of the drained fruit	5s. per cwt.	C — E 5s. per cwt.

	Rate of Import Duty (*if any*)	
Tariff Heading	*Full*	*Commonwealth* (C) *E.F.T.A.* (E)
20.06 Fruit otherwise prepared, etc.—*contd.*		
(O) Mixtures of fruit (including fruit pulp) other than mixtures falling within subheading (N) above, which contain not less than four separate descriptions of fruit, in which each of at least four descriptions constitutes at least 8 per cent., and no one description represents more than 50 per cent. by weight, of all the fruit in the mixture:		
(1) Where not less than 80 per cent. by weight of all fruit in the mixture consists of all or any of the following fruits, viz. peaches, nectarines, pears, apricots, cherries	—	—
(2) Other	5s. per cwt.	C — E 5s. per cwt.
(P) Other	15%	C — E 15%
20.07 Fruit juices (including grape must) and vegetable juices, whether or not containing added sugar, but unfermented and not containing spirit:		
(A) Citrus fruit juices:		
(1) Lemon juice:		
(*a*) Not containing more than 20 per cent. by weight of added sweetening matter	13%	C — E 13%
(*b*) Other	14½%	C — E 14½%
(2) Grapefruit juice; orange, clementine, mandarin or tangerine juice whether containing the detached cells of the fruit or not:		
(*a*) Not containing more than 20 per cent. by weight of added sweetening matter	—	—
(*b*) Other	3%	C — E 3%
(3) Other:		
(*a*) Not containing more than 20 per cent. by weight of added sweetening matter	15%	C — E 15%
(*b*) Other	18%	C — E 18%
(B) Pineapple juice; tomato juice ...	8%	C — E 8%
(C) Other	10%	C — E 10%

Chapter 21

Miscellaneous Edible Preparations

otes

1. This Chapter does not cover:

(*a*) Mixed vegetables of heading No. 07.04;

(*b*) Roasted coffee substitutes containing coffee in any proportion (heading No. 09.01);

(*c*) Products of headings Nos. 09.04 to 09.10; or

(*d*) Yeast put up as a medicament (heading No. 30.03).

2. Extracts of the substitutes referred to in Note 1 (*b*) above are to be classified in heading o. 21.02.

Tariff Heading	Rate of Import Duty (*if any*)	
	Full	*Commonwealth (C)* *E.F.T.A.* (*E*)
.01 Roasted chicory and other roasted coffee substitutes; extracts, essences and concentrates thereof:		
(A) Roasted chicory, unmixed	£1 2s. 3d. per cwt.	C £1 per cwt. E —
(B) Preparations consisting wholly or partly of extracts, essences or other concentrates of roasted chicory	£2 9s. 6d. per cwt. on the total dry weight of the goods	C £1 19s. 0d. per cwt. on the total dry weight of the goods E —
(C) Other	10%	
.02 Extracts, essences or concentrates, of coffee, tea or maté; preparations with a basis of those extracts, essences or concentrates:		
(A) Extracts, essences or concentrates of coffee; preparations with a basis of extracts, essences or concentrates of coffee	£2 9s. 6d. per cwt. on the total dry weight of the goods	C £1 19s. 0d. per cwt. on the total dry weight of the goods E —
(B) Other	10%	—
.03 Mustard flour and prepared mustard ...	10%	—
.04 Sauces; mixed condiments and mixed seasonings	10%	—
.05 Soups and broths, in liquid, solid or powder form:		
(A) Canned, but not including tomato soups or dried soups	7½%	—
(B) Other	10%	—
.06 Natural yeasts (active or inactive); prepared baking powders:		
(A) Natural yeasts	4s. per cwt.	—
(B) Prepared baking powders	10%	—

2t

Tariff Heading	Rate of Import Duty (if any)		
	Full	Commonwealth (C E.F.T.A. (E	
21.07 Food preparations not elsewhere specified or included:			
(A) Sweetfat (mixtures of edible fats and sugar)	10%	C E	— 10%
(B) Ice cream (containing fat) but not including ice cream powder	10%	C E	— 10%
(C) Mixtures of water and emulsifying agents with fat or oil (not including synthetic cream)	10%	C E	— 10%
(D) Coffee pastes (mixtures of ground, roasted coffee with vegetable fats, with or without other ingredients)	10%	C E	— 10%
(E) Ravioli, macaroni, spaghetti and the like, cooked (other than rice and other whole cereal grains), whether or not stuffed with other substances or admixed with tomato sauce:			
(1) Ravioli	8%	C E	— 8%
(2) Other	10%	C E	— 10%
(F) Yoghourt with added flavouring or fruit	10%	C E	— 10%
(G) Maize, including maize on cob (sweet corn), frozen or in airtight containers	8%	C	—
(H) Other	10%		—

Chapter 22

Beverages, Spirits and Vinegar

Notes

1. This Chapter does not cover:

(*a*) Sea water (heading No. 25.01);

(*b*) Distilled water or conductivity water (heading No. 28.58);

(*c*) Acetic acid of a concentration exceeding 10 per cent. by weight of acetic acid (heading No. 29.14);

(*d*) Medicaments of heading No. 30.03; or

(*e*) Perfumery or toilet preparations (Chapter 33).

2. For the purposes of headings Nos. 22.08 and 22.09, the alcoholic strength is to be taken to be that shown on test by Sikes' hydrometer.

Tariff Heading	Rate of Import Duty (*if any*)		
	Full	Commonwealth (*C*) E.F.T.A. (*E*)	
22.01 Waters, including spa waters and aerated waters; ice and snow:			
(A) Waters, including spa waters and aerated waters	8%	—	
(B) Other	—	—	
22.02 Lemonade, flavoured spa waters and flavoured aerated waters, and other non-alcoholic beverages, not including fruit and vegetable juices falling within heading No. 20.07	10%	—	
22.03 Beer made from malt:	—	--	
(A) Of any description (other than mum, spruce, black beer, Berlin white beer or other preparations of a similar character, of an original gravity of 1200° or more) where the worts thereof were before fermentation of a gravity: (1) Of 1030° or less (2) Exceeding 1030°			
(B) Of the descriptions called or similar to mum, spruce, black beer, Berlin white beer, or other preparations of a similar character, where the worts thereof were before fermentation of a gravity of 1200° or more			
22.04 Grape must, in fermentation or with fermentation arrested otherwise than by the addition of alcohol	10%	C E	— 10%

Tariff Heading	Rate of Import Duty (*if any*)		
	Full	*Commonwealth* (C) E.F.T.A. (E)	

22.05 Wine of fresh grapes (including grape must with fermentation arrested by the addition of alcohol):
(A) Light wine:
   (1) Still:
     (*a*) Not in bottle
     (*b*) In bottle
   (2) Sparkling
(B) Other wine:
   (1) Still:
     (*a*) Not in bottle
     (*b*) In bottle
   (2) Sparkling
" Light wine " means wine not exceeding 25 degrees or, in the case of wine qualifying for Commonwealth preference, 27 degrees of proof spirit
      —   —

22.06 Vermouths, and other wines of fresh grapes flavoured with aromatic extracts
      —   —

22.07 Other fermented beverages (for example, cider, perry and mead):

	Full	C / E	
(A) Beer	—	C	—
(B) Wine	—	E	—
(C) Cider and perry containing no added spirit or spirit derived from the addition of sugar	10%	C E	— 10%
(D) Other	10%	C E	— 10%

22.08 Ethyl alcohol (ethanol) or neutral spirits, undenatured, of a strength of one hundred and forty degrees proof or higher; denatured spirits (including ethyl alcohol (ethanol) and neutral spirits) of any strength:
(A) If warehoused 3 years or more
(B) If not warehoused, or warehoused less than 3 years
      —   —

22.09 Spirits (other than those of heading No. 22.08); liqueurs and other spirituous beverages; compound alcoholic preparations (known as " concentrated extracts ") for the manufacture of beverages:
(A) Liqueurs, cordials, mixtures and other preparations in bottle, entered in such a manner as to indicate that the strength is not to be tested:
   (1) If warehoused 3 years or more ...
   (2) If not warehoused, or warehoused less than 3 years
      —   —

Tariff Heading	Rate of Import Duty (if any)	
	Full	Commonwealth (C) E.F.T.A. (E)
.09 Spirits (other than those of heading No. 22.08), etc.—*contd*.		
(B) Other spirits (including spirituous beverages having the character of spirits, and liqueurs):		
(1) If warehoused 3 years or more ...	—	—
(2) If not warehoused, or warehoused less than 3 years	—	—
(C) Other	8%	—
.10 Vinegar and substitutes for vinegar ...	25%	C —
		E 25%

Chapter 23

Residues and Waste from the Food Industries; Prepared Animal Fodder

Tariff Heading	Rate of Import Duty (if any)		
	Full	Commonwealth (C) E.F.T.A. (E)	
23.01 Flours and meals, of meat, offals, fish, crustaceans or molluscs, unfit for human consumption; greaves:			
(A) Herring meal	—	—	
(B) Other	10%	—	
23.02 Bran, sharps and other residues derived from the sifting, milling or working of cereals or of leguminous vegetables	10%	C E	— 10%
23.03 Beet-pulp, bagasse and other waste of sugar manufacture; brewing and distilling dregs and waste; residues of starch manufacture and similar residues:			
(A) Bagasse	—	—	
(B) Other	10%	C E	— 10%
23.04 Oil-cake and other residues (except dregs) resulting from the extraction of vegetable oils:			
(A) Soya bean cake and soya bean meal ...	13%	C E	— 13%
(B) Other	10%	C E	— 10%
23.05 Wine lees; argol:			
(A) Wine lees	—	—	
(B) Other	—	—	
23.06 Vegetable products of a kind used for animal food, not elsewhere specified or included:			
(A) Dried apple pomace, unground ...	—	—	
(B) Dried citrus fruit waste	—	—	
(C) Other	10%	C E	— 10%
23.07 Sweetened forage; other preparations of a kind used in animal feeding:			
(A) Vitamin supplements:			
(1) Where the vitamin content consists of natural vitamin concentrates	8%	C E	— 8%
(2) Other	25% of the value of the vitamin content (other than natural vitamin concentrates) or 8%, whichever is the greater	C E	— 25% of the value of the vitamin content (other than natural vitamin concentrates) or 8%, whichever is the greater

Tariff Heading	Rate of Import Duty (if any)	
	Full	Commonwealth (C) E.F.T.A. (E)
3.07 Sweetened forage, etc.—*contd.*		
(B) Liquefied herring wholly of herring apart from preserving and liquefying ingredients	—	—
(C) Other:		
(1) Fish solubles	10%	—
(2) Other	10%	C — E 10%

Chapter 24

Tobacco

Tariff Heading	Rate of Import Duty (if any)	
	Full	*Commonwealth (E.F.T.A.*
24.01 Unmanufactured tobacco; tobacco refuse:	—	—
(A) Containing 10 per cent. or more by weight of moisture		
(B) Other		
24.02 Manufactured tobacco; tobacco extracts and essences:	—	—
(A) Manufactured tobacco: (1) Cigars (2) Cigarettes (3) Cavendish or negrohead: (*a*) Manufactured in bond (*b*) Other (4) Snuff and snuff work (including tobacco dust or powder and ground tobacco) (5) Other		
(B) Extracts and essences		

SECTION V

MINERAL PRODUCTS

Chapter 25

Salt; Sulphur; Earths and Stone; Plastering Materials, Lime and Cement

otes

1. Except where the context otherwise requires, the headings of this Chapter are to be
ken to apply only to goods which are in the crude state, or which have been washed
cluding washing with chemical substances to remove impurities provided that this does
t change the character of the product), crushed, ground, powdered, levigated, sifted,
eened, concentrated by flotation, magnetic separation or other mechanical or physical
ocesses (not including crystallisation) but not calcined or subjected to any further process
her than a process specially mentioned in any heading in respect of the goods described
erein.

2. This Chapter does not cover:

(a) Sublimed sulphur, precipitated sulphur or colloidal sulphur (heading No. 28.02);

(b) Ferrous earth colours containing 70 per cent. or more by weight of combined iron
    evaluated as Fe_2O_3 (heading No. 28.23);

(c) Pharmaceutical products falling within Chapter 30;

(d) Perfumery, cosmetics or toilet preparations (heading No. 33.06);

(e) Road and paving setts, flagstones, curbs, mosaic cubes, and roofing, facing and damp
    course slates, falling within heading No. 68.01, 68.02 or 68.03;

(f) Precious or semi-precious stones (Chapter 71);

(g) Cultured sodium chloride crystals (other than optical elements) weighing not less than
    two and a half grammes each, of heading No. 38.19; optical elements of sodium
    chloride (heading No. 90.01); or

(h) Writing, drawing, tailors' and billiards chalks (heading No. 98.05).

Tariff Heading	Rate of Import Duty (if any)	
	Full	Commonwealth (C) E.F.T.A. (E)
.01 Common salt (including rock salt, sea salt and table salt); pure sodium chloride; salt liquors; sea water:		
(A) Sodium chloride, pharmaceutical quality	22%	—
(B) Fishery salt, being salt in coarse crystals of a kind used for curing fish	—	—
(C) Other	8%	—
.02 Iron pyrites (including cupreous iron pyrites), unroasted	—	—
.03 Sulphur of all kinds, other than sublimed sulphur, precipitated sulphur and colloidal sulphur	—	—

Tariff Heading	Rate of Import Duty (if any)	
	Full	Commonwealth (C E.F.T.A. (E

25.04 Natural graphite:
   (A) Flake graphite containing not less than 83 per cent. by weight of carbon and of which not more than 15 per cent. by weight passes a sieve having a nominal width of aperture of 105 microns and conforming to British Standard 410:1962, and being graphite such that, if a cylindrical container with an internal diameter of 2 inches and a depth of 1$\frac{15}{16}$ inches is filled by funnelling the graphite through a circular orifice of $\frac{1}{2}$ inch diameter placed centrally 2$\frac{1}{2}$ inches above the top of the container, the contents of the container will have a density of less than 60 grammes per 100 cubic centimetres — —
   (B) Other ... ...   10% —

25.05 Natural sands of all kinds, whether or not coloured, other than metal-bearing sands falling within heading No. 26.01   8% —

25.06 Quartz (other than natural sands); quartzite, including quartzite not further worked than roughly split, roughly squared or squared by sawing:
   (A) Quartz:
     (1) Ground or powdered ... ...   8% —
     (2) Other ... ... — —
   (B) Quartzite ... ...   8% —

25.07 Clay (for example, kaolin and bentonite), andalusite, kyanite and sillimanite, whether or not calcined, but not including expanded clays falling within heading No. 68.07; mullite; chamotte and dinas earths:
   (A) Attapulgite clay of which not more than 0·1 per cent. by weight of the dry material is retained, after sieving in the wet state, on a sieve having a nominal width of aperture of 45 microns and conforming to British Standard 410:1962 — —
   (B) Other ... ...   6% —

25.08 Chalk:
   (A) Whiting .. ..   16% —
   (B) Other ... ...   8% —

25.09 Earth colours, whether or not calcined or mixed together; natural micaceous iron oxides   8% —

Tariff Heading	Rate of Import Duty (if any)	
	Full	Commonwealth (C) E.F.T.A. (E)
5.10 Natural mineral calcium phosphates, natural aluminium calcium phosphates, apatite and phosphatic chalk	—	—
5.11 Natural barium sulphate (barytes); natural barium carbonate (witherite), whether or not calcined	8%	—
5.12 Infusorial earths, siliceous fossil meals and similar siliceous earths (for example, kiesel-guhr, tripolite or diatomite), whether or not calcined, of an apparent specific gravity of 1 or less:		
(A) Not bagged or otherwise packed, containing not less than 35 per cent. by weight of moisture	—	—
(B) Other	6%	—
5.13 Pumice stone; emery; natural corundum, natural garnet and other natural abrasives, whether or not heat-treated:		
(A) Garnet	—	—
(B) Emery, not crushed, ground, powdered or graded	—	—
(C) Other	8%	—
5.14 Slate, including slate not further worked than roughly split, roughly squared or squared by sawing:		
(A) Blocks, slabs or sheets not less than ¾ inch in thickness	5%	—
(B) Other ... ..., ...	8%	—
5.15 Marble, travertine, ecaussine and other calcareous monumental and building stone of an apparent specific gravity of 2·5 or more and alabaster, including such stone not further worked than roughly split, roughly squared or squared by sawing	6½%	—
5.16 Granite, porphyry, basalt, sandstone and other monumental and building stone, including such stone not further worked than roughly split, roughly squared or squared by sawing:		
(A) Granite:		
(1) Not sawn	8 %	—
(2) Sawn on three or more sides:		
(a) Pieces of a volume not exceeding 30 cubic inches		

| Tariff Heading | Rate of Import Duty (if any) | |
	Full	Commonwealth (C E.F.T.A. (E

25.16 Granite, etc.—cont.
  (A) (2) Granite—cont.
      (b) Other   ...   .
      (3) Other   ...   .
  (B) Other ...   .
	
	28%
	10%
	8%
		
		—
		—
		—

25.17 Pebbles and crushed or broken stone (whether or not heat-treated), gravel, macadam and tarred macadam, of a kind commonly used for concrete aggregates, for road metalling or for railway or other ballast; flint and shingle, whether or not heat-treated; granules and chippings (whether or not heat-treated) and powder of stones falling within heading No. 25.15 or 25.16:
  (A) Flint, not crushed, ground or powdered
  (B) Chippings of calcareous stones falling within heading No. 25.15 or 25.16 and chippings of serpentine
  (C) Other   ...   .
	
	—
	
	—
	
	8%
		
		—
		
		—
		
		—

25.18 Dolomite, whether or not calcined, including dolomite not further worked than roughly split, roughly squared or squared by sawing; agglomerated dolomite (including tarred dolomite):
  (A) Calcined dolomite which, on boiling with 2N hydrochloric acid, yields not more than 0·3 per cent. by weight of insoluble residue
  (B) Other   ...   .
	
	—
	
	8%
		
		—
		
		—

25.19 Natural magnesium carbonate (magnesite), whether or not calcined:
  (A) Dead-burned ...   .
  (B) Other ...   .
	
	8%
	—
		
		—
		—

25.20 Gypsum; anhydrite; calcined gypsum, and plasters with a basis of calcium sulphate, whether or not coloured, but not including plasters specially prepared for use in dentistry	8%	—
25.21 Limestone flux and calcareous stone, com- monly used for the manufacture of lime or cement	8%	—
25.22 Quicklime, slaked lime and hydraulic lime	8%	—
25.23 Portland cement, high alumina cement, slag cement, supersulphate cement and similar hydraulic cements, whether or not coloured or in the form of clinker:		

Tariff Heading	Rate of Import Duty (if any)	
	Full	Commonwealth (C) E.F.T.A. (E)
5.23 Portland cement, etc.—cont.		
(A) Calcareous cement, not containing added colouring matter	5%	—
(B) Other	8%	—
5.24 Asbestos	10%	—
5.25 Meerschaum (whether or not in polished pieces) and amber; agglomerated meerschaum and agglomerated amber, in plates, rods, sticks or similar forms, not worked after moulding; jet	8%	—
5.26 Mica, including splittings; mica waste:		
(A) Blocks, films and splittings	—	—
(B) Other	8%	—
5.27 Natural steatite, including natural steatite not further worked than roughly split, roughly squared or squared by sawing; talc	—	—
5.28 Natural cryolite and natural chiolite ...	—	—
5.29 Natural arsenic sulphides	6%	—
5.30 Crude natural borates and concentrates thereof (calcined or not), but not including borates separated from natural brine; crude natural boric acid containing not more than 85 per cent. of H_3BO_3 calculated on the dry weight		
5.31 Felspar, leucite, nepheline and nepheline syenite; fluorspar:		
(A) Felspar:		
(1) Ground or powdered	4%	—
(2) Other	—	—
(B) Other	8%	—
5.32 Strontianite (whether or not calcined), other than strontium oxide; mineral substances not elsewhere specified or included; broken pottery:		
(A) Infusorial earths, siliceous fossil meals and similar siliceous earths, not bagged or otherwise packed, containing not less than 35 per cent. by weight of moisture	—	—
(B) Perlite, obsidian and pitchstone, crushed, ground, powdered or graded	—	—
(C) Rare earth minerals and concentrates thereof containing not less than 40 per cent., and not more than 95 per cent., by weight of rare earth compounds calculated as rare earth oxides	—	—
(D) Other	8%	—

Chapter 26

Metallic Ores, Slag and Ash

Notes

1. This Chapter does not cover:

(*a*) Natural magnesium carbonate (magnesite), whether or not calcined (heading No 25.19);

(*b*) Basic slag of Chapter 31;

(*c*) Slag wool, rock wool or similar mineral wools (heading No. 68.07);

(*d*) Goods falling within Chapter 71 (which relates, *inter alia*, to goldsmiths' and silver smiths' sweepings, residues and lemels); or

(*e*) Copper, nickel or cobalt mattes produced by any process of smelting (Section XV).

2. For the purposes of heading No. 26.01, the term " metallic ores " means minerals o those mineralogical species used for the extraction on an industrial scale of mercury, of th metals of heading No. 28.50 or of the metals of Section XIV or XV; minerals which hav undergone a process rendering them more suitable for a purpose other than the extractio of metal on an industrial scale are, however, excluded from the heading.

3. Heading No. 26.03 is to be taken to apply only to ash and residues of a kind used on a industrial scale either for the extraction of metals or as a basis for the manufacture o chemical compounds of metals.

Tariff Heading	Rate of Import Duty (*if any*)	
	Full	Commonwealth (C) E.F.T.A. (E)
26.01 Metallic ores and concentrates thereof; roasted iron pyrites, including roasted cupreous iron pyrites	—	—
26.02 Slag, dross, scalings and similar waste from the manufacture of iron or steel	—	—
26.03 Ash and residues (other than from the manufacture of iron or steel), containing metals or metallic compounds	—	—
26.04 Other slag and ash, including kelp ...	—	—

Chapter 27

Mineral Fuels, Mineral Oils and Products of their Distillation;
Bituminous Substances; Mineral Waxes

Notes

1. This Chapter does not cover:

(*a*) Separate chemically defined organic compounds, other than chemically pure methane which is to be classified in heading No. 27.11; or

(*b*) Medicaments (heading No. 30.03).

2. In heading No. 27.07 the expression " similar oils and products obtained by other processes " is to be taken to refer to products similar to those obtained by the distillation of high temperature coal tar but which are obtained by the distillation of low temperature coal tar or other mineral tars, by processing petroleum or by any other process, provided that the weight of the aromatic constituents exceeds that of non-aromatic constituents.

3. References in heading No. 27.10 to petroleum oils and oils obtained from bituminous minerals are to be taken to include not only petroleum oils and oils obtained from bituminous minerals but also similar oils obtained by any process, provided that the weight of the non-aromatic constituents exceeds that of the aromatic constituents.

4. Heading No. 27.13 is to be taken to include not only paraffin wax and the other products specified therein, but also similar products obtained by synthesis or by other processes.

Special note applying to subheadings only

Throughout this Schedule:

(*a*) " Hydrocarbon oils " means petroleum oils, coal tar, and oils produced from coal, shale, peat or any other bituminous substance, and all liquid hydrocarbons, but does not include such hydrocarbons or bituminous or asphaltic substances as are—

    (i) solid or semi-solid at a temperature of 60° F.; or

    (ii) gaseous at a temperature of 60° F. and under a pressure of one atmosphere.

The expression also includes products which, apart from small proportions of colouring matter or of additives, consist wholly of hydrocarbon oils as defined above. For this purpose, " additive " means any substance commonly added in small proportions to hydrocarbon oils for the purpose of improving or modifying their quality or characteristics as fuel or as lubricants.

(*b*) " Light oils " has the meaning given by section 195 (1) of the Customs and Excise Act 1952 as for the time being in force.

(*c*) Except as provided in paragraph (*a*) of this Note, references to hydrocarbon oils do not include mixtures or combinations of those oils with other substances.

Tariff Heading	Rate of Import Duty (if any)	
	Full	*Commonwealth (C)* *E.F.T.A.* *(E)*
27.01 Coal; briquettes, ovoids and similar solid fuels manufactured from coal	—	—
27.02 Lignite, whether or not agglomerated ...	—	—
27.03 Peat (including peat litter), whether or not agglomerated	12½%	—

Tariff Heading	Rate of Import Duty (if any)	
	Full	Commonwealth (C) E.F.T.A. (E)
27.04 Coke and semi-coke of coal, of lignite or of peat	—	—
27.05 Retort carbon	6%	—
27.05 (bis) Coal gas, water gas, producer gas and similar gases	6%	—
27.06 Tar distilled from coal, from lignite or from peat, and other mineral tars, including partially distilled tars and blends of pitch with creosote oils or with other coal tar distillation products:		
(A) Hydrocarbon oils	—	—
(B) Other	6%	—
27.07 Oils and other products of the distillation of high temperature coal tars and similar oils and products obtained by other processes (for example, benzole, creosote, cresylic acid and solvent naphtha):		
(A) Hydrocarbon oils	—	—
(B) Other	8%	—
27.08 Pitch and pitch coke, obtained from coal tar or from other mineral tars	8%	—
27.09 Petroleum oils and oils obtained from bituminous minerals, crude:		
(A) Solid and semi-solid petroleum oils...	—	—
(B) Other	—	—
27.10 Petroleum oils and oils obtained from bituminous minerals, other than crude; preparations not elsewhere specified or included, containing not less than 70 per cent. by weight of petroleum oils or of oils obtained from bituminous minerals, these oils being the basic constituents of the preparations:		
(A) Hydrocarbon oils	—	—
(B) Other:		
(1) Containing light oils	3%, in addition to any hydrocarbon oil duty	—
(2) Other	8%	—
27.11 Petroleum gases and other gaseous hydro-carbons:		
(A) Methane	—	—
(B) Other	8%	—

Tariff Heading	Rate of Import Duty (if any)	
	Full	Commonwealth (C) E.F.T.A. (E)
27.12 Petroleum jelly:		
(A) Hydrocarbon oils	—	—
(B) Other	8%	—
27.13 Paraffin wax, micro-crystalline wax, slack wax, ozokerite, lignite wax, peat wax and other mineral waxes, whether or not coloured:		
(A) Lignite (montan) wax	—	—
(B) Petroleum waxes containing not less than 10 per cent. by weight of oil when determined by the Institute of Petroleum Method No. 158/64T	—	—
(C) Paraffin wax and micro-crystalline wax	10%	—
(D) Other	8%	—
27.14 Petroleum bitumen, petroleum coke and other residues of petroleum oils or of oils obtained from bituminous minerals:		
(A) Petroleum coke, calcined, not containing by weight more than 0·8 per cent. of ash, 0·01 per cent. of manganese, 0·02 per cent. of nickel or of vanadium, one part per million of boron or 50 parts per million of titanium	—	—
(B) Hydrocarbon oils	—	—
(C) Other	8%	—
27.15 Bitumen and asphalt, natural; bituminous shale, asphaltic rock and tar sands	8%	—
27.16 Bituminous mixtures based on natural asphalt, on natural bitumen, on petroleum bitumen, on mineral tar or on mineral tar pitch (for example, bituminous mastics, cut-backs):		
(A) Hydrocarbon oils	—	—
(B) Other	8%	—

SECTION VI

PRODUCTS OF THE CHEMICAL AND ALLIED INDUSTRIES

Notes

1. (a) Goods (other than radio-active ores) answering to a description in heading No 28.50 or 28.51 are to be classified in those headings and in no other heading of this Schedule

(b) Subject to paragraph (a) above, goods answering to a description in heading No. 28.4 or 28.52 are to be classified in those headings and in no other heading of this Section.

2. Subject to Note 1 above, goods classifiable within heading No. 30.03, 30.04, 30.0! 32.09, 33.06, 35.06, 37.08 or 38.11 by reason of being put up in measured doses or for sale b retail are to be classified in those headings and in no other heading of this Schedule.

Chapter 28

Inorganic Chemicals; Organic and Inorganic Compounds of Precious Metals, of Rare Eart Metals, of Radio-Active Elements and of Isotopes

Notes

1. Except in so far as the context otherwise requires, the headings of this Chapter ar to be taken to apply only to:

(a) Separate chemical elements and separate chemically defined compounds, whether o not containing impurities;

(b) Products mentioned in (a) above dissolved in water;

(c) Products mentioned in (a) above dissolved in other solvents provided that the solutio constitutes a normal and necessary method of putting up these products adopted sole! for reasons of safety or for transport and that the solvent does not render the produc particularly suitable for some types of use rather than for general use;

(d) The products mentioned in (a), (b) or (c) above with an added stabiliser necessary fo their preservation or transport.

2. In addition to dithionites stabilised with organic substances and to sulphoxylate (heading No. 28.36), carbonates and percarbonates of inorganic bases (heading No. 28.42 cyanides and complex cyanides of inorganic bases (heading No. 28.43), fulminates, cyanate and thiocyanates, of inorganic bases (heading No. 28.44), organic products included i headings Nos. 28.49 to 28.52 and metallic and non-metallic carbides (heading No. 28.56 only the following compounds of carbon are also to be classified in the present Chapter

(a) Oxides of carbon; hydrocyanic, fulminic, isocyanic, thiocyanic and other simple o complex cyanogen acids (heading No. 28.13);

(b) Oxyhalides of carbon (heading No. 28.14);

(c) Carbon disulphide (heading No. 28.15);

(d) Thiocarbonates, selenocarbonates, tellurocarbonates, selenocyanates, tellurocyanate: tetrathiocyanatodiamminochromates (reineckates) and other complex cyanates, c inorganic bases (heading No. 28.48);

(e) Solid hydrogen peroxide (heading No. 28.54), carbon oxysulphide, thiocarbony halides, cyanogen, cyanogen halides and cyanamide and its metallic derivatives (headin No. 28.58) other than calcium cyanamide containing not more than 25 per cent. b weight of nitrogen, calculated on the dry anhydrous product (Chapter 31).

3. This Chapter does not cover:

(a) Sodium chloride or other mineral products falling within Section V;

(b) Organo-inorganic compounds other than those mentioned in Note 2 above;

(c) Products mentioned in Note 1, 2 ,3 or 4 of Chapter 31;

(d) Inorganic products of a kind used as luminophores (heading No. 32.07);

(e) Artificial graphite (heading No. 38.01); activated carbon (heading No. 38.03); products put up as charges for fire-extinguishers or put up in fire-extinguishing grenades, of heading No. 38.17; ink removers put up in packings for sale by retail, of heading No. 38.19; cultured crystals (other than optical elements) weighing not less than two and a half grammes each, of magnesium oxide or of the halides of the alkali or of the alkaline-earth metals, of heading No. 38.19;

(f) Precious or semi-precious stones (natural, synthetic or reconstructed) or dust or powder of such stones (headings Nos. 71.02 to 71.04), and precious metals falling within Chapter 71;

(g) The metals, whether or not chemically pure, falling within any heading of Section XV; or

(h) Optical elements, for example, of magnesium oxide or of the halides of the alkali or of the alkaline-earth metals (heading No. 90.01).

4. Chemically defined complex acids consisting of a non-metal acid falling within sub-Chapter II and a metallic acid falling within sub-Chapter IV are to be classified in heading No. 28.13.

5. Headings Nos. 28.29 to 28.48 inclusive are to be taken to apply only to metallic or ammonium salts or peroxysalts. Except where the context otherwise requires, double or complex salts are to be classified in heading No. 28.48.

6. Heading No. 28.50 is to be taken to apply only to:

(a) The following fissile chemical elements and isotopes:
natural uranium and uranium isotopes 233 and 235, plutonium and plutonium isotopes;

(b) The following radio-active chemical elements:
technetium, promethium, polonium, astatine, radon, francium, radium, actinium, protactinium, neptunium, americium and other elements of higher atomic number;

(c) All other radio-active isotopes, natural or artificial, including those of the precious metals and of the base metals of Sections XIV and XV;

(d) Compounds, inorganic or organic, of these elements or isotopes, whether or not chemically defined and whether or not mixed together;

(e) Alloys (other than ferro-uranium), dispersions and cermets, containing any of these elements or isotopes or their inorganic or organic compounds;

(f) Nuclear reactor cartridges, spent or irradiated.

The term " isotopes " mentioned above and in headings Nos. 28.50 and 28.51 includes " enriched isotopes ", but does not include chemical elements which occur in nature as pure isotopes nor uranium depleted in uranium-235.

7. Heading No. 28.55 is to be taken to include ferro-phosphorus containing 15 per cent. or more by weight of phosphorus and phosphor copper containing more than 8 per cent. by weight of phosphorus.

Tariff Heading	Rate of Import Duty (if any)	
	Full	Commonwealth (C) E.F.T.A. (E)
I. Chemical elements		
28.01 Halogens (fluorine, chlorine, bromine and iodine):		
(A) Fluorine; chlorine	8%	—
(B) Bromine; iodine	—	—

Tariff Heading	Rate of Import Duty (if any)	
	Full	Commonwealth (C E.F.T.A. (E
28.02 Sulphur, sublimed or precipitated; colloidal sulphur:		
(A) Colloidal sulphur	8%	—
(B) Other	—	—
28.03 Carbon, including carbon black, anthracene black, acetylene black and lamp black:		
(A) Acetylene black	14%	—
(B) Other	8%	—
28.04 Hydrogen, rare gases and other non-metals:		
(A) Silicon; selenium	—	—
(B) Other	8%	—
28.05 Alkali, alkaline-earth and rare earth metals; yttrium and scandium; mercury:		
(A) Mercury	—	—
(B) Other	8%	—
II. Inorganic acids and oxygen compounds of non-metals		
28.06 Hydrochloric acid and chlorosulphonic acid:		
(A) Hydrochloric acid:		
(1) Analytical reagent quality ...	22%	—
(2) Other	8%	—
(B) Chlorosulphonic acid	8%	—
28.07 Sulphur dioxide	8%	—
28.08 Sulphuric acid; oleum:		
(A) Sulphuric acid:		
(1) Analytical reagent quality ...	22%	—
(2) Other	8%	—
(B) Oleum	8%	—
28.09 Nitric acid; sulphonitric acids:		
(A) Nitric acid:		
(1) Analytical reagent quality ...	23%	—
(2) Other	12%	—
(B) Sulphonitric acids	8%	—
28.10 Phosphorus pentoxide and phosphoric acids (meta-, ortho- and pyro-):		
(A) Phosphorus pentoxide	25%	—
(B) Phosphoric acids:		
(1) Metaphosphoric acid	8%	—
(2) Other	20%	—

Tariff Heading	Rate of Import Duty (if any)	
	Full	Commonwealth (C) E.F.T.A. (E)
.11 Arsenic trioxide, arsenic pentoxide and acids of arsenic:		
(A) Arsenic trioxide	—	—
(B) Other	25%	—
12 Boric oxide and boric acid:		
(A) Boric oxide	25%	—
(B) Boric acid	14½%	—
.13 Other inorganic acids and oxygen compounds of non-metals (excluding water):		
(A) Carbon dioxide; carbon monoxide...	8%	—
(B) Chlorine dioxide	8%	—
(C) Fluorosulphonic acid	8%	—
(D) Hexafluorophosphoric acid	8%	—
(E) Hydrofluoric acid:		
(1) Analytical reagent quality ...	17%	—
(2) Other	8%	—
(F) Hydrogen fluoride; hydrogen sulphide	8%	—
(G) Metaboric acid	8%	—
(H) *di*Nitrogen tetroxide	8%	—
(IJ) Nitrosylsulphuric acid	8%	—
(K) Nitric oxide; nitrous oxide	8%	—
(L) Per*mono*sulphuric acid	8%	—
(M) Selenium dioxide	8%	—
(N) Silicic acid; silicon dioxide; silicon monoxide	8%	—
(O) Sulphur trioxide	8%	—
(P) Sulphurous acid	8%	—
(Q) Other	20%	—
III. Halogen and sulphur compounds of non-metals		
.14 Halides, oxyhalides and other halogen compounds of non-metals:		
(A) Boron trifluoride	8%	—
(B) Bromine pentafluoride; bromine trifluoride	8%	—
(C) Chlorine trifluoride	8%	—
(D) Nitrosyl chloride	8%	—
(E) Phosphoryl bromide	8%	—
(F) Selenium bromide	8%	—
(G) Sulphur chloride; sulphur dichloride; sulphur hexafluoride	8%	—
(H) Sulphuryl chloride	8%	—
(IJ) Thionyl bromide	8%	—
(K) Other	25%	—
.15 Sulphides of non-metals; phosphorus trisulphide:		
(A) Arsenic disulphide; arsenic pentasulphide; arsenic trisulphide	8%	—
(B) Phosphorus trisulphide	8%	—
(C) Other	20%	—

Tariff Heading	Rate of Import Duty (if any)	
	Full	Commonwealth (C) E.F.T.A. (E)
IV. Inorganic bases and metallic oxides, hydroxides and peroxides		
28.16 Ammonia, anhydrous or in aqueous solution	16%	—
28.17 Sodium hydroxide (caustic soda); potassium hydroxide (caustic potash); peroxides of sodium or potassium:		
(A) Sodium hydroxide	10%	—
(B) Sodium peroxide	25%	—
(C) Other	8%	—
28.18 Oxides, hydroxides and peroxides, of strontium, barium or magnesium:		
(A) Barium oxide and peroxide; strontium peroxide	8%	—
(B) Magnesium oxide:		
(1) Pharmaceutical quality	17%	—
(2) Other	8%	—
(C) Magnesium peroxide	20%	—
(D) Other	25%	—
28.19 Zinc oxide and zinc peroxide:		
(A) Zinc oxide	12%	—
(B) Zinc peroxide	25%	—
28.20 Aluminium oxide and hydroxide; artificial corundum:		
(A) Aluminium oxide:		
(1) Analytical reagent quality ...	23%	—
(2) Other	9%	—
(B) Aluminium hydroxide	$12\frac{1}{2}$%	—
(C) Artificial corundum	9%	—
28.21 Chromium oxides and hydroxides:		
(A) Chromic oxide	16%	—
(B) Other	20%	—
28.22 Manganese oxides	8%	—
28.23 Iron oxides and hydroxides; earth colours containing 70 per cent. or more by weight of combined iron evaluated as Fe_2O_3:		
(A) Iron oxides and hydroxides	$12\frac{1}{2}$%	—
(B) Earth colours	8%	—
28.24 Cobalt oxides and hydroxides:		
(A) Cobalt oxides	15%	—
(B) Cobalt hydroxides	24%	—

Tariff Heading	Rate of Import Duty (*if any*)	
	Full	*Commonwealth* (C) *E.F.T.A.* (E)
.25 Titanium oxides	12%	—
.26 Tin oxides (stannous oxide and stannic oxide)	16%	—
.27 Lead oxides; red lead and orange lead:		
(A) Lead oxides:		
(1) Lead dioxide	20%	—
(2) Lead monoxide:		
(*a*) Pharmaceutical quality ...	18%	—
(*b*) Other	9%	—
(3) Other	9%	—
(B) Red lead and orange lead	12½%	—
.28 Hydrazine and hydroxylamine and their inorganic salts; other inorganic bases and metallic oxides, hydroxides and peroxides:		
(A) Antimony oxides	£40 per ton or 25%, whichever is the greater	—
(B) Calcium oxide; calcium hydroxide ...	8%	
(C) Cupric or cuprous oxide; cupric hydroxide:		
(1) Cupric oxide, analytical reagent quality	17%	—
(2) Other	8%	—
(D) Germanium dioxide	16%	—
(E) Hydrazine, anhydrous	8%	—
(F) Hydroxylammonium nitrate	8%	—
(G) Lead hydroxide	8%	—
(H) Mercuric oxide	8%	—
(IJ) Metastannic acid	8%	—
(K) Nickel oxides	8%	—
(L) Rhenium dioxide ... ·	8%	—
(M) Sodium monoxide	8%	—
(N) Thallium hydroxide	8%	—
(O) Zinc hydroxide	8%	—
(P) Other	20%	—
V. Metallic salts and peroxysalts, of inorganic acids		
.29 Fluorides; fluorosilicates, fluoroborates and other complex fluorine salts:		
(A) Aluminium calcium fluoride; aluminium sodium fluoride	8%	—
(B) Ammonium copper fluorides ...	8%	—
(C) Antimony sodium fluoride; antimony trifluoride	8%	—
(D) Beryllium fluoride	8%	—

Tariff Heading	Rate of Import Duty (if any)	
	Full	Commonwealth (C) E.F.T.A. (E)
28.29 Fluorides; fluorosilicates, fluoroborates, etc.—cont.		
(E) Bismuth fluoride	8%	
(F) Cadmium fluoroborate	8%	
(G) Calcium fluoride	8%	
(H) Copper fluoroborates	8%	
(IJ) Lead fluoroborate	8%	
(K) Magnesium fluorosilicate	8%	
(L) Potassium hydrogen difluoride ...	8%	
(M) Sodium fluorotitanate; sodium fluorozirconate	8%	
(N) Stannous fluoroborate	8%	
(O) Zinc fluoroborate	8%	
(P) Other	20%	
28.30 Chlorides and oxide chlorides:		
(A) Aluminium chloride, other than anhydrous	8%	—
(B) Aluminium chlorohydrate	8%	—
(C) Ammonium chloride:		
(1) Pharmaceutical quality	24%	—
(2) Other	16%	—
(D) Barium chloride:		
(1) Analytical reagent quality ...	14%	—
(2) Other	8%	—
(E) Calcium chloride:		
(1) Pharmaceutical quality	24%	—
(2) Other	16%	—
(F) Ferric or ferrous chloride; ferric oxide chloride	8%	—
(G) Gallium trichloride	8%	—
(H) Lead chloride; lead oxide chloride ...	8%	—
(IJ) Magnesium chloride:		
(1) Analytical reagent quality ...	20%	—
(2) Other	—	—
(K) Magnesium oxide chloride	8%	—
(L) Manganous chloride:		
(1) Analytical reagent quality ...	22%	—
(2) Other	8%	—
(M) Stannic or stannous chloride; stannic oxide chloride:		
(1) Stannic or stannous chloride, analytical reagent quality	22%	—
(2) Other	8%	—
(N) Zinc chloride	8%	—
(O) Other	25%	—
28.31 Chlorites and hypochlorites	8%	—
28.32 Chlorates and perchlorates:		
(A) Ammonium chlorate	8%	—
(B) Barium chlorate	8%	—

Tariff Heading	Rate of Import Duty (if any)	
	Full	Commonwealth (C) E.F.T.A. (E)

.32 Chlorates and perchlorates:—cont.

(C) Ferrous perchlorate	8%	—
(D) Lead perchlorate	8%	—
(E) Lithium perchlorate	8%	—
(F) Magnesium perchlorate	8%	—
(G) Potassium chlorate	6½%	—
(H) Potassium perchlorate	8%	—
(IJ) Sodium chlorate; sodium perchlorate	8%	—
(K) Other	17½%	—

.33 Bromides, oxide bromides, bromates and perbromates, and hypobromites:

(A) Ferric or ferrous bromide	—	—
(B) Chromous bromide	8%	—
(C) Other	25%	—

.34 Iodides, oxide iodides, iodates and periodates:

(A) Cupric or cuprous iodide	—	—
(B) Barium periodate	8%	—
(C) Other	25%	—

.35 Sulphides; polysulphides:

(A) Sulphides:		
(1) Ammonium sulphide; ammonium hydrogen sulphide	8%	—
(2) Antimony pentasulphide; antimony trisulphide	12½%	—
(3) Barium sulphide	8%	—
(4) Cadmium sulphide	12½%	—
(5) Calcium sulphide; calcium hydrogen sulphide	8%	—
(6) Cupric or cuprous sulphide ...	8%	—
(7) Ferrous sulphide	8%	—
(8) Lead sulphide	8%	—
(9) Mercuric sulphide:		
(a) Red	12½%	—
(b) Other	8%	—
(10) Sodium sulphide; sodium hydrogen sulphide:		
(a) Sodium sulphide, analytical reagent quality	17%	—
(b) Other	8%	—
(11) Zinc sulphide	16%	—
(12) Other	20%	—
(B) Polysulphides	8%	—

.36 Dithionites, including those stabilised with organic substances; sulphoxylates:

(A) Zinc dithionite	8%	—
(B) Other	25%	—

Tariff Heading	Rate of Import Duty (*if any*)	
	Full	*Commonwealth* (C) *E.F.T.A.* (E)
28.37 Sulphites and thiosulphates:		
(A) Aluminium thiosulphate	8%	—
(B) Calcium sulphite; calcium hydrogen sulphite	8%	—
(C) Sodium sulphite; sodium hydrogen sulphite (aqueous solution):		
(1) Sodium sulphite, analytical reagent quality	22%	—
(2) Other	8%	—
(D) Sodium thiosulphate, other than photographic quality	8%	—
(E) Other	25%	—
28.38 Sulphates (including alums) and persulphates:		
(A) Sulphates (including alums):		
(1) Aluminium ammonium sulphate and aluminium potassium sulphate, other than pharmaceutical quality; aluminium sodium sulphate; aluminium sulphate, other than analytical reagent quality	5%	—
(2) Barium sulphate:		
(*a*) Pharmaceutical quality ...	24%	—
(*b*) Other	16%	—
(3) Calcium sulphate	16%	—
(4) Chromic sulphate	10%	—
(5) Chromic potassium sulphate ...	8%	—
(6) Cupric or cuprous sulphate, other than analytical reagent quality	8%	—
(7) Ferric or ferrous sulphate, other than pharmaceutical quality; iron sulphates, basic	8%	—
(8) Gallium sulphate	8%	—
(9) Lead sulphate	8%	—
(10) Lead sulphate, basic	12½%	—
(11) Magnesium sulphate, other than pharmaceutical quality	8%	—
(12) Manganic or manganous sulphate, other than analytical reagent quality	8%	—
(13) Potassium sulphate:		
(*a*) Analytical reagent quality ...	20%	—
(*b*) Other	—	—
(14) Sodium sulphate, other than pharmaceutical quality; sodium hydrogen sulphate, other than analytical reagent quality	8%	—
(15) Zinc sulphate, other than pharmaceutical quality	8%	—

Tariff Heading	Rate of Import Duty (if any)	
	Full	Commonwealth (C) E.F.T.A. (E)
8.38 Sulphates (including alums) and persulphates:—*contd.*		
(16) Other:		
(*a*) Pharmaceutical qualities of the following:	22%	
Aluminium ammonium sulphate		
Aluminium potassium sulphate		
Ferric or ferrous sulphate		
Magnesium sulphate		
Sodium sulphate		
Zinc sulphate		
Analytical reagent qualities of the following:		
Aluminium sulphate		
Cupric or cuprous sulphate		
Manganic or manganous sulphate		
Sodium hydrogen sulphate		
(*b*) Other	25%	—
(B) Persulphates	25%	—
8.39 Nitrites and nitrates:		
(A) Calcium nitrate	—	
(B) Ferric nitrate	8%	—
(C) Gallium nitrate	8%	—
(D) Lead nitrate:		
(1) Analytical reagent quality ...	22%	—
(2) Other	8%	—
(E) Potassium nitrate:		
(1) Synthetic	8%	—
(2) Other than synthetic	—	
(F) Sodium nitrate:		
(1) Synthetic	16%	—
(2) Other than synthetic	—	—
(G) Sodium nitrite:		
(1) Analytical reagent quality ...	22%	—
(2) Other	10%	—
(H) Stannic nitrate	8%	—
(IJ) Other	25%	—
8.40 Phosphites, hypophosphites and phosphates:		
(A) Aluminium metaphosphate	10%	—
(B) *di*Ammonium hydrogen orthophosphate; *tetra*ammonium pyrophosphate:		
(1) *di*Ammonium hydrogen orthophosphate, analytical reagent quality	23%	—
(2) Other	9%	—
(C) Antimony phosphate	10%	—
(D) Cadmium metaphosphate; *di*cadmium pyrophosphate	10%	—
(E) *tri*Calcium diorthophosphate ...	10%	—

Tariff Heading	Rate of Import Duty (if any)	
	Full	Commonwealth (C E.F.T.A. (E

28.40 Phosphites, hypophosphites and phosphates: —contd.

(F) Calcium hydrogen orthophosphate ...	10%	—
(G) Calcium hydroxyphosphate	10%	—
(H) Calcium metaphosphate; *di*calcium pyrophosphate	10%	—
(IJ) Calcium tetrahydrogen diorthophosphate, other than baking powder quality	10%	—
(K) Chromium metaphosphates	10%	—
(L) Magnesium dihydrogen pyrophosphate	10%	—
(M) *tri*Potassium orthophosphate; *penta*potassium triphosphate	10%	—
(N) *di*Sodium hydrogen orthophosphate:		
(1) Pharmaceutical quality	21%	—
(2) Other	2½%	—
(O) *tri*Sodium orthophosphate	2½%	—
(P) Other	25%	—

28.41 Arsenites and arsenates:

(A) Antimony arsenate	8%	—
(B) Barium arsenite; barium arsenate ...	8%	—
(C) Bismuth arsenate	8%	—
(D) Copper arsenites	8%	—
(E) Lead arsenite; lead arsenate ...	8%	—
(F) Sodium arsenite; sodium arsenate:		
(1) Sodium arsenate, analytical reagent quality	22%	—
(2) Other	8%	—
(G) Other	25%	—

28.42 Carbonates and percarbonates; commercial ammonium carbonate containing ammonium carbamate:

(A) Aluminium carbonate	8%	—
(B) Barium carbonate:		
(1) Analytical reagent quality ...	24%	—
(2) Other	16%	—
(C) Calcium carbonate:		
(1) Analytical reagent quality ...	22%	—
(2) Other	8%	—
(D) Chromous carbonate	8%	—
(E) Copper carbonates, basic	12½%	—
(F) Ferrous carbonate	8%	—
(G) Lead carbonate	8%	—
(H) Lead carbonate, basic	12½%	—
(IJ) Potassium carbonate:		
(1) Analytical reagent quality ...	20%	—
(2) Other	—	

Tariff Heading	Rate of Import Duty (if any)	
	Full	Commonwealth (C) E.F.T.A. (E)
.42 Carbonates and percarbonates, etc.—*contd.*		
(K) Sodium carbonate; sodium hydrogen carbonate; sodium percarbonate; sodium sesquicarbonate:		
(1) Sodium carbonate, analytical reagent quality; sodium hydrogen carbonate, pharmaceutical quality	22%	—
(2) Other	8%	—
(L) Zinc carbonate	8%	—
(M) Other	25%	—
.43 Cyanides and complex cyanides:		
(A) Calcium cyanide; calcium ferrocyanide; calcium potassium ferrocyanide	8%	—
(B) Copper sodium cyanides	8%	—
(C) Ferric ferrocyanide	16%	—
(D) Ferrous ferricyanide	16%	—
(E) Magnesium ferrocyanide	8%	—
(F) Potassium cyanide; potassium ferrocyanide; potassium zinc ferrocyanide:		
(1) Potassium cyanide and potassium ferrocyanide, analytical reagent quality	22%	—
(2) Other	8%	—
(G) Sodium cyanide; sodium ferrocyanide; sodium zinc cyanide	8%	—
(H) Zinc ferrocyanide	8%	—
(IJ) Other	25%	—
.44 Fulminates, cyanates and thiocyanates:		
(A) Aluminium thiocyanate	8%	—
(B) Barium thiocyanate	8%	—
(C) Cupric or cuprous thiocyanate ...	8%	—
(D) Strontium thiocyanate	8%	—
(E) Other	25%	—
.45 Silicates; commercial sodium and potassium silicates:		
(A) Barium silicate	17½%	—
(B) Cadmium silicate	17½%	—
(C) Chromic or chromous silicate ...	17½%	—
(D) Cobalt silicate	17½%	—
(E) Cupric or cuprous silicate	17½%	—
(F) Lead silicate	20%	—
(G) Magnesium silicate	20%	—
(H) Manganic or manganous silicate ...	17½%	—
(IJ) Nickel silicate	17½%	—
(K) Strontium silicate	17½%	—
(L) Zinc silicate	17½%	—
(M) Other	8%	—

Tariff Heading	Rate of Import Duty (if any)	
	Full	Commonwealth (C E.F.T.A. (E
28.46 Borates and perborates:		
(A) Cadmium borate	8%	—
(B) Calcium perborate	8%	—
(C) Cobalt borate	8%	—
(D) Ferric borate	8%	—
(E) Manganic or manganous borate ...	8%	—
(F) Potassium pentaborate	8%	—
(G) Sodium borates:		
(1) Sodium metaborate	20%	—
(2) diSodium tetraborate, such that reduced to the dry anhydrous form it would be of a purity not less than 99 per cent.:		
(a) Anhydrous	—	—
(b) Hydrated	14½%	—
(3) Other	8%	—
(H) Sodium perborate	8%	—
(IJ) Zinc borate	8%	—
(K) Other	25%	—
28.47 Salts of metallic acids (for example, chromates, permanganates, stannates):		
(A) Aluminium chromate	10%	—
(B) Ammonium perrhenate	8%	—
(C) Barium stannate; barium titanate; barium zirconate	8%	—
(D) Cadmium dichromate...	10%	—
(E) Caesium chromate; caesium dichromate	10%	—
(F) Calcium stannate; calcium titanate; calcium zirconate	8%	—
(G) Chromium chromates...	10%	—
(H) Cobalt aluminate; cobalt zincate ...	12½%	—
(IJ) Lead chromate; lead chromate, basic	13½%	—
(K) Lead titanate	12½%	—
(L) Lead dichromate	10%	—
(M) Lead zirconate	8%	—
(N) Lithium tungstate	8%	—
(O) Magnesium stannate; magnesium titanate; magnesium zirconate	8%	—
(P) Potassium dichromate:		
(1) Analytical reagent quality ...	19%	—
(2) Other	10%	—
(Q) Potassium manganate; potassium perrhenate	8%	—
(R) Rubidium dichromate	10%	—
(S) Sodium aluminate; sodium manganate; sodium permanganate; sodium stannate; sodium titanate; sodium zincate	8%	—
(T) Sodium chromate; sodium dichromate	10%	—
(U) Strontium stannate; strontium titanate; strontium zirconate	8%	—
(V) Zinc chromate; zinc tetroxychromate	13½%	—
(W) Other	20%	—

Tariff Heading	Rate of Import Duty (if any)	
	Full	Commonwealth (C) E.F.T.A. (E)
48 Other salts and peroxysalts of inorganic acids, but not including azides:		
(A) Salts of inorganic acids:		
(1) Aluminium selenate; aluminium potassium selenate; aluminium sodium silicate and other double or complex silicates; aluminium sulphamate; aluminium telluride	8%	—
(2) Ammonium chlorostannite; ammonium cobalt chloride; ammonium cobalt sulphate; ammonium copper carbonates; ammonium reineckate; ammonium sulphamate; ammonium zinc chloride; ammonium zinc phosphate	8%	—
(3) Ammonium cobalt phosphate ...	12½%	—
(4) Barium selenite	8%	—
(5) Caesium iodobismuthate	8%	—
(6) Calcium magnesium phosphate; calcium selenate; calcium sodium iodide	8%	—
(7) Cupric or cuprous lead arsenate; cupric or cuprous magnesium sulphate; cupric or cuprous sulphamate; cupric or cuprous zinc chromate	8%	—
(8) Ferric magnesium sulphate; ferric sodium phosphate	8%	—
(9) Ferrous selenate	8%	—
(10) Lead sulphamate	8%	—
(11) Lithium potassium sulphate ...	8%	—
(12) Magnesium potassium chloride; magnesium potassium sulphate; magnesium selenate	8%	—
(13) Manganese sulphamates	8%	—
(14) Potassium chlorostannate; potassium sodium sulphate; potassium thioantimonate; potassium tetrathionate	8%	—
(15) Sodium hydrogen selenite; sodium sulphamate; sodium thiostannate	8%	—
(16) Strontium selenate	8%	—
(17) Zinc selenite	8%	—
(18) Other	20%	—
(B) Peroxysalts of inorganic acids ...	8%	—

	Rate of Import Duty (if any)	
Tariff Heading	Full	Commonwealth (C E.F.T.A. (E

VI. Miscellaneous

28.49 Colloidal precious metals; amalgams of precious metals; albuminates, proteinates, tannates and similar compounds of precious metals, whether or not chemically defined; other salts and compounds, inorganic or organic, of precious metals:

(A) Colloidal precious metals	8%	—
(B) Amalgams of precious metals ...	8%	—
(C) Other:		
(1) Silver chloride and silver sulphide of purity of less than 95 per cent., excluding moisture	8%	—
(2) Other	25%	—

28.50 Fissile chemical elements and isotopes; other radio-active chemical elements and radio-active isotopes; compounds, inorganic or organic, of such elements or isotopes, whether or not chemically defined; alloys, dispersions and cermets, containing any of these elements, isotopes or compounds:

(A) Radium compounds; compounds of natural uranium, the following: Ammonium diuranate Magnesium diuranate Sodium diuranate *tri*Uranium octaoxide; mixtures consisting wholly or mainly of the foregoing	—	—
(B) Natural uranium:		
(1) Waste and scrap	—	—
(2) Other	8%	—
(C) Nuclear reactor cartridges, spent or irradiated	—	—
(D) Other	25%	—

28.51 Isotopes and their compounds, inorganic or organic, whether or not chemically defined, other than isotopes and compounds falling within heading No. 28.50

25%	—

28.52 Compounds, inorganic or organic, of thorium, of uranium depleted in uranium–235, of rare earth metals, of yttrium or of scandium, whether or not mixed together

25%	—

28.53 Liquid air (whether or not rare gases have been removed); compressed air

8%	—

Tariff Heading	Rate of Import Duty (if any)	
	Full	Commonwealth (C) E.F.T.A. (E)
8.54 Hydrogen peroxide (including solid hydrogen peroxide)	8%	—
8.55 Phosphides:		
(A) Calcium phosphide	8%	—
(B) Iron phosphides	8%	—
(C) Other	20%	—
8.56 Carbides (for example, silicon carbide, boron carbide, metallic carbides):		
(A) Calcium carbide	—	—
(B) Silicon carbide	—	—
(C) Molybdenum carbide	20%	—
(D) Vanadium carbide	25%	—
(E) Other	8%	—
8.57 Hydrides, nitrides and azides, silicides and borides:		
(A) Aluminium lithium hydride; aluminium nitride	8%	—
(B) Barium azide	8%	—
(C) Boron nitride	8%	—
(D) Calcium hydride; calcium boride ...	8%	—
(E) Calcium silicide	—	—
(F) Chromium borides	8%	—
(G) Lithium hydride	8%	—
(H) Niobium hydride	8%	—
(IJ) Potassium borohydride	8%	—
(K) Sodium hydride; sodium borohydride	8%	—
(L) Tantalum hydride	8%	—
(M) Titanium hydride; titanium nitride; titanium boride	8%	—
(N) Zirconium hydride; zirconium boride	8%	—
(O) Manganese nitrides containing not less than 4 per cent. by weight of nitrogen in all	—	—
(P) Other	25%	—
8.58 Other inorganic compounds (including distilled and conductivity water and water of similar purity); amalgams, except amalgams of precious metals:		
(A) Amalgams	8%	—
(B) Boron phosphate	8%	—
(C) Calcium cyanamide	—	—
(D) Cyanamide	8%	—
(E) Lead cyanamide	16%	—
(F) Thiocarbonyl chloride	8%	—
(G) Water, distilled, conductivity or of similar purity	8%	—
(H) Other	20%	—

Chapter 29

Organic Chemicals

Notes

1. Except in so far as the context otherwise requires, the headings of this Chapter are to be taken to apply only to:

(a) Separate chemically defined organic compounds, whether or not containing impurities;

(b) Mixtures of two or more isomers of the same organic compound (whether or not containing impurities), except mixtures of acyclic hydrocarbon isomers (other than stereoisomers), whether or not saturated (Chapter 27);

(c) The products of headings Nos. 29.38 to 29.42 inclusive, or the sugar ethers and sugar esters, and their salts, of heading No. 29.43, or the products of heading No. 29.44 whether or not chemically defined;

(d) Products mentioned in (a), (b) or (c) above dissolved in water;

(e) Products mentioned in (a), (b) or (c) above dissolved in other solvents provided that the solution constitutes a normal and necessary method of putting up these products adopted solely for reasons of safety or for transport and that the solvent does not render the product particularly suitable for some types of use rather than for general use;

(f) The products mentioned in (a), (b), (c), (d) or (e) above with an added stabiliser necessary for their preservation or transport;

(g) Diazonium salts, arylides used as couplers for these salts, and fast bases for azoic dyes, diluted to standard strengths.

2. This Chapter does not cover:

(a) Goods falling within heading No. 15.04, or glycerol (heading No. 15.11);

(b) Ethyl alcohol (ethanol) (heading No. 22.08 or 22.09);

(c) Methane (heading No. 27.11);

(d) The compounds of carbon mentioned in Note 2 of Chapter 28;

(e) Urea containing not more than 45 per cent. by weight of nitrogen, calculated on the dry anhydrous product (Chapter 31);

(f) Colouring matter of vegetable or animal origin (heading No. 32.04); synthetic organic dyestuffs (including pigment dyestuffs), synthetic organic products of a kind used as luminophores and products of the kind known as optical bleaching agents substantive to the fibre and natural indigo (heading No. 32.05) and dyes put up in forms or packings of a kind sold by retail (heading No. 32.09);

(g) Metaldehyde, hexamine and similar substances put up in forms (for example, tablets, sticks or similar forms) for use as fuels, and liquid fuels of a kind used in mechanical lighters in containers of a capacity not exceeding 300 cubic centimetres (heading No. 36.08);

(h) Products put up as charges for fire-extinguishers or put up in fire-extinguishing grenades, of heading No. 38.17; ink removers put up in packings for sale by retail of heading No. 38.19; or

(ij) Optical elements, for example, of 1,2-diaminoethane tartrate (heading No. 90.01).

3. Goods which could be included in two or more of the headings of this Chapter are to be classified in the latest of those headings.

4. In headings Nos. 29.03 to 29.05, 29.07 to 29.10 and 29.12 to 29.21 inclusive, any reference to halogenated, sulphonated, nitrated or nitrosated derivatives is to be taken to include a reference to any combinations of these derivatives (for example, sulphohalogenated, nitrohalogenated, nitrosulphonated and nitrosulphohalogenated derivatives).

Nitro and nitroso groups are not to be taken as nitrogen-functions for the purpose of heading No. 29.30.

5. (a) The esters of acid-function organic compounds falling within sub-Chapters I to VII with organic compounds of these sub-Chapters are to be classified with that compound which is classified in the heading placed last in the sub-Chapters.

(b) Esters of ethyl alcohol (ethanol) or glycerol with acid-function organic compounds f sub-Chapters I to VII are to be classified with the corresponding acid-function compounds.

(c) The salts of the esters referred to in paragraph (a) or (b) above with inorganic bases re to be classified with the corresponding esters.

(d) The salts of other acid- or phenol-function organic compounds falling within sub-hapters I to VII with inorganic bases are to be classified with the corresponding acid- or henol-function organic compounds.

(e) Halides of carboxylic acids are to be classified with the corresponding acids.

6. The compounds of headings Nos. 29.31 to 29.34 are organic compounds the molecules " which contain, in addition to atoms of hydrogen, oxygen or nitrogen, atoms of other on-metals or of metals (such as sulphur, arsenic, mercury or lead) directly linked to carbon oms.

Heading No. 29.31 (organo-sulphur compounds) and heading No. 29.34 (other organo-organic compounds) are to be taken not to include sulphonated or halogenated derivatives ncluding compound derivatives) which, apart from hydrogen, oxygen and nitrogen, only ave directly linked to carbon the atoms of sulphur and of halogens which give them their ature of sulphonated or halogenated derivatives (or compound derivatives).

7. Heading No. 29.35 (heterocyclic compounds) is to be taken not to include internal ethers, ternal hemi-acetals, methylene ethers of orthodihydric phenols, epoxides with three or ur member rings, cyclic acetals, cyclic polymers of aldehydes, of thioaldehydes or of dimines, anhydrides of polybasic acids, cyclic esters of polyhydric alcohols with polybasic ids, cyclic ureides, imides of polybasic acids, hexamine and hexahydro-1,3,5-trinitro-3,5-triazine.

pecial notes applying to subheadings only

1. Where any esters, salts or halides mentioned in Note 5 above fall within a heading of is Chapter divided into subheadings, they shall be classified in the final subheading unless entioned in any other subheading.

2. Throughout this Schedule where there is any reference to an organic compound which has normal isomer, that reference shall be taken to include only the normal isomer, unless e contrary intention appears.

Tariff Heading	Rate of Import Duty (if any)	
	Full	Commonwealth (C) E.F.T.A. (E)
I. Hydrocarbons and their halogenated, sulphonated, nitrated or nitrosated derivatives		
.01 Hydrocarbons:		
(A) " Hydrocarbon oils " as defined in paragraph (a) of the special note to Chapter 27:		
(1) The following:	—	—
Benzene, other than analytical reagent quality		
Dicyclopentadiene		
Dipentene		
Heptane		
Hexane		
Indene		
(+)-Limonene, (−)-limonene		
2-Methylbutane		
Octadecane		
Octane		

Tariff Heading	Rate of Import Duty (if any)		
	Full	Commonwealth (C) E.F.T.A. (E)	

29.01 Hydrocarbons:—*contd.*
   (A) "Hydrocarbon oils", etc.—*contd.*
     (1) The following:—*contd.*
       Pentane
       Pinene
       Terpinolene
       Toluene
       Xylene, mixed isomers

(2) Styrene monomer	8%, in addition to any hydrocarbon oil duty	—	
(3) Other	22%	—	

   (B) Other:
     (1) The following:
       Anthracene
       Butane
       Ethane
       Ethylene
       Naphthalene
       Phenanthrene
       Propane

The following:	8%	—	
(2) Buta-1,2-diene; buta-1,3-diene ...	16%	—	
(3) Other	25%	—	
29.02 Halogenated derivatives of hydrocarbons:			
(A) The following:	25%	C	20%
Bromoethane		E	—
Chloroethane			
Chloroform			
Iodoethane			
(B) Other	25%	—	
29.03 Sulphonated, nitrated or nitrosated derivatives of hydrocarbons	25%	—	

II. Alcohols and their halogenated, sulphonated, nitrated or nitrosated derivatives

29.04 Acyclic alcohols and their halogenated, sulphonated, nitrated or nitrosated derivatives:			
(A) Chloral hydrate	25%	C	20%
		E	—

Tariff Heading	Rate of Import Duty (*if any*)	
	Full	Commonwealth (C) E.F.T.A. (E)
9.04 Acyclic alcohols, etc.—*contd.*		
(B) Methanol:		
(1) Synthetic	21½%	—
(2) Other than synthetic	8%	—
(C) Other	25%	—
9.05 Cyclic alcohols and their halogenated, sulphonated, nitrated or nitrosated derivatives:		
(A) Menthol, not containing more than 10 per cent. by weight of isomers of menthol other than (−) menthol	—	—
(B) Other	25%	—
III. Phenols, phenol-alcohols, and their halogenated, sulphonated, nitrated or nitrosated derivatives		
9.06 Phenols and phenol-alcohols:		
(A) Cresol, mixed isomers	8%	—
(B) Phenol, other than synthetic or pharmaceutical quality	8%	—
(C) 2,2-Di-(4-hydroxyphenyl)propane ...	20%	—
(D) Other	25%	—
9.07 Halogenated, sulphonated, nitrated or nitrosated derivatives of phenols or phenol-alcohols	25%	—
IV. Ethers, alcohol peroxides, ether peroxides, epoxides with a three or four member ring, acetals and hemiacetals, and their halogenated, sulphonated, nitrated or nitrosated derivatives		
9.08 Ethers, ether-alcohols, ether-phenols, ether-alcohol-phenols, alcohol peroxides and ether peroxides, and their halogenated, sulphonated, nitrated or nitrosated derivatives:		
(A) Diethyl ether	29%	C 24% E —
(B) Other	25%	—
9.09 Epoxides, epoxyalcohols, epoxyphenols and epoxyethers, with a three or four member ring, and their halogenated, sulphonated, nitrated or nitrosated derivatives	25%	—

Tariff Heading	Rate of Import Duty (if any)	
	Full	Commonwealth (C) E.F.T.A. (E)
29.10 Acetals and hemiacetals and single or complex oxygen-function acetals and hemiacetals, and their halogenated, sulphonated, nitrated or nitrosated derivatives	25%	—
V. Aldehyde-function compounds		
29.11 Aldehydes, aldehyde-alcohols, aldehyde-ethers, aldehyde-phenols and other single or complex oxygen-function aldehydes	25%	—
29.12 Halogenated, sulphonated, nitrated or nitrosated derivatives of products falling within heading 29.11	25%	—
VI. Ketone-function compounds and quinone-function compounds		
29.13 Ketones, ketone-alcohols, ketone-phenols, ketone-aldehydes, quinones, quinone-alcohols, quinone-phenols, quinone-aldehydes and other single or complex oxygen-function ketones and quinones, and their halogenated, sulphonated, nitrated or nitrosated derivatives:		
(A) Camphor, natural or synthetic ...	8%	—
(B) Acetone	20%	—
(C) Other	25%	—
VII. Acids, acid anhydrides, acid halides, acid peroxides and peracids, and their halogenated, sulphonated, nitrated or nitrosated derivatives		
29.14 Monoacids and their anhydrides, acid halides, acid peroxides and peracids, and their halogenated, sulphonated, nitrated or nitrosated derivatives:		
(A) Ethyl acetate	26½%	C 21½% E —
(B) Ethyl butyrate; ethyl *iso*butyrate ...	29%	C 24% E —
(C) Lead acetate; lead acetate, basic ...	20%	—
(D) Chromic or chromous acetate ...	8%	—
(E) Cupric or cuprous acetate; copper acetates, basic:		
(1) Cupric or cuprous acetate, analytical reagent quality	22%	—
(2) Other	8%	—

Tariff Heading	Rate of Import Duty (if any)	
	Full	Commonwealth (C) E.F.T.A. (E)
9.14 Monoacids and their anhydrides, etc. —*contd.*		
(F) 2-Ethylbutyric acid	8%	—
(G) Ferric or ferrous acetate	8%	—
(H) Sodium acetate:		
(1) Analytical reagent quality ...	22%	—
(2) Other	8%	—
(IJ) Acrylic acid	20%	—
(K) Propionic acid	20%	—
(L) Sorbic acid	20%	—
(M) Other	25%	—
9.15 Polyacids and their anhydrides, acid halides, acid peroxides and peracids, and their halogenated, sulphonated, nitrated or nitrosated derivatives	25%	
9.16 Alcohol-acids, aldehyde-acids, ketone-acids, phenol-acids and other single or complex oxygen-function acids, and their anhydrides, acid halides, acid peroxides and peracids, and their halogenated, sulphonated, nitrated or nitrosated derivatives:		
(A) Calcium tartrate	—	—
(B) Calcium gluconate	21½%	—
(C) Methyl, ethyl and propyl 4-hydroxy-benzoate	20%	—
(D) Aluminium ammonium citrate ...	8%	—
(E) Antimony barium tartrate; antimony potassium tartrate; antimony strontium tartrate; antimony tartrate	8%	—
(F) Citric acid	8%	—
(G) Potassium dihydrogen citrate; *di*potassium hydrogen citrate	8%	—
(H) Potassium hydrogen tartrate ...	8%	—
(IJ) (+)-Tartaric acid	8%	—
(K) Other	25%	—
VIII. Inorganic esters and their salts, and their halogenated, sulphonated, nitrated or nitrosated derivatives		
9.17 Sulphuric esters and their salts, and their halogenated, sulphonated, nitrated or nitrosated derivatives	25%	—
9.18 Nitrous and nitric esters, and their halogenated, sulphonated, nitrated or nitrosated derivatives	25%	—
9.19 Phosphoric esters and their salts, including lactophosphates, and their halogenated, sulphonated, nitrated or nitrosated derivatives	25%	—

Tariff Heading	Rate of Import Duty (if any)	
	Full	Commonwealth (C E.F.T.A. (E
29.20 Carbonic esters and their salts, and their halogenated, sulphonated, nitrated or nitrosated derivatives	25%	—
29.21 Other esters of mineral acids (excluding halides) and their salts, and their halogenated, sulphonated, nitrated or nitrosated derivatives	25%	—
IX. Nitrogen-function compounds		
29.22 Amine-function compounds	25%	—
29.23 Single or complex oxygen-function amino-compounds:		
(A) Aluminium glutamate	8%	—
(B) Glutamic acid hydrochloride ...	8%	—
(C) Sodium hydrogen glutamate ...	8%	—
(D) Glycine	20%	—
(E) Triethanolamine	20%	—
(F) Other	25%	—
29.24 Quaternary ammonium salts and hydroxides; lecithins and other phosphoaminolipins:		
(A) Lecithins and other phosphoaminolipins	8%	—
(B) Other	25%	—
29.25 Amide-function compounds:		
(A) Urea	20%	—
(B) Other	25%	—
29.26 Imide-function compounds and imine-function compounds	25%	—
29.27 Nitrile-function compounds:		
(A) Dicyandiamide	—	—
(B) Other	25%	—
29.28 Diazo-, azo- and azoxy-compounds ...	25%	—
29.29 Organic derivatives of hydrazine or of hydroxylamine	25%	—
29.30 Compounds with other nitrogen-functions	25%	—
X. Organo-inorganic compounds and heterocyclic compounds		
29.31 Organo-sulphur compounds	25%	—
29.32 Organo-arsenic compounds	25%	—

Tariff Heading	Rate of Import Duty (if any)	
	Full	Commonwealth (C) E.F.T.A. (E)
9.33 Organo-mercury compounds	25%	—
9.34 Other organo-inorganic compounds ...	25%	—
9.35 Heterocyclic compounds; nucleic acids:		
(A) Amidopyrin	8%	—
(B) Catechin	8%	—
(C) Nucleic acids	8%	—
(D) Pyrrole	8%	—
(E) Santonin	8%	—
(F) 1, 6—Hexanolactam	16%	—
(G) Other	25%	—
9.36 Sulphonamides	20%	—
9.37 Sultones and sultams	25%	—

XI. Provitamins, vitamins, hormones and enzymes, natural or reproduced by synthesis

Tariff Heading	Full	C / E
9.38 Provitamins and vitamins, natural or re-produced by synthesis (including natural concentrates), derivatives thereof used primarily as vitamins, and intermixtures of the foregoing, whether or not in any solvent:		
(A) Natural vitamin concentrates ...	8%	—
(B) Other	25%	—
9.39 Hormones, natural or reproduced by synthesis, and derivatives thereof used primarily as hormones:		
(A) Insulin and its salts	—	
(B) Chorionic gonadotrophin; serum gonadotrophin	8%	—
(C) Corticotrophin; thyrotrophin ...	8%	—
(D) Other	25%	—
29.40 Enzymes	8%	—

XII. Glycosides and vegetable alkaloids, natural or reproduced by synthesis, and their salts, ethers, esters and other derivatives

Tariff Heading	Full	C / E
29.41 Glycosides, natural or reproduced by synthesis, and their salts, ethers, esters and other derivatives:		
(A) Aesculin	25%	—
(B) Aloin	25%	—
(C) Amygdalin	25%	—
(D) Arbutin; arbutin benzoate	25%	—
(E) Colocynthin	25%	—
(F) Digitalin	25%	—

Tariff Heading	Rate of Import Duty (if any)	
	Full	Commonwealth (C E.F.T.A. (E
29.41 Glycosides, natural or reproduced by synthesis, etc.—*contd.*		
(G) Digitonin	25%	—
(H) Digitoxin	25%	—
(IJ) Digoxin	25%	—
(K) Ouabain	25%	—
(L) Phloridzin	25%	—
(M) Rutin	25%	—
(N) Salicin	25%	—
(O) Salicylaldehyde glucoside	25%	—
(P) Sinigrin	25%	—
(Q) Other	8%	—
29.42 Vegetable alkaloids, natural or reproduced by synthesis, and their salts, ethers, esters and other derivatives:		
(A) Caffeine and its salts	16%	—
(B) Theobromine and its salts	16%	—
(C) Emetine and its salts	16%	—
(D) Nicotine; nicotine sulphate	16%	—
(E) Quinine sulphate of vegetable origin	8%	—
(F) Other:		
(1) Chemically defined compounds ...	25%	—
(2) Other	8%	—
XIII. Other organic compounds		
29.43 Sugars, chemically pure, other than sucrose, glucose and lactose; sugar ethers and sugar esters, and their salts, other than products of headings Nos. 29.39, 29.41 and 29.42:		
(A) Fructose	—	—
(B) Sugar ethers and sugar esters, and their salts:		
(1) Chemically defined compounds ...	25%	—
(2) Other	8%	—
(C) Other	25%	—
29.44 Antibiotics	20%	—
29.45 Other organic compounds:		
(A) Quassin	8%	—
(B) Sodium antimonylgluconate	8%	—
(C) Other	25%	—

Chapter 30

Pharmaceutical Products

Notes

1. For the purposes of heading No. 30.03, "medicaments" means goods (other than foods or beverages such as dietetic, diabetic or fortified foods, tonic beverages, spa water) not falling within heading No. 30.02 or 30.04 which are either:

(a) Products comprising two or more constituents which have been mixed or compounded together for therapeutic or prophylactic uses; or

(b) Unmixed products suitable for such uses put up in measured doses or in forms or in packings of a kind sold by retail for therapeutic or prophylactic purposes.

For the purposes of these provisions and of Note 3 (d) to this Chapter, the following are to be treated:

(A) As unmixed products:

(1) Unmixed products dissolved in water;

(2) All goods falling in Chapter 28 or 29; and

(3) Simple vegetable extracts falling in heading No. 13.03, merely standardised or dissolved in any solvent;

(B) As products which have been mixed:

(1) Colloidal solutions and suspensions (other than colloidal sulphur);

(2) Vegetable extracts obtained by the treatment of mixtures of vegetable materials; and

(3) Salts and concentrates obtained by evaporating natural mineral waters.

2. The headings of this Chapter are to be taken not to apply to:

(a) Aqueous distillates and aqueous solutions of essential oils, suitable for medicinal uses (heading No. 33.05);

(b) Dentifrices of all kinds, including those having therapeutic or prophylactic properties (heading No. 33.06); or

(c) Medicated soap of all kinds (heading No. 34.01).

3. Heading No. 30.05 is to be taken to apply, and to apply only, to:

(a) Sterile surgical catgut and similar sterile suture materials;

(b) Sterile laminaria and sterile laminaria tents;

(c) Sterile absorbable surgical haemostatics;

(d) Opacifying preparations for X-ray examinations and other diagnostic reagents (excluding those of heading No. 30.02) designed to be administered to the patient, being unmixed products put up in measured doses or products consisting of two or more constituents which have been mixed or compounded together for such uses;

(e) Dental alloys, dental cements and other dental fillings; and

(f) First-aid boxes and kits.

Tariff Heading	Rate of Import Duty (if any)	
	Full	Commonwealth (C) E.F.T.A. (E)
30.01 Organo-therapeutic glands or other organs, dried, whether or not powdered; organo-therapeutic extracts of glands or other organs or of their secretions; other animal substances prepared for therapeutic or prophylactic uses, not elsewhere specified or included	8%	—

Tariff Heading	Rate of Import Duty (if any)	
	Full	Commonwealth (C E.F.T.A. (E,
30.02 Antisera; microbial vaccines, toxins, microbial cultures (including ferments but excluding yeasts) and similar products	8%	—
30.03 Medicaments (including veterinary medicaments):		
(A) Products comprising two or more constituents which have been mixed or compounded together for therapeutic or prophylactic uses:		
(1) Insulin preparations	—	—
(2) Products not included above containing one or more constituents which have been used in their manufacture or preparation and have not lost their identity and which, if imported separately, would be classified in Chapter 28 or 29 and be chargeable with import duty amounting to 20 per cent. or more of the value of the constituent	8% or such greater rate as is equal to the amount or aggregate amount of the duty chargeable on such constituents	—
(3) Other	8%	—
(B) Unmixed products put up in measured doses or in forms or in packings of a kind sold by retail for therapeutic or prophylactic purposes	The rate applicable to the products when not put up in measured doses or in forms or in packings of a kind sold by retail	C E { The rate ap plicable to th products whe not put up i measured dose or in forms o in packings o a kind sold b retail
30.04 Wadding, gauze, bandages and similar articles (for example, dressings, adhesive plasters, poultices), impregnated or coated with pharmaceutical substances or put up in retail packings for medical or surgical purposes, other than goods specified in Note 3 to this Chapter:		
(A) Wadding:		
(1) Of cellulose	14%	—
(2) Of other materials	10%	—
(B) Other	16%	—
30.05 Other pharmaceutical goods:		
(A) First-aid boxes and kits	16%	—
(B) Dental alloys, dental cements and other dental fillings:		
(1) Containing base metal	16%	—
(2) Not containing base metal ...	10%	—
(C) Other	10%	—

Chapter 31

Fertilisers

1. Heading No. 31.02 is to be taken to apply, and to apply only, to the following goods provided that they are not put up in the forms or packings described in heading No. 31.05:

(*a*) Goods which answer to one or other of the descriptions given below:

(i) Sodium nitrate containing not more than 16·3 per cent. by weight of nitrogen;

(ii) Ammonium nitrate, whether or not pure;

(iii) Ammonium sulphonitrate, whether or not pure;

(iv) Ammonium sulphate, whether or not pure;

(v) Calcium nitrate containing not more than 16 per cent. by weight of nitrogen;

(vi) Calcium nitrate-magnesium nitrate, whether or not pure;

(vii) Calcium cyanamide containing not more than 25 per cent. by weight of nitrogen, whether or not treated with oil;

(viii) Urea containing not more than 45 per cent. by weight of nitrogen.

(*b*) Fertilisers consisting of any of the goods described in (*a*) above, but without quantitative criteria, mixed together.

(*c*) Fertilisers consisting of ammonium chloride or of any of the goods described in (*a*) or (*b*) above, but without quantitative criteria, mixed with chalk, gypsum or other inorganic non-fertilising substances.

(*d*) Liquid fertilisers consisting of the goods of sub-paragraphs 1 (*a*) (ii) or (viii) above, or of mixtures of those goods, in an aqueous or ammonia solution.

2. Heading No. 31.03 is to be taken to apply, and to apply only, to the following goods, provided that they are not put up in the forms or packings described in heading No. 31.05:

(*a*) Goods which answer to one or other of the descriptions given below:

(i) Basic slag;

(ii) Disintegrated (calcined) calcium phosphates (thermophosphates and fused phosphates) and calcined natural aluminium calcium phosphates;

(iii) Superphosphates (single, double or triple);

(iv) Calcium hydrogen phosphate containing not less than 0·2 per cent. by weight of fluorine.

(*b*) Fertilisers consisting of any of the goods described in (*a*) above, but without quantitative criteria, mixed together.

(*c*) Fertilisers consisting of any of the goods described in (*a*) or (*b*) above, but without quantitative criteria, mixed with chalk, gypsum or other inorganic non-fertilising substances.

3. Heading No. 31.04 is to be taken to apply, and to apply only, to the following goods, provided that they are not put up in the forms or packings described in heading No. 31.05:

(*a*) Goods which answer to one or other of the descriptions given below:

(i) Crude natural potassium salts (for example, carnallite, kainite and sylvinite);

(ii) Crude potassium salts obtained by the treatment of residues of beet molasses;

(iii) Potassium chloride, whether or not pure, except as provided in Note 6 (*c*) below;

(iv) Potassium sulphate containing not more than 52 per cent. by weight of K_2O;

(v) Magnesium sulphate-potassium sulphate containing not more than 30 per cent. by weight of K_2O.

(*b*) Fertilisers consisting of any of the goods described in (*a*) above, but without quantitative criteria, mixed together.

4. Ammonium phosphates containing not less than 6 milligrams of arsenic per kilogram are to be classified in heading No. 31.05.

5. For the purposes of the quantitative criteria specified in Notes 1 (*a*), 2 (*a*), 3 (*a*) and 4 above, the calculation is to be made on the dry anhydrous product.

6. This Chapter does not cover:

(a) Animal blood;

(b) Separate chemically defined compounds (other than those answering to the descriptions in Note 1 (a), 2 (a), 3 (a) or 4 above); or

(c) Cultured potassium chloride crystals (other than optical elements) weighing not less than two and a half grammes each, of heading No. 38.19; optical elements of potassium chloride (heading No. 90.01).

Tariff Heading	Rate of Import Duty (if any)	
	Full	Commonwealth (C) E.F.T.A. (E)
31.01 Guano and other natural animal or vegetable fertilisers, whether or not mixed together, but not chemically treated	8%	—
31.02 Mineral or chemical fertilisers, nitrogenous:		
(A) Calcium cyanamide; calcium nitrate; sodium nitrate, natural	—	—
(B) Ammonium sulphate (analytical reagent quality)	20%	—
(C) Urea, whether or not mixed with chalk, gypsum or other inorganic non-fertilising substances or in an aqueous or ammonia solution	20%	—
(D) Ammonium nitrate	12½%	—
(E) Other	19%	—
31.03 Mineral or chemical fertilisers, phosphatic:		
(A) Superphosphates	11%	—
(B) Other	6½%	—
31.04 Mineral or chemical fertilisers, potassic:		
(A) Potassium chloride (analytical reagent quality)	20%	—
(B) Other	—	—
31.05 Other fertilisers; goods of the present Chapter in tablets, lozenges and similar prepared forms or in packings of a gross weight not exceeding 10 kilograms: (A) Other fertilisers:		
(1) Ammonium dihydrogen orthophosphate containing not more than 0·5 per cent. by weight of material insoluble in water and containing not less than 59 per cent. by weight of phosphorus calculated as P_2O_5; diammonium dihydrogen pyrophosphate; triammonium orthophosphate	25%	—
(2) Fertilisers consisting solely of two or more potassic fertilising salts or of natural potassium nitrate and natural sodium nitrate	—	—
(3) Other	12½%	—

Tariff Heading	Rate of Import Duty (*if any*)	
	Full	*Commonwealth (C)* *E.F.T.A.* (*E*)
31.05 Other fertilisers, etc.—*contd.* (B) Goods of the present Chapter in tablets, lozenges and similar prepared forms or in packings of a gross weight not exceeding 10 kilograms	The rate applicable to the products when not in tablets, lozenges and similar prepared forms or when in packings of a gross weight exceeding 10 kilograms	—

Chapter 32

*Tanning and Dyeing Extracts; Tannins and their Derivatives; Dyes, Colours,
Paints and Varnishes; Putty, Fillers and Stoppings; Inks*

Notes

1. This Chapter does not cover:

(a) Separate chemically defined elements and compounds (except those falling withi
heading No. 32.04 or 32.05, inorganic products of a kind used as luminophores (headin
No. 32.07), and also dyes in forms or packings of a kind sold by retail falling withi
heading No. 32.09); or

(b) Tannates and other tannin derivatives of products falling within headings Nos. 29.3
to 29.42, 29.44 or 35.01 to 35.04.

2. Heading No. 32.05 is to be taken to include mixtures of stabilised diazonium salt
and coupling compounds for the production of insoluble azoic dyestuffs on the fibre.

3. Headings Nos. 32.05, 32.06 and 32.07 are to be taken to apply also to preparation
based on, respectively, synthetic organic dyestuffs (including pigment dyestuffs), colou
lakes and other colouring matter, of a kind used for colouring in the mass artificial plastics
rubber or similar materials or as ingredients in preparations for printing textiles. Th
headings are not to be applied, however, to prepared pigments falling within heading N
32.09.

4. Heading No. 32.09 is to be taken to include solutions (other than collodions) consistin
of any of the products specified in headings Nos. 39.01 to 39.06 in volatile organic solvent
if, and only if, the weight of the solvent exceeds 50 per cent. of the weight of the solution

5. The expression " colouring matter " in this Chapter does not include products of
kind used as extenders in oil paints, whether or not they are also suitable for colourin
distempers.

6. The expression " stamping foils " in heading No. 32.09 is to be taken to apply only t
products of a kind used for printing, for example, book covers or hat bands, and consisting of

(a) Thin sheets composed of metallic powder (including powder of precious metal), o
pigment, agglomerated with glue, gelatin or other binder; or

(b) Metal (for example, gold or aluminium), or pigment, deposited on paper, artificia
plastic material or other support.

Tariff Heading	Rate of Import Duty (if any)	
	Full	Commonwealth (C) E.F.T.A. (E)
32.01 Tanning extracts of vegetable origin: (A) **Gambier** (extract from *Uncaria gambier*) (B) Other	— 8%	— —
32.02 Tannins (tannic acids), including water-extracted gall-nut tannin, and their salts, ethers, esters and other derivatives	8%	—

Tariff Heading	Rate of Import Duty (if any)	
	Full	Commonwealth (C) E.F.T.A. (E)
32.03 Synthetic tanning substances, whether or not mixed with natural tanning materials; artificial bates for pre-tanning (for example, of enzymatic, pancreatic or bacterial origin)	8%	—
32.04 Colouring matter of vegetable origin (including dyewood extract and other vegetable dyeing extracts, but excluding indigo) or of animal origin:		
(A) Quercitron bark extract	—	—
(B) Pearl essence containing 5 per cent. or more by weight of guanine	—	—
(C) Other	8%	—
32.05 Synthetic organic dyestuffs (including pigment dyestuffs); synthetic organic products of a kind used as luminophores; products of the kind known as optical bleaching agents, substantive to the fibre; natural indigo:		
(A) Natural indigo	8%	—
(B) Luminophores consisting of synthetic organic dyestuffs (including pigment dyestuffs) dispersed or dissolved in artificial plastic material	16%	—
(C) Synthetic organic dyestuffs (including pigment dyestuffs) dispersed or dissolved in cellulose nitrate (plasticised or not)	16%	—
(D) Other	26%	—
32.06 Colour lakes	16%	—
32.07 Other colouring matter; inorganic products of a kind used as luminophores:		
(A) Other colouring matter:		
(1) Ultramarine blue	11%	—
(2) Mixtures consisting wholly of inorganic substances, containing not less than 94 per cent. by weight of titanium dioxide	12%	—
(3) Mixtures containing not less than 85 per cent. by weight of antimony oxides expressed as antimony trioxide	£40 per ton or 25%, whichever is the greater	—
(4) Other	16%	—
(B) Inorganic products of a kind used as luminophores:		
(1) Barium tungstate; calcium tungstate; magnesium tungstate	25%	—
(2) Other	8%	—

Tariff Heading	Rate of Import Duty (if any)	
	Full	Commonwealth (C) E.F.T.A. (E)
32.08 Prepared pigments, prepared opacifiers and prepared colours, vitrifiable enamels and glazes, liquid lustres and similar products, of the kind used in the ceramic, enamelling and glass industries; engobes (slips); glass frit and other glass, in the form of powder, granules or flakes:		
(A) Powder consisting of glass and poly-ethylene glycol wax, which contains not less than 85 per cent. by weight nor more than 95 per cent. by weight of glass and of which, after washing and drying, at least 80 per cent. by weight is capable of passing a sieve having a nominal width of aperture of 150 microns and conforming to British Standard 410:1962	10%	—
(B) Other	16%	—
32.09 Varnishes and lacquers; distempers; prepared water pigments of the kind used for finishing leather; paints and enamels; pigments in linseed oil, white spirit, spirits of turpentine, varnish or other paint or enamel media; stamping foils; dyes in forms or packings of a kind sold by retail:		
(A) " Hydrocarbon oils " as defined in paragraph (a) of the Special Note to Chapter 27	—	—
(B) Pearl essence:		
(1) Containing 5 per cent. or more by weight of guanine	—	—
(2) Other	12½%	—
(C) Stamping foils:		
(1) Consisting of precious metal, deposited on paper, artificial plastic material or other support	8%	—
(2) Other	12½%	—
(D) Other:		
(1) Varnishes, lacquers, paints and enamels:		
(a) Solutions of alkyd resins (whether modified or not)	7½%	—
(b) Other	10½%	—
(2) Dyes in forms or packings of a kind sold by retail:		
(a) Synthetic organic dyestuffs ...	26%	—
(b) Other	8%	—
(3) Goods referred to in Note 4 to this Chapter, other than varnishes and lacquers:		
(a) Solutions of alkyd resins (whether modified or not)	5%	—
(b) Other	8%	—

Tariff Heading	Rate of Import Duty (*if any*)	
	Full	*Commonwealth (C)* *E.F.T.A.* (*E*)

32.09 Varnishes and lacquers, etc.—*contd.*
(D) Other—*contd.*
   (4) Other:
     (*a*) Containing " light oils " as defined in paragraph (b) of the Special Note to Chapter 27
	15%	—

(*b*) Other	12½%	—
32.10 Artists', students' and signboard painters' colours, modifying tints, amusement colours and the like, in tablets, tubes, jars, bottles, pans or in similar forms or packings, including such colours in sets or outfits, with or without brushes, palettes or other accessories	16%	—
32.11 Prepared driers	8%	—
32.12 Glaziers' putty; grafting putty; painters' fillings; stopping, sealing and similar mastics, including resin mastics and cements	8%	—
32.13 Writing ink, printing ink and other inks: (A) Printing ink ... ... (B) Drawing ink ... ... (C) Other	10½% 12% 16%	— — —

Chapter 33

Essential Oils and Resinoids; Perfumery, Cosmetics and Toilet Preparations

Notes

1. This Chapter does not cover:

(*a*) Compound alcoholic preparations (known as "concentrated extracts") for the manufacture of beverages (heading No. 22.09);

(*b*) Soap falling within heading No. 34.01; or

(*c*) Spirits of turpentine or other products falling within heading No. 38.07.

2. Heading No. 33.06 is to be taken to apply, *inter alia*, to products (whether or not mixed), other than those of heading No. 33.05, suitable for use as perfumery, cosmetics or toilet preparations, put up in packings of a kind sold by retail for such use.

Tariff Heading	Rate of Import Duty (*if any*)	
	Full	*Commonwealth* (*C*) *E.F.T.A.* (*E*)
33.01 Essential oils (terpeneless or not); concretes and absolutes; resinoids:		
(A) Essential oils:		
(1) The following oils, not terpeneless:	—	—
Aniseed		
Attar (otto) of rose		
Bergamot		
Brown camphor		
Cananga		
Cassia		
Chenopodium		
Copaiba		
Geranium		
Lavandin		
Lavender		
Lemon		
Mandarin (tangerine)		
Neroli		
Peppermint		
Petitgrain		
Rosewood (bois de rose)		
Spearmint		
Spike lavender		
Vetiver (cuscus)		
Ylang-ylang		
(2) Hop oil	£1 per oz.	C 13s. 4d. per oz. E —
(3) Lime oil	25%	—
(4) Other	8%	—
(B) Concretes and absolutes; resinoids:		
(1) Jasmin	—	—
Lavandin		
Lavender		
Mimosa		
Mousse de chêne		
Orange flowers		
Rose		
Violet leaf (vert de violet)		
(2) Other	8%	—

Tariff Heading	Rate of Import Duty (*if any*)	
	Full	*Commonwealth (C)* *E.F.T.A.* *(E)*
33.02 Terpenic by-products of the deterpenation of essential oils	6½%	—
33.03 Concentrates of essential oils in fats, in fixed oils, or in waxes or the like, obtained by cold absorption or by maceration	8%	
33.04 Mixtures of two or more odoriferous substances (natural or artificial) and mixtures (including alcoholic solutions) with a basis of one or more of these substances, of a kind used as raw materials in the perfumery, food, drink or other industries:		
(A) Containing synthetic organic chemicals or natural isolates of essential oils	8%, or 25% of the value of the constituents referred to in Column 1, whichever is the greater	—
(B) Other	8%	
33.05 Aqueous distillates and aqueous solutions of essential oils, including such products suitable for medicinal uses	12%	
33.06 Perfumery, cosmetics and toilet preparations:		
(A) Perfumed spirits:	—	—
(1) In cask:		
(a) If warehoused 3 years or more		
(b) If warehoused 2 and less than 3 years		
(c) If not warehoused, or warehoused less than 2 years		
(2) In bottle:		
(a) If warehoused 3 years or more		
(b) If warehoused 2 and less than 3 years		
(c) If not warehoused, or warehoused less than 2 years		
(B) Bath salts and essences	20%	—
(C) Dental plate fixative preparations ...	9%	—
(D) Other	12%	—

Chapter 34

Soap, Organic Surface-Active Agents, Washing Preparations, Lubricating Preparations, Artificial Waxes, Prepared Waxes, Polishing and Scouring Preparations, Candles and Similar Articles, Modelling Pastes and "Dental Waxes"

Notes

1. This Chapter does not cover:

(*a*) Separate chemically defined compounds; or

(*b*) Dentifrices, shaving creams or shampoos containing soap or organic surface-active agents (heading No. 33.06).

2. Heading No. 34.01 is to be taken to apply only to soap, soluble in water, with or without the addition of other substances (for example, disinfectants, abrasive powders, fillers or medicaments).

3. The reference in heading No. 34.03 to petroleum oils and oils obtained from bituminous minerals is to be taken to apply to the products defined in Note 3 of Chapter 27.

4. In heading No. 34.04 the expression " prepared waxes, not emulsified or containing solvents " is to be taken to apply only to:

(A) Mixtures of animal waxes, mixtures of vegetable waxes or mixtures of artificial waxes;

(B) Mixtures of different classes of waxes (animal, vegetable, mineral or artificial); and

(C) Mixtures of waxy consistency not emulsified or containing solvents, with a basis of one or more waxes, and containing fats, resins, mineral substances or other materials.

The heading is to be taken not to apply to:

(*a*) Waxes falling within heading No. 27.13; or

(*b*) Separate animal waxes and separate vegetable waxes, merely coloured.

Tariff Heading	Rate of Import Duty (if any)	
	Full	Commonwealth (C) E.F.T.A. (E)
34.01 Soap, including medicated soap:		
(A) Shaving soap	13%	—
(B) Toilet soap	20%	—
(C) Other:		
(1) Soap flakes; soft soap	13%	—
(2) Hard soap (not including abrasive soap) in blocks, bars, tablets or similar forms	10%	—
(3) Other	16%	—
34.02 Organic surface-active agents; surface-active preparations and washing preparations, whether or not containing soap:		
(A) Products of the condensation of normal aliphatic alcohols containing eight or more carbon atoms in the molecule with epoxyalkanes or alkanediols, and preparations and mixtures containing not less than 90 per cent. by weight of such products	20%	

Tariff Heading	Rate of Import Duty (if any)	
	Full	Commonwealth (C) E.F.T.A. (E)
34.02 Organic surface active agents; etc.—contd. (B) Other: (1) Consisting solely of polyethylene glycol ethers or of polyethylene glycol ether-esters	—	—
(2) Other	10%	—
34.03 Lubricating preparations, and preparations of a kind used for oil or grease treatment of textiles, leather or other materials, but not including preparations containing 70 per cent. or more by weight of petroleum oils or of oils obtained from bituminous minerals: (A) Containing 50 per cent. or more by weight of siloxanes	8%	—
(B) Other: (1) Containing " light oils " as defined in paragraph (b) of the Special Note to Chapter 27	3%, in addition to any hydro-carbon oil duty	—
(2) Other	8%	
34.04 Artificial waxes (including water-soluble waxes); prepared waxes, not emulsified or containing solvents: (A) Consisting solely of polyethylene glycol ethers or of polyethylene glycol ether-esters	—	—
(B) Other ...	8%	—
34.05 Polishes and creams, for footwear, furniture or floors, metal polishes, scouring powders and similar preparations, but excluding prepared waxes falling within heading No. 34.04	8%	—
34.06 Candles, tapers, night-lights and the like...	16%	—
34.07 Modelling pastes (including those put up for children's amusement and assorted modelling pastes); preparations of a kind known as " dental wax " or as " dental impression compounds ", in plates, horse-shoe shapes, sticks and similar forms: (A) Modelling pastes put up for children's amusement	20%	—
(B) Other	8%	—

Chapter 35

Albuminoidal Substances; Glues

Note

This Chapter does not cover:

(*a*) Protein substances put up as medicaments (heading No. 30.03); or

(*b*) Gelatin postcards and other products of the printing industry (Chapter 49).

Tariff Heading	Rate of Import Duty (if any)		
	Full	Commonwealth (C) E.F.T.A. (E)	
35.01 Casein, caseinates and other casein derivatives; casein glues:			
(A) Casein glues	8%	—	
(B) Other	10%	C E	— 10%
35.02 Albumins, albuminates and other albumin derivatives	10%	—	
35.03 Gelatin (including gelatin in rectangles, whether or not coloured or surface-worked) and gelatin derivatives; glues derived from bones, hides, nerves, tendons or from similar products; fish glues; isinglass:			
(A) Gelatin derivatives; isinglass ...	8%	—	
(B) Gelatin and glue	16%	—	
35.04 Peptones and other protein substances and their derivatives; hide powder, whether or not chromed	8%	—	
35.05 Dextrins and dextrin glues; soluble or roasted starches; starch glues	10%	—	
35.06 Prepared glues, not elsewhere specified or included; products suitable for use as glues put up for sale by retail as glues in packages not exceeding a net weight of one kilogram:			
(A) Pastes and mucilages put up in packages not exceeding a net weight of one kilogram for sale by retail as stationery glues	13%	—	
(B) Other	16%	—	

Chapter 36

Explosives; Pyrotechnic Products; Matches; Pyrophoric Alloys;
certain Combustible Preparations

Notes

1. This Chapter does not cover separate chemically defined compounds other than those described in Note 2 (*a*) or (*b*) below.

2. Heading No. 36.08 is to be taken to apply only to:

(*a*) Metaldehyde, hexamine and similar substances, put up in forms (for example, tablets, sticks or similar forms) for use as fuels; fuels with a basis of alcohol, and similar prepared fuels, in solid or semi-solid form;

(*b*) Liquid fuels (for example, petrol, liquid butane) of a kind used in mechanical lighters, in containers of a capacity not exceeding 300 cubic centimetres; and

(*c*) Resin torches, firelighters and the like.

Tariff Heading	Rate of Import Duty (if any)	
	Full	Commonwealth (C) E.F.T.A. (E)
36.01 Propellent powders	8%	—
36.02 Prepared explosives, other than propellent powders	8%	—
36.03 Mining, blasting and safety fuses	16%	—
36.04 Percussion and detonating caps; igniters; detonators	16%	—
36.05 Pyrotechnic articles (for example, fireworks, railway fog signals, amorces, rain rockets):		
(A) Bengal matches	—	—
(B) Other	16%	—
36.06 Matches (excluding Bengal matches) ...	—	—
36.07 Ferro-cerium and other pyrophoric alloys in all forms:		
(A) In pieces weighing not more than 4 ounces	16%	—
(B) Other	8%	—
36.08 Other combustible preparations and products:		
(A) "Hydrocarbon oils" as defined in paragraph (a) of the Special Note to Chapter 27	—	—
(B) Metaldehyde and hexamine	25%	—
(C) Other	8%	—

Chapter 37

Photographic and Cinematographic Goods

Notes

1. This Chapter does not cover waste or scrap materials.

2. Heading No. 37.08 is to be taken to apply only to:

(a) Chemical products mixed or compounded for photographic uses (for example, sensitised emulsions, developers and fixers); and

(b) Unmixed substances suitable for such uses and put up in measured portions or put u for sale by retail in a form ready for use.

The heading does not apply to photographic pastes or gums, varnishes or similar products

Tariff Heading	Rate of Import Duty (if any)		
	Full	Commonwealth (C) E.F.T.A. (E)	
37.01 Photographic plates and film in the flat, sensitised, unexposed, of any material other than paper, paperboard or cloth	16%	—	
37.02 Film in rolls, sensitised, unexposed, perforated or not:			
(A) Of a length of 12 feet or more ...	9%	C	6%
		E	—
(B) Of a length less than 12 feet	16%	—	
37.03 Sensitised paper, paperboard and cloth, unexposed or exposed but not developed	16%	—	
37.04 Sensitised plates and film, exposed but not developed, negative or positive	—	—	
37.05 Plates, unperforated film and perforated film (other than cinematograph film), exposed and developed, negative or positive:			
(A) Microfilm, being film for optical projection, consisting wholly of microphotographs of books, publications or other documents, other than trade advertising material	—	—	
(B) Aerial survey film depicting only topographical features, of a kind suitable for use in making maps or charts	—	—	
(C) Plates and film imported in a packet not exceeding 8 ounces in gross weight which does not form part of a larger consignment	—	—	
(D) Other	8%	—	
37.06 Cinematograph film, exposed and developed, consisting only of sound track, negative or positive	—	—	

Tariff Heading	Rate of Import Duty (*if any*)	
	Full	*Commonwealth (C)* *E.F.T.A.* *(E)*
7.07 Other cinematograph film, exposed and developed, whether or not incorporating sound track, negative or positive: (A) Negative film ... ... (B) Positive film:	—	—
(1) Film of a width of less than 35 millimetres, depicting only private and personal records of a kind not suitable for public commercial exhibition or sale	—	—
(2) Film, without sound track of any description, in two or more lengths representing the same objects, imported together and designed for use as a set, each complementary to the other or others, in the production of a coloured film	—	—
(3) Film of a width of 16 millimetres, bearing not more than one frame across the width, with double perforation but without sound track of any description	—	—
(4) Film, not falling within subheading (B) (1), (B) (2) or (B) (3) of this heading, with or without incorporated sound track, bearing not more than one frame across the width	0·85d. per linear foot	C 0·19d. per linear foot E —
(5) Other	0·85d. per linear foot	C 0·19d. per linear foot E —
	for film of a width not greater than 35 millimetres, and for other film a rate increased in proportion to the extent to which the width is greater than 35 millimetres	
7.08 Chemical products and flash light materials, of a kind and in a form suitable for use in photography	12%	—

Chapter 38

Miscellaneous Chemical Products

Notes

1. This Chapter does not cover:

(a) Separate chemically defined elements or compounds with the exception of the following:

(1) Artificial graphite (heading No. 38.01); activated carbon (decolourising, depolarising or adsorbent) (heading No. 38.03);

(2) Disinfectants, insecticides, fungicides, weed-killers, anti-sprouting products, rat poisons and similar products put up as described in heading No. 38.11;

(3) Products put up as charges for fire-extinguishers or put up in fire-extinguishing grenades (heading No. 38.17);

(4) Products specified in Note 2 (a), 2 (c), 2 (d) or 2 (f) below.

(b) Medicaments (heading No. 30.03).

2. Heading No. 38.19 is to be taken to include the following goods which are to be taken not to fall within any other heading of this Schedule:

(a) Cultured crystals (other than optical elements) weighing not less than two and a half grammes each, of magnesium oxide or of the halides of the alkali or of the alkaline earth metals;

(b) Fusel oil;

(c) Ink removers put up in packings for sale by retail;

(d) Stencil correctors put up in packings for sale by retail;

(e) Ceramic firing testers, fusible (for example, Seger cones);

(f) Plasters specially prepared for use in dentistry; and

(g) Mixed alkylenes with a very low degree of polymerisation.

Tariff Heading	Rate of Import Duty (if any)	
	Full	Commonwealth (C E.F.T.A. (E
38.01 Artificial graphite; colloidal graphite, other than suspensions in oil	8%	
38.02 Animal black (for example, bone black and ivory black), including spent animal black	8%	
38.03 Activated carbon (decolourising, depolarising . or adsorbent); activated diatomite, activated clay, activated bauxite and other activated natural mineral products:		
(A) Activated carbon, not being of animal origin	20%	—
(B) Activated aluminium oxide	9%	—
(C) Other	8%	—
38.04 Ammoniacal gas liquors and spent oxide produced in coal gas purification	8%	—
38.05 Tall oil	8%	—
38.06 Concentrated sulphite lye	8%	—

	Rate of Import Duty (if any)	
Tariff Heading	Full	Commonwealth (C) E.F.T.A. (E)
38.07 **Spirits of turpentine (gum, wood and sulphate) and other terpenic solvents produced by the distillation or other treatment of coniferous woods; crude dipentene; sulphite turpentine; pine oil (excluding " pine oils " not rich in terpineol):**		
(A) " Hydrocarbon oils " as defined in paragraph (a) of the Special Note of Chapter 27	—	
(B) Other	8%	—
38.08 **Rosin and resin acids, and derivatives thereof other than ester gums included in heading No. 39.05; rosin spirit and rosin oils:**		
(A) " Hydrocarbon oils " as defined in paragraph (a) of the Special Note to Chapter 27	—	
(B) Other:		
(1) Rosin and resin acids	—	
(2) Disproportionated, hydrogenated, polymerised or oxidised rosin and resin acids	—	
(3) Other	8%	—
38.09 **Wood tar; wood tar oils (other than the composite solvents and thinners falling within heading No. 38.18); wood creosote; wood naphtha; acetone oil**	8%	—
38.10 **Vegetable pitch of all kinds; brewers' pitch and similar compounds based on rosin or on vegetable pitch; foundry core binders based on natural resinous products**	6½%	—
38.11 **Disinfectants, insecticides, fungicides, weedkillers, anti-sprouting products, rat poisons and similar products, put up in forms or packings for sale by retail or as preparations or as articles (for example, sulphurtreated bands, wicks and candles, flypapers):**		
(A) Unmixed products put up in forms or packings for sale by retail	The rate applicable to the products when not put up as mentioned in this heading	C E The rate applicable to the products when not put up as mentioned in this heading.
(B) Other:		
(1) Products containing one or more constituents which have been used in their manufacture or preparation and have not lost their identity and which, if imported separately, would be classified in Chapter 28 or 29 and be chargeable with import duty amounting to 20 per cent. or more of the value of the constituent	8% or such greater rate as is equal to the amount or aggregate amount of the duty chargeable on such constituents	—
(2) Other	8%	—

Tariff Heading	Rate of Import Duty (if any)	
	Full	Commonwealth (C E.F.T.A. (E
38.12 Prepared glazings, prepared dressings and prepared mordants, of a kind used in the textile, paper, leather or like industries	8%	—
38.13 Pickling preparations for metal surfaces; fluxes and other auxiliary preparations for soldering, brazing or welding; soldering, brazing or welding powders and pastes consisting of metal and other materials; preparations of a kind used as cores or coatings for welding rods and electrodes:		
(A) Soldering, brazing or welding powders and pastes consisting of metal and other materials	12½%	—
(B) Other	8%	—
38.14 Anti-knock preparations, oxidation inhibitors, gum inhibitors, viscosity improvers, anti-corrosive preparations and similar prepared additives for mineral oils:		
(A) " Hydrocarbon oils " as defined in paragraph (a) of the Special Note to Chapter 27	—	—
(B) Products containing one or more constituents which have been used in their manufacture or preparation and have not lost their identity and which, if imported separately, would be classified in Chapter 28 or 29 and be chargeable with import duty amounting to 20 per cent. or more of the value of the constituent	8% or such greater rate as is equal to the amount or aggregate amount of the duty chargeable on such constituents	
(C) Other	8%	—
38.15 Prepared rubber accelerators	25%	—
38.16 Prepared culture media for development of micro-organisms	8%	—
38.17 Preparations and charges for fire-extinguishers; charged fire-extinguishing grenades	8%	—
38.18 Composite solvents and thinners for varnishes and similar products:		
(A) " Hydrocarbon oils " as defined in paragraph (a) of the Special Note to Chapter 27	—	—

	Rate of Import Duty (*if any*)	
Tariff Heading	*Full*	*Commonwealth* (C) *E.F.T.A.* (E)
8.18 Composite solvents and thinners, etc.— *contd.*		
(B) Other:		
(1) Products containing one or more constituents which have been used in their manufacture or preparation and have not lost their identity and which, if imported separately, would be classified in Chapter 28 or 29 and be chargeable with import duty amounting to 20 per cent. or more of the value of the constituent:		
(*a*) Containing " light oils " as defined in paragraph (*b*) of the Special Note to Chapter 27	3% or such greater rate as is equal to the amount or aggregate amount by which the duty chargeable on such constituents exceeds 7%, in addition to any hydrocarbon oil duty	—
(*b*) Other	8% or such greater rate as is equal to the amount or aggregate amount of the duty chargeable on such constituents	—
(2) Other:		
(*a*) Containing " light oils " as defined in paragraph (*b*) of the Special Note to Chapter 27	3%, in addition to any hydrocarbon oil duty	—
(*b*) Other	8%	—
8.19 Chemical products and preparations of the chemical or allied industries (including those consisting of mixtures of natural products), not elsewhere specified or included; residual products of the chemical or allied industries, not elsewhere specified or included:		
(A) " Hydrocarbon oils " as defined in paragraph (a) of the Special Note to Chapter 27	—	—
(B) Getters and the like for vacuum tubes	25%	—
(C) Compounded extenders for paints ...	16%	—
(D) Silicon alloys containing not less than 90 per cent. by weight of silicon; products containing more than 99·9 per cent. by weight of silicon	—	—

Tariff Heading	Rate of Import Duty (if any)	
	Full	Commonwealth (C E.F.T.A. (E
38.19 Chemical products and preparations of the chemical or allied industries, etc.—*contd.*		
(E) Products consisting solely of polyethylene glycol ethers or of polyethylene glycol ether-esters	—	—
(F) Mixtures containing 50 per cent. or more by weight of siloxanes	8%	—

(G) Catalysts, containing platinum dispersed with alumina, or with alumina and silica, or with aluminium silicate, which contain by weight—
  not less than 0·10 per cent. nor more than 1·0 per cent. of platinum; and
  not less than 0·20 per cent. nor more than 8·0 per cent. of chlorine, or of fluorine, or of chlorine and fluorine together;
and are in the form of rods, pellets, granules or spheres, having no axial dimension less than 0·030 inch nor more than 1·0 inch
	2s. 2d. per lb.	—

(H) Pearl essence containing 5 per cent. or more by weight of guanine	—	—
(IJ) Other:		
(1) Products and preparations containing one or more constituents which have been used in their manufacture or preparation and have not lost their identity and which, if imported separately, would be classified in Chapter 28 or 29 and be chargeable with import duty amounting to 20 per cent. or more of the value of the constituent	8% or such greater rate as is equal to the amount or aggregate amount of the duty chargeable on such constituents	—
(2) Other	8%	—

SECTION VII

ARTIFICIAL RESINS AND PLASTIC MATERIALS, CELLULOSE ESTERS AND ETHERS, AND ARTICLES THEREOF; RUBBER, SYNTHETIC RUBBER, FACTICE, AND ARTICLES THEREOF

Chapter 39

Artificial Resins and Plastic Materials, Cellulose Esters and Ethers; Articles thereof

Notes

1. This Chapter does not cover:

(*a*) Stamping foils of heading No. 32.09;

(*b*) Artificial waxes (heading No. 34.04);

(*c*) Synthetic rubber, as defined for the purposes of Chapter 40, or articles thereof;

(*d*) Saddlery or harness (heading No. 42.01) or travel goods, handbags or other receptacles falling within heading No. 42.02;

(*e*) Plaits, wickerwork or other articles falling within Chapter 46;

(*f*) Man-made fibres (Section XI) or articles thereof;

(*g*) Footwear, headgear, umbrellas, sunshades, walking-sticks, whips, riding-crops, fans or parts thereof or other articles falling within Section XII;

(*h*) Imitation jewellery falling within heading No. 71.16;

(*ij*) Articles falling within Section XVI (machines and mechanical or electrical appliances);

(*k*) Parts of vehicles or aircraft (Section XVII);

(*l*) Optical elements of artificial plastics, spectacle frames, drawing instruments or other articles falling within Chapter 90;

(*m*) Goods falling within Chapter 91 (for example, clocks, watches and parts thereof);

(*n*) Musical instruments or parts thereof or other articles falling within Chapter 92;

(*o*) Furniture or parts of furniture (Chapter 94);

(*p*) Brushes or other articles falling within Chapter 96;

(*q*) Toys, games or sports requisites (Chapter 97); or

(*r*) Buttons, slide fasteners, combs, mouthpieces or stems for smoking pipes, cigarette-holders or the like, parts of vacuum flasks or the like, pens, propelling pencils or other articles falling within Chapter 98.

2. Headings Nos. 39.01 and 39.02 are to be taken to apply only to goods of a kind produced by chemical synthesis answering to one of the following descriptions:

(*a*) Artificial plastics including artificial resins;

(*b*) Silicones;

(*c*) Resols, liquid polyisobutylene, and similar artificial polycondensation or polymerisation products.

3. Headings Nos. 39.01 to 39.06 are to be taken to apply to materials in the following forms only:

(*a*) Liquid or pasty, including emulsions, dispersions and solutions (but not including solutions in which the weight of the volatile organic solvent exceeds 50 per cent. of the weight of the solution);

(*b*) Blocks, lumps, powders (including moulding powders), granules, flakes and similar bulk forms;

(*c*) Monofil of which any cross-sectional dimension exceeds 1 millimetre; seamless tubes, rods, sticks and profile shapes, whether or not surface-worked but not otherwise worked;

(*d*) Plates, sheets, strip, film and foil, whether or not printed or otherwise surface-worked but not cut to shape or otherwise worked, and rectangular articles cut therefrom, not further worked;

(*e*) Waste and scrap.

Tariff Heading	Rate of Import Duty (*if any*)	
	Full	*Commonwealth (C E.F.T.A. (*
39.01 Condensation, polycondensation and polyaddition products, whether or not modified or polymerised, and whether or not linear (for example, phenoplasts, aminoplasts, alkyds, poly(allyl esters) and other unsaturated polyesters, silicones):		
(A) Melamine-formaldehyde	18%	—
(B) Phenoplast and aminoplast moulding powders and laminates	15%	—
(C) Consisting solely of polyethylene glycol ethers	—	—
(D) Other:		
(1) Solutions of alkyd resins (whether modified or not)	5%	—
(2) Other	10%	—
39.02 Polymerisation and copolymerisation products (for example, polyethylene, polytetrahaloethylenes, polyisobutylene, polystyrene, poly(vinyl chloride), poly(vinyl acetate), poly(vinyl chloroacetate) and other poly (vinyl derivatives), poly(acrylic derivatives), poly(methacrylic derivatives), coumaroneindene resins):		
(A) " Hydrocarbon oils " as defined in paragraph (a) of the Special Note to Chapter 27	—	—
(B) Other:		
(1) Copolymers solely of acrylonitrile with 5-vinyl-2-picoline and containing not less than 40 per cent. and not more than 60 per cent. by weight of acrylonitrile	—	—
(2) Other:		
(*a*) Strip not exceeding 4 inches in width coated with adhesive, other than strip suitable for use with embossing devices of subheading 98.07 (B)	14½%	—
(*b*) Other	10%	—
39.03 Regenerated cellulose; cellulose nitrate, cellulose acetate and other cellulose esters, cellulose ethers and other chemical derivatives of cellulose, plasticised or not (for example, collodions, celluloid); vulcanised fibre:		
(A) Cellulose acetate, but not including transparent wrapping:		
(1) Not plasticised or otherwise compounded	25%	—
(2) Other:		
(*a*) Waste and scrap	23%	—

Tariff Heading	Rate of Import Duty (if any)	
	Full	Commonwealth (C) E.F.T.A. (E)
9.03 Regenerated cellulose, etc.—contd.		
(A) Cellulose acetate:—contd.		
(2) Other:—contd.		
(b) Photographic (including cinematograph) film base	1s. 2d. per lb. or 10%, whichever is the greater	—
(c) Strip not exceeding 4 inches in width coated with adhesive	14½%	—
(d) Other	9d. per lb. or 10%, whichever is the greater	—
(B) Cellulose ethers, not plasticised or otherwise compounded	23%	—
(C) Cellulose nitrate (collodion cotton) ...	14%	—
(D) Transparent wrapping:		
(1) Of plasticised ethylcellulose, or of plasticised cellulose esters (other than cellulose acetate)	12½%	—
(2) Of regenerated cellulose, of cellulose acetate or of other materials	16%	—
(E) Vulcanised fibre	10%	—
(F) Other:		
(1) Strip not exceeding 4 inches in width coated with adhesive	14½%	—
(2) Other	10%	—
9.04 Hardened proteins (for example, hardened casein and hardened gelatin)	8%	—
9.05 Natural resins modified by fusion (run gums); artificial resins obtained by esterification of natural resins or of resinic acids (ester gums); chemical derivatives of natural rubber (for example, chlorinated rubber, rubber hydrochloride, oxidised rubber, cyclised rubber)	10%	—
9.06 Other high polymers, artificial resins and artificial plastic materials, including alginic acid, its salts and esters; linoxyn:		
(A) Heparin	19%	—
(B) Alpha-cellulose in powder form, having a residue on ignition of more than 0·15 per cent. by weight	—	—
(C) Alginic acid and its salts and esters ...	8%	—
(D) Other	10%	—
9.07 Articles of materials of the kinds described in headings Nos. 39.01 to 39.06:		
(A) Clock and watch glasses	24%	C 13% E —
(B) Objects of personal adornment ...	17½%	—
(C) Articles of apparel and clothing accessories	16%	—

Tariff Heading	Rate of Import Duty (*if any*)	
	Full	Commonwealth (C E.F.T.A. (E
39.07 Articles of materials etc.—*contd.*		
(D) Lighting appliances and fittings ...	16%	—
(E) Bobbins, cones, cops, cores, spools and similar supports, of a kind used on textile machinery	16%	—
(F) Beads and bead trimmings:		
(1) Beads of a size and shape adapted for use in jewellery or imitation jewellery, not mounted, set or strung	—	
(2) Other:		
(*a*) Of vulcanised fibre, hardened proteins or chemical derivatives of rubber	12%	
(*b*) Of other materials	15%	
(G) Other	10%	

Chapter 40

Rubber, Synthetic Rubber, Factice, and Articles thereof

Notes

1. Except where the context otherwise requires, throughout this Schedule the expression " rubber " means the following products, whether or not vulcanised or hardened: natural rubber, balata, gutta-percha and similar natural gums, synthetic rubber, and factice derived from oils, and such substances reclaimed.

2. This Chapter does not cover the following products of rubber and textiles, which fall generally within Section XI:

(a) Knitted or crocheted fabric or articles thereof, elastic or rubberised (other than transmission, conveyor and elevator belts or belting, of rubberised knitted or crocheted fabric of heading No. 40.10); other elastic fabric or articles thereof;

(b) Textile hosepiping and similar textile tubing, internally coated or lined with rubber (heading No. 59.15);

(c) Woven textile fabrics (other than the goods of heading No. 40.10) impregnated, coated, covered or laminated with rubber:

    (i) Weighing not more than one and a half kilograms per square metre; or

    (ii) Weighing more than one and a half kilograms per square metre and containing more than 50 per cent. by weight of textile material;

    and articles of those fabrics;

(d) Felt impregnated or coated with rubber and containing more than 50 per cent. by weight of textile material, and articles thereof;

(e) Bonded fibre fabrics impregnated or coated with rubber, or in which rubber forms the bonding substance, irrespective of their weight per square metre, and articles thereof;

(f) Fabrics composed of parallel textile yarns agglomerated with rubber, irrespective of their weight per square metre, and articles thereof.

However, plates, sheets and strip, of expanded, foam or sponge rubber, combined with textile fabric, and articles thereof, are to be classified in Chapter 40 provided that the textile fabric is present merely for reinforcing purposes.

3. The following are also not covered by this Chapter:

(a) Footwear or parts thereof falling within Chapter 64;

(b) Headgear or parts thereof (including bathing caps) falling within Chapter 65;

(c) Mechanical or electrical appliances or parts thereof (including electrical goods of all kinds), of hardened rubber, falling within Section XVI;

(d) Articles falling within Chapter 90, 92, 94 or 96;

(e) Toys, games or other articles falling within Chapter 97; or

(f) Buttons, combs, smoking pipe stems, pens or other articles falling within Chapter 98.

4. In Note 1 to this Chapter and in headings Nos. 40.02, 40.05 and 40.06, the expression " synthetic rubber " is to be taken to apply to:

(a) Unsaturated synthetic substances which can be irreversibly transformed into non-thermoplastic substances by vulcanisation with sulphur, selenium or tellurium, and which, when so vulcanised as well as may be (without the addition of any substances such as plasticisers, fillers or reinforcing agents not necessary for the cross-linking), can produce non-thermoplastic substances which, at a temperature between fifteen and twenty degrees Centigrade, will not break on being extended to three times their original length and will return after being extended to twice their original length, within a period of two hours, to a length not greater than one and a half times the original length.

    Such substances include *cis*-polyisoprene, polybutadiene, polychlorobutadiene (GRM), polybutadiene-styrene (GRS), polychlorobutadiene-acrylonitrile (GRN), polybutadiene-acrylonitrile (GRA) and butyl rubber (GRI);

(b) Thioplasts (GRP); and

(c) Natural rubber modified by grafting or mixing with artificial plastic material, provided that it complies with the requirements concerning vulcanisation, elasticity and reversibility in (a) above.

5. Headings Nos. 40.01 and 40.02 are to be taken not to apply to:

(a) Natural or synthetic rubber latex (including pre-vulcanised rubber latex) compounde with vulcanising agents or accelerators, fillers or reinforcing agents, plasticisers, colourin matter (other than colouring matter added solely for the purpose of identification), with any other substance; however, latex merely stabilised or concentrated, an thermo-sensitive and electro-positive latex are to be classified in heading No. 40.01 40.02 as the case may be;

(b) Rubber which has been compounded with carbon black (with or without the additic of mineral oil) or with silica (with or without the addition of mineral oil) befo coagulation or with any substance after coagulation; or

(c) Mixtures of any of the products specified in Note 1 to the present Chapter, wheth or not compounded with any other substance.

6. Thread wholly of vulcanised rubber, of any cross-section of which any dimensic exceeds five millimetres, is to be classified as strip, rod or profile shape, falling within headir No. 40.08.

7. Heading No. 40.10 is to be taken to include transmission, conveyor or elevator bel or belting of textile fabric impregnated, coated, covered or laminated with rubber or mad from textile yarn or cord impregnated or coated with rubber.

8. For the purpose of heading No. 40.06, pre-vulcanised rubber latex is to be deemed be unvulcanised rubber latex.

For the purposes of headings Nos. 40.07 to 40.14, balata, gutta-percha and simil natural gums, and factice derived from oils, and such substances reclaimed, are to deemed to be vulcanised rubber whether or not they have been vulcanised.

9. In headings Nos. 40.05, 40.08 and 40.15, the expressions " plates ", " sheets " an " strip " are to be taken to apply, and to apply only, to plates, sheets and strip, wheth or not printed or otherwise surface-worked but not cut to shape or otherwise worked, an rectangular articles cut therefrom not further worked.

In heading No. 40.08 the expressions " rods " and " profile shapes " and in heading N 40.15 the expressions " rods ", " profile shapes " and " tubes " are to be taken to appl and to apply only, to such products, whether or not cut to length or surface-worked b not otherwise worked.

Tariff Heading	Rate of Import Duty (if any)	
	Full	Commonwealth (C E.F.T.A. (E
I. Raw rubber		
40.01 Natural rubber latex, whether or not with added synthetic rubber latex; pre-vulcanised natural rubber latex; natural rubber, balata, gutta-percha and similar natural gums:		
(A) Natural rubber latex:		
(1) Mixtures of natural rubber latex and synthetic rubber latex	6%	—
(2) Thermo-sensitive and electro-positive latex; pre-vulcanized latex	6%	—
(3) Other	—	—
(B) Natural rubber, balata, gutta-percha, and similar natural gums:		
(1) Natural rubber, balata in pieces not less than 2 inches thick, and gutta-percha	—	—
(2) Other	7½%	—

Tariff Heading	Rate of Import Duty (if any)	
	Full	Commonwealth (C) E.F.T.A. (E)
0.02 Synthetic rubber latex; pre-vulcanised synthetic rubber latex; synthetic rubber; factice derived from oils:		
(A) Pre-vulcanized synthetic rubber latex	7½%	—
(B) Other	6%	—
0.03 Reclaimed rubber	8%	—
0.04 Waste and parings of unhardened rubber; scrap of unhardened rubber, fit only for the recovery of rubber; powder obtained from waste or scrap of unhardened rubber	—	—
II. Unvulcanised rubber		
0.05 Plates, sheets and strip, of unvulcanised natural or synthetic rubber, other than smoked sheets and crepe sheets of heading No. 40.01 or 40.02; granules of unvulcanised natural or synthetic rubber compounded ready for vulcanisation; unvulcanised natural or synthetic rubber, compounded before or after coagulation either with carbon black (with or without the addition of mineral oil) or with silica (with or without the addition of mineral oil), in any form, of a kind known as masterbatch	8%	—
0.06 Unvulcanised natural or synthetic rubber, including rubber latex, in other forms or states (for example, rods, tubes and profile shapes, solutions and dispersions); articles of unvulcanised natural or synthetic rubber (for example, coated or impregnated textile thread; rings and discs):		
(A) Blocks and similar bulk forms; rods, tubes and profile shapes	8%	—
(B) Coated or impregnated thread of silk or man-made fibres	17% plus 6d. per lb. of silk and of man-made fibres	C 85% of the full rate E —
(C) Other	16%	—
III. Articles of unhardened vulcanised rubber		
0.07 Vulcanised rubber thread and cord, whether or not textile covered, and textile thread covered or impregnated with vulcanised rubber	12½%	—
0.08 Plates, sheets, strip, rods and profile shapes, of unhardened vulcanised rubber:		
(A) Sheet or strip coated with adhesive ...	16%	—

Tariff Heading	Rate of Import Duty (if any)	
	Full	Commonwealth (C E.F.T.A. (E
40.08 Plates, sheets, strip, etc.—*cont.* (B) Other: (1) Plates, sheets and strip, with a textile backing (2) Other	17½% 10%	— —
40.09 Piping and tubing, of unhardened vulcanised rubber	8%	—
40.10 Transmission, conveyor or elevator belts or belting, of vulcanised rubber: (A) Containing more than 20 per cent. by weight of man-made fibres (B) Containing more than 5 per cent. but not more than 20 per cent. by weight of man-made fibres (C) Other	27% 19% 9%	C 85% of the fu rate E — C 85% of the fu rate E — —
40.11 Rubber tyres, tyre cases, interchangeable tyre treads, inner tubes and tyre flaps, for wheels of all kinds: (A) Suitable for cycles (not mechanically propelled) (B) Suitable for motor vehicles ... ... (C) Other	19% 19% 16½%	— C 12½% E — —
40.12 Hygienic and pharmaceutical articles (including teats), of unhardened vulcanised rubber, with or without fittings of hardened rubber	16%	—
40.13 Articles of apparel and clothing accessories (including gloves), for all purposes, of unhardened vulcanised rubber: (A) Gloves ... ... (B) Other: (1) Containing more than 25 per cent. by weight of man-made fibres (2) Other	19% 19% 16½%	— C 85% of the fu rate E — —
40.14 Other articles of unhardened vulcanised rubber: (A) Articles of stationery of the following types, viz. bands and erasers (B) Other	12% 16%	— —

Tariff Heading	Rate of Import Duty (if any)	
	Full	Commonwealth (C) E.F.T.A. (E)
V. Hardened rubber (ebonite and vulcanite); articles made thereof		
40.15 Hardened rubber (ebonite and vulcanite), in bulk, plates, sheets, strip, rods, profile shapes or tubes; scrap, waste and powder, of hardened rubber	8%	—
40.16 Articles of hardened rubber (ebonite and vulcanite)	16%	—

SECTION VIII

RAW HIDES AND SKINS, LEATHER, FURSKINS AND ARTICLES THEREOF; SADDLERY AN͏
HARNESS; TRAVEL GOODS, HANDBAGS AND SIMILAR CONTAINERS; ÁRTICLES OF GU͏
(OTHER THAN SILK-WORM GUT)

Chapter 41

Raw Hides and Skins (other than Furskins) and Leather

Notes

1. This Chapter does not cover:

(*a*) Parings or similar waste, of raw hides or skins (heading No. 05.05 or 05.06);

(*b*) Birdskins or parts of birdskins, with their feathers or down, falling within headin͏
No. 05.07 or 67.01; or

(*c*) Hides or skins, with the hair on, raw, tanned or dressed (Chapter 43); the followin͏
are, however, to be classified in heading No. 41.01, namely, raw hides or skins, with th͏
hair on, of bovine cattle (including buffalo), of equine animals, of sheep and lamb
(except Persian, Astrakhan, Caracul and similar lambs, Indian, Chinese, Mongolia
and Tibetan lambs), of goats and kids (except Yemen, Mongolian and Tibetan goat
and kids), of swine (including peccary), of reindeer, of chamois, of gazelle, of deer, o͏
elk, of roebucks or of dogs.

2. Throughout this Schedule the expression " composition leather " is to be taken t
mean only substances of the kind referred to in heading No. 41.10.

Tariff Heading	Rate of Import Duty (*if any*)	
	Full	Commonwealth (C͏ E.F.T.A. (E
41.01 Raw hides and skins (fresh, salted, dried, pickled or limed), whether or not split, including sheepskins in the wool:		
(A) Goat and kid skins	6%	—
(B) Other hides and skins:		
(1) Split...	6%	—
(2) Not split	—	—
41.02 Bovine cattle leather (including buffalo leather) and equine leather, except leather falling within heading No. 41.06, 41.07 or 41.08:		
(A) Box and willow calf, box and willow sides and other chrome tanned leather, imported in skins or pieces weighing less than 4 lb. each, but not including wet blue chrome tanned leather	18%	—
(B) Other:		
(1) Dressed	13½%	—
(2) Other	9%	—

Tariff Heading	Rate of Import Duty (*if any*)	
	Full	*Commonwealth (C)* *E.F.T.A.* (E)
41.03 Sheep and lamb skin leather, except leather falling within heading No. 41.06, 41.07 or 41.08:		
(A) Dressed:		
(1) Chrome tanned and coloured black, of a thickness not exceeding 0·20 millimetre	—	—
(2) Other	13½%	—
(B) Other	9%	—
41.04 Goat and kid skin leather, except leather falling within heading No. 41.06, 41.07 or 41.08:		
(A) Dressed:		
(1) Glacé kid, being chrome tanned goat skin of smooth, polished finish	9%	—
(2) Other	13½%	—
(B) Other	9%	—
41.05 Other kinds of leather, except leather falling within heading No. 41.06, 41.07 or 41.08:		
(A) Dressed:		
(1) Reptile	12%	—
(2) Other	10%	—
(B) Other	9%	—
41.06 Chamois-dressed leather	13½%	—
41.07 Parchment-dressed leather	13½%	—
41.08 Patent leather and imitation patent leather; metallised leather:		
(A) Patent leather	7½%	—
(B) Imitation patent leather	15%	—
(C) Other	12%	—
41.09 Parings and other waste, of leather or of composition or parchment-dressed leather, not suitable for the manufacture of articles of leather; leather dust, powder and flour	—	—
41.10 Composition leather with a basis of leather or leather fibre, in slabs, in sheets or in rolls	8%	—

Chapter 42

Articles of Leather; Saddlery and Harness; Travel Goods, Handbags and Similar Containers;
Articles of Animal Gut (other than Silk-Worm Gut)

Notes

1. This Chapter does not cover:

   (a) Sterile surgical catgut and similar sterile suture materials (heading No. 30.05);

   (b) Articles of apparel and clothing accessories (except gloves), lined with furskin or artificial fur or to which furskin or artificial fur is attached on the outside except as mere trimming (heading No. 43.03 or 43.04);

   (c) String or net bags of Section XI;

   (d) Articles falling within Chapter 64;

   (e) Headgear or parts thereof falling within Chapter 65;

   (f) Whips, riding-crops or other articles of heading No. 66.02;

   (g) Strings, skins for drums and the like, and other parts of musical instruments (heading No. 92.09 or 92.10);

   (h) Furniture or parts of furniture (Chapter 94);

   (ij) Toys, games or sports requisites of Chapter 97; or

   (k) Buttons, studs, cuff-links, press-fasteners, including snap-fasteners and press-studs, and blanks and parts of such articles, falling within heading No. 98.01 or Chapter 71.

2. An incomplete or unfinished article is to be classified with the corresponding complete or finished article, provided it has the essential character of that complete or finished article.

3. For the purposes of heading No. 42.03, the expression " articles of apparel and clothing accessories " is to be taken to apply, *inter alia*, to gloves (including sports gloves), aprons and other protective clothing, braces, belts, bandoliers and wrist straps, including watch straps.

	Rate of Import Duty (if any)	
Tariff Heading	Full	Commonwealth (C) E.F.T.A. (E)
42.01 Saddlery and harness, of any material (for example, saddles, harness, collars, traces, knee-pads and boots), for any kind of animal	16%	—
42.02 Travel goods (for example, trunks, suit-cases, hat-boxes, travelling-bags, rucksacks), shopping-bags, handbags, satchels, brief-cases, wallets, purses, toilet-cases, tool-cases, tobacco-pouches, sheaths, cases, boxes (for example, for arms, musical instruments, binoculars, jewellery, bottles, collars, footwear, brushes) and similar containers, of leather or of composition leather, of vulcanised fibre, of artificial plastic sheeting, of paperboard or of textile fabric:		
(A) Women's handbags and pochettes of leather, material resembling leather, composition leather, artificial plastic sheeting or paperboard:		
(1) Without key locks and not exceeding 12 inches in length or width exclusive of the handle	1s. 6d. each or 13%, whichever is the greater	—

	Rate of Import Duty (if any)	
Tariff Heading	*Full*	*Commonwealth (C)* *E.F.T.A.* *(E)*

42.02 Travel goods, etc.—*contd.*
  (A) Women's handbags and pochettes, etc.
    —*contd.*
    (2) Other ... ...
	1s. 6d. each or
	16%, whichever
	is the greater
		—

(B) Other	16%	—

**42.03 Articles of apparel and clothing accessories,
of leather or of composition leather:**
  (A) Gloves, including gloves of leather and
    furskin or of leather and artificial fur
	28%	—

(B) Other	20%	—

**42.04 Articles of leather or of composition
leather of a kind used in machinery or
mechanical appliances or for industrial
purposes:**
  (A) Machinery belting (including conveyor
    and elevator bands)
	9%	—

(B) Other	16%	—
42.05 Other articles of leather or of composition leather	16%	—
42.06 Articles made from gut (other than silk- worm gut), from goldbeater's skin, from bladders or from tendons: (A) Catgut and articles thereof	16%	—
(B) Other	10%	—

Chapter 43

Furskins and Artificial Fur; Manufactures thereof

Notes

1. Throughout this Schedule references to furskins, other than to raw furskins of headir No. 43.01, are to be taken to apply to hides or skins of all animals which have bee tanned or dressed with the hair on.

2. This Chapter does not cover:

(*a*) Birdskins or parts of birdskins, with their feathers or down, falling within headir No. 05.07 or 67.01;

(*b*) Raw hides or skins, with the hair on, of a kind falling within Chapter 41 (*see* Note 1 ((to that Chapter);

(*c*) Gloves consisting of leather and furskin or of leather and artificial fur (headir No. 42.03);

(*d*) Articles falling within Chapter 64;

(*e*) Headgear or parts thereof falling within Chapter 65; or

(*f*) Toys, games or sports requisites of Chapter 97.

3. For the purposes of heading No. 43.02, the expression " plates, crosses and simila forms " means furskins or parts thereof (excluding " dropped " skins) sewn together i rectangles, crosses or trapeziums, without the addition of other materials. Other assemble skins ready for immediate use (or requiring only cutting to become ready for use), and skir or parts of skins sewn together in the form of garments or parts or accessories of garmen or of other articles fall within heading No. 43.03.

4. Articles of apparel and clothing accessories (except those excluded by Note 2) line with furskin or artificial fur or to which furskin or artificial fur is attached on the outsid except as mere trimming are to be classified under heading No. 43.03 or 43.04 as the cas may be.

5. Throughout this Schedule the expression " artificial fur " means any imitation (furskin consisting of wool, hair or other fibres gummed or sewn on to leather, woven fabr or other materials, but does not include imitation furskins obtained by weaving (headin No. 58.04, for example).

Tariff Heading	Rate of Import Duty (*if any*)	
	Full	*Commonwealth (C E.F.T.A.* *(E*
43.01 Raw furskins:		
(A) Goat and kid skins	6%	—
(B) Other	—	—
43.02 Furskins, tanned or dressed, including furskins assembled in plates, crosses and similar forms; pieces or cuttings, of furskin, tanned or dressed, including heads, paws, tails and the like (not being fabricated):		
(A) Furskins assembled in plates, crosses and similar forms	23%	—
(B) Other	9½%	—
43.03 Articles of furskin	23%	—
43.04 Artificial fur and articles made thereof ...	20%	—

SECTION IX

WOOD AND ARTICLES OF WOOD; WOOD CHARCOAL; CORK AND ARTICLES OF CORK; MANUFACTURES OF STRAW, OF ESPARTO AND OF OTHER PLAITING MATERIALS; BASKETWARE AND WICKERWORK

Chapter 44

Wood and Articles of Wood; Wood Charcoal

Notes

1. This Chapter does not cover:

(a) Wood of a kind used primarily in perfumery, in pharmacy, or for insecticidal, fungicidal or similar purposes (heading No. 12.07);

(b) Wood of a kind used primarily in dyeing or in tanning (heading No. 13.01);

(c) Activated charcoal (heading No. 38.03);

(d) Articles falling within Chapter 46;

(e) Footwear or parts thereof falling within Chapter 64;

(f) Goods falling within Chapter 66 (for example, umbrellas and walking-sticks and parts thereof);

(g) Goods falling within heading No. 68.09;

(h) Imitation jewellery falling within heading No. 71.16;

(ij) Goods falling within Section XVII (for example, wheelwrights' wares);

(k) Goods falling within Chapter 91 (for example, clocks and clock cases);

(l) Musical instruments or parts thereof (Chapter 92);

(m) Parts of firearms (heading No. 93.06);

(n) Furniture or parts thereof falling within Chapter 94;

(o) Toys, games or sports requisites or other articles falling within Chapter 97; or

(p) Smoking pipes or the like or parts thereof, buttons, pencils or other articles falling within Chapter 98.

2. Unless the context otherwise requires, articles of wood, whether or not comprising accessories or parts of glass, marble or other materials, imported unassembled or disassembled are to be classified as such articles, provided that the components are imported at the same time.

3. In this Chapter, the expression " improved wood " means wood which has been subjected to chemical or physical treatment (being, in the case of layers bonded together, treatment in excess of that needed to ensure a good bond), and which has thereby acquired increased density or hardness together with improved mechanical strength or resistance to chemical or electrical agencies.

4. Headings Nos. 44.19 to 44.28 are to be taken to apply to articles of the respective descriptions of plywood, cellular wood, " improved " wood or reconstituted wood as they apply to such articles of wood.

5. Heading No. 44.25 shall be taken not to apply to tools in which metal parts form the blade, working edge, working surface or other working part.

Tariff Heading	Rate of Import Duty (if any)	
	Full	*Commonwealth (C)* *E.F.T.A. (E)*
44.01 Fuel wood, in logs, in billets, in twigs or in faggots; wood waste, including sawdust	6%	—

Tariff Heading	Rate of Import Duty (if any)	
	Full	Commonwealth (C E.F.T.A. (E
44.02 Wood charcoal (including shell and nut charcoal), agglomerated or not	8%	—
44.03 Wood in the rough, whether or not stripped of its bark or merely roughed down:		
(A) Logs not exceeding 85 inches in length and 48 inches in girth at the narrower end and not being of ash	—	—
(B) Telegraph poles not less than 20 feet in length, not less than 5 inches in top diameter and not less than 6 inches in diameter 5 feet down from the butt end	—	—
(C) Other:		
(1) Of the following species, namely, species of *Acer, Betula, Fagus, Fraxinus, Juglans, Populus, Quercus* and *Ulmus; Castanea sativa; Eucalyptus diversicolor; Eucalyptus marginata*	6%	—
(2) Other	—	—
44.04 Wood, roughly squared or half-squared, but not further manufactured:		
(A) Of the following species, namely, species of *Acer, Betula, Fagus, Fraxinus, Juglans, Populus, Quercus* and *Ulmus; Castanea sativa; Eucalyptus diversicolor; Eucalyptus marginata*	6%	—
(B) Other	—	—
44.05 Wood sawn lengthwise, sliced or peeled, but not further prepared, of a thickness exceeding five millimetres:		
(A) Of the following species, namely, coniferous species; species of *Acer, Betula, Fagus, Fraxinus, Juglans, Populus, Quercus* and *Ulmus; Castanea sativa; Eucalyptus diversicolor; Eucalyptus marginata:*		
(1) Ash in straight lengths not less than 17 inches and not more than 108 inches, of uniform square cross-section of not less than $1\frac{1}{8}$ inches square and not more than $1\frac{3}{4}$ inches square	4%	—

Tariff Heading	Rate of Import Duty (if any)	
	Full	Commonwealth (C) E.F.T.A. (E)
44.05 Wood sawn lengthwise, sliced or peeled, but not further prepared, of a thickness exceeding five millimetres:—*contd.*		
(A) Of the following species, etc.—*contd.*		
(2) Feather-edged boards:		
(*a*) Of softwood	6%	—
(*b*) Of other wood	9½%	—
(3) Blocks of a length exceeding 18 inches but not exceeding 40 inches and of a sectional perimeter exceeding 18 inches but not exceeding 44 inches, roughly sawn to octagonal cross-section	5%	—
(4) Boxboards	8%	—
(5) Pencil slats:		
(*a*) Of incense cedar, not exceeding 7½ inches in length and 3 inches in width	—	—
(*b*) Other	8%	—
(6) Other:		
(*a*) Of coniferous species	—	—
(*b*) Other	6%	—
(B) Other	—	—
44.06 Wood paving blocks	6%	—
44.07 Railway or tramway sleepers of wood:		
(A) Of coniferous species	—	—
(B) Other	8%	—
44.08 Riven staves of wood, not further prepared than sawn on one principal surface; sawn staves of wood, of which at least one principal surface has been cylindrically sawn, not further prepared than sawn	6%	—
44.09 Hoopwood; split poles; piles, pickets and stakes of wood, pointed but not sawn lengthwise; chipwood; wood chips of a kind suitable for use in the manufacture of vinegar or for the clarification of liquids:		
(A) Hoopwood	8%	—

Tariff Heading	Rate of Import Duty (if any)	
	Full	Commonwealth (C) E.F.T.A. (E)
44.09 Hoopwood; split poles; piles, pickets and stakes of wood, pointed but not sawn lengthwise; chipwood; wood chips of a kind suitable for use in the manufacture of vinegar or for the clarification of liquids:—*contd.*		
(B) Pulpwood, in the form of chips, with a bulk density of not less than 10 lb. per cubic foot when measured by a loose weight method using the apparatus described in British Standard 812: 1960, and of which not more than 5 per cent. by weight passes a sieve having a nominal width of aperture of 2·00 millimetres and conforming to British Standard 410:1962, and imported in consignments of not less than 500 tons each	—	—
(C) Other	12½%	—
44.10 Wooden sticks, roughly trimmed but not turned, bent nor otherwise worked, suitable for the manufacture of walking-sticks, whips, golf club shafts, umbrella handles, tool handles or the like	8%	—
44.11 Drawn wood; match splints; wooden pegs or pins for footwear	16%	—
44.12 Wood wool and wood flour:		
(A) Wood wool	£2 4s. per ton	—
(B) Wood flour	12%	—
44.13 Wood (including blocks, strips and friezes for parquet or wood block flooring, not assembled), planed, tongued, grooved, rebated, chamfered, V-jointed, centre V-jointed, beaded, centre-beaded or the like, but not further manufactured:		
(A) Softwood boards (other than box-boards)	6½%	—
(B) Hardwood flooring blocks, strips and friezes, planed and tongued and grooved, or planed and otherwise manufactured	15%	—
(C) Other	8%	—

Tariff Heading	Rate of Import Duty (if any)	
	Full	Commonwealth (C) E.F.T.A. (E)
44.14 Wood sawn lengthwise, sliced or peeled, but not further prepared, of a thickness not exceeding five millimetres; veneer sheets and sheets for plywood, of a thickness not exceeding five millimetres:		
(A) Boxboards; veneer sheets and sheets for plywood	8%	—
(B) Pencil slats:		
(1) Of incense cedar, not exceeding 7½ inches in length and 3 inches in width	—	—
(2) Other	8%	—
(C) Other:		
(1) Of coniferous species	—	—
(2) Other	8%	—
44.15 Plywood, blockboard, laminboard, battenboard and similar laminated wood products (including veneered panels and sheets); inlaid wood and wood marquetry:		
(A) Plywood, blockboard, laminboard and battenboard, containing no material other than wood and bonding material	8%	—
(B) Other	16%	—
44.16 Cellular wood panels, whether or not faced with base metal	16%	—
44.17 " Improved " wood, in sheets, blocks or the like	8%	—
44.18 Reconstituted wood, being wood shavings, wood chips, sawdust, wood flour or other ligneous waste agglomerated with natural or artificial resins or other organic binding substances, in sheets, blocks or the like:		
(A) Flaxboard	10%	—
(B) Other	19%	—
44.19 Wooden beadings and mouldings, including moulded skirting and other moulded boards	12%	—
44.20 Wooden picture frames, photograph frames, mirror frames and the like:		
(A) Carved	12%	—
(B) Other	16%	—

Tariff Heading	Rate of Import Duty (if any)	
	Full	Commonwealth (C) E.F.T.A. (E)
44.21 Complete wooden packing cases, boxes, crates, drums and similar packings imported assembled, unassembled or partly assembled:		
(A) Imported unassembled, and consisting of softwood boxboards:		
(1) Dove-tailed, mortised or tenoned at the ends	10½%	—
(2) Other	8%	—
(B) Other	13%	—
44.22 Casks, barrels, vats, tubs, buckets and other coopers' products and parts thereof, of wood, other than staves falling within heading No. 44.08:		
(A) Sections of cask-heads not dowel-holed or pegged, and cask-heads consisting of a single circular sheet of wood	8%	—
(B) Empty palm oil casks, assembled, with staves not less than 39 inches and not more than 44 inches in length and heads not less than 34 inches and not more than 40 inches in diameter, which have been used to contain palm oil	8%	—
(C) Used casks and barrels of oak, whether assembled or not; staves and heads, being parts of such casks and barrels	—	—
(D) Other	12½%	—
44.23 Builders' carpentry and joinery (including prefabricated and sectional buildings and assembled parquet flooring panels):		
(A) Hardwood parquet flooring panels, assembled	15%	—
(B) Other	12%	—
44.24 Household utensils of wood:		
(A) Bath trays, bread boards, butter patters, clothes horses, clothes pegs, egg cups, plate racks, platters and dishes, pots and jars, rolling pins, spoons, forks and salad servers, and washing boards	16½%	—
(B) Other	18%	—

Tariff Heading	Rate of Import Duty (if any)	
	Full	Commonwealth (C) E.F.T.A. (E)
4.25 Wooden tools, tool bodies, tool handles, broom and brush bodies and handles; boot and shoe lasts and trees, of wood:		
(A) Tools and tool bodies	14½%	—
(B) Tool, broom and brush handles:		
(1) Fork, shovel and spade handles of the box or " D " type, whether riveted or not	—	—
(2) Straight pole handles of softwood not exceeding 54 inches in length or 1¼ inches in diameter	16%	—
(3) Other:		
(a) Of ash	10%	—
(b) Of other wood	11%	—
(C) Boot and shoe lasts and trees (including fillers):		
(1) Last blocks roughly shaped by sawing or turning, but not further manufactured	—	—
(2) Other	14½%	—
(D) Other	16%	—
4.26 Spools, cops, bobbins, sewing thread reels and the like, of turned wood:		
(A) Sewing thread reels and reel blocks, not exceeding 5 inches in length and 2¼ inches in diameter, punched longitudinally	4%	—
(B) Rough turned bobbin blocks, not exceeding 6 inches in length and 3¼ inches in diameter at the ends and 1¼ inches diameter in the barrel, punched longitudinally but not further manufactured	9%	—
(C) Other	12½%	—
4.27 Standard lamps, table lamps and other lighting fittings, of wood; articles of furniture, of wood, not falling within Chapter 94; caskets, cigarette boxes, trays, fruit bowls, ornaments and other fancy articles, of wood; cases for cutlery, for drawing instruments or for violins, and similar receptacles, of wood; articles of wood for personal use or adornment, of a kind normally carried in the pocket, in the handbag or on the person; parts of the foregoing articles, of wood:		

Tariff Heading	Rate of Import Duty (if any)	
	Full	Commonwealth (C E.F.T.A. (E
44.27 Standard lamps, etc.—contd.		
(A) Beads and bead trimming; carved pictures and wall plaques	12%	
(B) Caskets, cigarette boxes, trays, fruit bowls, ornaments (including statuettes and figures but not including candlesticks) and other fancy articles of wood:		
(1) Statuettes and figures of a kind used solely for ornamental or religious purposes	15%	—
(2) Other	18%	—
(C) Candlesticks	14½%	—
(D) Other	16%	—
44.28 Other articles of wood:		
(A) Pallets of a kind used with fork lift trucks having two-tongue forks	—	
(B) Softwood boxboards, other than those covered by headings Nos. 44.05, 44.13, 44.14 and 44.21, not dove-tailed, mortised or tenoned at the ends	8%	—
(C) Spring blind or shade rollers, whether with brackets or laths or not, and whether in sets or not, and rollers therefor bored at one or both ends or further manufactured	8%	—
(D) Stems of turned ash, being straight lengths of not less than 18 inches and not more than 42 inches, of circular cross-section of diameter (uniform throughout the length) not less than 1⅜ inches and not more than 1 11/16 inches, not further prepared or manufactured	8%	—
(E) Board consisting of an inner layer of thin strips of wood or of blocks of wood not exceeding 1 inch by 1¼ inches in cross-section, covered on both sides with one or more layers of paper or paperboard	15%	—
(F) Coat hangers and towel rails ...	16½%	—
(G) Other	18%	—

Chapter 45

Cork and Articles of Cork

Notes

1. This Chapter does not cover:

(a) Footwear or parts of footwear falling within Chapter 64;

(b) Headgear or parts of headgear falling within Chapter 65; or

(c) Toys, games or sports requisites (Chapter 97).

2. Natural cork roughly squared or deprived of the outer bark is to be taken to fall within heading No. 45.02 and not within heading No. 45.01.

Tariff Heading	Rate of Import Duty (if any)	
	Full	Commonwealth (C) E.F.T.A. (E)
45.01 Natural cork, unworked, crushed, granulated or ground; waste cork	—	—
45.02 Natural cork in the form of rectangular blocks, plates, sheets or strips (including cubes or square slabs, cut to size for corks or stoppers)	8%	—
45.03 Articles of natural cork:		
(A) Discs not exceeding $1\frac{3}{16}$ inches in diameter nor $\frac{3}{16}$ inch in thickness	—	—
(B) Stoppers containing no material other than natural cork, wax and adhesives	—	—
(C) Other:		
(1) Stoppers not containing metal, rubber or wood	8%	—
(2) Other	16%	—
45.04 Agglomerated cork (being cork agglomerated with or without a binding substance) and articles of agglomerated cork:		
(A) Stoppers not containing metal, rubber or wood	8%	—
(B) Tiles, not exceeding $\frac{3}{8}$ inch in thickness, and of which neither the length nor the width exceeds 13 inches, tongued and grooved and surface smoothed, but not further prepared or manufactured	8%	—
(C) Rectangular blocks, plates, sheets or strips, made wholly from cork	8%	—
(D) Other	16%	—

Chapter 46

Manufactures of Straw, of Esparto and of Other Plaiting Materials; Basketware and Wickerwork

Notes

1. In this Chapter the expression " plaiting materials " includes straw, osier or willow, bamboos, rattans, rushes, reeds, strips of wood, strips of vegetable fibre or bark, unspun textile fibres, monofil and strip of artificial plastic materials and strips of paper, but not strips of leather, of composition leather or of felt, human hair, horsehair, textile rovings or yarns, or monofil or strip of Chapter 51.

2. This Chapter does not cover:

(*a*) Twine, cordage, ropes or cables, plaited or not (heading No. 59.04);

(*b*) Footwear or headgear or parts thereof falling within Chapter 64 or 65;

(*c*) Vehicles and bodies for vehicles, of basketware (Chapter 87); or

(*d*) Furniture or parts thereof (Chapter 94).

3. For the purposes of heading No. 46.02, " plaiting materials bound together in parallel strands " means plaiting materials placed side by side and bound together, in the form of sheets, whether the binding materials are of spun textile fibre or not.

| | Rate of Import Duty *(if any)* | |
Tariff Heading	*Full*	*Commonwealth* (C) *E.F.T.A.* (E)
46.01 Plaits and similar products of plaiting materials, for all uses, whether or not assembled into strips	8%	—
46.02 Plaiting materials (other than products falling within heading No. 46.01) bound together in parallel strands or woven, in sheet form, including matting, mats and screens; straw envelopes for bottles:		
(A) Mats and matting, of rush, reed, straw or grass	4%	—
(B) Woven material and mats and matting, of raffia	8%	—
(C) Straw envelopes for bottles	8%	—
(D) Other	16%	—
46.03 Basketwork, wickerwork and other articles of plaiting materials, made directly to shape; articles made up from goods falling within heading No. 46.01 or 46.02; articles of loofah:		
(A) Baskets of osier, willow, cane or wicker	30%	—
(B) Handbags, shopping bags and similar receptacles of sisal	13%	—
(C) Baskets not comprised in subheading (A) above and shopping bags and similar receptacles not comprised in subheading (B) above	10%	—
(D) Mats and matting, of rush, reed, straw or grass	4%	—
(E) Other	16%	—

SECTION X

PAPER-MAKING MATERIAL; PAPER AND PAPERBOARD AND ARTICLES THEREOF

Chapter 47

Paper-making Material

Tariff Heading	Rate of Import Duty (if any)	
	Full	Commonwealth (C) E.F.T.A. (E)
47.01 Pulp derived by mechanical or chemical means from any fibrous vegetable material: (A) Wood pulp; straw pulp, bleached; bagasse pulp; pulp of esparto, albardin grass or diss (vine-tie) grass; reed or rush pulp, bleached	—	—
(B) Bleached fibrous hydroxyethylated cotton linter pulp, which is insoluble in water and in which the ethylene oxide which is combined with the cotton linters amounts to not less than 1·2 per cent. and not more than 7·5 per cent. by weight of the finished product	—	—
(C) Other	6%	—
47.02 Waste paper and paperboard; scrap articles of paper or of paperboard, fit only for use in paper-making	10%	—

Chapter 48

Paper and Paperboard; Articles of Paper Pulp, of Paper or of Paperboard

Notes

1. This Chapter does not cover:

   (a) Stamping foils of heading No. 32.09;

   (b) Perfume and cosmetic papers (heading No. 33.06);

   (c) Soap papers (heading No. 34.01), papers impregnated or coated with deterger (heading No. 34.02) and cellulose wadding impregnated with polishes, creams similar preparations (heading No. 34.05);

   (d) Paper or paperboard, sensitised (heading No. 37.03);

   (e) Paper-reinforced stratified artificial plastic sheeting (headings Nos. 39.01 to 39.06), vulcanised fibre (heading No. 39.03), or articles of such materials (heading No. 39.07

   (f) Goods falling within heading No. 42.02 (for example, travel goods);

   (g) Articles falling within any heading in Chapter 46 (manufactures of plaiting material

   (h) Paper yarn or textile articles of paper yarn (Section XI);

   (ij) Abrasive paper (heading No. 68.06) or paper-backed mica splittings (heading N 68.15) (paper coated with mica powder is, however, to be classified in heading No. 48.07

   (k) Paper-backed metal foil (Section XV);

   (l) Perforated paper or paperboard for musical instruments (heading No. 92.10); or

   (m) Goods falling within any heading in Chapter 97 (for example, toys, games and spor requisites) or Chapter 98 (for example, buttons).

2. Subject to the provisions of Note 3, headings Nos. 48.01 and 48.02 are to be taken include paper and paperboard which have been subjected to calendering, super-calenderin glazing or similar finishing, including tub-sizing or false water-marking and also to pap and paperboard coloured or marbled throughout the mass by any method. They do n apply to paper or paperboard which has been further processed, for example, by coating impregnation.

3. Paper or paperboard answering to a description in two or more of the headings No 48.01 to 48.07 is to be classified under that one of such headings which occurs latest in th Chapter.

4. Headings Nos. 48.01 to 48.07 are to be taken not to apply to paper, paperboard cellulose wadding:

   (a) In strips or rolls of a width not exceeding fifteen centimetres; or

   (b) In rectangular sheets (unfolded if necessary) of which no side exceeds thirty-si centimetres; or

   (c) Cut into shapes other than rectangular shapes.

Except that hand-made paper in any size or shape as made directly and having all its edg deckled remains classified, subject to the provisions of Note 3, within heading No. 48.0

5. For the purposes of heading No. 48.11 " wallpaper and lincrusta " are to be taken apply only to:

   (a) Paper in rolls, suitable for wall or ceiling decoration, being:

      (i) Paper with one or with two margins, with or without guide marks; or

      (ii) Paper without margins, surface-coloured or design-printed, coated or embosse of a width not exceeding sixty centimetres;

   (b) Borders, friezes and corners of paper, of a kind used for wall or ceiling decoratio

6. Heading No. 48.15 is to be taken to apply, *inter alia*, to paper wool, paper strip (wheth or not folded or coated) of a kind used for plaiting, and to toilet paper in rolls or packet but not to the articles mentioned in Note 7.

7. Heading No. 48.21 is to be taken to apply, *inter alia*, to cards for statistical machines, erforated paper and paperboard cards for Jacquard and similar machines, paper lace, shelf lging, paper tablecloths, serviettes and handkerchiefs, paper gaskets, moulded or pressed oods of wood pulp, and dress patterns.

8. Paper, paperboard and cellulose wadding, and articles thereof, printed with characters pictures which are not merely incidental to the primary use of the goods are regarded printed matter falling within Chapter 49.

Tariff Heading	Rate of Import Duty (*if any*)	
	Full	Commonwealth (C E.F.T.A. (E)
I. Paper and paperboard, in rolls or in sheets		
.01 Paper and paperboard (including cellulose wadding), machine-made, in rolls or sheets:		
(A) Weighing more than 220 grammes per square metre:		
(1) Board manufactured wholly of unbleached, undyed sulphate cel- lulose fibre, in reels	$11\frac{1}{2}\%$	—
(2) Strawboard, being board con- taining not less than 90 per cent. by weight of unbleached cereal straw pulp	$13\frac{1}{2}\%$	—
(3) Other	19%	—
(B) Weighing not more than 220 grammes per square metre:		
(1) Paper manufactured wholly of bleached or unbleached sulphate cellulose fibre	12%	—
(2) Machine glazed paper (excluding paper comprised in subheading (1) above and fully bleached white poster paper)	13%	—
(3) Other:		
(*a*) Tissue paper	16%	—
(*b*) Printing paper	16%	—
(*c*) Writing or duplicating paper in sheets	16%	—
(*d*) Strawpaper, being paper manu- factured entirely from unbleach- ed cereal straw pulp	16%	—
(*e*) Newsprint, that is to say, paper in rolls, having a water absorb- ency when tested by the one- minute Cobb method of not less than 45 grammes per square metre, containing not less than 70 per cent. of mechanical wood pulp and of a weight not less than 48 nor more than 62 grammes per square metre	—	—
(*f*) Other	19%	—

Tariff Heading	Rate of Import Duty (if any)	
	Full	Commonwealth (C) E.F.T.A. (E)
48.02 Hand-made paper and paperboard:		
(A) Writing or printing paper in sheets measuring more than 36 centimetres in either length or breadth	16%	—
(B) Tissue paper	16%	—
(C) Other	19%	—
48.03 Parchment or greaseproof paper and paperboard, and imitations thereof, and glazed transparent paper, in rolls or sheets:		
(A) Greaseproof paper and imitation greaseproof paper	13%	—
(B) Other	19%	—
48.04 Composite paper or paperboard (made by sticking flat layers together with an adhesive), not surface-coated or impregnated, whether or not internally reinforced, in rolls or sheets:		
(A) Weighing more than 220 grammes per square metre and, apart from adhesive, consisting wholly of strawboards containing not less than 90 per cent. by weight of unbleached cereal straw pulp	13½%	—
(B) Other	19%	—
48.05 Paper and paperboard, corrugated (with or without flat surface sheets), creped, crinkled, embossed or perforated, in rolls or sheets:		
(A) Of a weight when fully extended equivalent to not more than 220 grammes per square metre, not being corrugated with flat surface sheets:		
(1) Paper manufactured wholly of bleached or unbleached sulphate cellulose fibre	12%	—
(2) Machine glazed paper (excluding paper comprised in subheading (1) above and fully bleached white poster paper)	13%	—
(3) Other:		
(a) Tissue paper	16%	—
(b) Printing paper	16%	—
(c) Writing paper in sheets ...	16%	—
(d) Strawpaper, being paper manufactured entirely from unbleached cereal straw pulp	16%	—
(e) Greaseproof and imitation greaseproof paper	13%	—
(f) Other	19%	—

Tariff Heading	Rate of Import Duty (*if any*)	
	Full	*Commonwealth (C)* *E.F.T.A.* *(E)*
8.05 Paper and paperboards, etc.—*contd.*		
(B) Other:		
(1) Board manufactured wholly of unbleached, undyed sulphate cellulose fibre, in reels, not being corrugated with flat surface sheets	11½%	—
(2) Other	19%	—
8.06 Paper and paperboard, ruled, lined or squared, but not otherwise printed, in rolls or sheets:		
(A) Writing or duplicating paper in sheets	16%	—
(B) Printing paper	16%	—
(C) Other	19%	—
8.07 Paper and paperboard, impregnated, coated, surface-coloured, surface-decorated or printed (not being merely ruled, lined or squared and not constituting printed matter within Chapter 49), in rolls or sheets:		
(A) Weighing not more than 220 grammes per square metre:		
(1) Paper manufactured wholly of bleached or unbleached sulphate cellulose fibre	12%	—
(2) Machine glazed paper (excluding paper comprised in subheading (1) above and fully bleached white poster paper)	13%	—
(3) Other:		
(*a*) Tissue paper	16%	—
(*b*) Printing paper	16%	—
(*c*) Writing or duplicating paper in sheets	16%	—
(*d*) Strawpaper, being paper manufactured entirely from unbleached cereal straw pulp	16%	—
(*e*) Greaseproof and imitation greaseproof paper	13%	—
(*f*) Other	19%	—
(B) Weighing more than 220 grammes per square metre:		
(1) Board manufactured wholly of unbleached, undyed sulphate cellulose fibre, in reels, not being composite board	11½%	—
(2) Strawboard, being board containing not less than 90 per cent. by weight of unbleached cereal straw pulp	13½%	—
(3) Other	19%	—
8.08 Filter blocks, slabs and plates, of paper pulp	19%	—

Tariff Heading	Rate of Import Duty (if any)	
	Full	Commonwealth (C) E.F.T.A. (E
48.09 Building board of wood pulp or of vegetable fibre, whether or not bonded with natural or artificial resins or with similar binders	19%	—
II. Paper and paperboard cut to size or shape and articles of paper or paperboard		
48.10 Cigarette paper, cut to size, whether or not in the form of booklets or tubes	16%	—
48.11 Wallpaper and lincrusta; window transparencies of paper	16%	—
48.12 Floor coverings prepared on a base of paper or of paperboard, whether or not cut to size, with or without a coating of linoleum compound	13%	—
48.13 Carbon and other copying papers (including duplicator stencils) and transfer papers, cut to size, whether or not put up in boxes	19%	—
48.14 Writing blocks, envelopes, plain letter cards, plain postcards, correspondence cards; boxes, pouches, wallets and writing compendiums, of paper or paperboard, containing only an assortment of paper stationery	18%	—
48.15 Other paper and paperboard (including cellulose wadding), cut to size or shape: (A) Weighing not more than 220 grammes per square metre:		
(1) Toilet paper	19%	—
(2) Paper manufactured wholly of bleached or unbleached sulphate cellulose fibre, in strips, rolls or in square-cut or angle-cut sheets	12%	—
(3) Machine glazed paper (excluding paper comprised in subheadings (1) or (2) above and fully bleached white poster paper) in strips, rolls or in square-cut or angle-cut sheets	13%	—
(4) Greaseproof and imitation greaseproof paper in strips, rolls or in square-cut or angle-cut sheets	13%	—
(5) Other:		
(a) Tissue paper in strips, rolls or rectangular sheets	16%	—
(b) Writing or printing paper in parallelograms of which all sides exceed 36 centimetres	16%	—

Tariff Heading	Rate of Import Duty (if any)	
	Full	Commonwealth (C) E.F.T.A. (E)

48.15 Other paper and paperboard etc.—*contd.*
  (A) (5) Other—*contd.*
      (*c*) Strawpaper, being paper manu-
          factured entirely from un-
          bleached cereal straw pulp
      (*d*) Other ...   .
  (B) Weighing more than 220 grammes
      per square metre
	
	16%
	
	19%
	19%
		
		—
		
		—
		—

48.16 Boxes, bags and other packing containers, of paper or paperboard	16½%	—

**48.17 Box files, letter trays, storage boxes and
  similar articles, of paper or paperboard,
  of a kind commonly used in offices, shops
  and the like**
	16½%	—

**48.18 Registers, exercise books, note books,
  memorandum blocks, order books, receipt
  books, diaries, blotting-pads, binders (loose-
  leaf or other), file covers and other stationery
  of paper or paperboard; sample and other
  albums and book covers, of paper or
  paperboard:**
  (A) Printed book covers (other than trade
      advertising material) for books of a
      kind falling within heading No. 49.01,
      49.03, 49.04 or 49.05
  (B) Printed forms ...   .
  (C) Trade advertising material:
      (1) Material the primary purpose of
          which is to stimulate travel out-
          side the United Kingdom
      (2) Other   ...   .
  (D) Looseleaf binders of the ring, prong
      or post type
  (E) Other ...   .
	
	—
	
	—
	
	—
	
	13¼%
	14½%
	
	16%
		
		—
		
		—
		
		—
		
		—
		—
		
		—

48.19 Paper or paperboard labels, whether or not printed or gummed	19%	—

**48.20 Bobbins, spools, cops and similar supports
  of paper pulp, paper or paperboard
  (whether or not perforated or hardened)**
	16%	—

**48.21 Other articles of paper pulp, paper, paper-
  board or cellulose wadding:**
  (A) Paper dress patterns, including the
      paper envelopes in which they are
      enclosed
  (B) Face and hand towels, made wholly
      of paper weighing not less than 24
      grammes per square metre
	
	10%
	
	10%
		
		—
		
		—

Tariff Heading	Rate of Import Duty (*if any*)	
	Full	*Commonwealth* (C) *E.F.T.A.* (E)
48.21 Other articles of paper pulp, paper, paperboard or cellulose wadding—*contd.*		
(C) Serviettes and handkerchiefs, not printed, of an area not exceeding 2,580 square centimetres, made wholly of paper weighing not less than 17 grammes per square metre	10%	—
(D) Sanitary napkins of cellulose wadding	10%	—
(E) Cards, tapes and other articles on which information has been recorded by means of perforated holes and which are for use in statistical and other machines (but not including articles for use in Jacquard and similar machines)	—	—
(F) Other	19%	—

Chapter 49

*Printed Books, Newspapers, Pictures and other Products of the Printing Industry;
Manuscripts, Typescripts and Plans*

Notes

1. This Chapter does not cover:

(a) Paper, paperboard, or cellulose wadding, or articles thereof, in which printing is merely incidental to their primary use (Chapter 48);

(b) Playing cards or other goods falling within any heading in Chapter 97; or

(c) Original engravings, prints or lithographs (heading No. 99.02), postage, revenue or similar stamps falling within heading No. 99.04, antiques of an age exceeding 100 years or other articles falling within any heading in Chapter 99.

2. Newspapers, journals and periodicals which are bound otherwise than in paper, and sets of newspapers, journals or periodicals comprising more than one number under a single cover are to be treated as falling within heading No. 49.01 and not within heading No. 49.02.

3. Heading No. 49.01 is to be extended to apply to:

(a) A collection of printed reproductions of, for example, works of art or drawings, with a relative text, put up with numbered pages in a form suitable for binding into one or more volumes;

(b) A pictorial supplement accompanying, and subsidiary to, a bound volume; and

(c) Printed parts of books or booklets, in the form of assembled or separate sheets or signatures, constituting the whole or a part of a complete work and designed for binding.

However, printed pictures or illustrations not bearing a text, whether in the form of signatures or separate sheets, fall in heading No. 49.11.

4. Headings Nos. 49.01 and 49.02 are to be taken not to apply to publications issued for advertising purposes by or for an advertiser named therein, or to publications which are primarily devoted to advertising (including tourist propaganda). Such publications are to be taken as falling within heading No. 49.11.

5. For the purposes of heading No. 49.03, the expression " children's picture books " means books for children in which the pictures form the principal interest and the text is subsidiary.

6. For the purposes of heading No. 49.06, the expression " manuscripts and typescripts " is to be taken to extend to carbon copies or copies on sensitised paper of manuscripts and typescripts. References in this Chapter to printed matter of any kind include references to any matter of that kind which is reproduced by means of a duplicating machine.

7. For the purposes of heading No. 49.09, the expression " picture postcards " means cards consisting essentially of an illustration and bearing printed indications of their use.

Tariff Heading	Rate of Import Duty (if any)	
	Full	Commonwealth (C) E.F.T.A. (E)
9.01 Printed books, booklets, brochures, pamphlets and leaflets	—	—
9.02 Newspapers, journals and periodicals, whether or not illustrated	—	—

Tariff Heading	Rate of Import Duty (if any)	
	Full	Commonwealth (C E.F.T.A. (E
49.03 Children's picture books and painting books	—	—
49.04 Music, printed or in manuscript, whether or not bound or illustrated	—	—
49.05 Maps and hydrographic and similar charts of all kinds, including atlases, wall maps and topographical plans, printed; printed globes (terrestrial or celestial)	—	—
49.06 Plans and drawings, for industrial, architectural, engineering, commercial or similar purposes, whether original or reproductions on sensitised paper; manuscripts and typescripts	—	—
49.07 Unused postage, revenue and similar stamps of current or new issue in the country to which they are destined; paper impressed with such stamps; banknotes, stock, share and bond certificates and similar documents of title; cheque books and cheque forms	—	—
49.08 Transfers	16%	—
49.09 Picture postcards and pictorial greeting cards, printed, with or without trimmings: (A) Trade advertising material the primary purpose of which is to stimulate travel outside the United Kingdom (B) Other	— 13½%	— —

49.10 Calendars of any kind, of paper or paperboard, including calendar blocks:
(A) Trade advertising material:
  (1) Material the primary purpose of which is to stimulate travel outside the United Kingdom
  (2) Other   ...   .
(B) Other ...   .
	
	—
	
	12%
	16%
		
		—
		
		—
		—

49.11 Other printed matter, including printed pictures and photographs: (A) Trade advertising material, the following: (1) Catalogues and lists of books and publications offered for sale by publishers or booksellers established outside the United Kingdom	 —	 —

Tariff Heading	Rate of Import Duty (*if any*)	
	Full	*Commonwealth* (C) *E.F.T.A.* (E)
49.11 Other printed matter, etc.—*contd.*		
(A) Trade advertising material, etc.—*contd.*		
(2) Publications, illustrated or not, the primary purpose of which is to stimulate study or travel outside the United Kingdom, or to advertise exhibitions held outside the United Kingdom	—	—
(3) Other catalogues, lists, books, publications and documents:		
(*a*) Imported either in a packet not exceeding 2¼ lb. in gross weight or in a packet containing not more than one copy of any catalogue, list, book, publication or document, being in either case a postal packet or a packet which does not form part of a larger consignment	—	—
(*b*) Other	13½%	—
(4) Printed parts of catalogues, lists, books, publications and documents	13½%	—
(B) Less than full-size reproductions of articles falling within headings Nos. 49.01, 49.02, 49.03, 49.04, 49.05, 49.06, 49.07 or subheadings 49.09 (A), 49.10 (A) (1), 49.11 (A) (1), 49.11 (A) (2), 49.11 (C) (2) (*a*), 49.11 (C) (2) (*b*)	—	—
(C) Other:		
(1) Photographic prints:		
(*a*) Imported in a packet not exceeding 8 ounces in gross weight which does not form part of a larger consignment	—	—
(*b*) Other	8%	—
(2) Other printed matter:		
(*a*) Parts of books or booklets in the form of printed pictures or illustrations not bearing a text	—	—
(*b*) Printed documents, printed diagrams, and printed architectural, engineering and similar industrial designs or plans, not being trade advertising material	—	—
(*c*) Other	16½%	—

SECTION XI

TEXTILES AND TEXTILE ARTICLES

Notes

1. This Section does not cover:

(a) Animal brush making bristles or hair (heading No. 05.02); horsehair or horsehair waste (heading No. 05.03);

(b) Human hair or articles of human hair (heading No. 05.01, 67.03 or 67.04), except straining cloth of a kind commonly used in oil presses and the like (heading No. 59.17);

(c) Vegetable materials falling within Chapter 14;

(d) Asbestos (heading No. 25.24) or articles of asbestos (heading No. 68.13 or 68.14);

(e) Articles falling within heading No. 30.04 or 30.05 (for example, wadding, gauze bandages and similar articles for medical or surgical purposes, sterile surgical suture materials);

(f) Sensitised textile fabric (heading No. 37.03);

(g) Monofil of which any cross-sectional dimension exceeds 1 millimetre and strip (artificial straw and the like) of a width exceeding 5 millimetres, of artificial plastic material (Chapter 39) or plaits or fabrics of such monofil or strip (Chapter 46);

(h) Woven textile fabrics, felt or bonded fibre fabrics, impregnated, coated, covered or laminated with rubber, and articles thereof, falling within Chapter 40;

(ij) Skins with their wool on (Chapter 41 or 43) or articles of furskin, artificial fur or articles thereof, falling within heading No. 43.03 or 43.04;

(k) Articles falling within heading No. 42.01 or 42.02 (saddlery, harness, travel goods, haversacks, handbags and the like);

(l) Cellulose wadding (Chapter 48);

(m) Footwear or parts of footwear, gaiters or leggings or similar articles classified in Chapter 64;

(n) Headgear or parts thereof falling within Chapter 65;

(o) Hair nets of any kind (heading No. 65.05 or 67.04, as the case may be);

(p) Goods falling within Chapter 67;

(q) Abrasive-coated threads, cords or fabric (heading No. 68.06);

(r) Glass fibre or articles of glass fibre, other than embroidery with glass thread on a visible ground of fabric (Chapter 70);

(s) Articles falling within Chapter 94 (furniture and bedding); or

(t) Articles falling within Chapter 97 (toys, games and sports requisites).

2. (A) Goods classifiable in any heading in Chapters 50 to 57 and of a mixture of two or more different textile materials are to be classified according to the following rules:

(a) Goods containing more than 10 per cent. by weight of silk, noil or other waste silk or any combination thereof are to be classified in Chapter 50, and, for the purposes of classification in that Chapter, as if consisting wholly of that one of those materials which predominates in weight;

(b) All other goods are to be classified as if consisting wholly of that one textile material which predominates in weight over any other single textile material.

(B) For the purposes of the above rules:

(a) Metallised yarn is to be treated as a single textile material and its weight is to be taken as the aggregate of the weight of the textile and metal components, and, for the classification of woven fabrics, metal thread is to be regarded as a textile material;

(b) Where a heading refers to a particular form of a textile material (for example, carded sheep's or lambs' wool), that form is to be treated as a single textile material. However, where a heading refers to two or more textile materials (or different forms of the same textile material), all those materials are to be treated as a single textile material;

(c) Except as provided in (B) (a), the weight of constituents other than textile material is not to be included in the weight of the goods.

(C) The provisions of paragraphs (A) and (B) above are to be applied also to the yarns referred to in Notes 3 and 4 below.

3. (A) For the purposes of this Section, and subject to the exceptions in paragraph (B) below, yarns (single, multiple or cabled) of the following descriptions are to be treated as twine, cordage, ropes and cables ":

(a) Of silk, noil or other waste silk, or man-made fibres described in Note 1 (b) to Chapter 51 (including yarn of two or more monofil of Chapter 51), of a weight exceeding 2 grammes per metre (18,000 denier);

(b) Of man-made fibres described in Note 1 (a) to Chapter 51 (including yarn of two or more monofil of Chapter 51), of a weight exceeding 1 gramme per metre (9,000 denier);

(c) Of true hemp or flax:

    (i) Polished or glazed, of which the length per kilogram, multiplied by the number of constituent strands, is less than 7,000 metres;

    (ii) Not polished or glazed and of a weight exceeding 2 grammes per metre;

(d) Of coir, consisting of three or more plies;

(e) Of other vegetable fibres, of a weight exceeding 2 grammes per metre; or

(f) Reinforced with metal.

(B) Exceptions:

(a) Yarn of sheep's or lambs' wool or other animal hair and paper yarn, other than yarn reinforced with metal;

(b) Continuous filament tow of man-made fibres and man-made fibres in slivers or rovings;

(c) Silk worm gut, imitation catgut of silk or of man-made fibres, and monofil of Chapter 51;

(d) Metallised yarn, not being yarn reinforced with metal; and

(e) Chenille yarn and gimped yarn.

4. (A) For the purposes of Chapters 50, 51, 53, 54, 55 and 56, the expression " put up or retail sale " in relation to yarn means, subject to the exceptions in paragraph (B) below, yarn put up:

(a) In balls or on cards, reels, tubes or similar supports, of a weight (including support) not exceeding:

    (i) 200 grammes in the case of flax and ramie;

    (ii) 85 grammes in the case of silk, noil or other waste silk, and man-made fibres (continuous); or

    (iii) 125 grammes in other cases;

(b) In hanks or skeins of a weight not exceeding:

    (i) 85 grammes in the case of silk, noil or other waste silk, and man-made fibres (continuous); or

    (ii) 125 grammes in other cases;

(c) In hanks or skeins comprising several smaller hanks or skeins separated by dividing threads which render them independent one of the other, each of uniform weight not exceeding:

    (i) 85 grammes in the case of silk, noil or other waste silk, and man-made fibres (continuous); or

    (ii) 125 grammes in other cases.

(B) Exceptions:

(a) Single yarn of any textile material, except:

    (i) Single yarn of sheep's or lambs' wool or of fine animal hair, unbleached; and

    (ii) Single yarn of sheep's or lambs' wool or of fine animal hair, bleached, dyed or printed, of a length less than 2,000 metres per kilogram;

(b) Multiple or cabled yarn, unbleached:

    (i) Of silk, noil or other waste silk, however put up; or

    (ii) Of other textile material except sheep's or lambs' wool or fine animal hair, in hanks or skeins;

(c) Multiple or cabled yarn of silk, noil or other waste silk, bleached, dyed or printed of a length not less than 75,000 metres per kilogram, measured multiple; and

(d) Single, multiple or cabled yarn of any textile material:

    (i) In cross-reeled hanks or skeins; or

    (ii) Put up on supports indicating their use in the textile industry (for example, cops, twisting mill tubes, pirns, conical bobbins or spindles).

5. (a) For the purposes of heading No. 55.07, " gauze " means a fabric with a warp composed wholly or in part of standing or ground threads and crossing or doup threads which cross the standing or ground threads making a half turn, a complete turn or more to form loops through which weft threads pass.

(b) For the purposes of heading No. 58.08, " plain " means consisting solely of a single series of regular meshes of the same shape or size without any pattern or filling-in of the meshes. In applying this definition no account is to be taken of any minor open spaces which are inherent in the formation of the meshes.

6. For the purposes of this Section, the expression " made up " means:

(a) Cut otherwise than into rectangles;

(b) Made and finished by weaving and ready for use (or merely needing separation by cutting dividing threads) and not requiring sewing or further fabrication (for example, certain dusters, towels, table cloths, scarf squares and blankets);

(c) Hemmed or with rolled edges (except fabrics in the piece which have been cut from wider pieces and hemmed or rolled merely to prevent unravelling), or with a knotted fringe at any of the edges;

(d) Cut to size and having undergone a process of drawn thread work;

(e) Assembled by sewing, gumming or otherwise (other than piece goods consisting of two or more lengths of identical material joined end to end and piece goods composed of two or more fabrics assembled in layers, whether or not padded).

7. The headings of Chapters 50 to 57 and, except where the context otherwise requires, the headings of Chapters 58 to 60, are to be taken not to apply to goods made up within the meaning of Note 6 above. Chapters 50 to 57 are to be taken not to apply to goods falling within Chapter 58 or 59.

8. Any import duty at a rate fixed by reference to the weight of any silk or man-made fibres is to be calculated on the weight inclusive of any loading or dressing, but exclusive of any waterproofing; and in the case of goods containing both silk and man-made fibres, or other fibres in addition to silk or man-made fibres, the total weight of loading or dressing in the goods is to be apportioned between the different types of fibre in the goods according to their respective weights.

Chapter 50

Silk and Waste Silk

Tariff Heading	Rate of Import Duty (*if any*)	
	Full	*Commonwealth* (C) *E.F.T.A.* (E)
50.01 Silk-worm cocoons suitable for reeling ...	—	—
.02 Raw silk (not thrown)	—	—
50.03 Silk waste (including cocoons unsuitable for reeling, silk noils and pulled or garnetted rags):		
(A) Wholly of silk	—	—
(B) Other:		
(1) Not carded or combed:		
(*a*) In which the textile material which predominates in weight is man-made fibre	16%	C 85% of the full rate E —
(*b*) Other	—	—
(2) Carded or combed:		
(*a*) Containing man-made fibres	10%	C 85% of the full rate E —
(*b*) Not containing man-made fibres	10%	—
50.04 Silk yarn, other than yarn of noil or other waste silk, not put up for retail sale:		
(A) Containing more than 50 per cent. by weight of man-made fibres	19% or 7½d. per lb., whichever is the greater	C 85% of the full rate E —
(B) Other	19%	C 85% of the full rate E —
50.05 Yarn spun from silk waste other than noil, not put up for retail sale:		
(A) Containing more than 50 per cent. by weight of man-made fibres	19% or 7½d. per lb., whichever is the greater	C 85% of the full rate E —
(B) Other	19%	C 85% of the full rate E —
50.06 Yarn spun from noil silk, not put up for retail sale:		
(A) Containing more than 50 per cent. by weight of man-made fibres	19% or 7½d. per lb., whichever is the greater	C 85% of the full rate E —
(B) Other	19%	C 85% of the full rate E —
50.07 Silk yarn and yarn spun from noil or other waste silk, put up for retail sale:		
(A) Containing more than 50 per cent. by weight of man-made fibres	19% or 7½d. per lb., whichever is the greater	C 85% of the full rate E —
(B) Other	19%	C 85% of the full rate E —

Tariff Heading	Rate of Import Duty (if any)	
	Full	*Commonwealth* (C) *E.F.T.A.* (E)
50.08 Silk-worm gut; imitation catgut of silk:		
(A) Silk-worm gut	—	—
(B) Imitation catgut	19% or 7½d. per lb., whichever is the greater	C 85% of the full rate E —
50.09 Woven fabrics of silk or of waste silk other than noil:		
(A) Containing more than 50 per cent. by weight of silk or of silk and man-made fibres	20½% or 5d. per square yard, whichever is the greater, plus 1s. 4d. per lb. of silk plus 5d. per lb. of any man-made fibres	C 85% of the full rate E —
(B) Other	20½% plus 1s. 4d. per lb. of silk plus 5d. per lb. of any man-made fibres	C 85% of the full rate E —
50.10 Woven fabrics of noil silk:		
(A) Containing more than 50 per cent. by weight of silk or of silk and man-made fibres	20½% or 5d. per square yard, whichever is the greater, plus 1s. 4d. per lb. of silk plus 5d. per lb. of any man-made fibres	C 85% of the full rate E —
(B) Other	20½% plus 1s. 4d. per lb. of silk plus 5d. per lb. of any man-made fibres	C 85% of the full rate E —

Chapter 51

Man-made Fibres (Continuous)

Notes

1. Throughout this Schedule, the term " man-made fibres " means fibres or filaments of organic polymers produced by manufacturing processes, either:

(a) By polymerisation or condensation of organic monomers, for example, polyamides, polyesters, polyurethanes and polyvinyl derivatives; or

(b) By chemical transformation of natural organic polymers (such as cellulose, casein, proteins and algae), for example, viscose rayon, cuprammonium rayon (cupra), cellulose acetate and alginates.

2. Heading No. 51.01 is to be taken not to apply to continuous filament tow of man-made fibres falling within Chapter 56.

3. The expression " yarn of man-made fibres (continuous) " is to be taken not to apply to yarn (known as " ruptured filament yarn ") of which the majority of the filaments have been ruptured by passage through rollers or other devices (Chapter 56).

4. Monofil of man-made fibre materials of which no cross-sectional dimension exceeds millimetre is to be classified in heading No. 51.01 when of a weight less than $6 \cdot 6$ milligrams per metre (60 denier) and in heading No. 51.02 in other cases. Monofil of which any cross-sectional dimension exceeds 1 millimetre is to be classified in Chapter 39.

Strip (artificial straw and the like) of man-made fibre materials is to be classified in heading No. 51.02 when of a width not exceeding 5 millimetres and in Chapter 39 in other cases.

Tariff Heading	Rate of Import Duty (if any)	
	Full	Commonwealth (C) E.F.T.A. (E)
51.01 Yarn of man-made fibres (continuous), not put up for retail sale	14½% plus 4½d. per lb. of man-made fibres and of any silk, or 10d. per lb., whichever is the greater	C 85% of the full rate E —
51.02 Monofil, strip (artificial straw and the like) and imitation catgut, of man-made fibre materials	14½% plus 4½d. per lb., or 10d. per lb., whichever is the greater	C 85% of the full rate E —
51.03 Yarn of man-made fibres (continuous), put up for retail sale	14½% plus 4½d. per lb. of man-made fibres and of any silk, or 10d. per lb., whichever is the greater	C 85% of the full rate E —
51.04 Woven fabrics of man-made fibres (continuous), including woven fabrics of monofil or strip of heading No. 51.01 or 51.02: (A) Containing more than 75 per cent. by weight of man-made fibres or of man-made fibres and silk	17½% plus 3½d. per lb. of man-made fibres and of any silk, or 7d. per square yard, whichever is the greater	C 85% of the full rate E —

Tariff Heading	Rate of Import Duty (if any)	
	Full	Commonwealth (C) E.F.T.A. (E)
51.04 Woven fabrics of man-made fibres (continuous), etc.—*contd.* (B) Other ...　...　...　...　...	17½% plus 5d. per lb. of man-made fibres and of any silk, or 5d. per square yard, whichever is the greater	C 85% of the full rate E —

Chapter 52

Metallised Textiles

Tariff Heading	Rate of Import Duty (*if any*)	
	Full	*Commonwealth (C)* *E.F.T.A.* (E)
52.01 Metallised yarn, being textile yarn spun with metal or covered with metal by any process:		
(A) Containing silk or man-made fibres ...	14½% plus 4½d. per lb. of silk and of man-made fibres	C 85% of the full rate
(B) Not containing silk or man-made fibres	12½%	E —
52.02 Woven fabrics of metal thread or of metallised yarn, of a kind used in articles of apparel, as furnishing fabrics or the like:		
(A) Containing silk or man-made fibres	17½% plus 5d. per lb. of silk and of man-made fibres	C 85% of the full rate
(B) Not containing silk or man-made fibres	17½%	E —

Chapter 53

Wool and other Animal Hair

Note

In this Schedule, the expression "fine animal hair" means hair of alpaca, llama, vicuna, yak, camel, Angora, Tibetan, Kashmir and similar goats (but not common goats), rabbit (including Angora rabbit), hare, beaver, nutria and musk rat.

Tariff Heading	Rate of Import Duty (if any)	
	Full	*Commonwealth (C) E.F.T.A.* (E)
53.01 Sheep's or lambs' wool, not carded or combed:		
(A) Raw, cleaned, scoured or carbonised, but not otherwise worked	—	—
(B) Other	8%	—
53.02 Other animal hair (fine or coarse), not carded or combed:		
(A) Raw, cleaned, scoured or carbonised, but not otherwise worked	—	—
(B) Other:		
(1) Hatters' fur	—	—
(2) Other	8%	—
53.03 Waste of sheep's or lambs' wool or of other animal hair (fine or coarse), not pulled or garnetted:		
(A) Containing more than 33⅓ per cent. by weight of man-made fibres	12%	C 85% of the full rate
		E
(B) Other	—	—
53.04 Waste of sheep's or lambs' wool or of other animal hair (fine or coarse), pulled or garnetted (including pulled or garnetted rags):		
(A) Containing more than 33⅓ per cent. by weight of man-made fibres	12%	C 85% of the full rate
		E —
(B) Other	5%	—
53.05 Sheep's or lambs' wool or other animal hair (fine or coarse), carded or combed:		
(A) Containing man-made fibres ...	10%	C 85% of the full rate
		E
(B) Not containing man-made fibres ...	10%	—
53.06 Yarn of carded sheep's or lambs' wool (woollen yarn), not put up for retail sale:		
(A) Containing silk or man-made fibres	14½% plus 4½d. per lb. of silk and of man-made fibres	C 85% of the full rate
		E

Tariff Heading	Rate of Import Duty (if any)	
	Full	Commonwealth (C) E.F.T.A. (E)
53.06 Yarn of carded sheep's or lambs' wool, etc.—contd.		
(B) Not containing silk or man-made fibres	7½%	—
53.07 Yarn of combed sheep's or lambs' wool (worsted yarn), not put up for retail sale:		
(A) Containing silk or man-made fibres	14½% plus 4½d. per lb. of silk and of man-made fibres	C 85% of the full rate E —
(B) Not containing silk or man-made fibres	7½%	—
53.08 Yarn of fine animal hair (carded or combed), not put up for retail sale:		
(A) Containing silk or man-made fibres	14½% plus 4½d. per lb. of silk and of man-made fibres	C 85% of the full rate E —
(B) Not containing silk or man-made fibres	7½%	—
53.09 Yarn of horsehair or of other coarse animal hair, not put up for retail sale:		
(A) Containing silk or man-made fibres	14½% plus 4½d. per lb. of silk and of man-made fibres	C 85% of the full rate E —
(B) Not containing silk or man-made fibres	7½%	—
53.10 Yarn of sheep's or lambs' wool, of horsehair or of other animal hair (fine or coarse), put up for retail sale:		
(A) Containing silk or man-made fibres	14½% plus 4½d. per lb. of silk and of man-made fibres	C 85% of the full rate E —
(B) Not containing silk or man-made fibres	7½%	—
53.11 Woven fabrics of sheep's or lambs' wool or of fine animal hair:		
(A) Containing silk or man-made fibres	17½% plus 5d. per lb. of man-made fibres and of silk	C 85% of the full rate E —
(B) Not containing silk or man-made fibres	17½%	—

	Rate of Import Duty (if any)	
Tariff Heading	*Full*	*Commonwealth (C)* *E.F.T.A.* (E)
53.12 Woven fabrics of coarse animal hair other than horsehair:		
(A) Containing silk or man-made fibres	17½% plus 5d. per lb. of man-made fibres and of silk	C 85% of the full rate E —
(B) Not containing silk or man-made fibres	17½%	—
53.13 Woven fabrics of horsehair:		
(A) Containing silk or man-made fibres	17½% plus 5d. per lb. of man-made fibres and of silk	C 85% of the full rate E —
(B) Not containing silk or man-made fibres	17½%	—

Chapter 54

Flax and Ramie

Tariff Heading	Rate of Import Duty (if any)	
	Full	Commonwealth (C) E.F.T.A. (E)
54.01 Flax, raw or processed but not spun; flax tow and waste (including pulled or garnetted rags): (A) Flax, flax tow and flax waste, not hackled, carded or combed: (1) Containing more than 33⅓ per cent. by weight of man-made fibres	12%	C 85% of the full rate E —
(2) Other	—	—
(B) Other: (1) Containing man-made fibres ...	8%	C 85% of the full rate E —
(2) Not containing man-made fibres...	8%	—
54.02 Ramie, raw or processed but not spun; ramie noils and waste (including pulled or garnetted rags): (A) Ramie, ramie noils and ramie waste, not carded or combed: (1) Containing more than 33⅓ per cent. by weight of man-made fibres	12%	C 85% of the full rate E —
(2) Other	—	—
(B) Other: (1) Containing man-made fibres ...	8%	C 85% of the full rate E —
(2) Not containing man-made fibres...	8%	—
54.03 Flax or ramie yarn, not put up for retail sale: (A) Containing silk or man-made fibres...	14½% plus 4½d. per lb. of silk and of man-made fibres	C 85% of the full rate E —
(B) Not containing silk or man-made fibres: (1) Of flax, polished or glazed ...	10%	—
(2) Other	7½%	—
54.04 Flax or ramie yarn, put up for retail sale: (A) Containing silk or man-made fibres...	14½% plus 4½d. per lb. of silk and of man-made fibres	C 85% of the full rate E —
(B) Not containing silk or man-made fibres: (1) Of flax, polished or glazed ...	10%	—
(2) Other	7½%	—

Tariff Heading	Rate of Import Duty (if any)	
	Full	Commonwealth (C) E.F.T.A. (E)
54.05 Woven fabrics of flax or of ramie: (A) Containing silk or man-made fibres	17½% plus 5d. per lb. of man-made fibres and of silk	C 85% of the full rate E —
(B) Not containing silk or man-made fibres	17½%	

Chapter 55

Cotton

Tariff Heading	Rate of Import Duty (*if any*)	
	Full	Commonwealth (*C*) E.F.T.A. (*E*)
55.01 Cotton, not carded or combed:		
(A) Not bleached or dyed...	—	—
(B) Bleached or dyed	8%	—
55.02 Cotton linters:		
(A) Unbleached	—	—
(B) Bleached	6%	—
55.03 Cotton waste (including pulled or garnetted rags), not carded or combed:		
(A) Containing more than 33⅓ per cent. by weight of man-made fibres	12%	C 85% of the full rate
		E —
(B) Other	—	—
55.04 Cotton, carded or combed:		
(A) Containing man-made fibres ...	8%	C 85% of the full rate
		E —
(B) Not containing man-made fibres ...	8%	—
55.05 Cotton yarn, not put up for retail sale:		
(A) Containing more than 5 per cent. by weight of silk, of man-made fibres, or of both together	14½% plus 4½d. per lb. of silk and of man-made fibres	C 85% of the full rate
		E —
(B) Other	7½%	—
55.06 Cotton yarn, put up for retail sale:		
(A) Containing more than 5 per cent. by weight of silk, of man-made fibres, or of both together	14½% plus 4½d. per lb. of silk and of man-made fibres	C 85% of the full rate
		E —
(B) Other	7½%	—
55.07 Cotton gauze:		
(A) Containing silk or man-made fibres	25%	C 20%
		E —
(B) Not containing silk or man-made fibres	25%	—

Tariff Heading	Rate of Import Duty (if any)	
	Full	Commonwealth (C) E.F.T.A. (E
55.08 Terry towelling and similar terry fabrics, of cotton:		
(A) Containing silk or man-made fibres	17½% plus 5d. per lb. of man-made fibres and of silk	C 85% of the fu rate E —
(B) Not containing silk or man-made fibres	17½%	—
55.09 Other woven fabrics of cotton:		
(A) Containing silk or man-made fibres	17½% plus 5d. per lb. of man-made fibres and of silk	C 85% of the fu rate E —
(B) Not containing silk or man-made fibres	17½%	—

Chapter 56

Man-made Fibres (Discontinuous)

Note

Heading No. 56.02 is to be taken to apply only to continuous filament tow of man-made fibres, consisting of parallel filaments of a uniform length equal to the length of the tow, meeting the following specification:

(*a*) Length of tow exceeding 2 metres;

(*b*) Twist less than 5 turns per metre;

(*c*) Weight per filament less than 6·6 milligrams per metre (60 denier);

(*d*) In the case of filaments described in Note 1 (*a*) to Chapter 51, the tow must be drawn, that is to say, be incapable of being stretched by more than 100 per cent. of its length;

(*e*) Total weight of tow:

(i) In the case of filaments described in Note 1 (*b*) to Chapter 51, more than 0·5 grammes per metre (4,500 denier); or

(ii) In the case of filaments described in Note 1 (*a*) to Chapter 51, more than 1·66 grammes per metre (15,000 denier).

Tow of a length not exceeding 2 metres is to be classified in heading No. 56.01.

Tariff Heading	Rate of Import Duty (*if any*)	
	Full	*Commonwealth (C) E.F.T.A. (E)*
56.01 Man-made fibres (discontinuous), not carded, combed or otherwise prepared for spinning:		
(A) Of copolymerised vinyl chloride and vinyl acetate, in lengths not exceeding ¾ inch	—	—
(B) Man-made fibres produced by a process mentioned in Note 1 (*b*) to Chapter 51	5·9d. per lb.	C 85% of the full rate E —
(C) Other	7·8d. per lb.	C 85% of the full rate E —
56.02 Continuous filament tow for the manufacture of man-made fibres (discontinuous)	14½% plus 4½d. per lb., or 9d. per lb., whichever is the greater	C 85% of the full rate E —
56.03 Waste (including yarn waste and pulled or garnetted rags) of man-made fibres (continuous or discontinuous), not carded, combed or otherwise prepared for spinning	16%	C 85% of the full rate E —
56.04 Man-made fibres (discontinuous or waste), carded, combed or otherwise prepared for spinning	7d. per lb. of man-made fibres or 10%, whichever is the greater	C 85% of the full rate E —

Tariff Heading	Rate of Import Duty (if any)	
	Full	Commonwealth (C) E.F.T.A. (E)
56.05 Yarn of man-made fibres (discontinuous or waste), not put up for retail sale	14½% plus 4½d. per lb. of man-made fibres and of any silk, or 10d. per lb., whichever is the greater	C 85% of the full rate E —
56.06 Yarn of man-made fibres (discontinuous or waste), put up for retail sale	14½% plus 4½d. per lb. of man-made fibres and of any silk, or 10d. per lb., whichever is the greater	C 85% of the full rate E —
56.07 Woven fabrics of man-made fibres (discontinuous or waste):		
(A) Containing more than 75 per cent. by weight of man-made fibres or of man-made fibres and silk	17½% plus 3½d. per lb. of man-made fibres and of any silk, or 7d. per square yard, whichever is the greater	C 85% of the full rate E —
(B) Other	17½% plus 5d. per lb. of man-made fibres and of any silk, or 5d. per square yard, whichever is the greater	C 85% of the full rate E —

Chapter 57

Other Vegetable Textile Materials; Paper Yarn and Woven Fabrics of Paper Yarn

Tariff Heading	Rate of Import Duty (if any)	
	Full	Commonwealth (C) E.F.T.A. (E)
.01 True hemp (*Cannabis sativa*), **raw or processed but not spun; tow and waste of true hemp (including pulled or garnetted rags or ropes):**		
(A) True hemp, tow and waste of true hemp, not carded or combed:		
(1) Containing more than 33⅓ per cent. by weight of man-made fibres	12%	C 85% of the full rate E —
(2) Other	—	—
(B) Other:		
(1) Containing man-made fibres ...	8%	C 85% of the full rate E —
(2) Not containing man-made fibres...	8%	—
7.02 Manila hemp (abaca) (*Musa textilis*), **raw or processed but not spun; tow and waste of manila hemp (including pulled or garnetted rags or ropes):**		
(A) Manila hemp, tow and waste of manila hemp, not carded or combed	—	—
(B) Other	8%	—
7.03 Jute, raw or processed but not spun; tow and waste of jute (including pulled or garnetted rags or ropes):		
(A) Jute, tow and waste of jute, not carded or combed:		
(1) Containing more than 33⅓ per cent. by weight of man-made fibres	12%	C 85% of the full rate E —
(2) Other	—	—
(B) Other:		
(1) Containing man-made fibres ...	8%	C 85% of the full rate E —
(2) Not containing man-made fibres...	8%	—
7.04 Other vegetable textile fibres, raw or processed but not spun; waste of such fibres (including pulled or garnetted rags or ropes):		
(A) Coir fibre	10%	—
(B) Other:		
(1) Not carded or combed	—	—
(2) Carded or combed:		
(*a*) Containing man-made fibres ...	8%	C 85% of the full rate E —
(*b*) Not containing man-made fibres	8%	—

Tariff Heading	Rate of Import Duty (if any)		
	Full	Commonwealth (C E.F.T.A. (E	
57.05 Yarn of true hemp:			
(A) Containing man-made fibres ...	15% plus 4½d. per lb. of man-made fibres	C	85% of the f⸢ rate
		E	—
(B) Not containing man-made fibres:			
(1) Polished or glazed...	15%		—
(2) Other	7½%		—
57.06 Yarn of jute:			
(A) Containing man-made fibres ...	15% plus 4½d. per lb. of man-made fibres	C	85% of the f⸢ rate
		E	—
(B) Not containing man-made fibres:			
(1) Singles, not polished or glazed ...	10%		—
(2) Singles, polished or glazed; multiples, whether or not polished or glazed	15%		—
57.07 Yarn of other vegetable textile fibres:			
(A) Containing man-made fibres ...	15% plus 4½d. per lb. of man-made fibres	C	85% of the f⸢ rate
		E	—
(B) Not containing man-made fibres:			
(1) Hard fibre singles, polished or glazed singles and all multiples (but not including yarn of coir)	15%		
(2) Other	10%		
57.08 Paper yarn	16%		—
57.09 Woven fabrics of true hemp:			
(A) Containing man-made fibres	20%	C	15%
		E	—
(B) Not containing man-made fibres ...	20%		—
57.10 Woven fabrics of jute:			
(A) Containing man-made fibres	20%	C	15%
		E	—
(B) Not containing man-made fibres ...	20%		—
57.11 Woven fabrics of other vegetable textile fibres:			
(A) Containing man-made fibres	20%	C	15%
		E	—
(B) Not containing man-made fibres ...	20%		—
57.12 Woven fabrics of paper yarn	19%		—

Chapter 58

Carpets, Mats, Matting and Tapestries; Pile and Chenille Fabrics; Narrow Fabrics; Trimmings; Tulle and other Net Fabrics; Lace; Embroidery

Notes

1. The headings of this Chapter are to be taken not to apply to coated or impregnated fabrics, elastic fabrics or elastic trimmings, machinery belting or other goods falling within Chapter 59. However, embroidery on any textile base falls within heading No. 58.10.

2. In headings Nos. 58.01 and 58.02, the words " carpets " and " rugs " are to be taken to extend to similar articles having the characteristics of floor coverings but intended for use for other purposes. These headings are to be taken not to apply to felt carpets, which fall within Chapter 59.

3. For the purposes of heading No. 58.05, the expression " narrow woven fabrics " means:

(a) Woven fabrics of a width not exceeding 30 centimetres, whether woven as such or cut from wider pieces, provided with selvedges (woven, gummed or made otherwise) on both edges;

(b) Tubular woven fabrics of a flattened width not exceeding 30 centimetres; and

(c) Bias binding with folded edges, of a width when unfolded not exceeding 30 centimetres. Narrow woven fabrics in the form of fringes are to be treated as falling within heading No. 58.07.

4. Heading No. 58.08 is to be taken not to apply to nets or netting in the piece made of twine, cordage or rope, which are to be taken as falling within heading No. 59.05.

5. In heading No. 58.10, and elsewhere in this Schedule, the expression " embroidery " means, *inter alia*, embroidery with metal or glass thread on a visible ground of textile fabric, and sewn appliqué work of sequins, beads or ornamental motifs of textile or other materials. The heading is to be taken not to apply to needlework tapestry (heading No. 58.03).

6. The headings of this Chapter are to be taken to include goods of the descriptions specified therein when made of metal thread and of a kind used in apparel, as furnishings or the like.

Tariff Heading	Rate of Import Duty (*if any*)		
	Full	**Commonwealth (C) E.F.T.A.**	**(E)**
58.01 Carpets, carpeting and rugs, knotted (made up or not): (A) Hand-made: (1) Containing more than 20 per cent. by weight of silk, of man-made fibres, or of both together	4s. 6d. per sq. yd. exclusive of fringes or 33%, whichever is the greater	C E	27½% —
(2) Containing more than 5 per cent. but not more than 20 per cent. by weight of silk, of man-made fibres, or of both together	4s. 6d. per sq. yd. exclusive of fringes or 23%, whichever is the greater	C E	19% —
(3) Other	4s. 6d. per sq. yd. exclusive of fringes		—
(B) Other: (1) Containing more than 20 per cent. by weight of silk, of man-made fibres, or of both together	1s. per sq. yd. exclusive of fringes or 32%, whichever is the greater	C E	26½% —

Tariff Heading	Rate of Import Duty (if any)	
	Full	Commonwealth (C) E.F.T.A. (E)
58.01 Carpets, carpeting and rugs, etc.—contd.		
(B) Other—contd.		
(2) Containing more than 5 per cent. but not more than 20 per cent. by weight of silk, of man-made fibres, or of both together	1s. per sq. yd. exclusive of fringes or 25%, whichever is the greater	C 21% E —
(3) Other	1s. per sq. yd. exclusive of fringes or 19%, whichever is the greater	—
58.02 Other carpets, carpeting, rugs, mats and matting, and " Kelem ", " Schumacks " and " Karamanie " rugs and the like (made up or not):		
(A) Coir mats and matting	20%	—
(B) Other:		
(1) Containing more than 20 per cent. by weight of silk, of man-made fibres, or of both together	1s. per sq. yd. exclusive of fringes or 37%, whichever is the greater	C 31% E —
(2) Containing more than 5 per cent. but not more than 20 per cent. by weight of silk, of man-made fibres, or of both together	1s. per sq. yd. exclusive of fringes or 25%, whichever is the greater	C 21% E —
(3) Other	1s. per sq. yd. exclusive of fringes or 19%, whichever is the greater	—
58.03 Tapestries, hand-made, of the type Gobelins, Flanders, Aubusson, Beauvais and the like, and needle-worked tapestries (for example, petit point and cross stitch) made in panels and the like by hand:		
(A) Containing more than 20 per cent. by weight of silk, of man-made fibres, or of both together	33%	C 85% of the full rate E —
(B) Containing more than 5 per cent. but not more than 20 per cent. by weight of silk, of man-made fibres, or of both together	23%	C 85% of the full rate E —
(C) Other	23%	—
58.04 Woven pile fabrics and chenille fabrics (other than terry towelling or similar terry fabrics of cotton falling within heading No. 55.08 and fabrics falling within heading No. 58.05):		
(A) Containing silk or man-made fibres:		
(1) Containing more than 75 per cent. by weight of silk, of man-made fibres, or of both together	17½% or 5d. per sq. yd., whichever is the greater, plus 1s. 4d. per lb. of silk plus 3½d. per lb. of man-made fibres	C 85% of the full rate E —

Tariff Heading	Rate of Import Duty (if any)	
	Full	Commonwealth (C) E.F.T.A. (E)
8.04 Woven pile fabrics, etc.—contd.		
(A) Containing silk or man-made fibres—contd.		
(2) Other	17½% plus 5d. per lb. of silk and of man-made fibres	C 85% of the full rate E —
(B) Not containing silk or man-made fibres	17½%	—
8.05 Narrow woven fabrics, and narrow fabrics (bolduc) consisting of warp without weft assembled by means of an adhesive, other than goods falling within heading No. 58.06:		
(A) Containing silk or man-made fibres	17½% plus 5d. per lb. of silk and of man-made fibres	C 85% of the full rate E —
(B) Not containing silk or man-made fibres:		
(1) Consisting wholly of cotton, sheep's or lambs' wool, fine animal hair or flax, or any combination thereof	17½%	—
(2) Other	19%	—
8.06 Woven labels, badges and the like, not embroidered, in the piece, in strips or cut to shape or size:		
(A) Containing silk or man-made fibres:		
(1) Containing more than 10 per cent. by weight of silk, of man-made fibres, or of both together	20½% plus 1s. 4d. per lb. of silk plus 6½d. per lb. of man-made fibres	C 85% of the full rate E —
(2) Other	17½% plus 6½d. per lb. of silk and of man-made fibres	C 85% of the full rate E —
(B) Not containing silk or man-made fibres	17½%	—
8.07 Chenille yarn (including flock chenille yarn), gimped yarn (other than metallised yarn of heading No. 52.01 and gimped horsehair yarn); braids and ornamental trimmings in the piece; tassels, pompons and the like:		
(A) Chenille yarn and gimped yarn:		
(1) Containing silk or man-made fibres	14½% plus 4½d. per lb. of silk and of man-made fibres	C 85% of the full rate E —
(2) Not containing silk or man-made fibres:		
(a) Containing metal or paper ...	12½%	—
(b) Other	9%	—

Tariff Heading	Rate of Import Duty (if any)		
	Full	Commonwealth (C E.F.T.A. (E	

58.07 Chenille yarn, gimped yarn, etc.—contd.
  (B) Braids and ornamental trimmings in the piece:
    (1) Containing silk or man-made fibres:

(a) Containing more than 50 per cent. by weight of monofil of headings Nos. 51.01 and 51.02, of strip of heading No. 51.02, or of both together	17½% plus 1s. 4d. per lb. of silk plus 6½d. per lb. of man-made fibres	C E	85% of the fu rate —
(b) Containing more than 10 per cent. by weight of silk, of man-made fibres, or of both together, but not including goods comprised in subheading (a) above	20½% plus 1s. 4d. per lb. of silk plus 6½d. per lb. of man-made fibres	C E	85% of the fu rate —
(c) Other	17½% plus 6½d. per lb. of silk and of man-made fibres	C E	85% of the fu rate —
(2) Not containing silk or man-made fibres:			
(a) Consisting wholly of cotton, sheep's or lambs' wool, fine animal hair or flax, or any combination thereof	17½%		—
(b) Other	19%		—
(C) Tassels, pompons and the like:			
(1) Containing more than 20 per cent. by weight of silk, of man-made fibres, or of both together	33%	C E	85% of the fu rate —
(2) Containing more than 5 per cent. but not more than 20 per cent. by weight of silk, of man-made fibres, or of both together	23%	C E	85% of the fu rate —
(3) Other	20%		—
58.08 Tulle and other net fabrics (but not including woven, knitted or crocheted fabrics), plain: (A) Knotted: (1) Containing silk or man-made fibres:			
(a) Containing more than 10 per cent. by weight of silk, of man-made fibres, or of both together	6d. per sq. yd. or 24%, whichever is the greater	C E	85% of the fu rate —
(b) Other	23%	C E	85% of the fu rate —
(2) Not containing silk or man-made fibres	23%		—
(B) Other: (1) Containing silk or man-made fibres:			

Tariff Heading	Rate of Import Duty (*if any*)	
	Full	*Commonwealth (C)* *E.F.T.A.* (E)
8.08 Tulle and other net fabrics, etc.—*contd.*		
(B) Other—*contd.*		
(1) Containing silk or man-made fibres—*contd.*		
(*a*) Exceeding 30 centimetres in width and containing more than 75 per cent. by weight of silk, of man-made fibres, or of both together	23% or 4½d. per sq. yd., whichever is the greater	C 85% of the full rate E —
(*b*) Other	23%	C 17% E —
(2) Not containing silk or man-made fibres	23%	
8.09 Tulle and other net fabrics (but not including woven, knitted or crocheted fabrics), figured; hand or mechanically made lace, in the piece, in strips or in motifs:		
(A) Containing silk or man-made fibres:		
(1) Exceeding 30 centimetres in width and containing more than 75 per cent. by weight of silk, of man-made fibres, or of both together	23% or 4½d. per sq. yd., whichever is the greater	C 85% of the full rate E —
(2) Other	23%	C 17% E —
(B) Not containing silk or man-made fibres	23%	—
8.10 Embroidery, in the piece, in strips or in motifs:		
(A) Containing silk or man-made fibres:		
(1) Exceeding 30 centimetres in width and containing more than 75 per cent. by weight of silk, of man-made fibres, or of both together	23% or 4½d. per sq. yd., whichever is the greater	C 85% of the full rate E —
(2) Other	23%	C 17% E —
(B) Not containing silk or man-made fibres	23%	—

Chapter 59

Wadding and Felt; Twine, Cordage, Ropes and Cables; Special Fabrics; Impregnated and Coated Fabrics; Textile Articles of a kind suitable for Industrial Use

Notes

1. For the purposes of this Chapter, the expression "textile fabric" is to be taken to apply only to the textile fabrics of Chapters 50 to 57 and headings Nos. 58.04 and 58.05, the braids and trimmings in the piece of heading No. 58.07, the tulle and other net fabrics of headings Nos. 58.08 and 58.09, lace of heading No. 58.09 and the knitted and crocheted fabrics of heading No. 60.01.

2. Headings Nos. 59.08 and 59.12 are to be taken not to apply to fabrics in which the impregnation or coating is not apparent or is apparent only by reason of a resulting change of colour. Heading No. 59.12 is also to be taken not to apply to:

(a) Fabrics painted with designs (other than theatrical scenery, studio back-cloths and the like);

(b) Fabrics covered with flock, dust, powdered cork or the like and bearing designs resulting from these treatments; or

(c) Fabrics finished with normal dressings having a basis of amylaceous or similar substances.

3. In heading No. 59.11 "rubberised textile fabrics" means:

(a) Textile fabrics impregnated, coated, covered or laminated with rubber:
  (i) Weighing not more than 1½ kilograms per square metre; or
  (ii) Weighing more than 1½ kilograms per square metre and containing more than 50 per cent. by weight of textile material;

(b) Fabrics composed of parallel textile yarns agglomerated with rubber, irrespective of their weight per square metre; and

(c) Plates, sheets and strip, of expanded, foam or sponge rubber, combined with textile fabric, other than those falling in Chapter 40 by virtue of the last paragraph of Note 2 to that Chapter.

4. Heading No. 59.16 is to be taken not to apply to:

(a) Transmission, conveyor or elevator belting of a thickness of less than 3 millimetres; or

(b) Transmission, conveyor or elevator belts or belting of textile fabric impregnated, coated, covered or laminated with rubber or made from textile yarn or cord impregnated or coated with rubber (heading No. 40.10).

5. Heading No. 59.17 is to be taken to apply to the following goods which are to be taken as not falling within any other heading of Section XI:

(a) Textile products (other than those having the character of the products of headings Nos. 59.14 to 59.16), the following only:
  (i) Textile fabric, felt and felt-lined woven fabric, coated, covered or laminated with rubber, leather or other material, of a kind commonly used for card clothing, and similar fabric of a kind commonly used in machinery or plant;
  (ii) Bolting cloth;
  (iii) Straining cloth of a kind commonly used in oil presses and the like, of textile fibres or of human hair;
  (iv) Woven textile felts, whether or not impregnated or coated, of a kind commonly used in paper-making or other machinery, tubular or endless with single or multiple warp or weft, or flat woven with multiple warp or weft;
  (v) Textile fabrics reinforced with metal, of a kind commonly used in machinery or plant;
  (vi) Textile fabrics of the metallised yarn falling within heading No. 52.01, of a kind commonly used in paper-making or other machinery;
  (vii) Cords, braids and the like, whether or not coated, impregnated or reinforced with metal, of a kind commonly used in machinery or plant as packing or lubricating materials;

(b) Textile articles (other than those of headings Nos. 59.14 to 59.16) of a kind commonly used in machinery or plant (for example, gaskets, washers, polishing discs and other machinery parts).

Tariff Heading	Rate of Import Duty (if any)	
	Full	Commonwealth (C) E.F.T.A. (E)
9.01 Wadding and articles of wadding; textile flock and dust and mill neps: (A) Textile flock and dust: (1) Containing man-made fibres ...	6¼d. per lb. of man-made fibres	C 85% of the full rate E —
(2) Not containing man-made fibres...	—	—

(B) Other:
   (1) Containing man-made fibres:
     (a) Containing more than 10 per cent. by weight of man-made fibres
	19½% plus 6¼d. per lb. of man-made fibres	C 85% of the full rate
		E —

(b) Other	16½%	C 85% of the full rate E —
(2) Not containing man-made fibres...	8%	—

9.02 Felt and articles of felt, whether or not impregnated or coated:
(A) Felt, not made up:
   (1) Containing man-made fibres:
     (a) Containing more than 10 per cent. by weight of man-made fibres
	19% plus 5d. per lb. of man-made fibres	C 85% of the full rate
		E —

(b) Other	19%	C 85% of the full rate E —
(2) Not containing man-made fibres...	19%	—
(B) Articles of felt: (1) Containing more than 20 per cent. by weight of silk, of man-made fibres, or of both together	28%	C 85% of the full rate E —
(2) Containing more than 5 per cent. but not more than 20 per cent. by weight of silk, of man-made fibres, or of both together	23%	C 85% of the full rate E —
(3) Other	20%	—

9.03 Bonded fibre fabrics, similar bonded yarn fabrics, and articles of such fabrics, whether or not impregnated or coated:
(A) Bonded fibre fabrics and similar bonded yarn fabrics, not made up:
   (1) Containing man-made fibres:
     (a) Containing more than 10 per cent. by weight of man-made fibres
	19% plus 5d. per lb. of man-made fibres	C 85% of the full rate
		E —

(b) Other	19%	C 85% of the full rate E —
(2) Not containing man-made fibres...	19%	—

Tariff Heading	Rate of Import Duty (if any)	
	Full	Commonwealth (C E.F.T.A. (E
59.03 Bonded fibre fabrics etc.—_contd._		
(B) Articles of bonded fibre fabrics or of similar bonded yarn fabrics:		
(1) Containing more than 20 per cent. by weight of silk, of man-made fibres, or of both together	28%	C 85% of the fu rate E —
(2) Containing more than 5 per cent. but not more than 20 per cent. by weight of silk, of man-made fibres or of both together	23%	C 85% of the fu rate E —
(3) Other	20%	—
59.04 Twine, cordage, ropes and cables, plaited or not:		
(A) Containing silk or man-made fibres:		
(1) Multiple, cabled or plaited:		
(a) Containing more than 50 per cent. by weight of silk, of man-made fibres, or of both together	28%	C 85% of the fu rate E —
(b) Other	20%	C 85% of the fu rate E —
(2) Other	18%	C 85% of the fu rate E —
(B) Not containing silk or man-made fibres:		
(1) Of paper yarn	16%	—
(2) Of cotton, flax, ramie or coir ...	10%	—
(3) Of true hemp:		
(a) If singles, not polished or glazed	7½%	—
(b) Otherwise	15%	—
(4) Other	15%	—
59.05 Nets and netting made of twine, cordage or rope, and made up fishing nets of yarn, twine, cordage or rope:		
(A) Nets, including made up fishing nets:		
(1) Containing more than 20 per cent. by weight of silk, of man-made fibres, or of both together	37%	C 85% of the fu rate E —
(2) Containing more than 5 per cent. but not more than 20 per cent. by weight of silk, of man made fibres, or of both together	25%	C 85% of the fu rate E —
(3) Other	20%	—

Tariff Heading	Rate of Import Duty (if any)	
	Full	Commonwealth (C) E.F.T.A. (E)
9.05 Nets and netting made of twine, etc.—_contd._ (B) Netting: (1) Containing silk or man-made fibres: (a) Containing more than 10 per cent. by weight of silk, of man-made fibres, or of both together	6d. per sq. yd. or 22½%, whichever is the greater	C 85% of the full rate E —
(b) Other	20%	C 85% of the full rate E —
(2) Not containing silk or man-made fibres	20%	—
9.06 Other articles made from yarn, twine, cordage, rope or cables, other than textile fabrics and articles made from such fabrics: (A) Containing more than 20 per cent. by weight of silk, of man-made fibres, or of both together	35%	C 85% of the full rate E —
(B) Containing more than 5 per cent. but not more than 20 per cent. by weight of silk, of man-made fibres, or of both together	25%	C 85% of the full rate E —
(C) Other	20%	—
9.07 Textile fabrics coated with gum or amylaceous substances, of a kind used for the outer covers of books and the like; tracing cloth; prepared painting canvas; buckram and similar fabrics for hat foundations and similar uses: (A) Containing silk or man-made fibres	19%	C 85% of the full rate E —
(B) Not containing silk or man-made fibres	19%	—
9.08 Textile fabrics impregnated or coated with preparations of cellulose derivatives or of other artificial plastic materials: (A) Containing silk or man-made fibres: (1) Containing more than 10 per cent. by weight of silk, of man-made fibres, or of both together	19% plus 1s. 4d. per lb. of silk plus 5d. per lb. of man-made fibres	C 85% of the full rate E —
(2) Other	19%	C 85% of the full rate E —
(B) Not containing silk or man-made fibres	17½%	—

Tariff Heading	Rate of Import Duty (if any)	
	Full	Commonwealth (C E.F.T.A. (E
59.09 Textile fabrics coated or impregnated with oil or preparations with a basis of drying oil:		
(A) Containing silk or man-made fibres:		
(1) Containing more than 10 per cent. by weight of silk, of man-made fibres, or of both together	19% plus 1s. 4d. per lb. of silk plus 5d. per lb. of man-made fibres	C 85% of the fu rate E —
(2) Other	19%	C 85% of the fu rate E —
(B) Not containing silk or man-made fibres	17½%	—
59.10 Linoleum and materials prepared on a textile base in a similar manner to linoleum, whether or not cut to shape or of a kind used as floor coverings; floor coverings consisting of a coating applied on a textile base, cut to shape or not	14½%	—
59.11 Rubberised textile fabrics, other than rubberised knitted or crocheted goods:		
(A) Containing silk or man-made fibres:		
(1) Containing more than 10 per cent. by weight of silk, of man-made fibres, or of both together	19% plus 1s. 4d. per lb. of silk plus 5d. per lb. of man-made fibres	C 85% of the fu rate E —
(2) Other	19%	C 85% of the fu rate E —
(B) Not containing silk or man-made fibres	19%	—
59.12 Textile fabrics otherwise impregnated or coated; painted textile fabrics being theatrical scenery, studio back-cloths or the like:		
(A) Fabrics:		
(1) Containing silk or man-made fibres:		
(a) Containing more than 10 per cent. by weight of silk, of man-made fibres, or of both together	19% plus 1s. 4d. per lb. of silk plus 5d. per lb. of man-made fibres	C 85% of the fu rate E —
(b) Other	19%	C 85% of the fu rate E —
(2) Not containing silk or man-made fibres	19%	—
(B) Theatrical scenery, studio back-cloths or the like	19%	—

Tariff Heading	Rate of Import Duty (if any)	
	Full	*Commonwealth (C)* *E.F.T.A.* (E)
59.13 Elastic fabrics and trimmings (other than knitted or crocheted goods) consisting of textile materials combined with rubber threads: (A) Containing silk or man-made fibres: (1) Containing more than 10 per cent. by weight of silk, of man-made fibres, or of both together	19% plus 1s. 4d. per lb. of silk plus 5d. per lb. of man-made fibres	C 85% of the full rate E —
(2) Other	19%	C 85% of the full rate E —
(B) Not containing silk or man-made fibres	19%	
59.14 Wicks, of woven, plaited or knitted textile materials, for lamps, stoves, lighters, candles and the like; tubular knitted gas-mantle fabric and incandescent gas mantles: (A) Containing man-made fibres: (1) Containing more than 10 per cent. by weight of man-made fibres	22½%	C 85% of the full rate E —
(2) Other	19%	C 85% of the full rate E —
(B) Not containing man-made fibres ...	17½%	
59.15 Textile hosepiping and similar tubing, with or without lining, armour or accessories of other materials: (A) Containing more than 20 per cent. by weight of silk, of man-made fibres, or of both together	27%	C 85% of the full rate E —
(B) Containing more than 5 per cent. but not more than 20 per cent. by weight of silk, of man-made fibres, or of both together	22%	C 85% of the full rate E —
(C) Other	19%	—
59.16 Transmission, conveyor or elevator belts or belting, of textile material, whether or not strengthened with metal or other material: (A) Containing more than 20 per cent. by weight of silk, of man-made fibres, or of both together	27%	C 85% of the full rate E —
(B) Containing more than 5 per cent. but not more than 20 per cent. by weight of silk, of man-made fibres, or of both together	22%	C 85% of the full rate E —
(C) Other ... ... ·	14%	—

Tariff Heading	Rate of Import Duty (if any)	
	Full	Commonwealth (C) E.F.T.A. (E)
59.17 Textile products and textile articles, of a kind commonly used in machinery or plant:		
(A) Bolting cloth, not treated or operated upon, containing no other fibre than silk	—	—
(B) Woven textile felts of a kind used in paper-making machinery, in the form of tubes or endless bands, whether woven as such or assembled by splicing, sewing or otherwise, or in the form of flat fabrics fitted with eyelets or other means of fastening, ready for assembly into tubes or endless bands by such fastening	9½%	—
(C) Other textile fabrics; cords, braids and the like of a kind used as packing or lubricating materials:		
(1) Containing silk or man-made fibres:		
(a) Containing more than 10 per cent. by weight of silk, of man-made fibres, or of both together	19% plus 1s. 4d. per lb. of silk plus 5d. per lb. of man-made fibres	C 85% of the full rate E —
(b) Other	19%	C 85% of the full rate E —
(2) Not containing silk or man-made fibres	19%	—
(D) Other:		
(1) Containing more than 20 per cent. by weight of silk, of man-made fibres, or of both together	28%	C 85% of the full rate E —
(2) Containing more than 5 per cent. but not more than 20 per cent. by weight of silk, of man-made fibres, or of both together	23%	C 85% of the full rate E —
(3) Other	20%	—

Chapter 60

Knitted and Crocheted Goods

Notes

1. This Chapter does not cover:

(a) Crochet lace of heading No. 58.09;

(b) Knitted or crocheted goods falling within Chapter 59;

(c) Corsets, corset-belts, suspender-belts, brassières, braces, suspenders, garters or the like (heading No. 61.09);

(d) Old clothing or other articles falling within heading No. 63.01; or

(e) Orthopaedic appliances, surgical belts, trusses or the like (heading No. 90.19).

2. Headings Nos. 60.02 to 60.06 are to be taken to apply to:

(a) Articles of the kinds described therein (finished or unfinished, complete or incomplete) and parts thereof, knitted or crocheted directly to shape or made up from knitted or crocheted fabric; and

(b) Knitted or crocheted fabric shaped for making the goods referred to in (a) above.

3. For the purposes of heading No. 60.06, knitted or crocheted articles are not considered to be elastic articles only by reason of their containing rubber thread or elastic forming merely a supporting band.

4. The headings of this Chapter are to be taken to include goods of the descriptions specified therein when made of metal thread and of a kind used in apparel, as furnishings or the like.

5. For the purposes of this Chapter:

(a) " Elastic " means consisting of textile materials combined with rubber threads; and

(b) " Rubberised " means impregnated, coated or covered with rubber, or made with textile thread coated or impregnated with rubber.

Tariff Heading	Rate of Import Duty (if any)	
	Full	Commonwealth (C) E.F.T.A. (E)
60.01 Knitted or crocheted fabric, not elastic nor rubberised:		
(A) Net of a kind used in articles of apparel, furnishings or the like, and fabric resembling lace:		
(1) Containing silk or man-made fibres:		
(a) Exceeding 30 centimetres in width and containing more than 75 per cent. by weight of silk, of man-made fibres, or of both together	23% or 4½d. per sq. yd., whichever is the greater	C 85% of the full rate E —
(b) Other	23%	C 17% E —
(2) Not containing silk or man-made fibres	23%	—

Tariff Heading	Rate of Import Duty (if any)		
	Full	Commonwealth (C E.F.T.A. (E

60.01 Knitted or crocheted fabric, etc.—*contd.*

(B) Other fabric:

    (1) Containing silk or man-made fibres:

	Full	C/E	
(a) Exceeding 30 centimetres in width and containing more than 75 per cent. by weight of silk, of man-made fibres, or of both together	17½% plus 3½d. per lb. of silk and of man-made fibres, or 7d. per sq. yd., whichever is the greater	C E	85% of the fu rate —
(b) Exceeding 30 centimetres in width and containing more than 50 per cent. but not more than 75 per cent. by weight of silk, of man-made fibres, or of both together	17½% plus 5d. per lb. of silk and of man-made fibres, or 5d. per sq. yd., whichever is the greater	C E	85% of the fu rate —
(c) Other	17½% plus 5d. per lb. of silk and of man-made fibres	C E	85% of the fu rate —
(2) Not containing silk or man-made fibres	17½%		

60.02 Gloves, mittens and mitts, knitted or crocheted, not elastic nor rubberised:

	Full	C/E	
(A) Containing more than 20 per cent. by weight of silk, of man-made fibres, or of both together	6s. 6d. per lb. or 30%, whichever is the greater	C E	90% of the fu rate —
(B) Containing more than 5 per cent. but not more than 20 per cent. by weight of silk, of man-made fibres, or of both together:			
(1) Wholly or partly cut out of fabric containing cotton and sewn up (but excluding gloves known as astrakhan gloves and gloves, mittens and mitts in which the fabric containing cotton is present in the lining only)	2s. 6d. per lb. or 28%, whichever is the greater	C E	2s. 3d. per lb. c 20%, whicheve is the greater —
(2) Other	2s. 6d. per lb. or 22½%, whichever is the greater	C E	2s. 3d. per lb. c 20%, whicheve is the greater —
(C) Other:			
(1) Wholly or partly cut out of fabric containing cotton and sewn up (but excluding gloves known as astrakhan gloves and gloves, mittens and mitts in which the fabric containing cotton is present in the lining only)	28%		
(2) Other	20%		—

Tariff Heading	Rate of Import Duty (if any)	
	Full	Commonwealth (C) E.F.T.A. (E)
60.03 Stockings, under stockings, socks, ankle-socks, sockettes and the like, knitted or crocheted, not elastic nor rubberised:		
(A) Containing more than 20 per cent. by weight of silk, of man-made fibres, or of both together:		
(1) Where no component is silk and all the man-made fibres are of re-generated cellulose or cellulose acetate	6s. per dozen pairs or 25%, whichever is the greater	C 90% of the full rate E —
(2) Other	8s. 3d. per dozen pairs or 30%, whichever is the greater	C 90% of the full rate E —
(B) Containing more than 5 per cent. but not more than 20 per cent. by weight of silk, of man-made fibres, or of both together	21½%	C 19% E —
(C) Other	20%	—
60.04 Under garments, knitted or crocheted, not elastic nor rubberised:		
(A) Containing more than 20 per cent. by weight of silk, of man-made fibres, or of both together:		
(1) Containing more than 5 per cent. by weight of silk	11s. per lb. or 28%, whichever is the greater	C 90% of the full rate E —
(2) Other	6s. 6d. per lb. or 23%, whichever is the greater	C 90% of the full rate E —
(B) Containing more than 5 per cent. but not more than 20 per cent. by weight of silk, of man-made fibres, or of both together:		
(1) Containing embroidery, net, lace or material resembling lace	23%	C 19% E —
(2) Other	21½%	C 19% E —
(C) Other:		
(1) Containing embroidery, net, lace or material resembling lace	23%	—
(2) Other	20%	—

Tariff Heading	Rate of Import Duty (*if any*)	
	Full	*Commonwealth* (C) E.F.T.A. (E)
60.05 Outer garments and other articles, knitted or crocheted, not elastic nor rubberised: (A) Containing more than 20 per cent. by weight of silk, of man-made fibres, or of both together: (1) Articles of apparel: (*a*) Containing more than 5 per cent. by weight of silk:		
(i) Dresses	13s. 4½d. per lb. or 26%, whichever is the greater	C 90% of the full rate E —
(ii) Other	11s. per lb. or 28%, whichever is the greater	C 90% of the full rate E —
(*b*) Other: (i) Dresses trimmed with furskin or artificial flowers, foliage or fruit	7s. 4d. per lb. or 26%, whichever is the greater	C 90% of the full rate E —
(ii) Dresses containing embroidery, net, lace or material resembling lace, or trimmed with feathers (but not including dresses comprised in subheading (i) above)	7s. 4d. per lb. or 24½%, whichever is the greater	C 90% of the full rate E —
(iii) Other dresses	6s. 4d. per lb. or 23%, whichever is the greater	C 90% of the full rate E —
(iv) Skirts, other than divided skirts	6s. per lb. or 23%, whichever is the greater	C 90% of the full rate E —
(v) Other	6s. 6d. per lb. or 23%, whichever is the greater	C 90% of the full rate E —
(2) Bed linen, table linen, curtains and other furnishing articles	2s. 9d. per lb. or 28%, whichever is the greater	C 90% of the full rate E —
(3) Other	28%	C 90% of the full rate E —

Tariff Heading	Rate of Import Duty (if any)		
	Full	Commonwealth (C) E.F.T.A. (E)	
60.05 Outer garments and other articles, etc.—contd.			
(B) Containing more than 5 per cent. but not more than 20% by weight of silk, of man-made fibres, or of both together:			
(1) Articles of apparel:			
(a) Articles trimmed with furskin or artificial flowers, foliage or fruit	26%	C E	19% —
(b) Articles not comprised in sub-heading (a) above, containing embroidery, net, lace or material resembling lace, or trimmed with feathers	23%	C E	19% —
(c) Other	21½%	C E	19% —
(2) Other	23%	C E	19½% —
(C) Other:			
(1) Articles trimmed with furskin or artificial flowers, foliage or fruit	26%		—
(2) Other:			
(a) Articles of apparel, bed linen, table linen, curtains and other furnishing articles, containing embroidery, net, lace or material resembling lace, or trimmed with feathers	23%		—
(b) Other	20%		—
60.06 Knitted or crocheted fabric and articles thereof, elastic or rubberised (including elastic knee-caps and elastic stockings):			
(A) Fabric:			
(1) Containing silk or man-made fibres	19%	C E	85% of the full rate —
(2) Not containing silk or man-made fibres:			
(a) Elastic fabric	19%		—
(b) Rubberised fabric	17½%		—
(B) Made-up articles:			
(1) Containing more than 20 per cent. by weight of silk, of man-made fibres, or of both together	23%	C E	85% of the full rate —
(2) Containing more than 5 per cent. but not more than 20 per cent. by weight of silk, of man-made fibres, or of both together	21½%	C E	85% of the full rate —
(3) Other	20%		—

Chapter 61

Articles of Apparel and Clothing Accessories of Textile Fabric,
Other Than Knitted or Crocheted Goods

Notes

1. The headings of this Chapter are to be taken to apply to articles of the kinds described therein only when made up of any textile fabric (including felt, bonded fibre fabric, braid or trimmings of heading No. 58.07, tulle or other net fabrics and lace) or of fabric of metal thread, but not including articles of knitted or crocheted material other than those falling within heading No. 61.09.

2. The headings of this Chapter do not cover:

(a) Old clothing or other articles falling within heading No. 63.01; or

(b) Orthopaedic appliances, surgical belts, trusses or the like (heading No. 90.19).

3. For the purposes of headings Nos. 61.01 to 61.04:

(a) Articles which cannot be identified as either men's or boys' garments or as women's or girls' garments are to be classified in heading No. 61.02 or 61.04 as the case may be

(b) The expression " infants' garments " is to be taken to apply to:

(i) Garments for young children which are not identifiable as for wear exclusively by boys or by girls, and

(ii) Babies' napkins.

4. Scarves and articles of the scarf type, square or approximately square, of which no side exceeds 60 centimetres are to be classified as handkerchiefs (heading No. 61.05).

Handkerchiefs of which any side exceeds 60 centimetres are to be classified in heading No. 61.06.

5. The headings of this Chapter are to be taken to apply also to unfinished or incomplete articles of the kinds described therein and to shaped textile fabric for making such articles including knitted or crocheted fabric shaped for making articles classified in heading No. 61.09.

Tariff Heading	Rate of Import Duty (if any)		
	Full	Commonwealth (C) E.F.T.A. (E)	
61.01 Men's and boys' outer garments:			
(A) Containing more than 20 per cent. by weight of silk, of man-made fibres, or of both together:			
(1) Containing more than 5 per cent. by weight of silk	11s. per lb. or 28%, whichever is the greater	C E	90% of the full rate —
(2) Other	6s. 6d. per lb. or 23%, whichever is the greater	C E	90% of the full rate —
(B) Containing more than 5 per cent. but not more than 20 per cent. by weight of silk, of man-made fibres, or of both together	21½%	C E	19% —
(C) Other	20%		—

Tariff Heading	Rate of Import Duty (if any)		
	Full	Commonwealth (C) E.F.T.A. (E)	

1.02 Women's, girls' and infants' outer garments:

(A) Containing more than 20 per cent. by weight of silk, of man-made fibres, or of both together:

  (1) Containing more than 5 per cent. by weight of silk:

	Full	C/E	
(a) Dresses	13s. 4½d. per lb. or 26%, whichever is the greater	C	90% of the full rate
		E	—
(b) Other	11s. per lb. or 28%, whichever is the greater	C	90% of the full rate
		E	—

  (2) Other:

	Full	C/E	
(a) Dresses trimmed with furskin or artificial flowers, foliage or fruit	7s. 4d. per lb. or 26%, whichever is the greater	C	90% of the full rate
		E	—
(b) Dresses containing embroidery, net, lace or material resembling lace, or trimmed with feathers (but not including dresses comprised in subheading (a) above)	7s. 4d. per lb. or 24½%, whichever is the greater	C	90% of the full rate
		E	—
(c) Other dresses	6s. 4d. per lb. or 23%, whichever is the greater	C	90% of the full rate
		E	—
(d) Skirts, other than divided skirts	6s. per lb. or 23%, whichever is the greater	C	90% of the full rate
		E	—
(e) Other	6s. 6d. per lb. or 23%, whichever is the greater	C	90% of the full rate
		E	—

(B) Containing more than 5 per cent. but not more than 20 per cent. by weight of silk, of man-made fibres, or of both together:

	Full	C/E	
(1) Garments trimmed with furskin or artificial flowers, foliage or fruit	26%	C	19%
		E	—
(2) Garments, not comprised in subheading (1) above, containing embroidery, net, lace or material resembling lace, or trimmed with feathers	23%	C	19%
		E	—
(3) Other	21½%	C	19%
		E	—

(C) Other:

	Full	C/E	
(1) Garments trimmed with furskin or artificial flowers, foliage or fruit	26%		—
(2) Garments, not comprised in subheading (1) above, containing embroidery, net, lace or material resembling lace, or trimmed with feathers	23%		—
(3) Other	20%		—

Tariff Heading	Rate of Import Duty (if any)	
	Full	Commonwealth (C) E.F.T.A. (E)
61.03 Men's and boys' under garments, including collars, shirt fronts and cuffs:		
(A) Containing more than 20 per cent. by weight of silk, of man-made fibres, or of both together:		
(1) Containing more than 5 per cent. by weight of silk	11s. per lb. or 28%, whichever is the greater	C 90% of the full rate E —
(2) Other	6s. 6d. per lb. or 23%, whichever is the greater	C 90% of the full rate E —
(B) Containing more than 5 per cent. but not more than 20 per cent. by weight of silk, of man-made fibres, or of both together	21½%	C 19% E —
(C) Other	20%	
61.04 Women's, girls' and infants' under garments:		
(A) Containing more than 20 per cent. by weight of silk, of man-made fibres, or of both together:		
(1) Containing more than 5 per cent. by weight of silk	11s. per lb. or 28%, whichever is the greater	C 90% of the full rate E —
(2) Other	6s. 6d. per lb. or 23%, whichever is the greater	C 90% of the full rate E —
(B) Containing more than 5 per cent. but not more than 20 per cent. by weight of silk, of man-made fibres, or of both together:		
(1) Containing embroidery, net, lace or material resembling lace	23%	C 19% E —
(2) Other	21½%	C 19% E —
(C) Other:		
(1) Containing embroidery, net, lace or material resembling lace	23%	—
(2) Other	20%	—
61.05 Handkerchiefs:		
(A) Containing more than 20 per cent. by weight of silk, of man-made fibres, or of both together:		
(1) Containing more than 5 per cent. by weight of silk	11s. per lb. or 28%, whichever is the greater	C 90% of the full rate E —
(2) Other	6s. 6d. per lb. or 23%, whichever is the greater	C 90% of the full rate E —

Tariff Heading	Rate of Import Duty (*if any*)	
	Full	Commonwealth (C) E.F.T.A. (E)

51.05 Handkerchiefs—*contd.*
(B) Containing more than 5 per cent. but not more than 20 per cent. by weight of silk, of man-made fibres, or of both together:
  (1) Containing more than 5 per cent. by weight of silk:
    (*a*) Containing embroidery, net, lace or material resembling lace
	4s. per lb. or 23%, whichever is the greater	C 3s. 7d. per lb. or 19%, whichever is the greater
		E —

(*b*) Other	4s. per lb. or 21½%, whichever is the greater	C 3s. 7d. per lb. or 19%, whichever is the greater E —
(2) Other: (*a*) Containing embroidery, net, lace or material resembling lace	2s. 7½d. per lb. or 23%, whichever is the greater	C 2s. 3d. per lb. or 19%, whichever is the greater E —
(*b*) Other	2s. 7½d. per lb. or 21½%, whichever is the greater	C 2s. 3d. per lb. or 19%, whichever is the greater E —
(C) Other: (1) Containing embroidery, net, lace or material resembling lace	2s. 3d. per lb. or 23%, whichever is the greater	—
(2) Other	1s. 6d. per lb. or 20%, whichever is the greater	—
51.06 Shawls, scarves, mufflers, mantillas, veils and the like: (A) Containing more than 20 per cent. by weight of silk, of man-made fibres, or of both together: (1) Containing more than 5 per cent. by weight of silk	11s. per lb. or 28%, whichever is the greater	C 90% of the full rate E —
(2) Other	6s. 6d. per lb. or 23%, whichever is the greater	C 90% of the full rate E —
(B) Containing more than 5 per cent. but not more than 20 per cent. by weight of silk, of man-made fibres, or of both together	21½%	C 19% E —
(C) Other	20%	—

Tariff Heading	Rate of Import Duty (if any)	
	Full	Commonwealth (C) E.F.T.A. (E)
61.07 Ties, bow ties and cravats:		
(A) Containing more than 20 per cent. by weight of silk, of man-made fibres, or of both together:		
(1) Containing more than 5 per cent. by weight of silk	11s. per lb. or 28%, whichever is the greater	C 90% of the full rate E —
(2) Other	6s. 6d. per lb. or 23%, whichever is the greater	C 90% of the full rate E —
(B) Containing more than 5 per cent. but not more than 20 per cent. by weight of silk, of man-made fibres, or of both together	21½%	C 19% E —
(C) Other	20%	
61.08 Collars, tuckers, fallals, bodice-fronts, jabots, cuffs, flounces, yokes and similar accessories and trimmings for women's and girls' garments:		
(A) Containing more than 20 per cent. by weight of silk, of man-made fibres, or of both together:		
(1) Containing more than 5 per cent. by weight of silk	11s. per lb. or 28%, whichever is the greater	C 90% of the full rate E —
(2) Other	6s. 6d. per lb. or 23%, whichever is the greater	C 90% of the full rate E —
(B) Containing more than 5 per cent. but not more than 20 per cent. by weight of silk, of man-made fibres, or of both together	21½%	C 19% E —
(C) Other	20%	
61.09 Corsets, corset-belts, suspender-belts, brassières, braces, suspenders, garters and the like (including such articles of knitted or crocheted fabric), whether or not elastic:		
(A) Containing more than 20 per cent. by weight of silk, of man-made fibres, or of both together:		
(1) Containing more than 5 per cent. by weight of silk	11s. per lb. or 28%, whichever is the greater	C 90% of the full rate E —
(2) Other	6s. 6d. per lb. or 23%, whichever is the greater	C 90% of the full rate E —

Tariff Heading	Rate of Import Duty (*if any*)	
	Full	*Commonwealth (C)* *E.F.T.A.* *(E)*

61.09 Corsets, etc.—*contd.*

(B) Containing more than 5 per cent. but not more than 20 per cent. by weight of silk, of man-made fibres, or of both together:

(1) Containing embroidery, net, lace or material resembling lace	23%	C 19% E —
(2) Other	21½%	C 19% E —

(C) Other:

(1) Containing embroidery, net, lace or material resembling lace	23%	—
(2) Other:		
(a) Corsets and similar body-supporting under garments and brassières	15%	—
(b) Other	20%	—

61.10 Gloves, mittens, mitts, stockings, socks and sockettes, not being knitted or crocheted goods:

(A) Containing more than 20 per cent. by weight of silk, of man-made fibres, or of both together	6s. 6d. per lb. or 30%, whichever is the greater	C 90% of the full rate E —

(B) Containing more than 5 per cent. but not more than 20 per cent. by weight of silk, of man-made fibres, of or both together:

(1) Gloves, mittens and mitts wholly or partly cut out of fabric containing cotton and sewn up (but excluding gloves known as astrakhan gloves and gloves, mittens and mitts in which the fabric containing cotton is present in the lining only)	2s. 6d. per lb. or 28%, whichever is the greater	C 2s. 3d. per lb. or 20%, whichever is the greater E —
(2) Other	2s. 6d. per lb. or 22½%, whichever is the greater	C 2s. 3d. per lb. or 20%, whichever is the greater E —

(C) Other:

(1) Gloves, mittens and mitts wholly or partly cut out of fabric containing cotton and sewn up (but excluding gloves known as astrakhan gloves and gloves, mittens and mitts in which the fabric containing cotton is present in the lining only)	28%	—
(2) Other	20%	—

Tariff Heading	Rate of Import Duty (if any)	
	Full	Commonwealth (C) E.F.T.A. (E)
61.11 Made up accessories for articles of apparel (for example, dress shields, shoulder and other pads, belts, muffs, sleeve protectors, pockets): (A) Containing more than 20 per cent. by weight of silk, of man-made fibres, or of both together:		
(1) Containing more than 5 per cent. by weight of silk	11s. per lb. or 28%, whichever is the greater	C 90% of the full rate E —
(2) Other	6s. 6d. per lb. or 23%, whichever is the greater	C 90% of the full rate E —
(B) Containing more than 5 per cent. but not more than 20 per cent. by weight of silk, of man-made fibres, or of both together	21½%	C 19% E —
(C) Other	20%	—

Chapter 62

Other Made Up Textile Articles

Notes

1. The headings of this Chapter are to be taken to apply to the articles of the kinds described therein only when made up of any textile fabric (other than felt and bonded fibre fabric) or of the braids or trimmings of heading No. 58.07, not being knitted or crocheted goods.

2. The headings of this Chapter do not cover:
(a) Goods falling within Chapter 58, 59 or 61; or
(b) Old clothing or other articles falling within heading No. 63.01.

Tariff Heading	Rate of Import Duty (if any)	
	Full	*Commonwealth (C)* *E.F.T.A.* *(E)*
62.01 Travelling rugs and blankets:		
(A) Containing more than 20 per cent. by weight of silk, of man-made fibres, or of both together	28%	C 23½% E —
(B) Containing more than 5 per cent. but not more than 20 per cent. by weight of silk, of man-made fibres, or of both together	23%	C 19½% E —
(C) Other	20%	
62.02 Bed linen, table linen, toilet linen and kitchen linen; curtains and other furnishing articles:		
(A) Containing more than 20 per cent. by weight of silk, of man-made fibres, or of both together	2s. 9d. per lb. or 28%, whichever is the greater	C 85% of the full rate E —
(B) Containing more than 5 per cent. but not more than 20 per cent. by weight of silk, of man-made fibres, or of both together	23%	C 19½% E —
(C) Other:		
(1) Containing embroidery, net, lace or material resembling lace	23%	—
(2) Other:		
(a) Bedspreads, quilts, sheets, pillow cases, bolster cases, mattress cases, and face, hand and bath towels, wholly of cotton	17½%	—
(b) Other	20%	—
62.03 Sacks and bags, of a kind used for the packing of goods:		
(A) Used sacks and bags containing 85 per cent. or more by weight of jute	—	—
(B) Other:		
(1) Containing more than 20 per cent. by weight of silk, of man-made fibres, or of both together	30%	C 85% of the full rate E —
(2) Containing more than 5 per cent. but not more than 20 per cent. by weight of silk, of man-made fibres, or of both together	25%	C 85% of the full rate E —

Tariff Heading	Rate of Import Duty (if any)		
	Full	Commonwealth (C) E.F.T.A. (E)	
62.03 Sacks etc.—*contd.*			
(B) Other—*contd.*			
(3) Other:			
(a) Of a weight not less than 4 oz. and not more than 5 oz., measuring not less than 28 inches by 14 inches and not more than 30 inches by 15½ inches, made wholly of woven cotton fabric and indelibly marked with a trade mark covering an area of not less than 80 square inches	17½%	—	
(b) Other	20%	—	
62.04 Tarpaulins, sails, awnings, sunblinds, tents and camping goods:			
(A) Containing more than 20 per cent. by weight of silk, of man-made fibres, or of both together	28%	C 85% of the full rate E —	
(B) Containing more than 5 per cent. but not more than 20 per cent. by weight of silk, of man-made fibres, or of both together	20%	C 85% of the full rate E —	
(C) Other:			
(1) Tent roofs, each of a weight of not less than two tons	—	—	
(2) Other	20%	—	
62.05 Other made up textile articles (including dress patterns):			
(A) Containing more than 20 per cent. by weight of silk, of man-made fibres, or of both together:			
(1) Articles of apparel and dress patterns:			
(a) Containing more than 5 per cent. by weight of silk	9s. per lb. or 28%, whichever is the greater	C 90% of the full rate E —	
(b) Other	4s. 6d. per lb. or 23%, whichever is the greater	C 90% of the full rate E —	
(2) Other	28%	C 90% of the full rate E —	
(B) Containing more than 5 per cent. but not more than 20 per cent. by weight of silk, of man-made fibres, or of both together:			
(1) Articles of apparel and dress patterns	21%	C 90% of the full rate E —	
(2) Other	23%	C 90% of the full rate E —	
(C) Other	20%	—	

Chapter 63

Old Clothing and Other Textile Articles; Rags

Tariff Heading	Rate of Import Duty (*if any*)	
	Full	Commonwealth (C) E.F.T.A. (E)
63.01 Clothing, clothing accessories, travelling rugs and blankets, household linen and furnishing articles (other than articles falling within heading No. 58.01, 58.02 or 58.03), of textile materials, footwear and headgear of any material, showing signs of appreciable wear and imported in bulk or in bales, sacks or similar bulk packings	The rates applicable to the goods when new	C⎰ The rates E⎱ applicable to the goods when new
63.02 Used or new rags, scrap twine, cordage, rope and cables and worn out articles of twine, cordage, rope or cables:		
(A) Containing more than 55 per cent. by weight of man-made fibres	5d. per lb. or 16%, whichever is the greater	C 85% of the full rate
(B) Other	—	E —

SECTION XII

FOOTWEAR, HEADGEAR, UMBRELLAS, SUNSHADES, WHIPS, RIDING-CROPS AND
PARTS THEREOF; PREPARED FEATHERS AND ARTICLES MADE THEREWITH;
ARTIFICIAL FLOWERS; ARTICLES OF HUMAN HAIR; FANS

Chapter 64

Footwear, Gaiters and the like; Parts of such Articles

Notes

1. This Chapter does not cover:

(*a*) Footwear, without applied soles, knitted or crocheted (heading No. 60.03) or of other textile fabric (except felt or bonded fibre fabric) (heading No. 62.05);

(*b*) Old footwear falling within heading No. 63.01;

(*c*) Articles of asbestos (heading No. 68.13);

(*d*) Orthopaedic footwear or other orthopaedic appliances, or parts thereof (heading No. 90.19); or

(*e*) Toys and skating boots with skates attached (Chapter 97).

2. For the purposes of headings Nos. 64.05 and 64.06, the expression " parts " is to be taken not to include pegs, boot protectors, eyelets, boot hooks, buckles, ornaments, braid, laces, pompons or other trimmings (which are to be classified in their appropriate headings) or buttons or other goods falling within heading No. 98.01.

3. For the purposes of heading No. 64.01, the expression " rubber or artificial plastic material " is to be taken to include any textile fabric coated or covered externally with one or both of those materials.

Tariff Heading	Rate of Import Duty (*if any*)	
	Full	*Commonwealth (C)* *E.F.T.A.* (*E*)
64.01 Footwear with outer soles and uppers of rubber or artificial plastic material: (A) If made to cover the ankle: (1) Of a length (front of sole to heel tip) exceeding 11 inches	4s. per pair	—
(2) Other	1s. 6d. per pair	—
(B) If not made to cover the ankle: (1) Of a length (front of sole to heel tip) exceeding 9¼ inches	1s. per pair	—
(2) Other	10d. per pair	—
64.02 Footwear with outer soles of leather or composition leather; footwear (other than footwear falling within heading No. 64.01) with outer soles of rubber or artificial plastic material: (A) With outer soles of rubber or artificial plastic material and uppers of material other than leather: (1) Containing more than 5 per cent. by weight of silk, of man-made fibres, or of both together	17½%	C 15½% E —
(2) Other: (*a*) If made to cover the ankle: (i) Of a length (front of sole to heel tip) exceeding 11 inches	4s. per pair	—
(ii) Other	1s. 6d. per pair	—

Tariff Heading	Rate of Import Duty (*if any*)	
	Full	*Commonwealth (C)* *E.F.T.A.* *(E)*

4.02 Footwear with outer soles of leather, etc.—*contd.*
 (A) With outer soles of rubber etc.—*contd.*
    (2) Other—*contd.*
      (b) If not made to cover the ankle:
        (i) Of a length (front of sole to heel tip) exceeding 9¼ inches
	1s. per pair	—

(ii) Other	10d. per pair	—

(B) Other:
    (1) Containing more than 5 per cent. by weight of silk, of man-made fibres, or of both together:
      (a) Women's ... ...
	2s. 4d. per pair or 17½%, whichever is the greater	C 15½%
		 E

(b) Other	17½%	C 15½% E
(2) Other: (a) Women's	2s. 4d. per pair or 8%, whichever is the greater	—
(b) Men's	12%	—
(c) Other	16%	—
4.03 Footwear with outer soles of wood or cork: (A) Containing more than 5 per cent. by weight of silk, of man-made fibres, or of both together: (1) Women's	2s. 4d. per pair or 17½%, whichever is the greater	C 15½% E —
(2) Other	17½%	C 15½% E —
(B) Other: (1) Women's	2s. 4d. per pair or 8%, whichever is the greater	—
(2) Men's	12%	—
(3) Other	16%	—
4.04 Footwear with outer soles of other materials: (A) Containing more than 5 per cent. by weight of silk, of man-made fibres, or of both together: (1) Women's	2s. 4d. per pair or 17½%, whichever is the greater	C 15½% E —
(2) Other	17½%	C 15½% E —

Tariff Heading	Rate of Import Duty (if any)		
	Full	Commonwealth (C) E.F.T.A. (E)	
64.04 Footwear with outer soles of other material etc.—_contd._ (B) Other: (1) Women's	2s. 4d. per pair or 8%, whichever is the greater	—	
(2) Men's	12%	—	
(3) Other	16%	—	
64.05 Parts of footwear, removable in-soles, hose protectors and heel cushions of any material except metal: (A) Boot and shoe uppers, mounted on dummy lasts of wood or unmounted, and, in either case, perforated in at least two prominent places by the letters " S.P." so as to render them unsuitable for use as boot or shoe parts	—	—	
(B) Other: (1) Containing more than 5 per cent. by weight of silk, of man-made fibres, or of both together	17½%	C E	15½% —
(2) Other	16%	—	
64.06 Gaiters, spats, leggings, puttees, cricket pads, shin-guards and similar articles, and parts thereof	20%	—	

Chapter 65

Headgear and Parts thereof

Notes

1. This Chapter does not cover:

(*a*) Old headgear falling within heading No. 63.01;

(*b*) Hair nets of human hair (heading No. 67.04);

(*c*) Asbestos headgear (heading No. 68.13); or

(*d*) Dolls' hats or other toy hats, or carnival articles of Chapter 97.

2. Heading No. 65.02 is to be taken not to apply to hat-shapes made by sewing (other than hat-shapes made by the sewing in spirals of plaited or other strips).

3. For the purposes of headings Nos. 65.03 to 65.06, the expression " headgear " is to be taken to include hoods and hat-shapes not falling within headings Nos. 65.01 and 65.02.

Tariff Heading	Rate of Import Duty (*if any*)	
	Full	Commonwealth (C) E.F.T.A. (E)
65.01 Hat-forms, hat bodies and hoods of felt, neither blocked to shape nor with made brims; plateaux and manchons (including slit manchons), of felt:		
(A) Hat-forms and cone-shaped hat bodies:		
(1) Containing silk or man-made fibres	17½%	C 15% E —
(2) Not containing silk or man-made fibres	15%	
(B) Hat bodies (other than cone-shaped) and hoods:		
(1) Containing silk or man-made fibres	22%	C 13% E —
(2) Not containing silk or man-made fibres	22%	
(C) Plateaux and manchons (including slit manchons):		
(1) Containing silk or man-made fibres	19%	C 13% E —
(2) Not containing silk or man-made fibres	19%	
65.02 Hat-shapes, plaited or made from plaited or other strips of any material, neither blocked to shape nor with made brims:		
(A) Containing silk or man-made fibres (including monofil or strip of heading No. 51.01 or 51.02):		
(1) Containing more than 10 per cent. by weight of silk, of man-made fibres, or of both together	20½%	C 85% of the full rate E —
(2) Other	17½%	C 85% of the full rate E
(B) Not containing silk or man-made fibres:		
(1) Wholly of unspun buntal fibre ...	8%	—
(2) Other	12%	—

Tariff Heading	Rate of Import Duty (if any)		
	Full	Commonwealth (C) E.F.T.A. (E)	

Tariff Heading	Full	C	E
65.03 Felt hats and other felt headgear, being headgear made from the felt hoods and plateaux falling within heading No. 65.01, whether or not lined or trimmed:			
(A) Containing more than 20 per cent. by weight of silk, of man-made fibres, or of both together:			
(1) Lined or trimmed or decorated in any manner or with edges which have been cut to shape, hemmed or bound	28%	C E	25% —
(2) Other	27%	C E	22% —
(B) Containing more than 5 per cent. but not more than 20 per cent. by weight of silk, of man-made fibres, or of both together:			
(1) Lined or trimmed or decorated in any manner or with edges which have been cut to shape, hemmed or bound	23%	C E	19% —
(2) Other	22%	C E	16% —
(C) Other:			
(1) Lined or trimmed or decorated in any manner or with edges which have been cut to shape, hemmed or bound	23%		
(2) Other	22%		
65.04 Hats and other headgear, plaited or made from plaited or other strips of any material, whether or not lined or trimmed:			
(A) Containing more than 20 per cent. by weight of silk, of man-made fibres (including monofil or strip of heading No. 51.01 or 51.02), or of both together:			
(1) Lined or trimmed or decorated in any manner or with edges which have been cut to shape, hemmed or bound	28%	C E	25% —
(2) Other	27%	C E	85% of the full rate —
(B) Containing more than 5 per cent. but not more than 20 per cent. by weight of silk, of man-made fibres (including monofil or strip of heading No. 51.01 or 51.02), or of both together:			
(1) Lined or trimmed or decorated in any manner or with edges which have been cut to shape, hemmed or bound	23%	C E	19% —
(2) Other	20½%	C E	85% of the full rate —

Tariff Heading	Rate of Import Duty (*if any*)		
	Full	*Commonwealth (C) E.F.T.A.*	*(E)*
5.04 Hats and other headgear, plaited, etc. *—contd.*			
(C) Other:			
(1) Wholly of unspun buntal fibre, not lined, trimmed or decorated in any manner	8%	—	
(2) Other:			
(*a*) Lined or trimmed or decorated in any manner or with edges which have been cut to shape, hemmed or bound	23%	—	
(*b*) Other	12%		
5.05 Hats and other headgear (including hair nets), knitted or crocheted, or made up from lace, felt or other textile fabric in the piece (but not from strips), whether or not lined or trimmed:			
(A) Containing more than 20 per cent. by weight of silk, of man-made fibres, or of both together	28%	C	25%
		E	—
(B) Containing more than 5 per cent. but not more than 20 per cent. by weight of silk, of man-made fibres, or of both together	23%	C	19%
		E	—
(C) Other	23%		
5.06 Other headgear, whether or not lined or trimmed:			
(A) Bathing caps of rubber	16%	—	
(B) Headgear of furskin	26%	—	
(C) Other headgear	23%	—	
5.07 Head-bands, linings, covers, hat foundations, hat frames (including spring frames for opera hats), peaks and chinstraps, for headgear	19%	—	

Chapter 66

Umbrellas, Sunshades, Walking-sticks, Whips, Riding-crops and parts thereof

Notes

1. This Chapter does not cover:

(a) Measure walking-sticks or the like (heading No. 90.16);

(b) Firearm-sticks, sword-sticks, loaded walking-sticks or the like (Chapter 93); or

(c) Goods falling within Chapter 97 (for example, toy umbrellas and toy sunshades).

2. Heading No. 66.03 is to be taken not to apply to parts, trimmings or accessories of textile material, nor to covers, tassels, thongs, umbrella cases or the like, of any material. Such goods imported with, but not fitted to, articles falling within heading No. 66.01 or 66.02 are to be classified separately and are not to be treated as forming part of those articles.

Tariff Heading	Rate of Import Duty (*if any*)		
	Full	*Commonwealth (C.)* *E.F.T.A. (E.)*	
66.01 Umbrellas and sunshades (including walking-stick umbrellas, umbrella tents, and garden and similar umbrellas):			
(A) With covers or cases containing silk or man-made fibres	33%	C	27½%
		E	—
(B) Other	20%		
66.02 Walking-sticks (including climbing-sticks and seat-sticks), canes, whips, riding-crops and the like	16%		—
66.03 Parts, fittings, trimmings and accessories of articles falling within heading No. 66.01 or 66.02:			
(A) Whip centres of leather	10%		—
(B) Handles and parts incorporating handles	16%		—
(C) Other:			
(1) Wholly of wood	16%		
(2) Other	22%		

Chapter 67

Prepared Feathers and Down and Articles made of Feathers or of Down;
Artificial Flowers; Articles of Human Hair; Fans

Notes

1. This Chapter does not cover:

(a) Straining cloth of human hair (heading No. 59.17);

(b) Floral motifs of lace, of embroidery or other textile fabric (Section XI);

(c) Footwear (Chapter 64);

(d) Headgear (Chapter 65);

(e) Feather dusters (heading No. 96.04), powder-puffs (heading No. 96.05) or hair sieves (heading No. 96.06); or

(f) Toys, sports requisites or carnival articles (Chapter 97).

2. Heading No. 67.01 is to be taken not to apply to:

(a) Goods (for example, bedding) in which feathers or down constitute only filling or padding;

(b) Articles of apparel and accessories thereto in which feathers or down constitute no more than mere trimming or padding;

(c) Artificial flowers or foliage or parts thereof or made up articles of heading No. 67.02; or

(d) Fans (heading No. 67.05).

3. Heading No. 67.02 is to be taken not to apply to:

(a) Articles of glass (Chapter 70);

(b) Artificial flowers, foliage or fruit of pottery, stone, metal, wood or other materials, obtained in one piece by moulding, forging, carving, stamping or other process, or consisting of parts assembled otherwise than by binding, glueing or similar methods or to articles made of such artificial flowers, foliage or fruit.

Tariff Heading	Rate of Import Duty (if any)	
	Full	Commonwealth (C) E.F.T.A. (E)
67.01 Skins and other parts of birds with their feathers or down, feathers, parts of feathers, down, and articles thereof (other than goods falling within heading No. 05.07 and worked quills and scapes):		
(A) Skins and pieces thereof, with their down	13%	—
(B) Down	10%	—
(C) Other	16%	—
67.02 Artificial flowers, foliage or fruit and parts thereof; articles made of artificial flowers, foliage or fruit:		
(A) Containing more than 25 per cent. by weight of silk, of man-made fibres, or of both together	33½%	C 28% E —
(B) Other	20%	—

Tariff Heading	Rate of Import Duty (if any)	
	Full	Commonwealth (C E.F.T.A. (E
67.03 Human hair, dressed, thinned, bleached or otherwise worked; wool or other animal hair prepared for use in making wigs and the like	8%	—
67.04 Wigs, false beards, hair pads, curls, switches and the like, of human or animal hair or of textiles; other articles of human hair (including hair nets)	16%	—
67.05 Fans and hand screens, non-mechanical, of any material; frames and handles therefor and parts of such frames and handles, of any material	16%	—

SECTION XIII

ARTICLES OF STONE, OF PLASTER, OF CEMENT, OF ASBESTOS, OF MICA AND OF
SIMILAR MATERIALS; CERAMIC PRODUCTS; GLASS AND GLASSWARE

Chapter 68

Articles of Stone, of Plaster, of Cement, of Asbestos, of Mica and of Similar Materials

otes

1. This Chapter does not cover:

(*a*) Goods falling within Chapter 25;

(*b*) Coated or impregnated paper falling within heading No. 48.07 (for example, paper coated with mica powder or graphite, bituminised or asphalted paper);

(*c*) Coated or impregnated textile fabric falling within Chapter 59 (for example, mica-coated fabric, bituminised or asphalted fabric);

(*d*) Articles falling within Chapter 71;

(*e*) Tools or parts of tools, falling within Chapter 82;

(*f*) Lithographic stones of heading No. 84.34;

(*g*) Electrical insulators (heading No. 85.25) or fittings of insulating material falling within heading No. 85.26;

(*h*) Dental burrs (heading No. 90.17);

(*ij*) Goods falling within Chapter 91 (for example, clocks and clock cases);

(*k*) Articles falling within heading No. 95.07;

(*l*) Toys, games or sports requisites (Chapter 97);

(*m*) Goods falling within heading No. 98.01 (for example, buttons), No. 98.05 (for example, slate pencils) or No. 98.06 (for example, drawing slates); or

(*n*) Works of art, collectors' pieces or antiques (Chapter 99).

2. In heading No. 68.02 the expression " worked monumental or building stone " is to e taken to apply not only to the varieties of stone referred to in headings Nos. 25.15 and 5.16 but also to all other natural stone (for example, quartzite, flint, dolomite and steatite) imilarly worked; it is, however, to be taken not to apply to slate.

Tariff Heading	Rate of Import Duty (*if any*)	
	Full	Commonwealth (C) E.F.T.A. (E)
8.01 Road and paving setts, curbs and flagstones, of natural stone (except slate):		
(A) Granite flagstones	28%	—
(B) Other	10%	—
8.02 Worked monumental or building stone, and articles thereof (including mosaic cubes), other than goods falling within heading No. 68.01 or within Chapter 69:		
(A) Granite, and articles thereof:		
(1) Blocks in the form of rough cylinders, not less than 18 feet in length and not less than 28 inches in diameter, not further worked than scabbled	—	—

Tariff Heading	Rate of Import Duty (if any)	
	Full	Commonwealth (C E.F.T.A. (E
68.02 Worked momumental or building stone etc.—*contd.*		
(A) Granite, and articles thereof—*contd.*		
(2) Planed, or sawn and planed, on one or two sides only, but not further worked	15%	—
(3) Vases, inkstands (with or without trays or penholders), pen or pencil racks, stands and trays, blotters and letter openers, and bureau sets consisting of two or more of the foregoing articles	16%	—
(4) Other	28%	—
(B) Marble, ecaussine and similar calcareous stone of an apparent specific gravity of 2·5 or more, and articles thereof:		
(1) Tiles of which no side exceeds 2 feet in length; mosaic cubes	10%	—
(2) Other:		
(*a*) Sawn but not otherwise worked (apart from being roughly split or roughly squared)	8%	—
(*b*) Other	16½%	—
(C) Other	9%	—
68.03 Worked slate and articles of slate, including articles of agglomerated slate:		
(A) In rectangular blocks, ground or polished, but not further manufactured, and not less than ¾ inch in thickness	5%	—
(B) Other	8%	—
68.04 Millstones, grindstones, grinding wheels and the like (including grinding, sharpening, polishing, trueing and cutting wheels, heads, discs and points), of natural stone (agglomerated or not), of agglomerated natural or artificial abrasives, or of pottery, with or without cores, shanks, sockets, axles and the like of other materials, but not mounted on frameworks; segments and other finished parts of such stones and wheels, of natural stone (agglomerated or not), of agglomerated natural or artificial abrasives, or of pottery:		
(A) Of a diameter of not less than 54 inches, of agglomerated natural stone	8½%	—
(B) Other	11%	—

Tariff Heading	Rate of Import Duty (if any)	
	Full	Commonwealth (C) E.F.T.A. (E)
68.05 Hand polishing stones, whetstones, oil stones, hones and the like, of natural stone, of agglomerated natural or artificial abrasives, or of pottery	11%	—
68.06 Natural or artificial abrasive powder or grain, on a base of woven fabric, of paper, of paperboard or of other materials, whether or not cut to shape or sewn or otherwise made up:		
(A) On a base of paper or vulcanised fibre	9%	—
(B) Other	12½%	—
68.07 Slag wool, rock wool and similar mineral wools; exfoliated vermiculite, expanded clays, foamed slag and similar expanded mineral materials; mixtures and articles of heat-insulating, sound-insulating, or sound-absorbing mineral materials, other than those falling in heading No. 68.12 or 68.13, or in Chapter 69	8%	—
68.08 Articles of asphalt or of similar material (for example, of petroleum bitumen or coal tar pitch):		
(A) Pipes, couplings and pipe-fittings containing not less than 20 per cent. by weight of vegetable fibre and not less than 50 per cent. by weight of the asphalt or similar material	16%	—
(B) Other	8%	—
68.09 Panels, boards, tiles, blocks and similar articles of vegetable fibre, of wood fibre, of straw, of wood shavings or of wood waste (including sawdust), agglomerated with cement, plaster or with other mineral binding substances	16%	—
68.10 Articles of plastering material	8%	—
68.11 Articles of cement (including slag cement), of concrete or of artificial stone (including granulated marble agglomerated with cement), reinforced or not	8%	—
68.12 Articles of asbestos-cement, of cellulose fibre-cement or the like:		
(A) Articles of asbestos-cement, not made partly of wood or other vegetable fibre, the following: Sheets, plates, tiles, slates and roof cappings; tubes, pipes and pipe and tube fittings; gutters and fittings for gutters	10½%	—
(B) Other	12%	—

Tariff Heading	Rate of Import Duty (if any)	
	Full	Commonwealth (C E.F.T.A. (E
68.13 Fabricated asbestos and articles thereof (for example, asbestos board, thread and fabric; asbestos clothing, asbestos jointing), reinforced or not, other than goods falling within heading No. 68.14; mixtures with a basis of asbestos and mixtures of, or with a basis of, asbestos and magnesium carbonate, and articles of such mixtures:		
(A) Yarns	9%	—
(B) Clothing and parts thereof	16%	—
(C) Other	12%	—
68.14 Friction material (segments, discs, washers, strips, sheets, plates, rolls and the like) of a kind suitable for brakes, for clutches or the like, with a basis of asbestos, other mineral substances or of cellulose, whether or not combined with textile or other materials:		
(A) Unmounted linings suitable for brakes, clutches and other parts of motor vehicles	19%	C 12½% E —
(B) Other	12%	—
68.15 Worked mica and articles of mica, including bonded mica splittings on a support of paper or fabric (for example, micanite and micafolium)	10%	—
68.16 Articles of stone or of other mineral substances (including articles of peat), not elsewhere specified or included	8%	—

Chapter 69

Ceramic Products

otes

1. The headings of this Chapter are to be taken to apply only to ceramic products which ave been fired after shaping.   Headings Nos. 69.04 to 69.14 are to be taken to apply only such products other than heat-insulating goods and refractory goods.

2. This Chapter does not cover:

(*a*) Goods falling within Chapter 71 (for example, imitation jewellery);

(*b*) Cermets falling within heading No. 81.04;

(*c*) Electrical insulators (heading No. 85.25) or fittings of insulating material falling within heading No. 85.26;

(*d*) Artificial teeth (heading No. 90.19);

(*e*) Goods falling within Chapter 91 (for example, clocks and clock cases);

(*f*) Toys, games or sports requisites (Chapter 97);

(*g*) Smoking pipes, buttons or other articles falling within Chapter 98; or

(*h*) Original statuary, collectors' pieces or antiques (Chapter 99).

Tariff Heading	Rate of Import Duty (*if any*)	
	Full	*Commonwealth* (C) *E.F.T.A.* (E)
I. Heat-insulating and refractory goods		
.01 Heat-insulating bricks, blocks, tiles and other heat-insulating goods of infusorial earths, of kieselguhr, of siliceous fossil meal or of similar siliceous earths:		
(A) Bricks and blocks	6%	—
(B) Other	16%	—
.02 Refractory bricks, blocks, tiles and similar refractory constructional goods, other than goods falling within heading No. 69.01	8%	—
.03 Other refractory goods (for example, retorts, crucibles, muffles, nozzles, plugs, supports, cupels, tubes, pipes, sheaths and rods), other than goods falling within heading No. 69.01:		
(A) Laboratory wares	26½%	—
(B) Other	8%	—
II. Other ceramic products		
.04 Building bricks (including flooring blocks, support or filler tiles and the like)	8%	—
.05 Roofing tiles, chimney-pots, cowls, chimney-liners, cornices and other constructional goods, including architectural ornaments:		
(A) Roofing tiles	9½%	—
(B) Other	16%	—

Tariff Heading	Rate of Import Duty (if any)	
	Full	*Commonwealth (C E.F.T.A. (E*
69.06 Piping, conduits and guttering (including angles, bends and similar fittings)	16%	—
69.07 Unglazed setts, flags and paving, hearth and wall tiles	12%	—
69.08 Glazed setts, flags and paving, hearth and wall tiles:		
(A) Flat, rectangular, not figured or embossed:		
(1) All-white	2s. 3d. per sq. yd.	—
(2) Other	2s. 8d. per sq. yd. or 15%, whichever is the greater	—
(B) Other	2s. 3d. per sq. yd. or 24%, whichever is the greater	—
69.09 Laboratory, chemical or industrial wares; troughs, tubs and similar receptacles of a kind used in agriculture; pots, jars and similar articles of a kind commonly used for the conveyance or packing of goods:		
(A) Laboratory wares	26½%	—
(B) Other	16%	—
69.10 Sinks, wash basins, bidets, water closet pans, urinals, baths and like sanitary fittings	20%	—
69.11 Tableware and other articles of a kind commonly used for domestic or toilet purposes, of porcelain or china (including biscuit porcelain and parian):		
(A) Articles designed for fixing to or setting in the wall	20%	—
(B) Articles designed for use primarily in the storage, preparation, serving or consumption of food or drink, the following: Cups (including mugs and beakers) Saucers and plates Teapots and coffee pots Sets of articles of the kinds commonly known as morning sets, dinner sets, hors d'oeuvre sets, tea sets and coffee sets, and articles designed as parts of such sets Cooking utensils and kitchen ware	£1 per cwt.	—
(C) Washstand utensils and chamber pots	£1 per cwt.	—
(D) Other	£4 10s. per cwt.	—
69.12 Tableware and other articles of a kind commonly used for domestic or toilet purposes, of other kinds of pottery:		
(A) Fireproof non-vitrified earthenware cooking utensils	22%	—

Tariff Heading	Rate of Import Duty (*if any*)	
	Full	*Commonwealth* (C) *E.F.T.A.* (E)
9.12 Tableware and other articles, etc.—*contd.*		
(B) Articles designed for fixing to or setting in the wall	20%	—
(C) Articles designed for use primarily in the storage, preparation, serving or consumption of food or drink, the following:	£1 per cwt.	—
Cups (including mugs and beakers)		
Saucers and plates		
Teapots and coffee pots		
Sets of articles of the kinds commonly known as morning sets, dinner sets, hors d'oeuvre sets, tea sets and coffee sets, and articles designed as parts of such sets		
Cooking utensils, not comprised in subheading (A) above, and kitchen ware		
(D) Washstand utensils and chamber pots	£1 per cwt.	—
(E) Other	£4 10s. per cwt.	—
9.13 Statuettes and other ornaments, and articles of personal adornment; articles of furniture:		
(A) Statuettes and other ornaments ...	£4 10s. per cwt.	—
(B) Other	16%	—
9.14 Other articles	16%	—

Chapter 70

Glass and Glassware

Notes

1. This Chapter does not cover:

(*a*) Ceramic enamels (heading No. 32.08);

(*b*) Goods falling within Chapter 71 (for example, imitation jewellery);

(*c*) Electrical insulators (heading No. 85.25) or fittings of insulating material falling within heading No. 85.26;

(*d*) Hypodermic syringes, artificial eyes, thermometers, barometers, hydrometers, optically worked optical elements or other articles falling within Chapter 90;

(*e*) Toys, games, sports requisites, Christmas tree ornaments or other articles falling within Chapter 97 (excluding glass eyes without mechanisms for dolls or for other articles of Chapter 97); or

(*f*) Buttons, fitted vacuum flasks, complete scent or similar sprays or other articles falling within Chapter 98.

2. The reference in heading No. 70.07 to " cast, rolled, drawn or blown glass (including flashed or wired glass) cut to shape other than rectangular shape, or bent or otherwise worked (for example, edge worked or engraved), whether or not surface ground or polished " is to be taken to apply to articles made from such glass, provided they are not framed or fitted with other materials.

3. For the purposes of this Schedule, the expression " glass " is to be taken to extend to fused quartz and fused silica.

Tariff Heading	Rate of Import Duty (*if any*)	
	Full	*Commonwealth* (C) *E.F.T.A.* (E)
70.01 Waste glass (cullet); glass in the mass (excluding optical glass)	8%	—
70.02 Glass of the variety known as " enamel " glass, in the mass, rods and tubes	16%	—
70.03 Glass in balls, rods and tubes, unworked (not being optical glass):		
(A) Balls	8%	—
(B) Tubing of fused silica or fused quartz, of a kind suitable for use for scientific purposes	26%	—
(C) Other	18%	—
70.04 Unworked cast or rolled glass (including flashed or wired glass), whether figured or not, in rectangles	12%	—
70.05 Unworked drawn or blown glass (including flashed glass), in rectangles	12%	—
70.06 Cast, rolled, drawn or blown glass (including flashed or wired glass) in rectangles, surface ground or polished, but not further worked	12%	—
70.07 Cast, rolled, drawn or blown glass (including flashed or wired glass) cut to shape other than rectangular shape, or bent or otherwise worked (for example, edge worked or engraved), whether or not surface ground or polished; multiple-walled insulating glass; leaded lights and the like	12%	—

Tariff Heading	Rate of Import Duty (*if any*)	
	Full	*Commonwealth (C)* *E.F.T.A.* (E)
0.08 Safety glass consisting of toughened or laminated glass, shaped or not:		
(A) In sizes and shapes ready for incorporation in motor vehicles	16%	C 10½% E —
(B) Other:		
(1) Laminated safety glass	14½%	—
(2) Other	16%	—
0.09 Glass mirrors (including rear-view mirrors), unframed, framed or backed:		
(A) Suitable for motor vehicles	24%	C 16% E —
(B) Other	16%	—
0.10 Carboys, bottles, jars, pots, tubular containers and similar containers, of glass, of a kind commonly used for the conveyance or packing of goods; stoppers and other closures, of glass:		
(A) Syphon vases	17%	—
(B) Other	20%	—
0.11 Glass envelopes (including bulbs and tubes) for electric lamps, electronic valves or the like:		
(A) For filament lamps	8%	—
(B) For mercury arc rectifiers of the mercury pool cathode type	8%	—
(C) Other	20%	—
0.12 Glass inners for vacuum flasks or for other vacuum vessels, and blanks therefor	24%	—
0.13 Glassware (other than articles falling in heading No. 70.19) of a kind commonly used for table, kitchen, toilet or office purposes, for indoor decoration, or for similar uses:		
(A) Powder bowls or boxes	18%	—
(B) Stemmed drinking vessels	18%	—
(C) Other	21%	—
0.14 Illuminating glassware, signalling glassware and optical elements of glass, not optically worked nor of optical glass:		
(A) Optical elements:		
(1) Pressed or moulded lenses (except dioptric lenses) and prisms and pressed or moulded blanks of lenses or prisms, unmounted	20%	—
(2) Other	32%	—
(B) Miners' lamp glasses	10%	—

Tariff Heading	Rate of Import Duty (if any)	
	Full	Commonwealth (C) E.F.T.A. (E)
70.14 Illuminating glassware etc.—*contd.*		
(C) Oil lamp chimneys of which the top orifice is not larger than the bottom orifice and the height is not less than twice the maximum diameter	10%	—
(D) Other illuminating glassware and lighting panels, not of a kind used on cycles or motor vehicles	13%	—
(E) Other	16%	—
70.15 Clock and watch glasses and similar glasses (including glass of a kind used for sunglasses but excluding glass suitable for corrective lenses), curved, bent, hollowed and the like; glass spheres and segments of spheres, of a kind used for the manufacture of clock and watch glasses and the like:		
(A) Clock and watch glasses	26½%	C 17½% E —
(B) Other	8%	—
70.16 Bricks, tiles, slabs, paving blocks, squares and other articles of pressed or moulded glass, of a kind commonly used in building; multi-cellular glass in blocks, slabs, plates, panels and similar forms	8%	—
70.17 Laboratory, hygienic and pharmaceutical glassware, whether or not graduated or calibrated; glass ampoules:		
(A) Laboratory glassware; glass ampoules	26½%	—
(B) Other	21½%	—
70.18 Optical glass and elements of optical glass, other than optically worked elements; blanks for corrective spectacle lenses:		
(A) Optical glass and elements of optical glass, other than optically worked elements	32%	—
(B) Blanks for corrective spectacle lenses:		
(1) Of optical glass	32%	—
(2) Other	20%	—
70.19 Glass beads, imitation pearls, imitation precious and semi-precious stones, fragments and chippings, and similar fancy or decorative glass smallwares, and articles of glassware made therefrom; glass cubes and small glass plates, whether or not on a backing, for mosaics and similar decorative purposes; artificial eyes, of glass, including those for toys but excluding those for wear by humans; ornaments and other fancy articles of lamp-worked glass; glass grains (ballotini):		

Tariff Heading	Rate of Import Duty (if any)	
	Full	Commonwealth (C) E.F.T.A. (E)
0.19 Glass beads etc.—contd.		
(A) Glass beads, imitation pearls, imitation precious and semi-precious stones, fragments and chippings, and similar fancy or decorative glass smallwares:		
(1) Not mounted, set or strung, but including ungraded goods temporarily strung for convenience of transport	—	—
(2) Other	20%	—
(B) Articles of glassware made from the goods within subheading (A) above:		
(1) Bead trimmings	12%	—
(2) Other	20%	—
(C) Ornaments and other fancy articles of lamp-worked glass	20%	—
(D) Other	8%	—
0.20 Glass fibre (including wool), yarns, fabrics, and articles made therefrom	10%	—
0.21 Other articles of glass:		
(A) Glass gobs, being measured quantities of glass, in the form of discs, for the manufacture of pressed or moulded blanks for lenses	10%	—
(B) Other	16%	—

SECTION XIV

PEARLS, PRECIOUS AND SEMI-PRECIOUS STONES, PRECIOUS METALS, ROLLED PRECIOUS METALS
AND ARTICLES THEREOF; IMITATION JEWELLERY; COIN

Chapter 71

Pearls, Precious and Semi-Precious Stones, Precious Metals,
Rolled Precious Metals, and Articles thereof; Imitation Jewellery

Notes

1. Subject to Note 1 (*a*) to Section VI and except as provided below, all articles consisting wholly or partly:

(*a*) Of pearls or of precious or semi-precious stones (natural, synthetic or reconstructed), o

(*b*) Of precious metal or of rolled precious metal,

are to be classified within this Chapter and not within any other Chapter.

2. (*a*) Headings Nos. 71.12, 71.13 and 71.14 do not cover articles in which precious meta or rolled precious metal is present as minor constituents only, such as minor fittings o minor ornamentation (for example, monograms, ferrules and rims), and paragraph (*b*) o the foregoing Note does not apply to such articles.

(*b*) Heading No. 71.15 does not cover articles containing precious metal or rolled preciou metal (other than as minor constituents).

3. This Chapter does not cover:

(*a*) Amalgams of precious metal, and colloidal precious metal (heading No. 28.49);

(*b*) Sterile surgical suture materials, dental fillings and other goods falling in Chapter 30

(*c*) Goods falling in Chapter 32 (for example, lustres);

(*d*) Handbags and other articles falling within heading No. 42.02 or 42.03;

(*e*) Goods of heading No. 43.03 or 43.04;

(*f*) Goods falling within Section XI (textiles and textile articles);

(*g*) Footwear (Chapter 64) and headgear (Chapter 65);

(*h*) Umbrellas, walking-sticks and other articles falling within Chapter 66;

(*ij*) Fans and hand screens of heading No. 67.05;

(*k*) Coin (Chapter 72 or 99);

(*l*) Abrasive goods falling within headings Nos. 68.04, 68.05, 68.06 or Chapter 82, con taining dust or powder of precious or semi-precious stones (natural or synthetic) goods of Chapter 82 with a working part of precious or semi-precious stones (natura synthetic or reconstructed) on a support of base metal; machinery, mechanical appli ances and electrical goods, and parts thereof, falling within Section XVI, not being such articles wholly of precious or semi-precious stones (natural, synthetic or re constructed);

(*m*) Goods falling within Chapter 90, 91 or 92 (scientific instruments, clocks and watches or musical instruments);

(*n*) Arms or parts thereof (Chapter 93);

(*o*) Articles covered by Note 2 to Chapter 97;

(*p*) Articles falling within headings of Chapter 98 other than headings Nos. 98.01 an 98.12; or

(*q*) Original sculptures and statuary (heading No. 99.03), collectors' pieces (heading No 99.05) and antiques of an age exceeding 100 years (heading No. 99.06), other than pearls or precious or semi-precious stones.

4. (*a*) The expression " pearls " is to be taken to include cultured pearls.

(*b*) The expression " precious metal " means silver, gold, platinum and other metals o the platinum group.

(*c*) The expression " other metals of the platinum group " means iridium, osmium palladium, rhodium and ruthenium.

5. For the purposes of this Chapter, any alloy (including a sintered mixture) containing precious metal is to be treated as an alloy of precious metal if, and only if, any one precious metal constitutes as much as 2 per cent., by weight, of the alloy.

Alloys of precious metal are to be classified according to the following rules:

(a) An alloy containing 2 per cent. or more, by weight, of platinum is to be treated only as an alloy of platinum.

(b) An alloy containing 2 per cent. or more, by weight, of gold but no platinum, or less than 2 per cent., by weight, of platinum, is to be treated only as an alloy of gold.

(c) Other alloys containing 2 per cent. or more, by weight, of silver are to be treated as alloys of silver.

For the purposes of this Note, metals of the platinum group are to be regarded as one metal and are to be treated as though they were platinum.

6. Except where the context otherwise requires, any reference in these Notes or elsewhere in this Schedule to precious metal or to any particular precious metal is to be taken to include a reference to alloys treated as alloys of precious metal or of the particular metal in accordance with the rules in Note 5 above, but not to rolled precious metal or to base metal or non-metals coated or plated with precious metal.

7. The expression " rolled precious metal " means material made with a base of metal upon one or more surfaces of which there is affixed by soldering, brazing, welding, hot-rolling or similar mechanical means a covering of precious metal. The expression is also to be taken to cover base metal inlaid with precious metal.

8. In this Chapter the expression " articles of jewellery " means:

(a) Any small objects of personal adornment (gem-set or not) (for example, rings, bracelets, necklaces, brooches, ear-rings, watch-chains, fobs, pendants, tie-pins, cuff-links, dress-studs, religious or other medals and insignia); and

(b) Articles of personal use of a kind normally carried in the pocket, in the handbag or on the person (such as cigarette cases, powder boxes, chain purses, cachou boxes).

9. For the purposes of heading No. 71.13, the expression " articles of goldsmiths' or silversmiths' wares " includes such articles as ornaments, tableware, toilet-ware, smokers' requisites and other articles of household, office or religious use.

10. For the purposes of heading No. 71.16, the expression " imitation jewellery " means articles of jewellery within the meaning of paragraph (a) of Note 8 above, not incorporating pearls, precious or semi-precious stones (natural, synthetic or reconstructed) nor (except as plating or as minor constituents) precious metal or rolled precious metal, and composed:

(a) Wholly or partly of base metal, whether or not plated with precious metal; or

(b) Of at least two materials (for example, wood and glass, bone and amber, mother of pearl and artificial plastic material), no account being taken of materials (for example, necklace strings) used only for assembly, or of paint, varnish, pearl essence or similar coating materials.

However, heading No. 71.16 does not cover buttons, studs or cuff-links (heading No. 98.01), dress combs or hair slides (heading No. 98.12) or buckles, buckle clasps or clasps.

11. Cases, boxes and similar containers imported with articles of this Chapter are to be classified with such articles if they are of a kind normally sold therewith. Cases, boxes and similar containers imported separately are to be classified under their appropriate headings.

Tariff Heading	Rate of Import Duty (if any)	
	Full	Commonwealth (C) E.F.T.A. (E)

I. Pearls and precious and semi-precious stones

71.01 Pearls, unworked or worked, but not mounted, set or strung (except ungraded pearls temporarily strung for convenience of transport) — —

71.02 Precious and semi-precious stones, unworked, cut or otherwise worked, but not mounted, set or strung (except ungraded stones temporarily strung for convenience of transport):
  (A) Diamonds drilled so as to be adapted for use in wire-drawing dies — 16% — —
  (B) Piezo-electric quartz in the form of plates, bars or rods — 8% — —
  (C) Other ... ... — —

71.03 Synthetic or reconstructed precious or semi-precious stones, unworked, cut or otherwise worked, but not mounted, set or strung (except ungraded stones temporarily strung for convenience of transport):
  (A) Piezo-electric quartz in the form of plates, bars or rods — 8% —
  (B) Other ... ... — —

71.04 Dust and powder of natural or synthetic precious or semi-precious stones — —

II. Precious metals and rolled precious metals, unwrought, unworked or semi-manufactured

71.05 Silver, including silver gilt and platinum-plated silver, unwrought or semi-manufactured:
  (A) Silver bullion ... ... — —
  (B) Other ... ... — 8% —

71.06 Rolled silver, unworked or semi-manufactured — 8% —

71.07 Gold, including platinum-plated gold, unwrought or semi-manufactured:
  (A) Gold bullion ... ... — —
  (B) Other ... ... — 8% —

71.08 Rolled gold on base metal or silver, unworked or semi-manufactured — 8% —

Tariff Heading	Rate of Import Duty (if any)	
	Full	Commonwealth (C) E.F.T.A. (E)
71.09 Platinum and other metals of the platinum group, unwrought or semi-manufactured: (A) Platinum in grain, ingot, bar or powder; platinum sponge (B) Other	 — 8%	 — —
71.10 Rolled platinum or other platinum group metals, on base metal or precious metal, unworked or semi-manufactured	6½%	—
71.11 Waste and scrap (including goldsmiths', silversmiths' and jewellers' sweepings, residues and lemels) of precious metal, fit only for the recovery of metal or for use in the manufacture of chemicals	—	—
III. Jewellery, goldsmiths' and silversmiths' wares and other articles		
71.12 Articles of jewellery and parts thereof, of precious metal or rolled precious metal: (A) Powder boxes and parts thereof ... (B) Cigarette cases of rolled precious metal on a base of non-precious metal (C) Other	 17% 17% 20%	 — — —
71.13 Articles of goldsmiths' or silversmiths' wares and parts thereof, of precious metal or rolled precious metal, other than goods falling within heading No. 71.12: (A) Articles of rolled precious metal on a base of non-precious metal (B) Other: (1) Powder bowls, powder boxes and powder puffs, and parts thereof (2) Knives, forks and spoons and similar tableware (3) Manicure sets, manicure appliances, and parts thereof ... ... (4) Other	 16% 18% 21% 21% 24%	 — — — — —
71.14 Other articles of precious metal or rolled precious metal	16%	—
71.15 Articles consisting of, or incorporating, pearls, precious or semi-precious stones (natural, synthetic or reconstructed): (A) Diamond-set used or defective drill bits, reaming shells and other articles, being parts of tools, fit only for recovery of the diamonds set therein	 —	 —

Tariff Heading	Rate of Import Duty (if any)	
	Full	Commonwealth (C E.F.T.A. (E
71.15 Articles consisting of, or incorporating, pearls, etc.—*contd.*		
(B) Machinery and instrument parts made wholly of precious or semi-precious stones:		
(1) Bearings and parts of bearings prepared for mounting and setting:		
(a) Wholly of natural stones ...	—	—
(b) Other	9%	—
(2) Other:		
(a) Wholly of agate or wholly of natural or synthetic sapphire or ruby	12%	—
(b) Other	9%	—
(C) Other:		
(1) Made wholly or partly of jade, onyx, lapis lazuli, agate, rose quartz, cornelian or other similar stones; made partly of ivory, tortoise-shell, mother of pearl, amber or coral:		
(a) Stationery, powder bowls and boxes, manicure sets, manicure appliances; parts of the foregoing; vases of onyx	18%	—
(b) Other	24%	—
(2) Other:		
(a) Articles of jewellery and parts thereof	20%	—
(b) Other	17%	—
71.16 Imitation jewellery	20%	—

Chapter 72

Coin

Note   This Chapter does not cover collectors' pieces (heading No. 99.05)

Tariff Heading	Rate of Import Duty (*if any*)	
	Full	*Commonwealth (C)* *E.F.T.A.* (*E*)
72.01 Coin	—	—

SECTION XV

Base Metals and Articles of Base Metal

Notes

1. This Section does not cover:

(a) Prepared paints, inks or other products with a basis of metallic flakes or powder falling within heading No. 32.08, 32.09, 32.10 or 32.13;

(b) Ferro-cerium or other pyrophoric alloys (heading No. 36.07);

(c) Headgear or parts thereof falling within heading No. 65.06 or 65.07;

(d) Frames or parts of umbrellas, sunshades, walking-sticks or of other articles, falling within heading No. 66.03;

(e) Goods falling within Chapter 71 (for example, precious metal alloys, rolled precious metal and imitation jewellery);

(f) Subject to the operation of Note 1 (f) to Chapter 84, articles falling within Section XVI (machinery, mechanical appliances and electrical goods);

(g) Assembled railway or tramway track (heading No. 86.10) or other articles falling within Section XVII (vehicles, ships and boats, aircraft);

(h) Instruments or apparatus of base metal of a kind falling within Section XVIII, including clock and watch springs;

(ij) Lead shot prepared for ammunition (heading No. 93.07) or other articles falling within Section XIX (arms and ammunition);

(k) Articles falling within Chapter 94 (furniture and mattress supports);

(l) Hand sieves (heading No. 96.06);

(m) Articles falling within Chapter 97 (toys, games and sports requisites); or

(n) Buttons, pens, pencil-holders, pen nibs or other articles falling within Chapter 98.

2. Throughout this Schedule, the expression " parts of general use " means:

(a) Goods described in headings Nos. 73.20, 73.25, 73.29, 73.31 and 73.32 and similar goods of other base metals;

(b) Springs and leaves for springs, of base metal, other than watch and clock springs (heading No. 91.11); and

(c) Goods described in headings Nos. 83.01, 83.02, 83.07, 83.09, 83.12 and 83.14.

In Chapters 73 to 82 (but not in heading No. 73.29 or 74.13) references to parts of goods do not include references to parts of general use as defined above.

Subject to the preceding paragraph and to the Note to Chapter 83, the headings in Chapters 73 to 81 are to be taken not to apply to any goods falling within Chapter 82 or 83.

3. Classification of Alloys:

(a) An alloy of base metals containing more than 10 per cent., by weight, of nickel is to be classified as an alloy of nickel, except in the case of an alloy in which iron predominates by weight over each of the other metals or of a ferro-alloy or master alloy (as defined in Chapters 73 and 74).

(b) Ferro-alloys and master alloys (as defined in Chapters 73 and 74) are to be classified under headings Nos. 73.02 and 74.02, respectively.

(c) Any other alloy of base metals is to be classified as an alloy of the metal which predominates by weight over each of the other metals.

(d) An alloy, not being a ferro-alloy or a master alloy, composed of base metals of this Section and of elements not falling within this Section is to be treated as an alloy of base metals of this Section if the total weight of such metals equals or exceeds the total weight of the other elements present.

(e) In this Section the term " alloy " is to be taken to include sintered mixtures of metal powders and heterogeneous intimate mixtures obtained by melting.

4. Unless the context otherwise requires, any reference in this Schedule to a base metal is to be taken to include a reference to alloys which, by virtue of Note 3 above, are to be classified as alloys of that metal.

5. Classification of Composite Articles:

Except where the headings otherwise require, articles of base metal (including articles of mixed materials treated as articles of base metal under the Interpretative Rules) containing two or more base metals are to be treated as articles of the base metal predominating by weight.

For this purpose:

(a) Iron and steel, or different kinds of iron or steel, are regarded as one and the same metal, and

(b) An alloy is regarded as being entirely composed of that metal as an alloy of which, by virtue of Note 3, it is classified.

6. For the purposes of this Section, the expression " waste and scrap " means waste and scrap metal fit only for the recovery of metal or for use in the manufacture of chemicals.

7. In this Section, any reference to base metal, or to a particular base metal, is to be taken as including base metal plated with precious metal.

Chapter 73

Iron and Steel and Articles thereof

Notes

1. In this Chapter the following expressions have the meanings hereby assigned to them:

(a) **Pig iron and cast iron** (heading No. 73.01):

A ferrous product containing, by weight, 1·9 per cent. or more of carbon, and which may contain one or more of the following elements within the weight limits specified:
less than 15 per cent. phosphorus,
not more than 8 per cent. silicon,
not more than 6 per cent. manganese,
not more than 30 per cent. chromium,
not more than 40 per cent. tungsten, and
an aggregate of not more than 10 per cent. of other alloy elements (for example, nickel, copper, aluminium, titanium, vanadium, molybdenum).

However, the ferrous alloys known as "non-distorting tool steels", containing, by weight, 1·9 per cent. or more of carbon and having the characteristics of steel, are to be classified as steels, under their appropriate headings.

(b) **Spiegeleisen** (heading No. 73.01):

A ferrous product containing, by weight, more than 6 per cent. but not more than 30 per cent. of manganese and otherwise conforming to the specification at (a) above.

(c) **Ferro-alloys** (heading No. 73.02):

Alloys of iron which are not usefully malleable and are commonly used as raw material in the manufacture of ferrous metals and which contain, by weight, separately or together:
more than 8 per cent. of silicon, or
more than 30 per cent. of manganese, or
more than 30 per cent. of chromium, or
more than 40 per cent. of tungsten, or
a total of more than 10 per cent. of other alloy elements (aluminium, titanium, vanadium, molybdenum, niobium or other elements except copper),

and which do not contain, by weight, more than 90 per cent. (92 per cent. in the case of ferro-alloys containing manganese but no silicon or 96 per cent. in the case of ferro-alloys containing silicon) of non-ferrous alloy elements.

(*d*) **Alloy steel** (heading No. 73.15):

Steel containing, by weight, one or more elements in the following proportions:
more than 2 per cent. of manganese and silicon, taken together, or
2·00 per cent. or more of manganese, or
2·00 per cent. or more of silicon, or
0·50 per cent. or more of nickel, or
0·50 per cent. or more of chromium, or
0·10 per cent. or more of molybdenum, or
0·10 per cent. or more of vanadium, or
0·30 per cent. or more of tungsten, or
0·30 per cent. or more of cobalt, or
0·30 per cent. or more of aluminium, or
0·40 per cent. or more of copper, or
0·10 per cent. or more of lead, or
0·12 per cent. or more of phosphorus, or
0·10 per cent. or more of sulphur, or
0·20 per cent. or more of phosphorus and sulphur, taken together, or
0·10 per cent. or more of other elements, taken separately.

(*e*) **High carbon steel** (heading No. 73.15):

Steel containing, by weight, not less than 0·60 per cent. of carbon and having
content, by weight, less than 0·04 per cent. of phosphorus and sulphur taken separatel
and less than 0·07 per cent. of these elements taken together.

(*f*) **Puddled bars and pilings** (heading No. 73.06):

Products for rolling, forging or re-melting obtained either:
(i) By shingling balls of puddled iron to remove the slag arising during puddling, o
(ii) By roughly welding together by means of hot-rolling, packets of scrap iron o
steel or puddled iron.

(*g*) **Ingots** (heading No. 73.06):

Products for rolling or forging obtained by casting into moulds.

(*h*) **Blooms and billets** (heading No. 73.07):

Semi-finished products of rectangular section, of a cross-sectional area exceedin
1,225 square millimetres and of such dimensions that the thickness exceeds one quarte
of the width.

(*ij*) **Slabs and sheet bars (including tinplate bars)** (heading No. 73.07):

Semi-finished products of rectangular section, of a thickness not less than 6 milli
metres, of a width not less than 150 millimetres and of such dimensions that the thickne
does not exceed one quarter of the width.

(*k*) **Coils for re-rolling** (heading No. 73.08):

Coiled semi-finished hot-rolled products, of rectangular section, not less than 1·
millimetres thick, of a width exceeding 500 millimetres and of a weight of not les
than 500 kilograms per piece.

(*l*) **Universal plates** (heading No. 73.09):

Products of rectangular section, hot-rolled lengthwise in a closed box or universa
mill, of a thickness exceeding 5 millimetres but not exceeding 100 millimetres, an
of a width exceeding 150 millimetres but not exceeding 1,200 millimetres.

(*m*) **Hoop and strip** (heading No. 73.12):

Rolled products with sheared or unsheared edges, of rectangular section, of a thicknes
not exceeding 6 millimetres, of a width not exceeding 500 millimetres and of suc
dimensions that the thickness does not exceed one tenth of the width, in straight strips
coils or flattened coils.

(*n*) **Sheets and plates** (heading No. 73.13):

Rolled products (other than coils for re-rolling as defined in paragraph (*k*) above)
of any thickness and, if in rectangles, of a width exceeding 500 millimetres.

Heading No. 73.13 is to be taken to apply, *inter alia*, to sheets or plates which have
been cut to non-rectangular shape, perforated, corrugated, channelled, ribbed, polishe

or coated, provided that they do not thereby assume the character of articles of or products falling within other headings.

(*o*) **Wire** (heading No. 73.14):

Cold-drawn products of solid section of any cross-sectional shape, of which no cross-sectional dimension exceeds 13 millimetres. In the case of headings Nos. 73.26 and 73.27, however, the term " wire " is deemed to include rolled products of the same dimensions.

(*p*) **Bars and rods (including wire rod)** (heading No. 73.10):

Products of solid section which do not conform to the entirety of any of the definitions (*h*), (*ij*), (*k*), (*l*), (*m*), (*n*) and (*o*) above, and which have cross-sections in the shape of circles, segments of circles, ovals, isosceles triangles, rectangles, hexagons, octagons or quadrilaterals with only two sides parallel and the other sides equal.

The expression also includes concrete reinforcing bars which apart from minor indentations, flanges, grooves or other deformations produced during the rolling process correspond to the above definition.

(*q*) **Hollow mining drill steel** (heading No. 73.10):

Steel hollow bars of any cross-section, suitable for mining drills, of which the greatest external dimension exceeds 15 millimetres but does not exceed 50 millimetres, and of which the greatest internal dimension does not exceed one third of the greatest external dimension. Other steel hollow bars are to be treated as falling within heading No. 73.18.

(*r*) **Angles, shapes and sections** (heading No. 73.11):

Products, other than those falling within heading No. 73.16, which do not conform to the entirety of any of the definitions (*h*), (*ij*), (*k*), (*l*), (*m*), (*n*) and (*o*) above, and which do not have cross-sections in the form of circles, segments of circles, ovals, isosceles triangles, rectangles, hexagons, octagons or quadrilaterals with only two sides parallel and the other two sides equal, and which are not hollow.

2. Headings Nos. 73.06 to 73.14 are to be taken not to apply to goods of alloy or high carbon steel (heading No. 73.15).

3. Iron and steel products of the kind described in any of the headings Nos. 73.06 to 73.15 inclusive, clad with another ferrous metal, are to be classified as products of the ferrous metal predominating by weight.

4. Iron obtained by electrolytic deposition is classified according to its form and dimensions with the corresponding products obtained by other processes.

5. The expression " high-pressure hydro-electric conduits of steel " (heading No. 73.19) means riveted, welded or seamless circular steel tubes or pipes and bends therefor, of an internal diameter exceeding 400 millimetres and of a wall thickness exceeding 10·5 millimetres.

Tariff Heading	Rate of Import Duty (*if any*)	
	Full	Commonwealth (C) E.F.T.A. (E)
73.01 Pig iron, cast iron and spiegeleisen, in pigs, blocks, lumps and similar forms:		
(A) Pig iron, smelted wholly with charcoal	—	—
(B) Vanadium-titanium pig iron produced in an electric furnace	—	—
(C) Pig iron produced in an electric furnace and containing more than 0·1 per cent. by weight of cobalt but not more than 0·025 per cent. by weight of phosphorus and not more than 0·02 per cent. by weight of sulphur	—	—

Tariff Heading	Rate of Import Duty (*if any*)	
	Full	*Commonwealth (C)* *E.F.T.A.* *(E)*

73.01 Pig iron, etc.—*contd.*

(D) Pig iron produced in an electric furnace and containing not more than 0·025 per cent. by weight of phosphorus, not more than 0·02 per cent. by weight of sulphur and not more than 2·5 per cent. by weight of total carbon — —

(E) Other pig iron; cast iron ... ... | £2 6s. per ton or 9%, whichever is the greater | —

(F) Spiegeleisen ... ... | £3 13s. per ton or 9%, whichever is the greater | —

73.02 Ferro-alloys:

(A) Ferro-chromium ... ... — —

(B) Ferro-silicon containing not less than 20 per cent. by weight of silicon — —

(C) Silico-manganese ... ... — —

(D) Ferro-silico-chromium containing not less than 20 per cent. by weight of silicon and not less than 10 per cent. by weight of chromium — —

(E) Calcium-silicon containing not less than 20 per cent. by weight of calcium, not less than 55 per cent. by weight of silicon and not more than 5 per cent. by weight of aluminium, and otherwise consisting mainly of iron — —

(F) Calcium-manganese-silicon containing not less than 15 per cent. by weight of calcium, not less than 8 per cent. by weight of manganese and not less than 50 per cent. by weight of silicon, and otherwise consisting mainly of iron — —

(G) Silicon-manganese-zirconium coning not less than 55 per cent. by weight of silicon, not less than 4 per cent. by weight of manganese and not less than 4 per cent. by weight of zirconium, and otherwise consisting mainly of iron — —

(H) Ferro-nickel ... ... — —

(IJ) Ferro-manganese:

(1) Containing less than 3 per cent. by weight of carbon — —

(2) Other:

(*a*) Containing less than 65 per cent. by weight of manganese | £3 13s. per ton or 9%, whichever is the greater | —

(*b*) Other ... ... | £8 1s. per ton or 9%, whichever is the greater | —

Tariff Heading	Rate of Import Duty (if any)	
	Full	Commonwealth (C) E.F.T.A. (E)
73.02 Ferro-alloys—*contd.*		
(K) Ferro-molybdenum and ferro-vanadium	21%	—
(L) Ferro-tungsten	18%	—
(M) Ferro-titanium containing not more than 2 per cent. by weight of carbon	21%	—
(N) Other	8%	—
73.03 Waste and scrap metal of iron or steel ...	—	—
73.04 Shot and angular grit, of iron or steel, whether or not graded; wire pellets of iron or steel:		
(A) Shot and angular grit	9%	—
(B) Wire pellets	30%	—
73.05 Iron or steel powders; sponge iron or steel:		
(A) Sponge iron in the form of cakes, briquettes or powder, containing not less than 94 per cent. by weight of total iron and not more than 0·2 per cent. by weight of total carbon	—	—
(B) Other	8%	—
73.06 Puddled bars and pilings; ingots, blocks, lumps and similar forms, of iron or steel:		
(A) Puddled bars and pilings:		
(1) Of wrought iron produced by puddling with charcoal from pig iron smelted wholly with charcoal	—	—
(2) Other	£3 13s. per ton or 9%, whichever is the greater	—
(B) Ingots, blocks, lumps and similar forms:		
(1) Manufactured entirely from pig iron smelted wholly with charcoal	—	—
(2) Other	£2 19s. per ton or 9%, whichever is the greater	—
73.07 Blooms, billets, slabs and sheet bars (including tinplate bars), of iron or steel; pieces roughly shaped by forging, of iron or steel:		
(A) Blooms, billets, slabs and sheet bars	£3 13s. per ton or 9%, whichever is the greater	—
(B) Pieces roughly shaped by forging ...	13%	—
73.08 Iron or steel coils for re-rolling	£5 15s. per ton or 9%, whichever is the greater	—
73.09 Universal plates of iron or steel	£4 7s. per ton or 9%, whichever is the greater	—

Tariff Heading	Rate of Import Duty (if any)	
	Full	Commonwealth (C) E.F.T.A. (E)
73.10 Bars and rods (including wire rod), of iron or steel, hot-rolled, forged, extruded, cold-formed or cold-finished (including precision-made); hollow mining drill steel:		
(A) Bars and rods of wrought iron produced by puddling with charcoal from pig iron smelted wholly with charcoal	—	
(B) Cut bars of iron or steel, not exceeding 6 inches in length, 6 inches in width and 1¼ inches in thickness, and containing not more than 0·03 per cent. by weight of sulphur and not more than 0·025 per cent. by weight of phosphorus	—	
(C) Bright steel bars	£6 8s. per ton or 9%, whichever is the greater	—
(D) Other bars and rods; hollow mining drill steel	£4 2s. per ton or 9%, whichever is the greater	—
73.11 Angles, shapes and sections, of iron or steel, hot-rolled, forged, extruded, cold-formed or cold-finished; sheet piling of iron or steel, whether or not drilled, punched or made from assembled elements:		
(A) Fluted or U-section form sections of a kind suitable for use in the manufacture of umbrella ribs, whether or not hardened, tempered or annealed, cut into lengths not exceeding 36 inches but not further manufactured	12%	—
(B) Other angles, shapes and sections:		
(1) Not drilled, punched or otherwise fabricated	£4 2s. per ton or 9%, whichever is the greater	—
(2) Other	£6 18s. per ton or 9%, whichever is the greater	—
(C) Sheet piling	£4 2s. per ton or 9%, whichever is the greater	—
73.12 Hoop and strip, of iron or steel, hot-rolled or cold-rolled:		
(A) Bandsaw strip 10½ inches wide and over and from 16 to 12 gauge (Birmingham wire gauge) in thickness	—	—
(B) Other hoop and strip:		
(1) 3 millimetres or more in thickness	£4 7s. per ton or 9%, whichever is the greater	—

Tariff Heading	Rate of Import Duty (if any)	
	Full	Commonwealth (C) E.F.T.A. (E)
73.12 Hoop and strip, etc.—*contd.*		
(B) Other hoop and strip—*contd.*		
(2) Less than 3 millimetres in thickness:		
(*a*) Not plated, coated or clad, nor cold-rolled	£4 2s. per ton or 9%, whichever is the greater	
(*b*) Other	£6 8s. per ton or 9%, whichever is the greater	—
73.13 Sheets and plates, of iron or steel, hot-rolled or cold-rolled:		
(A) 3 millimetres or more in thickness ...	£4 7s. per ton or 9%, whichever is the greater	—
(B) Less than 3 millimetres in thickness:		
(1) Not plated, coated or clad ...	£5 15s. per ton or 9%, whichever is the greater	—
(2) Other	£6 13s. per ton or 9%, whichever is the greater	—
73.14 Iron or steel wire, whether or not coated, but not insulated:		
(A) Of a value exceeding £60 per ton	25%	—
(B) Other	30%	—
73.15 Alloy steel and high carbon steel in the forms mentioned in headings Nos. 73.06 to 73.14:		
(A) Bandsaw strip 10½ inches wide and over and from 16 to 12 gauge (Birmingham wire gauge) in thickness	—	—
(B) Machinery belting (including conveyor and elevator bands) of cold-rolled strip, exceeding 10 inches in width, imported in coils, of stainless steel or, hardened and tempered, of charcoal steel	9%	—
(C) Heat resisting wire, not plated, coated or covered, of metal alloy containing by weight the following:	13½%	—

	not less than per cent.	not more than per cent.
Chromium ...	19·5	26·0
Aluminium ...	3·5	6·5
Cobalt ...	1·5	4·0

and not more than a total of 3 per cent. by weight of substances other than chromium, aluminium, cobalt and iron

Tariff Heading	Rate of Import Duty (*if any*)	
	Full	Commonwealth (C) E.F.T.A. (E)
73.15 Alloy steel, etc.—*contd.*		
(D) Other:		
(1) Ingots, blocks, lumps and similar forms	£2 19s. per ton or 9%, whichever is the greater	—
(2) Blooms, billets, slabs and sheet bars	£3 13s. per ton or 9%, whichever is the greater	—
(3) Pieces roughly shaped by forging	13%	—
(4) Coils for re-rolling	£5 15s. per ton or 9%, whichever is the greater	—
(5) Universal plates	£4 7s. per ton or 9%, whichever is the greater	—
(6) Bars and rods (including wire rod):		
(a) Bright steel bars	£6 8s. per ton or 9%, whichever is the greater	—
(b) Other	£4 2s. per ton or 9%, whichever is the greater	—
(7) Hollow mining drill steel ...	£4 2s. per ton or 9%, whichever is the greater	—
(8) Angles, shapes and sections:		
(a) Not drilled, punched or otherwise fabricated	£4 2s. per ton or 9%, whichever is the greater	—
(b) Other	£6 18s. per ton or 9%, whichever is the greater	—
(9) Sheet piling	£4 2s. per ton or 9%, whichever is the greater	—
(10) Hoop and strip:		
(a) 3 millimetres or more in thickness	£4 7s. per ton or 9%, whichever is the greater	—
(b) Less than 3 millimetres in thickness:		
(i) Not plated, coated or clad, nor cold-rolled	£4 2s. per ton or 9%, whichever is the greater	—
(ii) Other	£6 8s. per ton or 9%, whichever is the greater	—
(11) Sheets and plates:		
(a) 3 millimetres or more in thickness	£4 7s. per ton or 9%, whichever is the greater	—

Tariff Heading	Rate of Import Duty (*if any*)	
	Full	*Commonwealth* (*C*) *E.F.T.A.* (*E*)
73.15 Alloy steel, etc.—*contd.*		
(D) Other—*contd.*		
(11) Sheets and plates—*contd.*		
(*b*) Less than 3 millimetres in thickness:		
(i) Not plated, coated or clad	£5 15s. per ton or 9%, whichever is the greater	—
(ii) Other	£6 13s. per ton or 9%, whichever is the greater	—
(12) Wire:		
(*a*) Of a value exceeding £60 per ton	25%	—
(*b*) Other	30%	—
73.16 Railway and tramway track construction material of iron or steel, the following: rails, check-rails, switch blades, crossings (or frogs), crossing pieces, point rods, rack rails, sleepers, fishplates, chairs, chair wedges, sole plates (base plates), rail clips, bedplates, ties and other material specialised for joining or fixing rails:		
(A) Rails, check-rails, switch blades, crossings (or frogs) and crossing pieces:		
(1) Used	—	—
(2) Unused	£3 18s. per ton or 9%, whichever is the greater	—
(B) Sleepers, fishplates and sole plates (base plates)	£5 1s. per ton or 9%, whichever is the greater	—
(C) Other	14%	—
73.17 Tubes and pipes, of cast iron	17%	—
73.18 Tubes and pipes and blanks therefor, of iron (other than of cast iron) or steel, excluding high-pressure hydro-electric conduits:		
(A) Cast tubes and pipes	17%	—
(B) Other tubes and pipes	18½%	—
73.19 High-pressure hydro-electric conduits of steel, whether or not reinforced	18½%	—
73.20 Tube and pipe fittings (for example, joints, elbows, unions and flanges), of iron or steel	17%	—

Tariff Heading	Rate of Import Duty (if any)	
	Full	Commonwealth (C) E.F.T.A. (E)
73.21 Structures, complete or incomplete, whether or not assembled, and parts of structures, (for example, hangars and other buildings, bridges and bridge-sections, lock-gates, towers, lattice masts, roofs, roofing frameworks, door and window frames, shutters, balustrades, pillars and columns), of iron or steel; plates, strip, rods, angles, shapes, sections, tubes and the like, prepared for use in structures, of iron or steel:		
(A) Door and window frames and casements	12%	—
(B) Tubes:		
(1) Of cast iron or steel	17%	—
(2) Other	18½%	—
(C) Other	9%	—
73.22 Reservoirs, tanks, vats and similar containers, for any material, of iron or steel, of a capacity exceeding 300 litres, whether or not lined or heat-insulated, but not fitted with mechanical or thermal equipment	13½%	—
73.23 Casks, drums, cans, boxes and similar containers, of sheet or plate iron or steel, of a description commonly used for the conveyance or packing of goods:		
(A) Churns for the conveyance of milk ...	13%	—
(B) Other	16%	—
73.24 Compressed gas cylinders and similar pressure containers, of iron or steel	10%	—
73.25 Stranded wire, cables, cordage, ropes, plaited bands, slings and the like, of iron or steel wire, but excluding insulated electric cables	18½%	—
73.26 Barbed iron or steel wire; twisted hoop or single flat wire, barbed or not, and loosely twisted double wire, of kinds used for fencing, of iron or steel	30%	—
73.27 Gauze, cloth, grill, netting, fencing, reinforcing fabric and similar materials, of iron or steel wire:		
(A) Galvanised hexagonal wire netting ...	18½%	—
(B) Woven or knitted mesh of a kind commonly used in the manufacture of pot scourers	18½%	—
(C) Other	24½%	—
73.28 Expanded metal, of iron or steel	9%	—

Tariff Heading	Rate of Import Duty (if any)		
	Full	Commonwealth (C) E.F.T.A. (E)	
73.29 Chain and parts thereof, of iron or steel:			
(A) Motor vehicle transmission chain, and parts thereof	19%	C	12½%
		E	—
(B) Jack chain (including mattress chain)	21½%		—
(C) Other:			
(1) Chain and parts thereof, manufactured of wire (other than welded or forged chain)	26½%		—
(2) Other	13%		—
73.30 Anchors and grapnels and parts thereof, of iron or steel	14½%		—
73.31 Nails, tacks, staples, hook-nails, corrugated nails, spiked cramps, studs, spikes and drawing pins, of iron or steel, whether or not with heads of other materials, but not including such articles with heads of copper	13½%		—
73.32 Bolts and nuts (including bolt ends and screw studs), whether or not threaded or tapped, and screws (including screw hooks and screw rings), of iron or steel; rivets, cotters, cotter-pins, washers and spring washers, of iron or steel:			
(A) Bolts, nuts, bolt ends, set screws and screw studs, and other screws for metal:			
(1) Not exceeding $\frac{9}{32}$ inch in maximum thread diameter:			
(a) Of a value not exceeding £16 per cwt.	16½%		—
(b) Of a value exceeding £16 per cwt.	13½%		—
(2) Exceeding $\frac{9}{32}$ inch but not exceeding $\frac{13}{32}$ inch in maximum thread diameter:			
(a) Of a value not exceeding £10 per cwt.	16½%		—
(b) Of a value exceeding £10 per cwt.	13½%		—
(3) Exceeding $\frac{13}{32}$ inch but not exceeding $\frac{9}{16}$ inch in maximum thread diameter:			
(a) Of a value not exceeding £6 5s. per cwt.	16½%		—
(b) Of a value exceeding £6 5s. per cwt.	13½%		—
(4) Exceeding $\frac{9}{16}$ inch in maximum thread diameter:			
(a) Of a value not exceeding £5 per cwt.	16½%		—
(b) Of a value exceeding £5 per cwt.	13½%		—
(B) Rivets, washers and spring washers...	13½%		—
(C) Other	16½%		—

Tariff Heading	Rate of Import Duty (if any)	
	Full	Commonwealth (C) E.F.T.A. (E)
73.33 Needles for hand sewing (including embroidery), hand carpet needles and hand anitting needles, bodkins, crochet hooks, knd the like, and embroidery stilettos, of iron or steel, including blanks	13%	—
73.34 Pins (excluding hatpins and other ornamental pins and drawing pins), hairpins and curling grips, of iron or steel	21½%	—
73.35 Springs and leaves for springs, of iron or steel:		
(A) Upholstery and mattress wire springs	21½%	—
(B) Other	13½%	—
73.36 Stoves (including stoves with subsidiary boilers for central heating or for hot water supply), ranges, cookers, grates, fires and other space heaters, gas-rings, plate warmers with burners, wash boilers with grates or other heating elements, and similar equipment, of a kind used for domestic purposes, not electrically operated, and parts thereof, of iron or steel:		
(A) Stoves for heating with solid fuel, and parts thereof	13%	—
(B) Other	16%	—
73.37 Boilers (excluding steam-generating boilers of heading No. 84.01) and radiators, for central heating, not electrically heated, and parts thereof, of iron or steel; air heaters and hot air distributors (including those which can also distribute cool or conditioned air), not electrically heated, incorporating a motor-driven fan or blower, and parts thereof, of iron or steel	16%	—
73.38 Articles of a kind commonly used for domestic purposes, builders' sanitary ware for indoor use, and parts of such articles and ware, of iron or steel:		
(A) Of wire, but not including boot and shoe trees	26½%	—
(B) Other:		
(1) Builders' sanitary ware for indoor use:		
(a) Baths, wrought enamelled or galvanised	16%	—
(b) Other	13%	—
(2) Other	17½%	—

Tariff Heading	Rate of Import Duty (if any)	
	Full	Commonwealth (C) E.F.T.A. (E)
73.39 **Iron or steel wool; pot scourers and scouring and polishing pads, gloves and the like, of iron or steel:**		
(A) Of wire, other than pot scourers of woven or knitted mesh	21½%	—
(B) Other	18½%	—
73.40 **Other articles of iron or steel:**		
(A) Empty ribbon spools adapted for use in typewriters (including electric type-writers), accounting, adding, listing, book-keeping and billing machines, cash registers, weighing machines or time recorders, and parts of such spools	7%	—
(B) Other:		
(1) Of wire:		
(a) Mattress hooks	25%	—
(b) Other	30%	—
(2) Other	13%	—

Chapter 74

Copper and Articles thereof

Notes

1. For the purposes of heading No. 74.02, the expression " master alloys " means alloys (except copper phosphide (phosphor copper) containing more than 8 per cent. by weight of phosphorus) of copper with other materials in any proportion, not usefully malleable and commonly used as raw material in the manufacture of other alloys or as de-oxidants, de-sulphurising agents or for similar uses in the metallurgy of non-ferrous metals.

(Copper phosphide (phosphor copper) containing more than 8 per cent. by weight of phosphorus falls within heading No. 28.55 and not within this Chapter).

2. In this Chapter the following expressions have the meanings hereby assigned to them:

(*a*) **Wire** (headings Nos. 74.03, 74.10 and 74.11):

Rolled, extruded or drawn products of solid section of any cross-sectional shape, of which no cross-sectional dimension exceeds six millimetres.

(*b*) **Wrought bars, rods, angles, shapes and sections** (heading No. 74.03):

Rolled, extruded, drawn or forged products of solid section, of which the maximum cross-sectional dimension exceeds six millimetres and which, if they are flat, have a thickness exceeding one tenth of the width. Also cast or sintered products, of the same forms and dimensions, which have been subsequently machined (otherwise than by simple trimming or de-scaling).

(*c*) **Wrought plates, sheets and strip** (heading No. 74.04):

Flat-surfaced, wrought products (coiled or not), of which the maximum cross-sectional dimension exceeds six millimetres, and of which the thickness exceeds $0·15$ millimetre but does not exceed one tenth of the width.

Heading No. 74.04 is to be taken to apply, *inter alia*, to such products, whether or not cut to shape, perforated, corrugated, ribbed, channelled, polished or coated, provided that they do not thereby assume the character of articles or of products falling within other headings.

(*d*) **Foil** (heading No. 74.05):

Products of a thickness (excluding any backing) not exceeding $0·15$ millimetre.

Heading No. 74.05 is to be taken to apply, *inter alia*, to such products whether or not embossed, cut to shape, perforated, coated, printed, or backed with paper or other reinforcing material.

3. Heading No. 74.07 is to be taken to apply, *inter alia*, to tubes, pipes and hollow bars which have been polished or coated, or which have been shaped or worked, such as bent, coiled, threaded, drilled, waisted, cone-shaped or finned. Heading No. 74.08 is to be taken to apply, *inter alia*, to tube and pipe fittings which have been similarly treated.

Tariff Heading	Rate of Import Duty (*if any*)	
	Full	Commonwealth (C) E.F.T.A. (E)
74.01 Copper matte; cement copper; unwrought copper (refined or not); copper waste and scrap:		
(A) Alloys of copper, not being waste and scrap:		
(1) Beryllium alloys	10%	—
(2) Other	8%	—
(B) Other		—
74.02 Master alloys:		
(A) Beryllium alloys	10%	—
(B) Other	8%	—

Tariff Heading	Rate of Import Duty (if any)	
	Full	Commonwealth (C) E.F.T.A. (E)
74.03 Wrought bars, rods, angles, shapes and sections, of copper; copper wire:		
(A) Of beryllium alloys	10%	—
(B) Other	9%	—
74.04 Wrought plates, sheets and strip, of copper:		
(A) Of beryllium alloys	15%	—
(B) Other	12%	—
74.05 Copper foil:		
(A) Of beryllium alloys	15%	—
(B) Other	12½%	—
74.06 Copper powders and flakes	16%	—
74.07 Tubes and pipes and blanks therefor, of copper; hollow bars of copper:		
(A) Of beryllium alloys	18%	—
(B) Other	16%	—
74.08 Tube and pipe fittings (for example, joints, elbows, sockets and flanges), of copper:		
(A) Of beryllium alloys	18%	—
(B) Other	16%	—
74.09 Reservoirs, tanks, vats and similar containers, for any material, of copper, of a capacity exceeding 300 litres, whether or not lined or heat-insulated, but not fitted with mechanical or thermal equipment	16%	—
74.10 Stranded wire, cables, cordage, ropes, plaited bands and the like, of copper wire, but excluding insulated electric wires and cables	16%	—
74.11 Gauze, cloth, grille, netting, fencing, reinforcing fabric and similar materials (including endless bands), of copper wire	16%	—
74.12 Expanded metal, of copper	16%	—
74.13 Chain and parts thereof, of copper ...	16%	—
74.14 Nails, tacks, staples, hook-nails, spiked cramps, studs, spikes and drawing pins, of copper, or of iron or steel with heads of copper	13½%	—
74.15 Bolts and nuts (including bolt ends and screw studs), whether or not threaded or tapped, and screws (including screw hooks and screw rings), of copper; rivets, cotters, cotter-pins, washers and spring washers, of copper:		
(A) Screws for wood (other than screw hooks and screw rings):		
(1) Up to and including 8 gauge ...	10%	—
(2) Over 8 gauge	7%	—
(B) Other	13½%	—

Tariff Heading	Rate of Import Duty (if any)	
	Full	Commonwealth (C) E.F.T.A. (E)
74.16 Springs, of copper	14%	—
74.17 Cooking and heating apparatus of a kind used for domestic purposes, not electrically operated, and parts thereof, of copper	16%	—
74.18 Other articles of a kind commonly used for domestic purposes, builders' sanitary ware for indoor use, and parts of such articles and ware, of copper	16%	—
74.19 Other articles of copper	16%	—

Chapter 75

Nickel and Articles thereof

Notes

1. In this Chapter the following expressions have the meanings hereby assigned to them:

(*a*) **Wire** (heading No. 75.02):

Rolled, extruded or drawn products of solid section of any cross-sectional shape, of which no cross-sectional dimension exceeds six millimetres.

(*b*) **Wrought bars, rods, angles, shapes and sections** (heading No. 75.02):

Rolled, extruded, drawn or forged products of solid section, of which the maximum cross-sectional dimension exceeds six millimetres and which, if they are flat, have a thickness exceeding one tenth of the width. Also cast or sintered products, of the same forms and dimensions, which have been subsequently machined (otherwise than by simple trimming or de-scaling).

(*c*) **Wrought plates, sheets and strip** (heading No. 75.03):

Flat-surfaced, wrought products (coiled or not), of which the maximum cross-sectional dimension exceeds six millimetres, and of which the thickness exceeds 0·15 millimetre but does not exceed one tenth of the width.

Heading No. 75.03 is to be taken to apply, *inter alia*, to such products, whether or not cut to shape, perforated, corrugated, ribbed, channelled, polished or coated, provided that they do not thereby assume the character of articles or of products falling within other headings.

(*d*) **Foil** (heading No. 75.03):

Products of a thickness (excluding any backing) not exceeding 0·15 millimetre.

Heading No. 75.03 is to be taken to apply, *inter alia*, to such products whether or not embossed, cut to shape, perforated, coated, printed, or backed with paper or other reinforcing material.

2. Heading No. 75.04 is to be taken to apply, *inter alia*, to tubes, pipes, hollow bars and tube and pipe fittings which have been polished or coated, or which have been shaped or worked, such as bent, coiled, threaded, drilled, waisted, cone-shaped or finned.

	Rate of Import Duty (*if any*)	
Tariff Heading	*Full*	*Commonwealth* (C) *E.F.T.A.* (E)
75.01 Nickel mattes, nickel speiss and other intermediate products of nickel metallurgy; unwrought nickel (excluding electro-plating anodes); nickel waste and scrap:		
(A) Alloys of nickel, not being waste and scrap:		
(1) Nickel-copper alloys containing more than 60 per cent. by weight of nickel	—	—
(2) Other	8%	—
(B) Other	—	—
75.02 Wrought bars, rods, angles, shapes and sections, of nickel; nickel wire:		
(A) Bars and rods, of nickel-copper alloy containing more than 60 per cent. by weight of nickel	—	—
(B) Other	9%	—

Tariff Heading	Rate of Import Duty (if any)	
	Full	Commonwealth (C) E.F.T.A. (E)
75.03 Wrought plates, sheets and strip, of nickel; nickel foil; nickel powders and flakes:		
(A) Plates, sheets and strip:		
(1) Of nickel-copper alloy containing more than 60 per cent. by weight of nickel	—	—
(2) Of other nickel alloys or of nickel:		
(a) Of an alloy in which copper predominates by weight over each of the other metals	12%	—
(b) Other	9%	—
(B) Foil:		
(1) Of nickel-copper alloy containing more than 60 per cent. by weight of nickel	—	—
(2) Other	12½%	—
(C) Powders	—	—
(D) Flakes	15%	—
75.04 Tubes and pipes and blanks therefor, of nickel; hollow bars, and tube and pipe fittings (for example, joints, elbows, sockets and flanges), of nickel:		
(A) Hollow bars and blanks for tubes and pipes, of nickel-copper alloy containing more than 60 per cent. by weight of nickel	—	—
(B) Tubes and pipes of an alloy in which copper predominates by weight over each of the other metals; tube and pipe fittings	16%	—
(C) Other	10%	—
75.05 Electro-plating anodes, of nickel, wrought or unwrought, including those produced by electrolysis:		
(A) Unwrought	—	—
(B) Wrought	9%	—
75.06 Other articles of nickel	16%	—

Chapter 76

Aluminium and Articles thereof

Notes

1. In this Chapter the following expressions have the meanings hereby assigned to them:

(*a*) **Wire** (headings Nos. 76.02, 76.12 and 76.13):

Rolled, extruded or drawn products of solid section of any cross-sectional shape, of which no cross-sectional dimension exceeds six millimetres.

(*b*) **Wrought bars, rods, angles, shapes and sections** (heading No. 76.02):

Rolled, extruded, drawn or forged products of solid section, of which the maximum cross-sectional dimension exceeds six millimetres and which, if they are flat, have a thickness exceeding one tenth of the width. Also cast or sintered products, of the same forms and dimensions, which have been subsequently machined (otherwise than by simple trimming or de-scaling).

(*c*) **Wrought plates, sheets and strip** (heading No. 76.03):

Flat-surfaced, wrought products (coiled or not), of which the maximum cross-sectional dimension exceeds six millimetres, and of which the thickness exceeds 0·20 millimetre but does not exceed one tenth of the width.

Heading No. 76.03 is to be taken to apply, *inter alia*, to such products, whether or not cut to shape, perforated, corrugated, ribbed, channelled, polished or coated, provided that they do not thereby assume the character of articles or of products falling within other headings.

(*d*) **Foil** (heading No. 76.04):

Products of a thickness (excluding any backing) not exceeding 0·20 millimetre.

Heading No. 76.04 is to be taken to apply, *inter alia*, to such products whether or not embossed, cut to shape, perforated, coated, printed, or backed with paper or other reinforcing material.

2. Heading No. 76.06 is to be taken to apply, *inter alia*, to tubes, pipes and hollow bars which have been polished or coated, or which have been shaped or worked, such as bent, coiled, threaded, drilled, waisted, cone-shaped or finned. Heading No. 76.07 is to be taken to apply, *inter alia*, to tube and pipe fittings which have been similarly treated.

Tariff Heading	Rate of Import Duty (if any)	
	Full	*Commonwealth* (*C*) *E.F.T.A.* (*E*)
.01 Unwrought aluminium; aluminium waste and scrap:		
(A) Alloys of aluminium, not being waste and scrap	8%	—
(B) Other	—	—
.02 Wrought bars, rods, angles, shapes and sections, of aluminium; aluminium wire	10½%	—
.03 Wrought plates, sheets and strip (including discs and circles), of aluminium	10½%	—
.04 Aluminium foil:		
(A) Of a thickness (excluding any backing) exceeding 0·15 millimetre	11½%	—
(B) Other	16%	—
.05 Aluminium powders and flakes	16%	—

Tariff Heading	Rate of Import Duty (if any)	
	Full	Commonwealth (C) E.F.T.A. (E)
76.06 Tubes and pipes and blanks therefor, of aluminium; hollow bars of aluminium	10½%	—
76.07 Tube and pipe fittings (for example, joints, elbows, sockets and flanges), of aluminium	12½%	
76.08 Structures, complete or incomplete, whether or not assembled, and parts of structures (for example, hangars and other buildings, bridges and bridge-sections, towers, lattice masts, roofs, roofing frameworks, door and window frames, balustrades, pillars and columns), of aluminium; plates, rods, angles, shapes, sections, tubes and the like, prepared for use in structures, of aluminium	16%	
76.09 Reservoirs, tanks, vats and similar containers, for any material, of aluminium, of a capacity exceeding 300 litres, whether or not lined or heat-insulated, but not fitted with mechanical or thermal equipment	16%	
76.10 Casks, drums, cans, boxes and similar containers (including rigid and collapsible tubular containers), of aluminium, of a description commonly used for the conveyance or packing of goods: (A) Churns for the conveyance of milk ... (B) Other	 13% 16%	 — —
76.11 Compressed gas cylinders and similar pressure containers, of aluminium	16%	—
76.12 Stranded wire, cables, cordage, ropes, plaited bands and the like, of aluminium wire, but excluding insulated electric wires and cables	16%	—
76.13 Gauze, cloth, grill, netting, reinforcing fabric and similar materials, of aluminium wire	14½%	—
76.14 Expanded metal, of aluminium	16%	—
76.15 Articles of a kind commonly used for domestic purposes, builders' sanitary ware for indoor use, and parts of such articles and ware, of aluminium	16%	—
76.16 Other articles of aluminium: (A) Lasts for boot and shoe making machines; boot and shoe trees (including fillers) (B) Other	 14½% 16%	 — —

Chapter 77

Magnesium and Beryllium and Articles thereof

Tariff Heading	Rate of Import Duty (if any)	
	Full	Commonwealth (C) E.F.T.A. (E)
7.01 Unwrought magnesium; magnesium waste (excluding shavings of uniform size) and scrap:		
(A) Magnesium, other than alloys of magnesium	6%	—
(B) Alloys of magnesium	8%	—
(C) Waste and scrap	—	—
7.02 Wrought bars, rods, angles, shapes and sections, of magnesium; magnesium wire; wrought plates, sheets and strip, of magnesium; magnesium foil; raspings and shavings of uniform size, powders and flakes, of magnesium; tubes and pipes and blanks therefor, of magnesium; hollow bars of magnesium:		
(A) Raspings and shavings of uniform size of alloys of magnesium; powder and flakes of alloys of magnesium	16%	—
(B) Other	9%	—
7.03 Other articles of magnesium	16%	—
7.04 Beryllium, unwrought or wrought, and articles of beryllium:		
(A) Waste and scrap	—	—
(B) Other	10%	—

Chapter 78

Lead and Articles thereof

Notes

1. In this Chapter the following expressions have the meanings hereby assigned to them

(*a*) **Wire** (heading No. 78.02):

Rolled, extruded or drawn products of solid section of any cross-sectional shape, which no cross-sectional dimension exceeds six millimetres.

(*b*) **Wrought bars, rods, angles, shapes and sections** (heading No. 78.02):

Rolled, extruded, drawn or forged products of solid section, of which the maximum cross-sectional dimension exceeds six millimetres and which, if they are flat, have thickness exceeding one tenth of the width. Also cast or sintered products, of the same forms and dimensions, which have been subsequently machined (otherwise than simple trimming or de-scaling).

(*c*) **Wrought plates, sheets and strip** (heading No. 78.03):

Flat-surfaced, wrought products (coiled or not), of which the maximum cross sectional dimension exceeds six millimetres, of which the thickness does not exceed one tenth of the width, and which are of a weight exceeding 1,700 grammes per square metre.

Heading No. 78.03 is to be taken to apply, *inter alia*, to such products, whether not cut to shape, perforated, corrugated, ribbed, channelled, polished or coated, provide that they do not thereby assume the character of articles or of products falling with other headings.

(*d*) **Foil** (heading No. 78.04):

Products of a weight per square metre (excluding any backing) not exceeding 1,700 grammes.

Heading No. 78.04 is to be taken to apply, *inter alia*, to such products whether or no embossed, cut to shape, perforated, coated, printed, or backed with paper or other reinforcing material.

2. Heading No. 78.05 is to be taken to apply, *inter alia*, to tubes, pipes, hollow bars and tube and pipe fittings which have been polished or coated, or which have been shaped worked, such as bent, coiled, threaded, drilled, waisted, cone-shaped or finned.

Tariff Heading	Rate of Import Duty (*if any*)	
	Full	*Commonwealth (C* *E.F.T.A.* *(E*
78.01 Unwrought lead (including argentiferous lead); lead waste and scrap:		
(A) Alloys of lead containing not more than 12 per cent. by weight of tin, not being waste and scrap	8%	—
(B) Other	—	—
78.02 Wrought bars, rods, angles, shapes and sections, of lead; lead wire	9%	—
78.03 Wrought plates, sheets and strip, of lead ...	9%	—
78.04 Lead foil; lead powders and flakes ...	16%	—

Tariff Heading	Rate of Import Duty (if any)	
	Full	Commonwealth (C) E.F.T.A. (E)
78.05 Tubes and pipes and blanks therefor, of lead; hollow bars, and tube and pipe fittings (for example, joints, elbows, sockets, flanges and S-bends), of lead	10%	—
78.06 Other articles of lead	16%	—

Chapter 79

Zinc and Articles thereof

Notes

1. In this Chapter the following expressions have the meanings hereby assigned to them

(*a*) **Wire** (heading No. 79.02):

Rolled, extruded or drawn products of solid section of any cross-sectional shape, which no cross-sectional dimension exceeds six millimetres.

(*b*) **Wrought bars, rods, angles, shapes and sections** (heading No. 79.02):

Rolled, extruded, drawn or forged products of solid section, of which the maximum cross-sectional dimension exceeds six millimetres and which, if they are flat, have thickness exceeding one tenth of the width. Also cast or sintered products, of the same forms and dimensions, which have been subsequently machined (otherwise than by simple trimming or de-scaling).

(*c*) **Wrought plates, sheets and strip** (heading No. 79.03):

Flat-surfaced, wrought products (coiled or not), of which the maximum cross-sectional dimension exceeds six millimetres, and of which the thickness exceeds 0·15 millimetre but does not exceed one tenth of the width.

Heading No. 79.03 is to be taken to apply, *inter alia*, to such products, whether or not cut to shape, perforated, corrugated, ribbed, channelled, polished or coated, provided that they do not thereby assume the character of articles or of products falling within other headings.

(*d*) **Foil** (heading No. 79.03):

Products of a thickness (excluding any backing) not exceeding 0·15 millimetre.

Heading No. 79.03 is to be taken to apply, *inter alia*, to such products whether or not embossed, cut to shape, perforated, coated, printed, or backed with paper or other reinforcing material.

2. Heading No. 79.04 is to be taken to apply, *inter alia*, to tubes, pipes, hollow bars and tube and pipe fittings which have been polished or coated, or which have been shaped or worked, such as bent, coiled, threaded, drilled, waisted, cone-shaped or finned.

Tariff Heading	Rate of Import Duty (*if any*)	
	Full	*Commonwealth (C E.F.T.A. (E*
79.01 Unwrought zinc; zinc waste and scrap:		
(A) Zinc, other than alloys of zinc ...	£1 10s. per ton	—
(B) Alloys of zinc	8%	—
(C) Waste and scrap	—	—
79.02 Wrought bars, rods, angles, shapes and sections, of zinc; zinc wire	9%	—
79.03 Wrought plates, sheets and strip, of zinc; zinc foil; zinc powders and flakes:		
(A) Foil and flakes	16%	
(B) Other:		
(1) Alloys of zinc	9%	—
(2) Zinc, other than alloys of zinc; zinc powders	12%	—
79.04 Tubes and pipes and blanks therefor, of zinc; hollow bars, and tube and pipe fittings (for example, joints, elbows, sockets and flanges), of zinc	10%	—

Tariff Heading	Rate of Import Duty (if any)	
	Full	Commonwealth (C) E.F.T.A. (E)
9.05 Gutters, roof capping, skylight frames, and other fabricated building components, of zinc	16%	—
9.06 Other articles of zinc	16%	—

Chapter 80

Tin and Articles thereof

Notes

1. In this Chapter the following expressions have the meanings hereby assigned to them:

(*a*) **Wire** (heading No. 80.02):

Rolled, extruded or drawn products of solid section of any cross-sectional shape of which no cross-sectional dimension exceeds six millimetres.

(*b*) **Wrought bars, rods, angles, shapes and sections** (heading No. 80.02):

Rolled, extruded, drawn or forged products of solid section, of which the maximum cross-sectional dimension exceeds six millimetres and which, if they are flat, have thickness exceeding one tenth of the width. Also cast or sintered products, of the same forms and dimensions, which have been subsequently machined (otherwise than by simple trimming or de-scaling).

(*c*) **Wrought plates, sheets and strip** (heading No. 80.03):

Flat-surfaced, wrought products (coiled or not), of which the maximum cross-sectional dimension exceeds six millimetres, of which the thickness does not exceed one tenth of the width, and which are of a weight exceeding one kilogram per square metre.

Heading No. 80.03 is to be taken to apply, *inter alia*, to such products, whether or not cut to shape, perforated, corrugated, ribbed, channelled, polished or coated, provided that they do not thereby assume the character of articles or of products falling within other headings.

(*d*) **Foil** (heading No. 80.04):

Products of a weight per square metre (excluding any backing) not exceeding one kilogram.

Heading No. 80.04 is to be taken to apply, *inter alia*, to such products, whether or not embossed, cut to shape, perforated, coated, printed, or backed with paper or other reinforcing material.

2. Heading No. 80.05 is to be taken to apply, *inter alia*, to tubes, pipes, hollow bars and tube and pipe fittings which have been polished or coated, or which have been shaped or worked, such as bent, coiled, threaded, drilled, waisted, cone-shaped or finned.

Tariff Heading	Rate of Import Duty (if any)	
	Full	Commonwealth (C) E.F.T.A. (E)
80.01 Unwrought tin; tin waste and scrap ...	—	—
80.02 Wrought bars, rods, angles, shapes and sections, of tin; tin wire	9%	—
80.03 Wrought plates, sheets and strip, of tin ...	9%	—
80.04 Tin foil; tin powders and flakes	16%	—
80.05 Tubes and pipes and blanks therefor, of tin; hollow bars, and tube and pipe fittings (for example, joints, elbows, sockets and flanges), of tin	10%	—
80.06 Other articles of tin	16%	—

Chapter 81

Other Base Metals employed in Metallurgy and Articles thereof

Note

Heading No. 81.04 is to be taken to apply only to the following base metals: antimony, bismuth, cadmium, chromium, cobalt, gallium, germanium, hafnium, indium, manganese, niobium (columbium), rhenium, thallium, thorium, titanium, uranium depleted in uranium-235, vanadium, zirconium. The heading also covers cobalt mattes, cobalt speiss and other intermediate products of cobalt metallurgy, and cermets.

Tariff Heading	Rate of Import Duty (if any)	
	Full	Commonwealth (C) E.F.T.A. (E)
81.01 Tungsten (wolfram), unwrought or wrought, and articles thereof	20%	—
81.02 Molybdenum, unwrought or wrought, and articles thereof	26½%	—
81.03 Tantalum, unwrought or wrought, and articles thereof:		
(A) Tantalum (other than alloys of tantalum) unwrought or in powder, sheets, plates, bars, wire, tubes and other semi-manufactured forms; waste and scrap	—	—
(B) Other	10%	—
81.04 Other base metals, unwrought or wrought, and articles thereof; cermets, unwrought or wrought, and articles thereof:		
(A) Antimony and articles thereof:		
(1) Antimony metal containing not less than 85 per cent. by weight of antimony	£40 per ton or 25%, whichever is the greater	—
(2) Other:		
(a) Waste and scrap	—	—
(b) Other	10%	—
(B) Bismuth and articles thereof:		
(1) Unwrought metal; waste and scrap	—	—
(2) Other	10%	—
(C) Chromium and vanadium and articles thereof	20%	—
(D) Cobalt and articles thereof:		
(1) Mattes, speiss and other intermediate products of cobalt metallurgy; waste and scrap	—	—
(2) Unwrought metal; powder:		
(a) Cobalt, other than alloys of cobalt	—	—
(b) Alloys of cobalt	8%	—
(3) Other	10%	—
(E) Germanium and articles thereof:		
(1) Waste and scrap	—	—
(2) Other	8%	—

Tariff Heading	Rate of Import Duty (if any)	
	Full	Commonwealth (C E.F.T.A. (E

81.04 Other base metals, etc.—*contd.*

Tariff Heading	Full	Commonwealth
(F) Manganese and articles thereof:		
(1) Waste and scrap	—	—
(2) Ferro-manganese containing less than 3 per cent. by weight of carbon, and silico-manganese	—	—
(3) Manganese metal, other than alloys, of a purity exceeding 99½ per cent.	—	—
(4) Other	10%	—
(G) Other metals and articles thereof:		
(1) Waste and scrap	—	—
(2) Uranium depleted in uranium-235	20%	—
(3) Other	10%	—
(H) Cermets and articles thereof	10%	—

Chapter 82

Tools, Implements, Cutlery, Spoons and Forks, of Base Metal; Parts thereof

Notes

1. Apart from blow lamps, portable forges, grinding wheels mounted on frameworks, manicure and chiropody sets, and goods classified in headings Nos. 82.07 and 82.15, the present Chapter covers only articles with a blade, working edge, working surface or other working part of:

(*a*) Base metal;

(*b*) Metallic carbides;

(*c*) Precious or semi-precious stones (natural, synthetic or reconstructed) on a support of base metal; or

(*d*) Abrasive materials on a support of base metal, provided that the articles have cutting teeth, flutes, grooves, or the like, of base metal, which retain their identity and function after the application of the abrasive.

2. Parts of base metal of the articles falling in the headings of this Chapter are to be classified with the articles of which they are parts, except parts separately specified as such and tool-holders for hand tools (heading No. 84.48). However, parts of general use as defined in Note 2 to Section XV are in all cases excluded from this Chapter.

Recognisable blanks of the articles falling in the headings of this Chapter and blanks of the parts of articles classified in this Chapter by virtue of the first part of this Note are to be classified with the articles or parts of which they are blanks except blanks separately specified as such.

Cutting plates for electric hair clippers are to be classified in heading No. 82.13 and blades and heads for electric shavers are to be classified in heading No. 82.11.

3. Sets (other than manicure or chiropody sets (heading No. 82.13)) comprising an assortment of tools, cutlery, spoons, forks or other articles of a kind falling within the different headings of this Chapter, fitted in cabinets, boxes, cases or the like, are to be classified as that one of the constituent articles which is chargeable with the highest rate of duty. For this purpose a specific rate of duty shall be converted into its *ad valorem* equivalent rate and where an *ad valorem* equivalent rate is the highest rate of duty, the set shall be charged as a whole at that rate.

4. Cases, boxes and similar containers imported with articles of this Chapter are to be classified with such articles if they are of a kind normally sold therewith. Cases, boxes and similar containers imported separately are to be classified under their appropriate headings.

Tariff Heading	Rate of Import Duty (if any)	
	Full	Commonwealth (C) E.F.T.A. (E)
82.01 Hand tools, the following: spades, shovels, picks, hoes, forks and rakes; axes, bill hooks and similar hewing tools; scythes, sickles, hay knives, grass shears, timber wedges and other tools of a kind used in agriculture, horticulture or forestry	12%	—
82.02 Saws (non-mechanical) and blades for hand or machine saws (including toothless saw blades): (A) Saws (non-mechanical): (1) Of a value of less than 3s. 9d. each (2) Of a value of 3s. 9d. or more each	14½% 13%	— —

Tariff Heading	Rate of Import Duty (if any)	
	Full	Commonwealth (C) E.F.T.A. (E)
82.02 Saws, etc.—*contd.*		
(B) Blades for saws:		
(1) Circular saws:		
(a) Fitted with toothed segments of metal:		
(i) Not exceeding 20 inches in maximum diameter	12½%	—
(ii) Exceeding 20 inches in maximum diameter	15%	—
(b) Diamond saws and abrasive saws	14½%	—
(c) Other	13%	—
(2) Hacksaw blades, bandsaw blades, jigsaw blades and fretsaw blades	13%	—
(3) Blanks for blades of hand panel saws, being blanks of tapered cross-section, but not including toothed blanks	13%	—
(4) Other blades for saws	14½%	—
(C) Parts of saws, other than blades; parts of blades for saws:		
(1) Toothed segments of metal for circular saws	10%	—
(2) Other	14½%	—
82.03 Hand tools, the following: pliers (including cutting pliers), pincers, tweezers, tinmen's snips, bolt croppers and the like; perforating punches; pipe cutters; spanners and wrenches (but not including tap wrenches); files and rasps:		
(A) Tweezers; tinmen's snips; perforating punches not of the plier type	14½%	—
(B) Other tools	11%	—
(C) Parts of the tools of subheadings (A) and (B) above, but not including files or rasps without handles:		
(1) Parts of pliers, pincers, nippers and the like (including bolt croppers and perforating punches of the plier type)	11%	—
(2) Other	14½%	—
82.04 Hand tools (including mounted glaziers' diamonds but not including needles, bodkins, crochet hooks, embroidery stilettos and the like) not falling within any other heading of this Chapter; blow lamps, anvils; vices and clamps, other than accessories for, and parts of, machine tools; portable forges; grinding wheels mounted on frameworks (hand or pedal operated):		
(A) Knife sharpeners	16%	—

Tariff Heading	Rate of Import Duty (*if any*)	
	Full	**Commonwealth (C)** **E.F.T.A.** **(E)**
2.04 Hand tools, etc.—contd.		
(B) Tyre levers and other appliances for fitting tyres	12%	—
(C) Other tools and appliances:		
(1) Of wire, but not including engineers', carpenters' and joiners' tools	26½%	—
(2) Other	11%	—
(D) Parts of the tools and appliances of subheadings (A), (B) and (C) above:		
(1) Parts of wire of the tools and appliances of subheading (C)(1) above	26½%	—
(2) Other	14½%	—
2.05 Interchangeable tools for hand tools, for machine tools or for power-operated hand tools (for example, for pressing, stamping, drilling, tapping, threading, boring, broaching, milling, cutting, turning, dressing, morticing or screw driving), including dies for wire drawing, extrusion dies for metal, and rock drilling bits:		
(A) Diamond dies for wire drawing ...	16%	—
(B) Threading dies and taps	10½%	—
(C) Other tools	11%	—
(D) Parts of the tools of subheadings (A), (B) and (C) above	14½%	—
2.06 Knives and cutting blades, for machines or for mechanical appliances:		
(A) Knives and cutting blades consisting of or tipped with any sintered preparation of metallic carbide	11%	—
(B) Other knives and cutting blades:		
(1) Diamond tools	11%	—
(2) Other	10%	—
2.07 Tool-tips and plates, sticks and the like for tool-tips, unmounted, of sintered metal carbides (for example, carbides of tungsten, molybdenum or vanadium)	14½%	—
2.08 Coffee-mills, mincers, juice-extractors and other mechanical appliances, of a weight not exceeding ten kilograms and of a kind used for domestic purposes in the preparation, serving or conditioning of food or drink:		
(A) Food grinders or slicers; fruit juice extractors	13%	—
(B) Other appliances	14½%	—
(C) Parts of the appliances of subheadings (A) and (B) above	14½%	—

Tariff Heading	Rate of Import Duty (if any)	
	Full	Commonwealth (C) E.F.T.A. (E)
82.09 Knives with cutting blades, serrated or not (including pruning knives), other than knives falling within heading No. 82.06:		
(A) Knives	2s. per dozen or 19%, whichever is the greater	—
(B) Parts of knives	18%	—
82.10 Knife blades	1s. per dozen or 18%, whichever is the greater	—
82.11 Razors and razor blades (including razor blade blanks, whether or not in strips):		
(A) Safety razor blades (including blanks):		
(1) Blanks, not ground	25%	—
(2) Other	18%	—
(B) Other	9½%	—
82.12 Scissors (including tailors' shears), and blades therefor	20%	—
82.13 Other articles of cutlery (for example, secateurs, hair clippers, butchers' cleavers, paper knives); manicure and chiropody sets and appliances (including nail files):		
(A) Manicure and chiropody sets and appliances	20%	—
(B) Sheep shearers and other animal hair clippers, flexible drive and vacuum operated types	11½%	—
(C) Secateurs	16%	—
(D) Other	14½%	—
82.14 Spoons, forks, fish-eaters, butter-knives, ladles, and similar kitchen or tableware	19%	—
82.15 Handles of base metal for articles falling within heading No. 82.09, 82.13 or 82.14	19%	—

Chapter 83

Miscellaneous Articles of Base Metal

Note

In this Chapter a reference to parts of articles is in no case to be taken as applying to cables, chains, nails, bolts, nuts, screws, springs or other articles of iron or steel of a kind described in heading No. 73.25, 73.29, 73.31, 73.32 or 73.35, nor to similar articles of other base metals (Chapters 74 to 81 inclusive).

Tariff Heading	Rate of Import Duty (*if any*)	
	Full	*Commonwealth* (C) *E.F.T.A.* (E)
83.01 Locks and padlocks (key, combination or electrically operated), and parts thereof, of base metal; frames incorporating locks, for handbags, trunks or the like, and parts of such frames, of base metal; keys for any of the foregoing articles, finished or not, of base metal:		
(A) Trunk, travelling bag, suitcase and attache case locks with the keys therefor not exceeding three per lock, and such locks without keys	14%	—
(B) Other	15½%	—
83.02 Base metal fittings and mountings of a kind suitable for furniture, doors, staircases, windows, blinds, coachwork, saddlery, trunks, caskets and the like (including automatic door closers); base metal hat-racks, hat-pegs, brackets and the like:		
(A) Hasps and staples	9%	—
(B) Other	13%	—
83.03 Safes, strong-boxes, armoured or reinforced strong-rooms, strong-room linings and strong-room doors, and cash and deed boxes and the like, of base metal	12%	—
83.04 Filing cabinets, racks, sorting boxes, paper trays, paper rests and similar office equipment, of base metal, other than office furniture falling within heading No. 94.03	12%	—
83.05 Fittings for loose-leaf binders, for files or for stationery books, of base metal; letter clips, paper clips, staples, indexing tags, and similar stationery goods, of base metal:		
(A) Indexers; list binders; fittings for files	13%	—
(B) Other	16%	—
83.06 Statuettes and other ornaments of a kind used indoors, of base metal	16%	—

Tariff Heading	Rate of Import Duty (if any)	
	Full	Commonwealth (C) E.F.T.A. (E)
83.07 Lamps and lighting fittings, of base metal, and parts thereof, of base metal (excluding switches, electric lamp holders, electric lamps for vehicles, electric battery or magneto lamps, and other articles falling within Chapter 85 except heading No. 85.22)	12½%	—
83.08 Flexible tubing and piping, of base metal ...	16%	—
83.09 Clasps, frames with clasps for handbags and the like, buckles, buckle-clasps, hooks, eyes, eyelets, and the like, of base metal, of a kind commonly used for clothing, travel goods, handbags, or other textile or leather goods; tubular rivets and bifurcated rivets, of base metal:		
(A) Bifurcated rivets of iron or steel ...	20%	—
(B) Handbag frames, not less than 5 inches and not more than 20 inches in length	9%	—
(C) Other	12%	—
83.10 Beads and spangles, of base metal ...	12%	—
83.11 Bells and gongs, non-electric, of base metal, and parts thereof of base metal:		
(A) Cycle bells; bell domes	24%	—
(B) Other	18%	—
83.12 Photograph, picture and similar frames, of base metal; mirrors of base metal	16%	—
83.13 Stoppers, crown corks, bottle caps, capsules, bung covers, seals and plombs, case corner protectors and other packing accessories, of base metal	12½%	—
83.14 Sign-plates, name-plates, numbers, letters and other signs, of base metal	15%	—
83.15 Wire, rods, tubes, plates, electrodes and similar products of base metal or of metal carbides, coated or cored with flux material, of a kind used for soldering, brazing, welding or deposition of metal or of metal carbides; wire and rods, of agglomerated base metal powder, used for metal spraying	12½%	—

SECTION XVI

MACHINERY AND MECHANICAL APPLIANCES ; ELECTRICAL EQUIPMENT ; PARTS THEREOF

Notes

1. This Section does not cover:

(a) Transmission, conveyor or elevator belts or belting, of artificial plastic material of Chapter 39, or of vulcanised rubber (heading No. 40.10); or other articles of a kind used on machinery, mechanical or electrical appliances, of unhardened vulcanised rubber (for example, washers) (heading No. 40.14);

(b) Articles of leather or of composition leather (heading No. 42.04) or of furskin (heading No. 43.03), of a kind used in machinery or mechanical appliances or for industrial purposes;

(c) Bobbins, spools, cops, cones, cores and similar supports, of a kind used on machinery, mechanical appliances or electrical goods, falling within Chapter 39, 40, 44 or 48 or Section XV;

(d) Perforated cards of paper or paperboard for Jacquard or similar machines, falling within heading No. 48.21;

(e) Transmission, conveyor or elevator belts of textile material (heading No. 59.16) or other articles of textile material of a kind commonly used in machinery or plant (heading No. 59.17);

(f) Articles wholly of precious or semi-precious stones (natural, synthetic or reconstructed), falling within heading No. 71.02, 71.03 or 71.15;

(g) Parts of general use, as defined in Note 2 to Section XV, of base metal (Section XV), or similar goods of artificial plastic materials (which are generally classified in heading No. 39.07);

(h) Endless belts of metal wire or strip (Section XV);

(ij) Articles falling within Chapter 83;

(k) Vehicles, aircraft, ships or boats, and parts thereof, of Section XVII;

(l) Articles falling within Chapter 90;

(m) Clocks, watches and other articles falling within Chapter 91;

(n) Brushes of a kind used as parts of machines, falling within heading No. 96.02; interchangeable tools falling within heading No. 82.05; similar interchangeable tools, which are to be classified according to the constituent material of their working part (for example, in Chapter 40, 42, 43, 45 or 59, or heading No. 68.04 or 69.09); or

(o) Articles falling within Chapter 97.

2. Subject to Notes 1 and 3 to this Section, Note 1 to Chapter 84 and to Note 1 to Chapter 85, parts of machines (not being parts of the articles described in headings Nos. 84.64, 85.23, 85.24, 85.25 and 85.27) are to be classified according to the following rules:

(a) Goods of a kind described in any of the headings of Chapters 84 and 85 (other than headings Nos. 84.65 and 85.28) are in all cases to be classified in their respective headings.

(b) Other parts, if suitable for use solely or principally with a particular kind of machine, or with a number of machines falling within the same heading (including a machine falling within heading No. 84.59 or 85.22) are to be classified with the machines of that kind. However, goods which are equally suitable for use principally with the goods of headings Nos. 85.13 and 85.15 are to be classified in heading No. 85.13.

(c) All other parts are to be classified in heading No. 84.65 or 85.28.

3. An incomplete machine is to be classified with the corresponding complete machine (and not with parts of such a machine if its parts are separately specified), provided it has the essential character of such a complete machine.

4. A machine (or an incomplete machine classified as if it were complete by virtue of the preceding Note 3) imported unassembled or disassembled is to be classified as a machine of the corresponding kind.

5. Unless the headings otherwise require, composite machines consisting of two or more machines fitted together to form a whole and other machines adapted for the purpose of performing two or more complementary or alternative functions are to be classified as if consisting only of that component or as being that machine which performs the principal function.

6. Motors and transmission, conveyor or elevator belts, for machinery or appliances to which they are fitted, or, if packed separately for convenience of transport, which are clearly intended to be fitted to or mounted on a common base with the machine or appliance with which they are imported, are to be classified under the same heading as such machinery or appliances.

7. For the purposes of these Notes, the expression " machine " means any machine, apparatus or appliance of a kind falling within Section XVI.

Chapter 84

Boilers, Machinery and Mechanical Appliances; Parts thereof

Notes

1. This Chapter does not cover:

(a) Millstones, grindstones and other articles falling within Chapter 68;

(b) Appliances and machinery (for example, pumps) and parts thereof, of ceramic material (Chapter 69);

(c) Laboratory glassware of heading No. 70.17; machinery and appliances and parts thereof, of glass (heading No. 70.20 or 70.21);

(d) Articles falling within heading No. 73.36 or 73.37 and similar articles of other base metals (Chapters 74 to 81);

(e) Hand tools or electro-mechanical domestic appliances, with self-contained electric motors, of heading No. 85.05 or 85.06; or

(f) Articles falling within Chapter 82, not being articles falling within heading No. 84.21, 84.22, 84.49 or 84.50.

2. Subject to the operation of Notes 5 and 6 to Section XVI, a machine or appliance which answers to a description in one or more of the headings Nos. 84.01 to 84.21 and at the same time to a description in one or other of the headings Nos. 84.22 to 84.60, is to be classified under the appropriate heading of the former group and not the latter.

Heading No. 84.17 is, however, to be taken not to apply to:

(a) Germination plant, incubators and brooders, falling within heading No. 84.28;

(b) Grain dampening machines falling within heading No. 84.29;

(c) Diffusing apparatus for sugar juice extraction falling within heading No. 84.30; or

(d) Machinery falling within heading No. 84.40 for the heat-treatment of textile yarns, fabrics or made up textile articles.

Heading No. 84.17 is also to be taken not to apply to machinery or plant, designed for a mechanical operation, in which the change of temperature, even if necessary, is subsidiary to the main function.

Heading No. 84.19 is to be taken not to apply to:

(a) Sewing machines (heading No. 84.41); or

(b) Office machinery of heading No. 84.54.

3. Heading No. 84.62 is to be taken to apply, *inter alia*, to polished steel balls, the maximum and minimum diameters of which do not differ from the nominal diameter by more than 1 per cent. or by more than 0·05 millimetre, whichever is less. Other steel balls are to be classified under heading No. 73.40.

4. A machine which is used for more than one purpose is, for the purposes of classification, to be treated as if its principal purpose were its sole purpose.

Subject to Note 2 to this Chapter and Note 5 to Section XVI, a machine whose principal purpose is not described in any heading or for which no one purpose is the principal purpose is, unless the context otherwise requires, to be classified in heading No. 84.59. Heading

No. 84.59 is also to be taken to cover machines for making rope or cable (for example, stranding, twisting or cabling machines) from metal wire, textile yarn or any other material or from a combination of such materials.

5. Heading No. 84.16 is to be taken to apply, *inter alia*, to machines for rolling into sheet form material fed to the rollers in a plastic condition.

Tariff Heading	Rate of Import Duty (if any)		
	Full	Commonwealth (C) E.F.T.A. (E)	
84.01 Steam and other vapour generating boilers (excluding central heating hot water boilers capable also of producing low pressure steam)	11%	—	
84.02 Auxiliary plant for use with steam and other vapour generating boilers (for example, economisers, superheaters, soot removers, gas recoverers and the like); condensers for vapour engines and power units	14%	—	
84.03 Producer gas and water gas generators, with or without purifiers; acetylene gas generators (water process) and similar gas generators, with or without purifiers	16%	—	
84.04 Steam engines (including mobile engines, but not steam tractors falling within heading No. 87.01 or mechanically propelled road rollers) with self-contained boilers	14%	—	
84.05 Steam and other vapour power units, not incorporating boilers	14%	—	
84.06 Internal combustion piston engines: (A) Engines: (1) Motor vehicle engines, but not including track-laying tractor engines:			
(a) Of a cylinder capacity exceeding 250 cubic centimetres	18½%	C E	12% —
(b) Other	20%	C E	13% —
(2) Other	12½%		
(B) Parts of engines: (1) Parts suitable for use in motor vehicles, but not including piston rings of a diameter of 5 inches or over when compressed or parts specialised for use in track-laying tractor engines:			
(a) Cylinder blocks, crankcases, cylinder heads, cylinders and liners, connecting rods and pistons	18½%	C E	12% —
(b) Other	20%	C E	13% —
(2) Other	11%	—	

Tariff Heading	Rate of Import Duty (if any)		
	Full	Commonwealth (C) E.F.T.A. (E)	
84.07 Hydraulic engines and motors (including water wheels and water turbines)	11%	—	
84.08 Other engines and motors:			
(A) Motor vehicle engines	19%	C E	12½%
(B) Musical instrument (including gramophone) motors	24%	C E	13%
(C) Camera and cinematograph motors ...	38%	—	
(D) Other	11%	—	
84.09 Mechanically propelled road rollers	12%	—	
84.10 Pumps (including motor pumps and turbo pumps) for liquids, whether or not fitted with measuring devices; liquid elevators of bucket, chain, screw, band and similar kinds	10½%	—	
84.11 Air pumps, vacuum pumps and air or gas compressors (including motor and turbo pumps and compressors, and free-piston generators for gas turbines); fans, blowers and the like:			
(A) Vacuum pumps and air or gas compressors	10%	—	
(B) Other pumps; fans, blowers and the like:			
(1) Parts and accessories of motor vehicles	19%	C E	12½%
(2) Other	10½%	—	
(C) Parts of the goods of subheadings (A) and (B) (2) above	10½%	—	
84.12 Air conditioning machines, self-contained, comprising a motor-driven fan and elements for changing the temperature and humidity of air	10%	—	
84.13 Furnace burners for liquid fuel (atomisers), for pulverised solid fuel or for gas; mechanical stokers, mechanical grates, mechanical ash dischargers and similar appliances	14%	—	
84.14 Industrial and laboratory furnaces and ovens, non-electric	11%	—	
84.15 Refrigerators and refrigerating equipment (electrical and other):			
(A) Electrically operated refrigerators ...	10%	—	
(B) Other refrigerators and refrigerating equipment	11%	—	

Tariff Heading	Rate of Import Duty (if any)	
	Full	Commonwealth (C) E.F.T.A. (E)
84.15 Refrigerators, etc.—contd.		
(C) Parts of refrigerators and refrigerating equipment:		
(1) Complete mechanical units ...	10½%	—
(2) Other	11%	—
84.16 Calendering and similar rolling machines (other than metal-working and metal-rolling machines and glass-working machines) and cylinders therefor	11%	
84.17 Machinery, plant and similar laboratory equipment, whether or not electrically heated, for the treatment of materials by a process involving a change of temperature such as heating, cooking, roasting, distilling, rectifying, sterilising, pasteurising, steaming, drying, evaporating, vapourising, condensing or cooling, not being machinery or plant of a kind used for domestic purposes; instantaneous or storage water heaters, non-electrical:		
(A) Electrical cooking and heating apparatus:		
(1) High frequency induction and dielectric apparatus	12½%	—
(2) Other	9%	—
(B) Other:		
(1) For the drying of hides, skins or leather, being dryers incorporating vertically suspended plates on which the material is pasted	7½%	—
(2) For the drying of textile fibres ...	10%	—
(3) Other	11%	—
(C) Parts of the goods of subheadings (A) (2) and (B) above	11%	—
84.18 Centrifuges; filtering and purifying machinery and apparatus (other than filter funnels, milk strainers and the like), for liquids or gases:		
(A) Centrifuges:		
(1) Dryers of the types used in dry cleaning and laundering	12%	—
(2) Cream separators	9%	—
(3) Other	14%	—
(B) Filtering and purifying machinery and apparatus:		
(1) Parts of motor vehicles	19%	C 12½% E —
(2) Other	14%	—
(C) Parts of the goods of subheadings (A) and (B) (2) above	11%	—

Tariff Heading	Rate of Import Duty (*if any*)	
	Full	*Commonwealth* (C) *E.F.T.A.* (E)
84.19 Machinery for cleaning or drying bottles or other containers; machinery for filling, closing, sealing, capsuling or labelling bottles, cans, boxes, bags or other containers; other packing or wrapping machinery; machinery for aerating beverages; dish washing machines:		
(A) Can casing machines; cappers, sealers (excluding carton sealing machines) and closers	10%	—
(B) Machines for filling containers, being machines incorporating devices which automatically control the quantity of material to be inserted into each container, but not including machines constructed for performing operations additional to filling and control of quantity	10%	—
(C) Tube filling machines, being machines for filling and closing collapsible metal containers	10%	—
(D) Other machines	11%	—
(E) Parts of the machines of subheadings (A) to (D) above	11%	—
84.20 Weighing machinery (excluding balances of a sensitivity of 5 centigrams or better), including weight-operated counting and checking machines; weighing machine weights of all kinds:		
(A) Weights of a kind used with the balances of heading No. 90.15	26½%	—
(B) Other	14%	—
84.21 Mechanical appliances (whether or not hand operated) for projecting, dispersing or spraying liquids or powders; fire extinguishers (charged or not); spray guns and similar appliances; steam or sand blasting machines and similar jet projecting machines:		
(A) Sand blast nozzles lined with material wholly or mainly of silicon carbide or tungsten carbide	9%	—
(B) Spraying machines incorporating an endless conveyor and one or more spray guns with a reciprocating or rotary motion and also incorporating mechanism which cuts off the spray automatically when the material is not directly beneath the gun or guns	7½%	—
(C) Other	11%	—

Tariff Heading	Rate of Import Duty (*if any*)	
	Full	*Commonwealth* (C) *E.F.T.A.* (E)
84.22 Lifting, handling, loading or unloading machinery, telphers and conveyors (for example, lifts, hoists, winches, cranes, transporter cranes, jacks, pulley tackle, belt conveyors and teleferics), not being machinery falling within heading No. 84.23:		
(A) Power operated machines, the following:	10%	—
Cranes		
Hoists		
Winches		
Lifts (elevators)		
Telphers		
Conveyor or transporter installations which operate on a fixed track		
Winders, being mining machines		
(B) Parts of power operated machines, the following:	10%	—
Conversion front end attachments for cranes		
Crane attachments for lorries or tractors		
(C) Non-portable lifting jacks	10%	—
(D) Parts of the goods of subheadings (A), (B) and (C) above	11%	—
(E) Rolling mill (metal working) machinery, the following:	20%	—
Working and transporter roller racks and tables; ingot, slab, bar and plate tilters and manipulators		
(F) Stacking machines designed for stacking hides, skins or leather of irregular lengths, and incorporating devices which adjust the stacking mechanism automatically according to the length of each piece of material	7½%	—
(G) Other	11%	
84.23 Excavating, levelling, tamping, boring and extracting machinery, stationary or mobile, for earth, minerals or ores (for example, mechanical shovels, coal-cutters, excavators, scrapers, levellers and bulldozers); pile-drivers; snow-ploughs, not self-propelled (including snow-plough attachments):		
(A) Power operated machines, the following:	10%	—
Excavators; motor graders; rippers; rooters; scrapers; trenching machines; ditchers; coal cutters		

Tariff Heading	Rate of Import Duty (if any)	
	Full	Commonwealth (C) E.F.T.A. (E)

84.23 Excavating, etc.—contd.
  (B) Parts of power operated machines, the
     following:
        Conversion front end attachments
        for excavators
        Shovel and dragline attachments for
        lorries or tractors
        Angledozer and bulldozer attach-
        ments
        Excavator buckets, including shovel
        dippers, dragline, clamshell, orange
        peel and grab buckets and rock
        grabs
	10%	—

(C) Parts of the goods of subheadings (A) and (B) above	11%	—
(D) Rotary snow-plough attachments not incorporating power units	9%	—
(E) Other	11%	—
84.24 Agricultural and horticultural machinery for soil preparation or cultivation (for example, ploughs, harrows, cultivators, seed and ferti- liser distributors); lawn and sports ground rollers	9%	—
84.25 Harvesting and threshing machinery; straw and fodder presses; hay or grass mowers; winnowing and similar cleaning machines for seed, grain or leguminous vegetables and egg-grading and other grading machines for agricultural produce (other than those of a kind used in the bread grain milling industry falling within heading No. 84.29):		
(A) Root topping machines, root lifters and root harvesters	8%	—
(B) Hay or grass mowers: (1) Rotary blade type	11%	—
(2) Other	10%	—

(C) Other:
     (1) Agricultural and commercial
        horticultural machines
	12%	—

(2) Other	11%	—
84.26 Dairy machinery (including milking mach- ines):		
(A) Cheese presses; milking machines ...	9%	—
(B) Churns for butter making and com- bined churns and butter workers	12%	—
(C) Other	13½%	—

Tariff Heading	Rate of Import Duty (if any)	
	Full	Commonwealth (C) E.F.T.A. (E)
84.27 Presses, crushers and other machinery, of a kind used in wine-making, cider-making, fruit juice preparation or the like	14%	—
84.28 Other agricultural, horticultural, poultry-keeping and bee-keeping machinery; germination plant fitted with mechanical or thermal equipment; poultry incubators and brooders:		
(A) Sheep shearers and other animal hair-clippers	10%	—
(B) Other	12%	—
84.29 Machinery of a kind used in the bread grain milling industry, and other machinery (other than farm type machinery) for the working of cereals or dried leguminous vegetables	14%	—
84.30 Machinery, not falling within any other heading of this Chapter, of a kind used in the following food or drink industries: bakery, confectionery, chocolate manufacture, macaroni, ravioli or similar cereal food manufacture, the preparation of meat, fish, fruit or vegetables (including mincing or slicing machines), sugar manufacture or brewing:		
(A) Gut cleaning machines, being slaughterhouse machinery; extruders, spreaders and coilers, being machines of the types used for preparing macaroni and similar cereal foods	10%	—
(B) Other machines	11%	—
(C) Parts of the machines of subheadings (A) and (B) above	11%	—
84.31 Machinery for making or finishing cellulosic pulp, paper or paperboard	11%	—
84.32 Book-binding machinery, including book-sewing machines	11%	—
84.33 Paper or paperboard cutting machines of all kinds; other machinery for making up paper pulp, paper or paperboard:		
(A) Box and carton making machines, the following: Sheet fed cutting and creasing platen presses	10%	—
(B) Parts of the machines of subheading (A) above	11%	—
(C) Other	11%	—

Tariff Heading	Rate of Import Duty (*if any*)	
	Full	*Commonwealth (C)* *E.F.T.A.* *(E)*
84.34 Machinery, apparatus and accessories for type-founding or type-setting; machinery, other than the machine-tools of heading No. 84.45, 84.46 or 84.47, for preparing or working printing blocks, plates or cylinders; printing type, impressed flongs and matrices, printing blocks, plates and cylinders; blocks, plates, cylinders and lithographic stones, prepared for printing purposes (for example, planed, grained or polished):		
(A) Typesetting machines	10%	—
(B) Parts of typesetting machines ...	11%	—
(C) Impressed flongs and matrices for the production of complete printed pages, each page, without margins, being not less than 20 inches long and not less than 15 inches wide	—	—
(D) Other	11%	—
84.35 Other printing machinery; machines for uses ancillary to printing:		
(A) Rotary newspaper printing machines, that is to say, rotary printing machines designed for the printing of newspapers and the like from reels of paper, and equipped with cutting and folding mechanism	10%	—
(B) Sheet fed printing machines, the following: Cylinder flat bed, platen or rotary presses, for either letterpress, lithographic, gravure or aniline printing, whether printing from flat formes or from curved plates or formes, whether hand fed or automatically fed	10%	—
(C) Magazine presses, whether flat bed, rotary sheet or web fed and with or without folding, stitching and cutting mechanism	10%	—
(D) Other machines	11%	—
(E) Parts of the machines of subheadings (A) to (D) above	11%	—
84.36 Machines for extruding man-made textiles; machines of a kind used for processing natural or man-made textile fibres; textile spinning and twisting machines; textile doubling, throwing and reeling (including weft-winding) machines: (A) Machines, the following: Opening machines Ragtearing machines Garnetting machines	10%	—

Tariff Heading	Rate of Import Duty (*if any*)	
	Full	*Commonwealth* (C) *E.F.T.A.* (E)
84.36 Machines for extruding man-made textiles, etc.—*contd.*		
(A) Machines, the following:—*contd.*		
Feeding machines		
Spreading machines		
Scutching machines		
Tenterhook Willeys (Fearnought machines)		
Burring machines		
Hackling machines		
Carding machines		
Lap forming machines		
Combing machines		
Gilling machines		
Carbonising machines		
Drawing frames		
Roving, flyer or speed frames		
Jute and hemp softening machines		
Beating machines		
Fibre cutting machines		
Spinning machines and twisting machines, including spinning frames and mules, but not including doubling machines		
(B) Other	11%	—
84.37 Weaving machines, knitting machines and machines for making gimped yarn, tulle, lace, embroidery, trimmings, braid or net; machines for preparing yarns for use on such machines, including warping and warp sizing machines	10½%	—
84.38 Auxiliary machinery for use with machines of heading No. 84.37 (for example, dobbies, Jacquards, automatic stop motions and shuttle changing mechanisms); parts and accessories suitable for use solely or principally with the machines of the present heading or with machines falling within heading No. 84.36 or 84.37 (for example, spindles and spindle flyers, card clothing, combs, extruding nipples, shuttles, healds and heald-lifters and hosiery needles):		
(A) Inset mails of a kind used in the manufacture of wire healds for textile looms	—	—
(B) Bearded needles, and narrowing points, running-on points and welt-hooks, adapted for use in conjunction therewith	32%	—
(C) Hosiery latch needles	26½%	—

Tariff Heading	Rate of Import Duty (*if any*)	
	Full	*Commonwealth* (C) *E.F.T.A.* (E)
84.38 Auxiliary machinery, etc.—*contd.*		
(D) Other	11%	—
84.39 Machinery for the manufacture or finishing of felt in the piece or in shapes, including felt-hat making machines and hat-making blocks	14%	—
84.40 Machinery for washing, cleaning, drying, bleaching, dyeing, dressing, finishing or coating textile yarns, fabrics or made-up textile articles (including laundry and dry-cleaning machinery); fabric folding, reeling or cutting machines; machines of a kind used in the manufacture of linoleum or other floor coverings for applying the paste to the base fabric or other support; machines of a type used for printing a repetitive design, repetitive words or overall colour on textiles, leather, wallpaper, wrapping paper, linoleum or other materials, and engraved or etched plates, blocks or rollers therefor:		

(A) Dry cleaning and laundering machines (other than hand operated machines of the types used for domestic purposes), the following:
      Cleaners and washers
      Dryers
      Wringers
      Ironing machines
	10%	—

(B) Other machines	11%	—
(C) Parts of the machines of subheadings (A) and (B) above	11%	—
84.41 Sewing machines; furniture specially designed for sewing machines; sewing machine needles	14%	—
84.42 Machinery (other than sewing machines) for preparing, tanning or working hides, skins or leather (including boot and shoe machinery):		
(A) Machines for preparing, tanning or finishing hides, skins or leather	7½%	—
(B) Other	11%	—
84.43 Converters, ladles, ingot moulds and casting machines, of a kind used in metallurgy and in metal foundries	11%	—

Tariff Heading	Rate of Import Duty (if any)	
	Full	Commonwealth (C) E.F.T.A. (E)
84.44 Rolling mills and rolls therefor:		
(A) Rolls for rolling mills, or iron or steel	13½%	—
(B) Other	16%	—
84.45 Machine-tools for working metal or metallic carbides, not being machines falling within heading No. 84.49 or 84.50:		
(A) Flying shears of a kind used in rolling mills	20%	—
(B) Other	9%	—
84.46 Machine-tools for working stone, ceramics, concrete, asbestos-cement and like mineral materials or for working glass in the cold, other than machines falling within heading No. 84.49:		
(A) Machines for cutting, shaping, dressing, or polishing natural building stone	12½%	—
(B) Glass-working machines of the types used for surface grinding, polishing and smoothing in the production of plate glass	12½%	—
(C) Other	14%	—
84.47 Machine-tools for working wood, cork, bone, ebonite (vulcanite), hard artificial plastic materials or other hard carving materials, other than machines falling within heading No. 84.49:		
(A) Machine-tools for working wood, the following: 　　Branding machines 　　Corrugated fastener driving machines 　　Peeling machines 　　Slicing machines 　　Splitting machines 　　Cooperage machines, the following: 　　　Stave hollowing and backing machines 　　　Stave bending machines 　　　Stave jointing machines 　　　Head rounding and bevelling machines 　　　Crozing machines; chiming and crozing machines; chiming, crozing and howelling machines 　　　Shive making and working machines	13½%	—
(B) Other	15%	—

Tariff Heading	Rate of Import Duty (if any)	
	Full	Commonwealth (C) E.F.T.A. (E)
84.48 Accessories and parts suitable for use solely or principally with the machines falling within headings Nos. 84.45 to 84.47, including work and tool holders, self-opening dieheads, dividing heads and other appliances for machine-tools; tool holders for any type of tool or machine-tool for working in the hand:		
(A) Parts of flying shears of a kind used in rolling mills	20%	—
(B) Accessories and parts of the machine-tools of subheading No. 84.45(B)	9%	—
(C) Other	12%	—
84.49 Tools for working in the hand, pneumatic or with self-contained non-electric motor:		
(A) Tools	10½%	—
(B) Parts of the tools of subheading (A) above	11%	—
84.50 Gas-operated welding, brazing, cutting and surface tempering appliances	11%	—
84.51 Typewriters, other than typewriters incorporating calculating mechanisms; cheque-writing machines:		
(A) Non-electric typewriters	7½%	—
(B) Cheque-writing machines	10%	—
(C) Other	12%	—
84.52 Calculating machines; accounting machines, cash registers, postage-franking machines, ticket-issuing machines and similar machines, incorporating a calculating device:		
(A) Cash registers	8%	—
(B) Electronic computers, complete electronic computing systems and central processing units	14%	—
(C) Other	11%	—
84.53 Statistical machines of a kind operated in conjunction with punched cards (for example, sorting, calculating and tabulating machines); accounting machines operated in conjunction with similar punched cards; auxiliary machines for use with such machines (for example, punching and checking machines):		
(A) Electronic computers, complete electronic computing systems and central processing units	14%	—
(B) Other	11%	—

Tariff Heading	Rate of Import Duty (if any)	
	Full	Commonwealth (C) E.F.T.A. (E)
84.54 Other office machines (for example, hecto-graph or stencil duplicating machines, addressing machines, coin-sorting machines, coin-counting and wrapping machines, pencil-sharpening machines, perforating and stapling machines):		
(A) Cash registers	8%	—
(B) Machines of the types used for the automatic production of typewritten correspondence	12%	—
(C) Other	11%	
84.55 Parts and accessories (other than covers, carrying cases and the like) suitable for use solely or principally with machines of a kind falling within heading No. 84.51, 84.52, 84.53 or 84.54:		
(A) Parts of the following machines (not being electronic machines or machines operated in conjunction with punched cards): Typewriters (including electric type-writers) Machines of the types used for the automatic production of type-written correspondence Accounting machines Calculating machines Adding machines Listing machines Book-keeping machines Billing machines Posting machines Cheque-writing machines	2s. 9d. per lb. or 12½%, whichever is the less	—
(B) Parts of cash registers	8%	—
(C) Parts of electronic computers... ...	14%	—
(D) Other	11%	—
84.56 Machinery for sorting, screening, separating, washing, crushing, grinding or mixing earth, stone, ores or other mineral substances, in solid (including powder and paste) form; machinery for agglomerating, moulding or shaping solid mineral fuels, ceramic paste, unhardened cements, plastering materials or other mineral products in powder or paste form; machines for forming foundry moulds of sand:		
(A) Brick presses	10½%	—
(B) Other	11%	—

Tariff Heading	Rate of Import Duty (if any)	
	Full	Commonwealth (C) E.F.T.A. (E)
84.57 Glass-working machines (other than machines for working glass in the cold); machines for assembling electric filament and discharge lamps and electronic and similar tubes and valves:		
(A) Automatic multi-head machines of the types used for bottle-making, for making glass stems for electric lamps or for exhausting electric lamps and valves	10%	—
(B) Other machines	11%	—
(C) Parts of the machines of subheadings (A) and (B) above	11%	—
84.58 Automatic vending machines (for example, stamp, cigarette, chocolate and food machines), not being games of skill or chance	11%	—
84.59 Machinery and mechanical appliances (except those suitable for use solely or principally as parts of other machines or apparatus), not falling within any other heading of this Chapter:		
(A) Strip coilers of a kind used in rolling mills	20%	—
(B) Other	11%	—
84.60 Moulding boxes for metal foundry; moulds of a type used for metal (other than ingot moulds), for metallic carbides, for glass, for mineral materials (for example, ceramic pastes, concrete or cement) or for rubber or artificial plastic materials	12½%	—
84.61 Taps, cocks, valves and similar appliances, for pipes, boiler shells, tanks, vats and the like, including pressure reducing valves and thermostatically controlled valves	12½%	—
84.62 Ball, roller or needle roller bearings	14%	—
84.63 Transmission shafts, cranks, bearing housings, plain shaft bearings, gears and gearing (including friction gears and gear-boxes and other variable speed gears), flywheels, pulleys and pulley blocks, clutches and shaft couplings	11%	—

Tariff Heading	Rate of Import Duty (if any)	
	Full	Commonwealth (C) E.F.T.A. (E)
84.64 Gaskets and similar joints of metal sheeting combined with other material (for example, asbestos, felt and paperboard) or of laminated metal foil; sets or assortments of gaskets and similar joints, dissimilar in composition, for engines, pipes, tubes and the like, put up in pouches, envelopes or similar packings	12½%	—
84.65 Machinery parts, not containing electrical connectors, insulators, coils, contacts or other electrical features and not falling within any other heading in this Chapter	13½%	

Chapter 85

Electrical Machinery and Equipment; Parts thereof

Notes

1. This Chapter does not cover:

(a) Electrically warmed blankets, bed pads, foot-muffs and the like; electrically warmed clothing, footwear and ear pads and other electrically warmed articles worn on or about the person;

(b) Articles of glass falling within heading No. 70.11 (for example, glass bulbs for electric lamps);

(c) Electrically heated furniture of Chapter 94.

2. Heading No. 85.01 is to be taken not to apply to goods described in heading No. 85.08, 85.09 or 85.21, other than metal tank mercury arc rectifiers which remain classified in heading No. 85.01.

3. Heading No. 85.06 is to be taken to apply only to the following electro-mechanical machines of types commonly used for domestic purposes:

(a) Vacuum cleaners, floor polishers, food grinders and mixers, fruit juice extractors and fans, of any weight;

(b) Other machines provided the weight of such other machines does not exceed 20 kilograms.

The heading does not, however, apply to dish washing machines (heading No. 84.19) centrifugal and other clothes washing machines (heading No. 84.18 or 84.40), roller and other ironing machines (heading No. 84.16 or 84.40), sewing machines (heading No. 84.41) or to electro-thermic appliances (heading No. 85.12).

Tariff Heading	Rate of Import Duty (if any)	
	Full	Commonwealth (C) E.F.T.A. (E)
85.01 Electrical goods of the following descriptions: generators, motors, converters (rotary or static), transformers, rectifiers and rectifying apparatus, inductors:		
(A) Motor and generator casings and unwound rotors and stators	8%	—
(B) Transformers rated at not less than 1 KVA on continuous load	11%	—
(C) Metal tank mercury arc rectifiers ...	12½%	—
(D) Inductors, calibrated	20%	—
(E) Generators, motors, synchros and rotary converters	13½%	—
(F) Other	16%	—
85.02 Electro-magnets; permanent magnets and articles of special materials for permanent magnets, being blanks of such magnets; electro-magnetic and permanent magnet chucks, clamps, vices and similar work holders; electro-magnetic clutches and couplings; electro-magnetic brakes; electro-magnetic lifting heads:		
(A) Chucks and vices	12%	—
(B) Other	16%	—

Tariff Heading	Rate of Import Duty (if any)	
	Full	Commonwealth (C) E.F.T.A. (E)
85.03 Primary cells and primary batteries:		
(A) Standard cells	20%	—
(B) Other	17%	—
85.04 Electric accumulators	12%	—
85.05 Tools for working in the hand, with self-contained electric motor	11%	—
85.06 Electro-mechanical domestic appliances, with self-contained electric motor:		
(A) Vacuum cleaners	12%	—
(B) Food mixers, grinders or slicers ...	12%	—
(C) Drink mixers and fruit juice extractors	12%	—
(D) Refuse disposal units	12%	—
(E) Other appliances	13½%	—
(F) Parts of the appliances of subheadings (A) to (E) above	13½%	--
85.07 Shavers and hair clippers, with self-contained electric motor:		
(A) Shavers and hair clippers	10½%	—
(B) Parts of shavers and hair clippers ...	14½%	—
85.08 Electrical starting and ignition equipment for internal combustion engines (including ignition magnetos, magneto-dynamos, ignition coils, starter motors, sparking plugs and glow plugs); dynamos and cut-outs for use in conjunction therewith:		
(A) Ignition magnetos	16%	—
(B) Other starting and ignition equipment and dynamos and cut-outs:		
(1) Parts of motor vehicles	19%	C 12½% E
(2) Other	14½%	—
85.09 Electrical lighting and signalling equipment and electrical windscreen wipers, defrosters and demisters, for cycles or motor vehicles:		
(A) Equipment for cycles (other than motor cycles):		
(1) Dynamo lighting sets, comprising dynamo and head lamp, with or without clips and wiring, and with or without rear lamp	22%	—
(2) Dynamos for lighting sets, with or without clips and wiring; and cases (or bodies) thereof, whether complete or not	22%	—
(3) Lamps designed for use on cycles; and cases (or bodies) thereof, whether complete or not	22%	—

Tariff Heading	Rate of Import Duty (if any)		
	Full	Commonwealth (C) E.F.T.A. (E)	
85.09 Electrical lighting, etc.—*contd.*			
(A) Equipment for cycles, etc.,—*contd.*			
(4) Other equipment	17½%		
(5) Parts (other than cases or bodies of dynamos and lamps)	17½%		
(B) Equipment for motor vehicles:			
(1) Defrosters and demisters	13½%	C E	9% —
(2) Other	19%	C E	12½% —
85.10 Portable electric battery and magneto lamps, other than lamps falling within heading No. 85.09	16%		
85.11 Industrial and laboratory electric furnaces, ovens and induction and dielectric heating equipment; electric welding, brazing and soldering machines and apparatus and similar electric machines and apparatus for cutting:			
(A) Welding machines or apparatus (other than tube-making machines or apparatus)	12%		
(B) Heating and cooking apparatus:			
(1) High frequency induction and dielectric apparatus	12½%	—	
(2) Other	9%	—	
(C) Other machines and apparatus ...	14½%	—	
(D) Parts of the goods of subheadings (A), (B) (2) and (C) above	14½%	—	
85.12 Electric instantaneous or storage water heaters and immersion heaters; electric soil heating apparatus and electric space heating apparatus; electric hair dressing appliances (for example, hairdryers, hair curlers, curling tong heaters) and electric smoothing irons; electro-thermic domestic appliances; electric heating resistors, other than those of carbon:			
(A) Heating and cooking apparatus:			
(1) High frequency induction and dielectric apparatus	12½%	—	
(2) Other	9%	—	
(B) Hairdryers; hand and face dryers ...	14½%	—	
(C) Other apparatus and appliances ...	16%	—	
(D) Parts of the goods of subheadings (A) and (C) above	16%	—	
85.13 Electrical line telephonic and telegraphic apparatus (including such apparatus for carrier-current line systems)	12%	—	

Tariff Heading	Rate of Import Duty (if any)	
	Full	Commonwealth (C) E.F.T.A. (E)
85.14 Microphones and stands therefor; loudspeakers; audio-frequency electric amplifiers:		
(A) Microphones and stands therefor; loudspeakers and amplifiers, not being sound amplification apparatus of a kind used for the reproduction of music	16%	—
(B) Other loudspeakers and amplifiers ...	16%	C 10½% E —
(C) Parts of the goods of subheadings (A) and (B) above	16%	—
85.15 Radiotelegraphic and radiotelephonic transmission and reception apparatus; radio-broadcasting and television transmission and reception apparatus (including those incorporating gramophones) and television cameras; radio navigational aid apparatus, radar apparatus and radio remote control apparatus:		
(A) Transmitting sets, receiving sets and combined transmitting and receiving sets:		
(1) Receiving sets of the domestic or portable type	18%	—
(2) Sets designed or adapted for fitting to motor vehicles	20%	C 13½% E —
(3) Other	16½%	—
(B) Parts of the sets of subheading (A) above	18%	—
(C) Radiogramophones; combined recorders and reproducers for magnetic sound recording on tape or wire, incorporated with radio receivers of the domestic type or with radio-gramophones	18%	C 12% E —
(D) Other	18%	—
85.16 Electric traffic control equipment for railways, roads or inland waterways and equipment used for similar purposes in port installations or upon airfields	16%	—
85.17 Electric sound or visual signalling apparatus (such as bells, sirens, indicator panels, burglar and fire alarms), other than those of heading No. 85.09 or 85.16	16%	—
85.18 Electrical capacitors, fixed or variable:		
(A) Laboratory and standard	20%	—
(B) Other	14½%	—

Tariff Heading	Rate of Import Duty (if any)	
	Full	Commonwealth (C) E.F.T.A. (E)
85.19 Electrical apparatus for making and breaking electrical circuits, for the protection of electrical circuits, or for making connections to or in electrical circuits (for example, switches, relays, fuses, lightning arresters, surge suppressors, plugs, lamp-holders, terminals, terminal strips and junction boxes); resistors, fixed or variable (including potentiometers), other than heating resistors; switchboards (other than telephone switchboards) and control panels:		
(A) Parts of motor vehicles	19%	C 12½% E —
(B) Resistors, precision, standard and laboratory	26½%	—
(C) Other	12½%	—
85.20 Electric filament lamps and electric discharge lamps (including infra-red and ultra-violet lamps); arc-lamps; electrically ignited photographic flashbulbs:		
(A) Discharge lamps	20%	—
(B) Arc-lamps for cinematograph projectors	20%	—
(C) Other	12½%	—
85.21 Thermionic, cold cathode and photo-cathode valves and tubes (including vapour or gas filled valves and tubes, cathode-ray tubes, television camera tubes and mercury arc rectifying valves and tubes); photocells; mounted transistors and similar mounted devices incorporating semi-conductors; mounted piezo-electric crystals:		
(A) Mercury arc rectifiers, being rectifiers with mercury pool cathodes	12½%	—
(B) Thermionic, cold cathode and photo-cathode valves and tubes other than those described in subheading (A) above	20%	—
(C) Photocells	23%	—
(D) Mounted piezo-electric crystals of quartz	8%	—
(E) Other	20%	—
85.22 Electrical goods and apparatus (except those suitable for use solely or principally as parts of other machines or apparatus), not falling within any other heading of this Chapter:		
(A) Standard signal generators, radio type; oscillators, laboratory and standard	26½%	—
(B) Other	12½%	—

Tariff Heading	Rate of Import Duty (if any)	
	Full	Commonwealth (C) E.F.T.A. (E)
85.23 Insulated (including enamelled or anodised) electric wire, cable, bars, strip and the like (including co-axial cable), whether or not fitted with connectors:		
(A) Cable core, whether bound with brass tape or not, produced by stripping used submarine cables	—	
(B) Wire and cable (but not including wire insulated only with enamel, varnish or lacquer)	11½%	—
(C) Other	12½%	—
85.24 Carbon brushes, arc-lamp carbons, battery carbons, carbon electrodes and other carbon articles of a kind used for electrical purposes:		
(A) Arc-lamp carbons and parts thereof:		
(1) Arc-lamp carbons which are externally covered with copper and do not exceed 14 millimetres in diameter and parts thereof	5s. 9d. per lb.	—
(2) Other	1s. 9d. per lb.	—
(B) Amorphous carbon electrodes, but not including primary battery carbons or arc-lamp carbons	20%	—
(C) Carbon brushes fitted with metal terminals or metal connectors	9½%	—
(D) Other:		
(1) Carbon electrodes:		
(a) Slabs in length exceeding 960 millimetres and not exceeding 1,040 millimetres, in width exceeding 168 millimetres and not exceeding 190 millimetres, and in thickness exceeding 48 millimetres and not exceeding 52 millimetres	9%	—
(b) Rods in length exceeding 288 millimetres and not exceeding 364 millimetres and in diameter exceeding 48 millimetres and not exceeding 52 millimetres	9%	—
(c) Other	12½%	—
(2) Other	12½%	—
85.25 Insulators of any material:		
(A) Porcelain insulators, whether or not incorporating metal fittings, of a weight exceeding 2 lb.	13%	—
(B) Other	16%	—

Tariff Heading	Rate of Import Duty (if any)	
	Full	Commonwealth (C) E.F.T.A. (E)
85.26 Insulating fittings for electrical machines, appliances or equipment, being fittings wholly of insulating material apart from any minor components of metal incorporated during moulding solely for purposes of assembly, but not including insulators falling within heading No. 85.25:		
(A) Parts of motor vehicles	19%	C 12½% E —
(B) Other	16%	—
85.27 Electrical conduit tubing and joints therefor, of base metal lined with insulating material	12½%	—
85.28 Electrical parts of machinery and apparatus, not being goods falling within any of the preceding headings of this Chapter	16%	—

SECTION XVII

VEHICLES, AIRCRAFT, AND PARTS THEREOF; VESSELS AND CERTAIN ASSOCIATED TRANSPORT EQUIPMENT

Notes

1. This Section does not cover articles falling within heading No. 97.01, 97.03 or 97.08, or bobsleighs, toboggans and the like falling within heading No. 97.06.

2. Throughout this Section the expressions " parts " and " parts and accessories " are to be taken not to apply to the following articles, whether or not they are identifiable as for the goods of this Section:

(a) Joints, washers and the like (classified according to their constituent material or in heading No. 84.64);

(b) Parts of general use, as defined in Note 2 to Section XV, of base metal (Section XV), or similar goods of artificial plastic materials (which are generally classified in heading No. 39.07);

(c) Articles falling within Chapter 82 (tools);

(d) Articles falling within heading No. 83.11;

(e) Machines and mechanical appliances and other articles falling within headings Nos. 84.01 to 84.59, 84.61 or 84.62 and parts of engines and motors falling within heading No. 84.63;

(f) Electrical machinery and equipment (Chapter 85);

(g) Articles falling within Chapter 90;

(h) Clocks (Chapter 91);

(ij) Arms (Chapter 93);

(k) Brushes of a kind used as parts of vehicles (heading No. 96.02).

3. References in Chapters 86 to 88 to parts or accessories are to be taken not to apply to parts or accessories which are not suitable for use solely or principally with the articles of those Chapters. A part or accessory which answers to a description in two or more of the headings of those Chapters is to be classified under that heading which corresponds to the principal use of that part or accessory.

4. Flying machines specially constructed so that they can also be used as road vehicles are classified as flying machines. Amphibious motor vehicles are classified as motor vehicles.

5. An incomplete or unfinished article of this Section is to be classified as the corresponding complete or finished article, provided it has the essential character of such complete or finished article.

6. Unless otherwise provided, an article of this Section (or an incomplete or unfinished article classified as if it were complete or finished by virtue of the preceding Note 5) imported unassembled is to be classified as an assembled article of the corresponding kind.

Chapter 86

Railway and Tramway Locomotives, Rolling-stock and Parts Thereof; Railway and Tramway Track Fixtures and Fittings; Traffic Signalling Equipment of All Kinds (Not Electrically Powered)

Notes

1. This Chapter does not cover:
   (a) Railway or tramway sleepers of wood (heading No. 44.07) or of concrete (heading No. 68.11);
   (b) Railway or tramway track construction material of iron or steel falling within heading No. 73.16; or
   (c) Electrically powered signalling apparatus falling within heading No. 85.16.

2. Heading No. 86.09 is to be taken to apply, *inter alia*, to:
   (a) Axles, wheels, metal tyres, hoops and hubs and other parts of wheels;
   (b) Frames, underframes and bogies;
   (c) Axle boxes; brake gear;
   (d) Buffers for rolling-stock; coupling gear and corridor connections;
   (e) Coachwork.

3. Subject to the provisions of Note 1 above, heading No. 86.10 is to be taken to apply, *inter alia*, to:
   (a) Assembled track, turntables, platform buffers, loading gauges;
   (b) Semaphores, mechanical signal discs, level crossing control gear, signal and point controls, whether or not they are fitted for electric lighting.

Tariff Heading	Rate of Import Duty (if any)	
	Full	Commonwealth (C) E.F.T.A. (E)
86.01 Steam rail locomotives and tenders ...	12½%	—
86.02 Electric rail locomotives, battery operated or powered from an external source of electricity	12½%	—
86.03 Other rail locomotives	12½%	—
86.04 Mechanically propelled railway and tramway coaches, vans and trucks; mechanically propelled track inspection trolleys	12½%	—
86.05 Railway and tramway passenger coaches and luggage vans; hospital coaches, prison coaches, testing coaches, travelling post office coaches and other special purpose railway coaches	12½%	—
86.06 Railway and tramway rolling-stock, the following: workshops, cranes and other service vehicles	12½%	—

Tariff Heading	Rate of Import Duty (*if any*)	
	Full	*Commonwealth (C) E.F.T.A. (E)*
86.07 Railway and tramway goods vans, goods wagons and trucks:		
(A) For use on railways not exceeding 3 feet in gauge	26½%	—
(B) Other	16%	—
86.08 Road-rail and similar containers specially designed and equipped to be equally suitable for transport by rail, road and ship	16%	—
86.09 Parts of railway and tramway locomotives and rolling-stock:		
(A) Of vans, wagons and trucks for use on railways not exceeding 3 feet in gauge	17%	—
(B) Other	13½%	—
86.10 Railway and tramway track fixtures and fittings; mechanical equipment, not electrically powered, for signalling to or controlling road, rail or other vehicles, ships or aircraft; parts of the foregoing fixtures, fittings or equipment	16%	—

Chapter 87

Vehicles, other than Railway or Tramway Rolling-stock, and parts thereof

Notes

1. For the purposes of this Chapter, tractors are deemed to be vehicles constructed essentially for hauling or pushing another vehicle, appliance or load, whether or not they contain subsidiary provision for the transport, in connection with the main use of the tractor, of tools, seeds, fertilisers or other goods.

2. Motor chassis fitted with cabs are to be treated as falling within heading No. 87.02 and not within heading No. 87.04.

3. Headings Nos. 87.10 and 87.14 are to be taken not to apply to children's cycles which are not fitted with ball bearings nor to children's cycles which, though fitted with ball bearings, are not constructed in the normal form of adults' cycles. Such children's cycles are to be treated as falling within heading No. 97.01.

4. The headings of this Chapter are to be taken not to apply to railway or tramway rolling-stock designed solely for running on rails.

Tariff Heading	Rate of Import Duty (if any)		
	Full	Commonwealth (C) E.F.T.A. (E)	
87.01 Tractors (other than those falling within heading No. 87.07), whether or not fitted with power take-offs, winches or pulleys:			
(A) Track-laying tractors:			
(1) Of a drawbar horsepower not exceeding 50	15%	—	
(2) Of a drawbar horsepower exceeding 50	12%	—	
(B) Other tractors:			
(1) One or two wheeled tractors ...	12%	—	
(2) Other:			
(a) Agricultural	12%	C E	12% —
(b) Other	22%	C E	15% —
87.02 Motor vehicles for the transport of persons, goods or materials (including sports motor vehicles, other than those of heading No. 87.09):			
(A) Dumpers designed solely for use in excavating and levelling operations	12%	—	
(B) Agricultural vehicles of a kind mainly used for hauling or pushing another vehicle, appliance or load	12%	C E	12% —
(C) Other:			
(1) Motor vehicles for the transport of persons including vehicles designed for the transport of both passengers and goods:			
(a) With a seating capacity of 15 or more and either a spark ignition engine of a cylinder capacity	22%	C E	15% —

Tariff Heading	Rate of Import Duty (if any)		
	Full	Commonwealth (C) E.F.T.A. (E)	

87.02 Motor vehicles for the transport of persons, etc.—*contd.*
  (C) Other—*contd.*
    (1) Motor vehicles etc.—*contd.*
      (*a*) With a seating capacity etc.—*contd.*
        of 2,800 cubic centimetres or more or a compression ignition engine of a cylinder capacity of 2,500 cubic centimetres or more

(*b*) Other	17½%	C	11½%
		E	—

    (2) Motor vehicles for the transport of goods or materials:
      (*a*) With either a spark ignition engine of a cylinder capacity of 2,800 cubic centimetres or more or a compression ignition engine of a cylinder capacity of 2,500 cubic centimetres or more

	22%	C	15%
		E	—
(*b*) Other	17½%	C	11½%
		E	—

87.03 Special purpose motor lorries and vans (such as breakdown lorries, fire-engines, fire-escapes, road sweeper lorries, snow-ploughs, spraying lorries, crane lorries, searchlight lorries, mobile workshops and mobile radiological units), but not including the motor vehicles of heading No. 87.02

	18½%	C	12½%
		E	—

87.04 Chassis fitted with engines, for the motor vehicles falling within heading No. 87.01, 87.02 or 87.03:
  (A) For track-laying tractors or the dumpers of subheading No. 87.02 (A)

	12%		—

  (B) Other:
    (1) For motor vehicles for the transport of persons including vehicles designed for the transport of both passengers and goods:
      (*a*) With a seating capacity of 15 or more and either a spark ignition engine of a cylinder capacity of 2,800 cubic centimetres or more or a compression ignition engine of a cylinder capacity of 2,500 cubic centimetres or more

	22%	C	15%
		E	—
(*b*) Other	17½%	C	11½%
		E	—

    (2) For other motor vehicles:
      (*a*) With either a spark ignition engine of a cylinder capacity of 2,800 cubic centimetres or more

	22%	C	15%
		E	—

Tariff Heading	Rate of Import Duty (if any)		
	Full	Commonwealth (C) E.F.T.A. (E)	

87.04 Chassis fitted with engines, etc.—contd.
  (B) Other—*contd.*
    (2) For other motor vehicles—*contd.*
      (*a*) With either a spark ignition engine etc.—*contd.*
        or a compression ignition engine of a cylinder capacity of 2,500 cubic centimetres or more

(*b*) Other	17½%	C	11½%
		E	—

87.05 Bodies (including cabs), for the motor vehicles falling within heading No. 87.01, 87.02 or 87.03

	18½%	C	12½%
		E	—

87.06 Parts and accessories of the motor vehicles falling within heading No. 87.01, 87.02 or 87.03:

(A) Of track-laying tractors, of one or two wheeled tractors, or of the dumpers of subheading No. 87.02 (A)	11%		
(B) Other:			
(1) Of safety glass	16%	C	11%
		E	—
(2) Other	17½%	C	11½%
		E	—

87.07 Works trucks, mechanically propelled, of the types used in factories or warehouses for short distance transport or handling of goods (for example, fork-lift trucks and platform trucks); tractors of the type used on railway station platforms; parts of the foregoing trucks and tractors

	14%		

87.08 Tanks and other armoured fighting vehicles, motorised, whether or not fitted with weapons, and parts of such vehicles:

(A) Track-laying vehicles and parts thereof	14½%		—
(B) Other vehicles and parts thereof ...	18%		—

87.09 Motor-cycles, auto-cycles and cycles fitted with an auxiliary motor, with or without side-cars; side-cars of all kinds:

(A) Motor-bicycles with internal combustion piston engines of a cylinder capacity of not less than 800 cubic centimetres	19%	C	19%
		E	—
(B) Other	20½%	C	20½%
		E	—

87.10 Cycles, not motorised ... ...

	20%		—

Tariff Heading	Rate of Import Duty (if any)	
	Full	Commonwealth (C) E.F.T.A. (E)
87.11 Invalid carriages, fitted with means of mechanical propulsion (motorised or not)	13½%	C 10½% E —
87.12 Parts and accessories of articles falling within heading No. 87.09, 87.10 or 87.11: (A) Of motor-cycles, side-cars, auto-cycles, cycles fitted with an auxiliary motor, or motorised invalid carriages	20%	C 12% E —
(B) Of cycles (not motorised), or invalid carriages (not motorised)	20%	—
87.13 Baby carriages and invalid carriages (other than motorised or otherwise mechanically propelled) and parts thereof	16%	—
87.14 Other vehicles (including trailers), not mechanically propelled, and parts thereof: (A) Trailer units of flexible or articulated motor vehicles and parts thereof	22%	C 15% E —
(B) Other	16%	—

Chapter 88

Aircraft and parts thereof; Parachutes; Catapults and similar Aircraft Launching Gear; Ground Flying Trainers

Tariff Heading	Rate of Import Duty (if any)	
	Full	Commonwealth (C) E.F.T.A. (E)
88.01 Balloons and airships	14%	—
88.02 Flying machines, gliders and kites; roto-chutes:		
(A) Helicopters of an empty weight of 2,000 kilograms or less	14%	—
(B) Other	11%	—
88.03 Parts of goods falling in heading No. 88.01 or 88.02	11%	—
88.04 Parachutes and parts thereof and accessories thereto:		
(A) Of silk or man-made fibres	26½%	C 22% E —
(B) Other	12½%	—
88.05 Catapults and similar aircraft launching gear; ground flying trainers; parts of any of the foregoing articles	13%	—

Chapter 89

Ships, Boats and Floating Structures

Note

A hull, unfinished or incomplete vessel, assembled or unassembled, or a complete vessel, unassembled, is to be classified as a vessel of a particular kind if it has the essential character of a vessel of that kind except that a hull or such a vessel for breaking up is to be classified in heading No. 89.04. In other cases such goods are to be classified within heading No. 89.01.

Special Note applying to subheadings only

References in this Chapter to gross tonnage are references thereto as ascertained in accordance with the Merchant Shipping Acts as for the time being in force or, where not capable of being ascertained under those Acts, as ascertained by such methods as the Commissioners of Customs and Excise may determine.

Tariff Heading	Rate of Import Duty (if any)	
	Full	*Commonwealth (C)* *E.F.T.A.* (E)
89.01 Ships, boats and other vessels not falling within any of the following headings of this Chapter:		
(A) Of a gross tonnage of 80 tons or more	—	—
(B) Fishing vessels of the kind commonly known as Danish-type seiners with a fuel carrying capacity of not less than 500 gallons	—	—
(C) Other	8%	—
89.02 Tugs:		
(A) Of a gross tonnage of 80 tons or more	—	—
(B) Other	8%	—
89.03 Light-vessels, fire-floats, dredgers of all kinds, floating cranes, and other vessels the navigability of which is subsidiary to their main function; floating docks:		
(A) Of a gross tonnage of 80 tons or more	—	—
(B) Other	8%	—
89.04 Ships, boats and other vessels for breaking up	The same rate as if not for breaking up	—
89.05 Floating structures other than vessels (for example, coffer-dams, landing stages, buoys and beacons)	12½%	—

SECTION XVIII

OPTICAL, PHOTOGRAPHIC, CINEMATOGRAPHIC, MEASURING, CHECKING, PRECISION, MEDICAL AND SURGICAL INSTRUMENTS AND APPARATUS; CLOCKS AND WATCHES; MUSICAL INSTRUMENTS; SOUND RECORDERS AND REPRODUCERS; TELEVISION IMAGE AND SOUND RECORDERS AND REPRODUCERS, MAGNETIC; PARTS THEREOF

Chapter 90

Optical, Photographic, Cinematographic, Measuring, Checking, Precision, Medical and Surgical Instruments and Apparatus; Parts Thereof

Notes

1. This Chapter does not cover:

   (a) Articles of a kind used in machines, appliances, instruments or apparatus, of unhardened vulcanised rubber, falling within heading No. 40.14, of leather or of composition leather falling within heading No. 42.04, or of textile material (heading No. 59.17);

   (b) Refractory goods of heading No. 69.03; laboratory, chemical or industrial wares of heading No. 69.09;

   (c) Glass mirrors, not optically worked, falling within heading No. 70.09, and mirrors of base metal or of precious metal, not being optical elements, falling within heading No. 83.12 or Chapter 71;

   (d) Goods falling within heading No. 70.07, 70.11, 70.14, 70.15, 70.17 or 70.18;

   (e) Parts of general use, as defined in Note 2 to Section XV, of base metal (Section XV), or similar goods of artificial plastic materials (which are generally classified in heading No. 39.07);

   (f) Pumps incorporating measuring devices, of heading No. 84.10; weighing machinery, including weight-operated counting and checking machinery, and separately imported weights for balances (heading No. 84.20); lifting and handling machinery of heading No. 84.22; fittings for adjusting work or tools on machine-tools, of heading No. 84.48, including fittings with optical devices for reading the scale (for example, " optical " dividing heads) but not those which are in themselves essentially optical instruments (for example, alignment telescopes); valves and other appliances of heading No. 84.61;

   (g) Searchlights and spotlights, of a kind used on motor vehicles, of heading No. 85.09, and radio navigational aid or radar apparatus of heading No. 85.15;

   (h) Cinematographic sound recorders, reproducers and re-recorders, operating solely by a magnetic process (heading No. 92.11); magnetic sound-heads (heading No. 92.13);

   (ij) Articles of Chapter 97; or

   (k) Capacity measures, which are to be classified according to the material of which they are made.

2. An incomplete or unfinished machine, appliance, instrument or apparatus is to be classified with the corresponding complete or finished machine, appliance, instrument or apparatus, provided it has the essential character of that complete or finished article.

3. Subject to Notes 1 and 2 above, parts or accessories which are suitable for use solely or principally with machines, appliances, instruments, or apparatus falling within any heading of this Chapter are to be classified as follows:

   (a) Parts or accessories constituting in themselves machines, appliances, instruments or apparatus (including optical elements of heading No. 90.01 or 90.02) of any particular heading of the present Chapter or of Chapter 84, 85 or 91 (other than headings Nos 84.65 and 85.28) are to be classified in that heading;

   (b) Other parts or accessories are to be classified in heading No. 90.29 if they answer to the terms of that heading; otherwise they are to be classified in the heading appropriate to the machine, appliance, instrument or apparatus itself.

4. Heading No. 90.05 is to be taken not to apply to astronomical telescopes of a kind unsuitable for terrestrial observation (heading No. 90.06), or to telescopic sights for fitting to firearms, periscopic telescopes for fitting to submarines or tanks, or to telescopes for machines, appliances, instruments or apparatus of this Chapter; such telescopic sights and telescopes are to be classified in heading No. 90.13.

5. Measuring or checking optical instruments, appliances or machines which, but for this Note, could be classified both in heading No. 90.13 and in heading No. 90.16, are to be classified in heading No. 90.16.

6. Heading No. 90.28 is to be taken to apply, and apply only, to the following goods which are to be taken not to fall within any other heading of this Schedule:

(a) Instruments or apparatus for measuring or checking electrical quantities;

(b) Machines, appliances, instruments or apparatus of a kind described in heading No. 90.14, 90.15, 90.16, 90.22, 90.23, 90.24, 90.25 or 90.27 (other than stroboscopes), the operation of which depends on an electrical phenomenon which varies according to the factor to be ascertained or automatically controlled;

(c) Instruments or apparatus for measuring or detecting alpha, beta, gamma, X-ray, cosmic or similar radiations; and

(d) Automatic regulators of electrical quantities, and instruments or apparatus for automatically controlling non-electrical quantities the operation of which depends on an electrical phenomenon varying according to the factor to be controlled.

7. Cases, boxes and similar containers imported with articles of this Chapter are to be classified with such articles if they are of a kind normally sold therewith. Cases, boxes and similar containers when imported separately are not to be treated as parts of or accessories to their articles but are to be classified within heading No. 42.02 or according to their constituent material as appropriate.

Tariff Heading	Rate of Import Duty (if any)	
	Full	Commonwealth (C) E.F.T.A. (E)
90.01 Lenses, prisms, mirrors and other optical elements, of any material, unmounted, other than such elements of glass not optically worked; sheets or plates, of polarising material	40%	—
90.02 Lenses, prisms, mirrors and other optical elements, of any material, mounted, being parts of or fittings for instruments or apparatus, other than such elements of glass not optically worked:		
(A) Lighthouse lenses of glass, being dioptric drum lenses of external diameter not less than 10 inches	30%	—
(B) Other	40%	—
90.03 Frames and mountings, and parts thereof, for spectacles, pince-nez, lorgnettes, goggles and the like	16%	—

Tariff Heading	Rate of Import Duty (if any)	
	Full	Commonwealth (C) E.F.T.A. (E)
90.04 Spectacles, pince-nez, lorgnettes, goggles and the like, corrective, protective or other	16%	—
90.05 Refracting telescopes (monocular and binocular), prismatic or not	32%	—
90.06 Astronomical instruments (for example, reflecting telescopes, transit instruments and equatorial telescopes), and mountings therefor, but not including instruments for radio-astronomy	32%	—
90.07 Photographic cameras; photographic flash-light apparatus:		
(A) Photographic cameras:		
(1) Of fixed focus with a single simple lens, excluding folding cameras	27%	—
(2) Other	32%	—
(B) Photographic flashlight apparatus ...	13½%	—
(C) Tripods and other stands for articles of this heading; pistol grips for cameras of this heading	16%	—
90.08 Cinematographic cameras, projectors, sound recorders and sound reproducers but not including re-recorders or film editing apparatus; any combination of these articles:		
(A) Tripods and other stands for articles of this heading; pistol grips for cameras of this heading	16%	—
(B) Cinematographic projectors	20%	—
(C) Cinematographic sound reproducers (photo-electric)	20%	C 13% E —
(D) Cinematographic projectors combined with sound reproducers (photo-electric or magnetic)	20%	—
(E) Cinematographic cameras:		
(1) For film of a width of 16 millimetres	23%	—
(2) Other	32%	—
(F) Other	32%	—

Tariff Heading	Rate of Import Duty (*if any*)	
	Full	*Commonwealth* (C) *E.F.T.A.* (E)
90.09 Image projectors (other than cinematographic projectors); photographic (except cinematographic) enlargers and reducers:		
(A) Tripods and other stands for image projectors	16%	—
(B) Image projectors	33½%	—
(C) Photographic enlargers and reducers	32%	—
90.10 Apparatus and equipment of a kind used in photographic or cinematographic laboratories, not falling within any other heading in this Chapter; photo-copying apparatus (contact type); spools or reels, for film; screens for projectors:		
(A) Cinematographic editing machines incorporating means of projection	28%	—
(B) Other:		
(1) Cinematographic enlargers and reducers (optical printers); re-recorders; other optical projection apparatus	32%	—
(2) Film viewing magnifiers	32%	—
(3) Re-winders for cinematograph film	12%	—
(4) Other	12½%	—
90.11 Microscopes and diffraction apparatus, electron and proton	26½%	—
90.12 Compound optical microscopes, whether or not provided with means for photographing or projecting the image:		
(A) Micro-manipulators	26½%	—
(B) Other	40%	—
90.13 Optical appliances and instruments (but not including lighting appliances other than searchlights or spotlights), not falling within any other heading of this Chapter:		
(A) Spotlights (non-focusing) and searchlights	20%	—
(B) Other	32%	—

Tariff Heading	Rate of Import Duty (*if any*)	
	Full	*Commonwealth* (C) *E.F.T.A.* (E)
90.14 Surveying (including photogrammetrical surveying), hydrographic, navigational, meteorological, hydrological and geophysical instruments; compasses; range-finders:		
(A) Instruments incorporating optical elements but not including instruments in which the optical element is for viewing a scale or for some other subsidiary function:		
(1) Rangefinders Surveying (including photogrammetrical surveying) instruments, the following: Theodolites and photo-theodolites, but not including kine-theodolites Tacheometers Telescopic alidades Transit instruments Levels, Abney Levels, dumpy Levels, telescopic Photogrammetrical stereo-plotting instruments	37%	—
(2) Parts and accessories of the instruments of subheading (1) above	40%	—
(3) Other	40%	—
(B) Other:		
(1) Compasses	26½%	—
(2) Surveying (including photogrammetrical surveying) and hydrographic instruments:		
(a) Clinometers; hypsometers; co-ordinatographs	20%	—
(b) Cross staff heads; plane tables	17%	—
(c) Other	14½%	—
(3) Navigational instruments:		
(a) Accelerometers; altimeters; horizons (artificial), gyroscopic type	20%	—
(b) Other	14½%	—
(4) Meteorological and hydrological instruments	17%	—
(5) Geophysical instruments:		
(a) Magnetometers; seismographs; variometers	20%	—
(b) Other	17%	—

Tariff Heading	Rate of Import Duty (*if any*)	
	Full	Commonwealth (C) E.F.T.A. (E)
0.15 Balances of a sensitivity of five centigrams or better, with or without their weights	26½%	—
0.16 Drawing, marking-out and mathematical calculating instruments (for example, drafting machines, pantographs, slide rules, disc calculators, centre punches, scribers and carpenters' marking gauges); measuring or checking instruments, appliances and machines, not falling within any other heading of this Chapter (for example, micrometers, callipers, gauges, measuring rods, balancing machines); profile projectors:		
(A) Instruments, appliances and machines incorporating optical elements but not including instruments, appliances or machines in which the optical element is for viewing a scale or for some other subsidiary function:		
(1) Profile projectors	33½%	—
(2) Other	40%	—
(B) Other instruments, appliances and machines:		
(1) Calculating cylinders, dials and rules; isographs; half sets; compasses (including beam compasses); dividers (including proportional dividers); bows; spring bows; ruling pens; pantographs and eidographs; slide rules	26½%	—
(2) Chronographs, barrel; clinometers; co-ordinatographs; dividing machines and engines, linear and circular; engine indicators; harmonic analysers (planimeter type); integraphs; integrators (planimeter type); opisometers; planimeters; spherometers	20%	—
(3) Curves; drafting machines; parallel rules; protractors; precision squares, set squares and T squares; scribing blocks of precision or surface gauges; straight edges; surface plates	20%	—
(4) Other:		
(*a*) Gauges and measuring instruments of precision of the types used in engineering machine shops and viewing rooms	20%	—
(*b*) Other	17%	—

Tariff Heading	Rate of Import Duty (if any)	
	Full	Commonwealth (C) E.F.T.A. (E)
90.17 Medical, dental, surgical and veterinary instruments and appliances (including electro-medical apparatus and ophthalmic instruments):		
(A) Instruments and appliances incorporating optical elements but not including instruments or appliances in which the optical element is for viewing a scale or for some other subsidiary function:		
(1) Mirrors, mouth, not optically worked	12½%	—
(2) Other	32%	—
(B) Other instruments and appliances:		
(1) Cardiographs; optometers; myographs	19%	—
(2) Glass barrelled hypodermic syringes	19%	—
(3) Other	13%	—
90.18 Mechano-therapy appliances; massage apparatus; psychological aptitude-testing apparatus; artificial respiration, ozone therapy, oxygen therapy, aerosol therapy or similar apparatus; breathing appliances (including gas masks and similar respirators):		
(A) Breathing appliances	12½%	—
(B) Other	9%	—
90.19 Orthopaedic appliances, surgical belts, trusses and the like; artificial limbs, eyes, teeth and other artificial parts of the body; deaf aids; splints and other fracture appliances	12%	—
90.20 Apparatus based on the use of X-rays or of the radiations from radio-active substances (including radiography and radiotherapy apparatus); X-ray generators; X-ray tubes; X-ray screens; X-ray high tension generators; X-ray control panels and desks; X-ray examination or treatment tables, chairs and the like	20%	—
90.21 Instruments, apparatus or models, designed solely for demonstrational purposes (for example, in education or exhibition), unsuitable for other uses	12½%	—

Tariff Heading	Rate of Import Duty (*if any*)	
	Full	*Commonwealth* (C) *E.F.T.A.* (E)
90.22 Machines and appliances for testing mechanically the hardness, strength, compressibility, elasticity and the like properties of industrial materials (for example, metals, wood, textiles, paper or plastics)	16%	—
90.23 Hydrometers and similar instruments; thermometers, pyrometers, barometers, hygrometers, psychrometers, recording or not; any combination of these instruments:		
(A) Pyrometers, optical	40%	—
(B) Other	20%	—
90.24 Instruments and apparatus for measuring, checking or automatically controlling the flow, depth, pressure or other variables of liquids or gases, or for automatically controlling temperature (for example, pressure gauges, thermostats, level gauges, flow meters, automatic oven-draught regulators), not being articles falling within heading No. 90.14; heat meters of a type used with central heating systems and the like	12½%	—
90.25 Instruments and apparatus for physical or chemical analysis (such as polarimeters, refractometers, spectrometers, gas analysis apparatus); instruments and apparatus for measuring or checking viscosity, porosity, expansion, surface tension or the like (such as viscometers, porosimeters, expansion meters); instruments and apparatus for measuring or checking quantities of heat, light or sound (such as photometers (including exposure meters), calorimeters); microtomes:		
(A) Instruments and apparatus incorporating optical elements but not including instruments or apparatus in which the optical element is for viewing a scale or for some other subsidiary function	32%	—
(B) Environmental test chambers ...	11%	—
(C) Other instruments and apparatus ...	26½%	—
90.26 Gas, liquid and electricity supply or production meters; calibrating meters therefor	12½%	—

Tariff Heading	Rate of Import Duty (if any)		
	Full	Commonwealth (C) E.F.T.A. (E)	
90.27 Revolution counters, production counters, taximeters, mileometers, pedometers and the like, speed indicators (including magnetic speed indicators) and tachometers (other than articles falling within heading No. 90.14); stroboscopes:			
(A) Stroboscopes	40%		—
(B) Mileometers, revolution indicators and speed indicators, suitable for use on motor vehicles	19%	C E	12½% —
(C) Other	16%		—
90.28 Electrical measuring, checking, analysing or automatically controlling instruments and apparatus:			
(A) Instruments and apparatus incorporating optical elements but not including instruments or apparatus in which the optical element is for viewing a scale or for some other subsidiary function	32%		—
(B) Ammeters, voltmeters, wattmeters, thermostats and thermo-regulators:			
(1) Precision types	20%		—
(2) Other	17%		—
(C) Telemetering instruments and apparatus	14½%		—
(D) Other instruments and apparatus:			
(1) Automatic voltage regulators and other automatic regulators of electrical quantities; automatic control instruments and apparatus for controlling non-electrical quantities but not including instruments and apparatus for automatic control of flow, depth, pressure, or other variables of liquids or gases, or of temperature	14½%		—
(2) Other	20%		
90.29 Parts or accessories suitable for use solely or principally with one or more of the articles falling within heading No. 90.23, 90.24, 90.26, 90.27 or 90.28	The rate of duty applicable to the article of which the goods are parts or accessories		—

Chapter 91

Clocks and Watches and Parts Thereof

Notes

1. For the purposes of headings Nos. 91.02 and 91.07, the expression " watch movements " means movements regulated by a balance-wheel and hairspring and not exceeding twelve millimetres in thickness measured with the plate and bridges.

2. Headings Nos. 91.07 and 91.08 are to be taken not to apply to spring-operated or weight-operated motors not fitted, nor adapted to be fitted, with escapements (heading No. 84.08).

3. Headings Nos. 91.09, 91.10 and 91.11 are to be taken not to include:

(a) Weights, clock or watch glasses, watch chains or straps, ball bearings or bearing balls;
(b) Electric motors, electro-magnets and other electrical parts of the kinds used both in clocks or watches and in other articles, whether or not suitable for use only in clocks or watches;
(c) Parts of general use, as defined in Note 2 to Section XV, of base metal (Section XV), or similar goods of artificial plastic materials (which are generally classified in heading No. 39.07).

Clock or watch springs are to be classified as clock or watch parts (heading No. 91.11).

4. Except as provided in Notes 2 and 3, movements and other parts suitable for use both in clocks or watches and in other articles (for example, precision instruments) are to be taken as falling within this Chapter and not within any other Chapter.

5. Cases, boxes and similar containers imported with articles of this Chapter are to be classified with such articles if they are of a kind normally sold therewith. Cases, boxes and similar containers imported separately are to be classified under their appropriate headings.

Tariff Heading	Rate of Import Duty (if any)		
	Full	Commonwealth (C) E.F.T.A. (E)	
91.01 Pocket-watches, wrist-watches and other watches, including stop-watches:			
(A) Watches capable of indicating the time of day	26½%	C	17½%
		E	—
(B) Other	16%		—
91.02 Clocks with watch movements (excluding clocks of heading No. 91.03):			
(A) Alarm clocks:			
(1) Of a value not less than 12s. each	3s 4½d. each or 17%, whichever is the greater	C	2s. 3d. each or 11%, whichever is the greater
		E	—
(2) Other	2s. 6d. each	C	1s. 8½d. each
		E	—
(B) Other	26½%	C	17½%
		E	—
91.03 Instrument panel clocks and clocks of a similar type, for vehicles, aircraft or vessels	26½%	C	17½%
		E	—

Tariff Heading	Rate of Import Duty (if any)	
	Full	Commonwealth (C) E.F.T.A. (E)
91.04 Other clocks: (A) Alarm clocks: (1) Of a value not less than 12s. each	3s. 4½d. each or 17%, whichever is the greater	C 2s. 3d. each or 11%, whichever is the greater E —
(2) Other	2s. 6d. each	C 1s. 8½d. each E —
(B) Other	26½%	C 17½% E —
91.05 Time of day recording apparatus; apparatus with clock or watch movement (including secondary movement) or with synchronous motor, for measuring, recording or otherwise indicating intervals of time: (A) Apparatus capable of indicating the time of day	26½%	C 17½% E —
(B) Other	16%	—
91.06 Time switches with clock or watch movement (including secondary movement) or with synchronous motor	16%	—
91.07 Watch movements (including stop-watch movements), assembled: (A) Movements suitable for articles capable of indicating the time of day	26½%	C 17½% E —
(B) Other	16%	—
91.08 Clock movements (including secondary movements), assembled: (A) Movements suitable for articles capable of indicating the time of day	26½%	C 17½% E —
(B) Other	16%	—
91.09 Watch cases and parts of watch cases, including blanks thereof	26½%	C 17½% E —
91.10 Clock cases and cases of a similar type for other goods of this Chapter, and parts thereof	26½%	C 17½% E —
91.11 Other clock and watch parts	26½%	C 17½% E —

Chapter 92

Musical Instruments; Sound Recorders and Reproducers; Television Image and Sound Recorders and Reproducers, Magnetic; Parts and Accessories of such Articles

Notes

1. This Chapter does not cover:

(*a*) Film wholly or partly sensitised for photographic or photo-electric recording or such film exposed, whether or not developed (Chapter 37);

(*b*) Parts of general use, as defined in Note 2 to Section XV, of base metal (Section XV), or similar goods of artificial plastic materials (which are generally classified in heading No. 39.07);

(*c*) Microphones, amplifiers, loudspeakers, head-phones, switches, stroboscopes and other accessory instruments, apparatus or equipment falling within Chapter 85 or 90, for use with but not incorporated in or housed in the same cabinet as instruments of the present Chapter; sound recorders or reproducers combined with a radio receiver (heading No. 85.15);

(*d*) Brushes (for cleaning musical instruments) falling within heading No. 96.02;

(*e*) Toy instruments (heading No. 97.03); or

(*f*) Collectors' pieces or antiques (heading No. 99.05 or 99.06).

2. For the purposes of this Chapter, an incomplete or unfinished instrument or apparatus is to be classified as the corresponding complete or finished article, provided it has the essential character of such a complete or finished article.

3. Bows and sticks and similar devices used in playing the musical instruments of headings Nos. 92.02 and 92.06 imported with such instruments in numbers normal thereto and clearly intended for use therewith, are to be classified in the same heading as the relative instruments.

Perforated music rolls (heading No. 92.10) and gramophone records and the like (heading No. 92.12) imported with an instrument are to be treated as separate articles and not as forming a part of such instrument.

4. Cases, boxes and similar containers imported with articles of this Chapter are to be classified with such articles if they are of a kind normally sold therewith. Cases, boxes and similar containers imported separately are classified elsewhere in this Schedule, in general according to their constituent material, and not under heading No. 92.10 or 92.13.

Tariff Heading	Rate of Import Duty (if any)	
	Full	Commonwealth (*C*) E.F.T.A.　　(*E*)
92.01 Pianos (including automatic pianos, whether or not with keyboards); harpsichords and other keyboard stringed instruments; harps but not including aeolian harps:		
(A) Harps	—	—
(B) Other	26½%	C　17½% E
92.02 Other string musical instruments	20%	C　13% E　—

Tariff Heading	Rate of Import Duty (*if any*)		
	Full	*Commonwealth (C)* *E.F.T.A.* (E)	
92.03 Pipe and reed organs, including harmoniums and the like:			
(A) Reed organs, including harmoniums	20%	—	
(B) Other	20%	C	13%
		E	—
92.04 Accordions, concertinas and similar musical instruments; mouth organs:			
(A) Piano accordions	12½%	C	8%
		E	—
(B) Other	16%	C	10½%
		E	—
92.05 Other wind musical instruments	20%	C	13%
		E	—
92.06 Percussion musical instruments (for example, drums, xylophones, cymbals, castanets)	26½%	C	17½%
		E	—
92.07 Electro-magnetic, electrostatic, electronic and similar musical instruments (for example, pianos, organs, accordions)	20%	C	13%
		E	—
92.08 Musical instruments not falling within any other heading of this Chapter (for example, fairground organs, mechanical street organs, musical boxes, musical saws); mechanical singing birds; decoy calls and effects of all kinds; mouth-blown sound signalling instruments (for example, whistles and boatswains' pipes):			
(A) Musical instruments:			
(1) Musical boxes	24%	C	16%
		E	—
(2) Other	26½%	C	17½%
		E	—
(B) Mechanical singing birds; decoy calls and effects of all kinds; mouth-blown sound signalling instruments	16%	—	
92.09 Musical instrument strings:			
(A) For keyboard instruments	26½%	C	17½%
		E	—
(B) Other	20%	C	13%
		E	—

Tariff Heading	Rate of Import Duty (if any)		
	Full	Commonwealth (C) E.F.T.A. (E)	

Tariff Heading	Full		
92.10 Parts and accessories of musical instruments (other than strings), including perforated music rolls and mechanisms for musical boxes; metronomes, tuning forks and pitch pipes of all kinds:			
(A) Parts and accessories of musical instruments (including pitch pipes and tuning forks of a kind designed for musical purposes):			
(1) Parts of organs (other than reeds) but not including parts of mouth organs	8%	C E	5% —
(2) Reeds, and reed plates incorporating reeds, not comprised in subheading (1) above	16%	C E	10½% —
(3) Drum head skins	12%		—
(4) Mechanical movements for musical boxes	20%	C E	13% —
(5) Other parts and accessories:			
(a) Specialised for use with concertinas, accordions, wind or string instruments	20%	C E	13% —
(b) Other	26½%	C E	17½% —
(B) Metronomes; tuning forks and pitch pipes not comprised in subheading (A) above	16%		
92.11 Gramophones, dictating machines and other sound recorders and reproducers, including record-players and tape decks, with or without sound-heads; television image and sound recorders and reproducers, magnetic:			
(A) Dictating machines, and reproducing machines adapted for use therewith (but not including machines suitable for the recording or reproduction of music)	10%		—
(B) Television image and sound recorders and reproducers, magnetic	12½%		—
(C) Other:			
(1) Gramophones with electrical amplification; combined recorders and reproducers (complete with electrical amplifiers); recorders without reproducing apparatus	16%	C E	10½% —
(2) Other	24%	C E	16% —

Tariff Heading	Rate of Import Duty (if any)	
	Full	Commonwealth (C) E.F.T.A. (E)

92.12 Gramophone records; other articles having recordings (whether of sound or not) or data embodied therein by means similar to those used for the recording of sound; matrices for the production of records, prepared record blanks, film for mechanical sound recording, prepared tapes, wires, strips and like articles of a kind commonly used for embodying recordings or data by means similar to those used for the recording of sound:

	Full	Commonwealth (C) / E.F.T.A. (E)
(A) Matrices, impressed	—	—
(B) Gramophone records for the reproduction of speech, specially adapted for the use of the blind	—	—
(C) Other:		
(1) Sound recordings for reproducing music:		
(*a*) Gramophone records	12%	C 8% E —
(*b*) Other	20%	C 13% E —
(2) Other	8%	—

92.13 Other parts and accessories of apparatus falling within heading No. 92.11:

	Full	Commonwealth (C) / E.F.T.A. (E)
(A) Record shaving machines adapted for use in connection with dictating machines	10%	—
(B) Parts and accessories of the apparatus of subheading No. 92.11(B)	12½%	—
(C) Gramophone needles or styli:		
(1) Of steel or fibre	13½%	C 9% E —
(2) Of other materials...	19%	C 12½% E —
(D) Other parts and accessories:		
(1) Of gramophones	24%	C 16% E —
(2) Other	16%	C 10½% E —

SECTION XIX

ARMS AND AMMUNITION; PARTS THEREOF

Chapter 93

Arms and Ammunition; Parts thereof

Notes

1. This Chapter does not cover:

(a) Goods falling within Chapter 36 (for example, percussion caps, detonators, signalling flares);

(b) Parts of general use, as defined in Note 2 to Section XV, of base metal (Section XV), or similar goods of artificial plastic materials (which are generally classified in heading No. 39.07);

(c) Armoured fighting vehicles (heading No. 87.08);

(d) Telescopic sights and other optical devices suitable for use with arms, unless mounted on a firearm or imported with the firearm on which they are designed to be mounted (Chapter 90);

(e) Bows, arrows, fencing foils or toys falling within Chapter 97; or

(f) Collectors' pieces or antiques (heading No. 99.05 or 99.06).

2. For the purposes of this Chapter, incomplete or unfinished arms are to be classified with the corresponding complete or finished articles, provided they have the essential character of such complete or finished articles.

3. In heading No. 93.07, the reference to " parts thereof " is to be taken not to include radio or radar apparatus of heading No. 85.15.

4. Cases, boxes and similar containers imported with articles of this Chapter are to be classified with such articles if they are of a kind normally sold therewith. Cases, boxes and similar containers imported separately are to be classified under their appropriate headings.

Tariff Heading	Rate of Import Duty (if any)	
	Full	Commonwealth (C) E.F.T.A. (E)
93.01 Side-arms (for example, swords, cutlasses and bayonets) and parts thereof and scabbards and sheaths therefor	20%	—
93.02 Revolvers and pistols, being firearms ...	16%	—
93.03 Artillery weapons, machine-guns, sub-machine-guns and other military firearms and projectors (other than revolvers and pistols)	16%	—

Tariff Heading	Rate of Import Duty (if any)	
	Full	Commonwealth (C) E.F.T.A. (E)
93.04 Other firearms, including Very light pistols, pistols and revolvers for firing blank ammunition only, line-throwing guns and the like:		
(A) Miniature, cadet and sporting rifles and carbines; sporting guns; pistols and revolvers for firing blank cartridges only	16%	—
(B) Other	13½%	—
93.05 Arms of other descriptions, including air, spring and similar pistols, rifles and guns:		
(A) Air, spring and similar pistols, rifles and guns	23%	—
(B) Other	16%	—
93.06 Parts of arms, including roughly sawn gun stock blocks and gun barrel blanks, but not including parts of side-arms:		
(A) Wooden stock blocks, roughly sawn or planed or polished but not further manufactured	8%	—
(B) Other parts	16%	—
93.07 Bombs, grenades, torpedoes, mines, guided weapons and missiles and similar munitions of war, and parts thereof; ammunition and parts thereof, including cartridge wads; lead shot prepared for ammunition	16%	—

SECTION XX

MISCELLANEOUS MANUFACTURED ARTICLES

Chapter 94

Furniture and parts thereof; Bedding, Mattresses, Mattress Supports, Cushions and similar Stuffed Furnishings

Notes

1. This Chapter does not cover:

(*a*) Pneumatic or water mattresses, pillows or cushions, falling within Chapter 39, 40 or 62;

(*b*) Standard lamps, table lamps, wall lamp brackets and other lighting fittings;

(*c*) Articles of stone or ceramic materials, used as chairs, seats, tables or columns, of the kind used in parks, gardens or vestibules, falling within Chapter 68 or 69;

(*d*) Mirrors designed for placing on the floor or ground (for example, cheval-glasses (swing-mirrors)) falling within heading No. 70.09;

(*e*) Parts of general use, as defined in Note 2 to Section XV, of base metal (Section XV), or similar goods of artificial plastic materials (which are generally classified in heading No. 39.07); and safes falling within heading No. 83.03;

(*f*) Furniture specially designed as parts of refrigerators of heading No. 84.15; furniture specially designed for sewing machines (heading No. 84.41);

(*g*) Furniture specially designed as parts of radio-gramophones, wireless sets or television sets (heading No. 85.15);

(*h*) Dentists' spittoons falling within heading No. 90.17;

(*ij*) Goods falling within Chapter 91 (for example, clocks and clock cases);

(*k*) Furniture specially designed as parts of gramophones, of dictating machines or of other sound reproducers or recorders, falling within heading No. 92.13; or

(*l*) Toy furniture (heading No. 97.03), billiard tables and other furniture specially constructed for games (heading No. 97.04) or for conjuring tricks (heading No. 97.05).

2. The references in headings Nos. 94.01 and 94.02 to chairs and other seats and in headings Nos. 94.02 and 94.03 to furniture are to be taken as not applying to articles which are not designed for placing on the floor or ground.

This provision is, however, to be taken not to apply to the following, even if they are designed to be fixed to the wall or to stand one on the other:

(*a*) Kitchen cabinets and similar cupboards;

(*b*) Folding seats and beds;

(*c*) Unit bookcases and similar unit furniture.

3. An article of furniture, whether or not comprising sheets, parts or fittings of glass, marble or other materials, imported unassembled, is to be treated as a single assembled article of furniture, provided that the components are imported together.

4. (*a*) In this Chapter references to parts of goods do not include references to sheets (whether or not cut to shape but not combined with other parts) of glass (including mirrors) or of marble or other stone.

(*b*) Goods described in heading No. 94.04, imported separately, are not to be classified in heading No. 94.01, 94.02 or 94.03 as parts of goods.

Tariff Heading	Rate of Import Duty (if any)	
	Full	Commonwealth (C) E.F.T.A. (E)
94.01 Chairs and other seats (other than those falling within heading No. 94.02), whether or not convertible into beds, and parts thereof:		
(A) Chairs and other seats:		
(1) Wholly of birchwood (other than plywood or bentwood), not stained, polished, painted or otherwise treated	14½%	—
(2) Other:		
(a) Of metal	13%	—
(b) Of other materials ...	16%	—
(B) Parts of the above	16%	—
94.02 Medical, dental, surgical or veterinary furniture (for example, operating tables, hospital beds with mechanical fittings); dentists' and similar chairs with mechanical elevating, rotating or reclining movements; parts of the foregoing articles:		
(A) Pedestal chairs with reclining movement:		
(1) Of metal	13%	—
(2) Of other materials	16%	—
(B) Other chairs and furniture	16%	—
(C) Parts of the above	16%	—
94.03 Other furniture and parts thereof:		
(A) Tables, stands, desks and counters, bookcases and bookshelves, drawers and cupboards, shelving, storage bins and storage racks, office letter racks, lockers and cabinets (including filing cabinets):		
(1) Of metal	13%	—
(2) Of other materials	16%	—
(B) Other furniture	16%	—
(C) Parts of the above	16%	—
94.04 Mattress supports; articles of bedding or similar furnishing fitted with springs or stuffed or internally fitted with any material, or of expanded, foam or sponge rubber or of expanded, foam or sponge artificial plastic material, whether or not covered (for example, mattresses, quilts, eiderdowns, cushions, pouffes and pillows):		
(A) Containing more than 20 per cent. by weight of silk, of man-made fibres, or of both together	33%	C 27½% E —
(B) Containing more than 5 per cent. but not more than 20 per cent. by weight of silk, of man-made fibres, or of both together	23%	C 19% E —
(C) Other	20%	—

Chapter 95

Articles and Manufactures of Carving or Moulding Material

Note

This Chapter does not cover:

(*a*) Articles falling within Chapter 66 (for example, parts of umbrellas, walking-sticks);

(*b*) Fans or hand screens, non-mechanical (heading No. 67.05);

(*c*) Articles falling within Chapter 71 (for example, imitation jewellery);

(*d*) Cutlery or other articles falling within Chapter 82, whether or not having handles or other parts of carving or moulding materials; the headings of the present Chapter apply, however, to separate handles or other parts of such articles;

(*e*) Articles falling within Chapter 90 (for example, spectacle frames);

(*f*) Articles falling within Chapter 91 (for example, clock or watch cases);

(*g*) Articles falling within Chapter 92 (for example, musical instruments and parts thereof);

(*h*) Articles falling within Chapter 93 (arms and parts thereof);

(*ij*) Articles falling within Chapter 94 (furniture and parts thereof);

(*k*) Brushes, powder-puffs or other articles falling within Chapter 96;

(*l*) Articles falling within Chapter 97 (toys, games and sports requisites);

(*m*) Articles falling within Chapter 98 (for example, buttons, cuff-links, smoking pipes, combs); or

(*n*) Collectors' pieces or antiques (Chapter 99).

Tariff Heading	Rate of Import Duty (*if any*)	
	Full	Commonwealth (C) E.F.T.A. (E)
95.01 Worked tortoise-shell and articles of tortoise-shell	24%	—
95.02 Worked mother of pearl and articles of mother of pearl:		
(A) Mother of pearl discs, cut from simply prepared shell, not polished or otherwise worked	8%	—
(B) Other	24%	—
95.03 Worked ivory and articles of ivory:		
(A) Statuettes and figures; vases, bowls and similar vessels	21%	—
(B) Other	24%	—
95.04 Worked bone (excluding whalebone) and articles of bone (excluding whalebone):		
(A) Unstrung beads	—	—
(B) Other	12½%	—

Tariff Heading	Rate of Import Duty (if any)	
	Full	Commonwealth (C E.F.T.A. (E
95.05 Worked horn, coral (natural or agglomerated) and other animal carving material, and articles of horn, coral (natural or agglomerated) or of other animal carving material:		
(A) Unstrung beads made of shells ...	—	—
(B) Unmounted cameos made of natural coral or of shell and of a size and shape suitable for use in articles of jewellery or imitation jewellery	—	—
(C) Other:		
(1) Coral (natural or agglomerated) and articles thereof	24%	—
(2) Other	12½%	—
95.06 Worked vegetable carving material (for example, corozo) and articles of vegetable carving material:		
(A) Unstrung beads made of seeds ...	—	—
(B) Other	12½%	—
95.07 Worked jet (and mineral substitutes for jet), amber, meerschaum, agglomerated amber and agglomerated meerschaum, and articles of those substances:		
(A) Unmounted cameos made of amber and of a size and shape suitable for use in articles of jewellery or imitation jewellery	—	—
(B) Other	18%	—
95.08 Moulded or carved articles of stearin, of natural gums or natural resins (for example, copal or rosin) or of other non-mineral substances, not elsewhere specified or included; moulded or carved articles of wax or of modelling pastes; worked, unhardened gelatin (except gelatin falling within heading No. 35.03) and articles of unhardened gelatin:		
(A) Bee comb foundations	13½%	—
(B) Other	16%	—

Chapter 96

Brooms, Brushes, Feather Dusters, Powder-puffs and Sieves

Notes

1. This Chapter does not cover:

(a) Articles falling within Chapter 71;

(b) Brushes of a kind specialised for use in dentistry or for medical, surgical or veterinary purposes, falling within heading No. 90.17; or

(c) Toys (Chapter 97).

2. In heading No. 96.03, the expression " prepared knots and tufts for broom or brush making " is to be taken to apply only to unmounted knots and tufts of animal hair, vegetable fibre or other material, which are ready for incorporation without division in brooms or brushes, or which require only such further minor processes as glueing or coating the butts, or trimming to shape at the top, to render them ready for such incorporation.

Tariff Heading	Rate of Import Duty (if any)	
	Full	Commonwealth (C) E.F.T.A. (E)
96.01 Brooms and brushes, consisting of twigs or other vegetable materials merely bound together and not mounted in a head (for example, besoms and whisks), with or without handles	16%	—
96.02 Other brooms and brushes (including brushes of a kind used as parts of machines); paint rollers; squeegees (other than roller squeegees) and mops:		
(A) Paint rollers, squeegees and mops ...	16%	—
(B) Brooms, household and toilet brushes:		
(1) With filling of man-made fibres (including monofil of heading No. 51.01 or 51.02)	28%	C 25% E —
(2) With filling of iron or steel wire ...	28%	—
(3) Other	6s. per gross or 20%, whichever is the greater	—
(C) Other:		
(1) Brushes with filling of man-made fibres (including monofil of heading No. 51.01 or 51.02)	26½%	C 24% E —
(2) Brushes with filling of iron or steel wire; pipe cleaners	26½%	—
(3) Other	18½%	—
96.03 Prepared knots and tufts for broom or brush making	16%	—
96.04 Feather dusters	16%	—
96.05 Powder-puffs and pads for applying cosmetics or toilet preparations	16%	—
96.06 Hand sieves and hand riddles	20%	—

Chapter 97

Toys, Games and Sports Requisites; Parts thereof

Notes

1. This Chapter does not cover:

(a) Christmas tree candles (heading No. 34.06);

(b) Fireworks or other pyrotechnic articles falling within heading No. 36.05;

(c) Yarns, monofil, cords or gut and the like for fishing, cut to length but not made up into fishing lines, falling within Chapter 39, heading No. 42.06 or Section XI;

(d) Rubber tyres (heading No. 40.11); sports bags or other containers of heading No. 42.02 or 43.03;

(e) Sports clothing or fancy dress, of textiles, falling within Chapter 60 or 61;

(f) Textile flags or bunting, or sails for boats or land craft, falling within Chapter 62;

(g) Sports footwear (other than skating boots with skates attached), cricket pads, shin-guards or the like, falling within Chapter 64, or sports headgear falling within Chapter 65;

(h) Climbing sticks, whips, riding crops or the like (heading No. 66.02), or parts thereof (heading No. 66.03);

(ij) Unmounted glass eyes for dolls or other toys, falling within heading No. 70.19;

(k) Parts of general use, as defined in Note 2 to Section XV, of base metal (Section XV), or similar goods of artificial plastic materials (which are generally classified in heading No. 39.07);

(l) Articles falling within heading No. 83.11;

(m) Sports vehicles (other than bobsleighs, toboggans and the like) falling within Section XVII;

(n) Children's cycles fitted with ball bearings and in the normal form of adults' cycles (heading No. 87.10);

(o) Sports craft such as canoes and skiffs (Chapter 89), or their means of propulsion (Chapter 44 for such articles made of wood);

(p) Spectacles, goggles and the like, for sports and outdoor games (heading No. 90.04);

(q) Decoy calls and whistles (heading No. 92.08);

(r) Arms or other articles of Chapter 93; or

(s) Racket strings, tents or other camping goods, or gloves (classified, in general, according to the material of which they are made).

2. The headings of this Chapter are to be taken to include articles in which pearls, precious or semi-precious stones (natural, synthetic or reconstructed), precious metals or rolled precious metals constitute only minor constituents.

3. In heading No. 97.02 the term " dolls " is to be taken to apply only to such articles as are representations of human beings.

4. An incomplete or unfinished article is to be classified with the corresponding complete or finished article, provided it has the essential character of that complete or finished article.

5. Subject to Note 1 above, parts and accessories which are suitable for use solely or principally with articles falling within any heading of this Chapter are to be classified with those articles.

Tariff Heading	Rate of Import Duty (*if any*)	
	Full	*Commonwealth (C)* E.F.T.A. (*E*)
97.01 Wheeled toys designed to be ridden by children (for example, toy bicycles and tricycles and pedal motor cars); dolls' prams and dolls' push chairs:		
(A) Containing more than 20 per cent. by weight of silk, of man-made fibres, or of both together	20%	C 16% E —
(B) Other	20%	—
97.02 Dolls:		
(A) Containing more than 20 per cent. by weight of silk, of man-made fibres, or of both together	20%	C 16% E —
(B) Other	20%	—
97.03 Other toys; working models of a kind used for recreational purposes:		
(A) Containing more than 20 per cent. by weight of silk, of man-made fibres, or of both together	20%	C 16% E —
(B) Other	20%	—
97.04 Equipment for parlour, table and funfair games for adults or children (including billiard tables and pintables and table-tennis requisites):		
(A) Playing cards, exceeding 1¾ inches in length and 1¼ inches in width, being any of the 13 cards of a conventional suit	½d. per pack (of 52 cards), and so in proportion for any other number of cards	C ½d. per pack (of 52 cards), and so in proportion for any other number of cards E —
(B) Coin or disc operated machines ...	16%	—
(C) Other	20%	—
97.05 Carnival articles; entertainment articles (for example, conjuring tricks and novelty jokes); Christmas tree decorations and similar articles for Christmas festivities, (for example, artificial Christmas trees, Christmas stockings, imitation yule logs, Nativity scenes and figures therefor):		
(A) Christmas tree decorations and similar articles for Christmas festivities, electrical	16%	—
(B) Other:		
(1) Containing more than 20 per cent. by weight of silk, of man-made fibres, or of both together	20%	C 16% E —
(2) Other	20%	—

Tariff Heading	Rate of Import Duty (if any)	
	Full	Commonwealth (C) E.F.T.A. (E)
97.06 Appliances, apparatus, accessories and requisites for gymnastics or athletics, or for sports and outdoor games (other than articles falling within heading No. 97.04):		
(A) Wooden golf club head blocks roughly shaped by sawing but not further manufactured	8%	—
(B) Rackets, exceeding 9 oz. in weight ...	5s. per racket or 23%, whichever is the greater	—
(C) Unstrung racket frames	3s. per frame or 23%, whichever is the greater	—
(D) Golf clubs of a value exceeding 12s. 6d. each; golf club shafts of a value exceeding 4s. 6d. each; rough turned wooden golf club shafts of any value; golf tees of wood	20%	—
(E) Skates	20%	—
(F) Other	23%	—
97.07 Fish-hooks, line fishing rods and tackle; fish landing nets and butterfly nets; decoy " birds " and similar lures:		
(A) Fishing rods of iron or steel	12%	—
(B) Fishing reels	15%	—
(C) Fish-hooks of iron or steel	18%	—
(D) Other	21%	—
97.08 Roundabouts, swings, shooting galleries and other fairground amusements; travelling circuses, travelling menageries and travelling theatres	20%	—

Chapter 98

Miscellaneous Manufactured Articles

Notes

1. This Chapter does not cover:

(a) Eyebrow and other cosmetic pencils (heading No. 33.06);

(b) Buttons, studs, cuff-links or other articles of a kind described in heading No. 98.01 or 98.12, if made wholly or partly of precious metal or rolled precious metal (subject to the provisions of Note 2 (a) to Chapter 71) or if containing pearls or precious or semi-precious stones (natural, synthetic or reconstructed) (Chapter 71);

(c) Parts of general use, as defined in Note 2 to Section XV, of base metal (Section XV), or similar goods of artificial plastic materials (which are generally classified in heading No. 39.07);

(d) Mathematical drawing pens (heading No. 90.16); or

(e) Toys falling within Chapter 97.

2. Subject to Note 1 above, the headings in this Chapter are to be taken to apply to goods of the kind described whether or not composed wholly or partly of precious metal or rolled precious metal or of pearls or precious or semi-precious stones (natural, synthetic or reconstructed).

3. Cases, boxes and similar containers imported with articles of this Chapter are to be classified with such articles if they are of a kind normally sold therewith. Cases, boxes and similar containers imported separately are to be classified under their appropriate headings.

Tariff Heading	Rate of Import Duty (*if any*)	
	Full	*Commonwealth* (C) *E.F.T.A.* (E)
98.01 Buttons and button moulds, studs, cuff-links, and press-fasteners, including snap-fasteners and press-studs; blanks and parts of such articles:		
(A) Buttons and button moulds, and parts and blanks thereof	28%	—
(B) Cuff-links and parts and blanks thereof:		
(1) Decorative glass smallwares, unmounted	—	—
(2) Decorative plastic smallwares, unmounted	10%	—
(3) Other	20%	—
(C) Press-fasteners of the dome type having not less than three parts to a set	9%	—
(D) Other	12%	—
98.02 Slide fasteners and parts thereof:		
(A) Slide fasteners	9½d. per dozen plus, for any length in excess of 2½ inches, 1½d. per dozen for each inch or part of an inch of such excess	—

Tariff Heading	Rate of Import Duty (if any)	
	Full	Commonwealth (C) E.F.T.A. (E)
98.02 Slide fasteners, etc.—_contd._ (B) Parts of slide fasteners: (1) Metal chain scoops mounted on tape or other material	1d. per foot length of single tape or 16%, whichever is the greater	—
(2) Unmounted metal chain scoops and all other metal components	2s. 4d. per lb. or 16%, whichever is the greater	—
(3) Other	8%	—
98.03 Fountain pens, stylograph pens and pencils (including ball point pens and pencils) and other pens, pen-holders, pencil-holders and similar holders, propelling pencils and sliding pencils; parts and fittings thereof, other than those falling within heading No. 98.04 or 98.05	16%	—
98.04 Pen nibs and nib points	12%	—
98.05 Pencils (other than pencils of heading No. 98.03), pencil leads, slate pencils, crayons and pastels, drawing charcoals and writing and drawing chalks; tailors' and billiards chalks: (A) Pencil leads and tailors' chalks ...	8%	—
(B) Pencils, slate pencils, drawing charcoals and billiards chalks	16%	—
(C) Crayons, pastels, writing and drawing chalks: (1) White	10%	—
(2) Coloured	13%	—
98.06 Slates and boards, with writing or drawing surfaces, whether framed or not	16%	—
98.07 Date, sealing or numbering stamps, and the like (including devices for printing or embossing labels), designed for operating in the hand; hand-operated composing sticks and hand printing sets incorporating such composing sticks: (A) Hand-operated daters and numberers with metal figures over 6 millimetres in height, and self-inking hand-operated daters and numberers with rubber letters or figures	9½%	—
(B) Devices for making labels by printing or embossing, otherwise than by stamping the whole legend simultaneously	11%	—
(C) Other	16%	—

Tariff Heading	Rate of Import Duty (if any)	
	Full	Commonwealth (C) E.F.T.A. (E)
98.08 Typewriter and similar ribbons, whether or not on spools; ink-pads, with or without boxes	16%	—
98.09 Sealing wax (including bottle-sealing wax) in sticks, cakes or similar forms; copying pastes with a basis of gelatin, whether or not on a paper or textile backing	16%	—
98.10 Mechanical lighters and similar lighters, including chemical and electrical lighters, and parts thereof, excluding flints and wicks:		
(A) Portable lighters, being portable mechanical, chemical, electrical or similar contrivances intended to provide a means of ignition, whether by spark, flame or otherwise, and parts thereof:		
(1) Portable lighters constructed solely for the purpose of igniting gas for domestic use, whether complete or incomplete (including stems of electrical lighters and rigid or spring frames of flint lighters)	—	—
(2) Other portable lighters, complete or incomplete (including bodies)	—	—
(3) Parts not specified above ...	16%	—
(B) Other lighters and parts thereof ...	16%	—
98.11 Smoking pipes; pipe bowls, stems and other parts of smoking pipes (including roughly shaped blocks of wood or root); cigar and cigarette holders and parts thereof:		
(A) Briar root blocks, roughly shaped by sawing but not further manufactured	—	—
(B) Cigar and cigarette holders	10½%	—
(C) Smoking pipes; parts of smoking pipes and parts of cigar and cigarette holders	12½%	—
98.12 Combs, hair-slides and the like	16%	—
98.13 Corset busks and similar supports for articles of apparel or clothing accessories	16%	—
98.14 Scent and similar sprays of a kind used for toilet purposes, and mounts and heads therefor:		
(A) Of glass, or containing precious metal (not including base metal rolled, coated or plated with precious metal)	24%	—
(B) Other	16%	—

Tariff Heading	Rate of Import Duty (if any)	
	Full	Commonwealth (C) E.F.T.A. (E)
98.15 Vacuum flasks and other vacuum vessels, complete with cases; parts thereof, other than glass inners:		
(A) Vacuum flasks and other vacuum vessels, complete with cases	24%	—
(B) Parts	18%	—
98.16 Tailors' dummies and other lay figures; automata and other animated displays of a kind used for shop window dressing	12½%	—

SECTION XXI

Works of Art, Collectors' Pieces, and Antiques

Chapter 99

Works of Art, Collectors' Pieces, and Antiques

Notes

1. This Chapter does not cover:

(*a*) Unused postage, revenue or similar stamps of current or new issue in the country to which they are destined (heading No. 49.07);

(*b*) Theatrical scenery, studio back-cloths or the like, of painted canvas (heading No. 59.12); or

(*c*) Pearls or precious or semi-precious stones (heading No. 71.01 or 71.02).

2. For the purposes of heading No. 99.02, the expression " original engravings, prints and lithographs " means impressions produced directly, in black and white or in colour, of one or of several plates wholly executed by hand by the artist, irrespective of the process or of the material employed by him, but not including any mechanical or photo-mechanical process.

3. Heading No. 99.03 is to be taken not to apply to mass-produced reproductions or works of conventional craftsmanship of a commercial character.

4. (*a*) Subject to Notes 1 to 3 above, articles falling within headings of this Chapter are to be classified in whichever of those headings is appropriate and not in any other heading of this Schedule.

(*b*) Heading No. 99.06 is to be taken not to apply to articles falling within any of the preceding headings of this Chapter.

5. Frames around paintings, drawings, pastels, engravings, prints or lithographs are to be treated as forming part of those articles, provided they are of a kind and of a value normal to those articles.

Tariff Heading	Rate of Import Duty (*if any*)	
	Full	*Commonwealth (C)* *E.F.T.A.* (E)
9.01 Paintings, drawings and pastels, executed entirely by hand (other than industrial drawings falling within heading No. 49.06 and other than hand-painted or hand-decorated manufactured articles)	—	—
9.02 Original engravings, prints and lithographs: (A) Of an age exceeding 100 years ... (B) Other	— 16%	— —

	Rate of Import Duty (*if any*)	
Tariff Heading	*Full*	*Commonwealth* (*C*) *E.F.T.A.* (*E*)
99.03 Original sculptures and statuary, in any material:		
(A) Of an age exceeding 100 years ...	—	—
(B) Other	16%	—
99.04 Postage, revenue and similar stamps (including stamp-postmarks and franked envelopes, letter-cards and the like), used, or if unused not of current or new issue in the country to which they are destined	—	—
99.05 Collections and collectors' pieces of zoological, botanical, mineralogical, anatomical, historical, archaeological, paleontological, ethnographic or numismatic interest		
99.06 Antiques of an age exceeding one hundred years		

LIST OF SECTION AND CHAPTER TITLES

Section I

Live Animals; Animal Products

Chapter

1 Live animals.
2 Meat and edible meat offals.
3 Fish, crustaceans and molluscs.
4 Dairy produce; birds' eggs; natural honey.
5 Products of animal origin, not elsewhere specified or included.

Section II

Vegetable Products

6 Live trees and other plants; bulbs, roots and the like; cut flowers and ornamental foliage.
7 Edible vegetables and certain roots and tubers.
8 Edible fruit and nuts; peel of melons or citrus fruit.
9 Coffee, tea, maté and spices.
10 Cereals.
11 Products of the milling industry; malt and starches; gluten; inulin.
12 Oil seeds and oleaginous fruit; miscellaneous grains, seeds and fruit; industrial and medical plants; straw and fodder.
13 Raw vegetable materials of a kind suitable for use in dyeing or in tanning; lacs; gums, resins and other vegetable saps and extracts.
14 Vegetable plaiting and carving materials; vegetable products not elsewhere specified or included.

Section III

Animal and Vegetable Fats and Oils and their Cleavage Products; Prepared Edible Fats; Animal and Vegetable Waxes

15 Animal and vegetable fats and oils and their cleavage products; prepared edible fats; animal and vegetable waxes.

Section IV

Prepared Foodstuffs; Beverages, Spirits and Vinegar; Tobacco

16 Preparations of meat, of fish, of crustaceans or molluscs.
17 Sugars and sugar confectionery.
18 Cocoa and cocoa preparations.
19 Preparations of cereals, flour or starch; pastrycooks' products.
20 Preparations of vegetables, fruit or other parts of plants.
21 Miscellaneous edible preparations.
22 Beverages, spirits and vinegar.
23 Residues and waste from the food industries; prepared animal fodder.
24 Tobacco.

Section V

Mineral Products

25 Salt; sulphur; earths and stone; plastering materials, lime and cement.
26 Metallic ores, slag and ash.
27 Mineral fuels, mineral oils and products of their distillation; bituminous substances; mineral waxes.

Section VI

Products of the Chemical and Allied Industries

Section VII

Artificial Resins and Plastic Materials, Cellulose Esters and Ethers, and Articles thereof; Rubber, Synthetic Rubber, Factice, and Articles thereof

Section VIII

Raw Hides and Skins, Leather, Furskins and Articles thereof; Saddlery and Harness; Travel Goods, Handbags and Similar Containers; Articles of Gut (other than Silk-Worm Gut)

Section IX

Wood and Articles of Wood; Wood Charcoal; Cork and Articles of Cork; Manufactures of Straw, of Esparto and of other Plaiting Materials; Basketware and Wickerwork

Section X

Paper-Making Material; Paper and Paperboard and Articles thereof

Section XI

Textiles and Textile Articles

Chapter

50	Silk and waste silk.
51	Man-made fibres (continuous).
52	Metallised textiles.
53	Wool and other animal hair.
54	Flax and ramie.
55	Cotton.
56	Man-made fibres (discontinuous).
57	Other vegetable textile materials; paper yarn and woven fabrics of paper yarn.
58	Carpets, mats, matting and tapestries; pile and chenille fabrics; narrow fabrics; trimmings; tulle and other net fabrics; lace; embroidery.
59	Wadding and felt; twine, cordage, ropes and cables; special fabrics; impregnated and coated fabrics; textile articles of a kind suitable for industrial use.
60	Knitted and crocheted goods.
61	Articles of apparel and clothing accessories of textile fabric, other than knitted or crocheted goods.
62	Other made-up textile articles.
63	Old clothing and other textile articles; rags.

Section XII

Footwear, Headgear, Umbrellas, Sunshades, Whips, Riding-crops and Parts thereof; Prepared Feathers and Articles made therewith; Artificial Flowers; Articles of Human Hair; Fans

64	Footwear, gaiters and the like; parts of such articles.
65	Headgear and parts thereof.
66	Umbrellas, sunshades, walking-sticks, whips, riding-crops and parts thereof.
67	Prepared feathers and down and articles made of feathers or of down; artificial flowers; articles of human hair; fans.

Section XIII

Articles of Stone, of Plaster, of Cement, of Asbestos, of Mica and of Similar Materials; Ceramic Products; Glass and Glassware

68	Articles of stone, of plaster, of cement, of asbestos, of mica and of similar materials.
69	Ceramic products.
70	Glass and glassware.

Section XIV

Pearls, Precious and Semi-Precious Stones, Precious Metals, Rolled Precious Metals, and Articles thereof; Imitation Jewellery; Coin

71	Pearls, precious and semi-precious stones, precious metals, rolled precious metals, and articles thereof; imitation jewellery.
72	Coin.

Section XV

Base Metals and Articles of Base Metal

73	Iron and steel and articles thereof.
74	Copper and articles thereof.
75	Nickel and articles thereof.
76	Aluminium and articles thereof.
77	Magnesium and beryllium and articles thereof.
78	Lead and articles thereof.
79	Zinc and articles thereof.
80	Tin and articles thereof.
81	Other base metals employed in metallurgy and articles thereof.
82	Tools, implements, cutlery, spoons and forks, of base metal; parts thereof.
83	Miscellaneous articles of base metal.

Section XVI

Machinery and Mechanical Appliances; Electrical Equipment; Parts thereof

Chapter

84 Boilers, machinery and mechanical appliances; parts thereof.
85 Electrical machinery and equipment; parts thereof.

Section XVII

Vehicles, Aircraft, and Parts thereof; Vessels and certain associated Transport Equipment

86 Railway and tramway locomotives, rolling-stock and parts thereof; railway and tramway track fixtures and fittings; traffic signalling equipment of all kinds (not electrically powered).
87 Vehicles, other than railway or tramway rolling-stock, and parts thereof.
88 Aircraft and parts thereof; parachutes; catapults and similar aircraft launching gear; ground flying trainers.
89 Ships, boats and floating structures.

Section XVIII

Optical, Photographic, Cinematographic, Measuring, Checking, Precision, Medical and Surgical Instruments and Apparatus; Clocks and Watches; Musical Instruments; Sound Recorders and Reproducers; Television Image and Sound Recorders and Reproducers, Magnetic; Parts thereof

90 Optical, photographic, cinematographic, measuring, checking, precision, medical and surgical instruments and apparatus; parts thereof.
91 Clocks and watches and parts thereof.
92 Musical instruments; sound recorders and reproducers; television image and sound recorders and reproducers, magnetic; parts and accessories of such articles.

Section XIX

Arms and Ammunition; Parts thereof

93 Arms and ammunition; parts thereof.

Section XX

Miscellaneous Manufactured Articles

94 Furniture and parts thereof; bedding, mattresses, mattress supports, cushions and similar stuffed furnishings.
95 Articles and manufactures of carving or moulding material.
96 Brooms, brushes, feather dusters, powder-puffs and sieves.
97 Toys, games and sports requisites; parts thereof.
98 Miscellaneous manufactured articles.

Section XXI

Works of Art, Collectors' Pieces, and Antiques

99 Works of art, collectors' pieces, and antiques.

SCHEDULE 2

IMPORT DUTIES (GENERAL) ORDERS REVOKED

Number and Year of Order					*Reference*
No. 11 of 1966	...	...	...	...	...	S.I. 1966/1555 (1966 III, p. 4405)
No. 1 of 1967	...	...	...	...	...	S.I. 1967/79 (1967 I, p. 159)
No. 2 of 1967	...	...	...	...	...	S.I. 1967/203 (1967 I, p. 342)
No. 3 of 1967	...	...	...	...	...	S.I. 1967/468 (1967 I, p. 1411)
No. 4 of 1967	...	...	...	...	...	S.I. 1967/469 (1967 I, p. 1413)
No. 5 of 1967	...	...	...	...	...	S.I. 1967/953 (1967 II, p. 2918)
No. 6 of 1967	...	...	...	...	...	S.I. 1967/1112 (1967 II, p. 3266)
No. 7 of 1967	...	...	...	...	...	S.I. 1967/1562 (1967 III, p. 4335)
No. 8 of 1967	...	...	...	...	...	S.I. 1967/1718 (1967 III, p. 4646)
No. 1 of 1968	...	...	...	...	...	S.I. 1968/77 (1968 I, p. 259)
No. 2 of 1968	...	...	...	...	...	S.I. 1968/642 (1968 I, p. 1476)
No. 3 of 1968	...	...	...	...	...	S.I. 1968/643 (1968 I, p. 1478)

EXPLANATORY NOTE

(This Note is not part of the Order.)

This Order has five main purposes: it consolidates; it implements the first instalment of the Kennedy Round tariff reductions; it effects some simplifications of the tariff which were agreed during the course of the Kennedy Round; it eliminates certain unnecessary tariff subheadings; and it substitutes import duties for the present revenue duties on hops and hop products.

Dealing in turn in more detail with each of the above purposes:

(1) It consolidates, as at 1st July 1968, the Import Duties (General) (No. 11) Order 1966 and the various Orders amending it.

(2) It reduces, in most cases as the first of a series of reductions to be completed by 1st January 1972, the full rate of import duty (and, where applicable, the Commonwealth preferential rate) on a wide range of goods in accordance with the undertakings given by the United Kingdom at Geneva and set out in the June 1967 Protocol to the General Agreement on Tariffs and Trade (the Kennedy Round; Cmnd. 3347), coupled, in a few instances, with the final stage of implementation of the undertakings set out in the July 1962 Protocol to that Agreement (the Dillon Round; Cmnd. 1804).

(3) It amalgamates, consequential upon the June 1967 (Kennedy) undertakings, certain tariff subheadings, thus effecting a degree of simplification in the tariff, and changes the basis on which duty is charged on some goods. The following are examples of such modifications:—

   (a) the Order amalgamates former subheadings Nos. 59.08(B)(1) and 59.08(B)(2) so that certain textile fabrics coated with plastic, some of which have been dutiable under the first at 2d. per lb. or 15%, whichever is the greater, and others under the second at 20%, all become dutiable at $17\frac{1}{2}\%$ under the single subheading No. 59.08(B);

   (b) it changes some rates of duty from a specific to an ad valorem basis, thus e.g., some unexposed film in subheading No. 37.02(A), hitherto dutiable at $\frac{1}{4}$d. per linear foot, becomes dutiable at 9% of its value;

(c) it changes the basis on which duty is charged on certain- textile products, e.g., garments of heading No. 61.01, containing silk or man-made fibres. Hitherto the rates for such goods have varied according to the percentage which the *value* of the silk or man-made fibre components has borne to the value of all the components. Under this Order, the rates vary according to the percentage which the *weight* of such components bears to the weight of the products as a whole.

(4) It eliminates a number of subheadings which have become unnecessary, and makes a number of other minor modifications, not directly consequential upon the Geneva undertakings.

(5) It imposes import duties on hops, hop oil and hop extracts to replace the existing revenue duties on these products. The rates of duty are unchanged except that such goods originating in and consigned from the Republic of Ireland become free of duty in accordance with the Agreement of December 1965 establishing a Free Trade Area between the United Kingdom and the Republic of Ireland.

1968 No. 680

SOCIAL SECURITY

The National Insurance (New Entrants Transitional) Amendment Regulations 1968

Made - - - -	*29th April* 1968
Laid before Parliament	*2nd May* 1968
Coming into Operation	*6th May* 1968

The Minister of Social Security, in conjunction with the Treasury, in exercise of powers conferred by paragraph 18 of Schedule 11 to the National Insurance Act 1965(**a**) and of all other powers enabling her in that behalf, and in consequence of the passing of section 1(1) of the Public Expenditure and Receipts Act 1968(**b**), hereby makes the following regulations :—

Citation and commencement

1. These regulations may be cited as the National Insurance (New Entrants Transitional) Amendment Regulations 1968 and shall come into operation on 6th May 1968.

Amendment of regulations

2. Schedule 2 to the National Insurance (New Entrants Transitional) Regulations 1949(**c**) as amended(**d**), which sets out the amounts payable by way of refund of contributions to persons who enter insurance too late to be able to satisfy the contribution conditions for widow's benefit or retirement pension, shall be amended by the addition, immediately after paragraph 6 thereof (which was added by regulation 3(2) of and Schedule M to the National Insurance (Increase of Benefit and Miscellaneous Provisions) Regulations 1967(**e**)), of the provisions contained in the Schedule to these regulations.

Judith Hart,
Minister of Social Security.

26th April 1968.

J. McCann,
Joseph Harper,
Two of the Lords Commissioners
of Her Majesty's Treasury.

29th April 1968.

(**a**) 1965 c. 51.　　　(**b**) 1968 c. 14.　　　(**c**) S.I. 1949/352 (1949 I, p. 2737).
(**d**) The relevant amending instruments are S.I. 1958/1239, 2124, 1960/2422, 1961/557, 1963/502, 676, 1965/40, 1967/1265 (1958 II, pp. 1661, 1666; 1960 II, p. 2169; 1961 I, p. 1228; 1963 I, pp. 578, 815; 1965 I, p. 47; 1967 II, p. 3673).
(**e**) S.I. 1967/1265 (1967 II, p. 3673).

Regulation 2

SCHEDULE

PROVISIONS TO BE ADDED TO SCHEDULE 2 TO THE NATIONAL INSURANCE (NEW ENTRANTS TRANSITIONAL) REGULATIONS 1949

7. Applicable (in substitution for the provisions of paragraph 6 of this Schedule) to contributions in respect of contribution weeks commencing on or after 6th May 1968.

Men

Age of man at expiration of period of currency of contribution card on which contribution was paid	Employed	Self-employed	Non-employed
	Portion of contribution to be refunded		
	pence 109	pence 164	pence 163
	Total number of pence to be refunded (including interest) in respect of each contribution		
(1)	(2)	(3)	(4)
65 and over ...	110	165	164
64 ...	112	168	167
63 ...	115	172	171
62 ...	117	177	176
61 ...	120	181	180
60 ...	123	185	184
59 ...	126	190	189

Women

Age of woman at expiration of period of currency of contribution card on which contribution was paid	Employed	Self-employed	Non-employed
	Portion of contribution to be refunded		
	pence 90	pence 120	pence 119
	Total number of pence to be refunded (including interest) in respect of each contribution		
(5)	(6)	(7)	(8)
60 and over ...	91	121	120
59 ...	92	123	122
58 ...	95	126	125
57 ...	97	129	128
56 ...	99	132	131
55 ...	102	136	135
54 ...	104	139	138

EXPLANATORY NOTE

(This Note is not part of the Regulations.)

These Regulations are made in consequence of the passing of section 1(1) of the Public Expenditure and Receipts Act 1968 and accordingly, by virtue of section 1(4) of that Act, no preliminary draft of them has been submitted to the National Insurance Advisory Committee.

The Regulations prescribe the amounts payable to persons who enter insurance too late to be able to satisfy the contribution conditions for widow's benefit or retirement pension, by way of refund of national insurance contributions in respect of contribution weeks commencing on or after the 6th May 1968.

S.I. Nos. 681 to 684 are local: particulars of them will be found in Part III of the Volume.

APPENDIX
OF CERTAIN INSTRUMENTS
NOT REGISTERED AS S.I.

Orders in Council,
Letters Patent
and Royal Instructions

relating to the Constitutions etc. of
Overseas Territories or to appeals to the Judicial
Committee,

Royal Proclamations, etc.

ROAD TRAFFIC

The Breath Test Device (Approval) (No. 1) Order 1968

In pursuance of the power conferred on me by section 7(1) of the Road Safety Act 1967(a), I, the Right Honourable James Callaghan, one of Her Majesty's Principal Secretaries of State, do by this order approve, for the purpose of breath tests as defined in the said section 7(1), the type of device described in the Schedule hereto.

James Callaghan,
One of Her Majesty's Principal
Secretaries of State.

Home Office,
    Whitehall.

9th February 1968.

SCHEDULE

The device known as the Alcotest, comprising an indicator tube (marked with the name "Alcotest"), mouth piece and measuring bag, and supplied to police forces in England and Wales in a container marked with the name "ALCOTEST®80".

(a) 1967 c. 30.

ROYAL WARRANT

To amend the Royal Warrant of 19th September 1964, concerning pensions and other grants in respect of disablement or death due to service in the military forces during the 1914 World War and after 2nd September 1939.

ELIZABETH R.

Preamble

WHEREAS We deem it expedient to amend Our Warrant of 19th September 1964(a), as amended (b), concerning pensions and other grants in respect of disablement or death due to service in the military forces during the 1914 World War and after 2nd September 1939 (hereinafter referred to as "the 1964 Warrant"):

Our Will and Pleasure is that, notwithstanding anything in the 1964 Warrant, the following provisions of this Our Warrant shall take effect accordingly and, except in the cases stated in the Warrant of Her Majesty Queen Victoria of 27th October 1884, and except as otherwise provided by statute, shall be established and obeyed as the sole authority in the matters herein treated of.

Amendment of Schedule 6 to the 1964 Warrant, and transitional provisions

1.—(1) In Schedule 6 to the 1964 Warrant (rates of allowances payable in respect of disablement) there shall be made the amendments set out in Part I of the Appendix hereto.

(2) Where, by virtue of the provisions of paragraph (1) of this Article, the aggregate rate of additional unemployability or treatment allowances (or allowances analogous thereto made by the Minister with the consent of the Treasury) and allowances, if any, under the Family Allowances Act 1965(c) or under any legislation in Northern Ireland or the Isle of Man corresponding to that Act, payable in respect of the children of a member of the military forces who qualify therefor at 8th April 1968 is, upon the coming into operation of the said paragraph, less than it was according to the rates in force on the said 8th April, then for the period for which the said aggregate rate in respect of those children or any remaining number of them continues to be less than it would have been had the said rates remained in force, the rate of additional unemployability or treatment allowances (or allowances analogous thereto) payable in respect of those children may be varied to the extent required to exclude the reduction in the said aggregate rate.

Amendment of Schedule 7 to the 1964 Warrant

2. In Schedule 7 to the 1964 Warrant (rates of pensions, other than widows' pensions, and allowances payable in respect of death) there shall be made the amendments set out at Part II of the Appendix hereto.

(a) S.I. 1964 III, p. 5257.   (b) The relevant amending Warrant is S.I. 1967 II, p. 3811.
(c) 1965 c. 53.

Commencement

3.—(1) Subject to the following provision of this Article, this Our Warrant shall come into operation in relation to an officer on 9th April 1968 and in relation to a soldier on 8th April 1968.

(2) Article 1 shall come into operation in relation to a soldier on 10th April 1968.

> Given at Our Court at St. James's, this twelfth day of February 1968, in the 17th Year of Our Reign.

> *By Her Majesty's Command.*

> *Judith Hart.*

APPENDIX

PART I

Amendment of Schedule 6 to the 1964 Warrant

1. In Schedule 6 paragraph 5 (unemployability allowances) for head (iii) of sub-paragraph (*b*) there shall be substituted the following head:—

"(iii) increased allowance under Article 17(4)(*f*)—

(*a*) in respect of the child, or the elder or eldest of the children, of a member ...	£72 16*s*. per annum	28*s*. per week
(*b*) in respect of the second child of a member	£33 16*s*. per annum	13*s*. per week
(*c*) in respect of each other child of a member ...	£30 per annum	11*s*. per week"

2. In Schedule 6 paragraph 9 (treatment allowances) for sub-paragraph (*d*) there shall be substituted the following sub-paragraph:—

"(*d*) increased additional allowance under Article 21(4) proviso (*b*)—

(i) in respect of the child, or the elder or eldest of the children, of a member ...	£72 16*s*. per annum	28*s*. per week
(ii) in respect of the second child of a member ...	£33 16*s*. per annum	13*s*. per week
(iii) in respect of each other child of a member ...	£30 per annum	11*s*. per week"

PART II

Amendment of Schedule 7 to the 1964 Warrant

In Schedule 7—

(*a*) for paragraph 5 (allowances in respect of children) there shall be substituted the following paragraph:—

"5. Allowances in respect of children—

(*a*) under Article 35(1)—

   (i) in respect of the child, or
the elder or eldest of the
children, of a member ... £136 16s. per annum 49s. 6d. per week

   (ii) in respect of each other
child of a member—

    (a) where the child qualifies
for a family allowance
under the Family
Allowances Act 1965
or under any legisla-
tion in Northern Ire-
land or the Isle of Man
corresponding to that
Act ... ... £118 12s. per annum 42s. 6d. per week

    (b) where the child does
not so qualify ... £129 per annum 46s. 6d. per week
  (b) under Article 35(3) ... £197 16s. per annum where the child is 15
             (maximum)   years of age or over—
                       72s. 6d. per week
                       (maximum)"

 (b) for paragraph 6 (pension under Article 36 to a motherless or fatherless child)
there shall be substituted the following paragraph:—

"6. Pension under Article 36 to a motherless or fatherless child—

    (a) in respect of the child,
or the elder or eldest of
the children, of a mem-
ber, and in respect of
each other child of a
member who does not
qualify for a family
allowance as aforesaid £197 16s. per annum (i) where the child is
                             under 15 years of
                             age—
                             49s. 6d. per week

                            (ii) where the child is
                             15 years of age or
                             over—
                             72s. 6d. per week

    (b) in respect of each other
child of a member who
qualifies for a family
allowance as aforesaid £179 12s. per annum (i) where the child is
                             under 15 years of
                             age—
                             42s. 6d. per week

                            (ii) where the child is
                             15 years of age or
                             over—
                             65s. 6d. per week"

EXPLANATORY NOTE

(This Note is not part of the Royal Warrant.)

This Royal Warrant further amends the Royal Warrant of 19th September 1964.

Articles 1 and 2 make amendments which take account of the increase in family allowances made by the Family Allowances and National Insurance Act 1967 from 9th April 1968 and have the effect—

(*a*) of varying the rates of allowances payable in respect of children of unemployable pensioners or of pensioners receiving treatment as defined in Article 21(8) so that the allowances and (where payable) family allowances together will normally provide a total of £72 16s. a year in respect of each child of an officer and 28s. a week in respect of each child of a soldier (instead of £65 or £70 4s. a year and 25s. or 27s. a week). In the case of existing awards, transitional provisions provide for the aggregate rate of these allowances to be maintained if, exceptionally, it would be reduced by the application of the new rates.

(*b*) in relation to children of deceased members of the military forces—

    (i) of increasing the rate payable in respect of the only, elder or eldest child (and certain other children who do not qualify for a family allowance) by £7 16s. a year in the case of a child of an officer and 3s. a week in the case of a child of a soldier;

    (ii) of adjusting the rate payable in respect of any child who also qualifies for a family allowance so that the total weekly amount provided is normally increased by £7 16s. a year in the case of a child of an officer and 3s. a week in the case of a child of a soldier.

ORDER BY HER MAJESTY

To amend the Order of 24th September 1964, concerning pensions and other grants in respect of disablement or death due to service in the air forces during the 1914 World War and after 2nd September 1939.

ELIZABETH R.

Preamble

WHEREAS by Section 2 of the Air Force (Constitution) Act 1917(a) it is provided that it shall be lawful for Her Majesty, by order signified under the hand of a Secretary of State, to make orders with respect to the government, discipline, pay, allowances and pensions of the Air Force, and with respect to all other matters and things relating to the Air Force, including any matter by that Act authorised to be prescribed or expressed to be subject to orders or regulations:

AND WHEREAS Her Majesty deems it expedient to amend the Order dated 24th September 1964(b), as amended (c), concerning pensions and other grants in respect of disablement or death due to service in the air forces during the 1914 World War and after 2nd September 1939 (hereinafter referred to as "the 1964 Order"):

NOW, THEREFORE, Her Majesty, in exercise of the powers conferred upon Her as aforesaid and of all other powers whatsoever Her thereunto enabling, is pleased to order, and it is hereby ordered that, notwithstanding anything in the 1964 Order, the following provisions of this Order shall take effect accordingly and, except in the cases stated in the Order by His Majesty King George V of 13th January 1922, and except as otherwise provided by statute, shall be established and obeyed as the sole authority in the matters herein treated of.

Amendment of Schedule 6 to the 1964 *Order, and transitional provisions*

1.—(1) In Schedule 6 to the 1964 Order (rates of allowances payable in respect of disablement) there shall be made the amendments set out in Part I of the Appendix hereto.

(2) Where, by virtue of the provisions of paragraph (1) of this Article, the aggregate rate of additional unemployability or treatment allowances (or allowances analogous thereto made by the Minister with the consent of the Treasury) and allowances, if any, under the Family Allowances Act 1965(d) or under any legislation in Northern Ireland or the Isle of Man corresponding to that Act, payable in respect of the children of a member of the air forces who qualify therefor at 8th April 1968 is, upon the coming into operation of the said paragraph, less than it was according to the rates in force on the said 8th April, then for the period for which the said aggregate rate in respect of those children or any remaining number of them continues to be less than it would have been had

---

(a) 7 & Geo. 5. c. 51.　　　　　(b) S.I. 1964 III, p. 5361.
(c) The relevant amending Order is S.I. 1967 II, p. 3831.　　(d) 1965 c. 53.

the said rates remained in force, the rate of additional unemployability or treatment allowances (or allowances analogous thereto) payable in respect of those children may be varied to the extent required to exclude the reduction in the said aggregate rate.

Amendment of Schedule 7 to the 1964 Order

2. In Schedule 7 to the 1964 Order (rates of pensions, other than widows' pensions, and allowances payable in respect of death) there shall be made the amendments set out at Part II of the Appendix hereto.

Commencement

3.—(1) Subject to the following provision of this Article, this Order shall come into operation in relation to an officer on 9th April 1968 and in relation to an airman on 8th April 1968.

(2) Article 1 shall come into operation in relation to an airman on 10th April 1968.

By Her Majesty's Command.

Denis Healey,

Secretary of State.

Judith Hart,

Minister of Social Security.

13th February 1968.

APPENDIX

PART I

Amendment of Schedule 6 to the 1964 Order

1. In Schedule 6 paragraph 5 (unemployability allowances) for head (iii) of sub-paragraph (*b*) there shall be substituted the following head:—

"(iii) increased allowance under
Article 17(4)(*f*)—

(*a*) in respect of the child, or the elder or eldest of the children, of a member ...	£72 16*s*. per annum	28*s*. per week
(*b*) in respect of the second child of a member ...	£33 16*s*. per annum	13*s*. per week
(*c*) in respect of each other child of a member ...	£30 per annum	11*s*. per week"

2. In Schedule 6 paragraph 9 (treatment allowances) for sub-paragraph (*d*) there shall be substituted the following sub-paragraph:—

"(*d*) increased additional allowance
under Article 21(4) proviso (*b*)—

(i) in respect of the child, or the elder or eldest of the children, of a member ...	£72 16*s*. per annum	28*s*. per week
(ii) in respect of the second child of a member ...	£33 16*s*. per annum	13*s*. per week

(iii) in respect of each other
child of a member   ...   £30 per annum   11s. per week"

PART II

Amendment of Schedule 7 to the 1964 Order

In Schedule 7—

(a) for paragraph 5 (allowances in respect of children) there shall be substituted the following paragraph:—

"5. Allowances in respect of children—

(a) under Article 35(1)—

   (i) in respect of the child, or the elder or eldest of the children, of a member   ...   £136 16s. per annum   49s. 6d. per week

   (ii) in respect of each other child of a member—

      (a) where the child qualifies for a family allowance under the Family Allowances Act 1965 or under any legislation in Northern Ireland or the Isle of Man corresponding to that Act   ...   .   £118 12s. per annum   42s. 6d. per week

      (b) where the child does not so qualify   ...   £129 per annum   46s. 6d. per week

(b) under Article 35(3)   ...   £197 16s. per annum (maximum)   where the child is 15 years of age or over— 72s. 6d. per week (maximum)"

(b) for paragraph 6 (pension under Article 36 to a motherless or fatherless child) there shall be substituted the following paragraph:—

"6. Pension under Article 36 to a motherless or fatherless child—

   (a) in respect of the child, or the elder or eldest of the children, of a member, and in respect of each other child of a member who does not qualify for a family allowance as aforesaid   £197 16s. per annum

      (i) where the child is under 15 years of age— 49s. 6d. per week

      (ii) where the child is 15 years of age or over— 72s. 6d. per week

(b) in respect of each other child of a member who qualifies for a family allowance as aforesaid	£179 12s. per annum	(i) where the child is under 15 years of age— 42s. 6d. per week (ii) where the child is 15 years of age or over— 65s. 6d. per week"

EXPLANATORY NOTE

(This Note is not part of the Order.)

This Order further amends the Order of 24th September 1964.

Articles 1 and 2 make amendments which take account of the increase in family allowances made by the Family Allowances and National Insurance Act 1967 from 9th April 1968 and have the effect—

(a) of varying the rates of allowances payable in respect of children of unemployable pensioners or of pensioners receiving treatment as defined in Article 21(8) so that the allowances and (where payable) family allowances together will normally provide a total of £72 16s. a year in respect of each child of an officer and 28s. a week in respect of each child of an airman (instead of £65 or £70 4s. a year and 25s. or 27s. a week). In the case of existing awards, transitional provisions provide for the aggregate rate of these allowances to be maintained if, exceptionally, it would be reduced by the application of the new rates.

(b) in relation to children of deceased members of the air forces—

  (i) of increasing the rate payable in respect of the only, elder or eldest child (and certain other children who do not qualify for a family allowance) by £7 16s. a year in the case of a child of an officer and 3s. a week in the case of a child of an airman;

  (ii) of adjusting the rate payable in respect of any child who also qualifies for a family allowance so that the total weekly amount provided is normally increased by £7 16s. a year in the case of a child of an officer and 3s. a week in the case of a child of an airman.

PENSIONS

At the Court at Buckingham Palace, the 14th day of February 1968

Present,

The Queen's Most Excellent Majesty in Council

WHEREAS by section 3 of the Naval and Marine Pay and Pensions Act 1865(a) it is enacted that all pay, wages, pensions, bounty money, grants or other allowances in the nature thereof, payable in respect of services in Her Majesty's naval or marine force to a person being or having been an officer, seaman or marine, or to the widow or any relative of a deceased officer, seaman or marine, shall be paid in such manner and subject to such restrictions, conditions and provisions, as are from time to time directed by Order in Council:

AND WHEREAS Her Majesty deems it expedient to amend the Order in Council dated 25th September 1964(b), as amended(c), concerning pensions and other grants in respect of disablement or death due to service in the naval forces during the 1914 World War and after 2nd September 1939 (hereinafter referred to as "the 1964 Order"):

NOW, THEREFORE, Her Majesty, in exercise of the powers conferred upon Her as aforesaid and of all other powers whatsoever Her thereunto enabling, is pleased, by and with the advice of Her Privy Council, to order, and it is hereby ordered that, notwithstanding anything in the 1964 Order, the following provisions of this Order shall take effect accordingly and, except in the cases stated in the Order in Council of 19th December 1881, and except as otherwise provided by statute, shall be established and obeyed as the sole authority in the matters herein treated of.

Amendment of Schedule 6 to the 1964 Order, and transitional provisions

1.—(1) In Schedule 6 to the 1964 Order (rates of allowances payable in respect of disablement) there shall be made the amendments set out in Part I of the Appendix hereto.

(2) Where, by virtue of the provisions of paragraph (1) of this Article, the aggregate rate of additional unemployability or treatment allowances (or allowances analogous thereto made by the Minister with the consent of the Treasury) and allowances, if any, under the Family Allowances Act 1965(d) or under any legislation in Northern Ireland or the Isle of Man corresponding to that Act, payable in respect of the children of a member of the naval forces who qualify therefor at 8th April 1968 is, upon the coming into operation of the said paragraph, less than it was according to the rates in force on the said 8th April, then for the period for which the said aggregate rate in respect of those children or any remaining number of them continues to be less than it would have been had the said rates remained in force, the rate of additional unemployability or treatment allowances (or allowances analogous thereto) payable in respect of those children may be varied to the extent required to exclude the reduction in the said aggregate rate.

(a) 28 & 29 Vict. c. 73.   (b) S.I. 1964 III, p. 5466.
(c) The relevant amending Order is S.I. 1967 II, p. 3851.   (d) 1965 c. 53.

Amendment of Schedule 7 to the 1964 Order

2. In Schedule 7 to the 1964 Order (rates of pensions, other than widows' pensions, and allowances payable in respect of death) there shall be made the amendments set out at Part II of the Appendix hereto.

Commencement

3.—(1) Subject to the following provision of this Article, this Order shall come into operation in relation to an officer on 9th April 1968 and in relation to a rating on 8th April 1968.

(2) Article 1 shall come into operation in relation to a rating on 10th April 1968.

W. G. Agnew.

APPENDIX

PART I
Amendment of Schedule 6 to the 1964 Order

1. In Schedule 6 paragraph 5 (unemployability allowances) for head (iii) of sub-paragraph (b) there shall be substituted the following head:—
" (iii) increased allowance under Article 17(4)(f)—

(a) in respect of the child, or the elder or eldest of the children, of a member... £72 16s. per annum 28s. per week

(b) in respect of the second child of a member ... ... £33 16s. per annum 13s. per week

(c) in respect of each other child of a member ... ... £30 per annum 11s. per week "

2. In Schedule 6 paragraph 9 (treatment allowances) for sub-paragraph (d) there shall be substituted the following sub-paragraph:—
" (d) increased additional allowance under Article 21(4) proviso (b)—

(i) in respect of the child, or the elder or eldest of the children, of a member... ... ... £72 16s. per annum 28s. per week

(ii) in respect of the second child of a member ... ... £33 16s. per annum 13s. per week

(iii) in respect of each other child of a member... ... ... £30 per annum 11s. per week "

PART II
Amendment of Schedule 7 to the 1964 Order

In Schedule 7—
(a) for paragraph 5 (allowances in respect of children) there shall be substituted the following paragraph:—
" 5. Allowances in respect of children—

(a) under Article 35(1)—

(i) in respect of the child, or the elder or eldest of the children, of a member ... ... (i) Commissioned Officer* or Nurse— £136 16s. per annum 49s. 6d. per week
(ii) Warrant Officer†— £130 16s. per annum

(ii) in respect of each other child of a member—

    (a) where the child qualifies for a family allowance under the Family Allowances Act 1965 or under any legislation in Northern Ireland or the Isle of Man corresponding to that Act ... ...

       (i) Commissioned Officer* or Nurse—£118 12s. per annum — 42s. 6d. per week
       (ii) Warrant Officer†—£112 12s. per annum

    (b) where the child does not so qualify... ... ...

       (i) Commissioned Officer* or Nurse—£129 per annum — 46s. 6d. per week
       (ii) Warrant Officer†—£123 per annum

(b) under Article 35(3)—

       (i) Commissioned Officer*—£197 16s. per annum (maximum) — where the child is 15 years of age or over—72s. 6d. per week (maximum)"

       (ii) Warrant Officer†—

         (a) where the child is under 15 years of age—£136 16s. per annum (maximum)

         (b) where the child is 15 years of age or over—£189 16s. per annum (maximum)

(b) for paragraph 6 (pension under Article 36 to a motherless or fatherless child) there shall be substituted the following paragraph:—

" 6. Pension under Article 36 to a motherless or fatherless child—

    (a) in respect of the child, or the elder or eldest of the children, of a member, and in respect of each other child of a member who does not qualify for a family allowance as aforesaid ... ...

       (i) Commissioned Officer* or Nurse—£197 16s. per annum — (i) where the child is under 15 years of age—49s. 6d. per week

       (ii) Warrant Officer†— — (ii) where the child is 15 years of age or over—72s. 6d. per week

         (a) where the child is under 15 years of age—£136 16s. per annum

         (b) where the child is 15 years of age or over—£189 16s. per annum

(b) in respect of each other child of a member who qualifies for a family allowance as aforesaid ... ...

(i) Commissioned Officer* or Nurse—£179 12s. per annum

(i) where the child is under 15 years of age—42s. 6d. per week

(ii) Warrant Officer†—

(a) where the child is under 15 years of age—£118 12s. per annum

(b) where the child is 15 years of age or over—£171 12s. per annum

(ii) where the child is 15 years of age or over—65s. 6d. per week "

EXPLANATORY NOTE

(This Note is not part of the Order.)

This Order further amends the Order of 25th September 1964.

Articles 1 and 2 make amendments which take account of the increase in family allowances made by the Family Allowances and National Insurance Act 1967 from 9th April 1968 and have the effect—

(a) of varying the rates of allowances payable in respect of children of unemployable pensioners or of pensioners receiving treatment as defined in Article 21(8) so that the allowances and (where payable) family allowances together will normally provide a total of £72 16s. a year in respect of each child of an officer and 28s. a week in respect of each child of a rating (instead of £65 or £70 4s. a year and 25s. or 27s. a week). In the case of existing awards, transitional provisions provide for the aggregate rate of these allowances to be maintained if, exceptionally, it would be reduced by the application of the new rates.

(b) in relation to children of deceased members of the naval forces—

(i) of increasing the rate payable in respect of the only, elder or eldest child (and certain other children who do not qualify for a family allowance) by £7 16s. a year in the case of a child of an officer and 3s. a week in the case of a child of a rating ;

(ii) of adjusting the rate payable in respect of any child who also qualifies for a family allowance so that the total weekly amount provided is normally increased by £7 16s. a year in the case of a child of an officer and 3s. a week in the case of a child of a rating.

BY THE QUEEN

A PROCLAMATION

DETERMINING NEW DESIGNS FOR CUPRO-NICKEL AND BRONZE COINS

ELIZABETH R.

Whereas under section 11 of the Coinage Act 1870(a), We have power, with the advice of Our Privy Council, from time to time by Proclamation to determine the design for any coin:

And Whereas it appears to Us desirable, in consequence of the passing of the Decimal Currency Act 1967(b), to determine designs for the coins hereinafter specified, being coins of the denominations described in Schedule 1 to that Act:

And Whereas, by virtue of section 2(4) of the said Act of 1967, We have power, by Proclamation under section 11 of the said Act of 1870, to direct that coins made in accordance with section 2 of the said Act of 1967 may be issued for use before the day appointed under section 1(2) of that Act as current coins of such denominations as may be specified:

We, therefore, in pursuance of section 11 of the Coinage Act 1870, as extended by section 2(4) of the Decimal Currency Act 1967, and of all other powers enabling Us in that behalf, do hereby, by and with the advice of Our Privy Council, proclaim, direct and ordain as follows:—

The designs for the cupro-nickel and bronze coins of the denominations described in Schedule 1 to the Decimal Currency Act 1967 shall be as follows:—

CUPRO-NICKEL COINS

(1) Ten new pence—Every ten new pence shall have for the obverse impression Our effigy with the inscription " D·G·REG·F·D·ELIZABETH·II " and the date of the year, and for the reverse a lion passant guardant royally crowned, being part of the crest of England, and the inscription " 10 NEW PENCE ". The coin shall have a graining upon the edge.

(2) Five new pence—Every five new pence shall have the same obverse impression and inscription as the ten new pence, and for the reverse a thistle royally crowned, being the badge of Scotland, and the inscription " 5 NEW PENCE ". The coin shall have a graining upon the edge.

BRONZE COINS

(1) Two new pence—Every two new pence shall have for the obverse impression Our effigy with the inscription " D·G·REG·F·D·ELIZABETH·II " and the date 1971, or of a succeeding year, and for the reverse the badge of the Prince of Wales, being three ostrich feathers enfiling a coronet of crosses pattée and fleurs de lys with the motto " ICH DIEN ", and the inscription " 2 NEW PENCE ". The coin shall have a plain edge.

(2) New penny—Every new penny shall have the same obverse impression and inscription as the two new pence, and for the reverse a portcullis with chains royally crowned, being a badge of King Henry VII and his successors, and the inscription " 1 NEW PENNY " The coin shall have a plain edge.

(a) 1870 c. 10.　　(b) 1967 c. 47.

(3) New halfpenny—Every new halfpenny shall have the same obverse impression and inscription as the two new pence, and for the reverse the Royal Crown, and the inscription " ½ NEW PENNY ". The coin shall have a plain edge.

The ten new pence and the five new pence may be issued for use before the day appointed under section 1(2) of the Decimal Currency Act 1967 as a florin and a shilling respectively.

This Proclamation shall come into force on the seventeenth day of February One thousand nine hundred and sixty-eight.

Given at Our Court at Buckingham Palace, this fourteenth day of February, in the year of our Lord One thousand nine hundred and sixty-eight, and in the seventeenth year of Our Reign.

GOD SAVE THE QUEEN

MAURITIUS

The Mauritius Independence Order 1968

At the Court at Buckingham Palace, the 4th day of March 1968

Present,

The Queen's Most Excellent Majesty in Council

Her Majesty, by virtue and in exercise of the powers enabling Her in that behalf, is pleased, by and with the advice of Her Privy Council, to order, and it is hereby ordered, as follows:—

1.—(1) This Order may be cited as the Mauritius Independence Order 1968.

Citation and commencement.

(2) This Order shall be published in the Gazette and shall come into force on the day on which it is so published (**a**):

Provided that section 4(2) of this Order shall come into force forthwith:

2.—(1) In this Order—

Interpretation.

"the Constitution" means the Constitution of Mauritius set out in the Schedule to this Order;

"the appointed day" means 12th March 1968;

"the existing Assembly" means the Legislative Assembly established by the existing Orders;

"the existing laws" means any Acts of the Parliament of the United Kingdom, Orders of Her Majesty in Council, Ordinances, rules, regulations, orders or other instruments having effect as part of the law of Mauritius immediately before the appointed day but does not include any Order revoked by this Order;

"the existing Orders" means the Orders revoked by section 3(1) of this Order.

(2) The provisions of sections 111, 112, 120 and 121 of the Constitution shall apply for the purposes of interpreting sections 1 to 17 of this Order and otherwise in relation thereto as they apply for the purpose of interpreting and in relation to the Constitution.

3.—(1) With effect from the appointed day, the Mauritius Constitution Order 1966(**a**), the Mauritius Constitution (Amendment) Order 1967(**b**) and the Mauritius Constitution (Amendment No. 2) Order 1967(**c**) and

Revocations.

(a) Day published 6.3.68.   (b) S.I. 1966 III, p. 5190.   (c) S.I. 1967 I, p. 2132.
(d) S.I. 1967 II, p. 3807.

the Mauritius Constitution (Amendment No. 3) Order 1967(a) are revoked.

(2) The Emergency Powers Order in Council 1939(b), and any Order in Council amending that Order, shall cease to have effect as part of the law of Mauritius on the appointed day :

Provided that if Part II of the Emergency Powers Order in Council 1939 is in operation in Mauritius immediately before the appointed day a Proclamation such as is referred to in paragraph (b) of section 19(7) of the Constitution shall be deemed to have been made on that day and to have been approved by the Assembly within seven days of that day under paragraph (a) of section 19(8) of the Constitution.

Establishment of Constitution.

4.—(1) Subject to the provisions of this Order, the Constitution shall come into effect in Mauritius on the appointed day.

(2) The Governor (as defined for the purposes of the existing Orders) acting after consultation with the Prime Minister (as so defined) may at any time after the commencement of this subsection exercise any of the powers conferred upon the Governor-General by section 5 of this Order or by the Constitution to such extent as may in his opinion be necessary or expedient to enable the Constitution to function as from the appointed day.

Existing laws.

5.—(1) The revocation of the existing Orders shall be without prejudice to the continued operation of any existing laws made, or having effect as if they had been made, under any of those Orders ; and any such laws shall have effect on and after the appointed day as if they had been made in pursuance of the Constitution and shall be construed with such modifications, adaptations, qualifications and exceptions as may be necessary to bring them into conformity with the Mauritius Independence Act 1968(c) and this Order.

(2) Where any matter that falls to be prescribed or otherwise provided for under the Constitution by Parliament or by any other authority or person is prescribed or provided for by or under an existing law (including any amendment to any such law made under this section) or is otherwise prescribed or provided for immediately before the appointed day by or under the existing Orders that prescription or provision shall, as from that day, have effect (with such modifications, adaptations, qualifications and exceptions as may be necessary to bring it into conformity with the Mauritius Independence Act 1968 and this Order) as if it had been made under the Constitution by Parliament or, as the case may require, by the other authority or person.

(3) The Governor-General may, by order published in the Gazette, at any time before 6th September 1968 make such amendments to any existing law (other than the Mauritius Independence Act 1968 or this Order) as may appear to him to be necessary or expedient for bringing that law into conformity with the provisions of this Order or otherwise for giving effect or enabling effect to be given to those provisions.

(4) An order made under this section may be amended or revoked by Parliament or, in relation to any existing law affected thereby,

(a) S.I. 1967 III, p. 5455.   (b) See S.I. 1952 I, p. 621.   (c) 1968 c. 8.

by any other authority having power to amend, repeal or revoke that existing law.

(5) It is hereby declared, for the avoidance of doubt, that, save as otherwise provided either expressly or by necessary implication, nothing in this Order shall be construed as affecting the continued operation of any existing law.

(6) The provisions of this section shall be without prejudice to any powers conferred by this Order or any other law upon any person or authority to make provision for any matter, including the amendment or repeal of any existing law.

6.—(1) Where any office has been established by or under the existing Orders or any existing law and the Constitution establishes a similar or an equivalent office any person who, immediately before the appointed day, holds or is acting in the former office shall, so far as is consistent with the provisions of the Constitution, be deemed to have been appointed on the appointed day to hold or to act in the latter office in accordance with the provisions of the Constitution and to have taken any necessary oaths under the Constitution and, in the case of a person who holds or is acting in the office of a judge of the Supreme Court, to have complied with the requirements of section 79 of the Constitution (which relates to oaths): *Existing offices.*

Provided that any person who under the existing Orders or any existing law would have been required to vacate his office at the expiration of any period or on the attainment of any age shall vacate his office under the Constitution at the expiration of that period or upon the attainment of that age.

(2) Section 113(1) of the Constitution shall have effect—

(a) in relation to the person holding the office of Electoral Commissioner immediately before the appointed day as if it permitted him to be appointed to that office on the appointed day for a term expiring on 30th November 1969 or such later date as may be determined by the Judicial and Legal Service Commission ; and

(b) in relation to the person holding the office of Commissioner of Police immediately before the appointed day as if it permitted him to be appointed to that office on the appointed day for a term expiring on such date (not being earlier than 31st March 1969 or later than 30th September 1969) as may be determined by the Police Service Commission ;

and those persons shall be deemed to have been appointed as aforesaid and, in relation to them, the reference in section 113(1) to the specified term shall be construed accordingly.

(3) The provisions of this section shall be without prejudice to any powers conferred by or under the Constitution upon any person or authority to make provision for the abolition of offices and for the removal from office of persons holding or acting in any office.

7.—(1) Until such time as it is otherwise provided under section 39 of the Constitution, the respective boundaries of the twenty constituencies in the Island of Mauritius shall be the same as those prescribed by the Mauritius (Electoral Provisions) Regulations 1966(a) for the twenty *Elections.*

(a) G. N. 1966/82.

electoral districts established by those Regulations in pursuance of the Mauritius (Electoral Provisions) Order 1966(a).

(2) If any election of a member of the Assembly is held in any constituency before 1st February 1969, and it is prescribed that any register of electors published before 1st February 1967 is to be used, then no person shall be entitled to vote in that constituency—

(a) in the case of a constituency in the Island of Mauritius, unless, in pursuance of the Mauritius (Electoral Provisions) Order 1966, he has been registered as an elector in the electoral district corresponding to that constituency ;

(b) in the case of Rodrigues, unless, in pursuance of the Mauritius (Electoral Provisions) Order 1965(b), he has been registered as an elector in Rodrigues as if Rodrigues had been established as an electoral district for the purposes of that Order.

The Legislative Assembly.

8.—(1) The persons who immediately before the appointed day were members of the existing Assembly shall as from the appointed day be members of the Assembly established by the Constitution as if elected as such in pursuance of section 31(2) of the Constitution and shall hold their seats in that Assembly in accordance with the provisions of the Constitution :

Provided that persons who immediately before the appointed day represented constituencies in the existing Assembly shall so hold their seats as if respectively elected to represent the corresponding constituencies under the Constitution.

(2) Any person who is a member of the Assembly established by the Constitution by virtue of the preceding provisions of this section and who, since he was last elected as a member of the existing Assembly before the appointed day, has taken the oath of allegiance in pursuance of section 49 of the Constitution established by the existing Orders shall be deemed to have complied with the requirements of section 55 of the Constitution (which relates to the oath of allegiance).

(3) The persons who immediately before the appointed day were unreturned candidates at the general election of members of the existing Assembly shall, until the dissolution of the Assembly next following the appointed day, be regarded as unreturned candidates for the purposes of paragraph 5(7) of Schedule 1 to the Constitution ; and for those purposes anything done in accordance with the provisions of Schedule 1 to the Constitution established by the existing Orders shall be deemed to have been done in accordance with the corresponding provisions of Schedule 1 to the Constitution.

(4) For the purpose of section 57(2) of this Constitution the Assembly shall be deemed to have had its first sitting after a general election on 22nd August 1967 (being the date on which the existing Assembly first sat after a general election).

Procedure of Legislative Assembly.

9. The rules and orders of the existing Assembly, as those rules and orders were in force immediately before the appointed day, shall, except as may be otherwise provided under section 48 of the Constitution, have effect after the appointed day as if they had been made under that section

---

(a) S.I. 1966 I, p. 1101.   (b) S.I. 1965 III, p. 6451.

but shall be construed with such modifications, adaptations, qualifications and exceptions as may be necessary to bring them into conformity with this Order.

10. If by virtue of section 10(1) of the Mauritius (Constitution) Order 1966 the person referred to in section 9(1) of the Mauritius (Constitution) Order 1964(a) is immediately before the appointed day holding the office of Speaker of the existing Assembly, then, with effect from the appointed day— The Speaker.

(a) that person shall be deemed to be a member of the Assembly and to have been elected Speaker of the Assembly under section 32 of the Constitution ; and

(b) the provisions of the Constitution (other than paragraphs (a), (b) and (e) of section 32(3)) shall apply to him accordingly,

until such time as he vacates the office of Speaker under paragraph (c) or (d) of section 32(3) of the Constitution or under section 32(5) of the Constitution or becomes a candidate for election as a member of the Assembly.

11. All proceedings commenced or pending before the Supreme Court, the Court of Civil Appeal or the Court of Criminal Appeal of Mauritius immediately before the appointed day may be carried on before the Supreme Court, the Court of Civil Appeal or the Court of Criminal Appeal, as the case may be, established by the Constitution. Pending proceedings.

12.—(1) Unless it is otherwise prescribed by Parliament, the Court of Appeal may exercise on and after the appointed day such jurisdiction and powers in relation to appeals from the Supreme Court of Seychelles as may be conferred upon it by or in pursuance of the Seychelles Civil Appeals Order 1967(b) or of any other law in that behalf for the time being in force in Seychelles. Jurisdiction of Court of Appeal in relation to Seychelles.

(2) The provisions of section 81 of the Constitution shall not apply in relation to decisions of the Court of Appeal given in the exercise of any jurisdiction and powers conferred upon it in relation to appeals from the Supreme Court of Seychelles, and appeals shall lie to Her Majesty in Council from such decisions in accordance with the Seychelles (Appeals to Privy Council) Order 1967(c) or any other law in that behalf for the time being in force in Seychelles.

(3) The Seychelles Civil Appeals Order 1967 and the Seychelles (Appeals to Privy Council) Order 1967 shall cease to form part of the law of Mauritius with effect from the appointed day.

13.—(1) Until such time as a salary and allowances are prescribed by Parliament, there shall be paid to the holder of any office to which section 108 of the Constitution applies a salary and allowances calculated at the same rate as the salary and allowances paid immediately before the appointed day to the holder of the office corresponding thereto. Remuneration of certain officers.

(2) If the person holding the office of Governor immediately before the appointed day becomes Governor-General his terms and conditions of service, other than salary and allowances, as Governor-General shall,

(a) S.I. 1964 I, p. 1163. (b) S.I. 1967 III, p. 5414. (c) S.I. 1967/1480 (1967 III, p. 4180).

until such time as other provisions are made in that behalf, be the same as those attaching to the office of Governor immediately before the appointed day.

Transitional provisions relating to existing Commissions.

14. Any power that, immediately before the appointed day, is vested in a Commission established by any of the existing Orders and that, under that Order, is then delegated to some other person or authority shall be deemed to have been delegated to that person or authority on the appointed day in accordance with the provisions of the Constitution ; and any proceedings commenced or pending before any such Commission immediately before the appointed day may be carried on before the appropriate Commission established by the Constitution.

Compulsory retirement to facilitate appointment of local candidates.

15.—(1) If the Prime Minister so requests, the authorities having power to make appointments in any branch of the public service shall consider whether there are more local candidates suitably qualified for appointment to, or promotion in, that branch than there are vacancies in that branch that could appropriately be filled by such local candidates ; and those authorities, if satisfied that such is the case, shall, if so requested by the Prime Minister, select officers in that branch to whom this section applies and whose retirement would in the opinion of those authorities cause vacancies that could appropriately be filled by such suitably qualified local candidates as are available and fit for appointment and inform the Prime Minister of the number of officers so selected ; and if the Prime Minister specifies a number of officers to be called upon to retire (not exceeding the number of officers so selected), those authorities shall nominate that number of officers from among the officers so selected and by notice in writing require them to retire from the public service ; and any officer who is so required to retire shall retire accordingly.

(2) A notice given under the preceding subsection requiring an officer to retire from the public service shall be not less than six months from the date he receives the notice, at the expiration of which he shall proceed on leave of absence pending retirement :

Provided that, with the agreement of the officer or if the officer is on leave when it is given, a notice may specify a shorter period.

(3) This section applies to any officer who is the holder of a pensionable office in the public service and is a designated officer for the purposes of the Overseas Service (Mauritius) Agreement 1961.

Appeals in respect of certain decisions affecting pensions benefits.

16.—(1) The provisions of this section shall have effect for the purpose of enabling an officer to whom this section applies or his personal representatives to appeal against any of the following decisions, that is to say :—

(a) a decision of the appropriate Commission to give such concurrence as is required by subsection (1) or (2) of section 95 of the Constitution in relation to the refusal, withholding, reduction in amount or suspending of any pensions benefits in respect of such an officer's service as a public officer ;

(b) a decision of any authority to remove such an officer from office if the consequence of the removal is that any pensions benefits cannot be granted in respect of the officer's service as a public officer ; or

(c) a decision of any authority to take some other disciplinary action in relation to such an officer if the consequence of the action is, or in the opinion of the authority might be, to reduce the amount of any pensions benefits that may be granted in respect of the officer's service as a public officer.

(2) Where any such decision as is referred to in the preceding subsection is taken by any authority, the authority shall cause to be delivered to the officer concerned, or to his personal representatives, a written notice of that decision stating the time, not being less than twenty-eight days from the date on which the notice is delivered, within which he, or his personal representatives, may apply to the authority for the case to be referred to an Appeals Board.

(3) If application is duly made within the time stated in the notice, the authority shall notify the Prime Minister in writing of that application and the Prime Minister shall thereupon appoint an Appeals Board consisting of—

(a) one member selected by the Prime Minister ;

(b) one member selected by an association representative of public officers or a professional body, nominated in either case by the applicant ; and

(c) one member selected by the two other members jointly (or, in default of agreement between those members, by the Judicial and Legal Service Commission) who shall be the chairman of the Board.

(4) The Appeals Board shall enquire into the facts of the case, and for that purpose—

(a) shall, if the applicant so requests in writing, hear the applicant either in person or by a legal representative of his choice, according to the terms of the request, and shall consider any representations that he wishes to make in writing ;

(b) may hear any other person who, in the opinion of the Board, is able to give the Board information on the case ; and

(c) shall have access to, and shall consider, all documents that were available to the authority concerned and shall also consider any further document relating to the case that may be produced by or on behalf of the applicant or the authority.

(5) When the Appeals Board has completed its consideration of the case, then—

(a) if the decision that is the subject of the reference to the Board is such a decision as is mentioned in paragraph (a) of subsection (1) of this section, the Board shall advise the appropriate Commission whether the decision should be affirmed, reversed or modified and the Commission shall act in accordance with that advice ; and

(b) if the decision that is the subject of the reference to the Board is such a decision as is referred to in paragraph (b) or paragraph

(c) of subsection (1) of this section, the Board shall not have power to advise the authority concerned to affirm, reverse or modify the decision but—

(i) where the officer has been removed from office the Board may direct that there shall be granted all or any part of the pensions benefits that, under any law, might have been granted in respect of his service as a public officer if he had retired voluntarily at the date of his removal and may direct that any law with respect to pensions benefits shall in any other respect that the Board may specify have effect as if he had so retired ; and

(ii) where some other disciplinary action has been taken in relation to the officer the Board may direct that, on the grant of any pensions benefits under any law in respect of the officer's service as a public officer, those benefits shall be increased by such amount or shall be calculated in such manner as the Board may specify in order to offset all or any part of the reduction in the amount of those benefits that, in the opinion of the Board, would or might otherwise be a consequence of the disciplinary action,

and any direction given by the Board under this paragraph shall be complied with notwithstanding the provisions of any other law.

(6) In this section—

" pensions benefits " has the meaning assigned to that expression in section 94 of the Constitution ; and

" legal representative " means a person lawfully in or entitled to be in Mauritius and entitled to practise in Mauritius as a barrister or as an attorney-at-law.

(7) This section applies to an officer who is the holder of a pensionable office in the public service and—

(a) who is a member of Her Majesty's Overseas Civil Service or of Her Majesty's Overseas Judiciary ;

(b) who has been designated for the purposes of the Overseas Service (Mauritius) Agreement 1961 ; or

(c) who was selected for appointment to any office in the public service or whose appointment to any such office was approved by a Secretary of State.

Alteration of this Order.

17.—(1) Parliament may alter any of the provisions of this Order in the same manner as it may alter any of the provisions of the Constitution not specified in section 47(2) of the Constitution:

Provided that section 6 and section 8(4) and this section may be altered by Parliament only in the same manner as the provisions so specified.

(2) Section 47(4) of the Constitution shall apply for the purpose of construing references in this section to any provision of this Order and to the alteration of any such provision as it applies for the purpose of construing references in section 47 of the Constitution to any provision of the Constitution and to the alteration of any such provision.

W. G. Agnew.

SCHEDULE TO THE ORDER

Section 2(1)

THE CONSTITUTION OF MAURITIUS

ARRANGEMENT OF SECTIONS

CHAPTER I

THE STATE AND THE CONSTITUTION

CHAPTER II

PROTECTION OF FUNDAMENTAL RIGHTS AND FREEDOMS OF THE INDIVIDUAL

CHAPTER III

CITIZENSHIP

CHAPTER IV

CHAPTER V

PARLIAMENT

PART I

The Legislative Assembly

PART II

Legislation and Procedure in Legislative Assembly

CHAPTER VI

THE EXECUTIVE

CHAPTER VII

THE JUDICATURE

CHAPTER VIII

SERVICE COMMISSIONS AND THE PUBLIC SERVICE

SCHEDULE 1 TO THE CONSTITUTION

Election of Members of Legislative Assembly

SCHEDULE 2 TO THE CONSTITUTION

Offices within Jurisdiction of Judicial and
Legal Service Commission

SCHEDULE 3 TO THE CONSTITUTION

Oaths

CHAPTER I

The State and the Constitution

1. Mauritius shall be a sovereign democratic State.   The State.

2. This Constitution is the supreme law of Mauritius and if any other   Constitution
law is inconsistent with this Constitution, that other law shall, to the   is supreme
extent of the inconsistency, be void.   law.

CHAPTER II

Protection of Fundamental Rights and Freedoms
of the Individual

3. It is hereby recognised and declared that in Mauritius there have   Fundamenta
existed and shall continue to exist without discrimination by reason of   rights and
race, place of origin, political opinions, colour, creed or sex, but subject   freedoms
to respect for the rights and freedoms of others and for the public   of the
interest, each and all of the following human rights and fundamental   individual.
freedoms, namely—

(a) the right of the individual to life, liberty, security of the person and
the protection of the law ;

(b) freedom of conscience, of expression, of assembly and association
and freedom to establish schools ; and

(c) the right of the individual to protection for the privacy of his home
and other property and from deprivation of property without
compensation,

and the provisions of this Chapter shall have effect for the purpose of
affording protection to the said rights and freedoms subject to such
limitations of that protection as are contained in those provisions, being
limitations designed to ensure that the enjoyment of the said rights and
freedoms by any individual does not prejudice the rights and freedoms
of others or the public interest.

4.—(1) No person shall be deprived of his life intentionally save in   Protection
execution of the sentence of a court in respect of a criminal offence of   of right
which he has been convicted.   to life.

(2) A person shall not be regarded as having been deprived of his life in contravention of this section if he dies as the result of the use, to such extent and in such circumstances as are permitted by law, of such force as is reasonably justifiable—

    (a) for the defence of any person from violence or for the defence of property ;

    (b) in order to effect a lawful arrest or to prevent the escape of a person lawfully detained ;

    (c) for the purpose of suppressing a riot, insurrection or mutiny ; or

    (d) in order to prevent the commission by that person of a criminal offence,

or if he dies as the result of a lawful act of war.

Protection of right to personal liberty.

5.—(1) No person shall be deprived of his personal liberty save as may be authorised by law in any of the following cases, that is to say—

    (a) in consequence of his unfitness to plead to a criminal charge or in execution of the sentence or order of a court, whether in Mauritius or elsewhere, in respect of a criminal offence of which he has been convicted ;

    (b) in execution of the order of a court punishing him for contempt of that court or of another court ;

    (c) in execution of the order of a court made to secure the fulfilment of any obligation imposed on him by law ;

    (d) for the purpose of bringing him before a court in execution of the order of a court ;

    (e) upon reasonable suspicion of his having committed, or being about to commit, a criminal offence ;

    (f) in the case of a person who has not attained the age of eighteen years, for the purpose of his education or welfare ;

    (g) for the purpose of preventing the spread of an infectious or contagious disease ;

    (h) in the case of a person who is, or is reasonably suspected to be, of unsound mind or addicted to drugs or alcohol, for the purpose of his care or treatment or the protection of the community ;

    (i) for the purpose of preventing the unlawful entry of that person into Mauritius, or for the purpose of effecting the expulsion, extradition or other lawful removal of that person from Mauritius or the taking of proceedings relating thereto ;

    (j) upon reasonable suspicion of his being likely to commit breaches of the peace ; or

    (k) in execution of the order of the Commissioner of Police upon reasonable suspicion of his having engaged in, or being about to engage in, activities likely to cause a serious threat to public safety or public order.

(2) Any person who is arrested or detained shall be informed as soon as reasonably practicable, in a language that he understands, of the reasons for his arrest or detention.

(3) Any person who is arrested or detained—

    (a) for the purpose of bringing him before a court in execution of the order of a court ;

(b) upon reasonable suspicion of his having committed, or being about to commit, a criminal offence ; or

(c) upon reasonable suspicion of his being likely to commit breaches of the peace,

and who is not released, shall be afforded reasonable facilities to consult a legal representative of his own choice and shall be brought without undue delay before a court ; and if any person arrested or detained as mentioned in paragraph (b) of this subsection is not tried within a reasonable time, then, without prejudice to any further proceedings that may be brought against him, he shall be released either unconditionally or upon reasonable conditions, including in particular such conditions as are reasonably necessary to ensure that he appears at a later date for trial or for proceedings preliminary to trial ; and if any person arrested or detained as mentioned in paragraph (c) of this subsection is not brought before a court within a reasonable time in order that the court may decide whether to order him to give security for his good behaviour then, without prejudice to any further proceedings that may be brought against him, he shall be released unconditionally.

(4) When a person is detained in pursuance of any such provision of law as is referred to in paragraph (k) of subsection (1) of this section, the following provisions shall apply, that is to say :—

(a) he shall, as soon as is reasonably practicable and in any case not more than seven days after the commencement of his detention, be furnished with a statement in writing in a language that he understands specifying in detail the grounds upon which he is detained ;

(b) not more than seven days after the commencement of his detention, a notification shall be published in the Gazette stating that he has been detained and giving particulars of the provision of law under which his detention is authorised ;

(c) not more than fourteen days after the commencement of his detention and thereafter during his detention at intervals of not more than thirty days, his case shall be reviewed by an independent and impartial tribunal consisting of a chairman and two other members appointed by the Judicial and Legal Service Commission, the chairman being appointed from among persons who are entitled to practise as a barrister or as an attorney-at-law in Mauritius ;

(d) he shall be afforded reasonable facilities to consult a legal representative of his own choice who shall be permitted to make representations to the tribunal appointed for the review of his case ;

(e) at the hearing of his case by the tribunal he shall be permitted to appear in person or by a legal representative of his own choice and, unless the tribunal otherwise directs, the hearing shall be held in public ;

(f) at the conclusion of any review by a tribunal in pursuance of this subsection in any case, the tribunal shall announce its decision in public, stating whether or not there is, in its opinion, sufficient cause for the detention, and if, in its opinion, there is not sufficient cause, the detained person shall forthwith be released and if during the period of six months from his release he is again detained as aforesaid the tribunal established as aforesaid for the review of his case shall not decide that, in its opinion, there is sufficient cause for the further detention unless it is satisfied that new and reasonable grounds for the detention exist.

(5) Any person who is unlawfully arrested or detained by any other person shall be entitled to compensation therefor from that other person.

(6) In the exercise of any functions conferred upon him for the purposes of subsection (1)(*k*) of this section, the Commissioner of Police shall not be subject to the direction or control of any other person or authority.

Protection from slavery and forced labour.

6.—(1) No person shall be held in slavery or servitude.

(2) No person shall be required to perform forced labour.

(3) For the purposes of this section, the expression " forced labour " does not include—

(*a*) any labour required in consequence of the sentence or order of a court ;

(*b*) labour required of any person while he is lawfully detained that, though not required in consequence of the sentence or order of a court, is reasonably necessary in the interests of hygiene or for the maintenance of the place at which he is detained ;

(*c*) any labour required of a member of a disciplined force in pursuance of his duties as such or, in the case of a person who has conscientious objections to service as a member of a naval, military or air force, any labour that that person is required by law to perform in place of such service ; or

(*d*) any labour required during a period of public emergency or in the event of any other emergency or calamity that threatens the life or well-being of the community, to the extent that the requiring of such labour is reasonably justifiable, in the circumstances of any situation arising or existing during that period or as a result of that other emergency or calamity, for the purpose of dealing with that situation.

Protection from inhuman treatment.

7.—(1) No person shall be subjected to torture or to inhuman or degrading punishment or other such treatment.

(2) Nothing contained in or done under the authority of any law shall be held to be inconsistent with or in contravention of this section to the extent that the law in question authorises the infliction of any description of punishment that was lawful in Mauritius on 11th March 1964, being the day before the day on which section 5 of the Constitution set out in Schedule 2 to the Mauritius (Constitution) Order 1964 came into force.

Protection from deprivation of property.

8.—(1) No property of any description shall be compulsorily taken possession of, and no interest in or right over property of any description shall be compulsorily acquired, except where the following conditions are satisfied, that is to say—

(*a*) the taking of possession or acquisition is necessary or expedient in the interests of defence, public safety, public order, public morality, public health, town and country planning or the development or utilisation of any property in such a manner as to promote the public benefit ; and

(*b*) there is reasonable justification for the causing of any hardship that may result to any person having an interest in or right over the property ; and

(c) provision is made by a law applicable to that taking of possession or acquisition—

    (i) for the prompt payment of adequate compensation ; and

    (ii) securing to any person having an interest in or right over the property a right of access to the Supreme Court, whether direct or on appeal from any other authority, for the determination of his interest or right, the legality of the taking of possession or acquisition of the property, interest or right, and the amount of any compensation to which he is entitled, and for the purpose of obtaining prompt payment of that compensation.

(2) No person who is entitled to compensation under this section shall be prevented from remitting, within a reasonable time after he has received any amount of that compensation, the whole of that amount (free from any deduction, charge or tax made or levied in respect of its remission) to any country of his choice outside Mauritius.

(3) Nothing contained in or done under the authority of any law shall be held to be inconsistent with or in contravention of the last preceding subsection to the extent that the law in question authorises—

(a) the attachment, by order of a court, of any amount of compensation to which a person is entitled in satisfaction of the judgment of a court or pending the determination of civil proceedings to which he is a party ;

(b) the imposition of reasonable restrictions on the manner in which any amount of compensation is to be remitted ; or

(c) the imposition of any deduction, charge or tax that is made or levied generally in respect of the remission of moneys from Mauritius and that is not discriminatory within the meaning of section 16(3) of this Constitution.

(4) Nothing contained in or done under the authority of any law shall be held to be inconsistent with or in contravention of subsection (1) of this section—

(a) to the extent that the law in question makes provision for the taking of possession or acquisition of property—

    (i) in satisfaction of any tax, rate or due ;

    (ii) by way of penalty for breach of the law or forfeiture in consequence of a breach of the law ;

    (iii) as an incident of a lease, tenancy, mortgage, charge, sale, pledge or contract ;

    (iv) in the execution of judgments or orders of courts ;

    (v) by reason of its being in a dangerous state or injurious to the health of human beings, animals, trees or plants ;

    (vi) in consequence of any law with respect to the limitation of actions or acquisitive prescription ;

    (vii) for so long only as may be necessary for the purposes of any examination, investigation, trial or inquiry or, in the case of land, the carrying out thereon—

        (A) of work of soil conservation or the conservation of other natural resources ; or

        (B) of agricultural development or improvement that the owner or occupier of the land has been required, and has, without reasonable and lawful excuse, refused or failed to carry out,

except so far as that provision or, as the case may be, the thing done under the authority thereof is shown not to be reasonably justifiable in a democratic society ; or

(b) to the extent that the law in question makes provision for the taking of possession or acquisition of—

(i) enemy property ;

(ii) property of a person who has died or is unable, by reason of legal incapacity, to administer it himself, for the purpose of its administration for the benefit of the persons entitled to the beneficial interest therein ;

(iii) property of a person adjudged bankrupt or a body corporate in liquidation, for the purpose of its administration for the benefit of the creditors of the bankrupt or body corporate and, subject thereto, for the benefit of other persons entitled to the beneficial interest in the property ; or

(iv) property subject to a trust, for the purpose of vesting the property in persons appointed as trustees under the instrument creating the trust or by a court or, by order of a court, for the purpose of giving effect to the trust.

(5) Nothing in this section shall affect the making or operation of any law so far as it provides for the vesting in the Crown of the ownership of underground water or unextracted minerals.

(6) Nothing in this section shall affect the making or operation of any law for the compulsory taking of possession in the public interest of any property, or the compulsory acquisition in the public interest of any property, or the compulsory acquisition in the public interest of any interest in or right over property, where that property, interest or right is held by a body corporate established by law for public purposes in which no moneys have been invested other than moneys provided from public funds.

Protection for privacy of home and other property.

9.—(1) Except with his own consent, no person shall be subjected to the search of his person or his property or the entry by others on his premises.

(2) Nothing contained in or done under the authority of any law shall be held to be inconsistent with or in contravention of this section to the extent that the law in question makes provision—

(a) in the interests of defence, public safety, public order, public morality, public health, town and country planning, the development or utilisation of mineral resources, or the development or utilisation of any other property in such a manner as to promote the public benefit ;

(b) for the purpose of protecting the rights or freedoms of other persons ;

(c) to enable an officer or agent of the Government or a Local Authority, or a body corporate established by law for a public purpose, to enter on the premises of any person in order to value those premises for the purpose of any tax, rate or due, or in order to carry out work connected with any property that is lawfully on those premises and that belongs to the Government, the Local Authority or that body corporate, as the case may be ; or

(d) to authorise, for the purpose of enforcing the judgment or order of a court in any civil proceedings, the search of any person or property by order of a court or the entry upon any premises by such order,

except so far as that provision or, as the case may be, the thing done under the authority thereof is shown not to be reasonably justifiable in a democratic society.

10.—(1) If any person is charged with a criminal offence, then, unless the charge is withdrawn, the case shall be afforded a fair hearing within a reasonable time by an independent and impartial court established by law.

Provisions to secure protection of law.

(2) Every person who is charged with a criminal offence—

(a) shall be presumed to be innocent until he is proved or has pleaded guilty ;

(b) shall be informed as soon as reasonably practicable, in a language that he understands and in detail, of the nature of the offence ;

(c) shall be given adequate time and facilities for the preparation of his defence ;

(d) shall be permitted to defend himself in person or, at his own expense, by a legal representative of his own choice or, where so prescribed, by a legal representative provided at the public expense ;

(e) shall be afforded facilities to examine, in person or by his legal representative, the witnesses called by the prosecution before any court, and to obtain the attendance and carry out the examination of witnesses to testify on his behalf before that court on the same conditions as those applying to witnesses called by the prosecution ; and

(f) shall be permitted to have without payment the assistance of an interpreter if he cannot understand the language used at the trial of the offence,

and, except with his own consent, the trial shall not take place in his absence unless he so conducts himself as to render the continuance of the proceedings in his presence impracticable and the court has ordered him to be removed and the trial to proceed in his absence.

(3) When a person is tried for any criminal offence, the accused person or any person authorised by him in that behalf shall, if he so requires and subject to payment of such reasonable fee as may be specified by or under any law, be given within a reasonable time after judgment a copy for the use of the accused person of any record of the proceedings made by or on behalf of the court.

(4) No person shall be held to be guilty of a criminal offence on account of any act or omission that did not, at the time it took place, constitute such an offence, and no penalty shall be imposed for any criminal offence that is severer in degree or description than the maximum penalty that might have been imposed for that offence at the time when it was committed.

(5) No person who shows that he has been tried by a competent court for a criminal offence and either convicted or acquitted shall again be tried for that offence or for any other criminal offence of which he could have been convicted at the trial of that offence, save

upon the order of a superior court in the course of appeal or review proceedings relating to the conviction or acquittal.

(6) No person shall be tried for a criminal offence if he shows that he has been granted a pardon, by competent authority, for that offence.

(7) No person who is tried for a criminal offence shall be compelled to give evidence at the trial.

(8) Any court or other authority required or empowered by law to determine the existence or extent of any civil right or obligation shall be established by law and shall be independent and impartial ; and where proceedings for such a determination are instituted by any person before such a court or other authority the case shall be given a fair hearing within a reasonable time.

(9) Except with the agreement of all the parties thereto, all proceedings of every court and proceedings for the determination of the existence or extent of any civil right or obligation before any other authority, including the announcement of the decision of the court or other authority, shall be held in public.

(10) Nothing in the last foregoing subsection shall prevent the court or other authority from excluding from the proceedings (except the announcement of the decision of the court or other authority) persons other than the parties thereto and their legal representatives to such extent as the court or other authority—

(a) may by law be empowered so to do and may consider necessary or expedient in circumstances where publicity would prejudice the interests of justice, or in interlocutory proceedings, or in the interests of public morality, the welfare of persons under the age of eighteen years or the protection of the privacy of persons concerned in the proceedings ; or

(b) may by law be empowered or required to do so in the interests of defence, public safety or public order.

(11) Nothing contained in or done under the authority of any law shall be held to be inconsistent with or in contravention of—

(a) subsection (2)(a) of this section, to the extent that the law in question imposes upon any person charged with a criminal offence the burden of proving particular facts ;

(b) subsection (2)(e) of this section, to the extent that the law in question imposes conditions that must be satisfied if witnesses called to testify on behalf of an accused person are to be paid their expenses out of public funds ;

(c) subsection (5) of this section, to the extent that the law in question authorises a court to try a member of a disciplined force for a criminal offence notwithstanding any trial and conviction or acquittal of that member under the disciplinary law of that force, so, however, that any court so trying such a member and convicting him shall in sentencing him to any punishment take into account any punishment awarded him under that disciplinary law.

(12) In this section " criminal offence " means a crime, misdemeanour or contravention punishable under the law of Mauritius.

11.—(1) Except with his own consent, no person shall be hindered in the enjoyment of his freedom of conscience, and for the purposes of this section the said freedom includes freedom of thought and of religion, freedom to change his religion or belief, and freedom, either alone or in community with others and both in public and in private, to manifest and propagate his religion or belief in worship, teaching, practice and observance.

Protection of freedom of conscience.

(2) Except with his own consent (or, if he is a minor, the consent of his guardian), no person attending any place of education shall be required to receive religious instruction or to take part in or attend any religious ceremony or observance if that instruction, ceremony or observance relates to a religion that he does not profess.

(3) No religious community or denomination shall be prevented from making provision for the giving, by persons lawfully in Mauritius, of religious instruction to persons of that community or denomination in the course of any education provided by that community or denomination.

(4) No person shall be compelled to take any oath that is contrary to his religion or belief or to take any oath in a manner that is contrary to his religion or belief.

(5) Nothing contained in or done under the authority of any law shall be held to be inconsistent with or in contravention of this section to the extent that the law in question makes provision—

(*a*) in the interests of defence, public safety, public order, public morality or public health ; or

(*b*) for the purpose of protecting the rights and freedoms of other persons, including the right to observe and practise any religion or belief without the unsolicited intervention of persons professing any other religion or belief,

except so far as that provision, or as the case may be, the thing done under the authority thereof is shown not to be reasonably justifiable in a democratic society.

12.—(1) Except with his own consent, no person shall be hindered in the enjoyment of his freedom of expression, that is to say, freedom to hold opinions and to receive and impart ideas and information without interference, and freedom from interference with his correspondence.

Protection of freedom of expression.

(2) Nothing contained in or done under the authority of any law shall be held to be inconsistent with or in contravention of this section to the extent that the law in question makes provision—

(*a*) in the interests of defence, public safety, public order, public morality or public health ;

(*b*) for the purpose of protecting the reputations, rights and freedoms of other persons or the private lives of persons concerned in legal proceedings, preventing the disclosure of information received in confidence, maintaining the authority and independence of the courts, or regulating the technical administration or the technical operation of telephony, telegraphy, posts, wireless broadcasting, television, public exhibitions or public entertainments ; or

(*c*) for the imposition of restrictions upon public officers, except so far as that provision or, as the case may be, the thing done under the authority thereof is shown not to be reasonably justifiable in a democratic society.

Protection of freedom of assembly and association.

13.—(1) Except with his own consent, no person shall be hindered in the enjoyment of his freedom of assembly and association, that is to say, his right to assemble freely and associate with other persons and in particular to form or belong to trade unions or other associations for the protection of his interests.

(2) Nothing contained in or done under the authority of any law shall be held to be inconsistent with or in contravention of this section to the extent that the law in question makes provision—

(a) in the interests of defence, public safety, public order, public morality or public health ;

(b) for the purpose of protecting the rights or freedoms of other persons ; or

(c) for the imposition of restrictions upon public officers,

except so far as that provision or, as the case may be, the thing done under the authority thereof is shown not to be reasonably justifiable in a democratic society.

Protection of freedom to establish schools.

14.—(1) No religious denomination and no religious, social, ethnic or cultural association or group shall be prevented from establishing and maintaining schools at its own expense.

(2) Nothing contained in or done under the authority of any law shall be held to be inconsistent with or in contravention of the preceding subsection to the extent that the law in question makes provision—

(a) in the interests of defence, public safety, public order, public morality or public health ; or

(b) for regulating such schools in the interests of persons receiving instruction therein,

except so far as that provision or, as the case may be, the thing done under the authority thereof is shown not to be reasonably justifiable in a democratic society.

(3) No person shall be prevented from sending to any such school a child of whom that person is parent or guardian by reason only that the school is not a school established or maintained by the Government.

(4) In the preceding subsection " child " includes a stepchild and a child adopted in a manner recognised by law ; and the word " parent " shall be construed accordingly.

Protection of freedom of movement.

15.—(1) No person shall be deprived of his freedom of movement, and for the purposes of this section the said freedom means the right to move freely throughout Mauritius, the right to reside in any part of Mauritius, the right to enter Mauritius, the right to leave Mauritius and immunity from expulsion from Mauritius.

(2) Any restriction on a person's freedom of movement that is involved in his lawful detention shall not be held to be inconsistent with or in contravention of this section.

(3) Nothing contained in or done under the authority of any law shall be held to be inconsistent with or in contravention of this section to the extent that the law in question makes provision—

(a) for the imposition of restrictions on the movement or residence within Mauritius of any person in the interests of defence, public safety, public order, public morality or public health ;

(b) for the imposition of restrictions on the right of any person to leave Mauritius in the interests of defence, public safety, public order, public morality or public health or of securing compliance with any international obligation of the Government particulars of which have been laid before the Assembly ;

(c) for the imposition of restrictions, by order of a court, on the movement or residence within Mauritius of any person either in consequence of his having been found guilty of a criminal offence under the law of Mauritius or for the purpose of ensuring that he appears before a court at a later date for trial in respect of such a criminal offence or for proceedings preliminary to trial or for proceedings relating to his extradition or other lawful removal from Mauritius ;

(d) for the imposition of restrictions on the movement or residence within Mauritius of any person who is not a citizen of Mauritius or the exclusion or expulsion from Mauritius of any such person ;

(e) for the imposition of restrictions on the acquisition or use by any person of land or other property in Mauritius ;

(f) for the removal of a person from Mauritius to be tried outside Mauritius for a criminal offence or to undergo imprisonment outside Mauritius in execution of the sentence of a court in respect of a criminal offence of which he has been convicted ; or

(g) for the imposition of restrictions on the right of any person to leave Mauritius in order to secure the fulfilment of any obligations imposed upon that person by law,

except so far as the provision or, as the case may be, the thing done under the authority thereof is shown not to be reasonably justifiable in a democratic society.

(4) If any person whose freedom of movement has been restricted in pursuance of any such provision of law as is referred to in paragraph (a) or (b) of the preceding subsection so requests, the following provisions shall apply, that is to say—

(a) he shall, as soon as is reasonably practicable and in any case not more than seven days after the making of the request, be furnished with a statement in writing in a language that he understands specifying the grounds for the imposition of the restriction ;

(b) not more than fourteen days after the making of the request, and thereafter during the continuance of the restriction at intervals of not more than six months, his case shall be reviewed by an independent and impartial tribunal consisting of a chairman and two other members appointed by the Judicial and Legal Service Commission, the chairman being appointed from among persons who are entitled to practise as a barrister or as an attorney-at-law in Mauritius ;

(c) he or a legal representative of his own choice shall be permitted to make representations to the tribunal appointed for the review of his case ;

(d) on any review by a tribunal in pursuance of this subsection in any case, the tribunal may make recommendations concerning the necessity or expediency of continuing the restriction in question to the authority by which it was ordered and that authority shall act in accordance with any recommendation for the removal or relaxation of the restriction:

Provided that a person whose freedom of movement has been restricted by virtue of a restriction that is applicable to persons generally or to general classes of persons shall not make a request under this subsection unless he has first obtained the consent of the Supreme Court.

Protection from discrimination on the grounds of race, etc.

16.—(1) Subject to the provisions of subsections (4), (5) and (7) of this section, no law shall make any provision that is discriminatory either of itself or in its effect.

(2) Subject to the provisions of subsections (6), (7) and (8) of this section, no person shall be treated in a discriminatory manner by any person acting in the performance of any public function conferred by any law or otherwise in the performance of the functions of any public office or any public authority.

(3) In this section, the expression " discriminatory " means affording different treatment to different persons attributable wholly or mainly to their respective descriptions by race, caste, place of origin, political opinions, colour or creed whereby persons of one such description are subjected to disabilities or restrictions to which persons of another such description are not made subject or are accorded privileges or advantages that are not accorded to persons of another such description.

(4) Subsection (1) of this section shall not apply to any law so far as that law makes provision—

(a) for the appropriation of revenues or other funds of Mauritius ;

(b) with respect to persons who are not citizens of Mauritius ; or

(c) for the application, in the case of persons of any such description as is mentioned in subsection (3) of this section (or of persons connected with such persons), of the law with respect to adoption, marriage, divorce, burial, devolution of property on death or other like matters that is the personal law applicable to persons of that description.

(5) Nothing contained in any law shall be held to be inconsistent with or in contravention of subsection (1) of this section to the extent that it makes provision with respect to standards or qualifications (not being standards or qualifications specifically relating to race, caste, place of origin, political opinions, colour or creed) to be required of any person who is appointed to any office in the public service, any office in a disciplined force, any office in the service of a Local Authority or any office in a body corporate established directly by any law for public purposes.

(6) Subsection (2) of this section shall not apply to anything which is expressly or by necessary implication authorised to be done by any such provision of law as is referred to in subsection (4) or (5) of this section.

(7) Nothing contained in or done under the authority of any law shall be held to be inconsistent with or in contravention of this section to the extent that the law in question makes provision whereby persons

of any such description as is mentioned in subsection (3) of this section may be subjected to any restriction on the rights and freedoms guaranteed by sections 9, 11, 12, 13, 14 and 15 of this Constitution, being such a restriction as is authorised by section 9(2), 11(5), 12(2), 13(2), 14(2) or 15(3) of this Constitution, as the case may be.

(8) Subsection (2) of this section shall not affect any discretion relating to the institution, conduct or discontinuance of civil or criminal proceedings in any court that is vested in any person by or under this Constitution or any other law.

17.—(1) If any person alleges that any of the foregoing provisions of this Chapter has been, is being or is likely to be contravened in relation to him, then, without prejudice to any other action with respect to the same matter that is lawfully available, that person may apply to the Supreme Court for redress. *Enforcement of protective provisions.*

(2) The Supreme Court shall have original jurisdiction to hear and determine any application made by any person in pursuance of the preceding subsection, and may make such orders, issue such writs and give such directions as it may consider appropriate for the purpose of enforcing, or securing the enforcement of, any of the foregoing provisions of this Chapter to the protection of which the person concerned is entitled:

Provided that the Supreme Court shall not exercise its powers under this subsection if it is satisfied that adequate means of redress for the contravention alleged are or have been available to the person concerned under any other law.

(3) The Supreme Court shall have such powers in addition to those conferred by this section as may be prescribed for the purpose of enabling that court more effectively to exercise the jurisdiction conferred upon it by this section.

(4) The Chief Justice may make rules with respect to the practice and procedure of the Supreme Court in relation to the jurisdiction and powers conferred upon it by or under this section (including rules with respect to the time within which applications to that court may be made).

18.—(1) Nothing contained in or done under the authority of a law shall be held to be inconsistent with or in contravention of section 5 or section 16 of this Constitution to the extent that the law authorises the taking during any period of public emergency of measures that are reasonably justifiable for dealing with the situation that exists in Mauritius during that period: *Derogations from fundamental rights and freedoms under emergency powers.*

Provided that no law, to the extent that it authorises the taking during a period of public emergency other than a period during which Mauritius is at war of measures that would be inconsistent with or in contravention of section 5 or section 16 of this Constitution if taken otherwise than during a period of public emergency, shall have effect unless there is in force a Proclamation of the Governor-General declaring that, because of the situation existing at the time, the measures authorised by the law are required in the interest of peace, order and good government.

(2) A Proclamation made by the Governor-General for the purposes of this section—

(*a*) shall, when the Assembly is sitting or when arrangements have already been made for it to meet within seven days of the date of the Proclamation, lapse unless within seven days the Assembly by resolution approves the Proclamation ;

(*b*) shall, when the Assembly is not sitting and no arrangements have been made for it to meet within seven days, lapse unless within twenty-one days it meets and approves the Proclamation by resolution ;

(*c*) shall, if approved by resolution, remain in force for such period, not exceeding six months, as the Assembly may specify in the resolution ;

(*d*) may be extended in operation for further periods not exceeding six months at a time by resolution of the Assembly ;

(*e*) may be revoked at any time by the Governor-General or by resolution of the Assembly:

Provided that no resolution for the purposes of paragraphs (*a*), (*b*), (*c*) or (*d*) of this subsection shall be passed unless it is supported by the votes of at least two-thirds of all the members of the Assembly.

(3) When a person is detained by virtue of any such law as is referred to in subsection (1) of this section of this Constitution (not being a person who is detained because he is a person who, not being a citizen of Mauritius, is a citizen of a country with which Mauritius is at war or has been engaged in hostilities against Mauritius in association with or on behalf of such a country or otherwise assisting or adhering to such a country) the following provisions shall apply, that is to say :—

(*a*) he shall, as soon as is reasonably practicable and in any case not more than seven days after the commencement of his detention, be furnished with a statement in writing in a language that he understands specifying in detail the grounds upon which he is detained ;

(*b*) not more than fourteen days after the commencement of his detention, a notification shall be published in the Gazette stating that he has been detained and giving particulars of the provision of law under which his detention is authorised ;

(*c*) not more than one month after the commencement of his detention and thereafter during his detention at intervals of not more than six months, his case shall be reviewed by an independent and impartial tribunal consisting of a chairman and two other members appointed by the Judicial and Legal Service Commission, the chairman being appointed from among persons who are entitled to practise as a barrister or as an attorney-at-law in Mauritius ;

(*d*) he shall be afforded reasonable facilities to consult a legal representative of his own choice who shall be permitted to make representations to the tribunal appointed for the review of the case of the detained person ; and

(*e*) at the hearing of his case by the tribunal appointed for the review of his case he shall be permitted to appear in person or by a legal representative of his own choice.

(4) On any review by a tribunal in pursuance of this section of the case of a detained person, the tribunal may make recommendations

concerning the necessity or expediency of continuing his detention to the authority by which it was ordered but, unless it is otherwise provided by law, that authority shall not be obliged to act in accordance with any such recommendations.

19.—(1) In this Chapter, unless the context otherwise requires— Interpretation and savings.

" contravention ", in relation to any requirement, includes a failure to comply with that requirement, and cognate expressions shall be construed accordingly ;

" court " means any court of law having jurisdiction in Mauritius, including Her Majesty in Council, but excepting, save in sections 4 and 6 of this Constitution and this section, a court established by a disciplinary law ;

" legal representative " means a person lawfully in or entitled to be in Mauritius and entitled to practise in Mauritius as a barrister or, except in relation to proceedings before a court in which an attorney-at-law has no right of audience, as an attorney-at-law ;

" member ", in relation to a disciplined force, includes any person who, under the law regulating the discipline of that force, is subject to that discipline.

(2) Nothing contained in section 5(4), 15(4) or 18(3) of this Constitution shall be construed as entitling a person to legal representation at public expense.

(3) Nothing contained in sections 12, 13 or 15 of this Constitution shall be construed as precluding the inclusion in the terms and conditions of service of public officers of reasonable requirements as to their communication or association with other persons or as to their movements or residence.

(4) In relation to any person who is a member of a disciplined force of Mauritius, nothing contained in or done under the authority of the disciplinary law of that force shall be held to be inconsistent with or in contravention of any of the provisions of this Chapter other than sections 4, 6 and 7.

(5) In relation to any person who is a member of a disciplined force that is not a disciplined force of Mauritius and who is present in Mauritius in pursuance of arrangements made between the Government of Mauritius and another Government or an international organisation, nothing contained in or done under the authority of the disciplinary law of that force shall be held to be inconsistent with or in contravention of any of the provisions of this Chapter.

(6) No measures taken in relation to a person who is a member of a disciplined force of a country with which Mauritius is at war and no law, to the extent that it authorises the taking of any such measures, shall be held to be inconsistent with or in contravention of any of the provisions of this Chapter.

(7) In this Chapter " period of public emergency " means any period during which—

(a) Mauritius is engaged in any war ; or

(b) there is in force a Proclamation by the Governor-General declaring that a state of public emergency exists ; or

(c) there is in force a resolution of the Assembly supported by the votes of a majority of all the members of the Assembly declaring that democratic institutions in Mauritius are threatened by subversion.

(8) A Proclamation made by the Governor-General for the purposes of the preceding subsection—

(a) shall, when the Assembly is sitting or when arrangements have already been made for it to meet within seven days of the date of the Proclamation, lapse unless within seven days the Assembly by resolution approves the Proclamation ;

(b) shall, when the Assembly is not sitting and no arrangements have been made for it to meet within seven days, lapse unless within twenty-one days it meets and approves the Proclamation by resolution ;

(c) may be revoked at any time by the Governor-General or by resolution of the Assembly:

Provided that no resolution for the purposes of paragraphs (a) or (b) of this subsection shall be passed unless it is supported by the votes of a majority of all the members of the Assembly.

(9) A resolution passed by the Assembly for the purposes of sub-section (7)(c) of this section—

(a) shall remain in force for such period, not exceeding twelve months, as the Assembly may specify in the resolution ;

(b) may be extended in operation for further periods not exceeding twelve months at a time by a further resolution supported by the votes of a majority of all the members of the Assembly ;

(c) may be revoked at any time by resolution of the Assembly.

CHAPTER III

CITIZENSHIP

Persons who become citizens on 12th March 1968.

20.—(1) Every person who, having been born in Mauritius, is on 11th March 1968 a citizen of the United Kingdom and Colonies shall become a citizen of Mauritius on 12th March 1968.

(2) Every person who, on 11th March 1968, is a citizen of the United Kingdom and Colonies—

(a) having become such a citizen under the British Nationality Act 1948(a) by virtue of his having been naturalised by the Governor of the former colony of Mauritius as a British subject before that Act came into force ; or

(b) having become such a citizen by virtue of his having been naturalised or registered by the Governor of the former colony of Mauritius under that Act,

shall become a citizen of Mauritius on 12th March 1968.

(3) Every person who, having been born outside Mauritius, is on 11th March 1968 a citizen of the United Kingdom and Colonies shall, if his father becomes, or would but for his death have become, a citizen of Mauritius by virtue of subsection (1) or subsection (2) of this section, become a citizen of Mauritius on 12th March 1968.

(4) For the purposes of this section a person shall be regarded as having been born in Mauritius if he was born in the territories which were comprised in the former colony of Mauritius immediately before

(a) 1948 c. 56.

8th November 1965 but were not so comprised immediately before 12th March 1968, unless his father was born in the territories which were comprised in the colony of Seychelles immediately before 8th November 1965.

21.—(1) Any woman who, on 12th March 1968, is or has been married to a person—

 (a) who becomes a citizen of Mauritius by virtue of the preceding section ; or

 (b) who, having died before 12th March 1968 would, but for his death, have become a citizen of Mauritius by virtue of that section,

shall be entitled, upon making application and, if she is a British protected person or an alien, upon taking the oath of allegiance, to be registered as a citizen of Mauritius :

Provided that, in the case of any woman who on 12th March 1968 is not a citizen of the United Kingdom and Colonies, the right to be registered as a citizen of Mauritius under this section shall be subject to such exceptions or qualifications as may be prescribed in the interests of national security or public policy.

(2) Any application for registration under this section shall be made in such manner as may be prescribed as respects that application.

Persons entitled to be registered, etc, as citizens.

22. Every person born in Mauritius after 11th March 1968 shall become a citizen of Mauritius at the date of his birth :

Provided that a person shall not become a citizen of Mauritius by virtue of this section if at the time of his birth—

 (a) his father possesses such immunity from suit and legal process as is accorded to an envoy of a foreign sovereign power accredited to Mauritius and neither of his parents is a citizen of Mauritius ; or

 (b) his father is an enemy alien and the birth occurs in a place then under occupation by the enemy.

Persons born in Mauritius after 11th March 1968.

23. A person born outside Mauritius after 11th March 1968 shall become a citizen of Mauritius at the date of his birth if at that date his father is a citizen of Mauritius otherwise than by virtue of this section or section 20(3) of this Constitution.

Persons born outside Mauritius after 11th March 1968.

24. Any woman who after 11th March 1968 marries a person who is or becomes a citizen of Mauritius shall be entitled, upon making application in such manner as may be prescribed and, if she is a British protected person or an alien, upon taking the oath of allegiance, to be registered as a citizen of Mauritius :

Provided that the right to be registered as a citizen of Mauritius under this section shall be subject to such exceptions or qualifications as may be prescribed in the interests of national security or public policy.

Marriage to citizen of Mauritius.

25.—(1) Every person who under this Constitution or any other law is a citizen of Mauritius or under any enactment for the time being in force in any country to which this section applies is a citizen of that country shall, by virtue of that citizenship, have the status of a Commonwealth citizen.

Common- wealth citizens.

(2) Every person who is a British subject without citizenship under the British Nationality Act 1948, continues to be a British subject under section 2 of that Act or is a British subject under the British Nationality Act 1965(a) shall, by virtue of that status, have the status of a Commonwealth citizen.

(3) Save as may be otherwise provided by Parliament, the countries to which this section applies are the United Kingdom and Colonies, Canada, Australia, New Zealand, India, Pakistan, Ceylon, Ghana, Malaysia, Nigeria, Cyprus, Sierra Leone, Tanzania, Jamaica, Trinidad and Tobago, Uganda, Kenya, Malawi, Malta, Zambia, The Gambia, Singapore, Guyana, Lesotho, Botswana, Barbados and Southern Rhodesia.

Powers of Parliament.

26. Parliament may make provision—

(a) for the acquisition of citizenship of Mauritius by persons who are not eligible or who are no longer eligible to become citizens of Mauritius by virtue of the provisions of this Chapter ;

(b) for depriving of his citizenship of Mauritius any person who is a citizen of Mauritius otherwise than by virtue of sections 20, 22 or 23 of the Constitution ;

(c) for the renunciation by any person of his citizenship of Mauritius ;

(d) for the maintenance of a register of citizens of Mauritius who are also citizens of other countries ; or

(e) for depriving of his citizenship of Mauritius any citizen of Mauritius who has attained the age of 21 years after 11th March 1968, and who, being a citizen of some other country, has not, within such period after his attainment of that age as may be prescribed, renounced his citizenship of that other country or, if the law of that other country does not permit him to renounce his citizenship of that other country, made such declaration as may be prescribed.

Interpretation.

27.—(1) In this Chapter " British protected person " means a person who is a British protected person for the purposes of the British Nationality Act 1948.

(2) Any reference in this Chapter to the father of a person shall, in relation to a person born out of wedlock, be construed as a reference to the mother of that person.

(3) For the purposes of this Chapter, a person born aboard a registered ship or aircraft, or aboard an unregistered ship or aircraft of the government of any country, shall be deemed to have been born in the place in which the ship or aircraft was registered or, as the case may be, in that country.

(4) Any reference in this Chapter to the national status of the father of a person at the time of that person's birth shall, in relation to a person born after the death of his father, be construed as a reference to the national status of the father at the time of the father's death ; and where that death occurred before 12th March 1968 and

the birth occurred after 11th March 1968 the national status that the father would have had if he had died on 12th March 1968 shall be deemed to be his national status at the time of his death.

CHAPTER IV

THE GOVERNOR-GENERAL

28. There shall be a Governor-General and Commander-in-Chief of Mauritius who shall be appointed by Her Majesty and shall hold office during Her Majesty's pleasure and who shall be Her Majesty's representative in Mauritius.

Establishment of office of Governor-General.

29. Whenever the office of Governor-General is vacant or the holder of the office is absent from Mauritius or is for any other reason unable to perform the functions of his office, those functions shall be performed by such person as Her Majesty may appoint or, if there is no such person in Mauritius so appointed and able to perform those functions, by the Chief Justice.

Acting Governor-General.

30. A person appointed to the office of Governor-General or assuming the functions of that office under the preceding section shall, before entering upon the duties of that office, take and subscribe to the oath of allegiance and the oath of office as prescribed by schedule 3 to this Constitution, such oaths being administered by the Chief Justice or such other judge of the Supreme Court as may be designated by the Chief Justice.

Oaths to be taken by Governor-General.

CHAPTER V

PARLIAMENT

Part I—The Legislative Assembly

31.—(1) There shall be a Parliament for Mauritius, which shall consist of Her Majesty and a Legislative Assembly.

Parliament of Mauritius.

(2) The Assembly shall consist of persons elected in accordance with schedule 1 to this Constitution, which makes provision for the election of seventy members.

32.—(1) The Assembly shall at its first sitting after any general election elect from among its members a Speaker and a Deputy Speaker.

Speaker and Deputy Speaker.

(2) A member of the Assembly shall not be qualified for election as Speaker or Deputy Speaker if he is a Minister or a Parliamentary Secretary.

(3) The office of the Speaker or the Deputy Speaker shall become vacant—

(a) if he ceases to be a member of the Assembly otherwise than by reason of a dissolution of the Assembly ;

(b) if, under the provisions of section 36 of this Constitution, he is required to cease to perform his functions as a member of the Assembly ;

(c) if he becomes a Minister or a Parliamentary Secretary ;

(*d*) if the Assembly passes a resolution supported by the votes of two-thirds of all the members thereof requiring his removal from office ;

(*e*) when the Assembly first sits after any general election ; or

(*f*) in the case of the Deputy Speaker, when the Assembly first sits after being prorogued.

(4) If the office of the Speaker or the Deputy Speaker becomes vacant at any time the Assembly shall, unless it is sooner dissolved, elect one of its members to fill the vacancy at its next sitting after the occurrence of the vacancy or as soon as practicable thereafter.

(5) A person holding the office of Speaker or Deputy Speaker may resign his office by writing under his hand addressed to the Assembly and the office shall become vacant when the writing is received by the Clerk to the Assembly.

(6) No business shall be transacted in the Assembly (other than the election of a Speaker) at any time when the office of Speaker is vacant.

Qualifications for membership.

33. Subject to the provisions of the next following section, a person shall be qualified to be elected as a member of the Assembly if, and shall not be so qualified unless, he—

(1) is a Commonwealth citizen of not less than twenty-one years of age ;

(2) has resided in Mauritius for a period of, or periods amounting in the aggregate to, not less than two years before the date of his nomination for election ;

(3) has resided in Mauritius for a period of not less than six months immediately before that date ; and

(4) is able to speak and, unless incapacitated by blindness or other physical cause, to read the English language with a degree of proficiency sufficient to enable him to take an active part in the proceedings of the Assembly.

Disqualifications for membership.

34.—(1) No person shall be qualified to be elected as a member of the Assembly who—

(*a*) is, by virtue of his own act, under any acknowledgement of allegiance, obedience or adherence to a power or state outside the Commonwealth ;

(*b*) is a public officer or a local government officer ;

(*c*) is a party to, or a partner in a firm or a director or manager of a company which is a party to, any contract with the Government for or on account of the public service, and has not, within fourteen days after his nomination as a candidate for election, published in the English language in the Gazette and in a newspaper circulating in the constituency for which he is a candidate a notice setting out the nature of such contract and his interest, or the interest of any such firm or company, therein ;

(*d*) has been adjudged or otherwise declared bankrupt under any law in force in any part of the Commonwealth and has not been discharged or has obtained the benefit of a *cessio bonorum* in Mauritius ;

(*e*) is a person adjudged to be of unsound mind or detained as a criminal lunatic under any law in force in Mauritius ;

(*f*) is under sentence of death imposed on him by a court in any part of the Commonwealth, or is serving a sentence of imprisonment (by whatever named called) exceeding twelve months imposed on him by such a court or substituted by competent authority for some other sentence imposed on him by such a court, or is under such a sentence of imprisonment the execution of which has been suspended ;

(*g*) is disqualified for election by any law in force in Mauritius by reason of his holding, or acting in, an office the functions of which involve—

   (i) any responsibility for, or in connection with, the conduct of any election ; or

   (ii) any responsibility for the compilation or revision of any electoral register ; or

(*h*) is disqualified for membership of the Assembly by any law in force in Mauritius relating to offences connected with elections.

(2) If it is prescribed by Parliament that any office in the public service or the service of a Local Authority is not to be regarded as such an office for the purposes of this section, a person shall not be regarded for the purposes of this section as a public officer or a local government officer, as the case may be, by reason only that he holds, or is acting in, that office.

(3) For the purpose of this section—

(*a*) two or more terms of imprisonment that are required to be served consecutively shall be regarded as a single term of imprisonment for the aggregate period of those terms ; and

(*b*) imprisonment in default of payment of a fine shall be disregarded.

35.—(1) The seat in the Assembly of a member thereof shall become vacant— *Tenure of office of members.*

(*a*) upon a dissolution of Parliament ;

(*b*) if he ceases to be a Commonwealth citizen ;

(*c*) if he becomes a party to any contract with the Government for or on account of the public service, or if any firm in which he is a partner or any company of which he is a director or manager becomes a party to any such contract, or if he becomes a partner in a firm or a director or manager of a company which is a party to any such contract:

Provided that, if in the circumstances it appears to him to be just to do so, the Speaker (or, if the office of Speaker is vacant or he is for any reason unable to perform the functions of his office, the Deputy Speaker) may exempt any member from vacating his seat under the provisions of this paragraph if such member, before becoming a party to such contract as aforesaid, or before or as soon as practicable after becoming otherwise interested in such contract (whether as a partner in a firm or as a director or manager of a company), discloses to the Speaker or, as the case may be, the Deputy Speaker the nature of such contract and his interest or the interest of any such firm or company therein ;

(*d*) if he ceases to be resident in Mauritius ;

(*e*) if, without leave of the Speaker (or, if the office of Speaker is vacant or he is for any reason unable to perform the functions of his office, the Deputy Speaker) previously obtained, he is absent from the sittings of the Assembly for a continuous period of three months during any session thereof for any reason other than his being in lawful custody in Mauritius ;

(f) if any of the circumstances arise that, if he were not a member of the Assembly, would cause him to be disqualified for election thereto by virtue of paragraph (a), (b), (d), (e), (g) or (h) of the preceding section ;

(g) in the circumstances mentioned in the next following section ; or

(h) in the case of a member who does not represent a constituency, if he is nominated for election to represent a constituency.

(2) A member of the Assembly may resign his seat therein by writing under his hand addressed to the Speaker and the seat shall become vacant when the writing is received by the Speaker or, if the office of Speaker is vacant or the Speaker is for any reason unable to perform the functions of his office, by the Deputy Speaker or such other person as may be specified in the rules and orders of the Assembly.

(3) If the seat in the Assembly of a member who represents a constituency becomes vacant otherwise than by reason of a dissolution of Parliament, the writ for an election to fill the vacancy shall, unless the Parliament is sooner dissolved, be issued within ninety days of the occurrence of the vacancy.

Vacation of seat on sentence.

36.—(1) Subject to the provisions of this section, if a member of the Assembly is sentenced by a court in any part of the Commonwealth to death or to imprisonment (by whatever name called) for a term exceeding twelve months, he shall forthwith cease to perform his functions as a member of the Assembly and his seat in the Assembly shall become vacant at the expiration of a period of thirty days thereafter :

Provided that the Speaker (or, if the office of Speaker is vacant or he is for any reason unable to perform the functions of his office, the Deputy Speaker) may, at the request of the member, from time to time extend that period of thirty days to enable the member to pursue any appeal in respect of his conviction or sentence, so however that extensions of time exceeding in the aggregate three hundred and thirty days shall not be given without the approval of the Assembly signified by resolution.

(2) If at any time before the member vacates his seat he is granted a free pardon or his conviction is set aside or his sentence is reduced to a term of imprisonment of less than twelve months or a punishment other than imprisonment is substituted, his seat in the Assembly shall not become vacant under the preceding subsection and he may again perform his functions as a member of the Assembly.

(3) For the purpose of this section—

(a) two or more terms of imprisonment that are required to be served consecutively shall be regarded as a single term of imprisonment for the aggregate period of those terms ; and

(b) imprisonment in default of payment of a fine shall be disregarded.

Determination of questions as to membership.

37.—(1) The Supreme Court shall have jurisdiction to hear and determine any question whether—

(a) any person has been validly elected as a member of the Assembly ;

(b) any person who has been elected as Speaker or Deputy Speaker was qualified to be so elected or has vacated the office of Speaker or Deputy Speaker as the case may be ; or

(c) any member of the Assembly has vacated his seat or is required, under the provisions of section 36 of this Constitution, to cease to perform his functions as a member of the Assembly.

(2) An application to the Supreme Court for the determination of any question under subsection (1)(a) of this section may be made by any person entitled to vote in the election to which the application relates or by any person who was a candidate at that election or by the Attorney-General and, if it is made by a person other than the Attorney-General, the Attorney-General may intervene and may then appear or be represented in the proceedings.

(3) An application to the Supreme Court for the determination of any question under subsection (1)(b) of this section may be made by any member of the Assembly or by the Attorney-General and, if it is made by a person other than the Attorney-General, the Attorney-General may intervene and may then appear or be represented in the proceedings.

(4) An application to the Supreme Court for the determination of any question under subsection (1)(c) of this section may be made—

(a) by any member of the Assembly or by the Attorney-General ; or

(b) by any person registered in some constituency as an elector,

and, if it is made by a person other than the Attorney-General, the Attorney-General may intervene and may then appear or be represented in the proceedings.

(5) Parliament may make provision with respect to—

(a) the circumstances and manner in which and the imposition of conditions upon which any application may be made to the Supreme Court for the determination of any question under this section ; and

(b) the powers, practice and procedure of the Supreme Court in relation to any such application.

(6) A determination by the Supreme Court in proceedings under this section shall not be subject to an appeal:

Provided that an appeal shall lie to Her Majesty in Council in such cases as may be prescribed by Parliament.

(7) In the exercise of his functions under this section, the Attorney-General shall not be subject to the direction or control of any other person or authority.

38.—(1) There shall be an Electoral Boundaries Commission which shall consist of a chairman and not less than two nor more than four other members appointed by the Governor-General, acting in accordance with the advice of the Prime Minister tendered after the Prime Minister has consulted the Leader of the Opposition. *Electoral Commissions.*

(2) There shall be an Electoral Supervisory Commission which shall consist of a chairman appointed by the Governor-General in accordance with the advice of the Judicial and Legal Service Commission and not less than two nor more than four other members appointed by the Governor-General, acting in accordance with the advice of the Prime Minister tendered after the Prime Minister has consulted the Leader of the Opposition.

(3) No person shall be qualified for appointment as a member of the Electoral Boundaries Commission or the Electoral Supervisory Commission if he is a member of, or a candidate for election to, the Assembly or any Local Authority or a public officer or a local government officer.

(4) Subject to the provisions of this section, a member of the Electoral Boundaries Commission or the Electoral Supervisory Commission shall vacate his office—

(a) at the expiration of five years from the date of his appointment ; or

(b) if any circumstances arise that, if he were not a member of the Commission, would cause him to be disqualified for appointment as such.

(5) The provisions of section 92(2) to (5) of this Constitution shall apply to a member of the Electoral Boundaries Commission or of the Electoral Supervisory Commission as they apply to a Commissioner within the meaning of that section.

Constitu-
encies.

39.—(1) There shall be twenty-one constituencies and accordingly—

(a) the Island of Mauritius shall be divided into twenty constituencies ;

(b) Rodrigues shall form one constituency :

Provided that the Assembly may by resolution provide that any island forming part of Mauritius that is not comprised in the Island of Mauritius or Rodrigues shall be included in such one of the constituencies as the Electoral Boundaries Commission may determine and with effect from the next dissolution of Parliament after the passing of any such resolution the provisions of this section shall have effect accordingly.

(2) The Electoral Boundaries Commission shall review the boundaries of the constituencies at such times as will enable them to present a report to the Assembly ten years, as near as may be, after the 12th August 1966 and, thereafter, ten years after presentation of their last report :

Provided that the Commission may at any time carry out a review and present a report if it considers it desirable to do so by reason of the holding of an official census of the population of Mauritius and shall do so if a resolution is passed by the Assembly in pursuance of the preceding subsection.

(3) The report of the Electoral Boundaries Commission shall make recommendations for such alterations (if any) to the boundaries of the constituencies as appear to the Commission to be required so that the number of inhabitants of each constituency is as nearly equal as is reasonably practicable to the population quota :

Provided that the number of inhabitants of a constituency may be greater or less than the population quota in order to take account of means of communication, geographical features, density of population and the boundaries of administrative areas.

(4) The Assembly may, by resolution, approve or reject the recommendations of the Electoral Boundaries Commission but may not vary them ; and, if so approved, the recommendations shall have effect as from the next dissolution of Parliament.

(5) In this section "population quota" means the number obtained by dividing the number of inhabitants of the Island of Mauritius (including any island included in any constituency in the Island of Mauritius by virtue of any resolution under subsection (1) of this section) according to the latest official census of the population of Mauritius by twenty.

40.—(1) There shall be an Electoral Commissioner, whose office shall be a public office and who shall be appointed by the Judicial and Legal Service Commission. Electoral Commissioner.

(2) No person shall be qualified to hold or act in the office of Electoral Commissioner unless he is qualified to practise as a barrister in Mauritius.

(3) Without prejudice to the provisions of the next following section, in the exercise of his functions under this Constitution the Electoral Commissioner shall not be subject to the direction or control of any other person or authority.

41.—(1) The Electoral Supervisory Commission shall have general responsibility for, and shall supervise, the registration of electors for the election of members of the Assembly and the conduct of elections of such members and the Commission shall have such powers and other functions relating to such registration and such elections as may be prescribed. Functions of Electoral Supervisory Commission and Electoral Commissioner.

(2) The Electoral Commissioner shall have such powers and other functions relating to such registration and elections as may be prescribed ; and he shall keep the Electoral Supervisory Commission fully informed concerning the exercise of his functions and shall have the right to attend meetings of the Commission and to refer to the Commission for their advice or decision any question relating to his functions.

(3) Every proposed bill and every proposed regulation or other instrument having the force of law relating to the registration of electors for the election of members of the Assembly or to the election of such members shall be referred to the Electoral Supervisory Commission and to the Electoral Commissioner at such time as shall give them sufficient opportunity to make comments thereon before the bill is introduced in the Assembly or, as the case may be, the regulation or other instrument is made.

(4) The Electoral Supervisory Commission may make such reports to the Governor-General concerning the matters under their supervision, or any draft bill or instrument that is referred to them, as they may think fit and if the Commission so requests in any such report other than a report on a draft bill or instrument that report shall be laid before the Assembly.

(5) The question whether the Electoral Commissioner has acted in accordance with the advice of or a decision of the Electoral Supervisory Commission shall not be enquired into in any court of law.

42.—(1) Subject to the provisions of the next following section, a person shall be entitled to be registered as an elector if, and shall not be so entitled unless— Qualifications of electors.

    (*a*) he is a Commonwealth citizen of not less than twenty-one years of age ; and (*b*) either he has resided in Mauritius for a period of not less than two years immediately before such date as may be prescribed by Parliament or he is domiciled in Mauritius and is resident therein on the prescribed date.

(2) No person shall be entitled to be registered as an elector—

(*a*) in more than one constituency ; or

(*b*) in any constituency in which he is not resident on the prescribed date.

Disqualifications of electors.

43. No person shall be entitled to be registered as an elector who—

(*a*) is under sentence of death imposed on him by a court in any part of the Commonwealth, or is serving a sentence of imprisonment (by whatever name called) exceeding twelve months imposed on him by such a court or substituted by competent authority for some other sentence imposed on him by such a court, or is under such a sentence of imprisonment the execution of which has been suspended ;

(*b*) is a person adjudged to be of unsound mind or detained as a criminal lunatic under any law in force in Mauritius ; or

(*c*) is disqualified for registration as an elector by any law in force in Mauritius relating to offences connected with elections.

Right to vote at elections.

44.—(1) Any person who is registered as an elector in a constituency shall be entitled to vote in such manner as may be prescribed at any election for that constituency unless he is prohibited from so voting by any law in force in Mauritius because—

(*a*) he is a returning officer ; or

(*b*) he has been concerned in any offence connected with elections ;

Provided that no such person shall be entitled so to vote if on the date prescribed for polling he is in lawful custody or (except in so far as may otherwise be prescribed) he is for any other reason unable to attend in person at the place and time prescribed for polling.

(2) No person shall vote at any election for any constituency who is not registered as an elector in that constituency.

Part II—Legislation and Procedure in Legislative Assembly

Power to make laws.

45.—(1) Subject to the provisions of this Constitution, Parliament may make laws for the peace, order and good government of Mauritius.

(2) Without prejudice to the generality of subsection (1) of this section, Parliament may by law determine the privileges, immunities and powers of the Assembly and the members thereof.

Mode of exercise of legislative power.

46.—(1) The power of Parliament to make laws shall be exercisable by bills passed by the Assembly and assented to by the Governor-General on behalf of Her Majesty.

(2) When a bill is submitted to the Governor-General for assent in accordance with the provisions of this Constitution he shall signify that he assents or that he withholds assent.

(3) When the Governor-General assents to a bill that has been submitted to him in accordance with the provisions of this Constitution the bill shall become law and the Governor-General shall thereupon cause it to be published in the Gazette as a law.

(4) No law made by Parliament shall come into operation until it has been published in the Gazette but Parliament may postpone the coming into operation of any such law and may make laws with retrospective effect.

(5) All laws made by Parliament shall be styled " Acts of Parliament " and the words of enactment shall be "Enacted by the Parliament of Mauritius ".

47.—(1) Subject to the provisions of this section, Parliament may alter this Constitution. *Alteration of Constitution.*

(2) A bill for an Act of Parliament to alter any of the following provisions of this Constitution, that is to say:—

(*a*) this section ;

(*b*) sections 28 to 31, 37 to 46, 56 to 58, 64, 65, 71, 72 and 108 ;

(*c*) Chapters II, VII, VIII and IX ;

(*d*) schedule 1 ; and

(*e*) Chapter XI, to the extent that it relates to any of the provisions specified in the preceding paragraphs,

shall not be passed by the Assembly unless it is supported at the final voting in the Assembly by the votes of not less than three-quarters of all the members of the Assembly.

(3) A bill for an Act of Parliament to alter any provision of this Constitution (but which does not alter any of the provisions of this Constitution as specified in subsection (2) of this section) shall not be passed by the Assembly unless it is supported at the final voting in the Assembly by the votes of not less than two-thirds of all the members of the Assembly.

(4) In this section references to altering this Constitution or any part of this Constitution include references—

(*a*) to revoking it, with or without re-enactment thereof or the making of different provision in lieu thereof ;

(*b*) to modifying it, whether by omitting or amending any of its provisions or inserting additional provisions in it or otherwise ; and

(*c*) to suspending its operation for any period, or terminating any such suspension.

48.—Subject to the provisions of this Constitution, the Assembly may regulate its own procedure and may in particular make rules for the orderly conduct of its own proceedings. *Regulation of procedure in Legislative Assembly.*

49. The official language of the Assembly shall be English but any member may address the chair in French. *Official language.*

50. The Speaker or in his absence the Deputy Speaker or in their absence a member of the Assembly (not being a Minister or a Parliamentary Secretary) elected by the Assembly for the sitting, shall preside at any sitting of the Assembly. *Presiding in Legislative Assembly.*

51. The Assembly may act notwithstanding any vacancy in its membership (including any vacancy not filled when the Assembly first meets after any general election) and the presence or participation of any person not entitled to be present at or to participate in the proceedings of the Assembly shall not invalidate those proceedings. *Legislative Assembly may transact business notwithstanding vacancies.*

Quorum.

52.—(1) If at any sitting of the Assembly a quorum is not present and any member of the Assembly who is present objects on that account to the transaction of business and, after such interval as may be prescribed by the Assembly, the person presiding at the sitting ascertains that a quorum is still not present, he shall adjourn the Assembly.

(2) For the purposes of this section a quorum shall consist of seventeen members of the Assembly in addition to the person presiding.

Voting.

53.—(1) Save as otherwise provided in this Constitution, all questions proposed for decision in the Assembly shall be determined by a majority of the votes of the members present and voting; and a member of the Assembly shall not be precluded from so voting by reason only that he holds the office of Speaker or Deputy Speaker or is presiding in the Assembly.

(2) If, upon any question before the Assembly that falls to be determined by a majority of the members present and voting, the votes cast are equally divided, the Speaker or other person presiding shall have and shall exercise a casting vote.

Bills, motions and petitions.

54. Except upon the recommendation of a Minister, the Assembly shall not—

(a) proceed upon any bill (including any amendment to a bill) that, in the opinion of the person presiding, makes provision for any of the following purposes—

(i) for the imposition of taxation or the alteration of taxation otherwise than by reduction ;

(ii) for the imposition of any charge upon the Consolidated Fund or other public funds of Mauritius or the alteration of any such charge otherwise than by reduction ;

(iii) for the payment, issue or withdrawal from the Consolidated Fund or other public funds of Mauritius of any monies not charged thereon or any increase in the amount of such payment, issue or withdrawal ; or

(iv) for the composition or remission of any debt to the Government ;

(b) proceed upon any motion (including any amendment to a motion) the effect of which, in the opinion of the person presiding, would be to make provision for any of those purposes ; or

(c) receive any petition that, in the opinion of the person presiding, requests that provision be made for any of those purposes.

Oath of allegiance.

55. No member of the Assembly shall take part in the proceedings of the Assembly (other than proceedings necessary for the purposes of this section) until he has made and subscribed before the Assembly the oath of allegiance prescribed in schedule 3 to this Constitution.

Sessions.

56.—(1) The sessions of the Assembly shall be held in such place and begin at such time as the Governor-General by Proclamation may appoint :

Provided that the place at which any session of the Assembly is to be held may be altered from time to time during the course of the session by a further Proclamation made by the Governor-General.

(2) A session of the Assembly shall be held from time to time so that a period of twelve months shall not intervene between the last sitting of the Assembly in one session and its first sitting in the next session.

(3) Writs for a general election of members of the Assembly shall be issued within sixty days of the date of any dissolution of Parliament and a session of the Assembly shall be appointed to commence within thirty days of the date prescribed for polling at any general election.

57.—(1) The Governor-General, acting in accordance with the advice of the Prime Minister, may at any time prorogue or dissolve Parliament:

Provided that—

(*a*) if the Assembly passes a resolution that it has no confidence in the Government and the Prime Minister does not within three days either resign from his office or advise the Governor-General to dissolve Parliament within seven days or at such later time as the Governor-General, acting in his own deliberate judgment, may consider reasonable, the Governor-General, acting in his own deliberate judgment, may dissolve Parliament ;

(*b*) if the office of Prime Minister is vacant and the Governor-General considers that there is no prospect of his being able within a reasonable time to appoint to that office a person who can command the support of a majority of the members of the Assembly, the Governor-General, acting in his own deliberate judgment, may dissolve Parliament.

Prorogation and dissolution of Parliament.

(2) Parliament, unless sooner dissolved, shall continue for five years from the date of the first sitting of the Assembly after any general election and shall then stand dissolved.

(3) At any time when Mauritius is at war Parliament may from time to time extend the period of five years specified in the preceding subsection by not more than twelve months at a time:

Provided that the life of Parliament shall not be extended under this subsection for more than five years.

(4) At any time when there is in force a Proclamation by the Governor-General declaring, for the purposes of section 19(7)(*b*) of this Constitution, that a state of public emergency exists Parliament may from time to time extend the period of five years specified in subsection (2) of this section by not more than six months at a time:

Provided that the life of Parliament shall not be extended under this subsection for more than one year.

(5) If, after a dissolution and before the holding of the election of members of the Assembly, the Prime Minister advises the Governor-General that, owing to the existence of a state of war or of a state of emergency in Mauritius or any part thereof, it is necessary to recall Parliament, the Governor-General shall summon the Parliament that has been dissolved to meet.

(6) Unless the life of Parliament is extended under subsection (3) or subsection (4) of this section, the election of members of the Assembly shall proceed notwithstanding the summoning of Parliament under the preceding subsection and the Parliament that has been recalled shall, if not sooner dissolved, again stand dissolved on the day before the day prescribed for polling at that election.

CHAPTER VI
THE EXECUTIVE

Executive
authority of
Mauritius.

58.—(1) The executive authority of Mauritius is vested in Her Majesty.

(2) Save as otherwise provided in this Constitution, that authority may be exercised on behalf of Her Majesty by the Governor-General either directly or through officers subordinate to him.

(3) Nothing in this section shall preclude persons or authorities other than the Governor-General from exercising such functions as may be conferred upon them by any law.

Ministers.

59.—(1) There shall be a Prime Minister who shall be appointed by the Governor-General.

(2) There shall be, in addition to the offices of Prime Minister and of Attorney-General, such other offices of Minister of the Government as may be prescribed by Parliament or, subject to the provisions of any law, established by the Governor-General, acting in accordance with the advice of the Prime Minister:

Provided that the number of offices of Minister other than the Prime Minister shall not be more than fourteen.

(3) The Governor-General, acting in his own deliberate judgment, shall appoint as Prime Minister the member of the Assembly who appears to him best able to command the support of the majority of the members of the Assembly, and shall, acting in accordance with the advice of the Prime Minister, appoint the Attorney-General and the other Ministers from among the members of the Assembly:

Provided that—

(a) if occasion arises for making an appointment while Parliament is dissolved a person who was a member of the Assembly immediately before the dissolution may be appointed ; and

(b) a person may be appointed Attorney-General notwithstanding that he is not (or, as the case may be, was not) a member of the Assembly.

Tenure of
office of
Ministers.

60.—(1) If a resolution of no confidence in the Government is passed by the Assembly and the Prime Minister does not within three days resign from his office the Governor-General shall remove the Prime Minister from office unless, in pursuance of section 57(1) of this Constitution, Parliament has been or is to be dissolved in consequence of such resolution.

(2) If at any time between the holding of a general election and the first sitting of the Assembly thereafter the Governor-General, acting in his own deliberate judgment, considers that, in consequence of changes in the membership of the Assembly resulting from that general election, the Prime Minister will not be able to command the support of a majority of the members of the Assembly, the Governor-General may remove the Prime Minister from office:

Provided that the Governor-General shall not remove the Prime Minister from office within the period of ten days immediately following the date prescribed for polling at that general election unless he is satisfied that a party or party alliance in opposition to the Government and registered for the purposes of that general election under paragraph 2 of schedule 1 to this Constitution has at that general election gained a majority of all the seats in the Assembly.

(3) The office of Prime Minister or any other Minister shall become vacant—

    (a) if he ceases to be a member of the Assembly otherwise than by reason of a dissolution of Parliament ; or

    (b) if, at the first sitting of the Assembly after any general election, he is not a member of the Assembly :

Provided that paragraph (b) of this subsection shall not apply to the office of Attorney-General if the holder thereof was not a member of the Assembly on the preceding dissolution of Parliament.

(4) The office of a Minister (other than the Prime Minister) shall become vacant—

    (a) if the Governor-General, acting in accordance with the advice of the Prime Minister, so directs ;

    (b) if the Prime Minister resigns from office within three days after the passage by the Assembly of a resolution of no confidence in the Government or is removed from office under subsection (1) or subsection (2) of this section ; or

    (c) upon the appointment of any person to the office of Prime Minister.

(5) If for any period the Prime Minister or any other Minister is unable by reason of the provisions of section 36(1) of this Constitution to perform his functions as a member of the Assembly, he shall not during that period perform any of his functions as Prime Minister or Minister, as the case may be.

61.—(1) There shall be a Cabinet for Mauritius, consisting of the Prime Minister and the other Ministers.

    The Cabinet.

(2) The functions of the Cabinet shall be to advise the Governor-General in the government of Mauritius and the Cabinet shall be collectively responsible to the Assembly for any advice given to the Governor-General by or under the general authority of the Cabinet and for all things done by or under the authority of any Minister in the execution of his office.

(3) The provisions of the last preceding subsection shall not apply in relation to—

    (a) the appointment and removal from office of Ministers and Parliamentary Secretaries, the assigning of responsibility to any Minister under the next following section, or the authorisation of another Minister to perform the functions of the Prime Minister during absence or illness ;

    (b) the dissolution of Parliament ; or

    (c) the matters referred to in section 75 of this Constitution (which relate to the prerogative of mercy).

62. The Governor-General, acting in accordance with the advice of the Prime Minister, may, by directions in writing, assign to the Prime Minister or any other Minister responsibility for the conduct (subject to the provisions of this Constitution and any other law) of any business of the Government, including responsibility for the administration of any department of government.

    Assignment of responsibilities to Ministers.

63.—(1) Whenever the Prime Minister is absent from Mauritius or is by reason of illness or of the provisions of section 60(5) of this Constitution unable to perform the functions conferred on him by this Constitution, the Governor-General may, by directions in writing,

    Performance of functions during absence or illness.

authorise some other Minister to perform those functions (other than the functions conferred by this section) and that Minister may perform those functions until his authority is revoked by the Governor-General.

(2) The powers of the Governor-General under this section shall be exercised by him in accordance with the advice of the Prime Minister:

Provided that if the Governor-General, acting in his own deliberate judgment, considers that it is impracticable to obtain the advice of the Prime Minister owing to the Prime Minister's absence or illness, or if the Prime Minister is unable to tender advice by reason of the provisions of section 60(5) of this Constitution, the Governor-General may exercise those powers without that advice and in his own deliberate judgment.

Exercise of Governor-General's functions.

64.—(1) In the exercise of his functions under this Constitution or any other law, the Governor-General shall act in accordance with the advice of the Cabinet or of a Minister acting under the general authority of the Cabinet except in cases where he is required by this Constitution to act in accordance with the advice of, or after consultation with, any person or authority other than the Cabinet or in his own deliberate judgment.

(2) Where the Governor-General is directed by this Constitution to exercise any function after consultation with any person or authority other than the Cabinet, he shall not be obliged to exercise that function in accordance with the advice of that person or authority.

(3) Where the Governor-General is required by this Constitution to act in accordance with the advice of or after consultation with any person or authority, the question whether he has in any matter so acted shall not be called in question in any court of law.

(4) During any period in which the office of Leader of the Opposition is vacant by reason that there is no such opposition party as is referred to in subsection (2)(a) of section 73 of this Constitution and the Governor-General, acting in his own deliberate judgment, is of the opinion that no member of the Assembly would be acceptable to the leaders of the opposition parties for the purposes of subsection (2)(b) of that section or by reason that there are no opposition parties for the purposes of that section, the operation of any provision of this Constitution shall, to the extent that it requires the Governor-General, the Prime Minister or the Public Service Commission to consult the Leader of the Opposition, be suspended.

Governor-General to be kept informed.

65. The Prime Minister shall keep the Governor-General fully informed concerning the general conduct of the government of Mauritius and shall furnish the Governor-General with such information as he may request with respect to any particular matter relating to the government of Mauritius.

Parliamentary Secretaries.

66.—(1) The Governor-General, acting in accordance with the advice of the Prime Minister, may appoint Parliamentary Secretaries from among the members of the Assembly to assist Ministers in the performance of their duties:

Provided that—

(a) the number of Parliamentary Secretaries shall not exceed five; and

(b) if occasion arises for making appointments while the Assembly is dissolved, a person who was a member of the Assembly immediately before the dissolution may be appointed as a Parliamentary Secretary.

(2) The office of a Parliamentary Secretary shall become vacant—

(*a*) if the Governor-General, acting in accordance with the advice of the Prime Minister, so directs ;

(*b*) if the Prime Minister resigns from office within three days after the passage by the Assembly of a resolution of no confidence in the Government or is removed from office under section 60(1) or (2) of this Constitution ;

(*c*) upon the appointment of a person to the office of Prime Minister ;

(*d*) if the holder of the office ceases to be a member of the Assembly otherwise than by reason of a dissolution of Parliament ; or

(*e*) if, at the first sitting of the Assembly after any general election, the holder of the office is not a member of the Assembly.

(3) If for any period a Parliamentary Secretary is unable by reason of the provisions of section 36(1) of this Constitution to perform his functions as a member of the Assembly, he shall not during that period perform any of his functions as a Parliamentary Secretary.

67. A Minister or a Parliamentary Secretary shall not enter upon the duties of his office unless he has taken and subscribed the oath of allegiance and such oath for the due execution of his office as is prescribed by schedule 3 to this Constitution.

Oaths to be taken by Ministers, etc.

68. Where any Minister has been charged with responsibility for the administration of any department of government, he shall exercise general direction and control over that department and, subject to such direction and control, any department in the charge of a Minister (including the office of the Prime Minister or any other Minister) shall be under the supervision of a Permanent Secretary or of some other supervising officer whose office shall be a public office :

Direction, etc., of government departments.

Provided that—

(*a*) any such department may be under the joint supervision of two or more supervising officers ; and

(*b*) different parts of any such department may respectively be under the supervision of different supervising officers.

69.—(1) There shall be an Attorney-General who shall be principal legal adviser to the Government of Mauritius.

Attorney-General.

(2) The office of Attorney-General shall be the office of a Minister.

(3) No person shall be qualified to hold the office of Attorney-General unless he is entitled to practise as a barrister in Mauritius, and no person who is not a member of the Assembly shall be qualified to hold the office if he is for any cause disqualified from membership of the Assembly :

Provided that a person may hold the office of Attorney-General notwithstanding that he holds or is acting in a public office (not being the office of Director of Public Prosecutions).

(4) If the person holding the office of Attorney-General is not a member of the Assembly, he shall be entitled to take part in the proceedings of the Assembly, and the provisions of this Constitution and any other law shall apply to him as if he were a member of the Assembly :

Provided that he shall not be entitled to vote in the Assembly.

(5) If the person holding the office of Attorney-General is for any reason unable to exercise the functions conferred upon him by or under any law, those functions may be exercised by such other person, being a person entitled to practise as a barrister in Mauritius (whether or not he is a member of the Assembly), as the Governor-General, acting in accordance with the advice of the Prime Minister, may direct.

Secretary to the Cabinet.

70.—(1) There shall be a Secretary to the Cabinet, whose office shall be a public office.

(2) The Secretary to the Cabinet shall be responsible, in accordance with such instructions as may be given to him by the Prime Minister, for arranging the business for, and keeping the minutes of, the Cabinet or any committee thereof and for conveying the decisions of the Cabinet or any committee thereof to the appropriate person or authority, and shall have such other functions as the Prime Minister may direct.

Commissioner of Police.

71.—(1) There shall be a Commissioner of Police, whose office shall be a public office.

(2) The Police Force shall be under the command of the Commissioner of Police.

(3) The Prime Minister, or such other Minister as may be authorised in that behalf by the Prime Minister, may give to the Commissioner of Police such general directions of policy with respect to the maintenance of public safety and public order as he may consider necessary and the Commissioner shall comply with such directions or cause them to be complied with.

(4) Nothing in this section shall be construed as precluding the assignment to a Minister of responsibility under section 62 of this Constitution for the organisation, maintenance and administration of the Police Force, but the Commissioner of Police shall be responsible for determining the use and controlling the operations of the Force and, except as provided in the preceding subsection, the Commissioner shall not, in the exercise of his responsibilities and powers with respect to the use and operational control of the Force, be subject to the direction or control of any person or authority.

Director of Public Prosecutions.

72.—(1) There shall be a Director of Public Prosecutions whose office shall be a public office and who shall be appointed by the Judicial and Legal Service Commission.

(2) No person shall be qualified to hold or act in the office of Director of Public Prosecutions unless he is qualified for appointment as a judge of the Supreme Court.

(3) The Director of Public Prosecutions shall have power in any case in which he considers it desirable so to do—

(a) to institute and undertake criminal proceedings before any court of law (not being a court established by a disciplinary law) ;

(b) to take over and continue any such criminal proceedings that may have been instituted by any other person or authority ; and

(c) to discontinue at any stage before judgment is delivered any such criminal proceedings instituted or undertaken by himself or any other person or authority.

(4) The powers of the Director of Public Prosecutions under the preceding subsection may be exercised by him in person or through other persons acting in accordance with his general or specific instructions.

(5) The powers conferred upon the Director of Public Prosecutions by paragraphs (b) and (c) of subsection (3) of this section shall be vested in him to the exclusion of any other person or authority:

Provided that, where any other person or authority has instituted criminal proceedings, nothing in this subsection shall prevent the withdrawal of those proceedings by or at the instance of that person or authority at any stage before the person against whom the proceedings have been instituted has been charged before the court.

(6) In the exercise of the powers conferred upon him by this section the Director of Public Prosecutions shall not be subject to the direction or control of any other person or authority.

(7) For the purposes of this section, any appeal from any determination in any criminal proceedings before any court, or any case stated or question of law reserved for the purposes of any such proceedings to any other court, shall be deemed to be part of those proceedings:

Provided that the power conferred on the Director of Public Prosecutions by subsection 3(c) of this section shall not be exercised in relation to any appeal by a person convicted in any criminal proceedings or to any case stated or question of law reserved except at the instance of such a person.

73.—(1) There shall be a Leader of the Opposition who shall be appointed by the Governor-General.

Leader of Opposition.

(2) Whenever the Governor-General has occasion to appoint a Leader of the Opposition he shall in his own deliberate judgment appoint—

(a) if there is one opposition party whose numerical strength in the Assembly is greater than the strength of any other opposition party, the member of the Assembly who is the leader in the Assembly of that party ; or

(b) if there is no such party, the member of the Assembly whose appointment would, in the judgment of the Governor-General, be most acceptable to the leaders in the Assembly of the opposition parties:

Provided that, if occasion arises for making an appointment while Parliament is dissolved, a person who was a member of the Assembly immediately before the dissolution may be appointed Leader of the Opposition.

(3) The office of the Leader of the Opposition shall become vacant—

(a) if, after any general election, he is informed by the Governor-General that the Governor-General is about to appoint another person as Leader of the Opposition ;

(b) if, under the provisions of section 36(1) of this Constitution, he is required to cease to perform his functions as a member of the Assembly ;

(c) if he ceases to be a member of the Assembly otherwise than by reason of a dissolution of Parliament ;

(d) if, at the first sitting of the Assembly after any general election, he is not a member of the Assembly ; or

(e) if his appointment is revoked under the next following subsection.

(4) If the Governor-General, acting in his own deliberate judgment, considers that a member of the Assembly other than the Leader of the Opposition has become the leader in the Assembly of the opposition party having the greatest numerical strength in the Assembly or, as the case may be, the Leader of the Opposition is no longer acceptable as such to the leaders of the opposition parties in the Assembly, the Governor-General may revoke the appointment of the Leader of the Opposition.

(5) For the purposes of this section " opposition party " means a group of members of the Assembly whose number includes a leader who commands their support in opposition to the Government.

Constitution of offices.

74. Subject to the provisions of this Constitution and of any other law, the Governor-General may constitute offices for Mauritius, make appointments to any such office and terminate any such appointment.

Prerogative of mercy.

75.—(1) The Governor-General may, in Her Majesty's name and on Her Majesty's behalf—

(*a*) grant to any person convicted of any offence a pardon, either free or subject to lawful conditions ;

(*b*) grant to any person a respite, either indefinite or for a specified period, of the execution of any punishment imposed on that person for any offence ;

(*c*) substitute a less severe form of punishment for any punishment imposed on any person for any offence ; or

(*d*) remit the whole or part of any punishment imposed on any person for an offence or of any penalty or forfeiture otherwise due to the Crown on account of any offence.

(2) There shall be a Commission on the Prerogative of Mercy (hereinafter in this section referred to as " the Commission ") consisting of a chairman and not less than two other members appointed by the Governor-General, acting in his own deliberate judgment.

(3) A member of the Commission shall vacate his seat on the Commission—

(*a*) at the expiration of the term of his appointment (if any) specified in the instrument of his appointment ; or

(*b*) if his appointment is revoked by the Governor-General, acting in his own deliberate judgment.

(4) In the exercise of the powers conferred upon him by subsection (1) of this section, the Governor-General shall act in accordance with the advice of the Commission.

(5) The validity of the transaction of business by the Commission shall not be affected by the fact that some person who was not entitled to do so took part in the proceedings.

(6) Whenever any person has been sentenced to death (otherwise than by a court martial) for an offence, a report on the case by the judge who presided at the trial (or, if a report cannot be obtained from that judge, a report on the case by the Chief Justice), together with such other information derived from the record of the case or elsewhere as may be required by or furnished to the Commission shall be taken into consideration at a meeting of the Commission which shall then advise the Governor-General whether or not to exercise his powers under subsection (1) of this section in that case.

(7) The provisions of this section shall not apply in relation to any conviction by a court established under the law of a country other than Mauritius that has jurisdiction in Mauritius in pursuance of arrangements made between the Government of Mauritius and another Government or an international organisation relating to the presence in Mauritius of members of the armed forces of that other country or in relation to any punishment imposed in respect of any such conviction or any penalty or forfeiture resulting from any such conviction.

CHAPTER VII
THE JUDICATURE

76.—(1) There shall be a Supreme Court for Mauritius which shall have unlimited jurisdiction to hear and determine any civil or criminal proceedings under any law other than a disciplinary law and such jurisdiction and powers as may be conferred upon it by this Constitution or any other law.

Supreme Court.

(2) Subject to the provisions of the next following section, the judges of the Supreme Court shall be the Chief Justice, the Senior Puisne Judge and such number of Puisne Judges as may be prescribed by Parliament:

Provided that the office of a judge shall not be abolished while any person is holding that office unless he consents to its abolition.

77.—(1) The Chief Justice shall be appointed by the Governor-General acting after consultation with the Prime Minister.

Appointment of judges of Supreme Court.

(2) The Senior Puisne Judge shall be appointed by the Governor-General acting in accordance with the advice of the Chief Justice.

(3) The Puisne Judges shall be appointed by the Governor-General, acting in accordance with the advice of the Judicial and Legal Service Commission.

(4) No person shall be qualified for appointment as a judge of the Supreme Court unless he is, and has been for at least five years, a barrister entitled to practise before the Supreme Court.

(5) Whenever the office of Chief Justice is vacant or the person holding that office is for any reason unable to perform the functions of the office, those functions shall be discharged by such one of the other judges of the Supreme Court as may from time to time be designated in that behalf by the Governor-General, acting in accordance with the advice of the person holding the office of Chief Justice:

Provided that if the office of Chief Justice is vacant or if the person holding that office is on leave of absence pending retirement or if the Governor-General, acting in his own deliberate judgment, considers that it is impracticable to obtain the advice of that person owing to that person's absence or illness, the Governor-General shall act after consultation with the Prime Minister.

(6) Whenever the office of Senior Puisne Judge is vacant or the person holding that office is acting as Chief Justice or is for any reason unable to perform the functions of the office, such one of the judges of the Supreme Court as the Governor-General, acting in accordance with the advice of the Chief Justice, may appoint shall act in the office of Senior Puisne Judge.

(7) If the office of any Puisne Judge is vacant or if a person holding the office of Puisne Judge is acting as Chief Justice or as Senior Puisne Judge or is for any reason unable to perform the functions of his office or if the Prime Minister, having been informed by the Chief Justice that the state of business in the Supreme Court requires that the number of judges should be temporarily increased and having consulted with the Chief Justice, requests the Governor-General to appoint an additional judge, the Governor-General, acting in accordance with the advice of the Judicial Service Commission, may appoint a person qualified for appointment as a judge of the Supreme Court to act as a Puisne Judge of that court:

Provided that a person may act as a Puisne Judge notwithstanding that he has attained the age prescribed for the purposes of section 78(1) of this Constitution.

(8) Any person appointed under this section to act as a Puisne Judge shall, unless he is removed from office under section 78 of this Constitution, continue to act for the period of his appointment or, if no such period is specified, until his appointment is revoked by the Governor-General, acting in accordance with the advice of the Chief Justice:

Provided that a person whose appointment to act as a Puisne Judge has expired or been revoked may, with the permission of the Governor-General, acting in accordance with the advice of the Chief Justice, continue to act as such for such a period as may be necessary to enable him to deliver judgment or to do any other thing in relation to proceedings that were commenced before him previously thereto.

Tenure of office of judges of Supreme Court.

78.—(1) Subject to the provisions of this section, a person holding the office of a judge of the Supreme Court shall vacate that office on attaining the retiring age:

Provided that he may, with the permission of the Governor-General, acting in his own deliberate judgment in the case of the Chief Justice or in any other case in accordance with the advice of the Chief Justice, continue in office for such period as may be necessary to enable him to deliver judgment or to do any other thing in relation to proceedings that were commenced before him before he attained that age.

(2) A judge of the Supreme Court may be removed from office only for inability to perform the functions of his office (whether arising from infirmity of body or mind or from any other cause) or for misbehaviour, and shall not be so removed except in accordance with the provisions of the next following subsection.

(3) A judge of the Supreme Court shall be removed from office by the Governor-General if the question of removing him from office has, at the request of the Governor-General made in pursuance of the next following subsection, been referred by Her Majesty to the Judicial Committee of Her Majesty's Privy Council under section 4 of the Judicial Committee Act 1833(a) or any other enactment enabling Her Majesty in that behalf and the Judicial Committee has advised Her Majesty that the judge ought to be removed from office for inability as aforesaid or misbehaviour.

(4) If the Chief Justice or, in relation to the removal of the person holding the office of Chief Justice, the Governor-General considers

(a) 1833 c. 41.

that the question of removing a judge of the Supreme Court from office for inability as aforesaid or misbehaviour ought to be investigated, then—

(a) the Governor-General shall appoint a tribunal, which shall consists of a chairman and not less than two other members, selected by the Governor-General from among persons who hold or have held office as a judge of a court having unlimited jurisdiction in civil and criminal matters in some part of the Commonwealth or a court having jurisdiction in appeals from any such court ;

(b) the tribunal shall enquire into the matter and report on the facts thereof to the Governor-General and recommended to the Governor-General whether he should request that the question of removing the judge from office should be referred by Her Majesty to the Judicial Committee; and

(c) if the tribunal so recommends, the Governor-General shall request that the question should be referred accordingly.

(5) If the question of removing a judge of the Supreme Court from office has been referred to a tribunal under subsection (4) of this section, the Governor-General may suspend the judge from performing the functions of his office ; and any such suspension may at any time be revoked by the Governor-General and shall in any case cease to have effect—

(a) if the tribunal recommends to the Governor-General that he should not request that the question of removing the judge from office should be referred by Her Majesty to the Judicial Committee ; or

(b) if the Judicial Committee advises Her Majesty that the judge ought not to be removed from office.

(6) The functions of the Governor-General under this section shall be exercised by him in his own deliberate judgment.

(7) The retiring age for the purposes of subsection (1) of this section shall be the age of sixty-two years or such other age as may be prescribed by Parliament:

Provided that a provision of any Act of Parliament, to the extent that it alters the age at which judges of the Supreme Court shall vacate their offices, shall not have effect in relation to a judge after his appointment unless he consents to its having effect.

79. A judge of the Supreme Court shall not enter upon the duties of his office unless he has taken and subscribed the oath of allegiance and such oath for the due execution of his office as is prescribed by schedule 3 to this Constitution. *Oaths to be taken by judges.*

80.—(1) There shall be a Court of Civil Appeal and a Court of Criminal Appeal for Mauritius, each of which shall be a division of the Supreme Court. *Courts of Appeal.*

(2) The Court of Civil Appeal shall have such jurisdiction and powers to hear and determine appeals in civil matters and the Court of Criminal Appeal shall have such jurisdiction and powers to hear and determine appeals in criminal matters as may be conferred upon them respectively by this Constitution or any other law.

(3) The judges of the Court of Civil Appeal and the Court of Criminal Appeal shall be the judges for the time being of the Supreme Court.

Appeals to Her Majesty in Council.

81.—(1) An appeal shall lie from decisions of the Court of Appeal or the Supreme Court to Her Majesty in Council as of right in the following cases:—

(a) final decisions, in any civil or criminal proceedings, on questions as to the interpretation of this Constitution;

(b) where the matter in dispute on the appeal to Her Majesty in Council is of the value of Rupees 10,000 or upwards or where the appeal involves, directly or indirectly, a claim to or a question respecting property or a right of the value of Rupees 10,000 or upwards, final decisions in any civil proceedings;

(c) final decisions in proceedings under section 17 of this Constitution; and

(d) in such other cases as may be prescribed by Parliament:

Provided that no such appeal shall lie from decisions of the Supreme Court in any case in which an appeal lies as of right from the Supreme Court to the Court of Appeal.

(2) An appeal shall lie from decisions of the Court of Appeal or the Supreme Court to Her Majesty in Council with the leave of the court in the following cases:—

(a) where in the opinion of the court the question involved in the appeal is one that, by reason of its great general or public importance or otherwise, ought to be submitted to Her Majesty in Council, final decisions in any civil proceedings; and

(b) in such other cases as may be prescribed by Parliament:

Provided that no such appeal shall lie from decisions of the Supreme Court in any case in which an appeal lies to the Court of Appeal, either as of right or by the leave of the Court of Appeal.

(3) The foregoing provisions of this section shall be subject to the provisions of section 37(6) of this Constitution and paragraphs 2(5), 3(2) and 4(4) of schedule 1 to this Constitution.

(4) In this section the references to final decisions of a court do not include any determination thereof that any application made thereto is merely frivolous or vexatious.

(5) Nothing in this section shall affect any right of Her Majesty to grant special leave to appeal to Her Majesty in Council from the decision of any court in any civil or criminal matter.

Supreme Court and subordinate courts.

82.—(1) The Supreme Court shall have jurisdiction to supervise any civil or criminal proceedings before any subordinate court and may make such orders, issue such writs and give such directions as it may consider appropriate for the purpose of ensuring that justice is duly administered by any such court.

(2) An appeal shall lie to the Supreme Court from decisions of subordinate courts in the following cases:—

(a) as of right from any final decision in any civil proceedings;

(b) as of right from any final decision in criminal proceedings whereby any person is adjudged to pay a fine of or exceeding such amount as may be prescribed or to be imprisoned with or without the option of a fine;

(c) by way of case stated, from any final decision in criminal proceedings on the ground that it is erroneous in point of law or in excess of jurisdiction ; and

(d) in such other cases as may be prescribed:

Provided that an appeal shall not lie to the Supreme Court from the decision given by a subordinate court in any case if, under any law—

(i) an appeal lies as of right from that decision to the Court of Appeal ;

(ii) an appeal lies from that decision to the Court of Appeal with the leave of the court that gave the decision or of some other court and that leave has not been withheld ;

(iii) an appeal lies as of right from that decision to another subordinate court ; or

(iv) an appeal lies from that decision to another subordinate court with the leave of the court that gave the decision or of some other court and that leave has not been withheld.

83.—(1) Subject to the provisions of sections 41(5), 64(3) and 101(1) of this Constitution, if any person alleges that any provision of this Constitution (other than Chapter II) has been contravened and that his interests are being or are likely to be affected by such contravention, then, without prejudice to any other action with respect to the same matter which is lawfully available, that person may apply to the Supreme Court for a declaration and for relief under this section. *Original jurisdiction of Supreme Court in constitutional questions.*

(2) The Supreme Court shall have jurisdiction, in any application made by any person in pursuance of the preceding subsection or in any other proceedings lawfully brought before the Court, to determine whether any provision of this Constitution (other than Chapter II) has been contravened and to make a declaration accordingly:

Provided that the Supreme Court shall not make a declaration in pursuance of the jurisdiction conferred by this subsection unless it is satisfied that the interests of the person by whom the application under the preceding subsection is made or, in the case of other proceedings before the Court, a party to these proceedings, are being or are likely to be affected.

(3) Where the Supreme Court makes a declaration in pursuance of the preceding subsection that any provision of the Constitution has been contravened and the person by whom the application under subsection (1) of this section was made or, in the case of other proceedings before the Court, the party in those proceedings in respect of whom the declaration is made, seeks relief, the Supreme Court may grant to that person such remedy, being a remedy available against any person in any proceedings in the Supreme Court under any law for the time being in force in Mauritius, as the Court considers appropriate.

(4) The Chief Justice may make rules with respect to the practice and procedure of the Supreme Court in relation to the jurisdiction and powers conferred on it by this section (including rules with respect to the time within which applications shall be made under subsection (1) of this section).

(5) Nothing in this section shall confer jurisdiction on the Supreme Court to hear or determine any such question as is referred to in section 37 of this Constitution or paragraph 2(5), 3(2) or 4(4) of

schedule 1 thereto otherwise than upon an application made in accordance with the provisions of that section or that paragraph, as the case may be.

Reference of constitutional questions to Supreme Court.

84.—(1) Where any question as to the interpretation of this Constitution arises in any court of law established for Mauritius (other than the Court of Appeal, the Supreme Court or a court martial) and the court is of opinion that the question involves a substantial question of law, the court shall refer the question to the Supreme Court.

(2) Where any question is referred to the Supreme Court in pursuance of this section, the Supreme Court shall give its decision upon the question and the court in which the question arose shall dispose of the case in accordance with that decision or, if the decision is the subject of an appeal to the Court of Appeal or Her Majesty in Council, in accordance with the decision of the Court of Appeal or, as the case may be, of Her Majesty in Council.

CHAPTER VIII

SERVICE COMMISSIONS AND THE PUBLIC SERVICE

Judicial and Legal Service Commission.

85.—(1) There shall be a Judicial and Legal Service Commission which shall consist of the Chief Justice, who shall be chairman, and the following members—

(a) the Senior Puisne Judge ;

(b) the chairman of the Public Service Commission ; and

(c) one other member (in this section referred to as " the appointed member ") appointed by the Governor-General, acting in accordance with the advice of the Chief Justice.

(2) The appointed member shall be a person who is or has been a judge of a court having unlimited jurisdiction in civil or criminal matters in some part of the Commonwealth or a court having jurisdiction in appeals from any such court.

(3) If the office of the appointed member is vacant or the appointed member is for any reason unable to perform the functions of his office, the Governor-General, acting in accordance with the advice of the Chief Justice, may appoint a person qualified for appointment as such a member to act as a member of the Commission and any person so appointed shall continue to act until his appointment is revoked by the Governor-General, acting in accordance with the advice of the Chief Justice.

Appointment, etc., of judicial and legal officers.

86.—(1) Power to appoint persons to hold or act in offices to which this section applies (including power to confirm appointments), to exercise disciplinary control over persons holding or acting in such offices and to remove such persons from office shall vest in the Judicial and Legal Service Commission.

(2) The offices to which this section applies are the offices specified in schedule 2 to this Constitution and such other offices as may be prescribed:

Provided that—

(a) if the name of any such office is changed, or any such office is abolished, the provisions of this section and that schedule shall have effect accordingly ;

(*b*) this section shall also apply to such other offices, being offices that in the opinion of the Judicial and Legal Service Commission are offices similar to those specified in schedule 2 to this Constitution, as may be prescribed by the Commission, acting with the concurrence of the Prime Minister.

87. The power to appoint persons to hold the offices of Ambassador, High Commissioner or other principal representative of Mauritius in any other country or accredited to any international organisation and to remove such persons from office shall vest in the Governor-General, acting in accordance with the advice of the Prime Minister: Appointments, etc., of principal representatives of Mauritius abroad.

Provided that before advising the Governor-General to appoint to any such office a person who holds or is acting in some other public office the Prime Minister shall consult the Public Service Commission.

88.—(1) There shall be a Public Service Commission, which shall consist of a chairman and four other members appointed by the Governor-General. Public Service Commission.

(2) No person shall be qualified for appointment as a member of the Public Service Commission if he is a member of, or a candidate for election to, the Assembly or any Local Authority, a public officer or a local government officer.

(3) Whenever the office of chairman of the Public Service Commission is vacant or the chairman is for any reason unable to perform the functions of his office, those functions shall be performed by such one of the other members of the Commission as the Governor-General may appoint.

(4) If at any time there are less than three members of the Public Service Commission besides the chairman or if any such member is acting as chairman or is for any reason unable to perform the functions of his office, the Governor-General may appoint a person qualified for appointment as a member of the Commission to act as a member, and any person so appointed shall continue to act until his appointment is revoked by the Governor-General.

(5) The functions of the Governor-General under this section shall be exercised by him after consultation with the Prime Minister and the Leader of the Opposition.

89.—(1) Subject to the provisions of this Constitution, power to appoint persons to hold or act in any offices in the public service (including power to confirm appointments), to exercise disciplinary control over persons holding or acting in such offices and to remove such persons from office shall vest in the Public Service Commission. Appointment, etc., of public officers.

(2) The Public Service Commission may, subject to such conditions as it thinks fit, delegate any of its powers under this section by directions in writing to any member of the Commission or to any public officer.

(3) The provisions of this section shall not apply in relation to any of the following offices—

(*a*) the office of Chief Justice or Senior Puisne Judge ;

(*b*) except for the purpose of making appointments thereto or to act therein, the office of Director of Audit ;

(*c*) the office of Ombudsman ;

(d) any office, appointments to which are within the functions of the Judicial and Legal Service Commission or the Police Service Commission ;

(e) any office to which section 87 of this Constitution applies ;

(f) any ecclesiastical office ;

(g) any office prescribed by the Public Service Commission acting with the concurrence of a Minister, being an office the emoluments attaching to which are paid at daily rates ; or

(h) any office of a temporary nature, the duties attaching to which are mainly advisory and which is to be filled by a person serving under a contract on non-pensionable terms.

(4) Before any appointment is made to the office of Secretary to the Cabinet, of Financial Secretary, of a Permanent Secretary or of any other supervising officer within the meaning of section 68 of this Constitution, the Public Service Commission shall consult the Prime Minister and no appointment to the office of Secretary to the Cabinet, of Financial Secretary or of a Permanent Secretary shall be made unless the Prime Minister concurs therein.

(5) Notwithstanding the preceding provisions of this section, the power to transfer any person holding any such office as is mentioned in the preceding subsection to any other such office, being an office carrying the same emoluments, shall vest in the Governor-General, acting in accordance with the advice of the Prime Minister.

(6) Before the Public Service Commission appoints to or to act in any public office any person holding or acting in any office the power to make appointments to which is vested in the Judicial and Legal Service Commission or the Police Service Commission, the Public Service Commission shall consult that Commission.

(7) Before making any appointment to any office on the staff of the Ombudsman, the Public Service Commission shall consult the Ombudsman.

(8) The Public Service Commission shall not exercise any of its powers in relation to any office on the personal staff of the Governor-General, or in relation to any person holding or acting in any such office, without the concurrence of the Governor-General, acting in his own deliberate judgment.

(9) References in this section to the office of Financial Secretary or of a Permanent Secretary are references to that office as established on 11th March 1968 and include references to any similar office established after that date that carries the same or higher emoluments.

Police Service Commission.

90.—(1) There shall be for Mauritius a Police Service Commission which shall consist of the chairman of the Public Service Commission as chairman, and four other members, who shall be appointed by the Governor-General.

(2) No person shall be qualified for appointment as a member of the Police Service Commission if he is a member of, or a candidate for election to, the Assembly or any Local Authority, a public officer or a local government officer.

(3) If at any time there are less than three members of the Police Service Commission besides the chairman or if any such member is

for any reason unable to perform the functions of his office, the Governor-General may appoint a person who is qualified for appointment as a member of the Commission to act as a member, and any person so appointed shall continue to act until his appointment to act is revoked by the Governor-General.

(4) The functions of the Governor-General under this section shall be exercised by him after consultation with the Prime Minister and the Leader of the Opposition.

91.—(1) Subject to the provisions of section 93 of this Constitution, power to appoint persons to hold or act in any office in the Police Force (including power to confirm appointments), to exercise disciplinary control over persons holding or acting in such offices and to remove such persons from office shall vest in the Police Service Commission: Appointment, etc., of Commissioner of Police and other members of Police Force.

Provided that appointments to the office of Commissioner of Police shall be made after consultation with the Prime Minister.

(2) The Police Service Commission may, subject to such conditions as it thinks fit, by directions in writing delegate any of its powers of discipline or removal from office to the Commissioner of Police or to any other officer of the Police Force, but no person shall be removed from office except with the confirmation of the Commission.

92.—(1) Subject to the provisions of this section, a person holding an office to which this section applies (hereinafter referred to as a " Commissioner ") shall vacate his office— Tenure of office of members of Commissions and the Ombudsman.

(a) at the expiration of three years from the date of his appointment ; or

(b) if any circumstances arise that, if he did not hold that office, would cause him to be disqualified for appointment thereto.

(2) A Commissioner may be removed from office only for inability to discharge the functions of his office (whether arising from infirmity of body or mind or any other cause) or for misbehaviour and shall not be so removed except in accordance with the provisions of this section.

(3) A Commissioner shall be removed from office by the Governor-General if the question of his removal from that office has been referred to a tribunal appointed under the next following subsection and the tribunal has recommended to the Governor-General that he ought to be removed from office for inability as aforesaid or for misbehaviour.

(4) If the Governor-General, acting in his own deliberate judgment, considers that the question of removing a Commissioner ought to be investigated, then—

(a) the Governor-General, acting in his own deliberate judgment, shall appoint a tribunal which shall consist of a chairman and not less than two other members, being persons who hold or have held office as a judge of a court having unlimited jurisdiction in civil and criminal matters in some part of the Commonwealth or of a court having jurisdiction in appeals from such a court ;

(b) that tribunal shall enquire into the matter and report on the facts thereof to the Governor-General and recommend to the Governor-General whether the Commissioner ought to be removed under this section.

(5) If the question of removing a Commissioner has been referred to a tribunal under this section, the Governor-General, acting in his own

deliberate judgment, may suspend the Commissioner from performing the functions of his office and any such suspension may at any time be revoked by the Governor-General, acting in his own deliberate judgment, and shall in any case cease to have effect if the tribunal recommends to the Governor-General that the Commissioner should not be removed.

(6) The offices to which this section applies are those of appointed member of the Judicial and Legal Service Commission, chairman or other member of the Public Service Commission and member of the Police Service Commission:

Provided that, in its application to the appointed member of the Judicial and Legal Service Commission, subsection (4) of this section shall have effect as if for the words "acting in his own deliberate judgment" there were substituted the words "acting in accordance with the advice of the Chief Justice".

(7) The provisions of this section shall apply to the office of Ombudsman as they apply to a person specified in subsection (6) of this section:

Provided that subsection (1) shall have effect as if the words "four years" were substituted for the words "three years".

Removal of certain officers.

93.—(1) Subject to the provisions of this section, a person holding an office to which this section applies shall vacate that office on attaining the retiring age.

(2) Any such person may be removed from office only for inability to discharge the functions of his office (whether arising from infirmity of body or mind or any other cause) or for misbehaviour and shall not be so removed except in accordance with the provisions of this section.

(3) Any such person shall be removed from office by the Governor-General if the question of his removal from that office has been referred to a tribunal appointed under the next following subsection and the tribunal has recommended to the Governor-General that he ought to be removed from office for inability as aforesaid or for misbehaviour.

(4) If the appropriate Commission considers that the question of removing any such person ought to be investigated, then—

(a) the Governor-General, acting in his own deliberate judgment, shall appoint a tribunal which shall consist of a chairman and not less than two other members, being persons who hold or have held office as a judge of a court having unlimited jurisdiction in civil and criminal matters in some part of the Commonwealth or a court having jurisdiction in appeals from such a court;

(b) that tribunal shall enquire into the matter and report on the facts thereof to the Governor-General and recommend to the Governor-General whether he ought to be removed under this section.

(5) If the question of removing any such person has been referred to a tribunal under this section, the Governor-General, acting in his own deliberate judgment, may suspend him from performing the functions of his office and any such suspension may at any time be

revoked by the Governor-General, acting in his own deliberate judgment, and shall in any case cease to have effect if the tribunal recommends to the Governor-General that he should not be removed.

(6) The offices to which this section applies are those of Electoral Commissioner, Director of Public Prosecutions, Commissioner of Police and Director of Audit.

(7) In this section "the appropriate Commission" means—

(a) in relation to a person holding the office of Electoral Commissioner or Director of Public Prosecutions, the Judicial and Legal Service Commission ;

(b) in relation to a person holding the office of Commissioner of Police, the Police Service Commission ;

(c) in relation to a person holding office of Director of Audit, the Public Service Commission.

(8) The retiring age for holders of the offices mentioned in subsection (6) of this section shall be the age of sixty years or such other age as may be prescribed :

Provided that a provision of any law, to the extent that it alters the age at which persons holding such offices shall vacate their offices, shall not have effect in relation to any such person after his appointment unless he consents to its having effect.

94.—(1) The law to be applied with respect to any pensions benefits that were granted to any person before 12th March 1968, shall be the law that was in force at the date on which those benefits were granted or any law in force at a later date that is not less favourable to that person. *Pensions laws and protection of pension rights.*

(2) The law to be applied with respect to any pensions benefits (not being benefits to which the preceding subsection applies) shall—

(a) in so far as those benefits are wholly in respect of a period of service as a public officer that commenced before 12th March 1968, be the law that was in force immediately before that date ; and

(b) in so far as those benefits are wholly or partly in respect of a period of service as a public officer that commenced after 11th March 1968, be the law in force on the date on which that period of service commenced,

or any law in force at a later date that is not less favourable to that person.

(3) Where a person is entitled to exercise an option as to which of two or more laws shall apply in his case, the law for which he opts shall, for the purposes of this section, be deemed to be more favourable to him than the other law or laws.

(4) All pensions benefits (except so far as they are a charge on some other fund and have been duly paid out of that fund to the person or authority to whom payment is due) shall be a charge on the Consolidated Fund.

(5) In this section "pensions benefits" means any pensions, compensation, gratuities or other like allowances for persons in respect of their service as public officers or for the widows, children, dependants or personal representatives of such persons in respect of such service.

(6) References in this section to the law with respect to pensions benefits include (without prejudice to their generality) references to the law regulating the circumstances in which such benefits may be granted or in which the grant of such benefits may be refused, the law regulating the circumstances in which any such benefits that have been granted may be withheld, reduced in amount or suspended and the law regulating the amount of any such benefits.

Power of Commissions in relation to pensions, etc.

95.—(1) Where under any law any person or authority has a discretion—

(a) to decide whether or not any pensions benefits shall be granted ; or

(b) to withhold, reduce in amount or suspend any such benefits that have been granted,

those benefits shall be granted and may not be withheld, reduced in amount or suspended unless the appropriate Commission concurs in the refusal to grant the benefits or, as the case may be, in the decision to withhold them, reduce them in amount or suspend them.

(2) Where the amount of any pensions benefits that may be granted to any person is not fixed by law, the amount of the benefits to be granted to him shall be the greatest amount for which he is eligible unless the appropriate Commission concurs in his being granted benefits of a smaller amount.

(3) The appropriate Commission shall not concur under subsection (1) or subsection (2) of this section in action taken on the ground that any person who holds or has held the office of Electoral Commissioner, Director of Public Prosecutions, judge of the Supreme Court, Commissioner of Police, Ombudsman or Director of Audit has been guilty of misbehaviour unless he has been removed from office by reason of such misbehaviour.

(4) In this section " the appropriate Commission " means—

(a) in the case of benefits for which any person may be eligible in respect of the service in the public service of a person who, immediately before he ceased to be a public officer, was subject to the disciplinary control of the Judicial and Legal Service Commission or that have been granted in respect of such service, the Judicial and Legal Service Commission ;

(b) in the case of benefits for which any person may be eligible in respect of the service in the public service of a person who, immediately before he ceased to be a public officer, was a member of the Police Force, the Police Service Commission ; and

(c) in any other case, the Public Service Commission.

(5) Any person who is entitled to the payment of any pensions benefits and who is ordinarily resident outside Mauritius may, within a reasonable time after he has received that payment, remit the whole of it (free from any deductions, charge or tax made or levied in respect of its remission) to any country of his choice outside Mauritius :

Provided that nothing in this subsection shall be construed as preventing—

(a) the attachment, by order of a court, of any payment or part of any payment to which a person is entitled in satisfaction of the judgment of a court or pending the determination of civil proceedings to which he is a party to the extent to which such attachment is permitted by the law with respect to pensions benefits that applies in the case of that person ; or

(b) the imposition of reasonable restrictions as to the manner in which any payment is to be remitted.

(6) In this section " pensions benefits " means any pensions, compensation, gratuities or other like allowances for persons in respect of their service as public officers or of the widows, children, dependants or personal representatives of such persons in respect of such service.

CHAPTER IX

THE OMBUDSMAN

96.—(1) There shall be an Ombudsman, whose office shall be a public office.

Office of Ombudsman.

(2) The Ombudsman shall be appointed by the Governor-General, acting after consultation with the Prime Minister, the Leader of the Opposition and such other persons, if any, as appear to the Governor-General, acting in his own deliberate judgment, to be leaders of parties in the Assembly.

(3) No person shall be qualified for appointment as Ombudsman if he is a member of, or a candidate for election to, the Assembly or any Local Authority or is a local government officer ; and no person holding the office of Ombudsman shall perform the functions of any other public office.

(4) The offices of the staff of the Ombudsman shall be public offices and shall consist of that of a Senior Investigations Officer and such other offices as may be prescribed by the Governor-General, acting after consultation with the Prime Minister.

97.—(1) Subject to the provisions of this section, the Ombudsman may investigate any action taken by any officer or authority to which this section applies in the exercise of administrative functions of that officer or authority, in any case in which a member of the public claims, or appears to the Ombudsman, to have sustained injustice in consequence of maladministration in connection with the action so taken and in which—

Investigations by Ombudsman.

(a) a complaint under this section is made ;

(b) he is invited to do so by any Minister or other member of the Assembly ; or

(c) he considers it desirable to do so of his own motion.

(2) This section applies to the following officers and authorities—

(a) any department of the Government ;

(b) the Police Force or any member thereof ;

(c) the Mauritius Prison Service or any other service maintained and controlled by the Government or any officer or authority of any such service ;

(d) any authority empowered to determine the person with whom any contract or class of contracts is to be entered into by or on behalf of the Government or any such officer or authority ;

(*e*) such other officers or authorities as may be prescribed by Parliament:

Provided that it shall not apply in relation to any of the following officers and authorities—

(i) the Governor-General or his personal staff ;

(ii) the Chief Justice ;

(iii) any Commission established by this Constitution or their staff ;

(iv) the Director of Public Prosecutions or any person acting in accordance with his instructions ;

(v) any person exercising powers delegated to him by the Public Service Commission or the Police Service Commission, being powers the exercise of which is subject to review or confirmation by the Commission by which they were delegated.

(3) A complaint under this section may be made by any individual, or by any body of persons whether incorporated or not, not being—

(*a*) an authority of the Government or a Local Authority or other authority or body constituted for purposes of the public service or local government ; or

(*b*) any other authority or body whose members are appointed by the Governor-General or by a Minister or whose revenues consist wholly or mainly of moneys provided from public funds.

(4) Where any person by whom a complaint might have been made under the last preceding subsection has died or is for any reason unable to act for himself, the complaint may be made by his personal representatives or by a member of his family or other individual suitable to represent him ; but except as aforesaid a complaint shall not be entertained unless made by the person aggrieved himself.

(5) The Ombudsman shall not conduct an investigation in respect of any complaint under this section unless the person aggrieved is resident in Mauritius (or, if he is dead, was so resident at the time of his death) or the complaint relates to action taken in relation to him while he was present in Mauritius or in relation to rights or obligations that accrued or arose in Mauritius.

(6) The Ombudsman shall not conduct an investigation under this section in respect of any complaint under this section in so far as it relates to any of the following matters, that is to say—

(*a*) any action in respect of which the person aggrieved has or had a right of appeal, reference or review to or before a tribunal constituted by or under any law in force in Mauritius ; or

(*b*) any action in respect of which the person aggrieved has or had a remedy by way of proceedings in any court of law:

Provided that—

(i) the Ombudsman may conduct such an investigation notwithstanding that the person aggrieved has or had such a right or remedy if satisfied that in the particular circumstances it is not reasonable to expect him to avail himself or to have availed himself of that right or remedy ; and

(ii) nothing in this subsection shall preclude the Ombudsman from conducting any investigation as to whether any of the provisions of Chapter II of this Constitution has been contravened.

(7) The Ombudsman shall not conduct an investigation in respect of any complaint made under this section in respect of any action if he is given notice in writing by the Prime Minister that the action was taken by a Minister or Parliamentary Secretary in person in the exercise of his own deliberate judgment.

(8) The Ombudsman shall not conduct an investigation in respect of any complaint made under this section where it appears to him—

(a) that the complaint is merely frivolous or vexatious ;

(b) that the subject-matter of the complaint is trivial ;

(c) that the person aggrieved has no sufficient interest in the subject-matter of the complaint ; or

(d) that the making of the complaint has, without reasonable cause, been delayed for more than twelve months.

(9) The Ombudsman shall not conduct an investigation under this section in respect of any matter if he is given notice by the Prime Minister that the investigation of that matter would not be in the interests of the security of Mauritius.

(10) In this section " action " includes failure to act.

98.—(1) Where the Ombudsman proposes to conduct an investigation under the preceding section, he shall afford to the principal officer of any department or authority concerned, and to any other person who is alleged to have taken or authorised the action in question, an opportunity to comment on any allegations made to the Ombudsman in respect thereof. *Procedure in respect of investigations.*

(2) Every such investigation shall be conducted in private but except as provided in this Constitution or as prescribed under section 102 of this Constitution the procedure for conducting an investigation shall be such as the Ombudsman considers appropriate in the circumstances of the case ; and without prejudice to the generality of the foregoing provision the Ombudsman may obtain information from such persons and in such manner, and make such enquiries, as he thinks fit, and may determine whether any person may be represented, by counsel or attorney-at-law or otherwise, in the investigation.

99.—(1) For the purposes of an investigation under section 97 of this Constitution the Ombudsman may require any Minister, officer or member of any department or authority concerned or any other person who in his opinion is able to furnish information or produce documents relevant to the investigation to furnish any such information or produce any such document. *Disclosure of information, etc.*

(2) For the purposes of any such investigation the Ombudsman shall have the same powers as the Supreme Court in respect of the attendance and examination of witnesses (including the administration of oaths and the examination of witnesses abroad) and in respect of the production of documents.

(3) No obligation to maintain secrecy or other restriction upon the disclosure of information obtained by or furnished to persons in the public service imposed by any law in force in Mauritius or any rule of law shall apply to the disclosure of information for the purposes of any such investigation ; and the Crown shall not be entitled in relation

to any such investigation to any such privilege in respect of the production of documents or the giving of evidence as is allowed by law in legal proceedings.

(4) No person shall be required or authorised by virtue of this section to furnish any information or answer any question or produce any document relating to proceedings of the Cabinet or any committee thereof ; and for the purposes of this subsection a certificate issued by the Secretary to the Cabinet with the approval of the Prime Minister and certifying that any information, question or document so relates shall be conclusive.

(5) The Attorney-General may give notice to the Ombudsman, with respect to any document or information specified in the notice, or any class of documents or information so specified, that in his opinion the disclosure of that document or information, or of documents or information of that class, would be contrary to the public interest in relation to defence, external relations or internal security ; and where such a notice is given nothing in this section shall be construed as authorising or requiring the Ombudsman or any member of his staff to communicate to any person for any purpose any document or information specified in the notice, or any document or information of a class so specified.

(6) Subject to subsection (3) of this section, no person shall be compelled for the purposes of an investigation under section 97 of this Constitution to give any evidence or produce any document which he could not be compelled to give or produce in proceedings before the Supreme Court.

Proceedings after investigation.

100.—(1) The provisions of this section shall apply in every case where, after making an investigation, the Ombudsman is of opinion that the action that was the subject-matter of investigation was—

(*a*) contrary to law ;

(*b*) based wholly or partly on a mistake of law or fact ;

(*c*) unreasonably delayed ; or

(*d*) otherwise unjust or manifestly unreasonable.

(2) If in any case to which this section applies the Ombudsman is of opinion—

(*a*) that the matter should be given further consideration ;

(*b*) that an omission should be rectified ;

(*c*) that a decision should be cancelled, reversed or varied ;

(*d*) that any practice on which the act, omission, decision or recommendation was based should be altered ;

(*e*) that any law on which the act, omission, decision or recommendation was based should be reconsidered ;

(*f*) that reasons should have been given for the decision ; or

(*g*) that any other steps should be taken,

the Ombudsman shall report his opinion, and his reasons therefor, to the principal officer of any department or authority concerned, and may make such recommendations as he thinks fit ; he may request that officer to notify him, within a specified time, of the steps (if any) that it is proposed to take to give effect to his recommendations ; and he shall also send a copy of his report and recommendations to the Prime Minister and to any Minister concerned.

(3) If within a reasonable time after the report is made no action is taken which seems to the Ombudsman to be adequate and appropriate, the Ombudsman, if he thinks fit, after considering the comments (if any) made by or on behalf of any department, authority, body or person affected, may send a copy of the report and recommendations to the Prime Minister and to any Minister concerned, and may thereafter make such further report to the Assembly on the matter as he thinks fit.

101.—(1) In the discharge of his functions, the Ombudsman shall not be subject to the direction or control of any other person or authority and no proceedings of the Ombudsman shall be called in question in any court of law. *Discharge of functions of Ombudsman.*

(2) In determining whether to initiate, continue or discontinue an investigation under section 97 of this Constitution the Ombudsman shall act in accordance with his own discretion ; and any question whether a complaint is duly made for the purposes of that section shall be determined by the Ombudsman.

(3) The Ombudsman shall make an annual report to the Governor-General concerning the discharge of his functions, which shall be laid before the Assembly.

102. There shall be such provision as may be prescribed for such supplementary and ancillary matters as may appear necessary or expedient in consequence of any of the provisions of this Chapter, including (without prejudice to the generality of the foregoing power) provision— *Supplementary and ancillary provision.*

   (a) for the procedure to be observed by the Ombudsman in performing his functions ;
   (b) for the manner in which complaints under section 97 of this Constitution may be made (including a requirement that such complaints should be transmitted to the Ombudsman through the intermediary of a member of the Assembly) ;
   (c) for the payment of fees in respect of any complaint or investigation ;
   (d) for the powers, protection and privileges of the Ombudsman and his staff or of other persons or authorities with respect to any investigation or report by the Ombudsman, including the privilege of communications to and from the Ombudsman and his staff ; and
   (e) the definition and trial of offences connected with the functions of the Ombudsman and his staff and the imposition of penalties for such offences.

CHAPTER X
FINANCE

103. All revenues or other moneys raised or received for the purposes of the Government (not being revenues or other moneys that are payable by or under any law into some other fund established for a specific purpose or that may by or under any law be retained by the authority that received them for the purposes of defraying the expenses of that authority) shall be paid into and form one Consolidated Fund. *Consolidated Fund.*

Withdrawals from Consolidated Fund or other public funds.

104.—(1) No moneys shall be withdrawn from the Consolidated Fund except—

(a) to meet expenditure that is charged upon the Fund by this Constitution or by any other law in force in Mauritius ; or

(b) where the issue of those moneys has been authorised by an Appropriation law or by a supplementary estimate approved by resolution of the Assembly or in such manner, and subject to such conditions, as may be prescribed in pursuance of section 106 of this Constitution.

(2) No moneys shall be withdrawn from any public fund of Mauritius other than the Consolidated Fund unless the issue of those moneys has been authorised by or under a law.

(3) No moneys shall be withdrawn from the Consolidated Fund except in the manner prescribed.

(4) The deposit of any moneys forming part of the Consolidated Fund with a bank or with the Crown Agents for Overseas Governments and Administrations or the investment of any such moneys in such securities as may be prescribed shall not be regarded as a withdrawal of those moneys from the Fund for the purposes of this section.

Authorisation of expenditure.

105.—(1) The Minister responsible for finance shall cause to be prepared and laid before the Assembly, before or not later than thirty days after the commencement of each financial year, estimates of the revenues and expenditure of Mauritius for that year.

(2) The heads of expenditure contained in the estimates for a financial year (other than expenditure charged upon the Consolidated Fund by this Constitution or any other law) shall be included in a bill, to be known as an Appropriation bill, introduced into the Assembly to provide for the issue from the Consolidated Fund of the sums necessary to meet that expenditure and the appropriation of those sums for the purposes specified in the bill.

(3) If in any financial year it is found—

(a) that the amount appropriated by the Appropriation law for the purposes included in any head of expenditure is insufficient or that a need has arisen for expenditure for a purpose for which no amount has been appropriated by the Appropriation law ; or

(b) that any moneys have been expended on any head of expenditure in excess of the amount appropriated for the purposes included in that head by the Appropriation law or for a purpose for which no amount has been appropriated by the Appropriation law,

a supplementary estimate showing the sums required or spent shall be laid before the Assembly and the heads of expenditure shall be included in a supplementary Appropriation bill introduced in the Assembly to provide for the appropriation of those sums, or in a motion or motions introduced into the Assembly for the approval of such expenditure.

(4) Where any supplementary expenditure has been approved in a financial year by a resolution of the Assembly in accordance with the provisions of the preceding subsection, a supplementary Appropriation bill shall be introduced in the Assembly, not later than the end of the financial year next following, providing for the appropriation of the sums so approved.

106. If the Appropriation law in respect of any financial year has not come into operation by the beginning of that financial year, the Minister responsible for finance may, to such extent and subject to such conditions as may be prescribed, authorise the withdrawal of moneys from the Consolidated Fund for the purpose of meeting expenditure necessary to carry on the services of the Government until the expiration of six months from the beginning of that financial year or the coming into operation of the Appropriation law, whichever is the earlier.

Authorisation of expenditure in advance of appropriation.

107.—(1) There shall be such provision as may be prescribed by Parliament for the establishment of a Contingencies Fund and for authorising the Minister responsible for finance, if he is satisfied that there has arisen an urgent and unforeseen need for expenditure for which no other provision exists, to make advances from that Fund to meet that need.

Contingencies Fund.

(2) Where any advance is made from the Contingencies Fund, a supplementary estimate shall be laid before the Assembly, and a bill or motion shall be introduced therein, as soon as possible for the purpose of replacing the amount so advanced.

108.—(1) There shall be paid to the holders of the offices to which this section applies such salaries and such allowances as may be prescribed.

Remuneration of certain officers.

(2) The salaries and any allowances payable to the holders of the offices to which this section applies shall be a charge on the Consolidated Fund.

(3) Any alteration to the salary payable to any person holding any office to which this section applies or to his terms of office, other than allowances, that is to his disadvantage shall not have effect in relation to that person after his appointment unless he consents to its having effect.

(4) Where a person's salary or terms of office depend upon his option, the salary or terms for which he opts shall, for the purposes of the last preceding subsection, be deemed to be more advantageous to him than any others for which he might have opted.

(5) This section applies to the office of Governor-General, chairman or other members of the Electoral Boundaries Commission or of the Electoral Supervisory Commission, Electoral Commissioner, Director of Public Prosecutions, Chief Justice, Senior Puisne Judge, Puisne Judge, appointed member of the Judicial and Legal Service Commission, chairman or other member of the Public Service Commission, appointed member of the Police Service Commission, Commissioner of Police, Ombudsman or Director of Audit.

109.—(1) All debt charges for which Mauritius is liable shall be a charge on the Consolidated Fund.

Public debt.

(2) For the purposes of this section debt charges include interest, sinking fund charges, the repayment or amortisation of debt, and all expenditure in connection with the raising of loans on the security of the revenues of Mauritius or the Consolidated Fund and the service and redemption of debt thereby created.

Director
of Audit.

110.—(1) There shall be a Director of Audit, whose office shall be a public office and who shall be appointed by the Public Service Commission, acting after consultation with the Prime Minister and the Leader of the Opposition.

(2) The public accounts of Mauritius and of all courts of law and all authorities and officers of the Government shall be audited and reported on by the Director of Audit and for that purpose the Director of Audit or any person authorised by him in that behalf shall have access to all books, records, reports and other documents relating to those accounts :

Provided that, if it is so prescribed in the case of any body corporate directly established by law, the accounts of that body corporate shall be audited and reported on by such person as may be prescribed.

(3) The Director of Audit shall submit his reports to the Minister responsible for finance, who shall cause them to be laid before the Assembly.

(4) In the exercise of his functions under this Constitution the Director of Audit shall not be subject to the direction or control of any other person or authority.

CHAPTER XI

MISCELLANEOUS

Interpretation.

111.—(1) In this Constitution, unless the context otherwise requires—

" the Assembly " means the Legislative Assembly established by this Constitution ;

" the Commonwealth " means Mauritius and any country to which section 25 of this Constitution for the time being applies, and includes the dependencies of any such country ;

" the Court of Appeal " means the Court of Civil Appeal or the Court of Criminal Appeal ;

" the Crown " means the Crown in right of Mauritius ;

" disciplinary law " means a law regulating the discipline—

(*a*) of any disciplined force ; or

(*b*) of persons serving prison sentences ;

" disciplined force " means—

(*a*) a naval, military or air force ;

(*b*) the Police Force ;

(*c*) a fire service established by any law in force in Mauritius ; or

(*d*) the Mauritius Prison Service ;

" financial year " means the period of twelve months ending on the thirtieth day of June in any year or such other day as may be prescribed by Parliament ;

" the Gazette " means the Government Gazette of Mauritius ;

" the Government " means Her Majesty's Government of Mauritius ;

" the Governor-General " means the Governor-General and Commander-in-Chief of Mauritius ;

" the Island of Mauritius " includes the small islands adjacent thereto ;

" Local Authority " means the Council of a town, district or village in Mauritius ;

" local government officer " means a person holding or acting in any office of emolument in the service of a Local Authority but does not include a person holding or acting in the office of Mayor, Chairman or other member of a Local Authority or Standing Counsel or Attorney of a Local Authority ;

" Mauritius " means the territories which immediately before 12th March 1968 constituted the colony of Mauritius ;

" oath " includes affirmation ;

" oath of allegiance " means such oath of allegiance as prescribed in schedule 3 to this Constitution ;

" Parliament " means the Parliament established by this Constitution ;

" the Police Force " means the Mauritius Police Force and includes any other police force established in accordance with such provision as may be prescribed by Parliament ;

" prescribed " means prescribed in a law:

Provided that—

(a) in relation to anything that may be prescribed only by Parliament, it means prescribed in any Act of Parliament ; and

(b) in relation to anything that may be prescribed only by some other specified person or authority, it means prescribed in an order made by that other person or authority ;

" public office " means, subject to the provisions of the next following section, an office of emolument in the public service ;

" public officer " means the holder of any public office and includes a person appointed to act in any public office ;

" the public service " means the service of the Crown in a civil capacity in respect of the government of Mauritius ;

" Rodrigues " means the Island of Rodrigues ;

" session " means the sittings of the Assembly commencing when Parliament first meets after any general election or its prorogation at any time and terminating when Parliament is prorogued or is dissolved without having been prorogued ;

" sitting " means a period during which the Assembly is sitting continuously without adjournment, and includes any period during which the Assembly is in committee ;

" subordinate court " means any court of law subordinate to the Supreme Court but does not include a court-martial.

(2) Save as otherwise provided in this Constitution, the Interpretation Act 1889(a) shall apply, with the necessary adaptations, for the purpose of interpreting this Constitution and otherwise in relation thereto as it applies for the purpose of interpreting and in relation to Acts of the Parliament of the United Kingdom.

(a) 1889 c. 63.

References to public office, etc.

112.—(1) In this Constitution, unless the context otherwise requires, the expression " public office "—

(a) shall be construed as including the offices of judges of the Supreme Court, the offices of members of all other courts of law in Mauritius (other than courts-martial), the offices of members of the Police Force and the offices on the Governor-General's personal staff ; and

(b) shall not be construed as including the office of Speaker or Deputy Speaker of the Assembly, Minister, Parliamentary Secretary, member of the Assembly or member of any Commission or tribunal established by this Constitution.

(2) For the purposes of this Constitution, a person shall not be considered as holding a public office or a local government office, as the case may be, by reason only that he is in receipt of a pension or other like allowance in respect of service under the Crown or under a Local Authority.

(3) For the purposes of sections 38(3), 88(2) and 90(2) of this Constitution, a person shall not be considered as holding a public office or a local government office, as the case may be, by reason only that he is in receipt of fees and allowances by virtue of his membership of a board, council, committee, tribunal or other similar authority (whether incorporated or not).

Appointments to certain offices for terms of years.

113.—(1) It shall be lawful for a suitably qualified person to be appointed (regardless of his age) to hold any office to which this section applies for such term (not being less than four years) as may be specified in the instrument of appointment and the provisions of this Constitution shall have effect in relation to any person so appointed as if he would attain the retiring age applicable to that office on the day on which the specified term expires.

(2) This section applies to the office of Electoral Commissioner, Director of Public Prosecutions, Chief Justice, Senior Puisne Judge, Puisne Judge, Commissioner of Police or Director of Audit.

Acting appointments.

114.—(1) In this Constitution, unless the context otherwise requires, a reference to the holder of an office by the term designating his office shall be construed as including a reference to any person for the time being lawfully acting in or exercising the functions of that office.

(2) Where power is vested by this Constitution in any person or authority to appoint any person to act in or perform the functions of any office if the holder thereof is himself unable to perform those functions, no such appointment shall be called in question on the ground that the holder of the office was not unable to perform those functions.

Reappointments and concurrent appointments.

115.—(1) Where any person has vacated any office established by this Constitution, he may, if qualified, again be appointed or elected to hold that office in accordance with the provisions of this Constitution.

(2) Where a power is conferred by this Constitution upon any person to make any appointment to any office, a person may be appointed to that office notwithstanding that some other person may be holding that office, when that other person is on leave of absence pending the relinquishment of the office ; and where two or more persons are holding the same office by reason of an appointment made in pursuance of this

subsection, then, for the purposes of any function conferred upon the holder of that office, the person last appointed shall be deemed to be the sole holder of the office.

116.—(1) References in this Constitution to the power to remove a public officer from his office shall be construed as including references to any power conferred by any law to require or permit that officer to retire from the public service and to any power or right to terminate a contract on which a person is employed as a public officer and to determine whether any such contract shall or shall not be renewed: Removal from office.

Provided that—

(a) nothing in this subsection shall be construed as conferring on any person or authority power to require any person to whom the provisions of section 78(2) to (6) or section 92(2) to (5) apply to retire from the public service ; and

(b) any power conferred by any law to permit a person to retire from the public service shall, in the case of any public officer who may be removed from office by some person or authority other than a Commission established by this Constitution, vest in the Public Service Commission.

(2) Any provision in this Constitution that vests in any person or authority power to remove any public officer from his office shall be without prejudice to the power of any person or authority to abolish any office or to any law providing for the compulsory retirement of public officers generally or any class of public officer on attaining an age specified therein.

117. Any person who has been appointed to any office established by this Constitution may resign from that office by writing under his hand addressed to the person or authority by whom he was appointed ; and the resignation shall take effect, and the office shall accordingly become vacant— Resignations.

(a) at such time or on such date (if any) as may be specified in the writing ; or

(b) when the writing is received by the person or authority to whom it is addressed or by such other person as may be authorised by that person or authority to receive it,

whichever is the later:

Provided that the resignation may be withdrawn before it takes effect if the person or authority to whom the resignation is addressed consents to its withdrawal.

118.—(1) Any Commission established by this Constitution may by regulations make provision for regulating and facilitating the performance by the Commission of its functions under this Constitution. Performance of functions of Commissions and tribunals.

(2) Any decision of any such Commission shall require the concurrence of a majority of all the members thereof and, subject as aforesaid, the Commission may act notwithstanding the absence of any member:

Provided that if in any particular case a vote of all the members is taken to decide the question and the votes cast are equally divided the chairman shall have and shall exercise a casting vote.

(3) Subject to the provisions of this section, any such Commission may regulate its own procedure.

(4) In the exercise of their functions under this Constitution, no such Commission shall be subject to the direction or control of any other person or authority.

(5) In addition to the functions conferred upon it by or under this Constitution any such Commission shall have such powers and other functions (if any) as may be prescribed.

(6) The validity of the transaction of business of any such Commission shall not be affected by the fact that some person who was not entitled to do so took part in the proceedings.

(7) The provisions of subsections (1), (2), (3) and (4) of this section shall apply in relation to a tribunal established for the purposes of section 5(4), 15(4), 18(3), 78(4), 92(4) or 93(4) of this Constitution as they apply in relation to a Commission established by this Constitution, and any such tribunal shall have the same powers as the Supreme Court in respect of the attendance and examination of witnesses (including the administration of oaths and the examination of witnesses abroad) and in respect of the production of documents.

Saving for jurisdiction of courts.
119. No provision of this Constitution that any person or authority shall not be subject to the direction or control of any other person or authority in the exercise of any functions under this Constitution shall be construed as precluding a court of law from exercising jurisdiction in relation to any question whether that person or authority has performed those functions in accordance with this Constitution or any other law or should not perform those functions.

Power to amend and revoke instruments, etc.
120. Where any power is conferred by this Constitution to make any order, regulation or rule, or to give any direction, the power shall be construed as including the power, exercisable in like manner, to amend or revoke any such order, regulation, rule or direction.

Consultation.
121. Where any person or authority other than the Governor is directed by this Constitution to exercise any function after consultation with any other person or authority, that person or authority shall not be obliged to exercise that function in accordance with the advice of that other person or authority.

Parliamentary control over certain subordinate legislation.
122. All laws other than Acts of Parliament that make any such provision as is mentioned in section 5(1) or section 15(3) of this Constitution or that establish new criminal offences or impose new penalties shall be laid before the Assembly as soon as is practicable after they are made and (without prejudice to any other power that may be vested in the Assembly in relation to any such law) any such law may be revoked by the Assembly by resolution passed within thirty days after it is laid before the Assembly:

Provided that

(a) if it is so prescribed by Parliament in relation to any such law, that law shall not be laid before the Assembly during a period of public emergency within the meaning of Chapter II of this Constitution:

(*b*) in reckoning the period of thirty days after any such law is laid before the Assembly no account shall be taken of any period during which Parliament is dissolved or prorogued or is adjourned for more than four days.

SCHEDULE 1 TO THE CONSTITUTION
Election of Members of Legislative Assembly

Section 31(2).

1.—(1) There shall be sixty-two seats in the Assembly for members representing constituencies and accordingly each constituency shall return three members to the Assembly in such manner as may be prescribed, except Rodrigues, which shall so return two members. *Elected members to be returned by constituencies.*

(2) Every member returned by a constituency shall be directly elected in accordance with the provisions of this Constitution at a general election or by-election held in such manner as may be prescribed.

(3) Every vote cast by an elector at any election shall be given by means of a ballot which, except in so far as may be otherwise prescribed in relation to the casting of votes by electors who are incapacitated by blindness or other physical cause or unable to read or understand any symbols on the ballot paper, shall be taken so as not to disclose how any vote is cast ; and no vote cast by any elector at any general election shall be counted unless he cast valid votes for three candidates in the constituency in which he is registered or, in the case of an elector registered in Rodrigues, for two candidates in that constituency.

2.—(1) Every political party in Mauritius, being a lawful association, may, within fourteen days before the day appointed for the nomination of candidates for election at any general election of members of the Assembly, be registered as a party for the purposes of that general election and paragraph 5(7) of this schedule by the Electoral Supervisory Commission upon making application in such manner as may be prescribed: *Registration of parties, etc.*

Provided that any two or more political parties may be registered as a party alliance for those purposes, in which case they shall be regarded as a single party for those purposes ; and the provisions of this schedule shall be construed accordingly.

(2) Every candidate for election at any general election may at his nomination declare in such manner as may be prescribed that he belongs to a party that is registered as such for the purposes of that general election and, if he does so, he shall be regarded as a member of that party for those purposes, while if he does not do so, he shall not be regarded as a member of any party for those purposes ; and where any candidate is regarded as a member of a party for those purposes, the name of that party shall be stated on any ballot paper prepared for those purposes upon which his name appears.

(3) Where any party is registered under this paragraph, the Electoral Supervisory Commission shall from time to time be furnished in such manner as may be prescribed with the names of at least two persons, any one of whom is authorised to discharge the functions of leader of that party for the purposes of the proviso to paragraph 5(7) of this schedule.

(4) There shall be such provision as may be prescribed requiring persons who make applications or declarations for the purposes of this paragraph to furnish evidence with respect to the matters stated in such applications or declarations and to their authority to make such applications or declarations.

(5) There shall be such provision as may be prescribed for the determination, by a single judge of the Supreme Court before the day

appointed for the nomination of candidates at a general election, -of any question incidental to any such application or declaration made in relation to that general election ; and the determination of the judge therein shall not be subject to appeal.

Communities.

3.—(1) Every candidate for election at any general election of members of the Assembly shall declare in such manner as may be prescribed which community he belongs to and that community shall be stated in a published notice of his nomination.

(2) Within seven days of the nomination of any candidate for election at any general election an application may be made by any elector in such manner as may be prescribed to the Supreme Court to resolve any question as to the correctness of the declaration relating to his community made by that candidate in connection with his nomination, in which case the application shall (unless withdrawn) be heard and determined by a single judge of the Supreme Court, in such manner as may be prescribed, within fourteen days of the nomination ; and the determination of the judge therein shall not be subject to appeal.

(3) For the purposes of this schedule, each candidate for election at any general election shall be regarded as belonging to the community to which he declared he belonged at his nomination as such or, if the Supreme Court has held in proceedings questioning the correctness of his declaration that he belongs to another community, to that other community ; but the community to which any candidate belongs for those purposes shall not be stated upon any ballot paper prepared for those purposes.

(4) For the purposes of this schedule, the population of Mauritius shall be regarded as including a Hindu community, a Muslim community and a Sino-Mauritian community ; and every person who does not appear, from his way of life, to belong to one or other of those three communities shall be regarded as belonging to the General Population, which shall itself be regarded as a fourth community.

Provisions with respect to nominations.

4.—(1) If it is so prescribed, every candidate for election as a member of the Assembly shall in connection with his nomination make a declaration in such manner as may be prescribed concerning his qualifications for election as such.

(2) There shall be such provision as may be prescribed for the determination by a returning officer of questions concerning the validity of any nomination of a candidate for election as a member of the Assembly.

(3) If a returning officer decides that a nomination is valid, his decision shall not be questioned in any proceedings other than proceedings under section 37 of this Constitution.

(4) If a returning officer decides that a nomination is invalid, his decision may be questioned upon an application to a single judge of the Supreme Court made within such time and in such manner as may be prescribed, and the determination of the judge therein shall not be subject to appeal.

Allocation of eight additional seats.

5.—(1) In order to ensure a fair and adequate representation of each community, there shall be eight seats in the Assembly, additional to the sixty-two seats for members representing constituencies, which shall so far as is possible be allocated to persons (if any) belonging to parties who have stood as candidates for election as members at the general election but have not been returned as member to represent constituencies.

(2) As soon as is practicable after all the returns have been made of persons elected at any general election as members to represent constituencies, the eight additional seats shall be allocated in accordance with

the following provisions of this paragraph by the Electoral Supervisory Commission which shall so far as is possible make a separate determination in respect of each seat to ascertain the appropriate unreturned candidate (if any) to fill that seat.

(3) The first four of the eight seats shall so far as is possible each be allocated to the most successful unreturned candidate (if any) who is a member of a party and who belongs to the appropriate community, regardless of which party he belongs to.

(4) When the first four seats (or as many as possible of those seats) have been allocated, the number of such seats that have been allocated to persons who belong to parties other than the most successful party shall be ascertained and so far as is possible that number of seats out of the second four seats shall one by one be allocated to the most successful unreturned candidates (if any) belonging both to the most successful party and to the appropriate community.

(5) In the event that any of the eight seats remains unfilled, then the following procedure shall so far as is possible be followed until all (or as many as possible) of the eight seats are filled, that is to say, one seat shall be allocated to the most successful unreturned candidate (if any) belonging both to the most successful of the parties that have not received any of the eight seats and to the appropriate community, the next seat (if any) shall be allocated to the most successful unreturned candidate (if any) belonging both to the second most successful of those parties and to the appropriate community, and so on as respects any remaining seats and any remaining parties that have not received any of the eight seats.

(6) In the event that any of the eight seats still remains unfilled, then the following procedure shall so far as is possible be followed (and, if necessary, repeated) until all (or as many as possible) of the eight seats are filled, that is to say, one seat shall be allocated to the most successful unreturned candidate (if any) belonging both to the second most successful party and to the appropriate community, the next seat (if any) shall be allocated to the most successful unreturned candidate (if any) belonging both to the third most successful part (if any) and to the appropriate community, and so on as respects any remaining seats and parties.

(7) If at any time before the next dissolution of Parliament, one of the eight seats falls vacant, the seat shall as soon as is reasonably practicable after the occurrence of the vacancy be allocated by the Electoral Supervisory Commission to the most successful unreturned candidate (if any) available who belongs to the appropriate community and to the party to whom the person to whom the seat was allocated at the last general election belonged:

Provided that, if no candidate of the appropriate community who belongs to that party is available, the seat shall be allocated to the most successful unreturned candidate available who belongs to the appropriate community and who belongs to such other party as is designated by the leader of the party with no available candidate.

(8) The appropriate community means, in relation to the allocation of any of the eight seats, the community that has an unreturned candidate available (being a person of the appropriate party, if the seat is one of the second four seats) and that would have the highest number of persons (as determined by reference to the results of the latest published official census of the whole population of Mauritius) in relation to the number of seats in the Assembly held immediately before the allocation of the seat by persons belonging to that community (whether as members elected to represent constituencies or otherwise), if the seat were also held by a person belonging to that community:

Provided that, if, in relation to the allocation of any seat, two or more communities have the same number of persons as aforesaid, preference shall be given to the community with an unreturned candidate who was more successful than the unreturned candidates of the other community or communities (that candidate and those other candidates being persons of the appropriate party, if the seat is one of the second four seats).

(9) The degree of success of a party shall, for the purposes of allocating any of the eight seats at any general election of members of the Assembly, be assessed by reference to the number of candidates belonging to that party returned as members to represent constituencies at that election as compared with the respective numbers of candidates of other parties so returned, no account being taken of a party that had no candidates so returned or of any change in the membership of the Assembly occurring because the seat of a member so returned becomes vacant for any cause; and the degree of success of an unreturned candidate of a particular community (or of a particular party and community) at any general election shall be assessed by comparing the percentage of all the valid votes cast in the constituency in which he stood for election secured by him at that election with the percentages of all the valid votes cast in the respective constituencies in which they stood for election so secured by other unreturned candidates of that particular community (or, as the case may be, of that particular party and that particular community), no account being taken of the percentage of votes secured by any unreturned candidate who has already been allocated one of the eight seats at that election or by any unreturned candidate who is not a member of a party:

Provided that if, in relation to the allocation of any seat, any two or more parties have the same number of candidates returned as members elected to represent constituencies, preference shall be given to the party with an appropriate unreturned candidate who was more successful than the appropriate unreturned candidate or candidates of the other party or parties.

(10) Any number required for the purposes of sub-paragraph (8) of this paragraph or any percentage required for the purposes of sub-paragraph (9) of this paragraph shall be calculated to not more than three places of decimals if it cannot be expressed as a whole number.

Section 86.

SCHEDULE 2 TO THE CONSTITUTION

OFFICES WITHIN JURISDICTION OF JUDICIAL AND LEGAL SERVICE COMMISSION

Solicitor-General.

Master and Registrar of the Supreme Court.

Senior Crown Counsel.

Magistrate (including the President or a Magistrate of the Intermediate Criminal Court or of the Industrial Court).

Crown Counsel.

Crown Attorney.

Assistant Crown Attorney.

SCHEDULE 3 TO THE CONSTITUTION

OATHS

Oath of Allegiance

I,   , do swear [or solemnly affirm] that
I will be faithful and bear true allegiance to Her Majesty Queen Elizabeth
II, Her Heirs and Successors, according to law. [So help me God.]

*Oath for the due execution of
the office of Governor-General.*

I,   , do swear [or solemnly affirm] that
I will well and truly serve Her Majesty Queen Elizabeth II, Her Heirs and
Successors, in the office of Governor-General. [So help me God.]

*Oath for the due execution of
the office of Prime Minister or
other Minister or Parliamentary
Secretary.*

I,   , being
appointed Prime Minister/Minister/Parliamentary Secretary, do swear [or
solemnly affirm] that I will to the best of my judgment, at all times when
so required, freely give my counsel and advice to the Governor-General
(or any other person for the time being lawfully performing the functions
of that office) for the good management of the public affairs of Mauritius,
and I do further swear [or solemnly affirm] that I will not on any account,
at any time whatsoever, disclose the counsel, advice, opinion or vote of any
particular Minister or Parliamentary Secretary and that I will not, except
with the authority of the Cabinet and to such extent as may be required
for the good management of the affairs of Mauritius, directly or indirectly
reveal the business or proceedings of the Prime Minister/Minister/
Parliamentary Secretary or any matter coming to my knowledge in my
capacity as such and that in all things I will be a true and faithful Prime
Minister/Minister/Parliamentary Secretary. [So help me God.]

Judicial Oath.

I,   , do swear
[or solemnly affirm] that I will well and truly serve Our Sovereign Lady
Queen Elizabeth II, Her Heirs and Successors, in the office of Chief
Justice/judge of the Supreme Court and I will do right to all manner of
people after the laws and usages of Mauritius without fear or favour,
affection or ill will. [So help me God.]

EXPLANATORY NOTE

(This Note is not part of the Order.)

By virtue of the Mauritius Independence Act 1968 Mauritius will attain fully responsible status within the Commonwealth on 12th March 1968. This Order makes provision for a Constitution for Mauritius to come into effect on that day, including provision for the legislature, executive government, the judicature and the public service. The Constitution also contains provisions relating to citizenship of Mauritius and fundamental rights and freedoms of the individual.

SEYCHELLES

The Seychelles Civil Appeals (Amendment) Order 1968

At the Court at Buckingham Palace, the 4th day of March 1968

Present,

The Queen's Most Excellent Majesty in Council

Her Majesty, in exercise of the powers enabling Her in that behalf, is pleased, by and with the advice of Her Privy Council, to order, and it is hereby ordered, as follows :—

1.—(1) This Order may be cited as the Seychelles Civil Appeals (Amendment) Order 1968.

(2) This Order shall be construed as one with the Seychelles Civil Appeals Order 1967(**a**) and this Order and that Order may be cited together as the Seychelles Civil Appeals Orders 1967 and 1968.

(3) This Order shall come into operation on the appointed day.

Citation, construction and commencement.

2. In this Order, unless the context otherwise requires—

" the appointed day " means 12th March 1968 ;

" Court " means the Court of Civil Appeal for Mauritius as from time to time established.

Interpretation.

3. Section 3 of the Seychelles Civil Appeals Order 1967 is amended by inserting the word " Civil " before the word " Appeal " in sub-section (1) thereof.

Amendment to section 3 of the Seychelles Civil Appeals Order 1967.

4.—(1) An appeal from any decision of the Supreme Court of Seychelles pending immediately before the appointed day in the Court may be continued and concluded after that day in the Court as if the appeal had been commenced in the Court after that day.

(2) A decision of the Court on an appeal from the Supreme Court of Seychelles given before the appointed day may be enforced or otherwise dealt with in Seychelles as if it were a decision of the Court given after that day on such an appeal.

Pending appeals and enforcement of decisions given before appointed day.

W. G. Agnew.

(**a**) S.I. 1967 III, p. 5414.

EXPLANATORY NOTE

(This Note is not part of the Order.)

This Order makes provision relating to appeals from the Supreme Court of Seychelles to the Court of Civil Appeal for Mauritius and the enforcement of decisions of the Mauritius Court on such appeals consequent on that Court being re-established by the Constitution of Mauritius set out in the Schedule to the Mauritius Independence Order 1968.

ROAD TRAFFIC

The Breath Test Device (Approval) (No. 2) Order 1968

In pursuance of the power conferred on me by section 7(1) of the Road Safety Act 1967(a), I, the Right Honourable Denis Healey, one of Her Majesty's Principal Secretaries of State, do by this order approve, for the purpose of breath tests as defined in the said section 7(1), the type of device described in the Schedule hereto.

Denis Healey,
One of Her Majesty's Principal
Secretaries of State.

Dated 13th March 1968.

SCHEDULE

The device known as the Alcotest, comprising an indicator tube (marked with the name "Alcotest"), mouth piece and measuring bag, and supplied to members of the provost staff (as defined in section 6(3) of the said Act of 1967) in a container marked with the name "ALCOTEST®80"

(a) 1967 c. 30.

Modifications to Legislation

Year and Number (or date)	Act or instrument	How affected
1843	Theatres Act 1843 (c. 68)	s. 6 **am.** (E. and W.) 1968/170, (S.) 1968/248
1847	Town Police Clauses Act 1847 (c. 89)	s. 46 **am.**, 1968/170
1860	Game Licences Act 1860 (c. 90) ...	ss. 2, 7, 13 **am.**, 1968/120
1871	Pedlars Act 1871 (c. 96)	s. 5 **am.**, 1968/170
1872	Pawnbrokers Act 1872 (c. 93) ...	s. 37 **am.**, 1968/120
1875	Explosives Act 1875 (c. 17)	ss. 15, 18, 21 **am.** (E. and W.) 1968/170, (S.) 1968/248
1876	Sheriff Courts (S.) Act 1876 (c. 70) ...	s. 45 **am.**, 1968/140
Instrt. not S.I. 1 Apr.	Public Works Loans Act 1875—Regs. (Rev. XVIII p. 899)	**r.**, 1968/458
1879 18 Dec.	Public Works Loans Act 1875—further Regs. (Rev. XVIII, p. 901)	**r.**, 1968/458
1881	Fugitive Offenders Act 1881 (c. 69) ...	**r.**, exc. s. 25 in pt. (Cayman Is.) 1968/112, (Falkland Is. and Dependencies) 1968/113, (British Indian Ocean Territory) 1968/183, (St. Helena) 1968/184, (Turks and Caicos Is.) 1968/185
1883	Customs and Inland Revenue Act 1883 (c. 10)	s. 5 **am.**, 1968/120
1888 19 Jan.	Bermuda L.P. 1888 (Rev. III, p. 119)	**r.**, 1968/182

Year and Number (or date)	Act or instrument	How affected
1889 31 May	Preparation, issue and cancellation of Treas. Bills—Minute (Rev. XXIII, p. 289)	**r.**, 1968/414
1890	Foreign Jurisdiction Act 1890 (c. 37)	sch. 1 **am.** (Cayman Is.) 1968/112, (Falkland Is. and Dependencies) 1968/113, (British Indian Ocean Territory) 1968/183, (St. Helena) 1968/184, (Turks and Caicos Is.) 1968/185
	Public Health Acts Amdt. Act 1890 (c. 59)	s. 51 para. 1 **am.**, 1968/170
1892	Burgh Police (S.) Act 1892 (c. 55) ...	ss. 275, 396, sch. 5 para. 2 **am.**, 1968/248
1897 884	Merchant Shipping Act 1894, exercise of powers of British Consular Officer in Gilbert and Ellice Is. and Solomon Is.—O. in C. 1897 (Rev. XIV, p. 687)	**r.**, 1968/293
1898	Merchant Shipping (Mercantile Marine Fund) Act 1898 (c. 44)	sch. 2 **am.**, 1968/580
1904 24 Jan.	Tenders for Treas. Bills — Amdg. Minute (H. of C. Paper 1) (2 Feb., 1904)	**r.**, 1968/414
1907	Public Health Acts Amdt. Act 1907 (c. 53)	s. 94 **am.**, 1968/170
1908 1318	Merchant Shipping Act 1894, exercise of powers of British Consular Officer in Gilbert and Ellice Is. and Solomon Is.—O. in C. 1908 (Rev. XIV, p. 688)	**r.**, 1968/293
1909	Cinematograph Act 1909 (c. 30) ...	s. 2 **am.** (E. and W.) 1968/170, (S.) 1968/248

Year and Number (or date)	Act or instrument	How affected
1915	Fugitive Offenders (Protected States) Act 1915 (c. 39)	**r.**, (Cayman Is.) 1968/112, (Falkland Is. and Dependencies) 1968/113, (British Indian Ocean Territory) 1968/183, (St. Helena) 1968/184, (Turks and Caicos Is.) 1968/184
13 Apr.	Preparation, issue and cancellation of Treasury Bills—Treas. Minute (H. of C. Paper 199 (15 Apr. 1915))	**r.**, 1968/414
25 Nov.	Bermuda R. Instructions 1915 ...	**r.**, 1968/182
1920	Official Secrets Act 1920 (c. 75) ...	s. 5 **am.** (E. and W.) 1968/170, (S.) 1968/248
1923	Fees (Increase) Act 1923 (c. 4) ...	s. 9 **am.**, 1968/656
1925	Performing Animals (Regulation) Act 1925 (c. 38)	s. 5 **am.** (E. and W.) 1968/170, (S.) 1968/248
	Theatrical Employers Registration Act 1925 (c. 50)	s. 3 **am.** (E. and W.) 1968/170, (S.) 1968/248
1926	Home Counties (Music and Dancing) Licensing Act 1926 (c. 31)	s. 3 **am.**, 1968/170
	Fertilisers and Feeding Stuffs Act 1926 (c. 45)	schs. 1–5 **replaced**, 1968/218
1927	Moneylenders Act 1927 (c. 21) ...	s. 1 **am.**, 1968/120
1184	Supreme Ct. Funds Rules 1927 (1927, p. 1638)	**am.**, 1968/106
1185	Land Charges Fees O. 1927 (Rev. XI, p. 814)	**r.**, 1968/677
1928	Petroleum (Consolidation) Act 1928 (c. 32)	sch. 1 **am.** (E. and W.) 1968/170, (S.) 1968/248
668	Agricultural Credits Fees O. 1928 (Rev. I, p. 94)	**r.**, 1968/678
1930 *Instrt. not S.I.* 9 June	Bermuda Addnl. Instructions 1930 ...	**r.**, 1968/182
1933	Local Govt. Act 1933 (c. 51)	s. 290 **am.**, 1968/656
	Road and Rail Traffic Act 1933 (c. 53)	s. 47 **am.**, 1968/656

Year and Number (or date)	Act or instrument	How affected
1933		
479	Scottish Milk Marketing Scheme (Approval) O. 1933 (Rev. I, p. 263)	**am.,** 1968/391
1149	Savings Certificates Regs. 1933 (Rev. XV, p. 309)	**am.,** 1968/425
1936	Petroleum (Transfer of Licences) Act 1936 (c. 27)	s. 1 **am.** (E. and W.) 1968/170, (S.) 1968/248
	Public Health Act 1936 (c. 49) ...	s. 187 **am.,** 1968/102
1937		
329	Public Health (Imported Food) Regs. 1937 (Rev. VIII, p. 118)	**r.,** 1968/97
1938	Nursing Homes Registration (S.) Act 1938 (c. 73)	s. 1 **am.,** 1968/248
1435	Foot and Mouth Disease (Controlled Areas Restrictions) General O. 1938 (1938 I, p. 169)	**am.,** 1968/51
1939 *Instrt. not S.I.* 9 Mar.	Emergency Powers O. in C. 1939 (1952 I, at p. 621)	**a.m.,** 1968/724 **r.** (Mauritius), O. 4.3.68
1943 *Instrt. not S.I.* 30 Aug.	Bermuda Addnl. Instructions 1943 ...	**r.,** 1968/182
1945		
248	County and Voluntary Schools (Notices) Regs. 1945 (Rev. VI, p. 375)	**r.,** 1968/615
698	Milk and Meals Regs. 1945	**am.,** 1968/534
722	Public Works Loan Act 1875, s. 41—Regs. (Rev. XVIII, p. 903)	**r.,** 1968/458
1947	Exchange Control Act 1947 (c. 14) ...	sch. 1 para. 21A **inserted,** 1968/333
	Local Govt. (S.) Act 1947 (c. 43) ...	s. 355 **am.,** 1968/656
1443	Petroleum (Inflammable Liquids and Other Dangerous Substances) O. 1947 (Rev. XVIII, p. 5)	**am.,** 1968/570
2043	Exchange Control (Deposit of Securities) (Exemption) O. 1947 (Rev. VI, p. 1041)	**r.,** 1968/79

Year and Number (or date)	Act or instrument	How affected
1947		
2866	Double Taxation Relief (Taxes on Income) (British Honduras) O., 1947 (Rev. X, p. 363)	**am.,** 1968/573
2869	Double Taxation Relief (Taxes on Income) (Montserrat) O. 1947 (Rev. X, p. 433)	**am.,** 1968/576
2874	Double Taxation Relief (Taxes on Income) (Virgin Is.) O. 1947 (Rev. X, p. 537)	**am.,** 1968/578
1948	National Assistance Act 1948 (c. 29) ...	s. 37 **am.** (E. and W.) 1968/102, (S.) 1968/248
886	Public Health (Imported Food) Amdt. Regs. 1948 (Rev. VIII, p. 118)	**r.,** 1968/97
1121	Public Health (Imported Food) (Amdt. No. 2) Regs. 1948 (Rev. VIII, p. 118)	**r.,** 1968/97
1261	National Insurance (Widows Benefit and Retirement Pensions) Regs. 1948 (Rev. XVI, p. 207)	**am.,** 1968/524
1278	National Insurance (General Benefit) Regs. 1948 (Rev. XVI, p. 179)	**am.,** 1968/524
1390	National Health Service (Appointment of Medical and Dental Officers) (S.) Regs. 1948 (Rev. XV, p. 854)	**am.,** 1968/225
1781	Town and Country Planning (Tree Preservation O.) (S.) Regs. 1948 (Rev. XXII, p. 895)	**am.,** 1968/435
2096	Town and Country Planning (Building Preservation O.) (S.) Regs. 1948 (Rev. XXII, p. 897)	**am.,** 1968/434
1949		
352	National Insurance (New Entrants Transitional) Regs. 1949 (1949 I, p. 2737)	**am.,** 1968/680
360	Double Taxation Relief (Taxes on Income) (Falkland Is.) O. (1949 I, p. 2262)	**am.,** 1968/575
404	Food and Drugs (Whalemeat) Regs. 1949 (1949 I, p. 1754)	**r.,** 1968/97
1417	Civil Defence Corps (S.) Regs. 1949 (1949 I, p. 645)	**r.,** 1968/547
1433	Civil Defence Corps Regs. 1949 (1949 I, p. 639)	**r.,** 1968/541
2058	County Cts. Districts O. 1949 (1949 I, p. 955)	**am.,** 1968/404
2120	Civil Defence (Fire Services) Regs. 1949 (1949 I, p. 658)	**am.,** 1968/542

Year and Number (or date)	Act or instrument	How affected
1949		
2167	Civil Defence (Fire Services) (S.) Regs. 1949 (1949 I, p. 659)	**am.**, 1968/548
1950		
145	Superannuation (Transfers between the Civil Service and Local Govt.) Rules 1950 (1950 II, p. 277)	**r.**, 1968/72
189	Food and Drugs (Whalemeat) (Amdt.) Regs. 1950 (1950 I, p. 757)	**r.**, 1968/97
1950		
748	Double Taxation Relief (Taxes on Income) (British Solomon Is. Protectorate) O. 1950 (1950 I, p. 997)	**am.**, 1968/574
749	Double Taxation Relief (Taxes on Income) (Fiji) O. 1950 (1950 I, p. 1029)	**am.**, 1968/308
750	Double Taxation Relief (Taxes on Income) (Gilbert and Ellice Is. Colony) O. 1950 (1950 I, p. 1036)	**am.**, 1968/309
1539	Superannuation (Transfers between the Civil Service and Public Bds.) Rules 1950 (1950 II, p. 291)	**am.**, 1968/471
1977	Double Taxation Relief (Taxes on Income) (Brunei) O. 1950 (1950 I, p. 1004)	**am.**, 1968/306
1951	Pet Animals Act 1951 (c. 35)	s. 1 **am.** (E. and W.) 1968/170, (S.) 1968/248
	Rag Flock and other Filling Materials Act 1951 (c. 63)	ss. 2, 6, 7 **am.** (E. and W.) 1968/99, (S.) 1968/248
1259	Civil Defence Corps (Scunthorpe) Regs. 1951 (1951 I, p. 256)	**r.**, 1968/541
1456	Food Standards (Fish Paste) O. 1951 (1951 III, p. 16)	**r.** (15.3.71), 1968/430
1457	Food Standards (Meat Paste) O. 1951 (1951 III, p. 20)	**r.** (15.3.71), 1968/430
2241	Food Standards (Fish Paste) (Amdt.) O. 1951 (1951 III, p. 18)	**r.** (15.3.71), 1968/430
2242	Food Standards (Meat Paste) (Amdt.) O. 1951 (1951 III, p. 22)	**r.** (15.3.71), 1968/430
1952	National Health Service Act 1952 (c. 25)	s. 2 **am** (E. and W.) 1968/544, (S.) 1968/557

Year and Number (or date)	Act or instrument	How affected
1952		
2209	Matrimonial Causes (Judgment Summons) Rules 1952 (1952 III, p. 3359)	**r.,** 1968/219
1953		
392	Merchant Shipping (Light Dues) O. 1953 (1953 I, p. 1065)	**am.,** 1968/580
1230	County and Voluntary Schools (Notices) Amdg. Regs. 1953 (1953 I, p. 604)	**r.,** 1968/615
Instrts. not S.I.		
16 May	Bermuda Addnl. Instructions 1953 ...	**r.,** 1968/182
9 Nov.	Bermuda (Amdt.) L.P. 1953 (1953 II, p. 2777)	**r.,** 1968/182
	Evidence)	
1955		
127	(E and	**am.,** 1968/422
127	Superannuation (Transfers between the Civil Service and Public Bds.) (Amdt.) Rules 1955 (1955 II, p. 1822)	
1369	Welfare Foods (G.B.) (Amdt.) O. 1955 (1955 II, p. 2511)	**am.,** 1968/471
1370	Welfare Foods (N.I.) (Amdt.) O. 1955 (1955 II, p. 2514)	**r.,** 1968/389
1542	Superannuation (Transfers between the Civil Service and Local Govt.) Amdt. Rules 1955 (1955 II, p. 1812)	**r.,** 1968/427
1796	Welfare Foods (G.B.) Amdt. (No. 2) O. 1955 (1955 II, p. 2512)	**r.,** 1968/72
Instrt. not S.I.		
25 Aug.	Bermuda (Amdt.) L.P. 1955 (1955 II, p. 3179)	**r.,** 1968/389
		r., 1968/182

Year and Number (or date)	Act or instrument	How affected
1956		
715	Ulster and Colonial Savings Certificates (Income Tax Exemption) Regs. 1956 (1956 I, p. 1086)	am., 1968/428
962	Foreign Compensation Rules 1956 (1956 I, p. 1021)	am., 1968/164
1130	Welfare Foods (G.B.) Amdt. O. 1956 (1956 II, p. 2266)	r., 1968/389
1466	Housing (Improvement Grants) (Rate of Interest) Regs. 1956 (1956 I, p. 1064)	r., 1968/234
1471	Water (Rate of Interest on Deposits) Regs. 1956 (1956 II, p. 2951)	r., 1968/230
1999	Police (S.) Regs. 1956 (1956 II, p. 1766)	am., 1968/50
1957	House of Commons Disqualification Act 1957 (c. 20)	sch. 1 Pts. I—III am., 1968/187
411	Welfare Foods (G.B.) Amdt. O. 1957 (1957 II, p. 2343)	r., 1968/389
415	Welfare Foods (N.I.) (Amdt.) O. 1957 (1957 II, p. 2346)	r., 1968/427
488	National Health Service (Designation of London Teaching Hospitals) O. 1957	am., 1968/490, 545
619	Matrimonial Causes Rules 19.. II, p. 2406)	r., 1968/219
1177	Matrimonial Causes (Maintenance Agreements) Rules 1957 (1957 II, p. 2462)	am., 1968/645
2202	Spring Traps (Approval) O. 1957 (1957 I, p. 146)	
2216	Adoption Act 1958 (7 & 8 Eliz. 2) (c. 5)	s. 30 am. (E. and W.) 1968/170, (S) 1968/248
1958	Petroleum (Carbon Disulphide) O. 1958 (1958 II, p. 1888)	am., 1968/571
257	Independent Schools Tribunal Rules 1958 (1958, I, p. 1006)	am., 1968/588
519	Fatstock (Protection of Guarantees) O. 1958 (1958 I, p. 84)	am., 1968/399
958	Spring Traps Approval (S.) O. 1958 (1958 I, p. 160)	am., 1968/676
1780		

Year and Number (or date)	Act or instrument	How affected
1958 2082	Matrimonial Causes (Amdt.) Rules 1958 (1958 II, p. 2294)	r., 1968/219
1959 258	Rate-product Rules 1959 (1959 II, p. 2288)	r., 1968/491
496	Agriculture (Calculation of Value for Compensation) Regs. 1959 (1959 I, p. 1528)	am., 1968/378
537	Foreign Service Fees O. 1959 (1959 I, p. 1411)	r., 1968/114
622	Foreign Service Fees Regs. 1959 (1959 I, p. 1420)	r., 1968/137
640	Foreign Compensation Commission (Egyptian Claims) Rules 1959 (1959 I, p. 1368)	am., 1968/163
833	Grant Aided Secondary Schools (S.) Grant Regs. 1959 (1959 I, p. 1104)	am., 1968/449
1253	Public Works Loan Commissioners (Officers' Powers) Regs. 1959 (1959 I, p. 306)	r., 1968/458
1432	General Optical Council (Registration and Enrolment Rules) O. of C. 1959/1959 II, p. 1984)	am., 1968/379
1960	Road Traffic Act 1960 (c. 16) ...	s. 249 **am.**, 1968/656
	Mental Health (S.) Act 1960 (c. 61) ...	s. 15 **am.**, 1968/248
250	Cycle Racing on Highways Regs. 1960 (1960 III, p. 3047)	am., 1968/188
477	Matrimonial Causes (District Registries) O. 1960 (1960 III, p. 3168)	r., 1968/219
544	Matrimonial Causes (Amdt.) Rules 1960 (1960 III, p. 3163)	r., 1968/219
1165	Fertilisers and Feeding Stuffs Regs. 1960 (1960 I, p. 185)	r. (1.10.70) 1968/218
1213	Matrimonial Causes (District Registries) (No. 2) O. 1960 (1960 III, p. 3169)	r., 1968/219
1261	Matrimonial Causes (Amdt.) (No. 2) Rules 1960 (1960 III, p. 3164)	r., 1968/219
1530	Rate-product Rules 1960 (1960 III, p. 2831)	r., 1968/491
2433	Town and Country Planning (Grants) (S.) Regs. 1960 (1960 III, p. 3300)	r., 1968/392
1961	Trustee Investments Act 1961 (c. 62) ...	sch. 1 Pt. I **am.**, 1968/470
64	Foreign Service Fees (Amdt.) O. ...	r., 1968/114
352	Welfare Foods (G.B.) Amdt. O. 1961...	r., 1968/389

Year and Number (or date)	Act or instrument	How affected
1961		
367	Welfare Foods (N.I.) (Amdt.) O. 1961	r., 1968/427
485	Traffic Regulation Orders (Procedure) (E. and W.) Regs. 1961	r., 1968/172
1082	Matrimonial Causes (Amdt.) Rules 1961	r. (exc. rule 8), 1968/219
1197	Foreign Service Fees (Amdt.) (No. 2) O. 1961	r., 1968/114
1214	Nurses Agencies Regs. 1961	am., 1968/101
1219	Nurses Agencies (S.) Regs. 1961 ...	am., 1968/247
1365	Dental Auxiliaries Regs. 1961... ...	r., 1968/357
1510	Foreign Service Fees (Amdt.) (No. 3) O. 1961	r., 1968/114
2074	Welfare Foods (N.I.) (Amdt. No. 2) O. 1961	r., 1968/427
2307	Supreme Ct. Fees O. 1961 ...	am., 1968/388
2364	Matrimonial Causes (Amdt. No. 2) Rules 1961	r., 1968/219
1962	Local Govt. (Financial Provisions etc.) (S.) Act 1962 (c. 9)	sch. 1 am., 1968/198
	Vehicles (Excise) Act 1962 (c. 13) ...	s. 2 am., 1968/439
	Commonwealth Immigrants Act 1962 (c. 21)	s. 4A mod. 1968/284 (Jersey), 1968/315
	Transport Act 1962 (c. 46)	s. 90 am., 1968/656
623	Approved Schools (Contributions by Local Authorities) Regs. 1962	am., 1968/407
824	Matrimonial Causes (Judgment Summons) (Amdt.) Rules 1962	r., 1968/219
839	Matrimonial Causes (Amdt.) Rules 1962	r., 1968/219
1340	Commonwealth Immigrants (Jersey) O. 1962	am., 1968/300
1341	Commonwealth Immigrants (Guernsey) O. 1962	am., 1968/301
1342	Commonwealth Immigrants (Is. of Man) O. 1962	am., 1968/302
2044	Building Societies (Authorised Investments) O. 1962	am., 1968/657
2615	Matrimonial Causes (District Registries) O. 1962	r., 1968/219
2713	Fertilisers and Feeding Stuffs (Amdt.) Regs. 1962	r. (1.10.70), 1968/218
Instrt. not S.I.		
10 Jan.	Bermuda L.P. 1962 (1962 I, p.1025) ...	r., 1968/182

Year and Number (or date)	Act or instrument	How affected
1963	Betting, Gaming and Lotteries Act 1963 (c. 2)	sch. 2 para. 11 3 para. 12 6 para. 4 7 paras. 3, 9 **am.** (E. and W.) 1968/170, (S.) 1968/248
	Weights and Measures Act 1963 (c. 31)	sch. 3 Pt. V **am.**, 1968/320
	London Government Act 1963 (c. 33)...	sch. 12 paras. 3, 6 **am.**, 1968/170
	Animal Boarding Establishments Act 1963 (c. 43)	s. 1 **am.** (E. and W.) 1968/170, (S.) 1968/248
	Local Govt. (Financial Provisions) Act 1963 (c. 46)	s. 6 **am.**, 1968/491
525	Abstract of Factories Act (Docks, etc.) O. 1963	**r.**, 1968/354
596	Companies Registration Office (Fees) (No. 2) O. 1963	**am.**, 1968/659
934	National Insurance (Industrial Injuries) (Colliery Workers Supplementary Scheme) Amdt. and Consolidation O. 1963	**am.**, 1968/83
989	Matrimonial Causes (Amdt.) Rules 1963	**r.**, 1968/219
1165	General Grant (Relevant Expenditure) (S.) Regs. 1963	**r.**, 1968/392
1283	Exchange Control (Deposit of Securities) (Exemption) (Amdt.) O. 1963	**r.**, 1968/79
1709	Measuring Instruments (Liquid Fuel and Lubricants) Regs. 1963	**am.**, 1968/267
1710	Weights and Measures Regs. 1963	**am.**, 1968/338
1711	Weights and Measures (Local Standards: Limits of Error) Regs. 1963	**am.**, 1968/339
1864	London Borough Council and Greater London Council Elections Rules 1963	**am.**, 1968/497
1990	Matrimonial Causes (Amdt. No. 2) Rules 1963	**r.**, 1968/219
1964	Riding Establishments Act 1964 (c. 70)	s. 1 **am.** (E. and W.) 1968/170, (S.) 1968/248
142	Fertilisers and Feeding Stuffs (Amdt.) Regs. 1964	**r.** (1.10.70), 1968/218
388	Prison Rules 1964	**am.**, 1968/440
404	Road Vehicles (Index Marks) Regs. 1964	**am.**, 1968/355

Year and Number (or date)	Act or instrument	How affected
1964		
409	Importation of Potatoes (Health) (G.B.) O. 1964	**am.,** 1968/165
454	London Borough Council and Greater London Council Elections Rules 1964	**am.,** 1968/497
463	Fatstock (Guarantee Payments) O. 1964	**am.,** 1968/398
504	National Insurance (Industrial Injuries) (Benefit) Regs. 1964	**am.,** 1968/92, 524
875	Town and Country Planning (Grants) Regs. 1964	**r.,** 1968/189
939	National Assistance (Professions Supplementary to Medicine) Regs. 1964	**am.,** 1968/271
940	National Health Service (Professions Supplementary to Medicine) Regs. 1964	**am.,** 1968/270
995	National Health Service (Professions Supplementary to Medicine) (S.) Regs. 1964	**am.,** 1968/279
996	National Assistance (Professions Supplementary to Medicine) (S.) Regs. 1964	**am.,** 1968/280
1071	Civil Aviation (Navigation Services Charges) Regs. 1964	**am.,** 1968/423
1125	Matrimonial Causes (District Registries) O. 1964	**r.,** 1968/219
1178	Road Vehicles (Registration and Licensing) Regs. 1964	**am.,** 1968/594
1212	Matrimonial Causes (Amdt.) Rules 1964	**r.,** 1968/219
1341	Composite Goods O. 1964	**am.,** 1968/405
1354	Building Societies (Designation for Trustee Investment) Regs. 1964	**am.,** 1968/480
1966	European Free Trade Association (Origin of Goods) Regs. 1964	**am.,** 1968/653
1979	Importation of Potatoes (Health) (G.B.) (Amdt.) O. 1964	**r.,** 1968/165
2030	Police (Common Police Services) (S.) O. 1964	**r.,** 1968/373
2077	Personal Injuries (Civilians) Scheme 1964	**am.,** 1968/176
Instrts. not S.I. 19 Sept.	Disablement and Death Pension etc. (Military), 1914 World War Service, and Service subsequent to 2 Sept. 1939, R. Warrant 1964 (1964 III, p. 5257)	**am.,** R. Warrant 12.2.68 (p. 1857)

Year and Number (or date)	Act or instrument	How affected
1964		
24 Sept.	Disablement and Death Pension etc. (Air Forces), 1914 World War Service, and Service subsequent to 2nd Sept. 1939, O. 1964 (1964 III, p. 5361)	am., O. 13.2.68 (p. 1861)
25 Sept.	Disablement and Death Pensions etc. (Naval Forces) 1914 World War Service, and Service subsequent to 2nd Sept. 1939 O. in C. 1964 (1964 III, p. 5466)	am., O. in C. 14.2.68 (p. 1865)
1965		
65	Plant Breeder's Rights Regs. 1965 ...	am., 1968/255, 622
66	Plant Breeders' Rights (Fees) Regs. 1965	r., 1968/619
225	Telephone Regs. 1965	am., 1968/593
318	Merchant Shipping (Light Dues) O. 1965	r., 1968/580
538	Police Regs. 1965	sch. 5 am. (*temp.*), remainder r. (exc. reg. 3, 62), 1968/26
577	Fire Services (Appointments and Promotion) Regs. 1965	am., 1968/614
584	Juvenile Cts. (London) O. 1965 ...	am., 1968/592
619	Police Federation Regs. 1965	am., 1968/24
621	London Authies. (Superannuation) O. 1965	am., 1968/488
722	Probation (Conditions of Service) Rules 1965	am., 1968/386
827	Matrimonial Causes (Amdt.) Rules 1965	r., 1968/219
1067	Merchant Shipping (Dangerous Goods) Rules 1965	am., 1968/332
1128	Repatriation Fees O. 1965	r., 1968/114
1216	Repatriation Fees Regs. 1965 ...	r., 1968/137
1392	Wages Regulation (Licensed Residential Establishment and Licensed Restaurant) O. 1965	r., 1968/54
1417	Sea Fisheries (S.) Byelaw (No. 72) 1965	r., 1968/600
1418	Sea Fisheries (S.) Byelaw (No. 73) 1965	r., 1968/238
1419	Sea Fisheries (S.) Byelaw (No. 74) 1965	r., 1968/239
1500	County Ct. Funds Rules 1965 ...	am., 1968/107
1707	Mayor's and City of London Ct. Funds Rules 1965	am., 1968/105
1722	Police (Amdt.) (No. 2) Regs. 1965 ...	r., 1968/26
1753	British Nationality Regs. 1965 ...	am., 1968/448
1920	British Indian Ocean Territory O. 1965	am., 1968/111
2029	Remuneration of Teachers (Farm Institutes) O. 1965	r., 1968/345

Year and Number (or date)	Act or instrument	How affected
1965		
2030	Remuneration of Teachers (Further Education) O. 1965	r., 1968/197
2073	Wages Regulation (General Waste Materials Reclamation) O. 1965	r., 1968/8
2137	Matrimonial Causes (Amdt.) (No. 2) Rules 1965	r., 1968/219
2169	Wages Regulation (Baking) (E. and W.) O. 1965	am., 1968/327
1966	Rating Act 1966 (c. 9)	s. 10 **am.**, 1968/491
	Prices and Incomes Act 1966 (c. 33) ...	sch. 2 **replaced**, 1968/616
43	Wages Regulation (Ostrich and Fancy Feather and Artificial Flower) O. 1966	**am.**, 1968/4
132	Police Federation (S.) Regs. 1966 ...	**am.**, 1968/590
146	Police (Amdt.) Regs. 1966	r., 1968/26
207	Fiduciary Note Issue (Extension of Period) O. 1966	r., 1968/259
518	Price Stability of Imported Products (Rates of Levy) O. 1966	r., 1968/551
551	Wages Regulation (Aerated Waters) (E. and W.) O. 1966	r., 1968/422
554	Wages Regulation (Road Haulage) O. 1966	**am.**, 1968/123
560	Matrimonial Causes (Amdt.) Rules 1966	r., 1968/219
635	Police (Amdt.) (No. 2) Regs. 1966 ...	r., 1968/26
641	Plant Breeder's Rights (Fees) (Amdt.) Regs. 1966	r., 1968/619
669	Wages Regulation (Hollow-ware) (Holidays) O. 1966	**am.**, 1968/626
709	Poison Rules 1966	r., 1968/75
779	Wages Regulation (Ready-made and Wholesale Bespoke Tailoring) O. 1966	r., 1968/660
820	Wages Regulation (Paper Box) O. 1966	r., 1968/260
831	Teacher's Salaries (S.) Regs. 1966 ...	r., 1968/420
854	Wages Regulation (Hair, Bars and Fibre) O. 1966	r., 1968/133
921	Import Duty Drawbacks (No. 6) O. 1966	**am.**, 1968/78, 251, 252 (*temp.*), 481, 644
1045	Firemen's Pension Scheme O. 1966 ...	**am.**, 1968/157, 397
1132	Rate-product (Amdt.) Rules 1966 ...	r., 1968/491
1156	Police (Amdt.) (No. 3) Regs. 1966 ...	r., 1968/26
1189	District Registries O. in C. 1966 ...	**am.**, 1968/579
1206	Salad Cream (S.) Regs. 1966	**am.**, 1968/263
1220	Import Duty Drawbacks (No. 8) O. 1966	**am.**, 1968/251
1224	Plant Breeder's Rights (Fees) (Amdt. No. 2) Regs. 1966	r., 1968/619

Year and Number (or date)	Act or instrument	How affected
1966		
1255	Air Navigation (Fees) Regs. 1966 ...	am., 1968/424
1288	Motor Vehicles (Construction and Use) Regs. 1966	am., 1968/362, 426, 523, 602
1289	Motor Vehicles (Authorisation of Special Types) General O. 1966	am., 1968/438
1302	Matrimonial Causes (District Registries) O. 1966	r., 1968/219
1471	Commons Registration (General) Regs. 1966	am., 1968/658
1481	European Free Trade Association (Drawback) Regs. 1966	am., 1968/100
1491	Wages Regulation (Aerated Waters) (E. and W.) Amdt. O. 1966	r., 1968/422
1493	Wages Regulation (Ready-made and Wholesale Bespoke Tailoring) (Holidays) O. 1966	am., 1968/660
1504	Wages Regulation (Dressmaking and Women's Light Clothing) (S.) (Holidays) O. 1966	r., 1968/173
1516	Wages Regulation (Milk Distributive) (E. and W.) O. 1966	r., 1968/525
1517	Wages Regulation (Paper Bag) O. 1966	r., 1968/328
1555	Import Duties (General) (No. 11) O. 1966	r., 1968/679
1572	Police (Amdt.) (No. 4) Regs. 1966 ...	r., 1968/26
1582	Police Pensions Regs. 1966	am., 1968/530
Instrt. not S.I. 21 Dec.	Mauritius Constitution O. 1966 (1966 III, p. 5190)	r., O. 4.3.68 (p. 1871)
1967	General Rate Act 1967 (c. 9)	s. 49 am., 1968/491
	National Insurance Act 1967 (c. 73) ...	s. 5 am., 1968/17
65	Probation (S.) Rules 1967	am., 1968/418
79	Import Duties (General) (No. 1) O. 1967	r., 1968/679
203	Import Duties (General) (No. 2) O. 1967	r., 1968/679
207	Approved Schools (Contribution by Education Authorities) (S.) Regs. 1967	r., 1968/196
270	Rate Support Grant (S.) O. 1967 ...	am., 1968/516
334	Approved Schools (Contributions by Local Authorities) Regs. 1967	r., 1968/407
446	Inner London (Needs Element) Regs. 1967	r. (*prosp.*), 1968/348
455	Milk (G.B.) O. 1967	am., 1968/457
468	Import Duties (General) (No. 3) O. 1967	r., 1968/679

Year and Number (or date)	Act or instrument	How affected
1967		
469	Import Duties (General) (No. 4) 1967...	**r.**, 1968/679
490	Police (Amdt.) Regs. 1967	**r.**, 1968/26
526	Poison (Amdt.) Rules 1967	**r.**, 1968/75
574	Composite Goods (Amdt.) O. 1967 ...	**r.**, 1968/405
578	Savings Certificates (Amdt.) Regs. 1967	**r.**, 1968/425
642	Prices and Incomes (General Considerations) O. 1967	**r.**, 1968/616
651	Import Duty Drawbacks (No. 4) O. 1967	**am.**, 1968/481
675	Export of Goods (Control) O. 1967 ...	**am.**, 1968/370
766	Police (Amdt.) (No. 2) Regs. 1967 ...	**r.**, 1968/26
815	Commonwealth Countries and Republic of Ireland (Immunities) (No. 2) O. 1967	**am.**, 1968/464
816	Mauritius (Appeals to Privy Council) O. 1967	**r.**, 1968/294
837	Matrimonial Causes (Amdt.) Rules 1967	**r.**, 1968/219
923	Police (Amdt.) (No. 3) Regs. 1967 ...	**r.**, 1968/26
937	National Health Service (General Dental Services) Regs. 1967	**am.**, 1968/443
953	Import Duties (General) (No. 5) O. 1967	**r.**, 1968/679
1078	Sausage and Other Meat Product (S.) Regs. 1967	**am.**, 1968/139
1112	Import Duties (General) (No. 6) O. 1967	**r.**, 1968/679
1113	Import Duty Drawbacks (No. 7) O. 1967	**am.**, 1968/251
1132	White Fish and Herring Subsidies (U.K.) Scheme 1967	**am.**, 1968/200
1148	Summer Time O. 1967	**am.**, 1968/117
1165	Redundancy Fund (Advances out of the Consolidated Fund) O. 1967	**r.**, 1965/599
1192	Police (Amdt.) (No. 4) Regs. 1967 ...	**r.**, 1968/26
1198	Wages Regulation (Hollow-ware) O. 1967	**r.**, 1968/626
1228	Family Allowances (Temporary Increase and Consequential Provisions) O. 1967	**am.**, 1968/17
1234	Criminal Justice Act 1967 (Commencement No. 1) O. 1967	**am.**, 1968/325
1265	National Insurance (Increase of Benefit and Miscellaneous Provisions) Regs. 1967	**am.**, 1968/524
1280	Wireless Telegraphy (Is. of Man) O. 1967	**am.**, 1968/118
1289	Criminal Justice Act 1967 (Commencement) (S.) O. 1967	**am.**, 1968/325

Year and Number (or date)	Act or instrument	How affected
1967		
1303	Fugitive Offenders (Extension) O. 1967	**r.** (Cayman Is.) 1968/112, (Falkland Is. and Dependencies) 1968/113
1385	Land Registration (District Registries) (No. 2) O. 1967	**r.,** 1968/344
1416	Inland Post Regs. 1967	**am.,** 1968/533
1455	Plant Breeders' Rights (Fees) (Amdt.) Regs. 1967	**r.,** 1968/619
1480	Seychelles (Appeals to Privy Council) O. 1967	**am.,** 1968/295
1562	Import Duties (General) (No. 7) O. 1967	**r.,** 1968/679
1583	Exchange Control (Authorised Dealers and Depositaries) O. 1967	**am.,** 1968/159, 668
1715	Betterment Levy (Waiver of Interest) (No. 2) Regs. 1967	**am.,** 1968/131
1718	Import Duties (General) (No. 8) O. 1967	**r.,** 1968/679
1747	Industrial Training Levy (Agricultural Horticultural and Forestry) O. 1967	**am.** (*temp.*), 1968/343
1765	Betterment Levy (Rate of Interest) (No. 5) O. 1967	**r.,** 1968/549
1810	Matrimonial Causes (Amdt. No. 2) Rules 1967	**r.,** 1968/219
1904	Fugitive Offenders (Bahamas Is.) O. 1967	**am.,** 1968/292
1905	Fugitive Offenders (Bermuda) O. 1967	**am.,** 1968/292
1906	Fugitive Offenders (British Honduras) O. 1967	**am.,** 1968/292
1907	Fugitive Offenders (British Solomon Is. Protectorate) O. 1967	**am.,** 1968/292
1908	Fugitive Offenders (Fiji) O. 1967 ...	**am.,** 1968/292
1909	Fugitive Offenders (Gibraltar) O. 1967	**am.,** 1968/292
1910	Fugitive Offenders (Gilbert and Ellice Is.) O. 1967	**am.,** 1968/292
1911	Fugitive Offenders (Hong Kong) O. 1967	**am.,** 1968/292
1912	Fugitive Offenders (Mauritius) O. 1967	**am.,** 1968/292
1913	Fugitive Offenders (Montserrat) O. 1967	**am.,** 1968/292
1914	Fugitive Offenders (Seychelles) O. 1967	**am.,** 1968/292
1915	Fugitive Offenders (Virgin Is.) O. 1967	**am.,** 1968/292
1916	Fugitive Offenders (Sovereign Base Areas of Akrotiri and Dhekelia) O. 1967	**am.,** 1968/292
1929	Land Registration. (District Registries) (No. 3) O. 1967	**r.,** 1968/344

Year and Number (or date)	Act or instrument	How affected
1967 *Instrts. not S.I.*		
12 Apr.	Mauritius Constitution (Amdt.) O. 1967 (1967 I, p. 2132)	r., O. 4.3.68 (p. 1871)
28 July	Mauritius Constitution (Amdt. No. 2) O. 1967 (1967 II, p. 3807)	r., O. 4.3.68 (p. 1871)
10 Oct.	Seychelles Civil Appeals O. 1967 (1967 III, p. 5414)	am., O. 4.3.68 (p. 1949)
28 Nov.	Mauritius Constitution (Amdt. No. 3) O. 1967 (1967 III, p. 5455)	r., O. 4.3.68 (p. 1871)
1968	Commonwealth Immigrants Act 1968 (c. 9)	s. 5 **am.** (Jersey) 1968/ 300, (Guernsey) 1968/ 301, (Is. of Man) 1968/302
26	Police Regs. 1968	**am.,** 1968/552
77	Import Duties (General) (No. 1) O. 1968	r., 1968/679
94	Foot-and-Mouth Disease (Imported Meat) O. 1968	r., 1968/585
112	Fugitive Offenders (Cayman Is.) O. 1968	**am.,** 1968/292
113	Fugitive Offenders (Falkland Is. and Dependencies) O. 1968	**am.,** 1968/292
137	Consular Fees Regs. 1968	r., 1968/456
182	Bermuda Constitution O. 1968 ...	**am.,** 1968/463
183	Fugitive Offenders (British Indian Ocean Territory) O. 1968	**am.,** 1968/292
184	Fugitive Offenders (St. Helena) O. 1968	**am.,** 1968/292
185	Fugitive Offenders (Turks and Caicos Is.) O. 1968	**am.,** 1968/292
251	Import Duty Drawbacks (No. 2) O. 1968	**am.,** 1968/644
256	Plant Breeders' Rights (Fees) (Amdt.) Regs. 1968	r., 1968/619
642	Import Duties (General) (No. 2) O. 1968	r., 1968/679
643	Import Duties (General) (No. 3) O. 1968	r., 1968/679

Index to Part I

SBN 11 840005 3